BLACKSTONE'S

EMPLOYMENT
LAW PRACTICE

BLACKSTONE'S

EMPLOYMENT LAW PRACTICE

2019

EDITOR

GAVIN MANSFIELD QC
Barrister, Littleton Chambers

CONTRIBUTORS

LYDIA BANERJEE
Barrister, Littleton Chambers

DAMIAN BROWN QC
Barrister

CHARLOTTE DAVIES
Barrister, Littleton Chambers

SIMON FORSHAW
Barrister, 11KBW

MARK HUMPHREYS
Barrister, Littleton Chambers

ANTHONY KORN
Barrister, No. 5 Chambers

ELEENA MISRA
Barrister, Old Square Chambers

BRIAN NAPIER QC
Faculty of Advocates and Barrister, Cloisters Chambers

DAVID READE QC
Barrister, Littleton Chambers

CATHERINE TAYLOR
Partner, Olswang LLP

CONSULTANT EDITOR

JOHN BOWERS QC
Barrister, Littleton Chambers
Principal of Brasenose College, Oxford

OXFORD
UNIVERSITY PRESS

OXFORD
UNIVERSITY PRESS

Great Clarendon Street, Oxford, OX2 6DP,
United Kingdom

Oxford University Press is a department of the University of Oxford.
It furthers the University's objective of excellence in research, scholarship,
and education by publishing worldwide. Oxford is a registered trade mark of
Oxford University Press in the UK and in certain other countries

First Edition published in 2006
Tenth Edition published in 2019

Impression: 1

Published in the United States of America by Oxford University Press
198 Madison Avenue, New York, NY 10016, United States of America

British Library Cataloguing in Publication Data
Data available

Library of Congress Control Number: 2019939277

ISBN 978–0–19–882421–3

Printed in Great Britain by
Bell & Bain Ltd., Glasgow

Foreword to the first edition

This is a very welcome addition to the employment law library, produced by a very distinguished and hard-working team of editors and contributors. The whole of the employment law field is, by dint of a great deal of thoughtful and sensible selection and summarization, squeezed into one volume. It will be of immense value for academics and practitioners, trade unions, employers, and employees alike. It does not shrink from making clear and well-researched assertions on the law and the procedure, not too cluttered by footnotes, and yet the source for such assertions can easily be identified. The authors do not restrict themselves to narrative, but include a good deal of well-informed comment. I have no doubt they will ensure that this book continues to keep up to date in this ever-changing legal environment: but, as of date of publication, it succeeds in giving an excellent view, both panoramic and detailed, of all that needs to be known to bring or defend an employment issue before the courts or tribunals. I dare say that we judges will feel the more comfortable as we see the tome on the desk in front of the advocate or litigant in person appearing before us.

Sir Michael Burton
President of the Employment Appeal Tribunal
Chairman of the Central Arbitration Committee
High Court Judge

Preface

The idea behind this book is very simple. It should contain everything you need to know to run an employment case at the employment tribunal, Employment Appeal Tribunal, and Central Arbitration Committee, as well as in the High Court and Court of Appeal in one accessible volume. It is slanted towards an analysis of the practice and procedure adopted by the tribunal. It also contains a summary of the substantive law in the areas most likely to arise day to day in tribunals. It does not attempt to cover every case but examines the key points which may arise at tribunal.

We have attempted to state the law as at 30 November 2018. We have where possible been able to make some minor updates after that at proof stage. Unfortunately, time and space did not permit us to revise the Employment Appeal Tribunal chapter, or the Appendices, to include reference to the new Practice Direction (Employment Appeal Tribunal – Procedure) 2018, which came into force on 19 December 2018. It can be found at https://www.judiciary.uk/wp-content/uploads/2013/07/eat-pd.pdf. The changes from the previous Practice Direction are not extensive, but readers should check our text against the 2018 Practice Direction.

We are delighted to welcome Charlotte Davies and Mark Humphreys, both of Littleton Chambers, to the writing team. The 2019 Edition is the tenth edition of the book. We recognise the great contributions to this work made by John Bowers QC (its former editor) and by Julia Palca. This book incorporates the earlier work *Employment Tribunal Practice & Procedure*, and we recognize the contribution of Geoffrey Mead to that earlier work. A large number of people have assisted with the work and have read chapters. We would particularly like to thank our colleagues at Littleton Chambers, many of whom have provided great assistance.

Gavin Mansfield QC
Littleton Chambers
London
24 April 2019

Acknowledgements

Extracts from pages 11 to 15 of Chapter 4 'Psychiatric and Psychological Damage' from *Guidelines for the Assessment of General Damages in Personal Injury Cases* by the Judicial College (Fourteenth Edition, 2017) are reproduced by permission of Oxford University Press © Judicial College 2017.

The AA Motoring Costs tables 2014–2016 are reproduced by permission of Automobile Association Developments Ltd © Automobile Association Developments Ltd 2011, 2012, and 2013. For the latest update, please see http://www.theaa.com/motoring_ advice/running_ costs/index.html.

Crown copyright material is reproduced with the permission of the Controller of Her Majesty's Stationery Office.

Acknowledgements

Contents—Summary

Contents

Table of Cases

Table of UK Legislation

STATUTORY INSTRUMENTS

Table of European and International Legislation

Codes of Practice
and Practice Directions

List of Abbreviations

ACAS	Advisory, Conciliation and Arbitration Service
ADR	alternative dispute resolution
All ER	All England Law Reports
BEIS	Department for Business, Energy and Industrial Strategy
BIS	(Department for) Business, Innovation and Skills
CA	Court of Appeal
CAC	Central Arbitration Committee
CO	certification officer
COET	Central Office of Employment Tribunals
CRE	Commission for Racial Equality
DA	Deregulation Act 2015
DC	Divisional Court of Queen's Bench Division
DDA	Disability Discrimination Act 1995
DRC	Disability Rights Commission
DRCA	Disability Rights Commission Act 1999
DWP	Department for Work and Pensions
EA	Employment Acts 1980–1989
EAT	Employment Appeal Tribunal
ECHR	European Convention on Human Rights
ECJ	European Court of Justice
ECtHR	European Court of Human Rights
EDT	effective date of termination
EOC	Equal Opportunities Commission
EPA	Employment Protection Act 1975
EPCA	Employment Protection (Consolidation) Act 1978
EqA	Equality Act 2010
EqPA	Equal Pay Act 1970
ERelA 1999	Employment Relations Act 1999
ERA	Employment Rights Act 1996
ERRA	Enterprise and Regulatory Reform Act 2013
ETA	Employment Tribunals Act 1996
ET(EC) Regs)	Employment Tribunals (Early Conciliation: Exemptions and Rules of Procedure) Regulations 2014
ETR	Employment Tribunals (Constitution and Rules of Procedure) Regulations 2013
EU	European Union
EV Rules	Employment Tribunals (Equal Value) Rules of Procedure
FCA	Financial Conduct Authority
FTER 2002	Fixed Term Employees (Prevention of Less Favourable Treatment) Regulations 2002
HC	High Court
HMCTS	Her Majesty's Courts and Tribunals Service
HMSO	Her Majesty's Stationery Office
HRA	Human Rights Act 1998
ICR	Industrial Cases Reports
ILJ	*Industrial Law Journal*
IRLR	Industrial Relations Law Reports
ITR	Industrial Tribunal Reports
LQR	*Law Quarterly Review*
LSG	*Law Society Gazette*
MLR	*Modern Law Review*
NIRC	National Industrial Relations Court
NLJ	*New Law Journal*

PHR	pre-hearing review
PRA	Prudential Regulation Authority
PTOs	preparation time orders
PTWR	Part-time Workers (Prevention of Less Favourable Treatment) Regulations 2000
ROET	Regional Office of Employment Tribunals
RPO	Redundancy Payments Office
RPS	Redundancy Payments Service
RRA	Race Relations Act 1976
RRO	restricted reporting order
SDA	Sex Discrimination Act 1975
SJ	*Solicitors Journal*
TUA	Trade Union Act 1913
TUC	Trades Union Congress
TULRA	Trade Union and Labour Relations Act 1974
TULR(A)A	Trade Union and Labour Relations (Amendment) Act 1976
TULR(C)A	Trade Union and Labour Relations (Consolidation) Act 1992
TUPE 2006	Transfer of Undertakings (Protection of Employment) Regulations 2006
TUPE 2014	Collective Redundancies and Transfer of Undertakings (Protection of Employment) (Amendment) Regulations 2014
TURERA	Trade Union Reform and Employment Rights Act 1993
WTR	Work Time Regulations 1998

PART A

Tribunal Procedure

1

Jurisdiction and Constitution

SUMMARY

(1) Employment tribunals are established and governed by statute to hear a wide range of employment law disputes.

(2) A tribunal must be chaired by a qualified lawyer, and also may include two lay members from panels drawn up by the Lord Chancellor. Tribunal decisions are usually unanimous, but a decision can be made by a majority.

(3) An employment judge may sit alone for case management discussions, pre-hearing reviews, and for hearings of defined classes of cases. In each of the latter two situations the judge may be required at least to consider sitting with two lay members.

(4) The tribunals are headed by the President of Employment Tribunals, and each region has a regional employment judge. Employment tribunal offices are found in most major cities in England and Wales.

(5) There are no restrictions on rights of audience in the tribunals.

A.   INTRODUCTION

Employment tribunals are created by and derive their powers from statute. The Employment **1.01** Tribunals Act 1996 establishes the tribunals; their jurisdiction derives from the various statutes which create substantive employment law rights (for example Employment Rights Act 1996). Detailed arrangements for the constitution and procedure of the tribunals are set out in regulations, the most recent of which are the Employment Tribunals (Constitution and Rules of Procedure) Regulations 2013, SI 2013/1237. Those Regulations, which came into effect on 29 July 2013, replaced the previous 2004 Regulations, and were the product of the *Employment Tribunal Rules: Review by Mr Justice Underhill*, BIS, July 2012 (the Underhill Review). Schedule 1 to the Regulations contains the Employment Tribunal Rules of Procedure 2013 (ETR 2013). The Regulations contain two further Schedules, which contain rules for national security cases (sch 2) and equal value claims (sch 3). Regulation 11 of the 2013 Regulations provides for the Presidents of Tribunals to make practice directions about the procedure of the tribunals; r 7 provides that the

Presidents may publish presidential guidance as to matters of practice and as to how the powers conferred by the rules may be exercised. At the time of writing, sevenPresidential Guidances have been issued dealing with postponements, r 21 judgments, general case management, statutory appeals, and judicial assessments under r 3 of the ETR, awards for injury to feelings and pension loss.

1.02 The 2013 rules are expressed in clearer, simpler terms than the old rules, but many of the principles of the previous rules are maintained. In this edition of *Blackstone's Employment Law Practice*, we have maintained commentary on cases dealing with earlier rules, where the principles from those cases is likely to be applicable to the new rules.

1.03 In 2013 the government introduced a requirement that a fee be paid to HM Courts and Tribunals Service on the presentation of claims (and appeals), and at certain subsequent points (Employment Tribunals and the Employment Appeal Tribunal Fees Order 2013). That scheme was held to be unlawful by the Supreme Court in *R (on the application of UNISON) v Lord Chancellor* [2017] IRLR 911. Since 2017 no fees have been charged by HM Courts and Tribunals Service, and fees paid between July 2013 and July 2017 can be reclaimed.

1.04 The original vision for the employment tribunals was that they should be 'easily accessible, informal, speedy and inexpensive' (Donovan Commission on Trade Unions and Employers' Associations 1965–68). However, although the tribunals continue to strive for these objectives, over the years the claims upon which the tribunals have been required to adjudicate have become more and more complex, and the rules of procedure for dealing with those cases have become more extensive. Hearings in the tribunal are conducted in a format very similar to that applied in the civil courts. In recent years, there has been a trend towards a case management approach more in line with the approach in the civil courts under the Civil Procedure Rules 1998, SI 1998/3132 (CPR). For some interesting observations on the increasingly complex task faced by employment tribunals in the current political and economic climate, see the judgment of Mummery LJ in *Gayle v Sandwell & West Birmingham Hospitals NHS Trust* [2011] IRLR 810, paras 9–22.

1.05 By ETR 2013, r 2 the overriding objective of the rules is to enable tribunals to deal with cases fairly and justly. Dealing with a case fairly and justly includes, so far as practicable:

(a) ensuring that the parties are on an equal footing
(b) dealing with cases in ways which are proportionate to the complexity and importance of the issues
(c) avoiding unnecessary formality and seeking flexibility in the proceeding
(d) avoiding delay, so far as compatible with proper consideration of the issues and
(e) saving expense.

1.06 The tribunal must seek to give effect to this overriding objective in interpreting or exercising any power under ETR 2013, r 41 also sets out principles of general importance to the tribunal's approach: the tribunal may regulate its own procedure and shall conduct hearings in the manner it considers fair having regard to the overriding objective; the tribunal shall seek to avoid undue formality; the tribunal is not bound by rules of law as to admissibility of evidence.

1.07 By s 2 of the Human Rights Act 1998 (HRA 1998), the tribunal must take into account any judgment or decision of the European Court of Human Rights (ECtHR) when considering any matter in respect of which a human rights issue has arisen. The employment tribunal is a public authority, and as such may not itself act in a manner incompatible with rights under the European Convention on Human Rights (ECHR). In its procedures, a tribunal must respect the right of all parties before it to a fair trial under ECHR, Article 6(1).

1.08 The tribunal must, so far as possible, read and give effect to legislation in a way which is compatible with Convention rights (HRA 1998, s 3). This may affect the substantive decision-making of the tribunal. In *Xv Y* [2004] EWCA Civ 662, [2004] IRLR 625 the Court of Appeal held that when considering the fairness of a dismissal under s 98(4) of the Employment Rights Act 1996 (ERA 1996) a tribunal was required to give effect to Convention rights under s 3 of the HRA 1998. See also *Copsey v WWB Devon Clays Ltd* [2005] EWCA Civ 932, [2005] IRLR 811.

A tribunal may not make a declaration that primary legislation is incompatible with the ECHR **1.09** (HRA 1998, s 4). That power is limited to the High Court, the Court of Appeal, and the Supreme Court. The Employment Appeal Tribunal (EAT) has held that neither the employment tribunal nor the EAT has jurisdiction to hear a submission as to the incompatibility of legislation with the ECHR (*Whittaker v P&D Watson (t/a P & M Watson Haulage)* [2002] ICR 1244, EAT). Nor may a tribunal hear a free-standing claim for interference with Convention rights under s 6 of the HRA 1998. Chapter 16 deals further with claims raising human rights issues.

The employment tribunals are not courts of record. However, for the purposes of the Contempt **1.10** of Court Act 1981 they are inferior courts, so that contempt of court in tribunal proceedings is punishable by the Divisional Court of the High Court (*Peach Grey & Co v Sommers* [1995] ICR 549, [1995] IRLR 363, DC).

B. MEMBERSHIP AND COMPOSITION OF EMPLOYMENT TRIBUNALS

A tribunal must be constituted in accordance with s 4 of the Employment Tribunals Act 1996 **1.11** (ETA 1996) and the 2013 Regulations. A tribunal must be chaired by an appropriately qualified lawyer, referred to as an employment judge. A tribunal may consist either of an employment judge alone, or an employment judge with lay members.

Members

Employment judges

An employment judge must have satisfied the judicial appointment eligibility condition within **1.12** the meaning of the Tribunals, Courts and Enforcement Act 2007 for a period of five years. In Scotland or Northern Ireland, the judge must be a barrister, advocate, or solicitor of five years' standing (2013 Regulations, reg 8(2)). An employment judge will either be salaried or fee-paid (ie part-time). Fee-paid judges will normally be practising solicitors or barristers. They may not appear as representatives before a tribunal in the region in which they have been appointed as a part-time judge.

Lay members

Lay members are selected one from a panel of 'employer representatives' and one from a panel of **1.13** 'employee representatives'. The panels are drawn up by the Lord Chancellor after consultation with such organizations or associations of organizations representing respectively employers and employees as the Lord Chancellor sees fit (2013 Regulations, reg 8(2)). In fact, the practice in modern times is that lay members are recruited by public advertisement and interview. This appears to have resulted in a broadening of the range of lay members, in particular an increase in the number of younger members, although with some loss of 'hands-on' industrial experience, particularly from the employee panel.

The lay members are not intended to be delegates of their respective organizations; rather they **1.14** should be independent and open-minded. They should, and do, judge each case on its merits without preconception, fear, or favour: see the remarks of Burton J in *Rabahallah v BT Group plc* [2005] ICR 440, [2005] IRLR 184, EAT, paras 13–14; see also *de Haney v Brent MIND* [2003] EWCA Civ 1637, [2004] ICR 348. The Lord Chancellor looks for candidates who have practical experience of industrial relations and who are capable of acting impartially in reaching decisions on facts presented to them. The lay members can be perceived as the safety valve of the employment adjudication system, deflecting much of the criticism of the unions that the system is biased against them. They reflect the tripartism, which has been a feature of British employment relations—as reflected in bodies such as the Advisory, Conciliation and Arbitration Service (ACAS).

1.15 Since 1999 lay members have been appointed for a renewable period of three years. During his period of appointment, a lay member in England and Wales may be removed upon a written notice from the Lord Chancellor upon five grounds (misbehaviour, incapacity, failure as to training, failure to satisfy the sitting requirements, and sustained failure to observe the standards reasonably to be expected of a holder of the office). The Lord Chancellor cannot remove a lay member unless, having first consulted with the President of the Employment Tribunals, he then notifies the Lord Chief Justice of his concern and requests him (in consultation with the President) to nominate a judge to investigate all the circumstances. Only if the report of the investigating judge is that grounds for removal are made out and if the Lord Chief Justice concurs in the removal can the Lord Chancellor then remove the member. A lay member will automatically be offered reappointment at the end of his term, unless specified grounds for non-renewal are made out. The Lord Chancellor's power of non-renewal is subject to judicial control similar to that in cases of removal.

1.16 There are no requirements in the rules for the composition of tribunals to suit particular types of employment or particular types of claim. It was held in *Halford v Sharples* [1992] ICR 146 that, apart from cases of sex and race discrimination, appointment to tribunals should be by random selection and not based on type of employment. The practice in England and Wales in race and sex discrimination cases is different. During the passage of the Bill which became the Race Relations Act 1976, the government (House of Lords, Lord Jacques, 15 October 1976) said that steps would be taken to appoint to the panel of lay members persons who, in addition to their general knowledge or experience of employment, also had special knowledge or experience of relations between persons of different racial groups in the employment field and that, wherever possible, one such member would sit in cases where racial discrimination is alleged by the claimant. This has always been the normal practice. However, failure to appoint such a person does not affect the legal validity of a tribunal's composition: *Habib v Elkington & Co Ltd* [1981] ICR 435, [1981] IRLR 344, EAT. Further, a certificate given by the President of the Employment Tribunals for England and Wales that one lay member 'was selected as having special knowledge or experience of relations between persons of different racial groups in the employment field' could not be challenged in the absence of any convincing evidence that what is certified is either wholly inaccurate or is false. In sex discrimination cases, steps are normally taken to ensure the tribunal includes at least one female member.

1.17 Although the judge is the sole legally qualified member, and will be responsible for the management of proceedings before the tribunal, all three members of the tribunal participate equally in the decision-making of the tribunal. All members of the tribunal must take part in every aspect of the questions that they have to decide. This was made clear by the National Industrial Relations Court in *Morris v Gestetner Ltd* [1973] ICR 587, where one member failed to agree with the majority view that, since the tribunal could take no account of pressure exercised by employees in a strike threat, the employee had been unfairly dismissed. Having taken this view on the main issue against the claimant, the dissentient took no part in the further decision of whether to make a recommendation for the employee's re-engagement. Sir John Donaldson, then President, however, rebuked the tribunal on the grounds that all must participate in the decisions accorded them by statute. Where members disagree as to the decision, ETR, r 49 provides for majority decisions; see further para 11.09.

Independence and impartiality

1.18 All members of a tribunal must be independent and impartial—bias, or the appearance of bias, must be avoided. Bias is dealt with in detail in Chapter 10.

Composition of tribunals

1.19 A tribunal may comprise either an employment judge sitting alone, or a panel consisting of an employment judge and two lay members. ETR 2013 uses the term 'full tribunal' for such a panel (see r 1(1)). In certain limited circumstances, a full tribunal may consist of an employment judge and one lay member. The requirements for the composition of the tribunal panel depend upon the type of claim and the type of hearing.

Preliminary hearings

Preliminary hearings are interim hearings, which may make case management decisions, but may **1.20** also make more substantial decisions concerning a case. For example, at a preliminary hearing the tribunal may strike out a case, or decide a preliminary issue. ETR 2013, r 53(1) sets out the powers that may be exercised at a pre-hearing review.

Rule 55 provides that a preliminary hearing shall be conducted by an employment judge alone, **1.21** except that where notice has been given that any preliminary issues are to be, or may be, decided at the hearing a party may request in writing that the hearing be conducted by a full tribunal, in which case an employment judge shall decide whether that would be desirable.

Two cases decided under the 2001 version of the Rules emphasized the importance of lay mem- **1.22** bers in certain types of preliminary hearing. In *Edusei v (1) Ledwith, (2) Nynex Cablecoms Ltd*, 27 February 1997, EAT/1326/95, the EAT said that in cases which raised difficult disputes of fact, or mixed fact and law, the judge should consider carefully the wisdom of sitting alone, since in those types of case the experience of the lay members may be especially valuable. In *Sutcliffe v Big C's Marine* [1998] ICR 913 the EAT said that tribunals should think carefully before dispensing with lay members and must bear in mind the interests of justice, and not simply the saving of expense, when making such decisions. In principle, this guidance remains relevant to the tribunal's exercise of its powers under r 55, but in the intervening years since those cases there has been an increasing move to reduce the role of lay members.

Final hearings

By ETA 1996, s 4(1) proceedings before a tribunal shall be heard by an employment judge with **1.23** two lay members (ie a full tribunal), but this broad principle is subject to substantial exceptions set out in s 4. Subsections 4(2)–(3) set out a long list of proceedings that must be heard by a judge alone, unless having regard to particular matters (s 4(5), set out below), it is appropriate for the case to be heard by a full tribunal. Of the cases listed in s 4(3), categories (a)–(d) concern particular jurisdictions of the tribunal, whilst categories (e) and (g) deal respectively with cases where the parties consent to a hearing by judge alone, or where the respondent does not contest the case. Of the jurisdictions covered by this section, the most significant are breach of contract claims under s 3 of the ETA 1996 and, since April 2012, claims for unfair dismissal under s 111 of the ERA 1996. The full list is as follows:

- proceedings under ss 68A or 87 of the Trade Union and Labour Relations (Consolidation) Act 1992 (TULR(C)A 1992) (right not to suffer deductions of unauthorized or excessive trade union subscriptions)
- proceedings under s 192 of TULR(C)A 1992 (claim to receive compensation for failure to inform and consult over collective redundancies)
- proceedings under ss 161, 165, or 166 of TULR(C)A 1992 (claims for interim relief in cases of dismissal for trade union membership or activities)
- proceedings under s 126 of the Pension Schemes Act 1993 (complaints that the Secretary of State has failed to make required payments of unpaid contributions to pension schemes)
- proceedings under s 11 of the ERA 1996 (right to a written statement of terms and conditions of employment)
- proceedings under s 23 of the ERA 1996 (unauthorized deductions from wages)
- proceedings under s 34 of the ERA 1996 (right to guarantee payments)
- proceedings under ss 64 and 70(1) of the ERA 1996 (right to remuneration during suspension on medical grounds)
- proceedings under s 111 of the ERA 1996 (unfair dismissal)
- proceedings under s 163 of the ERA 1996 (right to a redundancy payment)
- proceedings under s 170 of the ERA 1996 (right to a redundancy payment from the Secretary of State in the event of the employer's insolvency or refusal/failure to make the payment)
- proceedings under s 188 of the ERA 1996 (right to payment from the Secretary of State in the event of insolvency)

- proceedings under ss 128, 131, or 132 of the ERA 1996 (interim relief in certain unfair dismissal cases)
- appointment by a tribunal under s 206(4) of the ERA 1996 of a person to act on behalf of a deceased person before a tribunal
- proceedings under reg 15(10) of the Transfer of Undertakings (Protection of Employment) Regulations 2006, SI 2006/246 (to recover money ordered by a tribunal to be paid for failure to inform and consult over a transfer of an undertaking)
- proceedings on a complaint under s 11 of the National Minimum Wage Act 1998
- proceedings on an appeal under ss 19 or 22 of the National Minimum Wage Act 1998
- proceedings under reg 30 of the Working Time Regulations 1998 relating to an amount due under reg 14(2) or 16(1) of those Regulations (claims for holiday pay)
- proceedings under reg 18 of the Merchant Shipping (Working Time: Inland Waterways) Regulations 2003 relating to an amount due under reg 11 (claims for holiday pay)
- proceedings under reg 18 of the Civil Aviation (Working Time) Regulations 2004 relating to an amount due under reg 4 (claims for holiday pay)
- proceedings under reg 19 of the Fishing Vessels (Working Time: Sea-fishermen) Regulations 2004 relating to an amount due under reg 11 (claims for holiday pay)
- proceedings under s 3 of the ETA 1996and the Employment Tribunals Extension of Jurisdiction (England and Wales) Order 1994, SI 1994/1623 and the Employment Tribunals Extension of Jurisdiction (Scotland) Order 1994, SI 1994/1624 (claims for breach of contract or money owing under a contract)
- proceedings in which the parties have given their written consent to the proceedings being heard by judge alone (whether or not they have subsequently withdrawn it)
- proceedings in which each respondent does not, or has ceased to, contest the case.

1.24 Section 4(5) of the ETA 1996 provides that the proceedings listed in s 4(3) shall be heard by a full tribunal if the judge decides at any stage of the proceedings to do so, having regard to:

(a) whether there is a likelihood of a dispute arising on the facts which makes it desirable for the proceedings to be heard by a full tribunal

(b) whether there is a likelihood of an issue of law arising which would make it desirable for the proceedings to be heard by a judge alone

(c) any views of any of the parties as to whether or not the proceedings ought to be heard by a judge alone or by a full tribunal and

(d) whether there are other proceedings which might be heard concurrently but which are not proceedings specified in s 4(3).

1.25 In a case where the views and experience of the lay members are likely to be of assistance to the decision-making process, a judge should generally decide pursuant to s 4(5) that the case be heard by a full tribunal (*Post Office v Howell* [2000] ICR 913).

1.26 A judge must consider s 4(5) if the issue is raised by one of the parties. A judge must also actively consider whether he should exercise the discretion where proceedings involve a combination of causes of action of which one or more is listed under s 4(3) and one or more is not (*Birring v Rogers & Anor* [2015] ICR 1001). It is desirable for a judge to consider s 4(5) in any event, although it is not an error of law to fail to do so: *Morgan v Brith Gof Cyf* [2001] ICR 978, Lindsay J, departing from a number of earlier decisions (*Sogbetun v Hackney LBC* [1998] ICR 1264; *Post Office v Howell* [2000] ICR 913; *Professional Selection & Development Ltd v Wahab* EAT/64/00). In *Gladwell v Secretary of State for Trade and Industry* [2007] ICR 264, the EAT under Elias P followed the approach taken in *Morgan*, but added a second situation in which a judge is obliged actively to exercise his discretion: where one of the parties is a litigant in person, or at least a litigant in person who may not be aware of the possibility, or relative merits, of a differently constituted panel. Elias P also agreed with the EAT in *Clarke v Arriva Kent (Thameside) Ltd* [2001] All ER (D) 485 (Jul) that the discretion should be kept under review, as the circumstances may change from those existing at the time the decision was made. *Gladwell* has since been followed by a differently constituted EAT in *Sterling Developments (London) Ltd v Pagano* [2007] IRLR 471, HHJ Clark presiding.

Reconsiderations

The hearing of an application for reconsideration should, where practicable, be heard by the judge **1.27** or tribunal which made the decision under review (ETR 2013, r 72(3)). If the decision subject to reconsideration was made by a full tribunal, the reconsideration should be by that tribunal. If the reconsideration is of a decision of a judge sitting alone, then the reconsideration should be conducted by that judge sitting alone. See further paras 13.31–13.35.

Judge sitting with one lay member

A tribunal has power to sit with the judge and one lay member provided the parties consent (ETA **1.28** 1996, s 4(1)). This may occur, for example, in the event of illness or travel difficulties of a tribunal member. If one party does not give its consent to the hearing going ahead on this basis, it must be adjourned.

Where the tribunal proposes sitting with only one lay member, the tribunal must inform **1.29** the parties from which panel the absent member was taken (employer's panel or employee's panel): *Rabahallah v BT Group plc* [2005] ICR 440, [2005] IRLR 184, following *de Haney v Brent MIND* [2003] EWCA Civ 1637, [2004] ICR 348, where the Court of Appeal dealt with the identical situation in relation to the composition of the EAT. Absence of this information vitiates the consent of the parties. In *Rabahallah*, Burton J (para 35) suggested that it would be sensible for a form to be signed by the parties, giving consent to a case commencing or continuing before a panel of two rather than three. It should contain an express reference to the identity of the judge and one member who will try or continue to try the case, with a statement of the panel from which that member is drawn.

Where a tribunal consists of a judge and one lay member, the judge has a casting vote (ETR **1.30** 2013, r 49).

Legal officers and caseworkers

A succession of government proposals in recent years has aimed to reduce the burden on the **1.31** Tribunal Service by reducing the number of claims which reach hearings before employment judges and full tribunals. However, few of those proposals have been implemented. In 2012 the government proposed a 'rapid resolution service' where non-judicial legal officers may decide straightforward low-value claims without a hearing. To implement this policy, s 11 of the Enterprise and Regulatory Reform Act 2013 (ERRA 2013) amended s 4 of the ETA 1996 to provide for regulations to be made under which 'legal officers' may determine proceedings of certain kinds. The notion that certain interlocutory decisions could be taken by non-judicial legal officers has been mooted for some considerable time. Indeed, s 5 of the Employment Rights (Dispute Resolution) Act 1998 provided for such legal officers, but the provision was never implemented. The intention behind s 11 of the ERRA 2013 appears to be to give legal officers a wider remit than that provided by the 1998 Act, so that they can make substantive decisions on cases. However, at the time of writing no draft regulations have been proposed under s 11 of the ERRA 2013. Between December 2016 and February 2017, the government consulted on a number of proposals for reform of employment tribunals, including delegating to legally qualified caseworkers to make case management decisions. The government's response to that consultation was a statement of intention to introduce powers to delegate to case workers, but no such legislation has been brought forward at the date of writing.

The Employment Act 2008 introduced an amendment to the ETA 1996 in the form of a new subs **1.32** 3AA to s 7. The provisions allow regulations to be introduced to authorize a 'fast track' system for adjudicating certain disputes without a hearing if all the parties consent or the respondent has either presented no response or does not contest the claim. At the time of writing no such regulations have been made. The categories of cases for which the government believes this system would be suitable are claims for unlawful deduction from wages, breach of contract, redundancy pay, holiday pay, and national minimum wage.

C. JURISDICTION

1.33 The tribunal has only the jurisdiction given to it by statute. There are now over seventy statutory jurisdictions in respect of which the tribunal may hear claims. Most of these are to determine rights which are defined in some detail by statute. Others, however, amount to a statutory jurisdiction to determine a common law cause of action: ETA 1996, s 3, for example, gives the employment tribunal jurisdiction to hear certain claims of breach of contract (see Chapter 8). The tribunal's jurisdiction can be ousted by the High Court where a civil restraint order is issued (*Nursing & Midwifery Council and Anor v Harrold* [2015] EWHC 2254 (QB), [2016] IRLR 30). The interplay of the tribunal's jurisdiction and the jurisdiction of the civil courts is considered in Chapter 20.

1.34 Whether a tribunal has jurisdiction in respect of any particular claim is largely a matter of substantive law depending on the jurisdictional requirements of the particular statute upon which the claim is based. The tribunal has no power to determine any matter or give any remedy falling outside its specific statutory jurisdictions.

Territorial jurisdiction

1.35 It is increasingly common for questions to arise as to the territorial grasp of the legislation on which claims are based. In the modern workplace, there are often employment relationships with an international element involving one or more foreign jurisdictions, and the increased use of electronic communications to facilitate cross-border working tends to make the matter more complicated. There are two key questions:

(a) What is the legislative scope of the statutes which create employment rights? Are there territorial limits?

(b) What, if any, territorial limitations are imposed by the ETA 1996 and the regulations and rules made under that Act?

1.36 Identifying the legislative scope of a particular statute or statutory instrument is often not straightforward. It might be thought an obvious issue for legislators to address, but Parliament's approach has fluctuated over time. Section 196 of the ERA 1996 did appear to provide for a territorial limitation, but this section was repealed in October 1999. Prior to the Equality Act 2010, its predecessors included express territorial limitations: see, for example, Sex Discrimination Act 1975, ss 6 and 10; Race Relations Act 1976, s 8; Disability Discrimination Act 1995, s 68. However, the Equality Act 2010 contains no such provisions.

1.37 The courts have been ready to imply some territorial limitation on the scope of statutory rights; identifying what those limits are has been less straightforward. At one end of the scale, it is easy to see that some form of connection with Great Britain is necessary. It is easy to see that, for example, a Chinese citizen employed by a Chinese company working wholly in China would fall outside the protection of UK employment law. Formulating the applicable test in more complicated fact situations has proved difficult.

1.38 In *Lawson v Serco* [2006] UKHL 3, [2006] ICR 250 the House of Lords held that the ERA 1996 confers rights primarily upon claimants employed in Great Britain at the time of their dismissal, but also upon workers overseas in certain exceptional cases set out by Lord Hoffmann: peripatetic employees based in Great Britain; employees posted overseas for the purposes of a business based in Great Britain; and employees working in a political or social enclave abroad. However, the exact formulation of the test applicable to the 'exceptions' has been revisited by the Supreme Court on two occasions in the time since *Lawson*: see *Duncombe v SoS for Children Schools and Families* [2011] UKSC 36, [2011] ICR 1312 and *Ravat v Halliburton Manufacturing & Services Ltd* [2012] UKSC 1, [2012] ICR 389. In *Ravat*, the Supreme Court held that the categories identified by Lord Hoffmann in *Lawson* are merely examples of the application of the general principle that, in order for there to be jurisdiction, an employment must have much stronger connections both with Great Britain and with British employment law than with any other system of law. In general the place of employment will be decisive, and the question for the tribunal will always be, as a matter of fact and degree, whether, at the time of dismissal, the employee can show a sufficiently strong connection with Great Britain and British employment law such that it could be presumed that Parliament must have intended that the employment right should apply to them (*Dhunna v Creditsights Ltd* [2014] EWCA Civ 1238, [2015] ICR 105).

In *Bamieh v Eulex Kosovo and Others* [2018] UKEAT/0268/16 the EAT (Simler P) considered, apparently for the first time, the territorial scope of statutory employment rights from the perspective of respondents to claims. The claimant was employed by the Foreign & Commonwealth Office and seconded to work in Kosovo for Eulex, a multi-nation mission established by the EU Council. She brought whistle-blowing unfair dismissal and detriment claims against (among others) the Foreign Office and two Foreign Office employees who were also based in Kosovo. The Foreign Office accepted that the tribunal had jurisdiction to determine the claims against it, but the two individuals denied that they fell within the territorial scope of the ERA 1996. Simler P applied the *Ravat* test by analogy, and held that these claims were within scope, as the two individuals had a sufficiently strong connection to England and English employment law. It remains to be seen whether this approach will be followed. While there is a certain logic to applying the same test to claimants and respondents, there is some force in the argument advanced on the claimant's behalf that in a case where the claimant has a sufficient connection to England, and the employer is located in England there is no need for a further hurdle to be crossed in relation to the employer's employees. Arguably, the only remaining question should be (ERA, s 47B(1A)) whether the individual respondents were acting in the course of their employment for the English based employer. **1.39**

A different approach to that taken in respect of unfair dismissal may be required where the claims of employees are based on rights conferred by European Union laws, rather than domestic laws: see *Bleuse v MBT Transport* [2008] IRLR 264, where the EAT held that an employee's claims founded on EU legislation fell within the tribunal's jurisdiction, while those based on legislation with no origin in EU law did not (see paras 26.154 ff) The Court of Appeal has held (without reference to *Bleuse*), that the territorial reach of Pt 5 of the Equality Act 2010 should not be regarded as wider than that applying to unfair dismissal under the ERA (*R (on the application of Hottak) v Secretary of State for Foreign and Commonwealth Affairs* [2016] EWCA Civ 438). Consolidation around the unfair dismissal approach has also been seen in its application to protected disclosure dismissal (*Smania v Standard Chartered Bank* [2015] ICR 436, [2015] IRLR 271) and entitlement to pension auto-enrolment (*R (on the application of Fleet Maritime Services (Bermuda) Ltd) v Pensions Regulator* [2015] EWHC 3744 (Admin), [2016] IRLR 199). In *Jeffrey v Britih Council* [2019] IRLR 123 the Court of Appeal rejected an argument that the approach in whistleblowing cases should differ from the *Lawson/Ravat* approach. After the UK's departure from the EU there will no longer be a distinction between EU rights and domestic rights, so there will no longer be an argument for a wider approach to be taken. **1.40**

The second question identified above is whether the ETA 1996 and the tribunal Regulations add any further jurisdictional requirement. Regulation 19(1) of the 2004 Regulations provided that an employment tribunal in England and Wales shall only have jurisdiction to deal with proceedings where: **1.41**

(a) the respondent or one of the respondents resides or carries on business in England or Wales
(b) had the remedy been by way of action in the county court, the cause of action would have arisen wholly or partly in England and Wales
(c) the proceedings are to determine a question which has been referred to the tribunal by a court in England and Wales or
(d) in the case of proceedings to which sch 3, 4, or 5 applies, the proceedings relate to matters arising in England and Wales.

Regulation 19(2) contained an equivalent provision in respect of Scotland.

It was unclear whether this regulation presented a jurisdictional hurdle, or whether it was simply concerned with allocation of work between England and Wales on the one hand, and Scotland on the other. The regulation was held not to have been intended to define the legislative grasp of the ERA 1996 in *Jackson v Ghost Ltd* [2003] IRLR 824. However, in *Pervez v Macquarie Bank Ltd* [2011] ICR 266, [2012] IRLR 315 the EAT (Underhill J) held that the regulation was **1.42** jurisdictional, even if the draftsmen may not have had in mind the potential impact of the regulation on cases with a non-GB element.

1.43 On the facts of the case, the EAT in *Pervez* held that there was jurisdiction by a broad interpretation of 'carrying on business in England or Wales' (indeed, Underhill J himself described the interpretation as 'strained'): a company can carry on business in England and Wales by seconding an employee to work at a third party establishment here, even if the supply of workers to third parties is not part of its ordinary business. A company may carry on business in England and Wales for the purposes of reg 19(1)(a), even though its registered office is abroad: see *Knulty v Eloc Electro-Opteik and Communicatie BV* [1979] ICR 827.

1.44 Under the ETR 2013, there continues to be a provision which requires a connection with, respectively, England and Wales or Scotland: ETR 2013, r 8. The problem which arose in *Pervez* has been addressed by the Underhill Review not by abolishing the rule, but by widening and clarifying the language. So, r 8(2) provides that a claim may be presented in England and Wales if:

(a) the respondent, or one of the respondents, resides or carries on business in England and Wales

(b) one or more of the acts or omissions complained of took place in England and Wales

(c) the claim relates to a contract under which the work is or has been performed partly in England and Wales or

(d) the tribunal has jurisdiction to determine the claim by virtue of a connection with Great Britain and the connection is at least partly a connection with England and Wales.

Rule 8(3) makes similar provision for Scotland.

1.45 The Employment Protection (Offshore Employment) Order 1976, SI 1976/766 provides that the main employment legislation applies to any activities in British territorial waters (other than activities connected with a ship in the course of a navigational survey or a ship engaged in dredging or fishing), activities connected with the exploration of the sea bed, sub-soil, or the exploitation of their natural resources, and any activities connected with the exploration or exploitation of the Frigg gas field. The provisions confer jurisdiction on employment tribunals whether or not individual claimants or respondents are British subjects, and whether or not any respondent company is incorporated under the laws of the United Kingdom. Specific provisions, however, limit the application of key rights (eg s 199 of the ERA and the Equality Act 2010 (Work on Ships and Hovercraft) Regulations 2011, reg 3).

1.46 Cases can be transferred between England and Scotland by order of the President or regional employment judge if it appears to him or her that the case can be more conveniently tried on transfer, and if the 'transferee' President has consented to the transfer (ETR 2013, r 99).

D. ADMINISTRATION

1.47 The Lord Chancellor has a statutory duty to ensure that there is an efficient and effective system to support the carrying on of the business of the employment tribunals and the EAT, and to ensure that appropriate services are provided for the tribunals (Tribunals, Courts and Enforcement Act 2007, s 40). Employment tribunals and the EAT come under the auspices of the Senior President of Tribunals. Both are subject to the oversight of the Administrative Justice and Tribunals Council.

1.48 At the time this edition is being written, the future of the employment tribunals is uncertain. Administratively, the employment tribunals and the EAT have stood apart from the civil courts (the High Court and the county court), and also from the administrative tribunals. Over the course of 2015 and 2016 there has been considerable debate as to their future, in particular given the downturn in workload following the introduction of fees in 2013. There are a number of voices arguing (for a variety of reasons) that they cannot, or should not continue their separate existence. In England and Wales, the Civil Courts Structure Review, chaired by Briggs LJ, produced its final report in July 2016. At para 11.11 of the Review, Briggs LJ described the employment tribunals (and the EAT) as 'uncomfortably stranded' between the civil courts and the first tier and upper tribunals. Briggs LJ envisages a convergence between the employment tribunals and the civil courts in England and Wales, to create an Employment and Equalities Court, with a route of appeal to the EAT as a specialist appeal court. Briggs LJ regarded his remit to consider only 'boundary issues' and leaves the details of how such a court would operate to be determined in due course.

In September 2016, the Lord Chancellor, the Lord Chief Justice, and the Senior President of **1.49** Tribunals published a joint statement setting out intentions on transforming the justice system, outlining proposed reforms. In December 2016, the Ministry of Justice and BEIS issued a consultation as to how those reforms may be given effect in the employment tribunals. The consultation stated that the government has decided that action is needed to bring the processes in the employment tribunals and EAT into line with the rest of the justice system, but it does not consider that radical structural change is necessary to achieve this. The government stated that it will keep the separate nature of the employment tribunals and EAT 'under review'. The government responded to the consultation in February 2017. A Prison and Courts Bill 2017 included provisions to change the enabling powers for the employment tribunals. However, there was insufficient time to pass the Bill before the 2017 general election, and the Bill has not been reintroduced since then.

The future is thus unclear at the time of writing. What follows describes the current position as at **1.50** May 2018.

The overall heads of employment tribunals are the Presidents of Employment Tribunals; there is one **1.51** President for England and Wales, and one President for Scotland (see 2013 Regulations, reg 5). The President in England and Wales is appointed by the Lord Chancellor, and the President in Scotland is appointed by the Lord President of the Court of Session. Each President is responsible to secure, as far as practicable, the speedy and efficient disposal of proceedings (2013 Regulations, reg 7(1)). The President's duties include nominal responsibility for selection of judges and lay members for the hearing of particular cases, giving directions for their sittings, and determining the number of tribunals to be established. He also receives complaints about the conduct of employment judges and members. He may also sit as a judge of a tribunal himself, and is responsible for regional employment judges. Since the Tribunals, Courts and Enforcement Act 2007, the apex of the tribunal judiciary is the Senior President of Tribunals, who has responsibility not just for the employment tribunals and EAT, but for numerous other statutory tribunals falling within the remit of the Tribunals Service.

The employment tribunals operate through a number of offices in cities around England and **1.52** Wales, and Scotland. Most tribunals sit between 10 am and 4 or 4.30 pm, although practice varies in different parts of the country. Tribunal offices are open between 9 am and 5 pm on weekdays. Employment tribunals are grouped in regions comprising a number of tribunal offices and hearing centres, headed by a regional employment judge. Regional employment judges are drawn from the panel of full-time judges, and are appointed by the Lord Chancellor (2013 Regulations, reg 6). In Scotland, the role of Vice President performs the functions of a regional employment judge. As a matter of practice, claims are required to be presented at to a particular employment tribunal office by reference to the postcode of the claimant's place of work. However, that is only a matter of practice, and is not prescribed by either the ETR or any other rule. The regional employment judge has a discretion to transfer a claim between regions for any reason that seems good to the regional employment judge, subject only to any question of the transfer giving rise to injustice: see *Falaye v UK Mission Enterprise Ltd* [2010] UKEAT/0359/10/LA, para 15 (Underhill J).

Administrative matters for the tribunals are the responsibility of the Secretary of Employment **1.53** Tribunals. There is one Secretary for England and Wales and one for Scotland. Each employment tribunal office will have a person who exercises the powers of the Secretary for that office. Administrative support for employment tribunals and the EAT is provided by HM Courts & Tribunals Service, an agency of the Ministry of Justice.

E. REPRESENTATION

Employment tribunals are intended to be less daunting and cheaper for those appearing than are **1.54** the ordinary courts. Ideally, the parties should be able to dispense with legal representation. About

Part A Tribunal Procedure

two-thirds of claimants do appear unrepresented by lawyers. They may, however, receive help with their case from a trade union, law centre, Citizens Advice Bureau, or a friend more articulate than themselves. There are limited restrictions on the range of representation and, indeed, claimants are fully entitled to represent themselves, as frequently happens. Many employers are also tempted to represent themselves, and some human resources managers have acquired considerable expertise in doing so.

1.55 In recent years, tribunals have seen an increase in representation of employers by employment consultants, often as part of employer insurance schemes. Most are not covered by a code of professional conduct. In response to concerns over the highly variable quality of advice and representation being provided, a regulatory framework was introduced by the Compensation (Regulated Claims Management Services) Order 2006, SI 2006/3319, which came into force on 23 April 2007. Those who provide 'claims management services' must obtain authorization from the Regulator; a failure to do so is a criminal offence. There are a number of exemptions to the requirement for regulation: barristers; solicitors; charities; not-for-profit organizations; and independent trade unions provided that they comply with the code of practice for the provision of regulated claims management services by trade unions issued by the Secretary of State on 28 November 2006. Further detail about authorization can be found at https://www.gov.uk/government/groups/claims-management-regulator. Regulated claims managers are governed by the Conduct of Authorised Persons Rules 2013 https://www.gov.uk/guidance/claims-management-company-regulations-guidance-and-legislation.

1.56 For an interesting study on the effect of legal representation in tribunal proceedings, see P L Latreille, J A Latreille, and K G Knight, 'Making a Difference? Legal Representation in Employment Tribunal Cases: Evidence from a Survey of Representatives' (2005) 34 *Industrial Law Journal* 308.

1.57 Most employment judges actively assist an unrepresented party, for example, in cross-examining the witnesses of the other side. Kilner Brown J said in *Mortimer v Reading Windings Ltd* [1977] ICR 511: 'The little man, or the little woman, trying to put a case of grievance, should be given every assistance so that his or her case will have been put and properly considered'.

1.58 The EAT has deprecated representation by a member of management who has been involved in an internal appeal by the claimant employee. Phillips J stated in *Singh v London Country Bus Services Ltd* [1976] IRLR 176, 291:

> It can obviously give rise to misunderstanding if a man who has appeared as a member of an Appeal Board subsequently appears at a tribunal as an advocate, as it were, officially representing the respondent employer. To do so can give rise to misunderstanding, however ill-founded in the mind of the employee. We think that as far as possible such a course should be avoided.

1.59 Ultimately, however, the choice of representative is a matter for the party (subject only to authorization where that representative is a provider of claims management services). A party to proceedings indeed has a statutory right under s 6 of the ETA 1996 to be represented by the representative of his or her choice. In *Bache v Essex County Council* [2000] ICR 313, [2000] IRLR 251 the employment judge purported to 'sack' the claimant's representative on the grounds that he was not conducting the case competently. The Court of Appeal held that the tribunal had no power to do so; the tribunal's power to control the way in which a party conducts its case does not extend to the power to control the choice of representative. Further, in *Douglas v Dispatch Management Services (UK) Ltd* [2002] IRLR 389, the claimant was represented by solicitors who had previously acted for the respondent, and the tribunal held, following *Bache*, that it has no power to dismiss the solicitors from acting as a representative in the proceedings.

1.60 There is no legal aid available for representation in employment tribunals. Section 28 of the Equality Act 2006 gives the Equality and Human Rights Commission the power to give legal assistance to individuals in proceedings relating to the equality enactments. It may choose to offer assistance where a question of principle arises or where it is unreasonable, having regard to the complexity of the case, to expect the individual to deal with the case unaided.

2

Claim Form

SUMMARY

(1) Claims before employment tribunals must be made on prescribed forms.

(2) There are pre-acceptance procedures where a claim form is vetted to ensure that a claimant has supplied the required information.

(3) What has emerged from the EAT in relation to the 2004 Tribunal Rules demonstrates that some flexibility will be permitted and that access to justice remains a major principle outweighing technical or minor defaults. It is presumed that the same approach will continue to apply under the ETR 2013.

A. INTRODUCTION

There is a prescribed claim form that must be used in all cases, ETR 2013, r 8.   **2.01**

The claim form can be obtained online (https://hmctsformfinder.justice.gov.uk/HMCTS/   **2.02**
GetForm.do?original_id=3131) or from any local office of the Employment Tribunals Service. There is also guidance as to how to fill it in. If the form is being completed for multiple claimants the

form ET1A should be used (http://hmctsformfinder.justice.gov.uk/HMCTS/GetForm.do?court_forms_id=3130).

B. REQUIRED INFORMATION

2.03 The required minimum information is set out in ETR 2013, r 10(1)(b) and (c) as:

(a) each claimant's name;
(b) each claimant's address;
(c) the name of each person against whom the claim is made ('the respondent');
(d) each respondent's address; and
(e) an early conciliation number; confirmation that the claim does not institute any relevant proceedings; or confirmation that one of the early conciliation exemptions applies.

2.04 Rule 10(2) states that if the required information is not provided, or the claim is not on the prescribed form, the claim will not be accepted by the tribunal. The form will be returned to the claimant with a notice of rejection explaining the reason for the rejection and information on how to apply for the rejection to be reconsidered.

2.05 A claim shall be rejected if it is in a form which 'cannot sensibly be responded to', r 12(1)(b). It will therefore remain necessary to provide sufficient details to enable a respondent to address the claims brought. Mrs Justice Laing in *Trustees of the William Jones's School Foundation v Parry* [2016] ICR 1140 held that r 12(1)(b) was ultra vires, going beyond the power bestowed on the Secretary of State by s 7 Employment Tribunals Act 1996. The judgment suggests that the only part of r 12 which is authorized by s 7 is r 12(1)(a), which allows for rejection of a claim without a hearing where the tribunal have no jurisdiction. However, the Court of Appeal overturned Laing J and held the rule was not ultra vires (sub nom *Secretary of State for Business, Energy and Industrial Strategy* v *Parry* [2018] EWCA Civ 672). Bean LJ held that rejection of a claim under r 12(1)(b) was not a determination of proceedings under s 7, rather it is a recognition that no valid proceedings have been commenced. A rejection does not go to the substance of the claim or give rise to a cause of action or issue estoppel. Further, the Court of Appeal held that the claim could sensibly be responded to: although the claim form was filed without the background and details that were said to be in an attachment, the claim was for unfair dismissal, and the employer was in a position to file a response stating the reason for dismissal, and asserting the reasonableness of the decision. However, in a more complex case, such as a discrimination claim, a claim form without particulars might properly be rejected.

C. PRESENTATION OF THE CLAIM FORM

2.06 The claim can be presented by hand, post, or online (ETR 2013, r 85(2) and Presidential Practice Direction of 29 July 2013). A claim is presented online when it is successfully submitted online to the Employment Tribunals Service website—that is, it is submitted and accepted there even if it is not then forwarded by the website host to the tribunal office. In *McFadyen and Others v PB Recovery Ltd and Others* UKEATS/0072/08/BI, the Scottish Employment Appeal Tribunal (EAT) held that presenting a claim online is effective only for the tribunal to which the claim is directed and does not amount to effective presentation to all UK tribunals generally. The host server receiving online claims acts as an agent for the tribunal nearest to the address of the respondent provided on the form and it is this tribunal to which the form is submitted. A solicitor's error meant that the claim form was directed to the Bristol tribunal, where it was rejected, rather than the Glasgow tribunal. The EAT held that it was correct to use the date the form was resubmitted to Glasgow when considering if the claims were in time, rather than the date the claim was first presented online.

2.07 If a claim form is sent by post the EAT has stressed that there is a duty on claimants, and those representing them, to ensure that it has been received. In *Capital Foods Retail Ltd v Corrigan*

[1993] IRLR 430, the application was posted well within time but, for some unexplained reason, the tribunal did not receive it; the EAT was critical of the failure by the applicant's solicitor to pursue the tribunal to confirm receipt after a lengthy silence, and held that the application had not been presented and it was not right to extend the time. In *Camden and Islington Community Health Services NHS Trust v Kennedy* [1996] IRLR 351, the EAT stressed that the test laid down in *Corrigan* above is a stringent one. For a solicitor to act reasonably and without fault, there must be a system in place which enables the solicitor to find out contemporaneously whether the conduct of business is taking a normal course and to check, at or near the time, that replies which should have been received at a given date have in fact been received. A competent solicitor practising in this field must be taken to appreciate the vital importance of complying with time limits strictly and having in place a system designed to ensure that such limits are complied with at the time when they are supposed to be being complied with. In *Camden* the employment judge had erred in finding that a system which involved only a check several weeks after the solicitor expected an acknowledgement from the tribunal that the application had been received could be regarded as satisfying the requirement that solicitors should take all reasonable steps to see that an application was timeously presented.

For more on postal claims, see paras 3.49–3.53.   **2.08**

D. ACTIONS ON RECEIPT

On receipt the claim form is date stamped and retained along with the envelope and this is gen-   **2.09**
erally treated as the date of presentation. This can be rebutted, for example by showing that the claim form was posted physically through the tribunal letter box (see *Post Office v Moore* [1981] ICR 623).

E. ACCEPTANCE PROCEDURES

A claim will be rejected where the correct form has not been used or the minimum information   **2.10**
has not been supplied (ETR 2013, r 10) (see para 2.04). A claim shall be rejected if, after consid-
eration by a judge, it is considered that a claim or part thereof is one which the tribunal have no jurisdiction to consider or it is in a form which cannot sensibly be responded to or is otherwise an abuse of process (ETR 2013, r 12). In this context see the comments in 2.05 relating to the operation of r 12(1)(b).

If the judge thinks that further particulars are necessary, they can be ordered.   **2.11**

Claims lodged on or after 29 July 2013 required payment of a fee and a claim form would be   **2.12**
rejected unless it was accompanied by the relevant fee or a remission application. This position changed on 26 July 2017 from which time fees are not charged to claimants bringing employment tribunal claims (see para 2.36).

A claim form presented without compliance with the requirement for early conciliation under   **2.13**
s 18A of the ETA 1996 will be rejected unless it falls within one of the statutory exemptions. Outside the exemptions there is no discretion afforded to an employment judge as the requirement for ACAS early conciliation is absolute and strict (see *Cranwell v Cullen* UKEATPAS/0046/14/SM. See also paras 5.08–5.14). Except that, in the cases of rr 12(e) and 12(f), that is where the claim may be one which institutes relevant proceedings and the name of the claimant or respondent on the claim form is not the same as the name of the prospective claimant or respondent on the early conciliation certificate to which the early conciliation number relates, the Judge has a discretion to accept the claim if they consider that the claimant made a minor error in relation to a name or address and it would not be in the interests of justice to reject the claim (ETR r 12(2A)).

In any circumstance where a claim or part of it is being rejected the form shall be returned to   **2.14**
the claimant together with a notice of rejection giving the judge's reasons. If the claim is rejected

under rr 10 or 12 such notice will include information on how to apply to have the rejection reconsidered r 12(3).

2.15 A claimant whose claim has been rejected in whole or in part under rr 10 or 12 may apply for the rejection to be reconsidered on the basis that either the decision to reject was wrong or the defect can be rectified (ETR 2013, r 13(1)). Such an application must be made in writing within fourteen days of the notice of rejection being sent. The application must explain why the decision is said to be wrong or rectify the defect (ETR 2013, r 13(2)). A claimant may request an oral hearing of the application for reconsideration. Such a request must be made in the application (ETR 2013, r 13(2)). If no oral hearing is requested an Employment Judge will decide the application on paper. An Employment Judge may accept the application in full on paper without the need for an oral hearing, however if a hearing has been requested and the judge is not granting the application on paper, then a hearing will be held attended only by the claimant (ETR 2013, r 13(3)). If the original rejection was correct but the defect has been rectified then the claim is treated as presented on the date that the defect was rectified (ETR 2013, r 13(4)).

2.16 If a claim is accepted the tribunal will:

(a) send a copy of the claim to each respondent and record in writing the date on which it was sent

(b) assign the claim a case number which must from then on be referred to in all correspondence relating to the claim and provide the address to which notices and other communications to the Employment Tribunal Office must be sent, r 85(3)

(c) inform the respondent in writing about how to present a response to the claim, the time limit for doing so, what may happen if a response is not entered within the time limit, including the provision of the prescribed response form, r 15

(d) when any enactment relevant to the claim provides for conciliation, notify the parties that the services of a conciliation officer may be available to them, r 93 and

(e) if only part of the claim has been accepted, inform each respondent whether any part of the claim has been rejected, r 15.

2.17 Where the claim concerns a protected disclosure, the tribunal may also, where it considers it appropriate and with the consent of the claimant, send a copy of the claim, or part of it, to a regulator (ie a person listed in Schedule 1 to the Public Interest Disclosure (Prescribed Persons) Order 1999), r 14.

F. FILLING IN THE CLAIM FORM

2.18 The prescribed form reminds claimants to read the guidance notes and that items marked with an asterisk are mandatory. The sections of the form are described below. When the form is completed and submitted online, the form appears in a series of screens and it is not possible to progress to the next screen until all the required information has been submitted on the present screen. The sections referred to below are not labelled in this way when the form is completed online.

Section 1 'Your details'

2.19 The claimant must provide his or her first name, surname, and address. These are mandatory details. In addition, claimants must give their sex and date of birth, their telephone number, and their preference for communications—post is usually used but email is an option. If an address other than the claimant's home address is to be used for communications, then this should be provided. This can be changed by giving notice to the tribunal and the other parties (ETR 2013, r 86(2)).

Section 2 'Respondent's details' and Section 13 'Details of additional respondents'

2.20 The name and address of the employer, or person against whom relief is sought, is mandatory. The employer's telephone number should also be included and if the claimant worked at a different address from that given for the employer this should be provided along with the postcode. Up to three respondents may be detailed in section 2. Details of additional respondents against whom relief is sought may be provided in section 13. For each respondent it is necessary to provide a valid ACAS early conciliation certificate number. Particular problems may arise where the respondent is an unincorporated association. Although a trade union is an unincorporated association it may sue or be sued in its own name by virtue of statute (see TULR(C)A 1992, s 10(1)(b)). The correct respondent for all other such bodies is the individual officers who have effective control of the organization—usually either the management committee or the chairman and/or secretary (see *Affleck v Newcastle Mind* [1999] IRLR 405).

Where the respondent is a company in administration, tribunal proceedings may only be com- **2.21** menced with the permission of the High Court or the administrator (see *Carr v British International Helicopters Ltd* [1994] ICR 18 and Insolvency Act 1986, schedule B1 para 43(6)). If permission is not given, the proceedings will be stayed until it is obtained. The administrator may also be joined as an interested party but, in some circumstances, he or she may be personally liable because he or she has adopted the employee's contract of employment.

If the respondent is bankrupt the respondent's trustee in bankruptcy will have a clear interest in the **2.22** outcome of the proceedings and would be entitled to apply to be joined as a party. The Secretary of State will also be an interested party (since many payments will be met from the National Insurance Fund: see ERA 1996, s 182). Usually, the tribunal notifies the Department for Business, Enterprise and Regulatory Reform of the claim and asks whether the Secretary of State wishes to be joined.

Section 3 'Multiple cases' and Section 4 'Cases where the respondent was not your employer'

These sections deal with specific claims where further or specific information is required. For mul- **2.23** tiple claims the name of any other claimant is requested to enable the tribunal service to link the claims together. For claims against a non-employer, the type of claim must be specified with details provided later. If the claim form is being used to bring multiple claims, an additional section must be completed—Employment Tribunals—Multiple Claim form.

Section 5 'Employment details' and Section 6 'Earnings and Benefits'

These sections deal with the details concerning the claimant's employment with the re- **2.24** spondent—dates, pay, hours, etc. The information is not mandatory. It also asks about the type of work done by the claimant and whether there was a notice period and, if so, whether it was worked or paid.

Section 7 'If your employment with the respondent has ended, what has happened since?'

This section seeks details of any post-termination employment and earnings. This section is not **2.25** mandatory.

Section 8 'Type and details of claim'

In this section the claimant will set out the substance of the complaint. The case of *Ali v Office* **2.26** *for National Statistics* [2005] IRLR 201 shows the importance of completing claim forms thoroughly, and setting out all potential claims. Mr Ali had made a complaint of race discrimination when his application for employment was rejected by the Office for National Statistics (ONS). He initially succeeded in the tribunal in showing direct discrimination, although he failed in a victimization claim. The ONS appealed to the EAT, and the direct discrimination finding was overturned and the matter remitted to the tribunal. At this stage, Mr Ali sought leave to amend his claim form, to add a complaint of indirect race discrimination, in view of evidence that had come to light during disclosure and cross-examination in the first hearing.

The tribunal said this could be permitted as it was merely adding a different label. The EAT and Court of Appeal disagreed: it was a new claim, direct and indirect discrimination being distinct causes of action. The matter was remitted to the tribunal for consideration of whether it was just and equitable to allow the claim to be presented out of time. The earlier statement in *Quarcoopome v Sock Shop Holdings Ltd* [1995] IRLR 353 that an originating application that makes a claim for race discrimination incorporates any claim for race discrimination, whether direct or indirect, was disapproved.

2.27 The online form limits the contents of this section to seventy lines. For all but the most simple claims, this will not be sufficient room to set out in full the details of the claim. It is therefore appropriate to use a 'rider' and provide the details of claim as an attachment to the form. Attachments are added at the 'additional information' stage of the form. Attachments must be rtf files.

Section 9 'What do you want if your claim is successful?'

2.28 The claimant has an option to complete this section. If she specifies a figure she is asked to explain how that figure has been calculated. Specifying a figure at this stage does not prevent the claimant from later altering the amount claimed. Claimants are invited to use the rtf attachment process if there is insufficient room in this section of the form.

Section 10 'Information to regulators in protected disclosure cases'

2.29 In cases which include a claim of a protected disclosure under the Employment Rights Act 1996 (otherwise known as a whistle-blowing claim) the claimant is given the opportunity to indicate if he wants a copy of the form or the information within it to be forwarded on his behalf to any relevant regulator.

Section 11 'Your representative'

2.30 If the claimant has a representative, his or her name and address should be provided.

Section 12 'Disability'

2.31 This section asks the claimant whether he or she is disabled and what assistance will be required. If more space is needed, then an rtf may be attached in the additional information section.

Section 13 'Details of additional respondents'

2.32 See para 2.20.

Section 14 'Final Check'

2.33 This section asks the claimant to re-read the form, check he or she has entered all the relevant information and confirm that he or she has done so.

Section 15 'Additional information'

2.34 This section is not an opportunity to repeat information already set out in the claim form but it does provide space to address any matter not previously addressed. As set out above, this is the part of the process when the form is completed online, which allows for the attachment of any additional information by way of an rtf file.

Diversity monitoring questionnaire

2.35 This questionnaire is optional.

G. FEES

All claims and appeals lodged on or after 29 July 2013 required the payment of fees pursuant to *The* **2.36**
Employment Tribunals and the Employment Appeal Tribunal Fees Order 2013 (the Fees Order). The
Fees Order was declared to be unlawful, from the date of its introduction, by the Supreme Court
in *R (on the application of UNISON) v Lord Chancellor* [2017] UKSC 51. As a result, fees are not
charged to claimants bringing employment tribunal claims, or to appellants bringing appeals to
the Employment Appeal Tribunal. This has been the position since 26 July 2017, the date of the
judgment in *R (on the application of UNISON).*

H. CLAIMS BROUGHT ON BEHALF OF DECEASED PERSONS

On the death of an employee s 206 of the ERA 1996 provides that, in cases concerning unfair **2.37**
dismissal, redundancy, and other individual employment rights, proceedings can be instituted or
continued by a personal representative of the deceased employee, or where there is no personal
representative, by a person appointed by the tribunal.

Any award made in favour of a deceased employee may be enforced on behalf of his estate by **2.38**
his personal representative or any such person appointed by the tribunal (Employment Tribunals
Awards (Enforcement in Case of Death) Regulations 1976, SI 1976/663, regs 5 and 6).

Although there is no equivalent to s 206 of the ERA 1996 in the discrimination legislation, claims **2.39**
under the Equality Act 2010 can nevertheless be instituted or continued after the death of the
complainant by virtue of s 1(1) of the Law Reform (Miscellaneous Provisions) Act 1934 (see *Harris*
(Personal Representatives of Andrews (deceased)) v Lewisham and Guy's Mental Health NHS Trust
[2000] IRLR 320). A claim of discrimination being in the nature of a statutory tort (see *Sheriff*
v Klyne Tugs (Lowestoft) Ltd [1999] IRLR 481, [1999] ICR 1170) is a cause of action within the
meaning of s 1(1) of the 1934 Act, which will survive for the benefit of the complainant's estate
after death. The court held that there is nothing in the RRA 1976 (nor in the SDA 1975 or DDA
1995) which disapplies that section and precludes existing causes of action from vesting in the
deceased's estate. There is no reason to consider the position under the Equality Act 2010 to be
any different.

I. CLAIMS BY AND AGAINST BANKRUPT AND INSOLVENT PARTIES

A bankrupt is limited in the claims (and appeals) he can pursue, all claims 'for property' vesting in **2.40**
the trustee in bankruptcy. In the case of *Grady v HM Prison Service* [2003] IRLR 474 the Court
of Appeal held that unfair dismissal claims are personal in nature and can be pursued by a bankrupt—a finding influenced by the fact that, when addressing the question of remedy, a tribunal
must consider reinstatement and re-engagement (essentially personal remedies). In *Khan v Trident*
Safeguards Ltd [2004] EWCA Civ 624, [2004] ICR 1591, the Court of Appeal held that if a bankrupt pursuing a discrimination claim limits his claim for relief to a declaration and compensation
for injury to feelings, he is permitted to proceed. This is because the cause of action can be categorized as personal rather than a property claim.

For information about TUPE claims against employers who are in liquidation or administration **2.41**
see para 29.20.

3

Time Limits

SUMMARY

(1) Time limits for bringing claims are a matter of jurisdiction, and a failure to comply may result in a tribunal refusing to entertain a claim.

(2) The first question to consider is the date from when time starts to run; this will depend upon the wording of the specific statute under consideration.

(3) The second question is when the early conciliation process began and when it was completed.

(4) The date of presentation of the complaint is the final matter to consider; care should also be taken not to present a premature application.

(5) If an application is presented late there is normally a discretion to extend the time limit and again this depends upon the provisions of the relevant statute.

A. JURISDICTION

3.01 Time limits are expressed in mandatory terms in the various statutes; s 111 of the ERA 1996, for example, states that a tribunal 'shall not consider' a complaint unless it is presented within the time limit. The Court of Appeal confirmed in *Dedman v British Building & Engineering Appliances Ltd* [1973] IRLR 379 that time limits are a matter of jurisdiction in unfair dismissal claims (see also *Secretary of State for Employment v Atkins Auto Laundries Ltd* [1972] ICR 76). One consequence of this is that the tribunal may raise the question of its own volition, regardless of the parties' views. Secondly, questions of jurisdiction may be raised at any stage, even at the remedies hearing (see *Rogers v Bodfari (Transport) Ltd* [1973] IRLR 172) or, for the first time, on appeal.

B. WHEN TIME STARTS TO RUN—GENERALLY

The most important time limits are three months in the case of unfair dismissal and six months for **3.02** redundancy payments. The table setting out time limits and qualifying periods is at Appendix 6.

When time starts to run from a particular date, the general rule is that this means the whole period **3.03** of 24 hours from midnight to midnight, so that in general no account is taken of fractions of a day (*Trow v Ind Coope (West Midlands) Ltd* [1967] 2 QB 899). Thus, where the effective date of termination is 1 January, time runs from the start of that day and the claim form must be presented not later than midnight on 31 March (that is three months from the effective date of termination in a case of unfair dismissal; a month is defined in Sch 1, para 5 of the Interpretation Act 1978 as a calendar month). Where time runs from 31 January, the month ends on 28 February (or 29 February in a leap year).

Where the statute specifies that a claim must be brought 'beginning with' a date, that date is in- **3.04** cluded in the calculation of time (see *Hammond v Haigh Castle and Co Ltd* [1973] ICR 148); when a claim must be presented 'from', 'after', or 'of' a particular date that date is excluded from the calculation (see *Trow*). There is an exception where time runs from a day where there is no corres- ponding day in the later month, for example, time running from 31 January ends on 30 March (see *Pruden v Cunard Ellerman Ltd* [1993] IRLR 317 and *University of Cambridge v Murray* [1993] ICR 460).

More generally, under s 5 and Sch 1 of the Interpretation Act 1978, a 'month' means a **3.05** calendar month.

Where the last day of a month has no corresponding day in a following month—for example, a **3.06** dismissal on 30 November—then the previous day is to be taken—28 February. Care should be taken with a dismissal on 28 February—the corresponding date is 27 May.

C. SPECIFIC CASES

Unfair dismissal

The ERA 1996 defines the normal time limit of three months in such cases as running from **3.07** the effective date of termination (EDT) (see s 97(1)). In *Gisda CYF v Lauren Barratt* [2010] UKSC 41 the Supreme Court upheld the decision of the ET, EAT, and CA that a letter of dismissal, which had arrived by post at the recipient's address whilst she was away from home, did not become effective until the recipient read the letter. The Supreme Court held that, in a summary dismissal case where termination takes place in writing, the effective date of ter- mination is when the employee is informed of the dismissal, or when the employee has had a reasonable opportunity of discovering that she has been dismissed. They also held that it would be appropriate to include consideration of the behaviour of the employee in assessing whether the employee had had a reasonable opportunity to find out about the dismissal. The same approach was adopted for cases where dismissal was given on notice (*Newcastle Upon Tyne NHS Trust v Haywood* [2018] UKSC 22). Notice begins to run, absent express contrac- tual provision to the contrary, from the date at which notice is received by the employee and the employee has either read or had a reasonable opportunity of reading it. Where dismissal is by notice the effective date is the date of expiry of the notice, however, an exception is per- mitted such that a claimant can present a claim after notice has been given but before the EDT occurred (see ERA 1996, s 111(3)). Further, the time can be extended if it was not reasonably practicable to present in time and the presentation was within a reasonable period thereafter (see also paras 3.54–3.92).

In a constructive dismissal case the claimant may also give notice and present a claim before the **3.08** EDT (see ERA 1996, s 95(1)(c) and *Presley v Llanelli Borough Council* [1979] ICR 419).

3.09 In the case of a fixed term contract, its expiry on its due date is not a termination by notice and therefore an unfair dismissal complaint may only be presented after expiry of the term.

Written particulars and itemized pay

3.10 Claims arising from a failure by the employer to provide statements of employment particulars and itemized pay statements must be brought during employment or within three months of termination (ERA 1996, s 11). The time may be extended if it was not reasonably practicable to present in time and the presentation was within a reasonable period thereafter (see also paras 3.54–3.92).

Discrimination cases

3.11 The time limit for discrimination claims under s 120 of the Equality Act 2010 is three months starting with the date of the act to which the complaint relates (s 123(1)(a)). Extensions are permitted on a 'just and equitable' basis. Commonly, however, claimants rely upon the fact that there was an act extending over a period, in which case time will run from the date of the last act complained of. In the case of service personnel the time limit is six months from the act complained of and they must invoke the applicable Service Redress Procedure before presenting a claim. See Appendix 6 for the particular time limits and extensions permitted.

3.12 Three matters are important when considering discrimination time limits:

(a) An inclusion of a term in a contract that renders the making of the contract an unlawful act extends throughout the duration of the contract.
(b) Acts extending over a period are treated as having been done at the end of the period.
(c) A deliberate omission is treated as made when the person in question decided upon it.

3.13 The leading case on (b) above is *Barclays Bank plc v Kapur* [1991] IRLR 136 (HL), which concerned a term in a pension scheme introduced in 1970 that discriminated against employees whose previous service was in Africa rather than in Europe. The employees were able to bring claims in 1987 because the act extended over the period in question. Similarly, where the employer fails to remedy acts of racial harassment, time runs from the end of the period in which the employer failed to act (see *Littlewoods Organisation plc v Traynor* [1993] IRLR 154).

3.14 Confusion has arisen over the distinction between an act *extending over a period* and the *consequences* of such an act. This distinction was illustrated in a sex discrimination case where a man was promoted to a position over a woman and it was held that, in the absence of a policy of discrimination, the promotion was a single act of discrimination (*Amies v Inner London Education Authority* [1977] 2 All ER 100; see also *Sougrin v Haringey Health Authority* [1992] IRLR 416 and *Owusu v London Fire and Civil Defence Authority* [1995] IRLR 574 where the EAT cautioned against deciding on whether there is a continuing act or a series of single acts as often a succession of specific acts can indicate the existence of a practice: the same point was made by the Court of Appeal in *Hendricks v Commissioner of Police of the Metropolis* [2003] IRLR 96). In *Lyfar v Brighton & Hove University Hospitals Trust* [2006] EWCA Civ 1548, the Court of Appeal approved the practice of dealing with the question of whether acts extend over a period at a preliminary hearing, in general (although it declined to give guidance on the particular circumstances when it would be appropriate and when not). Where there is a factual dispute regarding the various incidents of alleged discrimination a preliminary hearing may not be the appropriate place to address the question since it would involve hearing evidence and making findings on the factual issues, a task better completed by a tribunal at a full hearing.

3.15 In *Owusu*, the EAT ruled that the statutory words 'an act extending over a period' required a 'policy, practice or regime'. In *Hendricks*, the Court of Appeal took a different view. In the words of Mummery LJ, the reference to a 'practice, policy or regime' was merely an example and was not intended to be exhaustive. He said that 'the burden is on (the applicant) to prove, either by direct evidence or by inference from primary facts, that the numerous alleged incidents of discrimination are linked to one another and that they are evidence of a discriminatory state of affairs'. The Court of Appeal in *Lyfar* ruled that the *Hendricks* test was the correct one.

In *Arthur v London Eastern Railway Ltd* [2007] ICR 193, IRLR 58, the Court of Appeal held that **3.16** a tribunal had erred in deciding whether acts were part of a series and therefore whether a claim of being subjected to a detriment for making a protected disclosure was brought in time without hearing any evidence, although stressing that the burden was on the claimant who must show a prima facie case.

In considering whether separate incidents form part of 'an act extending over a period' one relevant **3.17** but not conclusive factor is whether the same individuals or different individuals were involved in those incidents: see *British Medical Association v Chaudhary*, EAT, 24 March 2004 (unreported, UKEAT/1351/01/DA & UKEAT/0804/02DA) at para 208. Where a disciplinary process is ongoing although each stage can be considered separately for assessing complaints of discrimination they will form part of a continuing act for assessing time limits: *Hale v Brighton and Sussex University Hospitals NHS Trust* UKEAT/0342/16/LA.

The mere repetition of a request cannot convert a single managerial decision into a policy. See, **3.18** in particular, *Cast v Croydon College* [1998] ICR 500 in which the Court of Appeal judgment draws an important distinction between a decision which is a fresh consideration and one which is merely a reference back to an earlier determination, the latter falling outside of what constitutes a continuing act.

Where the issue involves a duty to make reasonable adjustments, the duty persists as long as the **3.19** state of affairs giving rise to it pertains. This means that an ongoing refusal to act can amount to a continuing act (*Jobcentre Plus v Jamil* UKEAT/0097/13/BA). Time starts to run from the end of the periods in which the respondent might reasonably have been expected to comply with the duty (s 123(3) and (4) of the Equality Act 2010). This is not the same as assessing when the duty has first been breached. A failure to comply may have begun at an earlier date pursuant to s 20(3): *Abertawe Bro Morgannwg University v Morgan* [2018] EWCA Civ 640.

In *Swithland Motors plc v Clarke* [1994] ICR 231, the EAT considered the time limits for an **3.20** omission to act. Section 76(6)(c) of the SDA 1975 stated that 'a deliberate omission shall be treated as done when the person in question decided upon it' (now found at s 123(3)(b) of the Equality Act 2010). The applicants were not offered new employment when their employer was bought from receivership because, they claimed, the purchaser had a policy of women-only sales staff. They were interviewed by the purchaser and some time later the purchase took place. The EAT held that time ran from the date the purchase took place, not the interviews, because that was the date when the purchasers were in a position to decide whether or not to re-employ the applicants.

In a discriminatory dismissal case time runs from the date of expiry of the notice—not, as one **3.21** might think, from the decision to dismiss. In *Lupetti v Wrens Old House Ltd* [1984] ICR 348, the applicant was given oral notice on 3 February 1983 that his employment would terminate on 28 February 1983. He did not present his claim for race discrimination until 19 May 1983. At the hearing, both parties accepted that the dismissal had taken place on 3 February, and that the complaint was out of time. On appeal, the employee argued that the dismissal in fact took place on the date of termination and not when notice was given. The EAT accepted the employee's argument that the proper date to consider was when the applicant found himself without a job, 28 February, and the application was in time.

There were special rules applying in a case of an appeal against dismissal and the date from which **3.22** time runs. If the contract provides that the employment or the contract continues pending the appeal, then the date on which the unsuccessful appellant is notified of the result is the date from which time runs (*Adekeye v The Post Office (No 2)* [1997] ICR 110). If the contract did not subsist pending the appeal then time runs from the date of dismissal. In *Rhys-Harper v Relaxion Group* [2003] IRLR 484 the House of Lords held that a tribunal does have jurisdiction in such circumstances and s 108 of the Equality Act 2010 provides protection where there is post-termination discrimination or harassment where that arises 'out of and is closely connected to a former employment relationship' (there was initially some doubt but see *Onu v Akwiku* [2013] IRLR 523).

3.23   Where the claim is based on a failure to promote an applicant, the tribunal looks to when the cause of action crystallized, not when the applicant felt that he was discriminated against (see *Clarke v Hampshire Electro-Plating Co Ltd* [1991] IRLR 490, where the EAT held that when an action crystallizes is a question of fact for the tribunal to find).

Interim relief

3.24   There is a short time limit in these cases because of the nature of the relief involved. The claim may be made involving trade union activity or membership cases, health and safety, protected disclosures, and the protected activities of employee representatives. Claims must be brought at any time up to seven days *immediately following* the EDT (for example, dismissal on Monday requires presentation the following Monday: ERA 1996, s 128). There is no discretion to extend time for the interim relief application in such claims.

Equal pay

3.25   In a standard case, claims for breach of an equality clause under the Equality Act 2010 should be brought during the existence of the contract or within six months of the employee leaving employment (see s 129(3)). The relevant consideration is neither the end of the job nor the employee leaving the employer but the end of the contract in respect of which the equality clause has been breached. *National Power v Young* [2001] IRLR 328 is authority for the proposition that time does not run from the end of a particular job, the tribunal having found (or proceeded on the assumption) that the claimant was employed under the same contract throughout each job change.

3.26   In addition to a standard case, there are three categories in which the normal six-month time limit is modified (s 129(3)). They are:

(a)   a case in which there is 'concealment'
(b)   an incapacity case and
(c)   a 'stable employment case'.

3.27   In order for the employee to rely upon the 'concealment' provisions, the employer must have deliberately concealed a fact which is relevant to the breach of the Act and without knowledge of which the worker could not reasonably have been expected to bring the proceedings, and that the worker did not discover (or could not with reasonable diligence have discovered) that fact until after the relevant day. There is thus a causative link that must be established as the worker must also show that, without knowledge of that fact, the proceedings could not have been commenced and the fact was not discovered until after the last day on which the worker was employed or the day on which the worker's 'stable employment relationship' ended (see further below).

3.28   If there has been concealment the claim must be presented within six months of the date on which the fact was discovered or could have been discovered using reasonable diligence.

3.29   An 'incapacity case' is one where the worker is not disabled under the Equality Act 2010 but where they were a minor or of unsound mind at any time during the six months after the date on which they ceased to be employed, their stable employment relationship ended, they discovered the concealed fact, or could have discovered it with reasonable diligence if that date was later than the last day of employment.

3.30   The time limit is then six months from that day after the day they ceased to be under an incapacity.

3.31   A 'standard case' is a case which is not one of the other types and proceedings must be brought within six months of the last date of employment.

3.32   Special rules apply where a worker is engaged on a series of fixed term contracts in a stable relationship. When a stable relationship arises depends in part upon the intention of the parties, but the features that characterize a 'stable employment relationship' are that there is a succession of short-term contracts, meaning three or more contracts for an academic year or shorter; concluded at regular intervals, in that they are clearly predictable and can be calculated precisely, or where the employee is called upon frequently whenever a need arises; relating to the same employment; and to which the same pension scheme applies. In such circumstances the termination of each of the contracts does not trigger the obligation to lodge a claim—only termination of the final contract does so (see *Preston v Wolverhampton NHS Trust (No 2)* [2001] IRLR 237). The point was specifically considered in *Slack v Cumbria County Council* [2009] IRLR 463, where the Court of Appeal was concerned with equal pay claims where women had worked under a series of contracts with the same local authority employer. Over the years the contents of their contracts had varied, and conditions had changed. The Council argued that the original contracts had terminated and been replaced by new contracts, and any arrears payable under the equal pay claim were limited to the period covered by the final contract. The Court of Appeal accepted that there was a 'stable employment relationship' where the same work continued to be done under a series of successive contracts, and where the only difference between contracts was a reduction in working hours. Where there were other changes of a more substantial nature, affecting the nature of the work done and other conditions of employment (such as the acquiring of a new right to sick pay), the question whether there was such a relationship was a matter of fact, to be decided by the tribunal.

Redundancy

Under s 164(1) of the ERA 1996, in a redundancy case the employee must show that within six months from the date of termination: **3.33**

(a) the redundancy payment has been agreed and paid
(b) a claim for the payment has been made in writing to the employer
(c) a question as to the right to the payment or the amount of it has been referred to an employment tribunal or
(d) a complaint of unfair dismissal has been made to an employment tribunal.

This means that, where the employer accepts the employee's right to a redundancy payment but disputes its amount, the employee is protected provided he has submitted a written claim for the payment within six months. The employee may then actually submit an application to a tribunal to settle any argument about the actual amount at any time (see *Bentley Engineering Co Ltd v Crown and Miller* [1976] ICR 225). This is satisfied by a letter provided it is clear that what is sought is a redundancy payment (see *Price v Smithfield & Zwanenburg Group Ltd* [1978] ICR 93). **3.34**

Section 164 goes on to provide that if the employee fails to take any of the steps within the initial six months, provided the employee refers a redundancy claim or makes a complaint of unfair dismissal to the tribunal within the *next* six months, the tribunal has a discretion to award a redundancy payment if it is just and equitable having regard to the reason shown by the employee for his failure to take one of the prescribed steps and all the other relevant circumstances. There is no discretion to extend time for taking the necessary steps beyond the second six months period, so any application even a day late will be out of time (*Secretary of State for Employment v Banks* [1983] ICR 48). **3.35**

Deduction of wages claims ERA 1996, s 23

In claims under s 23 of the ERA 1996 for deductions of wages, the time limit of three months commences from the date of payment of wages from which the deduction was made or the date on which the payment was received by the employee. Where there has been a series of deductions, time runs from the date the last deduction could have been made in accordance with the contract, and the entire series is recoverable (see *Group 4 Nightspeed v Gilbert* [1997] IRLR 398). **3.36**

Further, the time can be extended if it was not reasonably practicable to present in time and the presentation was within a reasonable period thereafter (see also paras 3.54–3.92). **3.37**

Other claims

Time runs from the date the act complained of was done in trade union and health and safety discrimination cases (TULR(C)A 1992, ss 66(2), 68A(1), 139(1), 147, and 175 and ERA 1996, ss 48–49). **3.38**

The time period is three months with the usual extension if it was not reasonably practicable to present in time and the presentation was within a reasonable period thereafter (see also paras 3.54–3.92).

European claims

3.39 Time limits under European claims are dealt with in Chapter 22.

D. ACAS EARLY CONCILIATION PROCESS

3.40 Since 6 May 2014 it has been compulsory to comply with early conciliation processes through ACAS (see further paras 5.08–5.14). Section 292A of the TULR(C)A provides for an automatic extension of the time limits for bringing a claim by effectively stopping the clock during the ACAS early conciliation process. The time period between the day on which the prospective claimant complies with the requirement to contact ACAS in the prescribed manner and the issuing of the certificate by ACAS is not counted in the calculation of any time limit. Section 207B of the ERA 1996 provides the formula for calculating how the extension of time operates. Two days are identified by the formula: day A is the day that the claimant contacts ACAS; day B is the day on which the claimant receives or, if earlier, is treated as receiving the certificate from ACAS. Once these two dates have been identified the usual time limits for the claims must be considered. If a time limit would expire during the period beginning with day A and ending one month after day B, the time limit expires not on the original date but one month after day B. In calculating the period ending one month after day B, a month is a calendar month and the corresponding date rule approved by the House of Lords in *Dodds v Walker* [1981] 1 WLR 1027 (HL) applies (see *Tanveer v East London Bus and Coach Company* UKEAT/0022/16/RN). This means that if day B is 30 June, then the period ending one month after day B is 30 July. If the extension applies, the claim must be presented by 30 July.

3.41 There was initially some ambiguity over whether, where s 207B(4) applies, it displaces s 207B(3), that is, whether the time limit referred to in s 207B(4) is the expiry of the original limitation date or the expiry of the limitation date as extended by s 207B(3). The EAT has now confirmed, in the case of *Luton Borough Council v Mr M Haque* UKEAT/0180/17/JOJ, that these sections are to be applied sequentially and not as alternatives. A claimant will therefore always get the benefit of the extension under s 207B(3) of the ERA. If such extended expiry date falls within the period specified in s 207B(4) of the ERA, he or she will also get the benefit of an extension under that section.

3.42 Where early conciliation is started before the time limit begins to run (e.g. before dismissal), only that part of the early conciliation period which falls after the time limit begins to run will count towards an extension of time under s 207B(3)—the limitation 'clock' cannot be stopped if it has not yet started: *Commissioners for HM Revenue and Customs Commissioners v Serra Garau* [2017] ICR 1121.

3.43 A second period of early conciliation, resulting in a second early conciliation certificate will have no bearing on the limitation date for presentation of the claim: see *Serra Garau* (cited above) and *Treska v Master and Fellows of University College Oxford* UKEAT/0197/16/JOJ.

E. PRESENTATION OF COMPLAINT: SPECIFIC PROBLEMS

Expiry of time outside office hours

3.44 Claims can now be made online at any time at https://employmenttribunals.service.gov.uk/apply.

3.45 The 'ordinary course of email', without any contrary indication that an email message has not been sent, is to expect delivery within a reasonable time thereafter, perhaps half an hour up to an hour (see *Initial Electronic Security Systems Ltd v Avdic* [2005] IRLR 671).

With the increased use of the online claim system or email submission issues over office hours **3.46** arise less frequently. Nevertheless, for applications being submitted by hand the following analysis remains relevant.

The expiry date for an application may be a day on which the tribunal offices are closed, because **3.47** it falls at the weekend or on a statutory holiday. The decisions of *Post Office v Moore* [1981] ICR 623 and *Hetton Victory Club v Swainston* [1983] ICR 139 shed some light on the problem. In *Swainston*, the Regional Office of Employment Tribunals (ROET) in Manchester was closed on a Sunday, which was the last day on which the applicant was entitled to present his claim for unfair dismissal and he therefore presented his complaint on the Monday. The EAT considered that an application was 'presented' when placed in the letter box or dealt with in some other way which was held out by the ROET as a means whereby it will receive communications.

The EAT held that the application was presented in time but the Court of Appeal disagreed, **3.48** deciding that the three-month time limit expired at midnight on the last day of the period even where that was not a working day. For the purposes of the rules, 'presentation' was complete when the application was put through the letter box, which the applicant could easily have done. The case of *Pritam Kaur v Russell & Sons* [1973] 1 QB 336 was distinguished on the grounds that, although in the High Court a writ that does not arrive on a working day, which is required as it must be issued by the court staff, receives an automatic extension to the next working day, 'presentation' does not require any action on the part of the body to whom the presentation is made. A submission that there would be injustice if the ROET did not have a letter box was dealt with by Waller J, who suggested that the applicant in such a case 'might be able to show that it was not reasonably practicable for him to present the complaint within the relevant period' (see further paras 3.54– 3.92). The Court of Appeal's judgment leaves a question mark over when an applicant can rely on the automatic extension and when he must argue that it was not reasonably practicable to present a complaint in time. The Court of Appeal was silent as to which rule would apply where there was no post box at the tribunal. This is perhaps resolved in *Ford v Stakis Hotels & Inns Ltd* [1988] IRLR 46, where the originating application was pushed under the door of the Cardiff ROET, which had no letter box, on a bank holiday which was the last day for presenting the complaint. The EAT decided that, in this case, time was automatically extended to the next day.

In *Lang v Devon General Ltd* [1987] ICR 4, there was evidence of a special arrangement between **3.49** the ROET and the Post Office, whereby post received for delivery on a Saturday would be kept until the Monday. The EAT held that the Post Office was thus made a bailee of the mail, and a letter which was actually received at the ROET on Monday could be treated as if received on the Saturday.

Premature applications

The Act requires 'termination' and so an application anticipating non-renewal of a fixed term con- **3.50** tract will be premature (see *Throsby v Imperial College of Science & Technology* [1977] IRLR 337). Where the application is made after notice of termination has been given, the fact that the employer subsequently summarily dismisses does not deprive the tribunal of jurisdiction (see *Patel v Nagesan* [1995] IRLR 370). See paras 3.07 and 3.08 dealing with applications following dismissal on notice, prior to the expiry of notice and the effective date of termination.

There is no equivalent for redundancy payment claims which must be made after the notice expires **3.51** (*Watts v Rubery Owen Conveyancer Ltd* [1977] IRLR 112). In *Banking Insurance and Finance Union v Barclays Bank plc* [1987] IRLR 495 the EAT held that it was not premature to bring a claim for failure to consult under reg 10 of the TUPE Regulations 1981, before the transfer had taken place.

Delays in the post

In *St Basil's Centre v McCrossan* [1992] ICR 140 it was suggested that the High Court procedure **3.52** as set out in CPR, r 6.7 (which provides that a first class letter takes two working days to arrive after posting—Saturdays, Sundays, bank holidays, Christmas Day, and Good Friday are excluded from this computation) should be applied in the tribunal. In *Metcalfe v Cygnet Healthcare* [2002] 3 All ER 801 the claimant's solicitors posted a letter on a Thursday in circumstances where the time limit was due to expire on Saturday at midnight and it was received by the tribunal on a Monday. The EAT held that applying the postal rule the letter was deemed delivered on the Saturday as that was a posting day. The approach in *St Basil's* was approved by the Court of Appeal in the case of *Consignia plc v Sealy* [2002] EWCA Civ 878, [2002] ICR 1193, where Brooke LJ set out (at para 31) the following guidance:

(1) Section 111(2) of the Employment Rights Act 1996 speaks of 'presenting' a complaint to a tribunal. It is now well established that a complaint is 'presented' when it arrives at the Central Office of Employment Tribunals or an Office of the tribunals (Office).

(2) If a complainant or his/her agent proves that it was impossible to present a complaint in this way before the end of the time prescribed by s 111(2)(a)—for example because the Office was found to be locked at a weekend and it did not have a letter-box—then it will be possible to argue that it was not reasonably practicable for the complaint to be presented within the prescribed period.

(3) If a complainant chooses to present a complaint by sending it by post, presentation will be assumed to have been effected, unless the contrary is proved, at the time when the letter would be delivered in the ordinary course of post (see, by analogy, s 7 of the Interpretation Act 1978).

(4) If the letter is sent by first class post, it is now legitimate to adapt the approach contained in CPR 6.7 and conclude that in the ordinary course of post it will be delivered on the second day after it was posted (excluding Sundays, bank holidays, Christmas Day, and Good Friday, being days when post is not normally delivered).

(5) If the letter does not arrive at the time when it would be expected to arrive in the ordinary course of post, but is unexpectedly delayed, a tribunal may conclude that it was not reasonably practicable for the complaint to be presented within the prescribed period.

(6) If a form is date-stamped on a Monday by a Tribunal Office so as to be outside a three-month period which ends on the Saturday or Sunday, it will be open to a tribunal to find as a fact that it was posted by first class post not later than the Thursday and arrived on the Saturday, alternatively to extend time as a matter of discretion if satisfied that the letter was posted by first class post not later than the Thursday.

(7) This regime does not allow for any unusual subjective expectation, whether based on inside knowledge of the postal system or on lay experience of what happens in practice, to the effect that a letter posted by first class post may arrive earlier than the second day (excluding Sundays etc: see (4) above) after it is posted. The 'normal and expected' result of posting a letter must be objectively, not subjectively, assessed and it is that the letter will arrive at its destination in the *ordinary* course of post. As the present case shows, a complainant knows that he/she is taking a risk if the complaint is posted by first class post on the day before the guillotine falls, and it would be absurd to hold that it was not reasonably practicable for it to be presented in time if it arrives in the ordinary course of post on the second day after it was posted. Nothing unexpected will have occurred. The post will have taken its usual course.

3.53 In *Initial Electronic Security Systems Ltd v Avdic* [2005] IRLR 671 and *Metcalfe* (cited above), the EAT reiterated that *Consignia* should be relied upon as establishing the test of objective reasonable expectation of a claimant sending his claim form to the ET: it does not impose an obligation to prove an 'unforeseen circumstance'. Only if the '*Consignia* escape route' is established, however, is a claimant free from justifying his or her delay during the three-month period.

3.54 Guidance on whether it is reasonable to rely on next day posting was given in *Beanstalk Shelving Ltd v Horn* [1980] ICR 273, where evidence that a letter posted first class from Liverpool could be expected to arrive in London the next day was heard, but it was also stated that 'it is an extremely dangerous practice for applicants to industrial tribunals to leave the posting of their application until the penultimate day' (see also *Sturges v AE Farr Ltd* [1975] ICR 356, where it was stressed that the tribunal will want to know the exact date and time when the application was posted).

A different issue arose in *Capital Foods Retail Ltd v Corrigan* [1993] IRLR 430, where the applica- **3.55** tion was posted well within time but, for some unexplained reason, the tribunal did not receive it. The EAT was critical of the failure by the applicant's solicitors to pursue the tribunal to confirm receipt after a lengthy silence and held that the application had not been presented and it was not right to extend the time (see also *Camden and Islington Community Health Services NHS Trust v Kennedy* [1996] IRLR 351).

For claims presented through the Employment Tribunals Service website, an application is pre- **3.56** sented when it was successfully submitted online and accepted by the website (see *Tyne & Wear Autistic Society v Smith* [2005] ICR 663).

F. EXTENSIONS

Not reasonably practicable

Many time limits allow the applicant an extension for a further period which the tribunal considers **3.57** 'reasonable in a case where it is satisfied that it was not reasonably practicable for a complaint to be presented before the end of the period' (ERA 1996, s 111(2)(b)). This applies to unfair dismissal and most other employment protection rights. The different provisions of the Equality Act 2010 are considered separately below.

The statutory test can be reduced to two distinct questions: **3.58**

(a) was it reasonably practicable to present the complaint in time, and
(b) if it was not, did the applicant bring the complaint within a further reasonable period?

It is for the claimant to prove that it was not reasonably practicable to bring the claim in time and **3.59** it is a question of fact for the tribunal to decide. The EAT and the Court of Appeal are reluctant to interfere with such a decision (see *Wall's Meat Co Ltd v Khan* [1979] ICR 52; *Riley v Tesco Stores Ltd* [1980] IRLR 103; and *Palmer and Saunders v Southend-on-Sea Borough Council* [1984] IRLR 119).

The question of practicability has been described as being whether something can be done (see **3.60** *Singh v Post Office* [1973] ICR 437). Lord Denning MR in the Court of Appeal, in *Dedman v British Building and Engineering Appliances Ltd* [1974] ICR 53 (at 61) considered practicability and stated that:

> if in the circumstances the man knew or was put on enquiry as to his rights, and as to the time limit then it was practicable for him to have presented his complaint within the [time limit] and he ought to have done so. But if he did not know and there was nothing to put him on enquiry, then it was not practicable and he should be excused If a man engages skilled advisers to act for him and they mistake the limit and present it too late—he is out. His remedy is against them.

More general consideration was given in *Palmer and Saunders v Southend-on-Sea Borough Council* **3.61** (cited above), where May LJ stated (at 125):

> to construe the words 'reasonably practicable' as the equivalent of reasonable is to take a view too favour-able to the employee. On the other hand 'reasonably practicable' means more than what is reasonably capable physically of being done in the context in which the words are used in the 1978 Consolidation Act, however inaptly as we think, they mean something between the two. Perhaps to read the word 'practicable' as the equivalent of 'feasible' and to ask colloquially and untrammelled by too much legal logic—was it reasonably feasible to present the complaint to the industrial tribunal within the relevant 3 months?—is the best approach to the correct application of the relevant subsection.

A number of factors were set out, although May LJ emphasized that they could not be exhaustive, **3.62** but should form a useful starting point, and the tribunal should consider, amongst other things:

(a) the manner in which, and the reason for which, the employee was dismissed, including any internal 'conciliatory appeals procedure'
(b) the substantial cause of the employee's failure to comply with the statutory time limit
(c) whether he knew he had the right to complain that he had been unfairly dismissed

(d) whether there had been any 'misrepresentation' about any relevant matter by the employer to the employee

(e) whether the employee was advised at any material time and, if so, by whom; the extent of the adviser's knowledge of the facts of the case and the advice given to the employee.

3.63 Other factors to be considered were suggested in *Wall's Meat* by Brandon LJ, where (at 60) he gave the following guidance:

> the performance of an act, in this case the presentation of a complaint, is not reasonably practicable if there is some impediment which reasonably prevents, or interferes with, or inhibits such performance. The impediment may be physical, for instance the illness of the complainant or a postal strike; or the impediment may be mental, namely, the state of mind of the complainant in the form of ignorance of, or mistaken belief with regard to essential matters. Such states of mind can, however, only be regarded as impediments making it not reasonably practicable to present a complaint within the period of three months, if the ignorance on the one hand, or the mistaken belief on the other, is itself reasonable. Either state of mind will, further, not be reasonable if it arises from the fault of his solicitors or other professional advisers in not giving him such information as they should reasonably in all the circumstances have given him ([1979] ICR 52, 60–61).

3.64 The EAT will rarely interfere with a tribunal's decision on reasonable practicability; however, it will do so where the tribunal has reached a decision that can be categorized as perverse (see *Birmingham Optical Group plc v Johnson* [1995] ICR 459, where the EAT reversed a tribunal decision that it was not reasonably practicable to submit an application because of ongoing commercial relations between the parties). We now consider in turn the factors set out by May LJ (see para 3.59).

The manner in which, and the reason for which, the employee was dismissed, including any internal 'conciliatory appeals procedure'

3.65 One frequently encountered explanation for delay is that internal disciplinary proceedings arising out of the dismissal were pending at the same time, and these often take several weeks or months to resolve. Tribunals have rejected the argument that the pursuit of such remedies generally post-pones the effective date of termination until their conclusion (*Savage v J Sainsbury plc* [1980] IRLR 109). In the absence of a delayed starting point, applicants have sought to use the extension of time discretion in those circumstances. In *Crown Agents for Overseas Governments and Administration v Lawal* [1979] ICR 103, Kilner Brown J said (at 109):

> Merely as a statement of general principle, it would seem to us that in cases where a person is going through a conciliation process or is taking up a domestic appeals procedure whether it be for discipline or whether it be for medical purposes that common sense would indicate that while he is going through something which involves him and his employer directly he should be able to say it was not reasonably practicable for me to lodge any application within three months.

3.66 This view has not, however, commanded universal acceptance. In *Bodha (Vishnudut) v Hampshire Area Health Authority* [1982] ICR 200, Browne-Wilkinson J reminded tribunals that the stat-utes set out the tests and they require the tribunal to have regard to what could be done, albeit approaching what is practicable in a common-sense way. The statutory tests are not satisfied just because it was reasonable not to do what could be done. The phrase 'reasonably practicable' means reasonably capable of being done:

> there may be cases where the special facts (additional to the bare fact that there is an internal appeal pending) may persuade an industrial tribunal, as a question of fact, that it was not reasonably practicable to complain to the industrial tribunal within the time limit. But we do not think that the mere fact of the pending appeal by itself, is sufficient to justify a finding of fact that it was not 'reasonably practicable' to present a complaint to the industrial tribunal ([1982] ICR 200, 205).

3.67 In that case it was held that it was reasonably practicable to present a complaint within the time limit, notwithstanding the internal appeals procedure. In *Palmer and Saunders*, the applicants were charged in 1980 with theft of fuel from Southend Airport, where they worked. They were imme-diately suspended on half-pay, and the letter stated that 'in the event that you are adjudged to be not blameworthy, your suspension will be lifted and you will be entitled to reimbursement of lost pay. On the other hand, a conviction by a court will establish gross misconduct which could lead to instant dismissal'. The two applicants were convicted of theft in April 1981 and their employment was summarily terminated. On 22 April 1981, their internal appeals were rejected but they were told that, if their criminal appeal succeeded, the employers would reconsider their positions. In December 1981, the Court of Appeal quashed the convictions but the employers refused to reinstate them. On 28 April, a year after the dismissal but only days after the successful appeal, the applicants presented their complaints to a tribunal. The tribunal, which was upheld by the EAT and the Court of Appeal, decided that it was reasonably practicable to have presented the complaints in time. The applicants' argument that they acted reasonably in waiting for the internal procedures to be exhausted was rejected by the tribunal, since they could have presented the complaints in time and postponed the tribunal hearing until the resolution of the criminal proceedings (it should be noted that the continuation of civil proceedings is also not usually relevant for similar reasons). The case must be distinguished from the situation in which the employer specifically requests the employee to refrain from making a tribunal application because there are ongoing negotiations (see *Owen v Crown House Engineering Ltd* [1973] ICR 511; contrast with *Times Newspapers Ltd v O'Regan* [1977] IRLR 101; and *Ruff v Smith* [1976] ICR 118), where the tribunal will nearly always grant extra time.

3.68 Problems have arisen in relation to the terms of disciplinary procedures. The fact that a procedure provides that a successful appellant will be reinstated with back-pay does not assist the unsuccessful appellant and the EDT remains the original date when termination becomes effective. In *Savage v J Sainsbury plc* the procedure stated that the employee was suspended pending appeal and would be reinstated with full back-pay if successful. Where the applicant was summarily dismissed, this did not keep the employment relationship alive until the date on which the appeal was refused because it was only if the appeal was successful that the employee was reinstated with back-pay in which case the earlier time limit applied. While several cases have held that, in the absence of a suspensory provision in the procedure an agreement in advance can remedy the problem (see, e.g., *Booth v USA* [1999] IRLR 16), in *London Probation Board v Kirkpatrick* [2005] IRLR 443 the EAT held that it is not necessary as a term can be implied and also that it is possible to have a retrospective agreement.

3.69 *John Lewis Partnership v Charman* [2011] UKEAT/0079/11/2403 restated the proposition that it may not be 'reasonably practicable' for an unfair dismissal claim to be presented within the time limit, if an employee is reasonably ignorant of the time limit prior to receiving the outcome of an internal appeal against dismissal and presents the claim within a reasonable period after the primary period for presentation has elapsed. The EAT reiterated that whether it is reasonably practicable for a claim to be brought within time is normally a question of fact for an employment tribunal and that a decision will only be overturned if it is found to be perverse.

The substantial cause of the employee's failure to comply with the statutory time limit

3.70 This means that the tribunal must examine the reasons proffered by the employee and must decide whether the delay was outside the applicant's control. Postal delays are commented upon above. Physical impediment, such as serious illness or absence abroad, will be relevant, as will the fact that the applicant was serving a prison sentence during some or all of the three-month period. In *Schultz v Esso Petroleum Ltd* [1999] IRLR 488 the Court of Appeal had to consider a case in which the claimant had been ill with depression towards the end of the time limit. The Court of Appeal held that, while there was a seven-week period at the start when the claimant could have presented his claim, it was not fair to give this the same weight as the later period and, accordingly, it had not been reasonably practicable to lodge the claim in time. In *Imperial Tobacco v Wright* [2005] All ER (D) 325 (Jul) an employee was incapable of lodging his claim in time owing to a relapse into drug abuse following his dismissal. The EAT accepted that a tribunal had correctly equated this with *Esso* (the employer on appeal wished to argue that, given that it is a criminal offence to be in possession of a controlled drug, and it is a general principle of common law that a party may not rely on his own wrong to secure a benefit, it would be wrong to allow the employee to rely on his drug use to excuse his late claim, but whilst it was arguable this had not been raised). On the other hand, in *Agrico v Ireland* EAT 0024/05, where a solicitor had left issuing an unfair dismissal claim to the last few days of the limitation period, his secretary's unexpected illness was not sufficient reason for the claim to be accepted a day late. An employment judge decided to accept the claim on the basis that it had not been reasonably practicable for the complaint to be presented in time. Given that there would have been nothing wrong with the application being presented on the last day, the judge focused on the last few days of the three-month period. He concluded that, in those days the solicitor had done everything he could by leaving the matter with his experienced secretary. The failure to present the claim in time arose from the secretary's unforeseen illness. On the employer's appeal, the EAT concluded that the judge had been wrong to focus entirely on the last three days of the three-month period. He had failed to take account of the fact that, although there is nothing wrong with a claim being presented on the last day of that period, a firm runs serious risks if it deliberately files claims so late. A competent solicitor must be taken to have appreciated the vital importance of complying with time limits strictly. To show that he or she acted reasonably, a solicitor must have a rather better system for ensuring that claims were issued in time when he or she was away from the office than simply relying on a secretary.

3.71 As there had been no evidence as to why the secretary had failed to contact the office to instruct someone else to issue the claim form there was no real evidence as to whether the solicitor's firm, as opposed to the individual solicitor, had done everything it could in the circumstances.

3.72 In *Churchill v A Yeates & Son Ltd* [1983] ICR 380, the applicant presented his claim for unfair dismissal after hearing that his previous job had apparently been filled, thus nullifying the employer's claim that he was redundant. The EAT held that it might not be reasonably practicable to bring a complaint of unfair dismissal until he had knowledge of a fundamental fact which rendered the dismissal unfair. It is irrelevant that the employee could have brought a claim on another ground of unfairness. The case was remitted to a tribunal to decide whether the applicant could 'demonstrate that until he was aware of the possibility of challenging the reason for dismissal given by the employers he reasonably took the view that he had no reasonable grounds to complain of unfair dismissal' (contrast this with *Borland v Independent Vegetable Processors Ltd* (CA, 9 December 1982), where, on similar facts, it was held that the employee did not make inquiries as to the situation at the company and ignorance of the true facts in those circumstances was not reasonable). See also *Cambridge & Peterborough NHS Trust v Crouchman* EAT 8/5/09, where the EAT held that it had not been reasonably practicable for a claimant to present an unfair dismissal claim within the time limit prescribed by the Employment Rights Act 1996, s 111(2), where written reasons for the dismissal of his internal appeal, delivered after the expiry of the time limit, differed from oral reasons delivered before the expiry of the time limit, such that they disclosed crucial facts making him reasonably and genuinely believe that he had grounds to pursue a claim.

Whether he knew that he had the right to complain that he had been unfairly dismissed

3.73 The mistaken belief or ignorance of an applicant as to his rights must be reasonable in order to support the claim that it was not reasonably practicable to present the application in time. The employee may be ignorant as to the existence of the right, the way to exercise it, or the time limit. In each case, that ignorance must be reasonable. A good illustration is the fact that an employee who knows of the right but not of the time limit will not be reasonable since he should be put on notice about claiming those rights (*W Press & Son Ltd v Hall* [1974] ICR 21; *Avon County Council v Haywood-Hicks* [1978] ICR 646; *House of Clydesdale Ltd v Foy* [1976] IRLR 391; and also *Trevelyans Ltd v Norton* [1991] ICR 488).

3.74 In *Dedman* (para 3.01), the Court of Appeal set out some of the relevant questions that tribunals might ask when considering a claim that the employee was ignorant as to his rights:

(a) what opportunities did the applicant have for finding out about his rights
(b) did he take them or
(c) was he misled or deceived (clearly this overlaps, to a degree, with item (d) of the *Palmer* guidance, considered at para 3.59).

3.75 In *Porter v Bandridge* [1978] ICR 943, the Court of Appeal stressed that pure and simple ignorance is not enough. The real issue is that the applicant ought to have known and tribunals will, in general, be reluctant to accept a claim that intelligent and well-educated individuals are unaware of their rights or that such ignorance is reasonable (as in the *Avon* case above). In some cases, the fact that an applicant had poor English is relevant but not decisive to this question (*Bhatt v Pioneer Plastic Containers Ltd* EAT/108/90).

It is important to distinguish between ignorance of the law and ignorance of material facts (as in the *Churchill* case, see para 3.72). In *Machine Tool Industry Research Association v Simpson* [1988] ICR 558, Simpson discovered that someone else was doing her former job shortly before the expiry of the unfair dismissal time limit, at which point she thought she might not have been dismissed for redundancy. The Court of Appeal upheld her claim that it had not been reasonably practicable to bring the claim in time and that the employee's subjective belief was the focus of the inquiry. Applicants in those sorts of cases must demonstrate three things: **3.76**

(1) It was not reasonable to expect the applicant to have been aware of the factual basis upon which a claim or complaint could have been brought during the time limit.
(2) The applicant gained the knowledge thereafter reasonably and it was crucial, fundamental, or important to the change in the applicant's belief that he now did have grounds for applying to a tribunal.
(3) The belief that there are grounds for an application must be reasonable and genuinely held.

This has been followed in *James W Cook & Co (Wivenhoe) Ltd v Tipper* [1990] IRLR 386 and by Mummery J in *Marley (UK) Ltd v Anderson* [1994] IRLR 152 (affirmed [1996] IRLR 163). After his redundancy, Anderson discovered that his former post still existed and that he had been dismissed for his work performance. The EAT accepted that these facts were capable of providing independent grounds justifying the late presentation of the application and that the applicant does not have to demonstrate the *truth* of the facts that cause him to change his mind. **3.77**

The analysis where an applicant is unaware of the right to make a claim is slightly different. The applicant in *Biggs v Somerset County Council* [1996] IRLR 203 was a part-time teacher who was dismissed in 1976. In 1994, the House of Lords declared that the restriction on part-time employees claiming unfair dismissal was contrary to EC law. Mrs Biggs brought her claim within three months of the House of Lords' judgment. However, her claim was dismissed on the basis that she could and should have sought to challenge the law in 1976 and it was not possible to claim that the law was only recently clarified as this would seriously undermine the principle of legal certainty. *Biggs* was a case involving the 'reasonably practicable' test and a slightly different approach was adopted in *British Coal Corporation v Keeble* [1997] IRLR 336, which dealt with the just and equitable extension. The EAT in that case held that the discretion applying the 'just and equitable' test is wide and comparable to that under s 33 of the Limitation Act 1980 and the court can consider prejudice to the parties, the length of any delay, and the excuse advanced for it, as well as the fact that, as a result of a change in the law, the applicant has a 'new' right. Each of these factors must be considered in turn by the tribunal. **3.78**

Whether there had been any 'misrepresentation' about any relevant matter by the employer to the employee

The facts of *Marley* are a good example of such misrepresentations. Other examples include the *Churchill* case cited at para 3.72. **3.79**

Whether the employee was advised at any material time, and if so, by whom; the extent of the adviser's knowledge of the facts of the case and the advice given to the employee

The starting point must be the famous passage in *Dedman* (para 3.57) where Lord Denning MR said: 'If a man engages skilled advisers to act for him and they mistake the limit and present it too late—he is out. His remedy is against them'. **3.80**

Skilled advisers include trade union representatives and voluntary advisers such as CAB workers and the Free Representation Unit (see *Croydon Health Authority v Jaufurally* [1986] ICR 4). In *Riley v Tesco Stores Ltd and Greater London Citizens Advice Bureaux Service Ltd* [1980] IRLR 103 **3.81** the Court of Appeal disapproved of the construction of 'skilled adviser' as if it were part of the statute and stated that the issue was one of fact. In *Wall's Meat Co Ltd v Khan* [1979] ICR 52, 57. Shaw LJ stated:

> the test is empirical and involves no legal concept. Practical common sense is the keynote and legalistic footnotes may have no better results than to introduce a lawyer's complication into what should be a layman's pristine province. These considerations prompt me to express the emphatic view that the forum to decide such questions is the industrial tribunal and that their decision should prevail unless it is plainly perverse or oppressive.

3.82 The *Dedman* principle has been doubted by the Court of Appeal in *London International College Ltd v Sen* [1993] IRLR 333, where the Master of the Rolls questioned the basis of any rule of law to the effect that consulting an adviser makes it reasonably practicable to present a complaint in time. In *Marks & Spencer v Williams Ryan* [2005] IRLR 562 the Court of Appeal upheld a tribunal's decision that it had not been reasonably practicable for an employee to bring an unfair dismissal claim in accordance with the applicable three-month time limit where, having received advice from a CAB, the employee had believed it necessary to exhaust the employer's internal appeal procedure before bringing her claim. A similar conclusion was reached in *DHL Supply Chain Limited v Fazackerley* UKEAT/0019/18/JOJ, where the employee contacted ACAS shortly after dismissal and was told to complete the internal appeal process. He then took no further steps until conclusion of the appeal, which was after the expiry of the time limit. The ET accepted that the erroneous ACAS advice rendered it not reasonably practicable to bring the claim within the time limit. HHJ Barklem in the EAT accepted that a different judge could have reached a different conclusion but that the finding was not perverse and therefore could not be disturbed on appeal.

3.83 The Court of Appeal concluded that whilst the decision of the tribunal was generous to the claimant it was not outside the ambit of conclusions available to it. It was not for the Court of Appeal to review findings of fact unless there was no basis for those findings or they were perverse. It noted that no authorities were referred to where the Court of Appeal had reversed a decision on the facts and the present case should not be a first. Further it was held that s 111(2) of the ERA 1996 should be interpreted liberally in favour of employees and the tribunal was entitled to reach the conclusion it had.

3.84 Where an applicant has missed the time limit because of erroneous or misleading advice from tribunal staff, tribunals are more sympathetic (see *Jean Sorelle Ltd v Rybak* [1991] IRLR 153 and *London International College Ltd v Sen* [1993] IRLR 333). In the *Sen* case, the applicant's solicitor told him the date for presenting the originating application and he confirmed it with a member of the tribunal staff. The date was one day out of time and he failed to present his claim within the time limit. The Court of Appeal stated that it was clear that the 'effective cause of the failure was the advice, on all the facts, of the industrial tribunal'.

Further period

3.85 If the applicant fails to establish that he did bring the claim in time, he should apply for an extension to bring it within 'such further period as the tribunal considers reasonable'. The tribunal's decision is, of course, a question of fact and successful challenges on appeal will be rare. Two cases offering guidance are *James W Cook & Co (Wivenhoe) v Tipper* [1990] IRLR 386, CA, and *Marley (UK) Ltd v Anderson* [1994] IRLR 152. In the former case the applicants were dismissed, but there were attempts to keep the shipyard open. After the expiry of the time limit the shipyard closed and two weeks later the applicants presented claims to the tribunal. This was held to be a reasonable further period. In the latter case, the tribunal had held that the applicant had delayed too long in bringing his complaint without focusing on the reasons for the delay, which must be relevant.

3.86 The principles upon which the discretion hinges will be similar to those in the 'reasonably practicable' cases. It will be rare for a tribunal to allow an extension where the applicant is represented by his trade union or has not pursued a claim through his own neglect.

Extension of time on a just and equitable basis

The test that applies in, for the main, the discrimination legislation potentially affords a tribunal **3.87** a far wider discretion than in the case of the reasonably practicable extension as emphasized in *Hutchison v Westward Television* [1977] IRLR 69 For the impact of that test see *British Coal Corporation v Keeble* [1997] IRLR 336, in which the EAT held that the discretion applying the 'just and equitable' test is wide and comparable to that under s 33 of the Limitation Act 1980, and the court can consider prejudice to the parties, the length of any delay and the excuse advanced for it, and the fact that as a result of a change in the law the applicant has a 'new' right. Each of these factors must be considered in turn by the tribunal. A suggestion that the discretion to extend time should be exercised in exceptional circumstances in *Robertson v Bexley Community Centre* [2003] IRLR 434, endorsed by the Court of Appeal in *Department of Constitutional Affairs v Jones* [2008] IRLR 128, was doubted by the Court of Appeal in *Chief Constable of Lincolnshire v Caston* [2010] IRLR 327, in which Sedley LJ held that there is no principle of law which dictates how generously or sparingly the power to enlarge time is to be exercised.

In *Chohan v Derby Law Centre* [2004] IRLR 685 Judge McMullen QC summarized the principles **3.88** from the authorities as follows (paras 12–16):

A tribunal demonstrably taking the wrong approach or not taking account of a fact which it should have done errs in law—see *Hutchison v Westward Television* [1977] IRLR 69 EAT.

The availability of legal advice is a relevant question—see *British Coal Corporation v Keeble* [1997] IRLR 336 EAT at paragraph 8 per Smith J.

The use of a check list under the Limitation Act is often useful: *British Coal Corporation v Keeble* EAT/ 413/94 unreported 6 July 1995 EAT Holland J at paragraph 10, upon which Mrs Justice Smith based her judgment above.

Although it is not a requirement that a tribunal go through the check list, failure to consider a significant factor will amount to an error of law: *London Borough of Southwark v Afolabi* [2003] IRLR 220 CA paragraph 33 per Peter Gibson LJ.

The failure by a legal adviser to enter proceedings in time should not be visited upon the claimant for otherwise the defendant would be in receipt of windfall: *Steeds v Peverel Management Services Ltd* [2001] EWCA Civ 419 pp 38–40.

The Limitation Act (1980) checklist requires the court to consider the prejudice which each party **3.89** would suffer as the result of the decision to be made and also to have regard to all the circumstances of the case and in particular to:

(a)   the length of and reasons for the delay
(b)   the extent to which the cogency of the evidence is likely to be affected by the delay
(c)   the extent to which the party sued had cooperated with any requests for information
(d)   the promptness with which the claimant acted once he or she knew of the facts giving rise to the cause of action and
(e)   the steps taken by the claimant to obtain appropriate professional advice once he or she knew of the possibility of taking action.

Whilst the Court of Appeal has held that it is not mandatory to go through the checklist (see **3.90** *London Borough of Southwark v Afolabi* [2003] EWCA Civ 15, [2003] IRLR 220) it is recommended that any witness evidence and/or skeleton arguments use the checklist as a template. In particular for respondents, the issue of specific prejudice—for example, that evidence has been destroyed—will most often be determinative (although there is no rule of law to this effect—see *Apelogun-Gabriels v London Borough of Lambeth* [2001] EWCA Civ 1853, [2002] IRLR 116). In addition, while the 'reason' for delay is a factor it is not a requirement that the Tribunal finds a good reason before exercising its discretion (see *Abertawe Bro Morgannwg University v Morgan* [2018] EWCA Civ 640).

Chohan was a case in which the EAT overruled the tribunal's decision that incorrect advice by the **3.91** claimant's solicitor did not amount to a just and equitable excuse. The tribunal had not been persuaded by the case of *Hawkins v Ball* [1996] IRLR 258 which only held that it was not a mistake in law to take the adviser's error in calculating time into account, but the EAT went further in following the *Steeds* case above. It is still the case, however, that the claimant's own delay in instructing lawyers or in issuing proceedings will be a relevant factor, as will the adviser's fault in simply failing to send the claim in time or any inexcusable delay. The EAT in *Virdi v Commissioner of Police of the Metropolis* [2007] IRLR 24 has confirmed that the fault of a solicitor will be a 'highly material' factor in deciding whether to extend time on a just and equitable basis to allow a complaint of discrimination to proceed out of time (see also *Benjamin-Cole v Great Ormond Street Hospital for Sick Children NHS Trust* [2010] All ER (D) 73 (Feb), which applied *Virdi*). Finally, there is no rule of law that a CAB adviser should be regarded as a 'skilled adviser', comparable to a solicitor, so as to fix the claimant with the adviser's fault (*Royal Bank of Scotland v Theobald* UKEAT/0444/06).

Specific examples

3.92 In *Berry v Ravensbourne National Health Service Trust* [1993] ICR 871, the applicant's claim of race discrimination was additional to, and overlapped with, an existing unfair dismissal complaint, which was made in time but had not yet been heard. The applicant was given notice of redundancy by her employers on 4 January 1992 and made a complaint of unfair dismissal, alleging that she had been unfairly selected for redundancy. Her employment terminated on 31 March 1992. At the end of August 1992, the applicant learnt that on 14 April 1992 the employers had advertised a vacancy for a pharmacist which they had not brought to her attention, although under the employer's redundancy procedure an employee who was made redundant was, where practicable, given preferential consideration for suitable vacant posts up to four weeks after the termination of employment. On 2 November 1992, she sought to amend her complaint to add a claim of racial discrimination.

3.93 An extension of time was granted to allow the race claim to be heard as there was the overlap, and she had not discovered the facts in relation to the discrimination claim immediately.

3.94 In *Robinson v Post Office* [2000] IRLR 804, a delay caused by a claimant invoking an internal grievance or disciplinary appeal procedure prior to commencing proceedings was held to justify the grant of an extension of time. However, this is merely one factor that must be weighed in the balance along with others that may be present (the case was approved by the Court of Appeal in *Apelogun-Gabriels v London Borough of Lambeth* above). On the facts of *Robinson*, the employee delayed making a disability discrimination claim whilst he pursued an internal disciplinary appeal. He was ultimately refused an extension of time as he knew of the time limit for bringing a discrimination claim and refused to take his union's advice to lodge the application in time. In *Apelogun-Gabriels*, the Court of Appeal rejected the earlier decision of Morison J in *Aniagwu v London Borough of Hackney* [1999] IRLR 303 that there is a general principle that an extension should always be granted where a delay is caused by a claimant invoking an internal grievance or appeal procedure, unless the employers could show some particular prejudice.

3.95 An extension of time was granted to a claimant who did not discover the evidence which led to his race discrimination claim (concerning the failure to appoint him to a particular grade) until nine years after the expiry of the time limit: *Southwark London Borough v Afolabi*, cited above. Factors taken into account were that he had no reason to discover the evidence earlier, that he presented his complaint within three months of discovering it, and that the nine-year delay would be equally prejudicial to both parties.

4

The Response

SUMMARY

(1) In the case of the response the time limit for entering it is twenty-eight days after the claim form has been sent to the respondent.

(2) Extensions of time are possible but, if the respondent fails to lodge a response within the specified or extended time, he is not entitled to take part in the proceedings except to a very limited degree.

A. INITIAL STEPS

The respondent has twenty-eight days after the claim form has been sent to submit his response. **4.01** A claim against a foreign state is governed by the State Immunity Act 1978, s 12(2) of which provides that the time limit is two months and provides special rules for service which are incompatible with, and therefore supersede, the provisions of ETR 2013. The twenty-eight-day period will be strictly construed as running from the date when the document was actually sent by the tribunal, and there is no scope for construing it as running from the date when it was received (see *Bone v Fabcon Projects Ltd* [2006] ICR 1421 and the ETR 2013, r 16(1)). The response must be on the prescribed form (see Appendix 5) and contain specified information. It may also be entered in respect of more than one respondent (ETR 2013, r 16(2)) provided that it responds to a single claim and all respondents resist, or admit, the claim on the same grounds. In addition it may respond to more than one claim if the claims are based on the same set of facts and the respondent resists, or admits, the claim on the same grounds (ETR 2013, r 16(3)).

If the tribunal accepts the response it will send a copy to all other parties (ETR, r 22). The case then **4.02** proceeds to an initial sift, where both the claim and response are considered by an employment judge (ETR 2013, r 26) (see para 6.01).

B. REJECTION OF RESPONSE

4.03 The response shall be rejected if (i) it is not on the prescribed form (ETR 2013, r 17(1)(a)), (ii) it does not contain the required information (ETR 2013, r 17(1)(b)), or (iii) it is received outside the twenty-eight-day period (or any extended period) (ETR 2013, r 18).

4.04 If the response is not on the prescribed form or does not contain all of the required minimum information the form will be returned to the respondent with a notice of rejection explaining why it has been rejected, and explaining what steps may be taken by the respondent, including the need (if appropriate) to apply for an extension of time, and how to apply for a reconsideration of the rejection (ETR 2013, r 17(2)). If the response is received outside the twenty-eight-day period (or any extension of that limit (see para 4.05) granted within the original limit) the response shall be returned to the respondent together with a notice of rejection explaining that the response has been presented late. The notice shall explain how the respondent can apply for an extension of time and how to apply for a reconsideration. However, if an application for extension has already been made, or the response includes or is accompanied by such an application, the response will not be rejected pending the outcome of the application (ETR 2013, r 18).

4.05 Rule 20 allows for an application for an extension of time. If an application to extend time is made under r 20 it should be in writing and copied to the claimant. Unless the time limit has already expired it should include a draft of the response and/or an explanation why a draft response is not possible and if the respondent wishes to request a hearing that should be requested in the application. If the application is opposed, the claimant has seven days from receipt of the application to give reasons in writing as to why the application is opposed. The matter may be determined by an employment judge without a hearing (ETR 2013 r 20(3)). If the extension is refused any previous rejection will stand and if it is granted any judgment made under r 21 will be revoked (see para 4.18).

C. CONTENTS OF THE RESPONSE

Boxes 1 to 3 'Claimant's name', 'Respondent's details', and 'ACAS early conciliation details'

4.06 These boxes seek basic contact details and information regarding the size of the respondent business. Box 3 requires the respondent to confirm whether the information from the claimant is correct in relation to early conciliation through ACAS. This helps identify any jurisdictional disputes at an early stage.

Boxes 4 and 5 'Employment details' and 'Earnings and benefits'

4.07 Confirmation of the claimant's employment dates is required here and if there is disagreement, reasons should be given. This is clearly in order to flush out any disputes concerning continuity and/or basic award at an early stage. The respondent is also asked whether the claimant's description of his or her job or job title are correct and if not, the respondent is requested to give the details he or she believes to be correct. Similarly, the respondent is asked to confirm whether the details provided by the claimant of his or her hours of work, earnings, information regarding payment for notice period, and other benefits are correct and, if not, the respondent is asked to provide the information he or she believes to be correct. Many of these sections are not mandatory for the respondent; in cases where worker/employee status is in dispute, it may be advisable to leave these sections blank.

Box 6 'Response'

4.08 It is mandatory to indicate whether the claim is resisted or not. If the claim is resisted, then details of the reasons for disputing the claim must be provided. Although the form provides some space to set out the response in all but the simplest claims this will not be adequate. It is standard practice simply to use this box to refer to an attached defence/response and to upload a full response at the end of the form.

Particular care should be taken in filling out the response in all cases but this is especially important **4.09** in discrimination cases as inferences may be drawn from an incorrect or ambiguous pleading (see *Dattani v Chief Constable of West Mercia Police* [2005] IRLR 327).

If the respondent seeks early orders for further information or for a preliminary hearing, details of **4.10** the reasons for the orders should be set out in the response. Similarly, any issue as to the correct identity of the employer or the need to join a further party should be clearly identified in the response.

Box 7 'Employer's contract claim'

Where the claimant has made a contract claim the employer may make a counterclaim and, if so, **4.11** this box should be completed.

Box 8 'Your representative'

The details of any representative including his or her preferred method of communication should **4.12** be included in this box.

D. RECONSIDERATION OF REJECTION

If the response has been rejected r 19(1) provides that the respondent can apply for reconsideration **4.13** on the basis that the decision was wrong, or where the rejection was on the basis that the wrong form was used or the prescribed information was not provided, that the defect can be remedied. The application must be made in writing within fourteen days of the date that the notice of rejection was sent, must explain why the decision is said to have been wrong or must rectify any defect, and must state whether the respondent requests a hearing. If the respondent does not request a hearing, or the employment judge decides, on considering the application, that the response will be accepted in full, the judge will determine the application without a hearing. Otherwise, the application will be considered at a hearing attended only by the respondent (ETR 2013, r 19(3)). Any decision resulting from such a hearing is not a judgment (ETR 2013, r 1(3)(b)) and cannot be subject to further review.

The employment judge may decide: **4.14**

(i) that the original decision was correct but the defect has been remedied and that the response should be treated as presented on the date that the defect was remedied (and may also extend time under r 5) r 19(4) or
(ii) that the decision to reject was wrong and the date of presentation will remain the same or
(iii) in the case of a response presented out of time the decision to reject was wrong: for example that the twenty-eight day period had been incorrectly calculated, or regard had not been paid to an extension that had been granted, or that an application for an extension had been made.

E. EXTENSION OF TIME

A respondent who has submitted a late response may apply for an extension of time either pro- **4.15** spectively (as set out above) or retrospectively. An application for an extension must:

(i) be in writing
(ii) explain the reason for the application
(iii) be copied to the claimant
(iv) in a retrospective case be accompanied by a draft response
(v) request a hearing if that is what is sought (ETR 2013, r 20) otherwise the employment judge can determine the matter without a hearing. The employment judge may decide to determine the matter without a hearing in any event.

4.16 The claimant may attend any hearing and oppose the application by giving reasons within seven days of receipt of the application unless he applies for an extension of this period under r 5 or the tribunal does so of its own volition. There is no time limit for making an application to extend time under ETR 2013 (as opposed to under the ETR 2004, which set the time limit at twenty-eight days). The changes in ETR 2013 are significant and r 20(4) envisages post-judgment applications being made with the consequence that a judgment is set aside (see also the general discretion under r 5 for extending or shortening time).

4.17 An extension of time will be determined in accordance with the principles in *Kwik Stores Ltd v Swain* [1997] ICR 49. The respondent must provide a full explanation as to the non-compliance and ensure that all relevant material (including any documents) is before the tribunal. The completeness of the explanation of the circumstances is especially important as the tribunal may dispense with a hearing so any letter may attach a skeleton argument. The material should include an explanation of the defence on the merits. The test to be applied by the employment judge is to take into account all of the relevant factors, which include the matters mentioned above and must be objectively justified on the grounds of reason and justice, including the prejudice to each party.

F. CONSEQUENCES OF FAILING TO ENTER A RESPONSE, REJECTION OF RESPONSE, OR UNCONTESTED APPLICATIONS

4.18 A respondent who fails to enter a response or whose response is not accepted or who does not wish to contest the proceedings is subject to r 21 of the ETR 2013. In any of these situations, an employment judge must decide whether to make a determination of the claim (whether in whole or in part) on the basis of the available material. The employment judge may require the parties to provide additional information (ETR 2013, r 21(2)). If the employment judge can make a determination on the material, then he should issue a judgment without a hearing. Otherwise, a hearing is required before a judge alone. The respondent is entitled to notice of any hearings and decisions of the tribunal but unless and until an extension of time is granted can only participate in any hearing to the extent permitted by the judge (ETR 2013, r 21(3)). The same limited right applies equally to a claimant who has not responded to an employer's contract claim (ETR 2013, r 25).

4.19 A decision under r 21(2) is a judgment and can be reconsidered under rr 70–73 where it is necessary in the interests of justice. Such a reconsideration can be at the employment judge's initiative or at the request of either party. Any such application must be made in writing (unless it has been made at a hearing) and presented to the tribunal along with copies to all other parties. It must be made within fourteen days of the date on which the written record (or written reasons if later) was sent to the parties. This time limit may be extended under r 5. The application must set out why the reconsideration of the original decision is necessary (ETR 2013, r 71). Where the judge proposes to reconsider the judgment on his own initiative he must inform the parties of the reason why the decision is being reconsidered. Unless a hearing is unnecessary in the interests of justice one should be held and the original decision can be confirmed, varied or revoked (ETR 2013, r 70).

4.20 The ETR 2004 process of issuing a default judgment generated some case law on the limits of that procedure. In *Eaton v Spencer, Cox, Da Vinci and Conroy t/a Wiggles Experience* UKEAT/0177/11/DA [2011] ICR D7, the EAT held that when determining remedy following such a judgment the tribunal cannot revisit issues of liability that have already been determined by the judgment itself. The same principles ought to apply to a judgment under r 21. The EAT held that while issues as to causation and the assessment of any damages will be considered at any such remedies hearing the default judgment is conclusive in determining liability.

G. COUNTERCLAIMS

4.21 If the claimant makes a complaint of breach of contract, the respondent employer may include a counterclaim (ETR 2013, r 23). The employer's claim may be rejected under r 12 in the same way as a claimant's claim may be rejected, for example if there is no jurisdiction or it is in a form which cannot sensibly be responded to or is otherwise an abuse of the process. Any such rejection can be reconsidered under r 13.

When the tribunal sends the response to the other parties it shall notify the claimant that the response includes an employer's contract claim and include information on how to submit a response to the claim, the time limit for doing so (which is twenty-eight days from the date that the employer's response was sent to the claimant) and the consequence if a response is not received within that time (ETR 2013, r 24). If no response is presented within the time limit the provisions for applying for an extension of time under r 20 apply and those relating to non-presentation of a response under r 21 also apply (ETR 2013, r 25).

4.22

Part A Tribunal Procedure

5

Conciliation and Settlement

SUMMARY

(1) ACAS has a duty to endeavour to promote settlement of disputes. Since 2014, mandatory early conciliation requires a claimant to involve ACAS before commencing a claim.

(2) Since 2013, the 'protected conversation' regime, which exists in parallel with the common law 'without prejudice' rules, has created an opportunity for employers to enter into pre-termination discussions with employees which, if they are conducted in prescribed circumstances, will make it impermissible for either party to refer to such negotiations in the course of tribunal proceedings.

(3) There are restrictions on contracting out of most statutory employment rights. A settlement of a dispute concerning a statutory employment right will not be effective unless it conforms to the requirements of an ACAS conciliated agreement, or the requirements for a settlement agreement, or unless a consent order is made by the tribunal.

(4) If a settlement agreement does not meet the requirements of an ACAS conciliated agreement or a settlement agreement, it will not prevent a claimant from pursuing a claim in the tribunal.

(5) If a party fails to perform a valid settlement agreement, the agreement can be enforced in the civil courts in an action for breach of contract. In limited circumstances, a claim for breach of the settlement agreement can be brought in the tribunal.

(6) A settlement agreement may be set aside on grounds of mistake, misrepresentation, illegality, duress, or undue influence.

A. INTRODUCTION

Most civil disputes are resolved by compromise. This is as true, if not more so, of disputes in the   **5.01** employment tribunal as it is of disputes conducted in the civil courts. The court and tribunal systems in recent years have increasingly encouraged settlement and alternative dispute resolution as a means of easing the burden of litigation on the public purse. In April 2014, the government moved from mere encouragement to actually imposing a positive requirement on claimants in most cases to try to settle before presenting a complaint in the tribunal, through the means of an early conciliation scheme. Further, once a claim has been issued, r 3 of the Employment Tribunals (Constitution and Rules of Procedure) Regulations 2013 rule provides that a tribunal shall, wherever practicable and appropriate, encourage the use by the parties of the services of ACAS, judicial or other mediation, or other means of resolving their disputes by agreement. This rule, which was first introduced in the ETR 2013, puts on an express and formal footing the tribunal's desire to encourage consensual resolution of disputes. Parties to a dispute may, in any event, view settlement as an attractive solution for a number of reasons:

(a) it avoids the uncertainty of the trial process
(b) there is a saving of cost, particularly relevant in the tribunal where costs are unlikely to be recovered even by the winning party
(c) a compromise will often lead to a quicker solution than a trial, and therefore may avoid litigation becoming a distraction
(d) a compromise may avoid publicity and
(e) the parties may agree between themselves terms which are outside the tribunal's power to order by way of remedy (for example, terms as to an agreed reference or a protocol as to future behaviour).

It is open to the parties to reach a settlement at any stage from the moment when the dispute arises,   **5.02** before proceedings commence, until the moment before judgment is entered by the tribunal. Even after that point, the parties may settle a case between the decision determining liability and compensation and the hearing of any pending appeal. Many disputes are settled without the need for tribunal proceedings to be issued at all. Even where a claim is issued, the majority of cases settle without the need for a determination at a hearing. Throughout each stage of a claim in the tribunal the parties are likely to be involved in a process of assessment of the benefit of settlement, in the context of an analysis of the merits of each party's case and the time and cost of pursuing the claim to a hearing.

Where settlement is considered as an option, the following questions arise: **5.03**

(a) By what process is settlement best achieved? There are a number of methods of alternative dispute resolution ('ADR'): private negotiation between the parties and their representatives; ACAS conciliation; ACAS arbitration; as well as other forms of commercially provided mediation.

(b) What terms of agreement can be negotiated?

(c) Once an agreement is reached, how should the parties best give effect to the agreement?

(d) Once agreement is reached, how should the proceedings be disposed of consistent with the terms of the agreement?

5.04 There are a number of special features which impact upon settlement of disputes in the employment tribunal:

(a) A system is provided for the intervention of ACAS to assist in conciliation of most tribunal claims and attempting to settle a dispute before bringing a claim is mandatory in most cases.

(b) As a matter of common law, an agreement to settle a claim is a contract like any other, and is subject to the normal rules of formation and interpretation of contracts. However, statute imposes stringent restrictions on contracting out of many statutory employment rights, and the capacity of the parties to compromise many statutory rights is limited by important procedural restrictions.

(c) In certain types of claim employers and employees will be able to enter into pre-termination of employment negotiations within 'protected conversations' which cannot be referred to in tribunal proceedings and may, therefore, encourage a full and frank discussion as an aid to resolving differences before any litigation arises.

5.05 We will outline the principles applicable to three methods of ADR (ACAS conciliation, ACAS arbitration, and mediation) before turning to consider in detail the statutory restrictions on settlements of statutory claims. A specimen settlement agreement and drafting notes for settlement agreements are contained at sections P and Q of this chapter.

B. THE ROLE OF ACAS

5.06 ACAS has a long-established role in conciliating disputes which fall within the employment tribunal's jurisdiction, pursuant to ss 18–19A of the ETA 1996. For many years, the involvement of ACAS typically arose once a claim had been issued (s 18(2)), although it was open to ACAS to take up a request for its services at an earlier stage (s 18(3)). Section 7 of the Enterprise and Regulatory Reform Act (ERRA) 2013 introduced a system of mandatory conciliation before proceedings are issued commonly referred to as 'early conciliation' (although the statute does not actually use that term). Sections 18A and 18B of the Employment Tribunals Act 1996 deal with early conciliation, and s 18C deals with conciliation after the institution of proceedings. The new sections are supplemented by the Employment Tribunals (Early Conciliation: Exemptions and Rules of Procedure) Regulations 2014 (SI 2014/254, as amended by SI 2014/847). The changes took effect on 6 April 2014. The following text sets out the law as amended by the ERRA 2013.

5.07 The conciliation regime applies to 'relevant proceedings' set out in s 18(1). These include all of the principal jurisdictions of the employment tribunal (unfair dismissal, workplace discrimination, redundancy pay, unlawful deduction from wages, rights to time off or flexible working, and equal pay).

Early conciliation

5.08 Section 18A(1) of the ETA 1996 provides that, before a prospective claimant presents an application to institute relevant proceedings in relation to any matter, he or she must provide ACAS with prescribed information in the prescribed manner, ie prescribed by employment tribunal procedure regulations. The Early Conciliation Notification form requires only basic information about the applicant and the employer, and does not require details of the claim.

5.09 ACAS must then send that information to a conciliation officer. The conciliation officer's duty is to endeavour to promote settlement during the prescribed period of one month (see Sch 1, r 6 of the ET(EC) Regulations). If settlement that avoids proceedings being issued is not possible in the officer's view, or if settlement is not reached within the prescribed period, then the officer must issue a certificate confirming this. A person who is subject to the requirements of s 18A(1) may not present an application to institute relevant proceedings without such a certificate. The tribunal has no discretion to hear a claim submitted without a certificate (*Cranwell v Cullen* UKEATPAS/0046/14/SM). However, in *Ahmed v Arearose Ltd* UKEAT/0314/15/LA, the EAT found that a reconsideration hearing should have been provided where there were issues in dispute around the certification requirement.

Where incorrect details of a certificate are recorded on a claim form this will result in its rejection. **5.10** If a fresh form with corrected details is not then provided until the claim is out of time, an application for an extension of time will be necessary (*Adams v British Telecommunications PLC* UKEAT/0342/15/LA and *Sterling v United Learning Trust* UKEAT/0439/14/DM).

This early conciliation requirement is automatically treated as complied with where an excep- **5.11** tion under s 18(7) of the ETA 1996 applies. These exceptions, specified by reg 3 of the ET(EC) Regulations are:

- multiple claims, where another person instituting proceedings has complied with the requirement in respect of the same matter (eg a collective redundancy case with multiple claimants arising out of the same matter)
- where proceedings not deemed to be relevant under s 18(1) of the ETA 1996 are instituted in the same claim
- where ACAS has already been contacted by a respondent under s 18B of the ETA 1996 in relation to the same dispute
- where an application to institute proceedings for unfair dismissal is accompanied by an application for interim relief under s 128 of the ERA 1996 or s 161 TULR(C)A or
- where the intended respondent is the Security Service, Secret Intelligence Service, or GCHQ.

Early conciliation under s 18A is only required once in relation to each 'matter'. As such, once a **5.12** claim has been issued, it is not necessary to conduct a further early conciliation exercise in order to amend the claim so as to add a new cause of action arising out of the same matter (*Science Warehouse Ltd v Mills* [2016] ICR 252, [2016] IRLR 96). Similarly, it is not necessary to commence a second early conciliation exercise where a claimant has issued a claim against the wrong respondent in relation to a particular matter. Once the claim has been issued, the claimant is no longer a 'prospective claimant' in relation to that 'matter' (*Drake International Systems Ltd & Others v Blue Arrow Ltd* [2016] ICR 445; *TIC International Ltd v Ali* UKEAT/0284/15/RN). An early conciliation certificate can cover matters that take place after it has been issued, provided a link can be established between such matters and those raised in early conciliation: *Compass Group UK & Ireland Ltd v Morgan* [2017] ICR 73, [2016] IRLR 924.

Section 18B sets out a procedure for early conciliation to be initiated by a prospective respondent **5.13** to relevant proceedings. The procedure is broadly similar to s 18A, save that there is no requirement on the ACAS officer under this section to issue a certificate. The duty under s 18B ceases once the prospective claimant takes the necessary steps to trigger s 18A.

In order to allow for this new compulsory procedure, Sch 2 of the ERRA provides for the extension **5.14** of limitation periods. For further details of the application and effect of such extensions to time limits see Chapter 3 paras 3.40 to 3.43.

Conciliation once a claim has been issued

Section 18C of the ETA 1996 provides that where a claim under one of the relevant statutory **5.15** jurisdictions has been presented before an employment tribunal, and a copy has been sent to a conciliation officer (which is required under s 19 and ETR 2013, r 93), then he must endeavour to promote a settlement if either (1) he receives a request from both parties to do so, or (2) he considers that he could act with a reasonable prospect of success of achieving such an outcome.

5.16 Rule 93 of the ETR 2013 provides that an ACAS conciliation officer may attend a preliminary hearing in connection with a case which is subject to conciliation enactments, subject to national security and privacy rules (rr 50 and 94).

'Endeavour to promote a settlement'

5.17 The role of the conciliation officer is to explain the conciliation process; encourage the use of internal disciplinary and grievance procedures; explain the way tribunals go about making a decision; help the parties understand each other's views of the issues; and discuss proposals for resolution. The conciliation officer may facilitate some bargaining and if settlement is reached it is the parties and not the conciliation officer who determine the settlement. The process normally does not involve any face-to-face meetings between the parties. Rather, conciliation officers relay the perspectives of one party to the other.

5.18 What does the ACAS conciliation officer actually have to do to endeavour to promote settlement and thus meet his statutory obligations? The officer's role is to try and help the parties reach a settlement; but not to act as an arbitrator on the merits. Further, the conciliation officer:

(a) has no duty, when promoting a financial settlement, to ensure that it is fair to both sides (see *Moore v Duport Furniture Products Ltd* [1982] ICR 84, [1982] IRLR 31 (HL) and *Clarke v Redcar & Cleveland Borough Council* [2006] ICR 897)

(b) does not have to explain to the parties the legislative framework in which the claim or potential claim is made and

(c) does not have to advise the employee on his rights and remedies, and in fact advising a party as to the worth of his/her claim could actually undermine the function of the conciliation officer (see *Clarke v Redcar & Cleveland Borough Council* [2006] ICR 897).

Provided that the conciliation officer has not acted in bad faith or adopted unfair methods, a conciliated settlement cannot be set aside because he has failed in his duty (see *Slack v Greenham (Plant Hire) Ltd* [1983] ICR 617 and *Clarke* (above)).

5.19 Where the claim which has been presented, or which might be presented, is for unfair dismissal, the conciliation officer may seek to promote reinstatement or re-engagement (ETA 1996, ss 18A(9), 18C(2)). However, where reinstatement or re-engagement is either not desired by the complainant, or is not practicable (and it will usually fall into one of these categories), the conciliation officer may seek to promote an agreement for the payment of a cash sum. In many cases it will be plain that reinstatement or re-engagement is not practicable, and in such cases, an officer is not 'compelled, with no possibility of his doing any good at all, to go through the motions of acting in a way which was wholly inappropriate to the circumstances of the particular case with which he is concerned' (*Moore*, cited above).

5.20 If conciliation is successful, the conciliation officer will record the settlement in an agreement in form COT3. A vital question is whether a conciliation officer is acting legitimately if he merely 'rubber stamps' an agreement which has already been reached before he came on the scene. In *Moore*, the House of Lords gave a wide construction of the words now found in ss 18A–18C of the ETA 1996 which require the officer to 'endeavour to promote a settlement'. Their Lordships said that the words were 'capable of covering whatever action by way of such promotion is applicable in the circumstances of the particular case'. In that case, the officer did not play any part in formulating the terms of the settlement. He suggested that the parties should meet and try to reach an agreement but was not present at the meeting. The House of Lords held that it was sufficient that once an agreement had been reached he recorded the terms on a COT3 form, and ensured that the parties understood those terms and the implications of signing them. The circumstances faced by the conciliation officer were that there was no prospect of reinstatement of the employee, and an amount of compensation had already been agreed. Therefore, action to promote reinstatement or to promote agreement as to the amount of compensation was futile and not applicable. In the circumstances of the case the acts taken by the conciliation officer did amount to a sufficient degree to endeavouring to promote a settlement.

Confidentiality

Anything communicated to the conciliation officer in connection with his endeavours to promote **5.21**
settlement is not admissible in evidence in any proceedings before an employment tribunal, except
with the consent of the party making the communication: ETA 1996, s 18(7). Whether this is an
absolute prohibition in respect of any and all communications, or whether the words in the subsection 'in connection with the performance of his functions under this section' imply a limitation
on the scope of the prohibition analogous to the scope of protection afforded to 'without prejudice'
communications, has not been the subject of any appellate decision.

Further, in *Freer v Glover* [2006] IRLR 521, it was held that communications with a conciliation **5.22**
officer will be protected from defamation proceedings under the common law of absolute privilege
and could not therefore be made use of in any proceedings. This case was determined under the
common law relating to absolute privilege rather than on a construction of ETA 1996, s 18(7).
In that case solicitors acting for the respondent to employment tribunal proceedings had written
to the claimant indicating that the respondent would not be prepared to settle on any terms and
that they would 'not be blackmailed by you and your friends'. The conciliation officer had been
copied into the correspondence and the claimant subsequently issued defamation proceedings in
the High Court against the respondent's solicitors. It was argued by the claimant that the relevant
communication was not protected by absolute privilege because it was not a communication which
was 'incidental to the dispute', since the respondent was indicating why it was not prepared to negotiate with the claimant on any terms. It was held, however, that the relevant communication was
covered by absolute privilege since the conciliation officer was under a duty to promote settlement
and in order to do so, it was necessary for her to understand why one or other of the parties was
not willing to enter into negotiations. Therefore, the communication was incidental to the employment tribunal proceedings and absolute privilege was 'practically necessary for the administration
of justice' and the situation fell within the scope of the rules of privilege as set out in *Lincoln v
Daniels* [1962] 1 QB 237.

C. THE ACAS ARBITRATION SCHEME

ACAS has responsibility for an arbitration scheme under the Employment Rights (Dispute **5.23**
Resolution) Act 1998 as a means to resolve claims of unfair dismissal and flexible working claims.
The arbitrator hears from both sides and then makes a binding decision. The decision is therefore
the arbitrator's and the parties lose their power over the settlement. The arbitrator's award is final
and the case cannot then proceed to a tribunal. Parties therefore make a choice between arbitration
and going to court.

The ACAS arbitration scheme was set up to offer a distinct alternative to tribunals, and one of its **5.24**
key features is that it is designed to be free of legalism. Hearings are private and confidential, and
inquisitorial rather than adversarial. No cross-examination is permitted and clarification or questioning is conducted only through the arbitrator and with the arbitrator's permission. The parties
are given the opportunity to state their own cases and comment on the case of the other side. The
arbitrator rules on procedural and evidential matters rather than directly on points of law. The
arbitrator can only make awards of compensation, reinstatement, and re-engagement, so the settlements reached are limited to those provided by law.

In the arbitration scheme there is no appeal in respect to the arbitrator's award, except on grounds **5.25**
of serious irregularities. The scheme is voluntary so both parties will have to opt for it.

D. MEDIATION

In mediation the mediator, an independent, neutral, third party, assists disputing parties to reach **5.26**
a settlement. The mediator is not a judge or arbitrator of the dispute before him and will not seek
to impose a solution. Mediation does not attempt to determine the rights and wrongs of the case

Part A Tribunal Procedure

but to identify and focus on the real issues, and seek to create 'win–win' options for resolution that satisfy the needs of both parties. It is the parties, not the mediator, who decide the terms of the agreement, keeping the outcome of the dispute firmly in their hands. Like all ADR processes, mediation is voluntary, private, and informal. The process usually involves bringing the parties together for at least one face-to-face meeting, but the degree to which the parties continue to meet in joint session will vary depending on the practice of the mediator and the willingness of the parties to have joint meetings. Mediators may give an opinion or make suggestions for settlement. They test the reality of the positions of the parties to a greater or lesser extent depending on the particular mediation. Giving an opinion on the merits is usually out of bounds. There are many commercial mediation providers in the market.

5.27 Mediation may be used for a range of non-statutory workplace disputes, such as disputes between employees or between employer and employee, and as a stage within an organization's grievance or complaints procedure. It may work especially well in harassment and discrimination cases which are the most intractable of the statutory rights and where the parties may have to continue to work together.

5.28 Mediation is thus flexible in terms of both process and outcomes and may be ideally suited for problems concerned with relationships or behaviour. Mediated agreements can include protocols about future behaviour, a written apology, an explanation of what took place, and decisions about what might happen in the future. None of these is within the direct power of an employment tribunal or the court.

5.29 The majority of mediations last for one day. Mediation may be particularly beneficial where the employee is still with the employer and all parties want to continue the relationship. The early resolution of problems coupled with the non-adversarial nature of mediation is more likely to restore and safeguard relationships.

5.30 A further key advantage of ADR for many parties is that it is private. While the public forum of an employment tribunal may be important in some cases, the parties may prefer the more supportive and private forum that ADR processes provide. Although the employment tribunal rules provide that there may be no reporting of sexual harassment cases (which are especially sensitive) during their hearings, the press may report such cases *after* the hearings are concluded, and there is no such restraint in other areas where embarrassing details may emerge.

5.31 In most cases, nothing said during mediation can be used against a party at a later time; the entire process is strictly 'without prejudice' to legal rights. If a satisfactory outcome is not reached through mediation, the parties can still pursue a grievance or bring a claim to an employment tribunal (subject to time limits).

5.32 The employment tribunals offer a judicial mediation scheme. Suitable cases for mediation are identified by an Employment Judge at a preliminary hearing at which the Employment Judge may advise the parties of the possibility of judicial mediation. If both parties agree, the Regional Employment Judge will decide whether to offer a mediation. The mediation is conducted at the employment tribunal premises with an Employment Judge acting as mediator.

When to begin mediation

5.33 The general principle is the earlier the better, not least in order that the issue does not become more bitter as time goes on, but also because the cost and time savings are the greatest. However, it is inappropriate to hold a mediation if further documents or information have to be provided by one party to enable the other party to understand the first party's allegations fully. Also, part of mediation's flexibility is that it can be used at any stage in a dispute and can run in parallel to a formal grievance or tribunal process. Sometimes, conversely, time is a healer and the best time to mediate will be some time after a claim has been lodged.

5.34 If mediation is part of an organization's internal grievance or complaints process, then raising the mediation option with the other side is relatively easy. If a judge or tribunal recommends that mediation be attempted, the task of persuading the other side is considerably easier since it has been raised in a neutral way.

If mediation is neither part of an internal grievance process nor court-referred, the only way for- **5.35** ward is to persuade the other side to try mediation. One party can approach the other party dir- ectly or indirectly. The direct approach is contact between the parties themselves or through their respective lawyers or representatives. The indirect approach to the other side is likely to be through a mediation provider, which has the advantage of giving the other party the opportunity to dis- cuss any concerns and be informed about the process in more detail. Which approach to use will depend on the particular circumstances and personalities of each case. One way to facilitate the path to the mediation table is to offer to meet in order to discuss mediation and this can include a representative from a mediation provider.

The mediation agreement

The terms on which the mediation is to take place are usually outlined in a short document that should **5.36** be agreed by the parties and the mediator. The mediation agreement sets out the practical details of the mediation such as the date, time, venue, selected mediator, etc. The agreement also establishes the legal features of the mediation such as its 'without prejudice' nature, confidentiality, mediator immunity, and authority to settle. The document should be simple and straightforward so that all parties will be willing to sign it. The mediation should be attended by those parties with first-hand knowledge of the issues and full authority to settle the dispute. If lawyers or other representatives do attend the mediation with their clients it is important that they understand that their role is not to represent their client in the traditional sense, but rather to support them in seeking a solution going forward.

It is common for the parties to submit to the mediator a brief summary of the dispute (preferably **5.37** agreed between them) highlighting the key issues from each of their perspectives. This can help the parties to focus on the real issues in dispute that they wish to address. In many disputes there will also be some relevant documentation which it is appropriate for the mediator to see in advance. The case summaries and relevant documents are then exchanged between the parties and copied to the medi- ator at an agreed date before the mediation. Parties may bring additional documents to the mediation for only the mediator to see or send such documents to the mediator before the mediation.

Length of the mediation

Most mediations (not including the pre-mediation meetings) take no longer than one day (ie about **5.38** eight hours), but, occasionally, mediations last two or three days for particularly complex cases. The parties will decide in advance how long they want the mediation to last. Even if the mediation is agreed at eight hours, the parties are usually keen for it to continue on the same day if there has been no settlement at the end of the eight hours and yet agreement is in sight. If so, the mediation will continue by consent either until the dispute is resolved or it is agreed that there will be no reso- lution. Occasionally, mediations are adjourned after they have started if, during the course of the mediation, it is agreed that the parties require further information and that the mediation cannot be resolved without that information.

Often, the parties use all the available time and do not make their best offer (or even close to their **5.39** best) until the final stage of these proceedings. The length of a mediation depends on what the par- ties feel comfortable with in terms of time and cost. Sometimes the mediator will meet both parties separately prior to the mediation. This provides an opportunity for the mediator to become more familiar with the case, to establish rapport with both parties, and to address any concerns that they may have. Pre-mediation meetings have the advantage of freeing up more time on the day of the mediation since some of the exploratory stage will have taken place.

Role of private meetings or caucuses

Private sessions between the mediator and the individual parties are a useful opportunity for open and **5.40** confidential discussion of the issues and settlement options. They can be used for a variety of reasons, such as to examine privately the strengths and weaknesses of a particular proposal, to build more trust with each party, or to challenge positions and judgments. Private meetings (sometimes called caucuses) are usually crucial to progress in a mediation, and the degree to which a mediator will use them will depend on the mediator's preference and on the circumstances as they arise. A key aspect of the private meeting is its confidential nature and mediators should always check what can and cannot be conveyed to another party. The danger of using caucus meetings is that the mediator will become a shuttle negotiator, moving back and forth between the two parties until agreement is reached. Joint meetings are important for building relations and necessary trust between the parties and encouraging the parties to see the process as one of working together to find a mutually acceptable agreement. As a result, many mediators encourage the parties to continue to have joint meetings throughout the day.

The settlement agreement

5.41 At the conclusion of the mediation, the mediator may assist the parties to prepare a list of the points they have agreed upon. Once the agreement has been written it can be signed and formally typed up later. No agreement will be considered to be legally binding until it is written down and signed by the parties or their authorized representatives in the form of a settlement agreement. It is important to ensure that the settlement which comes out of an employment mediation meets the criteria of settlement agreements within the Employment Rights Act 1996 because otherwise they will not restrain the employee from taking the issue to an employment tribunal (see sections F and H below).

Post-settlement issues

5.42 An important feature of mediation is that it may provide for a review process, which is not possible in the once and for all circumstance of the tribunal. This may be important in cases of, for example, alleged sexual harassment where the result may be that the 'harasser' is moved away from contact with the 'victim' or a protocol is agreed for future behaviour. In such cases it is important to build in a review mechanism after say six months with, possibly, provision for a further mediation session to be held then.

When is it suitable?

5.43 Any employment dispute, in theory, can be mediated; but mediation is not always the best option for resolving a dispute. The suitability of a case for mediation is determined less by the type of case and more by the circumstances of the individual case at the particular timeframe when the mediation takes place.

5.44 When there is a relationship to preserve, mediation is a better option since it is a non-adversarial process that unlike litigation or arbitration does not produce a winner and a loser but an acceptable settlement for both sides. Mediation is suitable especially when the parties want to save the time, money, and stress of a protracted dispute.

E. PRIVATE NEGOTIATIONS BETWEEN THE PARTIES

5.45 In addition to the formal methods of ADR set out above it is of course open to the parties to seek to settle their disputes between themselves, either directly party to party, or through their legal representatives. In seeking to negotiate an agreement there are two particular issues to which the parties and their advisers will need to have particular regard.

- To be an effective settlement, any agreement must comply with any applicable statutory requirements (see sections F and H below).
- The parties will need to consider the extent to which their discussions may later be used in evidence in later proceedings. This issue raises two legal principles: first, the rules applicable to 'without prejudice' communications; secondly, the statutory regime for protected conversations.

5.46 For consideration of the 'without prejudice' rule, see Chapter 6.

Protected conversations

The regime of protected settlement negotiations is found in s 111A of the ERA 1996 (in effect **5.47** from 29 July 2013).

The scope of s 111A is limited to (non-automatic) u nfair dismissal cases under the ERA 1996. Its **5.48** effect is that evidence of both the fact and content of pre-termination negotiations, including offers made, is inadmissible in proceedings for unfair dismissal save where a party expressly reserves the right to refer to the negotiations on the question of costs or expenses, in which case he or she may do so (s 111A(5) of the ERA 1996) (see *Faithorn Farrell Timms LLP v Bailey* [2016] ICR 1054, [2016] IRLR 839). This confidentiality cannot be waived. 'Pre-termination negotiations' refers to any discussions held or offers made with a view to terminating employment on mutually agreed terms (and unlike the common law without prejudice rule, there is no need for the parties to be in dispute for s 111A to apply). The EAT has held that there is an exception to this rule if the date of termination is in dispute: see *Basra v BJSS Limited* UKEAT/0090/17. The legislation also reserves a 'get out clause' for what is termed 'improper' things said or done, or 'improper behaviour', in which case the general confidentiality provision will only apply to the extent that the tribunal considers it 'just' (s 111A(4) of the ERA 1996). There is no statutory definition of impropriety, but practitioners may wish to have regard to the examples given by ACAS in its Code of Practice (see para 5.51 below). In cases involving a claim of unfair dismissal alongside discrimination claims, the evidence of pre-termination negotiations may be inadmissible for the unfair dismissal claim but admissible in the discrimination claims: *Faithorn Farrell Timms LLP* (as above).

Nothing in s 14 of the ERRA (which implemented this provision) or s 111A of the ERA 1996 itself **5.49** is intended to or has the effect of displacing the common law rules concerning 'without prejudice' communications, which will, presumably, be applied in parallel to the statutory regime. A critical difference between the two regimes is that the 'without prejudice' form of privilege has only been applied in cases where there is an extant dispute between the parties, whereas the statutory regime does not require such a dispute in order to apply. Further, the common law principle is that the 'without prejudice' cloak will be lost where there has been unambiguous impropriety in the conduct of such negotiations or communications. This is a stricter test than the statutory regime. In *Faithorn Farrell Timms LLP* (as above) the EAT confirmed that 'improper behaviour' will include but not be limited to that which constitutes 'unambiguous impropriety'. It is, of course, possible that in certain cases offers and/or negotiations pre-termination will be covered by both 'without prejudice' privilege *and* s 111A of the ERA 1996.

ACAS has published Guidance on Settlement Agreements. It can be found and downloaded **5.50** at: http://www.acas.org.uk/media/pdf/o/a/Settlement_agreements_(the_Acas_Guide)JULY2013. pdf. The Guide includes model letters for making offers at the start of pre-termination negotiations and templates for settlement agreements.

Additionally, practitioners should have regard to the Code of Practice issued pursuant to s 199 of **5.51** the TULR(C)A 1992, which, unlike the Guidance, has formal status in the tribunal and ought to be taken into account in any case to which it may apply. This, too, can easily be found online and downloaded: http://m.acas.org.uk/media/pdf/j/8/Acas-Code-of-Practice-on-Settlement-Agreements.pdf. This includes examples of how s 111A might apply and of what might amount to improper behaviour.

F. STATUTORY RESTRICTIONS ON SETTLEMENT OF CLAIMS

There are statutory restrictions on contracting out of or waiving most statutory employment rights. **5.52** The policy behind these restrictions is to ensure that employees, who may be in a vulnerable position vis-à-vis their employers, are not subjected to improper pressure to give up their rights. These restrictions apply until all questions of liability and remedy have been determined by a tribunal (*Courage Take Home Trade Ltd v Keys* [1986] ICR 874, [1986] IRLR 427, EAT). There are exceptions to these restrictions which permit contracting out in narrowly defined circumstances where it is considered that employees are adequately protected. In the context of compromise of claims, the relevant exceptions are (1) ACAS conciliated settlements and (2) settlement agreements meeting strict criteria. Prior to 29 July 2013, settlement agreements were referred to in various statutes as 'compromise agreements' or compromise contracts. Section 23 of the ERRA introduced the standardized term 'settlement agreement'.

5.53 Section 203 of the ERA 1996 renders any provision in an agreement (whether a contract of employment or not) void insofar as it purports to exclude or limit the operation of any provision of the ERA 1996, or to preclude a person from bringing any proceedings under ERA 1996 before an employment tribunal.

5.54 'Purports to exclude or limit' does not require a purpose or intention to exclude or limit the operation of a provision of s 203, but encompasses any term which has the effect of excluding such a provision, see *Joseph v Joseph* [1967] Ch 78, at 87F–G (Denning MR) and 89F–90D (Diplock LJ) (in the context of similar language in s 38 of the Landlord and Tenant Act 1964), cited by the EAT in *M&P Steelcraft Ltd v Ellis* [2008] ICR 578, [2008] IRLR 355.

5.55 In some cases, a difficult distinction may arise between a clause which purports to exclude a right, and a clause which forms part of the defining characteristics of a type of contract under which the rights never arise in the first place. On the one hand if, for example, a contract is not a contract of employment then a right not to be unfairly dismissed does not arise, and there are no rights which s 203 could protect. On the other hand, the courts look with caution on attempts to avoid s 203 by 'dressing up' an exclusion of rights which would otherwise arise as a contract under which the rights never arise in the first place, for example by a clause stating that an agreement (which would otherwise be a contract of employment) is not a contract of employment, or that it has no legal effect at all.

5.56 In *M&P Steelcraft* Elias J said that it would seriously weaken the policy objective which 's 203 was designed to achieve if employers could, by the simple expedient of including a clause denying an agreement legal effect, thereby avoid the extensive statutory rights conferred upon employees' (at 67). Elias J identified two questions, both of which must be satisfied if a clause is to fall foul of s 203. First, but for the clause, would rights under the ERA 1996 be enforceable? Secondly, is the only purpose of the clause to alter, or seek to alter, what would, absent that clause, be the legal effect of the contractual arrangements?

5.57 Similar provisions to s 203 in relation to compromises of statutory claims are found in TULR(C)A 1992, s 288; the Working Time Regulations 1998, SI 1998/1833, reg 35; the National Minimum Wage Act 1998, s 49; and the Transnational Information and Consultation of Employees Regulations 1999, SI 1999/3323, reg 41 See also the Part-time Workers (Prevention of Less Favourable Treatment) Regulations 2000, SI 2000/1551, reg 9 and the Fixed Term Employees (Prevention of Less Favourable Treatment) Regulations 2002, SI 2002/2034, reg 10, which apply s 203 of the ERA 1996 to those regulations. This chapter focuses on s 203 of the ERA 1996, the most commonly encountered of these provisions. The analysis of that section applies equally to these equivalent provisions.

5.58 The approach in relation to claims under the TUPE Regulations 2006 is complex. Regulation 18 of TUPE provides that s 203 of the ERA 1996 shall apply in relation to the TUPE Regulations 2006 as if they were contained in the ERA 1996, save that that section shall not apply in so far as the TUPE Regulations 2006 provide for an agreement (whether in a contract of employment or not) to exclude or limit the operation of the Regulations. A claim based upon the TUPE Regulations 2006 may arise in two ways:

(1) where a claim based on breach of the TUPE Regulations 2006 takes the form of a complaint under an existing jurisdiction of the ERA 1996 (such as unfair dismissal or unlawful deduction from wages), s 203 of the ERA 1996 applies in the usual way, as described above or

(2) where the claim is a free-standing claim under the TUPE Regulations 2006, such as a failure to notify employee liability information (reg 12), or failure to inform or consult (reg 15), s 18 of the ETA 1996 is deemed to apply to such a claim (reg 12(7) and reg 16(1)),

and the claim may thus be settled by an ACAS conciliated settlement under s 203(e) of the ERA 1996. However, it appears that such a claim cannot be compromised by a settlement agreement under s 203(2)(f) of the ERA 1996. Section 203(2)(f) applies only to claims under certain specified paragraphs of s 18 of the ETA 1996 (as listed in s 203(2)(f) itself), and claims under reg 12 and reg 15 of the TUPE Regulations 2006 are not included in the list. A similar problem existed under TUPE Regulations 1981: see *Solectron Scotland Ltd v Roper* [2004] IRLR 4.

The formulation in respect of discrimination claims is slightly different. The principle provisions **5.59** are found in ss 144 and 147 of the Equality Act 2010 (EqA 2010). Rather than rendering the relevant provision in an agreement void, s 144(3) EqA 2010 provides that a term of a contract is 'unenforceable by a person in whose favour it would operate insofar as it purports to exclude or limit a provision of or made under this Act'. There are also exceptions relating to conciliated settlements and settlement agreements similar to those under s 203 of the ERA 1996: see s 144(4)–(6) and s 147. When dealing with an agreement which predates the EqA 2010, reference to the similar provisions of the predecessor statutes will be necessary: see Sex Discrimination Act (SDA) 1975, s 77(3); Race Relations Act (RRA) 1976, s 72(2); Disability Discrimination Act (DDA) 1995, Sch 3A, para 1(3); the Employment Equality (Sexual Orientation) Regulations 2003, SI 2003/497, Sch 4, para 1(3); the Employment Equality (Religion or Belief) Regulations 2003, SI 2003/1660, Sch 4, para 1(3); and the Employment Equality (Age) Regulations 2006, SI 2006/1031, Sch 5, para 1(3).

Where these statutory restrictions apply, a dispute may be compromised in the following ways: **5.60**

(a) By an agreement reached as a result of an ACAS conciliation (ERA 1996, s 203(2)(e); EqA s 144(4)(a)).
(b) By an agreement complying with the requirements for a settlement agreement (ERA 1996, s 203(2)(f); EqA s 144(4)(b)).

Further, any claim can be compromised by the parties causing or permitting the tribunal to make **5.61** a judgment or order disposing of the proceedings by consent. Each of these methods of settlement will be considered in detail below.

There are no statutory restrictions on compromise of common law claims (ie breach of contract **5.62** claims) brought in the employment tribunals. Such claims may be settled by agreement in the same manner as any other civil proceedings. An agreement to compromise a contract claim may be valid even if it is contained in an agreement which also contains a void compromise of statutory claims (*Sutherland v Network Appliances Ltd* [2001] IRLR 12; *Lunt v Merseyside TEC* [1999] IRLR 458, EAT).

It would appear also that the statutory restrictions do not preclude an agreement to refrain from **5.63** appealing a decision to the EAT. The EAT in *Hoeffler v Kwik Save Stores* EAT/803/97 held that s 77 of the SDA 1975 did not restrict the rights of the parties to compromise a right of appeal to the EAT. The EAT also went on to hold that the agreement was in any event void as it also compromised the claimant's right to have a determination of remedy for a complaint of unfair dismissal, an agreement which undoubtedly was covered by s 203 of the ERA 1996. On the terms of the particular agreement before it, the EAT was unable to separate out the parts of the agreement dealing with sex discrimination and those concerning unfair dismissal. However, it is likely that the statutory restrictions do prohibit an attempt to require a party to resolve statutory employment claims by arbitration (other than through ACAS) rather than in the tribunal: *Clyde & Co LLP and Another v Van Winkelhof* [2011] IRLR 467.

The reasoning in *Hoeffler* in refusing to separate out parts of the challenged agreement is open to **5.64** doubt. As Lindsay J pointed out in *Sutherland*, the effect of s 203(1) is not that any agreement which includes a requirement in contravention of its terms is totally void. It is not even that the whole of any separately identifiable provision which includes a requirement in contravention of s 203 is void. What is rendered void is only that provision 'in so far as it purports' to exclude or preclude a right to claim in contravention of s 203. Where a provision in an agreement offends s 203 so far as it relates to statutory claims, we would suggest that there is no reason to sweep aside the whole contract.

5.65 Whether a settlement is contained in a conciliated agreement or in a settlement agreement, the determination whether the agreement applies to prohibit any particular claim by a claimant depends on two questions:

(a) As a matter of construction of the contract, does the agreement cover the claim?

(b) If, as a matter of contract, the agreement would settle the claim, is the agreement rendered ineffective by the statutory restrictions on contracting out?

We now consider both issues in turn.

G. CONSTRUCTION OF THE CONTRACT

5.66 Whether the settlement is contained in a settlement agreement or in a COT3 it will always be a question of construction of the agreement as to precisely what claims were intended by the parties to be settled by the agreement. As a matter of common law, a COT3 or settlement agreement will be interpreted in accordance with the normal principles of contractual interpretation. The general contractual principles summarized in *Investors Compensation Scheme Ltd v West Bromwich Building Society* [1998] 1 WLR 896 (HL), 912–13 (Lord Hoffmann) apply to the construction of such agreements: *BCCI v Ali* [2001] UKHL 8, [2002] 1 AC 251, para 8, (Lord Bingham). Note the restatement of the *Investors Compensation Scheme* principles by the House of Lords in *Chartbrook Ltd v Persimmon Homes Ltd* [2009] UKHL 38, [2009] 1 AC 1101.

5.67 The more clearly the claims are set out in the agreement, the less room there will be for uncertainty. In *BCCI v Ali* above, for example, the employee had signed a COT3 in the widest terms: in return for a sum of money the agreement was stated to be 'in full and final settlement of all or any claims of whatever nature that exist or may exist'. At the time of the COT3, the employee had no reason to believe that he had any basis for claiming stigma damages arising out of the corrupt manner in which it transpired that BCCI had conducted its business over many years. Later, in the wake of the decision in *Malik v BCCI* [1998] AC 20, [1997] ICR 606, to the effect that stigma damages might be claimed in such circumstances, he wished to bring such a claim. As the compromise concerned a contractual rather than a statutory claim, there was no *statutory* restriction on the employees contracting out of their rights. The issue was thus whether the employee had, as a matter of *contract*, compromised rights of which he was not and could not have been aware at the time of making the agreement. The House of Lords held that there was no reason in principle to prevent a party from compromising, in an agreement supported by valuable consideration, rights of which he was not and could not be aware. However, the courts will be slow to infer that he had done so in the absence of clear language to such effect. Despite the apparently wide language of the agreement, the House of Lords held that on its true construction neither party had intended to compromise claims which they could never have had in contemplation.

5.68 The Supreme Court has held that where a settlement agreement is ambiguous, without prejudice communications between the parties may be used as an aid to construction if they form part of the relevant 'factual matrix': *Oceanbulk Shipping & Trading SA v TMT Asia Ltd and Others* [2010] UKSC 44, [2011] 1 AC 662.

5.69 In Royal National Orthopaedic Trust v Howard [2002] IRLR 849, EAT, the claimant entered into a COT3 agreement under which she accepted a payment on the following terms (at para 2):

> In full and final settlement of these proceedings and of all claims which the claimant has or may have against the respondent (save for claims for personal injury and in respect of occupational pension rights) whether arising under her contract of employment or out of the termination thereof on 29 November 1998, or arising under the Employment Rights Act 1996, the Sex Discrimination Act 1975 or under European Community law.

5.70 She subsequently brought a claim of victimization under the SDA 1975, and alleged that the act of victimization occurred after the date of the COT3. The question was whether she had effectively compromised any claims in respect of future acts by the COT3. The EAT rejected an argument that as a matter of public policy the parties could not agree to settle claims of which they were unaware, or claims which had not yet come into existence. The question was thus a matter of interpretation of the agreement as to whether the parties had intended to compromise such claims. The EAT followed the approach in *Ali*:

> If the parties seek to achieve such an extravagant result that they release claims of which they have and can have no knowledge, whether those claims have already come into existence or not, they must do so in language which is absolutely clear and leaves no room for doubt as to what it is they are contracting for.

The EAT found that the agreement did not have the effect of compromising future claims, and that 'have or may have' did not suggest that the agreement included future claims. However, the EAT's comments that there is in principle no restriction on the ability to contract out of future claims were in the context of an analysis of the position at common law. Having decided that, as a matter of construction, the contract did *not* cover future claims, the EAT did not need to decide whether there was any statutory restriction on contracting out of future claims, and it declined to do so. The most that it was prepared to say was that it had 'some doubts' as to whether the tribunal had been right that a COT3 agreement made under s 18 of the ETA 1996 is not capable of compromising a future cause of action. The difficult issue of exclusion of future claims was also considered in *Hilton UK Hotels Ltd v McNaughton* UKEAT/0059/04, where a list of statutory claims covered by the agreement was prefaced by the words 'all claims that you believe you have against the company for …'. The reference to the employee's belief indicated that the agreement could not cover future claims, the existence of which the employee was unaware at the time of the agreement.

Difficult issues also arose in *University of East London v Hinton* [2005] EWCA Civ 532, [2005] IRLR 552 The relevant clause of a settlement agreement said that the agreement was: **5.71**

> in full and final satisfaction of all claims in all jurisdictions (whether arising under statute, common law or otherwise) which the employee has or may have against the University officers [*sic*] or employees arising out of or in connection with his employment with the University, the termination of his employment or otherwise including in particular the following claims which have been raised by or on behalf of the Employee as being claims which he may have for …

There then followed a long list of claims, which did not include the claim eventually brought by the claimant in the tribunal (a claim under s 47B of the ERA 1996 of detriment by reason of whistle-blowing).

The main interest in the decision in *Hinton* is the Court of Appeal's analysis of the requirement **5.72** under s 203 of the ERA 1996 that a settlement agreement must '*relate to* the particular proceedings'. This point is dealt with in para 5.78 However, the Court of Appeal also dealt with the contractual construction of the clause. Purely as a matter of contractual construction, the agreement covered the s 47B claim in general terms, even though the claim was not specifically referred to. It should be noted that, in contrast to the situations in *Ali* and *Royal National Orthopaedic Trust* above, the s 47B claim did arise on facts which occurred prior to the date of the agreement. The omission of express reference to it appears to have been a drafting error. However, the language of the clause was in very broad terms, and the list was illustrative, not exhaustive. Another example is *Palihakkara v British Telecommunications plc* UKEAT/0185/06, where a compromise of claims 'arising out of the termination of employment' did not compromise claims existing prior to the date of termination.

H. STATUTORY REQUIREMENTS FOR SETTLEMENT AGREEMENTS

It is possible for the parties to reach a binding settlement of statutory claims without the intervention of a conciliation officer but only by entering into a settlement agreement which has its own criteria which must be met. In order for a settlement agreement in relation to a claim under the ERA 1996 to be valid, it must fulfil the following conditions (ERA 1996, s 203(3)): **5.73**

(a) the agreement must be in writing
(b) the agreement must relate to the particular proceedings

(c)   the employee or worker must have received advice from a relevant independent adviser as to the terms and effect of the proposed agreement and in particular its effect on his ability to pursue his rights before a tribunal

(d)   the adviser must be covered by a contract of insurance or an indemnity provided for members of a profession or professional body in respect of any claim which may be brought by the employee in respect of loss caused by the advice

(e)   the agreement must identify the adviser

(f)   the agreement must state that the conditions regulating settlement agreements under the Act are satisfied.

5.74   The provisions in relation to discrimination claims are materially the same: s 147 of the EqA 2010 There are some differences in language, for example the second requirement under s 147(3) is that the agreement must relate to the particular 'complaint' rather than 'proceedings'. See sections P and Q of this chapter for a specimen settlement agreement and drafting notes.

Claims which may be covered by a settlement agreement

Agreement reached prior to the issue of proceedings

5.75   Although s 203(3)(b) refers to particular 'proceedings', a settlement agreement may be used to settle a cause of action where proceedings have not yet been issued: *University of East London v Hinton* [2005] EWCA Civ 532, [2005] ICR 1260, 1266, para 17(6). Section 203(2) refers to an agreement 'to refrain from instituting or continuing any proceedings'. If a settlement agreement could not be used before proceedings were issued the reference to refraining from 'instituting' proceedings could not be given effect; see also *Bennett v De Vere Hotels Ltd* EAT/1113/95, IDS Employment Law Brief 568, applying the same reasoning. The Court of Appeal in *Hinton* observed that no sensible or useful purpose would be served by requiring an employee to issue proceedings for the sole purpose of enabling a valid settlement agreement to be made.

5.76   The better view is that a settlement agreement can settle a complaint under the EqA 2010, even if tribunal proceedings have not been instituted: the section refers to complaints which 'may be presented to an employment tribunal' rather than that they 'have been presented'. Moreover, as a matter of policy, there is every reason why the various statutory provisions should be interpreted consistently. The Court of Appeal's reasoning in *Hinton* that it would be pointless to have to issue proceedings purely to be able to enter into a valid settlement agreement applies equally to cases of discrimination. The EAT in *McWilliam and Others v Glasgow City Council* [2011] IRLR 568 decided that a compromise contract could settle a complaint under the SDA 1975 even if no tribunal proceedings have been commenced. Section 144(4) of the EqA 2010 refers to a contract which settles a complaint 'within s 120', and s 147(3)(b) refers to a contract relating to the 'particular complaint' (the successor to s 63(1) of the SDA and its cognate sections). This section would appear to have the same effect as the previous regime (see s 63(1) and s 77(4)(aa) of the SDA 1975), and there is no suggestion in the Explanatory Notes that the EqA 2010 was intended to effect a change in the scope of the ability to enter into compromise contracts.

More than one complaint/proceedings

5.77   A single settlement agreement may be used to settle more than one cause of action or set of proceedings: *Lunt v Merseyside TEC Ltd* [1999] IRLR 458; and *Hinton* (above), para 17(7).

Relating to the particular proceedings

5.78   Section 203(3)(b) requires the agreement to relate to 'the particular proceedings' (the formulation in the discrimination statutes is 'the particular complaint': s 147(3)(b)). The legislative policy is to protect employees from signing away rights except where a number of closely defined conditions have all been satisfied. As the Court of Appeal commented in *Hinton*, the code of protection set out in the ERA 1996 would be worthless if it could be removed, at the stroke of a pen, by a general release or waiver. A settlement agreement cannot therefore be used to achieve a 'clean break' settlement of all conceivable claims, whether presently contemplated by the parties or not.

A settlement agreement thus cannot be made in respect of claims which have not been raised by **5.79** the employee, although until the decision of the Court of Appeal in *Hinton* a degree of latitude was allowed as to the complaints which would be regarded as having been raised and capable of settlement.

It may therefore be sufficient that a complaint has been made in correspondence. In *Lunt v* **5.80** *Merseyside TEC Ltd* [1999] ICR 17, [1999] IRLR 458, the claimant had raised a number of different complaints in correspondence. She later signed a settlement agreement expressed to be 'in full and final settlement of all claims that [she] may have, whether arising out of her employment or its termination'. The EAT held that the settlement agreement was effective in respect of those matters about which she had complained in correspondence, and expressly adopted a passage from *Harvey on Industrial Relations and Employment Law*:

> A [settlement] agreement cannot seek to exclude potential complaints that have not yet arisen on the off-chance that they might be raised. However, where a number of different claims have been raised by the employee, whether in an originating application or in correspondence prior to the issue of the proceedings, there does not seem to be any good reason why these should not all be disposed of in the one [settlement].

However, in *Hinton* the Court of Appeal held that *Lunt* could not be regarded as authority for the **5.81** proposition that the words 'relate to' in s 203(3)(b) simply refer to proceedings or claims which have been raised, as opposed to the necessity of setting them out in the body of the settlement agreement. The Court of Appeal said that *Lunt* was not directed to the 'particular proceedings' point arising under s 203(3)(b) and is not authority on it.

In *Byrnell v British Telecommunications plc* UKEAT/0383/04 the settlement agreement purported to be in full and final settlement of all claims 'both contemplated and not contemplated at the date hereof'. The EAT held that the subsequent claim for unfair dismissal and sex discrimination had been validly compromised, on the basis that prior to the agreement (1) the claimant had raised with his employers a potential claim for unfair dismissal, and the facts of the discrimination claim were closely linked to the unfair dismissal claim; and (2) he had received advice from his solicitor in relation to both unfair dismissal and sex discrimination, a fact recorded in the settlement agreement itself. The EAT declined to comment on whether the agreement to compromise claims 'not contemplated' could be valid, but it is difficult to see how such a provision could satisfy the statutory requirement that the agreement relate to a particular complaint.

The requirement that the agreement relate to 'particular proceedings' was given a restrictive **5.83** interpretation by the Court of Appeal in *Hinton*. In that case, the Court decided that, purely as a matter of contractual construction, the compromise was wide enough to cover the whistle-blowing claim brought by the claimant, even though the claim was not specifically referred to (see para 5.72). However, the agreement fell foul of s 203(3)(b). The Court of Appeal held that the agreement did not cover the whistle-blowing claim, because there was no reference to either the factual or statutory basis for such a claim. The effect of the decision of the Court of Appeal is that the proceedings will need to be clearly identified in the agreement itself in order to be sure that they have been compromised. A general waiver such as 'all statutory rights' or 'all claims' is not sufficient for this purpose. The agreement must instead identify the particular claims to be covered. Smith LJ, going further than Mummery LJ, stated that it would not be enough to refer to *all* rights provided for under a particular statute (at least where the particular statute includes a number of rights). Either the particular claim must be identified by description (for example, 'unfair dismissal') or by the section number of the statute under which it arises.

The Court of Appeal indeed went so far as to suggest that as a matter of good practice the agree- **5.84** ment should contain a brief factual and legal description of the nature of the allegations and the statute under which they are made or the common law basis for the claims, irrespective of whether the claim being compromised is the subject of proceedings, or whether or not proceedings have yet been issued.

Part A Tribunal Procedure

Independent adviser

5.85 A 'relevant independent adviser' is defined as one of the following (ERA 1996, s 203(3A)):

    (a) a qualified lawyer (ie a solicitor or barrister, or in Scotland an advocate)

    (b) a trade union officer, employee, or member who has been certified by the union as competent to give such advice and is authorized to do so on behalf of the union

    (c) a worker or volunteer at an advice centre who has been certified by the centre as competent to give advice, and is authorized to do so on behalf of the centre or

    (d) a person of a description specified in an order made by the Secretary of State (no order yet having been made).

5.86 However, an adviser is not independent:

    (a) if he is employed by or acting in the matter for the employer or

    (b) in the case of a union or advice centre, if the union or the advice centre is the employer or

    (c) in respect of advice from a worker at an advice centre, if the employee makes a payment for the advice received from that worker.

5.87 The government has previously consulted on a proposal to extend the scope of relevant independent advisers to include members of the Chartered Institute of Personnel and Development (see 'Dispute Resolution: Secondary legislation consultation', Department for Business, Enterprise and Regulatory Reform, July 2008). However, the response to the consultation was mixed and in December 2008 the Government indicated that they would not extend the scope of relevant independent advisers.

5.88 The EqA 2010 defines 'independent adviser', at s 147(4)–(5), in very similar terms to s 203(3A) of the ERA 1996.

The advice

5.89 The relevant independent adviser must give advice as to 'the terms and effect of the proposed agreement and in particular its effect on the claimant's ability to pursue his rights before a tribunal': ERA 1996, s 203(3)(c). In *McWilliam and Others v Glasgow City Council* [2011] IRLR 568, several former council employees attempted to bring equal pay claims under the SDA 1975, arguing that the settlement agreements they had signed in respect of their claims were invalid. The EAT upheld the decision of the ET and rejected the argument that the advice must include advice on whether the terms offered are 'a good deal', or even such advice as would enable the employee to make an informed decision whether to sign the agreement. The EAT held that, in order to comply with s 77 of the SDA 1975, advice as to the terms simply required an explanation of what they mean. The requirement as to advice on the effect of the terms was satisfied by advice as to the effect on the claimant's rights to bring claims covered by the agreement. The agreement is still valid even if, against the advice of the adviser, the employee signs it. In any event, the adviser does not have to *approve* the deal; he merely has to *advise* on it. Provided that advice is given by an appropriate adviser, the tribunal will not inquire into the nature or quality of the advice. The only issue is whether advice has been given. If the employee clearly acknowledges in the settlement agreement that such advice has been given, the agreement itself will be sufficient evidence that the requirements of the statute have been met: *Hilton UK Hotels Ltd v McNaughton* UKEAT/0059/04, para 22.

5.90 Further, there is no legal requirement that the adviser actually sign the agreement to confirm that he has given the advice. Section 203(3)(e) requires only that the agreement *identifies* the adviser. It is, however, considered good practice for the adviser to sign a declaration (usually as a schedule to the agreement) that he or she is a relevant legal adviser, is covered by appropriate insurance, and that he or she has given advice for the purposes of s 203(3).

5.91 As regards paying the adviser, there is no legal requirement on the employer to meet any costs incurred by the employee in obtaining the requisite advice, although many employers are prepared to do so.

I. ACAS CONCILIATED SETTLEMENTS

The role played by ACAS in facilitating settlement has been considered in section B above. This **5.92** section considers the requirements which must be satisfied for an agreement facilitated by ACAS to comply with s 203 of the ERA 1996 and its equivalents.

Effect of ACAS facilitated settlement

Section 203(2)(e) of the ERA 1996 and its equivalents provide that the rule rendering void an **5.93** agreement by an employee not to pursue his statutory rights 'does not apply to any agreement to refrain from instituting or continuing proceedings where a conciliation officer has taken action under any of ss 18A to 18C of the Employment Tribunals Act 1996'.

In discrimination cases, s 144(4)(a) of the EqA 2010 provides that s 144 does not apply to a con- **5.94** tract which settles a complaint within s 120 of the EqA 2010 if the contract 'is made with the assistance of a conciliation officer'.

Form of settlement

There are no special formal requirements for an agreement reached through an ACAS conciliation, **5.95** in contrast to the requirements for a valid settlement agreement set out in Section H above. Indeed, a settlement is binding once terms have been agreed orally with the conciliation officer, even if the COT3 is not subsequently signed by a party (*Gilbert v Kembridge Fibres Ltd* [1984] IRLR 52). Hence, the parties should be careful when discussing settlement terms with a conciliation officer, and if they have any doubts as to whether they wish to accept the terms that are being proposed, they ought to tell the officer that they wish to consider them further and then revert to him. In practice, the settlement agreement is almost invariably reduced to writing. Form COT3 is provided by ACAS for this purpose.

Scope of settlement

In contrast to a settlement agreement, an ACAS conciliated settlement need not relate to 'particular **5.96** proceedings', or to a 'particular complaint'. An ACAS conciliated settlement may indeed be used to achieve a full and final settlement of all claims arising out of the claimant's employment or its termination. However, care must be taken to identify the claims covered by the agreement properly, and the claims in respect of which the ACAS officer is taking steps.

An ACAS officer will not be presumed to be taking steps to conciliate all possible claims which **5.97** could arise between the parties, and unless the parties tell the officer they wish to achieve a final clean break, and provide for this in their agreement, then there is a risk that the agreement will be taken as settling only the immediate proceedings which were before the tribunal. In *Livingstone v Hepworth Refractories plc* [1992] IRLR 63, the EAT held that the ACAS officer is to be taken to be dealing with complaints within the presumed contemplation of the parties at the time of the agreement. It held that a COT3 agreement drawn up pursuant to s 203 of the ERA 1996 did not cover a claim under the SDA 1975 or the Equal Pay Act 1970 (EqPA 1970), unless expressly stated to do so. The COT3 agreement in *Livingstone* stated that it was 'in full and final settlement of all claims which the claimant may have against the respondent arising from his employment with the respondent or out of its termination' save for personal injury and pension exclusions. On the face of it, it is difficult to see why such wide language would not cover a claim under the discrimination legislation. It should be noted, however, that the particular claim which was held not to be covered by the agreement only became open to the claimant following a decision of the ECJ which post-dated the COT3: *Barber v Guardian Royal Exchange Assurance Group* [1990] IRLR 240. The decision is perhaps best explained on the basis that the parties should not be taken as having in their contemplation a future claim which is not open to the claimant at the time of the agreement being reached. In the light of *Livingstone*, whilst it is possible to achieve a 'clean break' in a COT3 form it would seem prudent to make as clear as possible the precise claims to which the settlement relates, preferably by reference to statutory provisions. We deal further with the construction of the meaning of settlements as a matter of common law in section G above.

J. EFFECT OF AN AGREEMENT WHERE THE STATUTORY REQUIREMENTS HAVE NOT BEEN MET

5.98 Where a settlement agreement does not meet the strict requirements of statute, the employee is not precluded from bringing an action in the employment tribunal. This is well illustrated by the EAT's decision in *Riverside Health Authority v Chetty* EAT/1168/95. In that case, the claimants had entered into an agreement in which they accepted payments 'in full and final settlement' of their unfair dismissal claims. However, the settlement agreement did not satisfy the conditions of being a settlement agreement. Both the tribunal and the EAT refused to strike out the claims.

5.99 If a settlement agreement fails in any respect to satisfy the statutory requirements, the employee is entitled to pursue proceedings, even if the failure is what might be regarded as a minor technicality. In *Lunt v Merseyside TEC Ltd* [1999] IRLR 458, an agreement dealing with a number of claims, including unfair dismissal and sex discrimination, failed to state that the conditions regulating compromise under the SDA 1975 had been satisfied, although it did state that the equivalent conditions under the ERA 1996 had been satisfied. The agreement was thus a valid compromise of the unfair dismissal complaint, but was void in relation to the sex discrimination complaint. See *Palihakkara v British Telecommunications plc* UKEAT/0185/06, to similar effect.

5.100 In *CPS v Bamieh* EAT/309/99, the parties had apparently concluded a settlement agreement (but not signed it) one working day before the tribunal hearing was due to commence. When the case was about to begin, however, the claimant indicated that she was not prepared to continue with the agreement. The tribunal found that it was in the interests of justice for the case to proceed, and the EAT rejected an appeal on the basis that, if it was necessary to conduct a 'trial within a trial' to determine whether the agreement was reached, the power to strike out should not be exercised. It was also held not to be necessary for the tribunal to recuse themselves because they had been made aware of the agreement.

5.101 In the cases mentioned above, the claimant changed his or her mind about the compromise *before* the proceedings were disposed of. Where the claimant agrees to a compromise, and on the basis of that compromise withdraws his claim or otherwise permits it to be dismissed by the tribunal, then the claimant will be bound by that dismissal, even though he would not have been bound by the agreement which led to it: see *Mayo-Deman v University of Greenwich* [2005] IRLR 845. There is nothing to prevent a party from voluntarily abandoning proceedings, but what cannot be done is to compel him to do so because of an agreement he made, if he changes his mind before he does so abandon them. Once proceedings are abandoned they cannot be resuscitated: see *Times Newspapers Ltd v Fitt* [1981] ICR 637; *Council of Engineering Institutions v Maddison* [1977] ICR 30. In relation to proceedings which are withdrawn but not dismissed, see para 5.113.

5.102 In *Carter v Reiner Moritz Ltd* [1997] ICR 881, the tribunal dealing with a remedy hearing found that there had been an agreement to compromise claims for a certain sum, but that the agreement fell foul of the predecessor to s 203 (the Employment Protection (Consolidation) Act 1978 (EP(C) A 1978), s 140). The tribunal nonetheless awarded compensation in the sum upon which the parties had agreed even though the claimant's solicitors had indicated almost immediately after the purported agreement that a mistake had been made in calculating the figure. The EAT held that s 140 did not preclude the parties from reaching an agreement, albeit that such an agreement has to be considered by the tribunal and would not become enforceable unless the tribunal exercised its discretion to make an order in the terms of the agreement. It must be doubted whether the tribunal would have a discretion to make an order in the terms of the agreement in such circumstances. If the agreement falls foul of s 203, then a party cannot be precluded from changing his mind and abandoning the agreement. If the agreement is not binding, and one party no longer consents to its terms, then the tribunal cannot, we consider, make an order by consent. If a tribunal has a discretion to give effect to an agreement which the claimant has rejected, then the claimant is deprived of the protection of s 203. It is difficult to see on what principles the tribunal could exercise such a discretion.

That is not to say that a tribunal will disregard the fact that a void agreement has been reached, if **5.103** sums have been paid under that agreement. Sums paid will be taken into account in the assessment of any compensation due if the claim succeeds. In *Courage Take Home Trade Ltd v Keys* [1986] ICR 874, for example, the claimant agreed a sum in settlement of his claim, received the agreed monies, and then continued with his claim. As the agreement was not a valid settlement agreement he could not be prevented from pursuing the claim, but the EAT held that, in assessing compensation (and taking into account the sums which he had already received), it would not be just and equitable to make any award of compensation. A claimant who proceeded in such circumstances but did not recover more than the sum originally agreed would be at risk of an order for costs.

K. ENFORCEMENT OF A SETTLEMENT AGREEMENT OR CONCILIATED SETTLEMENT

The options for enforcement of a settlement agreement are more limited than those for enforcing **5.104** an ACAS conciliated settlement. Where a party fails to comply with either form of agreement, the aggrieved party may sue in the civil courts in the normal way in an action for breach of contract. The aggrieved party may claim damages for that breach, and may be able to claim specific performance of the agreement. In a clear case of breach of a binding agreement, the aggrieved party may be able to obtain summary judgment from the court, but in any event, a claim in the courts is likely to be expensive and time consuming.

In some circumstances, it may be possible to sue under an agreement in the tribunal, but only **5.105** if the claim can be said to be a contract claim within the meaning of the Employment Tribunals Extension of Jurisdiction Orders 1994, SI 1994/1623 and SI 1994/1624. For the tribunal to have jurisdiction over a claim for breach of contract under the Order, the claim must be for breach of an employment contract, or a contract connected with employment. In *Rock-It Cargo v Green* [1997] IRLR 581, the EAT held that. where an employer failed to pay to a former employee the sums due under a settlement agreement, the settlement agreement could be sued on in the tribunal as an agreement connected with employment.

It should be noted, however, that under Art 3(c) of the 1994 Orders a further jurisdictional re- **5.106** quirement is that the claim arises or is outstanding on termination of employment. In *Rock-It Cargo* the settlement agreement was made and was breached *prior* to termination of employment, and it was thus conceded that the claim was outstanding on termination of employment. Where a settlement agreement is made *after* termination, the claim cannot be said to arise or be outstanding on the termination of employment. This was indeed the conclusion reached (albeit reluctantly) by the EAT in *Miller Bros & FP Butler Ltd v Johnston* [2002] IRLR 386. Further, given that the claim in the contract case arises from the breach of contract and not the formation of the contract, it would seem that where a settlement agreement is made prior to termination, but the breach does not occur until after termination, the conditions of Art 3(c) would not be satisfied.

The process of enforcing conciliated agreements is simplified by s 19 of the ETA 1996. This pro- **5.107** vides that any agreement reached following conciliation under ss 18A–18C of the ETA 1996 that is recorded by an ACAS conciliator in a COT3 (or in documents annexed to a COT3) will, in most circumstances, be enforceable as if the sums payable under the conciliated agreement were contained in an order of the county court. Instead of suing under the agreement, the claimant need only obtain a warrant of control through written application to the county court under s 85 of the County Courts Act 1984 (or, more commonly, instruct an enforcement officer to obtain one on their behalf). Under s 17(10A) of the ETA 1996, any term of a conciliated agreement purporting to prevent disclosure of the details of such an agreement to an enforcement officer is void. If a claimant does not wish to engage with an enforcement officer or the county court directly they

Part A Tribunal Procedure

may make use of the 'ACAS and Employment Tribunal Fast Track' scheme operated by the Registry Trust, a non-profit company which manages the Registry of Judgments, Orders, and Fines on behalf of the Ministry of Justice.

5.108 A final option which, whilst not a direct form of enforcement, is likely to be of similar, or greater, coercive value arises under the penalty scheme introduced by s 150 of the Small Business, Enterprise and Employment Act 2015 into ss 37A–37Q of the ETA 1996. This scheme is available in connection with conciliated agreements entered into since 6 April 2016. Where sums due under such agreements are not paid, the Department of Business, Energy and Industrial Strategy (BEIS) will pursue the employer for payment upon receipt of a standard notification form, which can be downloaded at http://www.gov.uk/government/publications/employment-tribunal-penalty-enforcement.

5.109 If a BEIS enforcement officer considers that an employer has failed to pay the 'relevant sum' in full by the date due, the officer may issue a 'warning notice' under s 37E of the ETA 1996, stating the officer's intention to impose a financial penalty if the relevant sum is not paid in full by a specified date (which must be more than twenty-eight days after the date of the warning notice). If the employer does not pay in full by the specified date, then a 'penalty notice' may be issued under s 37F of the ETA 1996, with the penalty amounting to 50 per cent of the relevant sum (with a minimum of £100 and a maximum of £5,000). If the employer pays 50 per cent of the full penalty to BEIS within fourteen days and also the relevant sum due under the agreement, then the full penalty will be deemed to have been satisfied. If not, then further warning and, if necessary, penalty notices may be issued after three months (s 37E(3)(A) of the ETA 1996). An employer may appeal against the issue of a penalty notice to the tribunal under s 37G of the ETA 1996. Interest is payable on unpaid penalties and penalties are themselves also enforceable on obtaining an order from the county court (s 37H of the ETA 1996).

L. CONSENT ORDERS

5.110 Very often, the parties reach settlement at the tribunal just before the hearing; it is indeed often because the parties realize the weakness of their case and start worrying about cross-examination by the other side. Settlement may hold added attractions for the claimant/employee who has received, before the hearing, substantial state benefit payments since, if an award is made by a tribunal, such benefits received must be paid back, but this is not required to be done in an out-of-court settlement (including where agreement as to the compensation to be paid to the claimant is reached after a finding by the tribunal on liability). Settlement in these circumstances may also have attraction for the respondent employer who may be able to reduce his liability for the same reason (see Chapter 34 for detailed consideration of the recoupment provisions).

5.111 In such cases, it may not be practicable to involve a conciliation officer, nor to enter into a settlement agreement (for example because one of the parties does not have access to independent legal advice). The normal practice when a late settlement is reached in this manner is to ask the tribunal to make a consent order. If both or all of the parties agree in writing, or orally at a hearing, upon the terms of any order or judgment to be made by the tribunal, the tribunal may decide accordingly (ETR 2013, r 64).

5.112 However, the tribunal may be reluctant to incorporate the parties' agreement into a decision entered by consent, to avoid the risk of an order for the payment of money being subject to the recoupment provisions referred to above. Arguably the recoupment provisions would not apply where a tribunal makes an order in the terms of an agreed sum, particularly if the sum is a single lump sum which does not separately identify the basic award, past loss of earnings, and future loss of earnings to be paid. In practice many practitioners, to avoid any risk of recoupment, ask the tribunal to dismiss the claim on withdrawal on the basis of terms agreed between the parties and contained in a schedule to the dismissal order (see further under the heading of 'Tomlin Orders' below). If confidentiality is required, terms of settlement may be merely endorsed on counsel's brief, or by a separate agreement by representatives.

A claimant may withdraw all or part of his claim at any time by notifying the tribunal (ETR 2013, **5.113** r 51). The proceedings are brought to an end (save in relation to costs, wasted costs, or preparation time). Where a claim is withdrawn the tribunal shall issue a judgment dismissing it, unless (a) the claimant has expressed at the time of withdrawal a wish to reserve the right to bring a further claim, and the tribunal is satisfied there is legitimate reason for him to do so; or (b) the tribunal believes that to issue a judgment would not be in the interests of justice (r 52). If the proceedings are dismissed, the claimant may not commence a further claim against the respondent for the same or substantially the same cause of action (r 52). Where proceedings are withdrawn but not dismissed, the proceedings cannot be continued, but there is no cause of action estoppel barring a second set of proceedings on the same cause of action (*Khan v Heywood & Middleton Primary Care Trust* [2006] EWCA Civ 1087, [2007] ICR 24). For cause of action estoppel see further Chapter 11 section F.

Once an order has been made dismissing the claim there is no scope to argue that the agreement **5.114** which led to the dismissal fell foul of s 203 of the ERA 1996 (or its equivalents in other legislation). A tribunal is not required to ensure that an agreement for proceedings to be dismissed complies with s 203 (or its equivalents) before it permits a claim to be dismissed: *Mayo-Deman v University of Greenwich* [2005] IRLR 845. Section 203 is designed to protect employees from entering into misguided bargains before their claim is heard by the tribunal; once the claim has come before the tribunal and has been disposed of, the purpose of the section is exhausted in the absence of fraud or misrepresentation (*Times Newspapers v Fitt* [1981] ICR 637).

M. 'TOMLIN' ORDERS

Dismissing the claim on terms agreed between the parties presents difficulties if the settlement goes **5.115** wrong for some reason: once the proceedings have been dismissed, they cannot be reopened, and the only remedy for the aggrieved party will be to attempt to sue on the settlement agreement, assuming that the agreement can be shown to be valid.

To avoid the risk of difficulties if the settlement goes wrong, tribunals are often willing to **5.116** order that all further proceedings on the claim be stayed, except for the purpose of carrying the terms agreed between the parties into effect, with liberty to apply for that purpose. This means that if things go wrong the parties may go back to the tribunal. The terms of settlement may be scheduled to the order. This practice is based on the terms of the 'Tomlin Order', much used in the civil courts. The tribunal will invariably include a further order (provided that the parties consent) that if no application is made under the liberty to apply within a fixed period (usually a short period after the date on which money is to be paid under the agreement) the proceedings will be dismissed on withdrawal. The purpose of such an order by the tribunal is to achieve a balance between, on the one hand, allowing the parties to apply if something goes wrong with the agreement and, on the other hand, achieving an efficient final disposal of the claim so that parties are not left in a state of uncertainty. The option of staying the proceedings, so that the parties may return to the tribunal if something goes wrong, was regarded as preferable to a simple dismissal of the claim by the EAT in *Hoeffler v Kwik Save Stores* EAT/803/97.

In the civil courts, the effect of a Tomlin Order is to replace the party's original cause of action **5.117** with rights arising under the settlement agreement scheduled to the Tomlin Order (assuming the statutory provisions rendering an agreement void do not apply). In the civil courts once the compromise has been reached the court has no further power to deal with the original cause of action and the same applies in the tribunal. In *Green v Rozen* [1955] 1 WLR 741, the leading case in the civil courts, Slade J said (at 746):

> the Court has no further jurisdiction in respect of the original cause of action, because it has been superseded by the new agreement between the parties to the action, and if the terms of the new agreement are not complied with the injured party must seek his remedy upon the new agreement.

5.118 If a party defaults on the agreement (for example, the defendant fails to pay monies agreed) the innocent party's remedy is not to reopen the proceedings, but to sue on the agreement comprised in the schedule to the Tomlin Order. In the civil courts, there is no jurisdictional difficulty in a party doing so under the liberty to apply which is regularly contained in the Tomlin Order.

5.119 The analogous position in the tribunal is dictated by two factors:

(1) The restrictions on the settlement of most statutory claims may impinge on the validity of an agreement made at the door of the tribunal.

(2) The tribunal's jurisdiction in relation to claims for breach of contract is limited by statute.

5.120 If the 'agreement' is a void compromise of statutory claims (because it fails to comply with the requirements of s 203 of the ERA 1996 or its equivalents), it would not prevent the claimant from pursuing a hearing of his claim, and the claimant may apply to continue the proceedings under the liberty to apply provision. In *Milestone School of English v Leakey* [1982] IRLR 3 the tribunal made an order adjourning the proceedings generally on terms agreed between the parties; when the respondent failed to pay, the claimant was permitted to have his claim heard as the agreement fell foul of the predecessor to s 203. Indeed, if the agreement fails to satisfy the relevant statutory requirements it is open to the claimant to change his mind even if the other party is still prepared to abide by the agreement or has already abided by it: the agreement cannot be effective to exclude the claimant's right to a determination of the statutory claims. Therefore, whenever possible it is prudent for the parties to enter into a s 203 compliant settlement agreement, even where the agreement is entered at the door of the tribunal, to avoid the risk of a change of mind, or to ask the tribunal to make a consent order in the agreed amount.

5.121 On the other hand, if the agreement is valid but one party fails or refuses to comply with it:

(a) The aggrieved party cannot apply to have the case reopened. The position is the same as that in the civil courts: the underlying cause of action has been replaced by a right to sue on the contract which comprises the settlement agreement.

(b) The aggrieved party can sue on the contract in the courts, but would be unlikely to be able to sue on it in the tribunal: whilst the contract claim may be connected with the contract of employment, it does not arise on the termination of employment so that any enforcement would be in the county court (see paras 5.104–5.106, and see in particular *Miller Bros & FP Butler Ltd v Johnston* [2002] ICR 744, [2002] IRLR 386).

N. AUTHORITY OF REPRESENTATIVES TO COMPROMISE

5.122 Parties to tribunal proceedings will often have appointed advisers (often, but not always, solicitors) to act for them, including dealing with a conciliation officer to seek to settle the case. Where someone, such as a solicitor, is named as a representative and holds himself out as such, the other party is entitled to assume that he does indeed have authority so to act, unless he receives notice indicating to the contrary. This general principle applies to non-qualified representatives, as it does to legally qualified representatives. See *Freeman v Sovereign Chicken Ltd* [1991] ICR 853, [1991] IRLR 408, where the EAT held that the respondents were entitled to rely on an agreement signed by a Citizens Advice Bureau worker on behalf of the claimant. However, the representative must act with the actual or ostensible authority of the party. Ostensible authority arises from the party himself holding out that a person is authorized to act on his behalf, not from a holding out by the representative (see *Gloystarne & Co Ltd v Martin* [2001] IRLR 15). If there is such ostensible authority but the representative did not in fact have authority to do what he did, then the party whom he was 'representing' may have an action against him, but the resulting agreement still stands. In practical terms, those advising the parties should ensure that the party has seen and approved settlement terms before the representative formally agrees to them.

O. OVERTURNING AGREEMENTS

A settlement, whether reached through an ACAS officer or by settlement agreement, may be set **5.123** aside on the same grounds as any other contract: incapacity of the parties, mistake, misrepresentation, illegality, duress, and undue influence.

In *Hennessy v Craigmyle & Co Ltd and ACAS* [1986] IRLR 300, the Court of Appeal decided that **5.124** s 203 did not provide an exhaustive code of situations in which an agreement is valid or void and that the agreement could be set aside on the normal grounds of invalidity. The EAT in *Spikas & Son v Porter* EAT/927/96 considered what amounts to unlawful duress in the context of the settlement of employment claims. The employee argued that the settlement of his wages claim was signed only after the employer had applied improper pressure on him, namely refusing to make the payment until he agreed to accept a lesser amount than his full entitlement. The EAT rejected the employee's submission, noting that when negotiating to settle a dispute, it is quite common for each party to seek to exploit the weaknesses of the other. The EAT also noted that the individual had a 'cheap and quick procedure' for enforcing his claims, namely recourse to the tribunal. This case demonstrates just how difficult it will be for an employee to overturn a settlement agreement on the grounds of alleged economic duress.

In practice, particular difficulties may exist in seeking to set aside an agreement reached through a **5.125** conciliation officer. The EAT has said that if the conciliation officer acted in bad faith or adopted unfair methods when promoting a settlement, 'the agreement might be set aside and might not operate as a bar of the proceedings' (*Slack v Greenham (Plant Hire) Ltd* [1983] IRLR 271, 275, affirmed in *Clarke v Redcar & Cleveland Borough Council* [2006] ICR 897). There is, however, no reported case of a successful application on this basis.

There are inconsistent authorities as to whether a common law or equitable challenge to the val- **5.126** idity of a settlement agreement can be raised in the tribunal, rather than in the civil courts. We suggest that the better view is that such challenges can be raised in the tribunal. This is the more recent view of the EAT, although there are a number of earlier authorities which state that the tribunal does not have jurisdiction to determine such issues: *Hirsch v Ward & Goldstone plc* [1984] 280 IDS Employment Law Brief 9, COIT 1535/15 (misrepresentation); *Larkfield of Chepstow Ltd v Milne* [1988] ICR 1 (mistake of fact); *Byrnell v British Telecommunications plc* EAT/0383/ 04 (total failure of consideration). In each case, a claim within the tribunal's jurisdiction (eg unfair dismissal) was defeated on grounds that the claim was precluded by a settlement agreement, and the EAT declined jurisdiction to consider whether there were common law or equitable grounds to avoid the agreement. The reasoning of the EAT in these cases is open to doubt. In *Byrnell*, for example, the EAT held that the tribunal had jurisdiction only to determine whether the statutory requirements for a settlement agreement in s 203(2)(f) of the ERA 1996 were satisfied. Any common law challenge to the validity of the agreement was a matter for the civil courts. However, s 203(2)(f) provides that the restriction on contracting out of claims does not apply to 'any *agreement* to refrain from instituting or continuing … any proceedings' (emphasis added) of a kind to which the subsection applies 'if the conditions regulating settlement agreements under this Act are satisfied in relation to the agreement'. It would seem open to the tribunal to determine whether there is an agreement at common law, and not just whether the statutory requirements for such an agreement are met. This was the conclusion reached in the EAT in *Hennessy v Craigmyle* [1985] ICR 879: a tribunal can investigate the circumstances in which it is alleged that an agreement, within the meaning of what is now s 203 of the ERA 1996, is liable to be avoided at common law or in equity. This principle was not disputed (although not expressly affirmed) in the Court of Appeal (cited above). The EAT reached the same conclusion in *Greenfield v Robinson* EAT/811/95, and followed it in *Industrious Ltd v Horizon Ltd and Vincent* [2010] ICR 491, [2010] IRLR 204 and *Zinda v Ark Schools* UKEAT/0251/14/LA.

Statements of fact by one or other of the parties may form pre-contractual representations, or may **5.127** be included within the settlement agreement as warranties. As a matter of practice, settlement agreements often include warranties on the part of the employee as a condition of payment under the agreement. Thus, in a settlement agreement in which a claim relating to termination of employment is compromised for a payment of money, the employee may warrant that there are no circumstances which would have entitled the employer to dismiss summarily without payment. The employer may be able to withhold payment under the agreement if it later discovers that the facts were not as warranted: see, for example, *Collidge v Freeport plc* [2008] EWCA Civ 485, [2008] IRLR 697. See further the specimen settlement agreement and drafting notes at sections P and Q of this chapter.

5.128 The EAT has no power to entertain an appeal by a party from a settlement, according to the EAT in *Eden v Humphries and Glasgow Ltd* [1981] ICR 183, where the employee sought to appeal against the amount of compensation awarded on his unfair dismissal. On the day when the appeal was due to be heard he announced that he withdrew it on the understanding that the employers would pay an additional sum and offer him a testimonial. Later, the employee changed his mind about the settlement and sought to appeal against it, but the EAT determined that it had no power to set aside such a compromise and that it was a matter for the courts.

5.129 In some circumstances, an otherwise valid settlement agreement may be attacked on grounds that it contains a penalty clause. Often employers may wish to attempt to enforce confidentiality obligations (or indeed other obligations such as post-termination restrictions on competition) written into a settlement agreement by means of a 'claw-back' provision. By this provision, the employer is entitled to recover a proportion of the contractual consideration paid in respect of the compromise where obligations of confidentiality are not met. Such clauses may be unenforceable as they may be considered as penalty clauses. The position was considered in the Court of Appeal in *CMC Group plc v Zhang* [2006] EWCA Civ 408, where it was held that a 'claw-back' provision was unenforceable as amounting to a penalty clause since it was repayable on a breach of contract irrespective of the loss occasioned. The Court of Appeal gave helpful guidance on identifying penalty clauses in *Murray v Leisureplay* [2005] IRLR 946. It is first necessary to identify the amount payable under the contract on breach by a party. Further, it is necessary to identify the loss occasioned by the other party on breach. To the extent that there is a difference between the two, the court must then consider why there is a difference. Where there is no reasonable explanation, it is likely that the clause in question is not a genuine pre-estimate of loss and is a penalty clause. However, the Supreme Court has since taken a new approach to penalty clauses, which allows greater consideration of the commercial context of the impugned clause. In *Cavendish Square Holding BV v El-Makdessi* [2015] UKSC 67, [2015] 3 WLR 1373, the Supreme Court said that the test is whether the impugned clause constitutes a secondary obligation imposing a detriment on a contract-breaker out of all proportion to any legitimate interests of the innocent party in the enforcement of the primary obligation. That may assist an employer who seeks to impose a claw back of settlement sums where there is a breach of post-termination restrictive covenants, even though the losses flowing from the range of possible breaches may not be great. See also *Iman-Sadeque v Bluebay Asset Management* [2013] IRLR 344.

P. SAMPLE SETTLEMENT AGREEMENT

5.130 [On employer's headed notepaper]

STRICTLY PRIVATE AND CONFIDENTIAL
[Name]
[Address]
[Date]
WITHOUT PREJUDICE AND SUBJECT TO CONTRACT
Dear []
Termination of your employment with [   ]
This letter sets out the terms that have recently been discussed in relation to the termination of your employment with [   ] ('Company').

You [allege that you] have potential claims arising from your employment and its termination [*insert brief details of the relevant circumstances of termination*] which include: [all claims in the Proceedings (as defined in clause 3.8 below),] unfair dismissal, wrongful dismissal, [sex][race][disability][discrimination][equal pay] [*insert brief description of the other relevant potential claims*] ('Employment Claims').[1]

This Agreement settles the Employment Claims. In addition, it reflects the intention of both you and the Company [and all Group Companies] that this Agreement should also settle any other claim(s) that you may have against the Company [or any Group Company (defined as [   ])] [or its officers or employees], subject to and in accordance with the terms set out in this letter. [The Company enters this Agreement for itself and as agent and trustee for all Group Companies and it is authorized to do so. It is the parties' intention that each Group Company should be able to enforce any rights it has under this Agreement, subject to and in accordance with the Contracts (Rights of Third Parties) Act 1999].

1   Termination
    1.1 Your employment with the Company [will terminate] [terminated] on [*date*] ('Termination Date') [by reason of []. Your P45 [will be] [has been] issued [shortly after the Termination Date].
    1.2 The payments provided for by this Agreement are made without admission of liability but are in full and final settlement of any claims made or to be made by you as more fully set out in clause [3].
2   Payments
    2.1 You [will] [have] receive[d] your salary up to and including the Termination Date (less applicable tax and employee's National Insurance contributions [and less a repayment to the Company of £[] in respect of holiday taken by you in excess of your accrued entitlement [and you confirm your consent to this deduction]]).
    2.2 The Company will pay, without admission of liability, within 14 days of the later of: the Termination Date, the issue of your P45[,] [and] receiving a copy of this Agreement, signed by all the parties and your Adviser (as defined below), the following:
        2.2.1 a payment of £[] (less applicable income tax and employee's National Insurance contributions) in lieu of your [] notice
        2.2.2 a payment of £[] (less applicable income tax and employee's National Insurance contributions) in lieu of [] [day's] [days'] holiday accrued but untaken as at the Termination Date
        2.2.3 [a payment of £[] (less applicable income tax and employee's National Insurance contributions) as compensation for loss of your contractual benefits during your notice period]
        2.2.4 [a redundancy payment of £[], [which includes a statutory redundancy payment of £[]] ('Statutory Redundancy Payment')]. [The Statutory Redundancy Payment has been calculated as set out in Schedule [2]] [and]
        2.2.5 [a payment of £[] (less applicable tax and employee's National Insurance contributions) in consideration of your obligations set out in [any clauses containing post-termination restrictions] and]
        2.2.6 a payment of £[] as compensation for the termination of your employment ('Compensation Payment').
    2.3 For the avoidance of doubt, your entitlement to all salary and benefits [including [*specify PHI, private medical cover, life insurance, pension, etc*]] [will end] [ended] on the Termination Date.
3   Claims against the Company and warranties
    3.1 Subject to clause 3.2, you accept the terms of this Agreement in full and final settlement of all and any claims, costs, expenses, or rights of action of any kind, whether contractual, statutory, or otherwise arising out of circumstances of which the parties were aware before, on or after the date of this Agreement, and whether having already occurred or arising in the future [in the United Kingdom or in any other country in the world,] which you have or may have against the Company [or any Group Company] (or its [or their] shareholders, directors, officers, consultants, workers, or employees) from time to time, which arise out of or in connection with your employment by the Company [or any Group Company] or its termination including (but not limited to) any claim: [*Consider deleting obviously irrelevant claims from the list below.*]
        3.1.1 which is an Employment Claim
        3.1.2 in relation to notice or pay in lieu of notice
        3.1.3 for unauthorized deductions from wages, for detriment in employment (on any ground), for detriment or dismissal or selection for redundancy on grounds related to having made a protected disclosure, for paid time off for ante-natal care, for the right to time off for dependants, for the right to a written statement of reasons for dismissal, for unfair dismissal, for automatically unfair dismissal (on any ground), for a redundancy

---

[1] Use extreme care when completing this paragraph as you risk alerting the employee to claims they may not know they have.

payment, for automatically unfair selection for redundancy on any ground, and any other claim under the Employment Rights Act 1996

3.1.4   under the Employment Act 2002

3.1.5   for equal treatment under the Equal Pay Act 1970

3.1.6   for direct and/or indirect sex discrimination, discrimination on the grounds of gender reassignment, direct and/or indirect discrimination against married persons, discrimination by way of victimization, and any other claim under the Sex Discrimination Act 1975

3.1.7   for direct and/or indirect discrimination, discrimination by way of victimization, harassment, and any other claim under the Race Relations Act 1976

3.1.8   for discrimination, harassment, failure to make adjustments, and any other claim under the Disability Discrimination Act 1995

3.1.9   for refusal of employment, action short of dismissal, dismissal and/or other detriment on grounds related to trade union membership, for failure to comply with collective consultation obligations and/or to pay a protective award and/or any other claim under the Trade Union and Labour Relations (Consolidation) Act 1992

3.1.10   for the national minimum wage and/or additional remuneration, failure to allow access to records and detriment in employment on grounds related to the national minimum wage under the National Minimum Wage Act 1998

3.1.11   for the right to be accompanied and for detriment and/or dismissal on the grounds relating to the right to be accompanied under the Employment Relations Act 1999

3.1.12   for dismissal for reasons related to a relevant transfer, for failure to inform and/or consult, and/or any other claim under the Transfer of Undertakings (Protection of Employment) Regulations 2006

3.1.13   for compensation for entitlement to annual leave, payment in respect of annual leave, refusal to give paid annual leave, daily and/or weekly and/or compensatory rest and/or rest breaks, and any other claim under the Working Time Regulations 1998

3.1.14   relating to any rights to and/or during any period of maternity leave and/or parental leave, relating to the right to return after maternity and/or parental leave, detriment relating to maternity and/or paternity rights, automatic unfair dismissal on maternity or parental grounds, contractual rights to and/or during maternity and/or parental leave under the Maternity and Parental Leave etc Regulations 1999

3.1.15   under the Transnational Information and Consultation of Employees Regulations 1999

3.1.16   under the Information and Consultation of Employees Regulations 2004

3.1.17   for less favourable treatment, for the right to receive a written statement of reasons for less favourable treatment, automatic unfair dismissal and/or detriment in employment under the Part-time Workers (Prevention of Less Favourable Treatment) Regulations 2000

3.1.18   for less favourable treatment, for the right to receive a written statement of reasons for less favourable treatment, automatic unfair dismissal and/or detriment in employment under the Fixed Term Employees (Prevention of Less Favourable Treatment) Regulations 2002 or

3.1.19   for any rights to and/or during paternity and/or adoption leave, the right to return after paternity and/or adoption leave, for detriment relating to paternity and/or adoption leave, automatic unfair dismissal and/or contractual rights to and/or during paternity and/or adoption leave under the Paternity and Adoption Leave Regulations 2002 and/or the Statutory Paternity Pay and Adoption Pay (General) Regulations 2002

3.1.20   for detriment and/or dismissal or failure to allow the right to be accompanied under the Flexible Working (Procedural Requirements) Regulations 2002

3.1.21   for discrimination, victimization, and/or harassment on grounds of religion and/or belief under the Employment Equality (Religion or Belief) Regulations 2003

3.1.22   for discrimination, victimization, and/or harassment on grounds of sexual orientation under the Employment Equality (Sexual Orientation) Regulations 2003

3.1.23   for discrimination, victimization, and/or harassment on grounds of age under the Employment Equality (Age) Regulations 2006

3.1.24   for any prohibited conduct under the Equality Act 2010

3.1.25   in relation to any breach of your contract of employment including (but not limited to) unpaid wages, unpaid holiday pay and/or unpaid sick pay, permanent health insurance, private medical insurance, bonus or commission, or any other contractual or discretionary benefit, and any other contractual and/or tortuous claim

3.1.26   in relation to any office or directorship(s) of the Company [or any Group Company] you may hold

3.1.27   in relation to any share option scheme, bonus scheme, or other profit-sharing scheme or arrangement between you and the Company [or any Group Company] [including (but not limited to) [*specify scheme name*]

3.1.28   in relation to the conduct of the Company [or any Group Company] in relation to any retirement benefits scheme (as defined in s 611 of the Income and Corporation Taxes Act 1988) of which you are or claim to be a member including, without limitation, the payment of contributions to, the accrual of benefits under, or the exercise of any powers or discretion in relation to such a scheme

3.1.29   under the Protection from Harassment Act 1997

3.1.30   in respect of which a Conciliation Officer is authorized to act; 3.1.30 under European Union law [or]

3.1.31   [in the Proceedings (as defined in clause [3.8])] [or]

3.1.32   any other statutory claim or claim for breach of statutory duty.

3.2   For the purposes of clause [3.1], 'claim' excludes [any claim for personal injury [that has been notified to the Company in writing before the Termination Date]] that may be brought in a county court or the High Court and] [pension rights accrued up to the Termination Date under any occupational pension scheme (as defined in Pension Schemes Act 1993) operated by the Company [or any Group Company] and of which you are a member ('Pension Rights')]. [You undertake and warrant that, to the best of your knowledge, information and belief, after due and careful inquiry, you have [no claim for personal injury and][no claim against the Company [or any Group Company] in respect of Pension Rights] as at the date of this Agreement.]

3.3   For the purposes of clause [3.1], 'claim' includes (without limitation):

3.3.1   any claim of which, at the date of this Agreement, neither the Company nor you is aware and

3.3.2   any claim of which, at the date of this Agreement, you are aware but neither the Company [nor any Group Company] nor any of its [or their] consultants, directors, employees, officers, shareholders, or workers is aware.

3.4   You represent, warrant, and undertake that:

3.4.1   before entering this Agreement you have received advice from [] of [] ('Adviser') who is a relevant independent adviser (within the meaning of s 203 of the Employment Rights Act 1996 as amended) as to the terms and effect of this Agreement and in particular its effect on your ability to pursue your rights before an employment tribunal or any other court

3.4.2   you were advised by the Adviser that there was in force, at the time you received the advice referred to above, a contract of insurance, or an indemnity provided for members of a professional body, covering the risk of a claim by you in respect of loss arising in consequence of that advice

3.4.3   you [have not presented or brought and] will not present or bring any [other] complaint, proceedings, action, or claim before any court, employment tribunal or other judicial body in England or any other jurisdiction in connection with, relating to, or arising out of your employment and/or its termination and nor has nor will anyone acting on your behalf

3.4.4   [the Adviser has advised you as to whether you have any claim of any kind arising out of or in connection with your employment by the Company [or any Group Company] or the termination of any such employment and, to the extent that you have or may have any such claims, these have been asserted or intimated to the Company by you or the Adviser on your behalf prior to the date of this Agreement and this Agreement and the waiver and release in clause [3.1] above expressly relate to each and every one of those claims;] [OR] [any claims of any kind that you may have arising out of or in connection with your employment by the Company [or any Group Company] or the termination of such employment have been asserted or intimated to the Company by you or the Adviser on your behalf prior to the date of this Agreement and this Agreement and the waiver and release in clause [3.1] above expressly relate to each and every one of those claims]

3.4.5   except for those claims asserted as indicated in paragraph [3.4.4] above, you have no other complaints or claims of any nature against the Company [or any Group Company] or any of its [or their] directors, officers, consultants, employees, agents, workers, or shareholders

3.5 You accept that the Company [(on behalf of itself, and its Group Companies)] is entering into this Agreement in reliance upon the representations, warranties and undertakings provided by you in this clause [3].

3.6 You agree that the conditions regulating compromise agreements, compromise contracts or settlement agreements contained in the Sex Discrimination Act 1975, the Race Relations Act 1976, the Disability Discrimination Act 1995, the Employment Rights Act 1996, the National Minimum Wage Act 1998, the Working Time Regulations 1998, the Transnational Information and Consultation of Employees Regulations 1999, the Part-time Workers (Prevention of Less Favourable Treatment) Regulations 2000, the Fixed Term Employees (Prevention of Less Favourable Treatment) Regulations 2002, the Employment Equality (Religion or Belief) Regulations 2003, the Employment Equality (Sexual Orientation) Regulations 2003, the Employment Equality (Age) Regulations 2006, and the Equality Act 2010 are intended to be and have been satisfied.

3.7 [The Company agrees to pay, directly to the Adviser's firm, the Adviser's firm's reasonable legal fees incurred by you exclusively for advice given to you in relation to the termination of your employment and the terms of this agreement up to a maximum of £[] (inclusive of VAT) after receipt by the Company of an appropriate invoice from the Adviser's firm addressed to you and marked payable by the Company.]

3.8 [It is a condition of this Agreement that within three working days of the date of this Agreement you notify the [] Employment Tribunal (in writing, copied to the Company, in the form set out in Schedule [3]) that the whole claim against the Company [and all other respondents] lodged under case number [] ('Proceedings') has been settled, and is immediately withdrawn by you and should be dismissed.]

4 The validity, construction, and performance of the terms set out in this Agreement shall be governed by and construed in accordance with English law. Each of the parties irrevocably submits to the exclusive jurisdiction of the courts of England.

5 This Agreement, although marked 'without prejudice/subject to contract', will upon signature by us both and upon the Adviser signing the acknowledgement in Schedule [1] be treated as an open document evidencing an agreement binding on us both.

Please confirm your agreement to the terms set out in this Agreement by signing, dating, and returning to me both of the enclosed copies. Please note that it is a condition of this Agreement that your Adviser signs the acknowledgement at Schedule [1].

I look forward to hearing from you.

Yours sincerely

[   ]

Duly authorized for and on behalf of the Company

I have read and understood and agree to the terms of this Agreement.

....

....

[*Name of Employee*]   [*Dated*]

SCHEDULE 1

ADVISER'S ACKNOWLEDGEMENT

I [   ], confirm that I have given independent legal advice to [] of [] ('Employee') as to the terms and effect of this Agreement and in particular its effect on the Employee's ability to pursue the Employee's rights before an employment tribunal and any other court.

I confirm that I am a qualified lawyer within the meaning of section 203(4) of the Employment Rights Act 1996 (as amended) holding a current practising certificate and that I am neither employed by nor acting for [*name of employer*][, nor acting in this matter for any Group Company]. I confirm that there is, and was at the time I gave the advice referred to above, in force a contract of insurance or indemnity provided for members of a professional body covering for the risk of a claim by the Employee in respect of any loss arising in consequence of the advice referred to above.

Signed .... Dated ....

SCHEDULE 2

STATEMENT OF CALCULATION OF STATUTORY REDUNDANCY PAYMENT

Name:

Date of birth:

Date on which continuous employment commenced://

Effective date of termination of employment://

Number of completed years' service

(subject to statutory maximum of 20 years): Years

Week's pay (subject to statutory maximum): £

Calculated as follows:

- For every year during the whole of which you were 41 or over 1.5 × week's pay
- For every earlier year during the whole of which you were 22 or over 1.0 × week's pay
- For every earlier year (years under the age of 18 do not count) 0.5 × week's pay

So:

[   ] × 1.5 × [£] =

[   ] × 1.0 × [£] =

[   ] × 0.5 × [£] =

Total =

[Set out any reduction here.]

SCHEDULE 3

LETTER TO EMPLOYMENT TRIBUNAL

The Chairman

[   ] Employment Tribunal

[Address]

[Date]

Dear Sir

[Case Number] [Name of Case]

We write to confirm that settlement terms have been agreed in this matter and a settlement agreement has been signed.

The Claimant therefore wishes to withdraw [all] [his/her] claim[s] against [all] [the] Respondent[s] and confirms that there is no reason why the claim[s] should not be dismissed.

We look forward to receiving a notice of withdrawal accordingly.

Yours faithfully

[Adviser]

cc: [The Company]

[The Company's solicitors]

Q. DRAFTING NOTES FOR A SETTLEMENT AGREEMENT

This section proceeds on the basis that you are advising the employer in the drafting of a settlement **5.131** agreement. It should be read together with the checklist of issues below, which covers many of the practical issues you should consider when drafting a settlement agreement. See also the form of settlement agreement above. This contains the main substantive provisions which should be included in a settlement agreement to ensure it is binding on the employee.

General considerations

5.132 As a starting point, consider the contractual documents (contract of employment, handbook, benefit documents, share benefit documents). See the checklist section below for the type of issues that may arise from this consideration.

5.133 Be particularly careful to ensure you identify the correct employer, especially if an employee is employed by one group company but working for another one. Also, if an individual employee has been named as a respondent in discrimination proceedings, should he or she be a party to the settlement agreement too? Are share options or other benefits granted by a different company within the group? If so, the relevant company will also need to be joined as a party. Is there a TUPE transfer in the background, which means that the transferor or transferee should also be a party to the agreement?

5.134 Consider also the background to the dispute. Are there any specific points which need to be considered in the full and final settlement clause as a result? Should the settlement agreement also cover the withdrawal of any grievances, statutory questionnaires, or requests under the Data Protection Act 1998?

5.135 Generally the agreement should be marked 'without prejudice and subject to contract' until it is actually executed.

Taxation consideration

5.136 See generally Chapter 36 for the tax treatment of sums paid pursuant to a settlement agreement.

Termination date and reason

5.137 Preferably, the settlement agreement should be signed *after* the termination date. If the agreement is signed before the termination date, HM Revenue & Customs can argue that the agreement in fact represents a variation of the employee's contract of employment (or is a new fixed term contract of employment) and that the £30,000 exemption from tax (under s 401 of the Income Tax (Earnings and Pensions) Act 2003 (ITEPA 2003)) that usually applies to termination payments will not apply. In practical terms, this is less likely if the agreement is signed only days in advance of termination.

5.138 Reference to termination by mutual consent should be avoided wherever possible. A termination by mutual consent constitutes a discharge of a contract, not a breach. A breach is now required by HM Revenue & Customs before any termination payment is treated as damages (see *Tax Bulletin*, Issue 63 on Payments in Lieu of Notice (PILON) treatments). HM Revenue & Customs will most likely consider a mutual consent termination to be a variation of contract, so that the £30,000 exemption will not apply. Attempt, therefore, to agree an acceptable reason for dismissal, but the employer should beware of any attempt to collude with the employee, for example in a fraudulent claim for income support following 'redundancy', etc. There are proposed legislative changes in the treatment of termination payments, which are intended to take effect from 6 April 2018. These are addressed in Chapter 36. The changes, if implemented, will remove much of the distinction between contractual and non-contractual PILON clauses in that employees will always be taxed on payments which are calculated to reflect the basic pay they would have received over their notice period if, in fact, they have not served notice. It will, however, remain important to retain care over the use of language as the changes only impact on the treatment of what would have been the basic pay over the notice period.

Tax indemnity

5.139 An employer should consider including a tax indemnity whereby, if the employer is ordered to pay additional tax to HM Revenue & Customs because s 403 of the ITEPA 2003 does not apply and the £30,000 exemption from tax or some other tax exemption is not available, the employee will indemnify the employer for that tax and any fines or penalties imposed on the employer as a result of late payment. The primary liability for the deduction of tax in the situation where the £30,000 exemption from tax does not apply will be that of the employer, and usually HM Revenue & Customs will treat the amount paid as the net amount and gross it up to determine the tax which should have been deducted. A tax indemnity may, therefore, give the employer some comfort, although the indemnity will only be as good as the employee's ability to pay. As to the termination payment itself, there is a special tax code for termination payments, which the employer should apply to any payments which are not taxed as earnings. The employer deducts and pays to HMRC the tax that is then due which may, in practical terms, be more than the employee is eventually liable for and the employee may seek a recoupment at the end of the tax year. This means that there is an advantage for the employee in having the payment made before the P45 is issued as it will then be included in the 'pay to date' calculation and automatically be taken into account if the employee starts employment again within the tax year.

Tax treatment of the repayment provision

Settlement agreements sometimes include a provision whereby the employee will have to repay **5.140** any amounts of compensation if he breaches the terms of the compromise agreement, brings a claim against the employer, or otherwise claims the settlement agreement is invalid (see para 5.153 for further information on this type of provision). There are tax implications if such clauses are included. Certain tax inspectors considered that the inclusion of clauses such as this rendered the compensation payment (and possibly other payments under the agreement) fully taxable. HM Revenue & Customs has now, helpfully, confirmed that the inclusion of a repayment clause will not ordinarily, of itself, mean that the whole or part of the settlement payment should be attributed to the undertaking.

Practical arrangements, payment, and benefits

There are many general practical considerations and issues relating to benefits. See the checklist **5.141** below in relation to this. However, note that the employee is also likely to be entitled to the continued provision of other benefits during the notice period or compensation for their loss if termination is immediate. Consider: bonus entitlement (or other deferred payments), car allowance, other allowances, payments to personal pension schemes, holiday pay (and pay in lieu of untaken entitlement accrued to the termination date), private health insurance, PHI schemes, life assurance, use of company mobile, Blackberry, laptop, etc, and share options. It should be noted that the continued receipt of such benefits will still be taxable.

Post-termination restrictions

Most settlement agreements will include a confidentiality clause. This will restrict the employee **5.142** from discussing the terms of settlement and, in some cases, it will go further and also restrict discussion of the reasons for the termination of employment or events during the employment. In the latter case, both employer and employee will need to consider whether there needs to be a separate agreement or exclusions about announcements and responses to third party queries or discussions with legal advisers or family members. No such clause can preclude the employer making required disclosures to regulatory authorities (*Zinda v Ark Schools* UKEAT/0251/14) or the employee disclosing details of the settlement to a court appointed enforcement officer (s 17(10A) of the ETA 1996).

Many settlement agreements include a provision that the departing employee will not make or **5.143** publish any disparaging or derogatory or defamatory statements concerning the company or any of its officers or employees. This has obvious advantages for an employer in terms of controlling an employee's statements. However, it usually results in the employee's lawyers requiring a parallel undertaking from the company. Such a parallel undertaking must be carefully drafted to avoid depriving the company of defences which would be available under the law of defamation and imposing on the employer a higher burden than any which would otherwise apply. It is particularly important to bear in mind the necessity for executives of the employer to be able to speak freely in their internal discussions without laying themselves open to a claim if the departing employee finds out about their discussions. The departing employee need not concern himself about the intricacies of the law of defamation but would simply sue for breach of contract under the settlement agreement. If such a restriction is being demanded of the employer, you should always advise the employer that this is more onerous than the standard position under the law.

5.144 The employee may also request a reference. If he does, the employer needs to consider whether it is prepared to give one at all and, if so, whether it will be a 'dates only' reference, or something which is in fuller form. If it is the latter, the employee should seek to annex the form of reference to the agreement. The employer should include in the agreement details of a specified person who will be responsible for issuing the reference and may wish to retain the right to alter the terms of the reference if new facts about the employee's performance come to light. The employer should also include a standard disclaimer in the reference, to protect it from claims from future employers in relation to the contents of the reference.

5.145 Consider whether it is desirable to include any other post-termination restrictions controlling competition, dealings with clients, dealings with employees, and representations about the employee's involvement with the business. If so, the easiest way to address this may be to refer back to such restrictions in the original agreement, if they are likely to be enforceable. If not, bear in mind that these provisions will be subject to all the usual rules of restraint of trade which apply to post-termination restrictions in the employment context. Unless the settlement agreement merely restates the post-termination obligations under the contract of employment, there will be a tax implication of imposing restrictions, whether in the form of confidentiality or modified or enlarged post-termination restrictions. Payments for such obligations are taxable as earnings and, to ensure the consideration is separate from the termination payments, separate consideration should be identified for the obligations.

Full and final settlement

Settlement of 'all or any claims'—general release

5.146 Consider the following:

(1) Bear in mind, for the purposes of compliance with s 203 of the ERA 1996, the general guidance that using a rolled-up expression such as 'all statutory rights' is not sufficient: identifying the proceedings only by reference to the statute under which they may arise, for example 'under the ERA', is not sufficient, and the particular claims or potential claims to be covered must be identified, either by a generic description such as 'unfair dismissal' or by the section of the statute giving rise to the claim (see clause 3.1 of the settlement agreement above).

(2) Consider including a brief description of the complaints alleged in the body of the agreement (see the second paragraph of the sample settlement agreement, above). The employer may not wish to do this, particularly where it fears it may be alerting the employee to claims of which he or she was not aware, but it is preferable to do so. In any case, the employer can always do this without any admission of liability.

(3) Ensure the full and final settlement clause in the settlement agreement is specifically tailored to the situation; do not merely include a shopping list of each and every claim an employee could bring.

Warranties

5.147 Note also that, although the case of *Lunt v Merseyside TEC Ltd* [1999] ICR 17, [1999] IRLR 458 was doubted by the Court of Appeal in *Hinton v University of East London* [2005] EWCA Civ 532, [2005] ICR 126 on other issues, it is likely to continue to influence the drafting of settlement agreements in relation to warranties. *Lunt* stated that only those claims 'indicated' by the employee could be validly compromised in a settlement agreement. The EAT approved the statement as an accurate statement of the law: 'A compromise agreement cannot, therefore, seek to exclude poten-tial complaints that have not arisen on the off chance that they may be raised'. Many employers will therefore continue to include a specific warranty to deal with this (see clause 3.4.4 of the settlement agreement), notwithstanding *Hinton*.

Consider using full form warranties about future claims if this is of crucial importance (see clause 3.3 of the settlement agreement). Note that the employee may as a result become aware of further claims which may lead to demands for increased compensation. In practice, the likelihood of a settlement agreement being set aside is small. **5.148**

Note that any attempt to contract out of liability under an occupational pension scheme is void and unenforceable by virtue of the Pensions Act 1995 and so a carve-out from the settlement for such claims will be one it is proper to request (see clause 3.2 of the settlement agreement). If the employer has no occupational pension scheme, however, this carve-out will not be relevant and should not be included. **5.149**

It is usual for the employee's adviser to require a carve-out of personal injury claims. This is not usu-ally unreasonable, but consider requiring a warranty that the employee is not aware of claims at the termination date to give the employer some comfort (see clause 3.2 of the settlement agreement). **5.150**

As the employer, you may also wish to include a warranty from the employee that he has not obtained and is not about to obtain another job. This will then give the employer some comfort at least that the employee's negotiating position in relation to mitigation is accurate, although such a provision may be very strongly resisted by the employee concerned. **5.151**

The employer could also include a warranty by the employee in relation to breaches of his employ-ment and/or fiduciary duties. Such a warranty may, however, trigger a request from the employee for a waiver of all claims the employer may have against him. An employer should think carefully about granting such a waiver where the employee is senior, and any such waiver should be accom-panied by the warranty described above. Where the employee is a statutory director, the employer also needs to consider the limitations imposed by company law. **5.152**

The employer could include a provision which allows it to require the employee to repay some or all of the compensation paid on the occurrence of certain events, for example, breach of a material provision of the settlement agreement, the assertion of a claim against the employer which has supposedly been waived under the terms of the agreement, or other assertion that the settlement agreement is void. Such clauses may be enforceable, but the drafting must be done carefully or the provision may be void as a penalty clause (*CMC Group plc v Zhang* [2006] EWCA Civ 408). **5.153**

Any warranty restricting what the employer can say about the claimant to a third party cannot preclude the employer from complying with statutory duties to report misconduct to a regulatory body (*Zinda v Ark Schools* UKEAT/0251/14). Any warranty expressly purporting to preclude such a disclosure is void on the basis that it is contrary to public policy. **5.154**

If employment tribunal proceedings are ongoing it is necessary to ensure that they are properly withdrawn and dismissed, and provisions should be included in the agreement dealing with this (see clause 3.8 of the settlement agreement). **5.155**

It is traditional but not obligatory to pay the legal fees of the employee's adviser, or at least a con-tribution to those fees. In relation to this, see the tax requirements above and clause 3.7 of the settlement agreement. The adviser should sign an acknowledgement in the form of Sch 1 to the settlement agreement above. **5.156**

Company law considerations

Remember that a statutory director whose employment has ended remains entitled to notice of and to attend board meetings until he or she resigns or is removed as a director. If the statutory director is not given due notice, the business of the meeting is invalid. Consider the articles of as-sociation carefully. **5.157**

Part A Tribunal Procedure

5.158 Sections 215–222 of the Companies Act 2006 require that a compensatory payment to a director for 'loss of office' or upon retirement from office must be disclosed to and approved by the shareholders, unless the payment is made in good faith in discharge of a legal obligation, in payment of damages for breach of the director's employment contract, in compromise of a claim relating to termination of employment or loss of office, or by way of a contribution to pension to reflect past services.

5.159 Remember that a resolution from a holding company to terminate a directorship or approve a compensation payment will only operate as against that company, and separate resolutions must be proved in relation to directorships of subsidiary companies.

5.160 Consider also the Stock Exchange Rules: a relevant company must notify the Company Announcements Office of the UK Listing Authority upon the resignation or removal of a director. Placing a director on garden leave is arguably such a notifiable event if it is likely that, should the decision become public information, it would be price sensitive. Consider the City Code on Takeovers and Mergers: variations in contracts or 'poison pills' in contracts with companies 'in play' may require further consideration. Seek specialist corporate law advice if necessary.

5.161 Consideration should also be given to best practice in terms of corporate governance concerning termination packages. Is consultation with a remuneration committee or an investor protection committee appropriate? Public opinion may also be an issue.

5.162 Take note of the fiduciary duties of the departing director and those remaining. Breach of that duty is a risk if the directors approve a particularly generous or complex severance package. Any actual or potential conflict of interest must also be avoided (Companies Act 2006, ss 175 and 182).

CHECKLIST OF ISSUES

General considerations

Review copy of current contract of employment, any relevant handbook provisions, and relevant benefit documents. Check:

- Who is the correct employer? Consider also the definition of Group Company.
- The salary and benefits—have these been changed since the contract was drafted? Are there further non-contractual benefits you wish to include/exclude?
- Is there a PILON clause? If so, this will affect the tax treatment of any payment.
- Are there post-termination restrictions? Do you wish to rely on them—in which case are they enforceable?
- Does any other company and/or individual need to be a party to the agreement? For example, the entity granting any share benefits, any individual listed as a respondent in the employment tribunal, those involved in TUPE situations.

Consider the reason for termination of employment and relevant background. What reason will be stated in the agreement? Is the employer prepared to state a 'neutral' reason? (See also full and final settlement below.) Is the agreement marked 'without prejudice/subject to contract'? It should be.

Tax considerations

Does the employee wish to sign the agreement before the termination date? Beware as this may have adverse tax consequences and may bring the validity of the settlement agreement into question.

Does the employee wish to specify that the termination is by mutual consent? Beware of this as it may have adverse tax consequences.

Is the employee being made redundant? If so, the statutory redundancy payment will take up some of the £30,000 exemption and should be properly documented in the settlement agreement (see Sch 2 to the settlement agreement above).

Is there a PILON clause in the contract of employment? If so, the employer should deduct tax and NICs in respect of the PILON. As noted, if tax changes are implemented as proposed in 2018 basic notice pay will always have to be taxed as normal earnings.

Has the P45 been issued or will it be issued shortly? Under the new tax regime, it may be advantageous to make the payments before the issue of the P45 as this will enable automatic adjustment for any overpaid tax when an employee starts employment with a new employer.

Do you wish to include an indemnity obligation on the employee for any tax which becomes payable by the employer? If so, bear in mind that the indemnity will only be as effective as the employee's ability to pay.

Is the employee at or near retirement age? If so, consider the particular tax consequences which may arise. Is there to be a contribution towards the employee's legal fees? If so, it may be possible for them to be paid without tax liability for the employee under an HM Revenue & Customs concession. However, to qualify, there are very specific rules which must be adhered to.

Are there post-termination restrictions in the settlement agreement? If so, and they are not simply a re-statement of those which appeared in the contract of employment, beware as this may mean that the £30,000 exemption to tax may not apply and to avoid that, separate consideration should be identified for those post-termination restrictions and tax deducted as if an emolument of employment.

Is this an ill-health dismissal? A specific tax exemption may apply.

Has the employee any service abroad with the employer? A tax exemption may apply to compensation relevant to that service.

Practical considerations

Is the employee currently on garden leave or otherwise excluded from the company's premises? Does the company wish to include a provision that the employee will not contact or attempt to contact employees, customers, etc?

Will the employee be expected to attend the office as required to effect a handover? If so, include a pro-vision dealing with this in the agreement.

Does the employee have any company property which must be returned, for example documents con-taining confidential information, mobile, laptop, company car, etc? If so, include a provision to deal with this in the agreement.

What are the arrangements for payment of salary up to and including the termination date?

Benefits

Are there any outstanding loans, loans for relocation expenses, season ticket loans? Will the final salary payment be sufficient to meet repayment of these or will alternative arrangements be necessary?

Are there any outstanding expenses? What are the arrangements for the payment/approval of these?

Does the employee have any accrued but untaken holiday? The company will need to pay in lieu of annual leave in accordance with the Working Time Regulations 1998 and may have to pay in lieu of all of it under the relevant contractual provisions.

Equally, has the employee taken more than their accrued holiday entitlement? In this case the employer may be able to claw back payment in respect of the excess holiday if there is an appropriate contractual provision to this effect.

Does the employee have a company car? What are the arrangements for its retention or return? Consider issues such as insurance and running costs.

Is the employee going to buy the car? If so and even if the car is going to be transferred to the employee at no cost, for tax reasons the fair market value of the car will need to be ascertained.

If the car is leased, consider arrangements for obtaining consent of the leasing company etc. Note that it may be a breach of the leasing agreement for an employee to keep the car after employment has terminated.

What are the current pension arrangements and what is proposed in relation to these? Consider contri-butions to a personal pension scheme, rights under any occupational pension scheme, additional pension contributions by the company, the use of funded unapproved retirement benefit schemes, etc.

Does the employee hold any vested but unexercised share options? It is necessary to see the relevant share option scheme to determine what can be done in relation to them. Are there any arrangements in place to finance the exercise of the options? Is it proposed that the employer procure that the scheme's committee use its discretion to permit exercise?

What is proposed in relation to other benefits? Note that in many cases the company will have already paid the relevant annual premium to the service provider and, subject to the rules of the scheme(s), may be able to extend cover beyond the termination date at no additional cost which is likely to be an attractive incentive to the employee. Consider:

- private health care
- directors' and officers' liability insurance
- life insurance
- permanent health insurance.

Note that other contractual benefits may cease automatically under their terms on the termination date, for example life insurance, death in service benefit. You will need to check these issues and clarify the position in the agreement.

Termination benefits

Will the company pay for outplacement counselling and assistance for the employee? Up to what limit? (Note that this can be relatively expensive but is advantageous tax-wise.)

Is the company prepared to contribute to legal expenses? Up to what limit?

Ongoing arrangements

Is the company likely to wish to call on the employee at a later date, for example in relation to an ongoing project, litigation, etc? If so, consider the inclusion of a clause providing for this future assistance to the company.

Does the employer require the terms of the events leading up to the termination of employment and/or the settlement agreement to be kept confidential? Is it prepared to keep them confidential? If so, include a confidentiality provision but be ready for the employee to ask for a parallel undertaking from the employer.

Does the employer wish to prevent the employee:

- making derogatory statements about it and its employees, directors, etc
- making representations on behalf of the company?

If so, include the relevant provision but be ready for the employee to ask for a parallel undertaking from the employer.

What (if anything) is proposed by the company in relation to a reference? Will it provide a 'dates only reference' or something more detailed?

Are the employee's existing restrictions in his service agreement concerning confidentiality, intellectual property, and post-termination restrictions adequate and enforceable? If not, consider the inclusion of new ones in the settlement agreement but note the possible tax implications.

Is there to be an agreed announcement regarding the employee's departure?

Full and final settlement

If known, who will be advising the employee? Is he or she an independent solicitor or a trade union adviser?

Is the employer prepared to insert brief details of the complaints alleged by the employee? If so, do so as it will make the full and final settlement clause more likely to be enforceable.

Has the list of statutory clauses been properly edited to ensure it refers to each of the possible claims properly and to prevent allegations of a 'shopping list' settlement clause?

Has a warranty been included that these are all the claims the employee is asserting to prevent allegations that *Lunt v Merseyside TEC Ltd* [1999] ICR 17, [1999] IRLR 458, EAT applies?

Is this an exceptional case where the company is prepared to waive claims it may have against the employee? (Note: it is very rare to include this in first draft.)

Has the employee already presented a complaint to the employment tribunal? If so, the existing complaint will need to be withdrawn on settlement and an application for its dismissal made.

Does the employer require a warranty that the employee has not obtained employment elsewhere? This can be useful to ensure that what the employee is saying about mitigation is correct.

Does the employer want a provision requiring the employee to repay the payments made under the agreement should the employee breach any material term under the agreement and/or bring a claim in relation to the issues purportedly waived under the terms of the agreement? If so, bear in mind that such a provision must be carefully drafted to ensure it is enforceable as a penalty clause.

Does the employer require the employee to withdraw a grievance, grievance appeal, statutory questionnaire, or a request under the Data Protection Act 1998? If so, you should include drafting to cover this off.

Company law considerations

Is the employee a director/company secretary of the company or any group company? If so the employee will need to sign the relevant resignation forms, etc.

Does the employee hold any nominee/founder shares in the company? If so, it is necessary to include provision for their transfer back to the company.

Does the compensation package require board or other approval? Consider Stock Exchange and corporate governance requirements.

6

Case Management

SUMMARY

(1) Tribunals have the power to make interim orders and directions on a wide variety of matters.

(2) Applications for case management orders may be dealt with by written submissions without a hearing.

(3) If a hearing is needed, applications are generally dealt with by a judge alone at a preliminary hearing.

A. PRELIMINARY CASE MANAGEMENT AND THE SIFT

6.01 Tribunals have a number of procedures and powers to enable them to case manage proceedings with a view to managing costs, allocating a proportionate amount of court resources, ensuring cases are heard within a reasonable time and seeking to achieve a just result. Case management begins with the procedures for accepting or rejecting the claim form and response. These procedures are addressed in Chapter 2 in relation to the claim form (paras 2.10 to 2.16) and in Chapter 4 in relation to the response (paras 4.02 to 4.06). If the claim and response are accepted then they proceed to the 'sift'.

6.02 The sift is a process whereby as soon as possible after acceptance of the response an employment judge is required to consider all the documents held by the tribunal in relation to the claim to confirm whether there are arguable complaints and defences within the jurisdiction of the tribunal: ETR 2013, r 26. The employment judge can order further information from a party in order to enable him or her to assess the case. If the employment judge confirms that there are arguable complaints and defences, then he or she will proceed to make case management directions (see further below). If the employment judge is not satisfied then, under r 27 or 28, he or she may dismiss a claim or response in whole or in part.

6.03 Where an employment judge considers that the tribunal has no jurisdiction or that the claim or response, in whole or in part, has no reasonable prospect of success, the tribunal shall send notice to the parties setting out the judge's view and the reasons for it and ordering that the relevant pleading or part thereof be dismissed on a specified future date unless the affected party has presented written representations to the tribunal explaining why it should not be dismissed. Where the response is being challenged, the tribunal must set out the consequences of the response being dismissed and the claim will be treated under r 21 as if no response had been presented. If no written representations are presented, then the tribunal will write to the parties to confirm the dismissal of the relevant claims or defence.

On receipt of the written representation the judge may accept them and permit the claim or re-   **6.04** sponse to proceed or the judge may fix a hearing for the purpose of deciding the issue. The affected party should attend to make oral representations. The other party may, but need not, attend and participate in the hearing.

B. CASE MANAGEMENT AND PRELIMINARY HEARINGS

If a claim and response are accepted the tribunal will then proceed to case manage the claim to   **6.05** ensure that it is prepared for a hearing. The modern practice in employment tribunals is for case management to be judge led, although parties frequently apply for specific orders to meet specific circumstances. Case management can be conducted on paper or case management orders may be given at a preliminary hearing. A preliminary hearing may take place on either the application of a party or at the judge's own motion (ETR 2013, r 54). Discrimination claims and other complex cases are routinely called in for a preliminary hearing, which may be conducted by telephone conference or in person at the tribunal, to ensure that the issues are clearly identified and for appropriate case management orders to be made. A case management preliminary hearing is held by a judge alone and shall be held in private. In very complex cases there may be several preliminary hearings for the effective case management of proceedings. A preliminary hearing may also be held to determine preliminary issues such as applications for strike-out or a deposit. These preliminary issues are addressed in Chapter 7. The remainder of this chapter focuses on case management.

The Presidential Guidance on General Case Management was first issued in March 2014, and was   **6.06** reissued on 22 January 2018 to take account of the abolition of fees in the Tribunal. The Guidance contains general guidance on case management, together with specific Guidance Notes on a wide range of case management situations. In some regions a standard form of agenda for the preliminary hearing is sent to the parties with the notice of hearing which the parties are required to complete and exchange and copy to the tribunal for use by the judge during the preliminary hearing. The purpose is to reduce the areas of disagreement to be dealt with at the preliminary hearing and to encourage the parties to discuss the case prior to the preliminary hearing.

In all case management decisions the tribunal should have at the forefront the overriding objective   **6.07** that it is to deal with cases justly (ETR 2013, r 2) and this includes, so far as is practicable: (a) ensuring that the parties are on an equal footing; (b) dealing with cases in ways which are proportionate to the complexity and importance of the issues; (c) avoiding unnecessary formality and seeking flexibility in the proceedings; (d) avoiding delay, so far as compatible with proper consideration of the issues; and (e) saving expense. A tribunal or judge must seek to give effect to the overriding objective either when exercising any power given to it or them by the regulations or the rules in the schedules, or when interpreting any of the regulations or rules. There is also an obligation on the parties to assist the tribunal to further the overriding objective (ETR 2013, r 2).

Tribunals have a general power to manage proceedings and make case management orders (ETR   **6.08** 2013, r 29). The employment judge is likely to play a leading role in clarifying the issues for determination by the tribunal at the final hearing with a view to ensuring that costs are not wasted on pursuing extraneous matters. A timetable for agreeing a bundle and for exchange of witness statements and for the hearing itself is likely to be set. The question of whether judicial mediation may be appropriate might also be explored, ETR 2013, r 53(1)(e). ETR 2013, r 3 requires the tribunal, wherever practicable and appropriate, to encourage the parties to use the Advisory, Conciliation and Arbitration Service (ACAS), judicial or other mediation, or other means to resolve the dispute by agreement. The rules are clear that the tribunal may regulate its own procedure and shall conduct hearings in the manner it considers fair, having regard to the principles contained in the overriding objective (ETR 2013, r 41). Some specific powers are set out in the rules but these do not limit the general power (ETR 2013, r 29). The orders and powers include:

(a) power to extend or shorten any time limit specified in the rules or in any decision (ETR 2013, r 5)

(b) power to order a preliminary or final hearing (ETR 2013, r 26(2))

(c) power to vary, suspend or set aside an earlier case management order (ETR 2013, r 29)

(d) power to order any person in Great Britain to disclose documents or information to a party or to allow a party to inspect such material as might be ordered by a county court (or in Scotland, by a sheriff) (ETR 2013, r 31)

(e) power to order any person in Great Britain to attend a hearing to give evidence, produce documents, or produce information (ETR 2013, r 32)

(f) power to use the procedures for obtaining evidence prescribed in Council Regulation (EC) No 1026/2001 of 28 May 2001 on cooperation between the courts of the Member States in the taking of evidence in civil or commercial matters (ETR 2013, r 33)

(g) power to add or remove any person as a party, by way of substitution or otherwise (ETR 2013, r 34)

(h) power to permit any person to participate in proceedings, on such terms as may be specified (ETR 2013, r 35)

(i) power to specify one or more claim as the lead claim (ETR 2013, r 36)

(j) power to strike out all or part of a claim or response on any of the following grounds: (a) it is scandalous or vexatious or has no reasonable prospect of success; (b) the manner in which proceedings have been conducted by or on behalf of a party has been scandalous, unreasonable, or vexatious; (c) for non-compliance with any of the rules or an order of the tribunal; (d) that it has not been actively pursued; or (e) that the tribunal considers that it is no longer possible to have a fair hearing (ETR 2013, r 37)

(k) power to order that unless an order is complied with by a specified date a claim or response will be dismissed without further order (ETR 2013, r 38)

(l) power to order that a deposit be paid as a condition of permitting a party to continue with an allegation or argument (ETR 2013, r 39)

(m) power to timetable proceedings including imposing limits on the time that a party may take in presenting evidence, questioning witnesses or making submissions (ETR 2013, r 45)

(n) power to make an order with a view to preventing or restricting the public disclosure of any part of proceedings (ETR 2013, r 50).

6.09 Although the list of powers previously found in ETR 2004, r 10 has not been reproduced in ETR 2013, there is nothing to suggest that any of the powers have been removed from the tribunal. Therefore, the power to require written answers; to stay proceedings; to postpone or adjourn hearings; to give leave to amend a claim or response; and giving directions as to the use of experts or interpreters in the proceedings are all powers which the tribunal will continue to have at their disposal to manage proceedings. Any of these orders would fall within the tribunal's wide powers under ETR 2013, rr 29 and 41.

6.10 The EAT and other appellate courts have emphasized the importance of effective case management particularly in complex cases. Cases involving multiple parties, multiple claims, complex factual scenarios, or allegations spanning a considerable time period may give rise to particular difficulties. The complexity of such cases makes case management difficult but also essential and cost effective, saving time in the long run.

(1) In *Martins v Marks & Spencer plc* [1998] IRLR 326, Mummery LJ suggested that, in most cases, it would be good practice to hold a meeting for directions in order to identify the issues

before the hearing of the case began. The judge could then consider making directions on such matters as the issues falling for determination and, if appropriate, the exchange of witness statements in advance of the substantive hearing. It would be important to obtain from the parties a reliable time estimate of the length of the hearing, which the parties should be asked to justify by reference to the number of documents which the tribunal was likely to be asked to examine and to the number of witnesses who were likely to be called to give evidence on the relevant issues. It should then be possible for the regional office 'to allot a realistic slot in the list to ensure an uninterrupted hearing of the whole case, without damaging disruptions which had occurred in the present and other cases'.

(2) In *Hendricks v Metropolitan Police Commissioner* [2003] IRLR 96, para 54, Mummery LJ gave the following guidance for dealing with discrimination cases which involve numerous incidents by many people over a long period (in that case over eleven years):

> Before the applications proceed to a substantive hearing, the parties should attempt to agree a list of issues and to formulate proposals about ways and means of reducing the area of dispute, the number of witnesses and the volume of documents. Attempts must be made by all concerned to keep the discrimination proceedings within reasonable bounds by concentrating on the most serious and the more recent allegations. The parties' representatives should consult one another about their proposals before requesting another directions hearing before the chairman. It will be for him to decide how the matter should proceed, if it is impossible to reach a sensible agreement.

(3) In *Goodwin v Patent Office* [1999] IRLR 4, [1999] ICR 302 the EAT emphasized the importance of this approach in disability discrimination cases. In cases where the parties have not identified the real questions at issue in the claim and response, the tribunal should either give standard directions or arrange for a directions hearing in order to clarify the issues, as 'generally, it will be unsatisfactory for the disability issue to remain unclear and unspecific until the hearing itself'.

(4) *ALM Medical Services Ltd v Bladon* [2002] IRLR 807, [2002] ICR 1444 suggested that a hearing is needed in protected disclosure cases 'in order to identify the issues and ascertain what evidence the parties intend to call on those issues'. The reason for this is that the protected disclosure provisions of the ERA 1996 require a number of different elements to be established on the evidence before a claimant can succeed in his or her claim; including for example, whether he or she has made a qualifying disclosure under s 43B, which is made in accordance with any of ss 43C to 43H.

(5) In *HSBC Asia Holdings BV v Gillespie* [2011] IRLR 209 Underhill J considered the grounds on which a tribunal may, in the course of case management, make a decision that certain evidence will be excluded from the final hearing. The question was whether the evidence was sufficiently relevant for its admission to be justified. Whether a pre-hearing ruling on admissibility should be made depends on the circumstances of the case, but there may be advantages, in terms of managing disclosure and witness statements, to a ruling on admissibility at an early stage. This case demonstrates the importance and the difficulty of effectively case managing complex discrimination cases. See in particular Underhill J's consideration of the possibility of proceeding to a hearing on sample allegations.

6.11 Although the tribunals are empowered and encouraged to manage cases to ensure that they are dealt with efficiently and effectively the appellate courts have been wary of very robust practices where a tribunal has required a claimant to limit the claims which they are bringing by placing an arbitrary limit on the claim. The more proportionate way to address the situation is through discussion, careful distillation of the issues, and, if appropriate, costs: *McKinson v Hackney Community College & Others* [2011] UKEAT/0237/11 and *Fairbank v Care Management Group* [2012] UKEAT/0139/12.

6.12 There is a special case management procedure to follow in equal pay cases, which is set out in Chapter 27. The aim is to reduce the delays that occur in such claims and various timetables are set out.

C. APPLYING FOR ORDERS AND DIRECTIONS AT A PRELIMINARY HEARING

6.13 The Presidential Guidance on General Case Management contains guidance as to the content and timing of applications (see paras 12–17) and should be considered before making applications. An application for an order may be made at a hearing or in writing. It is good practice for an application for an order or direction to identify with precision the orders sought and the reasons for the order, including how the order will assist the judge in dealing with the proceedings efficiently and fairly.

6.14 If an application is made in writing then notice of the application must be sent to all parties along with notice that any objection should be made as soon as possible. The tribunal may address the application in writing or order that it is addressed at a preliminary or final hearing (ETR 2013, r 30).

D. VARYING OR SETTING ASIDE ORDERS

6.15 A party may apply for an order to be issued, varied or revoked at any stage in the proceedings (ETR 2013, r 29).

6.16 An application under r 30 may be made to vary, suspend, or set aside an earlier case management order where it is necessary, in the interests of justice and, in particular, where a party affected by the earlier order did not have a reasonable opportunity to make representations before it was made (ETR 2013, r 29).

6.17 An order made or refused by one judge cannot simply be revisited by another. If there is a subsequent application, tribunals should follow the same principles applicable under the CPR and only set aside or vary such an order where there has been a change in the circumstances since it was made (see CPR 29PD, para 6.4). In *Goldman Sachs Services Ltd v Montali* [2002] ICR 1251 a tribunal reversed an interim order (made by a different tribunal) providing for a limitation issue to be heard at a directions hearing, and instead ordered it to be dealt with at the substantive hearing. It was held on appeal that, in the absence of any change of circumstances, this was both 'a wrong exercise of discretion and wrong in principle'.

E. COMMON ORDERS AND DIRECTIONS

6.18 As set out at para 6.08, particular examples of orders which may be made are found throughout the rules and the principles governing common types of interim orders and directions are considered below.

Additional information

6.19 *General*

(a) A tribunal may order a party to provide further details of the allegations in a claim or response.
(b) The tribunal can so order at the request of a party or at the tribunal's own motion either before or at a hearing.
(c) Parties should try to avoid long and complicated requests and the earlier that such requests are made the more likely they are to be granted.
(d) The purpose of a request for further information is to inform the other side of the case that they have to meet, to prevent parties from being taken by surprise by enabling them to prepare rebutting evidence, and to define the issues in dispute.
(e) A party who fails to comply with an order to provide further information may find his claim or response, or relevant parts, dismissed or struck out although tribunals are naturally reluctant to take this draconian step (see paras 6.110–6.114).

The employer may request further information before the response has been entered in cases where **6.20** the claim is very obscure. A claim form may be rejected if it is in a form which cannot sensibly be responded to (ETR 2013, r 12). Rather than rejecting the claim the tribunal may order the provision of additional information to rectify the defect. Additional information may also be sought by the tribunal under r 26 as part of the sift process.

Tribunals are, in general, anxious that cases do not become a complex battle of pleadings and there- **6.21** fore seek to avoid unnecessarily pedantic applications for further information.

Important guidance on the proper scope of orders for further information was given in *White v* **6.22** *University of Manchester* [1976] ICR 419, 423, by Phillips J, who said:

> We do not wish to say anything to encourage unnecessary legalism to creep into the proceedings of Industrial Tribunals; but, while that should be avoided, it should not be avoided at the expense of falling into a different error, namely that of doing injustice by a hearing taking place when the party who has to meet the allegations does not know in advance what those allegations are. The moral of all this is that everybody involved, whether it be solicitors, counsel, non-professional representatives or the parties themselves where not represented, should bring to the problem commonsense and goodwill. This involves, or may involve in anything except the simplest cases, giving, when it is asked, reasonable detail about the nature of complaints which are going to be made at the Tribunal.

The EAT thus required particulars of the generalized allegation made by the employers that the **6.23** employee, a typist, was 'unable to cope with her job duties'. This guidance was echoed by Wood J in *Byrne v Financial Times* [1991] IRLR 417:

> General principles affecting the ordering of further and better particulars include that the parties should not be taken by surprise at the last minute; that particulars should only be ordered when necessary in order to do justice in the case or to prevent adjournment; that the Order should not be oppressive; that particulars are for the purposes of identifying the issues, not for the production of the evidence; and that complicated pleadings battles should not be encouraged.

An employer was also held to be entitled to particulars of an allegation that the employer condoned **6.24** fraudulent claims for expenses so that it should know precisely the case which was going to be put against it and to enable it to prepare its evidence (*International Computers Ltd v Whitley* [1978] IRLR 318). An interesting issue arose in the case of *P&O European Ferries (Dover) Ltd v Byrne* [1989] IRLR 254 as to when particulars should be revealed of the identity of a 'relevant employee' who had taken part in industrial action but had not been dismissed. This was essential in the case because the tribunal had at the time no jurisdiction to hear a case if all the employees taking part in the industrial action had been dismissed (TULR(C)A 1992, s 238(2)). The employers argued that the identity of the individual should be revealed as it was an oversight that he had not been dismissed if he had taken part in the industrial action and they would remedy it once they knew the employee's name. The Court of Appeal held that the employers were entitled to particulars to enable them to know the case they had to meet, even though this would result in the identification of a witness, since this was outweighed by the ability of the employers to take the jurisdictional point.

An order for further information will, however, be refused where it is unnecessary, overly onerous, **6.25** or oppressive. Part of the overriding objective relates to proportionality in any event. Thus, a request for details of incidents that occurred many years ago may be refused as both unnecessary and onerous, since the witnesses are unlikely to recall the matters. Requests that are very detailed and relate to statistical or other matters may also fail on the grounds that they are too onerous.

Where actual or constructive knowledge of a particular fact is alleged, for example, 'the applicant **6.26** knew he would be dismissed for fighting', further information would normally be ordered to discover how the applicant knew this; was he told, was it a rule derived from custom and practice, etc.

Form of application

It is good practice for an informal request for further information to be made before an order **6.27** from the tribunal is sought. The application to the tribunal should be brief and should enclose the previous request and reply (if any) and should state clearly why the order is sought. The request for further information should be set out clearly and preferably in a separate document.

The employment judge, who may often be the duty judge in the particular tribunal office and not normally the person ultimately hearing the case, may then simply tick off such requests as are granted and strike out those that he thinks impermissible. Where unrepresented parties are involved on the other side, it is useful to send two copies of the request (one for them to keep) and to set out the request with space beneath for the reply, thus ensuring that each of the requests is answered.

6.28 If the request is in relation to a pleading, it should identify the specific part of the other side's pleading that is being questioned, usually by setting out the phrase that is under consideration, and setting out the details required.

6.29 The tribunal will state the time within which the further information should be provided. This time can be extended and a party can apply to vary or set aside the order for further information.

6.30 The representative of a party subject to a request for further information should send a copy of it to his client, preferably retyped with space for the client's response to the requests. They may then be edited.

Further requests for further information

6.31 If the replies that come back from the other party are still vague or raise even more issues, the party in receipt is entitled to make a further request for further information (although whether an order will be made for its production is a matter for the discretion of the tribunal). Before making such an application, however, a party should bear in mind the general guidance set out above and the risk of a party who asks for more being criticized for unnecessarily complicating the process.

Inferences in discrimination cases

6.32 A Tribunal may draw adverse inferences if the employer deliberately omits to respond to a discrimination pleading or is misleading, evasive, or equivocal in the replies. If the tribunal considers it just and equitable to do so, they may infer that this failure or refusal is evidence that the employer has committed the unlawful act in question (see *King v Great Britain-China Centre* [1991] IRLR 513; *Virdee v ECC Quarries Ltd* [1978] IRLR 295; *Chapman v Simon* [1994] IRLR 124; *Igen Ltd v Wong* [2005] ICR 931, [2005] IRLR 258; and *Madarasy v Nomura* [2007] IRLR 246). The EAT in *Dattani v Chief Constable of West Mercia Police* [2005] IRLR 327 expressly extended these cases relying on the former questionnaire procedure to ET3 and other documents.

Written answers

6.33 The power to order further information is not limited to the pleadings and the tribunal can, of its own motion or on application, require a party to provide a written answer to a question. This power was specifically provided in ETR 2004, r 10(f). Although there is no reference to the provision of written answers in ETR 2013, there is no reason why the tribunal should not continue to have the power to require answers under its general powers in r 29. The power will be exercised where it appears to the tribunal that such an answer would clarify matters and it would assist the progress of the proceedings for that answer to be available before the hearing. The written answer is not evidence but is treated in the same way as written submissions.

6.34 The advantage of the written answer over requests for further information is that the former are not tied to the 'pleadings' and the material facts contained in them. So, for example, when a party claims that he was pressurized into resigning (in a witness statement or other than in the claim form), a written answer can be sought asking what pressure was allegedly brought to bear and by whom. The power may also be used in order to clarify the authorship of a document that has emerged in disclosure or whether a particular document was received by a party.

6.35 Any written answers that are provided are not direct evidence but may nonetheless form the basis of cross-examination if inconsistent answers are given.

Amendments

6.36

(1) Both the claimant and respondent can seek to amend their pleadings and in deciding whether to grant any such amendment the tribunal should attempt to do justice between the parties.
(2) Amendment can include the addition of new claims, in limited circumstances, even where the time limit for the new claim has expired.
(3) Similarly, respondents can add new grounds of resistance with relative ease where there is simply a change of legal label put on the facts alleged.
(4) Where amendment leads to an adjournment of the hearing, the party at fault will frequently have to pay the costs incurred.

Selkent principles

The leading authority is *Selkent Bus Co Ltd v Moore* [1996] ICR 836. The EAT there stated that, **6.37** when faced with an application to amend, a tribunal's discretion should be exercised in a way which is consistent with the requirements of 'relevance, reason, justice, and fairness consistent in all judicial discretions'. *Selkent* is considered further at paras 6.40 to 6.47.

Amending the claim

The claimant may amend his claim only with the leave of the tribunal once the primary time limit **6.38** for presenting the claim has expired. This is so even where the claimant seeks to add a new claim on the same or very similar facts, for example, for a redundancy payment in addition to a claim for unfair dismissal, *Home Office v Bose* [1979] ICR 481.

In exercising its discretion whether to allow an amendment, however, the tribunal should **6.39** consider in particular 'any injustice or hardship which may be caused to any of the parties if the proposed amendment were allowed or, as the case may be, refused' (*Cocking v Sandhurst (Stationers) Ltd* [1974] ICR 650). That case sets out (at 656–7) a useful checklist for tribunals to follow when considering amendments to the originating application (and was followed in *British Newspaper Printing Corporation (North) Ltd v Kelly* [1989] IRLR 222):

(a) Does the unamended claim form comply with the rules for presentation of a claim form?
(b) If it does not, a new claim form should probably be presented.
(c) If it does comply, was the claim presented within the time for the proposed amendment? This is not determinative of the issue, however, but is simply a factor to put in the scales (*British Newspaper Printing Corporation (North) Ltd v Kelly*, above).
(d) If it was in time, does the tribunal have the discretion to allow an amendment?
(e) If the amendment involves adding or substituting a new respondent or other party, this should only be allowed if the tribunal is satisfied that the non-inclusion was a genuine mistake and was not misleading or such as to cause reasonable doubt as to the identity of a party; a tribunal may at any time of its own volition or at the application of any person add a respondent (this is considered further below).
(f) The tribunal should have regard to the injustice or hardship which may be caused to any of the parties if the proposed amendment were allowed or, as the case may be, refused as stated above.
(g) The tribunal may make costs a condition of the amendment being granted.

In *Selkent Bus Co Ltd v Moore* [1996] ICR 836, Mummery J suggests that there are a number of **6.40** different types of amendment, some attracting the time limits, others not. The following were the matters that were suggested for consideration:

(1) the nature of the amendment, see paras 6.41–6.42
(2) the applicability of time limits, see paras 6.43–6.44
(3) the timing and manner of the application, see paras 6.45–6.47.

The nature of the amendment

6.41 Applications to amend are of many different kinds: on the one hand, the correction of clerical and typing errors, the addition of factual details to existing allegations, and the addition or substitution of other labels for facts already pleaded; and, on the other hand, the making of entirely new factual allegations which change the basis of the existing claim. The tribunal has to decide whether the amendment which is sought is one of the minor matters or is a substantial alteration pleading a new cause of action (see eg *New Star Asset Management Holdings Ltd v Evershed* [2010] EWCA Civ 870). In *Smith v Zeneca (Agrochemicals) Ltd* [2000] ICR 800 Charles J concluded that a claim of direct discrimination is different and separate from both a claim of indirect discrimination and of victimization, and so cannot be deemed to include either of those claims. The point at issue in *Smith* was not whether an amendment should have been allowed, for no application was made to amend, but whether the pleaded case that the employers were vicariously liable for acts of sexual harassment by a fellow employee was wide enough to cover an additional claim raised at the hearing that the employers' handling of the complaint itself amounted to direct sexual discrimination by them. The tribunal held that it had no jurisdiction to consider this additional point as there had been no application to amend. The EAT held that the new point was a separate claim and could not be regarded as simply putting a different label on facts already asserted. If an application had been made to amend, the time limit would have had to be considered as the new claim was a separate 'act complained of' for the purpose of SDA 1975, s 76(1). The fact that it was a further allegation of sex discrimination could not prevent time running. *Smith* was followed in *Ali v Office for National Statistics* [2005] IRLR 201 Mr Ali had sought leave to amend his claim form after a successful appeal by the Office for National Statistics in order to add a complaint of indirect race discrimination in light of evidence that had come to light during disclosure and cross-examination in the first hearing. The Court of Appeal overturned the decision of the tribunal that the claimant was merely applying a new label to the same claim, holding that direct and indirect discrimination are distinct causes of action and the amendment therefore amounted to a new claim. The matter was remitted to the tribunal for consideration of whether it was just and equitable to allow the claim to be presented out of time. The facts of *Selkent* itself provide another good illustration—a late application to amend an unfair dismissal claim to allege that the reason for dismissal was trade union activities was refused as this was an application to add a fresh cause of action rather than a change of label. In *Reuters Ltd v Cole* [2018] UKEAT/0258/17/BA the EAT held that an application to add a direct disability discrimination claim to an existing claim for disability related discrimination was more than a re-labelling of existing facts, and would require a wider factual enquiry.

6.42 In *BMA v Chaudhary* [2003] EWCA Civ 645 the Court of Appeal held that it was permissible for a claimant to amend a claim to raise allegations post-dating the original complaint (at paras 79–82) although the basis is far from clear from the judgment which largely related to issue estoppel. In *Prakash v Wolverhampton City Council* UKEAT/0140/06 the EAT held that it is permissible to amend a claim form, so as to include a claim which did not exist at the time the claim form was originally presented. This can be done by the employment tribunal exercising its discretion to allow a claim to be amended so as to permit a second claim to be included that could not have been included when the claim form was originally presented, because the second claim had accrued at a later date.

The applicability of time limits

6.43 If a new substantive complaint or cause of action is proposed to be added by way of amendment, it is essential for the tribunal to consider whether that complaint is out of time and, if so, whether the time limit should be extended under the applicable statutory provisions. An amendment of a claim form to add a new head of complaint which in itself would be out of time was only allowed if the grounds already given in the claim form clearly reveal the requisite causal connection between the original complaint and the amendment. The claimant in *Housing Corporation v Bryant* [1999] ICR 123 brought a claim for unfair dismissal (in time) and sex discrimination (out of time). The tribunal refused to allow the amendment to plead victimization because there was no suggestion of it in the unfair dismissal action and it was not just and equitable to extend time, and this approach was upheld by the Court of Appeal (see also *Ashworth Hospital Authority v Liebling* UKEAT/1436/96).

However, in *Lehman Brothers v Smith* UKEAT/0486/05 the EAT contrasted the tightly drawn provisions of the CPR dealing with amendment with those applicable in the tribunal and held, at para 43, that: **6.44**

> Whilst the question as to whether an amendment application seeking to add a new claim (as opposed to a minor amendment) is itself made out of time, is an important factor, it is not determinative of the question. The balance of hardship and justice as between the parties must always be considered in carrying out the exercise of discretion to grant or refuse the amendment.

The EAT reasoned that had Parliament wished to restrict tribunals' powers to amend where the new claim was out of time it would have so legislated. Where the proposed amendment is made within the limitation period, the fact that it could be commenced as a fresh claim is normally a significant factor in favour of allowing the amendment. It is likely to be more efficient, in terms of time and cost to allow the amendment rather than to require a separate claim to be issued. However, this is not a conclusive factor, and the tribunal may refuse the amendment in an appropriate case if, for example, it is made late and would disrupt a pending hearing: see *Patka v BBC* [2018] UKEAT/0190/17/DM, *Gillett v Bridge 86 Ltd* [2017] UKEAT/0051/17. In *Galilee v The Commissioner of Police of the Metropolis* [2018] ICR 634, HHJ Hand found that amendments to pleadings in the ET which introduce new claims or causes of action take effect, for the purposes of limitation, at the time permission is given to amend and there is no doctrine of 'relation back' in the ET to treat them as brought at the time of the original claim. HHJ Hand also concluded that in cases involving arguments of continuing act or a just and equitable extension permission to amend can precede decisions as to whether or not any new claim is in time, alternatively the decision in relation to whether or not to grant permission to amend can be postponed to after evidence.

The timing and manner of the application

An application should not be refused solely because there has been a delay in making it unless the delay has caused prejudice. There are no time limits laid down in ETR 2013 for the making of amendments. The amendments may be made at any time—before, at, and even after the hearing of the case. Delay in making the application is, however, a discretionary factor. It is relevant to consider why the application was not made earlier and why it is now being made: for example, the discovery of new facts or new information appearing from documents disclosed. In taking any factors into account, the paramount considerations are the relative injustice and hardship involved in refusing or granting an amendment. Questions of delay, as a result of adjournments, and additional costs, particularly if they are unlikely to be recovered by the successful party, are relevant in reaching a decision. In *Berry v Ravensbourne National Health Service Trust* [1993] ICR 871 a claimant was allowed to amend the claim alleging race discrimination even though more than three months had passed since the last act complained of, because she was unaware of the act until the time limit had expired. Further, she had acted promptly on discovering this and the facts of the complaint were similar to her existing unfair dismissal claim and it was therefore just and equitable to extend time. **6.45**

Although there is no obligation to hold an oral hearing to deal with every application for leave to amend, if the refusal of an application would lead to a claimant's case failing a hearing should be held (see *Smith v Gwent District Health Authority* [1996] ICR 1044, although in *Selkent* (above), which is now the most frequently cited decision on the point, Mummery J suggested that a failure to hold a hearing will not necessarily amount to an error of law). **6.46**

An amendment to change the nature of the relief sought is often a simple matter, particularly where the claimant seeks to add a claim for reinstatement or re-engagement, since ERA 1996 allows the claimant to choose remedies once liability has been determined, but it is clearly best practice to choose the appropriate remedy as soon as possible, as the employer might fill vacancies without notice of the claimant's claim. **6.47**

Adding/dismissing respondents

6.48 An application to amend which has the effect of adding or removing respondents raises particular issues. A tribunal or judge may add a respondent on the application of any person, or on its own initiative, at any time. Rule 34 specifically envisages that a party may be added where it appears that there are issues between that person and any of the existing parties falling within the jurisdiction of the tribunal, which it is in the interests of justice to have determined in the proceedings. Further any party apparently wrongly included may be removed.

6.49 In *Watts v Seven Kings Motor Co Ltd* [1983] ICR 135, an application to amend by the respondent was allowed even after the tribunal had reached its decision, on the proviso that the new respondent had appropriate safeguards, such as an opportunity to enter a response or apply for a review (see also *Linbourne v Constable* [1993] ICR 698). The effect of delay was again stressed to be merely a factor in the absence of time limits for amendments in *Gillick v BP Chemicals Ltd* [1993] IRLR 437 and *Linbourne*, both of which concerned amendments to add new respondents against whom new claims would be time-barred. The fact that two respondent companies are related is again only a factor and not the grounds upon which the discretion is exercised (see *Gillick*).

6.50 The EAT in *Linbourne* stressed that where it is evident during the tribunal hearing that the wrong respondent is present, the tribunal should make this clear to the applicant and invite an application to amend. However, potential new respondents should be given the chance to address the tribunal on the issue of whether joinder should be permitted (see *Gillick*).

6.51 It may not be appropriate for a party to be, or continue to be, a respondent in the proceedings where no remedy could be sought against it (*Sandhu v Department of Education & Science* [1978] IRLR 208).

6.52 The addition of a new respondent by way of amendment to an existing claim does not require completion of fresh ACAS Early conciliation (*Drake International Systems Ltd and Others v Blue Arrow* UKEAT/0282/15/DM).

Amending the response

6.53 A response can also be amended at any time with the leave of the tribunal, although the later that an amendment is left the less likely it is to be granted and the less likely any factual claim made in the amendment is to have credibility. An example of a late application that was refused is *Kapur v Shields* [1976] ICR 26, where the respondents sought to amend at the hearing from a defence that the claimant had asked for dismissal to assist in an application for a council flat, to a defence of capability and conduct. The application was refused on the grounds of lateness and fairness (see also *Ready Case Ltd v Jackson* [1981] IRLR 312, where the application was refused as the application was late, the respondents had professional advice, and they had not complied with a request for further information). If there is no prejudice to the claimant and no new evidence is needed, the application is far more likely to be granted.

Witnesses

Directions for witness statements

6.54 The ET will normally make provision for the evidence in chief of witnesses to be given by witness statements, and for those statements to be exchanged on a certain date ahead of the Hearing. See paras 9.22–9.25 for the preparation of witness statements, and paras 9.126–9.128 for their use at hearings.

Witness orders

6.55 Under a witness order, witnesses may be compelled to attend the tribunal and to produce documents, either on application by the parties or by the tribunal of its own motion. For a witness order to be made, the witness must be relevant to the proceedings and must be unwilling to attend unless compelled.

Either party may apply to an employment tribunal for a witness order against a person in any part **6.56** of Great Britain to attend the employment tribunal and for that person to produce any documents in his or her possession. The power generally corresponds to the witness summons power in the ordinary civil courts. The tribunal may order the attendance of a witness of its own motion and in such circumstances the witness should be called by the tribunal, with both parties having an opportunity to cross-examine. In Dada v Metal Box Co Ltd [1974] IRLR 251 it was stated that, before issuing a witness order, tribunals should satisfy themselves that:

(a) the witness prima facie can give evidence which is relevant to the issues in dispute and
(b) it is necessary to issue a witness order to compel attendance (that is because the witness has refused to come voluntarily, for example, because his employer objects).

It is an error of law to refuse a witness order where the witness has relevant documents in his pos- **6.57** session (see *Wilcox v Humphreys & Glasgow Ltd* [1975] IRLR 211). However, the Court of Appeal emphasized in *Noorani v Merseyside TEC Ltd* [1999] IRLR 184 that tribunals have a wide discretion in deciding whether to issue a witness order.

The attendance of the witness should be requested by letter before an order is sought. The witness **6.58** may claim travelling expenses to and from the tribunal from the Employment Tribunals Service. Failure without reasonable excuse to comply with a witness order may result in a fine not exceeding level 3 on the standard scale (ETA 1996, s 7(4)).

Expert evidence

If expert evidence is to be called, directions should be given at an early stage, as it would be un- **6.59** desirable for any such evidence to be given without proper advance notice to the other party and the early provision of a copy of any expert report to be referred to.

If the degree of impairment required for disability is an issue, tribunals are encouraged to use **6.60** the directions procedure to remind the parties, particularly where they are unrepresented, of the need, in most cases, for qualified and informed medical evidence to be obtained (see *De Keyser Ltd v Wilson* [2001] IRLR 324). It is not necessary to have an examination for the purposes of discovering the causes of an alleged disability but it may be legitimate to investigate whether a claimed impairment is genuine (see *Hospice of St Mary of Furness v Howard* [2007] IRLR 944). In *De Keyser*, Lindsay P (at para 36) set out the following guidance when considering the instruction of expert witnesses:

(a) Careful thought needs to be given before any party embarks upon instructions for expert evidence. It by no means follows that because a party wishes such evidence to be admitted that it will be. A prudent party will first explore with the employment tribunal at a directions hearing or in correspondence whether, in principle, expert evidence is likely to be acceptable.
(b) Save where one side or the other has already committed itself to the use of its own expert (which is to be avoided in the absence of special circumstances), the joint instruction of a single expert is the preferred course.
(c) If a joint expert is to be instructed, the terms which the parties need to agree include the incidence of that expert's fees and expenses. Nothing precludes the parties *agreeing* that they will abide by such a view as the tribunal shall later indicate as to that incidence (though the tribunal will not be obliged to give any such indication), but the tribunal has no *power* as to costs beyond the general provisions of ETR 2013, rr 74–84.
(d) If the means available to one side or another are such that in its view it cannot agree to share or to risk any exposure to the expert's fees or expenses, or if, irrespective of its means, a party refuses to pay or share such costs, the other party or parties can reasonably be expected to prefer to require their own expert but, even in such a case, the weight to be attached to that expert's evidence (a matter entirely for the tribunal to judge) may be found to have been increased if the terms of his instruction shall have been submitted to the other side, if not for agreement then for comment, ahead of their being finalized for sending to the expert.

(e) If a joint expert is to be used, tribunals, lest parties dally, may fix a period within which the parties are to seek to agree the identity of the expert and the terms of a joint letter of instruction and the tribunal may fix a date by which the joint expert's report is to be made available.

(f) Any letter of instruction should specify, in as much detail as can be given, any particular questions the expert is to be invited to answer and all more general subjects which he is to be asked to address.

(g) Such instructions are as far as possible to avoid partisanship. Tendentiousness, too, is to be avoided. Insofar as the expert is asked to make assumptions of fact, they are to be spelled out. It will, of course, be important not to beg the very questions to be raised. It will be wise if the letter emphasizes that in preparing his evidence the expert's principal and overriding duty is to the tribunal rather than to any party.

(h) Where a joint expert is to be used, the tribunal may specify, if his identity or instructions have not been agreed between the parties by a specified date, that the matter is to be restored to the tribunal, which may then assist the parties to settle that identity and those instructions.

(i) In relation to the issues to which an expert is or is not to address himself (whether or not he is a joint expert) the tribunal may give formal directions as it does generally in relation to the issues to be dealt with at the main hearing.

(j) Where there is no joint expert the tribunal should, in the absence of appropriate agreement between the parties, specify a timetable for disclosure or exchange of experts' reports and, where there are two or more experts, for meetings (see below).

(k) Any timetable may provide for the raising of supplementary questions with the expert or experts (whether there is a joint expert or not) and for the disclosure or exchange of the answers in good time before the hearing.

(l) In the event of separate experts being instructed, the tribunal should encourage arrangements for them to meet on a without prejudice basis with a view to their seeking to resolve any conflict between them and, where possible, to their producing and disclosing a schedule of agreed issues and of points of dispute between them.

(m) If a party fails, without good reason, to follow these guidelines and if in consequence another party or parties suffer delay or are put to expense which a due performance of the guidelines would have been likely to avoid, then the tribunal may wish to consider whether, on that party's part, there has been unreasonable conduct as to costs.

There is also considerable guidance in CPR Part 35 (Experts and Assessors), and the associated practice direction (PD), which ought to be carefully considered by all those seeking to rely upon expert evidence. This includes reminding parties in the High Court that the late production of expert evidence or the unavailability of a chosen expert will not usually be grounds to vary directions and/or a trial date. For example, in *Rollinson v Kimberley Clark Ltd* [2000] CP Rep 85, the Court of Appeal held that it was not acceptable for a solicitor to instruct an expert shortly before trial without checking on his availability.

6.61 Generally the use of expert evidence should be limited to that which is reasonably required to resolve the proceedings (CPR r 35.1) and it is the duty of the expert to assist the court rather than the parties (CPR r 35.3). This latter point may need to be emphasized when the expert is someone who treats, or has care for, a party. The expert's report, whether joint or a party's own, should comply with the practice direction which includes setting out the basis of instructions and expressly acknowledging the duty to the court.

Disclosure

6.62 Each party may need documents which are currently in the possession of the other party in order to prove its case. The general rule is that there is no obligation to disclose any document unless and until an order is made, however any party who chooses to make voluntary disclosure of any documents in his possession or power must not be unfairly selective in his disclosure. In *Birds Eye Walls Ltd v Harrison* [1985] IRLR 47, para 36, Waite J stated the general principle that:

> No party is under any obligation, in the absence of an order upon the Industrial Tribunal, to give discovery in the Tribunal proceedings. That is subject, however, to the important qualification that any

party who chooses to make voluntary discovery of any documents in his possession or power must not be unfairly selective in his disclosure. Once, that is to say, a party has disclosed certain documents (whether they appear to him to support his case or for any other reason) it becomes his duty not to withhold from discovery any further documents in his possession or power (regardless of whether they support his case or not) if there is any risk that the effect of withholding them might be to convey to his opponent or to the tribunal a false or misleading impression as to the true nature, purport or effect of any disclosed document.

A tribunal may, on the application of a party or of its own motion, order a party to grant disclosure **6.63** or inspection of a document to another party (ETR 2013, r 31). The tribunal's powers in relation to disclosure are the same as the powers of the county court or sheriff's court.

County court powers are found in the CPR and in particular Part 31, along with its practice dir- **6.64** ection. The principles of standard disclosure under the CPR require a party to disclose those documents on which he relies, any documents which support or adversely affect his or another party's case, and any other documents which a party is required to disclose pursuant to a relevant practice direction.

Document is defined in CPR Part 31.4 to mean anything in which information of any description **6.65** is recorded. This includes paper documents, photographs, electronic files, videos, text messages, voicemail and other audio files, faxes, photocopies, emails etc.

In addition to standard disclosure a judge may make an order for specific disclosure of a particular **6.66** document or category of document. Recent changes to CPR Part 31 enable the judge to consider a range of different disclosure orders, including disclosure on an issue-by-issue basis, sequential disclosure, disclosure of documents on which a party intends to rely or any combination of such orders. These provisions are relatively new and there is at present a degree of flux as parties and the courts consider and use the new orders. CPR 31PD, para 5.4 states that in deciding whether to make an order for specific disclosure the court will take into account all of the circumstances of the case and, in particular, the overriding objective (to deal with cases justly and in a cost-effective manner). The documents sought must be relevant and be necessary to be disclosed for the fair disposal of the proceedings (*Dolling Baker v Merrett* [1990] 1 WLR 1205).

CPR 31PD, para 2A requires parties to search for and disclose documents held in electronic form **6.67** as well as on paper. The definition of such a 'document' includes not only files stored on servers and back-up systems but also those that have been deleted. It also covers additional information stored and associated with electronic documents called 'metadata'—the data that describe the structure and workings of an organization's use of information, and which describe the systems it uses to manage that information. Parties in civil cases are required to give details of the steps they have taken to search for electronic documents (eg the devices—PCs, databases, back-ups, mobile phones, PDAs) and where they have not searched for types of documents to say so (eg spreadsheets, calendars, mail files).

Just as in a search for a paper document, the extent of a search is not without limit and will **6.68** depend upon:

(a) the number of documents involved
(b) the nature and complexity of the proceedings
(c) the ease and expense of retrieval of any particular document: this includes accessibility and location of documents and data including emails, servers, back-up systems, and other devices or media (eg phones, flash cards, portable USBs, PDAs), the likelihood of retrieving the data, the cost of it, and the significance of any document located in the search.

When any such document is sought, the PD stresses the importance of the parties discussing any **6.69** electronic search prior to the first case management conference (a preliminary hearing in the tribunal). This may involve the parties providing information about:

(a) the categories of documents under their control
(b) the computer systems, electronic devices, and media on which they may be held

    (c) the storage systems maintained and their document retention policies—this is particularly useful as it will give an indication of the shelf life of documents and when it is reasonable to destroy them.

6.70 In cases involving a large amount of documentation it may be necessary to use keyword searches and this costly procedure places a particular onus on the parties to narrow the area of dispute and to discuss:

    (a) the types and format of documents to be searched and disclosed (eg metadata, deleted data, back-up data)

    (b) the likely volume of documentation to be reviewed and/or disclosed

    (c) the categories of documentation to be aggregated before the keyword search

    (d) the terms of the keyword search

    (e) the method of exchanging the documents (printed or electronic)

    (f) the basis of charging for the process.

6.71 Not all of this will be relevant or immediately applicable in tribunals, and certainly not in straightforward claims, but where it is, the PD should be followed as closely as possible.

6.72 The general approach in employment tribunals has been set out by Wilkie J in *South Tyneside Metropolitan Borough Council v Anderson* EAT/0002/05 (the facts of which are considered below at para 6.73). When faced with an application for disclosure the tribunal should order disclosure of such documents as appear relevant at that stage and then later, if necessary, consider applications for specific disclosure—as opposed to order mass disclosure and leaving it to the parties to determine relevance later. If specific disclosure is then sought it would be sensible if the party applying produced either evidence or a skeleton argument as to why the disclosure already ordered was insufficient for the purpose of disposing of the issues at the hearing. In certain circumstances, an application for an order for disclosure will be refused, or granted with limitations, if to grant it may lead to such significant expenditure of time and cost to the respondent as to be oppressive (see *Perera v Civil Service Commission* [1980] ICR 699, see also para 6.76).

Equal pay cases

6.73 In *Clwyd CC v Leverton* [1985] IRLR 197, the employee, a female nursery nurse, was held to be entitled to discovery of the job descriptions of male clerical workers employed by the appellants in certain grades of the local government clerical scale, even though she had not yet named her male comparator on the grounds that all she needed to show was a prima facie case. However, in *South Tyneside Metropolitan Borough Council*, the EAT had to consider an application for disclosure by 218 claimants in an equal pay claim where it was contended that the employer's job evaluation scheme was not valid and they sought disclosure of the scoring, rankings, and bandings, as well as what had been agreed and what remained to be agreed in respect of the job evaluation study. The employment judge who dealt with the application at a CMD considered r 10(4) of the Employment Tribunal Rules of Procedure 2001 (ETR 2001) and ordered disclosure of a large amount of documents commenting that the parties could, once they had seen them, then determine what was relevant between them. On appeal, the EAT (Wilkie J) held that any order for disclosure should only be as much as 'but no more than necessary for' the effective disposal of the litigation and that step-by-step disclosure is often to be preferred. The essential issue in this case was whether the study was agreed and this could be determined, initially at least, by looking at the relevant minutes and/or correspondence. Accordingly, Wilkie J ordered only disclosure of the second category of documentation and criticized the judge's approach which had the effect of disclosing all documents and then leaving it to the parties to determine relevance. The correct approach is to order disclosure of such documents as appear relevant at that stage and then later to consider applications for specific disclosure.

Discrimination cases

6.74 The tribunal will only order that confidential personnel reports be revealed in cases where it is reasonably necessary to do so. In *Science Research Council v Nassé* [1979] IRLR 465, the employees sought details of employment records of all other persons interviewed for jobs they had sought but to which they had not been appointed, including service records, personal history forms, personal assessment records, and details of commendations, together with their application forms for the particular posts advertised. This presented a clear conflict between the principles of facilitating proof of discrimination and preserving the confidentiality of staff reports. All members of the House of Lords agreed that there was no general proposition of law that documents are protected from discovery by reason of confidentiality alone; their relevance, although a necessary condition, was not by itself sufficient. The true test was whether discovery 'is necessary for fairly disposing of the proceedings'. Lord Wilberforce stated this principle (at 468):

> The process is to consider fairly the strength and value of the interest in preserving confidentiality and the damage which may be caused by breaking it, then to consider whether the objective to dispose fairly of the case can be achieved without doing so and only in the last resort to order discovery.

6.75 Where the court or tribunal is impressed with the need to preserve confidentiality in a particular case, it should consider carefully whether the necessary information has been or can be obtained by other means not involving a breach of confidence. In especially sensitive cases, the court or tribunal may cover up parts of the relevant documents (known as redaction), insert anonymous references, or proceed in private. The tribunal may also review the documents in private to assess for relevance (see *British Railways Board v Natarajan* [1979] 2 All ER 794) or hear evidence on particular documents in private while the remainder of the hearing is in public. Anonymity orders or restricted reporting orders can be issued where persons affected by the case would otherwise suffer an infringement of their right to a private and family life under Art 8 of the ECHR.

6.76 In *Perera v Civil Service Commission* [1980] ICR 699, the EAT gave the *Nassé* principle further consideration. In order to prove that he had been turned down several times for jobs with the Civil Service on the grounds of his race, the applicant sought discovery of all documents relating to those applications. Notwithstanding that the assembly of all the relevant information would be difficult and expensive since there were 1,600 applicants, Slynn J called for sufficient material to be disclosed so that the applicant could pursue his relevant inquiry where other candidates had as high qualifications as he possessed. In particular, he called for the application forms of seventy-eight candidates interviewed in 1977 to be revealed, together with details of their nationality and fathers' nationalities and their final reports and assessment, with identifying material covered over. See also *Beck v Canadian Imperial Bank of Commerce* [2009] EWCA Civ 619, CA.

6.77 In *Selvarajan v Inner London Education Authority* [1980] IRLR 313, the claimant sought to refer, in support of his discrimination claim, to a series of incidents between 1961 and 1976 concerning abortive applications for jobs with the respondents. The EAT held that these could be logically probative and disagreed with the tribunal's cut-off point of 1973. Since the request was limited to the application forms of the appointed candidates, minutes of appointment, and Selvarajan's own file, no unfairness or oppression would result to the respondents.

6.78 A particularly contentious question has been the power to order a summary of the persons of various ethnic groups who were appointed by a respondent during a particular period. In *Jalota v Imperial Metal Industries (Kynoch) Ltd* [1979] IRLR 313, the EAT thought that such material need not be disclosed. The position was reviewed in *West Midlands Passenger Transport Executive v Singh* [1987] IRLR 351, where Popplewell J rejected the contention that the fact of previous discrimination could have no probative value as to present discrimination, especially since the code of practice on race relations recommends that employers monitor the ethnic background of their employees. On appeal, the Court of Appeal [1988] IRLR 186 set out the following principles for guidance when considering discovery applications in race or sex discrimination cases:

(a) There is normally no overt evidence of discrimination, and the claimant has an uphill struggle.

(b) The evidence adduced in a discrimination case does not need to prove decisively that the respondent acted on racial grounds.

(c) Direct discrimination involves unfavourable treatment because the claimant is a member of a group. Statistical evidence may establish a pattern in the treatment of that group, for example under-representation at the workplace, and this is why ethnic monitoring is recommended.

(d) Where a practice is being operated against a group, in the absence of a satisfactory explanation it is reasonable to infer that there has been discrimination. Evidence of discriminatory behaviour towards a group may be more persuasive than discrimination against the claimant as the latter may be motivated by personal dislike.

(e) Employers often adduce evidence that they employ both black and white employees to demonstrate that they do not discriminate and there is no reason why evidence that the employer is generally discriminatory or the ethnic breakdown of the workforce is imbalanced should not have the same probative effect.

(f) The suitability of candidates can rarely be measured objectively. Subjective judgments are often made and if there is a high failure rate for members of an ethnic group this may indicate a conscious or unconscious racial attitude involving stereotyped assumptions.

6.79 When ordering the release of application forms of other candidates the tribunal should limit disclosure to relevant details on the claim before it and should try and ensure that comparators are not identified (see, eg, *Oxford v Department of Health and Social Security* [1977] IRLR 225). In *Williams v Dyfed County Council* [1986] ICR 449, Wood J pointed to the balance that must be maintained between the essential maintenance of trust and confidence between employer and employee and the necessary information to be supplied to the claimant so as to ensure that he has a fair hearing. The matters which would be relevant to a discrimination claim relating to failure to gain the appointment on the grounds of sex would be the sex of other applicants, their age, qualifications, and work experience. The matter should be dealt with by the regional chairman and any matters which go to identify the other applicants should be kept to a minimum. In *Meister v Speech Design Carrier Systems* [2012] ICR 1006 the ECJ held that EU law does not require an employer facing a discrimination claim by an unsuccessful job applicant to disclose information about the successful candidate. However, an employer's refusal to grant access to such information may be taken into account by the national court when deciding whether the claimant has established facts from which direct or indirect discrimination may be inferred for the purposes of the burden of proof provisions.

Redundancy selection

6.80 To what extent is an individual selected for redundancy who claims that selection is unfair entitled to disclosure of the documents of the retained employees? This is a question grappled with by a number of courts over recent years. The first point to emphasize is that there must be an issue on the pleaded case that makes disclosure of such documents relevant (see *Green v British Aerospace* [1995] IRLR 433). So, the claimant must allege that either the whole or a particular part of the selection process was unfair in the claim form or risk a tribunal refusing disclosure. *Green* suggested that such general disclosure of other employee's documents would be exceptional. However, in *FDR Ltd v Holloway* [1995] IRLR 400 (concerning the need to make one employee redundant out of a workforce of eight) the EAT granted disclosure of documents relating to the assessments of all eight employees as being necessary in order to dispose of the issue whether the selection criteria had been fairly applied.

6.81 However, there have been reminders not to enter into an exercise of re-marking each candidate's assessment, in particular where the initial process was subjective and depended on value judgements (see also *Eaton v King* [1996] IRLR 199).

Medical reports

6.82 In *Department of Health and Social Security v Sloan* [1981] ICR 313, the employee wanted discovery of medical reports about herself. The employers, in response to the applicant's claim for unfair dismissal, stated that she had been retired on medical grounds because she was incapable of doing her work. The tribunal granted discovery of certain medical reports prepared by doctors on behalf of the employers, but, with the consent of the employee's legal advisers, restricted the circulation of the documents to the employee's solicitor and general practitioner. Her solicitors then applied for a variation of the order, since they wished to refer to the reports at the hearing. A different judge considered the employers' submission that disclosure to the applicant would be harmful to her health, and held that, since a litigant was entitled to see all the relevant documents unless there was a principle of law preventing it, they should be made available to the employee.

On appeal, the EAT held that, where it was agreed that certain evidence might be harmful to an **6.83** applicant if revealed, the proper course for the party's legal adviser was to cooperate to ensure that the applicant was protected, but that since it was not clear whether or not there was a fact in issue as to her medical state in this case, the decision as to whether the medical reports were relevant and ought to be disclosed would be postponed for consideration by the party's legal advisers when the employee's own medical report had been obtained.

In *Ford Motor Co v Nawaz* [1987] IRLR 163, the EAT agreed with a tribunal that had ordered the **6.84** respondent to reveal medical reports on the applicant notwithstanding that it was the employer's policy never to disclose medical reports to lay people. The fact that in ill-health cases the management are entitled to act on the advice of their medical advisers does not absolve the management from carrying out, through their medical advisers, the proper investigation which is required in any dismissal case. In deciding whether the medical expert had sufficient material before him on which to advise, the tribunal had to see the medical material itself. Thus, the employers had to disclose the consultant's report on the applicant, instructions given to him prior to the examination, and the notes made by the in-house doctor.

The EAT has decided that there will be no breach of a person's right to respect for private and **6.85** family life under Art 8 of the ECHR where he or she is obliged to attend a medical examination or disclose medical records for the purpose of a claim for personal injury (*De Keyser v Wilson* [2001] IRLR 324).

The Access to Medical Records Act 1988 gives employees a statutory right of access to medical **6.86** reports prepared for employment purposes by a medical practitioner who has been responsible for the employee. This does not include one-off reports or those of independent consultants.

If an employer wants access to a report prepared by the employee's doctor, he must notify the **6.87** employee and obtain his consent. The employee is allowed access to the report and may refuse to forward it to the employer. He can also amend the report and attach his own views to it. The principle of non-disclosure where it would have harmful effects on the employee's physical or mental health is embodied in s 7(1) of the 1988 Act. Similarly, where disclosure would be likely to reveal information about another person without his consent or would reveal the identity of a source of information (other than a health professional) disclosure will not be allowed (s 7(2)).

Disclosure by non-parties

A tribunal may make an order, either on application or of its own motion, requiring a person who **6.88** is not a party to attend (see witness orders, at paras 6.55 to 6.58) and to produce any document relating to the matter to be determined. This will be particularly useful in (a) insolvency cases as it means the liquidator can be required to attend and to bring important documents that the former employer and employee are unlikely to have; and (b) transfer of undertaking cases where an alleged transferee may require documents from the possession of the transferor. A similar power exists in the civil courts, which is much used.

Form of application

The party requiring the information should initially approach the other side by letter. If the other **6.89** side refuses a reasonable request an order for disclosure should be sought from the tribunal (in accordance with r 30). The letter should set out the documents sought and the request may be facilitated by a schedule or draft order identifying the documents sought, and the judge considering the application can simply tick off the documents to be disclosed.

Failure to comply with an order for disclosure

A refusal, without reasonable excuse, to comply with an order for disclosure may lead to a fine **6.90** (ETA 1996, s 7(4)) although this rarely happens or the party's claim or response may be struck out.

The party at risk of having his pleading struck out must be given notice under r 37(2), which also provides that the party be given a reasonable opportunity to make representations, either in writing or, if requested by the party at a hearing.

Grounds to withhold disclosure

Confidentiality

6.91 In *Nassé* (para 6.74), it was held that where a party claims that it is not appropriate to disclose a document, the tribunal may inspect the document and decide whether the claim is valid. As we have seen, confidentiality in *Nassé* was a consideration, but not a determinative factor, and the test should be whether disclosure was necessary for disposing fairly of the proceedings. There is no rule whereby confidential documents are excluded from disclosure merely because they are confidential. This was emphasized in *Alfred Compton Amusement Machines Ltd v Customs & Excise Commissioners (No 2)* [1974] AC 405, where it was stated that, in the absence of some additional factor, such as the fact that the claimant is exercising a statutory function which would be impeded by disclosure, confidentiality would not justify the non-disclosure of a document.

6.92 When considering an informant's information the principles of confidentiality may be relevant. In *British Steel Corporation v Granada Television Ltd* [1981] AC 1096, the House of Lords stated that the courts have a discretion to order the disclosure of the name of an informer but this must be balanced against other interests in the case.

Public interest immunity

6.93 Another possible ground for withholding a document is that it would damage the public interest (see CPR r 31.19). Public interest immunity arises in a number of ways and is usually claimed on the basis that withholding documents is necessary for the proper functioning of the public service. The public interest is not static and the categories 'are not closed and must alter from time to time whether by restriction or extension as social conditions and social legislation develop' (*D v NSPCC* [1977] 1 All ER 589). This must, however, be balanced in each case against the public interest in the fair administration of justice (*D v NSPCC* and *Evans v Chief Constable of Surrey* [1989] 2 All ER 594). The requirement of a fair trial under Art 6 of the ECHR is relevant to this balancing exercise.

6.94 In *Conway v Rimmer* [1968] AC 910 the courts reasserted their right, over that of the executive, to decide whether in any case disclosure is in the public interest. The principles in *Conway* were applied in *Halford v Sharples* [1992] ICR 146, EAT (affirmed [1992] ICR 583, CA), where it was stated that tribunals should use the power to inspect documents with extreme care and it was stressed that the onus to justify exclusion is a heavy one. The person claiming that a document attracts public interest immunity is acting under a duty and the immunity can extend to the contents of particular documents or to a class of documents (see *Campbell v Tameside Metropolitan Borough Council* [1982] QB 1065).

6.95 Evidence is sometimes excluded in employment tribunals on the grounds of national security, the defence of the realm, or good diplomatic relations. In *Balfour v Foreign and Commonwealth Office* [1994] ICR 277, for example, the Court of Appeal held that disclosure of certain diplomatic information was precluded by certificates signed by the Foreign Secretary and the Home Secretary claiming public interest immunity. The courts were not qualified to evaluate a minister's claim that national security would be damaged by disclosure and the request was refused.

6.96 In cases where a Minister of the Crown is of the opinion that the disclosure of information would be injurious to national security the information must not be disclosed (ERA 1996, s 202). The cases to which the provisions apply are those involving the giving of employment particulars, health and safety cases, ante-natal and maternity cases, written statements of reasons for dismissal, and unfair dismissal cases under Part I, ss 44 and 47, 48, and 49, 55–57, 61–63, 66–68, 69, and 70; Part VIII, ss 92 and 93; ss 99(1)–(3), 100, or 103 of the ERA 1996.

Diplomatic immunity

Where diplomatic immunity is claimed, embassy documents are protected by absolute privilege **6.97** from disclosure. Even where a respondent has waived that privilege the immunity can be claimed by the embassy concerned (*Fayed v Al-Tajir* [1987] 2 All ER 396).

Legal professional privilege

Communications between a party and his solicitor are privileged from disclosure provided that **6.98** they are confidential and made for the purpose of obtaining and giving legal advice (*Balabel v Air India* [1988] 2 All ER 246). Communications between a party and his lawyer and third parties (such as expert witnesses) are also privileged, provided the dominant purpose is the preparation for contemplated or pending litigation (*Waugh v British Railways Board* [1979] 2 All ER 1169).

The scope of legal professional privilege was somewhat extended in *Three Rivers Council and* **6.99** *BCCI v Bank of England* [2004] UKHL 48, [2005] 1 AC 610 in which the House of Lords held that legal privilege covered legal advice privilege and litigation privilege, and that only litigation privilege was restricted to proceedings or anticipated proceedings in a court of law. Legal advice privilege covered advice and assistance in relation to public law rights, liabilities, and obligations as well as private law rights, and for policy reasons should not be confined to telling the client the law, and had to include advice as to what should prudently and sensibly be done in the relevant legal context.

The communication must have been confidential and if not actually made during the legal relation- **6.100** ship it must have been made with a view to establishing one (see *Minter v Priest* [1930] AC 558).

There is no rule of law which prevents the disclosure of the fact that there has been correspondence **6.101** between the lawyer and client and/or that there have been meetings, only the advice given at those meetings is protected.

Initially, it was thought that privilege could be claimed by non-lawyers appearing before tribu- **6.102** nals (see *M&W Grazebrook v Wallens* [1973] IRLR 139) but in *New Victoria Hospital v Ryan* [1993] IRLR 202, the EAT refused to extend privilege beyond legally qualified members of professional bodies to a firm of industrial relations consultants. This should be contrasted with *Scotthorne v Four Seasons Conservatories (UK) Ltd* UKEAT 0178/10 where it was held that advice given by an employer's insurance adviser (a non-lawyer) in relation to contemplated litigation was protected by litigation privilege. The matter is beyond dispute with the Supreme Court finding in *R (on the application of Prudential plc and Another) v Special Commissioner of Income Tax and Another* [2013] UKSC 1 that legal advice privilege only extends to members of the legal professions.

It is possible to waive privilege by disclosing any part of the document in question in compliance **6.103** with a general order for disclosure (*Pozzi v Eli Lilly & Co* Times, 3 December 1986) and if part of a privileged document is read to the tribunal without further qualification that amounts to a waiver of privilege even if the party has not expressly authorized it (*Great Atlantic Insurance Co v Home Insurance Co* [1981] 2 All ER 485), although the document may still be excluded on the grounds of relevance (see *GE Capital Corporate Finance Group v Bankers Trust Co* [1995] 1 WLR 172). If the client raises in evidence something that he said to his solicitor on one occasion he may be questioned about what was said about the same matter on other occasions (*George Doland Ltd v Blackburn, Robson, Coates & Co* [1972] 1 WLR 1338). However, a mere reference to a privileged document does not amount to waiver (*Tate & Lyle International Ltd v Government Trading Corporation* Times, 24 October 1984).

Self-incrimination

Section 14 of the Civil Evidence Act 1968 provides that a party does not have to give disclosure if **6.104** it would tend to incriminate him or his spouse or expose them to proceedings which might lead to a penalty.

Part A Tribunal Procedure

'Without prejudice' communications

6.105 Communications between the parties made with a view to seeking a settlement are not generally admissible documents (see *Rush and Tompkins v Greater London Council* [1989] AC 1280). In *Independent Research Services v Catterall Ltd* [1993] ICR 1, Knox J, in the EAT, stated that the guiding principle on admissibility of 'without prejudice' communications is whether the negotiations are genuine and, if they are not, the documents should be admitted. There, an employee claimed a breakdown of trust and confidence and subsequently wrote a letter seeking further employment on different terms. The employers understandably wished to adduce the letter as evidence that trust and confidence had not broken down, but the EAT held it did not come within the exceptions to the 'without prejudice' rule, as it could not be said to be dishonest. There was nothing, however, to prevent the employers referring to the correspondence or the fact of the negotiations: it was only the contents of the documents so produced that were excluded.

6.106 The label 'without prejudice' is not itself determinative one way or the other of whether a document is really written without prejudice. The tribunal has to decide whether the communications were bona fide attempts at settlement before exercising the discretion to exclude them. In *BNP Paribas v Mezzotero* [2004] IRLR 508 the EAT upheld the decision of a tribunal that a meeting which the employer expressed to be without prejudice at which sexually discriminatory comments were allegedly made could be referred to in the proceedings, referring to the unequal relationship of the parties, the vulnerable position of the applicant, and the fact that the suggestion was made by the employer only once the meeting had begun. In *Vaseghi v Brunel University* [2006] EWCA Civ 1681 highly material without prejudice evidence was allowed as in discrimination claims the necessity of revealing the truth of what had occurred, and the public interest in the eradication of discrimination, tipped the scales as against the necessity of protecting the without prejudice privilege. In *Woodward v Santander* [2010] IRLR 834 the EAT refused to allow a relaxation to the without prejudice rule simply because discrimination was alleged, and held that where the privilege is to be relaxed because of 'unambiguous impropriety' that must be applied strictly.

Communications with ACAS

6.107 Communications with an ACAS conciliation officer, whether written or oral, are not subject to disclosure unless the privilege is expressly waived by the party who communicated with the officer (ETA 1996, s 18(7)).

Disclosure by mistake

6.108 If a privileged document is mistakenly sent to the opposing party it does not necessarily become properly disclosed and its return should be sought once the mistake is realized. However, the question as to whether a disclosure has been made by mistake is decided by primarily looking at the context in which the disclosure took place—for example it is easier to conclude that it was a mistake where there is one privileged document disclosed amongst many that cannot be so described. The test to determine whether privilege is lost is if it would not be obvious to a reasonable solicitor that a mistake had been made, the onus being on the party mistakenly disclosing to show this (see *Al Fayed v Commissioner of Police of the Metropolis* [2002] EWCA Civ 780 and *ISTIL Group Inc v Zahoor* [2003] EWHC 165). In *Pizzey v Ford Motor Company Limited* [1994] PIQR P15 a similar situation arose where the claimant's solicitors mistakenly sent a privileged document to the defendants. The same test is to be applied—whether it is evident to a reasonable person with the qualities of the recipient that there had been a mistake—even though the mistake is not in fact evident to the recipient. If so, the documents should be returned (see *Breeze v John Stacey & Sons Limited* [2000] CP Rep 77). This is to be contrasted with a waiver of privilege which can occur where the contents of the document are referred to during the proceedings. The principles underlying mistaken disclosure were summarized in *ISTIL* at para 74, as follows:

> First, it is clear that the jurisdiction to restrain the use of privileged documents is based on the equitable jurisdiction to restrain breach of confidence Second, after a privileged document has been seen by the opposing party, the court may intervene by way of injunction in exercise of the equitable jurisdiction if the circumstances warrant such intervention on equitable grounds. Third, if the party into whose hands

the document has come (or his solicitor) either (a) has procured inspection of the document by fraud or (b) on inspection, realises that he has been permitted to see the document only by reason of an obvious mistake, the court has the power to intervene by the grant of an injunction in exercise of the equitable jurisdiction. Fourth, in such cases the court should ordinarily intervene, unless the case is one where the injunction can properly be refused on the general principles affecting the grant of a discretionary remedy, e.g. on the ground of delay.

If a party wishes to recover documents mistakenly disclosed an application to the tribunal should be made promptly and/or an application may be made for an injunction to restrain improper use. **6.109**

F. SANCTIONS FOR NON-COMPLIANCE

If a party does not comply with a rule or an order made by the tribunal, a judge or tribunal may take such action as it considers just, which may include all or any of the following (ETR 2013, r 6): **6.110**

(1) waiving or varying the requirement
(2) striking out the claim or the response, in whole or in part, in accordance with r 37
(3) barring or restricting a party's participation in the proceedings, including, for example, making an 'unless' order under r 38 In such cases the striking out automatically follows the non-compliance, and the whole of the claims subject to the 'unless' order must be struck out even if there has only been a partial breach of it (see *Royal Bank of Scotland v Abraham* UKEAT/305/09 (26 August 2009))
(4) awarding costs in accordance with rr 74 to 84.

As soon as a strike-out under rr 6 and 37 takes effect it may be reviewed; it becomes a final determination of the proceedings and, therefore, a 'judgment' and may be reconsidered by the tribunal of its own initiative or on the application of a party (ETR 2013, rr 70 and 71). This is so even where it is for default of an unless order (see *Neary v Governing Body of St. Alban's Girls School* [2010] ICR 473, [2010] IRLR 124). When conducting a reconsideration a tribunal is not required or expected to follow the same approach as the civil courts by applying the CPR. The overriding objective requires tribunals to deal with cases fairly and justly. Consideration may involve some of the factors expressly referred to in the CPR but it does not need to do so in order to be fair: *Harris v Academies Enterprise Trust & Ors* UKEAT/0097/14/KN. See also *Opara v Partnerships In Care Ltd* UKEAT 0368/09 as to when a hearing should be held in relation to applications for relief from sanctions. **6.111**

An employer whose response is struck out is liable to have a default judgment issued just as if he had failed to present a response in the first place. The process is governed by r 21. A respondent may apply for reconsideration of the strike out order under rr 29 and 30 but, given that the striking out of the response is not judgment on the claim, the decision cannot be reconsidered under rr 70 and 71. **6.112**

In *James v Blockbuster Entertainment* [2006] IRLR 630, the claimant failed to provide adequate further particulars of his claims, refused to allow his employer to photocopy his disclosure documents, and attended the tribunal on day one of a six-day hearing with previously unseen documents (including an undisclosed tape recording of an important conversation). In addition to the above breaches of tribunal orders, he also refused to sign his witness statement, and attended on the morning of the hearing having made changes without notice to the employer. The tribunal struck his claim out. On appeal, the Court of Appeal held that, despite this set of breaches, the power to strike out should be exercised sparingly. Sedley LJ gave the following guidance: that the first object of any system of justice is to get triable cases tried and it does not necessarily matter if the litigant is difficult and uncooperative. He further observed that it is undesirable for a strike-out application to be made (or granted) on the first day of a six-day hearing. If non-compliance is serious enough to warrant a strike-out application, this ought to be clear before the trial begins—although it is not clear what the employer ought to have done here. Notwithstanding this, the EAT has continued to strike out claims for non-compliance with directions or orders. **6.113**

6.114 In *Essombe v Nandos Chickenland Ltd* UKEAT/0550/06, the EAT struck out Mr Essombe's claims against Nandos under ETR 2004, r 18(7)(e). A tribunal concluded that Mr Essombe had deliberately refused to comply with its disclosure order (for tape recordings he made during a disciplinary hearing). In *EB v BA* UKEAT/0139/08 and UKEAT/0138/08, the EAT confirmed the tribunal's decision to strike out a claim where the claimant had complied with a 'literal construction' of the tribunal's order but, having understood the intention behind the order, had 'deliberately flouted' it. Finally, in *Fariba v Pfizer Ltd* UKEAT/0605/10/CEA, the EAT upheld a tribunal judgment striking out a claim in part for the claimant's conduct and also for non-compliance with orders requiring her to particularize her claim. This went beyond mere failure to comply with orders. The EAT observed:

> This is not, therefore, a case of the (not uncommon) kind where a litigant in person fails to meet deadlines and/or behaves unreasonably or offensively but is nevertheless doing his or her misguided best to comply with the directions set by the tribunal in order to get to trial. Instead, the scatter of allegations of misconduct, the applications for a stay, the pursuit of other proceedings, the threats of resort to criminal or regulatory sanctions, clearly indicated that the Appellant's focus was entirely elsewhere and that if the case remained live she would, if I may use my own language, continue to thrash around indefinitely. That is why, and the sense in which, the Judge concluded that a fair trial was impossible.

7

Interim Applications: Striking Out and Other Preliminary Issues

SUMMARY

(1) A preliminary hearing is designed to consider case management orders and determine preliminary issues namely any substantive issues which may determine liability.

(2) A claim or response or part of one may be struck out at a preliminary hearing.

(3) A deposit order may also be made at a preliminary hearing.

(4) Preliminary hearings are usually held by a judge sitting alone, but can also be held by a full tribunal.

A. PRELIMINARY HEARINGS

Rule 53 of the ETR 2013 provides that at preliminary hearings the tribunal may do one of the following matters: **7.01**

(a) conduct a preliminary consideration of the claim with the parties and make a case management order
(b) determine any preliminary issue (namely any substantive issue which may determine liability, eg jurisdictional issues or whether an employee was dismissed (ETR 2013, r 53(3))
(c) consider whether a claim or response, or any part, should be struck out under r 37
(d) make a deposit order under r 39
(e) explore the possibility of settlement or alternative dispute resolution (including judicial mediation).

Preliminary hearings for the purpose of case management are addressed in Chapter 6. This chapter is concerned with preliminary hearings, which deal with striking out, deposit orders, and the determination of preliminary issues. **7.02**

7.03 A preliminary hearing can be directed by the tribunal on its own initiative following its initial consideration under r 26 (see Chapter 6) or at any time thereafter on application by a party (ETR 2013, r 54). Rule 30 of the ETR 2013 sets out the procedure for applying for case management orders (on which see paras 6.13–6.14). The application must identify any orders sought.

7.04 The tribunal, when it fixes a preliminary hearing, will give the parties reasonable notice of the date of the hearing (at least fourteen days' notice if any preliminary issues are to be resolved at the hearing) and the notice will specify the preliminary issues that are to be, or may be, decided at the hearing.

7.05 Preliminary hearings are conducted by a judge sitting alone unless a party makes a written request for the hearing to be conducted by a full tribunal in the event that preliminary issues are to be decided at the hearing. A judge will consider the written request and decide whether it would be desirable for the preliminary hearing to be conducted by a full tribunal (r 55). It should be noted that, where a preliminary hearing is held in front of a full panel of three, the subsequent order cannot be made by the employment judge alone: *South Lanarkshire Council v Russell and others* UKEAT 0067/09.

7.06 Preliminary hearings are typically held in private unless a preliminary issue is being determined or a strike-out is being considered, in which case any part of the hearing relating to that determination will be in public (subject to restricted reporting orders or issues of national security) and the tribunal can direct that the entirety of the hearing be in public (ETR 2013, r 56). There is discretion for the judge to convert a preliminary hearing into a final hearing (and vice versa) if there is no injustice to the parties (r 48). This discretion might be used, for example, in cases where at the time of the preliminary hearing there is no need for further witness evidence to determine liability.

B. DETERMINATION OF PRELIMINARY ISSUES

7.07 Tribunals can hold hearings on a wide range of preliminary issues including matters of jurisdiction and questions of law. Such hearings may be in the form of a preliminary hearing under r 53, or a final hearing under r 57, where the tribunal has determined that part of the proceedings be dealt with separately. A preliminary hearing may be appropriate for deciding the following issues: employment status, whether a claim was presented in time, whether the claimant has sufficient service to bring the claim, whether the claimant is/was disabled at the relevant time, and whether or not there has been a transfer of undertakings. However, in a case of constructive dismissal, for example, it will not normally be appropriate to determine whether or not there has been a dismissal because the question of who caused the dismissal is the central issue in the case. House of Lords authority indicates (by way of *obiter* comments) that a preliminary hearing should not be held unless there is a 'succinct knock-out point' (*SCA Packaging Ltd v Boyle* [2009] UKHL 37, [2009] IRLR 746). Therefore, a party should only apply for a preliminary hearing where there is an isolated issue, the resolution of which has the potential to dispose of the case or a significant part thereof. The specific issue to be determined must be capable of resolution separate to the substantive case (*Post Office Counters v Malik* [1991] ICR 355).

7.08 There are a number of EAT judgments warning of the dangers inherent in determining issues at a preliminary stage (see eg *Secretary of State for Education v Birchall* [1994] IRLR 630). While it may be superficially a cheaper and faster course of action to isolate an issue, it is often better to find all the facts first and then to decide matters of law (see *Smith v Gardner Merchant* [1998] IRLR 510). As a result there may be only one appeal to the EAT rather than a whole series of appeals, which may throw out the timescale and be more costly for the parties. In *Smith v Gardner Merchant Ltd* [1998] IRLR 510, Ward LJ said (at para 5):

> I would discourage industrial tribunals from trying to identify preliminary points of law in cases in which the facts are in dispute and when it is far from clear what facts will ultimately be found by the tribunal and what facts should be assumed to be necessary to form the basis of the proposed point of law.

Issues of jurisdiction are, however, commonly determined as preliminary issues. An example may **7.09** be to determine who is the transferor or transferee in transfer of undertakings cases and whether there has been a transfer of an undertaking and if so which (see *Allan v Stirling District Council* [1994] IRLR 208). Without these matters being clearly determined, the remainder of the structure of the hearing cannot be determined. The distinction between jurisdictional and substantive issues may nevertheless be difficult to draw. In *Warren v Wylie & Wylie* [1994] IRLR 316 the judge, sitting alone, held a preliminary hearing on whether the claimant had qualifying service to bring a claim for unfair dismissal. The facts in the case were not in dispute and the matter was a pure question of law. There are many appellate authorities warning against attempting to determine matters such as continuing acts of discrimination or the existence of a practice or policy of discrimination at such hearings. *Hendricks v Metropolitan Police Commissioner* [2003] IRLR 96 stresses that determining whether matters are out of time in a case of continuing discrimination is not suitable for preliminary determination as there are disputes of fact involved.

C. STRIKING OUT

A claim or response or any part of one can be struck out for any one or more of the reasons listed **7.10** in ETR 2013, r 37 namely:

(a) it is scandalous or vexatious or has no reasonable prospects of success (r 37(1)(a))
(b) the manner in which the proceedings have been conducted by or on behalf of the claimant or respondent has been scandalous, unreasonable, or vexatious (r 37(1)(b))
(c) non-compliance with the tribunal rules or with a tribunal order (r 37(1)(c))
(d) it has not been actively pursued (r 37(1)(d))
(e) the tribunal considers that it is no longer possible to have a fair hearing in respect of the claim or response (or the part to be struck out) (r 37(1)(e)).

This power is substantially the same as the old power under r 18(7) of the ETR 2004. As such, the **7.11** cases under the old rules will continue to apply.

This list is exhaustive, and tribunals' general case management powers do not extend to striking out **7.12** for any other reason (*Care First Partnership Ltd v Roffey* [2001] IRLR 85). The distinction between a strike-out and a dismissal for want of jurisdiction is that the former requires an exercise of judicial discretion (to some extent) and the latter is a jurisdictional barrier imposed by law.

An application for an order striking out a claim or response should be made in accordance **7.13** with r 30 and can be made at any point in the proceedings. However, it should be noted that an application to strike out a response, or part of one, halfway through proceedings may be met with difficulties (see *Timbo v Greenwich Council for Racial Equality* UKEAT/0160/12/SM; *Castlemilk Practice v Chakrabarti* UKEAT 0065/08; *Wiggan v RN Wooler & Co Ltd* UKEAT 0542/06).

Under the new rules, notice does not have to be given of the application to strike out to the other **7.14** party. However, the party in question must be given a reasonable opportunity to make representations, either in writing or, if requested by the party, at a hearing (r 37(2)). In practice, this will mean applying for a strike-out in good time before the preliminary hearing, although in some cases it may be possible to apply for a strike-out at the preliminary hearing itself successfully (providing the other party is given, at the preliminary hearing, a reasonable opportunity to make representations).

Scandalous or vexatious claim or response

A scandalous claim or response is one which is both irrelevant and abusive to the other side (but **7.15** see *De Keyser Ltd v Wilson* [2001] IRLR 324, where the EAT emphasized that caution must be exercised in such cases; if there can still be a fair hearing strike-out is likely to be disproportionate).

A vexatious claim or defence is one which is not pursued with the expectation that it will be successful but with the intention of harassing the other side out of some improper motive.

7.16 In *Ashmore v British Coal Corp* [1990] ICR 485 the Court of Appeal in an employment case expressed the view that:

> A litigant has the right to have his claim litigated, provided it is not frivolous, vexatious or an abuse of process. What may constitute such conduct must depend on all the circumstances of the case; the categories are not closed and considerations of public policy and the interests of justice may be very material.

No reasonable prospect of success

7.17 'No reasonable prospect of success' presents a lower threshold than 'no prospect of success'; it is not an issue of deciding whether a case is hopeless, but rather the question is whether an argument has a realistic as opposed to a merely fanciful prospect of success (see *Balamoody v United Kingdom Central Council for Nursing, Midwifery and Health Visiting* [2002] IRLR 288 at para 46, *Eszias v North Glamorgan NHS Trust* [2007] ICR 1126 at paras 25–26). In *Eszias* the Court of Appeal emphasized that a claim should not be struck out on this basis where the central facts are in dispute, unless exceptional circumstances exist, such as where the contemporaneous documentation is inconsistent with the facts asserted by one party. This should be contrasted with cases where there is 'little reasonable prospect of success' and the tribunal can make a deposit order under r 39 of the ETR(see para 7.35 below).

7.18 Applications to strike out on the basis that there is no reasonable prospect of success should only be made in the most obvious and plain cases in which there is no factual dispute and the applicant can clearly cross the threshold of showing that there are no reasonable prospects of success. In *QDOS Consulting Ltd & Others v Swanson* UKEAT/0495/11, HHJ Serota QC observed:

> Applications that involve prolonged or extensive study of documents and the assessment of disputed evidence that may depend on the credibility of the witnesses should not be brought under rule 18(7)(b) but must be determined at a full hearing. Applications under rule 18(7)(b) that involve issues of discrimination must be approached with particular caution. In cases where there are real factual disputes the parties should prepare for a full hearing rather than dissipate their energy and resources, and those, I would add, of Employment Tribunals, on deceptively attractive shortcuts. Such applications should rarely, if ever, involve oral evidence and should be measured in hours rather than days.

7.19 In *Balls v Downham Market High School & College* [2011] IRLR 217 the EAT held that the employment tribunal should also look at its own file to see if there is any correspondence or other document that is relevant to the issue of whether the claim has no reasonable prospects of success. If there is any such document, it should be shown to the parties and they should be invited to make submissions on it.

Scandalous, unreasonable, or vexatious conduct

7.20 Tribunals have no power to commit for contempt of court; the power to strike out on this ground may be seen as a means of regulating the behaviour of unruly litigants in person following the difficulties highlighted in *O'Keefe v Southampton City Council* [1988] ICR 419, although the Court of Appeal sounded a note of caution in *James v Blockbuster* [2006] IRLR 630 at para 5 (see below at para 7.30).

7.21 The EAT set out in *Bolch v Chipman* [2004] IRLR 140 the stages that must be undertaken by a tribunal in considering any application to strike out on grounds of conduct of the proceedings:

(a) There must be a conclusion by the tribunal not simply that a party has behaved unreasonably but that the proceedings have been conducted by or on his behalf unreasonably. The EAT commented that this proposition is supported by the decision of the Court of Appeal in *Bennett v Southwark London Borough Council* [2002] IRLR 407, where the conclusion was that conduct in the tribunal by an advocate, by way of aberrant and offensive behaviour (saying to the tribunal 'If I were an Oxford educated white barrister with a plummy voice

I would not be put in this position') was not, in those circumstances, relevant conduct within the rule. In *Harmony Healthcare plc v Drewery* UKEAT 866/00 the EAT upheld a decision to strike out a response where the respondent's representative assaulted the claimant's representative in the tribunal waiting room.

(b) Assuming there is a finding that the proceedings have been conducted scandalously, unreasonably, or vexatiously, that is not the final question so far as leading on to an order that the response must be struck out. What is required before there can be a strike-out of a response or indeed a claim is a conclusion as to whether a fair trial is or is not still possible (see *Force One Utilities Ltd v Hatfield* [2009] IRLR 45, EAT, where a case was struck out because the intimidation of the claimant by a director of the respondent outside of the tribunal meant a fair trial was no longer possible).

(c) Once there has been a conclusion, if there has been, that the proceedings have been conducted unreasonably etc, and that a fair trial is not possible, there still remains the question as to what remedy the tribunal considers appropriate, which is proportionate to its conclusion.

A good example of the application of the principles in *Bolch* arose in *Force One Utilities v Hatfield* **7.22** [2009] IRLR 45, where a respondent was struck out for intimidating the claimant as they left the hearing. The witness was in real fear for his safety and Elias J held that this conduct went to the root of the tribunal's ability to assess the evidence. He further held that there was no requirement to conduct the usual balancing exercise in these circumstances and that strike-out was entirely proportionate. In *Chidzoy v BBC* [2018] UKEAT 0097 the claimant during an adjournment in her evidence, spoke to a reporter about the case and her evidence. The tribunal struck out her claim on the basis that it was a proportionate response as it felt it could no longer fairly try the case. Interestingly the EAT did not interfere with the Tribunal's decision that it would not be proportionate to recuse itself and for a second Tribunal to hear the case, given the stage proceedings had reached. In addition, the EAT rejected an argument that the tribunal erred by deciding the strike out application without hearing oral evidence as to what had been said to the journalist. Although there were conflicts of evidence the tribunal had felt able to determine the matter on paper and with submissions, and to have done so fell within the tribunal's power to regulate its own procedure.

The claim has not been actively pursued

This ground ties in with whether or not a fair hearing is possible. A claim may be struck out on **7.23** this ground where, for example, there has been a considerable delay as a result of the claimant's illness and there is no prognosis as to when they may be fit to give evidence (see *Peixoto v British Telecommunications plc* UKEAT 0222/07, 22 January 2008). However, such an order should only be used in exceptional cases. In *Abegaze v Shrewsbury College of Arts and Technology* [2010] IRLR 238 the Court of Appeal reversed an EAT decision striking out a claim following a finding for a claimant on liability after a seven-year delay on the claimant's part in taking necessary steps for the holding of a remedy hearing. It was held that rigorous case management orders could assist a fair hearing on remedy; therefore, striking out the claim was considered to be a disproportionate sanction in the circumstances. See also *Miller v Lambert Primary Care Trust* [2009] All ER (D) 147 (Sep).

Fair hearing not possible

As indicated above, whether or not a fair hearing could still be held was always a condition in con- **7.24** sidering whether or not to strike out a claim on the basis of one of the parties' conduct. However, it has now been elevated to a ground for strike-out in and of itself, highlighting that it is both a necessary and sufficient condition. Tribunals generally follow the same guidelines as apply under CPR r 3.4, which gives the civil courts an unqualified discretion to strike out a claim where a party has failed to comply with a fixed time limit or order or practice direction. However, the prospect of a fair trial no longer being possible is a high threshold to attain. The Court of Appeal has stressed, in any event, that usually other alternatives to strike-out may be more appropriate such as costs (see *Biguzzi v Rank Leisure plc* [1999] 1 WLR 1926).

7.25 In *Evans' Executors v Metropolitan Police Authority* [1992] IRLR 570, however, the Court of Appeal accepted that when applying the old High Court principles to tribunals the courts would be less tolerant of delay than in other civil proceedings because there is a shorter limitation period and tribunals ought to decide cases quickly. The Court of Appeal stressed that prejudice must be shown and this is often obvious since memories get worse over time. This will not be so obvious when the case turns on pure law (as it did in *Evans' Executors*, which concerned equality in pensions).

Failure to comply with an order

7.26 Rule 6 provides that a failure to comply with an order (save for those in relation to time limits for presentation of the claim and response, employer's contract claim and claimant's response and a strike-out order or order to pay a deposit) does not render void the proceedings or any step in the proceedings but can lead to the tribunal waiving or varying the requirement, and/or striking out the claim or response in whole or in part (in accordance with r 37) and/or barring or restricting a party's participation in the proceedings and/or awarding costs (in accordance with rr 74–84). In the case of the exceptions outlined above, there are specific sanctions provided for in the rules.

7.27 An order to strike out does not need to be made at a hearing provided the party subject to it has been given the opportunity to make written representations and has not requested a hearing (ETR 2013, r 37(2)).

7.28 The tribunal will be guided by the overriding objective in r 2, which includes considering all of the circumstances of the case, and whether the default is the responsibility of a party or solicitor (see *Weir Valves and Control v Armitage* [2004] ICR 371). A key factor is whether a fair hearing is still possible as a result of the default as the purpose of the order is not, in the ordinary course of events, to punish, but to secure compliance with orders of the employment tribunal.

7.29 Any strike-out order made is a judgment within the meaning of r 1(3)(b) and therefore potentially subject to reconsideration in the interests of justice under r 70.

Other sanctions for non-compliance with an order

7.30 In *James v Blockbuster Entertainment* [2006] IRLR 630, the Court of Appeal stressed the necessity to consider other sanctions before striking out a claim on the ground of non-compliance with orders, given the extreme nature of the sanction. It would seem that such caution should be exercised in any case where strike-out is being considered as a result of a party's conduct (see *De Keyser Ltd v Wilson* [2001] IRLR 324), but the same does not hold true for r 37(1)(a) or (b). It would seem too that an 'unless' order would usually be a more appropriate sanction (*Abegaze v Shrewsbury College of Arts and Technology* [2010] IRLR 238). However, it is in line with the overriding objective and the tribunal is entitled to say enough is enough (see *Governing Body of St Albans Girls' School v Neary* [2010] IRLR 124 at para 64). An example of a case being struck out for non-compliance is *Bennet v London Probation Service* UKEAT 0194/09, where the claimant indicated that she would never disclose medical reports, despite being ordered to do so. See also *Pik v Goldman Sachs Services Ltd* [2009] All ER (D) 110 (Jan).

D. UNLESS ORDERS

7.31 Rule 38 of the ETR 2013 provides that a judge may make an 'unless' order, namely an order specifying that if it is not complied with by the date specified, the claim or response, or part of it, will be dismissed without further order. An 'unless' order is a conditional judgment and there is no discretion to do other than confirm dismissal of a claim or response in the event of non-compliance (*Scottish Ambulance Service v Laing* UKEATS/0038/12).

7.32 The rules contain a procedure for setting aside dismissal of a claim or response for breach of an 'unless' order (r 38(2)).

An application to set aside must be made in writing within fourteen days of the date that notice **7.33** of dismissal was sent. The application must state why it is in the interests of justice for dismissal to be set aside. Tribunals can determine such applications in a hearing (if requested) or on the basis of written representations. The ground on which the tribunal may set aside any dismissal is that it is in the interests of justice to do so. In *Governing Body of St Albans School v Neary* [2010] IRLR 124 the Court of Appeal departed from the earlier practice adopted by tribunals in considering the nine factors listed in CPR r 3.9(1) and held that the prime consideration is the overriding objective and that whilst employment judges may find it useful to refer to the CPR factors they are not obliged to consider each factor separately. The approach of the judge must be to determine the case rationally and not capriciously and consider relevant factors while excluding irrelevant ones.

As a footnote CPR r 3.9(1) has been amended and the nine factors removed (see Civil Procedure **7.34** (Amendment) Rules 2013, SI 2013/262). The factors now to be considered are all the circumstances of the case, so as to enable the Court to deal justly with the application, including the need for litigation to be conducted efficiently and at proportionate cost and to enforce compliance with rules, practice directions, and orders. The new provision was considered in *Michael and Another v Middleton and Another* [2013] EWHC 2881 (Ch), where the claimants applied for relief from sanctions under CPR r 3.9 following the striking out of their case. One of the issues the judge had to consider was whether any of the old r 3.9 applied or just the new rule. In his judgment, the judge referred to the judgment by Hildyard J in *Tavataba Thevarajah and Others v Riordan and Others* on 9 August 2013 (unreported), in which relief from sanctions against the defendants was refused, and concluded that, although the old r 3.9 checklist had been removed, nonetheless the checklist factors still represented matters that continued to be relevant for the court in its overall assessment required by the new rule, albeit that the new rule was more rigorous and that the courts should be slow to conclude that relief was appropriate and just. This has been reinforced by the Court of Appeal decision in *Andrew Mitchell MP v News Group Newspapers* [2013] EWCA Civ 1537, where the Court of Appeal stressed that a tougher approach would be adopted towards those in breach of the CPR, practice directions, and orders, as litigation needs to be conducted efficiently and at proportionate cost. If non-compliance is trivial and an application for relief is made promptly, relief will usually be given but, where the court considers the default not trivial, the burden of persuading the court to grant relief will fall on the defaulting party. The Court of Appeal held that overlooking deadlines, in particular, would be unlikely to justify relief. The application of *Mitchell* was considered by the Court of Appeal in *Denton v TH White Ltd & Others* and the Court of Appeal gave guidance as to the correct three-stage approach: (1) Is the breach serious or significant including consideration of the effect on other litigation? (2) Was there a good reason for the breach? A good reason will tend to justify granting relief from sanctions; (3) considering the factors in r 3.9 and all the circumstances of the case, should relief be granted?

E. PAYMENT OF A DEPOSIT

Rule 39 of the ETR 2013 provides that a judge may make an order in a preliminary hearing that a **7.35** party pay a deposit of an amount up to £1,000 as a condition of continuing to advance any specific allegation or argument, where he considers that the contentions put forward by that party have little reasonable prospect of success. This is a change to the power under the old rules in r 20 of the ETR 2004, where a deposit order was only payable on condition of being permitted to take part in the proceedings relating to that matter. Under the new rules, it is possible to obtain multiple deposit orders against a party in respect of specific parts of a claim or response.

In *Van Rensbury v Royal Borough of Kingston-upon-Thames* UKEAT/95/07, the EAT pointed out **7.36** the 'little reasonable prospects of success' test allows a tribunal greater leeway to take such a course than would be permissible under the 'no reasonable prospects of success' test for a strikeout but that the tribunal 'must have a proper basis for doubting the likelihood of the party being able to establish facts essential to the claim or response'.

7.37 The judge must make reasonable enquiries into the paying party's ability to pay the deposit and take that into account when deciding the amount of the deposit. A deposit order should be an order that is capable of being complied with, and the party subject to the deposit order should not be ordered to pay a sum that they are unlikely to be able to raise (see *Hemdan v Ishmail* [2017] IRLR 228). A deposit order will not necessarily be made just because an interim relief order has been made: *Blitz v Vectone Group Holdings Ltd* UKEAT 0306/09.

7.38 The deposit must be paid within twenty-one days of the order for payment being sent to the party. An extension of a further fourteen days may be allowed if the party against whom the order is made applies within the twenty-one days. Failure to pay will result in the part of the claim or response to which the order relates being struck out. This is mandatory under r 39(4). The order to pay the deposit cannot be reconsidered because r 39 (like its predecessor ETR 2004, r 20) is an order and not a judgment (see *Sodexho v Gibbons* [2005] ICR 1647).

7.39 If at any stage following the making of a deposit order the tribunal decides the specific allegation or argument against the paying party for substantially the same reasons given in the deposit order, the paying party shall be treated as having acted unreasonably in pursuing that specific allegation or argument for the purposes of r 76 (the rule addressing when a costs order or preparation time order shall be made), unless the contrary is shown, and the deposit will be paid to the other party, otherwise the deposit shall be refunded (r 39(5)).

7.40 See Chapter 12 in relation to orders for costs or preparation time orders where a deposit has been paid.

8

Contractual Claims

SUMMARY

(1) A narrowly defined range of claims for breach of contract can be brought in the employment tribunal.

(2) The tribunal may award damages for breach of contract up to a maximum of £25,000

(3) The time limit for a claim is three months, and may be the subject of extension on grounds that it was not reasonably practicable to claim in time.

(4) An employer may counterclaim for breach of contract only if the employee has brought a claim for breach of contract. The restrictions on the type of claim an employer may bring mirror those applying to employee claims.

(5) The relationship between contractual claims in the tribunal and in the civil courts requires careful tactical consideration.

A. INTRODUCTION

The Employment Tribunals Extension of Jurisdiction (England and Wales) Order 1994, SI 1994/ **8.01** 1623 (1994 Order) permits tribunals to hear certain specified claims for breach of contract.

B. CONDITIONS FOR A CONTRACT CLAIM

The effect of s 3(2) of the ETA 1996 and the 1994 Order is to give an employment tribunal a **8.02** jurisdiction to hear a narrowly defined class of claims for breach of contract. A number of types of contract claim which may commonly arise in the employment context are excluded from the tribunal's jurisdiction. Once it is determined that a claim falls within the terms of the 1994 Order, the tribunal's jurisdiction is concurrent with the civil courts' common law jurisdiction to hear claims of breach of contract (see ETA 1996, s 3(4)), and the claims fall to be determined applying normal common law principles of contract law. The overlap between the jurisdictions of the tribunal and the courts is considered at para 8.31 and in Chapter 20.

8.03 If an employee brings a contract claim a tribunal may also consider a contract claim brought by an employer (Art 4 of the 1994 Order); in effect a counterclaim. An employer has no independent right to sue in the tribunal for breach of contract. Employers' claims are dealt with at para 8.21.

8.04 The conditions for an employee's contract claim are as follows (Art 3 of the 1994 Order):

(1) The claim must be of one of the following types (ETA 1996, s 3(2)):
   (a) a claim for damages for breach of a contract of employment or other contract connected with employment
   (b) a claim for a sum due under such a contract
   (c) a claim for the recovery of a sum in pursuance of any enactment relating to the terms or performance of such a contract.
(2) The claim must be one which a court in England, Wales, or Scotland would have jurisdiction to hear and determine (ETA 1996, s 3(2)).
(3) The claim must arise or be outstanding on the termination of the employee's employment (Art 3(c) of the 1994 Order).
(4) The claim must not be in respect of personal injuries (ETA 1996, s 3(3)).
(5) The claim must not fall within the categories of claim excluded by Art 5 of the 1994 Order.

Contract claim

8.05 The tribunal's jurisdiction covers claims for damages for breach of contract and claims for sums due under the contract (or under an enactment relating to the terms or performance of such a contract) (ETA 1996, s 3(2)). The jurisdiction is therefore limited to money claims, whether in debt or damages. The employment tribunal is not given jurisdiction to grant injunctions, order delivery up of property, or make declarations, even if the civil courts could do so on the same facts. A maximum of £25,000 can be awarded in respect of each claim; this is discussed in more detail at paras 8.31–8.34.

8.06 The tribunal does not have jurisdiction to determine common law or equitable claims which are not founded on contract. There is therefore no jurisdiction to determine tortious claims (for example negligence or economic torts) or equitable claims (for example breach of fiduciary duty, or claims relating to trusts over an employer's property).

8.07 In *Pilley v British Steel Engineering Steels UK Ltd* EAT/182/99 the claimants complained that they had entered into a redundancy agreement on the basis of misrepresentations made by their employer. The EAT held that whatever the precise juridical basis of the claim for damages for misrepresentation it was not a claim for damages for breach of contract, and was therefore outside the tribunal's statutory jurisdiction. It should be noted, however, that the EAT remitted the case to the tribunal on the claimants' amended claim that the representations amounted to a collateral contract. There was a possibility that such a collateral contract would be a contract connected with employment for the purposes of s 3(2) of the ETA 1996.

Contract connected with employment

8.08 A claim must be for breach of an employment contract, or a contract connected with employment (ETA 1996, s 3(2)(a)). A claim may only be brought against the employer, not a third party: *Oni v Unison* [2018] IRLR 806.

8.09 A settlement agreement entered into between an employer and an employee in respect of the employee's employment is a contract connected with employment. Thus a party to the agreement may sue in the tribunal for damages for breach of such an agreement: see *Rock-It Cargo v Green* [1997] IRLR 581, EAT. However, in relation to settlement agreements careful consideration should be given to whether the claim arises or is outstanding on termination of employment (see para 8.16). In the light of *Pilley* (above), a contract collateral to a collective redundancy agreement may also be a contract connected with employment. Section 3(2) does not extend jurisdiction to allow a claim against a person who is not the employer: *Oni v Unison* [2018] UKEAT/0092/17. In that case, the employee's claim against her union for breach of her union membership agreement was held not to be an 'other contract connected with employment' for the purposes of s 3(2).

Jurisdiction of the courts of England and Wales

The tribunal's territorial jurisdiction in respect of contract claims is the same as the jurisdiction of **8.10** the courts (ETA 1996, s 3(2)). See further Chapter 1 for the territorial jurisdiction of employment tribunals.

Arising or outstanding on the termination of employment

Article 3(c) of the 1994 Order provides that the claim must 'arise or is outstanding on the termin- **8.11** ation of the employee's employment'. The word 'on' is used in a temporal sense: that is, the claim must be outstanding on the date of termination, or arise on that date (*Miller Bros & FP Butler Ltd v Johnston* [2002] IRLR 386, EAT).

A claim cannot be brought while the employee is still employed (see eg *Southern Cross Healthcare* **8.12** *Ltd v Perkins* [2011] IRLR 247, CA). The tribunal has no jurisdiction to hear a contract claim which is lodged before the date of termination of employment, even if the employment has terminated by the date of the hearing (*Capek v Lincolnshire County Council* [2000] ICR 878, CA).

Conversely, provided the claim arises or is outstanding on termination, a claim may be brought **8.13** even if the termination occurred before the employee started work under the contract: *Sarker v South Tees Acute Hospitals NHS Trust* [1997] IRLR 328, EAT. There is no minimum qualifying period for bringing a claim under the 1994 Order: *Masiak v City Restaurants Ltd* [1999] IRLR 780, EAT.

Where dealing with a claim for bonuses or commission, particular care must be taken to analyse **8.14** whether the claimant's entitlement arises or is outstanding on termination. If the sum claimed fell due on a date after termination of employment, then the tribunal will not have jurisdiction in respect of the claim. For example, in *Peninsula Business Services Ltd v Sweeney* [2004] IRLR 49, EAT, under the terms of a commission scheme, commission due on work carried out during the claimant's employment did not fall due for payment until a date after termination of his employment. The EAT held that as at the date of termination he had no more than a prospective right to payment, which had not yet matured, and so his claim neither arose on termination, nor was it outstanding on termination. The EAT held that a claim will only be 'outstanding' on the date of termination if it is in the nature of a claim which, as at that date, was immediately enforceable but remained unsatisfied.

As the Court of Appeal pointed out in *Capek*, where there is no jurisdiction to hear a contract claim **8.15** because employment has not been terminated, it may be possible for the claimant to formulate his claim as one for an unlawful deduction from wages under Part II of the ERA 1996.

As noted at para 8.09 above a settlement agreement will be regarded as a contract connected with **8.16** employment. However, the timing of when a settlement is made may exclude the tribunal's jurisdiction. In *Rock-It Cargo* the settlement agreement was made *prior* to termination of employment, and the breach of contract also occurred prior to termination of employment; it was thus conceded that the claim was outstanding on the termination of employment. By contrast, where a settlement agreement is made *after* the termination of employment, whilst the contract may, on the authority of *Rock-It*, be connected with the employment, the claim in respect of it cannot be said to arise or be outstanding on the termination of employment (Art 3(c) of the 1994 Order). The EAT in *Miller Bros & FP Butler Ltd v Johnston* (above) decided that there was no jurisdiction to hear a claim in relation to a contract where negotiations had begun prior to the termination of employment, but had not been concluded until after termination. However, the EAT clearly had some reservations about the undesirable practical consequences of this decision, given that there is little reason in principle to distinguish between settlements concluded before and after the termination of employment. One further point has not yet been canvassed by the authorities: given that the cause of action in the contract claim arises from the *breach* of contract, it is arguable that where a settlement agreement is made prior to termination, but breach does not occur until after termination, the conditions of Art 3(c) would not be satisfied.

Claims in respect of personal injuries

8.17 A claim cannot be brought in the tribunal for damages, or a sum due, in respect of personal injuries (ETA 1996, s 3(3); Art 3 of the 1994 Order). 'Personal injuries' includes any disease and any impairment of a person's physical or mental condition.

8.18 The exclusion is of potentially wide application. Obvious examples include claims in respect of injuries sustained at work as a result of the employer's culpable act or omission, the traditional territory of personal injury litigation. However, there is no requirement in s 3(3) that the claim need be one where the claimant is alleging that the personal injuries are the fault of the defendant. Where an employee's entitlement to a contractual benefit depends upon the employee demonstrating that he has suffered personal injury, then the claim is likely to fall within the exclusion, irrespective of whose fault the injury was, or indeed, by whom it was caused. In *Flatman v London Borough of Southwark* [2003] EWCA Civ 1610 the employer operated a personal injury allowance scheme in respect of injuries sustained during the course of work. The claimant's complaint was not that his employers had caused his injury, but that they had refused to pay him an allowance to which he was entitled, having satisfied the conditions for payment. He claimed for an award under the scheme, or for the loss of a chance of being awarded a sum. The Court of Appeal held that this was a claim for damages in respect of personal injuries, and was excluded from the tribunal's jurisdiction under s 3(3). Similar reasoning is likely to apply in respect of benefits under long-term disability and permanent health insurance schemes, although given their typically high value, such claims are unlikely to be suitable for the tribunal in any event.

8.19 The rationale for the exclusion would appear to be that claims in respect of personal injury invariably involve consideration of expert medical evidence, and as such raise matters which are thought unsuitable to determination in the tribunal (see for example *Flatman* above, at para 38 (Schiemann LJ)). There is less force in this rationale now than there would have been at the time that the predecessor of s 3 of the ETA 1996 was enacted. Tribunals now regularly have to deal with medical evidence in disability discrimination claims, and also in assessing damages for personal injury as a head of loss caused by discrimination.

Claims excluded by Article 5

8.20 Article 5 of the 1994 Order also excludes claims for breach of a contractual term of any of the following descriptions:

(1) a term requiring the employer to provide provision or occupation of living accommodation, or a term imposing obligations on the employer or employee in connection with the provision of living accommodation
(2) a term relating to intellectual property
(3) a term imposing an obligation of confidence
(4) a term which is a covenant in restraint of trade.

C. EMPLOYER COUNTERCLAIM

8.21 An employer may bring a claim for breach of contract against the employee (Art 4 of the 1994 Order). The conditions setting out the nature of the claim are the same as those applicable to an employee's claim, ie the claim must fall within s 3(2) of the ETA 1996; the claim must not fall within the excluded categories set out above; and the claim must arise or be outstanding on the termination of the employment of the employee against whom it is made.

There are, however, important further restrictions in relation to employers' claims. The tribunal **8.22** will only entertain a complaint which arises out of a contract with the employee (Art 8(b) of the 1994 Order), and only if the employee has brought a contract claim (Art 4(d) of the 1994 Order). An employer can only present a claim at a time when there is before the tribunal a complaint in respect of a contract claim of the employee which has not been settled or withdrawn (Art 8(a) of the 1994 Order). In other words, an employer's claim can only be brought by way of counterclaim.

When, however, a valid employer's claim has been presented, the tribunal will have jurisdiction to **8.23** determine it, even if the employee's claim is subsequently withdrawn or settled. This was held to be the case from the wording of Art 8 in *Patel v RCMS Ltd* [1999] IRLR 161, EAT. In *Patel* the EAT went so far as to hold that there was jurisdiction to entertain an employer's claim even though the employee's claim was not presented in time, and therefore could not proceed in the tribunal. This was because the presentation of a form IT1 (now ET1) in respect of an out-of-time claim was not a nullity, and therefore, in the language of Art 4(d), proceedings in respect of a claim of the employee had been *brought before an employment tribunal*.

The employee is in a vulnerable position, since at the time of making the initial claim he may not **8.24** know that the employer may seek to counter it. As a consequence, the employee may actually refrain from making the initial contract claim, especially if the claim is for a relatively small amount. If the employer can substantiate a counterclaim in respect of serious breaches by the employee, or breaches going back over a long period, the counterclaim may indeed significantly exceed the original claim. If the employee claims only unfair dismissal, the employer will not be able to counterclaim for breach of contract. However, if the employee adds in a claim for wrongful dismissal, no matter how short the notice period, he exposes himself to a risk of a counterclaim for damages of up to £25,000. It should be noted that in the case of *Ridge v HM Land Registry* UKEAT/0485/12/ DM, the EAT held that even though the employer's contract claim was submitted out of time such that the tribunal had no jurisdiction to hear it, the employer could still run a defence of set-off in respect of the claimant's contract claim.

On the other hand, the circumstances in which the employer can bring a contract claim in the tri- **8.25** bunal are all dependent on the claims the employee chooses to pursue. Even if the employee brings a contract claim, the employer may need to act swiftly in submitting a counterclaim, to avoid the risk of the employee withdrawing his claim before the counterclaim is presented.

D. COMMENCEMENT AND TIME LIMITS

Article 7 of the 1994 Order provides that the complaint shall be presented to a tribunal within **8.26** three months of the effective date of termination or, if there is no such date, the last day of the relevant employment. In cases where it is not reasonably practicable to present it within that time, it must be presented within such further period as the tribunal considers reasonable. For the purposes of Art 7, no definition of effective date of termination is given, but tribunals normally adopt the definition contained in s 97(1) of the ERA 1996. This view is reinforced by the fact that Art 2 defines the effective date of termination in terms of s 97(1).

Rule 23 of the ETR 2013 provides that any counterclaim by the employer must be made as part of **8.27** the employer's response to the claimant's claim, and must be presented in accordance with the time limit for a response under r 16, ie within twenty-eight days of the date that a copy of the claim was sent by the tribunal. This represents a tightening of the time limit, which, prior to the ETR 2013, was six weeks. It is unclear whether, in additional to the time limit in Art 7, the normal limitation period of six years pursuant to the Limitation Act 1980 also applies to claims in the tribunal. If so, that would prevent a claim in relation to a breach that was more than six years old, even if Art 7 was satisfied. There are two conflicting tribunal decisions on this issue: *Taylor v Central Manchester University Hospitals NHS Foundation Trust* ET/2405066/12 held that the Limitation Act does apply; *Gristanti v NBC News Worldwide Inc* ET/2200964/15 held that it does not.

8.28 An employer's counterclaim may be rejected by the tribunal under r 12, on the same grounds that a claim form may be rejected: ie the tribunal has no jurisdiction to consider the claim; the claim is in a form which cannot reasonably be responded to; or the claim is an abuse of process. For rejection of claims and reconsideration of rejections, see Chapters 2 and 13.

8.29 A claimant must present a response to an employer's contract claim within twenty-eight days of the date the employer's response was sent to the claimant (ETR 2013, r 25). If the claimant fails to do so in time, rr 20 (application for an extension of time) and 21 (judgment) apply.

E. HEARING OF A CONTRACT CLAIM

8.30 An employment judge sitting alone may hear any contractual claim (ETA 1996, s 4(3)(d)). In deciding whether to hear a case alone or with lay members, the judge must take into account whether there are other proceedings which might be heard concurrently. If there are other such proceedings which would warrant a full tribunal, this may weigh against having a judge sitting alone. See further paras 1.23–1.26.

F. COMPENSATION LIMITS AND RELATIONSHIP WITH THE CIVIL COURTS

8.31 As has been stated, all of the claims falling within the contractual jurisdiction may also be brought in the ordinary courts; a claimant thus faces a choice whether to bring a claim in the tribunal or in the High Court or the county court. A number of factors are likely to be relevant in choosing where to proceed:

(a) The value of the claim: will the claim exceed the £25,000 cap imposed in the tribunal?

(b) Remedy: does the claimant seek a remedy other than a monetary award (for example an injunction, an order for delivery up or an account)? If so, the court is the appropriate forum.

(c) Other claims: does the claim stand alone, or is it to be brought alongside other claims? If there are other claims, are they to be brought in the tribunal (for example unfair dismissal or discrimination) or in the courts (for example personal injury or restrictive covenant claims)? There may well be an advantage in having the contract claim determined along with the other claims, if this is possible.

(d) Speed: the tribunal is likely to provide a quicker remedy than the courts.

(e) Cost: court proceedings are more procedurally complex and are normally likely to cost more. The tribunal claim is likely to be determined on the basis that each side will bear its own costs—in the courts the claimant is likely to recover his costs if he wins, but risks paying the other side's costs if he loses.

(f) Limitation: the tribunal claim must be brought within three months (subject to extension), whereas a claim can be brought in the courts within the normal six-year limitation period for a claim for breach of contract.

8.32 One aspect is the level of award that may be made in the employment tribunal for a contract claim. Article 10 of the 1994 Order provides that the tribunal: 'shall not in proceedings in respect of a contract claim, or in respect of a number of contract claims relating to the same contract, order the payment of an amount exceeding £25,000'. This compensation limit has not been changed since 1994. In *Fraser v HLMAD Ltd* [2006] EWCA Civ 738, [2006] IRLR 687, Mummery LJ remarked that the time might have arrived for the Secretary of State to reconsider the limit, particularly in the light of the tribunal's experience of dealing with high value compensation claims in discrimination cases (see paras 5–6 and 33). A law society survey of members between 19 March and 2 April 2009 showed that 70 per cent of members responding felt that the cap should be removed or increased: http://www.lawsociety.org.uk/documents/downloads/employ-tribunal-survey-results-may09pdf.

The tribunal is entitled as a matter of fact to determine that the amount of loss or debt is a sum **8.33** in excess of £25,000, but can only award a capped sum of £25,000 (as in the analogous position of the statutory cap for unfair dismissal). Where a contract claim exceeds £25,000, it is not permissible to sue for the first £25,000 in the tribunal, and then claim the excess in the civil courts. The reason for this is the civil law doctrine of merger. If the tribunal adjudicates on the contract claim, the cause of action becomes merged into the judgment. Once judgment is given, there is no remaining cause of action upon which the claimant can sue. *Fraser v HLMAD* (above) was an application of the doctrine of merger in this context; see also *Republic of India v India Steamship Co Ltd* [1993] AC 410 and *Clarke v Yorke* (1882) 52 LJ Ch 32. It is important to note that the operation of the doctrine of merger is strict. Unlike abuse of process, there is no scope for discretionary factors to be taken into account. In *Fraser*, the claimant brought claims in the tribunal for unfair dismissal and breach of contract. He obtained judgment on both claims. His ET1 recognized that his contract claim exceeded £25,000, and expressly put the respondent on notice that he intended to claim in the High Court for the excess. Indeed, his court proceedings were commenced (but not concluded) before the tribunal judgment. The tribunal assessed his breach of contract damages at £80,000, but applied the statutory cap. His claim in the courts to recover the shortfall was struck out. The Court of Appeal expressed sympathy for his position: if the claimant had withdrawn his contract claim from the tribunal, not only would he have been entitled to pursue it in the High Court, but the tribunal's findings would have operated as an issue estoppel in his favour. There was no prejudice to the respondent. However, the application of the doctrine of merger was strict, and there was no scope to take into account matters such as prejudice (or absence of it) (see paras 29–30 (Mummery LJ)).

In practice a problem often arises where proceedings have been started in the tribunal but it sub- **8.34** sequently transpires that the cap of £25,000 will prevent full recovery of the value of the claim in the tribunal. This may be because the claimant commenced proceedings in person and was unaware of the cap, or it may be that the claim is difficult to evaluate, and it is only after disclosure of documents that it emerges that the claim is worth more than £25,000. In these circumstances, the claimant may wish to abandon the tribunal proceedings and pursue his claim in the civil courts. The approach of the courts to the appropriate procedure for bringing the tribunal proceedings to an end has been complicated. The position is considered in detail at paras 11.70 ff below. See also Chapter 20 in relation to the overlap of claims between the employment tribunal and the civil courts.

9

The Hearing

SUMMARY

(1) The rules distinguish between preliminary hearings and final hearings. There may be more than one of each type of hearing in a particular case.

(2) Parties are entitled to fourteen days' notice of a final hearing, or a preliminary hearing involving a preliminary issue. Parties are expected to do their utmost to adhere to listing timetables, but the tribunal has the power to postpone or adjourn any hearing.

(3) The tribunal has a broad discretion to conduct hearings in a manner most appropriate for the just handling of the proceedings. Tribunals should avoid formality as far as appropriate and are not bound by the rules of evidence. In many respects, however, hearings will be conducted in a manner similar to court proceedings.

(4) A final hearing and a preliminary hearing at which a preliminary issue is determined or a strike-out application considered will normally be in public. There are limited powers to depart from the principle of open justice, for example by sitting in private, anonymizing the record of proceedings, or restricting reporting of proceedings.

A. INTRODUCTION

There may be one or more hearings during a claim. The ETR 2013 distinguishes between two **9.01** principal types of hearing: preliminary hearings and final hearings. The structure of the ETR 2013 regarding hearings is as follows:

- rules 41–50 are rules common to all kinds of hearings
- rules 53–56 deal with preliminary hearings
- rules 57–59 deal with final hearings.

Rule 53 provides that a preliminary hearing is a hearing at which the tribunal may do one or more **9.02** of the following:

(a) conduct a preliminary consideration of the claim with the parties and make a case management order (including an order relating to the conduct of the final hearing)
(b) determine any preliminary issue
(c) consider whether a claim or response, or any part, should be struck out under r 37
(d) make a deposit order under r 39
(e) explore the possibility of settlement or alternative dispute resolution (including judicial mediation).

Rules 53–56 also apply to the hearing of applications for interim relief. At such hearings the tri- **9.03** bunal shall not hear evidence unless it directs otherwise: r 95.

Preliminary hearings replace two different types of hearing which existed under the previous **9.04** rules: case management discussions and pre-hearing reviews. The new rules give the tribunal more flexibility as to the steps that it may take at a particular hearing. The old rules were inflexible as to the types of orders which could be made at a case management discussion, and those which could only be made at a pre-hearing review. However, in complex cases there is often more than one preliminary hearing: some more focused on case management, and some more focused on dealing with substantive questions, such as determining a preliminary issue. Rule 53(2) provides that there may be more than one preliminary hearing in any case.

A preliminary hearing shall be in private, unless the hearing involves a determination of a prelim- **9.05** inary issue, or an application to strike out all or part of a claim or response: r 56. In those cases, any part of the hearing relating to such a determination shall be in public, and the tribunal may direct that the entirety of the hearing is in public.

Rule 57 defines a final hearing as a hearing at which the tribunal determines the claim or such **9.06** parts as remain outstanding following the initial sift under r 26 or any preliminary hearing. There may be different final hearings for different issues (for example liability, remedy, or costs). A final hearing shall be in public subject to rr 50 and 94 (see paras 9.177 ff below).

It would appear that a reconsideration hearing under r 72 falls into neither category. Under the **9.07** ETR 2004, a review hearing was a distinct category of hearing. Rules 41–50 will apply to reconsideration hearings, as they apply to all kinds of hearing.

This chapter deals primarily with preparation and conduct of the final hearing. However, many **9.08** of the principles, particularly in relation to natural justice and practical steps to prepare evidence, may apply to preliminary hearings where evidence is to be heard and where issues in the case are to be determined.

For the composition of tribunals for particular types of hearing, see paras 1.19 ff. **9.09**

B. LISTING AND NOTICE OF HEARING

9.10 The tribunal shall give the parties not less than fourteen days' notice of a final hearing (r 58) and of a preliminary hearing involving a preliminary issue. The tribunal must give the parties 'reasonable notice' of any other preliminary hearing, although listing practice can vary in different regions. The requirements and methods of notice and the date of deemed delivery of such notice are set out in rr 86 and 90 respectively.

9.11 In most cases the parties will have the opportunity to have input into the time estimate for the hearing. If there is a preliminary hearing, the judge will fix a hearing based on a time estimate which has been discussed with the parties. In a case with no preliminary hearing, a judge will normally make an estimate on the basis of the papers available to him, but may give the parties a short period of time to make representations to the tribunal if the time estimate is inadequate.

9.12 The parties should attempt to assess the likely length of hearing as realistically as possible, in order to avoid hearings overrunning their allotted time and having to be adjourned 'part-heard' for long periods before the same panel can sit together again (see comments of the Court of Appeal in *Martins v Marks and Spencer plc* [1998] IRLR 326, paras 60 and 61). This means that there is a risk that tribunal members will forget the evidence heard on the first hearing date. Problems arise in particular where hearings are spread out, with the result that it may be difficult for the tribunal to remember the demeanour of a witness or its impression of the evidence. The problem is exacerbated in cases where the judge is a part-time judge and thus only sits irregularly. In *Barnes v BPC (Business Forms) Ltd* [1975] ICR 390, the High Court stated that:

> unfortunately, all courts and tribunals have from time to time to adjourn, and not infrequently, but too frequently, the adjourned dates are often far apart. The real answer is that it cannot be helped particularly in the case of tribunals such as this which include part-time members ... I am sure that as many steps as possible ought to be taken so that consecutive hearings may be obtained.

In *Shashi Kumar v University of Strathclyde* EATS/0003/02, The Times, 19 July 2002, the EAT considered that it was unsatisfactory for a final hearing before an employment tribunal to be listed deliberately with gaps between every day of the hearing and such scheduling should be avoided unless absolutely necessary.

9.13 Tribunals may take the availability of legal representatives into consideration when listing a hearing, particularly when the case in question is long or complex, has been remitted on appeal, or has involved legal representatives in the past, but, generally, greater priority is given to the availability of the members of the employment tribunal and the parties themselves.

C. PREPARATION FOR THE HEARING

9.14 In many cases, all of the important case management decisions for preparation of a case will have been taken prior to the commencement of the hearing. Either a preliminary hearing will have taken place, or the tribunal may have issued directions of its own motion (following the decision of the EAT in *Hassan v Barts Health NHS Trust and Others* UKEAT/0042/16/RN, the practice of some tribunals to list a preliminary hearing after receipt of the ET1 but before receipt of the ET3 should be changed). The directions should set out the timetable for disclosure of documents, preparation of bundles, exchange of witness statements, and expert reports (if applicable). An estimate for the length of the hearing will have been made (either with or without the views of the parties), and the case will be listed accordingly. Case management is dealt with in more detail in Chapter 6. If there has been a preliminary hearing, the issues to be determined at a hearing should have been defined. The need for interim applications should have been identified, and by the time of the final hearing these interim applications should have been dealt with. Interim applications are dealt with in Chapter 7.

The following paragraphs outline the main steps to be considered in preparation for a hearing **9.15** (subject of course to any specific directions given by the tribunal). The guidance document entitled 'Presidential Guidance—General Case Management' (March 2014) produced by the President of the Employment Tribunals (England and Wales) sets out helpful practical guidance, particularly as to bundles and witness statements.

Bundles

A bundle of documents should be agreed between the parties and exchanged ahead of time. An **9.16** employment tribunal may place a limit on the number of pages to be allowed in such a bundle, allowing the parties to seek permission to exceed the total number when appropriate.

The guidance on preparation of bundles in civil proceedings is pertinent in the tribunal: see CPR **9.17** Practice Direction 39A, para 3. The following provisions are worthy of note:

3.3 The originals of the documents contained in the trial bundle, together with copies of any other court orders should be available at the trial. In practice, it is rare that an original document is required and therefore it is likely to be sufficient that a party is able to obtain originals if required, rather than to bring all originals to the hearing.

3.5 The trial bundle should be paginated in the bottom right corner (continuously) throughout, and indexed with a brief description of each document and the page range. Where the total number of pages is more than 100, numbered dividers should be placed at intervals between groups of documents. Unless otherwise directed, pages should be single-sided.

3.6 The bundle should normally be contained in a ring binder or lever arch file. Where more than one bundle is supplied, they should be clearly distinguishable, for example, by different colours or letters. If there are numerous bundles, a core bundle should be prepared containing the core documents essential to the proceedings, with references to the supplementary documents in the other bundles.

3.7 For convenience, experts' reports may be contained in a separate bundle and cross-referenced in the main bundle.

3.8 If a document to be included in the trial bundle is illegible, a typed copy should be included next to it in the bundle, suitably cross-referenced. Similarly, any documents not in English should be translated by a professional translator into a language that can be understood by the parties, their legal representatives and the tribunal (in the tribunals of England and Wales the default language will be English).

3.9 The contents of the trial bundle should be agreed where possible.

3.10 The party filing the trial bundle should supply identical bundles to all the parties to the proceedings and for the use of the witnesses.

The *Chancery Guide 2016*, paras 21.34 to 21.72, whilst not directly applicable to hearings in the **9.18** tribunal, provides useful detailed and practical guidance on preparation of bundles. A badly organized bundle can waste a great deal of tribunal time, and be confusing both for tribunal members and witnesses. Following the spirit of CPR Practice Direction 39A, para 3.1, a sensible order for the bundle in most cases is as follows:

(a) claim form and response
(b) any responses to requests for further information
(c) questionnaires
(d) orders and directions by the tribunal
(e) documents. Whilst there are various ways of organizing the documents depending on the issues in the case, in most cases a single chronological sequence of documents is most helpful; however, variations from this structure may be appropriate; for example, it may be convenient to put contract documents and employer's handbooks and policies in a separate section if they are voluminous
(f) witness statements and expert evidence. Such statements may most conveniently be grouped together in a separate volume.

9.19 All documents on which each party will rely should be included in the bundle but unnecessary documents should be excluded. The fact that a bundle is agreed between the parties does not mean that the parties admit the contents of the documents, but merely that it is agreed that those documents may go before the tribunal. The truth of any material contained in the document may need to be proved by oral evidence but documents generally do not have to be formally proved.

9.20 If a question arises as to whether a particular document should be excluded from a party's bundle of documents (or an agreed bundle), the judge should decide whether the document should be excluded or not, either at a separate preliminary hearing or at the outset of the hearing. There is no requirement that such matters should be dealt with in advance of the hearing. If the admissibility of the document is determined at the hearing and there is a fear of potential prejudice arising from the lay members seeing the disputed document in advance, the judge may direct that they shall not be given the bundle until the issue has been decided (*X v Z Ltd* [1998] ICR 43, CA).

9.21 Six copies of the bundle should be brought to the tribunal on the day of the hearing in cases in which a full tribunal (ie three panel members) is sitting. This includes a copy for the claimant and respondent. Additional copies will be necessary in cases with multiple claimants or respondents. Fewer copies are required where the case is to be heard by a judge sitting alone, ie the absence of two lay members means two copies fewer. Note that one bundle may be made available to members of the public or the press once the material has been adduced in evidence in the public domain, although they are not allowed to take it away from the tribunal room or to copy it.

Witnesses and witness statements

9.22 Witness statements should be exchanged in advance. If the hearing is in front of a full panel, six copies should be brought to the tribunal to account for the judge, two lay members, the witness table copy and one each for the claimant and the respondent, plus one further copy marked 'Not to be removed from the tribunal', to be made available to the public or press. For cases in front of a judge sitting alone, only four copies are needed, plus a copy available to the public. The statements should have been signed by the maker prior to exchange, although it is not uncommon for witnesses to sign their statements on the morning of the hearing. Some judges are more particular about this than others.

9.23 Once the notice of hearing has been received, witnesses should be warned of the dates when they are likely to be needed and advised to keep themselves available for those dates. If witnesses are unwilling to attend, witness orders may be obtained from the tribunal.

9.24 Representatives should ensure that each witness reads his witness statement shortly prior to the hearing and is happy with its content. Witnesses should also be given the opportunity to familiarize themselves with the bundle of documents. It may be helpful, if time and cost permit, for each witness to be given a brief explanation of the procedure that will be followed in the tribunal. Some witnesses may choose to attend a public hearing in another case to familiarize themselves with the tribunal environment and procedure. If witnesses have the time, this can prove helpful.

9.25 It is, of course, inappropriate for a representative to 'coach' a witness in preparation for the hearing, and inappropriate to practise cross-examination on the evidence in the case. English practice here differs from that common in the United States. There has been a recent trend in large value cases to make use of 'witness familiarization' programmes, where professional trainers carry out a *mock* tribunal and give training on the giving of evidence. This is permissible within prescribed limits, designed to prevent contamination of the evidence. The familiarization must take place in a context unrelated to the proceedings. Any case study should not be based on the facts of the case, nor similar facts. The legal representatives in the case should never be involved in the training. For detailed guidance in the context of the criminal courts see *R v Momodou* [2005] EWCA Crim 177, [2005] 1 WLR 3442. For an application of that guidance in civil proceedings see *Ultraframe (UK) Ltd v Fielding; Northstar Systems Ltd v Fielding* [2005] EWHC 1638 at paras 21–31 (Lewison J). There is guidance available at the Bar Standards Board website http://www.barstandardsboard.org.uk.

Special arrangements

9.26 Representatives should consider whether special arrangements are necessary for the hearing. For example:

(a) If audio or video recordings or links are to be used in evidence, the parties should liaise with the tribunal so that arrangements can be made to ensure that there are facilities for the recordings to be played. It may be necessary for the representatives to provide equipment. The hearing may be conducted by use of electronic communications provided that the tribunal considers it just and equitable to do so, and provided that the parties and members of the public attending the hearing are able to hear what the tribunal hears and see any witness as seen by the tribunal: ETR 2013, r 46. The formulation of r 46 would appear to be narrower than the old r 15(2) of the ERT 2004. Under the new rule, the public must be able to see a witness 'as seen by the tribunal': ie the public must see no less than the tribunal. This leaves open the possibility that neither judge nor public sees the witness (for example, if the witness is heard by audio link only). Old r 15(2) imposed a positive requirement that the public be allowed to see and hear all parties to the communication when witness evidence is heard.

(b) If a professional interpreter is needed, the tribunal office dealing with the case should be notified and arrangements should be made for an interpreter to be engaged.

(c) If any party or witness suffers from a disability, representatives should check access to the tribunal, and should take steps to ensure that he or she is able to participate and follow the proceedings. Will a deaf witness need a signer? Will a witness with a condition causing poor concentration or energy levels need extra breaks? In *Rackham v NHS Professionals Limited* UKEAT/0110/15 (judgment handed down on 15 and 16 December 2015) the President of the EAT, Mr Justice Langstaff, confirmed that tribunals as 'organs of the state' are required to make reasonable adjustments for disabled claimants and highlighted the guidance in the Equal Treatment Bench Book, which may also assist in civil proceedings.

9.27 All of these arrangements are likely to have an effect on the time estimate, and the listing should take these factors into account. Where a case has been listed, parties should inform the tribunal as soon as they are aware of any special features which may affect the time estimate.

Chronology, skeleton, and authorities

9.28 A chronology of main events is helpful for the tribunal in all but the most simple case. This should be agreed between the parties if possible and provided to the tribunal prior to the commencement of the hearing. Occasionally, the tribunal will make an order for the parties to produce a chronology.

9.29 In a complex case, the tribunal may be assisted by an opening skeleton argument of modest length or at least a list of issues (if these have not already been defined at a preliminary hearing). Again, the tribunal sometimes makes an order for skeleton arguments.

9.30 Legal authorities should be exchanged between the parties on the morning of the hearing unless the parties have agreed otherwise. In a complex case where exchange of skeleton arguments has been directed, representatives should exchange lists of authorities, along with the skeleton arguments. Again, as with hearing bundles, it is useful, if possible, to agree a joint bundle of authorities with an index and dividers, although unlike the hearing bundle continuous pagination should not be added to the authorities bundle. It is usually unnecessary to produce authorities for each and every trite proposition of law and parties should seek to keep the number of authorities within reasonable and sensible bounds.

Review of time estimate

9.31 The parties should review the time estimate for the case in the light of each stage of its progress, in particular following disclosure and exchange of witness statements. The tribunal should be notified as soon as possible if it appears that the time estimate is inadequate. The tribunal is more likely to be able to find extra days for the hearing the earlier it is aware of the problem. Similarly, if it appears that the original listing is excessively long, the tribunal should be informed so that it can list other matters on the days which will not be needed. It is important to remember that sufficient time should be factored into any estimate for the tribunal to read the papers before the oral hearing begins, and for deliberation and judgment after closing submissions.

Settlement

9.32 The parties should inform the tribunal in writing as soon as possible after any settlement is reached. Parties should confirm whether attendance is required if settlement has been reached. This may depend on the timing of the agreement and its proximity to the beginning of a listed hearing.

D. ADJOURNMENT AND POSTPONEMENT

General considerations

9.33 The tribunal has a wide discretion whether or not to postpone or adjourn a hearing: this power falls within its general powers to make case management orders and to regulate its own procedure (ETR 2013, rr 29 and 41). In the case of late (ie less than seven days before the hearing date) or repeated (ie two or more in the same proceedings by the same party) applications for postponements, the discretion is limited, at least in cases presented on or after 6 April 2016 (see para 9.39 below). Where the tribunal has a discretion, it is to be exercised judicially (ie not arbitrarily or capriciously and after taking into account the representations of the parties), and may grant an adjournment if there is a good, reasonable ground to do so (*Jacobs v Norsalta Ltd* [1977] ICR 189). There is no rule that says the tribunal should exercise its discretion only in exceptional cases. Instead, a tribunal should assess what is required in the best interests of justice in each case (*Carter v Credit Change Ltd* [1979] ICR 908, [1979] IRLR 361, CA). Particular considerations may arise where a party or witness is unwell or, for example, mentally impaired, eg *U v Butler & Wilson* UKEAT/0354/13/DM: the EAT held that the employment tribunal ought to have adjourned a hearing of its own volition in circumstances in which the claimant stated he was experiencing a psychotic episode and the judge, who observed he was exhibiting symptoms of being unwell, nonetheless went on to deal with an application for a review, which she determined against him.

9.34 In exercising their discretion to postpone hearings, tribunals should seek to weigh in the balance the need for speedy determinations, especially in the interests of claimants, against the requirement that, for example, witnesses be available at the hearing to enable justice to be done to all parties.

9.35 The procedure for applying for a postponement is the subject of Presidential Guidance (December 2013). An application should normally be made in writing, and should be discussed with the other parties. The application should explain the reason why it is made, and why the application is in accordance with the overriding objective. Supporting documents should be presented where available (ie a medical note explaining illness).

9.36 The tribunal is only required to provide brief reasons when allowing or dismissing an application of this nature, but it is required to demonstrate that the key points put forward in the application and any other essential factors have been considered in its decision: *British Security Industry Association v Brown* UKEAT/0228/15/BA.

9.37 The tribunal has the power to make costs orders in respect of costs incurred as a result of a postponement or adjournment. Rule 76(2) of the ETR 2013 is not subject to the more stringent conditions of r 76(1), so it is not necessary to show that a party has behaved vexatiously, abusively, disruptively, or otherwise unreasonably; the tribunal has a broad discretion to make any such order for costs as befits the justice of the case. In practice, however, tribunals are unlikely to make an order for costs on an adjournment unless there has been some unreasonable behaviour on the part of the party applying for the adjournment.

The tribunal has no power to attach conditions to an adjournment, and so should not make an adjournment dependent on the payment of costs which the party seeking the adjournment has been ordered to pay (*Cooper v Weatherwise (Roofing and Walling) Ltd* [1993] ICR 81, EAT). **9.38**

From 6 April 2016, applications for postponement have been governed by a new r 30A of the ETR 2013. The new rule applies in relation to proceedings which are presented to the employment tribunal on or after 6 April 2016. In summary, r 30A provides that: **9.39**

a) applications for postponement should be made and communicated to the other parties as soon as possible after the need for a postponement becomes known
b) where an application is made less than seven days before the hearing it will *only* be granted if:
    a. the parties all consent *and* it is practicable and appropriate for the purpose of giving the parties the opportunity to resolve their disputes by agreement or it is otherwise in accordance with the overriding objective or
    b. the application has been necessitated by the act or omission of another party or of the tribunal or
    c. there are exceptional circumstances;
c) where the tribunal has ordered two or more postponements in the same proceedings on the application of the same party then a further postponement will *only* be granted where the same conditions as above are fulfilled.

Rule 30A(4) provides that exceptional circumstances may include ill-health relating to an existing long-term health condition or disability. The purpose of that rule is not clear. The use of 'may' suggests that this is not a comprehensive definition of exceptional circumstances. Indeed, it would be absurd to attempt to define exceptional circumstances in such a limited manner and clearly there will be other exceptional circumstances outside the narrow scenario described in r 30A(4). It is difficult to see what purpose the sub-rule serves. **9.40**

Late and repeat applications for postponements are now subject to a strict, formalized regime. In the writer's view, there was little need for the rule, and its formulation is unnecessarily prescriptive. **9.41**

Proceedings pending in another forum

Applications for a postponement or a stay often arise where proceedings relating to the same employment are pending in the High Court, County Court, or Crown Court (*Jacobs v Norsalta Ltd* [1977] ICR 189). These would most commonly concern claims for breach of confidence, damages for wrongful dismissal, a criminal charge, or an action for unfair prejudice as a shareholder of a company pursuant to s 994 of the Companies Act 2006. An adjournment may be granted in respect of proceedings pending in a foreign jurisdiction (*JMCC Holdings Ltd v Conroy* [1990] ICR 179). **9.42**

The question to be considered is essentially in which court the action is most conveniently and appropriately to be tried, bearing in mind all the surrounding circumstances. There is no legal presumption in favour of or against adjournments when other proceedings are afoot (*Carter v Credit Change Ltd* [1980] 1 All ER 252). It is not an error of law to refuse an adjournment of a tribunal when High Court proceedings are pending, bearing in mind the need for speed in tribunals (*Automatic Switching Ltd v Brunet* [1986] ICR 542). **9.43**

The following factors were identified in *First Castle Electronics Ltd v West* [1989] ICR 72, 78 (Wood J) as relevant to the exercise of the discretion to adjourn: **9.44**

(a) The degree of overlap of the issues in the court proceedings and the tribunal proceedings.
(b) The complexity of the issues and the evidence.
(c) The amounts at stake in the respective proceedings.
(d) The risk of findings by the tribunal which will bind the High Court: 'findings of fact by the tribunal on issues coming before both proceedings in the High Court could prove embarrassing to the trial judge in the High Court clear findings of fact in a judgment from a High Court judge could well prove helpful to a tribunal at a later hearings'.

(e) The procedural complexity of the case: High Court procedure is better suited to dealing with procedural and evidential complexities, for example expert evidence, large-scale disclosure, or disputes about privilege.

(f) The rules of evidence: 'in a complicated matter such as the present it is probably best that the strict rules of evidence as applied in the High Court are more suitable—excessive informality can lead to injustice to one side or the other'.

(g) Delay: the claimant may be prejudiced by the delay in that receipt of compensation is delayed and may make reinstatement or re-engagement impracticable. Either party may potentially be prejudiced by delay in resolving issues which put the parties' reputations and integrity at stake.

See also *Bowater plc v Charlwood* [1991] ICR 798; *Warnock v Scarborough Football Club* [1989] ICR 489; *Cahm v Ward and Goldstone Ltd* [1979] ICR 574. The applicable principles were stated by the EAT in *Mindimaxnox LLP v Gover and Another* UKEAT/0225/10/DA, which was referred to with approval by the Court of Appeal in *Halstead v Paymentshield Group Holdings Ltd* [2012] IRLR 586.

9.45 In *Chorion plc v Lane*, The Times, 7 April 1999, the High Court ordered an employee involved in High Court and tribunal proceedings to apply for a stay of the tribunal proceedings or to consent to the employer's application for a stay. There was a significant overlap between the proceedings with both involving alleged breaches of fiduciary duty and breach of contract. Since allegations of dishonesty were made it was preferable for the matters to be heard in the High Court. In *GFI Holdings Ltd v Camm* UKEAT/0321/08/DA, [2008] All ER (D) 74 (Sep), the EAT held that a tribunal had erred when refusing to grant a stay on the grounds that there was no overlap of issues with High Court proceedings. A finding of dismissal was an important first stage in both sets of proceedings, and there was also a real risk that the tribunal would make findings going to the implied term contended for in the High Court. A stay should therefore be ordered.

9.46 Although it will usually be in the interests of the employer and not in the employee's interest to postpone tribunal proceedings, delay may also (but less frequently) suit a claimant employee if, for example, he expects to be acquitted of a criminal charge, and thus wishes the magistrate or the Crown Court to adjudicate before the unfair dismissal case is heard. In particular, he will not wish to be cross-examined in the employment tribunal in advance of a criminal trial.

9.47 In appropriate circumstances the tribunal will be prepared to stay or postpone tribunal proceedings even where High Court proceedings on the same facts have only been threatened but not yet issued. However, much depends on the context in which the High Court claim is threatened. Postponements ought normally to be granted where the claimant wishes to pursue a High Court claim, and has indicated that he only instituted tribunal proceedings as a protective measure to avoid being debarred by reason of the time limit. If proceedings are brought on this basis, claimants should make this clear in their originating applications and they can then easily be dealt with accordingly (see *First Castle* and *Warnock*). In *Halstead v Paymentshield*, the claimant had written a letter before action indicating what his future High Court claims might be. The respondent argued that the tribunal claim should be stayed pending the threatened High Court claim. The claimant wished to proceed with the tribunal claim first and had only raised the High Court claim in an effort to negotiate a settlement of all his claims against the respondent. The Court of Appeal held that correspondence short of proceedings did not deprive the claimant of the right to proceed in the tribunal.

9.48 Tribunals have stressed that claimants are entitled to an early hearing of their applications in the interests of justice and tribunals should go ahead where there are straightforward issues of fact which they were competent to determine. They are generally reluctant to grant postponements without good reason; see, for example, *Bastick v James Lane (Turf Accountants) Ltd* [1979] ICR 778, where an adjournment was refused because the issues in the tribunal were not sufficiently closely linked to those in parallel criminal proceedings. Where, however, it was essential that a witness's credibility be challenged in a criminal case, the tribunal has granted a postponement, even though the claimant was not himself the subject of the prosecution (*Smith-Evans v Wyre Forest District Council* COIT 1590/129).

It may, in some circumstances, be appropriate to stay a High Court claim pending the outcome **9.49** of tribunal proceedings. In *BUQ v HRE* [2012] EWHC 2827 QB (15 October 2012), the High Court postponed the trial of a claim for a privacy injunction pending determination of tribunal claims. The claims in the High Court overlapped with the claims in the tribunal, but the common claims formed part of a wider set of interrelated claims in the tribunal, whereas the High Court claim was narrower in scope. In that context, it appears the tribunal was better placed to determine the claims as a whole. In *Vaughan v London Borough of Lewisham* [2013] IRLR 720, the High Court ordered a stay of a claim under the Protection from Harassment Act 1997 pending determination of tribunal proceedings. The tribunal was the first seised, and a great deal of time and resource had been dedicated to the tribunal proceedings. A refusal of a stay in the High Court would likely lead to a stay of the tribunal proceedings, causing unacceptable delay and wasted time and costs. The judge also stated that the tribunal was the obvious place for resolution of the claimant's claims relating to her employment.

The tribunal will examine carefully the degree of overlap between the sets of proceedings in each **9.50** case. In *BUPA Care Homes (CFC Homes) Ltd v Muscolino* [2006] ICR 1329, the claimant was dismissed for gross misconduct, having been found asleep while on duty. The employers applied to adjourn the unfair dismissal claim pending the claimant's appeal to the Care Standards Tribunal against a determination made by the Secretary of State that she was unsuitable to work with vulnerable adults. The EAT upheld the employment tribunal's rejection of that application. The EAT did not consider that the overlap between the different issues which the two statutory tribunals were to decide was sufficiently great. It should also be noted that the tribunal's findings of fact would not be binding on the Care Standards Tribunal, by reason of the particular statutory provisions governing that tribunal. Similarly, in *Firouzian v Metroline Limited* UKEAT/0233/12/CEA, 23 May 2012, the EAT held that the tribunal had been entitled to refuse a postponement of a preliminary hearing, even though criminal proceedings were pending. The hearing was to consider the question of disability only, and there was no risk of a breach of the claimant's privilege against self-incrimination.

Inability of party, witness, or representative to attend

General

In exercising their discretion to postpone hearings, tribunals seek to weigh in the balance the need **9.51** for speedy determinations against the requirements of a fair hearing. Delay caused by adjournment potentially causes prejudice to both sides. The adjournment usually causes additional expense. There is prejudice from an unresolved dispute hanging over the parties, particularly in cases of discrimination. In unfair dismissal cases where reinstatement is sought, the longer the proceedings take, the less likely reinstatement will be a practical solution. Adjournments also entail a waste of the tribunal's limited resources.

However, the tribunal must not sacrifice the right of the parties to a fair trial in the interests of **9.52** speed and efficiency. An adjournment should normally be granted where a refusal would deny a fair trial. This most frequently arises if a party or important witness is unable to attend the hearing. In *Teinaz v London Borough of Wandsworth* [2002] IRLR 721, paras 20–21, Peter Gibson LJ said:

> [A]lthough an adjournment is a discretionary matter, some adjournments must be granted if not to do so amounts to a denial of justice. Where the consequences of the refusal of an adjournment are severe, such as where it will lead to the dismissal of the proceedings, the tribunal or court must be particularly careful not to cause an injustice to the litigant seeking an adjournment …

> A litigant whose presence is needed for the fair trial of a case, but who is unable to be present through no fault of his own, will usually have to be granted an adjournment, however inconvenient it may be to the tribunal or court and to the other parties. That litigant's right to a fair trial under Article 6 of the ECHR demands nothing less. But the tribunal or court is entitled to be satisfied that the inability of the litigant to be present is genuine, and the onus is on the claimant for an adjournment to prove the need for such an adjournment.

Absence of a witness

9.53 In most cases, the tribunal will send out a listing letter well in advance of a potential hearing date, asking the parties to indicate what dates are inconvenient for witnesses and representatives, and if a party has accepted a date as convenient, the tribunal is unlikely to accept an adjournment because it has at a later stage become inconvenient.

9.54 The parties are well advised to apply for an adjournment as soon as they become aware that a witness will not be able to attend the hearing, and to give reasons for the absence, and reasons why the adjournment application could not have been made sooner. Factors relevant to the tribunal's decision will include the importance of the evidence of the witness who cannot attend, the reasons for the witness's absence, the prejudice likely to be caused by delay, and whether the party seeking the adjournment had acted promptly in seeking the adjournment. In *Tillingbourne Bus Co Ltd v Norsworthy* EAT/947/99, the EAT said that the tribunal should have regard to the conduct of the parties such as whether they have complied with time limits and how much warning has been given of the application to adjourn. The tribunal should look at the reason for the application and how pressing it is. If an important witness cannot be present, it is necessary to consider whether the evidence might be presented in some other manner.

Ill-health

9.55 Requests for adjournments are often made on grounds that a party, or a witness, is unable to attend the hearing due to ill-health. If a party is genuinely unfit to attend the hearing, then, in line with general guidance in *Teinaz v London Borough of Wandsworth* (paras 20–22) an adjournment ought to be granted. In certain circumstances, a tribunal may be required to consider an adjournment due to ill-health even where a party has not applied for one, although these situations are likely to be very rare: see *Shui v University of Manchester* UKEAT/0230/16.

9.56 Where an application to adjourn is made, an adjournment ought generally to be granted, however late the application is made, as ill-health is not only unavoidable, but frequently unforeseen. Where there are grounds to criticize the ill party for not applying sufficiently quickly once it is known that he or she will not be able to attend, however, the appropriate remedy is in costs and it would not be appropriate to proceed in the absence of the ill party.

9.57 The practical problem for the tribunal is in assessing the medical reason upon which the application for an adjournment is based. From time to time, for their own reasons, parties are reluctant to attend hearings, and from time to time the unscrupulous may advance a false or exaggerated medical ground for non-attendance.

9.58 Save for cases of extreme emergency (for example if a party is taken ill or involved in an accident immediately before the hearing), a tribunal will not normally allow an adjournment without cogent medical evidence of the fact that the party is unable to attend. What is to be expected of the evidence will depend very much on the circumstances, and upon the time available between the onset of the incapacity and the hearing.

9.59 Assessing the genuineness of the evidence presents a difficult practical problem for the tribunal. Where the tribunal has doubts about the genuineness or sufficiency of the medical evidence, it may give directions to assist in resolving its doubts. In *Teinaz* above, Peter Gibson LJ (at para 22) suggested some possible approaches which may be suitable depending on the circumstances of the case. One possibility is to direct for further medical evidence to be provided promptly. Another is to invite the party seeking the adjournment to authorize the other side's representatives to have access to the doctor who provided the evidence. A short adjournment may be appropriate for further inquiries to be made (per Arden LJ in *Teinaz*, at para 43).

9.60 The results of these further inquiries may assist the tribunal in the exercise of the discretion. Further medical evidence may reinforce the initial advice that the party was unfit to attend; or the absence of further evidence may justify the tribunal in reaching the conclusion that the ill-health is not genuine or not sufficient to warrant an adjournment. In *Andreou v Lord Chancellor's Department* [2002] IRLR 728, the tribunal took the view that the medical evidence originally submitted was inadequate. The tribunal gave directions for further evidence to be provided and spelt out the matters which it wished to see medical evidence about. The further medical evidence was wholly inadequate compliance with the direction. The Court of Appeal (consisting of two of the same judges who sat in *Teinaz*) said that the tribunal was entitled to have regard to the fact that the party seeking the adjournment had had time to produce sufficient evidence and had failed to do so as justifying its inference that the ill-health was not so serious as to warrant an adjournment.

Andreou is also a useful reminder that the key question for the tribunal is whether the party is fit to **9.61** attend the hearing. This is not the same as whether the party is fit to attend work. An illness may frequently render a party both unfit to work and unfit to attend a hearing, but this is not automatically so. Whether it is the case is a matter of evidence.

Parties applying for an adjournment on grounds of ill-health should therefore ensure that their **9.62** medical evidence:

(a) gives a full account of the nature of the illness and its symptoms;
(b) specifically addresses the question of whether the person is fit to attend a hearing;
(c) sets out the period over which the person has suffered from the illness—if an application is made at the last minute on the basis of a condition that had been known of for some time, the party applying will have to explain the delay;
(d) if possible, sets out the prognosis for recovery, which will assist the parties and the tribunal in re-listing the case. In an urgent case this may not be possible.

If a party chooses not to attend, this is material to the exercise of the discretion to adjourn. However, **9.63** if a doctor has advised his patient not to attend on medical grounds, it is unfair to describe the party as 'choosing' not to attend. The party cannot be expected to attend the hearing to demonstrate the fact that he is not fit (*Teinaz*). In *Asim v University Hospital Birmingham NHS Foundation Trust* UKEAT/0094/10/SM, the EAT allowed an appeal by a claimant whose race discrimination claim was dismissed after he had failed to attend the hearing, saying that he was unwell. He had not produced any evidence of his ill-health before the tribunal but later submitted a credible doctor's letter to the EAT to support his explanation.

These principles should apply to ill-health of a witness as well as to ill-health of a party. However, **9.64** there are some further considerations in relation to witnesses: how important to the case is the evidence of the witness? Have reasonable steps been taken by the party to produce evidence from an alternative witness? The more peripheral the evidence of the witness, and in particular if another witness can give evidence as to the same matter, the less likely an adjournment will be granted. If, however, the evidence is important to the case, and there is no other witness who can cover the evidence, then an adjournment should be granted so as not to deprive the party of a fair chance to advance his or her case (see eg *Rotherham Metropolitan Borough Council v Jones* UKEAT/0726/04).

Where a party advances a false reason in support of an application to adjourn, he risks the tribunal **9.65** striking out his claim, regardless of whether a fair trial would still be possible: see, for example, *Carter v Highway Express* UKEAT/0813/01, where the claimant had falsely claimed that he could not attend the hearing on grounds of ill-health. It should be noted that in *Carter* the tribunal had found that the claimant had intentionally misled the tribunal and the EAT appears to have treated the case as equivalent to 'contumelious default'. This conclusion was reached by the EAT in *Rolls Royce Plc v Riddle* [2008] IRLR 873, where a misrepresentation about the claimant's health had been made to the tribunal which he knew to be false and took no steps to correct subsequently. Short of contumelious default, a strike-out will not normally be appropriate on grounds of unreasonable conduct if a fair trial is still possible (see *Bolch v Chipman* [2004] IRLR 140, EAT; *De Keyser Ltd v Wilson* [2001] IRLR 324, EAT and *Abegaze v Shrewsbury College of Articles and Technology* [2010] IRLR 238).

Lack of representation

In *Masters of Beckenham Ltd v Green* [1977] ICR 535, the EAT decided that the tribunal should **9.66** have granted an adjournment when told that the company secretary who had represented the company at the prior hearing had recently left their employ, and no one else at that stage knew the details of the case. A similar decision was reached in *Smith v Alsecure Guards Ltd* EAT/264/82, where the employee wanted to be represented by his local welfare rights office. The EAT has, however, decided that there is no general rule of law that tribunals should permit a request for postponement made merely because a party's legal representative will not be available on the listed date: *Hewson v Travellers Club* EAT/338/85. In most tribunal regions now, the listing offices and employment judges, if an application is made to them, will not accept the inconvenience of a date for the party's representatives as a reason for adjourning a hearing.

Interpreters

9.67 The unavailability of an interpreter in circumstances in which insufficient notice of a hearing has been given or in other circumstances in which a reasonable opportunity has not been afforded to the party requiring such assistance to make arrangements for an interpreter to attend is likely to be a good reason for postponing or adjourning a hearing. However, a party who wants an interpreter and proceeds in the absence of one, having been given the choice of continuing or seeking an adjournment, should be careful as being given such a choice is, according to the EAT in *Hak v St Christopher's Fellowship* [2016] IRLR 342, likely to provide a reasonable opportunity to the party in question to have an interpreter. Each case is fact specific, but the EAT considered it to be 'a useful test for a tribunal to consider while making such an assessment in circumstances in which it is called for' was to 'ask whether the litigant's command of language is sufficient to enable him to give the best account to the tribunal which he would wish to give relating to the matters in dispute'.

Cases where interim relief is available

9.68 Where interim relief is available under s 128 of the ERA 1996 (dismissals for trade union and employee representative activities and whistle-blowing), s 128(5) provides that the tribunal shall not postpone the hearing unless it is satisfied that special circumstances exist which justify it in doing so. Speed in such cases is of the essence such that a tribunal shall not entertain an application for interim relief unless it is presented to the tribunal before the end of the period of seven days immediately following the effective date of termination: s 128(2), see further para 3.24.

Appeals against adjournment decisions

9.69 The EAT is reluctant to interfere with the employment tribunal's discretion in the matter of adjournment. In *Bastick v James Lane (Turf Accountants) Ltd* [1979] ICR 778, it was held that before the EAT could overturn a tribunal's decision it was necessary to show either that it had improperly taken into account some matter in exercising its discretion to adjourn, or that its decision was perverse in all the circumstances. In *O'Cathail v Transport for London* [2013] ICR 614, the Court of Appeal affirmed this approach. Mummery LJ said (para 44):

> [I]n relation to case management the ET has exceptionally wide powers of managing cases brought by and against parties who are often without the benefit of legal representation. The ET's decisions can only be questioned for error of law. A question of law only arises in relation to their exercise, when there is an error of legal principle in the approach or perversity in the outcome. That is the approach, including failing to take account of a relevant matter or taking account of an irrelevant one, which the EAT should continue to adopt.

9.70 The Court of Appeal rejected an argument (derived from the civil court case of *Terluk v Berezovsky* [2010] All ER (D) 270 (Nov) CA) that the appellate body should ask itself whether the decision below was unfair, not whether it lay within the band of judicial discretion.

E. NON-ATTENDANCE BY A PARTY

9.71 From time to time, a party fails to attend the hearing. This may of course be for a variety of reasons. There may have been a last-minute difficulty preventing him from attending (eg ill-health, childcare problems, or transport problems); it may transpire that he had not received notice of the hearing, or made a mistake as to the date for the hearing. Occasionally litigants, particularly unrepresented litigants, simply decide to abandon their claim without telling the tribunal or the other side. Some litigants see non-attendance as a tactic for achieving an adjournment in situations where their case is not ready.

The tribunal faces a choice. It may adjourn the hearing to give the absent party the opportunity to attend. Or it may dismiss or dispose of the proceedings in the absence of the party: ETR 2013, r 47. The powers under r 47 may arise not just where a party fails to attend at the beginning of a hearing, but also where he fails to return during the course of a hearing: see *Smith v Greenwich London Borough Council* [2011] ICR 277, decided under the ETR 2004. **9.72**

Rule 47 provides that before proceeding with a hearing in a party's absence the tribunal shall consider any information which is available to it, having made any enquiries that may be practicable, about the reasons for the party's absence. Rule 47 applies to all kinds of hearing. It goes without saying that the reason for absence is unlikely to be known to the tribunal, or the other party, at the time the tribunal must make its decision as to how to deal with the case. The tribunal and the other party face a dilemma as to the most efficient and cost-effective way of dealing with the case. On the one hand, an adjournment may do an injustice to the party who has prepared and attended and will face another day's costs on the adjourned hearing. If the absent party has indeed abandoned his case, then that second day too will be wasted. Whilst the party not at fault can in theory be compensated in costs, costs orders cannot be enforced against an impecunious claimant. On the other hand, if the tribunal proceeds with the hearing, it risks injustice to the absent party if there is a good reason for absence. Further, there is a risk of further time and cost for the other party in dealing with any review or appeal subsequently brought by the absent party. **9.73**

Before making a decision whether to adjourn or proceed the tribunal should consider trying to telephone the party or his representative to ascertain the reason for absence. In *Cooke v Glenrose Fish Company* [2004] IRLR 866, EAT, Burton J said that, although the tribunal does not have to telephone the absent litigant in every case where there is an absent party, such a call should always be considered. Where solicitors were on record as representing the absent party, there would have to be a very good reason why a telephone call was not made (see also *London Borough of Southwark v Bartholomew* [2004] ICR 358, EAT). **9.74**

In *Cooke*, Burton J went on to say that where a tribunal takes a stringent attitude to a party's absence, it is a necessary concomitant that there be a less stringent attitude on a review if that party comes forward with a genuine and full explanation and shows that the original hearing was not one from which he deliberately absented himself. **9.75**

If the tribunal chooses not to adjourn, it may dismiss the claim or proceed with the hearing in the absence of the non-attending party (ETR 2013, r 47). In doing so, r 47 appears to give the tribunal considerable discretion as to how to proceed. The language of r 47 is different from that of r 27(5)–(6) of the ETR 2004. First, r 27(5) provided that the tribunal 'may dismiss or dispose of the proceedings' whereas the new rule refers to dismissing or proceeding with the hearing. Secondly, the old r 27(6) provided that, if it wished to dismiss or dispose of proceedings, the tribunal should first consider any information in its possession which had been made available to it by the parties. The new r 47 does refer to consideration of information available but only in the context of the decision whether or not to adjourn. However, it seems likely that the tribunal should still consider material available to it before dismissing or making a decision on the claim. **9.76**

Under the old rules, the tribunal's consideration of the case had to take account of the material referred to in r 27(6) and its predecessors, but the tribunal was not obliged to conduct a full hearing in the absence of the party. In *Roberts v Skelmersdale College* [2004] IRLR 69, Mummery LJ said (at paras 15–16) that the rule did not impose on the tribunal a duty to investigate the case, nor to be satisfied that, on the merits, the respondent to a case has established a good defence to the claim of the absent claimant. In the exercise of its discretion, the tribunal would be entitled to require the respondent to produce evidence, but the rule did not impose any duty on the tribunal to follow that course. At para 15 he gave the following example: **9.77**

[F]or example, in an unfair dismissal case where, as here, it is common ground that there has been dismissal, the burden of establishing the reason for the dismissal is on the respondent/employer. But rule 9(3) does not require the employment tribunal to hear evidence from the respondent in order to determine for itself substantively the reason for the dismissal, or to satisfy itself as to whether, if the dismissal was for a potentially fair reason, it was fair and reasonable to dismiss the claimant/employee for that reason.

9.78 If it decides to proceed with the hearing in the absence of the claimant, the tribunal is entitled to make findings of fact that are adverse to the respondent and will not be bound to dismiss the claim simply because the claimant is not available for cross-examination: *Duffy v George* UKEAT/0517/11, 19 October 2012.

F. WRITTEN REPRESENTATIONS

9.79 The parties may, if they wish, submit written representations to the tribunal if they are presented not less than seven days before the hearing: ETR 2013, r 42. A clear distinction must be drawn between written representations which must comply with the requirements of r 42 to be admissible, and written evidence (such as witness statements) or aids to an oral submission (such as a skeleton argument). In practice tribunals will accept written aids to oral submissions, such as skeleton arguments, lists of issues, and chronologies on the day of the hearing, and will not regard them as written representations falling within r 42. In most cases the tribunal will give directions for the date when witness statements are to be exchanged.

9.80 The tribunal will naturally pay rather less attention to written representations than oral evidence, since the latter (unlike the former) can be challenged by cross-examination. Where both parties submit written representations and there is an acute conflict of fact, the tribunal is in an impossible position, and should call the parties for oral evidence (*Tesco Stores Ltd v Patel*, The Times, 15 March 1986). Where there is no substantial conflict of fact, written representations on the law may be more appropriate.

G. CONDUCT OF THE HEARING

General considerations

9.81 The judge has a wide degree of discretion as to how the hearing should be conducted. The rules provide for a great degree of informality in tribunal procedure. However, tribunals must observe the overriding objective of dealing with cases justly, and must ensure that all parties are afforded a fair trial.

9.82 The employment tribunal has no duty to be inquisitorial in its approach, although it has a large measure of discretion, as set out above, which includes asking questions where it considers it appropriate to do so: *Joseph v Brighton & Sussex University Hospitals NHS Trust* UKEAT/0001/15/JOJ, applying *Mensah v East Hertfordshire NHS Trust* [1998] IRLR 531, CA and *Muschett v HM Prison Service* [2010] IRLR 451, CA.

Informality

9.83 Rule 41 of the ETR 2013 provides:

The Tribunal may regulate its own procedure and shall conduct the hearing in the manner it considers fair, having regard to the principles contained in the overriding objective. The following rules do not restrict that general power. The Tribunal shall seek to avoid undue formality and may itself question the parties or any witnesses as far as appropriate in order to clarify the issues or elicit the evidence. The Tribunal is not itself bound by any rule of law relating to the admissibility of evidence in proceedings before the courts.

The judge's discretion as to the conduct of the hearing is not, however, unfettered; the judge must conduct the proceedings in accordance with the overriding objective; and the parties' right to a fair trial, both under Art 6 of the ECHR, and at common law.

The tension between informality on the one hand and ensuring a fair hearing on the other hand is **9.84** constantly present in employment tribunals. In *Aberdeen Steak Houses Group plc v Ibrahim* [1988] ICR 550, the EAT indicated that too much informality may be counter-productive and may lead to actual or perceived unfairness to a party, and it was important that the parties should know in advance what rules are to apply.

Whilst the vast majority of cases are conducted along the lines of adversarial court proceedings, a **9.85** more inquisitorial approach may from time to time be appropriate. In *Ridley v GEC Machines Ltd* (1978) 13 ITR 195, 196, the EAT said:

> The cases which are heard by industrial tribunals are very different from ordinary cases heard by regular courts, and the litigation of necessity takes—or certainly at all events ought to take—something of the form of an enquiry; so that ordinary customary legal proceedings need to be applied with that requirement in mind. It is really essential that at the end of the day the parties should feel that the whole of the facts had been investigated.

The overriding objective

The overriding objective (ETR 2013, r 2) is to deal with cases fairly and justly. This includes as far **9.86** as practicable:

(a) ensuring that the parties are on an equal footing
(b) dealing with cases in ways which are proportionate to the complexity and importance of the issues
(c) avoiding unnecessary formality and seeking flexibility in the proceedings
(d) avoiding delay, so far as compatible with proper consideration of the issues;
(e) saving expense.

Whenever a tribunal exercises a power or interprets a provision of the ETR 2013, it should seek to **9.87** give effect to the overriding objective. The parties are under a duty to assist the tribunal to further the overriding objective, and shall cooperate generally with each other and with the tribunal. The overriding objective underpins the exercise of the tribunal's discretion in the matters covered in this chapter.

The right to a fair trial

An employment tribunal is a public authority for the purposes of the Human Rights Act 1998. **9.88** Therefore:

(a) the tribunal must, so far as possible, read and give effect to legislation in a way which is compatible with Convention rights (s 3)
(b) the tribunal must not itself act in a way which is incompatible with Convention rights (s 6).

Article 6(1) of the ECHR provides: **9.89**

> In the determination of his civil rights and obligations or of any criminal charge against him, everyone is entitled to a fair and public hearing within a reasonable time by an independent and impartial tribunal established by law.

The tribunal should ensure so far as possible equality of arms between the parties. **9.90**

Quite apart from Art 6, the right to a fair trial is a fundamental principle of the common law. The **9.91** Court of Appeal has said that Art 6 reflects the pre-existing approach of the common law: *R v Lord Chancellor, ex parte Witham* [1998] QB 575; *Ebert v Venvil* [2000] Ch 484, 497. The common law has long recognized the right to a hearing by an independent and impartial tribunal, and the right to be heard (often referred to as the principles of natural justice).

Part A Tribunal Procedure

The order of the hearing

Normal sequence of events

9.92 In the vast majority of cases, the order of events and the calling of evidence follows the format of the civil courts, save that opening speeches are rare in the tribunal. Normally, the sequence of events will be as follows:

(a) Discussion of opening and preliminary matters between the parties' representatives and the judge.

(b) Reading time for the tribunal to read the witness statements and key documents.

(c) Calling of witnesses: each witness will in turn give evidence in chief, and then answer questions in cross-examination from the other party/parties, and from the tribunal. The party's representative may then re-examine. Local practice varies as to whether re-examination takes place before or after the tribunal's questions.

(d) Closing submissions.

The right to go first

9.93 The normal rule in the civil courts is that the party bearing the burden of proof on the main issue in the case has the right to open (ie to go first)—this principle is followed in the tribunal (*Gill v Harold Andrews Sheepbridge Ltd* [1974] IRLR 109, [1974] ICR 294, NIRC).

9.94 In an unfair dismissal case where dismissal is admitted, the respondent will normally go first, as the employer must prove the reason for dismissal. Where dismissal is denied (for example in a constructive dismissal case) then the claimant must prove the dismissal, and accordingly the claimant will normally go first. The claimant will normally go first in discrimination cases: see *Hawker Siddeley Power Engineering Ltd v Rump* [1979] IRLR 425. In cases involving claims of both unfair dismissal and discrimination, it is sensible for the parties to seek to agree the running order in advance of the hearing. Although in such cases, the running order is ultimately a decision for the tribunal, judges are frequently willing to accept any agreement between the parties.

9.95 The normal rule is that the right to go first carries with it the right to the last word in closing submissions. So, for example, in an ordinary unfair dismissal case, the respondent will call its witnesses first, then the claimant and his witnesses will be called. When it comes to submissions, the claimant will go first, and then the respondent.

Opening and preliminary matters

9.96 Most tribunals read the claim form and the response before the beginning of the hearing, but representatives should never assume that this has happened. It is rare that a tribunal has had the opportunity to read the bundles of documents or witness statements before the beginning of the hearing unless some reading time has been allocated. It is important for representatives to ensure at this early stage that the tribunal has before it all the necessary material and that nothing is missing.

9.97 It is not the practice in most tribunals to allow the parties opening speeches. The party going first may get the opportunity to make a short opening address outlining the nature of the case, particularly in a complex case. Many tribunals are impatient with long introductions, and are usually eager to start the evidence. However, this eagerness should be balanced by the need to manage the hearing efficiently, and in modern practice it is common for the tribunal to spend some time before hearing evidence going through preliminary and housekeeping matters and identifying the issues to be determined.

9.98 The judge will usually identify what materials the tribunal has been provided with. The representatives should ensure that all members of the tribunal and the witness table are provided with all relevant documents (bundles, witness statements, skeletons, chronologies, etc).

9.99 The judge will usually outline his understanding of the main issues in the case, and ask the parties' representatives what they see the issues as being. In complex cases in particular it is helpful to prepare a list of issues for the beginning of the case, or to include such a list of issues in a skeleton argument. Some judges have been known to adjourn for a short period on the first morning whilst the parties' representatives draw up an agreed list of issues.

If it is not obvious from the judge's opening comments, the representatives should seek to ascertain **9.100** what documents the tribunal has had the chance to read before the hearing.

Correct identification of the issues at the outset of the hearing is important as it is the duty of the **9.101** parties, and not the tribunal, to ensure that all relevant issues are raised and that all relevant evidence is put before the tribunal. This is so even when one of the parties is not legally represented (*Kumchyk v Derby County Council* [1978] ICR 1116, EAT). This was confirmed in *Mensah v East Hertfordshire NHS Trust* [1998] IRLR 531, CA, where the Court of Appeal held that the tribunal had no duty to consider a part of the claim not raised by the claimant. However, the EAT has held that there are some matters which are so well established that they should be considered by a tribunal even if a party does not raise them, for example the principal criteria for an unfair redundancy (see *Langston v Cranfield University* [1998] IRLR 172, EAT). However, although judges should provide all possible help to litigants in person or those represented by unqualified friends, such assistance has to be balanced against the need to ensure fairness to the opposing party. In *Birmingham City Council v Laws* UKEAT/0360/06/MAA, the EAT held that in formulating an additional issue at the closing submissions stage, the tribunal had overstepped the boundary of providing proper assistance so that an injustice was suffered by the respondent.

Rule 45 of the ETR 2013 provides that a tribunal may impose limits on the time that a party may **9.102** take in presenting the evidence, questioning witnesses, or making submissions, and may prevent the party from proceeding beyond any time so allotted. The judge may seek to impose a timetable for the hearing, including time taken for hearing evidence from each witness and reading documents referred to in the evidence; time for cross-examination of each witness, and time for closing submissions. This may be discussed and a timetable set at a preliminary hearing on case management. If not, then representatives should be prepared to give such time estimates on the first morning of the final hearing. Some judges use a timetable as a guide; others are stricter and will impose a 'guillotine' if a representative goes materially beyond his estimate.

In addition to identifying the issues and timetabling the case, there may be contested preliminary **9.103** matters which may need to be resolved at the outset of the hearing. By the time the date of the final hearing comes around, the result of the case management decisions should be that the issues are clearly defined, the evidence and documents are in order, and the parties and the tribunal are ready to get on with hearing the case. In practice, this is often not the case, and case management decisions will need to be taken at the beginning of the hearing. The following issues commonly need to be dealt with at the beginning of the hearing:

(a) Definition or redefinition of the issues.
(b) Applications to admit or exclude witness evidence produced after the date for exchange of witness statements or late disclosed documents.
(c) Applications for late amendments of the parties' cases.
(d) Issues arising from the non-attendance of witnesses or parties.

Each of these issues is, at the very least, likely to give rise to timetabling questions, and may give **9.104** rise to applications for adjournment. Often issues such as these may arise after the hearing has commenced, for instance prompted by the evidence given by a witness, or by questions from the tribunal. The tribunal will have to decide how to deal with such issues as and when they arise. The principles that apply to such applications are dealt with in more detail in Chapters 6–7 dealing with case management and interim applications.

Split hearings; defining the issues

In a number of contexts tribunals may split a case so that different issues are dealt with at different **9.105** stages. Even in a straightforward case, tribunals generally deal separately with questions of liability and the appropriate remedies (*Copson v Eversure Accessories Ltd* [1974] ICR 636). It is common for a case to be listed so that the tribunal may deal with liability, give its decision, and then immediately proceed to deal with remedy. It is not uncommon for there to be insufficient time once a liability decision is reached for remedy to be dealt with. In this situation, directions will be given for remedy to be dealt with at a later hearing. In a complex case, particularly if there are multiple causes of action, there may be reasons why the tribunal will deal with some issues at one hearing, leaving other issues to a later hearing. However, the tribunal should take care to see that evidence on issues which are closely related should be heard in one go. In *Salford Royal NHS Foundation Trust v Roldan* [2010] IRLR 721, Elias LJ said that it is normally inappropriate for witnesses

> [t]o give evidence first on the question of liability, and then separately and at a later date, to give similar, if not identical, evidence to deal with the question of contributory fault. An economic and efficient approach, in line with the overriding objective, would normally require witnesses to deal with all relevant evidence they have to give on one occasion.

Notwithstanding those comments, it may often make sense for discrete issues of assessment of remedy (as opposed to *Polkey* or contributory fault) to be left to a later stage, particularly if, for example, expert evidence will be required to determine the remedy.

9.106   The tribunal should ensure that all parties are fully aware of what aspects are to be argued at what stage and that the parties have a proper opportunity to address all relevant points (*Slaughter v C Brewer & Sons Ltd* [1990] ICR 730; *Ferguson v Gateway Training Centre Ltd* [1991] ICR 658). Care should be taken to ensure that it is clear at the beginning of the hearing what issues are to be dealt with at the liability stage, and what is being left over to the remedy stage, so that the parties know what evidence needs to be called at which stage. Tribunals may refuse to allow evidence to be revisited at the remedies stage (see *Iggesund Converters Ltd v Lewis* [1984] IRLR 431; *King v Eaton (No 2)* [1998] IRLR 686, Court of Session).

The evidence

Exclusion of evidence

9.107   The tribunal has the power under rr 41, 43, and 45 to control the way a party or his representative conducts his case before the tribunal. The tribunal is not bound by the rules of evidence which apply in civil and criminal courts. The tribunal can exclude irrelevant evidence and argument and stop lines of questioning and submissions which do not assist the tribunal: *Bache v Essex County Council* [2000] IRLR 251, CA.

9.108   Where a dispute arises as to the admissibility of evidence the primary question is whether the evidence is relevant to the issues in the case. Evidence which is irrelevant to the issues is inadmissible as a matter of the law of evidence, and ought not to be admitted in tribunal proceedings; see *XXX v YYY* [2004] IRLR 471, where the Court of Appeal upheld the tribunal's decision to refuse to admit certain video evidence on the ground that it had no probative value.

9.109   Whilst a party is entitled to adduce evidence which is relevant to the issues in the case, it is, of course, a matter for the tribunal as to whether evidence is in fact relevant or not. In *ALM Medical Services Ltd v Bladon* [2002] IRLR 807, the Court of Appeal decided that the tribunal had wrongly held that the evidence which the respondent wished to call (and in respect of which witness statements had been submitted) was irrelevant. Mummery LJ said (at para 15):

> A party is entitled to adduce evidence relevant to the issues in the case and to put questions on relevant matters to the other party and to his witnesses. It is for the tribunal, with the assistance of the parties and their representatives, to identify the relevant issues for decision and to exercise its discretionary case management powers to decide whether the evidence adduced or the questions put to the witnesses in cross-examination are relevant. The exercise of the discretion will rarely be disturbed on appeal: it can only be successfully challenged if it can be shown that the tribunal has exercised it contrary to legal principle or otherwise in a manner which is plainly wrong.

9.110   In the later case of *Davies v Sandwell Metropolitan Borough Council* [2013] IRLR 374, Mummery LJ emphasized the necessity for tribunals to concentrate on the relevant and eliminate the irrelevant. He said that tribunals are 'not obliged to read acres of irrelevant materials nor do they have to listen, day in and day out, to pointless accusations or discursive recollections which do not advance the case'. Further, he said that tribunals should not hesitate to use their case management powers to prevent irrelevant cross-examination.

Although these statements by the Court of Appeal are clear in principle, the question of whether **9.111** evidence is relevant or irrelevant is often not clear cut. This is particularly so in discrimination claims where parties may rely on a wide array of evidence in support of, or to counter, an inference of discrimination. There is a risk that the tribunal may become bogged down with evidence which, although not completely irrelevant, is of marginal relevance. The EAT in *Digby v East Cambridgeshire District Council* [2007] IRLR 585 held that a tribunal does have a discretion, in accordance with the overriding objective, to exclude relevant evidence which is, for example, unnecessarily repetitive or of only marginal relevance in the interests of proper, modern day case management. In *HSBC Asia Holdings BV & Anor v Gillespie* [2011] IRLR 209, the EAT held that the employment judge had erred in *not* exercising his discretion to exclude (as irrelevant) 'background' evidence of a culture of discrimination dating back to many years before the acts of sex discrimination alleged by the claimant took place. However, that discretion must be exercised judicially. It may properly be challenged on appeal on *Wednesbury* principles. The guiding principle is to ensure justice between the parties. he tribunal has the power under r 45 to impose time limits on the presentation of evidence, which necessarily implies that relevant evidence may be excluded if it cannot be fitted within the time limit.

In a rare instance of a majority EAT judgment (Langstaff P dissenting) in *Kalu v Brighton & Sussex* **9.112** *NHS Trust* UKEAT/0609/12, the EAT held that it was incumbent upon the employment tribunal to investigate the relevance of any evidence before excluding it.

At the other end of the spectrum, the tribunal must take care not to cross the line between impartiality and acting as advocate and should not conduct internet research or its own investigations **9.113** into matters, as r 41 does not permit a tribunal 'to make enquiries on its own behalf into evidence which was never volunteered by either party': *East of England Ambulance Service v Sanders* [2015] ICR 293.

Hearsay evidence

Although there is no strict rule against hearsay evidence, the EAT in *Aberdeen Steak Houses Group* **9.114** *plc* (cited above) sounded a note of caution in relation to hearsay, in saying that, whilst a tribunal can and should on occasion admit hearsay, it must be remembered that rules of procedure and evidence have been built up over many years in order to guide courts and tribunals in the fairest and simplest way of dealing with and deciding issues.

Where a witness upon whose evidence a party wishes to rely cannot attend the hearing, a statement **9.115** should be submitted on behalf of the witness, together with an explanation as to why the witness is not available to give live evidence. The tribunal will assess the weight to be attached to the evidence. Inevitably, evidence untested by cross-examination will carry less weight than the evidence of witnesses whom the tribunal has seen questioned at the hearing. In assessing the weight to be attached to such hearsay evidence, it is suggested that the factors to be considered in the civil courts set out in s 4 of the Civil Evidence Act 1995 are relevant:

(1) In estimating the weight (if any) to be given to hearsay evidence in civil proceedings the court shall have regard to any circumstances from which any inference can reasonably be drawn as to the reliability or otherwise of the evidence.
(2) Regard may be had, in particular, to the following:
  (a) whether it would have been reasonable and practicable for the party by whom the evidence was adduced to have produced the maker of the original statement as a witness
  (b) whether the original statement was made contemporaneously with the occurrence or existence of the matters stated
  (c) whether the evidence involves multiple hearsay
  (d) whether any person involved had any motive to conceal or misrepresent matters

(e) whether the original statement was an edited account, or was made in collaboration with another or for a particular purpose

(f) whether the circumstances in which the evidence is adduced as hearsay are such as to suggest an attempt to prevent proper evaluation of its weight.

Without prejudice communications

9.116 Without prejudice communications between the parties and their representatives are privileged and may not be put in evidence: *Rush and Tompkins v Greater London Council* [1989] AC 1280. The principle extends to all negotiations genuinely aimed at settling the matters in dispute between the parties, and applies to both oral and written communications. The key question is whether the communication forms part of a genuine negotiation of a settlement: *Independent Research Services v Caterall* [1993] ICR 1. See further paras 6.105–6.106 in relation to without prejudice conversations and paras 5.47–5.51 in relation to protected conversations.

9.117 Questions of putting without prejudice communications in evidence will normally be resolved at the stage of disclosure, or in preparation of the bundle for the hearing. References to without prejudice communications in witness statements should be excised before the hearing. Not infrequently, however, a witness may start to refer to without prejudice communications in the course of evidence. Most judges are astute to issues of privilege, and will stop the witness as soon as it is apparent that he is about to give evidence of privileged matters. The same can be said of matters which are subject to legal privilege. A tribunal should not take account of evidence of without prejudice negotiations referred to in evidence absent a clear waiver by both parties: *Gallop v Newport City Council* [2013] IRLR 23, EAT (overturned on appeal on unrelated grounds).

9.118 Whether a communication is without prejudice or not depends upon the substance of the communication: ie whether it forms part of a genuine attempt to settle. Therefore, whilst it is common practice to label documents produced for the purpose of negotiation 'without prejudice', such a label is neither necessary nor sufficient: the label will not attach privilege to a document which is not without prejudice in nature, and the absence of the label will not deprive a true without prejudice communication of privilege.

9.119 In an employment dispute, it can often be difficult to ascertain the point at which without prejudice begins to apply. An employer may seek to start without prejudice discussions at an early stage: for example, where the employer is contemplating a dismissal, he may seek to have a without prejudice discussion to explore a consensual departure without the need to dismiss. If such a meeting is protected by without prejudice privilege, then the tribunal may see an incomplete picture of the events leading to dismissal, and of the reason for dismissal. Further still, it is possible, in a discrimination claim, for the events in the without prejudice meeting themselves to be acts of discrimination. This was the case in *BNP Paribas v Mezzotero* [2004] IRLR 508, EAT. The employee had raised a grievance whilst on maternity leave, and was called to a meeting with her employers. At the start of the meeting, the employers said that they wanted the discussions to be 'without prejudice' and suggested that it would be best for the business and for her if she terminated her employment. The EAT held that the tribunal was right to admit evidence of what occurred at the meeting. At the point that the meeting occurred, there was no dispute between the parties, and therefore the meeting could not have been in furtherance of settlement of a dispute. No privilege therefore attached to the contents of the meeting. In *Framlington Group Ltd v Barnetson* [2007] ICR 1439, the Court of Appeal addressed the question of when, in exchanges between employer and employee, a 'dispute' can be said to have arisen such as to engage the 'without prejudice' rule. The Court stated that what was important was the subject matter of the exchanges, rather than how long before the threat, or start, of litigation they were aired. The crucial consideration was whether in the course of negotiations the parties contemplated or might reasonably have contemplated litigation if the dispute could not be resolved. See also *A v B* [2013] UKEAT/0092/13/RN, 10 April 2013.

9.120 The privilege may be waived, but it must be waived by both parties, as the privilege is that of both parties. In *Chaudhary v Secretary of State for Health* [2006] EWCA Civ 1648, the Court of Appeal decided that the fact that a 'without prejudice' communication had been openly referred to in a tribunal case did not automatically mean that it could be referred to in a subsequent appeal. The question was whether the person claiming the privilege had waived it (which on the facts the Department of Health had not done) rather than whether the material had already been referred to in other proceedings. In *Brunel University v Webster* [2007] IRLR 592, both parties had given evidence of the allegedly privileged communications in an internal grievance meeting which had been conducted by an independent panel and amounted, in effect, to a mini-trial. The Court of Appeal held that privilege had been waived, although it stressed that the waiver arose in the context of the particular nature of the internal hearing. The Court of Appeal also held that privilege had been waived when each party referred to the without prejudice communications in the ET1 and the ET3.

Privilege will be lost if there is 'unambiguous impropriety' and an abuse of the without prejudice   **9.121** occasion: *Unilever plc v Procter & Gamble* [2000] 1 WLR 2436; *Savings & Investment Bank Ltd v Fincken* [2004] 1 WLR 667. There has been some suggestion by the EAT that privilege may more easily be lost in a discrimination case if it is necessary for the tribunal to hear evidence of without prejudice communications in order to fully investigate the allegations: that was the view of the EAT in *Brunel University v Webster* UKEAT/0307/06, purporting to follow certain *obiter* comments of Cox J in *Mezzotero* to that effect. However, the Court of Appeal in *Brunel*, whilst declining to decide the point, did not endorse the EAT's approach. In *Brodie v Nichola Ward t/a First Steps Nursery* EAT 0526/07, the EAT declined an invitation to widen the 'unambiguous impropriety' exception to allow a claimant to rely on a solicitor's letter offering a compromise agreement as the 'last straw' in her constructive dismissal claim: the letter had been a proper attempt to settle a dispute and as such was privileged. In *Woodward v Santander* [2010] IRLR 834, Underhill J said that no special rule applies to discrimination cases, but that Cox J's comments in *Mezzotero* could be explained as an application of the 'unambiguous impropriety' rule. The unambiguous impropriety exception is only one of a number of exceptions to the without prejudice rule. For other exceptions to the without prejudice rule see *Oceanbulk Shipping & Trading SA v TMT Asia Ltd and Others* [2011] 1 AC 662, in particular paras 30–36 (Lord Clarke). Many of the exceptions arise where there are issues as to whether a settlement agreement has been concluded, or as to its interpretation, and may therefore be less likely to arise in tribunal proceedings than in court proceedings.

Admissibility of evidence and human rights

In deciding whether to admit or exclude evidence, the court may on occasion have to weigh in the   **9.122** balance the right of the party seeking to rely on the evidence to a fair trial under Art 6 of the ECHR, with a competing Convention right of the other party. Most commonly, this will be the right to private life under Art 8. See, for example, *XXX v YYY* [2004] IRLR 471—although the Court of Appeal decided the case on grounds of relevance, it accepted that had the evidence been relevant there would have needed to be a weighing up of the competing human rights, on the one hand the right to a fair trial, and on the other the right to privacy.

Convention rights are not absolute, and most provide for legitimate restrictions. Article 8(2)   **9.123** permits interference with the right to private life in pursuit of a number of defined legitimate interests. Notable in the current context is the protection of rights and freedoms of others, which would include the right of another person to a fair trial under Art 6. Both the Court of Appeal and the EAT have been willing to allow in evidence material which is otherwise admissible and probative, even though the material was obtained by a party in a manner which interfered with the privacy of the other party. Thus, in *Jones v University of Warwick* [2003] 1 WLR 954, a personal injury claim, evidence obtained by covert video surveillance was admitted. In *City and County of Swansea v Gayle* [2013] IRLR 768, the EAT held that covert video surveillance of an employee in public, during working hours, was admissible and was not a breach of Art 8. Evidence of a recorded telephone conversation was admitted in *Avocet Hardware plc v Morrison* EAT/0417/02; given that the telephone call was the evidence relied on by the employer in deciding to dismiss the employee, the employer could not have had a fair trial without being able to put the evidence before the tribunal. In *Amwell View School Governors v Dogherty*

[2007] IRLR 198, the claimant covertly recorded disciplinary proceedings against her, both the open hearings and the panel's private deliberations. The EAT allowed the recordings of the open hearing in evidence, holding that no right to privacy was engaged. The recordings of the private deliberations were held to be inadmissible on the grounds of the public interest in maintaining the integrity of the private deliberations of adjudicating bodies. However, in balancing this interest against the claimant's right to a fair trial, the EAT expressly relied on the fact that the agreed procedure was that the panel would deliberate in private and then give full reasons for the decision. Further, the EAT indicated that the decision may have been different in a discrimination claim where the recording showed the only, and incontrovertible evidence of discrimination. The court must weigh the competing interests of fair trial and privacy in the circumstances of each case (see *Jersild v Denmark* (1995) 19 EHRR 1). In *Punjab National Bank v Gosain* UKEAT/0003/14, the EAT held that the balance was in favour of admitting such evidence and, distinguishing *Amwell v Dogherty*, allowed recordings of private deliberations to be admitted. Finally, it should be noted that if a party requests that secret recordings are admitted in evidence, that party must be prepared to provide a transcript of those recordings for consideration: *Vaughan v London Borough of Lewisham* UKEAT/0534/12.

Witness evidence

Provisions of the rules

9.124 Evidence is given on oath or affirmation (ETR 2013, r 43). If a witness needs an interpreter, there is a special interpreters' oath that is used. As evidence is given on oath, the law in relation to perjury applies to evidence given to the tribunal.

9.125 Rule 43 provides that the tribunal may exclude from the hearing any person who is to appear as a witness in the proceedings until such time as they have given their evidence if it considers it is in the interests of justice to do so. In practice, this power is rarely exercised in tribunals in England and Wales.

Witness statements

9.126 It is standard practice for a witness's evidence to be given by witness statement. Rule 43 further provides that any witness statement ordered by the tribunal shall stand as that witness's evidence in chief unless the tribunal orders otherwise. The new rule reflects an increasing trend over a number of years to take statements as read, rather than having them read out by the witness, which had been the older practice. The tribunal retains a discretion under r 43 to have statements read out. The EAT judgment in *Mehta v Child Support Agency* [2011] IRLR 305, although decided under the old rules, may still provide useful guidance on how tribunals should exercise their discretion on whether witness statements should be read aloud. The EAT said that there may in particular circumstances be good reason for a statement, particularly of an unrepresented party, being read out in whole or in part. The decision is a matter for the tribunal in exercise of its case management powers. A tribunal should try as much as possible to proceed by agreement. Witness statements of all witnesses on either side do not necessarily have to be treated the same way: there may be good reasons for a difference in treatment.

9.127 A tribunal will normally allow a witness to give some oral evidence to amplify his witness statement or to give evidence as to additional matters, for example to comment on matters arising from the other side's evidence in chief. In the civil courts a witness giving oral evidence at trial may, with the permission of the court, amplify his witness statement and give evidence in relation to new matters which have arisen since the witness statement was served on the other parties. The court will only give such permission if it considers that there is good reason not to confine the evidence of the witness to the contents of his witness statement (CPR r 32.5). An employment tribunal is not bound by this approach and, in practice, a certain latitude is allowed, especially for unrepresented parties. However, there are dicta to the effect that tribunals should be parsimonious in giving the parties leave to amplify their statements (*Shahronki v NATFHE* EAT/486/99). Sometimes, however, it may be helpful to amplify matters, and it may be necessary to deal with matters arising since exchange of statements.

In public hearings (ie in the vast majority of hearings) at least one copy of each witness statement **9.128** should be made available to be left at the back of the tribunal room marked 'Not to be removed from the tribunal'. These copies are available for inspection by the public. Directions during case management may sometimes provide for this, but even if there is no direction, copies should be provided in any event. It is an aspect of a public hearing that the public should be entitled to know what evidence is given by a witness, regardless of whether it was given orally or in a witness statement (see the High Court case of *Cox v Jones* [2004] EWHC 1006 (Ch), [2004] All ER (D) 385 (Mann J)).

Examination in chief

During any additional examination in chief a representative of the party calling the witness should **9.129** not ask leading questions which presuppose a particular answer. The witness evidence should be confined to matters of fact, and the witness should not be asked to give opinion evidence, or to speculate about matters outside his knowledge. Where the witness's evidence is hearsay, it will be admissible in the tribunal, as the rules of evidence do not apply, but the source of the hearsay should be identified so that the tribunal may assess the weight of the evidence.

Witnesses are not normally permitted in court proceedings to read notes when giving evidence. **9.130** A clean copy of the witness statement will be available on the witness table, and the witness will not normally be allowed to use his own marked-up copy of his statement. However, the EAT held in *Watson-Smith v Tagol Ltd (t/a Alangate Personnel)* EAT/611/81, that where parties represent themselves at hearings before employment tribunals they should be allowed to refer to notes. This takes account of the fact that a solicitor or barrister or other skilled representative will normally have a statement from a witness to assist in his cross-examination.

A problem can arise for a party where the witness attends under a witness order and gives evidence **9.131** that is unfavourable to the party who has called him. The general rule applicable in both criminal and civil cases is that a party cannot challenge the credibility of his own witness. There are, however, two situations that must be distinguished and they involve the unfavourable witness and the hostile witness. An unfavourable witness is one who, although he does not display any hostility to the party calling him, fails to come up to proof (that is, does not give the evidence expected of him) or gives evidence unfavourable to the party who has called him. The only avenue left open to the party is to call other evidence to make good his case, but he cannot challenge the witness directly (see *Ewer v Ambrose* (1825) 3 B & C 746).

A hostile witness is one who has no desire to tell the truth and displays hostility to the party calling **9.132** him. The tribunal must be invited to find that the witness is hostile and the party who has called him may be permitted to cross-examine him. The tribunal can take into account the attitude and demeanour displayed by the witness, his willingness to cooperate, and inconsistent prior statements. If cross-examination is allowed, the party who called the witness may ask leading questions but cannot present evidence to show that the witness cannot be believed on oath.

Cross-examination

After examination in chief, the other party or parties may cross-examine the witness. The aims of **9.133** cross-examination are to challenge the material parts of the evidence in chief; to elicit new evidence that may be helpful to the cross-examining party; and to undermine the credit of the witness. As a rule of practice, the party cross-examining must put his case to the witness, insofar as the matter is within the witness's knowledge. That is to say that the material facts which form part of the cross-examining party's case, and which are in issue, must be put to the witness so that he can respond to them. It is particularly important in discrimination cases and whistle-blowing cases, where it is often necessary for the tribunal to draw inferences as to the reason why individuals acted in a particular manner, that these matters are put to the witness under cross-examination in order that they are given the opportunity to comment on them. Thus, where it is alleged by a respondent in a whistle-blowing case that the claimant's disclosure was not made in good faith, the allegations of bad faith must be made clear to the claimant and the claimant must be given an opportunity to comment on them (see *Lucas v Chichester Diocesan Housing Association Limited* UKEAT/0713/04).

Similarly, in *Doherty v British Midland Airways Limited* [2006] IRLR 90 EAT, the tribunal found that the claimant was malicious without that allegation having been put to the claimant under cross-examination. An appeal was allowed and the matter was remitted to a fresh employment tribunal for determination.

9.134 The tribunal may impose restrictions on the cross-examination of witnesses under its general case management powers, and in furtherance of the overriding objective. By analogy with the High Court, limits may be imposed on cross-examination in two ways. A limit may be imposed on the issues explored in cross-examination (see *Watson v Chief Constable of Cleveland* [2001] EWCA Civ 1547); or a time limit on cross-examination may be imposed (see *Hayes v Transco plc* [2003] EWCA Civ 1261), leaving the advocate to decide how best to use his time.

9.135 A party does not have an absolute right to cross-examine come what may. The tribunal is not obliged to allow lengthy and detailed cross-examination on matters that do not appear to the tribunal to be of assistance, and has a duty to keep the inquiry before it within proper bounds (*Gulson v Zurich Insurance Co* [1998] IRLR 118, EAT (Kirkwood J), approved by the Court of Appeal in *Bache v Essex County Council* [2000] IRLR 251). A refusal to allow cross-examination may be compatible with Art 6(1) of the ECHR if the cross-examination would not assist the court: *X v Austria* (1972) 42 CD 145, ECommHR. In civil proceedings (as opposed to criminal proceedings), there is no express right to cross-examine, and a party does not have a right to confront and cross-examine any particular witness. He may, of course, make submissions as to the admissibility and weight of evidence if the other side fails to call a witness or offer a witness for cross-examination: see *Power v Greater Manchester Police* UKEAT/0087/10.

9.136 However, the employment judge must tread a delicate line between efficient case management, entailing the avoidance of wasted time and costs, and the need to ensure that the hearing is fair and can be seen to be fair. In *McBride v British Railways Board* (1972) 7 ITR 84, the employee was not given a chance to cross-examine witnesses, as the tribunal felt that this would be a waste of time. On appeal, the NIRC felt it doubtful that any different decision would have been reached had the cross-examination actually taken place, but it thought in all the circumstances that justice had not been seen to be done, and remitted the case for further consideration. Whilst it would be rare in modern times to find a case where a party was denied all right to cross-examine, excessive limitation of, or interference with, cross-examination may amount to a denial of a fair trial, and render the tribunal's decision liable to be set aside. See, for example, *Moir v Heart of England Housing & Care Ltd* UKEAT/0918/04.

Tribunal questions and re-examination

9.137 After cross-examination the employment tribunal may then ask questions of its own. Either before or after the tribunal's questions (depending on local tribunal practice), the representative calling the witness may re-examine.

9.138 The role of re-examination of one's own witness (which can be a very powerful weapon if used wisely) is to clear up misleading answers to questions or responses when the witness did not fully understand the nature and extent of the question. The limits of re-examination are often not well understood by laymen appearing in the tribunal. First, re-examination should be limited to matters arising out of cross-examination; it is not an opportunity for a 'second bite of the cherry' in evidence in chief. Secondly, as with examination in chief, the representative should not lead the witness.

Recalling witnesses

9.139 Witnesses are normally released so they can leave the tribunal after they have given evidence and are then free to leave the tribunal, although in exceptional circumstances they may be ordered to be recalled but only because some evidence is given which could not have been anticipated when the decision to release was made. These matters are within the general discretion of the employment tribunal to regulate its own procedures (see eg *Aberdeen Steak Houses Group plc v Ibrahim* [1988]

ICR 550). The parties should always ask the tribunal whether a particular witness can be released; they will usually be told that they can.

Party's decision as to what witnesses to call and the order in which they are called

It should normally be a matter for the parties, and not the tribunal, to determine how they call **9.140** their evidence. In *Barnes v BPC (Business Forms) Ltd* [1975] ICR 390, the employer's solicitor was instructed by the judge to call witnesses in a certain order to prevent their long absence from work. Phillips J reprimanded the judge and said that: 'solicitors and counsel are entitled to conduct, within the rules of court or of procedure, the proceedings as they think fit and, in particular, to call witnesses in the order they wish, subject to any particular rules which may apply... it was an unwise decision for the Chairman to have made and one which I hope would not be repeated by other Chairmen on other occasions'.

The EAT reached a contrary view in *Snowball v Gardner Merchant Ltd* [1987] IRLR 397, 399. **9.141** *Barnes* was, however, subsequently approved by the EAT (Wood J) in *Aberdeen Steak Houses Group plc* (cited above).

It is the parties' responsibility to ensure that all relevant issues are raised, and that all relevant evi- **9.142** dence is put before the tribunal (*Kumchyk v Derby County Council* [1978] ICR 1116, EAT). This was confirmed in *Mensah v East Hertfordshire NHS Trust* [1998] IRLR 531, CA.

Tribunal calling witness of own motion

Under r 14(3) of the ETR 2004, the predecessor to r 41, a judge or tribunal had a power to call **9.143** witnesses of their own motion, including parties to the proceedings. Although the wording of r 41 is not identical to that of the old r 14(3), the tribunal's powers remain similarly broad, and it is likely that the tribunal retains the power to call witnesses of its own motion. Where it does so, each party has a right to cross-examine the witness. In *Clapson v British Airways plc* [2001] IRLR 184, the EAT, however, warned that tribunals should be 'very cautious' before deciding to call a witness whom neither of the parties wishes to call, and should be particularly wary where the witness is one of the parties to the case. In ordinary circumstances, where there was a dispute of fact, the tribunal would deal with the situation by drawing an adverse inference against the party who had not given evidence.

Documents

For the preparation and composition of bundles, see paras 9.16 ff. **9.144**

The tribunal will not normally have read the documents in the bundle (other than the claim **9.145** form and the response) prior to the commencement of the hearing, and any documents on which a party wishes to rely must be read by the tribunal during the course of the hearing. Practice varies from judge to judge, and will depend on the circumstances of the particular case. Normally, documents are introduced during the course of the evidence of witnesses who deal with them. The tribunal may take time to adjourn and read the documents, either before the witness takes the witness stand, or during the course of the witness's evidence. This may be fitted into a timetable agreed during case management so that the tribunal has a reading day before the parties need attend. An alternative and common approach is for the tribunal at the beginning of the hearing to adjourn after the preliminary discussion to read the witness statements and essential documents referred to in them. A variation on this is for the tribunal to adjourn for a short period before each witness to read that witness's statement and the documents to which it refers.

Whichever course is adopted, the representatives must ensure that they and their clients understand **9.146** the procedure that is being followed, and that all documents upon which the party relies are drawn to the tribunal's attention. Representatives must be prepared to assist the tribunal at the beginning of the hearing by agreeing a key reading list with the other side. Representatives should note what documents are read by the tribunal during the course of the hearing, so that, after his client's last witness has given evidence, any documents not already referred to can be drawn to the tribunal's attention.

Submission of no case to answer

9.147 An application of no case to answer is made at 'half-time' in the case: ie after the evidence of the party bearing the burden of proof is complete, but before hearing evidence from the other party. It is an opportunity for the party going second to argue that the other party cannot succeed even on his own evidence, so that the second party should not be put to the expense of continuing with the hearing. The procedure is established in the civil courts and, more particularly, in the criminal courts (where of course the standard of proof is higher).

9.148 It is possible to make a submission of no case to answer in the employment tribunal, but such submissions have never been encouraged, see for example *Ridley v GEC Machines Ltd* (1978) 13 ITR 195; *Coral Squash Clubs Ltd v Matthews and Matthews* [1979] IRLR 390; and *George A Palmer Ltd v Beeby* [1978] ICR 196.

9.149 In *Logan v Commissioners of Customs & Excise* [2004] ICR 1 at paras 18–19, Ward LJ said that it should be rare for a submission of no case to answer to be made and rarer for it to succeed. He summarized the law as follows (by reference to *Clarke v Watford Borough Council*, 4 May 2000, EAT (Judge Peter Clark)):

(a) There is no inflexible rule of law and practice that a tribunal must always hear both sides, although that should normally be done (*Ridley v GEC Machines Ltd* (1978) 13 ITR 195).

(b) The power to stop a case at 'half-time' must be exercised with caution (*Coral Squash Clubs Ltd v Matthews and Matthews* [1979] IRLR 390).

(c) It may, however, be a complete waste of time to call upon the other party to give evidence in a hopeless case (*Ridley v GEC Machines Ltd*).

(d) Even where the onus of proof lies on the claimant, as in discrimination cases, it will only be in exceptional or frivolous cases that it would be right to take such a course (*Oxford v Department of Health* [1977] ICR 884; *Owen & Briggs v James* [1981] IRLR 133; *British Gas plc v Sharma* [1991] IRLR 101, 106). (This proposition applies to whistle-blowing cases, which to some extent are treated as a form of discrimination cases (see *Boulding v Land Securities Trillium (Media Services) Ltd* UKEAT/0023/06, applying *Logan*). This proposition applies also to constructive dismissal cases.)

(e) Where there is no burden of proof, as under s 98(4) of the ERA 1996, it will be difficult to envisage arguable cases where it is appropriate to terminate the proceedings at the end of the first party's case.

(f) Where a party makes an unsuccessful submission of no case to answer, he will not be regarded as having elected to call no evidence (*Walker v Josiah Wedgwood & Sons Ltd* [1978] ICR 744, 753). However, he will be bound by a specific statement that he will not call evidence (*Stokes v Hampstead Wine Co Ltd* [1979] IRLR 298). In civil and criminal proceedings, the party wishing to make a submission of no case to answer is generally put to his election whether he will call evidence or not (see *Alexander v Rayson* [1936] 1 KB 169, CA; *Miller (t/a Waterloo Plant) v Cawley* [2002] EWCA Civ 1100).

9.150 Similarly, an application to strike out a claim mid-hearing on grounds that it has no reasonable prospect of success would succeed only in exceptional circumstances. The approach in *Logan* should be followed whether the application is characterized as a submission of no case to answer, or an application to strike out: *Timbo v Greenwich Council for Racial Equality* [2013] ICR D7. In a case where the evidence of the party going first is weak it will normally be better, and simpler, for the tribunal to hear the remainder of the evidence, rather than using time to deal with a strike-out application: *Williams v Real Care Agency Limited* [2012] ICR D27, EAT (Scotland).

Closing submissions

9.151 After all of the evidence has been concluded, each party's representative may make a closing speech. The party bearing the burden of proof has the last word. Many employment judges discourage long closing speeches and welcome closing remarks in writing in longer cases in particular. Some impose time limits for oral submissions. The ECtHR has recognized that it is generally for national courts to regulate their own procedure, including the time allowed for oral submissions: *Brown v UK* (1999) 28 EHRR CD 233.

Skeleton arguments

A written skeleton argument, or outline of submissions, is often helpful to the tribunal, particularly **9.152** in a complex case, or in a case where there will be little time for oral submissions. Sometimes, the tribunal may have ordered skeleton arguments to be filed or may have invited the submission of skeletons during the course of the hearing. A skeleton argument (as opposed to full written submissions) is not intended as a substitute for oral argument, and should be as brief as the nature of the issues permits. A skeleton argument should identify concisely:

(a) the nature of the case generally, and the background facts insofar as they are relevant
(b) the propositions of law relied upon with references to the relevant authorities
(c) the submissions of fact to be made with reference to the evidence.

It is important for representatives to make a skeleton as easy to use for a tribunal as possible. **9.153** Paragraphs should be numbered, and appropriate use made of section headings and sub-headings. Cross-references to the evidence are helpful, as they mean the judge does not have to make a note of references during the oral submissions. Abbreviations and appropriate defined terms are to be encouraged. These principles are adapted from the *Chancery Guide 2016*, para 21.80.

In the President of the EAT's Practice Statement 2015 (see Appendix 2), the use of over-lengthy **9.154** skeleton arguments is deprecated. This is likely to be instructive in relation to the use of skeleton arguments in the tribunal as well.

Use of authorities

A representative can assume that the tribunal will be familiar with the leading cases, such as **9.155** *Devis v Atkins* [1977] AC 931, *British Home Stores v Burchell* [1978] IRLR 379, and *Polkey v Dayton* [1988] 1 AC 344. Any authorities upon which the party wishes to rely should be copied for the tribunal members and for the other side. Authorities should be handed up to the tribunal at the beginning of the hearing, having been exchanged between the parties' representatives beforehand by agreement between the representatives. Authorities should be suitably marked up wherever possible (adopting the usual convention of sidelining relevant passages). As discussed above, bundles of authorities, unlike hearing bundles, should not have continuous pagination. Instead, each authority will maintain its own internal pagination.

Written submissions

Not infrequently the tribunal will adjourn at the end of the evidence for written submissions. This **9.156** can arise because the evidence has used up all the listed time and there is no time left to do justice to oral submissions. The parties may prefer to prepare written submissions for use by the tribunal when deliberating, rather than to return for a further day of hearing. Alternatively, written submissions may be thought appropriate because the case is a long or complex one and the tribunal would prefer the assistance of written submissions before reaching its judgment. Where the parties are to provide written submissions, this may either be in substitution for any oral submissions, or to supplement them.

In *London Borough of Barking & Dagenham v Oguoko* [2000] IRLR 179, the EAT gave guidance to **9.157** employment tribunals on the correct procedure to be adopted for written closing submissions, if the parties are not to return to the tribunal to make oral submissions:

(a) The procedure for written submissions should be implemented only with the consent of all parties.
(b) It is the judge's responsibility to ensure that the procedure adopted complies with natural justice.

(c) Upon receipt of both sets of submissions, the tribunal should serve each party with the written submission of the other.

(d) Each party should be informed that if they have any appropriate comment to make on the submission of their opponent, they should send those comments to the tribunal within a further fixed period. They should be warned that if, within that time, no comment is received back by the tribunal, it will be assumed they have no comment to make and the tribunal will proceed to make its decision on the basis of the submissions already tendered.

9.158 In *Sinclair Roche & Temperley v Heard* [2004] IRLR 763, EAT, Burton J considered the position where written submissions were filed prior to a further day of hearing for closing submissions. Burton J remarked that an 'American system of briefs' was valuable but not intended to be a substitute for oral argument. His *obiter* remarks must be seen in the context of the type of long, complex case with which he was dealing. It is doubtful that he intended to suggest that there were not cases where it was appropriate to take written submissions without additional oral submissions: indeed, as noted above, in many cases (particularly simpler ones) the parties may feel that such an approach is the most efficient and cost-effective way of dealing with the submissions in the case.

9.159 Burton J's real concern was with the timescale in which the tribunal had required submissions to be produced in such a complex case. After twelve days of evidence, the tribunal heard oral closing submissions effectively on the next working day (with only the Easter weekend in between). He thought that the value of written submissions is lost if neither the parties nor the tribunal has time to read and assimilate the submissions before the commencement of oral submissions. Burton J said that, in a long case where written submissions were ordered, the following procedure should be followed:

(a) The timescale for preparation of the submissions must be a sensible one to allow the representatives time to prepare their submissions without unfair pressure.

(b) It is essential that the timescale should provide for the submissions to be provided to the other party in sufficient time before the oral submissions for the other party to be able to read them so that that party can, in his oral submissions, comment upon, address, and seek to answer them.

(c) It is equally, if not more, essential that the tribunal has had the opportunity to read the submissions before the oral submissions.

9.160 Where the tribunal agrees with the parties that they will file written submissions, but it then only receives one party's submissions, the tribunal should not proceed to decide the case without trying to find out why the absent submissions were not lodged. This can be done by a telephone call, just as in the case of a failure of a party to attend a hearing. Failure to do so may be a serious procedural irregularity leading to a rehearing if the party can show that there was a real possibility that the submissions may have made a difference to the decision: *Quashie v Methodist Homes Housing Association* UKEAT/0422/11, 16 January 2012.

H. CONTEMPT OF COURT

9.161 An employment tribunal is an inferior court for the purposes of CPR Part 81, and thus a person may be found guilty of contempt of court in connection with tribunal proceedings: *Peach Grey & Co v Sommers* [1995] IRLR 363. The contempt is punishable on committal by the Divisional Court (see also *dicta* in *Attorney-General v British Broadcasting Corporation* [1978] 1 WLR 477 (reversed on appeal on unrelated grounds).

9.162 A wide variety of different acts and omissions may be in contempt of court. The following may be particularly relevant in the tribunal:

(a) Contempt in the face of the court: this covers a wide variety of forms of disrespectful and disruptive behaviour in the tribunal.

(b) Words (written or spoken) scandalizing the court.

(c) Publication of matter which creates a substantial risk that the course of justice in proceedings which are active will be impeded or prejudiced.

(d) Publication of matter which the court has decided should be kept confidential in the interests of justice.

(e) Acts calculated to prejudice the course of justice, for example interference with witnesses.

(f) Further consideration is outside the scope of this work; interested parties and representatives should consult specialist works on civil procedure or contempt of court (eg CPR Part 81; *Borrie and Lowe: The Law of Contempt* (4th edn, LexisNexis 2009)).

In cases of disruptive behaviour by a party or his representative during the course of the hearing, **9.163** contempt proceedings before the Divisional Court are unlikely to be a practical solution. The tribunal has powers within its own rules to deal with such situations: the tribunal may at an stage of proceedings strike out all or part of a claim or response on the grounds that the proceedings have been conducted by a party or his representative in a manner which is scandalous, unreasonable, or vexatious (ETR 2013 r 37(1)(b)) (see Chapter 7). The tribunal may make an order for costs against a party or his representative, if behaviour at the hearing has led to costs being wasted (see Chapter 12). A tribunal may not, however, refuse to allow a party his choice of representative (*Bennett v London Borough of Southwark* [2002] IRLR 407, following *Bache v Essex County Council* [2000] IRLR 251). Nor does the tribunal have the power to ask the Official Solicitor to investigate the mental capacity of a litigant, however apparently delusional, or to appoint a litigation friend: *Johnson v Edwardian International Hotels Ltd* UKEAT 0588/07. Faced with disruptive behaviour the judge should first try to defuse the situation, by pointing out the potential consequences if the behaviour continues, and perhaps by allowing the parties a short break to reflect on their positions.

I. RESTRICTIONS ON PUBLICITY AND DISCLOSURE

Public hearings

Rule 59 of the ETR 2013 provides that any final hearing shall be in public, subject to two specific **9.164** powers: r 50 (privacy and restrictions on disclosure) and r 94 (national security). A preliminary hearing will normally be held in private, unless the hearing will determine a preliminary issue or consider a strike-out application. In either of those cases the hearing shall be in public, subject again to rr 50 and 94.

Where the rules provide for a hearing to be public, the requirement is a stringent one, as stressed **9.165** in *Storer v British Gas plc* [2000] IRLR 495. In that case, there was a coded door lock restricting entry to the part of the tribunal building where the hearing took place. The hearing was held not to have been in public, as the public did not have access to the hearing, even though there was no evidence that any person who wished to attend had been prevented from attending. Henry LJ stated that 'the obligation to sit in public was fundamental to the function of an employment tribunal'. Where a hearing (or part of it) is conducted by electronic means, r 46 of the ETR 2013 provides for public access to the hearing.

Restrictions on publicity

Sections 10–12 ETA 1996 provide for employment tribunal regulations to make restrictions on **9.166** publicity in certain cases. Under the ETR 2004, a tribunal had a number of powers to restrict the principle that hearings should be heard and reported on publicly:

(a) A tribunal could conduct a hearing, or part of it, in private in circumstances defined by r 16 of the ETR 2004 and s 10A of the ETA 1996.

(b) A tribunal could impose restricted reporting orders in cases involving allegations of sexual misconduct, or disability cases involving sensitive personal information (ETR 2004, r 50, ETA 1996, ss 11–12).

(c) Special procedures for private hearings applied to cases involving national security (ETR 2004, r 54).

(d) A tribunal could make a 'permanent anonymity order' or 'register deletion order' (RDO) under r 49 of the ETR 2004 requiring deletion from the register or judgment of material which would identify a person affected by or making an allegation of a sexual offence.

9.167 Following the introduction of the HRA 1998, there have been a number of cases which have considered the delicate relationship between open justice (as an element of both the right to a fair trial under Art 6 of the ECHR, and the right to freedom of expression under Art 10) and the right to private and family life (under Art 8). The rules under the ETR 2004 and its predecessors were rigid and technical, and there were a number of situations where Art 8 rights were engaged which were not catered for by the rules. Accordingly, the tribunals and EAT developed powers to restrict publicity outside the narrow confines of the rules. The Underhill Review (June 2012) felt that it was important that the tribunal rules were brought more into line with the requirements of the HRA 1998 and the jurisprudence of the ECtHR. The old rules were felt to be too prescriptive (Underhill Review, para 13). The purpose of the new rules relating to privacy, according to the Underhill Review, was to provide 'a more flexible regime which allows tribunals to take appropriate steps to balance the important principles of open justice and freedom of expression on the one hand and of privacy and effective justice on the other'.

9.168 Accordingly, the ETR 2013 contains new rules which simplify and broaden the powers to restrict publicity. Rule 50 draws together powers to hold hearings in private, anonymize references to parties and witnesses, and make restricted reporting orders. National security cases are dealt with separately in r 94 of the ETR 2013 and Sch 2 (National Security Rules of Procedure).

9.169 Rule 50 is more flexible than the old rules, and less burdened with technical jurisdictional requirements. In devising r 50, the Underhill Review expressly recognized that the rule went beyond existing rule-making powers (para 13): 'The rule goes beyond the explicit rule making powers conferred by the 1996 Act but we have no doubt that it is within your powers under the Human Rights Act'.

9.170 The government response to the Underhill Review (BIS March 2013) at paras 45–49 made clear that it accepted the need for the rules to be less prescriptive, and more in line with the requirements of the HRA 1998. Paragraph 47 of the response states:

> Whilst the suggested changes to the rules widen the existing legislative provisions in this area, and give judges more discretion and flexibility in the rules for deciding when anonymity or restricted reporting orders are required, such power already exists (see the case of *F v G* [2012] ICR 246).

9.171 Rule 50(1) provides that a tribunal may, at any stage of the proceedings, either of its own initiative or on application, make an order 'with a view to preventing or restricting the public disclosure of any aspect of those proceedings'. The tribunal may make such an order 'so far as it considers necessary' in the interests of justice, or in order to protect the ECHR rights of any person, or in the circumstances identified in s 10A of the ETA 1996. In considering whether to make an order under r 50, the tribunal 'shall give full weight' to the principle of open justice and to the ECHR right to freedom of expression.

9.172 Rule 50(3) sets out the type of provisions that an order under r 50(1) *may* include.

- an order that a hearing be conducted in whole or in part in private
- an order that the identities of specified parties, witnesses or other persons referred to in the proceedings should not be disclosed to the public, by the use of anonymization or otherwise, whether in the course of the hearing or in its listing, or in any documents entered on the register or otherwise forming part of the public record
- an order for measures preventing witnesses at a public hearing being identifiable by members of the public
- a restricted reporting order within the terms of ETA 1996, ss 11 or 12.

9.173 Thus, the tribunal may make an order under r 50, so far as it considers it necessary, on one or more of three grounds:

(a) in the interests of justice or

(b) in order to protect Convention rights of any person (Convention rights bearing the meaning it is given under s 1 of the HRA 1998: see r 50(6)) or

(c) in the circumstances identified in s 10A of the ETA 1996.

Section 10A of the ETA 1996 provides that tribunal procedure regulations may enable a tribunal **9.174** to sit in private for the purpose of hearing evidence from any person, which in the opinion of the tribunal is likely to consist of:

(a) information which he could not disclose without contravening a prohibition imposed by or by virtue of any enactment

(b) information which has been communicated to him in confidence or which he has otherwise obtained in consequence of the confidence reposed in him by another person or

(c) information the disclosure of which would, for reasons other than its effect on negotiations with respect to any of the matters mentioned in s 178(2) of the Trade Union and Labour Relations (Consolidation) Act 1992, cause substantial injury to any undertaking of his or in which he works.

Under r 50, the power to make each of the orders under r 50(3) is subject to the same overarching **9.175** test, as set out in r 50(1)–(2). Although the powers to sit in private, to make a RDO, and to make a restricted reporting order (RRO) existed under the old rules, each was subject to its own particular jurisdictional requirements. For instance, s 10A of the ETA (and r 16 of the ETR 2004 made pursuant to it) is a provision relating only to the hearing of evidence in private. The confidentiality grounds in those provisions did not entitle the tribunal to make an RRO or a RDO. Yet the grounds in s 10A may now be used as the basis for any of the orders listed in r 50(3).

As the grounds in r 50(1) are alternatives, each being separated by 'or', it would appear that an **9.176** order under r 50 can be made on the simple ground that the tribunal considers it to be in the interests of justice to do so. That represents a considerable widening of the tribunal's powers, although the tribunal must of course give full weight to the principles of open justice and freedom of expression (r 50(2)). In a case where neither a Convention right, nor a matter covered by s 10A of the ETA is engaged, it is difficult to see what 'interests of justice' would require a restriction of open justice and freedom of expression.

Private hearings

Under r 16 of the old ETR 2004, a hearing which would otherwise be held in public could have **9.177** been held in private only if evidence or representations were likely to consist of information of defined types derived from s 10A of the ETA 1996: information which could not be disclosed without breaching a statutory prohibition; confidential information; or information which, if disclosed, would cause substantial injury to an undertaking. The current r 50(1) of the ETR 2013 specifically refers to s 10A of the ETA 1996, so those categories will continue to be relevant, but it is clear that the power to sit in private is widened to include cases where it is necessary in the interests of justice to do so to protect a Convention right of any person.

In deciding whether to sit in private, r 50(2) requires the tribunal to give full weight to the prin- **9.178** ciple of open justice, and to the Convention right of freedom of expression. Open justice is a matter of public interest, and therefore the decision whether to sit in private is not simply a matter of agreement between the parties. The principle of open justice was established in the common law long before the HRA 1998: see *Scott v Scott* [1913] AC 417 in which Lord Shaw described open justice as 'one of the surest guarantees of our liberties' (at 476). In the same case, Lord Atkinson said (at 439) that, in order to justify an order for a hearing in camera, it must be shown that the paramount object of securing that justice is done would really be rendered doubtful of attainment if the order were not made. Since the HRA 1998, the approach of the courts has been to balance the potentially competing rights under Art 6 (fair trial), Art 8 (privacy), and Art 10 (freedom of speech). There is no general exception to the principle of open justice where privacy or confidentiality are in issue. Cases should be heard in private if and to the extent that the court is satisfied that by nothing short of the exclusion of the public can justice be done. In the High Court, in the context of 'super-injunctions' to protect privacy, Lord Neuberger of Abbotsbury MR has said that exclusions must be no more than the minimum necessary to ensure justice is done (see *Practice Guidance (Interim-Non-Disclosure Orders)* [2012] 1 WLR 1003). For a summary of the principles applicable in the High Court context see *Global Torch Ltd v Apex Global Management Ltd* [2013] 1 WLR 2993 at paras 13–22 (Kay LJ).

9.179 It is suggested that those principles are of equal application in the employment tribunals. Even under the ETR 2004, there had been some recognition by the appeal courts of the need to balance the competing rights of privacy and of freedom of expression. *XXX v YYY* [2004] IRLR 471 concerned a dispute as to the admissibility of a video recording showing the claimant (a nanny), her employer, and the child of her employer. An argument arose as to the protection of the right to privacy of the child. The EAT held that the evidence was potentially relevant and that to refuse to admit it may infringe X's right to a fair trial, but to play it in public would infringe the child's right to privacy. The EAT reconciled the competing rights by directing that the tribunal receive the evidence in a private hearing. The Court of Appeal overturned this decision, holding that the evidence was not relevant and therefore not admissible. However, the Court of Appeal noted that there was no challenge to the EAT's power to direct that the tribunal view the video in private. The EAT held that the jurisdiction to hear the evidence in private was in what is now r 50(2): playing the video in public would infringe the child's Art 8 rights, and the tribunal has an obligation to act in accordance with those rights under s 6 of the Human Rights Act 1998. The evidence would be likely to consist of information which could not be disclosed without contravening a prohibition imposed by or by virtue of an enactment.

9.180 When a case is heard in private, the husband of the claimant was entitled to attend. The extent of the persons so entitled to attend was a matter of fact and degree (*Fry v Foreign and Commonwealth Office* [1997] ICR 512).

Anonymisation orders

9.181 Rule 49 of the ETR 2004 gave the tribunal a limited power (derived from s 11(1)(a) of the ETA 1996) to omit from the register, or delete from the register or any judgment, document, or record of the proceedings which is available to the public, any identifying matter which is likely to lead members of the public to identify any person affected by or making an allegation of the commission of a sexual offence. Such an order was described as a RDO by Burton J in *X v Commissioner for Police for the Metropolis Stevens* [2003] ICR 1031, and that term has been used over a number of years, although Underhill J described the term as a misnomer in *F v G* [2012] ICR 246. In both *X* and *F v G*, the EAT held that a wider power existed to make such an order in order to protect a person's Convention rights, or to give effective protection to an EU right, such as a right under the Equal Treatment Directive.

9.182 Rule 50(3)(b) of the ETR 2013 gives the tribunal a much wider power to make anonymisation orders. Such an order may be made when it is in the interests of justice to do so in order to protect the Convention rights of any person. There is no limitation to particular types of claim, or particular subject matter. The rule is not limited to anonymisation in relation to parties; it extends to anonymising the identities of witnesses and persons referred to in the proceedings. The tribuna does not have power to make an order that a decision should not be published on the public register: *Ameyaw v PriceWaterhouseCoopers Services Ltd* [2018] UKEAT 0244/18.

9.183 The rule makes clear that the steps required to anonymize the identity of persons may extend not just to the judgment and the register (ie documents created at the end of proceedings), but to steps taken in the course of the hearing or the listing of a hearing.

Restricted reporting orders

Introduction

9.184 Rule 50(3) provides that one of the things an order made under r 50(1) may include is an RRO 'within the terms of' s 11 or 12 of the ETA 1996. The effect of such an RRO is to prohibit the media from publishing information which is likely to identify specified persons involved in the proceedings. An RRO is defined in each of ss 11 and 12 to mean an order made in exercise of a power conferred by regulations made under those sections prohibiting the publication in Great Britain of identifying matter in a written publication available to the public, or in a relevant programme.

Cases in which a restricted reporting order may be made

The circumstances in which an RRO may be made remain, unfortunately, unclear. Under s 11 **9.185** and s 12 of the ETA 1996, an RRO may be made in narrow circumstances: certain cases involving allegations of sexual misconduct (s 11(1)(b)) and, in certain cases, of disability discrimination (s 12(1)). However, case law had decided over the course of the 2000s that RROs (or orders analogous to them) may be made in wider circumstances than those dealt with by ss 11–12 (see para 9.199 below). It is clear from the Underhill Review, and from the government's response to it, that the new r 50 was intended to reflect the need for a wider power to make RROs in order to protect rights protected by the HRA 1998. However, r 50(3) speaks of RROs 'within the terms of' ss 11 and 12; those sections have not been amended, and there is no express power in r 50 to make an RRO, other than as provided by r 50(3). The question then arises as to what r 50 means when it says 'within the terms of' ss 11–12. One possibility is that ss 11 and 12 are referred to simply to define the meaning of an RRO, but the rule is not meant to refer to the conditions in those sections for the grant of an order. Another possibility is that r 50(3) is referring to an order complying with all of the conditions imposed by ss 11 and 12. The latter, which may seem a more natural meaning, is clearly contrary to the intention of the Underhill Review and the government, and contrary to the direction of case law in recent years. However, separating out the meaning of an RRO and the circumstances in which it may be made in ss 11 and 12 is no easy matter as, in each section, an RRO is defined by reference to the subject matter, which cannot be identified. The solution may rest in the fact that r 50(1) gives the tribunal a very wide power, and that r 50(3) does not give an exhaustive list of the orders which can be made: ie it is possible that an RRO type of order can be made in cases outside ss 11–12, even though such an order is not listed. Such a solution would seem to be in line with the intention of the Underhill Review.

The situation appears to have been clarified in *Fallows v News Group Newspapers Ltd* [2016] ICR 801, where Simler J noted at para 41:

> Provided an order is considered necessary in the interests of justice or necessary to protect Convention rights, and the tribunal considering whether to make an order gives full weight to the principle of open justice and the right to freedom of expression, rule 50(1) enables an order to be made in circumstances that do not fall strictly within sections 11 and 12 of the 1996 Act, or that extends beyond the end of the proceedings (whether they otherwise fall within sections 11 and 12 or not). This is not to create a power in order to give effect to the article 8 rights of parties to tribunal proceedings; but is a question of the proper construction of an express power given in rule 50(1) of the 2013 Rules.

In *Fallows*, Simler J held that an RRO, unlike under ss 11 and 12, which limited the duration of such an order to the promulgation of the tribunal's decision, r 50(1) of the ETR 2013 provided tribunals with a wider power enabling them to make restricted reporting orders without any temporal or other limitation and that, provided an order was considered necessary in the interests of justice or to protect rights under the Convention for the Protection of Human Rights and Fundamental Freedoms, and full weight was given to the principle of open justice and the right to freedom of expression, an order could be made under r 50(1) that extended beyond the end of the proceedings.

Scope

Cases involving allegations of sexual misconduct

Under s 11, the power to make an RRO arises in cases involving allegations of sexual misconduct. **9.186** Sexual misconduct means (ETA 1996, s 11(6)):

> the commission of a sexual offence, sexual harassment, or other adverse conduct (of whatever nature) related to sex, and conduct is related to sex whether the relationship with sex lies in the character of the conduct or in its having reference to the sex or sexual orientation of the person at whom the conduct is directed.

9.187 Such allegations will typically arise in cases of sex discrimination; however, s 11 of the ETA 1996 is not limited to claims under the EqA 2010 or its predecessor, the SDA 1975. For example, a claim of constructive unfair dismissal may be brought on the basis of allegations of sexual harassment, or a claimant in an unfair dismissal claim may have been dismissed for the reason that his employer believed him to have sexually harassed a co-worker. In each of these examples, the case involves an allegation of sexual misconduct, regardless of the cause of action relied on.

9.188 Conversely, there may be claims brought of sex discrimination which involve no allegation of sexual misconduct, and where, therefore, s 11 does not apply. In *Chief Constable of West Yorkshire Police v A* [2000] IRLR 465, the EAT held that 'sexual misconduct' did not extend so far as to cover the case of a claimant who alleged that she was rejected for a job on the grounds of her status as a transsexual. If all that was required for 'sexual misconduct' was that it was conduct which was 'adverse' and was 'related to sex' by way of having reference to the sex or sexual orientation of the person to whom it was directed, every case of sex discrimination would be a case of 'sexual misconduct'.

9.189 A case may involve allegations of sexual misconduct even if those allegations do not form the basis of the cause of action in the claim, and even if the allegations may not be central to the tribunal's decision-making. A legalistic analysis of the pleadings is not necessary, nor is proof of the allegations. Thus, for example, in *X v Commissioner of Police of the Metropolis* [2003] IRLR 411 the claim was that the claimant had been denied a vacancy because of her status as a post-operative transsexual. The respondent denied that this was the reason that the claimant was denied the vacancy, and alleged a number of reasons for the decision, including an unproven suspicion that the claimant had in the past been involved in a sexual assault. The EAT (Burton J) held that the tribunal would need to hear some evidence which touched on the suspected assault and that the claim therefore involved an allegation of sexual misconduct.

9.190 In sexual misconduct cases, the legislation is aimed at preventing identification of a person affected by or a person making the allegation.

9.191 There are certain categories of person who may naturally be thought to fall within the scope of an RRO: principally victims, alleged perpetrators, and witnesses. However, the statute does not define the concept of 'affected by' and the courts have declined to place a gloss on its meaning. In *R v London (North) Industrial Tribunal, ex parte Associated Newspapers Ltd* [1998] ICR 1212, Keene J said that each case must be viewed on its particular facts to ascertain whether the person in respect of whom an RRO is being sought is a person affected by the allegations.

9.192 An RRO should, however, be no wider in scope than is necessary to achieve the purposes of the legislation. The judge must consider the extent of the RRO on the basis of each individual of whom it is sought to prevent reporting. A blanket approach to such a prohibition is improper (see *ex parte Associated Newspapers* cited above). In *Scottish Daily Record and Sunday Mail Ltd v McAvoy* EATS/1271/01, the EAT held that the tribunal had erred in making a blanket order in respect of all the witnesses in the case, when some of those witnesses were not persons 'affected by' the allegation of sexual harassment at all.

9.193 It is necessary to appreciate two different ways in which the reporting of the identity of, or evidence of, a person may be covered by an RRO:

(1) Who is a person making or affected by the allegation of sexual misconduct? Such a person is the permissible subject of an RRO.
(2) What constitutes identifying matter ie matter which is likely to lead to identification of a person affected by, or making an allegation?

9.194 It is quite possible that the publication of the identity of, or evidence of, a witness who is not himself an affected person would be likely to cause identification of an affected person. In this situation, the witness is not a person affected, but the press may not report his evidence in a way which would lead to identification of someone who *is* a person affected. Such a person may be included in the RRO: *Tradition Securities & Futures SA v Times Newspapers Ltd* [2009] IRLR 354. Rule 50(3)(c) of the ETR 2013 now specifically provides for orders preventing witnesses at a public hearing being identified by members of the public, but it is unclear whether the measures to which the rule refers include restrictions on reporting the identity of witnesses.

For example: **9.195**

(a) X brings a claim against the company employing her (Y), alleging sexual harassment by her line manager (A); she alleges the managing director (B) failed properly to deal with her complaint about the harassment. She intends to call as a witness a co-worker (C) who witnessed some instances of harassment.

(b) X may be a person identified in an RRO as the person making an allegation of sexual misconduct.

(c) So too may A: he is the alleged perpetrator, and therefore a person affected by the allegation.

(d) B (the investigating manager), however, is not the maker of the allegation, nor is he affected by it. He is not entitled to have his identity protected. The press must be cautious, however, in reporting B's evidence to ensure that matter is not reported which would be likely to lead to the identification of X or A.

(e) C, as a witness to the harassment, may be affected by the allegation (see eg *ex parte Associated Newspapers* cited above).

(f) The position of Y, as a body corporate, requires further consideration: see para 9.201.

In *ex parte Associated Newspapers*, Keene J stated (at para 12) that it is unnecessary for an RRO **9.196** itself to ban the identification of one person simply on the basis that it is likely to lead to the identification of the person whose identity it is truly sought to protect or conceal: it is for the press to exercise its judgment as to what is likely to lead to such identification, and powerful sanctions exist if they transgress: see also Staughton LJ in *X v Z Ltd* [1998] ICR 43, 46.

Disability cases

A tribunal may make an RRO on a complaint of disability discrimination in which evidence of **9.197** a personal nature is likely to be heard (ETA 1996, s 12(1)). Evidence of a personal nature means (ETA 1996, s 12(7)) 'any evidence of a medical, or other intimate, nature which might reasonably be assumed to be likely to cause significant embarrassment to the complainant if reported'. An RRO may prohibit publication of 'identifying matter' likely to lead to identification of the complainant 'or such other persons (if any) as may be named in the order': ETA 1996, s 12(7).

There is no express qualification of the power to name other persons in the order. The proper scope **9.198** of the provision is unclear. Clearly the main intention of the provision is to protect publication of the identity of the complainant about whom evidence of a personal nature is likely to be heard. It is suggested that other persons may be named only to the extent necessary to protect the identity of the complainant. Given the importance of freedom of the press and open justice, and given the degree of dispute as to the scope of the (older) provisions under s 11, it seems unlikely that Parliament intended the tribunal to have an unfettered power to protect the identity of persons other than the complainant.

Cases of RRO outside ss 11 and 12

The EAT has recognized in a series of cases that the tribunal's and the EAT's powers to make **9.199** an RRO (and to anonymize the register) are wider than provided for by rr 49 and 50 of the ETR 2004 and ss 11–12 of the ETA, most recently in *Fallows* (discussed above). In particular, where an order is sought to protect the Art 8 right to a private life, or to protect rights of equal treatment conferred by EU law, the tribunal's powers did not have to be derived from rr 49–50 of the ETR 2004. The tribunal had wide powers (under its general case management powers) to take appropriate steps unconstrained by the specific terms of those rules. Rules 49–50 of the ETR 2004 remained a valuable source of terminology, and as regards questions of ancillary procedure see *F v G* [2012] ICR 246, particularly at paras 19–25 (Underhill J); *A v B* [2010] ICR 849 (Underhill J); *X v Commissioners of Police of the Metropolis* [2003] ICR 1031 (Burton J).

Part A Tribunal Procedure

9.200 Before *Fallows*, in *EF and Another v AB and Others* UKEAT/0525/13/DM, the EAT confirmed that the tribunal has the power to make RROs extending beyond the end of the proceedings and such power derives from the ECHR rather than r 50 itself. In that case, there had been allegations of sexual misconduct against the CEO of a company and his wife, which were of a lurid nature, and the tribunal had refused to extend an RRO beyond the end of proceedings, on the basis that the other employees had a right to know what was going on in the company in which they worked. The EAT criticized the employment tribunal below for failing to consider and balance the competing Convention rights of the applicants and respondents in connection with the RRO and held that an extended RRO should have been made.

Bodies corporate

9.201 There have been conflicting decisions as to whether the persons to whom an order may apply may include corporate bodies. In *M v Vincent* [1998] ICR 73, it was held that a 'person', the word used in the statute, could include a corporate body so that an order was made in respect of a company. In *ex parte Associated Newspapers* (see para 9.192), Keene J doubted that a local authority could be a person within the meaning of s 11. He pointed out, however, that reporting of the identity of a corporate body may in effect be restricted if, for example, reporting the name of the body is likely to lead to the identification of an individual himself covered by an RRO. In *Leicester University v A* [1999] ICR 701, the EAT, preferring the approach of Keene J in *ex parte Associated Newspapers*, held that the words 'person affected by the allegation' in s 11(6) of the ETA 1996 could only apply to an individual and not to a corporate body. The EAT said it was not the intention of Parliament to provide anonymity for corporate respondents who may be vicariously liable for acts of sexual misconduct in order to protect their commercial reputation.

Multiple proceedings

9.202 Where an RRO has been made in respect of a complaint, and that complaint is being heard together with any other proceedings as part of the same hearing, the tribunal or judge may order that the RRO applies in relation to those other proceedings or part of them (ETR 2013, r 50(5)(d)).

9.203 Rule 50(5)(d) reflects the earlier r 50(9) of the ETR 2004, which was a new provision in the ETR 2004. The provision applies to both sexual misconduct cases and disability cases. The provision is underpinned by express statutory provision in relation to disability claims (ETA 1996, s 12(2)(b)), but it is interesting to note that there is no such equivalent provision in s 11 of ETA 1996.

9.204 The power is apparently wide-ranging. However, it should be borne in mind that the statutory power under ss 11–12 remains unaltered. So, to take the example of sexual misconduct cases, the power under s 11 is limited to prohibiting information which is likely to reveal the identity of a person making an allegation of sexual misconduct or affected by the allegation. Where two sets of proceedings are being heard together, one raising an allegation of sexual misconduct (the first proceedings), the other not (the second proceedings), it is suggested the position is as follows:

(a) Rule 50(5)(d) permits the tribunal to make an order in respect of both proceedings. It is not a ground of objection to making an order in the second proceedings that no allegation of sexual misconduct is involved in those proceedings.

(b) However, the tribunal should satisfy itself that publication of matter from the second proceedings would be likely to lead to the identification of a person who is properly protected by an RRO in the first proceedings.

(c) Mindful of the interests of public justice and freedom of the press, the tribunal will need to examine carefully whether, and to what extent, it is necessary to restrict publication of matter relating to the second proceedings in order to protect the identity of the complainant in the first proceedings.

The effect of a restricted reporting order

9.205 An RRO is an order which prohibits the publication in Great Britain of 'identifying matter' in a written publication available to the public or its inclusion in a relevant programme for reception in

Great Britain. A relevant programme is defined in the Sexual Offences (Amendment) Act 1978 for the purpose of s 11(6), and in the Broadcasting Act 1990 for the purpose of s 12.

'Identifying matter' in relation to a person is defined as follows: **9.206**

(a) sexual misconduct cases: 'any matter likely to lead members of the public to identify him as a person affected by, or as the person making, the allegation' (ETA 1996, s 11(6))
(b) disability cases: 'any matter likely to lead members of the public to identify the complainant or such other persons (if any) as may be named in the order' (ETA 1996, s 12(7)).

Where a tribunal makes an RRO it must specify the persons whose identity is protected, and may **9.207** specify particular matters of which publication is prohibited as likely to lead to that person's identification (ETR 2013, r 50(5)(a)).

In *F v G* [2012] ICR 246 at para 24, Underhill J said that where an RRO is made under the wider **9.208** powers he identified in that case, the format or the order may not be much different from that used in a case under r 50 of the ETR 2004. However, he contemplated that there may be cases where the relief available may be too narrow and, if so, a wider order than that permitted by that rule may be made, for example an order of longer duration. The effect of a restricted reporting order is not to prevent a case from being reported, or to suppress allegations; rather, it prevents publication of material likely to identify the persons who are the subjects of the order.

The ETR 2004 permitted a tribunal to make either a temporary RRO or a full RRO. Each was **9.209** governed by different rules as to duration and the circumstances in which they could be made. The ETR 2013 scraps those distinctions, and gives a tribunal much more flexibility. An RRO may be made at any stage of the proceedings (r 50(1)); the tribunal must state the duration of the RRO in the order itself (r 50(5)(b)). Beyond those provisions, the duration of the order would appear to be a matter of discretion for the tribunal, having regard to the competing rights identified in r 50(1) and (2). As mentioned above, ss 11(1)(b) and 12(2)(b) ETA 1996 limited the duration of an RRO made under those sections until promulgation of the decision of the tribunal. However, Underhill J in *F v G* and Simler J in *Fallows* held that an order may last beyond the end of proceedings (whether by promulgation of the decision or withdrawal of the claim) when necessary to protect a Convention right.

In *R v Southampton Industrial Tribunal, ex parte INS News Group Ltd and Express Newspapers plc* **9.210** [1995] IRLR 247, Brooke J said (at para 22) that tribunals should make such orders as clear as they can so that the press is left in no doubt about what it may and may not do.

Exercise of the discretion

In exercising its discretion whether to make an RRO, a tribunal must balance a number of com- **9.211** peting human rights interests: the right to a fair trial (including the need for a public judgment); the right to respect for private life; and the right to freedom of expression.

In relation to allegations of sexual misconduct there is a delicate balance between: **9.212**

(1) the importance of stamping out sexual harassment and thus encouraging those with a proper grievance to bring claims to the attention of the employment tribunal and
(2) the principles of open justice in a democratic society.

In *ex parte Associated Newspapers* cited above, Keene J stated that an RRO was an infringement of **9.213** freedom of the press; any interference with such a basic constitutional right should be narrowly construed. Therefore, an RRO should extend so far as, and no further than, is necessary to achieve the purpose of the legislation (at para 45). The purpose of the legislation (based on consideration of *Hansard*) was to enable complaints of sexual harassment in the workplace to be brought and witnesses to give evidence without being deterred by fear of intimate sexual details about them being published (at para 36).

Women who have potential claims for sexual harassment were often shy of making them for fear of **9.214** damaging publicity. Potential claimants were being discouraged from bringing complaints through fear that they would suffer identification, adverse publicity, the trauma of giving evidence, and meeting the perpetrator of the harassment in the stressful situation of the employment tribunal room. Such discouragements are not, of course, confined to sexual harassment claims, but they are particularly acute in such circumstances.

9.215 The dangers in terms of publicity are also not, of course, confined to the *victim* of sexual harassment. Some employers are pushed into making large settlements because of the fear of lurid publicity, and are in effect open to 'blackmail' claims because of the likelihood of publicity at the hearing. Some claimants do alert the press in advance of a hearing, in order to embarrass the employer, and to force a better settlement.

9.216 Publicity for sexual harassment cases, on the other hand, may be seen to have some advantages as a matter of public interest to some degree for the following reasons:

(a) It may cause the issue to obtain a greater degree of public awareness. Harassment is still seen by some as a fact of working life which women have no choice but to suffer. If women see that other women are complaining about it to tribunals by those facts being reported widely, and that those complaints are being taken seriously (with large awards against the perpetrators), they too may be made aware of their legal rights and seek to enforce them. In essence, the press, in responsibly reporting such cases, can be put to good use in getting this matter dealt with, not only in the workplace, but also in a wider arena.

(b) It is important that the public become aware of which employers are guilty of harassing staff.

9.217 The tribunal will have to weigh each of these matters on the facts of the particular case:

(a) The wishes of each party for privacy or publicity.

(b) The fact that each of the parties had previously put aspects of the allegations in the public domain may be a relevant factor weighing against making an RRO: *Scottish Daily Record and Sunday Mail Ltd v McAvoy*, citing *Cinderella Bowyer v Armajit Singh Sandhu* ET/S/102262/99.

Application for restricted reporting order

9.218 An order may be made on the application of either party in cases involving allegations of sexual misconduct. In disability cases, only the complainant may apply for an order (s 12(2)(a)). In either case, an order may be made by the tribunal of its own motion (r 50(1), s 11(1)(b), s 12(2)(a)). The application may be made in writing or orally at a hearing.

Challenge to a restricted reporting order by a non-party

9.219 The groups most interested in challenging the making of restricted reporting orders are naturally the press and media organizations, who have an interest in reporting cases, and who may wish to object to an RRO on grounds of freedom of the press and freedom of speech.

9.220 Rule 50(4) of the ETR 2013 provides that any party, or person with a legitimate interest, who has not had a reasonable opportunity to make representations before an order under r 50(1) is made may apply in writing to the tribunal for the order to revoked or discharged, either on the basis of written representations or at a hearing.

9.221 Rule 50(4) provides a mechanism for the press (or other person with a legitimate interest) to make representations about an RRO which *has* been made. However, what the ETR 2013 lacks is any mechanism for the press to object to an order *before* it is made, or to participate in the hearing at which an RRO is sought by a party. This is in contrast to r 50 of the ETR 2004, under which the press could be heard on an application to make a full RRO. On the other hand, the ETR 2004 was unclear as to whether a non-party could apply to have an RRO discharged or varied, something which is now clear under r 50(4) of the ETR 2013.

Procedure at the hearing

9.222 The fact that an RRO has been made will be displayed on the noticeboard of the tribunal, and on the door of the room in which the hearing takes place (r 50(5)(c)) to ensure that the press is fully aware of the risks it runs if it breaches the order. As a matter of practice, the judge will normally remind all present of the existence of the RRO at the commencement of the hearing.

Penalties for breach of a restricted reporting order

Contravention of an RRO made under ss 11 or 12 of the ETA 1996 is a criminal offence, pun- **9.223** ishable in the criminal courts on summary conviction by a fine (ETA 1996, ss 11(2) and 12(3)). Sections 11(2) and 12(3) set out in detail the persons (both individual and corporate) who may commit an offence in respect of a publication in breach of an RRO (for example the editor, publisher, or proprietor of a newspaper). There is a defence for any such person if he 'proves that at the time of the alleged offence he was not aware, and neither suspected nor had reason to suspect, that the publication or programme in question was of, or included, identifying matter' (ETA 1996, ss 11(3) and 12(4)). In *F v G* [2012] ICR 246, Underhill J at para 22 recognized that if an RRO is made outside the scope of those sections, there may be 'complications' about the applicability of criminal sanctions, but he was not called upon to decide that issue. It is difficult to see how a criminal sanction could apply to an order made outside the strict definitions of ss 11 or 12. Although the line of cases of which *F v G* is a part expand the circumstances in which a tribunal may choose to make an RRO, they do not identify any means of enforcing such an order against a non-party, nor of applying sanctions to such a person, although it may be that a breach of such an order would be a contempt of court (see section H above).

National security

National security proceedings are governed by a special set of rules. National security proceedings **9.224** are proceedings in relation to which a direction is given or an order is made under r 94 of the ETR 2013 (defined in reg 3 of the ETR 2013). By r 94(1), where, in relation to particular Crown employment proceedings, a minister considers that it would be expedient in the interests of national security, the minister may direct a tribunal:

(a) to conduct all or part of the proceedings in private
(b) to exclude a person from all or part of the proceedings
(c) to take steps to conceal the identity of a witness in the proceedings.

The tribunal may take any of these steps of its own motion if it considers it expedient in the inter- **9.225** ests of national security to do so (r 94(2)(a)). A tribunal may also in such a case make directions limiting the persons to whom documents may be disclosed (r 94(2)(b)). Rule 94(3)–(10) contains provisions ancillary to the power to make orders under r 94(2). In exercising its functions the tribunal must ensure that information is not disclosed contrary to the interests of national security (r 94(10)).

Rules for the conduct of national security proceedings are set out in the Employment Tribunals **9.226** (National Security) Rules of Procedure 2013 (comprising Sch 2 of the ETR 2013). Those rules modify the ETR 2004 in cases where a power is exercised under r 94 of the ETR 2013. Rule 5 of Sch 2 provides that a hearing shall be in public, subject to any order under r 50 or 94 of the ETR 2013.

Of particular note is the procedure for the Attorney-General to appoint a special advocate to rep- **9.227** resent the interests of a claimant if either he or his representative is excluded from the proceedings (Sch 2, r 4). The Supreme Court rejected a challenge to these rules, which alleged that they were contrary to EU law or to Art 6 of the ECHR (*Tariq v Home Office* [2011] UKSC 35). In the same case, the Supreme Court also rejected the conclusion of the Court of Appeal that there was an absolute duty to make reasonable disclosure to the claimant (and not simply to the special advocate) in order to allow the claimant to know the gist of the case against him: the disadvantage to the claimant of not allowing such disclosure had to be balanced against the requirements of national security.

10

Bias and Improper Conduct
of the Hearing

SUMMARY

(1) All parties are entitled to a fair trial, and the tribunal must ensure the parties have a fair opportunity to put their case and to answer the case against them. The tribunal must avoid bias or the appearance of bias.

A. INTRODUCTION

10.01 Tribunals must conform to the general principles of natural justice, act fairly, and refrain from bias. Article 6(1) of the ECHR provides that:

> In the determination of his civil rights and obligations everyone is entitled to a fair and public hearing within a reasonable time by an independent and impartial tribunal established by law.

10.02 Article 6 is given effect in English law by virtue of s 6 of the Human Rights Act 1998. An employment tribunal is a public body for the purposes of s 6, and thus must not act in a manner that breaches a litigant's rights under Art 6(1). The rights to a fair hearing, to a public hearing, and to a hearing within a reasonable time are separate and distinct rights from the right to a hearing before an independent and impartial tribunal established by law. This means that a complaint that one of these rights was breached cannot be answered by showing that the other rights were not breached.

B. BIAS

The parties are entitled to a hearing by an independent and impartial tribunal. In *Findlay v UK* **10.03**
(1997) 24 EHRR 221, 244–45 (para 73) the ECtHR said:

> The Court recalls that in order to establish whether a tribunal can be considered as 'independent', regard
> must be had *inter alia* to the manner of appointment of its members and their term of office, the exist-
> ence of guarantees against outside pressures and the question whether the body presents an appearance
> of independence. As to the question of 'impartiality', there are two aspects to this requirement. First, the
> tribunal must be subjectively free from personal prejudice or bias. Secondly, it must also be impartial
> from an objective viewpoint, that is, it must offer sufficient guarantees to exclude any legitimate doubt in
> this respect. The concepts of independence and objective impartiality are closely linked.

The existence or appearance of bias on the part of any person sitting in a judicial capacity will **10.04**
ordinarily lead to the disqualification of that person from sitting, or, if the proceedings have
been concluded, to the hearing being declared a nullity and the decision set aside. In considering
whether to recuse himself, the judge has no discretion to weigh different factors in the balance.
Either there is the appearance of bias, in which case the judge must recuse himself; or there is not,
in which case there is no valid objection to the judge hearing the case (see *AWG Group Limited v
Morrison* [2006] 1 WLR 1163).

The general principles as to bias set out below relate to hearings before employment tribunals as **10.05**
they do to courts. The EAT has on occasions thus remitted a case to another employment tribunal
because of material irregularity in the procedure of the first hearing. Very few allegations of bias
have been proved, which can itself be seen as a testimony to the success of tribunals in dealing with
hard-fought industrial issues, notwithstanding that a majority of their members come from the
two sides of employment.

Bias can be divided for legal purposes into two categories: actual bias and the appearance of bias. **10.06**
Apparent bias can itself be divided into two 'sub-categories': presumed bias, and other cases of apparent bias (see *Locabail (UK) Ltd v Bayfield Properties Ltd* [2000] IRLR 96, CA).

Cases of actual bias on the part of a judge are rare, not least because its existence is difficult to prove. **10.07**

The fundamental principle in relation to the appearance of bias is that 'justice should not only **10.08**
be done, but should manifestly and undoubtedly be seen to be done' (*R v Sussex Justices, ex parte
McCarthy* [1924] 1 KB 256, 259). The cases on the appearance of bias identify two categories (see
R v Bow Street Metropolitan Stipendiary Magistrate, ex parte Pinochet Ugarte (No 2) [2000] 1 AC
119, 132G-133C (Browne-Wilkinson LJ):

(1) Where a judge is a party to proceedings or has a financial or proprietary interest, other than
    de minimis, in the outcome of a case, bias is presumed and disqualification is automatic. The
    leading case is *R v Bow Street Metropolitan Stipendiary Magistrate, ex parte Pinochet Ugarte (No 2)*
    [2000] 1 AC 119.
(2) The conduct or behaviour of a judge may give rise to a suspicion that he is not impartial. Here
    the test for apparent bias in *Porter v Magill* [2001] UKHL 67, [2002] 2 AC 357 should be
    applied.

In *Lawal v Northern Spirit Ltd* [2003] UKHL 35, [2003] ICR 856, the House of Lords stated (at **10.09**
para 22) that the indispensable requirement of public confidence in the administration of justice
requires higher standards today than was the case even a decade or two decades ago. What the
public was content to accept many years ago is not necessarily accepted in the world of today.

Appearance of bias: presumed bias

Where a judge has a direct personal interest, other than *de minimis*, in the outcome of a case, bias **10.10**
is presumed and disqualification is automatic. The fundamental principle is that a man may not
be judge in his own cause.

10.11 Such an interest will arise where the judge is a party to the action, or has a financial or proprietary interest in the outcome of the action. However, the principle is not limited to cases of pecuniary interest. The principle applies where the judge's decision would lead to promotion of a cause in which the judge was actively involved together with one of the parties (see *R v Bow Street Metropolitan Stipendiary Magistrate, ex parte Pinochet Ugarte (No 2)* [2000] 1 AC 119, where the judge was a director of Amnesty International, which took part in the proceedings). However, *Pinochet* was clearly an exceptional case, and Lord Browne-Wilkinson was at pains not to overstate the scope of relevant non-financial interests. Rejecting the suggestion that judges would be unable to sit in cases involving charities with whose work they were involved, he said that a judge should only be concerned to recuse himself, or disclose his position, where he took an active role as trustee or director of a charity closely allied to and acting with a party to the proceedings (at 134).

10.12 In *Meerabux v The Attorney-General of Belize* [2005] UKPC 9, [2005] 2 AC 513, Lord Hope, giving the opinion of the Privy Council, said that the decision in *Pinochet* 'appears, in retrospect, to have been a highly technical one' (at para 21). *Meerabux* concerned the judge of a tribunal, which had been convened to investigate complaints by the Bar Association of Belize against a judge. It was alleged that a presumption of bias had arisen because the judge was a member of the Bar Association, which brought the complaints. The Privy Council rejected the bias argument. Mere membership of an organization by which proceedings were brought would not automatically disqualify a member from sitting in the proceedings, but active involvement in the institution of the particular proceedings would.

10.13 The test is whether the outcome could realistically affect the judge's interest, allowing for a *de minimis* exception (*Locabail (UK) Ltd v Bayfield Properties Ltd* [2000] IRLR 96, paras 8–10). For example, if a judge has a small number of shares in a large company, and the sums at stake in the litigation are not so large that the litigation could affect the value of the shares or the dividend payable (*Locabail*, at para 8), the interest would be *de minimis* and would have no effect.

10.14 The relevant interest must be a direct interest of the judge's: see *Jones v DAS Legal Expenses Insurance Co Ltd* [2004] EWCA Civ 1071, [2004] IRLR 218, where no presumption of bias arose where the employment judge's husband was a barrister who received instructions from time to time from one of the parties. The judge's interest was only indirect and, in any event, even her husband's interest was in his own wellbeing, not in the fortunes of DAS.

10.15 Where a judge is a party to the action, or has a relevant interest in the proceedings, the judge is disqualified from hearing the case without any investigation of whether there was a likelihood or suspicion of bias.

Appearance of bias: other cases

10.16 The test for apparent bias is set out by the House of Lords in *Porter v Magill* [2001] UKHL 67, [2002] 2 AC 357, para 102 (Hope LJ), a case concerning alleged misconduct by councillors and an inference of apparent bias by the council auditor which approved the approach of the Court of Appeal in *Re Medicaments (No 2)* [2001] 1 WLR 700. The test requires that:

(a) the court must first ascertain all the circumstances which have a bearing on the suggestion that the judge was biased
(b) it must then ask whether those circumstances would lead a fair-minded and informed observer to conclude that there was a real possibility that the tribunal was biased.

10.17 The appearance of bias may arise from the nature of any connection between the tribunal members and anyone involved in the case; or the appearance of bias may arise from the way in which the tribunal members conduct themselves during the course of the hearing. The appearance of bias is judged from the standpoint of the fair-minded and informed observer whose impressive qualities are discussed at length by Lord Hope in *Helow v Secretary of State for the Home Department & Anor* [2008] 1 WLR 2416.

Material circumstances

What forms part of the material circumstances will of course depend on the facts of each **10.18** particular case.

In *Locabail (UK) Ltd v Bayfield Properties Ltd* [2000] IRLR 96, the Court of Appeal held that in **10.19** cases in the second category of apparent bias (as opposed to presumed bias) the reviewing court might properly inquire whether the judge knew of the matter alleged to undermine his impartiality, as ignorance would preclude a danger of bias.

Any explanation given by the judge may form part of the material circumstances. In *Re Medicaments* **10.20** *(No 2)* [2001] 1 WLR 700, para 86, the Court of Appeal said:

> The material circumstances will include any explanation given by the judge under review as to his knowledge or appreciation of those circumstances. Where that explanation is accepted by the claimant for review it can be treated as accurate. Where it is not accepted, it becomes one further matter to be considered from the viewpoint of a fair-minded observer. The court does not have to rule whether the explanation should be accepted or rejected. Rather it has to decide whether or not the fair-minded observer would consider that there was a real danger of bias notwithstanding the explanation advanced.

Fair-minded and informed observer

The fair-minded and informed observer is taken as being a person both with knowledge of the **10.21** litigation process, and with knowledge of the particular case. Other factors in ascertaining who is an informed observer are:

(a) The informed observer is 'not one who made his judgment after a brief visit to the court but was familiar with the detailed history of the proceedings and with the way cases of the present kind were tried' (*Arab Monetary Fund v Hashim (No 8)* The Times, 4 May 1993, (1994) 6 Admin LR 348). See also *Sengupta v Holmes* [2002] EWCA Civ 1104.

(b) The informed observer will be taken as being aware of the legal tradition and culture of the jurisdiction (*Taylor v Lawrence* [2003] QB 528, para 61). This entails awareness of the oath of office taken by judges to administer justice without fear or favour, and their ability to carry out that oath by reason of their training and experience (*Locabail (UK) Ltd v Bayfield Properties Ltd* [2000] IRLR 96, para 21).

(c) However, the informed observer is not to be taken to be wholly uncritical of the legal culture and system, and should be taken to be 'neither complacent nor unduly sensitive or suspicious' (*Lawal v Northern Spirit Ltd* [2003] UKHL 35, [2003] IRLR 538, paras 14 and 22).

In the specific context of the employment tribunal, it is irrelevant that any individual accused of **10.22** bias forms part of a panel of three members (despite some earlier views to the contrary). The following points should be noted:

(1) In *Jones v DAS Legal Expenses Insurance Co Ltd* [2004] EWCA Civ 1071, [2004] IRLR 218, para 28, the Court of Appeal held that it was a relevant circumstance that the tribunal was a panel of three. The charge of impartiality has to lie against the tribunal and this tribunal consisted not only of its judge but also of two independent wing members who were equal judges of the facts as the judge was. The Court of Appeal noted that their impartiality was not in question and their decision was unanimous. This may be taken to suggest that it will be harder to establish bias where one member of three is subject to the allegation of bias, than it would be to establish bias against a single judge.

(2) However, in the House of Lords in *Lawal* above it was said that the reasonable observer is likely to approach the matter on the basis that lay members look to the judge (in the EAT context) for guidance on the law, and can be expected to develop a fairly close relationship of trust and confidence with the judge (at para 21).

(3) In *Lodwick v Southwark LBC* [2004] EWCA Civ 306, [2004] IRLR 554 the fact that the judge was only one of three members all with an equal vote was said not to be a good reason for the judge to refuse to recuse himself. As the legally qualified and presiding member of the

tribunal, the judge's position was an important one, and any apparent bias was not nullified by the presence of two lay members (at para 20).

(4) It would appear, therefore, that despite the comments in *Jones v DAS*, an appearance of bias will not be dispelled by the fact that only one member of the tribunal is alleged to have shown bias, at least where that member is the judge.

Apparent bias: particular examples

10.23 In the employment tribunal questions of bias may arise more commonly than in the courts due to the composition of an employment tribunal. It is part of the very nature of the system that lay members will have business or professional interests outside their role as a tribunal member. Further, it is common for tribunals to be chaired by part-time judges who carry on practice as solicitors or barristers. These interests increase the chances of a case being listed in front of a member with some connection with one of the parties.

10.24 In *Locabail (UK) Ltd v Bayfield Properties Ltd* [2000] IRLR 96, the Court of Appeal, whilst acknowledging that each case must turn on an examination of all the material circumstances, gave some examples of the types of relationships which may or may not be likely to give rise to an appearance of bias:

(1) It was 'inconceivable' that an objection could be soundly based on the religion, ethnic or national origin, gender, age, class, means, or sexual orientation of the judge.

(2) Nor, ordinarily and without more, would an appearance of bias arise from the judge's:

   (a) social or educational or service or employment background or history, nor that of any member of the judge's family

   (b) previous political associations, membership of social or sporting or charitable bodies, or Masonic associations

   (c) previous judicial decisions or extra-curricular utterances (whether in textbooks, lectures, speeches, articles, interviews, reports, or responses to consultation papers)

   (d) previous receipt of instructions to act for or against any party, solicitor, or advocate engaged in a case before him

   (e) membership of the same Inn, circuit, local Law Society, or chambers

   (f) the fact that a judge, earlier in the same case or in a previous case, had commented adversely on a party or a witness, or found the evidence of a party or witness to be unreliable would not without more give rise to the appearance of bias.

(3) On the other hand, an appearance of bias may arise from the following circumstances (at para 25):

> By contrast, a real danger of bias might well be thought to arise if there were personal friendship or animosity between the judge and any member of the public involved in the case; or if the judge were closely acquainted with any member of the public involved in the case, particularly if the credibility of that individual could be significant in the decision of the case; or if, in a case where the credibility of any individual were an issue to be decided by the judge, he had in a previous case rejected the evidence of that person in such outspoken terms as to throw doubt on his ability to approach such person's evidence with an open mind on any later occasion; or if on any question at issue in the proceedings before him the judge had expressed views, particularly in the course of the hearing, in such extreme and unbalanced terms as to throw doubt on his ability to try the issue with an objective judicial mind ...; or if, for any other reason, there were real ground for doubting the ability of the judge to ignore extraneous considerations, prejudices and predilections and bring an objective judgment to bear on the issues before him.

Professional connections of judge

10.25 Traditionally it has been not uncommon for judges to have appearing before them members of the Bar and solicitors who are known to them (and with whom they may have been in chambers), without any concern as to bias.

10.26 Barristers in private practice are independent self-employed practitioners and do not have responsibility for, or (usually) detailed knowledge of, the affairs of other members of the same chambers (*Locabail* above, at para 20). The fact that a party is represented by a barrister who is from the same chambers as the judge or employment judge does not, of itself, give rise to an appearance of bias. See *Birmingham City Council v Yardley* [2004] EWCA Civ 1756 applying *Locabail* in the context of a recorder with counsel from his chambers appearing before him. Further, in *Smith v Kvaerner Cementation Foundations Ltd* [2006] EWCA Civ 242, [2007] 1 WLR 370, the Court of Appeal cited *Yardley* in finding that, ordinarily, the fact that a judicial officer was a barrister and was a member of the same chambers as one or both of the advocates did not prevent that judicial officer from hearing the case. However, it was pointed out, *obiter dicta*, by the Court of Appeal that the position may be different where one or more of the advocates is acting under a conditional fee agreement since, in those circumstances, the success or failure of that party may have an effect on the financial standing of the set of chambers as a whole.

In *Jones v DAS Legal Expenses Insurance Co Ltd* [2004] EWCA Civ 1071, [2004] IRLR 218, the **10.27** employment judge's husband was a barrister who received instructions from time to time from the respondent. The Court of Appeal rejected the presumption of bias on grounds that the judge did not herself have an interest in the outcome of the proceedings. The Court of Appeal also held that in the circumstances there was no apparent bias. The fair-minded and informed observer, proceeding on the basis that the judge knew in general how the employers' system of appointing barristers operated and that her husband was to some extent a beneficiary of it, would not conclude that the judge herself, still less the tribunal as the decision-making body, was biased.

The position of a solicitor as judge (or employment judge) is more difficult since, in contrast to **10.28** barristers in chambers, a solicitor in a partnership has a common financial interest with his partners. As a partner, the solicitor will owe duties to clients of whom he may personally know nothing (*Locabail* above, at para 20). The judge should consider whether there is any conflict of interest, which would have prevented him from acting against any party to the proceedings. However, the Court of Appeal rejected an inflexible rule that if there is such a conflict the judge must recuse himself. All the circumstances must be considered: *Locabail* above, at para 58.

An appearance of bias arose in *Cleveland Transit v Walton* EAT/578/91 from the fact that the em- **10.29** ployers had sought tenders from firms of solicitors to act as their legal advisers and one of those submitting an unsuccessful tender was the firm of which the employment judge was a senior partner.

The effect of a judge's former role as a partner in a firm of solicitors was considered in *BCCI v Ali* **10.30** (Ch D, 3 December 2001). Lawrence Collins J was assigned to determine costs sharing between employees involved in litigation against BCCI. An allegation of bias was made on the ground that the judge had been a partner in a firm of solicitors that had acted for BCCI's auditors in claims brought against the auditors by some of the employees in the instant proceedings. The judge refused to recuse himself. There was no presumption of bias: although the auditors might have an interest in the former employees being ordered to pay costs, that could not give a partner in the solicitors' firm representing them a financial interest in their success. In any event, as a *former* partner in that firm, it was clear that the judge could have no financial or other interest in the success or failure of the proceedings against the auditors. The judge also rejected the allegation of apparent bias: the auditors were not parties to the instant proceedings; the judge had not represented the auditors in the previous action by the employees and was no longer a partner in the firm that had represented them.

In *Howell v Lees Millais* [2007] EWCA Civ 720, one of the parties was a partner in a firm of soli- **10.31** citors. The judge had recently had unsuccessful negotiations to join the firm. The judge refused to recuse himself, but the Court of Appeal overturned his decision. However, the fact of the judge's contact with the firm was not the only factor that had given rise to the appearance of bias. The Court of Appeal attached weight to the judge's apparent irritation at the failure of the negotiations, and to the judge's intemperate conduct towards the firm during the recusal application. See also *Emerald Supplies Ltd v British Airways* [2015] EWHC 2201 (Ch), in which the same judge was to hear a case in which British Airways was the defendant, having previously made his own complaint about lost baggage to the chairman of British Airways. The judge recused himself for what he characterized as pragmatic reasons, rather than the alleged bias. This provided the backdrop for another

Part A Tribunal Procedure

165

bias challenge in the case of *Harb v Prince Abdul Aziz* [2016] EWCA Civ 556, in which the judge wrote a stingingly critical letter to the well-known head of chambers of the set at which two of the counsel appearing in the case were members. While on the facts bias was not established, the Court of Appeal was itself highly critical of the approach taken by the judge.

10.32 In *South Lanarkshire Council v Burns and Others* UKEATS/0040-42/12/BI, the EAT rejected an argument that the judge should have recused himself by reason of his daughter being a partner in the firm which represented one of the claimants, which fact was not disclosed. Of note was the fact that the judge's daughter did not have conduct of the proceedings or any involvement in the case, which was, in the event, insurance backed so that her firm would be paid whether or not the client won or lost in the case.

10.33 In *Singh v Glasgow University and Gusterson* UKEATS/0006/11 (Scotland), 10 July 2012 the claimant alleged that the tribunal was biased because one of the respondents was the chairman of the Judicial Appointments Board for Scotland. It was held by the EAT that the allegation of bias was fanciful as no fair-minded and well-informed bystander would think that a Scottish employment judge would be influenced by this fact.

Fee-paid judges (non-salaried)

10.34 Fee-paid judges sit part time, and are likely to be in practice as solicitors or barristers. This is likely to give rise to a greater risk that the fee-paid judge may have a connection with a party or a witness. The most recent terms and conditions of service for fee-paid judges (February 2013) provide that a fee-paid judge should not, as a general principle, sit as a judicial office holder or appear before a tribunal at a particular hearing if they are liable to be embarrassed in either capacity by doing so. They should not become involved in the preparation or representation of employment tribunal cases in any part of the region to which they have been assigned to sit. Finally, they are expected to refrain from any activity (including of a political nature) that would conflict with their judicial office or be seen to compromise their impartiality.

10.35 In *Lawal v Northern Spirit Ltd* (see para 10.09), apparent bias arose out of the fact that counsel appearing for one of the parties before the EAT sat as a part-time judge of the EAT, and had sat with one or more of the lay members in the past. Both the EAT and the Court of Appeal (by a majority) held that there was no apparent bias; the House of Lords held that there was an appearance of bias. The lay members are likely to look to the judge for guidance on the law, and to develop a relationship of trust and confidence with the judge. The informed observer would also be likely to consider the fact that a part-time judge of the employment tribunal cannot appear at all in the region in which he sits. The House of Lords directed that EAT practice should be assimilated to that in the employment tribunal by introducing a restriction on part-time judges appearing as counsel before a panel of the EAT consisting of one or two lay members with whom they had previously sat.

10.36 In *Peninsula Business Services and Another v Rees and Others* UKEAT/0333/08/RN (EAT 23 July 2009, Slade J), a part-time employment judge was a member of and employment specialist in a small Barnsley law firm, which took out an advertisement in the press denigrating non-solicitor employment consultants. Although the appellant was not named, it was a well-known national firm of such consultants. The EAT held that this constituted apparent bias adopting the *Porter v Magill* test of the fair-minded, informed observer.

Tribunal member having previously adjudicated on a case involving a party or representative

10.37 The mere fact that a judge, earlier in the same case or in a previous case, had commented adversely on a party or a witness, or found the evidence of a party or witness to be unreliable, would not without more found a sustainable claim of apparent bias (*Locabail* above, at para 25). This is the case even in circumstances where there are outstanding complaints against a tribunal member resulting from the conduct of previous litigation in which one or more of the parties were involved. Thus, in *Ansar v Lloyds TSB Bank plc* [2006] EWCA 1462, [2007] IRLR 211, the Court of Appeal approved the decision of an employment judge not to recuse himself from hearing a pre-hearing review in circumstances where he had previously heard litigation between the parties which had resulted in an appeal to the EAT and the making of complaints against the judge by one of the parties. See also *Henry v London Metropolitan University* EAT/0252/06, where the EAT refused the recusal of a lay member on the grounds that he had expressed a view on the live issue in the case during an earlier appeal in the same case. There must be something more which is of substance and which would lead the fair-minded and informed observer to conclude that there is a real possibility that the decision-maker who is impugned will not be able to bring an open mind and objective judgment to bear.

This principle also applies with at least as much force to previous adverse comments upon a party's **10.38** representative (*Lodwick v Southwark London Borough Council* [2004] EWCA Civ 306, [2004] ICR 884).

Tribunal having previously adjudicated on the same case

Rather unusually, in *Menzies Distribution Limited v Mendes* UKEAT/0497/13/JOJ UKEAT/0498/ **10.39** 13, the EAT was asked to determine whether a judge who had decided and given an oral determination that a claimant was disabled, but then mislaid the tape of the preliminary hearing so as to be unable to promulgate his reasons and then reheard the matter had acted in error. The EAT found that a fair-minded observer would consider that there was a real possibility that the employment judge could not consider the issue impartially second time around, but would be bound to be influenced by his earlier decision.

Judge's previous legislative role

In *Davidson v Scottish Ministers* [2004] UKHL 34, (2004) HRLR 34, however, the House of Lords **10.40** held that where a judge was required to rule on the meaning of legislation which he had previously been involved in drafting or promoting, there was a real risk of apparent bias. The informed observer would conclude that there was a real possibility that the judge would subconsciously strive to avoid a conclusion that undermined advice the judge had given to Parliament during the promotion of the legislation.

Connection between lay members and parties

Where a lay member has business connections with, or has been employed by one of the parties, **10.41** there may be a risk of the appearance of bias, and such connections should be disclosed to the parties at the outset of the proceedings. Further, pending or proposed applications by lay members for employment with a party may well give rise to the appearance of bias.

The *Medicaments* case (para 10.16) concerned the Restrictive Practices Court, which in common **10.42** with the employment tribunal has lay membership. One of the lay members applied for a job with the firm of economic consultants who were giving expert evidence for one of the parties in the case. The member disclosed the application to the President of the Restrictive Practices Court who notified the parties; the firm of economic consultants indicated that there were no vacancies available; and the member undertook initially not to pursue an application until after the trial, and then not to do so until two years after trial. The Court of Appeal held that the fair-minded observer may nevertheless be concerned that the member may still harbour hopes of working for the consultants, and that this may affect her ability to make an impartial appraisal of the expert evidence. In *London Underground v Ayanbadejo* EAT/1160/97, a lay member of the tribunal had worked for, and for a time been in dispute with, a predecessor of the employers, but did not disclose the connection. The EAT made clear that the fact should have been disclosed but was not prepared to overturn the decision ultimately reached.

In *Gillies v Secretary of State for Work and Pensions* [2006] UKHL 2, [2006] ICR 267 the House of **10.43** Lords considered the membership of the Disability Appeal Tribunal, which, like the employment tribunals and the EAT, has a legally qualified judge and two wing members. One of the members of the Disability Appeal Tribunal is a 'medical member' who has medical expertise. The claimant alleged that there was the appearance of bias on the part of the medical member of the panel given that that member was a doctor and had spent many years providing reports as an examining practitioner for the Benefits Agency. The House of Lords held that there was no appearance of bias and that the reasonable and right minded observer would conclude that the medical member would approach the evidence objectively and, in the light of her own knowledge and expertise, would not prefer the evidence of the examining medical practitioner to the other available evidence simply because of that member's relationship with the Benefits Agency.

10.44 The appearance of bias may arise from a wide variety of contacts between tribunal members and the parties. In *University College Swansea v Cornelius* [1988] ICR 735, EAT, for example, a lay member was the mother-in-law of one of the respondents (remarkably, a fact which did not come to light until after judgment in the claim). In *Source Publications v Ellison* EAT/872/83, apparent bias arose from the fact that a member of the tribunal had recently been in dispute with the employers about a bill.

10.45 The EAT held there to be an appearance of bias in *Halford v Sharples* [1992] ICR 146, where a lay member had been chosen for the case which involved the Assistant Chief Constable of Merseyside Police because of his relevant experience, in that he was employed by another police force as an equal opportunities officer. He had interviews with members of that force who were involved in the instant proceedings, and had knowledge of a number of officers involved in the case.

10.46 On the other hand, in *ASI v Glass Processing Ltd*, 27 April 1999, CA, the employment tribunal refused to review a decision on the ground that having lost, the employer found that one of the lay members knew the respondent. The point could have been taken before but was not so taken; no satisfactory explanation was given for the review application being long out of time; the objection was misconceived because the connection was tenuous and did not give rise to a real danger of bias.

10.47 In *Colback v Ena Ferguson* [2001] EWCA Civ 1027, although it was said that it had been unwise for two lay members of a tribunal to accept a lift in a taxi with one of the parties, it had not created a real risk or danger of bias. In *British Car Auctions Ltd v Adams* UKEAT/0159/12, 23 April 2013, a lay member's failure to disclose his connections with one of the parties when another lay member had disclosed a lesser connection was considered and it was held by the EAT that it would cause a fair-minded observer to think that there was a real risk that the non-disclosing lay member was consciously hiding those connections and conclude that there was a real possibility that the tribunal was biased. At the start of the hearing, the employment judge told the parties that one of the lay members had played a part in instructing the respondent's counsel in an earlier case, but the parties raised no objection and the hearing proceeded. Despite this, the other lay member did not reveal that he lived close to the respondent's site, that his son worked there and that, although he did not know the claimant, he did know another employee who had been named in the ET1 and in the response. He asserted that he had informed the employment judge; the EAT concluded that he had not.

10.48 In *Hamilton v GMB (Northern Region)* [2007] IRLR 391, the EAT held that a tribunal member should have stood down from the hearing of a claim involving the legality of the GMB's equal pay strategy. The fact that she had previously held a senior position in a union with an identical policy was sufficient to justify a finding of apparent bias. The court found that a reasonable person might conclude that she would have had a natural desire to uphold the legality of that policy. In *City & County of Swansea v Honey* EAT/0030/08/RN, the EAT allowed a bias appeal where a wing member was a union member who had been involved in a campaign against the employer and had a negative view of the employer council as a whole.

C. IMPROPER CONDUCT AND PROCEDURAL IRREGULARITIES

10.49 Both Art 6 of the ECHR and the common law concept of natural justice require a tribunal to afford parties a fair hearing. The requirements of a fair hearing are not fixed, but will depend on the circumstances of each case. Essential elements are the right to be heard on the issues in the case, and the right to be placed on an equal footing with the other parties.

The tribunal's overriding objective and procedural rules are designed to achieve a fair trial for all **10.50** parties. Interim decisions of the tribunal and the conduct of the tribunal at the hearing may give rise to a concern that a party has been denied a fair trial. A wide range of case management decisions both prior to and at the hearing may lead to an allegation that a party has been deprived of a fair trial: for example a refusal to allow an amendment, or the late admission, or refusal to admit evidence (see eg *Yellow Pages Ltd v Garton* EAT/0375/02). Many of these situations have been dealt with already in this chapter. This section considers specifically cases where the conduct of the tribunal at the hearing may be said to be improper or procedurally irregular so as deny a party a fair hearing, and the related issue of cases where the conduct of the tribunal at the hearing may give rise to the appearance of bias.

Interventions by the tribunal

The tribunal must take care to ensure in its conduct of the proceedings that all parties feel that they **10.51** have the opportunity to bring forward their case, and the tribunal must refrain from any expression which may appear partial. The tribunal must avoid conducting the hearing in a manner that indicates a closed mind.

Avoidance of immoderate language and personal comment

In *Tchoula v Netto Foodstores Ltd* EAT/1378/98, the EAT stressed that the tribunal should avoid **10.52** making and expressing judgments on the claimant in person. The tribunal should in particular avoid any appearance of being patronizing towards a litigant in person when issues of law were being considered. In *Diem v Crystal Services plc* UKEAT/0398/05, the employment judge, in the course of enquiring whether the claimant was seeking to depart from her case, questioned the claimant about her skin colour and made comparisons between his own skin colour and hers. The EAT found that the judge's enquiry would lead a fair-minded observer to conclude that there was a real possibility of unconscious bias on the part of the judge. In *Fraser v University and College Union* UKEAT/0266/14/DM, the claimant brought proceedings against his union for failing to provide support to him in his dispute with his employer, which he said was an act of race discrimination. During the full hearing, a lay member of the tribunal asked the claimant why he had not told the union that he thought that it was being discriminatory, to which he answered that he was seeking to be conciliatory. The member then asked him, 'So you are Mr Nice Guy, are you?'. The claimant relied on this in making an application to the tribunal to recuse itself from hearing the union's costs application after his claims of discrimination were dismissed by a majority. The EAT upheld his appeal, the ET having refused to recuse itself, again by a majority. The comments were deemed to be over the line in this instance and gave rise to the appearance of bias.

The importance of courtesy being shown by a tribunal was stressed by the EAT in *Laher v London* **10.53** *Borough of Hammersmith & Fulham* EAT/215/91. Immoderate or intemperate language should be avoided by tribunals, according to the EAT in *Kennedy v Metropolitan Police Commissioner*, The Times, 8 November 1990. Wood J commented that 'what could be tolerated by the Bar could give the wrong impression [of bias] to a layman'.

The tribunal must maintain a particularly difficult balance where one party is unrepresented. On **10.54** the one hand, it is proper for the judge to assist an unrepresented party to ensure that he brings out his case; on the other hand, the judge must not act in such a way as to allow the appearance of bias, or to restrict the other party in the conduct of its case. This point was stressed in *Riverside Restaurants Ltd (t/a Harry Ramsden) v Tremayne* EAT/1168/95.

Tribunal cross-examining a party or witness

While it is entirely usual for a tribunal to ask questions of a party or a party's witness, usually **10.54A** after evidence in chief and cross-examination, those questions ought not to amount to cross-examination which is a classic example of an inappropriate intervention. For example, in *Nawaz v Docklands Buses Limited* UKEAT/0104/15/DM, the judge made a number of interventions which were held to amount to cross-examination of the claimant and his witnesses. In particular, Singh J

Part A Tribunal Procedure

was concerned that the questions posed in the middle of the cross-examination of the claimant by the respondent's barrister were 'not asked by way of open questions to elicit and clarify' evidence but 'to put points to him and with which he would not necessarily agree but with a view to trying to persuade him that he should agree'. Singh J reminded the court that: 'That is what advocates do; it is not what Tribunals should do'.

Statements indicating predisposition against a party

10.55 Comments made by the employment judge may give rise to an appearance of bias. In *Harada Ltd (t/a Chequepoint UK Ltd) v Turner (No 1)* [2001] EWCA Civ 599, the Court of Appeal held that there was a real danger that the judge would not approach the case with an open mind in the light of comments made by him at the beginning of the hearing that the respondent did not come to the hearing with a clean slate, and criticisms of the respondent's conduct of other proceedings which had been before the same tribunal. In *Breeze Benton Solicitors v Weddell* UKEAT/0873/03, the judge listed to hear a nine-day case against the respondent firm had, a year previously, heard a case involving the same respondent, where he was alleged to have made disparaging remarks about the partner who represented the respondent—the respondent had subsequently written to complain to the regional chairman and to the Lord Chancellor's Department, although the complaints had not been pursued. Even though the disparaging remarks were disputed, the EAT held that there was a real possibility of bias, and the chairman should have recused himself. Accordingly, the case was remitted for rehearing by a different tribunal. However, the significance in *Breeze Benton* attached to the mere fact of the former complaint has been disapproved in *Ansar v Lloyds TSB Bank plc* [2006] EWCA 1462, [2007] IRLR 211.

Statements indicating prejudgment of the issues

10.56 In many cases, the tribunal, through the judge, may make comments indicating the difficulties which a party may face on one or more of the issues. It is inevitable that a tribunal will react to what is put before it, and the judge is entitled to try to obtain answers from the party to points which trouble the judge as being matters of great relevance: *BLP UK Ltd v Marsh* [2003] EWCA Civ 132. Whilst the judge cannot be expected to sit in silence through the hearing (and in most cases parties would not be assisted by the judge keeping his concerns to himself), care must be taken to avoid the appearance of prejudgment.

10.57 Allegations of prejudgment often arise where the tribunal has sought to encourage the parties to settle. Such encouragement is quite common in practice, and in giving such encouragement the tribunal may indicate its preliminary views of the case based on the evidence heard thus far. There are benefits to such an approach in terms of achieving amicable resolution for the parties, a saving of costs, and a saving of tribunal time. However, such comments can leave the lingering suspicion with one or more of the parties that tribunal members have already made up their minds on the issue.

10.58 There is no impropriety in a tribunal encouraging the parties to settle; nor is there anything wrong in principle with the tribunal expressing a provisional view on the case for the purposes of assisting the parties: *Jiminez v London Borough of Southwark* [2003] IRLR 477; *Harada Ltd (t/a Chequepoint UK Ltd) v Turner (No 1)* [2001] EWCA Civ 599; *AM (Fair Hearing) Sudan* [2015] UKUT 656 (IAC).

10.59 In *Harada*, Pill LJ stated that judges may make remarks at the beginning or in the course of hearings which indicate the difficulties a party faces upon one or more of the points at issue. Provided a closed mind is not shown, such comments are permissible. Such comments from the bench are at the very heart of the adversarial procedure by way of oral hearing. It enables the party to focus on the point and to make such submissions as he properly can. In principle there is nothing wrong with a judge, having explored the difficulties on the facts or legal issues of the case with counsel, giving an opportunity for settlement discussions. Pill LJ's comments were cited and followed in *Jiminez*.

Where comments are made as to the merits of the case while the case is ongoing, the key distinction, emphasized by *Harada* and *Jiminez*, is between the expression of a provisional view, and the expression of a concluded view or closed mind. Whether any particular statement by the tribunal falls on one side of the line will depend on the circumstances of the case, the manner in which the statement is made, and the stage of the hearing at which the statement is made. **10.60**

If a judge expresses a view too forcefully, or too early, or without making clear that the view is provisional, there is a risk that the appellate court may decide that the tribunal's mind was closed. So, for example: **10.61**

(a) In *Peter Simper & Co Ltd v Cooke* [1986] IRLR 19, unqualified remarks hostile to the employer's case were made by the judge during the course of cross-examination of the employee on the opening day, before the employer had led any evidence. The EAT held that this was not the appropriate time for such strongly expressed views.

(b) Similarly, in *Graham v Ivan Boardley* EAT/444/84, when, at the end of the examination in chief of the second witness, the tribunal announced that it was completely satisfied that a redundancy situation existed. The EAT thought that it could not have formed a concluded view of fairness at this stage, and remitted the case to another tribunal for rehearing.

(c) A rehearing was also ordered in *Mortimer v Reading Windings Ltd* [1977] ICR 511, where the judge, in introducing the case, said: 'Why are we here today, because you have obviously resigned'. He also continually pushed the claimant to finish his case.

(d) In *Chris Project v Hutt* UKEATS/0065/06, before any evidence was called the employment judge made a comment that the appellant employer faced an uphill struggle with its case. As a result of the comment the employer's lay representative conceded that the employee had been unfairly dismissed. The EAT held that the tribunal had appeared to be biased by giving the impression that the case had been prejudged; further the comment was such that an observer would have considered that it put undue pressure on the employer's representative to refrain from advancing the defence.

(e) In *Ezsias v North Glamorgan NHS Trust* [2007] EWCA Civ 330, (2007) 104(12) LSG 34, the Court of Appeal held that the fact that the employment judge had expressed a view of the claimant's prospects in concluded terms at an earlier hearing led to an appearance of bias. In the circumstances it was reasonable for a fair-minded and informed observer to take the view that the judge, at the second hearing, had a closed mind as to the claimant's prospects of success.

(f) In contrast, in *Jiminez* the judge's views were expressly said to be provisional, and at a stage when the bulk of the evidence had been heard.

(g) In *Advance Security UK Limited v Musa* UKEAT/0611/07, the tribunal had stated, immediately after hearing closing submissions, that they expected to reach their decision within twenty minutes. The EAT rejected an argument that this was unfair. In the circumstances, where the tribunal had heard only one day of evidence, an indication that a decision would or might be made in twenty minutes would not show to an impartial observer that the tribunal may have been treating unfairly one party or the other.

(h) In *Oni v NHS Leicester City (formerly Leicester City Primary Care Trust)* [2013] ICR 91, EAT, the tribunal, before any application for costs had been made by the respondent in the proceedings, expressed the view that: 'In our view, not only was the bringing of the various claims unreasonable but the manner in which they have been conducted was also unreasonable'. The respondent subsequently (and unsurprisingly) applied for costs and was awarded the whole of its costs. The EAT held that the tribunal had the threshold test for costs (under the old rules) in mind and held a concluded view and should, accordingly, have recused itself on the ground that there was a real possibility that it had prejudged the question of costs.

Remarks made after the conclusion of the hearing may be seen in a different light. In *Greenway Harrison Ltd v Wiles* [1994] IRLR 380, the judge was alleged to have said 'that will teach them not to settle when I tell them'. The EAT held that, even if this had been said, it was after the conclusion of the proceedings and would not amount to bias since it was a casual remark made at the conclusion of the hearing and not during the tribunal's deliberations. **10.62**

10.63 The EAT will look at the evidence as to the handling of the proceedings by the judge in the context of the proceedings as a whole, and of the issues raised by the parties; see, for example, *Anthony v Governors of Hillcrest School* EAT/1193/00, where comments from the judge which on their own suggested that he had prejudged the claimant's case did not give rise to the appearance of bias when seen in the context of the four-day hearing as a whole.

Reliance on matters not canvassed at the hearing

10.64 The tribunal should exercise caution if it wishes to consider matters not raised before it by the parties, in the pleadings, witness statements, and submissions. There are two relevant principles:

(1) The tribunal has jurisdiction to determine issues raised in the claim form (and any amendment allowed to the claim form). It does not have jurisdiction to determine a complaint which is not included in the claim form: *Chapman v Simon* [1994] IRLR 124, CA.

(2) Even if a particular claim falls within the tribunal's jurisdiction, the right to a fair hearing requires notice to be given to the parties of all material matters of fact and law upon which the tribunal intends to rely.

10.65 In *Hereford & Worcester County Council v Neale* [1986] IRLR 168, 175, Ralph Gibson LJ said that an employment tribunal should not rely on matters which occur to it *after* the hearing and which have not been mentioned or treated as relevant without the party against whom the point is raised having an opportunity to deal with it, unless the tribunal could be entirely sure that the point is so clear that the party could not make any useful comment or explanation. (See to similar effect *Laurie v Holloway* [1994] ICR 32; *British Gas v McCaull* [2001] IRLR 60, EAT; *Bradford Hospital NHS Trust v Al-Shabib* [2003] IRLR 4, EAT.) If, after the hearing and before reaching its judgment, the tribunal becomes concerned by a new point, it should recall the parties and give them the opportunity for further submissions on the point: *Vauxhall Motors Ltd v Ghafoor* [1993] ICR 376.

10.66 The steps that the tribunal must take to give the parties the opportunity to be heard on the new point will depend on the nature of the point, and its significance to the case as a whole. In some cases, it may be sufficient for the tribunal to give the parties the opportunity to submit further written submissions on the point, for example if the tribunal wants submissions on a new legal authority. However, where the tribunal's point is more fundamental, and may affect the evidence, which the parties would want to put before the tribunal, the tribunal should reconvene a hearing. In *Easter v Governing Body of Notre Dame High School* UKEAT/0615/04, the tribunal during its deliberations rejected gross misconduct as the reason for dismissal (which had been the reason advanced by the employer throughout) but decided instead that the reason was some other substantial reason. It was held by the EAT that it was insufficient simply to invite written submissions on this new reason: the hearing should have been reconvened and the parties given the opportunity to submit more evidence.

10.67 For further cases concerning the denial of opportunity to make representations see *Murphy v Epsom College* [1984] IRLR 271; *Ellis v Ministry of Defence* [1985] ICR 257; and *Hotson v Wisbech Conservative Club* [1984] IRLR 422. For more recent examples see also *Tarbuck v Sainsbury's Supermarkets Ltd* [2006] IRLR 184, para 62 and *Lewis v HSBC Bank plc* [2006] UKEAT 0364/06. More recently, in *Sheibani v Elan & Co LLP* UKEAT/0133/12, 13 July 2012, the EAT (Langstaff P) emphasized that where a matter is likely to be decisive then it is all the more important that the parties are alerted in clear terms of the importance the tribunal attaches to it. The tribunal's decision to reject the claimant's complaints of unfair dismissal and breach of contract, together with a counterclaim, on the basis of illegality, was overturned on appeal as neither the question of illegality nor the authorities to which the tribunal ultimately referred had been raised with the parties in the course of the hearing, hence no submissions had been made. This was, according to the EAT, not merely an irregularity but a breach of natural justice.

10.68 None of the above will, however, affect the general principle that appeals that are purely academic will not be entertained, for example if there is some other 'knock-out blow' which means that notwithstanding the reliance on matters not canvassed at the hearing, the outcome would have been just the same.

New evidence raised late in the hearing

A party may be denied a fair hearing if a matter is raised at the hearing in a way that does not give the party proper opportunity to deal with it. In *Panama v London Borough of Hackney* [2003] EWCA Civ 273, [2003] IRLR 278, evidence concerning fraud on the part of the claimant, which the tribunal later found relevant to the question of compensation, was not raised for the first time until cross-examination of the claimant. The Court of Appeal approved a statement by the EAT in *Hotson* that once dishonesty is introduced into a case, the relevant allegation has to be put with sufficient formality and at an early enough stage to provide a full opportunity for answer. It is suggested that the same principle should apply whenever new evidence, which is highly relevant to the tribunal's decision comes to light late in the hearing. The tribunal should ensure that the parties are given adequate opportunity to deal with the new evidence even if that means considering an adjournment. **10.69**

Reliance by the tribunal on authorities not canvassed with the parties

In *Albion Hotel (Freshwater) Ltd v Maia e Silva* [2002] IRLR 200, EAT, the employment tribunal had erred in relying on authorities which had not been cited by the parties' advocates. Where an employment tribunal considers that an authority is relevant, significant, and material to its decision, but the parties have not referred to it, the tribunal should refer that authority to the parties and invite their submissions before concluding its decision. Failure to do so may amount to a breach of natural justice and of the right to a fair hearing. See *Sheibani* (para 10.67). **10.70**

The limits of this principle must be recognized. The mere fact that a tribunal relies in its decision on authorities that have not been cited at the hearing does not give an automatic right of appeal. The Court of Appeal in *Stanley Cole Wainfleet Ltd v Sheridan* [2003] EWCA Civ 1046, [2003] IRLR 885 identified two elements before a decision can be said to be unfair by reason of failure to draw authority to the parties' attention: **10.71**

(1) The authority must be central to the tribunal's decision, in the sense of 'relevant, significant and material'. Ward LJ said (at para 32):

> the authority must alter or affect the way the issues have been addressed to a significant extent so that it truly can be said by a fair-minded observer that the case was decided in a way which could not have been anticipated by a party fixed with such knowledge of the law and procedure as it would be reasonable to attribute to him in all the circumstances.

(2) It must be shown that a material injustice has resulted. The hearing will not have been unfair if it causes no substantial prejudice to the party complaining.

Reliance by tribunal on information given by a third party

The EAT has provided guidelines to tribunals as to the approach to be adopted when third parties give the tribunal information. In *Begraj and Another v Heer Manak Solicitors and Others* UKEAT/0496/13/BA, police officers approached the judge part way through a lengthy hearing and provided information prejudicial to a party and subsequently asked her, in the presence of the regional judge, not to disclose the information. She did not. When an application for recusal was made after this became known (the judge having a week later asked to see legal representatives in private) she acceded to that application. The decision to recuse was challenged on appeal, which appeal was dismissed. The following guidance was given: **10.72**

(1) Where a third party proffers information or opinion about the merits of a case, or the parties in it, to a tribunal, without being invited to do so, the parties should be made aware of what has happened without delay. This plainly does not cover a request by a third party for information about the arrangements for the case (such as when a case is likely to be heard), but the

principle of judicial independence is such that it applies however influential or authoritative the communicant appears to be.

(2) There may be many good reasons for third parties to communicate with a tribunal, not about the substance of the case, but in respect of issues surrounding it which are of no direct relevance to the decision. In particular, the police or security services, security guards, and others generally responsible for the security and welfare of those participating in a tribunal may, for instance, wish to give advice, or warn of particular risks. It may well be self-defeating for such information to be revealed outside the members of the tribunal. Nothing in this judgment should affect communications relating to the administration of the case, and the security of those concerned in it. Judges should expect to be warned of risk even if that is said to arise from one party: the parties should expect judges to put that information to one side when reaching a decision upon the merits of the claim before it, as Judges are accustomed to doing. No adverse inference should emerge from keeping such communications quiet.

(3) An employment tribunal judge or lay member, however inexperienced they may be, is fulfilling a judicial role. Their impartiality is critical. It is inextricably linked with their independence from state or other third party interference. A judge approached by those apparently in authority should be clear as to the purpose of the approach, and should rebuff (and if appropriate report) any which appears to interfere with that independence.

(4) If in any doubt, the judge should be free to raise a concern with more senior Judges and discuss the issue with them. As with advice about administrative arrangements and security, the purpose of seeking and being given any advice from those consultees does not relate to the merits of the case and a judge is not to be thought to be acting improperly to be seeking it and considering it, when thinking through what the principles of open justice, fair trial, impartiality, independence, integrity, propriety, and equality require.

(5) There may sometimes be information which one party, or another on their behalf, wishes to give whilst requesting that it remains confidential to the decision-maker(s). Generally, the tribunal cannot accept information on such terms.

(6) There are some exceptions to (5) which are provided for by rule and by statute—for instance, in cases involving national security.

(7) There may be other exceptions to (5), such as those in which there may be a serious risk to the security of the individual (such as in cases where there are credible grounds for thinking there may have been domestic violence, or slavery) or where revelation would be a significant breach of the privacy to which that party may be entitled (eg where to reveal full medical records may reveal embarrassing personal details which have no direct relevance to the case). These may require a balance to be struck between the potential for interference with the fundamental rights involved and the requirements of transparent justice, itself a fundamental right.

(8) However, in cases such as those in (5) and (7) there should usually be little difficulty in informing the parties that an approach has been made, and/or that information has been received, together with a request to keep it confidential, which the tribunal proposes for good reason to honour. If that is done, then if the tribunal gives an assurance that the information imparted is not directly relevant to the issues it has to determine this must generally be respected, and will not give rise to any question of recusal.

(9) Finally, the guidance above is merely that: just guidance. It cannot hope to prescribe for all the many circumstances which may unexpectedly occur. Their applicability will depend heavily upon the particular circumstances. That said, I do not think Judges will go far wrong if they ask how they would wish to be treated if they were in the position of either of the parties, and act accordingly.

Use by members of industrial experience

10.73 The requirements of natural justice may also come into conflict with the desirability of the use by the lay members of their industrial experience. In *Hammington v Berker Sportcraft Ltd* [1980] ICR 248, a claimant complained that a lay member had used his personal knowledge in reaching a conclusion on compensation, and had thus not confined himself to the evidence placed before the employment tribunal. The EAT stated that if the lay member was minded to do this, it was not only necessary to indicate to the parties that the tribunal member was a specialist in the field, but also to bring facts known by him to the attention of the parties, so they could deal with them by calling other evidence if necessary.

This approach was reiterated in *Halford v Sharples* [1992] ICR 146, where it was held that it was **10.74** improper for lay members to make investigations of their own into a case, since it was impossible for either party to know the circumstances on which their decision was based. It was important that the findings of fact were based on the evidence heard by the tribunal, and not on investigations carried out by the members themselves. Here, a lay member had been chosen for the case, which involved the Assistant Chief Constable of Merseyside Police, because of his relevant experience, in that he was employed by another police force as an equal opportunities officer and he had interviews with members of that force who were involved in the instant proceedings.

Tribunal member asleep

The parties may be denied a fair hearing where a member of the tribunal falls asleep, or other- **10.75** wise fails to pay attention to the hearing. See, for example, *Whitehart v Raymond Thompson Ltd* EAT/910/83; *Red Bank Manufacturing Co Ltd v Meadows* [1992] ICR 204, EAT; and *Kudrath v Ministry of Defence* EAT/422/97 (where the EAT criticized the employment judge's practice of closing his eyes to indicate that an advocate was not being persuasive). A hearing by a tribunal which includes a member who has been drinking alcohol to the extent that he appeared to fall asleep and not to be concentrating on the case does not give the appearance of the fair hearing to which every party is entitled. Public confidence in the administration of justice would be damaged if the court took the view that such behaviour by a member of an employment tribunal did not matter: *Stansbury v Datapulse plc* [2003] EWCA Civ 1951, [2004] IRLR 466. In *Fordyce v Hammersmith & Fulham Conservative Association* [2006] UKEAT 0390/05, the parties raised the issue with the tribunal that one of the wing members appeared to be asleep but agreed to continue with the hearing. The wing member appeared to resume sleeping but the issue was not raised again by either of the parties. The losing party appealed and a rehearing was ordered. It was emphasized by the EAT that the decision of the tribunal was a decision of all three members and where one of the members was asleep, that member could not play a full part in the decision-making process.

D. RAISING AN ALLEGATION OF BIAS OR PROCEDURAL IMPROPRIETY

Issues of bias or unfairness in the conduct of the hearing may arise during the course of the hearing **10.76** itself, or they may arise after the tribunal has given its decision. If they are raised before the tribunal decision, the tribunal has the power to recuse itself and to direct that the proceedings should be re-heard before a differently constituted tribunal. If raised after the decision, the allegations may form the basis of an appeal, it having been made clear by the EAT in *Papajak v Intelligo Group Limited and Others* UKEAT/0124/12/JOJ that allegations of bias should not be dealt with by way of an application for review or reconsideration. There is conflicting case law as to the extent to which such allegations should be raised during the hearing.

The tribunal's power to recuse itself

It is clear that the tribunal has power to recuse itself and to order a rehearing by a differently con- **10.77** stituted tribunal: see *Charman v Palmers Scaffolding Ltd* [1979] ICR 335, where the EAT held that, although there was no specific reference to rehearings in the ETR 1993, the power fell within the tribunal's general power to give directions on any matter arising in connection with the proceedings and to regulate its own procedure. However, where a tribunal finds that the principle of judicial impartiality has been breached it must recuse itself. In this regard the power is exercised in a different manner to other case management decisions. The tribunal cannot decide to continue with the hearing weighing all the considerations in the balance (see *AWG Group Limited v Morrison* [2006] EWCA Civ 6, [2006] 1 WLR 1163).

Disclosure by the tribunal and waiver by the parties

10.78 Judges, chairmen, and tribunal members are under a duty to raise matters which may disqualify them from hearing a particular case. The Court of Appeal in *Locabail (UK) Ltd v Bayfield Properties Ltd* [2000] IRLR 96 stated that, in cases of personal embarrassment or automatic disqualification, the judge should recuse himself at the earliest possible stage; in any other case, where a judge became aware of a matter which could give rise to a real danger of bias, he should disclose this to the parties as soon as possible.

10.79 The party affected then has the opportunity to ask for the judge to recuse himself. A party could waive a right to call for a judge to be disqualified provided the waiver was clear and unequivocal and is given in full knowledge of the relevant facts (*Pinochet* [2000] 1 AC 119, 137 (Lord Browne-Wilkinson)). Where, following appropriate disclosure by the judge, no objection was taken to his hearing the case, no subsequent complaint of bias could be made in respect of the matter disclosed (see *Locabail* above, at paras 15 and 20; and see also *Adamson v Swansea University* UKEAT/0486/09/ZT). A party may waive any right to complain of presumed bias or apparent bias (*Jones v DAS* [2004] EWCA Civ 1071, [2004] IRLR 218, para 30). However, in circumstances where a party has not been made aware of all the relevant information, an apparent waiver of the right to object will not amount to a proper waiver (see *Smith v Kvaerner Cementation Foundations Ltd* [2006] EWCA Civ 242, [2007] IWLR 370). In the *Kvaerner* case, the party had not been made aware of how long it would take for a new trial date to be obtained and counsel acting for the party had sought to influence the decision of the party by making reference to the costs which would be thrown away.

10.80 Knowledge of the full facts does not mean that every single fact has to be known in order for a waiver to be effective. In *Bhardwaj v First Division Association* [2016] EWCA Civ 800, the claimant's appeal on grounds of bias failed before the EAT and before the Court of Appeal. The appeal proceeded on the basis that there was an appearance of bias arising from the fact that during the course of proceedings one of the respondents was appointed as a lay member in the region hearing the case. During the employment tribunal hearing, the claimant was told of this fact but agreed to proceed. She later argued on appeal that there had been no valid waiver, as she had not been informed of material facts. The employment judge had disclosed what he knew, but there were various matters of which he was not aware. Rimer LJ reviewed the authorities referred to in para 10.76 above. He attached weight to the point made in *Locabail* that the extent of disclosure that is appropriate depends on the stage the matter has reached. Before a hearing has begun the judge should enquire into the full facts, if ascertainable. However, if the issue comes to light during the hearing it is sufficient that the judge discloses what he knows. The reason for the lower standard is that it is generally undesirable that hearings should be aborted unless the reality or appearance of justice requires it. Rimer LJ also attached weight to the common sense point that if the claimant considered she needed more information than the employment judge had disclosed, she could have asked for it. Rimer LJ also rejected an argument that the claimant had been influenced by costs considerations; he found that she had given

> a free and unpressured decision, one primarily influenced by the investment to date of her own funds that she made in the proceedings. I well understand how that consideration would have weighed heavily with her—and how, in the event, it carried the day. As the EAT said, it did not, however, prevent her decision being a free and fully informed one.

Guidance on disclosure

10.81 In *Jones v DAS* the Court of Appeal gave the following guidance (at para 35):

(i) If there is any real as opposed to fanciful chance of objection being taken by that fair-minded spectator, the first step is to ascertain whether or not another judge is available to hear the matter. It is obviously better to transfer the matter than risk a complaint of bias. The judge should make every effort in the time available to clarify what his interest is which gives rise to this conflict so that the full facts can be placed before the parties.

(ii) Some time should be taken to prepare whatever explanation is to be given to the parties and, if one is really troubled, perhaps even to make a note of what one will say.

(iii) Because thoughts that the court may have been biased can become festering sores for the disappointed litigants, it is vital that the judge's explanation be mechanically recorded or carefully noted where that facility is not available. That will avoid the kind of controversy about what was or was not said which has bedevilled this case.

(iv) A full explanation must be given to the parties. That explanation should detail exactly what matters are within the judge's knowledge which give rise to a possible conflict of interest. The judge must be punctilious in setting out all material matters known to him. Secondly, an explanation should be given as to why the problem had only arisen so late in the day. The parties deserve also to be told whether it would be possible to move the case to another judge that day.

(v) The options open to the parties should be explained in detail. Those options are, of course, to consent to the judge hearing the matter, the consequence being that the parties will thereafter be likely to be held to have lost their right to object. The other option is to apply to the judge to recuse himself. The parties should be told it is their right to object, that the court will not take it amiss if the right is exercised and that the judge will decide having heard the submissions. They should be told what will happen next. If the court decides the case can proceed, it will proceed. If on the other hand the judge decides he will have to stand down, the parties should be told in advance of the likely dates on which the matter may be relisted.

(vi) The parties should always be told that time will be afforded to reflect before electing. That should be made clear even where both parties are represented. If there is a litigant in person the better practice may be to rise for five minutes. The litigant in person can be directed to the Citizens Advice Bureau if that service is available and if he wishes to avail of it. If the litigant feels he needs more help, he can be directed to the chief clerk and/or the listing officer. Since this is a problem created by the court, the court has to do its best to assist in resolving it.

In giving this guidance, the Court of Appeal emphasized that it was guidance, and not a definitive **10.82** checklist, and may not be applicable in every case. For an example of the guidance in action, see *Adamson v Swansea University* UKEAT/0486/09/ZT (para 10.79).

Dangers of inappropriate recusal

Whilst the recent trend may have been towards fuller disclosure in order to avoid the risk of allegations of bias, there is potential injustice in a tribunal acceding too readily to a request for a rehearing before a differently constituted tribunal. A rehearing will cause the parties additional costs and the further delay may affect the reliability of the evidence when the case is reheard. Particularly where the application for recusal arises out of conduct at the hearing, there is a risk that a party may manipulate the procedure in order to achieve a change to what he perceives may be a more favourable tribunal. There is a danger in complaints of bias or impropriety becoming 'self-fulfilling'. The Court of Appeal in *Dobbs v Triodos Bank NV* [2005] EWCA Civ 468 warned against judges too readily recusing themselves in the face of criticism (para 7 (Chadwick LJ)): **10.83**

> If judges were to recuse themselves whenever a litigant—whether it be a represented litigant or a litigant in person—criticised them (which sometimes happens not infrequently) we would soon reach the position in which litigants were able to select judges to hear their cases, simply by criticising all the judges they did not want to hear their cases. It would be easy for a litigant to produce a situation in which a judge felt obliged to recuse himself simply because he had been criticised—whether that criticism was justified or not.

In *Locabail* the court said that if an objection was made, it would be the duty of the judge to **10.84** consider the objection and exercise his judgment upon it, but 'he would be as wrong to yield to a tenuous or frivolous objection as he would to ignore an objection of substance'. In *BCCI v Ali*, 3 December 2001, Ch D, following *Locabail*, Lawrence Collins J said that it is important that judges discharge their duty to sit and do not, by acceding too readily to complaints of bias, encourage parties to believe that they may have their case tried by someone thought to be more sympathetic.

10.85 In *Taylor v Lawrence* [2003] QB 528, the Court of Appeal said that judges should be circumspect about disclosing relationships where no possibility of bias could arise in the mind of the fair-minded and impartial observer. If a relationship existed which might give rise to such a possibility, and in a borderline case, the relationship should be disclosed to the parties. The judge had been under no obligation to disclose the fact that a party's solicitor had acted for the judge in a personal matter: it was unthinkable that such a relationship would give rise to a possibility of bias in the mind of the fair-minded and impartial observer. In *Automobile Proprietary Ltd v Healy* [1979] ICR 809, the tribunal, whilst rejecting the allegation of bias, decided that it could not properly proceed with the case if the employee had no confidence in it, and thus ordered a rehearing before a different tribunal. The EAT criticized it for this action, on the ground that the lack of confidence was insufficient to form a ground for a rehearing.

10.86 The appropriateness of a tribunal's decision to recuse itself was raised before the Court of Appeal in *Bennett v London Borough of Southwark* [2002] EWCA Civ 223, [2002] IRLR 407, where the tribunal had recused itself after the claimant's representative had suggested racial bias on the part of the tribunal; the tribunal concluded that it could not hear a race discrimination case in which it had been accused of racism. When faced with allegations of this nature from a representative, the tribunal should first invite the representative to withdraw the comments. If he does so, the case can continue. If he does not withdraw, the tribunal must consider the justification for the comments. If no proper justification is offered, the tribunal will need to consider whether, given the potential injustice to the other side and the public expense which recusing itself will bring, it cannot continue with the hearing with an unclouded mind.

10.87 However, the EAT's decision in *Breeze Benton Solicitors v Weddell* UKEAT/0873/03 suggested an approach more favourable to recusal. Cox J stated the following principles (at paras 44 and 53):

(a) The tribunal is required to recuse itself if there is a real possibility of bias (according to the test in *Porter* and *Lawal* and see also the helpful summary in *Alubankudi* (appearance of bias) [2015] UKUT 542 (IAC)[7]). If such a risk is found, the tribunal is not entitled to balance against that risk considerations of prejudice to the other party resulting from delay.

(b) If in any case there is a real ground for doubt, that doubt should be resolved in favour of recusal.

(c) It is no answer to a recusal application to say that the judge was only one of three members (following *Lodwick*).

(d) The claim of the person asked to recuse himself that he will not be or is not partial is of no weight because of 'the insidious nature' of bias.

(e) If the application for recusal is well founded, the fact that it could have been made at an earlier interlocutory stage is relevant only to the question of costs and not to the question of recusal.

10.88 In *Breeze Benton* one factor alleged to give rise to the appearance of bias was that the judge was aware of a complaint made against him by the respondent (see para 47). There must be some caution in relation to this factor; as noted above, it is undesirable for applications for recusal to become self-fulfilling. *Bennett* (at para 19) and *Dobbs* cited above clearly show that tribunals should avoid manipulation, whether intentional or otherwise. *Bromley Appointments.com Ltd v Mackinnon* UKEAT/0640/04 (Bean J) concerned a complaint of bias on the part of the judge arising out of an interim decision made between the liabilities hearing and the remedies hearing. The employer complained about the judge to the regional chairman (even threatening proceedings against the ETS) and applied for the judge to recuse himself from the remedies hearing. The EAT found that no appearance of bias arose from the interim decision. The fact of the complaint did not give grounds for recusal: it would be a recipe for chaos if a party dissatisfied with an interlocutory decision of a tribunal could achieve a recusal by threat to sue the ETS, where a recusal was not otherwise appropriate (at para 29). The Court of Appeal in *Ansar v Lloyds TSB Bank plc* [2006] EWCA Civ 1462, [2007] IRLR 211 followed the robust approach in *Dobbs*, holding that the mere fact of complaint could not give rise to a decision to recuse.

10.89 In *AWG v Morrison* [2006] EWCA Civ 6, [2006] 1 WLR 1163, the Court of Appeal observes that in many of the cases the allegation of bias arose during the course of the trial or hearing. Where the issue arises prior to the commencement of the trial, there is room for 'the sensible application of the precautionary principle' on the basis that it is better to be safe than sorry (para 9). The Court's comments must, however, have been pragmatic: the test for the appearance of bias is clear and there can be no difference in the test applied depending upon the stage in the proceedings when the bias allegation is made. However, if the court can avoid an argument as to recusal, and the risk of disturbing the efficient case management of the case, there is sense in trying to do so. The Court of Appeal in *El Farargy v El Farargy* [2007] EWCA Civ 1149 took a similar approach, at para 32 (Ward LJ):

> It is invidious for a judge to sit in judgment on his own conduct in a case like this but in many cases there will be no option but that the trial judge deal with it himself or herself. If circumstances permit it, I would urge that first an informal approach be made to the judge, for example by letter, making the complaint and inviting recusal. Whilst judges must heed the exhortation in *Locabail* not to yield to a tenuous or frivolous objections, one can with honour totally deny the complaint but still pass the case to a colleague. If a judge does not feel able to do so, then it may be preferable, if it is possible to arrange it, to have another judge take the decision, hard though it is to sit in judgment of one's colleague, for where the appearance of justice is at stake, it is better that justice be done independently by another rather than require the judge to sit in judgment of his own behaviour.

Application for recusal

The ETR 2013 does not contain any express rules or procedures for the handling of allegations **10.90** or concerns about bias. It seems likely that the principles derived from earlier cases will continue to apply. Of course, the overriding objective enshrines the principle that cases must be dealt with fairly and justly (r 2). Where an application for a recusal and rehearing is made by one of the parties during the course of the hearing itself on the grounds of bias, it should be considered by all members of the tribunal and not by the judge alone (*West LB AG (London Branch) v Pan* UKEAT/0308/ 11). An opportunity must also be given to the other parties in the case to consider the grounds of the application, and to be heard on it, since a rehearing may result in injustice and would certainly increase the costs of that other party (see *Peter Simper & Co Ltd v Cooke* [1986] IRLR 19, EAT).

Where the tribunal discloses material which may give rise to the appearance of bias, the party af- **10.91** fected has a clear choice of whether or not to object to the hearing proceeding. Where an allegation of bias or denial of a fair hearing arises from the conduct of the tribunal during the course of the hearing the party affected has a more difficult decision whether to raise the matter in the course of the hearing, or to wait until the decision and use the bias allegation as a ground of appeal.

There is no hard and fast rule as to whether an objection must be taken at the hearing (so that **10.92** failure to do so means that the objection cannot be raised as a ground of appeal), or whether the objection may be raised for the first time in an appeal. In *Stansbury v Datapulse plc* [2003] EWCA Civ 1951, [2004] IRLR 466, the Court of Appeal allowed a complaint concerning a sleeping tribunal member to be raised on appeal for the first time. A failure to raise an objection before the employment tribunal should be considered against the test of reasonableness in all the circumstances of the case. Whilst it is always desirable that a point on the behaviour of the employment tribunal should be raised at the tribunal in the course of the hearing, it is unrealistic not to recognize the difficulty, even for legal representatives, in raising with the tribunal a complaint about the behaviour of one of its members who, if the complaint is not upheld, may yet be part of the tribunal deciding the case. Hence, in *Healey v Wincanton Group* UKEAT/0303/12, 12 December 2012, the claimant's failure to raise the issue of bias at the tribunal hearing was not criticized. His justification for not making an application for recusal was that he did not know that he himself could make such an application and that he thought that it would be very antagonistic for him and those he was representing if he raised his prior connection with the judge. The EAT held he had not waived his right to complain.

Similarly, in *Peter Simper & Co Ltd v Cooke* (above), Peter Gibson J stated (at para 21) that such **10.93** complaints should not be raised during the hearing:

> Save in extraordinary circumstances, it cannot be right for a litigant, unhappy with what he believes to be the indications from the Tribunal as to how the case is progressing, to apply, in the middle of the case, for

Part A Tribunal Procedure

a re-hearing before another Tribunal. It is undesirable that the Tribunal accused of giving the opinion [*sic*] of bias should be asked itself to adjudicate on that matter. The dissatisfied litigant should ordinarily await the decision and then, if he thinks it appropriate, he would make his dissatisfaction with the conduct of the Tribunal a ground of appeal.

10.94 However, some caution must be exercised in treating this as a statement of general principle. As was made clear in *Stansbury*, much depends upon the circumstances of the particular case, and the particular matter about which complaint is made. In *Harada Ltd (t/a Chequepoint UK Ltd) v Turner (No 1)* [2001] EWCA Civ 599, after the judge's preliminary comments, the respondent invited the tribunal to recuse itself, and when the tribunal refused to do so, it withdrew from any further part in the hearing. Pill LJ, whilst acknowledging the force of the approach in *Peter Simper*, stated that the appropriate procedure depends upon all the circumstances, including the subject matter of the case, the statement of which complaint is made, and the circumstances in which it is made. There may be cases where the alleged conduct of the tribunal is such, or where there is to be a long hearing and the point arises at a very early stage, that it would not be appropriate simply to carry on with the case and then take the point on appeal.

10.95 Where the complaint is of a matter which might be remedied at the hearing, both principle and common sense dictate that the party should raise it at the hearing; it will not be right for parties to await the outcome of the decision and only at that stage raise such transient matters (*Red Bank Manufacturing Co Ltd v Meadows* [1992] ICR 204, EAT). However, the EAT in *Kudrath v Ministry of Defence* EAT/422/97 noted that, whilst it was preferable to raise the matter during the course of the hearing, it is unrealistic to expect this always to be sensible or practicable.

10.96 *Anthony v Governors of Hillcrest School* EAT/1193/00 is another decision which indicates that a party may lose the right to complain of bias if it fails to raise the issue at the time of the conduct complained of, but instead waits to see whether it has won or lost. In *Anthony* the allegation of bias arose from the comments of the judge during the course of the hearing, and interference with cross-examination by the claimant's representative. The EAT held, in a case which it described as borderline, that the judge's comments did not give rise to the appearance of bias. The EAT also held that the claimant had effectively waived the right to complain: the comments had been made early in a four-day hearing, yet neither the claimant nor his representative complained during the hearing, nor during submissions, nor at any time until after the reserved decision had been given. It is perhaps doubtful that the same result would now be reached in the light of *Stansbury*, but clearly under the principles set out in *Stansbury* much will depend on the circumstances of the particular case.

Approach of the EAT

10.97 Where on appeal it is found that there was actual or apparent bias, the normal course will be to remit the matter for rehearing. It is not clear whether the decision *must* be set aside, or whether in some circumstances the court may allow the decision to stand if it can be said to be plainly right. In *Re Medicaments (No 2)* [2001] 1 WLR 700, the effect of the decisions of the ECtHR was said to be that the decision of the judge must be set aside. In *Turner v Harada* above, Pill LJ considered it to follow from that proposition that once the legitimate fear that the judge might not have been impartial is established, the decision of the judge must be set aside; if it ever can be otherwise, it would be an exceptional case. He did not give any guidance as to what might amount to an exceptional case. Mantell LJ, whilst agreeing with Pill LJ, said that irrespective of the correctness or otherwise of the decision which was eventually reached, what is at stake in cases of bias is public confidence in the administration of justice.

10.98 The EAT in *Anthony*, purporting to follow Pill LJ in *Turner v Harada*, said that the test was that once a real danger of bias is shown, except in exceptional cases, the decision must be set aside. It is not sufficient to establish exceptional circumstances to show that the decision would inevitably have been the same. The case must be one where it can be said with certainty that to permit the decision to stand would not affect confidence in the administration of justice. The EAT found that the facts of *Anthony* would give rise to such an exceptional case; however, as the EAT also found that there was no appearance of bias, its decision on this point is *obiter*.

Where any complaint is to be made on appeal to the EAT alleging bias or misconduct on the part **10.99** of the employment tribunal, full particulars of such matters must be set out in the grounds of appeal. Reference should be made to the EAT Practice Direction 2013, para 13.

The bright line between the role of advocate and witness must be respected by those representing **10.100** parties and care must be taken to decide when it is appropriate for someone who has been acting as an advocate or legal representative to assume the role of a witness of fact in an appeal, as it is never appropriate for an advocate to give evidence of that which occurred below on appeal.

Part A Tribunal Procedure

11

Judgments, Decisions, and Orders

SUMMARY

(1) A tribunal's decision finally determining a claim (or part of it) or an issue which is capable of disposing of a claim (or part of it) is given in a judgment. A tribunal's decision in relation to the conduct of proceedings is a case management order.

(2) A decision may be unanimous, or by a majority. Where a tribunal comprises a judge and only one lay member, the judge has a casting vote.

(3) A tribunal must give reasons for any decision, though the reasons given shall be proportionate to the significance of the issues determined.

(4) A tribunal may give its judgment or order, or the reasons for it, orally at a hearing, or may reserve its decision to a later date. Reasons will be given in writing if so requested by a party at the hearing, or within fourteen days of being sent the judgment.

(5) Reasons should be in sufficient detail to explain to the parties why they have won or lost. Reasons should contain an outline of the story which has given rise to the complaint and a summary of the tribunal's basic factual conclusions and a statement of the reasons which have led them to reach the conclusion which they do on those basic facts.

(6) There are limited grounds to challenge a decision before registration.

(7) A judgment is binding on the parties and may give rise to *res judicata* or issue estoppel in subsequent proceedings. Raising a claim in proceedings which could or should have been raised in earlier proceedings between the parties may be an abuse of process.

A. CLASSIFICATION OF JUDGMENTS AND ORDERS

Rule 1(3) of the ETR 2013 provides that an order or other decision of a tribunal is either: **11.01**

(a) a 'case management order', being an order or decision of any kind in relation to conduct of the proceedings, not including the determination of any issue which would be the subject of a judgment or

(b) a 'judgment', being a decision made at any stage of the proceedings which finally determines (i) a claim, or part of a claim, as regards liability, remedy or costs (including preparation time and wasted costs); or (ii) any issue which is capable of finally disposing of any claim, or part of a claim, even if it does not necessarily do so (for example, an issue whether a claim should be struck out or a jurisdictional issue). Decisions under rr 13 and 19 (reconsiderations of rejection of a claim or response) are specifically excluded from the definition of judgments.

Some caution is required when referring to authorities dealing with judgments or orders under **11.02**
previous versions of the rules: the ETR 2004 defined 'judgments' and 'orders' in rather different terms to the ETR 2013 definitions. There was a considerable lack of clarity under the old rules as to the correct classification of certain decisions of the tribunal. See previous editions of this work for the meaning of those terms under the ETR 2004. The 2013 Rules represent an improvement, but leave some uncertainty: it would appear from the language, for example, that a deposit order does not fall within the definition of a judgment, so would therefore be classified as a case management order, although this is not clear. The classification of an 'unless' order (see r 38) is also unclear. Under the ETR 2004, an 'unless' order was categorized as a final determination where a claimant failed to comply (as in *Uyamnawa Odu v Schools Offices Services Ltd* UKEAT/0294/05/ZT and *McMichael v East Sussex CC* UKEAT/0091/11/SM, but not where a respondent failed to do so in *North Tyneside Primary Care Trust v Aynsley* [2009] ICR 1333, where the respondent was otherwise liable to have a default judgment entered in any event).

B. PROCEDURAL REQUIREMENTS FOR JUDGMENTS AND ORDERS

Form and content of judgments and orders

Rules 60–61 recognize that decisions may be made either with or without a hearing. Where a decision is made without a hearing, the decision shall be communicated in writing to the parties, identifying the employment judge who made the decision (r 60). This will commonly occur in practice when case management directions are made without a hearing, but may also apply in other instances where parties request applications to be dealt with on paper only. **11.03**

Where there is a hearing, the tribunal may either announce its decision in relation to any issue at **11.04**
the hearing or reserve it to be sent to the parties as soon as practicable in writing (r 60(1)). If the decision is announced at the hearing a written record (eg a judgment if appropriate) shall be provided to the parties as soon as practicable (r 60(2)). Rule 60(2) further provides that a decision concerned only with the conduct of the hearing need not be identified in the record of the hearing unless a party requests that a specific decision is so recorded. This would apply, for example, to a decision as to the admissibility of a document, or as to the time limit for a witness's evidence.

Whether a decision is given orally at the end of the hearing or reserved to be given in writing has **11.05**
always been a matter of discretion for the judge or tribunal. The approach taken will depend on the complexity of the issues in the case, and the time of the day at which the hearing ends.

The written record shall be signed by the employment judge (r 60(3)). Where it is impossible or **11.06**
not practicable for a judge to sign the written record or reasons, due to death, incapacity, or absence, either a lay member may sign, or, if the judge dealt with the case sitting alone, the regional employment judge, Vice-President, or President may sign (r 63).

11.07 If the parties agree in writing or orally at a hearing upon the terms of any order or judgment, a tribunal may, if it thinks fit, make such order or judgment, in which case it shall be identified as having been made by consent (r 64). See further para 5.110 in relation to consent orders.

Delay in giving judgment or reasons

11.08 Under Art 6 of the European Convention on Human Rights a litigant has the right to the determination of a tribunal within a reasonable time: *Porter v Magill* [2001] UKHL 67, [2002] 2 AC 357, para 108 (Lord Hope). The consequences of unreasonable delay in promulgating a decision after a hearing was considered by the Court of Appeal in *Bangs v Connex South Eastern Ltd* [2005] EWCA Civ 14, [2005] IRLR 389. The case is considered more fully in Chapter 18 in the context of considering the EAT's approach to delay as a ground of appeal. In *Bangs* Mummery LJ also said that unreasonable delay may result in a breach of Art 6 and possibly give rise to state liability to pay compensation to the victim of the delay. In the subsequent decision of *Carpenter v City of Edinburgh Council* UKEATS/0038/07/MT, a delay of over three years was held to have given rise to a real risk that the claimant had been denied his Art 6 right to a fair trial. By contrast, in *Abbey National plc and Another v Chagger* [2009] ICR 624 (a decision partially reversed by the Court of Appeal on unrelated grounds) Underhill J, as he then was, held that there was no real risk that the substance of the right to a fair trial had been denied where a tribunal, which had provided an oral decision and outline reasons immediately after the liability hearing, only promulgated its formal judgment and full reasons eight months later.

Majority decisions

11.09 A tribunal may consist of a judge sitting alone, or of a panel. A panel will normally consist of a judge and two lay members (see paras 1.19–1.30 for situations in which a judge may sit alone or with one lay member only).

11.10 Where a tribunal is composed of three persons, any order or judgment may be made or issued by a majority. Where a tribunal is composed of two persons only, the judge has a second or casting vote (r 49).

11.11 In practice, the vast majority of judgments and orders are unanimous. The Court of Appeal has indeed said that it is undesirable for tribunals to reach split decisions, and all efforts should be made to achieve unanimity: *Anglian Home Improvements Ltd v Kelly* [2004] EWCA Civ 901, [2004] IRLR 793.

11.12 Where the tribunal is split, it is preferable for the tribunal to reserve the decision, rather than to give an oral decision at the hearing (*Anglian Home Improvements*, approving the approach in *Holden v Bradville Ltd* [1985] IRLR 483. This allows the judge to write a draft decision, recording both majority and minority views, and to circulate it to the lay members, ensuring that the lay members' views are properly expressed, and also allowing for reflection on the areas of disagreement.

11.13 Where the judge is in the minority, he must not sign the judgment until the majority have seen and approved the text: *Maure v Macmillan Distribution Ltd* (transcript 24 January 1997, Court of Appeal, 1997 WL 1105769). The majority and minority views should be set out clearly in separate paragraphs (*Parkers Bakeries Ltd v Palmer* [1977] IRLR 215, approved in *Anglian Home Improvements* (cited above). In *Eyitene v Wirral Metropolitan Borough Council* [2014] EWCA Civ 1243, [2014] IRLR 944, Underhill LJ set out, at 11, the typical approach to collective decision-making in the tribunal. He observed that whilst key passages may be settled during deliberations it is the employment judge's job as chairperson to draft the bulk of the judgment and, unless a member requests, or there is a split decision, a draft of the reasons will not normally be circulated prior to promulgation.

11.14 The fact that a majority and a minority of a tribunal came to differing views on the evidence before them does not, however, of itself amount to a ground of appeal; indeed, it may serve to emphasize the care with which the tribunal has considered the matter (*Chief Constable of Thames Valley Police v Kellaway* [2000] IRLR 170).

C. THE TRIBUNAL'S REASONS

The duty to give reasons

Rule 62 deals with the tribunal's duty to give reasons. The tribunal shall give reasons for its deci- **11.15**
sion on any disputed issue, whether substantive or procedural. This is expressly stated to include a
decision on an application for reconsideration or for orders for costs, preparation time, or wasted
costs. That list is clearly not meant to be exhaustive, nor to limit the general rule, but rather to
make clear the position in relation to types of decision where there may perhaps have been doubt
as to the application of the rule.

The ETR 2013 considerably simplified the previous rules as to the duty to give reasons. Under **11.16**
the previous rules, different rules applied to reasons for judgments and reasons for orders, see r 30
of the ETR 2004 and paras 11.10–11.14 of the 2012 edition of this work, but under r 62 of the
ETR 2013 applies to all decisions on disputed issues. Crucially, however, r 62(4) provides that the
reasons given for a decision shall be proportionate to the significance of the issue and for decisions
other than judgments may be very short.

Procedure for giving reasons

Rule 62 provides for the manner in which reasons are given as follows: **11.17**

(a) Where a decision is given in writing the reasons shall be given in writing (r 62(2)).
(b) Where a decision is announced at a hearing, the reasons may either be given orally at the
hearing or reserved to be given in writing later. The written reasons may be, but need not be,
part of the written record (r 62(2)).
(c) Where reasons are given orally, the employment judge shall announce that written reasons will
not be provided unless they are asked for by a party at the hearing or within fourteen days of
the sending of the written record. If there is no such request, the tribunal shall provide written
reasons only if asked to do so by the EAT or a court (r 62(3)).

When written reasons are given they shall be signed by the employment judge (see r 63, and para **11.18**
11.06 where the employment judge cannot sign the reasons).

The content of the reasons: general principles

It has always been the duty of the tribunal to give reasons for its decision. However, the EAT **11.19**
and Court of Appeal have had to grapple repeatedly with the question of what is entailed by
this duty: how detailed must the tribunal's reasons be? What are the consequences of a failure
to give adequate reasons? Rule 62 contains two important provisions as to the contents of the
reasons. First, r 62(4) provides that the reasons given for any decision shall be proportionate
to the significance of the issue. Secondly, r 62(5) provides that, in the case of a judgment, the
reasons shall:

(a) identify the issues which the tribunal has determined
(b) state the findings of fact made in relation to those issues
(c) concisely identify the relevant law
(d) state how that law has been applied to those findings in order to decide the issues.

Where the judgment includes a financial award, the reasons shall identify (by means of a table or
otherwise) how the amount to be paid has been calculated. Reasons must also be provided for the
application and level of any deductions to awards. In *Contract Bottling Ltd v Cave* [2015] ICR 146
the EAT twice allowed appeals in the same action following two differently constituted tribunals
failing to provide sufficient reasons in relation to the determination of a *Polkey* reduction.

The predecessor to r 62(5), r 30(6) of the ETR 2004, was in similar but wider terms. The reasons **11.20**
were required to include information as to (a) 'the issues which the tribunal or judge has identified
as being relevant to the claim' and (b) 'if some identified issues were not determined, what those

issues were and why they were not determined'. This clearly goes beyond the requirement in new r 62(5) to identify the issues which have been determined.

11.21 The EAT (HHJ Hand QC presiding) in *Greenwood v NWF Retail Ltd* [2011] ICR 896 held that r 30(6) of the ETR 2004 was mandatory, and it was an error of law not to comply with it. Rule 62(5) of the ETR 2013 is in similarly mandatory language. A judgment will not be defective simply because the structure of the rule is not visible on the surface of the decision, so long as its constituent parts can be unearthed from the material beneath. More is needed than a formal statement paying lip service to the rule: the judgment must demonstrate substantial compliance.

11.22 Rule 62 must be seen in the context of the existing body of case law concerning the scope and content of the duty to give reasons. The requirement for reasons arises not just in the employment tribunals, but across the whole range of judicial decision-making. The duty to provide reasons arises under the common law, as an aspect of natural justice and the right to a fair trial, and is also required by Art 6 of the ECHR (given effect in England and Wales by the Human Rights Act 1998). Article 6(1) requires that adequate and intelligible reasons must be given for judicial decisions (see *Ruiz Torija v Spain* (1994) 19 EHRR 553; *Garcia Ruiz v Spain* (2001) 31 EHRR 22).

11.23 The leading authority on the content of judicial reasons is *English v Emery Reimbold & Strick* [2002] EWCA Civ 605, [2003] IRLR 711. The case concerned the adequacy of reasons given by judges in High Court trials, but the Court of Appeal's guidance was plainly meant to be of general application. The Court of Appeal gave the following guidance (at paras 18–22 (Lord Phillips MR)):

(a) It is the duty of a judge to produce a judgment that gives a clear explanation for his or her order.

(b) The judgment should make it apparent to the parties why they have won or lost, and should enable the appellate court to understand why the judge reached his decision.

(c) There is no duty on a judge to deal with every argument presented to him, and a judgment need not be lengthy. While a judgment may often need to refer to evidence or submissions, it may be unnecessary to detail or even summarize the evidence or submission.

(d) However, issues which are vital to the judge's conclusion should be identified and the manner in which they are resolved should be explained. The judgment should identify and record the matters which are critical to the decision.

(e) If the critical issue is one of fact, it may be enough to say that one witness was preferred to another because he manifestly had a clearer recollection, or the other gave answers which demonstrated that his recollection could not be relied upon.

(f) Where there is a conflict of expert evidence, the judge should provide an explanation as to why he accepted the evidence of one expert and rejected that of another.

11.24 The Court of Appeal also dealt with the approach to amplification of a judge's reasons. This topic is dealt with at paras 11.53 ff.

11.25 Obviously, whether a particular judgment gives adequate reasons depends on the facts and circumstances of the particular case (*English* (para 11.23 above), at para 17; see also *Flannery v Halifax Estate Agencies Ltd* [2000] 1 WLR 377, 381–2 (Henry LJ), approved in *English*). The *English* guidance leaves room for argument as to whether a particular judgment complies with the guidance or not (see also Chapter 18).

11.26 The leading authority on reasons relating specifically to the employment tribunals has for many years been *Meek v City of Birmingham District Council* [1987] IRLR 250 In *Meek*, Bingham LJ said (at 251) that reasons should:

> contain an outline of the story which has given rise to the complaint and a summary of the tribunal's basic factual conclusions and a statement of the reasons which have led them to reach the conclusion which they do on those basic facts. The parties are entitled to be told why they have won or lost. There should be sufficient account of the facts and of the reasoning to enable the EAT or, on further appeal, this court to see whether any question of law arises; and it is highly desirable that the decision of an [employment] tribunal should give guidance both to employers and trade unions as to practices which should or should not be adopted.

In his judgment, Bingham LJ also approved and applied two earlier passages from decisions of the **11.27** Court of Appeal. First, in *Union of Construction, Allied Trades & Technicians v Brain* [1981] ICR 542, 551, Donaldson LJ (as he then was) stated that:

> Industrial tribunals' reasons are not intended to include a comprehensive and detailed analysis of the case, either in terms of fact or in law. Their purpose remains what it has always been, which is to tell the parties in broad terms why they lose, or as the case may be, win. I think it would be a thousand pities if these reasons began to be subjected to a detailed analysis and appeals were to be brought based upon such analysis. This, to my mind, is to misuse the purpose for which reasons are given.

Secondly, in *Martin v MBS Fastenings (Glynwed) Distribution Ltd* [1983] IRLR 198, 202, Sir John **11.28** Donaldson MR said:

> The duty of an Industrial Tribunal is to give reasons for its decision. This involves making findings of fact and answering a question or questions of law. So far as the findings of fact are concerned, it is helpful to the parties to give some explanation of them, but it is not obligatory. So far as the questions of law are concerned, the reasons should show expressly or by implication what were the questions to which the Industrial Tribunal addressed its mind and why it reached the conclusions which it did, but the way in which it does so is entirely a matter for the Industrial Tribunal.

In *Martin* the Court of Appeal rejected the contention that it was the tribunal's duty to state the **11.29** law, its primary findings of fact, secondary findings of fact, and conclusions. See also to similar effect *Kearney & Trecker Marwin v Varndell* [1983] IRLR 335 (Eveleigh LJ). This passage from *Martin* should not now be interpreted too broadly. The modern trend in the cases has been to require fuller reasons to be given by the tribunal, and r 62(5) now expressly requires reasons to contain a statement of the findings of fact, the applicable law, and conclusions drawn.

The guidance in *English* has swiftly been adopted by the EAT and the Court of Appeal as applying **11.30** to appeals against decisions of the employment tribunals: see *Logan v Commissioners of Customs & Excise* [2003] EWCA Civ 1068, [2004] IRLR 63, para 25, where Ward LJ regarded the principles in *English* as an authoritative statement of a test already embodied in *Meek*; see also *Burns v Consignia (No 2)* [2004] IRLR 425, where Burton P described *English* as 'a seminal decision' plainly intended to be of universal application.

The guidance in *Meek* has been followed repeatedly in subsequent cases as the touchstone for the **11.31** content of reasons: see, for example, *High Table v Horst* [1997] IRLR 513; *Miriki v General Council of the Bar* [2002] ICR 505; *Tran v Greenwich Vietnam Community* [2002] IRLR 735; and *Anya v University of Oxford* [2001] EWCA Civ 405, [2001] ICR 847. Indeed, the EAT and Court of Appeal have come to describe the question of adequacy of a tribunal's reasons as whether those reasons are '*Meek* compliant' (see *Tran*, at para 17 (Sedley LJ)). In *Greenwood* HHJ Hand QC explained that the ongoing utility of *Meek* since the introduction of r 30(6) of the ETR 2004 is in determining whether there has been substantial compliance with the rule: ie whether the judgment has sufficient detail in respect of each of its components as to enable a party to understand the conclusions reached and how their application has resulted in the outcome. HHJ Hand QC's analysis applies with equal force to r 62 of the ETR 2013. In *Vairea v Reed Business Information Ltd* UKEAT/0177/15/BA [2017] ICR D9, HHJ Hand QC held that the language of r 62(5) of the ETR 2013 made no difference to the requirements of *Meek* and *Greenwood*.

Whether the tribunal's reasons are adequate to satisfy the tests in *Meek* and *English* will depend **11.32** upon the particular issues and circumstances of each case and no hard and fast guidelines can be given.

The appellate courts have repeatedly discouraged overlong and elaborate decisions. They will gen- **11.33** erally give a generous interpretation to the tribunal's reasoning, and will not apply the standards to be expected of a judgment from a High Court judge. Lord Nicholls in *Shamoon v Chief Constable of the Royal Ulster Constabulary* [2003] ICR 337, at 59, said:

> It has also been recognized that a generous interpretation ought to be given to a tribunal's reasoning. It is to be expected, of course, that the decision will set out the facts. That is the raw material on which any view of its decision must be based. But the quality which is to be expected of its reasoning is not

that to be expected of a High Court Judge. Its reasoning ought to be explained, but the circumstances in which a tribunal works should be respected. The reasoning ought not to be subjected to an unduly critical analysis.

Particular aspects of the duty to give reasons

Dealing with the issues

11.34 The reasons should set out the issues which the tribunal is to determine. The modern practice is for those issues to have been defined before the evidence is heard: either at a case management discussion, or at the beginning of the hearing. Often the parties' representatives are asked to agree those issues.

11.35 Whilst a tribunal must consider all that is relevant, it need only deal with the points which are seen to be in controversy relating to those issues, and then only with the principal important controversial points: *High Table Ltd v Horst* [1998] ICR 409, [1997] IRLR 513, 518 (Peter Gibson LJ). Peter Gibson LJ repeated this proposition in *Comfort v Lord Chancellor's Department* [2004] EWCA Civ 349, [2004] All ER (D) 313 (Mar), in finding that a tribunal's reasons were defective because they failed to make findings on an important factual dispute. A tribunal must make findings upon the factual issues essential to its conclusions; it does not, however, have to explore the circumstances of every event in the evidence placed before it: *Wheeler and Newton v Durham County Council* [2001] EWCA Civ 844, paras 50, 54, and 55; *Anya v University of Oxford* [2001] ICR 847, 862; *Madarassy v Nomura International plc* [2007] EWCA Civ 33, [2007] IRLR 246. Similarly, in *Deman v Association of University Teachers* [2003] EWCA Civ 329, para 37, Potter LJ said that each case must be decided in the light of its own particular circumstances. It cannot be right that in every case the tribunal must make findings on every piece of circumstantial evidence, however peripheral, merely because the claimant chooses to make it the subject of complaint.

11.36 In *Miriki v General Council of the Bar* [2002] EWCA Civ 1973, [2002] ICR 505, it was argued that *Anya* set a higher standard for reasons, in that even on peripheral matters of complaint it is for the tribunal to state its findings and its reasons for rejecting the complaint. Peter Gibson LJ (at para 46) rejected this argument. What is required of the reasons depended on the circumstances of each particular case. He reiterated the approach that he had first set out in *High Table v Horst* [1997] IRLR 513.

Dealing with findings of fact

11.37 Although tribunals are not required to set out their reasons in great detail, they should set out their main findings of fact. This is required by r 62(5).

11.38 There is no need to recite all of the evidence in the case. The tribunal should state its findings of fact in a sensible order (often chronological) indicating in relation to any significant finding the nature of the conflicting evidence and the reason why one version has been preferred to another (*Tchoula v Netto Foodstores Ltd* EAT/1378/98). The ET should seek to present a coherent but neutral narrative of the facts. In *Co-operative Group Ltd v Baddeley* [2014] EWCA Civ 658 Underhill LJ, at 25, was critical of a tribunal's use of 'frequently rhetorical, not to say tabloid' language and observed that:

> [T]here is nothing wrong in principle in an employment tribunal being strongly critical of a party where the facts justify it; and there is no requirement that such criticism be expressed only in bland terms. But the trouble with using language of the type quoted is that it has an unprofessional flavour, which tends to give the impression that the tribunal has lost its objectivity.

11.39 Where a tribunal is faced with a conflict of evidence on a significant issue of fact, its view of the evidence must be made plain and discernible from the reasons (*Levy v Marrable & Co Ltd* [1984] ICR 583). The tribunal should state which evidence it believes or prefers (*British Gas plc v Sharma* [1991] IRLR 101; *Wadman v Carpenter Farrer Partnership* [1993] IRLR 374). The tribunal should avoid bald statements that it prefers the evidence of one party rather than another: reasons should be given for such a conclusion (*Tchoula v Netto Foodstores Ltd* above, approved in *Anya v University of Oxford* and *Deman v Association of University Teachers*).

An uncritical belief in the witnesses' credibility without proper examination of the relevant evidential issues through to a reasoned conclusion will not be sufficient: *Anya v University of Oxford* above, at para 25. Conversely, the tribunal is obliged to elaborate on its reasons for rejecting evidence where the basis is effectively a finding of bad faith (*Co-operative Group Ltd v Baddeley*, above, para 58). **11.40**

The degree of detail required will depend on the nature of the case. Discrimination claims **11.41** can raise particularly complicated issues, in that they will frequently turn on the inferences to be drawn from primary facts. A tribunal should take care to set out its findings of primary fact, and then to explain the inferences which it draws, and why it draws them. In *Deman v Association of University Teachers*, the Court of Appeal (at para 44) contrasted an unfair dismissal case on the one hand with a racial discrimination and victimization case on the other hand. In the first case, once the primary facts are found, the case turns upon applying objective and accepted standards of fairness; in the latter, the case will often depend on assessing nuances and drawing inferences as to the true reason underlying particular actions. The latter type of case will usually involve the necessity for a more careful and elaborate statement of reasons than the former in order for the parties to understand why they have won or lost, and in order for the EAT to know that there has been no error of law (see also *Chapman v Simon* [1994] IRLR 124).

As to the importance of the tribunal making findings of fact before drawing inferences, see *Anya* **11.42** *v University of Oxford* [2001] EWCA Civ 405, [2001] IRLR 377; *Bahl v The Law Society* [2004] EWCA Civ 1070, [2004] IRLR 799. As to the drawing of inferences in discrimination cases generally, see *King v The Great Britain-China Centre* [1991] IRLR 513, CA and *Glasgow City Council v Zafar* [1997] 1 WLR 1659, [1998] IRLR 36, HL, and in relation to the statutory reversal of the burden of proof in discrimination cases, see *Igen Ltd v Wong* [2005] EWCA Civ 142, [2005] IRLR 258; *Barton v Investec Henderson Crosthwaite Securities Ltd* [2003] ICR 1205, EAT; and *EB v BA* [2006] EWCA Civ 132, [2006] IRLR 471.

The tribunal should not simply set out the relevant evidential issues, but should follow them **11.43** through to a reasoned conclusion. If the tribunal feels it unnecessary to state a conclusion on an issue, it should explain why (*Anya*). It is insufficient merely to recite the background and then state a conclusion. The reasons should show how the tribunal got from its findings of fact to its conclusion (*Tran*, at para 17 (see para 11.31)).

Dealing with disputed expert evidence

Where an issue turns on expert evidence, the tribunal is under a duty to summarize and take into **11.44** account the expert evidence, and if it rejects the evidence, to explain why: *Edwards v Mid Suffolk DC* [2001] ICR 616, [2001] IRLR 190.

Dealing with the law

Rule 62(5) requires a concise statement of the applicable law. It is of course difficult for an appellate **11.45** court to determine whether the tribunal has made any error of law if the tribunal does not state the legal principles it has applied. In *Conlin v United Distillers* [1994] IRLR 169, the EAT had stressed the importance of setting out the applicable statutory provisions and the correct statutory test in an unfair dismissal case.

Some of the earlier cases discouraged detailed treatment of legal authorities in tribunals' reasons. In **11.46** *Anandarajah v Lord Chancellor's Department* [1984] IRLR 131, Waite J stated that industrial tribunals are not required to and should not be invited to subject the authorities to the same analysis as a court of law searching in a plethora of precedent for binding or persuasive authority. However, this does not reflect the reality of the exercise facing many tribunals in modern times. The tribunal's jurisdiction has expanded significantly since the 1980s, both in relation to the legal questions the tribunal must address, and the potential sums that it may be invited to award by way of compensation. In many cases, the tribunal has no choice but to grapple with complex legal issues, often where authorities conflict or are unclear. A tribunal would not discharge its duty to explain how it reaches its decision if it does not state the principles of law it applies, and in some cases this may require detailed consideration of the authorities.

Dealing with guidance and codes of practice

11.47 In a number of areas, the tribunal is obliged to have regard to statutory guidance and codes of practice. In *Goodwin v Patent Office* [1999] ICR 302, [1999] IRLR 4 (a disability discrimination case), Morison J emphasized the importance of express reference to guidance and to codes.

11.48 However, Burton P in *Steel v Chief Constable of Thames Valley Police* UKEAT/0793/03, pointed out that Morison J gave that guidance at a stage when the DDA 1995 was in its early period of operation; as employment tribunals become more familiar and comfortable with the operation of these procedures, express reference to particular provisions becomes less significant. Burton P said (at para 40):

> We do not conclude that there is any need in every case for spelling out, by reference to every paragraph of a relevant code, a conclusion as to whether there has been breach, and whether there is an inference to be drawn one way or the other from that breach, where a tribunal does not conclude that such breach or such inference is central, or essential, or significant to its conclusion, or at any rate where an appeal court, on looking at the matter, does not so conclude.

11.49 Similarly, in *McDonald v London Borough of Ealing* EAT/406/99, Charles J stated (at para 33) that it was not necessary, where there was an allegation of breach of a code of practice, for the provisions of the code of practice to be expressly referred to in the tribunal's reasons, if none of them pointed to a different conclusion or approach from that reached and taken by the tribunal.

Reasons for interim orders

11.50 In *English v Emery Reimbold & Strick* [2002] EWCA Civ 605, [2003] IRLR 710, paras 13–14, Lord Phillips MR observed that Strasbourg jurisprudence in relation to Art 6 of the ECHR acknowledged that there were some decisions where fairness does not demand that the parties should be informed of the reasoning underlying the decision. He gave interim decisions in the course of case management as 'an obvious example'. Rule 62 makes it clear that reasons must be given for all decisions. However, the reasons for decisions which are not judgments may be very short.

Reasons for costs orders

11.51 In *English* (above), Lord Phillips MR (at paras 14 and 27–30) noted that costs orders in the civil courts were often given in summary form without reasons. Whilst it remains in the interests of justice that a judge should be able to dispose of costs applications in a speedy and uncomplicated way, a costs order without reasons would only comply with Art 6 of the ECHR if the reason for the order was implicit from the circumstances of the case. In the normal case, in the civil courts costs follow the event (ie the winner gets his costs paid by the loser) and the reasoning will be plain. If the reasons for the costs order are not obvious, in particular if the costs order departs from the norm, a brief explanation should be given. The Court of Appeal will only give permission to appeal on grounds of inadequate reasons if no explanation is given, and there is no obvious explanation.

11.52 The same approach, in principle, should apply to the making of orders for costs in the tribunal. Indeed, there is likely to be a greater need for reasons in the tribunal. The tribunal's jurisdiction to make an order for costs is narrower than that of the civil courts, and the tribunal will at least need to explain briefly why the jurisdictional requirements of the rules are met, and why it is exercising its discretion, both in principle and as to amount.

Amplification of the reasons

Jurisdiction

11.53 For now, it appears settled that the EAT may remit a case to the tribunal to amplify its reasons: such a practice is provided for in the EAT Practice Direction 2004. The practice was recognized and approved in *Burns v Consignia plc (No 2)* [2004] IRLR 425, and *Burns* itself was approved by the Court of Appeal in *Barke v SEETEC Business Technology Centre Ltd* [2005] EWCA Civ 578, [2005] IRLR 633 and *Bone v London Borough of Newham* [2008] EWCA Civ 435, [2008] IRLR 546. See further Chapter 18.

Request for clarification by the parties

Rather than appeal a decision and seek a remission for further reasons, the parties may request **11.54** clarification of a decision from the tribunal. If there has been a material omission in the tribunal's findings of fact or in its consideration of the issues of fact and law before it, parties should ask the tribunal to amplify its reasons, either when oral reasons are given or as soon as possible after receiving written reasons: *Bansi v Alpha Flight Services (Note)* [2007] ICR 308, approved in *Royle v Greater Manchester Police Authority* [2007] ICR 281.

D. ANONYMIZATION OF JUDGMENTS AND TRIBUNAL RECORDS

In certain cases the tribunal may make an order requiring the identities of parties, witnesses, or **11.55** other persons to be anonymized in the written record or reasons (ETR 2013, r 50). See further paras 9.181 ff.

E. CHANGING THE DECISION

After registration

There are two situations in which a tribunal may change its decision after registration (other than **11.56** as a result of a successful appeal):

(1) The tribunal may reconsider its own decision under rr 70–73 of the ETR 2013.
(2) The tribunal may alter its decision or reasons under the 'slip rule' (ETR 2013, r 69), which provides that clerical mistakes and errors arising from an accidental slip or omission may at any time be corrected by the judge by certificate.

Reconsiderations and corrections under the slip rule are dealt with more fully in Chapter 13. **11.57**

Before registration

There are a number of apparently conflicting authorities on the question of the tribunal's powers **11.58** to recall and alter a decision after an oral decision has been given, but before the decision has been registered. Many of the decisions pre-date the introduction of the tribunal's power to review its own decision, first introduced in the ETR 1993. The power of review, currently contained in rr 70–73 of the ETR 2013, means that the power to recall is now of limited relevance, save where the formalities for seeking a review have not been complied with. That the power of recall had survived at least as far as the ETR 2004 was, however, confirmed by the EAT in *The Cadogan Hotel Partners Ltd v Ms J Ozog* [2014] EqLR 691. At 36, HHJ Eady QC held that: 'it might be appropriate for a Tribunal to recall its Judgment, rather than formally reviewing it, where an obvious error or omission comes to light soon after the hearing but before the order was drawn up. Save for such unusual cases, the oral Judgment of the Tribunal must stand as its final Judgment'.

In the civil courts there is a power to recall a decision before it has been perfected. The court is **11.59** not *functus officio* until the order carrying the judgment into effect has been drawn up and perfected (by sealing (CPR r 40(2))) (see *Re Barrell Enterprises* [1973] 1 WLR 19; *Robinson v Bird* [2003] EWCA Civ 1019; *In Re L (Children) (Preliminary Finding: Power to reverse)* [2013] UKSC 8, [2013] 1 WLR 634). A number of cases establish a limited power in the employment tribunal to recall a decision prior to registration. In *Hanks v Ace High Productions Ltd* [1978] ICR 1155, [1979] IRLR 32, Phillips J adopted the approach taken in the civil courts and held there was a power to recall. *Hanks* departed from the earlier EAT decision in *Jowett v Earl of Bradford* [1977]

ICR 342, which had held that a decision was binding as soon as it was orally announced. In *Hanks* Phillips J said (at 33):

> It is that class of case, where the error or omission is obvious and comes to light soon after the hearing and before the order is drawn up, which is suitable to be dealt with in this way, rather than by way of review. Putting the matter negatively, it would obviously be wrong to make use of the power, in effect to re-hear the case, or merely to hear further argument on matters of fact with the possibility of changing the mind of the tribunal on the facts, when already a clear decision has been reached upon them. It is intended for the simple error which can be put right and matters of that sort.

11.60 In *Lamont v Fry's Metals Ltd* [1985] ICR 566, [1985] IRLR 470, the tribunal gave an oral decision, and then changed its mind before the written reasons were completed or registered. The EAT held ([1983] IRLR 434) that the tribunal had the power to recall its decision before the decision was registered, and to invite further argument upon it. In the Court of Appeal Lawton LJ assumed, without deciding, that a tribunal could recall its judgments before they have been perfected, and that a decision of a tribunal is not perfected until it is registered in accordance with the regulations.

11.61 Subsequent decisions recognized the power to recall but followed the narrow approach of *Hanks* as to the circumstances in which the power may be exercised. It is doubtful whether the power would extend to allow the tribunal to reopen the case as it tried to do in *Lamont* The EAT (presided over by Underhill J) followed *Hanks* in *CK Heating Ltd v Doro* [2010] ICR 1449, in holding that the power to recall should be used sparingly, as a general principle, but that *Hanks* laid down no absolute rule. The ultimate question is whether it is necessary to recall the decision in the interests of justice, having regard to the overriding objective, in the circumstances of the particular case. The power to recall was useful in that case as the procedural requirements for a review had not been complied with.

11.62 It is important to preserve the principle that the tribunal should never contemplate departing from its previous oral decision without giving the parties the opportunity to make representations: *Arthur Guinness Son & Co (GB) Ltd v Green* [1989] ICR 241, [1989] IRLR 288 (as endorsed in *The Cadogan Hotel Partners Ltd* at 36). In *Spring Grove Services Group v Hickinbottom* [1990] ICR 111, the EAT held that the power to recall did not, however, allow the tribunal to invite argument on a new authority reported after the oral decision was handed down.

11.63 The above cases concerned the recall of final orders: there is authority that the position differed in respect of interim orders. An interim order is effective as soon as it is announced, and it would appear that there can never be a recall of it: *Casella London Ltd v Banai* [1990] ICR 215. However, an interim decision can subsequently be varied or revoked, so the power of recall is, for practical purposes, unnecessary.

11.64 It is far from clear that the EAT in *Doro* was right to proceed on the basis that a judgment is not perfected until it is entered on the register. At the time of *Hanks*, the Tribunal Rules then applicable (the 1974 version) were loosely worded and allowed the EAT to adopt the approach taken in the civil courts. However, the 2004 ETR (the relevant rules by the time of *Doro*) use the language of a judgment being 'issued' orally: r 28(3) of the ETR 2004 provided: 'At the end of a hearing the Employment Judge (or as the case may be, the tribunal) shall either issue any order or judgment orally or shall reserve the judgment or order to be given in writing at a later date'. The use of the language 'issue orally' suggests that the judgment is effective from the moment it is given orally. Rule 32 provided that a judgment shall be entered in the register, but it did not provide that the judgment was not completed or perfected until it was entered on the register. A tribunal judgment does not need to be sealed (as an order does in the civil courts). It does, however, need to be recorded in a written record signed by the employment judge (under both the ETR 2004 and the ETR 2013). The better analysis may be that the power to recall exists between oral announcement and the signing of the written record by the employment judge.

11.65 The ETR 2013 provides at r 65 that a judgment or order takes effect from the day when it is given or made, or on such later date as specified by the tribunal. Although this rule did not appear in previous versions of the rules, it is unlikely that its introduction changes the position in relation to the power to recall. Rule 65 mirrors the existing CPR r 40.7. The same rule in the CPR has not prevented the courts from recognizing the power to recall in the civil courts. The requirement to enter the judgment in the register (ETR 2004, r 32) does not feature in the ETR 2013, presumably being one of the elements of the old rules that the Underhill Review regarded as administrative and therefore unnecessary.

F. *RES JUDICATA*, ISSUE ESTOPPEL, AND ABUSE OF PROCESS

Introduction

The question of the effect of previous decisions of courts or tribunals involving the same or similar **11.66** parties arises from time to time in all civil litigation (see also Chapter 20). In the most straightforward case, a party seeks to bring proceedings which relitigate a matter which the court or tribunal has already decided on. Employment litigation creates particular difficulties with respect to the effect of earlier decisions because of the overlapping jurisdiction of the tribunal and the civil courts. There are a number of situations in which issues raised in tribunal proceedings may overlap with issues which may be raised in the civil courts (Chapter 20). For example, issues raised in an unfair dismissal complaint may also be raised in High Court breach of contract proceedings. Further, the tribunals and the courts have concurrent jurisdiction in relation to certain claims for breach of contract. Damages may be claimed in the tribunals in respect of personal injuries caused by unlawful discrimination. There may be an overlap between such a claim and a claim for damages for personal injury arising out of the employer's negligence, which may be pursued in the courts. As a result of these overlaps it will often be necessary for a court or tribunal to determine the effect of an earlier decision on related issues.

In *Virgin Atlantic Airways Ltd v Zodiac Seats UK Ltd* [2014] AC 160, Lord Sumption described *res* **11.67** *judicata* as a 'portmanteau' term, which is used to describe a number of different legal principles with different juridical origins (para 17). He identified five principles:

(1) *Cause of action estoppel* A final adjudication against a party on a particular cause of action will be conclusive in subsequent proceedings involving the same parties and the same cause of action as to all points decided in the previous judgment.

(2) The principle that where a claimant succeeds in the first action and does not challenge the outcome he may not bring a further action on the same cause of action, for example for further damages.

(3) *The doctrine of merger* A cause of action is extinguished once a judgment is given on it, and the claimant's sole right is a right on the judgment.

(4) *Issue estoppel* A judgment which includes a decision on a particular issue forming a *necessary* ingredient in the cause of action will be binding as to that particular issue if it arises in subsequent proceedings between the same parties or related parties where that issue is relevant, subject to narrow exceptions.

(5) *Abuse of process* It may be an abuse of process to make a claim which could and should have been brought forward as part of earlier proceedings.

Lord Sumption went on to identify the House of Lords decision in *Arnold v National Westminster* **11.68** *Bank plc* [1991] 2 AC 93 as authority for the following propositions (*Virgin Airways*, para 22):

(1) Cause of action estoppel is absolute in relation to all points which had to be and were decided in order to establish the existence or non-existence of a cause of action.

(2) Cause of action estoppel also bars the raising in subsequent proceedings of points essential to the existence or non-existence of a cause of action which were not decided because they were not raised in the earlier proceedings, if they could with reasonable diligence and should in all the circumstances have been raised.

(3) Except in special circumstances where this would cause injustice, issue estoppel bars the raising in subsequent proceedings of points which (i) were not raised in the earlier proceedings or (ii) were

raised but unsuccessfully. If the relevant point was not raised, the bar will usually be absolute if it could with reasonable diligence and should in all the circumstances have been raised.

11.69 He went on to describe *res judicata* and abuse of process as 'distinct although overlapping principles with the common underlying purpose of limiting abusive and duplicative litigation'. That purpose, he said, made it necessary to qualify the absolute character of both cause of action estoppel and issue estoppel when the conduct is not abusive (para 25).

Application of principles of estoppel to tribunal decisions

11.70 A decision of the employment tribunal may give rise to an issue estoppel, or to *res judicata* in High Court proceedings, so that no evidence may be led in High Court proceedings to contradict the decision of the tribunal (*Green v Hampshire County Council* [1979] ICR 861, Ch D; *Munir v Jang Publications Ltd* [1989] IRLR 224, [1989] ICR 1, CA; *Soteriou v Ultrachem Ltd* [2004] IRLR 870, EWHC, approved in *Fraser v HLMAD* [2006] EWCA Civ 738, [2006] IRLR 687 at para 28).

Cause of action and issue estoppel

Conditions for cause of action and issue estoppel

11.71 The following conditions apply to both forms of estoppel:

(a) There must be a *final* adjudication on the merits (see paras 11.70–11.79).
(b) The parties must be the same, or privies to the original parties (see para 11.80).
(c) The subject matter must be the same (see paras 11.81–11.88).

Final decision on the merits

11.72 A potential trap frequently arises when a party has started proceedings in the employment tribunal, but later decides to abandon those proceedings in favour of a claim in the High Court. A decision may be a decision on the merits even if there has been no argument upon it. In the employment tribunals, a dismissal on withdrawal by a claimant has been treated as a decision on the merits, giving rise to a cause of action estoppel. In *Barber v Staffordshire CC* [1996] IRLR 209, the Court of Appeal held that the principles of cause of action or issue estoppel apply to the dismissal of an application by a tribunal following its withdrawal by the claimant. The court stated that there is nothing which stipulates that the doctrine of estoppel can only apply in cases where a tribunal has given a reasoned decision on the issues of fact and law. This principle has presented problems in the tribunals for a number of years, as there has been no procedure in the tribunal for discontinuance. Unwary litigants and their representatives, therefore, on numerous occasions found themselves debarred from having their case determined on the merits through failing to appreciate the consequences of a dismissal on withdrawal. Rule 25 of the ETR 2004 sought to solve this problem, but the opaque language of the rule created its own problems of interpretation, and the rule was amended with effect from 6 April 2009. Withdrawal is now dealt with by rr 51 and 52 of the ETR 2013.

11.73 An order dismissing a complaint upon withdrawal is a judicial decision rather than a mere administrative act. Rule 51 provides that where a claimant informs the tribunal, either in writing or in the course of a hearing that a claim or part of it is withdrawn, the claim or part 'comes to an end' subject to any application the respondent may make for costs, preparation time, or wasted costs.

11.74 Rule 52 provides that where a claim or part of it has been withdrawn under r 51, the tribunal shall issue a judgment dismissing it (which means that the claimant may not commence a further claim against the respondent raising the same, or substantially the same complaint) unless:

(a) the claimant has expressed at the time of withdrawal a wish to reserve the right to bring such a further claim and the tribunal is satisfied that there would be a legitimate reason for doing so or
(b) the tribunal believes that to issue such a judgment would not be in the interests of justice.

The rule leaves open the possibility for proceedings to be withdrawn under r 51 but not dismissed **11.75**
under r 52. Whilst that distinction might seem opaque, it arises out of the quite separate issues
of (a) what happens to the proceedings which are being withdrawn; and (b) whether a new set of
proceedings can be issued on the same facts. The original version of r 25 of the ETR 2004 was
interpreted by the Court of Appeal (*Khan v Heywood & Middleton Primary Care Trust* [2006]
EWCA Civ 1087) as follows (and it is suggested these principles apply equally to rr 51–52 of the
ETR 2013):

(1) The purpose of the distinction between a withdrawal and a dismissal is to cover the lacuna that
there is no procedure in the tribunal for a discontinuance.

(2) Where proceedings are withdrawn and subsequently dismissed the principle in *Barber* applies,
and a cause of action estoppel arises out of the dismissal.

(3) Where the proceedings are withdrawn, but are not dismissed, no cause of action estoppel
arises, as proceedings are brought to an end automatically by operation of r 25(3), not by judicial decision. The claimant would therefore be free to pursue subsequent proceedings based
on the same facts.

(4) However, once the proceedings are withdrawn it is not possible for the tribunal to revoke or
set aside the withdrawal and continue with the original proceedings. The rule states that the
proceedings are brought to an end (save for certain specified purposes). Had the draftsman
intended there to be a power to set aside the withdrawal, the Rules would have needed to make
provision for such a procedure.

Prior to the introduction of r 25 of the ETR 2004, the Court of Appeal in a number of cases sought **11.76**
to avoid the consequences of *Barber* by holding that a dismissal on withdrawal in the tribunal did
not give rise to a cause of action estoppel if the withdrawal was in order to commence proceedings in the civil courts (because, for example, a claimant realized their contract claim exceeded the
£25,000 cap): see in particular *Ako v Rothschild Asset Management Ltd* [2002] EWCA Civ 236,
[2002] IRLR 348; and *Enfield LBC v Sivanandan* [2005] EWCA Civ 10. It was held by the EAT
in *British Association for Shooting and Conservation v Cokayne* [2008] ICR 185, that the route taken
in the *Ako* line of cases was no longer available to tribunals following the introduction of r 25 of the
ETR 2004. According to HHJ Richardson (para 35), the underlying principle illustrated by *Ako*
is that there may be exceptions to the application of cause of action estoppel where it is necessary
to do justice. The approach taken in *Ako* was only necessary when the tribunal rules had no mechanism for withdrawing proceedings without dismissing them. Given that a tribunal may permit
withdrawal without dismissal under r 25, if the tribunal goes the extra step and dismisses the claim,
then the claim must be taken as dismissed for all purposes, and it is not open to a claimant to avoid
the application of cause of action estoppel by reliance on *Ako*.

However, the EAT in *Cokayne* went on to note that a trap still remains for an unrepresented **11.77**
litigant who does not appreciate the significance of the distinction between dismissal and withdrawal under what are now rr 51–52 of the ETR 2013. The EAT recommended that the tribunal,
when faced with an application to withdraw by an unrepresented claimant, should itself consider
whether there is material on file which would suggest that it is unjust to dismiss the claim (para 37).
Further, if the claim is dismissed in cases where the claimant intends to commence fresh proceedings, the claimant's remedy is to seek an application for review of the dismissal. On the review, the
tribunal can consider whether it would be an abuse of process to set aside the dismissal, opening
the way for the claimant to commence fresh proceedings (para 36).

Rule 25 created a further difficulty, in that on its face it offers no guidance as to how the power to **11.78**
dismiss under r 25(4) should be operated. The power would appear to be discretionary, but there
is no indication as to the principles upon which the discretion is to be exercised. This problem was
considered by the EAT in *Verdin v Harrods Ltd* [2006] IRLR 339. The EAT confirmed that the
power under r 25(4) was discretionary, and gave some guidance as to when it should be exercised.
Once again, the key to the rule lay in the application of the principles of estoppel and abuse of
process to decisions of the tribunal. A respondent will generally be entitled to have the proceedings
dismissed. There may, however, be circumstances in which it would be just to refuse to dismiss the

proceedings if the dismissal is for the purpose of pursuing other proceedings. The questions for the tribunal to determine are those identified in *Ako*. Is the withdrawing party intending to abandon the claim? If the withdrawing party is intending to resurrect the claim in fresh proceedings, would it be an abuse of process to allow that to occur? If the answer to either of these questions is yes, then it will be just to dismiss the proceedings. If the answer to both questions is no, it will be unjust to dismiss the proceedings. The reasoning in *Verdin* as to the legislative intent of the rule was approved by the Court of Appeal in *Khan*.

11.79 Rule 52 of the ETR 2013 makes the position somewhat clearer. The starting position is that a withdrawn claim should be dismissed, unless one or other of the conditions are satisfied: either the claimant wishes to preserve the right to bring a further claim, and the tribunal considers it legitimate that they should do so; or a dismissal would not be in the interests of justice. It is difficult to see what situations may render it contrary to the interests of justice to dismiss the claim.

11.80 The decisions which do not give rise to a cause of action estoppel are set out below:

(a) A decision on the grounds of lack of jurisdiction (although in reaching its decision a court may decide issues which give rise to an issue estoppel on those issues (see, eg, *The Sennar No 2* [1985] 1 WLR 490, HL)). A dismissal on the grounds that a claim was out of time does not give rise to an issue estoppel (*Nayif v High Commissioner of Brunei Darussalam* [2014] EWCA Civ 1521, [2015] ICR 517).

(b) A refusal to allow an amendment to permit a claim to be brought (*Air Canada v Basra* [2000] IRLR 683, EAT, para 39).

(c) A 'decision' of the tribunal recording the terms of a settlement between the parties, but which does not order a sum to be paid or dismiss the claim is not a decision at all and therefore cannot give rise to a *res judicata* (*Dattani v Trio Supermarkets Ltd* [1998] IRLR 240, CA).

11.81 The 'underlying principle', as summarized by Elias LJ in *Nayif*, at 27, is that:

there should be finality and matters which have been litigated, or would have been but for a party being unwilling to put them to the test, should not be reopened' but that there was 'no justification for the principle applying in circumstances where there has been no actual adjudication of any issue and no action by a party which would justify treating him as having consented, either expressly or by implication, to having conceded the issue by choosing not to have the matter formally determined'.

In *Srivatsa v Secretary of State for Health* [2018] EWCA Civ 936 (Lewison LJ), the Court of Appeal followed the approach in cases such as *Sajid*, *Ako*, and *Nayif* in looking at the claimant's intention at the time he had withdrawn his tribunal claim: whether the circumstances showed and intention to abandon the claim or cause of action. The subsequent Supreme Court decision in *Virgin Atlantic* was consistent with the approach in those cases, as it indicated that even cause of action estoppel was not absolute where there was no abusive conduct, and in the claimant's case his conduct in withdrawing his claim had not been abusive. In *Srivatsa* the claimant had withdrawn his claim, and then sought (unsuccessfully) to reopen it after the respondent applied for costs. His subsequent High Court claim was issued before the tribunal dismissed his claim under the then applicable r 25(4) of the ETR 2004. Although he had not stated an intention to pursue a High Court claim at the time he withdrew the claim, by the time of the dismissal this was known, as he had commenced the High Court claim and had sought to reopen the tribunal claim.

Same parties or their privies

11.82 Privies may be privy to the parties by blood, title, or identity of interest (*Carl Zeiss Stiftung v Rayner and Keeler Ltd* [1967] 1 AC 853, 910 (Lord Reid)). So, for example, a judgment against a person will be binding on his heirs and executors. Further examples include office holders and their successors and members of a representative class in representative proceedings. Privity of interest arises where a party has sufficient involvement in proceedings to which he is not a party that it is just for the decision in those proceedings to be binding upon him. The circumstances giving rise to privity of interest are not well defined. The mere fact that a company's commercial success depended on the outcome of proceedings is not sufficient, nor is the fact that a person has provided a witness statement in the proceedings. Some element of control of the proceedings or the matters in issue in the proceedings is likely to be required. See in addition to the *Carl Zeiss* case, *Gleeson v Wippell & Co* [1977] 1 WLR 510, Ch D and *Kirin-Amgen Inc v Boehringer Mannheim GmbH* [1997] FSR 289, CA.

Same subject matter

Where cause of action estoppel is relied on, the cause of action in the subsequent case must be the **11.83** *same* as the cause of action determined in the first case.

Where issue estoppel is relied on, the issue in the second proceedings must be the same as the issue **11.84** in the first proceedings. Further, the issue must have been an issue which was necessarily determined in the first case. A party will not be bound by a finding of fact which it was not necessary for the tribunal in the first case to have decided in reaching its decision.

It is necessary to take some care in determining whether the cause of action or issue is indeed identical in the two sets of proceedings. **11.85**

In *Jones v Mid-Glamorgan County Council* [1997] ICR 815, [1997] IRLR 685: **11.86**

(a) County court proceedings were brought for breach of contract in relation to pension benefits. The key issue was whether, in accepting voluntary retirement terms, an employee had been acting under duress. The court held that he had not been subjected to duress, but that he had in fact retired voluntarily on the agreed terms.

(b) In a subsequent unfair dismissal complaint, the issue for the employment tribunal was whether the employee had been dismissed. The tribunal, having heard evidence, concluded that he had not been dismissed (thus in effect reaching the same conclusion as the county court), but in its reasons it referred to the county court's findings on the question of voluntary retirement as being 'binding' on it.

(c) The EAT and the Court of Appeal held that no issue estoppel arose. The issue in the county court was whether, under the law of contract, duress had vitiated the employee's acceptance of the early retirement offer, whereas, in the tribunal, the relevant question was whether the threat of dismissal was the operative factor in the employee accepting early retirement. As the two issues were quite different, requiring different analyses, the question of issue estoppel did not arise.

(d) The Court of Appeal, however, overturned the EAT's decision and upheld the tribunal's decision, finding that on a true construction of the reasons the tribunal had decided the issues itself, and had not applied an issue estoppel (but see Browne-Wilkinson J in *O'Laoire v Jackel International Ltd* [1991] ICR 718).

In *Friend v Civil Aviation Authority* [2001] EWCA Civ 1204, [2002] ICR 525: **11.87**

(a) The claimant was dismissed after complaining about certain safety procedures. In employment tribunal proceedings his dismissal was found to have been procedurally unfair, but his conduct was held to have contributed 100 per cent to his dismissal and he received no compensation.

(b) He later issued High Court proceedings claiming wrongful dismissal and various employment-related torts.

(c) The Court of Appeal held that no issue estoppel arose from the finding of contributory conduct. A decision under s 123(6) of the ERA 1996 that the claimant's conduct contributed to his dismissal, and that it would be just and equitable to reduce the amount of the compensatory award by 100 per cent, cannot be regarded as a decision that any loss resulting from the dismissal was not caused by any tort or breach of contract of the employers but by the claimant's own behaviour.

In *British Airways v Boyce* [2001] IRLR 157, Court of Session: **11.88**

(a) The claimant brought a race discrimination complaint, alleging that he had been discriminated against on grounds of his English *ethnic* origins. The complaint was dismissed, because the English were not an ethnic group.

Part A Tribunal Procedure

(b) The claimant brought a second race discrimination complaint on identical facts, the only difference being that he claimed discrimination on grounds of his English *national* origins.

(c) The Court of Session regarded the complaint as *res judicata*. The type of complaint, and the facts alleged were the same. The change reflected no more than a different legal approach in support of the same underlying proposition. The proper approach was to ask what was litigated and what was decided. Lord Marnoch said (at 159):

> The *media concludendi* should in general be taken as covering everything in the legislation, both in its legal and factual aspects, which is pertinent to the act or acts of the employer made subject of the complaint—here the act of the employer in refusing the respondent's job application on allegedly racial grounds.

11.89 In *Bainbridge v Redcar & Cleveland Borough Council* [2008] EWCA Civ 885, [2008] IRLR 776:

(a) The claimants brought equal pay claims relating to a period of time in respect of which earlier equal pay claims had already been determined, albeit in relation to different comparators. The respondents argued that a cause of action estoppel arose.

(b) The respondent categorized the cause of action as being the alleged breach of the equality clause in respect of the claimants for the particular period of time.

(c) The EAT, by a majority, had rejected this argument and instead found in favour of the claimants. The reasoning of the majority in the EAT was that a promise to pay A the same as B is not the same as a promise to pay A the same as C: a single contractual term may contain a number of contractual obligations.

(d) The Court of Appeal, dismissing an appeal from the EAT's decision, held that, although the equal pay claim was for contravention of a term of a contract, the content of the term was determined by the terms of the statute and not by agreement of the parties. The cause of action was asserted pursuant to statute. Within and by virtue of the statute there was more than one cause of action. Accordingly, there was nothing in the doctrine of *res judicata* which restricted the claimants to confine themselves to one way of putting their case.

11.90 In *Foster v Bon Groundwork Ltd* [2012] EWCA Civ 252, [2012] ICR 1027, the claimant was laid off, and subsequently dismissed purportedly for reason of retirement. The claimant brought a first claim for a redundancy payment, on grounds that he had been laid off. The claim failed, the tribunal finding that the claimant had been dismissed for retirement. The claimant brought a second claim for unfair dismissal. The Court of Appeal held that neither the fact of dismissal nor the reason for it was a necessary ingredient in the cause of action for a redundancy payment, and therefore no *res judicata* arose in relation to these issues in the unfair dismissal claim. A finding of fact by an earlier court which is not a necessary ingredient in the earlier cause of action will not give rise to a 'fact estoppel'. A finding of fact cannot be a necessary ingredient of a cause of action if the earlier court or tribunal did not have jurisdiction to decide the matter. An exception to this principle is where a court makes an express finding as to jurisdiction which is not appealed. The finding is binding, even if subsequently shown to be wrong (see *Bon Groundwork*, paras 5–6 (Elias LJ)).

Issue estoppel—special circumstances

11.91 A cause of action estoppel is an absolute bar to further proceedings based on the same cause of action. The principle of issue estoppel, however, is more flexible. There is an exception to the rule of issue estoppel in the special circumstances where further material has become available to a party which was relevant to the correct determination of the point involved in the earlier proceedings but which could not by reasonable diligence have been adduced in those proceedings: *Arnold v National Westminster Bank plc* [1991] 2 AC 93. In *Watt (formerly Carter) v Ahsan* [2007] UKHL 51, [2008] 2 WLR 17, [2008] ICR 82 the House of Lords held that it would be unjust to allow a party to one action (A) to rely on this exception where it had in unrelated proceedings appealed on the point of law decided against it in action A but made no attempt to stay action A pending the hearing of the appeal in the unrelated proceedings. Thus, even though the unrelated appeal later succeeded, the tribunal and the parties in action A remained bound by the earlier tribunal decision, however incorrect in law that had now proven to be.

The principle in *Henderson v Henderson*

General principle

In general, a litigant must raise all relevant points at the trial of the complaint he has brought. The **11.92** courts have long adhered to the principle that when a litigant brings a case he must bring forward his whole case and will not, except in special circumstances, be permitted to bring fresh proceedings in respect of a matter which could and should have been litigated in earlier proceedings. The starting point for this principle is the decision of the Court of Appeal in *Henderson v Henderson* (1843) 3 Hare 100. Sir James Wigram VC said (at 115):

> Where a given matter becomes the subject of litigation in, and of adjudication by, a court of competent jurisdiction, the court requires the parties to that litigation to bring forward their whole case, and will not (except under special circumstances) permit the same parties to open the same subject of litigation in respect of matter which might have been brought forward as part of the subject in contest, but which was not brought forward, only because they have, from negligence, inadvertence, or even accident, omitted part of their case. The plea of res judicata applies, except in special cases, not only to points upon which the court was actually required by the parties to form an opinion and pronounce a judgment, but to every point which properly belonged to the subject of litigation, and which the parties, exercising reasonable diligence, might have brought forward at the time.

Application in the employment sphere

The principle in *Henderson v Henderson* above presents a particular trap in employment litigation **11.93** because of the potential for claims which could be brought, either in the employment tribunal or in the courts.

In *Sheriff v Klyne Tugs (Lowestoft) Ltd* [1999] ICR 1170, [1999] IRLR 481:   **11.94**

(a) The claimant claimed to have been subjected to racial harassment as a result of which he suffered a nervous breakdown.
(b) He brought a claim of race discrimination in the employment tribunal which was dismissed on withdrawal after terms of settlement were reached between the parties.
(c) The claimant subsequently brought proceedings in the county court claiming that his psychiatric injury had been caused by abusive and detrimental treatment by his employer. The particulars relied on were substantially the same matters alleged in the tribunal claim.
(d) The Court of Appeal held that damages for personal injury arising out of unlawful race discrimination could have been recovered in the tribunal proceedings.
(e) Relying on the rule in *Henderson v Henderson* the Court of Appeal struck out the county court claim on the basis that the claimant could and should have brought forward his whole claim in the tribunal proceedings.
(f) The Court of Appeal rejected the argument that procedural differences between the tribunal and the court (limitation periods, costs regimes, power to award interim payments, and provisional damages) amounted to special circumstances. The fact that the medical condition was undiscovered at the time of the tribunal hearing may amount to a special circumstance.
(g) The Court of Appeal also held that the terms of the compromise reached in the tribunal proceedings had compromised any claim in relation to personal injuries. The relevant provision of the settlement provided:

> The Applicant accepts the terms of this agreement in full and final settlement of all claims which he has or may have against the respondent arising out of this employment or the termination thereof being claims in respect of which an industrial tribunal has jurisdiction.

A strict application of the principle can lead to harsh results. It was not clear as a matter of law that **11.95** the tribunal could award damages for personal injury in a discrimination claim until *Sheriff* itself, yet the claimant was precluded from bringing a court action because he should have raised such a claim in the tribunal. See also *Barber v Staffordshire County Council* [1996] ICR 379.

The principle may apply even though a party may have little time to decide whether to pursue a **11.96** claim in the earlier set of proceedings. In *Divine-Borty v London Borough of Brent* [1998] ICR 886,

[1998] IRLR 525, during the hearing of a claim for unfair dismissal, evidence from one of the employer's witnesses suggested that the claimant's race may have been a factor in the dismissal. No application was made to bring a claim under the Race Relations Act 1976. The tribunal dismissed the unfair dismissal application, making no express finding as to the racial issue.

11.97 The claimant issued a second tribunal application alleging race discrimination. The Court of Appeal held, on the basis of *Henderson v Henderson*, that the second complaint should not be allowed to proceed. The fact that the evidence upon which the race claim was based emerged during the hearing of the unfair dismissal was not a special circumstance. The race discrimination complaint should have been raised at the hearing, or if necessary an adjournment sought.

11.98 *Sheriff* was followed by the Court of Appeal in *Enfield LBC v Sivanandan* [2005] EWCA Civ 10. In striking out a High Court claim for breach of contract, the primary reasoning of the Court of Appeal in *Sivanandan* was that the same claim had been raised in the tribunal and had been struck out on the grounds of vexatious conduct. However, the Court of Appeal considered, and accepted, an alternative argument: even if the contract claim had been withdrawn from the tribunal proceedings prior to the strike-out, it was an abuse of process to 'reinvent' in the guise of a breach of contract a claim that was really the same as the race discrimination claim that had been struck out in the employment tribunal.

11.99 In so deciding, the Court of Appeal was influenced by the following:

(a) The facts giving rise to the breach of contract claim were encompassed by the race discrimination claim.

(b) The loss claimed in the contract claim could have been recovered in the race discrimination claim.

11.100 The Court of Appeal therefore closely followed *Sheriff* in holding that the second claim arose out of the same facts, and claimed the same losses as were claimed in the first claim, therefore the second claim was an abuse. Note, however, it was clear that the Court of Appeal regarded Sivanandan's conduct of the proceedings as unreasonable (see in particular Buxton LJ's judgment), and it was a relevant factor that in order to bring the contract claim she had significantly changed her position as to if and when her employment was terminated ([2005] EWCA Civ 10, para 138 (Peter Gibson LJ).

Relaxation of the strictness of the rule

11.101 The civil courts have in recent years taken a more liberal approach to the principle of *Henderson v Henderson*. In *Parker v Northumbrian Water Ltd* [2011] ICR 1172, [2011] IRLR 652, the EAT held that tribunals considering the application of the principle should adopt the merits-based approach of the House of Lords in *Johnson v Gore Wood & Co (No 1)* [2002] 2 AC 1, [2001] 2 WLR 72 (as detailed below), rather than the approach adopted by the Court of Appeal in *Divine-Borty*.

11.102 In *Johnson v Gore Wood Ltd*, the House of Lords made clear that, although closely connected with cause of action estoppel and issue estoppel, the principle in *Henderson v Henderson* is a form of abuse of process. Two important points arise, which alleviate the strict application of the principle: (1) a broad merits based approach, taking into account all the circumstances, should be taken; (2) the onus is on the defendant to show abuse, rather than on the claimant to show special circumstances why the claim should be allowed to proceed. Lord Bingham of Cornhill said (at 90):

> The bringing of a claim or the raising of a defence in later proceedings may, without more, amount to abuse if the court is satisfied (*the onus being on the party alleging abuse*) that the claim or defence should have been raised in the earlier proceedings if it was to be raised at all. I would not accept that it is necessary, before abuse may be found, to identify any additional element such as a collateral attack on a previous decision or some dishonesty, but where those elements are present the later proceedings will be much more obviously abusive, and there will rarely be a finding of abuse unless the later proceeding involves what the court regards as unjust harassment of a party. It is, however, wrong to hold that because a matter could have been raised in early proceedings it should have been, so as to render the raising of it in later proceedings necessarily abusive. That is to adopt too dogmatic an approach to what should in my opinion be *a broad, merits based judgment which takes account of the public and private interests involved*

and also takes account of all the facts of the case, focusing attention on the crucial question whether, in all the circumstances, a party is misusing or abusing the process of the court by seeking to raise before it the issue which could have been raised before (emphasis added).

The courts have resisted attempts to define or categorize what may be an abuse of process. However, **11.103** a number of elements which would be likely to render relitigation an abuse were identified by Auld LJ in *Bradford & Bingley Society v Seddon* [1999] 1 WLR 1482, CA, as:

(a) a collateral attack on an earlier judicial decision
(b) dishonesty
(c) successive actions amounting to harassment of the defendant
(d) pursuit of a claim after having pursued a mutually exclusive alternative claim
(e) pursuit of a claim which had previously been abandoned.

In *Stuart v Goldberg Linde (a firm)* [2008] EWCA 2, the Court of Appeal provided further guid- **11.104** ance on the question of abuse of process:

(a) The broad merits based approach to which *Johnson* referred related to the merits of the argument that it was an abuse of process to bring a second claim, not to the substantive merits of the claim itself. It would only be in an extreme case that the merits of the case would be relevant (for example, where the merits were such that summary judgment was appropriate, in which case the necessary application can be made for that purpose: *Walbrook Trustees (Jersey) Ltd v Fattal* [2009] EWCA Civ 297, para 6).
(b) Delay of itself is not relevant (absent questions of limitation).
(c) There is no general duty on the claimant to exercise reasonable diligence in finding out facts going to whether or not he has a new claim, and, as a general rule, a claimant's failure to exercise such diligence is not relevant to the question of abuse of process.

The more liberal approach, following *Johnson v Gore Wood Ltd* above, can be seen in the employ- **11.105** ment context in *Bon Groundwork Ltd v Foster* [2012] IRLR 517, *Friend v Civil Aviation Authority* [2001] IRLR 819, CA, *Chaudhary v Royal College of Surgeons* [2003] ICR 1510, paras 70–83; see also *Bradford & Bingley Building Society v Seddon* [1999] 1 WLR 1482, CA. It should be noted that *Seddon* was not cited in *Sheriff* and neither *Seddon* nor *Johnson v Gore Wood* were referred to in *Sivanandan*. In *University of London v Tariquez-Zaman* [2010] EWHC 908, Slade J rejected an argument that a High Court breach of contract claim was a *Henderson* abuse because the claimant had previously brought a tribunal discrimination claim, in which he claimed the same remedies as in the contract claim. Following *Johnson*, Slade J found no 'unjust harassment' of the defendant. She characterized both *Sheriff* and *Sivanandan* as turning on their own facts. In *Bon Groundwork*, Elias LJ emphasized that the central question is whether the later proceedings involve unjust harassment of a party; that condition is not satisfied merely because a claim could have been brought in the earlier proceedings but was not. For a recent application see also *Ochieng v Stantonbury Campus* UKEAT/0304/15/RN.

In Scotland, the doctrine of *res judicata* differs from that in England and Wales and does not go so **11.106** far as does the rule in *Henderson* in England and Wales. However, in *British Airways v Boyce* [2001] IRLR 157, the Court of Session held that the general principle of *res judicata* should apply to tribunal proceedings in Scotland, and a broad approach be taken to what was litigated and what was decided so that, in practice, the practical outcome of cases should be similar in both jurisdictions.

Other instances of abuse of process

Res judicata and issue estoppel will only arise where a dispute is relitigated between the same **11.107** parties. Similarly, in *Johnson v Gore Wood Ltd*, Lord Millett said that the principle in *Henderson v Henderson* only applies where a claim is brought between parties who had been parties to the previous proceedings.

However, there may be circumstances in which proceedings are held to be an abuse of process be- **11.108** cause of their close connection with an earlier dispute, even if the party claiming abuse was not a

Part A Tribunal Procedure

party to the previous proceedings. Quite apart from the interests of a defendant in not being sued twice over the same matter, there is a general public interest in the same issue not being litigated over again. There is a policy interest in finality, and also in avoiding inconsistent decisions. This policy can be used to justify the extension of the rules of issue estoppel to cases in which the parties are not the same but the circumstances are such as to bring the case within the spirit of the rules (see *Arthur J Hall & Co v Simons* [2000] 3 WLR 543, HL).

11.109 In *Ashmore v British Coal Corp* [1990] 2 QB 338, [1990] ICR 485, A was one of 1,500 women employees of the respondent who made equal pay complaints to the tribunal. The tribunal decided to hear fourteen sample cases, six selected by the employees and eight by the employers, to lay down general principles according to which the others could be decided. The tribunal decided all the cases adversely to the applicants on grounds which were equally applicable to A's application. She then asked for a separate hearing of her case. The Court of Appeal decided that it should be struck out as an abuse of the process of the court. A had not been a party to the sample proceedings but the sensible procedure there adopted would be undermined if all other members of the group were entitled to demand a separate hearing.

11.110 Similarly, in *Acland v Devon CC* EAT/1220/98, in 1997, 145 home care workers employed by three councils had brought claims for breach of contract claiming that they were not bound by the terms of a collective agreement. They also brought equal pay claims. These claims were settled but the underlying dispute continued. In 1998, 130 home care assistants, all members of the same unit for whom two unions were bargaining agents, claimed equal pay. There was no *res judicata* as the parties were not the same. The 1997 proceedings had been brought by named individuals on behalf of the bargaining unit. The tribunal dismissed the applications as an abuse of process because substantially the same workforce was reopening the same issue.

11.111 In *Dexter Ltd v Vlieland-Boddy* [2003] EWCA Civ 14, the Court of Appeal recognized that successive actions based on similar facts, but brought against different defendants who were not privies, could be an abuse of process. However, on the facts, applying the 'broad merits based approach' advocated in *Johnson v Gore Wood Ltd*, the circumstances did not amount to an abuse.

11.112 In *Mills v London Borough of Brent* UKEAT/0545/11, 12/2/13, the claimant withdrew claims brought against the primary school in which she worked. She then brought a further claim against Brent, as the local education authority, based on the same facts as the earlier claims. The earlier claims had been withdrawn but not dismissed, so no estoppel arose. The EAT held that it was an abuse of process to bring a new claim based on the same facts as the earlier claim which had been withdrawn three days into a four-day hearing. There was held to be privity of interest between the school and the local education authority, not least as the latter would have paid any compensation ordered against the school in the first claim.

11.113 It may be an abuse of process to bring proceedings for the purpose of mounting a collateral attack on a final decision made against a party by another court of competent jurisdiction in previous proceedings, in which the party had a full opportunity to contest the decision in the court by which it was made (see *Hunter v Chief Constable of West Midlands Police* [1982] AC 529, 541 (Lord Diplock)).

12

Costs

SUMMARY

(1) Costs are not usually awarded in tribunals.

(2) Tribunals have the power to order costs not only against a party but also their representative ('wasted costs') and also in favour of in-house representatives and litigants in person preparation time orders (PTOs).

(3) A tribunal can award either a fixed sum, up to a maximum of £20,000, which is agreed or summarily assessed by an employment judge or the costs can be determined in the county court or by an employment judge applying the same principles to assessment as the county court.

(4) This chapter addresses costs in the tribunal only.

A. INTRODUCTION

An important distinction between proceedings in the courts and those in the tribunal is that the **12.01** tribunal's powers to award costs to a successful party are very limited. In a civil claim the losing party will invariably have to pay the winner's costs at least in part; in the tribunal this will usually not be the case, and each side will bear its own costs. It is important, therefore, to assess the likely costs of pursuing or defending any claim at an early stage with this in mind.

Statistically, costs have tended to be awarded more frequently as the tribunal rules have changed **12.02** and the amounts of orders made have also increased over the years. For example, in the year 2000/01 there were 247 awards of costs out of 129,725 cases disposed of. The average amount of costs awarded was £295 (ETS Annual Report 2000/01). By the time of the 2011/12 Annual Report there were 612 costs orders made and the average award made was £2,973.

12.03 Tribunals may sometimes indicate to a party during the hearing that they are at risk of costs. In *Gee v Shell* [2003] IRLR 82, the Court of Appeal held that a tribunal should only give a costs warning where there is a real risk that an order for costs will be made against an unsuccessful claimant at the end of the hearing. The court recognized that there is a line to be drawn between 'robust, effective and fair case management', on the one hand, and inappropriate pressure, on the other. In deciding which category the behaviour is in, a number of factors must be considered, such as the circumstances in which the warning was given, the strength of the case against the party, the nature and extent of the warning (for example, whether it referred to the possibility of a summary or a detailed assessment being made), and the manner in which it was given. Note, however, that if a party puts the other side on notice it is important not to be 'oppressive' as that has led to aggravated damages in some discrimination cases: it is all a matter of degree and tone.

12.04 The engagement of the costs regime does not automatically mean that it would be appropriate for a tribunal to make a costs award, they must still be satisfied that it is appropriate to make such an order: *Robinson and Another v Hall Gregory Recruitment Ltd* UKEAT/0425/13.

B. OVERVIEW

12.05 Costs orders can be made in the following circumstances:

(a) where a hearing has been postponed or adjourned on the application of a party (ETR 2013, r 76(2))

(b) where an adjournment is occasioned by a failure to adduce evidence to deal with a request for reinstatement or re-engagement (ETR 2013, r 76(3))

(c) in the event of vexatious, abusive, disruptive, or otherwise unreasonable conduct (see paras 12.14–12.28) (ETR 2013, r 76(1)(a))

(d) where there has been a failure to comply with an order or practice direction (ETR 2013, r 76(2))

(e) where a party has been ordered to pay a deposit as a condition of being permitted to continue to participate in the proceedings and the tribunal or judge has found against that party (ETR 2013, r 49(5))

(f) where the claim or response had no reasonable prospect of success (ETR 2013, r 76(1)(b))

(g) for the payment of fees associated with a successful application (ETR 2013, rr 76(4) and 75(1)(b))—this provision is currently redundant with the revocation of the fees regime.

12.06 Preparation time orders (PTOs) can be made in similar circumstances where the party has not been legally represented at, for example, the hearing (see further para 12.43). Wasted costs orders may be made against a party's legal representatives in certain circumstances (see further para 12.48).

12.07 A tribunal cannot make a costs order under ETR 2013, r 75(1)(a) and a PTO in favour of the same party in the same proceedings (r 75(3)). This does not preclude a tribunal making a costs order under r 75(1)(b) or (c) in relation to witness expenses alongside a PTO. If a tribunal makes a costs order or a PTO before the proceedings are determined it can decide to make the award for costs or preparation time after the proceedings have been determined—effectively reserving the final determination on costs.

C. KEY TERMS

12.08 'Paying party' means the party against whom an order for costs is made. 'Receiving party' means the party in favour of whom costs are made. A 'costs order' is known in Scotland as an 'expenses order'. A costs order (or expenses order in Scotland) can be made only when the receiving party is legally represented (r 75(1)). Where the party is unrepresented, a PTO may be made.

D. TIMING OF ORDERS

An order can be made at any stage in the proceedings. An application which is made at the end of **12.09** a hearing can either be oral or in writing. In each case it must be made within twenty-eight days after the date on which the judgment finally determining the proceedings in respect of the party applying was sent to the parties (r 77). No order may be made unless the paying party has had a reasonable opportunity to make representations in writing or at a hearing (at the direction of the tribunal).

Where a tribunal makes a costs order or PTO it should provide written reasons for doing so if a **12.10** request for written reasons is received within fourteen days of the date of the order (ETR 2013, r 62(3)).

E. WHEN ORDERS MUST BE MADE

An order for costs (as opposed to a PTO) must be made against a respondent in an unfair **12.11** dismissal case where the claimant has expressed a wish to be reinstated or re-engaged which has been communicated to the respondent not less than seven days before the hearing and the respondent has obtained an adjournment based on its inability to adduce reasonable evidence as to the availability of the job from which the claimant was dismissed or comparable or suitable employment. The respondent can avoid such an order if the request was made less than seven days before the hearing and it can show a 'special reason' as to why it could not adduce the evidence. In many cases claimants will tick the box on the claim form indicating that they are seeking reinstatement/re-engagement. It is difficult to envisage circumstances in which a respondent will not have had at least seven days' notice as the schedule of loss and/or witness statements may also contain such an indication. In all other circumstances the order is discretionary.

F. DISCRETIONARY ORDERS

A party who has paid a deposit as a condition of being permitted to continue proceedings (under r **12.12** 39) shall be treated as having acted unreasonably if the tribunal finds against him for substantially the reasons given in the deposit order unless the contrary is proven. It will not automatically follow that costs will be awarded, the tribunal retains a discretion. If a costs order is made then the deposit will be forfeit as part of this costs order.

The tribunal has a discretion whether to order costs where there has been an adjournment of a **12.13** hearing. The order will be against the party which has caused the adjournment.

There is also the discretion to order costs against a party who has in bringing the proceedings acted **12.14** vexatiously, abusively, disruptively, or otherwise unreasonably. Costs may also be ordered against the paying party where any claim or response had no reasonable prospect of success.

Costs may be ordered against the party or his representative where they have acted vexatiously, **12.15** abusively, disruptively, or otherwise unreasonably in the conduct of the proceedings. In *Health Development Agency v Parish* [2004] IRLR 550, the EAT held that the conduct of a party prior to proceedings, or unrelated to proceedings, cannot form the basis of an order for costs (see also *Davidson v John Calder (Publishers) Ltd and Calder Educational Trust Ltd* [1985] IRLR 97—prior conduct can be relevant to an assessment of whether it was reasonable to bring or defend the claim, but it cannot be treated as the act of vexatiousness or unreasonableness upon which an award of costs can be founded). However, in *McPherson v BNP Paribas* [2004] IRLR 558, the Court of Appeal held that there is no requirement for the causal link between the party's unreasonable behaviour and the costs incurred by the receiving party. The tribunal should have regard to the nature, gravity, and effect of the unreasonable conduct as factors relevant to the exercise of its discretion but there is no need to link the conduct to any specific loss (this was followed in *Salinas v Bear Stearns Holdings Inc* [2005] ICR 1117). In [2017] *Sunuva Ltd v Martin* UKEAT/ 0174/17 the EAT held that the approach to causation set out in *McPherson* remains good law under the 2013 ETR, despite the changes in wording to the costs provisions.

Vexatious

12.16 The formulation used to describe conduct attracting an award of costs in the rules before 1993 was 'frivolous and vexatious' and the classic description of this was given by Sir Hugh Griffiths in *Marler (ET) Ltd v Robertson* [1974] ICR 72, 76:

> If the employee knows that there is no substance in his claim and that it is bound to fail, or if the claim is on the face of it so manifestly misconceived that it can have no prospect of success, it may be deemed frivolous and an abuse of the procedure of the tribunal to pursue it. If an employee brings a hopeless claim not with any expectation of recovering compensation but out of spite to harass his employers or for some other improper motive or acts vexatiously and likewise abuses the procedure [his action is vexatious].

12.17 Where claims are struck out for jurisdictional reasons the tribunal may not have considered the facts or legal merits. In these circumstances the Court of Appeal upheld the tribunal's decision not to make a costs order in *Dean & Dean Solicitors v Dionissiou-Moussaoui* [2011] EWCA Civ 1332.

No reasonable prospect of success

12.18 The categorization extends not only to a party who knows that there is no merit in the case but also to one who ought to have known that the case had no merit. Note in the 2004 rules it was a ground for considering costs if the bringing or conducting of proceedings was misconceived. Misconceived was defined to include claims which have no reasonable prospects of success, therefore many of the cases on this issue will continue to apply under the 2013 rules. In *Cartiers Superfoods Ltd v Laws* [1978] IRLR 315, the EAT held that a tribunal should inquire as to what a party knew or ought to have known had he gone about the matters sensibly. The question of whether a party knew or ought to have known that a claim was without merit should be considered throughout the hearing and not just at the time of commencement. So, while it might be reasonable to commence proceedings, it may later become clear that they have no reasonable prospect of success. In *Beynon v Scadden* [1999] IRLR 700, the EAT suggested that it may be unreasonable conduct to fail to seek further information, written answers, or disclosure in order to assess the merits of the case (at para 28). In that case, the EAT also said (at para 20): 'one does not necessarily judge a party who has had the benefit of advice as one would a lay person left only to his own perhaps inadequate devices'.

12.19 The fact that a party has sought legal advice is a relevant factor but not determinative of itself. The tribunal ought, however, to be wary of the dangers of hindsight. The fact that a party loses before the tribunal does not mean that the case had no reasonable prospect of success or was vexatious. What becomes clear to the parties, for example after cross-examination, at the end of the proceedings may not have been clear at the start.

12.20 A judge may also order costs against a party who has not complied with an order or a Practice Direction (r 76(2)) (see Chapter 6).

Collateral or improper purposes

12.21 In *Beynon* above, the employees pursued a TUPE claim which the union knew or ought to have known had no prospect of success. One reason for awarding costs was that the claims were proceeded with for the collateral purpose of forcing the employer to recognize the union. Similarly, in *Kovacs v Queen Mary & Westfield College* [2002] IRLR 414, the tribunal awarded costs on the basis, amongst other things, that there was no real claim against the respondent and they had been dragged in as part of a vendetta against the principal witness.

Otherwise unreasonably

Even if a party's case is meritorious, the way in which it is handled by the party or his advisers may **12.22** be unreasonable. Late disclosure of documents or late withdrawals often form the basis of an application for costs under this heading. The rule also covers conduct during the hearing or outside it including intimidating witnesses.

When considering whether an award of costs should be made against a claimant who withdraws his **12.23** claim, the crucial question is whether he has acted unreasonably in the conduct of the proceedings, not whether the withdrawal of the claim is itself unreasonable (*McPherson v BNP Paribas* [2004] IRLR 558). Mummery LJ at para 28 gave this guidance:

> [it would be] legally erroneous if, acting on a misconceived analogy with the CPR, tribunals took the line that it was unreasonable conduct for employment tribunal claimants to withdraw claims and that they should accordingly be made liable to pay all the costs of the proceedings.

In the next paragraph, however, he recognized the equal weight to be given to the principle of **12.24** discouraging speculative claims with a hope of a settlement.

Withdrawal is not in itself to be equated with unreasonableness and in each case it must be shown **12.25** that the claimant's conduct of the proceedings has been unreasonable. This is determined by looking at the conduct overall. If it is adjudged to have been unreasonable, then costs can be awarded but only in respect of the period after the conduct became unreasonable. However, the receiving party does not have to show that any particular item of expense after that was actually caused by the unreasonable conduct (*McPherson*, above and *Yerrakalva v Barnsley MBC* [2012] IRLR 78). The EAT in *G4S Services v Rondeau* UKEAT/0207/09/DA held that a failure by a party to consider a reasonable settlement offer, even if just by making a reasonable counter-offer, can amount to unreasonable conduct and justify a costs order. The claimant was resisting the appeal, and settled just before the hearing, accepting an offer he had turned down some months previously. The EAT held that not accepting the initial offer, and/or failing to make a reasonable counter-offer, was unreasonable conduct which justified a costs award, even in the EAT. Burton J observed that a party is entitled to resist an appeal unless and until there is an outcome or an offer which requires consideration, and described making and considering settlement offers as 'part and parcel of any litigation proceedings'.

Dishonesty may well be evidence of unreasonable conduct. In *Daleside Nursing Home Limited v* **12.26** *Mathew* UKEAT/0519/08 the tribunal found that the claim was based on a lie but declined to make an order for costs. The EAT held that having made such a finding the tribunal should have gone on to conclude that the claimant had acted unreasonably and order costs (see also *Dunedin Canmore Housing Association v Donaldson* UKEATS/0014/09 in which the EAT held that it was perverse for the tribunal to have refused to award costs where the claimant's assertions that she had not disclosed details of her compromise agreement in breach of a confidentiality clause were false). Similarly, in *Arrowsmith v Nottingham Trent University* [2012] ICR 648 the Court of Appeal held that an employment tribunal had correctly considered on the facts that a claimant had conducted her claim for sex discrimination unreasonably by relying on untrue assertions that job interviewers knew about her pregnancy when deciding not to offer her the job, and had properly exercised its discretion to order costs against her. However, a finding of dishonesty does not automatically make conduct unreasonable. In *Arrowsmith* the Court of Appeal endorsed the statement of the EAT in *HCA International Limited v May-Bheemul* EAT 0477/10 that 'a lie on its own will not necessarily be sufficient to found an award of costs. It will always be necessary for the tribunal to examine the context and to look at the nature, gravity and effect of the lie in determining the unreasonableness of the alleged conduct'.

Historically the position has been that it is not unreasonable to bring a claim simply for a declar- **12.27** ation of unfair dismissal even where the employer offered to pay the maximum award (*Telephone Information Services Ltd v Wilkinson* [1991] IRLR 148). However, the Scottish EAT in *Nicolson Highlandwear Ltd v Nicolson* UKEATS/0058/09 appears to have held differently, although *Telephone Information Services* was not cited. Admittedly the facts of *Nicolson* are extreme. The employer applied for costs based on Mr Nicolson's unreasonable behaviour in bringing the case. He had (among other things) defrauded them through false accounting, run his own business out of the employer's premises, and diverted customers to that business. His claim for unfair dismissal was successful as the employer had not followed a fair procedure, but the tribunal awarded him no compensation because the dismissal was 100 per cent attributable to his own fraudulent conduct. The tribunal refused to order costs, pointing out, among other things, that Mr Nicolson had not lied to the tribunal (although he had lied to the employer); that he had succeeded in showing that the dismissal was unfair; that claimants are entitled to seek 'simple findings of unfair dismissal' without the objective of compensation; and that unrepresented claimants should not be discouraged from asserting their rights where the applicable law is hard to understand.

12.28　The EAT overturned this decision as perverse as Mr Nicolson had persisted in a claim in which he knew that he had acted dishonestly, and that this had caused his dismissal. That he was successful in all or part of his claim did not necessarily mean it was not unreasonable of him to bring it. The employment judge was also wrong to say it was open to pursue a claim purely for the purpose of obtaining a declaration of unfair dismissal. Unlike in a discrimination case, a tribunal has no power to make such a declaration in an unfair dismissal case; its powers are limited to awarding remedies. Different principles may well apply in discrimination cases as it is arguable that there is a public interest in those claims being aired (although that principle cannot be limitless—see *Kovacs* for example).

G. *CALDERBANK* LETTERS

12.29　In proceedings in the civil courts, a winning party who fails to do better than an offer made to him by the losing party will usually expect to pay the losing party's costs from the date of the offer (see generally CPR Part 36). The use of '*Calderbank* letters' is common—an offer to settle without prejudice, save as to costs. The letter is not revealed to the court until the end of the trial. Initially the practice of *Calderbank* letters was not looked upon favourably in tribunals (see Lindsay J in *Monaghan v Close Thornton Solicitors* EAT/3/01). In *Kopel v Safeway Stores plc* [2003] IRLR 753, it was held that a failure by a party to beat a *Calderbank* offer will not, by itself, result in an award of costs against him. What must be shown is 'that the conduct of an appellant in rejecting the offer was unreasonable before the rejection becomes a relevant factor in the exercise of its discretion under [rule 76]' (at para 18). On the facts of that case, the EAT upheld a tribunal's award of £5,000 costs against the claimant where she had failed in her unfair dismissal and sex discrimination claims, and had not only turned down a 'generous' offer to settle the case but had persisted in alleging breaches of the provisions of the ECHR prohibiting torture and slavery, which the tribunal categorized as 'frankly ludicrous' and 'seriously misconceived'. In the circumstances, the EAT held that the tribunal was entitled to find that the rejection of the offer was unreasonable conduct of the proceedings justifying the award of costs that was made.

12.30　In *Power v Panasonic* EAT/439/04, the EAT again stressed that the rule in *Calderbank v Calderbank* [1976] Fam 93 has no place in the employment tribunal jurisdiction and cited with approval *Kopel v Safeway Stores plc* [2003] IRLR 753, paras 17–18. However, where a party has obstinately pressed for some unreasonably high award despite its excess being pointed out and despite a warning that costs might be asked for against that party if it were persisted in, the tribunal could, in appropriate circumstances, take the view that party had conducted the proceedings unreasonably. In *Peat & Others v Birmingham City Council* [2012] UKEAT/0503/11/CEA, the EAT held a failure to engage with a costs warning letter was unreasonable conduct.

H. COSTS AGAINST RESPONDENTS

12.31　In *Cartiers Superfoods Ltd v Laws* [1978] IRLR 315, the EAT stated that great care should be exercised by tribunals before awarding costs against respondents as they must be entitled to defend proceedings. However, the proceedings must still be defended reasonably.

I. AMOUNT

Where it has been decided to make a costs order against a party, a tribunal or judge may make one **12.32**
of the following orders (see r 78(1)):

(a) An order for a specified sum not exceeding £20,000.
(b) An order that the whole or a specified part of the costs be determined by way of a detailed
assessment in accordance with the CPR or, in Scotland, as taxed according to such part of the
table of fees prescribed for proceedings in the sheriff court as shall be directed by the order.
A detailed assessment is where the court will assess whether the amounts claimed as costs are
reasonable in relation to the length of time spent on any work and the hourly rate, for example, claimed by a party's representative, see para 12.37. Such an assessment may be carried
out either by a county court, or, since the introduction of ETR 2013, by an employment judge
applying the same principles as the county court. This is a change from the 2004 rules and
gives the employment judge wider powers in assessing costs.
(c) An order that the paying party pay expenses for a witness or another party.
(d) An order for costs in the sum agreed by the parties.

Orders under (b) to (d) may exceed £20,000. When considering either whether to make an **12.33**
order, or the amount of the order, the tribunal may have regard to the paying party's ability to
pay, r 84 (conversely, the receiving party's means are irrelevant). It is not mandatory to take
means into account and it may be that the tribunal cannot, in some circumstances, ascertain
what those means are. In *Jilley v Birmingham & Solihull Mental Health NHS Trust* [2008] All
ER (D) 35 (Feb) the EAT held that r 41(1) and (2) of the ETR 2004 were, taken together, wide
enough to allow a tribunal to take account of ability to pay by placing a cap on an award of
costs even where it ordered a detailed assessment. If a tribunal was satisfied that a paying party
had not been frank as to his means, it might be positively desirable to do so as it might render it
unnecessary to go through the expense of a detailed assessment, or assist parties to reach terms
of payment. In *Doyle v North West London Hospitals NHS Trust* [2012] UKEAT/0271/11/RN,
the EAT found that the tribunal had erred in failing to have regard to the claimant's ability to
pay. The tribunal was expected to raise the question of its own motion. If a tribunal decided not
to take ability to pay into account, it had to say why. If it decided to take into account ability
to pay, it should set out its findings about ability to pay, state what impact that had had on its
decision whether to award costs or on the amount of costs, and explain why. The extent of those
means was held to extend to all of the claimant's assets in *Shields Automotive v Greig* UKEATS/
0024/10/BI, although in that case, because the claimant had given misleading evidence about
his assets, the tribunal could not properly assess them and therefore it was proper to disregard
them. In *Herry v Dudley MBC* UKEAT/0100/16/LA the EAT noted that if a tribunal were to
make an award based on future earning capacity then the party applying for costs ought to say
if it intends to serve a statutory demand or commence bankruptcy proceedings since these actions will affect the ability of the paying party to meet the award. Similarly, an award based on
future earning capacity ought to consider the current statutory interest rate, which may also
affect ability to pay in such a case.

Even if means are taken into account, the Court of Appeal in *Kovacs* quoted with approval the **12.34**
principle set out by the tribunal (at 417):

> It does not appear, on the face of the relevant Regulations, that it was intended that poor litigants may
> misbehave with impunity and without fearing that any significant costs order will be made against them,
> whereas wealthy ones must behave themselves because otherwise an order will be made.

In *Walker v Heathrow Refuelling Services Co Ltd* EAT/0366/04, the EAT had to consider its own **12.35**
power to award costs under r 34B(2) of the EAT (Amendment) Rules 2004, which provides that
the appeal tribunal may have regard to the paying parties' ability to pay when considering the
amount of the costs order. The EAT in that case took into account the fact that the claimant was
backed by his union when having regard to his ability to pay.

12.36 A costs order includes the legal costs and the allowances paid by the Secretary of State for witnesses' allowances (r 74(1)) and those fees, charges, disbursements, or expenses incurred by or on behalf of a party in the proceedings. Solicitors', counsels', and experts' fees, letter-writing, conferences, and written advice, travelling time, and hearing time are all within this description. In *Verma v Harrogate NHS Trust* 2009 UKEAT 0155, a costs order was made pursuant to dismissal of a 'hopeless' strike out application made by the respondent. The EAT held that in such circumstances it is perverse to allow recovery of Counsel's fees for attending the prehearing review (PHR) (now preliminary hearing) and drafting a skeleton argument, whilst excluding recovery of the solicitor's costs of preparation for the hearing and attendance on counsel at the hearing.

J. ASSESSMENT

12.37 An assessment is the process by which the court or tribunal decides the amount of any costs orders made. An assessment can either be summary or detailed, the former usually an assessment of the costs performed by the tribunal and the latter by a costs officer in the county court or High Court (although wasted costs orders are assessed by the judge making the order). Under the 2013 Rules, the tribunal can also carry out a detailed assessment applying the principles of the CPR. In either case it is advisable for a party to prepare a schedule of costs and, wherever possible, serve it on the paying party so that he can make representations on it.

K. COSTS SCHEDULES

12.38 There is guidance on the format for a schedule of costs in CPR Practice Direction to Part 44 (and *Health Development Agency v Parish* [2004] IRLR 550 states that regard should be had to CPR principles). Of particular note is para 4.6, which sets out the various headings that can be claimed which include:

(a) attendances on the court
(b) attendances on and communications with the receiving party
(c) attendances on and communications with witnesses
(d) communications with the court and counsel
(e) work done on documents
(f) work done in connection with negotiations.

12.39 The summary should show the total profit costs and disbursements claimed separately from the VAT claimed.

12.40 In the tribunal, r 74(1) provides that costs include 'fees, charges, disbursements or expenses incurred by or on behalf of the receiving party (including expenses that witnesses incur for the purpose of, or in connection with, attendance at a Tribunal hearing)'.

12.41 VAT should only be claimed where a party is unable to reclaim it as input tax—in many cases the VAT will be reclaimable and therefore the receiving party would effectively be overcompensated (*Raggett v John Lewis* [2012] IRLR 906).

L. WITNESS ALLOWANCES

12.42 If an order is made for the payment of witness allowances they will usually cover the loss of wages, travel costs, and other expenses incurred by the individual concerned. Section 5(3) of the ERA 1996 sets out the fixed scales that are applicable for each head.

M. PREPARATION TIME ORDERS

In *Kingston Upon Hull City Council v Dunnachie (No 3)* [2003] IRLR 843, the EAT held that **12.43** under the 2001 Rules there was no jurisdiction to award costs in favour of a litigant in person. The 2004 and 2013 Rules provide that the circumstances in which a PTO must now be made and those in which it is discretionary are the same as those relating to orders for costs. In both sets of circumstances the PTO may only be made in favour of a receiving party who has not been legally represented at a hearing or in proceedings determined without a hearing where the party has not been represented when the proceedings are determined. A tribunal cannot make *both* a PTO and a costs order in the same proceedings but may defer the decision as to which order to make until a later stage of proceedings (r 75(3)), save as under r 75(1)(b) and (c). This provides that the costs for witness expenses may be recovered as costs and a PTO may be applied for in relation to other matters. The choice as to which order to apply for is initially that of the applicant. A common problem is the situation where a party has been represented for part of the litigation. In *Duhoe v Support Services Group Ltd* [2015] UKEAT/0102/15, the EAT gave guidance on the procedure: the applicant in such a case should not have to make a choice between which type of order to apply for and after applying for both it is for the tribunal to decide which order to make.

It would appear that employment consultants do not count as legal representatives because of the **12.44** definition in r 74(2), which covers only those with (a) rights of audience in any part of the Senior Courts of England and Wales, county courts or magistrates' courts; (b) advocates and solicitors in Scotland; and (c) solicitors and barristers in Northern Ireland. Note: for solicitors to be a legal representative within this rule the individual must hold a current practising certificate (*Ramsay and Others v Bowercross Construction Ltd and Another* UKEAT/0534/07).

Preparation time

Preparation time is the time spent by the receiving party or his employees or advisers carrying out **12.45** preparatory work directly relating to the proceedings. Preparation time covers that spent up to the hearing, but not the hearing itself. The time spent by advisers must relate to the conduct of the proceedings so it would not cover any advice given at a stage before proceedings were commenced.

The amount of a preparation time order

Once it has decided to make a PTO the tribunal has to assess the number of hours spent on **12.46** preparation. It is directed to do so using information provided by the receiving party and its own assessment of what is a reasonable and proportionate amount of time bearing in mind the complexity of the proceedings, the number of witnesses, and the documentation required. This figure is then applied to an hourly rate (£33 and increasing by £1 each year after 6 April 2013). There is no maximum for a PTO.

The tribunal may have regard to the paying party's ability to pay when considering whether to **12.47** make the order and how much it should be.

N. WASTED COSTS

Tribunals can make a wasted costs order against a party's representative. Representatives include **12.48** legal or other representatives (r 80(2)). Wasted costs means any costs incurred by a party as a result of any improper, unreasonable, or negligent act or omission, or any costs incurred by such conduct which the tribunal considers it unreasonable for a party to pay.

It seems clear that a party may apply for the wasted costs order against his own, or the other side's, **12.49** representative (see r 80(3)). It is now clear that the tribunal may also make such an order of its own motion (ETR 2013, r 82).

12.50 The tribunals will draw on the principles in the civil cases of *Ridehalgh v Horsefield* [1994] Ch 205 and *Medcalf v Weatherill* [2002] UKHL 27: see *Ratcliffe Duce & Gammer v (1) L Binns (t/a Parc Ferme) (2) N McDonald* [2008] UKEAT/0100/08 in which the EAT confirmed this approach. Simler P confirmed the approach in *Wentworth-Wood v Maritime Transport Ltd* [2018] UKEAT/0184/17/JOJ, at para 32.

12.51 According to Simler J, the approach to be adopted in the tribunal is:

(i)   to recognize that wasted costs is an exceptional jurisdiction to be exercised with great care adopting a staged approach, and requiring consideration of what specific conduct is said to be improper, unreasonable or negligent

(ii) to consider whether the particular conduct caused the opposing party unnecessary costs

(iii) to consider whether in all the circumstances it is just to order the legal representative to compensate the receiving party for the whole or any part of those costs.

12.52 Improper conduct includes that which is very serious under the representative's professional code of conduct (*Medcalf*). Negligent is to be defined in the normal sense of failing to act with reasonable competence but also something akin to abuse of process (see *Persaud (Luke) v Persaud (Mohan)* [2003] EWCA Civ 394 and *Charles v Gillian Radcliffe & Co* 5 November 2003, Ch D). Problems of privilege have arisen, for example, where a hopeless case has been pursued. A representative against whom the application is made does not have to waive privilege on advice given (and indeed the client may not allow him to do so). The Court of Appeal has held that it cannot be inferred from those circumstances that the representative has advised the course of action taken. The task for the court is to ask whether or not a reasonably competent legal adviser would have evaluated the chances of success such as to continue with it, but the judge may only come to a conclusion adverse to the party's advisers if he has seen their advice (*Dempsey v Johnstone* [2003] EWCA Civ 1134). In *Hafiz & Haque Solicitors v Mullick* [2015] ICR 1085 the claimants' claims were dismissed by the employment tribunal as ill-conceived. The respondent applied for wasted costs under r 80 on the basis that his solicitors had submitted a 'grossly exaggerated schedule of loss', which raised the claimants' expectations preventing acceptance of offers to settle and were awarded their costs.

12.53 The EAT applied *Medcalf* and held tribunals should be slow to conclude representatives have insufficient material to submit particular pleadings in cases where legal professional privilege prevents revelation of instructions. Employment judges may make wasted costs order if satisfied (a) there is an improper, unreasonable, or negligent act or omission; (b) the costs were incurred as a result of it, and (c) the case is one where the tribunal could say with confidence there was no room for doubt. That seems to set a fairly high threshold.

12.54 The order may be one, or a combination, of the following:

(a) the representative pays costs to another party

(b) the representative pays costs to his own client

(c) the representative pays any witness allowances of any person who has attended the tribunal by reason of the representative's conduct of the proceedings.

12.55 'Representatives' means a party's legal or other representatives and any employee of such representatives (r 80(2)). Excluded from wasted costs orders are representatives who do not act in pursuit of profit—principally law centres and Citizens Advice representatives—although those acting under conditional fee arrangements are deemed to be acting in pursuit of profit. Wasted costs orders against representatives who are the employees of a party may not be made. They can be made in favour of a party, regardless of whether he or she is legally represented. In *Wilsons Solicitors v Johnson and Others* UKEAT/0515/10/DA, the EAT upheld the decision of an employment judge who made a wasted costs order against a representative under ETR 2004, r 48 arising from the conduct of a telephone Case Management Discussion (CMD). The solicitors acted for two employees who raised a wide variety of claims in their ET1. The pleadings were obscure and lacked detail. Amended particulars were filed before the CMD but they were still not satisfactory and still not clarified at the CMD itself. The tribunal decided the respondents incurred wasted costs as a result of the claimants' solicitors' unreasonable and negligent acts and omissions and that the CMD had been a waste of time.

When can wasted costs orders be made?

An order does not have to be made at the end of the case but the party's representative should be given the notice in writing of the wasted costs proceedings and any order made. The representative should be given a reasonable opportunity to make oral or written representations as to why the order should not be made. The tribunal may have regard to the representative's ability to pay when considering whether to make an order or the amount. **12.56**

Amount

There is no limit to the amount of a wasted costs order and the order should specify the amount to be paid or disallowed which is decided by the tribunal (as opposed to the county court). In *Casqueiro v Barclays Bank* [2012] UKEAT/0085/12/MAA, the EAT confirmed that there is no power to refer a wasted costs order to the county court. The tribunal may take into account the representatives' ability to pay (ETR 2013, r 84). The tribunal should give written reasons for any order provided a request for them has been made within fourteen days of the date of the order. **12.57**

13

Reconsideration of Judgments

SUMMARY

(1) A tribunal may of its own volition or on receipt of an application by either party reconsider any judgment where it considers it necessary to do so in the interests of justice (ETR 2013, r 70).

(2) On reconsideration, a decision may be confirmed, varied, or revoked.

(3) An application for reconsideration must be made in writing within fourteen days of the decision (or written reasons if they follow later) being sent to the parties, except where it is made during the course of a hearing (r 71).

(4) A decision to reject a claim or response can also be reconsidered (rr 13 and 19).

A. INTRODUCTION

13.01 There are a number of circumstances in which a tribunal may reconsider or change its decisions. Different types of decision of the tribunal may be challenged in different ways.

(a) A rejection of a claim form or response may be reconsidered under rr 13 and 19 (see para 13.04).
(b) A judgment may be reconsidered under r 70 (see paras 13.12–13.31).
(c) A case management order may not be reconsidered, but may be varied, suspended, or set aside under r 29 (see para 13.09).
(d) An 'unless' order made under r 38 may be set aside under r 38(2) (see paras 6.108–6.111).
(e) Minor or clerical errors in a judgment or case management order may be remedied under the slip rule (r 69) (see para 13.36).
(f) Further, there remains the potential for a judgment or case management order to be recalled under the principle in *Hanks v High Ace Productions Ltd* [1979] IRLR 32 (see paras 11.58 ff).

13.02 In an appropriate case, of course, a decision of the tribunal may be subject to an appeal to the EAT. Appeals are dealt with in Chapter 18.

This chapter is concerned primarily with the various forms of reconsideration provided for by the **13.03** ETR 2013. Reconsideration takes the place of the review mechanism provided for under previous versions of ETR, most recently ETR 2004, r 34. Although the language of the new rules is simpler, the procedure for reconsideration is very similar to the procedure for a review. The principal difference between reconsideration and review relates to the grounds for the application. The sole ground for reconsideration is that reconsideration is 'necessary in the interests of justice'; ETR 2004, r 34 provided for five grounds for review, of which 'interests of justice' was one. It remains to be seen whether the old grounds will be treated as aspects of the new 'necessary interests of justice' ground.

B. DECISIONS THAT MAY BE RECONSIDERED

Decisions to reject a claim form or response

A decision by the tribunal to reject a claim form (under rr 10 and 12) or to reject a response under **13.04** rr 17–18, whether in either case in whole or in part, may be reconsidered on application by a party (ETR 2013, rr 13 and 19). An application may be made on the basis that the decision to reject was wrong or that the defect that led to rejection can be rectified.

A decision to reject a claim because it not accompanied by a tribunal fee or a remission application **13.05** cannot be reconsidered under r 13, as the rule makes no provision for such a reconsideration. It is unclear whether a decision under r 11 can be reconsidered under r 70. The question is whether a rejection is a judgment. On the one hand, the fact that there is a separate mechanism for reviewing rejections on substantive grounds tends to suggest that a rejection is not to be reviewed under r 70 On the other hand, a rejection does finally determine the claim, and there would appear to be no other mechanism for review. In *Butlins Skyline Ltd v Beynon* [2007] ICR 121, EAT, Burke J held that an erroneous rejection of a response amounted to a decision within ETR 2004, r 34(1)(a), and was therefore reviewable. He found that: 'although the decision was not one reached by a chairman, it was a decision which had the effect of bringing the part which could be played by the respondents in the proceedings to an end'.

Judgments

Under r 70, 'any' judgment may be reconsidered by the tribunal. **13.06**

Rule 1(3) defines a 'judgment' as any decision of the tribunal (other than a decision under rr 13 or **13.07** 19), which finally determines a claim (or part of a claim) as to liability, remedy, or costs, at any stage in the proceedings, or any issue which is capable of disposing of the claim (or part of the claim) such as jurisdiction (though it need not actually dispose of the claim). A judgment expressly includes a decision whether to strike out a claim. A dismissal of the claim at the initial consideration under rr 26–28 would also be a judgment amenable to reconsideration under r 70.

A strike-out for failure to pay a deposit under a deposit order was amendable to review under ETR **13.08** 2004: *Sodexho v Gibbons* [2005] ICR 1647, as was a strike-out for failure to comply with an 'unless' order: *Uyamnawa-Odu v Schools Offices Services Ltd* UKEAT/0294/05. It is likely that the same approach will be taken under ETR 2013. However, it seems arguable that the decision to make an 'unless' or deposit order, as opposed to the subsequent striking out pursuant to them, would not be judgments, as in themselves they do not finally determine any issue. They would, however, likely be reviewable as case management orders (see below).

Case management orders

In contrast, the other type of decision provided for by r 1(3) is a case management 'order', which is **13.09** an order or decision of any kind relating to the conduct of proceedings as opposed to any matter of substance. It cannot be reconsidered under r 70. That 'orders' or other rulings of the employment tribunal are not reviewable has previously been confirmed by the EAT in *Hart v English Heritage*

[2006] ICR 655 under the predecessor regime (ETR 2004). This does not, therefore, represent an altered position.

13.10   A case management order that is not amenable to reconsideration under r 70 may be challenged by an application to vary or revoke under the tribunal's case management powers. In *Onwuka v Spherion Technology UK Ltd* [2005] ICR 567, the EAT held that a judge has the power to vary or revoke an order under r 10(2)(n), r 11(1), and r 12(2)(b) of the ETR 2004, and a judge also has the power to vary or revoke an earlier case management decision (such as a refusal to grant an amendment). However, the EAT held that it would not ordinarily expect such a power to be exercised in the absence of a material change of circumstances. See also *Goldman Sachs Services Ltd v Mantali* [2002] ICR 1251, EAT, *Kuttapan v London Borough of Croydon* [1999] IRLR 349, EAT, and *Nikitas v Metropolitan Borough of Solihull* [1986] ICR 291. That is likely to be the position under ETR 2013 and the correct method for challenging a case management order will be to make an application for further case management directions pursuant to r 29, which allows the tribunal to vary, suspend, or set aside an earlier case management order where it is necessary in the interests of justice to do so.

Bias

13.11   Allegations of bias should be dealt with by way of an appeal (assuming that they are not dealt with at the hearing itself in an application for recusal) and not an application for reconsideration (see Chapter 10).

C. GROUNDS FOR RECONSIDERATION

Summary of grounds

13.12   An application for reconsideration may be made under r 70 ETR 2013 on the basis that it is 'necessary in the interests of justice' to do so. The previous rule, r 34(3) ETR 2004, provided five grounds for review, one of which was that the interests of justice require a review. The four additional grounds (now omitted) were:

  (a) the decision was wrongly made as a result of an administrative error
  (b) a party did not receive notice of the proceedings leading to the decision
  (c) the decision was made in the absence of a party and
  (d) new evidence has become available, the existence of which could not have been reasonably known of or foreseen at the time of the hearing.

13.13   The 2013 ETR elevates the 'interests of justice' test from a residual category to an overriding principle in respect of reconsideration. The principle is wide and some of the previous authorities on the interests of justice sub-category contained in r 34 of the ETR 2004 may be of assistance. It seems unlikely that the Underhill Review intended to narrow the scope of reconsideration, and it is likely that old grounds (a) to (d) would be regarded by a tribunal as specific instances which may satisfy the interests of justice test. Of those specific grounds, the 'new evidence' ground is likely to remain the most significant.

Interests of justice

13.14   In *Flint v Eastern Electricity Board* [1975] IRLR 277, the EAT held that the ground of interests of justice was intended to confer a wide discretion on the employment tribunals; however, the importance of finality of litigation militates against the discretion being exercised too readily. The discretion is not open ended and should be exercised in a principled way, having regard to the earlier case law: *Ministry of Justice v Burton* [2016] ICR 1128 at para 21 (Elias LJ).

13.15   In *Trimble v Supertravel Ltd* [1982] IRLR 451, the EAT stated that the old review procedure should only be available in exceptional circumstances. This approach was adopted over many years; see, for example, *Moncrieff (DG) (Farmers) v MacDonald* [1978] IRLR 112, EAT. In *Williams v*

Ferrosan [2004] IRLR 607, however, the EAT doubted the requirement of 'exceptional circumstances' because, first, there is no such requirement in the rule, the language of which ('in the interests of justice') is in broad terms. Secondly, since 2001 the Employment Tribunals Regulations and Rules have contained an overriding objective of dealing with cases justly, now found in r 2 of the ETR 2013.

In an appropriate case it may be in the interests of the overriding objective to reconsider a case rather than pursue the slower and more expensive route of an appeal. The more flexible approach in *Williams v Ferrosan* under the review regime was followed and endorsed by the EAT in *Sodexho Ltd v Gibbons* [2005] IRLR 836, EAT and *Newcastle upon Tyne City Council v Marsden* [2010] ICR 743. In *Marsden* Underhill J stated that it was desirable, in exercising a broad statutory discretion, to avoid resorting to phrases or labels from previous cases, rather than making a careful assessment of what justice required in a particular case. **13.16**

Reconsideration on grounds of the interests of justice may also be an appropriate way for a party to seek relief from the consequences of his failure to comply with a rule or order or where a claim has been struck out for non-compliance with an order of the tribunal. In dealing with such an application for review, the judge may have regard to the factors listed in CPR 3.9, however he is not under a positive duty to do so (*The Governing Body of St Albans Girls' School v Neary* [2010] IRLR 124). These factors are as follows: (a) the interests of the administration of justice; (b) whether the application for relief has been made promptly; (c) whether the failure to comply was intentional; (d) whether there is a good explanation for the failure; (e) the extent to which the party in default has complied with other rules, practice directions, court orders, and any other relevant pre-action protocol; (f) whether the failure to comply was caused by the party or his legal representative; (g) whether the trial date or the likely date can still be met if relief is granted; (h) the effect which the failure to comply had on each party; and (i) the effect which the granting of relief would have on each party. **13.17**

Applications for reconsideration in the interests of justice may involve complaints of errors of law, which raises an issue as to when it is appropriate to reconsider, and when it is appropriate to appeal. Whilst in the normal case an error of law on the face of the tribunal's decision should be challenged by way of appeal, it has been held not to be appropriate for a tribunal to refuse to review a decision simply because the review involved consideration of an error of law: *Trimble v Supertravel Ltd* [1982] IRLR 451. In *British Midland Airways Ltd v Lewis* [1978] ICR 782, the EAT said that review is appropriate when the tribunal makes a mistake and soon realizes the error. That is the case even if the mistake results in an error of law. In *Trimble*, the true distinction perceived by the EAT between appeal and review was not between minor and major errors of law, but whether or not a decision alleged to be erroneous in law has been reached after there has been a procedural mishap ([1982] IRLR 451, 453): **13.18**

> If the matter has been ventilated and properly argued, then errors of law of that kind fall to be corrected by this appeal tribunal. If, on the other hand, due to an oversight or to some procedural occurrence one or other party can with substance say that he had not had a fair opportunity to present his argument on a point of substance, then that is a procedural shortcoming in the proceedings before the tribunal which in our view can be correctly dealt with by a review however difficult the point of law or fact may be. In essence, the review procedure enables errors occurring in the course of the proceedings to be corrected but would not normally be appropriate when the proceedings had given both parties a fair opportunity to present their case and the decision had been reached in the light of all relevant argument.

This distinction, whilst still helpful, should not be seen as a hard and fast rule: *Williams v Ferrosan* [2004] IRLR 607, EAT, which made it clear that the power under the old r 34(3)(e) of the ETR 2004 (interests of justice sub-category of review) was a broad one to be exercised in the interests of justice and in accordance with the overriding objective. **13.19**

Applications for review on this ground have been successful under previous procedural rules where a procedural mishap occurred which deprived a party of a fair opportunity to present his case. For example, in *Trimble v Supertravel Ltd* [1982] IRLR 451, the party applying for a review was denied the opportunity to address the tribunal on the question of mitigation of loss. In *Harber v* **13.20**

North London Polytechnic [1990] IRLR 190, a claimant's representative withdrew a claim on the basis of a mistaken belief that the claimant did not meet the jurisdictional requirements for the claim. Whilst that was a mistake on the part of the representative, it was brought about in part by the respondent's failures during disclosure, and in part by a misapplication of the law by the Employment Judge. The Court of Appeal held that a review was in the interests of justice. There is no reason to suppose that this approach, as in the case of other examples of the courts or tribunals reviewing on the interests of justice ground, would not be permissible, in principle, under r 70 of the ETR 2013.

13.21 On the other hand, an application for reconsideration is not likely to be the appropriate method of dealing with a representative's failure. In *Ironside Ray & Vials v Lindsay* [1994] IRLR 318, Mummery J said that to permit a review on grounds of the inadequacy of a representative's presentation of a case was 'a dangerous path to follow'. He stated that it involved the risk of encouraging a disappointed claimant to seek to reargue his case by blaming his representative for the failure of his claim. That may involve the tribunal in inappropriate investigations into the competence of the representative. Similarly, in *Dhedhi v United Lincolnshire Hospitals NHS Trust* [2003] All ER (D) 366, the EAT observed that in the absence of a procedural short-coming, a decision should not be reviewed simply because a party's representative had made inadequate submissions.

13.22 In *Williams v Ferrosan* [2004] IRLR 607, EAT, the parties had not been denied an opportunity to present their case. An error arose in the decision because both the parties and the tribunal pro-ceeded on a mistaken belief as to the incidence of taxation on an award of compensation for loss of future earnings in a discrimination claim. The EAT held that a review should have been allowed: al-though it did not fall within the procedural mishap category, there was an error in the decision, which had resulted from the mistake of the parties and the judge. Whilst the decision could have been challenged by way of an appeal, it was in accordance with the overriding objective to follow the quicker and cheaper route of a review.

13.23 It has hitherto been unusual for a review application to succeed on the basis of events that post-date the decision in question, but this is possible and will remain possible on the right facts. For example, subsequent events could include a change in the law (*Griffin v City & Islington College* UKEAT/0459/06). A review was also held not to be appropriate on the basis that the tribunal had underestimated the amount of time a claimant would be out of work for the compensatory award (see *Brennan and Ging v Elward (Lancs) Ltd* [1976] IRLR 378). However, where the employee got another job after the hearing at a much higher rate of pay, a review was deemed to be appropriate (see *Yorkshire Engineering v Burnham* [1973] IRLR 316 and *Help the Aged v Vidler* [1977] IRLR 104). Those decisions do not necessarily sit easily with each other, but do reiterate that, as with all exercise of judicial discretion, the ambit of challenge is never set in stone.

New evidence

13.24 When considering a review on grounds of new evidence under the previous rules, tribunals follow the approach taken by the Court of Appeal in determining whether to permit fresh evidence on appeal: *Ladd v Marshall* [1954] 1 WLR 1489. Therefore, to be admissible on review or appeal such evidence must satisfy three conditions (see *Wileman v Minilec Engineering Ltd* [1988] IRLR 144; note that the case concerned admission of new evidence on appeal, but the EAT indicated that the same approach should be adopted on appeal and on review (at para 14), cf *Borden (UK) Ltd v Potter* [1986] ICR 647):

(1) the evidence could not have been obtained with reasonable diligence for use at the trial (as provided in r 34(3)(d) of the ETR 2004) and

(2) the evidence must be such that if given it would probably have an important influence on the result of his case, though it need not be decisive and

(3) the evidence must be apparently credible.

For examples of decisions on this ground see *Moncrieff (DG) (Farmers) v MacDonald* [1978] IRLR **13.25** 112; *Ladup v Barnes* [1982] IRLR 7; *Qureshi v Burnley Borough Council* EAT/916/92; and *Burnley Borough Council v Qureshi* EAT/917/92.

A party seeking to introduce fresh evidence on a review ought to lodge a statement of the evidence **13.26** on which he seeks to rely: *Vauxhall Motors Ltd v Henry* (1978) 13 ITR 432; *Drakard (PJ) & Sons Ltd v Wilton* [1977] ICR 642. The party will also need to give an explanation as to why the evidence was not relied on prior to the decision under review.

A number of the cases of review in the interests of justice concerned attempts to rely on new evi- **13.27** dence which would not fall within r 34(3)(d) of the ETR 2004, usually because the new evidence was, or should have been, available at the hearing. In such cases, r 34(3)(e) was not to be used to 'outflank' the requirements of r 34(3)(d). A review in the interests of justice could in these circumstances only arise by reason of some circumstance or mitigating factor relating to the failure to bring the evidence sought now to be adduced: *General Council of British Shipping v Deria* [1985] ICR 198. Failure on the part of the party's representative to identify or rely on relevant evidence was unlikely to amount to such a circumstance: see, for example, *Stanley Cole (Wainfleet) Ltd v Sheridan* [2003] IRLR 885. The tribunal should continue to apply *Ladd v Marshall* principles, save in exceptional circumstances, as confirmed by the EAT in *Outasight VB Limited v Brown* UKEAT/0253/14/LA (in confirming the general principle that *Ladd* holds good further to the new ET Rules).

D. PROCEDURE FOR RECONSIDERATION

Application by a party

A party may apply for reconsideration of a judgment during the course of a hearing, or within four- **13.28** teen days of the sending of the written record or written communication of the decision or written reasons, if they follow later: r 71 ETR 2013.

Late application

It will be an error of law for the tribunal not to allow the respondent to a late application for re- **13.29** consideration to make submissions as to whether the application should be allowed: *The Practice Surgeries Limited v Surrey PCT (now SS for Health)* UKEAT/0212/15/RN.

Reconsideration by the tribunal on its own initiative

Where no application has been made but the decision is being reconsidered on the initiative of the **13.30** tribunal, it will inform the parties of the reasons why it will reconsider the decision and proceed as though an application has been made and not refused in accordance with r 72(2). See r 73 of the ETR 2013. Reconsideration by the tribunal on its own initiative is an alternative to reconsideration on the application of a party. The tribunal cannot undertake both at the same time or conduct a hybrid of the two: *TCO In-Well Technologies Ltd. v Stuart* [2017] ICR 1175.

Hearing or paper only determination

An employment judge will consider the application and if there is no reasonable prospect of the **13.31** decision being varied or revoked (including, in particular, if the substance of the application is repetitive of an earlier application) then the tribunal will write to the parties informing them of the refusal: r 72(1). There is, at this stage, no further avenue for the disappointed applicant save to appeal.

Otherwise, the tribunal will write to the parties with notice of a deadline for a response from the **13.32** respondent to the application and the views of the parties as to whether a hearing is required. The judge's preliminary views on the application may be set out: r 72(2).

13.33 The application will be determined at a hearing unless the judge considers that it is not necessary in the interests of justice; if so there will be a reasonable opportunity for further written representations to be supplied by the parties: r 72(2).

13.34 The initial consideration under r 72(1) shall be by the judge who made the original decision, unless this is not practicable. The hearing of the application is before the judge and, if applicable, other members of the tribunal that made the original decision: r 72(3).

13.35 A tribunal which or judge who reviews a decision may confirm, vary, or revoke the decision. If the decision is revoked, the tribunal or judge must order the decision to be taken again. When an order is made that the original decision be taken again, if the original decision was taken by a judge without a hearing the new decision may be taken without hearing the parties and if the original decision was taken at a hearing, a new hearing must be held. Where a decision is varied, the tribunal should give a judgment explaining clearly which aspects of the original judgments and of their reasoning are being varied on review, and why: *Pressure Coolers Ltd v Molloy* [2011] IRLR 630, paras 42–47.

E. CORRECTIONS UNDER THE SLIP RULE

13.36 An employment judge may at any time correct any clerical mistake or other accidental slip or omission in any order, judgment, or other document produced by a tribunal pursuant to r 69 ETR 2013. Any published version of the document will also be corrected and a copy of the corrected version, signed by the judge, shall be sent to all the parties.

13.37 The Civil Procedure Rules 1998 contain a similar power to correct an accidental slip or omission: see CPR, r 40.12. The Court of Appeal has held that the predecessor rule, r 37 of the ETR 2004, should be interpreted consistently with the equivalent CPR provision. The rule should only be used to correct genuine slips or omissions, and should not be used to alter the substance of the court or tribunal's decision, *Markos v Goodfellow* [2002] EWCA Civ 1542. If the need for correction is such that the tribunal in fact issues what amounts to a fresh judgment, this may amount to a reconsideration by the tribunal on its own initiative under the old r 34 of the ETR 2004 (see *Aziz-Mir v Sainsbury's Supermarket plc* UKEATPA/0537/06/JOJ), although the principles are likely to apply to r 70 of the ETR 2013 as well). The slip rule should not be used to allow the tribunal to have second thoughts, or for the parties to seek to persuade the tribunal to do so. Whilst the tribunal may not change the substance of a decision under the slip rule, the slip rule may be used to alter a judgment or order to give clear meaning and effect to the tribunal's intention: *Bristol-Myers Squibb v Baker Norton Pharmaceuticals Inc* [2001] EWCA Civ 414; *Foenander v Foenander* [2004] EWCA Civ 1675. The slip rule should not be used by a tribunal to add a fresh finding on an important matter of substance to their decision: *Bone v London Borough of Newham* [2008] IRLR 546. The unusual circumstances of that case were that the tribunal made a finding of unfair dismissal, but omitted to record a decision that the dismissal had also been an act of sex discrimination and victimization. The tribunal had intended so to find, and purported to correct its decision under the slip rule. The Court of Appeal held that this was an inappropriate use of the slip rule, and allowed an appeal against the tribunal's order. However, in order for the tribunal to be able to reach the decision it had apparently intended to reach, the case was remitted to the tribunal under the *Burns/Barke* procedure (see *Barke v Seetec Business Technology Centre Ltd* [2005] IRLR 633, CA) with a direction that the tribunal should formally announce and give in writing its reasons for concluding that the constructive dismissal was an act of direct sex discrimination and victimization. Whilst the decision in *Bone* achieves justice on the unusual facts of the case, it is open to question whether the use of the *Burns/Barke* procedure was appropriate: the tribunal was not being asked to supplement its reasons for a judgment already made, but to make a fresh finding which had not formed part of its original judgment.

14

Enforcement of Tribunal Awards

SUMMARY

(1) Tribunals cannot enforce their own awards.

(2) Awards for money can be enforced against the respondent in the county court.

(3) From April 2016, fines can be imposed on employers who do not comply with financial awards made by employment tribunals or ACAS conciliated settlement agreements.

A. INTRODUCTION

It is a curious feature of the system that the tribunals do not have their own power of enforcement. **14.01** Instead, the machinery of the county court is used (ETA 1996, s 15(1), (2)) in respect of any sum payable in pursuance of a decision of an employment tribunal in England and Wales which has been registered in accordance with the regulations. Two important things must be noticed about this formulation:

(a) The county court has no power to enforce orders or agreements other than for the payment of money, for example reinstatement orders or agreements to provide a reference to the county court, even in respect of the monetary aspects of a reinstatement order (*O'Laiore v Jackel International Ltd* [1990] ICR 97, [1990] IRLR 70, CA).

(b) The order cannot be enforced against anyone other than the respondent mentioned in the order of the employment tribunal (*Stow v John Bell*, 29 July 1985, Aldershot County Court).

An applicant can apply to the county court to enforce an employment tribunal judgment even **14.02** though an appeal is outstanding to the Employment Appeal Tribunal (EAT, or the other appellate courts): *Zabaxe v Nicklin* (The Times, 30 October 1990). In determining whether or not to grant a stay of enforcement action, the county court (or High Court where a writ of *fieri facias* or writ of control is issued) will consider the risk of injustice to each of the parties of granting/refusing a stay of enforcement action: see *Hammond Suddard Solicitors v Agrichem International Holdings Limited* [2001] EWCA Civ 2026, *Wilson v Church (No 2)* [1879] 12 Ch D 454. It was suggested in a previous edition of this work that a stay of enforcement action would usually be granted on an employer's appeal to the EAT. However, in *Bibi-Hudson v J Sainsbury plc* [2012] EWHC 4189 (QB), Stuart-Smith J was not prepared to stay enforcement action altogether pending the employer's appeal, even in circumstances where (i) the employer was solvent and had offered to pay the judgment debt into an escrow account pending determination of the appeal; (ii) the appeal had passed through 'the sift' at the EAT; (iii) the judgment of the employment tribunal was a majority judgment where the Employment Judge was in the minority; and (iv) the claimant was unemployed and her only real asset was some equity in the claimant's house. Stuart-Smith J ordered a stay of enforcement only on the condition that £15,000 of the judgment debt was paid immediately to the claimant with the remainder being paid into court pending the employer's appeal to the EAT.

14.03 From 1 April 2009, any legal person who has an employment tribunal judgment registered against them by the County Court will have their name entered in the Register of Judgments, Orders and Fines (see the Register of Judgments, Orders and Fines Regulations 2005, SI 2005/3595). The register is available for inspection by members of the public as well as institutions wishing to consider the creditworthiness of such persons for the purpose of extending credit to them.

B. METHODS OF ENFORCEMENT

14.04 The methods by which enforcement of money judgments may take effect are set out in the Practice Direction to CPR Part 70 by:

(a) a writ of control or warrant of control (see CPR Parts 83 and 84)
(b) a third party debt order (see CPR Part 72)
(c) a charging order, stop order, or stop notice (see CPR Part 73)
(d) in the county court, an attachment of earnings order (see CCR Order 27)
(e) by the appointment of a receiver (see CPR Part 69).

The CPR procedures apply to monetary awards, including costs, but not to ACAS arbitration awards.

C. FORM OF APPLICATION

14.05 The successful party seeking to enforce the judgment may present an application to the county court, together with a copy of the award. This should be done in the district in which the defaulting party resides or carries on business.

14.06 The application may be heard and determined by any 'proper officer' and the order on the application must be in form N322A of the county court forms. Fixed costs apply (CPR, r 45.6). If interest is being claimed, details of the interest must also be included (CPR, r 70.5 and CPR PD70).

14.07 Where an employee has been awarded compensation by an employment tribunal and that money has been paid into the county court on the taking of enforcement proceedings, the money should remain in court if a High Court action is pending in respect of an employer's claim for a larger amount (*Schofield v Church Army* [1986] 2 All ER 715, CA).

D. ENFORCEMENT IN THE CASE OF DEATH

14.08 On the death of an employee in cases concerning unfair dismissal, redundancy, and other individual employment rights, under the ERA 1996 proceedings may be instituted or continued by a personal representative of the deceased employee, or, where there is no personal representative, by a person appointed by the tribunal (ERA 1996, s 206). Further, rights accruing under the ERA 1996 after the death of the employee devolve to the deceased's estate as if they had accrued before death. In such cases, an award made in favour of a deceased employee may be enforced on behalf of his estate by his personal representatives or any such person appointed by the tribunal (Employment Tribunals Awards (Enforcement in Cases of Death) Regulations 1976, SI 1976/663, regs 5 and 6). Although there are no provisions equivalent to s 206 in the discrimination legislation, a discrimination claim can be instituted or continued after the death of the complainant by the personal representatives of his estate pursuant to s 1(1) of the Law Reform (Miscellaneous Provisions) Act

1934 (*Harris (Personal Representatives of Andrews (deceased)) v Lewisham and Guy's Mental Health NHS Trust* [2000] ICR 1170, [2000] IRLR 320; *Executors of the Estate of Gary Soutar, Deceased v (1) James Murray and Co (Cupar) Ltd, (2) Scottish Provident Institution* [2000] IRLR 22).

E. FINES FOR FAILURE TO PAY TRIBUNAL AWARDS

From April 2016, where employers fail to pay awards (including costs awards) or sums payable **14.09** pursuant to ACAS conciliated settlement agreements, then warning notices and fines can be issued by High Court enforcement officers (see ETA 1996, Part 2A). The fine will be 50 per cent of the unpaid amount, save that it cannot be less than £100 and cannot be more than £5,000 (see s 37F of the ETA 1996). Before a penalty notice is issued, the High Court enforcement officer will issue a 'warning notice' (see s 37E of the ETA 1996).

Part A Tribunal Procedure

15

Special Jurisdictions

SUMMARY

Tribunals have a number of special jurisdictions. The rules in relation to these special jurisdictions been simplified by the ETR 2013, but some differences in the various regimes remain.

A. NATIONAL SECURITY

15.01   Rule 94(1) ETR 2013 provides for a Minister of the Crown to direct a tribunal or Employment Judge, in relation to Crown employment proceedings, to (a) conduct proceedings in private; (b) exclude a person from all or part of the proceedings; (c) take steps to conceal the identity of a witness in the proceedings where he considers it would be expedient in the interests of national security.

15.02   Rule 94(2) permits an employment tribunal to make the same orders if it considers it to be expedient and in the interests of national security. In addition, an employment tribunal may restrict disclosure of documents pursuant to r 94(2) ETR 2013 Such an order must be kept under review by the employment tribunal. As to such an order:

(a) Where the employment tribunal considers that it may be necessary to make such an order, the tribunal may consider any material provided by any party, or by a Minister (where the Minister is not a party) without providing that information to any other person. The employment tribunal must only consider that material in deciding whether or not to make the order, however, unless the material is subsequently used as evidence in the proceedings by a party.

(b) Where a Minister considers that it would be appropriate for the employment tribunal to make such an order, the Minister is entitled to apply to the employment tribunal for such an order. The employment tribunal, on such an application, can make 'interim orders' in the same form as is provided for in r 94(1)–(2) ETR 2013 pending the determination of the application. Where a Minister has made an application seeking the exclusion of a person from all or part of the proceedings, then such a person shall not be sent a copy of the response pending a decision on the Minister's application: see r 94(6) ETR 2013.

15.03   The use of these types of 'closed material' procedure (that is where the claimant is excluded from all or part of Crown employment proceedings) was challenged as being unlawful in *Home Office v Tariq* [2011] UKSC 35, [2011] IRLR 843. In that case the employee was an immigration officer and had had 'security clearance' removed by the Home Office. The background to the decision was that some of the employee's family members had been arrested in relation to a plot to mount a terrorist attack on a transatlantic flight. The employee alleged race discrimination and discrimination on grounds of religion or belief in relation to the removal of his security clearance. The Secretary of State contended that the decision to remove the employee's security clearance had been taken for reasons relating to national security. A 'closed material' procedure was ordered by the tribunal. The employee contended that this was inconsistent with his Art 6 right to a fair trial and with the European directives prohibiting discrimination, because the effect of the 'closed material' procedure was that the employee was unable to understand properly the case against him and therefore to respond to it adequately. In a review of the tribunal's 'closed material' procedures, the Supreme Court considered the 'closed material' procedure not to be in breach of the relevant European directives, nor to be in breach of Art 6 of the European Convention on Human Rights even in circumstances where an employee was not provided with the 'gist' of the case against him.

15.04 Schedule 2 to the Employment Tribunals (Constitution and Rules of Procedure) Regulations 2013 applies to proceedings in relation to which a direction is given, or order is made, under r 94 of the ETR 2013. Schedule 2 modifies the general rules provided for in Sch 1 to the Employment Tribunals (Constitution and Rules of Procedure) Regulations 2013.

Serving of documents

15.05 The employment tribunal will not send a copy of any response to proceedings issued in the employment tribunal to any 'excluded person' (that is a person who has been excluded from all or part of the proceedings by virtue of a direction under r 94 of the ETR 2013): see Sch 2, r 1(3).

Witness orders and disclosure of documents

15.06 Where a person is an 'excluded person' in proceedings, and a tribunal is considering whether to make an order under r 31 of the ETR 2013 (a disclosure order), or a witness order under r 32 of the ETR 2013, a minister may make an application to the tribunal objecting to that order. If such an order has been made, the Minister may make an application to vary or set aside the order. The tribunal shall determine the minister's application in private and the minister shall be entitled to address the tribunal: see Sch 2, r 3.

Special advocate

15.07 In any proceedings in which there is an excluded person the employment tribunal shall inform the Attorney-General (or in Scotland, the Advocate General) of the proceedings with a view to the Attorney-General (or the Advocate General in Scotland) deciding whether to appoint a special advocate to represent the interests of the claimant in respect of those parts of the proceedings from which:

(a) any representative of his is excluded
(b) both he and his representative are excluded or
(c) he is excluded and is unrepresented: see Sch 2, r 4(1)–(2).

15.08 A special advocate shall be a person who has a right of audience in relation to any class of proceedings in any part of the senior courts or all proceedings in county courts or magistrates' courts, or shall be an advocate or a solicitor admitted in Scotland: Sch 2, r 4(3).

15.09 Where the excluded person is the claimant, he shall be permitted to make a statement to the employment tribunal before the commencement of the proceedings, or the part of the proceedings, from which he is excluded: Sch 2, r 4(4).

15.10 There are special rules as to the conduct of special advocates. In particular, the special advocate may communicate, directly or indirectly, with an excluded person at any time before receiving closed material from a Minister: Sch 2, r 4(5). After receiving closed material, the special advocate must not communicate with any person about any matter connected with the proceedings other than:

(a) the tribunal; the minister or his or her representative; the relevant law officer or his or her representative; or any other person save for the excluded person or his or her representative with whom it is necessary for administrative purposes to communicate about matters not connected with the substance of the proceedings: Sch 2, r 4(7);

(b) with the excluded person where the tribunal has authorized such communication (on an application on notice to the minister): Sch 2, r 4(8). Other than in circumstances where the tribunal has authorized communication (in the manner set out above), the special advocate may only receive written communications from the excluded person and must not reply to them other than to send written acknowledgement of receipt to the legal representative: Sch 2, r 4(9).

Hearings

15.11 Unless there is a direction or order as discussed above, or made under ETR 2013 any hearing shall take place in public and any party may attend and participate in the hearing: Sch 2, r 5(1).

15.12 In a private hearing a member of the Administrative Justice and Tribunals Council is not entitled to attend: Sch 2, r 5(2).

Reasons in national security proceedings

15.13 The tribunal's reasons may be subject to restrictions also. Before the employment tribunal sends a copy of the full written reasons to any party, or enters them in the register, he must send a copy of the full written reasons to the minister. If the minister considers it expedient in the interests of national security he can direct that the written reasons:

(a) shall not be disclosed to persons specified in the direction ('the specified persons'), and require the employment tribunal to prepare a further document ('the edited reasons') setting out the reasons for the decision, but with the omission of such of the information as is specified in the direction

(b) direct the tribunal or judge that the full written reasons shall not be disclosed to the specified persons, but that no further document setting out the tribunal or judge's reasons should be prepared: Sch 2, r 6(3).

15.14 In addition, where the employment tribunal considers it expedient in the interests of national security it may make an order that steps are taken to keep secret all or part of the written reasons: Sch 2, r 6(2).

15.15 Where the minister has directed the tribunal or judge in accordance with (a) above, the edited reasons should be signed by the judge and initialled in each place where an omission has been made: Sch 2, r 6(4).

15.16 Where a direction has been made that edited reasons should be supplied the employment tribunal should:

(a) send a copy of the edited reasons to the specified persons

(b) send the edited reasons and the written reasons (i) to the parties and their representatives (provided that they are not specified persons); (ii) any special advocate appointed in the proceedings; and (iii) where the proceedings were referred to the employment tribunal by a court, to that court and

(c) enter the edited reasons in the register, but omit from the register the full written reasons: Sch 2, r 6(5) to (7).

15.17 Where a direction has been made that no further document should be prepared the employment tribunal shall send a copy of the full written reasons to the persons listed in (a) above, but it shall not enter the full written reasons in the register.

Correction of written reasons

Where written reasons (whether 'full' or 'edited' as above) have been omitted from the register, the **15.18** secretary shall send a copy of the corrected reasons to the same persons who had been sent the original set of reasons: see Sch 2, r 6(8).

B. EMPLOYMENT TRIBUNAL LEVY ASSESSMENT APPEALS

The Industrial Training Act 1982 provides for assessments of a levy to be made by the various **15.19** Industrial Training Boards (ITBs).

ETR 2013, r 104 provides that the rules in Sch 1 to the Employment Tribunal (Constitution and **15.20** Rules of Procedure) Regulations 2013 apply to levy assessment appeals. Appropriate amendments should be read into the rules so that 'claim or claimant shall be read as references to a levy appeal or to an appellant in a levy appeal'.

C. APPEALS AGAINST HEALTH AND SAFETY IMPROVEMENT AND PROHIBITION NOTICES

Rule 105 of the ETR 2013 provides that the rules in Sch 1 to the Employment Tribunal **15.21** (Constitution and Rules of Procedure) Regulations 2013 apply to appeals against a health and safety improvement or prohibition notice with some amendments. The words 'claims' or 'claimants' in the ETR 2013 should be read as 'appeal' or 'appellant' as appropriate and 'respondent' should be read as 'the inspector appointed under section 19(1) of the Health and Safety Act who issued the notice which is the subject of the appeal'.

An appeal must be issued by the presentation of a claim to a tribunal office before the end of the **15.22** period of twenty-one days beginning with the date of the service of the relevant notice or within such further period as the employment tribunal considers reasonable where it is satisfied it was not reasonably practicable for an appeal to be presented within that time. This is the same test as is found in s 111 of the Employment Rights Act 1996 and which is discussed in Chapter 3 of this work.

D. APPEALS AGAINST UNLAWFUL ACT NOTICES

Unlawful act notices can be issued under s 21 of the Equality Act 2006. **15.23**

Rule 106 of the ETR 2013 provides that the rules in Sch 1 to the Employment Tribunal **15.24** (Constitution and Rules of Procedure) Regulations 2013 apply to appeals against unlawful act notices with appropriate amendments. Claims or claimants should be read as notice of appeal or appellant against an unlawful act notice as appropriate and response should be read as 'the Commission for Equality and Human Rights'.

16

Human Rights Claims

SUMMARY

(1) The main practical effect of the Human Rights Act 1998 (HRA) was that those seeking to rely upon the European Convention on Human Rights (ECHR) could proceed in domestic courts rather than in the European Court of Human Rights (ECtHR) in Strasbourg.

(2) Tribunals, however, do not have jurisdiction to hear free-standing complaints under the HRA.

(3) Human rights jurisprudence has been important in developing employment case law:
   (a) in relation to procedural fairness Art 6 of the ECHR
   (b) in cases involving a claimant's private and/or family life under Art 8 of the ECHR
   (c) in cases involving religious discrimination under the Employment Equality (Religion or Belief) Regulations 2003, now the Equality Act 2010, and Art 9 of the ECHR
   (d) in cases involving trade union freedom and freedom of association under Art 11 of the ECHR.

A. CLAIMS UNDER THE HUMAN RIGHTS ACT 1998

16.01 The employment tribunal does not have jurisdiction to hear freestanding claims under ss 7–10 of the HRA or otherwise. It does not have the power to make a declaration of incompatibility under s 4 of the HRA. However,

- an employment tribunal owes direct duties under s 6(3) of the HRA as a 'public authority' as regards its own procedure;
- furthermore, in all cases it does have a duty under s 3 of the HRA to interpret legislation and subordinate legislation so far as it is possible to do so in such a way as is compatible with the Convention rights;
- it has a duty under s 2 of the HRA in determining a question which has arisen in connection with a Convention right to take account of judgments of the European Court of Human Rights, the Commission, and the Committee of Ministers.

16.02 It is therefore still open to rely upon Convention rights in order to aid interpretation or in order to ensure that the tribunal's own conduct and procedure conform to, for example, human rights obligations, in particular Art 6. The following are the more likely Articles of the ECHR to be engaged in employment cases (although not necessarily tribunals):

Article 4 prohibiting forced labour.
Article 6 right to a fair trial.
Article 8 right to respect for private and family life.
Article 9 freedom of thought, conscience, and religion.
Article 10 freedom of expression.
Article 11 freedom of assembly and association.
Article 14 prohibition of discrimination.

Article 6: fair trial

Since the enactment of the HRA, Art 6 has been argued in employment cases both in relation to the **16.03** employment tribunal's own procedure and more broadly in relation to procedural fairness. Article 6 has separate levels of protection for individuals charged and tried in criminal cases, and those whose 'civil rights and obligations' are determined in civil proceedings. In the employment context, it would be very unusual for the enhanced guarantees of Art 6 (criminal) to apply unless the disciplinary proceedings have a 'substantial influence or effect' on those civil rights and obligations (see *R (on the application of G) v Governors of X School and Y City Council* [2011] 756 IRLR 756).

Under Art 6 (civil)   **16.04**

> In the determination of his civil rights and obligations or of any criminal charge against him, everyone is entitled to a fair and public hearing within a reasonable time by an independent and impartial tribunal established by law..

Where Art 6(1) civil is relied on it is important in each case to identify:

- the determination of civil rights and obligations in issue. In cases where the tribunal's own procedure is in question, the determination of civil rights and obligations will usually be obvious—ie the substantive cause of action pursued in the tribunal. However, this issue is not straightforward in cases where the potentially determining public authority is the employer rather than the tribunal
- what the requirements of fairness are for the hearing of that determination
- whether the requirements for public access are satisfied
- whether the determining public authority is impartial
- whether the determining public authority is sufficiently independent
- whether there is a further public judicial authority which has full jurisdiction over the matter, which might be capable of curing any earlier defect of fairness.

Article 6 and the employer's procedure

An ordinary dismissal from employment is not a determination of civil rights and obligations: Art **16.05** 6 (see eg *R (on the application of G) v Governors of X School and Y City Council* [2011] IRLR 756). This means that the Art 6 guarantees to a fair and public hearing by an independent and impartial tribunal do not automatically apply when a public authority dismisses an employee. However, dismissal may have a 'decisive' or 'substantial influence or effect' on an individual's 'ability to practice a profession'. The right to practice a particular profession has been held to be a civil right or obligation (*Le Compte, Van Leuven and De Meyere v Belgium* (1981) 4 EHRR 1). Also capable of attracting Art 6 would be a dismissal which involved:

- a system of provisional listing, as used to exist under legislation protecting vulnerable adults and children (*R (on the application of Wright) v Secretary of State for Health* [2009] UKHL 3, [2009] All ER 129) or
- the sending of alert letters to all NHS trusts in the context of a doctor's dismissal (*Kulkarni v Milton Keynes NHS Trust* [2009] EWCA Civ 789, [2009] IRLR 829).

There has been large amount of case law concerning the question of whether a dismissal or other **16.06** disciplinary proceedings are 'decisive' of an employee's civil right to practice in a certain profession, or to be employed at all.

Part A Tribunal Procedure

16.07 In *Kulkarni v Milton Keynes NHS Trust* [2009] EWCA Civ 789, [2009] IRLR 829, a junior doctor was suspected of serious sexual misconduct. Suspension or dismissal would have resulted in an alert letter being sent out to all other NHS trusts, warning them of the suspected misconduct. The Court of Appeal held that the effect of the alert letter would have prevented any other NHS trust from employing Dr Kulkarni. The effect of this would have been that he would have been unable to finish his foundation year training as a junior doctor. Such training would not have been available in the private sector. The Court of Appeal held that Dr Kulkarni was entitled to legal representation at his disciplinary hearing on contractual grounds, but went on to consider Art 6. Smith LJ stated (*obiter*) that the dismissal of Dr Kulkarni in these circumstances would have been a determination of his civil rights and obligations such as to engage Art 6 of the ECHR. In the context of the serious allegations made against him, Art 6(1) (which is the civil limb) required that he be entitled to legal representation at his disciplinary hearing.

16.08 In *R (on the application of G) v Governors of X School and Y City Council* [2010] IRLR 222, the Court of Appeal considered this question again. Laws LJ for the Court held that it was sufficient for a decision of the public employer to have 'substantial influence or effect' on a later decision by a separate public authority as to whether the claimant could practice his profession as a teaching assistant. Laws LJ held that the factual evaluations made by a school within their internal employment disciplinary process would have a substantial influence or effect on the decision of the Independent Safeguarding Authority (ISA) as to whether the claimant should be entered onto the list of those deemed unsuitable to work with children. The school's findings might irretrievably prejudice the ISA proceedings. As the ISA's decision to list the claimant on the list of those unsuitable to work with children was potentially so serious, Art 6 required that he be entitled to legal representation at his internal disciplinary hearing at the school. In a passage of *dicta*, Laws LJ also considered that it would be difficult to see how a rational internal disciplinary hearing could deny the legal representative the right to cross examine witnesses (para 55). It did not matter that the claimant could bring an unfair dismissal case in the tribunal or could challenge the ISA's listing in the Upper Tribunal. The Supreme Court, however, allowed the school's appeal holding, as set out above, that Art 6(1) will apply to proceedings where the decision, although it is not strictly determinative, is likely to have a 'substantial influence or effect' on the outcome in proceedings.

16.09 The scope (and correctness) of the 'substantial influence or effect' test will be approached on a case-by-case basis. However, from these cases the following principles emerge:

- the employer must be a public authority within s 6 of the HRA
- it is necessary to identify some Art 6 determination other than the mere fact of dismissal (*G* para 26; see also *AB's application* [2010] NIQB 19), eg the right to practise a profession, professional misconduct proceedings by the relevant regulatory body, or listing on a list of those unsuitable to work with children/vulnerable adults
- the internal disciplinary proceedings within the public employer must consider those factual issues which would have the substantial effect on the Art 6 civil right or obligation. It will not be enough if the public employer will not make factual findings relevant to the Art 6 civil right (see *R (Kirk) v Middlesborough Council and Others* [2010] EWHC 1035 Admin, where the employer was not making factual findings in relation to proceedings in the General Care Council—the employee was dismissed because she had failed to inform the employer of those proceedings)
- whether legal representation will be required will depend on the nature of the misconduct alleged and the nature of the link with the proceedings capable of determining the civil right or obligation at stake
- it is unlikely that there will be a requirement that the public authority pay for the legal representation (*Botham v MOD* [2010] EWHC 646 (QB))
- if Art 6 requires legal representation, it may also be necessary to consider whether it requires, especially:
  - an independent and impartial panel to hear the disciplinary hearing
  - public access
  - what a hearing 'within a reasonable time' may require.

Each of these has attendant problems within the domestic disciplinary arena.

Although *G* and *Kulkarni* are Art 6 cases, tribunals have begun to read across a right to legal rep- **16.10**
resentation and Art 6 standards into an evaluation of fairness in unfair dismissal under s 98 of
the ERA (eg in Northern Ireland in *Connelly v Western Health and Social Care Trust* [2010] NIIT
4119_ 09IT). The jurisprudential basis for reading across Art 6 standards of fairness into s 98 is
unclear. It is more likely that Art 6 cases will be relied on in parallel with s 98 'fairness' where the
features in the above paragraph are met.

In *Stevens v University of Birmingham* [2015] EWHC 2300, the High Court held that a university's **16.11**
refusal to allow a representative of a professional defence organization to accompany an employee
at an investigation meeting concerning serious allegations of misconduct, was unfair and a breach
of the implied term of trust and confidence. Although the terms of the contractual disciplinary
procedure allowed a trade union representative or a staff member to attend as a companion (in
accordance with s 10 of the ERA 1999), the court held that these terms were modified by the overriding obligation of trust and confidence. The facts may be specific to the contractual terms under
review but there may be scope for wider application. The claimant was subject to two contracts
of employment: he had an academic role with the university and a clinical role with the NHS
Foundation Trust. The alleged misconduct related to the conduct of clinical trials, which was governed by both contracts. The trust's disciplinary procedure permitted him to have, amongst others,
a representative of his professional body in any disciplinary proceedings. However, the university,
which initiated the disciplinary proceedings, only permitted a fellow staff member or trade union
representative. He was not a trade union member and had few contacts within the university but
he was a member of the professional body which represented doctors. Whilst there was no express
right to a companion from his professional organization, the University had a discretion governed
by the implied term of trust and confidence and in the circumstances should have allowed his representative to attend.

Article 6 and the employment tribunal

As with the CPR the employment tribunal's rules contain an obligation to comply with the over- **16.12**
riding objective which includes the principle of proportionality. There have been many cases in
which the EAT and Court of Appeal have considered Art 6 in relation to powers exercised under
the employment tribunal's rules.

One of the early cases in which Art 6 was argued in relation to the procedural fairness of the em- **16.13**
ployment tribunal's rules was *Teinaz v Wandsworth London Borough Council* [2004] EWCA Civ
104 [2002] ICR 1471, [2002] IRLR 721. The Court of Appeal held that a litigant whose presence
is needed for the fair trial of a case but who is unable to be present through no fault of his own
will usually have to be granted an adjournment, however inconvenient it may be to the tribunal or
court and to the other parties. However, the tribunal or court is entitled to be satisfied that the inability of the litigant to be present is genuine, and the onus is on the applicant for an adjournment
to prove the need for such adjournment (para 21). Specific medical evidence is required, not just
of unfitness to work. The evidence must deal specifically with the witnesses' unfitness to attend and
give evidence to the tribunal: *Andreou v Lord Chancellors Department* [2002] EWCA Civ 1192,
[2002] IRLR 728.

The question of whether the right to a fair trial (Art 6) had been infringed by a delay of a year be- **16.14**
tween the tribunal hearing a case and the decision being promulgated was considered by the Court
of Appeal in *Bangs v Connex South Eastern Ltd* [2005] EWCA Civ 14, [2005] IRLR 389. The court
considered that unreasonable delay is generally a matter of fact, not law, and it does not in itself
constitute an independent ground of appeal. In order to succeed in such a challenge, it would be
necessary to satisfy the notoriously difficult perversity test. There may, however, be exceptional
cases in which unreasonable delay can properly be treated as a serious procedural error, giving rise
to a question of law, where a party is deprived of the substance of his or her right to a fair trial.
On the facts of this case, won by the appellant employee, the employer had not been deprived of
a fair hearing.

16.15 Article 6 has had a bearing in a number of cases concerning the composition and procedure of the employment tribunal:

- *AG v Wheen* [2001] IRLR 91: vexatious litigant order did not conflict with Art 6.
- *Scafuture v Secretary of State for Trade & Industry* [2001] IRLR 416: the employment tribunal now constituted is an independent and impartial tribunal within the meaning of Art 6(1) for the purposes of claims to which the Secretary of State is a party.
- *Lawal v Northern Spirit* [2003] IRLR 538, in which the House of Lords held that there is no difference between the common law test for bias and the requirements of Art 6: accordingly counsel appearing before the EAT ought not to have previously sat there in a judicial capacity as there was a real risk of bias. See also Chapters 9 and 10.
- *Stansbury v Datapulse plc* [2004] IRLR 466, in which the Court of Appeal held that an allegation that a member of a tribunal did not appear to be alert during the hearing may cause that hearing to be held to be unfair, both under English law and under Art 6(1).
- *Williams v Cowell* [2000] ICR 85, where it was held that a challenge to the exercise of the discretion under s 20(2) of the ETA 1996 to refuse to conduct a hearing in Wales, and therefore in Welsh, was not invalidated by any of the provisions of the Welsh Language Act 1993 or of Arts 6 and 14 (linguistic equality was argued for).

Article 8: private and family life

16.16 Article 8 has been considered most often in cases involving some degree of covert surveillance or recording. Article 8 was considered in *McGowan v Scottish Water* [2005] IRLR 167, where Mr McGowan had been the subject of covert surveillance. His employers suspected, and the surveillance confirmed, that he was falsifying his timesheets. Given that the movements of all the inhabitants of his home were being tracked, an issue for determination was whether there had been a breach of his right to a private and family life (Art 8). While the EAT considered that there was a 'strong presumption' of infringement, it upheld the tribunal's decision to reject Mr McGowan's complaint. Lord Johnston, sitting in Edinburgh, considered the employer's actions to have been justified and proportionate under Art 8(2) in circumstances where it was protecting its assets and investigating what in effect was a criminal activity.

16.17 In *Pay v UK* [2009] IRLR 139 the ECtHR considered Art 8 in the context of the dismissal of a probation officer discovered to have in his spare time pursued a business selling sadomasochistic and bondage products. In the context of his work as a probation officer working with sexual offenders, the dismissal was held to be a proportionate infringement. The claimant's conduct affected the employer's reputation and the confidence of the general public.

16.18 *Chairman and Governors of Amwell School v Dogherty* [2007] IRLR 198 concerned the use of covert surveillance by employees. The claimant had covertly recorded her disciplinary hearing and the deliberations of the panels on her mobile phone without asking for the panel's consent. She wished to rely on the recording in the employment tribunal. The employer sought to argue that the panel members' Art 8 rights were infringed. The EAT held that there was no infringement of Art 8.

16.19 In *De Keyser v Wilson* [2001] IRLR 324, it was argued that references to the claimant's private life in a letter of instruction to an expert witness amounted to a breach of her right to respect for her private and family life under Art 8. This was rejected as the material was not confidential and because the claimant's right would also conflict with the employer's right to a fair trial under Art 6.

16.20 In *X v Y* [2004] IRLR 625, Mummery LJ held that HRA (and Convention) rights could only be raised in the tribunals by way of interpretation of UK statutes and statutory instruments.

16.21 Mummery LJ set out the following framework for tribunals:

(a) Do the circumstances of the dismissal fall within the ambit of one or more of the Articles of the Convention? If they do not, the Convention right is not engaged and need not be considered.

(b) If they do, does the state have a positive obligation to secure enjoyment of the relevant Convention right between private persons? If it does not, the Convention right is unlikely to affect the outcome of an unfair dismissal claim against a private employer.

(c) If it does, is the interference with the employee's Convention right by dismissal justified? If it is, proceed to (e) below.

(d) If it is not, was there a permissible reason for the dismissal under the ERA 1996, which does not involve unjustified interference with a Convention right? If there was not, the dismissal will be unfair for the absence of a permissible reason to justify it.

(e) If there was, is the dismissal fair, tested by the provisions of s 98 of ERA 1996, reading and giving effect to them under s 3 of THE HRA 1998 so as to be compatible with the Convention right?

Article 9: religious freedom

The Employment Equality (Religion or Belief) Regulations 2003 implemented the Framework Directive on Equality 2000/73. The 2003 Regulations were repealed and replaced by the Equality Act 2010. The Framework Directive expressly refers in the recitals to the ECHR. Tribunals regularly refer to jurisprudence of the ECHR when interpreting the Regulations. In *Nicholson v Grainger plc* [2010] ICR 360, [2010] IRLR 4, Burton J held that the jurisprudence of the ECHR must be referred to in determining what constituted a 'philosophical belief' protected by reg 2. Applying *Campbell v United Kingdom* (1982) 4 EHRR 293, in order to be protected the following limitations to the term 'philosophical belief' apply: (i) the belief must be genuinely held; (ii) it must be a belief and not an opinion or viewpoint based on the present state of information available; (iii) it must be a belief as to a weighty and substantial aspect of human life and behaviour; (iv) it must attain a certain level of cogency, seriousness, cohesion, and importance; and (v) it must be worthy of respect in a democratic society, be not incompatible with human dignity, and not conflict with the fundamental rights of others. **16.22**

Article 11: freedom of association

The rights of both trade unions and their members are protected by Art 11 of the ECHR (*ASLEF v UK* [2007] IRLR 361). Article 11 protections include the right to form and join a trade union, the prohibition of closed-shop agreements, and the right for a trade union to seek to persuade the employer to hear what it has to say on behalf of its members (see *Demir v Turkey* [2009] IRLR 766 para 145 (Grand Chamber)). **16.23**

The 'right to strike' has been recognized by the ECJ as a fundamental principle of European Community law (Case C-438/05 *International Transport Workers' Federation v Viking Line* [2008] IRLR 143, para 44). **16.24**

However, there has been a reluctance of the English courts to find that the restrictions and conditions applied to trade unions' right to strike under TULR(C)A 1992 to be disproportionate (*Metrobus v Unite the Union* [2009] EWCA Civ 829—applied in *British Airways v Unite the Union* [2010] IRLR 423). **16.25**

17

Group Litigation

SUMMARY

(1) In the civil courts group litigation orders may be applied for in the case of mass claims.

(2) In the employment tribunal r 36 makes specific provisions in relation to lead cases.

A. INTRODUCTION

17.01 Where claims are brought by more than one claimant or against several respondents, which give rise to common issues of fact or law, all the claims should be dealt with on a group basis whether in the civil court or employment tribunal. Such an approach could include managing all the claims from one court centre or in one tribunal region, staying some claims while appropriately selected test cases are tried, and/or trying common issues as preliminary issues.

17.02 The civil courts have specific provision in the CPR to make group litigation orders to manage such litigation. The ETR 2013 introduced some limited provisions in relation to lead cases and other matters of case management fall within the general powers of the tribunal.

B. GROUP LITIGATION ORDERS IN THE CIVIL COURTS

17.03 Since 2000 procedures have been in place for the management of multi-party claims in the civil courts. The rules promote the following objectives recommended by Lord Woolf's *Final Access to Justice Report* (July 1996, Chapter 7, para 2):

(a) to provide access to justice where large numbers of people have been affected by another's conduct, but individual loss is so small that it makes an individual action economically unviable

(b) to provide expeditious, effective, and proportionate methods of resolving cases, where individual losses are large enough to justify individual action but where the number of claimants and the nature of the issues involved mean that the cases cannot be managed satisfactorily in accordance with normal procedure

(c) to achieve a balance between the normal rights of claimants and defendants, to pursue and defend claims individually, and the interests of a group of parties to litigate the action as a whole in an effective manner.

The rules establish a procedural framework to provide the flexibility for the court to deal with the **17.04** particular characteristics of these sorts of cases. They provide a mechanism to manage group litigation, for identifying generic issues applicable to the entire group, and for resolving cases at a cost that is proportionate to the value of an individual claim. They are located at CPR rr 19.10–19.15, and in CPR 19BPD.

A group litigation order (GLO) is defined in CPR r 19.10 as 'an order made under r 19.11 to pro- **17.05** vide for the case management of claims which give rise to common or related issues of fact or law ('the GLO issues')'. The court may make such a GLO where there are, or are likely to be, a number of claims giving rise to GLO issues (CPR, r 19.11).

The special procedural rules that then apply to GLO cases essentially provide for the following: **17.06**

(a) either before or after the commencement of litigation, a party may apply for a GLO
(b) the GLO will identify the issues to be managed as part of the group litigation ('the GLO issues') and any individual claim must raise these issues to fall under the terms of the order ('a GLO claim')
(c) a register of GLO claims will be maintained and a specified court will be given responsibility for managing them
(d) the managing court has wide case management powers to ensure the effective coordination and resolution of the GLO claims
(e) a judgment on any GLO issue will bind all other GLO claims.

In the general field of employment, situations that might merit the use of such a procedure dedi- **17.07** cated to the handling of civil claims involving multiple parties include personal injury claims arising from industrial disease or accident; financial loss arising from mishandling of pension schemes; disputes as to terms and conditions of employment after business transfers; claims for similar contractual debts; or claims for enhanced redundancy payments due under contract.

Preliminary matters

Before applying for a GLO, the solicitor acting for the proposed applicant should consult the Law **17.08** Society's Multi Party Action Information Service in order to obtain information about any other cases giving rise to the proposed GLO issues (CPR 19BPD, para 2.1).

The Practice Direction also recommends that the claimant's solicitors form a group, appoint one **17.09** of their number to be the lead solicitor, and carefully define in writing the lead solicitor's role and relationship with other members of the group (CPR 19BPD, para 2.2).

Application for a GLO

Any application for a GLO must be made in accordance with CPR Part 23 (CPR 19BPD, para **17.10** 3.1). The following information should be included in the application notice or in written evidence filed in support (CPR 19BPD, para 3.2):

(1) a summary of the nature of the litigation
(2) the number and nature of claims already issued
(3) the number of parties likely to be involved
(4) the common issues of fact or law that are likely to arise in the litigation and
(5) whether there are any matters that distinguish smaller groups of claims within the wider group.

The application for the GLO should be made to the Senior Master in the Queen's Bench Division **17.11** or the Chief Chancery Master in the Chancery Division. For claims that are proceeding or are likely to proceed in a specialist list (such as the Commercial Court), the application should be made to the senior judge of that list (CPR 19BPD, para 3.5). Outside London, the application should be made to a Presiding Judge or a Chancery Supervising Judge of the Circuit in which the District Registry which has issued the application notice is situated (CPR 19BPD, para 3.6). County court applications should be made to the designated civil judge for the area in which the county court which has issued the application notice is situated (CPR 19BPD, para 3.7).

17.12 The court may also make a GLO of its own initiative (CPR 19BPD, para 4), although this is rarely done.

17.13 A GLO may only be made with the consent of the following individuals: in the Queen's Bench Division, the Lord Chief Justice; in the Chancery Division, the Vice Chancellor; and in the county court, the Head of Civil Justice. The court will seek the necessary permission as part of its own administration of the application (CPR 19BPD, para 3.3).

Characteristics of a group litigation order

17.14 The GLO must:

    (a)   contain directions about the establishment of a 'group register' on which the claims managed under the GLO will be entered

    (b)   specify the GLO issues which will identify the claims to be managed under the GLO and

    (c)   specify the court which will manage the claims on the group register (CPR, r 19.11).

17.15 In addition, the GLO may:

    (a)   in relation to claims which raise one or more of the GLO issues direct their transfer to the management court (that is the court where the claims will be heard), order their stay until further order, and direct their entry onto the group register

    (b)   direct that from a specified date claims which raise one or more of the GLO issues should be started in the management court and entered on the group register and

    (c)   give directions for publicizing the GLO (CPR r 19.11).

The group register

17.16 Once a group register has been established, any party to a particular case may apply for the case to be entered on to it, but such an order will only be granted if the case gives rise to at least one of the GLO issues (CPR 19BPD, para 6). Rule 19.14 provides that a party entered on the group register may apply to the management court for the claim to be removed from the register, and if it does make such an order the court is given the power to give directions about the future management of that claim. In the Queen's Bench Division the senior master arranges for details of GLOs to be published on the court service website (http://www.gov.uk/guidance/group-litigation-orders).

Allocation

17.17 Every claim entered onto the group register will be automatically allocated, or reallocated, to the multi-track, and any case management directions that have been given by a court other than the management court will be set aside (CPR 19BPD, para 7).

Case management

17.18 Practice Direction 19B envisages one judge having responsibility for case management throughout the life of the group litigation case. A Master or District Judge may be appointed to deal with procedural matters, which he will do in accordance with any directions given by the managing judge (CPR 19BPD, para 8).

17.19 The management court will also normally require all new claims to be commenced in it, although failure to comply will not invalidate such a claim; instead it should be transferred to the management court to be entered on the group register as soon as possible (CPR 19BPD, para 9).

In addition to the general management powers of the court contained in CPR Part 3, r 19.13 states **17.20** that the following directionsmay be given by the management court, directions:

(a) varying GLO issues
(b) providing for one or more claims on the group register to proceed as test claims (which is the great advantage of the GLO)
(c) appointing the solicitor of one or more parties to be the lead solicitor for the claimants or defendants
(d) specifying the details to be included in a statement of case in order to show that the criteria for entry of the claim on the group register have been met
(e) specifying a date after which no claim may be added to the group register unless the court gives permission and
(f) entering any particular claim which meets one or more of the GLO issues on the group register.

The management court may direct that the GLO claimants serve 'Group Particulars of Claim' **17.21** which set out the various claims of all the claimants on the group register at the time of filing the particulars. Such particulars of claim will usually contain general allegations relating to all claims and a schedule containing entries relating to each individual claim specifying which of the general allegations are relied on and any specific facts relevant to the claimant (CPR 19BPD, para 14).

Test claims, which are not defined by the CPR, are specifically addressed by CPR, r 19.15. Where **17.22** a direction has been given for a claim on the group register to proceed as a test claim and that claim is settled, the management court may order that another claim on the register be substituted as the test claim. Where such an order is made, any order made in the test case before the date of substitution is binding on the substituted claim unless the court orders otherwise.

There are other methods of managing group litigation than using test cases as such, and these in- **17.23** clude division of the group into sub-groups, identification of common issues, trial of preliminary issues, investigation of a sample or all individual claims.

Judgments and orders

Under CPR r 19.12, where a judgment or order is given or made in a claim on the group register **17.24** in relation to one or more GLO issues:

(a) that judgment or order will be binding on the parties to all other claims on the group register at the time it is made, unless the court orders otherwise; and
(b) the court may give directions as to the extent to which that judgment or order is binding on the parties to any claim which is subsequently entered on the group register.

Any party who is adversely affected by a judgment or order binding on him may seek permission **17.25** to appeal the order, unless a party to a claim which was entered onto the group register after that judgment or order was given, in which case that party may not appeal it or apply for it to be set aside, varied, or stayed, but may apply to the court for an order that the judgment or order is not binding on him (CPR, r 19.12(2) and (3)).

CPR, r 19.12(4) provides that unless the court orders otherwise, disclosure of any document re- **17.26** lating to the GLO issues by a party to a claim on the group register is disclosure of that document to all parties to the claims who are at the time on the group register and those who are subsequently entered onto it.

Trial

The management court may give directions about the trial of common issues and of individual **17.27** issues. Common issues or test cases will normally be tried at the management court although it may be convenient for the parties to have other issues tried at courts located elsewhere (CPR 19BPD, para 15).

Costs

17.28 Costs will be apportioned between the parties taking account of those costs relating to common issues and those that relate to issues in particular cases. CPR r 46.6 provides a basic framework for costs where the court has made a GLO. The following principles have been established by authorities on some of the issues of assessment that may arise:

(1) Costs payable by those parties who discontinue their litigation before its conclusion should not be determined until after the outcome of the common issues part of the proceedings has been completed: *Afrika v Cape plc* [2001] EWCA Civ 2017, CA.

(2) No costs-sharing order had been made regarding five test cases (out of 369), but all parties were ordered to share the claimant's costs equally: *BCCI SA v Ali* (*Assessment of Costs*) [2000] 2 Costs LR 243.

(3) The importance of the courts' exercise of case management powers to limit costs was stressed in *Griffiths v Solutia UK Ltd* [2001] EWCA Civ 736.

(4) There may be joint and several liability of unsuccessful claimants in actions involving closely related claims tried together but where no GLO had been made: *Bairstow v Queens Moat Hotels plc* (*Assessment of Costs*) [2001] CP Rep 59.

17.29 Given that many mass claims are funded by groups of individuals paying in to a fund, the claimants may want to consider seeking a costs capping order under CPR, r 3.19. This limits the amount of future costs including disbursements which a party may recover pursuant to an order for costs subsequently made. Such an order may be in respect of the whole litigation or any issues which are ordered to be tried separately: CPR, r 3.19(4). The court may make such an order if it is in the interests of justice to do so, there is a substantial risk that without such an order costs will be disproportionately incurred, and it is not satisfied that this risk can be adequately controlled by other case management directions or orders and detailed assessment of costs, CPR, r 3.19(5).

C. MANAGEMENT OF GROUP LITIGATION IN EMPLOYMENT TRIBUNALS

17.30 Group litigation in the employment tribunal is most likely to involve similar claims for equal pay (eg, *Newcastle City Council v Allan* [2005] ICR 1170); arising out of the TUPE Regulations 2006; for deductions from wages; or where many employees are dismissed on a business reorganization or during a strike. It is believed that the largest ever single group actions were by those dismissed during the Wapping News International dispute in 1984–85 and 12,000 claims brought by retained fire-fighters under the Part Time Workers Regulations. Equal pay claims against NHS trusts from all over the UK have been centralized in the Newcastle region, at least for the purposes of case management directions. This has the advantage of a common approach being taken to such issues.

17.31 Rule 36 of the ETR 2013 enables a tribunal to specify lead cases where it considers that two or more claims give rise to common or related issues of fact or law. Where lead cases are specified all other related cases are stayed, or in Scotland sisted. Rules 36(2) and 36(3) specify that when a tribunal makes a decision in respect of the common or related issues it shall send a copy of that decision to each party in each of the related cases. Parties in related cases are given twenty-eight days in which to apply for an order that the decision does not apply to and is not binding on them. Such an application must be made in writing. If no application is made then the decision binds the parties in the related cases on the expiration of the twenty-eight-day time limit. Where a lead case is withdrawn before the tribunal makes a decision in respect of the common or related issues the tribunal shall make an order as to whether another claim is to be specified as the lead case and whether any order affecting the related cases should be set aside or varied.

17.32 Employment judges are encouraged to manage cases actively and this is required more for mass claims than elsewhere. The tribunal have all the usual case management tools available to them in dealing with lead cases; case management is addressed in more detail in Chapter 6. The issues which frequently arise in mass claims are:

(a) The centralization of cases—sometimes claims in relation to the same issue are lodged in many different regions because they are brought against a single employer which has many different places of business. The appropriate course is to write to the President of Employment Tribunals to ask him to make an order that all cases are heard in one region. Thus, in the thousands of cases arising out of part-time pensions litigation, the hearings were centralized in London Central region.

(b) It is important that, as far as possible, multiple appeals at different stages are avoided since this has the effect of postponing the conclusion of the litigation. The cases should therefore be managed in such a way that one case is taken to appeal and the others await the outcome of that appeal.

(c) It is often appropriate that an end date be stated after which new cases will not be treated as part of the multiple. This is done in order to avoid a situation where the cases are being prepared for trial and then new cases are added, which extends the preparation time for them and may lead to adjournments. However, in most cases the claims which are outside the multiple will fall in line with the decision in principle reached in the multiple in accordance with cases such as *Ashmore v British Coal* [1990] ICR 485.

(d) A clear register should be drawn up of those involved in the group litigation so that it is clear whose cases are covered by orders and decisions made in the litigation without further ado.

Case management is often needed very early on in these cases and regular discussion should be en- **17.33** couraged between representatives and ET judges (with active involvement by the administration) and most appropriately often by telephone (although the large number of representatives involved in some such cases may render this logistically difficult). Early active case management can save endless time and cost later on. Early identification of lead cases and common issues is helpful where possible. Once they are identified it is easier to move to further directions about further information, disclosure, and witness statements.

Where more than one claim is being pursued within a mass claim, eg unfair dismissal, discrimin- **17.34** ation, and/or breach of contract, and the generic claim is not applicable to all, claimant representatives should clearly identify at the outset which of the claims each claimant is pursuing and what structure of hearings is desired.

The same employment judge should deal throughout if possible with the mass claims in order **17.35** to achieve continuity. A senior clerk should also be appointed to deal with all claims and ensure continuity of treatment.

Frequently, there are similar issues arising in different mass claims going on around the country **17.36** but there is no clear information system (save informal discussion) which allows these matters to be tracked, still less to be reviewed to check whether such issues could be centralized. It would be sensible for all other cases to be stayed and for bulletins to then be issued to practitioners as to the progress on those lead cases with appropriate directions made on a national basis. This would be similar to the approach taken in the part-time pensions cases but not apparently in other cases.

D. FEES FOR GROUP LITIGATION IN THE EMPLOYMENT TRIBUNAL

From 29 July 2013, fees were payable for the issue of claims in the employment tribunal, including **17.37** group fees payable in respect of group litigation, pursuant to The Employment Tribunals and the Employment Appeal Tribunal Fees Order 2013 (Fees Order). The Fees Order was declared to be unlawful, from the date of its introduction, by the Supreme Court in *R (on the application of UNISON) v Lord Chancellor* [2017] UKSC 51. As a result, fees are not charged to claimants bringing employment tribunal claims, or to appellants bring appeals to the Employment Appeal Tribunal. This has been the position since 26 July 2017, the date of the judgment in *R (on the application of UNISON)*.

18

Employment Appeal Tribunal

SUMMARY

(1) A party may appeal to the EAT, subject to the payment of an appropriate fee, on the grounds that an employment tribunal has wrongly applied a principle of law, misunderstood a statute, reached a decision that no reasonable tribunal could have reached (perversity), or come to a conclusion that was perverse since there was no evidence whatever to support it.

(2) The EAT is reluctant to overturn tribunal decisions on fairness unless an error of law can clearly be identified.

(3) The EAT will not hear academic appeals which do not affect the decision in the case, nor will it allow, save in exceptional circumstances, new points of law to be raised which were not taken in the tribunal from which the appeal is brought.

(4) The EAT will only in exceptional circumstances overturn awards of compensation and it has no jurisdiction to set aside an agreement to compromise an appeal.

(5) New evidence which was not before the tribunal will be allowed to be relied on only in exceptional circumstances.

(6) Interim matters may be heard before the main hearing usually in preliminary hearings, and the EAT has the power to award costs and to review its own decisions in ways which are similar to that exercised by the employment tribunal.

(7) A party which is unsuccessful in the EAT may appeal to the Court of Appeal, but only with permission of the EAT or the Court of Appeal, and an application for permission should be made before the EAT as soon as possible after the hearing from which the appeal is brought and within four weeks of the date when the decision, judgment, or order was entered, perfected, or signed.

A. INTRODUCTION

Those litigants who are not satisfied with either the outcome of their case in the employment tribunal or alternatively, the way in which their case was dealt with by the tribunal have the right to appeal to the Employment Appeal Tribunal (EAT) but only on a point of law. The EAT's jurisdiction is now provided for by the Employment Tribunals Act 1996 (ETA 1996) and is limited, on the whole, to jurisdiction over individual disputes. **18.01**

The EAT has a division which sits in Scotland but it remains part of the same EAT. The EAT has occasionally sat in Wales since 2001. This was as a result of the decision of the Court of Appeal in *Williams v Cowell (t/a The Stables)* [2000] ICR 85. In that case, the Court of Appeal held that there was no requirement that the EAT permit the use of Welsh since an appeal heard by the EAT in England did not amount to 'legal proceedings in Wales' within s 22(1) of the Welsh Language Act 1993, even though an appeal might be from an employment tribunal which sat in Wales. In Northern Ireland, appeals from the decisions of the employment tribunals are brought by way of case stated to the Northern Ireland Court of Appeal and there is no equivalent to the EAT. **18.02**

Cases are usually heard within nine months of the notice of appeal being presented. **18.03**

B. CONSTITUTION AND PROCEDURAL RULES

Although titled a tribunal, the EAT is in fact a superior court of record consisting of a High Court or county court judge. Since 2013, cases in the EAT have usually been heard by a judge sitting alone (ETA 1996, s 28(2)). Before that cases were heard by a judge sitting with union and management lay members with industrial relations knowledge and experience (ETA 1996, s 22). The EAT can still sit with lay members (ETA 1996, s 28(3)) where a judge directs that proceedings are to be so heard. In such cases, the EAT usually sits as a three-member court but where cases of particular difficulty are dealt with four lay members may sit (see eg *Government Communications Staff Federation v Certification Officer* [1993] ICR 163). **18.04**

Several High Court judges are assigned to the tribunal, although typically only two sit on any one day. Circuit judges have also sat in the jurisdiction since 1991 Phillips J was the first President of the EAT and he was succeeded by Slynn J, Browne-Wilkinson J, Waite J, Popplewell J, Wood J, Mummery J, Morison J, Lindsay J, Burton J, Elias J, Underhill J, Langstaff J, and Simler J. The **18.05** present President of the EAT is Simler J. In Scotland, Lord Macdonald, a judge of the Court of Session, presided between 1974 and 1986. His successors have been in turn Lords Mayfield, Coulsfield, Johnson, Lady Smith, and Lady Wise. Applications for lay members are sought as and when they are required, mainly from trade unions and employer organizations.

18.06 The EAT's decision may be given on a majority basis and as such, since the EAT member has just one vote, the judge may be outvoted by the lay members. This is a unique position within the appellate courts and rarely happens but did, for example, in the cases of *Inner London Education Authority v Nash* The Times, 18 November 1978 and *Smith v Safeway plc* [1995] ICR 472. The judgment is always given by the judge, even if he is in the minority, although he will express the minority view in the judgment as well as the dominant majority view.

18.07 The administration of the EAT is headed by the registrar, presently Ms J Johnson, with a small staff.

18.08 On a typical day, two, three, or four divisions of the EAT sit in London and one in Scotland. The address of the EAT for England and Wales is Second Floor, Fleetbank House, 2–6 Salisbury Square, London EC4Y 8JX and in Scotland 52 Melville Street, Edinburgh EH3 7HF.

The procedural rules

18.09 The EAT has been governed since 16 December 1993 by the Employment Appeal Tribunal Rules 1993, SI 1993/2854. These rules have been amended by the Employment Appeal Tribunal (Amendment) Rules 2001, SI 2001/1128, the Employment Appeal Tribunal (Amendment) Rules 2004, SI 2004/2526, and the Employment Appeal Tribunal (Amendment) Rules 2013. However, the EAT retains a general power to regulate its own procedure under s 30(3) of the ETA 1996. As such, the EAT has issued a number of important Practice Directions. The most recent of these is the Practice Direction which came into force on 29 July 2013 (the 2013 Practice Direction). By para 1.1 of the 2013 Practice Direction, it supersedes all other Practice Directions. In *Zinda v Governing Body of Barn Hill Community High* [2011] ICR 174, the EAT reiterated that where there were tensions between the EAT Rules and (the then in force 2008) Practice Direction, the former would prevail. Presumably, the position will be the same in relation to the 2013 Practice Direction.

18.10 Paragraph 1.5 of the 2013 Practice Direction requires and enables the EAT to apply the overriding objective which is also contained in the EAT Rules. That objective is to deal with cases justly. Dealing with cases justly includes, so far as is practicable:

(a) ensuring that the parties are on an equal footing
(b) dealing with cases in ways which are proportionate to the importance and complexity of the issues
(c) ensuring that a case is dealt with expeditiously and fairly
(d) saving expense.

18.11 Paragraph 1.6 of the 2013 Practice Direction also provides that dealing with a case justly includes safeguarding the resources of the EAT so that each case gets its fair share of available time, but no more. The parties are required to help the EAT to further the overriding objective by virtue of para 1.7 of the 2013 Practice Direction so that a representative may be penalized in costs if she or he does not do so and instead is obstructive toward the EAT.

C. JURISDICTION

18.12 The EAT's jurisdiction is set out exhaustively in s 21 of the ETA 1996, which states that an appeal lies to the EAT in respect of 'any question of law arising from any decision of, or arising in any proceedings before an employment tribunal'. Further, s 21 requires that the appeal be in respect of a question of law arising under or by virtue of one of the following statutes or statutory instruments:

(a) Trade Union and Labour Relations (Consolidation) Act 1992
(b) Employment Rights Act 1996

(c) Employment Tribunals Act 1996

(d) National Minimum Wage Act 1998

(e) Employment Relations Act 1999

(f) Working Time Regulations 1998, SI 1998/1833

(g) Transnational Information and Consultation of Employees Regulations 1999, SI 1999/3323

(h) Part-time Workers (Prevention of Less Favourable Treatment) Regulations 2000, SI 2000/1551

(i) Fixed Term Employees (Prevention of Less Favourable Treatment) Regulations 2002, SI 2002/2034

(j) Merchant Shipping (Working Time: Inland Waterways) Regulations 2003, SI 2003/3049

(k) European Public Limited-Liability Company Regulations 2004, SI 2004/2326

(l) Fishing Vessels (Working Time: Sea-fishermen) Regulations 2004, SI 2004/1713

(m) Information and Consultation of Employees Regulations 2004, SI 2004/3426

(n) Equality Act 2006

(o) European Cooperative Society (Involvement of Employees) Regulations 2006

(p) Schedule to Occupational and Personal Pension Schemes (Consultation by Employers and Miscellaneous Amendment) Regulations 2006

(q) Companies (Cross-Border Mergers) Regulations 2007

(r) Cross-border Railway Services (Working Time) Regulations 2008;

(s) Pensions Act 2008

(t) European Public Limited-Liability Company (Employee Involvement) (Great Britain) Regulations 2009

(u) Employment Relations Act 1999 (Blacklists) Regulations 2010

(v) Equality Act 2010 (and its predecessor legislation)

(w) Agency Workers Regulations 2010, SI 2010/93.

In addition to the general jurisdiction conferred by s 21 of the ETA 1996, appeals lie to the **18.13** EAT on questions of law arising from the Transfer of Undertakings (Protection of Employment) Regulations 2006.

The EAT also has jurisdiction to hear appeals from the decision of the certification officer **18.14** under the Trade Union and Labour Relations (Consolidation) Act 1992 (see para 23.41). Section 9 of TULR(C)A 1992 provides jurisdiction for the EAT to hear appeals relating to the refusal of a certification officer to enter an organization's name in the list of trade unions or a refusal to issue a certificate of independence. Similarly, s 126 of TULR(C)A 1992 allows the EAT to hear appeals from the decision of a certification officer in respect of the entry of an organization's name on the list of employers' associations. Section 45D provides jurisdiction in respect of ss 25, 31, and 45C, which deal with the administration of trade unions. Appeals from the decision of the certification officer as to Part IV of TULR(C)A 1992, which deals with trade union elections, lie to the EAT by virtue of s 56A. Similarly, appeals lie to the EAT from the certification officer under Chapter VI (application of funds for political purposes), Chapter VIIA (breach of rules), and s 103 (resolutions approving union amalgamations or transfers). These decisions of the certification officer can be appealed by virtue of ss 95, 108C, and 104 respectively.

The EAT has no jurisdiction to hear appeals from the Central Arbitration Committee (CAC) **18.15** in respect of its main function of resolving statutory trade union recognition disputes under the ERA 1996, or indeed any of its functions; save that the EAT has a limited appellate jurisdiction over the CAC in respect of its decisions with regard to European Works Councils, under the Transnational Information and Consultation of Employees Regulations 1999 and in relation to the Information and Consultation of Employees Regulations 2004, the Companies (Cross-Border Mergers) Regulations 2007, the European Cooperative Society (Involvement of Employees) Regulations 2006, and the European Public Limited-Liability Company (Employee Involvement) (Great Britain) Regulations 2009. Any challenge to the CAC's decisions, save in that limited respect, lies by way of judicial review to the Administrative Court.

18.16 Where the EAT has no jurisdiction to hear an appeal from a decision of the employment tribunal such as improvement or prohibition notices (see Chapter 15), appeals on questions of law still lie with the High Court by virtue of s 11 of the Tribunals and Inquiries Act 1992. However, there are very few appeals from the employment tribunals which are heard by the High Court. In those cases, the appeal is governed by CPR, r 52 and RSC Order 94, r 8. The appellant's notice of appeal must be served on the employment tribunal and the respondent within forty-two days of the decision of the employment tribunal.

Original jurisdiction of the Employment Appeal Tribunal

18.17 In addition to its appellate jurisdiction, the EAT has original jurisdiction in certain circumstances:

(a) to hear complaints under regs 20(1) and 21(1) of the Transnational Information and Consultation Regulations 1999, which relate to failures to establish European Works Councils or information or consultation procedures, and disputes relating to the operation of the above. The EAT has the power to issue a written penalty notice to the relevant central management which requires it to pay a penalty to the Secretary of State in respect of the failure unless it is satisfied that the failure resulted from a reason beyond its control, or that it has some other reasonable excuse. In addition, the EAT may decide that the central management has not complied with the terms of an agreement setting up a European Works Council or consultation procedure. In that instance the EAT may order a defaulter to take steps that are necessary to comply;

(b) to hear applications under reg 22 of the Information and Consultation of Employees Regulations 2004 for a penalty notice to be issued following the CAC's declaration that there has been a failure to comply with a negotiated agreement or the standard information and consultation provisions. If issued with a penalty notice the employer will have to pay a penalty to the Secretary of State unless he is able to show that the failure resulted from circumstances beyond the employer's control or that he has some other reasonable excuse for his failure;

(c) to hear applications under reg 22 of the European Cooperative Society (Involvement of Employees) Regulations 2006 for a penalty notice to be issued following the CAC's declaration that there has been a failure to comply with the terms of an employee involvement agreement or with the standard information and consultation procedures;

(d) to hear applications under the Companies (Cross-Border Mergers) Regulations 2007 for a penalty notice to be issued following the CAC's declaration that there has been a failure to comply with the terms of an employee participation agreement or the standard rules of employee participation, or there has been a misuse of procedures;

(e) to hear applications under reg 20 of the European Public Limited-Liability Company (Employee Involvement) Regulations 2009 for a penalty notice to be issued following the CAC's declaration that there has been a failure to comply with an employee involvement agreement of the standard rules on employee involvement. An employer who is issued with a penalty notice will have to pay a penalty to the Secretary of State unless he is able to show that the failure resulted from circumstances beyond the employer's control or that he has some other reasonable excuse for his failure.

D. GROUNDS OF APPEAL

Appeal on a point of law

18.18 Appeals lie to the EAT (pursuant to ETA 1996, s 21) generally on any question of law arising out of those specified statutes and statutory instruments which the EAT has jurisdiction to hear appeals from. Appeals lie to the EAT in relation to such matters, with regard to all decisions made by tribunals whether or not the decision under appeal was made by an employment judge: see *Paw v Revenue and Customs Commissioners* [2011] WL 6329405. To succeed in an appeal on a point of law, an appellant must be able to establish that:

the employment tribunal has wrongly applied a principle of law; misunderstood a statute; reached a decision that no reasonable tribunal could have reached; or come to a conclusion that was perverse since there was no evidence whatever to support it (*Watling v William Bird & Son Contractors* (1976) 11 ITR 70).

If a tribunal has properly directed itself as to the law and has reached a permissible conclusion on the facts, its use of language in its decision which may appear to be inconsistent with the direction of its reasoning will not necessarily amount to an error of law (*Jones v Mid Glamorgan CC* [1997] ICR 815, 826). As Lord Denning MR stated in *Hollister v National Farmers' Union* [1979] ICR 542, 552:

> Parliament has expressly left the determination of all questions of fact to the industrial tribunals themselves. An appeal to the appeal tribunal lies only to a point of law; and from the tribunal to this Court only on a point of law. It is not right that points of fact should be dressed up as points of law so as to encourage appeals.

There are certain categories of cases in which the EAT and the Court of Appeal have stated that in general no points of law are likely to be raised since the matters in question are essentially matters of fact. This includes but is not limited to the following: **18.19**

(a) whether or not there has been a direct dismissal (*Western Excavating (ECC) Ltd v Sharp* [1978] IRLR 27, EAT)
(b) whether there has been a constructive dismissal (*Woods v WM Car Services (Peterborough) Ltd* [1982] IRLR 413; *Pederson v Camden London Borough Council* [1981] ICR 674)
(c) the assessment of fairness in unfair dismissal cases (*Earl v Slater & Wheeler (Airlyne) Ltd* [1973] 1 All ER 145)
(d) whether a person is employed or an independent contractor (*O'Kelly v Trust House Forte plc* [1983] IRLR 413; *Pederson v Camden London Borough Council* [1981] ICR 674)
(e) the assessment of contributory fault (*Hollier v Plysu Ltd* [1983] IRLR 260; *Warrilow v Robert Walker Ltd* [1984] IRLR 304)
(f) whether a person has taken part in industrial action (*Naylor v Orton & Smith Ltd* [1987] IRLR 233; *Faust v Power Packing Casemakers Ltd* [1983] IRLR 117)
(g) whether an employee has resigned (*Makin v Greens Motors (Bridport) Ltd* The Times, 18 April 1986)
(h) whether and when there has been a transfer of an undertaking for the purposes of the TUPE provisions (*Apex Leisure Hire v Barratt* [1984] IRLR 224)
(i) whether or not litigants had behaved abusively, vexatiously, disruptively, or otherwise unreasonably such that an award of costs might be appropriate: see *Barnsley v Yerrakalva* [2011] EWCA Civ 797; *Jackson v Walsall MBC* UKEAT/1430/10/JOJ.

The EAT has not tended, historically, to interfere with the amounts of compensation which are awarded to successful claimants before the employment tribunals since there is a recognition on the part of the EAT that damages are calculated making use of a broad brush approach (*Fougere v Phoenix Motor Co Ltd* [1977] 1 All ER 237). However, there has of late been a recognition, particularly with regard to discrimination cases, that awards should reflect compensation that would be made for injury to feelings in personal injury cases (*Vento v Chief Constable of West Yorkshire Police* [2002] IRLR 177, EAT). As such, the award of compensation has become a more exact science and therefore appeal points are more likely to be taken and to be successful. If they are to be successful appellants will still have to demonstrate that the assessment of compensation amounts to an error of law on the part of an employment tribunal rather than merely being a reasonable exercise of the employment tribunal's discretion. **18.20**

Perversity

The EAT will only interfere with a finding of fact made by the employment tribunal where that finding is perverse since a perverse finding of fact amounts to an error of law. Perversity is a difficult ground of appeal to establish since the test is a very high hurdle to overcome. In *Chiu v British Aerospace plc* [1982] IRLR 56 the EAT pointed out that a finding of an employment tribunal could only be described as perverse where no tribunal, properly directed in law, could have reached the **18.21**

Part A Tribunal Procedure

decision which the particular tribunal had reached. It would not be enough that the finding was 'contrary to the weight of the evidence' or that 'the tribunal heard evidence it is hard to believe'.

18.22 The classic statement of perversity as a ground of appeal can be found in *Neale v County Council of Hereford and Worcester* [1986] IRLR 168. The EAT had overturned the employment tribunal's decision relating to the fairness of the dismissal. However, the EAT decision was overturned by the Court of Appeal and it was rebuked for substituting its own view as to the fairness of the dismissal for that of the 'industrial jury'. May LJ stated at para 45 of his judgment:

> An [employment] tribunal has been described as an 'industrial jury', and so in many ways it is. It knows its area; it comprises a lawyer, a representative of employees and a representative of employers within that district; each has substantial experience of industrial problems and they are hearing this type of case regularly. Their job is to find the facts, to apply the relevant law and to reach the conclusion to which their findings and their experience lead them. It will not, in my opinion, be often that when an industrial tribunal has done just that, and with the care, clarity and thoroughness which the Industrial Tribunal in the present case displayed, that one can legitimately say that their conclusion 'offends reason', or that their conclusion was one to which no reasonable industrial tribunal could have come. Deciding these cases is the job of industrial tribunals and when they have not erred in law neither the EAT nor this Court should disturb their decision unless one can say in effect: 'My goodness, that was certainly wrong'.

18.23 However, the *Neale* formulation of perversity, despite frequently being cited by appellate courts, is not universally accepted. In *Piggott Brothers v Jackson* [1992] ICR 85, Lord Donaldson MR was of the view that the *Neale* formulation was liable to confuse appellate courts since the EAT, for example, could fall into error by deciding that it would have come to a different conclusion to that reached by the employment tribunal. It might then decide that the decision of an employment tribunal was certainly wrong. A decision of the employment tribunal is not perverse merely because an appellate court would have come to a different view. Lord Donaldson MR therefore proposed that the test be stricter. Appellate courts should look to see if the finding of fact could be supported by *any* evidence at all or alternatively whether there was a clear misdirection in law by the tribunal. If the tribunal's decision was not open to criticism on either of these grounds, then the appellate court might wish to reconsider whether the decision of the employment tribunal was perverse.

18.24 In *Stewart v Cleveland Guest (Engineering) Ltd* [1994] IRLR 443, Mummery P reviewed the authorities relating to perversity and stated:

> [The EAT] should only interfere with the decision of the Industrial Tribunal where the conclusion of that Tribunal on the evidence before it is 'irrational', 'offends reason', 'is certainly wrong' or 'is very clearly wrong' or 'must be wrong' or 'is plainly wrong' or 'is not a permissible option' or 'is fundamentally wrong' or 'is outrageous' or 'makes absolutely no sense' or 'flies in the face of properly informed logic'. This variety of phraseology is taken from a number of well-known cases which describe the circumstances in which this Tribunal (and higher courts) have characterised perversity. The result is that it is rare or exceptional for an appeal to succeed on the grounds of perversity.

18.25 This was reiterated by the Court of Appeal in *Yeboah v Crofton* [2002] EWCA Civ 794, [2002] IRLR 634. The court explained that 'even where the appeal tribunal had grave doubts about the decision it had to proceed with great care' where allegations of perversity were made. Mummery LJ said (at para 93):

> Such an appeal [perversity appeal] ought only to succeed where an overwhelming case is made out that the Employment Tribunal reached a decision which no reasonable tribunal, on a proper appreciation of the evidence and the law, would have reached. Even in cases where the Appeal Tribunal has 'grave doubts' about the decision of the Employment Tribunal it must proceed with 'great care'. (See also *James v LB of Greenwich* [2008] IRLR 302 paragraph 7; *McGregor v Intercity East Coast* [1998] SC 440.)

18.26 For an example of a case where it was found that an employment tribunal had come to a perverse finding, see the decision of the EAT (sitting in Scotland) in *United Distillers v Conlin* [1992] IRLR 502 In that case the claimant was dismissed from his job for having engaged in fraud against his employer while under a final written warning for the same offence. It was accepted that the procedure adopted by the employer was fair but the employment tribunal found the dismissal to be unfair in substance given the low value of the fraud and inconsistency in the approach by the employer. The EAT overturned the decision of the employment tribunal as being a perverse decision in the sense that the decision was not a permissible option in all the circumstances (see also *Anglian Home Improvements Ltd v Kelly* [2005] ICR 242 at para 32).

Paragraph 3.8 of the Practice Direction 2013 states with regard to the drafting of a notice of appeal **18.27** in cases of perversity appeals that:

> an appellant may not state as a ground of appeal simply words to the effect that 'the judgment or order was contrary to the evidence', or that 'there was no evidence to support the judgment or order', or that 'the judgment or order was one which no reasonable Tribunal could have reached and was perverse' unless the Notice of Appeal also sets out full particulars of the matters relied on in support of those general grounds.

It is thus important to set out very clearly precisely what findings it is said are perverse and why with reference to the evidence if necessary. The Court of Appeal reiterated this point recently in *Bowater v Northwest London Hospitals NHS Trust* [2011] IRLR 331 where Longmore LJ said (para 19):

> It is the ET to whom Parliament has entrusted the responsibility of making what are, no doubt sometimes, difficult and borderline decisions in relation to the fairness of dismissal. An appeal to the EAT only lies on a point of law and it goes without saying that the EAT must not under the guise of a charge of perversity substitute its own judgment for that of the ET.

See also *Fuller v LB of Brent* [2011] IRLR 414.

Examples of perversity: finding of fact unsupported by any evidence

The EAT will allow an appeal where the employment tribunal makes a finding of fact which is not **18.28** supported by any evidence. This form of appeal is really a subset of perversity since if a tribunal makes a finding of fact which is unsupported by any evidence, that is, in effect, the same as saying that the tribunal has made a finding of fact which no tribunal, properly directed in law could have made. It will not be enough for an appellant to show that the weight of evidence was against a particular finding of fact since the weight that a tribunal attached to evidence is a matter for itself (see *Eclipse Blinds Ltd v Wright* [1992] ICR 723, 733). The appellant must show that there was no evidence at all which could enable the tribunal to make a finding of fact that it has made, which usually means producing notes of evidence.

Therefore, in *British Telecommunications plc v Sheridan* [1990] IRLR 27, the Court of Appeal ex- **18.29** plained that it was not enough, in order to constitute a ground of appeal, that the employment tribunal had misunderstood or misapplied the facts. The error of the tribunal had to be more serious and it must have come to a conclusion for which there was absolutely no evidence in order to convert a finding of fact into an error of law.

Inadequate reasoning

The EAT is also entitled to interfere with the decision of an employment tribunal in circumstances **18.30** where it is of the view that the tribunal's reasons are inadequate. The extent of the reasons required will depend on the circumstances of the case. In *Meek v City of Birmingham DC* [1987] IRLR 250, para 8, the Court of Appeal classically explained what was required of an employment tribunal:

> It has on a number of occasions been made plain that the decision of an Industrial Tribunal is not required to be an elaborate formalistic product of refined legal draftsmanship, but it must contain an outline of the story which has given rise to the complaint and a summary of the Tribunal's basic factual conclusions and a statement of the reasons which have led them to reach the conclusion which they do on those basic facts. The parties are entitled to be told why they have won or lost. There should be sufficient account of the facts and of the reasoning to enable the EAT or, on further appeal, this court to see whether any question of law arises; and it is highly desirable that the decision of an Industrial Tribunal should give guidance both to employers and trade unions as to practices which should or should not be adopted.

Subsequently, in *English v Emery Reimbold & Strick Ltd* [2002] EWCA Civ 605, [2003] IRLR 710 **18.31** (which was not an employment case), the Court of Appeal stated that, as a matter of law arising both from (a) Art 6 of the European Convention on Human Rights, and (b) the common law duty to provide reasons, a judgment must contain sufficient reasoning so that the parties know why one won and the other lost. Further, any appellate court or tribunal in asking whether it is apparent to the parties why they have won or lost should not merely refer to the judgment as it appears on its face. Rather it must look at the judgment of the tribunal in the context of the material evidence and submissions which were placed before that tribunal. Similarly, if on the broad brush approach the judgment is plainly inadequate then detailed legal arguments should not be employed to repair it. Thus, in *Anya v University of Oxford* [2001] IRLR 377, Sedley LJ stated that it was not appropriate 'to comb through a patently deficient decision for signs of the missing elements and to try and amplify these by argument into an adequate set of reasons'.

18.32 In the final analysis, the extent to which detailed reasoning will be required may depend on the nature of the case in hand. Thus, the Court of Appeal stated in *Deman v Association of University Teachers* [2003] EWCA Civ 329 that more would be expected from an employment tribunal in a detailed race or sex discrimination case which required the tribunal to draw inferences in order to determine a person's true motivation for behaving in a particular manner than would be required if the tribunal were simply applying an objective norm to a set of facts as the tribunal does when it decides whether a dismissal is fair in all the circumstances.

18.33 Where an appeal is allowed by the EAT on the grounds that the employment tribunal has not given sufficient reasons for its decision, the matter will normally be remitted to the same tribunal in order that it can complete its statutory duty or alternatively to a different tribunal for rehearing (on the principles to be applied see paras 11.23–11.38). It will not simply be overturned by the EAT unless it is convinced that whatever the further reasoning it will reveal another error by the employment tribunal (see, eg, *Burns v Consignia Ltd No 2* [2004] IRLR 425 and *Barke v SEETEC* [2005] EWCA Civ 578, [2005] IRLR 633 discussed at paras 18.201–18.204).

Delay

18.34 The EAT may in certain limited cases intervene in situations where there has been excessive delay by an employment tribunal in promulgating its decision. The jurisprudential basis for such intervention has been the subject of some debate in the case law and the Court of Appeal diverged from the approach taken by the EAT itself.

18.35 In *Kwamin v Birmingham City Council* [2004] IRLR 516, the EAT held that an independent ground of appeal would arise in the case of delay where the decision of a tribunal was unsafe. A decision would become unsafe when the delay in promulgating the decision had led to a tribunal falling into error even if such error would not have resulted in the tribunal's decision being perverse and therefore amounting to an error of law.

18.36 The *Kwamin* appeal was made up of a number of conjoined appeals. One of those was subsequently appealed to the Court of Appeal and the appeal became known as *Bangs v Connex South Eastern Ltd* [2005] EWCA Civ 14, [2005] 2 All ER 316. The leading judgment of Mummery LJ did not accept the EAT's reasoning in *Kwamin* Mummery LJ held that the following principles govern appeals to the EAT where the ground of appeal is that the employment tribunal has delayed unreasonably in promulgating its decision:

(a) Appeals could only be brought before the EAT on questions of law by virtue of s 21 of the ETA 1996. No appeals could be brought in respect of findings of fact which were made by the employment tribunal.

(b) Unreasonable delay was ordinarily a matter of fact and not a question of law. No independent ground of appeal existed simply because a decision was unsafe as a result of factual errors or omissions which had been caused by the delay.

(c) If an appellant was to succeed in arguing that an appeal ought to succeed as a result of an employment tribunal unreasonably delaying the promulgation of its decision, it would need to be shown that the tribunal had come to a perverse decision in respect of its overall conclusion or in respect of specific matters of fact or credibility.

(d) There may be situations in which an appellant could argue that unreasonable delay can be treated as a procedural error or material irregularity giving rise to a question of law in the proceedings of the tribunal. Such a situation would occur if the appellant could show that the failure to promulgate the decision within a reasonable time gave rise to a real risk that the appellant had been deprived of his right to a fair trial under Art 6 of the ECHR.

In the light of *Bangs v Connex* it is unlikely that there will be many successful appeals on the sole **18.37** basis that litigants have experienced delays in the promulgation of a decision by the employment tribunal. Most delays are unlikely to be severe enough to deprive litigants of their Art 6 right to a fair trial—indeed, that was the conclusion of the Court of Appeal on the facts in *Bangs v Connex* itself. Moreover, if the delay leads to a perverse decision, an appellant will be able to rely on perversity as a ground of appeal without making reference to the delay.

Allegations of bias or procedural impropriety

Allegations of bias or procedural impropriety levelled against a tribunal (see Chapter 10) can raise a **18.38** question of law provided that they are not obviously so lacking in substance that there is, in reality, no challenge to the tribunal's decision. This point was investigated in *Lodwick v Southwark London Borough Council* [2004] EWCA Civ 306, [2004] IRLR 544, where the EAT had declined jurisdiction over a bias appeal on the basis that it raised no question of law and therefore the EAT had no jurisdiction. Pill LJ stated, however, at para 15 of his judgment that all but the most unfounded allegations of bias would raise a question of law and therefore the EAT would have jurisdiction to entertain such appeals:

> While there may be cases in which, upon findings of fact by the tribunal, the allegation of bias disappears, the appeal against the ruling of the employment tribunal was in my judgment an appeal on a question of law arising from a decision of the tribunal. The Employment Appeal Tribunal had jurisdiction unless the allegation of bias was on its face so lacking in substance that it could not be said to amount to a real challenge to the decision.

Moreover, the effect of Art 6 of the ECHR (restated in the overriding objective as the duty to act **18.39** fairly) is to place a tribunal under a duty to conduct a proper hearing without any form of prejudice (see *Kraska v Switzerland* (1993) 18 EHRR 188, 200, para 30). A breach of Art 6 would amount to an error of law on the part of the tribunal and therefore invoke the jurisdiction of the EAT.

The EAT has developed rules of practice for dealing with appeals where allegations of bias or pro- **18.40** cedural impropriety are made in the 2013 Practice Direction.

The appellant must include in the notice of appeal full particulars of each complaint made (2013 **18.41** Practice Direction, para 13.1). It is particularly important that a party making an allegation of bias or procedural impropriety sets out clearly the allegations made about the conduct of the employment tribunal. Thus, if the allegations are not set out adequately the registrar or a judge may direct that the appellant or his representative provide an affidavit setting out full particulars of all allegations of bias or misconduct relied upon (2013 Practice Direction, para 13.2). It is unusual now to require an affidavit but its use here stresses the degree of certainty that there should be before such a criticism is made.

If the appeal is allocated to the preliminary hearing track or the full hearing track, then the EAT **18.42** may take the following steps (as set out at para 13.3 of the 2013 Practice Direction):

(a) require the appellant or a representative to provide, if not already provided, an affidavit (it is thought that a witness statement is insufficient because of the gravity of the allegations)

(b) require any party to give an affidavit or to obtain a witness statement from any person who has represented any of the parties at the tribunal hearing, and any other person present at the tribunal hearing or a relevant part of it, giving their account of the events set out in the affidavit of the appellant or the appellant's representative

(c) seek comments, upon all affidavits or witness statements received, from the judge of the employment tribunal from which the appeal is brought, and may seek such comments from the lay members of the tribunal

(d) the EAT will on receipt supply to the parties copies of all affidavits, statements, and comments received.

18.43 Paragraph 13.6 of the 2013 Practice Direction provides that:

(a) the EAT will not permit complaints of bias or procedural impropriety to be raised or developed at the hearing of the appeal unless this procedure has been followed (and this is in practice strictly adhered to)

(b) the EAT recognizes that, pursuant to the Employment Tribunal (Constitution and Rules of Procedure) Regulations 2004 (which have now been replaced by the ETR 2013, although this has not been updated in the 2013 Practice Direction), judges and employment tribunals are themselves obliged to observe the overriding objective and are given wide powers and duties of case management, so appeals in respect of their conduct of employment tribunals, which is pursuant to these provisions, are less likely to succeed

(c) unsuccessful pursuit of an allegation of bias or improper conduct, particularly in respect of case management decisions, may put the party raising it at risk of an order for costs.

18.44 The EAT issued a Conciliation Protocol on 9 December 2004, which may apply to any appeal which is amenable to conciliation, but it is expressed to be likely to apply to complaints of bias or procedural irregularity on the part of the employment tribunal. The Protocol states at para 10 that the EAT can stay an appeal for a period of '(say) 28 days' in order that the parties might make use of the conciliation services of ACAS. If ACAS is successful in negotiating a settlement, the appeal may be dismissed on withdrawal by the appellant or alternatively the appeal may be allowed by consent. If the appeal is to be allowed by consent then the judge will give directions under para 18 of the 2013 Practice Direction. Further, in June 2007 ACAS announced that it would extend its conciliation services to selected cases referred to it by the EAT. The cases which are expected to be referred by the EAT include in particular:

(a) cases where the parties' employment relationship is ongoing

(b) cases which could be referred back to the employment tribunal

(c) appeals relating to monetary awards.

18.45 An appeal on grounds of bias or procedural impropriety may appear to draw the EAT into a position where it has to adjudicate upon factual disputes as to precisely what has occurred before the tribunal from which the appeal is brought, but naturally the EAT has tried to avoid being drawn into such a role. As such, in *Kennedy v Metropolitan Police Commissioner* The Times, 8 November 1990, the EAT was of the view that if there is a dispute as to what happened at a hearing before the employment tribunal, the practice of the EAT should be to 'accept the word and the evidence and comments of the learned chairman unless there is clearly a mistake'.

18.46 The decision of the EAT in *Facey v Midas Retail Security* [2000] IRLR 812, however, indicates that the EAT may have to determine factual disputes since the resolution of such disputes may well resolve the question of whether the judge or tribunal was biased or prejudiced. In *Facey* the appellant sought to bring the tribunal members to the EAT to give evidence as to what had occurred before the tribunal. The EAT decided that the procedure it ought to adopt in determining such matters of primary fact was that while the judge and lay members may be requested to provide sworn written evidence as to matters of primary fact and adverse inferences can be drawn in a suitable case from their failure to do so, they can neither voluntarily submit themselves for cross-examination, nor can they be compelled to answer questions under cross-examination.

18.47 Moreover, in *Stansbury v Datapulse plc* [2003] EWCA Civ 1951, [2004] IRLR 466, the Court of Appeal accepted the EAT's view as expressed in *Facey*, that in situations where there was a factual dispute, the EAT may well have to assume the role of being judges of fact. An acute case of this was seen in *Stansbury*; the allegation was that one of the wing members had fallen asleep and had appeared drunk during the hearing. Needless to say, there was a substantial dispute as to what had, in fact, occurred. The EAT had found that it was not necessary for it to resolve the issues of fact since even if the wing member had fallen asleep during the tribunal hearing, that would not render the hearing unfair since the tribunal had reserved its decision, which in the event, had been unanimous. The Court of Appeal disagreed. Peter Gibson LJ stated (at para 26): 'If the hearing was unfair because of the misbehaviour of a member of the ET the decision is not saved from being unfair by the fact that the decision was unanimous and reserved'. Thus, the Court of Appeal found that it was not only appropriate, but indeed necessary, for the EAT to resolve the issues of fact which would enable it to determine whether or not the hearing was fair.

Guidance as to whether or not an appeal on grounds of bias is likely to succeed was given to tribunals by the Court of Appeal in *Locabail (UK) Ltd v Bayfield Properties Ltd* [2000] IRLR 96. Paragraph 25 of the judgment sets out a number of factors which might lead to a successful appeal on grounds of bias and sets out other grounds which would ordinarily not lead to a successful appeal: **18.48**

> It would be dangerous and futile to attempt to define or list the factors which may or may not give rise to a real danger of bias. Everything will depend on the facts, which may include the nature of the issue to be decided. We cannot, however, conceive of circumstances in which an objection could be soundly based on the religion, ethnic or national origin, gender, age, class, means or sexual orientation of the judge. Nor, at any rate ordinarily, could an objection be soundly based on the judge's social or educational or service or employment background or history, nor that of any member of the judge's family; or previous political associations; or membership of social or sporting or charitable bodies; or Masonic associations; or previous judicial decisions; or extra-curricular utterances (whether in textbooks, lectures, speeches, articles, interviews, reports or responses to consultation papers); or previous receipt of instructions to act for or against any party, solicitor or advocate engaged in a case before him; or membership of the same Inn, circuit, local Law Society or chambers. By contrast, a real danger of bias might well be thought to arise if there were personal friendship or animosity between the judge and any member of the public involved in the case; or if the judge were closely acquainted with any member of the public involved in the case, particularly if the credibility of that individual could be significant in the decision of the case; or if, in a case where the credibility of any individual were an issue to be decided by the judge, he had in a previous case rejected the evidence of that person in such outspoken terms as to throw doubt on his ability to approach such person's evidence with an open mind on any later occasion; or if on any question at issue in the proceedings before him the judge had expressed views, particularly in the course of the hearing, in such extreme and unbalanced terms as to throw doubt on his ability to try the issue with an objective judicial mind; or if, for any other reason, there were real ground for doubting the ability of the judge to ignore extraneous considerations, prejudices and predilections and bring an objective judgment to bear on the issues before him.

Successful challenges to tribunal decisions on grounds of bias have been in fact few (see also paras 18.38 ff). **18.49**

In *Ansar v Lloyds TSB Bank plc* [2007] IRLR 211, the Court of Appeal, upholding the judgment of Burton J, decided that the EAT should test the employment tribunal's decision as to recusal by considering the proceedings which had taken place before the tribunal as a whole and should decide whether a perception of bias had arisen from the conduct of those proceedings. The mere fact that a judge or employment judge or member earlier in the same case or in a previous case had commented adversely on the conduct of a party or a witness or had found the evidence of a party or witness to be unreliable would not, without something more, found a sustainable objection. Here the claimant had sought to rely on the fact that he had already made a complaint about the particular judge, and thus sought his recusal from the case, but the Court of Appeal held that a mere complaint could not give rise to an automatic decision to recuse. **18.50**

E. RESTRICTIONS ON THE SCOPE OF APPEAL

There are certain types of appeal which the EAT has indicated are unlikely to be successful, even though the decision of the employment tribunal contains an error of law. These are: **18.51**

(a) academic points of appeal
(b) points of law which were not argued in the employment tribunal
(c) appeals in relation to settlement agreements.

Academic points

18.52 The EAT takes the same approach to academic appeals as does the Court of Appeal. This is that in order for the appeal to be considered, it must affect the actual decision in the case. Thus, if an appeal relates to an aspect of the reasoning of an employment tribunal which, even if overturned, would not affect the result of the case, then the EAT will not hear the appeal. The classic statement of the principle is to be found in the House of Lords decision of *Ainsbury v Millington* [1987] 1 WLR 379, where Lord Bridge stated (at 381):

> It has always been a fundamental feature of our judicial system that the courts decide disputes between the parties before them; they do not pronounce on abstract questions of law when there is no dispute to be resolved.

18.53 The principle was applied by the Court of Appeal to an employment case in *Riniker v University College London* [2001] EWCA Civ 597, in which Miss Riniker had succeeded in establishing sufficient continuity of service to bring her claim, but was concerned about the date of termination of certain contracts of employment as determined by the EAT and in particular the problems that this might cause her for future proceedings. Since Miss Riniker had established sufficient continuity of service and therefore an appeal would make no difference to the result of Miss Riniker's case, the Court of Appeal refused her permission to appeal.

18.54 In *Riniker*'s case, the Court of Appeal expressly approved the EAT's treatment of the principle relating to academic appeals in *Harrod v Ministry of Defence* [1981] ICR 8. In that case, the appellant sought to challenge a finding of fact made by the employment tribunal that there was no mobility clause in the appellant's contract of employment. Before the appeal the appellant's solicitor wrote to the EAT and explained that the appellant did not wish to challenge the employment tribunal's overall decision that he had not been constructively dismissed. The EAT declined jurisdiction to hear the appeal. May J stated (at 11):

> it is inherent in any appeal that the Appellant must be seeking to set aside the decision, judgment or order, whatever it may have been of the tribunal below and it would need very clear words to entitle a party to any proceedings to appeal to an appellate tribunal on the basis that, although the decision below was right, nevertheless the reasons for it were wrong.

18.55 Similarly, in *Carter v Tower Hamlets LBC* EAT/1073/99 an employee who had been a swimming instructor was found work as a classroom helper but was paid at a higher rate of pay of a swimming instructor. A complaint of unfair dismissal was upheld by the employment tribunal and an order was made as to re-engagement. The tribunal then ordered at a further hearing that it would not be reasonably practicable for the employment tribunal to comply with the order for reengagement and that she was not entitled to compensation since she had failed to take reasonable steps to mitigate her loss. The employee sought to appeal in respect of the order for re-engagement but the EAT was satisfied that there could be no benefit to the employee in pursuing an appeal and that, therefore, it would be inappropriate for the EAT to hear it.

18.56 It should be noted that since the decision of the House of Lords in *Ainsbury v Millington* (see para 18.52) both the Court of Appeal and House of Lords have sometimes taken the view that they should hear certain academic appeals where they raise points of general public importance. Thus, in *Don Pasquale v HM Customs and Excise* [1990] 1 WLR 1108, the Court of Appeal was prepared to hear an appeal in relation to the assessment of value added tax despite the fact that no live issue remained between the parties. In addition, in *R v Secretary of State for the Home Department, ex parte Salem* [1999] 2 All ER 42, the House of Lords accepted that its decision in *Ainsbury v Millington* only applied to questions of private rights and therefore the House of Lords was free to hear an appeal on a point of public law, even though there was no issue between the parties (see also *Rolls-Royce v Unite the Union* [2009] IRLR 576).

18.57 The EAT has so far declined to hear academic appeals. However, in the light of the retreat of the Court of Appeal and the House of Lords from the strictness of the principle set out in *Ainsbury v Millington*, the EAT might choose to do so in the future. There is nothing in the EAT's rules that would prevent it doing so since the jurisdiction provided for in s 21 of the EAT 1996 is invoked whenever the employment tribunal falls into an error of law.

Points of law which were not argued in the employment tribunal

It is very unusual that a party will be able to argue a point on appeal which was not argued in the **18.58** employment tribunal. The general principle was set out by the EAT in *Kumchyk v Derby County Council* [1978] ICR 1116. In that case a car park attendant was dismissed after he refused to work in a different place from his usual place of work. His claim for unfair dismissal failed before the tribunal on the basis that there was an express mobility clause in this contract of employment. He sought to argue on appeal that there was an implied term in his contract of employment which restricted the express mobility clause. The point had not, however, been argued below. The EAT found that there was nothing in the statute which prevented the EAT from taking new points on appeal. However, in most cases it would be unjust to do so. It may be just to allow a new point where there had been some deception on the part of the respondent to the appeal which entitled the appellant to say:

> This really is a case in which we were headed off from running the point which we are now seeking to run before the appellate court by conduct which cannot possibly be condoned in justice by the appellate court.

However, the EAT (Arnold J presiding) went on to state that (at 1123):

> It certainly is not enough, in our judgment, that the point was not taken owing to a wrong, or what turns out in the light of events to have been a wrong, tactical decision by the appellant or his advocate. It would certainly not be enough that the omission was due to the lack of skill or experience on the part of the advocate. It would certainly not, we think, be enough that the omission could have been made good had the industrial tribunal chosen to suggest the point for consideration to the appellant or his advocate.

The basis for the rule set out in *Kumchyk* is that there is a public interest in the finality of litigation **18.59** and this is especially acute in employment cases with their short time limits and lack of a costs jurisdiction. This rationale was set out by Robert Walker LJ in *Jones v Governing Body of Burdett Coutts School* [1998] IRLR 521, para 29, where he stated:

> the search for justice requires some difficult reconciliations of conflicting principles, and there is a strong public interest in finality in litigation. The rule or practice embodied in [*Kumchyk*] is not regarded as a matter of technicality, but of justice to a respondent who may be plunged into yet more litigation.

The rule set out in *Kumchyk* is of wide-ranging application and it will be generally difficult for ap- **18.60** pellants to introduce points of law before the EAT which were not argued before the employment tribunal. The rule is more strictly applied in the EAT than in the Court of Appeal. However, the rule is subject to certain exceptions:

(a) The rule will not be applied where the appellant was prevented from arguing a point before the employment tribunal by a deception on the part of the respondent to the appeal (see *Kumchyk*).

(b) It was held by the EAT in *House v Emerson Electrical Industrial Controls* [1980] ICR 785 that, where a point is related to the employment tribunal's jurisdiction to hear the issue, the *Kumchyk* principle should not be applied.

The extent to which the exception to the *Kumchyk* principle set out in *House* ought to be applied **18.61** has been considered by the EAT and Court of Appeal on a number of occasions since. In *Glennie v Independent Magazines (UK) Ltd* [1999] ICR 38, argument had taken place before the tribunal on a preliminary issue as to whether the claim was brought in time or not. The effective date of termination was agreed between the parties at the employment tribunal hearing. Ms Glennie, having lost before the employment tribunal, sought to argue before the EAT that the effective date of termination was a different date on the basis that her contract of employment had a provision requiring notice. The EAT allowed her to present that argument but its decision was overturned by the Court of Appeal ([1999] IRLR 719), which reasoned that:

(a) There was a conflict between the decision of the EAT in *House* which suggested that any jurisdictional issue could be taken as a new point on appeal and the subsequent authorities of *Russell v Elmdon Freight Terminal Ltd* [1989] ICR 629 and *Barber v Thames Television plc* [1991] IRLR 236. Those authorities held that not all jurisdictional points which were not raised before the tribunal of first instance could be taken on appeal before the EAT and that in each case the EAT had to decide whether justice required that the new point be taken. The EAT would be particularly reluctant to allow a point to be argued where new evidence was required for it to be properly considered. As was stated by Knox J in *Barber* (at 268):

> It does not however follow from this that all jurisdictional points must be allowed at any stage even if they involve a further hearing to establish further facts. In our view in each case the appeal tribunal has to decide on balance whether justice requires that the new point should be allowed to be taken. If it appears on existing evidence that the decision appealed from is a nullity that will be a consideration of overwhelming strength. Where what is relied upon is a chance of establishing a lack of jurisdiction by calling fresh evidence which was always available the case is far less straightforward.

(b) In the *Barber* case, Knox J had been wise to leave open the possibility that, in the case of an unrepresented party, justice might demand that the EAT put right what appeared to be a glaring injustice, even though, strictly, the evidence on which the unrepresented party sought to rely would have been available before the tribunal. However, Knox J had not envisaged the possibility that, when a represented party has fought and lost a jurisdictional issue on agreed facts before the tribunal, it should then be allowed to resile from its agreement and seek a new tribunal hearing in order to adduce evidence which would then be challenged, and invite the tribunal to decide the question of jurisdiction all over again on new facts.

(c) The Court of Appeal appeared to be impressed by the fact that the appellant in the *Glennie* case would not be deprived of relying on an 'obvious knock-out point' by its refusal to allow the point to be run.

18.62 In the light of the *Glennie* decision, it will be difficult for appellants who were represented before the employment tribunal to run jurisdictional points before the EAT which were not run below. They will have to show some exceptional reason why they should be permitted to run the argument. The EAT will be more likely to allow such points where they would not require a fresh analysis of evidence by the employment tribunal or where there was an 'obvious knock-out point' which had not been taken. Litigants who were unrepresented below will have an easier task of convincing the EAT to allow them to run fresh jurisdictional points, particularly in circumstances where there has been a 'glaring injustice' as a result of the failure of the litigant in person to take a point (see also *Vakante v Governing Body of Addey* and *Stanhope School (No 2)* [2005] ICR 231; *Atkins v Coyle Personnel plc* [2008] IRLR 420).

18.63 An exceptional case where the EAT did allow new arguments to be made was *O'Connell v Thames Water Utilities plc*, EAT/903/98. That case turned on a complicated issue where the employment tribunal wrongly held that the matter was covered by the Water Reorganization (Pensions) Regulations 1989, SI 1989/1161.

18.64 Where the EAT allows a new point to be taken on appeal, it must give reasons for doing so and, in *Jones v Governing Body of Burdett Coutts School* [1998] IRLR 521, the Court of Appeal overturned the decision of the EAT to do so because it had not given reasons, and unusually the decision fell outside the range within which the appeal tribunal could reasonably exercise its discretion.

18.65 The Court of Appeal in *Hellyer Bros Ltd v McLeod* [1987] ICR 526 suggested that while it was for the EAT to regulate its own procedure, it was surprising that the EAT adopted a more stringent rule than that which was applied by the Court of Appeal, although this hint that a more relaxed view should be taken has not in fact been taken up. The Court of Appeal practice was set out in *Wilson v Liverpool Corporation* [1971] 1 WLR 302, where it was stated that a new point may be taken (at 307):

> if the [Court of Appeal] is in possession of all the material necessary to enable it to dispose of the matter finally, without injustice to the other party and without recourse to a further hearing below.

In *Secretary of State for Health v Rance* [2007] IRLR 665 Judge McMullen collected the authorities **18.66** together as follows at para 50:

> I regard those two passages as key statements of the law, together with the interpretation by Brooke LJ of previous judgments of the EAT dealing with concessions. From the authorities reviewed in those cases, I draw the following principles of law:
>
> (1) There is a discretion to allow a new point of law to be argued in the EAT. It is tightly regulated by authorities; *Jones* paragraph 20.
> (2) The discretion covers new points and the re-opening of conceded points; ibid.
> (3) The discretion is exercised only in exceptional circumstances; ibid.
> (4) It would be even more exceptional to exercise the discretion where fresh issues of fact would have to be investigated; ibid.
> (5) Where the new point relates to jurisdiction, this is not a trump card requiring the point to be taken; *Barber v Thames Television plc* [1991] IRLR 236, EAT Knox J and members at paragraph 38; approved in *Jones*. It remains discretionary.
> (6) The discretion may be exercised in any of the following circumstances which are given as examples:
>> (a) It would be unjust to allow the other party to get away with some deception or unfair conduct which meant that the point was not taken below; *Kumchyk v Derby City Council* [1978] ICR 1116, EAT Arnold J and members at 1123.
>> (b) The point can be taken if the EAT is in possession of all the material necessary to dispose of the matter fairly without recourse to a further hearing; *Wilson v Liverpool Corporation* [1971] 1 WLR 302, 307, per Widgery LJ.
>> (c) The new point enables the EAT plainly to say from existing material that the Employment Tribunal judgment was a nullity, for that is a consideration of overwhelming strength; *House v Emerson Electric Industrial Controls* [1980] ICR 795 at 800, EAT Talbot J and members, followed and applied in *Barber* at paragraph 38 In such a case it is the EAT's duty to put right the law on the facts available to the EAT; *Glennie* paragraph 12 citing *House*.
>> (d) The EAT can see a glaring injustice in refusing to allow an unrepresented party to rely on evidence which could have been adduced at the Employment Tribunal; *Glennie* paragraph 15.
>> (e) The EAT can see an obvious knock-out point; *Glennie*, paragraph 16.
>> (f) The issue is a discrete one of pure law requiring no further factual enquiry; *Glennie* para 17 per Laws LJ.
>> (g) It is of particular public importance for a legal point to be decided provided no further factual investigation and no further evaluation by the specialist Tribunal is required; Laws LJ in *Leicestershire* para 21[.]
> (7) The discretion is not to be exercised where by way of example:
>> (a) What is relied upon is a chance of establishing lack of jurisdiction by calling fresh evidence; *Barber* para 20 as interpreted in *Glennie* para 15.
>> (b) The issue arises as a result of lack of skill by a represented party, for that is not a sufficient reason; *Jones* para 20.
>> (c) The point was not taken below as a result of a tactical decision by a representative or a party; *Kumchyk* at page 1123, approved in *Glennie* at para 15.
>> (d) All the material is before the EAT but what is required is an evaluation and an assessment of this material and application of the law to it by the specialist first instance Tribunal; *Leicestershire* para 21.
>> (e) A represented party has fought and lost a jurisdictional issue and now seeks a new hearing; *Glennie* para 15. That applies whether the jurisdictional issue is the same as that originally canvassed (normal retiring age as in *Barber*) or is a different way of establishing jurisdiction from that originally canvassed (associated employers and transfer of undertakings as in *Russell v Elmdom Freight Terminal Ltd* [1989] ICR 629, EAT Knox J and members). See the analysis in *Glennie* at paras 13 and 14 of these two cases.
>> (f) What is relied upon is the high value of the case; *Leicestershire* para 21.

On the facts of the particular case, the EAT held that: **18.67**

(a) it is relevant to ask what the period of time has been since the date of the judgment or possibly from the date of the 'concession'. A short period of time, or a short period of time in the context of very protracted litigation, would point in favour of the respondents.

(b) It is relevant to ask what the reason was for the change of position. An administrative mistake, or an oversight by a lawyer doing a routine audit of a very substantial number of files, is more venal than a tactical decision made by a representative in the proceedings. A mistake which arises in the course of handling 11,000 cases according to protocols directed by the employment tribunal from the centre should not readily be held against the respondents, even if the number is upwards of 120 out of the 11,000.

(c) genuine attempts were made to raise the matter on review before the tribunals which were unsuccessful is also a relevant factor, as is the reason for the tribunal's refusal. It would generally be unjust to allow the re-opening of a concession if the claimant had made an agreement to forego any part of her claim in exchange for the conceded point, unless the matter could be put right entirely on a financial settlement.

18.68 In *Lipscombe v Forestry Commission* [2007] EWCA Civ 428 the EAT allowed a new point to be argued where the employee was a litigant in person and the new point arose from an EAT decision which was issued after the decision of the tribunal and no further evidence was required.

18.69 The 2013 Practice Direction lays down a process for dealing with such challenges. Where a respondent intends to contend at the full hearing of an appeal that the appellant has raised a point which was not argued below, the respondent should inform the EAT within fourteen days of receiving the notice of appeal in a case where a preliminary hearing has been ordered and in a case which is set down for a full hearing without need for a preliminary hearing, in the respondent's answer (2013 Practice Direction, para 10.6). In the event of a dispute between the parties as to whether a point was argued before the employment tribunal, the employment judge will be asked for his comments. This in fact rarely happens as it should be obvious from the decision of the employment tribunal, especially now that tribunals are encouraged to set out what are the issues they decided.

18.70 In a surprising result, the EAT accepted (Mitting J presiding) in *Atos Origin IT Services UK Ltd v Haddock* [2005] IRLR 20 that a respondent who failed to enter a response before the employment tribunal and was therefore not allowed to take any part in the tribunal proceedings might still appeal the decision of the tribunal. The EAT held that r 3(3) of the ETR 2001 (which stated that 'a respondent who has not entered an appearance shall not be entitled to take part in any proceedings') applied only to proceedings before the tribunal and not to proceedings before the EAT. The EAT held that it governed its own procedure and that there was nothing in the ETA 1996 or in the EAT Rules which would restrict the right of a respondent who had not entered a notice of appearance from participating in an appeal. Moreover, para 19 of the 2013 Practice Direction provides a procedure for a situation where an appellant has not presented an ET3 to the tribunal. That procedure is strict, however, and requires the submission of a witness statement explaining in detail why no ET3 was submitted to the tribunal as well as a draft ET3.

Settlement agreements

18.71 The EAT has no jurisdiction to set aside an agreement by which the appellant has compromised his appeal before the EAT since the jurisdiction of the EAT is purely statutory and is confined to hearing appeals (see *Eden v Humphries and Glasgow Ltd* [1981] ICR 183; cf *Hirsch v Ward & Goldstone plc* COIT 1535/15). Any action brought on the settlement agreements must be brought as a contractual claim in the civil courts. However, where the parties settle the remedy or quantum part of an unfair dismissal claim that does not prevent an appeal as to the fairness of the dismissal since this will usually be entered into without prejudice to the issue of fairness (*Associated Tyre Specialists (Southern) Ltd v Lewis* 233 Industrial Relations Information Bulletin 13).

F. PRECEDENT

18.72 It might be expected that the doctrine of precedent applied to the EAT with the same rigour as in other civil appellate bodies (as to precedent in the Court of Appeal see *Davis v Johnson* [1979] AC 264). However, the EAT approaches the doctrine in a somewhat flexible manner. For example, in recent years there has been a willingness to depart from previous decisions where it is considered that those decisions are wrongly decided, although this will only be done 'in exceptional circumstances or where there are previous inconsistent decisions' (*Secretary of State for Trade & Industry v Cook* [1997] IRLR 150).

The EAT indicated in *Digital Equipment Co Ltd v Clements (No 2)* [1997] IRLR 140 that its approach in the face of inconsistent decisions would be to try and reconcile such decisions in order to preserve consistency but if this could not be done then to direct tribunals which of the inconsistent authorities ought to be followed. An example of this practice in action is in the decision of the EAT in *Woodward v Abbey National plc (No 2)* [2005] ICR 1702, in which the EAT directed employment tribunals to no longer follow the decision of the EAT in *Midland Packaging v Clark* [2005] 2 All ER 266. **18.73**

In *Clarke v Frank Staddon* [2004] EWCA Civ 422, a decision on rolled-up holiday pay and the Working Time Regulations 1998, the Court of Appeal dealt with the question of whether decisions of the Scottish Court of Session were binding on the EAT. In that case, there was authority in the form of a decision of the EAT sitting in Scotland in *MPB Structures Ltd v Munro* [2003] IRLR 350, which was inconsistent with the decision of the EAT sitting in London in *Marshalls Clay Products v Caulfield* [2004] ICR 436. The Court of Appeal held that there was no rule of law binding on any court in England or Wales to follow a decision of a court whose jurisdiction runs in Scotland only. Thus, although as a matter of pragmatic good sense, the EAT ought to follow decisions of the Scottish Court of Session (the equivalent of the Court of Appeal) where the point of law before them is indistinguishable from the point of law dealt with in the Scottish case, the EAT and Court of Appeal are not obliged to (*Airbus UK Ltd v Webb* [2008] IRLR 309). In the event, the Court of Appeal in *Clarke* preferred the approach set out in *Marshalls Clay Products* to that in *Munro*. **18.74**

G. APPEALS AGAINST INTERIM ORDERS

The EAT's jurisdiction to hear appeals against interim orders by employment tribunals is the same as the EAT takes in dealing with final orders and judgments. As such, there must be found to be an error of law in order to invoke the jurisdiction of s 21 of the ETA 1996 and therefore allow the EAT to intervene. This approach was set out by the EAT in *Adams v West Sussex CC* [1990] ICR 546. Wood J stated (at 551–52): **18.75**

> It seems to us desirable, and indeed we would have expected, that the same principle would apply to interlocutory appeals as for final appeals even though the former will in the main be the result of the exercise of a discretion. Thus, in examining an interlocutory order of an industrial tribunal or of a chairman sitting alone we would define three issues: (a) Is the order made one within the powers given to the tribunal? (b) Has the discretion been exercised within guiding legal principles? (e.g. as to confidential documents in discovery issues); (c) Can the exercise of the discretion be attacked on the principles in *Associated Provincial Picture Houses Ltd v Wednesbury Corporation* [1948] 1 KB 223?

The same principles apply to an appeal against the refusal on the part of a tribunal to review its decision. Generally, the EAT avoids interfering with the tribunal's exercise of its case management powers.

The approach adopted by the EAT in *Adams v West Sussex CC* amounted to a change in approach. Previously, the EAT in *British Library v Palyza* [1984] ICR 504 indicated that the EAT would be prepared to take a more interventionist approach to supervising the exercise of discretion on the part of the employment tribunals in interim matters. The same principles apply to an appeal against the refusal on the part of a tribunal to review its decision. (See also *Amey Services Ltd v Cardigan* [2008] IRLR 279). In *Xv Z Ltd* [1998] ICR 43, Waite LJ at para 54 said in regard to case management decisions: **18.76**

> the tribunals themselves are the best judges of the case management decisions which crop up every day as they perform the function of trying to do justice with the maximum of flexibility and the minimum of formality.

H. COMMENCING AN APPEAL

The notice of appeal

18.77 The appellant must present a notice of appeal to the EAT in a specified form depending upon which tribunal the appeal is in respect of. Appeals as to decisions of the employment tribunal should be completed in the form of 'Form 1', which is attached to the 2013 Practice Direction. This requires copies of the ET1 and the ET3 to be filed with the notice of appeal or alternatively an explanation as to why such documents are not included. Appeals from decisions of the CAC should be completed in the form of 'Form 1A' and appeals from a decision of a certification officer should be completed in the form of 'Form 2'. Forms 1A and 2 are attached to the EAT Rules.

18.78 The formal printed notice of appeal need not always be used and both the EAT Rules and the 2013 Practice Direction allow for a notice of appeal which is presented substantially in the prescribed form. However, appellants should exercise caution in making use of a document other than the prescribed forms. Such a document would have to include sufficiently defined grounds of appeal (2013 Practice Direction, paras 3.5–3.6) and in *Martin v British Railways Board* [1989] ICR 27, the EAT held that a letter merely indicating a wish to appeal was not sufficient to commence proceedings.

18.79 Paragraph 3.5 of the 2013 Practice Direction requires that the notice of appeal sets out the order which the appellant will ask the EAT to make. This might be overturning the decision of the tribunal or a remission of the case to the same tribunal or a differently constituted tribunal for reconsideration. These orders may be sought in the alternative.

18.80 On 16 June 2015, the EAT issued a Practice Statement because 'many notices of appeal are simply too long'. The Practice Statement stated that notices of appeal should usually be no more than two sides of A4 paper and are not intended to be skeleton arguments. The Practice Statement suggested that if the terms of the Practice Statement were not followed there were risks that: (i) a judge would send back notices of appeal, to be shortened; (ii) that a preliminary hearing would be directed; or (iii) that the EAT might consider a party to have engaged in unreasonable conduct of litigation, so as to invoke the EAT's costs jurisdiction.

18.81 By para 3.1 of the 2013 Practice Direction, the notice of appeal must have the following documents attached to it:

(a) a copy of the judgment, decision, or order appealed against and of the tribunal's written reasons and

(b) a copy of the ET1 and the ET3 or

(c) if any documents are not attached then a written explanation as to why they are not attached must be provided.

In addition, the notice of appeal must include a postal address at which the appellant can be contacted. If the notice of appeal is presented without these documents para 3.1 of the 2013 Practice Direction states that it will not be validly lodged: see also *Trafalgar Construction Corp Limited v Singh* UKEATPA/1502/13/BA. In cases where a written explanation is provided as to why the notice of appeal does not have a copy of the judgment, decision, or order appealed against attached, at the time of lodging the notice of appeal the appellant must apply in writing to the EAT to exercise its discretion to hear the appeal without written reasons or to request that the EAT exercises its power to request written reasons for the judgment from the tribunal.

18.82 Following the decision of Burton P in *Kanapathiar v Harrow LBC* [2003] IRLR 571, the registrar of the EAT adopted a strict approach and refused to accept notices of appeal which do not have the required documents attached. In that case the appellant had posted a notice of appeal with the relevant documentation attached to the EAT the day before the time limit for presentation expired. In addition, on the day that the deadline expired the appellant attended the EAT in person, despite there being concerns about his health, and lodged a copy of the notice of appeal but without any attached documentation. Burton P held that the registrar had not erred in granting the appellant a one-day extension of time to lodge the relevant documents in the circumstances of Mr Kanapathiar's case. However, Burton P wished to make it clear that the somewhat lax approach of permitting notices of appeal would no longer be adopted. He stated (at para 14):

> it is equally clear that, in the discretion of the Registrar, this was an appropriate case, not only because of the particular compassionate circumstances, but also because this would be the case used as an affirmative signal of the end of the previous lax practice, for the grant of what is, after all, only a one-day extension.

Indeed, on 3 February 2005 a Practice Statement was handed down by the President of the EAT ([2005] ICR 660) making it clear that notices of appeal would not be accepted without the required documents. This Practice Statement is now included at para 3.1 of the 2013 Practice Direction. **18.83**

Paragraph 3.10 of the 2013 Practice Direction provides that no party may reserve the right to amend, alter, or add to a statement of case (such as the notice of appeal). Any application to amend should be made in the usual way. **18.84**

It is not uncommon for an appellant to seek to pursue both an appeal before the EAT and a review of an employment tribunal's decision. If this course is adopted, the application to the employment tribunal for review should be attached to the notice of appeal. If the employment tribunal has dealt with the application for review, the judgment and written reasons should also be attached. In other cases, a statement should be provided stating that judgment is awaited (2013 Practice Direction, para 3.2). **18.85**

Paragraph 3.9 of the 2013 Practice Direction restates the position as set out in r 3(7)–(10) of the EAT Rules that a judge or the registrar may decide that no further action should be taken in respect of a notice of appeal which discloses either no reasonable grounds for the bringing of the appeal, or that the appeal is an abuse of the EAT's process or is otherwise likely to obstruct the just disposal of proceedings. In these circumstances, the registrar will notify the appellant setting out written reasons for his decision. The appellant may (unless the appeal is certified as being 'totally without merit' apply for an oral hearing under r 3(10) of the EAT Rules. In order to do this, the appellant must 'express dissatisfaction' with the reasons which have been given and request a hearing before a judge. The appellant has twenty-eight days from the date that written reasons were sent by the EAT to do this (EAT Rules, r 3(10)). However, where a judge or the registrar has taken a decision under r 3(7) and considers that the appeal is 'totally without merit' then there is no right to an oral hearing: see r 3(7ZA) of the EAT Rules (inserted by the Employment Appeal Tribunal (Amendment) Rules 2013). Although the terminology 'totally without merit' is new, from 2013, to the EAT Rules, it is familiar legal parlance since the same test is applied by the Court of Appeal (in determining whether to deprive an appellant of the right to an oral hearing where an appellant seeks permission to appeal to the Court of Appeal), and it is also the test which is made use of in the civil courts when considering the civil courts' jurisdiction to make 'civil restraint orders'. **18.86**

No fee payable for commencing an appeal

There is no fee payable for presenting an appeal to the EAT. Although such fees were introduced by the Employment Tribunals and the Employment Appeal Tribunal Fees Order 2013 this was found to be unlawful by the Supreme Court in *R (on the application of Unison) v Lord Chancellor* [2017] ICR 1037. The government has had to refund fees paid under this scheme and (at the date of writing) has not indicated that it will attempt to introduce further such fees in the future. **18.87**

Time limits for commencing an appeal

Rule 3(3) of the EAT Rules and para 5 of the 2013 Practice Direction require a notice of appeal to be filed within the following time limits: **18.88**

(a) In a case where the appeal is against an order, direction, or decision of the tribunal then the appeal must be commenced within forty-two days of the order, direction, or decision. The EAT treats the date of an order, direction, or decision as being the date on which it was sent to the parties: see para 5.2 of the 2013 Practice Direction.

(b) If the appeal is against a judgment of an employment tribunal the appeal must be instituted within forty-two days of the date on which the written record of the judgment was sent to the parties unless written reasons were requested orally at the hearing, in writing within fourteen days of the written record of the judgment being sent to the parties or if the tribunal reserved its reasons and gave them subsequently in writing. In these cases, the time limit will be forty-two days from the date when written reasons were sent to the parties.

18.89 The date on which the extended reasons were sent to the appellant is the date on which the document was transmitted to the party concerned and not when it was received by him. The position has been placed beyond doubt by the decision of the Court of Appeal in *Gdynia American Shipping Lines (London) Ltd v Chelminski* [2004] EWCA Civ 871, [2004] IRLR 725, where the Court of Appeal affirmed the EAT's decisions in *Sian v Abbey National* [2004] IRLR 185 and *Hammersmith & Fulham London Borough Council v Ladejobi* [1999] ICR 673 and found that the EAT's decisions in *Immigration Advisory Service v Oomen* [1997] ICR 683 and *Scotford v Smith Kline Beecham* [2002] ICR 264 to the contrary were wrongly decided. That was because the parties could not in this case, where the rules were clear on their face, rely on s 7 of the Interpretation Act 1978, that is the presumption that a document sent by first class post would arrive the following day. The Court of Appeal found that the deeming rules which were set out in the Interpretation Act 1978 had no bearing on the application of the EAT Rules which simply referred to the date on which the reasons were sent. The Court of Appeal, while viewing the question of law principally as a matter of statutory construction, also accepted Burton P's conclusion in *Sian v Abbey National* that it was more administratively convenient for the date from which the forty-two days ran to be the date on which the decision was transmitted to the parties by the employment tribunal. Burton P considered that the opposite result would cause great uncertainty, in particular, to the respondent, since it would never be clear from which date time ran.

18.90 *Sian v Abbey National* is an instructive example of the strictness with which the rules relating to time limits can be applied by the registrar. The appellant did not receive the written reasons of the tribunal at all until after the expiry of the 42-day period in which the appellant was required to appeal. The appellant's solicitor wrote to the employment tribunal asking for an extension of time in which to appeal and was told that the tribunal had no jurisdiction to grant such a request. The appellant then made an application to the EAT seeking an extension of time in which to appeal and arguing that the appeal had been brought within time. The registrar not only found that the notice of appeal had not been lodged within time but refused to grant an extension of time to the appellant. *Sian* was cited with approval in *Carroll v Mayor's Office for Policing and Crime* [2015] ICR 835, a case where the employment tribunals reasons had been improperly addressed and had not been received by the claimant's representatives.

18.91 Rule 37(1A) of the EAT Rules states that a notice of appeal must be lodged by 4 pm on the relevant day. This has raised problems as to what happens when a notice of appeal is partially presented, for example by fax, before 4 pm and partially after 4 pm. The EAT considered that question in *Midland Packaging v Clark* [2005] 2 All ER 266 Burton P found that:

(a) in circumstances where a notice of appeal was received by the EAT's fax machine prior to 4 pm on the relevant day, that such a notice of appeal would have been lodged in time even if the EAT's fax machine did not print it off until after the 4 pm time limit.

(b) a notice of appeal which had started to be delivered to the EAT's fax machine by the 4 pm deadline would be validly lodged within time.

Burton P concluded (at para 23):

> I say nothing as to what would happen if, for example, there were to be communication by e-mail, and someone was still typing an e-mail, halfway through it, at 4.00 pm, and as to whether that would count, but it seems to follow by analogy that such would not be sufficient, in that it is the communication which is crucial, though not the printing out—a printer could be jammed or overloaded. Where the document has in fact been completed, it is in either electronic or readable form, and is in the process of dispatch, and the dispatch has, on the balance of probabilities, started at the time of the expiry of the deadline, in my judgment that should count as good service or lodgment of the document.

However, in *Woodward v Abbey National plc (No 2)* [2005] ICR 1702, the EAT (Burton P presiding) **18.92** found that *Midland Packaging v Clark* was wrongly decided and that all of the notice of appeal and accompanying documentation must be lodged at the EAT by 4 pm on the relevant day in order that the notice of appeal is lodged in time. In cases where the notice of appeal is faxed, the time at which it is lodged will be determined with reference to the EAT's fax log and the fax containing the notice of appeal and its accompanying documents must be complete. In making this decision Burton P was influenced both by the wording of the EAT's own 2008 Practice Direction and CPR 5PD (Court Documents). Neither of these had been before the EAT in *Midland Packaging v Clark*. (On time limits for response see *Echendu v Wm Morrison Supermarkets plc* UKEATPA/1675/07.)

Application for an extension of time to lodge the notice of appeal

Under r 37(1) of the EAT Rules, the EAT has a discretion to extend time for a notice of appeal to **18.93** be presented, although in practice this is rarely granted. Therefore, if a notice of appeal is presented out of time, it must be accompanied by an application for an extension of time, setting out in detail the reason for the delay. It is not possible for a party to seek to extend time prior to the presentation of a notice of appeal since para 5.5 of the 2013 Practice Direction states that an application for an extension of time can only be considered once the notice of appeal has been received by the EAT.

Paragraph 5.6 of the 2013 Practice Direction sets out the procedure which will be adopted by the **18.94** EAT on receipt of an application to extend time. The application must be made as an interim application to the registrar who will determine whether to grant an extension of time having considered written representations from each side. The registrar will seek to decide this type of question in an expeditious manner and the parties will typically be given a relatively short amount of time in which to prepare written representations. Having received representations from the parties, the registrar will determine whether or not time ought to be extended.

An appeal from such a decision of the registrar lies to a judge and as with other interim appeals be- **18.95** fore the EAT, the EAT must be notified of the appeal within five days of the date that the registrar's decision was sent to the parties. Appeals in relation to applications to extend time are often heard at preliminary hearings (see para 18.111), although a potential respondent has the right to be heard, unlike the practice at a normal preliminary hearing.

Paragraphs 5.7 and 5.8 of the 2013 Practice Direction set out the principles by which the registrar **18.96** will exercise the discretion granted to him by r 37(1) of the EAT Rules and therefore by which an application to extend time will be determined. These principles have been developed by in turn the NIRC, EAT, and Court of Appeal. The paragraphs state:

> 5.7 In determining whether to extend the time for appealing, particular attention will be paid to whether any good excuse for the delay has been shown and to the guidance contained in the decisions of the EAT and the Court of Appeal, as summarised in cases such as *United Arab Emirates v Abdelghafar* [1995] ICR 65; *Aziz v Bethnal Green City Challenge Co Ltd* [2000] IRLR 111; and *Jurkovska v HLMAD* [2008] EWCA Civ 231, [2008] ICR 842.

> 5.8 It is not usually a good reason for late lodgment of a Notice of Appeal that (a) an application for litigation support from public funds has been made, but not yet determined; or that support is being sought from, but has not yet been provided by, some other body, such as a trade union, employers' association or the Equality and Human Rights Commission; (b) that the appellant was waiting for the result of an application for reconsideration; (c) that negotiations between the parties were occurring.

The EAT in *Marshall v Harland & Wolff* [1972] ICR 97 decided that the fact that a party is seeking **18.97** support to fund an appeal is not, of itself, a good reason for the EAT to exercise its discretion to extend time. The 2013 Practice Direction advises appellants, at para 5.9, to lodge a notice of appeal in time in 'any case of doubt or difficulty' and then to make an application to the registrar for directions.

Since para 5.7 of the 2013 Practice Direction refers specifically to the summaries of case law pro- **18.98** vided by the EAT and Court of Appeal in *Abdelghafar* and *Aziz*, some analysis of these leading decisions is required.

18.99 In *Abdelghafar*, Mummery P set out a summary of the authorities which deal with extensions of time generally and concluded that they showed that:

(a) It is necessary to weigh up or balance all the relevant factors when making a decision to extend a time limit. In particular, it was necessary to weigh on the one hand the public interest in promoting the expeditious dispatch of litigation and on the other hand the principle that litigants should not be denied an adjudication on the merits of their claim as a result of a procedural default.

(b) Where a party seeks an extension of time to present an appeal, that party will already have enjoyed a judicial determination of his or her claim and therefore the public interest and interest of the parties in having finality in the proceedings may make the court stricter about the application of time limits. Therefore, an extension of time may be refused even though the failure to observe the time limit had not caused prejudice to any party to the proceedings.

(c) No party is entitled to an extension and therefore it is incumbent upon any party seeking an extension of time that he or she provides the court with a 'full, honest and acceptable' explanation of the reasons for the delay.

18.100 Applying those general principles to the specific context of the EAT and to applications for an extension of the time limits for the presentation of a notice of appeal, Mummery P adumbrated the following guidelines:

(1) Although sympathy may be extended to an unrepresented litigant who may be in ignorance of the time limit or may not appreciate the importance of complying with it, the time limit will only be relaxed in rare cases where the EAT is satisfied that there is a reason which justifies departure from the limits.

(2) The EAT will not exercise its discretion unless it is provided with a full and honest explanation of the reason for the non-compliance with the time limit. The following explanations have been rejected by the EAT in the past and therefore are unlikely to excuse a failure to comply with the time limit:
   (a) ignorance of the time limit
   (b) oversight of the passing of the limit as a result of, for example, pressure of work
   (c) prior notification to the EAT, the employment tribunal, or to the other party of intent to appeal
   (d) the existence of pending applications for review of the decision or for remedies (see the 2013 Practice Direction, para 5.8) and
   (e) delay in the processing of an application for legal aid or of an application for advice or support from elsewhere.

(3) If an explanation for the delay is offered, then any number of factors may be considered by the EAT. The EAT will be particularly astute about any evidence of procedural abuse or wilful non-compliance. In addition, while the length of the delay, the merits of the appeal, and any prejudice which has been occasioned to the other party may be considered, they are unlikely to be very important in determining whether or not the EAT ought to exercise its discretion.

18.101 Mummery P concluded, therefore, that the questions which the EAT must ask itself are: '(a) what is the explanation for the default? (b) does it provide a good excuse for the default? (c) are there circumstances which justify the tribunal taking the exceptional step of granting an extension out of time?'

18.102 In *Abdelghafar*, the EAT was prepared to extend time for the presentation of an appeal despite the fact that no acceptable excuse had been put forward because the case unusually raised particular issues relating to the State Immunity Act 1978 and that Act bound all courts and tribunals to give effect to the immunity conferred by it. *Abdelghafar* itself demonstrates therefore that it is difficult to set out exhaustive guidelines explaining how the EAT will exercise a general discretion as to which of any number of factors could be relevant.

18.103 In *Aziz v Bethnal Green City Challenge Company* [2000] IRLR 111, the Court of Appeal affirmed the guidance given by the EAT in *Abdelghafar*, even though the Court recognized that the result was that the approach in the EAT was stricter than that adopted in the Court of Appeal itself. The Court of Appeal accepted that there were differences in the manner in which the EAT and the Court of Appeal approached appeals since the two courts had different jurisdictions on appeal. In any case, the Court of Appeal recognized that there was a trend in favour of applying time limits in a stricter manner in the civil courts and, therefore, the Court of Appeal itself may have to adopt a stricter approach in the future.

In *Woods v Lambeth Service Team Ltd* EATPA/251/99 the EAT extended time for a notice of appeal **18.104** which was received one day out of time on the basis that the function of the EAT was wider than that arising in the specific case. Morison P decided that the EAT's supervisory jurisdiction over employment tribunals required it to ensure that procedural mishaps did not occur which would render the proceedings defective. While this case demonstrates the breadth of factors which might be taken into account by the EAT in deciding whether to extend time and the fact that those will inevitably differ from case to case, it must, respectfully, be doubted as a general proposition. The strictness of the rules has been emphasized in a series of decisions of the EAT including that in *Sian v Abbey National plc* [2004] IRLR 185, where Burton P stated that the EAT's 'discretion is to be used sparingly'. The EAT will look at the whole period of delay before lodging in deciding why the notice of appeal was not lodged in time but this may require a different analysis of the reasons to be applied to different parts of the time (*Muschett v London Borough of Hounslow* EATPA/0/281/07; see also *Waller v Bromsgrove DC* EATPA/00/19/07). An excuse might not be sufficient to explain delay if it failed to explain why a notice was not lodged throughout the entirety of the period, although it was not fatal that an appellant was able to comply during part of the time (*Muschett v Hounslow LBC* [2009] ICR 424).

It is well established that a change in the case law by an appellate court will not usually tempt **18.105** the EAT to exercise its discretion to extend time limits in order to consider an appeal. In *Setiya v East Yorkshire HA* [1995] IRLR 348 a notice of appeal was served two years after the employment tribunal's decision was reached. The notice of appeal was filed in response to the landmark decision of the House of Lords in *R v Secretary of State for Employment, ex parte EOC* [1994] ICR 317. The EAT was not prepared to extend time in order to consider Dr Setiya's appeal merely as a result of a change in the law since it was of the view that Dr Setiya could have taken the arguments which ultimately succeeded in the *EOC* case. Mummery P concluded (at 352) that: 'Life, including law, is subject to the chance of change. Dr Setiya's claim against the authority was subject to the "hazards of time" inherent in change'.

In *Jurkovska v HLMAD* [2008] EWCA Civ 231, [2008] ICR 842 the Court of Appeal upheld a **18.106** decision of the EAT judge to extend time by thirty-three minutes when the notice of appeal had been presented in time but not the written reasons for decision. They rejected an argument that the introduction of the overriding objective into the EAT required a more relaxed approach to EAT time limits generally. Rimer LJ expressed the view that any explanation for delay should be provided in a witness statement by someone who could speak to the relevant facts (para 32). An extension of time was also granted by HHJ McMullen QC in *Fazal v Thames Water Utilities* UKEATPA/ 0058/12/JOJ. In that case, the reason why the appeal had been filed out of time was that there was out-of-date and inaccurate information on the EAT's website. However, the EAT declined to extend time by one day and that decision was upheld by the Court of Appeal in *Ojikutu v Camden LBC* [2014] EWCA Civ 978. In that case, the reasons why an extension of time was sought were that the appellant had miscalculated the deadline at a time when she was suffering from stress and a bereavement. The Court of Appeal found that it was 'simply a case where her problem was created by her own carelessness'.

I. THE SIFT AND THE SETTING OF DIRECTIONS

The sift

The present process for case management in the EAT was introduced by the 2002 Practice Direction **18.107** and was maintained with minimal amendments in the 2004, 2008, and 2013 Practice Directions.

The approach, pursuant to paras 11.1–11.2 of the 2013 Practice Direction, essentially involves sorting cases (including cross-appeals) and placing them on one of four tracks. Those tracks are:

(a)   r 3(7) (of the EAT Rules) cases (including those which are wholly without merit)
(b)   preliminary hearing cases
(c)   full hearing cases
(d)   fast-track full hearing cases.

18.108 An appeal (or cross-appeal) will be sorted or sifted onto one of these tracks by a judge or by the registrar in order to determine the most effective way in which to manage the case. The track on which the case is placed will usually determine the nature of the directions which are issued with regard to the appeal. However, there is no set manner in which directions should be given under the 2013 Practice Direction and the EAT has scope to give such directions as are appropriate in any particular case.

18.109 In r 3(7) cases, the judge or registrar may consider on the papers that the notice of appeal does not contain any grounds of appeal which have a reasonable prospect of success. Alternatively, it may be decided (although this will be highly unusual) that the notice of appeal amounts to an abuse of process or will otherwise obstruct the just disposal of proceedings. If a judge or the registrar forms the view that the case is thus a r 3(7) case, summary reasons will be sent to the appellant for this view. No further action will be taken unless the appellant requests an oral hearing before a judge pursuant to r 3(10). Where the appeal is certified as having been totally without merit, then the appellant will not be permitted any oral hearing pursuant to r 3(7ZA).

18.110 Paragraph 11.8 of the 2013 Practice Direction sets out the purpose of a preliminary hearing before the EAT as being to determine whether the notice of appeal gives rise to:

11.8.1 reasonable grounds to appeal ie a reasonable prospect of success at an FH; or

11.8.2 some other compelling reason that the appeal should be heard, eg that the appellant seeks a declaration of incompatibility under the Human Rights Act 1998; or to argue that a decision binding on the EAT should be considered by a higher court.

18.111 Prior to any preliminary hearing, automatic directions will be given pursuant to para 11.9 of the 2013 Practice Direction. By this paragraph, such directions may require, but in any event will enable, the respondent(s) to serve written submissions within fourteen days of the seal date of the order for a preliminary hearing. These written submissions are not themselves a respondent's answer. That will only be produced if the case is set down for a full hearing. Rather they are submissions which are directed to demonstrating that there is no point of law raised in the appeal. If the respondent is to cross-appeal, then the grounds for such cross-appeal must be accompanied by written notice to that effect and must be served within fourteen days of service of the notice of appeal. The respondent to the appeal must set out whether the cross-appeal is an unconditional cross-appeal, or a conditional cross-appeal: see para 11.10 of the 2013 Practice Direction. The respondent will be entitled to attend the preliminary hearing and will be able to make submissions which will also amount to a preliminary hearing on any cross-appeal: see para 11.10 of the 2013 Practice Direction.

18.112 At the preliminary hearing, the EAT will either:

(a)   dismiss the appeal wholly or in part and give a judgment setting out the reasons for doing so or
(b)   permit the appeal to go to a final hearing on all grounds in which case a reasoned judgment will not usually be given: see para 11.17 of the 2013 Practice Direction.

18.113 Where the EAT is only allowing an appellant's appeal to proceed to a full hearing on some of the grounds of appeal it should make clear which grounds are permitted to proceed and which are not (*IPC Magazines Ltd v Clements* EAT/456/99). However, in an exceptional case the EAT might exercise its general case management powers at the hearing to allow an appellant to depart from those points. In *Miriki v General Council of the Bar* [2002] ICR 505, the Court of Appeal stated that this might be permitted where:

(a) the point was raised before the employment tribunal
(b) the appellant explained why he did not appeal against the limiting of the grounds of appeal at the preliminary stage and
(c) the EAT gave full opportunity to the respondent to argue against the departure and explained its reasons for allowing the departure.

In *Vincent v MJ Gallagher Construction Ltd* [2003] EWCA 640, the appellant put forward six **18.114** grounds but the EAT allowed an appeal to proceed only in respect of two of them. The Court of Appeal considered that the other grounds were arguable. Pill LJ urged the EAT (at para 15) to act with great care when allowing appeals to proceed on one ground but not others when 'the entire compass of the case is a narrow one'. Further, if the matter was raised before the EAT at the preliminary hearing and the EAT which sat on that occasion refused to give directions to enable the appeal to proceed, the EAT hearing the full appeal would have to be satisfied that there was some material change of circumstances or other good reason to allow the additional ground of appeal to proceed.

In only a few cases has the Court of Appeal allowed an appeal from the conclusion of the EAT that **18.115** there was no point of law which raised a reasonable prospect of success at a full hearing. The Court of Appeal in *Lambe v 186K Ltd* [2005] ICR 307, where this occurred, had to consider whether in this case the appeal should be remitted to the EAT or be heard by the Court of Appeal and decided that the latter was the appropriate course.

In *Zinda v Governing Body of Barn Hill Community High* [2011] ICR 174, Judge Hand QC dealt **18.116** with the question of repeat applications. He found that r 3 of the EAT Rules was quite clear that once a determination under r 3(7) had been made that there were no reasonable grounds for an appeal and that there should be no further action taken on the appeal, there could be no further consideration of the same notice of appeal on paper. There could only be an oral hearing under r 3(10). Further, whilst a review of a r 3(7) order was possible under r 33, such a review would be carried out only very rarely since there was an alternative procedure, that is, an oral hearing. It might indeed be an abuse of process to seek such a review.

Where an appeal is permitted to continue to a full hearing it will be assigned a listing category. **18.117** This will be P where the appeal is recommended to be heard in the President's list, A where the appeal is complex and raises points of law which are of public importance, and B in any other case. The President reserves the discretion to alter any relevant category as circumstances require (2013 Practice Direction, para 11.19).

Pursuant to para 11.21 of the 2013 Practice Direction, a judge of the EAT or the registrar will al- **18.118** locate cases to the fast-track full hearing track, where such cases involve:

(a) appeals where the parties have made a reasoned case on the merits for an expedited hearing
(b) appeals against interim orders or decisions of the employment tribunal, particularly those which involve the taking of a step in proceedings within a specified period, for example adjournments, further information, amendments, disclosure, and witness orders
(c) appeals on the outcome of which other applications to the employment tribunal or the EAT or the civil courts depend
(d) appeals in which a reference to the Court of Justice of the European Union (CJEU), or a declaration of incompatibility under the Human Rights Act 1998, is sought
(e) appeals involving reinstatement, re-engagement, or interim relief.

Applications for expedition should be made with reasons to the registrar.

In addition, the EAT has a power to allocate category B cases which are estimated to take two hours **18.119** or less to the fast track (2013 Practice Direction, para 11.22).

Case management and directions

Paragraph 14 of the 2013 Practice Direction considers case management. Paragraph 14.1 pro- **18.120** vides that: 'Consistent with the overriding objective, the EAT will seek to give directions for case management so that the appeal can be dealt with quickly, or better considered, and in the most effective and just way'.

18.121 Generally the judge who considers an appeal on the sift will give directions for case management (see para 14.2 of the 2013 Practice Direction). However, directions can be given at any time (see 2013 Practice Direction at para 14.4) by a judge or by the registrar (with an appeal to a judge). An application for directions must be made on notice to all parties (2013 Practice Direction, para 14.3).

18.122 Failure to comply with the EAT's orders may result in an appeal being struck out, or may result in an order debarring a party from taking part in proceedings further, or may result in an order for costs: r 26 of the EAT Rules. However, the strike-out power will only be exercised after the issuing of a notice, usually in the 'unless order' form: para 14.4 of the 2013 Practice Direction. Any application to vary or discharge an order, or for an extension of time, should be submitted to the EAT on notice to all of the other parties, within the time fixed for compliance: see para 14.5 of the 2013 Practice Direction.

J. RESPONDENT'S ANSWER AND CROSS-APPEALS

18.123 If, but only if, an appeal is set down for a full hearing, the EAT will send a copy of the notice of appeal to all named respondents to the appeal along with any submissions or skeleton arguments lodged by the appellant. Within fourteen days of the seal date of the EAT order the respondent must lodge at the EAT and serve on all the other parties a respondent's answer (2013 Practice Direction, para 12.2). In cases where an appeal is set down for preliminary hearing, the respondent(s) will be given the opportunity to produce written submissions prior to the preliminary hearing but will only be required to lodge and serve a respondent's answer if the appeal is set down for a full hearing. This is often not understood by litigants who lodge the respondent's answer if, for example, they are sent a notice of appeal by the appellant merely as a matter of courtesy. This is not necessary until the case has proceeded through the sift.

18.124 Rule 6(2) of the EAT Rules requires that the respondent must answer the notice of appeal in accordance, or substantially in accordance with the specified form which is to be found in 'Form 3' appended to the EAT Rules. If a respondent fails to deliver an answer (or indeed a response where the EAT exercises its original jurisdiction) the EAT may order that the respondent is debarred from taking any further part in the proceedings by virtue of r 26 of the EAT Rules. The respondent's answer may only be a short document if the reasons given by the employment tribunal are relied on and nothing beyond, as will often be the case. A respondent may not wish to give succour to the appellant by itself criticizing the employment tribunal's reasoning, albeit from a different direction. Indeed, in its June 2015 Practice Statement, the EAT noted that respondents were 'not obliged to respond in any answer to contention made in any text which accompanies the notice of appeal. Unless it has additional reasons to add, it is enough to say it relies on the Reasons of the Tribunal'.

18.125 A cross-appeal is an appeal by the respondent against part or the whole of the tribunal's decision; it is not properly so called where the respondent wishes to uphold the conclusion on other grounds. Rather, it is putting forward a different conclusion on a particular cause of action: see, for example, *Wolfe v North Middlesex University Hospital NHS Trust* [2015] ICR 960 (where it was suggested by a successful party that an argument raised by that party had not been determined by the employment tribunal, and the proper approach was to invite the tribunal to determine that point, rather than to issue a cross-appeal in the EAT). If the respondent wishes to cross-appeal, it may do so, but it is not bound to do so. If it does, it includes a statement of grounds within the respondent's answer. For example, where an appeal is set down for a preliminary hearing at the sift, respondents should include a cross-appeal within the written submissions which a respondent must lodge and serve within fourteen days of service of the notice of appeal (2013 Practice Direction, para 11.10). Strangely, other than where a case is set down for a preliminary hearing, there is no time limit for the service of a cross-appeal, although, in practice, litigants tend to include a cross-appeal together with the respondent's answer and should do so speedily, given the turnaround time of the EAT and the risk that a cross-appeal which a party seeks to launch just before the hearing will be disallowed. Should a respondent not wish to contest the appeal, pursuant to r 6(5) of the EAT Rules, the parties can agree a draft order to be placed before the EAT for approval, although it is a matter for the EAT whether it will approve such an arrangement (see para 18.215).

Where the respondent's answer contains a cross-appeal, the appellant must within fourteen days of **18.126** service lodge at the EAT and serve on the other parties a reply (2013 Practice Direction, para 12.2).

K. AMENDMENTS TO THE NOTICE OF APPEAL OR RESPONDENT'S ANSWER

Paragraph 3.10 of the 2013 Practice Direction deals with amendments to the notice of appeal or **18.127** respondent's answer:

> A party cannot reserve the right to amend, alter or add to a Notice of Appeal or a Respondent's Answer. No party has the right to amend any Notice of Appeal or Answer without the prior permission of the EAT. Any application for permission to amend must be made as soon as practicable and must be accompanied by a draft of the amended Notice of Appeal or amended Answer which makes clear the precise amendments for which permission is sought.

Paragraph 14.6 of the 2013 Practice Direction sets out the form in which applications to amend **18.128** the notice of appeal or the respondent's answer are to be made:

> An application to amend a Notice of Appeal or Respondent's Answer must include the text of the original document with any changes clearly marked and identifiable, for example with deletions struck through in red and the text of the amendment either written or underlined in red. Any subsequent amendments will have to be in a different identifiable colour. Where provided from a computer print-out, the deleted wording should be struck through, and new wording put in italics. Where reamendment is made, the new wording must be in bold italics or a distinctive and easily readable font.

In practice, amendments are permitted quite readily, although the trend may be towards a more **18.129** rigorous approach as foreshadowed in *Khudados v Leggate* [2005] IRLR 540. The EAT held that the usual principles that applied to amendments to statements of case (which had been set out by the Court of Appeal in *Cobbold v London Borough of Greenwich* [1999] EWCA Civ 2074—that they should generally be permitted provided that the prejudice to the other party can be compensated for in costs and the public interest in the efficient administration of justice is not significantly harmed) ought not to be applied when dealing with applications to amend notices of appeal for a number of reasons:

(a) The approach of the EAT in ensuring that the parties deal with proposed appeals expeditiously is stricter than the approach taken by the Court of Appeal. This was noted by the Court of Appeal in the *Aziz* case.

(b) The EAT takes a strict view of anything which might delay a hearing. That approach is consistent with a desire to ensure that proceedings must be brought before an employment tribunal quickly and the usual three-month period in which claimants must present a claim is significantly less than the limitation periods in most civil claims.

(c) The EAT's regime is, for the most part, a cost-free regime and costs can only be awarded in very limited circumstances.

The EAT in *Khudados* also drew attention to the fact that, under the 2002 Practice Direction, **18.130** amendments had to be made 'as soon as the need for amendment is known' and that there was no equivalent provision in the CPR. However, the requirement for amendments to be made as soon as the need is known by the relevant party has been removed from the 2004 Practice Direction and has not been reintroduced in either the 2008 or 2013 Practice Directions. Amendments must be made, pursuant to the 2013 Practice Direction, as soon as it is practicable to do so.

The EAT concluded at para 86 of *Khudados* that the following matters would be relevant in **18.131** determining whether an appellant should be given permission to amend their notice of appeal:

(a) Whether or not the appellant is in breach of the EAT Rules or a relevant Practice Direction. In this vein the EAT referred again to the requirement in the 2002 Practice Direction that the amendment be made as soon as the need for amendment is known and explained that 'the requirement is not simply aspirational or an expression of hope'. Presumably, the requirement that amendments be made as soon as practicable imports a little more flexibility into the criterion.

(b) Any extension of time is an indulgence and the EAT is entitled to a full, honest, and acceptable explanation for any delay of failure to comply with the EAT, the Rules, or the Practice Direction.

(c) The extent to which, if the amendment was allowed, it would cause a delay. The EAT explained that crisp new points of law closely related to existing grounds are more likely to be allowed than new perversity points which will require an analysis of complex factual material.

(d) The extent to which allowing an amendment will cause prejudice to the opposite party and the extent to which refusing an amendment will do prejudice to the appellant by depriving him of fairly arguable points of law.

(e) It may be necessary to consider the merits of a proposed amendment. They must raise a point of law which gives the appeal a reasonable prospect of success.

(f) Regard must be had to the public interest in ensuring that business in the EAT is conducted expeditiously and that resources are used efficiently.

18.132 The 2013 Practice Direction suggests that the same principles should be applied to amendments in respect of the respondent's answer as to the notice of appeal. However, it is noteworthy that many of the concerns expressed above apply with less force to amendments to the respondent's answer than they would to notices of appeal.

L. INTERIM MATTERS

18.133 There are various interim matters which may come before the EAT in the course of an appeal. The most important of these are dealt with below.

Interim applications

18.134 Paragraph 6 of the 2013 Practice Direction states:

> Interim applications should be made in writing (no particular form is required) and will be initially referred to the Registrar who after considering the papers may deal with the case or refer it to a judge. The judge may dispose of it himself or refer it to a full EAT hearing. Parties are encouraged to make any such applications at a Preliminary Hearing or an Appointment for Directions if one is ordered (see paras 11.8–11.19 and 12.4).

18.135 There is a wide variety of interim applications which could be made to the EAT. The EAT Rules specifically provide for some powers which might be exercised on an interim application. Thus, the EAT can (a) debar a party from proceeding in relation to the appeal because of a failure to comply with its orders by r 26, (b) order the production of documents or the attendance of a witness by r 27, (c) join parties by r 18, (d) extend or abridge time by r 37, and (e) waive procedural requirements in the interests of justice by r 39.

18.136 An appeal lies from the decision of the registrar on an interim application to a judge. Such an appeal must be notified to the EAT within five days of the date on which the registrar's decision was sent to the parties by virtue of para 6.3 of the 2013 Practice Direction.

Conciliation

18.137 Since the insertion of r 36 in the EAT Rules by the Employment Appeal Tribunal (Amendment) Rules 2004 and the issuing of the Conciliation Protocol on 9 December 2004, the EAT has the power to stay appeals for a period of '(say) 28 days' while the parties make use of the services of

ACAS. This procedure is likely to be made use of in cases which involve allegations of bias and procedural impropriety (see para 2 of the Conciliation Protocol), but pursuant to para 8 of the Conciliation Protocol:

> Other appeals may also be amenable to conciliation, particularly those relating to monetary awards only, or where the overwhelmingly likely result of a successful appeal would be a remission to the ET.

Where conciliation is successful, the appeal may be dismissed on withdrawal or alternatively allowed by consent. Where the appeal is allowed by consent, a judge will give directions in accordance with the 2013 Practice Direction, para 18. The judge may need an explanation as to why an appeal should be allowed even where the parties consent.

M. VEXATIOUS LITIGANTS

Section 33(1) of the ETA 1996 states: **18.138**

> If, on an application made by the Attorney General or the Lord Advocate under this section, the Appeal Tribunal is satisfied that a person has habitually and persistently and without any reasonable ground—
>
> (a) instituted vexatious proceedings, whether before the Certification Officer, in any employment tribunal or before the Appeal Tribunal, and whether against the same person or against different persons, or
> (b) made vexatious applications in any proceedings, whether before the Certification Officer, in any employment tribunal or before the Appeal Tribunal,
>
> the Appeal Tribunal may, after hearing the person or giving him an opportunity of being heard, make a restriction of proceedings order.

This is based on a long-established practice in the civil courts but it was only introduced in the **18.139** employment tribunal and the EAT in 1998 as a result of the passage into law of the Employment Rights (Dispute Resolution) Act 1998. In *Attorney-General v Wheen* [2000] IRLR 461, the EAT considered the operation of s 33 of the ETA 1996. Mr Wheen had instituted fifteen sets of proceedings against various respondents alleging discrimination on the grounds of race, sex, disability, and marital status. The cases all followed the same pattern, which is that Mr Wheen had applied for a job with the respondent, had been turned down, and had then instituted proceedings in the employment tribunal. The majority of the claims had been struck out by the tribunal as being frivolous, vexatious, or an abuse of process. Drawing on a passage of Lord Bingham CJ in *Attorney-General v Barker* [2000] 1 FLR 759, the EAT clarified that the meaning of vexatious proceedings is that it has little or no basis in law (or at least no discernible basis), that whatever the intention of the proceedings may be, its effect is to subject the respondent to inconvenience, harassment, and expense out of all proportion to any gain likely to accrue to the claimant, and that it involves an abuse of process of the court, that is the use of the court process for a purpose or in a way that is significantly different from the ordinary and proper use of that process.

Mr Wheen appealed to the Court of Appeal. The Court of Appeal ([2001] IRLR 91) held that: **18.140**

(a) The fact that eighteen months had elapsed between Mr Wheen's most recent submission of an originating application and the Attorney-General's application under s 33 of ETA 1996 did not prevent the EAT from properly concluding that an order should be made against Mr Wheen.
(b) The s 33 order did not breach Art 6 of the ECHR on fair trial since access to the courts was not prohibited but rather was provided for on certain terms. The Court of Appeal indeed described it as 'wholly unarguable' that s 33 conflicted with the ECHR.

Where an order is made under s 33 of ETA 1996, the vexatious litigant is required to gain leave **18.141** of the EAT before commencing further proceedings (s 33(2)). Orders may be made indefinitely or for a specified period (s 33(3)). The Attorney-General and Lord Advocate have not applied for many of these orders.

N. LISTING THE CASE

18.142 The listing arrangements are now set out in para 15 of the 2013 Practice Direction.

18.143 Generally, a date will be fixed for a hearing as soon as practicable after the sift has taken place. In cases which are allocated to the preliminary hearing track, the preliminary hearing will be fixed for a hearing as soon as practicable after the sift and then will be listed for a full hearing, if necessary, after the preliminary hearing. The listing officer will generally consult the parties on dates and will try to accommodate reasonable requests but is not bound to do so (2013 Practice Direction, para 15.5). Once a date is fixed the appeal will be set down in the list.

18.144 If a party wishes to change the date fixed for an appeal, they should inform the EAT listing officer and may apply for it to be changed but must give the reasons why they wish this to be done. This will only occur if the date listed causes serious difficulties and a party must notify all the other parties of such an application and the reasons for it (2013 Practice Direction, para 15.5).

18.145 In addition to the usual process for the listing of appeals, the EAT maintains a 'warned list'. This list is ordinarily made up of short cases or cases which require expedition. Once a case is placed in the warned list, the parties are, in effect, on notice that the case will be listed at short notice. As much notice as possible will then be given to the parties of the intention to list the case for hearing but the 2013 Practice Direction suggests that this might well be fewer than seven days. The parties can object to the listing of their case at first instance to the listing officer and then on appeal to the registrar or a judge. The parties may also apply for a fixed date for the hearing. Other cases may be placed in the warned list such as cases which are settled or withdrawn, or cases which will appear to take less time than was originally anticipated. (See paras 1.7 and 15.8 of the 2013 Practice Direction as to the operation of the warned list.)

The bundle of papers for use at the hearing

18.146 By para 8.1 of the 2013 Practice Direction, ultimate responsibility for the bundle lies with the appellant and, pursuant to para 8.1 of the 2013 Practice Direction, the bundle must include only those documents which are relevant to the points of law raised in the appeal and which are likely to be referred to at the hearing. It is the responsibility of the parties to retain copies of all documents including hearing bundles sent to the EAT.

18.147 Paragraph 8.2 of the 2013 Practice Direction states:

> 8.2 The documents in the core bundle should be numbered by item, then paginated continuously and indexed, in the following order:
>
> 8.2.1 Judgment, decision or order appealed from and written reasons
> 8.2.2 Sealed Notice of Appeal
> 8.2.3 Respondent's Answer if a Full Hearing RESPONDENT'S Submissions if a PH
> 8.2.4 ET1 Claim (and any Additional Information or Written Answers)
> 8.2.5 ET3 Response (and any Additional Information or Written Answers)
> 8.2.6 Questionnaire and Replies (discrimination and equal pay cases)
> 8.2.7 Relevant orders, judgments and written reasons of the Employment Tribunal
> 8.2.8 Relevant orders and judgments of the EAT
> 8.2.9 Affidavits and Employment Tribunal comments (where ordered)
> 8.2.10 Any documents agreed or ordered.

18.148 The total number of pages in addition to the core documents must not exceed 50 unless the permission of the registrar or a judge is granted. If permitted or ordered, further pages may follow with consecutive pagination in additional bundles (2013 Practice Direction, para 8.3). In complex cases, the registrar will usually give that permission but the parties should be prepared to explain why it is necessary to do so. It is sometimes helpful to divide the papers into a core and non-core bundle.

18.149 The rules relating to the preparation of the bundles depend on the track to which the case is allocated (see 2013 Practice Direction, paras 8.5–8.6):

(a) In preliminary hearings, appeals from an order of the registrar, r 3(10) hearings, and appointments for directions, the appellant should prepare and lodge two copies of the bundle (or four if the judge is sitting with lay members) as soon as possible after the service of the notice of appeal and no later than twenty-eight days from the seal date of a relevant order unless otherwise directed.

(b) In final hearings the parties must cooperate in agreeing a bundle of papers for the hearing. By no later than twenty-eight days from the seal date of a relevant order, unless otherwise directed, the appellant is responsible for ensuring that two copies of a bundle (four if the judge is sitting with lay members) agreed by the parties is lodged at the EAT. This must be complied with even in a case where a preliminary hearing took place since the EAT will not retain papers from a preliminary hearing.

(c) In fast-track final hearing cases, the bundles should be lodged as soon as possible with the EAT and in any event within seven days of being notified that the case has been expedited (unless the hearing date is within seven days).

Where there is a disagreement between the parties as to the preparation of the bundles, the registrar may give directions on an application by the parties or on the registrar's own initiative (2013 Practice Direction, para 8.8). All documents should be legible and unmarked (2013 Practice Direction, para 8.4). The question of what documents should go into the bundle often becomes heated between the parties but is rarely of influence on the final outcome of the appeal. Brevity is welcomed by the EAT and it is clear that only those documents relevant to the point of law to be argued should be before the EAT. **18.150**

O. SKELETON ARGUMENTS

Skeleton arguments must be provided in all hearings before the EAT (other than in Scotland, as to which see para 16.13 of the 2013 Practice Direction) unless the EAT is notified by a party or representative that the notice of appeal or respondent's answer contains the full argument which a party wishes to advance on paper (2013 Practice Direction, para 16.2). This will be a rare case in fact. **18.151**

Pursuant to para 16.11 of the 2013 Practice Direction, skeleton arguments must be lodged at the EAT and exchanged in a case where both parties have been ordered to be present. **18.152**

(a) in the case of a preliminary hearing, appeal against an order of the registrar, a r 3(10) hearing, or appointment for directions, not less than ten days before the hearing, or, if the hearing is fixed at less than seven days' notice, as soon as possible after the hearing date has been notified

(b) not less than twenty-one days before a full hearing (although this is often reduced to fourteen days by order)

(c) in the case of warned list and fast-track final hearing cases, as soon as is possible and in any event (unless the hearing date is less than seven days later) within seven days of the parties having been notified that the case is expedited or in the warned list.

Paragraph 16.10 of the 2013 Practice Direction provides that the parties may submit skeleton arguments with the notice of appeal or respondent's answer (as occurs in the Court of Appeal). **18.153**

Where a party does not comply with the procedure with regard to skeleton arguments, it may lead to an adjournment of the appeal or alternatively (and unusually) a dismissal for non-compliance with the Practice Direction and to an award of costs. The party in default may also have to attend the EAT to explain their failure (2013 Practice Direction, para 16.12) which is likely to prove embarrassing. Often, the parties will attach a bundle of authorities to the skeleton argument but this may also be done separately. In *Sage UK Ltd v Bacco* EAT/597/06 the EAT laid down a practice direction that bundles of authorities should contain IRLR or ICR reports when the case is reported so as to avoid wasteful pre-reading (paras 15 to 17). This is now included at para 17.4 of the 2013 Practice Direction. The parties should also note that the EAT maintains a list of familiar cases. Where one of these is relied upon, there is no need to produce a copy of the relevant authority for the EAT. The EAT maintains a folder containing copies of all familiar cases for the use of judges and the parties. A list of **18.154** the familiar cases can be found on the EAT's website. Where authorities are relied on by a party, they should be marked up to show the passages which were intended to be relied upon before the EAT: see *East of England Ambulance Service NHS Trust v Sanders* [2015] ICR 293. The EAT has warned that a failure to do so could result in an adjournment, with a consequential application for costs.

18.155 A party in default should immediately despatch any delayed skeleton argument to the EAT by hand, fax, or email (londoneat@hmcts.gsi.gov.uk or edinburgheat@hmcts.gsi.gov.uk) and, unless notified by the EAT to the contrary, bring to the hearing a minimum of four copies (or six if the judge is sitting with lay members) of the skeleton argument and any authorities referred to. Paragraph 16.12 of the 2013 Practice Direction makes clear that the EAT staff will not be responsible for copying or supplying authorities or skeletons on the morning of the hearing.

18.156 A skeleton argument should:

(a) be concise (2013 Practice Direction, para 16.3)

(b) identify and summarize the points of law relied on (2013 Practice Direction, para 16.3)

(c) identify and summarize the steps in the legal argument and the statutory provisions and authorities to be relied on, identifying them by name, page, and paragraph and stating the legal proposition sought to be derived from them (2013 Practice Direction, para 16.3)

(d) refer to the parties by name as they appeared in the employment tribunal, that is Claimant (C) and Respondent (R); see 2013 Practice Direction at para 16.4

(e) state the form of the order which the party will ask the EAT to make at the hearing (2013 Practice Direction, para 16.5); this is very important given the wide range of disposals of the case which may be available in a particular case (the question whether a case if remitted should be remitted to the same or a different tribunal should be addressed)

(f) in the case of the appellant's argument, be accompanied by a chronology of events, to be agreed if possible (2013 Practice Direction, para 16.6)

(g) be prepared, unless impracticable, using the pagination in the index to the appeal bundle (2013 Practice Direction, para 16.7).

18.157 At para 16.8 of the 2013 Practice Direction, represented parties are informed that they must 'give the instructions necessary for their representatives to comply with this procedure within the time limits'. Further, it is no excuse for the failure of a party to produce a skeleton argument that conciliation or settlement negotiations were being conducted (2013 Practice Direction, para 16.9).

18.158 Skeleton arguments are merely an opportunity for the parties to set out the steps of their legal argument on paper and should not be used as an opportunity to argue the case in detail (2013 Practice Direction, para 16.3). The parties also should not cite an unnecessary number of authorities in skeleton arguments. It is, however, the first document which the EAT is likely to read in a case so it is vital to set out the party's contentions clearly.

P. HEARING LENGTH

18.159 The parties are required to ensure that time estimates are as accurate as possible, particularly in cases where lay members sit. A time estimate should take into account that the EAT will have pre-read the papers, but there must be time available for the giving of judgment orally on the day: paras 15.1 and 15.2 of the 2013 Practice Direction. If a judge considers that the time estimate is insufficient, he may guillotine submissions: see para 15.3 of the 2013 Practice Direction. In addition, a judge may hear submissions in any order and within whatever time limit he thinks fit. Different time limits may be prescribed for different parties: see para 15.4 of the 2013 Practice Direction.

Q. RESTRICTED REPORTING ORDERS

18.160 The EAT has the power to make restricted reporting orders under the EAT Rules where the case involves an appeal as to the grant of such an order or the refusal of an employment tribunal to grant an order (see ETA 1996, ss 31(2) and 32(1)). In addition, the EAT can make a restricted reporting order in any appeal from an interim decision of the employment tribunal where the employment tribunal has made a restricted reporting order which has not been revoked. It is to be noted that a decision of the tribunal on liability is not considered to be an interim decision even where quantum is yet to be determined. Rule 23 of the EAT Rules deals with cases where allegations of sexual misconduct have been made or where the commission of a sexual offence is relevant. Rule 23A deals with disability discrimination cases.

In addition, if an appeal appears to raise allegations of a sexual offence having been committed, the registrar must omit from the register or delete from any order, judgment, or other document which is available to the public any material which is likely to lead members of the public to identify any person affected by or making the allegation (EAT Rules, r 23(2)). **18.161**

In *X v Commissioner of Police of the Metropolis* [2003] ICR 1031, the EAT (Burton P presiding) considered the phrase 'appeared to involve allegations of the commission of a sexual offence' in the EAT Rules—the same phrase appears in ETR 2004. The EAT considered that in determining whether or not the case appeared to involve such allegations it was not limited to a consideration of the pleadings. The EAT or employment tribunal had to make a determination on the basis of everything that it had read as to whether or not the case would involve such allegations. **18.162**

The EAT will not usually make a restricted reporting order unless it has given the parties opportunity to advance oral argument at a hearing (EAT Rules, r 23(5)). However, the EAT need not comply with that requirement in the case of a temporary order and may make one pursuant to r 23(5A), even without the need for a hearing. Where a temporary order has been made the registrar will inform the parties of it as soon as possible. The parties may then apply within fourteen days to have the temporary order revoked or converted into a full order (EAT Rules, r 23(5B)). If no such application is made, then the temporary order will cease to have effect on the fifteenth day after it was made. If an application is made, it will continue in effect until the hearing takes place at which the application is considered (EAT Rules, r 23(5C)). **18.163**

Interested parties of the media may be joined as parties to a case in order that they are able to make representations as to whether or not a restricted reporting order should be made. The power to join parties to proceedings before the EAT is contained within r 18 of the EAT Rules. However, the press will have to show good cause to be joined as such joinder will not occur automatically (*A v B, ex p News Group Newspapers Ltd* [1998] ICR 55, 66). **18.164**

The discretion of the EAT to make a restricted reporting order will be exercised by reference to whether or not the making of the order is in the public interest. In *X v Z Ltd* [1998] ICR 43, 46–7, Staughton LJ explained: **18.165**

> It is important that those who have to exercise that power should realise that it is not to be exercised automatically at the request of one party, or even at the request of both parties. The industrial tribunal still has to consider whether it is in the public interest that the press should be deprived of the right to communicate information to the public if it becomes available. It is not a matter which is to be dealt with on the nod so to speak. *Scott v Scott* [1913] AC 417, 438 establishes that, when both sides consent to an order prohibiting publication, that is exactly the moment when a court ought to examine with particular care whether, as a matter of discretion, such an order should be made.

The EAT has been invited to find, on a number of occasions, that its powers to make a restricted reporting order are wider than the extent which is set out in the ETA 1996 and the EAT Rules. In *A v B, ex p News Group Newspapers* the EAT was asked to find that it had an inherent jurisdiction to make a restricted reporting order. The EAT (Morison P presiding) saw the force of the argument that the EAT had an inherent jurisdiction to make a restricted reporting order but was not prepared, on the facts of that case, to cut through the statutory regime provided for by the ETA 1996 and the EAT Rules by issuing a restricted reporting order. **18.166**

The EAT considered the issue again in *X v Commissioner of Police of the Metropolis* [2003] ICR 1031. In that case the appellant, who had undergone gender reassignment surgery, brought a claim for sex discrimination as a result of the rejection of her application to join the police force. **18.167**

The police alleged that the appellant was suspected of criminal offences and that was part of the reason that her application was rejected. The appellant's application before the tribunal for a restricted reporting order had been declined as not being a case which fell within the rules by which the employment tribunal could make a restricted reporting order. The appellant appealed to the EAT. The EAT (Burton P presiding) declined to offer conclusive guidance as to whether or not the EAT has an inherent jurisdiction to make a restricted reporting order. In that case, it was unnecessary for the EAT to do so since the EAT found that it could make a restricted reporting order by a different route, even though the case was not covered by the statutory provisions. The EAT's reasoning was that:

(a) The employment tribunal and the EAT have a power and are under a duty to apply the provisions of the Equal Treatment Directive (Council Directive 76/207/EEC [1976] OJ L39/40). In particular, Art 6 of the Directive requires Member States to ensure that judicial and administrative procedures are put in place to ensure the enforcement of obligations under the Directive and to ensure that all those people who consider themselves wronged by a failure to apply the principle of equal treatment are able to make use of such procedures.

(b) Both the employment tribunals and the EAT have the power to regulate their own procedure. That must include, where a claimant would otherwise be deterred from bringing a claim, the making of a restricted reporting order in order to ensure the confidentiality in respect of the identity of the claimant.

(c) As such, the EAT concluded at para 56 of its decision:

> In those circumstances, we conclude that both in the employment tribunal and in the appeal tribunal there is a power for those bodies to regulate their own procedure, so as to include, in a proper case, a restricted reporting order or a register deletion order or other order analogous to them or to make some provision in respect of confidentiality of the identity of the applicant, or, no doubt in an appropriate case, a respondent, not limited by the precise terms of the existing Rules.

18.168 Where material is published in contravention of a restricted reporting order, the punishment on summary conviction is a fine not exceeding level 5 on the standard scale (see ETA 1996, s 31(3)). In *A v B* [2010] ICR 849, it was held by the EAT that it could, like the ET, make a permanent anonymity order by reason of its general power to regulate its own procedure. This could be done by interpreting its powers pursuant to s 6 of the HRA 1998 since the loss of the claimant's anonymity would involve a breach of his right to the protection of honour and reputation under Art 8 of the European Convention.

R. NATIONAL SECURITY APPEALS

18.169 Rules 30A and 31A of the EAT Rules provide that where a minister of the Crown considers it to be expedient in the interests of national security, he may in Crown employment proceedings direct the EAT to sit in private for all or part of a hearing, exclude the party who was the claimant before the employment tribunal and his representative, and take steps to conceal the identity of particular witnesses.

18.170 Further, the EAT may choose to exercise its own authority and make any of the orders referred to above of its own volition (r 30A(2)). In addition, the EAT may prevent disclosure of documents (including any decision) to any excluded person such as the claimant or his representative or alternatively to any person who has been excluded from a private hearing. The EAT may also take steps to keep secret all or any part of the reasons for any order which it makes. In the case of a claimant or his representative being excluded from the proceedings, the EAT must pursuant to r 30A(4) and (5) inform the Attorney-General who may appoint a special advocate to represent the interests of the claimant. The special advocate must not communicate directly or indirectly with anyone including the excluded applicant about any of the grounds of appeal or the basis on which the appeal is resisted. Neither may the special advocate communicate any matter referred to during the private sitting pursuant to r 30A(7).

A minister may also, where he considers it expedient in the interests of national security, direct that **18.171** a document is prepared containing the reasons for a decision of the EAT but with material omitted from it for the benefit of a person who was excluded from the proceedings. Alternatively, a minister may simply state that no separate document should be prepared but that no reasons are disclosed to a party who was excluded from the proceedings. These powers are contained in r 31A(2)–(5) of the EAT Rules.

S. EVIDENCE

Notes of evidence

The vast majority of the work undertaken by the EAT involves the EAT exercising its appellate **18.172** jurisdiction and usually, in order for it to exercise such jurisdiction, there is no need for it to consider the evidence heard by the employment tribunal. However, where an appellant seeks seriously to argue that a finding of fact of the employment tribunal cannot be supported with reference to any of the evidence heard by the employment tribunal, it might be necessary for the EAT to consider the precise evidence which the employment tribunal heard. The only way in which evidence before the employment tribunal is formally recorded is in the form of a note taken by the judge. The parties may keep their own record of proceedings but there is no requirement on them to do so and those representing themselves will find this difficult to do. The judge's note need not, however, contain an account of all proceedings—there is no need for the note to contain the detail of an advocate's submissions, for example. However, the note should be a verbatim or near verbatim account of the witness evidence.

An application for the use of the judge's note should only be made by a party in appropriate cir- **18.173** cumstances. In particular, it should not be used merely to seek further grounds of appeal which are not apparent on the face of the tribunal's decision. In *Webb v Anglian Water Authority* [1981] IRLR 494 (decided under the old practice but still authoritative on this point) the EAT stated that notes should not be provided to a party unless the notice of appeal raised a ground of attack relating to the findings of fact made by the employment tribunal. Such grounds will be likely to be perversity appeals and in particular those perversity appeals where it is suggested that there was no evidence at all on which the employment tribunal could have properly reached a finding of fact. This principle is now succinctly enshrined in para 9.7 of the 2013 Practice Direction:

> A note of evidence is not to be produced and supplied to the parties to enable the parties to embark on a 'fishing expedition' to establish grounds or additional grounds of appeal or because they have not kept their own notes of evidence. If an application for such a note is found by the EAT to have been unreasonably made the party behaving unreasonably is at risk of being ordered to pay costs.

The EAT is naturally reluctant to allow access to the notes of evidence on the basis that it adds cost **18.174** to appeals and inevitably delays them, and an appellant which seeks access to the notes will usually find that the point must be argued orally before the EAT save in a very clear case.

An appellant who considers that a point raised in the notice of appeal cannot be argued without **18.175** reference to the evidence heard by the employment tribunal should submit an application with the notice of appeal (2013 Practice Direction, para 9.1). Where the application is not made at the same time as the notice of appeal it should be made:

(a) in the skeleton or written submissions lodged prior to the preliminary hearing in cases where there is a preliminary hearing;
(b) if no preliminary hearing is ordered and the case is sent straight to a final hearing then an application should be made within fourteen days of the seal date of the order which provides for such hearing.

The complexity of this sub-paragraph was criticized by the Court of Appeal in *Wheeler v Quality Deep Ltd* [2005] ICR 265 at paras 65–8 on the basis that litigants in person would not be able to understand it. Hooper LJ invited the EAT President to consider whether the judge who conducts the sift and orders a full hearing should consider in each case whether judge's notes should be required.

18.176 An application for the evidence heard by the employment tribunal to be used at the appeal hearing should include the following by virtue of para 9.2 of the 2013 Practice Direction:

(a) the issue in the notice of appeal or respondent's answer to which the matter is relevant

(b) the names of the witnesses whose evidence is considered relevant, alternatively the nature of the evidence the absence of which is considered relevant

(c) (if applicable) the part of the hearing when evidence was given

(d) the gist of the evidence (or absence of evidence) alleged to be relevant and

(e) (if the party has a record), saying so and by whom it was made, or producing an extract from a witness statement given in writing at the hearing.

The more detail that can be given in the application the better and the party must give as much background to the case to enable the registrar to master the issues arising on the application.

18.177 By para 9.3 of the 2013 Practice Direction the application may be considered on the papers or alternatively by the registrar or a judge at a preliminary hearing. Usually it will be ordered that the party seeking to place employment tribunal evidence before the EAT give notice to the other parties to the appeal, although orders determining the application or alternatively giving directions for written representations may be made. Where such notice is ordered, it will require the parties to cooperate and use best endeavours to agree a note of the relevant evidence or alternatively a statement that there was no such evidence within twenty-one days. Paragraph 9.7 of the 2013 Practice Direction threatens uncooperative parties with the prospect of payment of costs. Paragraph 9.4 of the 2013 Practice Direction further provides that where it proves impossible to agree the evidence within twenty-one days any party can apply to the EAT for directions within seven days. The directions might include:

> the resolution of the disagreement on the papers or at a hearing; the administration by one party to the others of, or a request to the Chairman to respond to, a questionnaire; or, if the EAT is satisfied that such notes are necessary, a request that the Chairman produce his/her notes of evidence in whole or in part.

18.178 Where a party disputes the contents of the employment judge's note of evidence the procedure set out in *Dexine Rubber Co Ltd v Alker* [1977] ICR 434 will be made use of. Any party who seeks to criticize the note should submit his criticism to the advocate for the other party in order to determine whether or not both sides agree that the note is inaccurate and then send his criticisms to the employment judge. If the judge replies, stating that after consideration of the matter he is satisfied that his note is correct, then the judge's conclusion must be accepted.

18.179 An unusual situation arose in *Houston v Lightwater Farms Ltd* [1990] ICR 502, where the employment judge refused to provide his note of evidence to the EAT on its request stating that it was an aide-memoire for his use and need only be supplied to the EAT out of courtesy. The EAT was of the view that since a judge sat in a judicial capacity and had a judicial duty to make notes the judge had to comply with the EAT's request.

Introducing new evidence

18.180 The EAT has a discretion (rarely exercised in fact) to admit fresh evidence which was not placed before the employment tribunal. Paragraph 10.3 of the 2013 Practice Direction states:

> 8.2 In exercising its discretion to admit any fresh evidence or new document, the EAT will apply the principles set out in *Ladd v Marshall* [1954] 1 WLR 1489, having regard to the overriding objective, ie:
>
> 8.2.1 the evidence could not have been obtained with reasonable diligence for use at the Employment Tribunal hearing;
>
> 8.2.2 it is relevant and would probably have had an important influence on the hearing;
>
> 8.2.3 it is apparently credible.

Accordingly the evidence and representations in support of the application must clearly address these principles.

Thus, the EAT has borrowed the strict principles as regards the admissibility of fresh evidence **18.181** which are used in the Court of Appeal. This is consistent with the EAT as a body which deals only with points of law and not fact. In *Ladd v Marshall* itself, the Court of Appeal refused to allow fresh evidence to be called where a witness admitted that she had lied at the original trial. The judges accepted that such evidence was relevant and would have an important influence on the hearing but declined to accept that such evidence was credible:

> A confessed liar cannot usually be accepted as credible. To justify the reception of the fresh evidence, some good reason must be shown why a lie was told in the first instance, and good ground given for thinking the witness will tell the truth on the second occasion. If it were proved that the witness had been bribed or coerced into telling a lie at the trial, and was now anxious to tell the truth, that would, I think, be a ground for a new trial, and it would not be necessary to resort to an action to set aside the judgment on the ground of fraud.

However, the EAT has discouraged the introduction of fresh evidence from its earliest days (*Bagga* **18.182** *v Heavy Electricals (India) Ltd* [1972] ICR 118, 120) and it is clear that where a party chooses not to raise a category of evidence at trial, he cannot seek to reopen that issue by calling the evidence on appeal (*Bingham v Hobourn Engineering Ltd* [1992] IRLR 298). Furthermore, the EAT has opined on several occasions that where new evidence is sought to be introduced, this should be done by means of an application for a review made to the employment tribunal, and not by means of an appeal: see, for example *Korashi v Abertawe Bro Morgannwg University Local Health Board* [2012] IRLR 4 The 2013 Practice Direction states, at para 10.1:

> The Employment Tribunal as the fact-finding body, which has heard relevant witnesses, is the appropriate forum to consider 'fresh evidence' and in particular the extent to which (if at all) it would or might have made a difference to its conclusions. It remains open to an intending appellant to contend that there has been an error of law if the Employment Tribunal is in error of law in refusing to reconsider its decision, and if so then to refer to evidence which was not placed before the Employment Tribunal at the time it made its initial decision but was placed before that Tribunal for the purposes of seeking or hearing a reconsideration of its decision.

In spite of the strict approach taken by the EAT, in *Borden (UK) Ltd v Potter* [1986] ICR 647, **18.183** Popplewell J explained that the EAT would look more favourably on the failure of a litigant in person to adduce evidence at trial than on the part of professional representatives. In that case the employer dismissed the claimant in circumstances where it was alleged that he had assaulted a fellow employee. A tribunal found that the dismissal was unfair and the employer sought to appeal that finding by introducing medical evidence to discredit the claimant. The EAT declined to admit the fresh evidence since no reasonable explanation was given as to why it had not been obtained and placed before the tribunal.

Similarly, in *Wileman v Minilec Engineering Ltd* [1988] ICR 318, the EAT declined to admit fresh **18.184** evidence. In that case the employer lost a claim for sexual harassment and sought to introduce before the EAT a photograph which had been published in a newspaper of the claimant posing in a 'flimsy costume' after the employment tribunal hearing. The employer argued that the photograph demonstrated that the claimant did not suffer a detriment as a result of the harassment. Although the evidence could not have been available at the hearing, the EAT was not convinced that it was relevant or probative.

However, fresh evidence is sometimes accepted by the EAT. One such case is *Photostatic Copiers* **18.185** *(Southern) Ltd v Okuda & Japan Office Equipment Ltd (In Liquidation)* [1995] IRLR 11. The claimant admitted before the EAT that he had been in receipt of a payment from the employer's business rival. The evidence had become available since the tribunal hearing and its existence could not have been known or foreseen by the employer. Moreover, the existence of the evidence was likely to have an impact on the result of the case albeit only on remedies.

As with the EAT's exercise of discretion in other areas (see *United Arab Emirates v Abdelghafar* **18.186** [1995] ICR 65) special considerations may arise in certain circumstances. For example, under the State Immunity Act 1978 there is an overriding duty on the EAT under the Act which overrides the usual rules (*Egypt v Gamal-Eldin* [1996] ICR 13).

Part A Tribunal Procedure

18.187   The procedure for admitting new evidence is that it should be filed with the EAT at the same time as the notice of appeal or respondent's answer along with an application to admit such new evidence (2013 Practice Direction, para 10.2). A party who wishes to resist an application to admit new evidence should submit written representations to the EAT and the other parties within fourteen days of the application being sent to them (2013 Practice Direction, para 10.4). The application will then be considered by the registrar or a judge of the EAT (2013 Practice Direction, para 10.5).

T. ORDERS OF THE EMPLOYMENT APPEAL TRIBUNAL

18.188   Where the EAT allows an appeal, it may, pursuant to s 35 of the ETA 1996:

(a)   exercise any of the powers of the body or officer from whom the appeal was brought or
(b)   remit the case to the body or officer from whom the appeal was brought.

18.189   In the case of the employment tribunals, therefore, the usual orders made by the EAT when allowing an appeal are to substitute its own decision for that of the tribunal, remit the case to the same tribunal for reconsideration or further reasoning, or, alternatively, remit the case to a differently constituted tribunal for rehearing on some or all points. In addition, the EAT has the power to accept an agreed order, to grant permission to appeal to the Court of Appeal, to review its own decision, or to make a reference to the Court of Justice of the European Union (see Chapter 22).

18.190   The EAT has no power to make a declaration of incompatibility under the Human Rights Act 1998 (HRA 1998) since it is not a court as defined in s 4(5) of the HRA 1998 This question was considered in *Whittaker v P&D Watson* [2002] ICR 1244, where the EAT, presided over by Lindsay P, commented (at 1249):

> It is to be noted that definition of 'court' does not include the employment tribunal or the Employment Appeal Tribunal. The effect is a little odd so far as concerns the Employment Appeal Tribunal because were I to be sitting alone, 500 yards away, in my erstwhile role in the Chancery Division, and were a corresponding question to come in front of me, I would be able to make a declaration of incompatibility in an appropriate case. But here, where I am assisted by a carefully balanced panel to represent both sides of industry, I cannot so decide.

This is a curious lacuna. It might be that the correct approach is for the EAT to dismiss the appeal in hand but then to grant permission to appeal. The Court of Appeal then has the power to make a declaration of incompatibility (see also Chapter 16).

Substitution

18.191   It was thought to be the case that the EAT could, having detected an error of law, reach its own determination and substitute that for the determination of the employment tribunal, where the answer was plain and required no further evidence. Thus, in *McLeod v Hellyer Brothers Ltd* [1987] IRLR 234, Slade LJ stated:

> If [the Employment Appeal Tribunal] are satisfied that a conclusion reached as a result of a misdirection is plainly and unarguably wrong upon the facts found by the industrial tribunal and those facts do not require further amplification or re-investigation, then we are entitled and bound to substitute our own conclusion as to what those findings require in law.

In *Dobie v Burns International Security Services (UK) Ltd* [1984] IRLR 329, Sir John Donaldson MR set out the test (at para 18) as follows:

> Once you detect that there has been a misdirection, and particularly that there has been an express misdirection of law, the next question to be asked is not whether the conclusion of the Tribunal is plainly wrong, but whether it is plainly and unarguably right, notwithstanding that misdirection, that the decision can stand. If the conclusion was wrong or might have been wrong, then it is for the appellate tribunal to remit the case to the only tribunal which is charged with making findings of fact.

18.192   However, in *Jafri v Lincoln College* [2014] ICR 920, Laws LJ stated (at para 21):

I must confess with great respect to some difficulty with the 'plainly and unarguably right' test elaborated in *Dobie* It is not the task of the EAT to decide what result is 'right' on the merits. That decision is for the ET, the industrial jury. The EAT's function is (and is only) to see that the ET's decisions are lawfully made. If therefore the EAT detects a legal error by the ET, it must send the case back unless (a) it concludes that the error cannot have affected the result, for in that case the error will have been immaterial and the result as lawful as if it had not been made; or (b) without the error the result would have been different, but the EAT is able to conclude what it must have been. In neither case is the EAT to make any factual assessment for itself, nor make any judgment of its own as to the merits of the case; the result must flow from findings made by the ET, supplemented (if at all) only by undisputed or indisputable facts. Otherwise, there must be a remittal.

It is somewhat difficult to detect a difference between the approach of Laws LJ in *Jafri* and that adopted in *McLeod* and in *Dobie*. Indeed, in *Burrell v Micheldever Tyre Services Limited* [2014] ICR 935, Maurice Kay LJ referred to the approach in *Jafri* as 'reaffirming the conventional approach' (see para 16).

The EAT can, of course, substitute its view for that of the employment tribunal where the parties **18.193** expressly consent to the EAT disposing of the case: see *Jafri* at para 47 (Underhill LJ) and *Kuznetsov v Royal Bank of Scotland* [2017] IRLR 350 at para 34.

Remission

Where the EAT exercises its power to remit a case to the employment tribunal and limits its scope **18.194** to redetermine all issues, the tribunal is only entitled to reconsider the case to the limited extent that is ordered by the EAT. Sometimes the EAT is not crystal clear about the scope of remission; the parties should be prepared to argue before the EAT as to precisely what subjects should be dealt with on such a remitted hearing and whether fresh evidence may be given or simply submissions to be made. Where the scope of the EAT's remission is unclear, the proper course is for an employment judge to adjourn the matter and seek guidance from the EAT. Generally, however, the EAT will only remit matters to a tribunal for a consideration of one or more of the issues that were under appeal: *LTRS Estates Limited v Hamilton* UKEAT/0230/12/KN (although pursuant to para 23 of the 2013 Practice Direction, the parties should raise any uncertainty in relation to an order for remission with the EAT). In *Aparau v Iceland Frozen Foods* [2000] IRLR 196, the Court of Appeal allowed an employee's appeal against the decision of an employment tribunal which had allowed a respondent employer to amend a response so as to add alternative potentially fair reasons for a dismissal once the matter had been remitted on a much narrower question. The Court of Appeal explained that the tribunal has no jurisdiction to hear or determine other matters and no power to allow a party to amend its case to raise new matters.

The EAT is entitled to remit to the same employment tribunal or to a differently constituted tri- **18.195** bunal. The EAT has given important guidance as to how it should determine whether to remit to the same tribunal (*Sinclair, Roche & Temperley v Heard* [2004] IRLR 763). The following factors will be relevant:

(a) Proportionality must be considered and in particular the amount of money at stake must be weighed against the cost and distress to the parties of ordering a complete rehearing.
(b) It is necessary to consider whether or not the same tribunal will remember the case. If the tribunal will have forgotten the case, then it should not be sent back to it. Whether or not the tribunal will remember the case is likely to depend on how much time has passed since the hearing as against the length of the hearing when it occurred.
(c) It would not be appropriate to send cases back to the same tribunal where the EAT had found that the tribunal was biased or there was a risk of pre-judgment or partiality.
(d) The EAT must have confidence that the tribunal, with appropriate guidance, can get the matter right on a reconsideration of the case. Therefore, where the first hearing was totally flawed or where there was complete mishandling of the case, the EAT should send the matter back to a differently constituted tribunal.
(e) There must be careful consideration not to provide the tribunal with what has been described as a 'second bite at the cherry'. The EAT must not send a case back to the same tribunal where

it does not have confidence that the tribunal will be able to consider the matter again and look at such further matters as are required and, if necessary, come to a different conclusion.

(f) On balance, in the ordinary case it is likely that the EAT will consider that the tribunal below is capable of taking a professional approach to dealing with the matter on remission (see also *HM Prison Service v Johnson* [2007] IRLR 951, para 126).

There are some cases where the EAT finds that the tribunal's approach to the case has been so poor that the party which lost cannot have confidence that justice will be done on remission. This is a matter of 'feel' for the EAT.

18.196 Pursuant to para 11.3 of the 2013 Practice Direction, the EAT can adjourn an appeal for up to twenty-one days and in effect remit an appeal to the employment tribunal:

> pending the making or the conclusion of an application by the appellant to the Employment Tribunal (if necessary out of time) for a review or pending the response by the Employment Tribunal to an invitation from the judge or Registrar to clarify, supplement or give its written reasons.

Therefore, that the EAT can remit an appeal to the employment tribunal in order that the tribunal clarifies or supplements its reasoning is now beyond doubt as a result of the 2013 Practice Direction and the cases of *Burns v Consignia plc (No 2)* [2004] IRLR 425 and *Barke v SEETEC Business Technology Centre Ltd* [2005] EWCA Civ 578, [2005] IRLR 633. Prior to the terms of the 2008 Practice Direction and these authorities, the power to remit for further reasons had been subject of conflicting authority (see eg *Tran v Greenwich Vietnam Community* [2002] IRLR 735 and the cases referred to therein).

18.197 In *Burns v Consignia plc (No 2)* [2004] IRLR 425, the claimant had issued an application alleging sex and race discrimination which had subsequently been withdrawn. After the withdrawal, she issued a second application making the same allegations of sex and race discrimination but in addition alleging constructive unfair dismissal. The employment tribunal struck out her application as an abuse of process. The EAT would have been prepared to allow her appeal in respect of the constructive unfair dismissal claim but noted that the tribunal had failed to consider whether, given Mrs Burns' behaviour, a fair trial was still possible. The EAT therefore adjourned the appeal and remitted the matter back to the employment tribunal. On the adjourned hearing of the appeal, Burton P upheld the decision to remit the matter to the ET.

The EAT did, however, issue this warning ([2004] IRLR 425, para 13 (Burton P):

> Of course there are dangers in remitting to the original tribunal a case where the ground of appeal is inadequacy of reasoning, and there will be some cases in which the reasoning is so inadequate that it would be unsafe to remit to the same tribunal. Equally, there will be the potential danger of giving the opportunity to a court below to reconsider its decision on an entirely different basis.

18.198 In *Barke v SEETEC Business Technology Centre Ltd* [2005] EWCA Civ 578, [2005] IRLR 633, the Court of Appeal found that even if there was no power for the employment tribunal to clarify or supplement its reasons under its own rules, the EAT had the power to regulate its own procedure under s 30(3) of the ETA 1996 Therefore, the Court of Appeal went on to uphold the *Burns* procedure—which is now codified in para 11.3 of the 2013 Practice Direction—of remitting cases to the employment tribunals in order for them to elaborate on their reasoning. However, the Court of Appeal agreed with Burton P that there would be some occasions when the procedure would not be appropriate, for example, when there was an allegation of bias against a member of the employment tribunal or:

> where the inadequacy of reasoning is on its face so fundamental that there is a real risk that supplementary reasons will be reconstructions of proper reasons rather than unexpressed actual reasons for the decision. The Employment Appeal Tribunal should always be alive to the danger that an employment tribunal might tailor its response to a request for explanations or further reasons (usually subconsciously rather than deliberately) so as to put the decision in the best possible light. (*Barke v SEETEC* para 46, *per* Dyson LJ)

18.199 Dyson LJ also stated that the Court of Appeal would be slow to interfere with the EAT's exercise of the power to remit to the employment tribunal for clarification or supplementation since the power was a discretionary case management power which should be left to the employment appeal tribunal to apply (*Barke v SEETEC* above, at para 49). There are indeed some dangers with the overuse of the process. Thus, in *Woodhouse School v Webster* [2009] IRLR 568, Mummery LJ emphasized that the purpose of the *Burns/Barke* procedure was to give the tribunal the opportunity of fulfilling its duty to provide adequate reasons, but the tribunal should do no more than answer the specific request. It should not advance arguments in defence of the decision against the grounds of appeal. The EAT might before it finally decides the appeal refer specific questions to the employment tribunal at the preliminary hearing of the appeal requesting it to clarify or supplement its reasons. It is not desirable for the tribunal to do more than answer the request. It should not advance arguments in defence of its decision and against the grounds of appeal. It must not reengage or appear to be engaged in advocacy rather than adjudication.

U. PERMISSION TO APPEAL

Appeals from the EAT lie to the Court of Appeal in England and Wales. Permission to appeal **18.200** is required and may be granted by order of the EAT. Pursuant to para 25.1 of the 2013 Practice Direction permission must be sought at the end of the hearing or when a reserved judgment is handed down. If permission is refused, then it may be sought from the Court of Appeal within fourteen days of the sealed order. Pursuant to para 25.2 of the 2013 Practice Direction where a party seeks permission to appeal it must first state the point of law to be advanced and the grounds of appeal.

In Scotland, an appeal lies from the EAT to the Court of Session. Permission must be sought from **18.201** the EAT to appeal to the Court of Session within forty-two days of the date of the hearing where judgment is delivered (2013 Practice Direction, para 25.3).

There are no rules which govern the EAT's discretion to give permission to appeal. However, per- **18.202** mission to appeal is likely to be granted by the EAT only if the appeal raises an important point of principle or practice or if there is some other compelling reason for the appeal court to hear the appeal.

The EAT has no power to grant a party permission to appeal straight to the House of Lords. This **18.203** was noted by the EAT (presided over by Bean J) in *Botham v Ministry of Defence* UKEAT/0503/04 (one of the appeals subsequently joined with *Lawson v Serco* [2006] UKHL 3, [2006] IRLR 289). In that case, the EAT stated (at para 23):

> We note that if the hearing before us had been in the High Court an application could have been made (with the consent of all parties) for a certificate under section 12 of the Administration of Justice Act 1969 permitting a petition to be presented to their Lordships for leave to bring a 'leapfrog' appeal direct to the House the power applies only in proceedings before a single judge of the High Court or a Divisional Court. We venture to suggest that consideration be given to whether the Employment Appeal Tribunal, which did not exist in 1969, might be brought within the scope of the section.

V. AGREED ORDER

An order may be agreed between the parties in an attempt to achieve one of two results. The parties **18.204** might agree that the appeal will be withdrawn by way of settlement. Alternatively the parties might agree that an appeal is allowed by way of settlement.

The situation in which the parties agree that an appeal should be withdrawn as part of a settlement **18.205** is dealt with by para 18.3 of the 2013 Practice Direction:

> If the parties reach an agreement that the appeal should be allowed by consent, and that an order made by the Employment Tribunal should be reversed or varied or the matter remitted to the Employment Tribunal on the ground that the decision contains an error of law, it is usually necessary for the matter to be heard by the EAT to determine whether there is a good reason for making the proposed order. On notification by the parties, the EAT will decide whether the appeal can be dealt with on the papers or by

a hearing at which one or more parties or their representatives should attend to argue the case for allowing the appeal and making the order that the parties wish the EAT to make.

18.206 This reflects the position established by the case law. In *British Newspaper Publishing Ltd v Fraser* [1987] ICR 517, Popplewell J set out the practice by which settlement of an appeal could be reached by correspondence if the EAT was satisfied that both parties were agreed. However, it was made clear that the EAT may, in its discretion, refuse to approve a settlement insofar as it overturns a decision of the employment tribunal. In that situation the EAT may well want full argument as to why the appeal should be allowed because the agreement not only affects the interests of the parties but also the role of the employment tribunal.

18.207 In any case, in order for an appeal to be allowed by consent, the settlement must truly dispose of the matter. Mummery J stated in *Sainsbury's v Moger* [1994] ICR 800 that where the parties' agreement did not truly dispose of the matter it would have to be fully argued with reasons given by the EAT for a remission or allowing of the appeal. The EAT follows the practice of the Court of Appeal in this respect.

18.208 Any withdrawal of an appeal should take place as soon as is practicable since if an appeal is withdrawn close to the hearing date the EAT may require the attendance of the appellant and/or a representative to explain the reasons for delaying in making the decision not to pursue the appeal (2013 Practice Direction, para 18.5).

W. REVIEW OF THE EMPLOYMENT APPEAL TRIBUNAL'S JUDGMENT OR ORDER

18.209 Paragraph 24 of the 2013 Practice Direction sets out the procedure by which an application for review by the EAT is made:

> Where an application is made for a review of a judgment or order of the EAT, it will normally be considered by the judge or judge and lay members who heard the appeal in respect of which the review is sought, who may exercise any power of case management as seems appropriate. If the original judgment or order was made by the judge together with lay members, then the judge may, pursuant to Rule 33, consider and refuse such application for review on the papers. If the judge does not refuse the application, he or she may make any relevant further order, but will not grant the application without notice to the opposing party and reference to the lay members, for consideration with them, either on paper or in open court. A request to review a judgment or order of the EAT must be made within 14 days of the seal date of the order, or must include an application, for an extension of time, with reasons, copied to all parties.

18.210 By r 33 of the EAT Rules, the EAT may of its own motion, or by application of one of the parties made within fourteen days of the order, review its order where:

(a) the order was wrongly made as a result of an error on the part of the EAT or its staff
(b) a party did not receive proper notice of the proceedings leading to the order or
(c) the interests of justice require such a review.

18.211 The scope of the power to review is therefore limited and reviews have ordinarily only been successful where there have been issues of jurisdiction, where there have been fundamental process errors, where there has been a fraud which appears soon after the decision, or in simple cases of minor error or omission such as where the EAT had acted on the first occasion under a misapprehension of fact.

18.212 However, the EAT made use of its power to review in the unusual case of *O'Neill v Governors of St. Thomas More Roman Catholic Voluntary Aided Upper School* [1997] ICR 33. The employment tribunal had dismissed Mrs O'Neill's complaint for sex discrimination in circumstances where she had been dismissed from a Roman Catholic school, having had a baby by a Roman Catholic priest who had some connection with the school. On 10 February 1995, Mrs O'Neill's solicitors withdrew her appeal. However, subsequently, Mrs O'Neill sought advice from the European Commission who referred her to case law dealing with 'mixed motives' in discrimination claims and indicated that she might succeed in an appeal. On 4 April 1995, Mrs O'Neill sought to re-instate her appeal stating that before she had withdrawn her appeal, her solicitors had not advised her as to the availability of legal aid. The EAT treated the application as an application for a review of their original decision to allow withdrawal of the appeal. In the event the EAT allowed the appeal to be reinstated, although it stressed that the case was unusual and that no general rule should be seen to be promulgated by the decision. Future applications to review an order withdrawing a case would require 'an unusual and exceptional case' in order to be successful. Indeed, the EAT was influenced in part by the fact that the case gave rise to an interesting and novel point of law and therefore it was in the public interest to permit the issue to be reopened. It is of some note that, at the full hearing, the appeal was successful.

Similarly, in *Brain v Corby BC* EAT/376/04, the appellant's solicitors withdrew an appeal but **18.213** then wrote to the EAT prior to the issuing of the sealed order by the EAT. They explained that their client had had a 'mini breakdown' when he instructed his solicitors that the appeal should be withdrawn. The EAT relied on *O'Neill v Governors of St Thomas More School* and permitted the withdrawal of a withdrawal of an appeal but the EAT once again emphasized that this would only be permitted in an exceptional case.

As a superior court of record, the EAT has an inherent power to reconsider its judgment at any **18.214** time before it is perfected. Therefore, in *Bass Leisure Ltd v Thomas* [1994] IRLR 104, the EAT was prepared to seek further argument from the parties in a case where there had been no appearance from the respondent. It was argued by the *amicus curiae* that in the light of r 26 of the EAT Rules, that the EAT should be slow to review a decision where a party had not appeared. However, the EAT considered that it was entitled as a superior court of record to reconsider its judgment at any time prior to an order being perfected and in the circumstances of that case, whilst finality and the question of costs were clearly relevant, there was a legitimate interest in not promulgating an avoidable error. The EAT stressed that, although it was prepared to exercise its discretion in that case, its discretion should be exercised sparingly and with caution.

The EAT, in *Asda Stores Ltd v Thompson, Pullan* & *Caller* [2004] IRLR 598, considered whether **18.215** or not the EAT was entitled to reopen its own decisions in a similar manner to the Court of Appeal is able. It was decided by the Court of Appeal in *Taylor v Lawrence* [2003] QB 528 that the Court of Appeal could exercise such a power in limited situations such as in the case of apparent bias, discovery of any new matter, or of any fraud. The appeal in *Asda v Thompson* arose from a dismissal following an investigation into allegations that the claimants were using illegal drugs. Witness statements were obtained by a number of informants but the employers refused to disclose the witness statements on the basis that promises of confidentiality had been made to the informants that their identities would not be revealed. The employment tribunal made an order that the witness statements had to be disclosed to the claimants but the employers appealed to the EAT. The EAT (Wall J presiding) remitted the matter back to the tribunal in order that it could re-examine the documents and make such order as was appropriate for discovery and inspection with appropriate safeguards for the fair disposal of the case. The tribunal made such directions as it considered to be appropriate but the respondent was not happy with those directions on the basis that:

(a) the respondent felt that it was important that it made submissions to the tribunal since only the respondent would understand why a particular redaction was sought; and

(b) the respondent opposed the idea that the parties could only make such applications to the tribunal following the tribunal's provision to the parties of its reasons and the statements redacted accordingly.

The respondent made an application to the EAT and attacked the previous decision of the EAT **18.216** presided over by Wall J on the basis that it was ambiguous and alternatively that it was wrong. Either way, it was argued that the EAT should substitute the decision for a new decision. Counsel for the respondent sought to argue that the EAT had jurisdiction to overrule one of its earlier decisions, or to indicate that it should not be followed in the event that it was of the view that the earlier decision of the EAT was wrong and sought to draw an analogy with the jurisdiction of the

Part A Tribunal Procedure

Court of Appeal. However, the EAT found that if it did have such jurisdiction it was not prepared to exercise it in that case since:

(a) the EAT is not a final court of appeal
(b) there was nothing to prevent the unsuccessful respondent in the case from appealing the judgment of Wall J to the Court of Appeal
(c) if there were any ground of reconsideration of this question, it would not be based on apparent bias, or discovery of any new matter, or any fraud which has taken its time to be revealed but rather would be because a point had not been argued.

18.217 As such it is unclear whether or not, in an appropriate case, the EAT may overturn an earlier decision in the same case. It seems unlikely that the EAT will choose to exercise such jurisdiction in any case where the route of appeal to the Court of Appeal was open to the unsuccessful party. The decision in *Asda v Thompson* has recently been affirmed by the EAT (Burton P presiding) in *Vakante v Governing Body of Addey* and *Stanhope School (No 2)* [2004] ICR 279.

X. COSTS

Circumstances in which costs may be awarded

18.218 Rule 34 of the EAT Rules provides the EAT with a general discretion to award costs against a party. Costs are defined by r 34(2) as including 'fees, charges, disbursements, expenses, reimbursement allowed to a litigant in person, or remuneration incurred by or on behalf of a party in relation to the proceedings'. The EAT's discretion to award costs against a party may be exercised in the circumstances set out in r 34A(1) of the EAT Rules:

> Where it appears to the Appeal Tribunal that any proceedings brought by the paying party were unnecessary, improper, vexatious or misconceived or that there has been unreasonable delay or other unreasonable conduct in the bringing or conducting of proceedings by the paying party, the Appeal Tribunal may make a costs order against the paying party.

18.219 Rule 34A(2) indicates three examples of cases where the EAT might exercise its discretion to award costs in particular. Those are where a party has not complied with a direction of the EAT, where a party has amended a pleading, or where a party has caused an adjournment of proceedings.

18.220 Case law provides further examples of when a party is at risk of having to pay the other side's costs:

(a) Where an appeal was abandoned shortly before the day of the hearing (*Maroof v JB Battye & Co Ltd* (1973) 8 ITR 489) or where there was unreasonable delay in communicating the decision to withdraw an appeal (*TVR Engineering Ltd v Johnson* [1978] IRLR 556) costs have been awarded. Thus, in *Rocha v Commonwealth Holiday Inns of Canada Ltd* EAT/13/80, the EAT stated: 'Applicants to industrial tribunals and appellants to the EAT must take notice that if they withdraw their allegations at a late stage they will be at risk of an application being made for costs. If they desire to contest that application it is their duty to appear before the industrial tribunal or EAT in order to do so'.
(b) Where there was no point of law involved in the appeal costs have been awarded against the appellant (*Redland Roof Tiles Ltd v Eveleigh* [1979] IRLR 11).
(c) Where the appellant was absent from the hearing and was unrepresented it has been held that the appellant had behaved unreasonably (*Croydon v Greenham (Plant Hire) Ltd* [1978] ICR 415).

18.221 In *Sodexho Ltd v Gibbons* [2005] IRLR 836 it was accepted by the EAT (Judge Peter Clark sitting alone) that the term 'misconceived' in r 34A includes the appeal having 'no reasonable prospect of success' since this was the definition as set out in reg 2 of ETR 2004. Therefore, the term 'misconceived' ought to be interpreted in the same manner in both the employment tribunals and the EAT.

18.222 However, no hard and fast rules can be enunciated as to when costs will be awarded against a party and when they will not. This is necessarily so since the EAT is bound to exercise its discretion before awarding such costs. Thus, while the EAT has been ready to award costs on many occasions where the appeal is abandoned shortly before the hearing, in *McPherson v BNP Paribas* [2004] IRLR 558, the Court of Appeal held that the question for employment tribunals and the EAT was whether in all the circumstances the claimant/appellant had conducted the proceedings reasonably and not whether or not the withdrawal of the claim/appeal was unreasonable.

Appellants ought not to feel that they will avoid an award of costs simply because the appeal has **18.223** progressed past a preliminary hearing or even in a case when the appeal is set down for a full hearing straight away. While it may appear that there is an arguable point of law at first sight, that might appear to be incorrect on a complete consideration of the case and therefore an award of costs might be appropriate (*Clifton Clinic Ltd v Monk* EAT/582/84; *Tesco Stores Ltd v Wilson* UKEAT/0749/98).

Assessment of costs

The 2013 Practice Direction provides at para 22.2 that a party may make an application for costs at **18.224** the end of a hearing or alternatively within fourteen days of the seal date of the relevant order of the EAT. The party seeking the order must set out clearly the legal ground on which the application is based and must show how the costs have been incurred. The production of a schedule of costs is the usual way of doing this. If an application for costs is made by paper, then the EAT may resolve the application on the papers provided that it has allowed all relevant parties to make representations in writing (2013 Practice Direction, para 22.4).

Rule 34B of the EAT Rules provides for three methods of assessing costs: **18.225**

(1) summary assessment by the EAT
(2) an order of the EAT ordering to be paid a sum which has been agreed between the parties
(3) detailed assessment in the High Court in accordance with the CPR.

If the assessment of costs takes place on a summary basis, then the EAT will look at the figures **18.226** for fees charged and will compare them with the schedules in Appendices I and II of the Schedule to Part 48 of the CPR, which contains notes on the applicable rates which might be charged by solicitors of various levels of experience and in various parts of the country. Barristers' fees are determined according to counsel's date of call. Summary assessments are carried out on a broad brush approach and therefore it is likely that the EAT will hear submissions and will then reduce any award of costs by either deducting some items claimed or alternatively by simply reducing by a percentage figure. On a summary assessment, the EAT may have regard to the ability of the paying party to pay costs when making an order (EAT Rules, r 34B(2)). Where a summary assessment of costs is undertaken, the EAT might order that the costs orders are 'set off' against cross-costs orders or orders for damages: see *Basildon and Thurrock NHS Foundation v Weerasinghe* [2016] ICR 305 and *Colletti v Borealis Driver Services Limited* UKEAT/0203/15/RN.

Alternatively, if the EAT feels that a detailed assessment of costs is more appropriate the matter will **18.227** be referred to the High Court and a costs judge will assess costs using the procedure set out in CPR Part 47. An appeal lies from the order of a costs judge to a High Court judge, although permission to appeal is required.

Rule 34D of the EAT Rules creates a special regime where costs are awarded in favour of a litigant **18.228** in person. The litigant in person is able to make a claim for costs of work undertaken by him or her and disbursements made by a legal representative. However, those two items are treated differently. Costs of work which the litigant in person has undertaken are limited to two-thirds of the amount which would have been allowed if the litigant in person had been represented by a legal representative. Thus, it is necessary to calculate the amount of loss by reference, for example, to the number of hours which the litigant in person has had to take off work in order to prepare the appeal. It is then necessary to work out the rate which would have been charged by a legal representative. The litigant in person's loss is then capped at two-thirds of the amount that the legal representative would have charged. In a case where the litigant in person has incurred no financial loss in the preparation of the appeal he or she may make a claim for the time which the EAT considers was reasonably spent preparing the appeal at a rate of £25 per hour. That rate was increased to £26 per hour from 6 April 2006 and is increased by £1 each subsequent year from that date. Disbursements, on the other hand, can be claimed in full, although they are subject to the usual cost rules and therefore must be reasonably incurred.

Wasted costs orders

18.229 The EAT can make a wasted costs order against a party's representative. Wasted costs are defined by r 34C of the EAT Rules:

> 'Wasted costs' means any costs incurred by a party (including the representative's own client and any party who does not have a legal representative):
>
> (a) as a result of any improper, unreasonable or negligent act or omission on the part of any representative; or
> (b) which, in the light of any such act or omission occurring after they were incurred, the Appeal Tribunal considers it reasonable to expect that party to pay.

18.230 Wasted costs may only be awarded against a party's representative as defined in r 34C(4). That definition only applies to representatives who are acting in pursuit of profit with regard to the proceedings. Therefore, those individuals who are acting on a *pro bono* basis, be that as a voluntary sector representative while acting for a law centre or the Free Representation Unit, or a friend or relative of one of the parties, could not be ordered to pay wasted costs.

18.231 When an order is to be made against a representative, the representative must be given an opportunity to make oral or written submissions setting out why such an order should not be made by virtue of r 34C(5). Although there is no requirement on the EAT to provide oral reasons for the making of a wasted costs order, it is likely that the EAT will do so. If the EAT does not do so, then a request for written reasons can be made within twenty-one days of the date of the order. Written reasons will then be sent to all parties (EAT Rules, r 34C(8)).

18.232 The EAT may have regard to the representative's ability to pay a wasted costs order when determining the amount of such an order (EAT Rules, r 34C(5)). In *Gill v Humanware Europe Ltd* [2010] ICR 1343, the Court of Appeal held that r 34C conferred a discretion on the EAT as to how it proceeded on an application for a wasted costs order including whether or not to hold an oral hearing. In the present case, however, because of the conflict as to facts giving rise to the application and that it involved a finding that a professionally qualified advocate had acted in an improper way, there should have been a hearing and an order should not have been made without providing counsel, who was criticized, with an opportunity to make further representations. The Court of Appeal also emphasized the need for the improper, unreasonable, or negligent conduct which was found to have caused the wasted costs for an order to be appropriate.

19

Tribunal Procedure and Appeals in Scotland

A. INTRODUCTION

The Employment Tribunal Rules of Procedure 2013 (ETR 2013) apply to both England and Wales, **19.01** and to Scotland. Provision is made in r 8(3) setting out the circumstances in which there is jurisdiction to bring a claim in Scotland. By a Presidential Practice Direction of 14 December 2016, claims may be presented in Scotland either online by using the online form submission service, accessible at www.employmenttribunals.service.gov.uk; or by post to Employment Tribunals Central Office (Scotland), PO Box 27105, GLASGOW, G2 9JR. A claim may also be presented, in the alternative, by hand to one of the four Employment Tribunal Offices (in Glasgow, Edinburgh, Dundee, and Aberdeen) details of which are listed in the schedule to this Practice Direction.

It was stated some time ago by the EAT (*Odeco (UK) Inc v Peacham* [1979] ICR 823 (Bristow J)) **19.02** that:

> The statutes which established the [employment] tribunals and gave them jurisdiction apply equally in England and in Scotland. There is no jurisdictional distinction between an [employment] tribunal sitting in Scotland and an [employment] tribunal sitting in England. This appeal tribunal can, and does, sit indifferently in England and in Scotland exercising the identical jurisdiction. Therefore the division which produces the problem in this case is not a true jurisdictional division at all; it is simply a division of the administrative structure into English and Scottish for administrative convenience.

That remains the position today, although there are significant changes afoot for the system of employment tribunals in Scotland, different to those facing tribunals in England and Wales. Section 39 of the Scotland Act 2016 devolves the administration of employment tribunals (a matter previously reserved to the UK Parliament) to the Scottish Parliament. That is in fulfilment of what was proposed by the Smith Commission, the body tasked with suggesting further devolution of powers in the post-referendum debate over law-making powers within the UK. The Commission proposed (para 63) that 'all powers over the management and operation of all reserved tribunals' should be transferred to the Scottish Parliament with limited exceptions (not extending to employment tribunals), and s 39 gives legislative expression to that proposal. What is devolved, it should be noted, is the *administration* of tribunals, not the substantive legal rights that they apply. These rights (and the determination of the policy that stands behind them) remain reserved matters. The details of this devolution, however, remain to be clarified. It was originally hoped that the practical impact of devolution would be seen in 2020, a timetable that left scope for developments and changes in what had been announced. The major change that was envisaged is the transfer of the functions of employment tribunals in Scotland to the First-tier Tribunal for Scotland, a body established under the Tribunals (Scotland) Act 2014. As and when this reform takes effect, it will mean that employment tribunals will, in Scotland, undergo a change of both name and status. This is very different to the changes being considered for England and Wales. While discussion in England and Wales contemplates the creation of a separate Employment and Equalities Court, in Scotland the proposals are for employment tribunals to move to sit within a structure alongside other adjudicatory bodies that deal primarily with disputes between the state and its citizens. If the proposals are carried through in their original form, employment tribunals will lose their separate identity and become part of the Scottish First-tier Tribunal, alongside the Lands Tribunal for Scotland, the Mental Health Tribunal for Scotland, and the Private Rented Housing Panel. At the same time, employment judges may lose their judicial status and tenure of office. Alongside these changes there will also be a number of associated procedural and substantive reforms. Appeal from the First-tier Tribunal will no longer be to the EAT, but to the Upper Tribunal, and is likely to be subject to the granting of leave.

19.03 In 2016, the Scottish government stated its intention to abolish the fees that were at that time imposed on those seeking to bring tribunal claims. That policy objective at the time marked a significant difference to the policy being pursued by the UK government for England and Wales, but it was overtaken by the Supreme Court's decision in R v Lord Chancellor [2017] UKSC 51 requiring the removal of fee charging in both England and Wales and Scotland. That makes much less likely the practice of 'forum-shopping' between jurisdictions as and when devolution of tribunal administration takes place, though differences in the rules and practices of tribunals may mean that in some respects one jurisdiction may be seen as more advantageous than the other.

19.04 Unsurprisingly, proposed changes in how the tribunal system operates have given rise to controversy within the Scottish legal community, and the consultation exercise undertaken by the Scottish Government has attracted many criticisms from interested parties. Despite devolution not extending to substantive rights, the practical differences that are likely to emerge in bringing and pursuing claims in Scotland seem likely to encourage a much greater separation between the operation of tribunals (and access to justice in employment matters) in the two jurisdictions.

19.05 Some developments in England and Wales have not, as yet, been adopted within the Scottish system of tribunals. In particular, the arrangements for judicial assessment, which came into force in England and Wales in October 2016 and allow for the possibility of early assessment of the merits of a claim and a response, have no counterpart in Scotland. Although there has been an expression of interest by the Scottish President of Employment Tribunals in developing a similar procedure, this has not at the time of writing (October 2017) materialized into formal reforms.

B. TRIBUNAL PROCEDURE

19.06 There is no reason why a party who has knowledge of the conduct of tribunal proceedings in England and Wales should have particular concerns about bringing a claim before a Scottish tribunal, though it should be noted there are separate Practice Directions which are specific to proceedings in the Scottish tribunals (see below). The same comment applies to the taking of appeals from decisions of tribunals to the Employment Appeal Tribunal (EAT), which sits separately in Scotland and is chaired by a Scottish judge of the Court of Session (equivalent to an English High Court judge). The EAT's Practice Directions apply to the EAT wherever it is sitting, although there are certain modifications in the former relevant to appeals held in Scotland. These are noted below. There are, however, certain differences in how hearings before employment tribunals proceed. As already noted, there is no procedure equivalent to the judicial assessment of tribunal claims introduced in England and Wales as part of the case management regime from October 2016. There are also differences in the legal terminology governing tribunal procedure, and (to a more limited extent) in the substantive law and practice that the tribunals apply.

A full discussion of the nature and extent of differences between England and Wales and Scotland in the substantive law of employment lies outside the scope of this chapter, but the following general comments may be of assistance. Insofar as tribunal claims turn upon questions of common law, it should be remembered that the common law of Scotland in matters of contract, tort (delict), and in public law is not identical to that of England and Wales. There is, for example, no doctrine of consideration known to Scots contract law, and there are also, inter alia, differences in the rules of estoppel (personal bar) and *res judicata*. The law relating to prescription and limitation is different. Not only is the maximum claim for arrears of pay in equal pay cases five years in Scotland (as against six in England and Wales) but the underlying concept of *prescription* (the doctrine that applies in Scotland) is different to that of *limitation* (the doctrine found in England and Wales). Whereas the right itself expires under the Prescription and Limitation (Scotland) Act 1975 after the appropriate period has elapsed, in England under the Limitation Act 1980 it is only the means of pursuing the right that expires. Another difference is found in the law of unfair dismissal, in the definition of what amounts to a dismissal. The law of constructive (unfair) dismissal incorporates elements of the doctrine of mutuality of contract, which does not exist in English law: see *McNeill v Aberdeen City Council (No 2)* [2014] IRLR 102, IH. **19.07**

While in the interpretation and application of statutory rights these differences are usually not important, there will be occasions, especially when considering contractual and other common law entitlements, when an understanding of the technical rules of Scots law is necessary in order to present or defend a tribunal claim. The more one is required to consider technical issues of the law of procedure or evidence in their application to proceedings in employment tribunals, the less likely it is that the detailed rules of English law will apply, although often the end result is very similar. (See eg *Renfrewshire Council v Adamson* UKEATS/0013/07/MT, a case dealing with the circumstances in which there is a right to withdraw a concession made in the course of proceedings.) The point is illustrated by the existence of situations where the powers of the tribunal are assimilated to those of a sheriff (in Scotland) or county court (in England). (See eg ETR 2013, Sch 1, r 78, which deals with the amount of a costs or expenses order.) Similarly, under r 31 of the ETR 2013 the power which a tribunal has in Scotland to require the disclosure of documents or information is the same as the power enjoyed by a sheriff under the general rules of civil procedure (it should be remembered that there is no rule providing for automatic discovery in the employment tribunal in Scotland). The Scottish regime for the recovery of expenses (costs) in the employment tribunal is different from that found in England and Wales, and it should be noted, in particular, that there is no provision for the recovery of expenses on an indemnity basis under Scots law. Neither is the concept of exemplary damages known in Scotland. Differences of lesser importance occur in terminology; 'costs' are usually referred to as 'expenses' in Scotland; the papers lodged in tribunal alongside the formal pleadings are referred to as 'productions', and the English term 'stay' is, in Scots legal terminology, a 'sist'. **19.08**

In a number of situations where the Employment Judge has a discretion, cases under previous versions of the ETR have stated that regard should be had to Civil Procedure Rules principles in exercising the discretion. See, for example, the power to strike out: see *McGuire v Centrewest London Buses Ltd* UKEAT/0576/06. The Civil Procedure Rules are not, of course, applicable to civil proceedings in Scotland, and it is less than obvious why they should provide authoritative guidance to employment tribunals in that jurisdiction, though the point has not to date arisen for decision. **19.09**

As a matter of formal hierarchy, while decisions of the EAT (being a court which has jurisdiction throughout Great Britain) have equal status within Great Britain, decisions of the Court of Appeal are not formally binding within Scotland. Similarly, decisions of the Court of Session in appeals from the EAT are not binding on English tribunals. Nevertheless, as a matter of practice it would be wholly exceptional for a decision of the Court of Appeal on a matter where there is no difference in the substantive law between the two jurisdictions not to be followed. In practice, decisions of the Court of Appeal are regularly cited and followed within the Scottish tribunal system and in **19.10** the EAT. And the same applies in the reverse. The point was well put by Laws LJ in *Clarke v Frank Staddon Ltd; Caulfield v Marshalls Clay Products Ltd* [2004] ICR 1502, when he said (at para 31):

> As a matter of pragmatic good sense the ET and the EAT in either jurisdiction will ordinarily expect to follow decisions of the higher appeal court in the other jurisdiction (whether the Court of Session or the Court of Appeal) where the point confronting them is indistinguishable from what was there decided.

That approach was foreshadowed by remarks made in 1992 by Lord Mayfield, a Scottish EAT judge, in the following terms: 'this Court, being part of a United Kingdom body in the field of employment law, would only depart from an opinion of the Court of Appeal on a matter which was purely related to a particular aspect of Scots Law' (*Brown v Rentokil Ltd* [1992] IRLR 302, EAT, at para 17).

19.11 What, however, would be the position in the event of there being a difference between a decision of the EAT (sitting in England) and a decision of the Court of Session (sitting in Scotland, on an appeal from the EAT)? While it is unlikely that such direct conflict will arise, it is not impossible that it could, especially in the event of one court being unaware of the decision of the other. The scope for conflict is apparent in the differences between the reasoning of the EAT in *Sharma v Manchester CC* [2008] IRLR 336 and that of the Court of Session (Inner House) in *McMenemy v Capital Systems Ltd* [2007] IRLR 400. While the point has never had to be decided, it is thought that in such a situation an employment tribunal in Scotland would be bound to follow the decision of the Court of Session in preference to that of the EAT.

19.12 Appeals from the EAT sitting in Scotland go to the Court of Session (Inner House) and thence (with leave) to the Supreme Court. In the event of considering an appeal to the Court of Session, it would always be appropriate to take advice from advisers qualified in Scots law. The Rules of the Court of Session (applicable to all proceedings before the Court of Session) are wholly different from the Civil Procedure Rules. Only party-litigants and those with rights of audience in the higher courts (ie advocates and solicitor-advocates) may appear in the Court of Session, unlike the EAT (where English-qualified barristers and solicitors regularly appear). Under Rules of Court 41.2 and 41.20, an applicant who seeks leave to appeal has forty-two days from the date when he receives intimation of the decision of the EAT. In *Francis v Pertemps Recruitment Partnership Ltd* [2011] CSIH 40, the Court of Session confirmed that where the EAT refuses leave to appeal to the Court of Session, that decision is itself one which can be appealed by reference to s 37(1) of the Employment Tribunals Act 1996 (ETA 1996); judicial review is not competent. The same decision also confirmed that a decision under the sift procedures found in r 3 of the Employment Appeal Tribunal Rules was a decision of the EAT (and so susceptible in principle to appeal, under s 37(1)), even though taken by a judge sitting alone.

19.13 In the past, employment tribunals in Scotland have generally tended to adopt a less formalistic approach to proceedings than their counterparts in England and Wales. There are signs that this relative informality may be changing, particularly as there has been, since 2004, a common set of regulations for both jurisdictions. As already mentioned, there are a number of separate Scottish Practice Directions currently in force. Two of them are made under the 2004 Regulations, and date from December 2006 Practice Direction No 1 requires the intimation of lists of documents fourteen days in advance of hearing where a party is legally represented. Practice Direction No 2 makes provision for the sist (stay) of proceedings where parties are agreed to do so in order to allow mediation to go ahead. (A third Practice Direction under the 2004 Rules dealing with counterclaims was revoked with effect from February 2014.) Practice directions have also been made under the current (2013) Regulations. These cover diverse matters arising in respect of holiday pay claims, presentation of claims to tribunals, and (jointly with England and Wales) principles for compensating pension loss.

19.14 Under the 2013 Rules, provision is also made (r 7) for the issue of Presidential Guidance where this is seen as appropriate. Employment judges and employment tribunals are expected to have regard to such Guidance, without being formally bound by it. The first Presidential Guidance for Scotland dates from effect from 1 February 2014 and this sets out guidance on appropriate practice where a postponement of a tribunal hearing is sought. There also exists Presidential Guidance on statutory appeals in the employment tribunal and a range of other matters (see below). Notwithstanding these recent regulatory interventions, practitioners coming from England and Wales may still expect to find in Scotland a less regulated regime, with more control left to the parties in the organization and presentation of their cases. It is worth emphasizing, in particular, that the Presidential Guidance on general case management, issued by the President of Employment Tribunals has no application in Scotland and no equivalent guidance exists. The full list of issued Presidential Practice Directions and Guidance is now quite extensive, covering the following matters:

Presidential Guidance Vento Bands
Employment Tribunals (Scotland) Practice Direction No. 1: Providing a List of Documents 14 days before a Hearing.
Employment Tribunals (Scotland) Practice Direction No 2: Sist for Mediation
Employment Tribunals (Scotland) Direction of the President: Holiday Pay
Employment Tribunals (Scotland) Direction of the President: Holiday Pay Direction 27 March 2015
Holiday Pay Direction 27 March 2015: Accompanying Note
Making a Statutory Appeal (Scotland)
Presidential Practice Direction (Scotland): Presentation of Claims
Presidential Guidance (Scotland): Seeking a postponement of a hearing
Presidential Practice Direction (Scotland)—Addresses for serving documents in special cases
Case Management Order of the President of the Employment Tribunals (Scotland) re Unison
Presidential Guidance Pension Loss
Principles for Compensating Pension Loss
Case Management Order of the President of the Employment Tribunals (Scotland) re Unison

Witness statements

While the rules for Scotland allow for the use of witness statements they are still very much the exception. In general, unless a tribunal has previously ruled to the contrary, it should be assumed that witness statements will neither be expected nor acceptable, and that witnesses will give their evidence in chief by answering questions from the party's representative. If a party wishes to make use of a witness statement, then it is important to ascertain in advance whether this would be acceptable to the tribunal. The absence of witness statements means of course there is a risk that the full case being argued by a party will not be known to his or her opponent until the hearing itself. For this reason, the use of the power to obtain further information of the claimant's case in advance of the hearing (part of the tribunal's general case management power under r 29 ETR 2013), is particularly important within the Scottish system. Should a party be taken by surprise by unexpected and important evidence given at the hearing, of which notice has not been given, then application to the tribunal should of course be made for adjournment or other appropriate procedure to allow for investigation and answer. **19.15**

Witnesses

During the course of the hearing witnesses are, in kept outside the tribunal until they have given their evidence. That is the general rule. In special circumstances (for example, where the party giving instructions to the legal representative is also a witness in the case or the witness is a director of the company) leave may be sought from the tribunal to permit the attendance of the individual before he or she gives evidence. **19.16**

Hearing

Separate hearings dealing with the issue of liability and remedy are not as common in Scotland as they are in England. Care should therefore be taken to ascertain the position at the start, and parties should generally assume that they will be required to deal with both aspects at the scheduled hearing unless the contrary is stated. **19.17**

Part A Tribunal Procedure

Closing speeches

19.18 In contrast to the position in England in which the party who starts the case presents their closing speech last, in Scotland the closing speeches will usually follow the order in which the evidence was led. But practice varies and confirmation of the wishes of the particular tribunal should be sought.

Opening speeches

19.19 It is very unusual for there to be any opening speech in tribunal proceedings, though where a matter is especially complex or technical some explanatory remarks may be appropriate. Where the differences between the parties are largely dependent on questions of law or on narrowly focused issues of fact, it is increasingly common, with the approval of the tribunal, to submit agreed summaries of facts, sometimes referred to as 'joint minutes', which may eliminate or substantially reduce the need for witness evidence. It is also common, especially in complex cases to have a list of issue agreed between the parties..

Disclosure of documents

19.20 The process of disclosure—finding and obtaining documents in the hands of another party—is known as recovery in Scotland. As noted above, there is no automatic disclosure required in Scotland. But, by Practice Direction No 1, where a party is legally represented, their representative must provide the other party or parties or their representative (if they are represented) with a list of the documents that it intends to rely on at any hearing on the merits of a claim, not less than fourteen days before any such hearing.

Use of documents at hearing

19.21 The documents are known as productions and each document is numbered, rather than the pages of the bundle. It is not uncommon for each party to produce its own productions as opposed to a bundle, but this of course is subject to any particular directions to the contrary that may be given in a particular case by a tribunal.

Costs

19.22 A costs order in Scotland is known as an expenses order.

Enforcement of awards

19.23 In Scotland the tribunal issues a certificate and any award can be enforced directly without having to go to the Sheriff Court (ETA 1996, s 15(1), (2)).

C. APPEALS

19.24 Appeals from the employment tribunal to the EAT are governed, as in England and Wales, by the provisions of the ETA 1996. It should be noted, however, that aspects of the EAT practice in Scotland are different to those in England and Wales, and attention should be paid to the EAT Practice Direction which explains where differences lie. It is, for example, not general practice for skeleton arguments to be submitted to the EAT in advance of the hearing, although increasingly these are required by specific direction of the court. In complex cases it is common for closing oral submissions to be supplemented by written submissions. (Part 13 of the EAT Practice Direction 2008, which governs skeleton arguments, states that it does not apply to an appeal heard in Scotland unless there is a contrary direction by the EAT in Edinburgh.) Appeals from the EAT are made to the Inner House of the Court of Session. Leave to appeal is required, as in England, and this may be obtained either from the EAT or, where the EAT has refused leave, from the Court of Session itself. In addition to raising a point of law, it is a requirement that *probabilis causa* be shown: see *Campbell v Dunoon & Cowal Housing Association* [1992] IRLR 528, para 3 (Lord

Murray). It has also been emphasized by the Court of Session that no appeal should be allowed to proceed on grounds other than those in respect of which leave has been granted: see *Hynd v (1) Armstrong; and (2) Messrs Bishops* [2005] CSIH 12. Further appeal to the Supreme Court is subject to the granting of leave either by the Inner House or the Supreme Court itself.

Staying or sisting proceedings

Proceedings in the tribunal may be sisted, which is the equivalent of a stay in English proceedings. **19.25**

'Without prejudice' documents

It should not be assumed that the English rules regarding use of documents marked 'without **19.26** prejudice' apply in Scotland. Although letters and communications used in attempts to settle disputes are regularly marked in this way, the legal effect is not the same. For a recent survey of the Scottish rules see *In the Petition of Sovereign Dimensional Survey Ltd* [2008] CSOH 85. The Scottish rule is narrower than the English one, in that while offers or concessions made for the purpose of settlement may not be used in proceedings, statements of fact are treated differently. Thus, a statement which is identified as a clear and unequivocal statement of fact, even though made in the course of negotiations between parties and even though contained in a document marked 'without prejudice', does not attract privilege and may be relied upon: see *Daks Simpson Group plc v Kuiper* 1994 SLT 689. This is an important point to keep in mind when, for example, the drawing up of settlement agreements for the settlement of disputes over dismissal is in hand.

Part A Tribunal Procedure

PART B

Procedure in Other Jurisdictions

20

Employment Litigation in the Civil Courts

SUMMARY

(1) Certain types of employment law claims may be brought in the civil courts. Some disputes may only be brought in the civil courts; others may be brought either in the courts or in the tribunal.

(2) Where a claim may be brought in either venue, or where there are multiple claims in different venues, careful consideration is necessary as to which venue is the most appropriate with reference to effects of the principles of *res judicata*, issue estoppel, and abuse of process.

(3) Claims in the High Court and county court are governed by the Civil Procedure Rules 1998 (CPR). There are many similarities between practice in the courts and tribunals. Claims in the courts are characterized by a greater emphasis on pre-action work, greater formality, and a wider range of remedies, particularly interim remedies. Costs orders are the norm rather than the exception.

A. INTRODUCTION

Certain types of employment dispute may fall to be litigated in the civil courts, either in the High **20.01** Court or in the county courts. This chapter will consider:

(a) Tactical and procedural issues which arise from the potential overlap of claims in the tribunal and in the civil courts.
(b) The procedure for bringing claims in the civil courts pursuant to the CPR.

B. JURISDICTION OF THE COURTS AND THE EMPLOYMENT TRIBUNALS

Claims in the employment tribunal

20.02 The jurisdiction of the tribunal is statutory, and the tribunal may not hear claims in respect of which it is not specifically given jurisdiction. A full list of claims falling within the tribunal's jurisdiction is at the end of Chapter 1. The vast majority of claims in the tribunal concern statutory rights. Generally, those rights can only be enforced in the tribunal and not in the civil courts. For example, a claim of unfair dismissal, or a claim of sex discrimination by an employee in relation to her employment, can only be brought in the tribunal. The rights upon which such claims are based are statutory and do not give rise to contractual rights which can be enforced in the civil courts: *Doherty v BMI* [2006] IRLR 90, EAT, paras 25–7 (although some statutory provisions do expressly and directly affect contractual terms, see, for example, the equality clause provided for by the Equal Pay Act 1970, and certain provisions of the National Minimum Wage Act 1998 and the Working Time Regulations 1998, SI 1998/1833).

Claims in the civil courts

20.03 A number of claims which are common in the context of employment fall outside the tribunal's general jurisdiction.

Breach of contract

20.04 See Chapter 30 for consideration of the substantive principles relevant to contract claims which commonly arise in the employment context. The Employment Tribunals Extension of Jurisdiction (England and Wales) Order 1994, SI 1994/1623 gives to the tribunal limited jurisdiction over claims of breach of contract. Contract claims in the tribunal are considered in detail in Chapter 8. Claims of breach of contract which cannot be brought in the tribunal, and can only be brought in the civil courts include the following:

(a) claims which exceed the tribunal's jurisdictional limit of £25,000;

(b) claims in respect of restrictive covenants in restraint of trade or confidential information;

(c) claims in respect of personal injuries.

See *Fraser v HLMAD Ltd* [2006] EWCA Civ 738, [2006] IRLR 687 and *University of London v Tariquez-Zaman* [2010] EWHC 908 (QB) at [59].

Equitable claims

20.05 The tribunal has no equitable jurisdiction, and therefore cannot deal with claims of breach of fiduciary duty or restitutionary claims.

20.06 Whatever the nature of the claim, the tribunal has no jurisdiction to grant equitable remedies, so if an injunction is sought, or an account of profits, this must be pursued in the civil courts.

Tortious claims

20.07 The tribunal has no jurisdiction to deal with claims in tort other than the statutory torts which specifically fall within its jurisdiction. Common law claims, such as claims in negligence, can only be pursued in the civil courts. Many statutory torts also do not fall within the tribunal's jurisdiction, such as claims under the Protection from Harassment Act 1997.

Personal injuries

20.08 Claims in respect of personal injuries based upon negligence, breach of contract, or breach of statutory duty not falling within the tribunal's jurisdiction, cannot be pursued in the tribunal. Damages for personal injury can however be claimed as a head of loss in discrimination claims (see *Sheriff v Klyne Tugs (Lowestoft) Ltd* [1999] IRLR 481; *Essa v Laing Ltd* [2004] EWCA Civ 2, [2004] IRLR 31).

Discrimination outside the employment field

Discrimination claims outside the employment field fall within the exclusive jurisdiction of the **20.09** county courts (and then only the county courts designated for this purpose). These include claims under Parts 3, 4, 6, and 7 of the Equality Act 2010 [EqA 2010], which are discrimination claims relating to services and public functions, premises, education, and associations. For a full list of the county court jurisdiction under the EqA 2010 see s 114 of the Act.

C. OVERLAPPING CLAIMS

In a number of situations, a claimant may face the potential to bring a claim either in the tribunal **20.10** or in the courts.

There is one situation where a claimant may bring exactly the same claim, based on the same cause **20.11** of action and claiming the same loss, in either the court or the tribunal, ie a breach of contract claim for less than £25,000. This may be brought in the tribunal (assuming the conditions of the Employment Tribunal (Extension of Jurisdiction) Orders 1994, SI 1994/1623, and SI 1994/1624 are met) or in the courts.

Other circumstances arise where the claimant may have different causes of action arising out of the **20.12** same facts, some of which may be brought in the courts, and some in the tribunal.

The claimant may have suffered a number of different losses arising under different causes of ac- **20.13** tion, but all arising out of the same broad set of facts. For example, a director of a company who is ousted in a boardroom coup may have claims in relation to unfair dismissal (tribunal), unlawful deduction from wages in relation to a previous year's bonus (tribunal), wrongful dismissal (court or tribunal depending on value), and in relation to his directorship and ownership of shares in the company (court). The right to a bonus may be the basis of a claim for the bonus in the High Court or county court or for loss of the ability to earn it in the employment tribunal.

Alternatively, the same loss could be attributed to different causes of action which fall to be liti- **20.14** gated in different venues. For example, a claimant complaining about his summary dismissal and consequent loss of earnings may be able to frame his claim both as an unfair dismissal (within the exclusive jurisdiction of the tribunal) or as a wrongful dismissal. If the wrongful dismissal claim is worth more than £25,000 it can only be brought in the civil courts. In each claim he could recover in respect of loss of earnings, although sums recovered in one claim will have to be accounted for in the other claim in order to prevent double recovery. An employee must choose his jurisdiction carefully. An employee with a breach of contract claim worth more than £25,000 cannot bring a claim in the tribunal for the first £25,000 and then claim in the courts for the balance of the same claim: *Fraser v HLMAD Ltd* [2006] EWCA Civ 738, [2006] IRLR 687 and see Chapter 8 at para 8.33.

A particularly difficult situation can arise where, for example, an employee has been subjected to **20.15** a course of harassment by his fellow employees, as a result of which he sustains personal injury. The claimant may have a claim of discrimination, if the harassment was on grounds which consti- tute unlawful discrimination, or he may have claims which can only be brought in the courts: for instance, for negligence, or under the Protection from Harassment Act 1997 (according to the House of Lords in *Majrowski v Guys and St Thomas' NHS Trust* [2006] UKHL 34, [2006] WLR 125, [2006] IRLR 695, the employer may be liable for harassment under the 1997 Act committed by an employee). One problem is that the employee will not necessarily know what the reason for the treatment is at the time he is deciding what claims to pursue.

Whichever proceedings are determined first, the decision in those proceedings will bind the court **20.16** or the tribunal in the later proceedings. A decision of the civil courts may give rise to an issue estoppel, or *res judicata* in tribunal proceedings, and vice versa (*Green v Hampshire County Council* [1979] ICR 861, Ch D; *Munir v Jang Publications Ltd* [1989] IRLR 224, [1989] ICR 1, CA). There are three relevant doctrines which are considered in more detail at paras 11.66–11.111:

(1) *Res judicata*, or cause of action estoppel: a final adjudication against a party on a particular cause of action will be conclusive in later proceedings involving the same parties and the same cause of action as to all points decided in the previous judgment.

(2) Issue estoppel: a judgment which includes a decision on a particular issue forming a necessary ingredient in the cause of action will be binding as to that particular issue if it arises in subsequent proceedings between the same parties or related parties where that issue is relevant, subject to narrow exceptions.

(3) Abuse of process: it may be an abuse of process to make a claim which could and should have been brought forward as part of earlier proceedings: *Henderson v Henderson* (1843) 3 Hare 100.

20.17 The practical problems in this area do not ordinarily arise from cause of action estoppel: the fact that there are two sets of proceedings tends to be because there are two separate causes of action. The problems arise either from issue estoppel, where an issue decided in the first proceedings binds the court in the second proceedings, or from the abuse identified in *Henderson*, where it is argued that the claim in the second set of proceedings should have been brought in the first proceedings.

20.18 In *Sheriff v Klyne Tugs (Lowestoft) Ltd* [1999] IRLR 481, the claimant's personal injury claim against his former employers was struck out in the county court. The Court of Appeal held that damages claimed could and should have been claimed in earlier race discrimination proceedings in the tribunal. Those proceedings had been withdrawn on settlement. The county court claim was held to be a *Henderson* abuse. In *Enfield LBC v Sivanandan* [2005] EWCA Civ 10, the Court of Appeal appeared similarly alert to prevent the claimant from having a second bite at the cherry by recasting a failed claim under a different cause of action in a different forum.

20.19 Given the risk of the claimant being bound by or restricted to the outcome of the claims he brings in his first set of proceedings, it is important to set a clear strategy at an early stage wherever there is the potential for overlapping claims. The following questions should be considered:

(a) What losses has the claimant suffered?

(b) What causes of action can be relied on to recover those losses?

(c) In what forum can those claims be pursued? Can all of the causes of action be sued upon in a single forum, or are two sets of proceedings inevitable?

(d) What are the merits of the various causes of action? Where do the real strengths of the case lie?

(e) What remedies will be available for the various claims?

(f) Which claims have the higher monetary value?

(g) Consider the availability of remedies: is this a case where an injunction or an account of profits may be sought?

(h) Consider interim remedies: is this a case where use may be made of the wider range of interim remedies in the courts (for example summary judgment)?

(i) What is the best strategy for the sequence in which the claims should be resolved? Consider the risks of a decision in one forum prejudicing the claim in the other, on the basis of *res judicata*, issue estoppel, or abuse of process.

(j) Are there limitation issues which will potentially interfere with the best sequence for resolution of the claims?

20.20 The best tactical approach in any case will depend on the particular circumstances of the case, and upon the priorities of the particular claimant.

20.21 Where two sets of proceedings are inevitable (for example, where a claimant has a claim for unfair dismissal and a high value wrongful dismissal claim), and assuming both claims have potential merit, it may be thought desirable to leave the High Court judge as unfettered as possible by findings of the tribunal.

Where there are to be two sets of proceedings the tribunal claim is likely to be heard well before **20.22** any civil claim. The limitation period for claims in the tribunal is much shorter; the civil court proceedings will have to be preceded by more extensive pre-action steps in order to avoid the risk of adverse costs orders; the procedural timetable in the courts is likely to be longer, although this depends on the claim (and the procedural steps to be taken). This problem can potentially be avoided by staying the tribunal claim pending resolution of the High Court claim. Stays of proceedings for this purpose are dealt with at paras 9.42–9.50.

D. PROCEEDINGS IN THE CIVIL COURTS

Introduction

The civil courts system

Civil claims may be brought in the High Court or the county court. The High Court of Justice **20.23** is based at the Royal Courts of Justice, The Strand, London WC2A 2LL. There are district registries of the High Court in the major cities of England and Wales. The High Court forms part of the Senior Courts of England and Wales (along with the Crown Court and the Court of Appeal). The Senior Courts Act 1981 (SCA 1981) deals with the High Court's powers and jurisdiction. The county courts are established by the County Courts Act 1984 (CCA 1984). County courts are arranged into districts, and most cities and large towns have a county court.

Procedure in the High Court and county courts is governed by the Civil Procedure Rules 1998 **20.24** (CPR). Most of the rules are supplemented by detailed practice directions. Some rules from the old regime which existed prior to the introduction of the CPR (Rules of the Supreme Court and County Court Rules 1981) still apply, and are to be found in appendices to the CPR.

For a detailed exposition of the CPR, a specialist text on civil procedure should be consulted; see, **20.25** for example, *Blackstone's Civil Practice*; the following is a brief outline.

Key distinctions between the civil courts and the tribunals

The following features of litigation in the civil courts mark it out from litigation in the tribunals: **20.26**

(a) There is a greater emphasis in the courts on pre-action steps to avoid litigation. In the tribunals there are measures to avoid unnecessary litigation including a mandatory conciliation period with ACAS and the overriding objective which seeks to encourage proportionate use of resources. However, the court system has a more formalized system of protocols governing steps to be taken to share information before proceedings are commenced.

(b) The normal position in civil proceedings is that the loser will pay the winner's legal costs. In the Employment Tribunal, the normal position is that no order is made as to costs and so each side bears their own costs.

(c) There are substantial court fees for the issue of proceedings and applications. In the Employment Tribunal, since 26 July 2017, no fees are payable by claimants for bringing claims.

(d) Civil proceedings offer a greater opportunity to determine a claim before trial, for example by summary judgment or strike-out.

(e) Most interim remedies, such as injunctions or orders for delivery up, are available only in the courts.

(f) Court procedure is more complex and more formal, both in terms of case management and at trial, and legal representation may be considered more appropriate.

(g) The rules of evidence apply to proceedings in the courts.

(h) The majority of cases are dealt with by a judge sitting alone, rather than by the tribunal's 'industrial jury', which is still used for discrimination claims.

(i) There is a wider range of final remedies in the civil courts, for example injunction, account of profits, restitutionary, and proprietary remedies. On the other hand, only the tribunal can make orders for reinstatement or re-engagement, or make protective awards.

(j) Lay representation is rarer in these courts than in the tribunals.

Pre-action steps

20.27 A number of features of the CPR are designed to assist and encourage settlement.

20.28 One key element is an encouragement to greater openness in communication between the parties at an earlier stage. Pre-action protocols set out procedures for the parties to identify their cases and share essential information before commencing proceedings, to promote the potential for settlement without litigation.

20.29 There are now several protocols dealing with disputes in a variety of common claims. Apart from the personal injury protocol, none are likely to impact directly on litigation in the employment field. However, the Protocol Practice Direction contains general guidance as to pre-action behaviour which covers both protocol and non-protocol cases (Protocol Practice Direction, para 4).

20.30 The court will expect the parties to act reasonably in exchanging information and documents relevant to the claim and generally in trying to avoid the necessity for the start of proceedings. A reasonable pre-action procedure should normally include:

(a) the claimant writing to give details of the claim
(b) the defendant acknowledging the claim letter promptly
(c) the defendant giving within a reasonable time a detailed written response and
(d) the parties conducting genuine and reasonable negotiations with a view to settling the claim economically and without court proceedings.

20.31 Paragraph 2 of Annex A of the Protocol Practice Direction sets out detailed guidance as to the contents of a claimant's letter before action. The letter should not only set out concisely the details of the proposed claim, but should enclose with it copies of the essential documents upon which the claimant relies. Similarly, the defendant's response should give detailed reasons why the claim is not accepted, and should enclose documents: both those sought by the claimant and the essential documents relied on by the defendant. For the full guidance, see Annex A Protocol Practice Direction, paras 3 and 4.

Commencement of proceedings

High Court or county court?

20.32 In addition to the SCA 1981 and the CCA 1984, the High Court and County Courts Jurisdiction Order 1991, SI 1991/724 deals with the jurisdiction of, and allocation of business between, the two courts.

20.33 Most employment-related claims fall within the jurisdiction of both the county court and the High Court. Section 15 of the CCA 1984 gives the county court general jurisdiction in relation to claims in contract and tort. Section 23 gives the county court jurisdiction over certain equitable claims (including partnership matters) up to a limit of £30,000. Where both the High Court and the county court have jurisdiction to hear a claim, the claim may be commenced in either court. A money claim in respect of which both courts have jurisdiction may only be commenced in the High Court if its value exceeds £25,000. A claim for damages for personal injuries may only be brought in the High Court if the value of the claim is £50,000 or more (1991 Order, Art 5).

20.34 Whilst the county court may grant injunctions, it should be noted that the county court does not have jurisdiction to grant freezing orders (other than in matrimonial proceedings) or search orders (CCA 1984, s 38 and the County Court Remedies Regulations 1991 (SI 1991/1222)).

20.35 On the other hand, as noted at para 20.09, certain claims under the discrimination legislation may only be brought in the county court.

In the High Court, most employment-related claims are suited for the Queen's Bench Division. If **20.36** a claim raises issues concerning confidential information or intellectual property rights, company law issues, or pension issues, the Chancery Division may be more appropriate.

Claim form and particulars of claim

There are two ways in which proceedings can be started in the civil courts: **20.37**

(a) by issuing a claim form (CPR, Part 7)
(b) by issuing a claim under the alternative procedure in CPR, Part 8.

The great majority of claims are commenced using the Part 7 claim form procedure. Part 8 claims **20.38** are appropriate where a decision is sought on a dispute which is unlikely to involve a substantial dispute of fact, or for certain types of proceedings where a rule or a practice direction requires or permits a Part 8 claim (see CPR, 8PD).

It will be appropriate to use the normal Part 7 claim form procedure for the majority of employ- **20.39** ment disputes which are likely to be litigated in the civil courts. Part 8 claims are not considered further in this chapter.

Tribunal awards may be enforced through the county court. The procedure for enforcement is in **20.40** CPR, Part 70, and is commenced by the issue of an application notice in form N322A.

There is a prescribed claim form, form N1. A claim form must be issued by the court office of the **20.41** court in which the proceedings are to be brought. A fee is payable on issue, the amount of which depends on the type and amount of the claim.

Once issued a claim form must be served on the defendant within four months (CPR, r 7.5), al- **20.42** though the court may grant an extension of time (CPR, r 7.6). An application for extension of time should be made before the time limit for service has expired. Although the court has the power to extend time after the expiry of the time limit, the grounds upon which it may do so are more limited (see CPR, r 7.6(3)). The application may be without notice, and must be supported by evidence (CPR, r 7.6(4)). The evidence should be in the form of a witness statement, and should explain all the circumstances relied on; the date of issue of the claim, the expiry date of any previous extension, and a full explanation of why the claim has not been served (CPR, 7APD, para 8). It is prudent also to explain the reason for the particular duration of the extension sought.

In a very simple case, the particulars of claim can be included in the space provided on the claim **20.43** form. In most cases the claim form should contain brief particulars of the nature of the claim and the full detail of the claim should be set out in the particulars of claim. Particulars of claim may be served with the claim form or within fourteen days of service of the claim form (but in any event no later than the last day for serving the claim form) (CPR, r 7.4).

Detailed provisions about service of the claim form are contained in CPR, Part 6, in particular at **20.44** rr 6.1–6.17.

Acknowledgement of service and defence

This is dealt with at CPR, Parts 9–11, 14, and 15. Once served with particulars of claim, a defendant **20.45** may file an admission (CPR, Part 14), an acknowledgement of service (CPR, Part 10), or a defence (CPR, Part 15). The time limit for doing so is fourteen days from service of the particulars of claim.

An acknowledgement of service is a short standard form (Form N9) in which a defendant indi- **20.46** cates that he has been served with the particulars of claim and that he intends to dispute the claim in whole or in part. If the defendant intends to contest the jurisdiction of the court, he should indicate this in the acknowledgement of service. In filing an acknowledgement, the defendant does not lose the right to contest the jurisdiction of the court (CPR, r 11.1(3)). The defendant must, however, make an application to dispute the jurisdiction within fourteen days of filing the acknowledgement.

Part B Procedure in Other Jurisdictions

20.47 The defence is the full response to the matters pleaded in the particulars of claim. A defence must be served within fourteen days of service of the particulars of claim, or, if an acknowledgement of service is filed, within twenty-eight days of the service of the particulars of claim (CPR, r 15.4). The parties may agree to extend time for filing a defence by up to twenty-eight days (CPR, r 15.5).

20.48 A claimant may respond to a defence in a reply. A reply is optional, as failure to file a reply is not taken as an implied admission of the defence. A reply may be appropriate if the claimant wishes to allege matters in response to the defence which were not included in the particulars of claim. See CPR, rr 15.8 and 16.7.

Default judgment

20.49 CPR, Parts 12 and 13 set out a detailed regime for judgment in default of filing a defence or acknowledgement of service, and for applying to set aside such default judgments.

20.50 Judgment in default of acknowledgement of service can be obtained where the defendant has failed to file an acknowledgement of service, and the time for doing so has expired (CPR, r 12.3(1)). Judgment in default of defence can be obtained where an acknowledgement of service has been filed, but the defendant fails to serve a defence within the time limit for doing so (CPR, r 12.3(2)). It should be noted that judgment in default is also available where a claimant fails to file a defence to counterclaim in the time provided for doing so (CPR, r 12.3(2)(b)). A default judgment may not be obtained if the defendant has made an application for a strike-out or summary judgment; or has made an admission of a claim for money but has requested time to pay (CPR, r 12.3(3)). There are some categories of case where judgment in default is not obtainable (CPR, r 12.2) but none is likely to arise in employment litigation.

20.51 There are two types of process for obtaining judgment in default. In a money claim, either for a specific sum or an amount to be assessed, judgment can be obtained by filing a request (CPR, r 12.4(1)). Judgment is then given as an administrative act. If the judgment is for a sum to be assessed the court will give directions for the assessment of damages (CPR, r 12.7). Where any other remedy is sought, for example, an injunction, judgment can only be obtained by application (CPR, r 12.4(2)). There are other categories of case where judgment can only be obtained on application which are set out at CPR, r 12.9 and r 12.10; of note are judgments for costs only (other than fixed costs) (r 12.9) and judgments where the proceedings have been served out of the jurisdiction without leave (r 12.10(b)). Where an application is made for judgment, the court will make such judgment as it appears to the court the claimant is entitled to on his statement of case (CPR, r 12.11(1)).

20.52 CPR, Part 13 deals with applications to set aside default judgments. The court must set aside judgment in default if the judgment was wrongly entered, either because the conditions in CPR, r 12.3(1), (2), or (3) were not satisfied, or if the whole claim was satisfied before the judgment was entered (CPR, r 13.1). So if the claim was not served, or if the time limit for service of a defence had not expired at the point of judgment, the judgment must be set aside. In any other case, the court has a discretion to set aside the judgment if the defendant has a real prospect of success, or it appears to the court there is some other good reason why judgment should be set aside or varied, or the defendant should be allowed to defend the claim. The test is the same as that for summary judgment.

Counterclaims

20.53 A defendant may counterclaim against a claimant. The procedure for counterclaims is set out in CPR, Part 20. In the employment tribunal, a respondent's entitlement to counterclaim is very limited. A counterclaim can only be brought where the claimant has brought a contract claim within the Employment Tribunals Extension of Jurisdiction (England and Wales) Order 1994 for certain defined types of contract claim. There are no such limits on counterclaims in the civil courts. A defendant may even, with permission of the court, bring a counterclaim against a person other than the claimant (CPR, r 20.5) (what used to be referred to as 'third party proceedings'). The court has the power to determine that a Part 20 claim should be heard separately to the main claim, and will take into account the connection between the main claim and the counterclaim, and where a third party is introduced, the connection between the relief sought, and the connection between the issues in the various claims (see CPR, r 20.9).

Statements of case generally

The particulars of claim, defence, defence and counterclaim, reply and defence to counterclaim **20.54** are all described as statements of case by the CPR. Prior to the CPR they were referred to as pleadings. General rules as to the form and content of statements of case are set out in CPR, Part 16. A statement of case must be verified by a statement of truth (CPR, r 22.1), in which the party states that he believes the facts stated in the statement of case are true. As an alternative, the party's solicitor may make a statement of truth, to the effect that the party believes the facts to be true. Rules as to the requirements for statements of truth are set out in CPR, Part 22 See also CPR, Parts 17 and 19 in relation to amendments to statement of case and addition of further parties.

Case management

Allocation and tracks

There are three tracks to which a claim may be allocated. The court will allocate the claim to the **20.55** appropriate track after taking into account a number of factors including the financial value of the claim, the complexity of the issues, the number of parties, the amount of oral and expert evidence, and the remedy sought. The general rule is as follows:

(a) Small claims track: claims not more than £10,000, or, personal injury cases not more than £1,000.
(b) Fast track: claims more than £10,000 but not more than £25,000; normally appropriate for trials expected to last not more than one day. For claims issued before 6 April 2009 the upper limit was £15,000.
(c) Multi-track: claims more than £25,000.

CPR, Part 26 contains detailed rules as to allocation. To assist the court in allocating a case an **20.56** allocation questionnaire is sent out to all parties once a defence is filed. A fee is payable by the claimant on filing of the allocation questionnaire, in all cases where the value of the claim is more than £1,000.

Small claims track

The small claims track is a streamlined procedure appropriate for dealing with claims of limited **20.57** financial value (CPR, Part 27). Standard directions are given; there are very rarely preliminary hearings. Expert evidence is not allowed without permission of the court, and the court may limit the evidence of witnesses and their cross-examination at the hearing. Hearings are conducted more informally than in trials on the other tracks, and the rules of evidence do not apply. The court need not take evidence on oath. Lay representatives are allowed. The recovery of costs is very limited: a party will normally recover only the fixed costs related to issuing the proceedings unless the other party has behaved unreasonably (CPR, r 27.14(2)).

Fast track

The fast-track procedure is contained in CPR, Part 28. The procedure is designed to provide a pro- **20.58** portionate way of dealing with claims which are more substantial than those on the small claims track, but are still of relatively limited value. Standard directions are normally given. Trial is limited to one day, and the management of the trial will be tightly timetabled. Whilst there is provision for disclosure and (if appropriate) expert evidence, these are kept within carefully controlled limits. Recovery of costs of trial is itself generally subject to limits (see CPR, Part 45).

Multi-track

20.59 The multi-track is the normal track for all cases where the small claims or fast track are not appropriate, due either to their value or complexity.

20.60 Case management of multi-track cases is dealt with in CPR, Part 29. Normally, a case management conference (CMC) will be listed before a master (or district judge in the county court) after the allocation questionnaires have been filed. At the CMC the master will consider the issues in the case and fix an appropriate timetable of directions to take the claim through to trial. Each claim has a designated master, appointed on issue, who will deal with all case management issues in the case (until close to trial when the trial judge may deal with certain case management issues). The parties may avoid the need for a CMC by submitting an appropriate set of agreed directions for approval by the master. Any applications the parties wish to make should be made, if possible, at the same time as the CMC, or in any event as soon as possible. A useful checklist of matters which may need to be dealt with at a CMC is contained in the pro forma order for case management directions in the multi-track, Queen's Bench Practice Form 52.

20.61 The court may order a pre-trial review, to be held close in time to the trial date, to ensure that the case is properly prepared and ready for trial.

Interim applications

20.62 A distinguishing feature of litigation in the courts from proceedings in the tribunal is the greater range of interim remedies that may be sought. In most employment-based civil litigation, one may encounter applications of two types:

(1) Applications which dispose of the proceedings, or of issues in proceedings, without trial: for example default judgment, strike-out, and summary judgment.

(2) Applications which give interim relief pending trial: for example injunctions, or delivery-up orders. Applications for interim injunctions are a primary area where the employment lawyer may become involved in High Court proceedings.

20.63 The general rules governing applications are found in CPR, Part 23 and its practice direction. These are to be read in conjunction with: CPR, Part 3.4, 3.5, and 3PD (Striking Out), CPR, Part 24 and 24PD (Summary Judgment), and CPR, Part 25 and 25PD (Interim Remedies and Security for Costs). See also the Queen's Bench Guide at 7.11 (Hearings), 7.12 (Applications), 7.13 (Interim Remedies), 9.5 (Interim Hearings List), and 9.7 (Listing before Interim Applications Judge); Chancery Guide, Chapter 5 (Applications).

Strike-out of statement of case

20.64 The court may strike out a statement of case on the following grounds: (CPR, r 3.4(2)):

(a) the statement of case discloses no reasonable grounds for bringing or defending the claim

(b) the statement of case is an abuse of process or is otherwise likely to obstruct the just disposal of the proceedings or

(c) there has been a failure to comply with a rule, practice direction, or court order.

20.65 In addition, CPR, r 3.4(2) does not limit the court's inherent jurisdiction to strike out a statement of case: CPR, r 3.4(5). The court retains an inherent power to strike out for any abuse of process which does not fall within r 3.4(2), for example, where a party's conduct puts the fairness of the trial in jeopardy.

20.66 There is therefore a distinction between grounds relating to the content of the claim or the defence (CPR, r 3.4(2)(a) and, in part, (b)), and the manner in which the claim has been conducted (CPR, r 3.4(2)(c) and, in part (b)) and the court's inherent jurisdiction.

Applications based on the content of the claim or the defence

In determining whether the respondent to the application has reasonable grounds for bringing **20.67** or defending the claim (CPR, r 3.4(2)(a)), the court will examine the party's case as formulated on its statement of case. For the purposes of the application, the facts as pleaded will be treated as true: the question is whether the claim or defence, taken at face value, has a reasonable prospect of success. Thus strike-out is appropriate where the statement of case is defective on its face; this may be because even on the assumed facts the party's position is wrong in law; or it may be because there are no facts, or incoherent facts relied on to support an essential ingredient of a cause of action. Where the claim or defence is not on its face bound to fail, but turns on questions of fact, then a strike-out under this rule is not appropriate. However, if the party's case on the issue of fact is sufficiently weak, an application for summary judgment may still be appropriate.

Even if a statement of case on its face has reasonable grounds to succeed, it may yet be an abuse **20.68** of process. The categories of abuse of process are not fixed or defined (*Ashmore v British Coal Corporation* [1990] ICR 485). The court has a good degree of latitude in determining what amounts to an abuse of process. The abuse may lie in the nature of the claim, for example, attempts to re-litigate matters which have been raised or should have been raised in earlier proceedings (see further paras 11.105–11.111); or conduct of proceedings inconsistent with proceedings in another forum. Alternatively, the abuse may lie in the pursuit of proceedings with an improper ulterior motive, or use of repeated proceedings to vex or harass the other side (see eg *Grovit v Doctor* [1997] 1 WLR 640).

A number of issues arising in employment litigation may come to be resolved on a strike-out appli- **20.69** cation. For example, a strike-out application may be the suitable forum to resolve issues concerning the scope of a contractual duty, or a common law duty of care. A strike-out application will also be the appropriate stage to raise issues such as *res judicata* and estoppel arising out of earlier tribunal claims, or to raise arguments that the claim has been compromised by a compromise agreement or ACAS settlement.

A statement of case should not be struck out if it raises serious issues of fact which can only be **20.70** properly determined by oral evidence at trial or if it is in an area of developing jurisprudence, since decisions as to novel points of law should be based on actual findings of fact.

There is an overlap between an application to strike out under CPR, r 3.4 and an application for **20.71** summary judgment under CPR, Part 24; an application can be brought relying on both rules in the alternative.

Applications based on the conduct of the parties

The conduct of the parties in the proceedings may result in a failure to comply with a rule, prac- **20.72** tice direction, or order, so as to fall within r 3.4(2)(c); or it may amount to an abuse of process under r 3.4(2)(b). An abuse of process in this case may entail conduct designed to prevent a fair trial, for example, forgery of documents (see, eg, *Arrow Nominees Inc v Blackledge* [2000] 2 BCLC 167).

Where the strike-out application is based on the conduct of the other party in the course of the **20.73** litigation, the court will have to consider whether strike-out is the appropriate sanction, or whether some lesser sanction is appropriate: for example, (indemnity) costs, payment into court, penalty in interest on the sum found to be due. See *Biguzzi v Rank Leisure plc* [1999] 1 WLR 1926. Both in cases of non-compliance with a rule or order, and in cases of abuse of process, the court should regard a strike-out as a last resort, and consider whether a lesser sanction is consistent with the overriding objective, and whether a fair trial can still take place.

In the majority of cases of failure to comply with a rule, practice direction, or order, the party in **20.74** default will apply for relief from sanction under CPR, r 3.9. The application must be supported by evidence. When deciding whether or not to grant relief from sanctions under CPR, r 3.9(1), the court will consider all the circumstances of the case so as to enable it to deal justly with the application, including the need for litigation to be conducted efficiently and at proportionate cost, and to enforce compliance with rules, practice directions, and orders. The wording set out was introduced in 2013, replacing a list of nine factors for the court to consider. The change in wording reflects a greater emphasis on strict case management in the civil courts, see *Mitchell v News Group Newspapers* [2013] EWCA Civ 1537, a recent example of the strict approach in action.

Procedure for application

20.75 An application to strike out is governed by the general principles in relation to interim applications, contained in CPR, Part 23. The application should be made on an application notice N244, setting out the grounds for the application and the order sought, and should be supported by a witness statement, which should be served with the application notice.

20.76 There are no specific rules relating to the timing of the application in CPR, r 3.4 (in contrast to the rules dealing with summary judgment in Part 24). Therefore, the general rules in CPR, Part 23 apply:

- The application should be made as soon as it becomes apparent that it is necessary or desirable to make it (23PD, para 2.7). Where the application is based on the statements of case, the application should be made soon after the service of the relevant statement of case.
- The application should be brought on at least three days' notice. However, for a contested application, the respondent will be likely to seek (and obtain) an extension of time in which to prepare and file evidence in response.

Summary judgment

20.77 CPR, Part 24 deals with summary judgment. This procedure, which is not available in the employment tribunal, is a powerful tool by which a party may obtain judgment, or defeat a claim against him by a court considering the case on the papers only, without the expense of a full trial.

20.78 Summary judgment may be obtained either against the claimant or the defendant. Summary judgment may be given in respect of the whole of a claim, part of a claim, or a particular issue on which the claim in whole or part depends (see CPR, r 24.1.2 and 24PD, para 1.2).

Grounds

20.79 The court may grant summary judgment if it considers (CPR, r 24.2) that:

(a) the claimant has no real prospect of succeeding on the claim or issue; or that the defendant has no real prospect of successfully defending the claim or issue and

(b) there is no other compelling reason why the case or issue should be disposed of at trial.

20.80 An application for summary judgment may be based on a point of law (including a question of construction of a document); the evidence which can reasonably be expected to be available at trial (or lack of it); or a combination of the two (CPR, 24PD, para 1.3).

Timing of application

20.81 A claimant may not apply until the defendant against whom the application is made has filed an acknowledgement of service or defence unless the court gives permission, or a practice direction provides otherwise (CPR, r 24.4(1)). If an application for summary judgment is made by a claimant before the defence is filed, the defendant need not file a defence before the hearing of the application (CPR, r 24.4(2)). In most cases in practice there is little point in a claimant making an application for summary judgment before a defence is filed. It is difficult to assess whether there is a real prospect in a defence succeeding before one knows what that defence is.

There is, however, no limitation on the time when a defendant can make an application for sum- **20.82** mary judgment. Whilst there is no express rule or practice direction governing how late in proceedings an application can be made, parties are encouraged to make applications before or upon filing allocation questionnaires. Certainly where the summary judgment application arises from matters known at the time this should be so, as a matter of efficient disposal of proceedings. However, where the applicant's view that summary judgment is appropriate is based on disclosure (or even the exchanged witness statements) the application could be made at a later stage.

Procedure for application

The procedure for an application for summary judgment is dealt with in CPR, rr 24.4 and 24.5, **20.83** and in 24PD, para 2. The general rules for interim applications in CPR, Part 23 are also relevant.

(a) The application should be made by notice on Practice Form N244 CPR, Part 24PD, para 2 sets out the following requirements for the application notice:
   (i) State that the application is brought under CPR, Part 24 for summary judgment.
   (ii) Identify the order that is sought, and upon what grounds. Either the application notice or the witness statement in support (see below) must identify the point of law or provision in a document upon which the applicant relies; and/or state that the applicant believes that on the evidence the respondent has no real prospect of succeeding on the claim or issue (or of defending the claim or issue); and that the applicant knows of no other reason why the disposal of the claim should await trial.
   (iii) Identify the written evidence upon which the applicant relies.
   (iv) Draw the respondent's attention to the provisions of CPR, r 24.5, which deals with filing of evidence by the respondent.
(b) The application should be supported by a witness statement. The witness statement should be served on the respondent with the application notice, and filed with the court (CPR, Part 23PD, para 9).
(c) A summary judgment application is normally heard before a master (or district judge in a district registry case). A master can direct that the application be heard by a judge (CPR, Part 24PD, para 3). If the applicant wishes to have the application heard before a judge, a direction to this effect should be sought in the application notice.
(d) The respondent must be given at least fourteen days' notice of the date fixed for the hearing and the issues which it is proposed the court will decide at the hearing (CPR, r 24.4(3)).
(e) A respondent must file and serve any evidence upon which he intends to rely at least seven days before the hearing. An applicant must file and serve any evidence in reply at least three days before the hearing (CPR, r 24.5).

The court's powers

The court may (CPR, Part 24PD, para 5) give judgment on the claim; strike out or dismiss the **20.84** claim; dismiss the application, permitting the claim to proceed to trial; make a conditional order, permitting the claim to proceed to trial on condition that a party pay money into court or take a specified step. The court is likely to consider a conditional order where there is a real, but improbable prospect of success (CPR Part 24PD, para 4).

Where the court dismisses the application, or makes an order which does not entirely dispose of **20.85** the claim, it will give case management directions at the hearing of the application (CPR, r 24.6).

The court's approach

The key question is whether there is sufficient in the impugned claim or defence to amount to a **20.86** real prospect of success at trial. Often this will involve an assessment of whether factual evidence is of sufficient merit to give a real prospect of success, or whether factual assertions can be shown to be unmeritorious even on paper. A real prospect of success means better than merely an arguable prospect, but does not require the respondent to show he will probably succeed. The term is meant to exclude false, fanciful, or imaginary claims/defences: *ED&F Man Liquid Products Ltd v Patel*

[2003] EWCA Civ 472; *Swain v Hillman* [2001] 1 All ER 91; *Three Rivers District Council v Bank of England (No 3)* [2001] 2 All ER 513, HL. The court will not conduct a mini-trial of disputed evidence on a summary judgment application, but will not be bound to accept all evidence on its face, no matter how lacking in credibility.

20.87 The court must consider also whether there is any other 'compelling reason' for a trial.

20.88 What constitutes a 'compelling reason' for trial, other than the potential merits of the case, is unclear. Examples include cases where a defendant needs to interrogate or cross-examine the claimant (*Harrison v Bottenheim* (1878) 26 WR 362); cases where the defendant has been unable to contact key witnesses, or needs disclosure of documents within the claimant's possession, although the court is astute not to allow cases to continue to trial on the basis that 'something may turn up' (see *Miles v Bull* [1969] 1 QB 258 and *Lady Ann Tennant v Associated Newspapers* (1979) FSR 298); or cases where the allegations are such that they demand resolution in a public trial. Although cases based on allegations of bad faith will normally need to be resolved at trial, there is no rule that this must be the case, and in some circumstances summary judgment based on allegations of bad faith may be appropriate: *Wrexham AFC Ltd v Crucialmove Ltd* [2006] EWCA Civ 237.

20.89 Where the application gives rise to a short point of law or construction, and if the court is satisfied that it has all the evidence necessary for a proper determination of the question and the parties have had an adequate opportunity to address it, the court should determine the point, rather than merely considering whether the point has a real prospect of success. Where a point of construction is said to turn on further documents or oral evidence, the court must consider whether the relevant facts, if established at trial, would have a bearing on the outcome: *ICI Chemicals & Polymers Ltd v TTE Training Ltd* [2007] EWCA Civ 725, paras 12–14.

20.90 The burden is on the applicant to show that the grounds for summary judgment are made out: see the *ED&F Man Liquid Products Ltd* case, cited above.

Tactical considerations

20.91 The tactical considerations under CPR, Part 24 involve a careful weighing of any disputed evidence and the relevance of that evidence to the merits of the case.

   (a) Does the claim turn on the law, or on disputed matters of fact?
   (b) Can the evidence relied on by the respondent be shown to be demonstrably false on paper?
   (c) Is the legal question upon which the case turns 'fact sensitive' or in a developing area of law?
   (d) Is there a real cost-benefit in making an application? How complex are the issues? What extra preparation will be required for trial? Would it be as cheap and efficient to pursue the matter to trial? Are there discrete issues that can be disposed of, leading to a saving in trial preparation?
   (e) Are there other advantages in making an application? For example, early sight of the other side's case; avoidance of exploration of issues orally at trial.

Interim injunctions

20.92 The employment tribunal does not have the power to grant injunctive relief. There are limited powers for a tribunal to order interim relief requiring an employer to continue to employ an employee where it is alleged that the dismissal has been for various prescribed reasons—notably trade union activities or public interest disclosure-related reasons (see ERA 1996, ss 128–32). Outside of these cases tribunals are not generally concerned with interim relief.

20.93 The civil courts have wide powers to grant interim relief pending trial: mandatory and prohibitory injunctions; orders for delivery up of property; search and seizure orders; orders for pre-action or early disclosure and inspection of documents.

20.94 Applications for injunctive relief will most commonly arise for employment practitioners in 'employee competition' disputes or those where the employee wishes the employer to comply with the contract in, for example, a disciplinary situation. In the former case, where an employee leaves, or threatens to leave, an employer to work in competition with the employer, there are a number of situations which may commonly give rise to the need for an injunction (either interim or final):

(a) The employee may have post-termination restrictive covenants in his contract of employment.

(b) The employee may threaten to work for a competitor during his notice period, prompting the employer to apply for 'a garden leave' injunction, whereby the employee is not permitted to work either for the employer or for a competitor for the duration of his notice period.

(c) The employee may threaten to misuse the employer's confidential information, prompting an application for an injunction to restrain misuse of confidential information, together with ancillary orders in support of such an order, eg delivery up of information, inspection of computers and electronic storage devices, destruction of electronic copies or hard copies of information.

(d) An employee may already have acted in breach of his obligations to the employer, and may be seeking to obtain further advantage, in a competing business, of an unlawful head start obtained by his breaches of duty; such a situation may warrant a 'springboard' injunction to deprive the wrongdoer of taking further advantage of his unlawful actions.

The substantive legal principles relating to such injunctions are addressed in Chapter 30. The following is a brief outline of the procedural principles applicable to injunction applications generally. Detailed consideration of interim injunctions, and in particular in the employment field, are outside the scope of this work, and specialist practitioner works should always be consulted. **20.95**

Section 37(1) of the SCA 1981 gives the High Court power to grant injunctions (whether interim or final) in all cases in which it appears to the court to be 'just and convenient' to do so. The equivalent provision in the county court is s 38 of the CCA 1984 (as amended by s 3 of the Courts and Legal Services Act 1990). County courts cannot grant freezing orders or search orders. CPR, Part 25 and its Practice Direction deal with interim remedies and security for costs. The range of interim remedies that the court may grant are set out at CPR, r 25.1(1). **20.96**

The general rules governing applications are found in CPR, Part 23 and its practice direction. See also the Queen's Bench Guide at 7.11 (Hearings), 7.12 (Applications), 7.13 (Interim Remedies), 9.5 (Interim Hearings List), and 9.7 (Listing before Interim Applications Judge); and the Chancery Guide, Chapter 5 (Applications). **20.97**

The grant of an injunction is a matter of discretion. In interim applications evidence is almost always by way of written statement without the court having the benefit of seeing the evidence tested by cross-examination. The court is required to 'hold the ring' as best it can. To obtain an interim injunction the claimant must give a cross-undertaking in damages so that in the event of the court at trial concluding that an injunction ought not to have been granted, the defendant can be compensated for any losses he has suffered by the grant of the injunction. The basic principles for grant of interim injunctions are set out in *American Cyanamid Co v Ethicon Ltd* [1975] AC 396, HL. **20.98**

(a) The claimant must show a good arguable claim: a 'serious issue to be tried' (*American Cyanamid Co v Ethicon Ltd* [1975] AC 396, 407 (Lord Diplock)) and that damages will not be an adequate remedy.

(b) Does the balance of convenience (the 'balance of the risk of doing an injustice'—see May LJ in *Cayne v Global Natural Resources* [1984] 1 All ER 225, 237) favour the grant or refusal of the injunction? Will more harm be done by the granting or refusal of an interim injunction? The court's aim at the interim stage is to take the course which runs the least risk of causing damage if it turns out to be wrong (in the sense that a different decision is reached at trial): *Films Rover International Ltd v Cannon Film Sales* [1987] 1 WLR 670, 680D–F (Hoffmann J).

(c) Where everything else is evenly balanced 'it is a counsel of prudence to take such measures as are calculated to preserve the status quo' said Lord Diplock in *Cyanamid*. For cases involving issues of the right to free speech (which may include, for example, cases concerning use of confidential information) see also *Cream Holdings v Banerjee* [2004] UKHL 44, [2004] 1 AC 253.

20.99   In the employment field, a claimant is likely to need to apply for an injunction to enforce such provisions on an urgent interim basis: modern restrictive covenants are seldom more than twelve months long, and notice periods (such as may be enforced by a garden leave injunction) are often shorter. Further, the interim battle is frequently decisive of the dispute as a whole; few cases in fact reach a speedy trial, as most are settled between the interim injunction application and the trial.

20.100 So far as 'ordinary' restrictive covenant cases are concerned the following principles can be distilled from *Lawrence David Ltd v Ashton* [1989] IRLR 22; *Lansing Linde v Kerr* [1991] IRLR 80; and *Arbuthnot v Rawlings* [2003] EWCA Civ 518:

(a)   If, without detailed examination of the factual background to the matter, it can be seen that the covenants relied upon plainly will not stand up or do not apply to restrict the employee from the activity in which he is engaged or proposes to be engaged, then that is an end of the matter and the court can, at an interim stage, dismiss the application for an injunction (*Arbuthnot*, at paras 20–30). Although the analysis of the particular covenant in *Arbuthnot* has been disapproved in *Safety Net Security Ltd v Coppage* [2013] EWCA Civ 1176, the general approach to assessing the validity of the covenant was not criticized.

(b)   If a speedy trial can be heard within the period of the restriction, then the court is unlikely to conduct a detailed examination of the strength of the respective cases of the parties; unless there is a compelling reason to do otherwise, then an interim injunction will ordinarily be granted and a speedy trial (with timetable) ordered.

(c)   In such a case, a defendant should give serious consideration to giving appropriate undertakings until the determination of a speedy trial, to avoid the need for an unnecessary interlocutory battle: *Lawrence David*, para 54.

(d)   If on the other hand a speedy trial cannot be heard within that period a more detailed examination of the strength of the respective cases may be required: *Lansing*, at paras 13–23; *Lawrence David*, at paras 50–1.

Application with or without notice

20.101 The general rule is that notice must be given of an application with a copy of the application notice being served on every defendant (CPR, r 23.4). Three clear days' notice is normally required of any application, although the court can abridge time under CPR, r 23.7(4) and/or r 3.1(2)(a). In an appropriate case, the court may hear an application and grant an interim injunction without notice (formerly known as '*ex parte*'). In cases of real urgency, applications can be made out of hours, and even by telephone. Applications without notice are only appropriate for cases of real urgency where there has been a true impossibility of giving notice; or cases where it is essential to maintain secrecy. Where possible (except in cases where secrecy is essential), short informal notice should be given: CPR, Part 25PD, para 4.3(3).

20.102 It is the duty of the claimant and legal advisers on a without notice application to ensure that full and frank disclosure is made of all relevant matters. CPR, Part 25PD, para 3.3 provides that the claimant's evidence must include 'all material facts of which the court should be aware'. This includes adverse evidence and extends to a duty to make reasonable investigation.

20.103 Where an application is made without notice, any order will normally be made for a short period of time only, over to a 'return date' on which the court considers, with notice to all parties, whether the relief granted without notice should be continued.

Documents in support of the application

20.104 When making an application for interim relief, the applicant will need an application notice; a draft order; one or more witness statements setting out the evidence supporting the application (an affidavit is necessary if a search order is being sought); a claim form and, if there is time, particulars of claim; and a skeleton argument. In urgent cases an order can be granted before issue of the claim form, provided an undertaking is given to issue and serve the claim form as soon as reasonably practicable after the injunction hearing.

Disclosure

20.105 CPR, Part 31 distinguishes between two types of disclosure: standard disclosure (CPR, r 31.6) and specific disclosure (CPR, r 31.12). An order for disclosure will be an order for standard disclosure unless the court directs otherwise (CPR, r 31.5). Once standard disclosure has been given, the parties may need to consider whether any application for specific disclosure is required. In multitrack claims other than those which include a claim for personal injury, r 31.5(3) to (8) set out a specific process for agreeing disclosure. The parties are required to serve a disclosure report not less than fourteen days before the first CMC; not less than seven days before the first CMC the parties are required to seek to agree a proposal in relation to disclosure; the court may approve the proposal or may make directions addressing disclosure. The range of orders is set out in CPR, r 31.5(7) and r 31.5(8) and includes disclosure by issue, disclosure of documents on which reliance is placed, standard disclosure, or an order dispensing with disclosure. In most cases it is anticipated that standard disclosure will be ordered, perhaps on a staged basis if there is a discrete preliminary issue.

20.106 The rules also distinguish between disclosure and inspection. Disclosure requires a statement that a document exists, conventionally by reference to it on a disclosure list. In most cases, a party has a right to inspect a document disclosed to him, but there are circumstances in which inspection may be withheld: because the document is no longer in the disclosing party's possession; because there is a right to withhold disclosure (most commonly on grounds of privilege); or because inspection would be disproportionate (CPR, r 31.2). Whilst in the employment tribunal disclosure and inspection are often elided, in court proceedings directions normally provide for inspection to follow a number of days after disclosure by list.

20.107 The principles applicable to disclosure, and in particular the right to withhold inspection, are relevant in the employment tribunal and are dealt with in Chapter 6, and are not repeated in detail here.

Standard disclosure

20.108 Standard disclosure (CPR, r 31.6) is disclosure of:

- the documents on which the party relies and
- the documents which adversely affect the party's, or another party's case or support another party's case and
- the documents required to be disclosed under a relevant practice direction.

20.109 The duty of disclosure (standard or specific) relates to documents in the party's control; these are documents that: are or were in the party's physical possession; of which he has a right to possession; or of which he has or has had a right to inspect or take copies (CPR, r 31.8).

20.110 The duty to search for documents when giving standard disclosure is limited by reasonableness (CPR, r 31.7). The factors relevant in deciding the reasonableness of a search include: the number of documents involved; the nature and complexity of the proceedings; the ease and expense of retrieval of any particular document; the significance of any document which is likely to be located in the search.

20.111 The manner in which standard disclosure is to be carried out is set out in CPR, r 31.10. A party's disclosure list must be supported by a disclosure statement, unless the parties agree or the court directs otherwise. The appropriate form of disclosure statement is set out in CPR, Part 31PD.

Specific disclosure

20.112 Specific disclosure and inspection (CPR, r 31.12) can be ordered in respect of documents or classes of document specified in the order. The court may require a party to carry out a search to the extent stipulated in an order and to disclose any documents located as a result of that search.

Part B Procedure in Other Jurisdictions

20.113 An application may be made by a party if the disclosure of documents is 'inadequate' (CPR, r 31.12). In reaching its decision, the court will take into account all of the circumstances of the case and the overriding objective. If the court concludes that the party from whom specific disclosure is sought has failed to comply with the obligations imposed by an order for disclosure, including by failing to make a sufficient search, the court will make such order as is necessary to ensure that the obligations are complied with.

Pre-action disclosure

20.114 The court has the power, under CPR, r 31.16, to order disclosure prior to the commencement of proceedings in the following circumstances:

- the respondent is likely to become a party to proceedings
- the applicant is also likely to be a party to those proceedings
- if proceedings had started, the respondent's duty by way of standard disclosure, set out in CPR, r 31.6, would extend to the documents or classes of document of which disclosure is sought and
- disclosure before proceedings have started is desirable in order to:
  - dispose fairly of the anticipated proceedings
  - assist the dispute to be resolved without proceedings; or
  - save costs.

20.115 It is not necessary to show a likelihood that proceedings will be commenced, only that if proceedings are commenced, the applicant and respondent may well be parties to them: *Black v Sumitomo Corp* [2001] EWCA Civ 1819, [2001] 1 WLR 1562. The court only has jurisdiction to make an order if there is a real prospect of an order being fair to the parties if proceedings are commenced, or assisting resolution of the dispute without proceedings, or saving costs. Once the jurisdictional threshold is satisfied, the court has a discretion whether to make an order (and if so what order to make) to be exercised in the light of all the circumstances: see *Black*, para 81. In determining the application, the court need only take a broad view of the merits of the case, and need not investigate legally complex issues: *Total v Edmonds* [2007] EWCA Civ 50.

Third party disclosure

20.116 The court may make an order for disclosure against a person who is not a party to the proceedings under CPR, r 31.17 where:

- the documents of which disclosure is sought are likely to support the case of the applicant or adversely affect the case of one of the other parties to the proceedings and
- disclosure is necessary in order to dispose fairly of the claim or to save costs.

20.117 An order under this rule must specify the documents or the classes of documents which the respondent must disclose, and require the respondent, when making disclosure, to specify any of those documents which are no longer in his control, or in respect of which he claims a right or duty to withhold inspection. Such an order may require the respondent to indicate what has happened to any documents which are no longer in his control; and specify the time and place for disclosure and inspection.

20.118 The court's power to order disclosure against a non-party is not limited to the power under CPR, r 31.17: see CPR, r 31.18.

20.119 Disclosure may also be obtained against a non-party by obtaining a witness summons under CPR, r 34.2 requiring the witness to attend court to produce documents to the court, either on the date fixed for a hearing or on such date as the court may direct. Under the provisions in CPR, r 34.3(2), a party must obtain permission from the court where he wishes to have a summons issued for a witness to attend a hearing or produce documents on any date except the date fixed for the trial.

20.120 Further, the court has the power to order disclosure against a non-party for the purposes of disclosing the identity of a wrongdoer: a 'Norwich Pharmacal order': see *Norwich Pharmacal v*

Customs & Excise Commissioners [1974] AC 133. The *Norwich Pharmacal* jurisdiction is an exceptional one and one which is only exercised by the courts with caution, not least because the order may engage the respondent's right to privacy under Art 8 of ECHR.

Evidence and witnesses

Rules concerning evidence and witnesses are in CPR, Parts 32–4. Expert evidence is dealt with in CPR, Part 35. The general principles, insofar as they are relevant to tribunal claims, have been touched on in Chapter 6 dealing with case management, and in relation to witnesses in Chapter 9, dealing with the hearing. Reference should be made to specialist works on civil procedure for the detailed principles as applied in the civil courts. **20.121**

A notable distinction between the tribunal and the civil courts is that the strict rules of evidence apply in the civil courts. The rules of evidence are a mixture of substantive and procedural law. CPR, Parts 32–34 deal with procedural issues in relation to evidence. **20.122**

Trial

CPR, Part 39 states the rules applicable to trials and other hearings. Hearings are normally held in public, unless the hearing falls within one of the categories in CPR, r 39.2, which are similar to the cases in which private hearings may be held in the tribunal. **20.123**

A trial in the civil courts will normally be conducted by a judge sitting alone. There are categories of civil trial which may be heard by judge and jury (for example, defamation, false imprisonment) but these are unlikely to arise in the employment context. In discrimination cases heard in the county court the judge must sit with expert assessors unless there are good reasons for not doing so (EqA 2010, s 114(7) and s 114(8)). As to the role of assessors, see *Ahmed v Governing Body of the University of Oxford* [2002] EWCA Civ 1907, [2003] 1 WLR 995. **20.124**

Generally, a trial will be listed in a trial window, that is a period of days or weeks during which the case may come on for trial, rather than having a fixed date. Parties can apply for a fixture in an appropriate case. **20.125**

Rights of audience in the High Court and county court are limited: see Access to Justice Act 1999, Part III and Courts and Legal Services Act 1990, Part II. Barristers and solicitors with appropriate rights of audience may appear in the courts. Fellows of the Institute of Legal Executives engaged in particular types of work may appear in certain hearings in the county court (County Courts (Right of Audience) Direction 1978). Lay representation is not widely permitted. The Lay Representatives (Rights of Audience) Order 1999, SI 1999/1225 enables lay representatives to appear in cases on the small claims track, but not in other cases. It used to be the case that, under the Courts and Legal Services Act 1990, s 27, the court retained a power to permit a lay representative rights of audience in exceptional cases. However, this was repealed by the Legal Services Act 2007, Sch 21, para 84, which came into force on 1 January 2010. A litigant may appear in person. In the case of a company which is party to proceedings, it may appear by a director or employee pursuant to CPR, r 39.6. **20.126**

The conduct of trials is more formal in the civil courts than the conduct of hearings in the tribunal. Unless the judge directs otherwise, legal representatives are robed (although increasingly this formality is dispensed with in county courts). Strict court procedure as to the order of speeches and evidence is adopted. The strict rules of evidence apply, as indicated above. There is a requirement on the parties to have filed and exchanged bundles and skeleton arguments prior to trial. Whilst opening speeches may be made, in modern practice the judge will normally have read the skeletons, statements of case, and key documents prior to trial, and therefore in many cases the opening may be quite short. The witness statements stand as evidence in chief and are taken as read. Very limited additional examination in chief will be permitted. **20.127**

Costs

20.128 The treatment of costs marks a great difference between proceedings in the employment tribunal and proceedings in the civil courts. Whereas in the tribunal costs orders remain the exception rather than the rule (see ETR 2013, rr 74–84, considered in Chapter 12), in the civil courts, the court has a wide discretion as to costs, and traditionally the normal rule has been that costs follow the event, that is, the loser pays the winner's costs.

20.129 The main provisions relating to costs are set out in CPR, Parts 44–47, together with their associated practice directions. Part 44 deals with general provisions in relation to costs. Part 45 concerns fixed costs and fast-track costs. Part 46 addresses costs in special cases. The following commentary concerns cases proceeding on the multi-track.

20.130 Following the Jackson report significant changes were made to the CPR to encourage tighter management of costs and, in appropriate cases, the use of costs budgets. Costs budgets apply in multi-track cases and must be produced on a standard form (Precedent H). Costs budgets are required before the first CMC and may be ordered at any stage in proceedings (CPR, r 3.13). Judges may approve or limit the costs budget (CPR, rr 3.15, 3.19, and 3.20) and may take the last approved budget into account when considering orders for costs at the end of proceedings (CPR, r 3.18).

General principles

20.131 By CPR, r 44.2 the court has a discretion as to whether costs are payable by one party to another; the amount of those costs; when they are to be paid; and whether costs are to be paid on a standard or indemnity basis.

20.132 The general rule is that the unsuccessful party will be ordered to pay the costs of the successful party, but the court is entitled to make a different order. When exercising that discretion, the court must have regard to all of the circumstances and in particular:

(a) The conduct of all of the parties. CPR, r 44.2(5) sets out some detailed aspects of conduct to be taken into consideration.

(b) Whether a party has succeeded on part of his case.

(c) Any payment into court or other admissible offer to settle made by a party which is drawn to the court's attention (whether or not it is an offer in accordance with Part 36).

20.133 Under CPR, r 44.2(6), the court has considerable margin of discretion to award a party part only of his costs, in order to do justice. The court may, for example, make an order that the winning party recovers a percentage of his total costs, or costs in respect of a particular period, or the costs of a distinct part of the proceedings.

Costs and ADR

20.134 One aspect of the parties' conduct which has become increasingly important in recent years is the attempt each party has made to resolve their dispute without recourse to the courts (CPR, r 44.4(3)), and in particular the parties' approach to alternative dispute resolution (ADR; see further Chapter 5). A refusal on the part of one party to take part in ADR can affect an award of costs under CPR, r 44.2(4)(a) since that party may be found to have conducted themselves unreasonably, see *Halsey v Milton Keynes NHS Trust* [2004] 1 WLR 3002. One of the key features of the CPR has been its encouragement of ADR methods, and the imposition of sanctions in costs has been one of the main tools by which the courts have given such encouragement.

Part 36 offers

20.135 An offer to settle made in accordance with the provisions of CPR, Part 36 is referred to as a Part 36 offer.

20.136 Part 36 contains detailed provisions for the form and timing of Part 36 offers, and for the timing of acceptance. The rules repay detailed consideration. The acceptance or non-acceptance of a valid Part 36 offer can have important costs consequences. The following outlines the key provisions.

A Part 36 offer must be in writing. It must (CPR, r 36.2): **20.137**

- state that it is intended to have the consequences of Part 36
- specify a period of not less than twenty-one days within which the offeror will be liable for the offeree's costs if the offer is accepted
- state whether it relates to the whole of the claim or part of it
- state whether it takes into account any counterclaim.

An offer by a defendant to pay a sum of money should be a single sum of money, and should be **20.138**
to pay the money within fourteen days following the date of acceptance. If an offer is not in such terms, and the offer is not accepted the offer will not be treated as a Part 36 offer. However, if the offer is accepted, the normal costs consequences of acceptance of a Part 36 offer will apply (CPR, r 36.4).

A Part 36 offer may be made at any time, including prior to the commencement of proceed- **20.139**
ings. It may be made at any time up to the end of the trial itself, although the costs consequences of an offer made less than twenty-one days before trial differ from those applicable in the normal case.

The Part 36 procedure relies on the concept of the 'relevant period' in the rules applicable to **20.140**
acceptance, withdrawal, and the costs consequences of any offer. This term is defined in CPR, r 36.2(1)(c). Where an offer is made not less than twenty-one days before trial, the relevant period is the period stated in the offer, or such other period agreed between the parties. Where an offer is made less than twenty-one days before trial, the relevant period is the period up to the end of the trial, or such other period as the court has determined.

Party accepts Part 36 offer

Pursuant to CPR, r 36.10 where a claimant accepts a Part 36 offer within the relevant period he **20.141**
will be entitled to his costs of the proceedings up to the date of service of notice of acceptance of the offer (CPR, r 36.10).

The court's permission is required to accept a Part 36 offer after commencement of the trial (CPR, **20.142**
r 36.9(3)).

Where a Part 36 offer is accepted after the expiry of the relevant period, or where an offer made **20.143**
less than twenty-one days before trial is accepted, the court will make an order for costs. Whilst the court has a discretion as to the appropriate order, the 'starting point' is that the offeree will be entitled to his costs up to the expiry of the relevant period, and the offeree will be liable for the offeror's costs between that date and the date of acceptance (CPR, r 36.10(5)).

On acceptance of a Part 36 offer, the proceedings are stayed, save for enforcement of the offer and **20.144**
costs (CPR, r 36.11). Where the offer included an offer to pay a single sum of money, the sum must be paid within fourteen days of acceptance (CPR, r 36.11(6)). If the sum is not paid in time, the offeree may enter judgment (CPR, r 36.11(7)).

Claimant refuses defendant's offer, and fails to beat it at trial

Where a claimant fails to beat a Part 36 offer at trial then, unless it considers it unjust to do so, **20.145**
the court will order the claimant to pay the defendant's costs from the date on which the relevant period expired, together with interest on those costs (CPR, r 36.14(2)).

In considering whether it would be unjust to make such orders, the court shall consider all the **20.146**
circumstances, including:

- the terms of any Part 36 offer
- the stage in the proceedings when the Part 36 offer was made
- the information available to the parties when the Part 36 offer was made
- the conduct of the parties with regard to giving or refusing to give information for the purposes of evaluating the offer.

Defendant fails to beat claimant's Part 36 offer at trial

20.147 Where judgment against a defendant is at least as advantageous to the claimant as the proposals in the claimant's Part 36 offer, the court may 'punish' the defendant by (CPR, r 36.14(3)):

(a) awarding interest on the whole or part of any sum of money awarded to the claimant at a rate not exceeding 10 per cent above the base rate for some or all of the period starting with the date when the relevant period expired and

(b) the court may also order that the claimant is entitled to costs on an indemnity basis from the date on which the relevant period expired and

(c) interest on those costs at a rate not exceeding 10 per cent above the base rate.

20.148 In determining whether it would be unjust to make any of the orders referred to in the previous paragraph, the same factors apply as referred to in para 20.146.

Costs against non-parties

20.149 Costs may be awarded in favour of, or against, a non-party to the proceedings as part of the general discretion to award costs under s 51 of the SCA 1981. CPR, r 46.2 states that if this discretion is to be exercised, then the individual must be added as a party to the proceedings and the individual must be given a reasonable opportunity to attend the hearing; see *Symphony Group plc v Hodgson* [1993] 4 All ER 143, CA.

Wasted costs orders

20.150 CPR, r 46.8 permits the court to make a wasted costs order against a party's legal representative; see as to employment tribunals Chapter 12. The test was set out by the Court of Appeal in *Ridehalgh v Horsefield* [1994] Ch 205. An order may be made if:

(a) the representative, of whom the complaint has been made, has acted improperly, unreasonably, or negligently

(b) such conduct has caused the applicant to incur unnecessary costs

(c) in all the circumstances it is just to order the legal representative to compensate the applicant for the whole or part of the relevant costs.

Assessment of costs

Standard or indemnity basis

20.151 The court can assess the amount of costs under CPR, r 44.3 on either a standard basis or an indemnity basis:

(a) Where costs are assessed on the standard basis, the court will allow costs which are proportionate to the matters in issue but any doubt as to whether the costs were reasonably incurred or are reasonable and proportionate in amount will be resolved in favour of the paying party.

(b) In contrast, where costs are assessed on the indemnity basis, the court will resolve any doubt as to whether costs were reasonably incurred or were reasonable in amount in favour of the receiving party.

Summary or detailed assessment

20.152 The court may assess costs either by summary assessment or detailed assessment (CPR, r 44.6). The terms are defined in CPR, rr 44.1.

(a) A summary assessment will be carried out by the judge who heard the trial or application and made the costs order, normally at the end of the trial or application. The assessment will be based on a summary statement of costs following form N260. The procedure for summary assessment is set out in CPR, PD44, paras 8 and 9.

(b) A detailed assessment will be carried out by a costs judge, on the basis of a detailed bill of costs. Detailed assessment is a whole contentious procedure in itself. The procedure to be followed on a detailed assessment is set out in CPR, Part 47.

The factors relevant to the decision whether to order summary or detailed assessment are set out in paras 8 and 9 of CPR, 44PD. As a general rule, the court should summarily assess costs at the end of a fast-track trial and at the end of any hearing (trial or application) which has lasted not more than one day. Where a detailed assessment is ordered, a payment on account of costs can be made prior to assessment pursuant to CPR, r 44.2(8). **20.153**

Security for costs

A defendant may apply for security for costs pursuant to CPR, r 25.12. An order for security for costs requires the party against whom it is made to pay an amount into court in respect of the other party's costs as a condition of proceeding with the claim. The court has a discretion to make such an order if it believes it to be just to do so in all the circumstances in certain specific situations set out in CPR, r 25.12. The most common circumstances are cases where the claimant is outside the jurisdiction and not resident in a state covered by the EU Judgments Regulation, or the claimant is a company or other body and there is reason to believe that it will be unable to pay the defendant's costs if ordered to do so. **20.154**

CHECKLIST OF STEPS UP TO COMPLETION OF STATEMENTS OF CASE

- Claimant's pre-action letter: the letter should give a reasonable period for response, for many claims one month may be reasonable (Practice Direction Pre-Action Conduct para 7.2).
- Defendant's acknowledgement of claimant's pre-action letter: within fourteen days of receipt (Practice Direction Pre-Action Conduct para 7.2). The acknowledgement should state when the defendant will give a full response. If the period is longer than that suggested by the claimant, the defendant should give reasons.
- Defendant's full response to pre-action letter: within the period stated by the claimant, or otherwise within a reasonable period.
- Issue of claim form: CPR, r 7.2.
- Service of claim form: within four months of the date of issue (six months where the claim form is to be served out of the jurisdiction (CPR, r 7.5)), subject to extension by order of the court (CPR, r 7.6).
- Particulars of claim: if not served with claim form, to be served within fourteen days of service of claim form (CPR, r 7.4(1)). Must be served no later than the latest date for serving the claim form (CPR, r 7.4(2)).
- Defendant's Acknowledgement of Service: to be filed within fourteen days after the service of the claim form, or fourteen days after service of the Particulars of Claim (where the Particulars of Claim are served subsequently) (CPR, r 10.3(1)). Special rules apply where the claim form is served out of the jurisdiction (CPR, r 10.3(2)).
- Defendant's application to dispute jurisdiction: must be made within fourteen days after filing an Acknowledgement of Service (CPR, r 11(4)).
- Defence: to be filed and served by fourteen days after service of the Particulars of Claim, or within twenty-eight days, if the defendant has filed an acknowledgement of service (CPR, r 15.4(1)). A defendant need not file a defence if he disputes the court's jurisdiction (CPR, r 11).
- Counterclaim: to be filed and served with the defence, or at any other time with permission of the court (CPR, r 20.4).

- Allocation questionnaire: to be served by the court on each party when a defence is filed (CPR, r 26.3(1)).
- Completed allocation questionnaires: to be filed by each party on the date specified in the questionnaire, which must be at least fourteen days after the deemed date of service (CPR, r 26.3(6)).
- Reply: to be filed and served when the claimant files his allocation questionnaire (CPR, r 15.8).
- Defence to counterclaim: to be filed and served by fourteen days after service of the counterclaim (CPR, r 15.4). However, the court will normally order that the defence to counterclaim must be filed by the same date as any reply (15PD, para 3.2A).

CHECKLIST OF MATTERS FOR CONSIDERATION AT CMC

- Allocation to a track (if this has not already been done).
- Transfer: is the case in the appropriate court or division?
- Alternative dispute resolution: one standard direction on the PF 52 form is a stay for ADR at an early stage of case management. The parties should consider whether this is appropriate, and if so, at what stage of the proceedings.
- Addition of parties.
- Consolidation with other cases: this involves consideration of Part 20 claims brought by the defendant, and unrelated claims, for example, claims brought by other claimants against the same defendant raising similar issues or evidence.
- Amendments to the statements of case, and/or provision of further information.
- Interim applications/trial of preliminary issues: are any such hearings appropriate? If so, they should be listed and a timetable of directions for those applications provided for.
- Disclosure.
- Witness statements.
- Expert evidence: the parties should be prepared to discuss the discipline(s) in which expert evidence is necessary, whether a joint expert is appropriate, the formulation of instructions, facilities for disclosure and examination, the date for service of reports, the mechanism for experts to attempt to agree or narrow the issues.
- Listing for trial: this will require consideration of the length of trial, the window in which it is to be listed, and its categorization as A, B, or C (in descending order of seriousness and complexity).
- Pre-trial review: this permits the court to ensure that the case will be ready for trial, but in many cases is now dispensed with.
- Preparation for trial: agreed lists of issues, bundles, skeleton arguments, agreed trial timetable.
- Settlement: the parties should notify the court immediately on settlement.
- Costs budgets.
- Costs of the CMC: the usual order is costs in the case.

21

Court of Appeal

SUMMARY

(1) An appeal to the Court of Appeal may only be made with the permission of the EAT or the Court of Appeal.

(2) In employment cases the Court of Appeal is a second-tier appeal.

A. GENERAL PRINCIPLES

An application for permission to appeal to the Court of Appeal must be made, unless the EAT **21.01** orders otherwise, at the hearing or when a reserved judgment is handed down or in writing within seven days thereafter as provided in EAT PD 21.5 (EAT PD, para 25.1). If this is not done, or an application is refused, any later application must be made to the Court of Appeal within twenty-one days of the date of the EAT's sealed order. The Court of Appeal may well want an explanation as to why it was not done earlier (*Balmoral Group v Borealis (UK) Ltd* [2006] EWHC 2228).

Appeal to the Court of Appeal may only be made with the permission of the EAT or the Court **21.02** of Appeal (ETA 1996, s 37(1), (2)). The rules are set out in CPR, r 52 supplemented by CPR, 52PD. In June 2016, the Civil Procedure Rules Committee undertook a consultation into proposed changes to Part 52 and CPR, 52PD. At the time of writing the response to the consultation is not known. What follows is a summary of the unamended rules and Practice Direction. The key points are as follows:

(1) permission will be given only if the EAT or the Court of Appeal decides that the appeal:
   (a) would have a real prospect of success or
   (b) there is some other compelling reason why the appeal should be heard (CPR, r 52.3(6)). 'Real prospect of success' means realistic and not fanciful (*Tanfern Ltd v Cameron MacDonald* [2000] 1 WLR 1311).
(2) An application is first made orally to the EAT and preferably on the day the appeal is heard or when judgment is given if later. It is not essential to do this before seeking permission to appeal from the Court of Appeal but it is advisable to do so. The Court of Appeal must take into account the overriding objective, which includes the need for the court to ensure that an appropriate share of the court's resources is allotted to a case, while taking into account the need to allot resources to other cases. This means dealing with cases justly and at proportionate cost (CPR, r 1.2).

(3) If the application is refused, an application may be made direct to the Court of Appeal (CPR, r 52.3(2)). This should be made within fourteen days of the date of the sealed order of the EAT.

(4) The Court of Appeal usually considers the application first without a hearing (CPR, 52BPD.8, para 7.1).

(5) If permission is refused without a hearing, a request may be made for reconsideration of that refusal at an oral hearing (CPR, 52BPD.8, para 7.2); this must be requested within seven days after service of the notice that permission has been refused (CPR, 52PDB.8 para 7.4).

(6) Service of the notice of appeal must be made on the respondents as soon as practicable, and no later than seven days after it is filed.

(7) A notice of appeal must be accompanied by a skeleton argument or if this is not possible within this period, this has to be done within fourteen days of filing the notice of appeal (CPR, 52CPD3 para 3(3)(g)11, para 5.9(2)).

(8) The respondent's skeleton argument must be served no later than fourteen days after the respondent receives the appellant's skeleton argument, although the court may make different directions in a particular case (CPR, 52PD.9, para 9).

(9) The parties may not agree between themselves to any extension of the time stated, but the Court of Appeal itself may vary any part of this timetable (CPR, r 52.6).

(10) The refusal by the Court of Appeal to give permission to appeal is not itself appealable.

B. SPECIAL FEATURES ABOUT EMPLOYMENT APPEALS

21.03 There are certain features of employment litigation in the Court of Appeal which are different from general cases in other areas. These are set out below.

Second-tier appeal

21.04 One of the primary issues where practice in employment law is different from the norm is that in employment cases the Court of Appeal is a second-tier appeal, the matter having already been heard by the employment tribunal and EAT. The Court of Appeal is 'primarily concerned to review the proceedings in and the decision of the ET in order to determine whether a question of law arises from them', according to Mummery LJ in *Yeboah v Crofton* [2002] IRLR 634, para 12; see also *Hennessy v Craigmyle & Co Ltd and ACAS* [1986] ICR 461, 470; *Campion v Hamworthy Engineering Ltd* [1987] ICR 966, 972; *Vento v Chief Constable of West Yorkshire Police* [2003] ICR 318 at para 25; and *Lambe v 186K Ltd* [2005] ICR 307 at para 80. This means that if the decision of the ET is correct in law the Court of Appeal will not allow the appeal because the EAT erred in its analysis in between.

21.05 This has always been applied with some flexibility since there may be fresh arguments or fresh evidence at the EAT.

21.06 In *Gover v Propertycare Limited* [2006] EWCA Civ 286, [2006] ICR 1073, para 9; however, Buxton LJ expressed 'some reserve' about the guidance in previous cases. He thought there was in no realistic sense an appeal from the employment appeal tribunal on a point of law, as the ETA 1996, s 37(1) expressly provided, if the Court of Appeal was only concerned with whether the tribunal was right. He said further: 'As to the business of this court, the assumption that we in effect repeat the exercise already performed by the expert appeal tribunal, of reviewing the decision of the employment tribunal, tends in practice to impose on this court an exercise that is inappropriate both in its nature and in its extent.' The argument in *Gover* was not full on this point, which was not raised during the hearing.

21.07 Without reference to *Gover*, Sir Peter Gibson in *Balfour Beatty v Wilcox* [2007] IRLR 63 soon afterwards, reiterated the *Hennessy* approach and stressed that the fact that the EAT had 'erred in its reasoning will not necessarily be conclusive as to the outcome of the appeal'. This was not to suggest, however, that the judgment of the EAT must be ignored (para 71). Buxton LJ, however, expressed views similar to those he had expressed in *Gover* and set out above.

The Court of Appeal will only rarely remit a case to the EAT for further consideration (*Lambe v* **21.08**
186K Ltd [2005] ICR 307) but examples have included a conclusion that the EAT lacked jurisdiction to hear the appeal (*Grady v Prison Service* [2003] ICR 1293) and where the Court of Appeal identified at the permission stage grounds which had not been put before the EAT although the circumstances of the case were unusual (*Sukul Lennard v Croydon PCT* The Times, 22 July 2003).

Other procedural issues

This does not purport to be a complete guide to procedure in the Court of Appeal but we consider **21.09**
some aspects which are important for those who may appear there for the first time:

(1) Where a respondent wishes only to request that the court upholds the judgment or order of the lower court, for the reasons given in the lower court, no permission is required nor is a respondent's notice necessary (CPR, 52, para 8), but if the respondent seeks to ask the court to uphold it for different or additional grounds a respondent's notice must be filed (CPR, 52CPD.8, para 8.1).

(2) The appeal bundle should be prepared in accordance with CPR, 52CPD, para 27(1)–(3), which sets down the general contents of bundles.

(3) When the parties have been notified of the hearing date the appellant's advocate must after consulting his opposite number file a bundle containing photocopies of the authorities; this should be filed at least seven days before the hearing or where the period of notice of hearing is less than seven days immediately; relevant passages should be marked down the side so that the judges may carry out the relevant pre-reading (CPR, 52CPD, para 29); the bundle should not exceed ten authorities unless the issues require more extensive citation and must be certified as complying with the Practice Direction.

(4) Any supplementary skeleton argument for the appellant must be strictly necessary and filed as soon as possible (CPR, 52CPD, para 32); skeleton arguments lodged later than seven days before the hearing will only exceptionally be allowed.

(5) There will be summary assessment of costs when appeals are listed for one day or less and parties must be prepared for this with schedules of costs swapped at least one day in advance of the hearing.

Costs

Normally if the Court of Appeal overturns the decision of the court below it will award costs of the **21.10**
appeal in the court below, but as the EAT is normally a costs-free jurisdiction it will not do so here, but the normal civil rules of costs apply to the Court of Appeal hearing itself. In *Governing Body of St Albans Girls' School v Neary* [2010] IRLR 124, the Court of Appeal for the first time considered the position on costs where the employee started proceedings in a cost free jurisdiction. On the state of authority at the time he won but the school wished to overturn the line of authority and appealed to the Court of Appeal. It was right that there should be no order for costs. The Jackson Reforms led to a new provision in CPR, r 52.19, which expressly permits the Court of Appeal to make an order that the recoverable costs of an appeal will be limited to the extent which the court specifies, in proceedings in which costs recovery is normally limited or excluded at first instance. An application for such an order must be made as soon as practicable and will be determined without a hearing unless the court orders otherwise. This is likely to apply frequently to appeals in employment matters.

22

European Union Law and References to the European Court of Justice

A. EU LAW

22.01 The treatment of EU law in this book is necessarily summary but addresses the key principles which ultimately derive from EU law with which employment lawyers need to be familiar. The ongoing role of the CJEU and EU law has been much discussed in the media coverage of the impact of the decision to leave the EU. At the time of writing it is too early to know what the position will be after the UK's departure from Europe. The UK's notice to leave the EU pursuant to Art 50 of the TFEU expired in March 2019 but at the time of writing no formal agreement has been reached, when the UK's notice to leave the EU pursuant to Art 50 of the TFEU expires. In the meantime, employment lawyers need to be familiar with:

(a) sources of EU law and general principles
(b) when and how EU law can be invoked in the employment tribunal
(c) references to the ECJ under Art 267 TFEU (ex Art 234 EC).

B. SOURCES OF EU LAW

The Treaties

22.02 The current Treaty, the Treaty on the Functioning of the European Union (TFEU; Treaty of Lisbon) entered into force on 1 December 2009. The TFEU replaces both the EU Treaty and EC Treaty and alters the numbering of the Treaty provisions.

22.03 Key provisions of the TFEU which employment lawyers should be aware of include:

- Article 8—promotion of equality between men and women
- Article 10—combating discrimination on sex, racial or ethnic origin, religion or belief, disability, age, or sexual orientation
- Article 18—prohibition of discrimination on grounds of nationality
- Article 157—equal pay for men and women

- Article 45—free movement of workers
- Articles 49 and 56—other free movement provisions in relation to establishment and services
- Articles 151–161—Legislative competences in the social chapter
- Article 267—references to the Court of Justice (ECJ)
- Article 263—challenges to Community institutions.

EU legislation

The TFEU empowers the Community legislative organs to enact various different types of legisla-   **22.04**
tive instruments including (under Art 288):

- Regulations and
- Directives.

These legislative instruments set out the exact mechanism by which the Member State must enact/   **22.05**
give effect to a measure within the individual Member State. Regulations are automatically 'directly
applicable' within each Member State. This means that individuals can rely on them, regardless
of whether they have actually been enacted domestically. The most important Regulation in the
employment sphere is the Jurisdiction and Judgments Regulation (Regulation 44/2001 Council
Regulation on Jurisdiction and the Recognition and Enforcement of Judgments in Civil and
Commercial Matters) which supersedes the previous Brussels Convention on the conflicts of laws.

Directives are the more common instrument of choice in employment matters. Key examples in-   **22.06**
clude the Equal Treatment Framework Directive 2000/78/EC; the Race Directive 2000/43/EC; the
Working Time Directive 93/104/EC; the Fixed Term Workers and Part Time Workers Directives
97/81/EC; the Posted Workers Directive 96/71/EC; the Data Protection Directive 95/46/EC; and
the Trade Secrets Directive 2016/244/EU.

Directives set out the aim to be achieved by the Member State, but leave that Member State some   **22.07**
degree of freedom to choose the method of implementation into the law of that State.

For employment lawyers it is important to remember the following features about Directives: **22.08**

- They can confer rights directly on individuals which have 'direct effect' provided they are expressed
  to be sufficiently clear and precise (Cases C-397/01 to C-403/01 *Pfeiffer* [2005] ICR 1307). With
  Directives this is restricted generally to 'vertical' direct effect (unlike the Treaty)—ie rights which
  can be relied upon directly against organs of a Member State (defined by reference to the criteria in
  Foster v British Gas [1991] 2 AC 306). However, in so far as a provision of a Directive gives effect to
  a horizontally applicable general principle of EU law (eg non-discrimination) they may be relied on
  in cases between purely private parties (Case C-555/07 *Seda Kucukdeveci v Swedex GmbH & Co KG*
  [2010] IRLR 346, seeking to apply Case C-144/04 *Mangold v Helm* [2006] IRLR 143, ECJ).
- Not all provisions of a Directive will have direct effect.
- As Directives permit the Member State some degree of freedom in the manner in which they
  have been implemented, Directives have both a date of publication in the Official Journal of
  the European Communities, and a date by which they must be implemented. This principle is
  subject to the following conditions:
  o in the time prior to implementation the Member State must not do anything which is inconsistent
    with the Directive (the *Inter-Environnement Wallonie* principle [1998] Env LR 623 and Case C-
    427/06 *Bartsch v Bosch and Siemens Hausgeräte (BSH) Altersfürsorge GmbH* [2008] ECR I-7245)
  o the European Commission may bring proceedings under Art 256 TFEU against a Member
    State which has failed to implement a Directive in time
  o an individual may rely on any directly effective rights conferred by the Directive in an action
    against a public body once the time for implementation has passed
  o National legislation must be interpreted consistently with a Directive from the date of pub-
    lication of that Directive, not just from the date for implementation (*Pfeiffer*, above; Case
    C-106/89 *Marleasing* [1990] ECR I-4135; Case C-268/06 *Impact* [2008] All ER (D) 194).
- If a Member State completely fails to implement a Directive on time, this is generally speaking
  a sufficiently serious breach which would enable an individual to bring a damages action against

Part B Procedure in Other Jurisdictions

the State for the State's breach of Community law in not enacting legislation in time (under the principle in *Francovich v Italy* [1991] ECR 5357). This will only be a remotely desirable option in cases which involve either:

- a Directive which has been implemented late (and there is no national legislation to be interpreted consistently so as to protect those rights) for provisions which do not have direct effect. These were the facts of *Francovich* or
- as for the first option, where the provision does have direct effect, but the individual lost the chance of a cause of action against a non-public entity.

22.09 It is important to consider the Treaty competence for legislation (ie the Article in the Treaty which gives the Community institutions the power to enact the legislation). This determines both:

- the procedure (ie whether it is adopted by qualified majority voting and whether the 'social partners' are involved) and
- the principles behind the substantive rights (eg principles of non-discrimination/free movement).

General principles of Community law

22.10 As in ordinary English common law, in EU law the sources of rights are not restricted to those under the EU Treaty directly or under legislation. There are also various 'general principles of Community law' which have been recognized/declared by the ECJ and CJEU (its successor) over the years.

22.11 From an employment lawyer's perspective it is important to remember the following two key features about the doctrines of consistent interpretation and direct effect.

- In all cases there is a duty on the national court to interpret national legislation consistently with EU law insofar as it is possible to do so. This is a powerful principle which permits the national court or tribunal to read out words in a national statute (or read words into one) where to do so would not go against a fundamental feature of the national legislation (for a recent summary of the principle see *Byrne v Motor Insurers Bureau* [2008] EWCA Civ 574).
- In a case involving a public body/emanation of the State, if it is not possible to interpret the national legislation compatibly with the relevant Directive/Treaty provision, it must be disapplied (eg *Marshall v Southampton & SW Hampshire HA (No 2)* [1994] 1 AC 530). Disapplication must also apply in cases where the article relied upon has horizontal direct effect, for example in equal pay—(Case C-200/91 *Coloroll Pension Trustees Limited v James Russell and Others* [1994] ECR I-04389). Following the ECJ's judgment in Case C-555/07 *Seda Kucukdeveci v Swedex GmbH & Co KG.* above, in horizontal employment discrimination cases where the prohibition is provided for in the relevant Directives, it appears that disapplication must apply.

Other international instruments

22.12 Sometimes there is confusion between the European Convention on Human Rights and the European Community. A full analysis is beyond the scope of this book, but the practical points to remember are:

- The EU is not a party to the ECHR. Crucially, directly effective provisions of EC law have the capability of automatically disapplying legislation. Provisions which are incompatible with the ECHR are not disapplied. They can only be declared incompatible (but this has no legislative effect).
- The duty of consistent interpretation/indirect effect, however, is very similar under both the Human Rights Act 1998 and the European Communities Act 1972. It is not unusual in HRA cases that EC cases are cited, and vice versa (see eg *Ghaidan v Godin Mendoza* [2004] 2 AC 557).
- The ECJ often makes reference to judgments of the ECHR when considering fundamental rights (eg *Viking v ITWF* [2008] ICR 741) and sometimes vice versa.
- Some legislation refers expressly to the ECHR (eg recitals 1 and 4 of the Framework Directive 2000/78 EC).

C. EU LAW IN THE EMPLOYMENT TRIBUNAL

Does the tribunal have jurisdiction?

The starting point is that employment tribunals are creatures of statute. They have no inherent **22.13** jurisdiction other than that provided by statute. The primary source of this is s 2 of the ETA 1996, which provides: 'employment tribunals shall exercise the jurisdiction conferred on them by or by virtue of this Act or any other Act, whether passed before or after this Act'.

However, under r 100 of the ETR the power is clearly set out: **22.14**

> Where a Tribunal decides to refer a question to the Court of Justice of the European Union for a preliminary ruling under Article 267 of the Treaty on the Functioning of the European Union, a copy of that decision shall be sent to the registrar of that court.

Under the previous rules a reference could only be made after the time limit for appealing had expired, or an appeal had been heard. Now there is no restriction under the 2013 Rules as to when the reference may be made. **22.15**

Since 1996 there has been an increase in Regulations conferring jurisdiction on the employment **22.16** tribunal which wholly implement European legislation, for instance:

- Part-time Workers (Prevention of Less Favourable Treatment) Regulations 2000
- Fixed-term Employees (Prevention of Less Favourable Treatment) Regulations 2002
- Employment Equality (Sexual Orientation) Regulation 2003
- Transfer of Undertakings (Protection of Employment) Regulations 2006
- Employment Equality (Age) Regulations 2006.

Pre-existing legislation has also more recently been amended to bring it into line with European le- **22.17** gislation, for instance the Sex Discrimination Act 1975, the Race Relations Act 1976, the Disability Discrimination Act 1995, and the Equality Act 2010.

Historically, the employment tribunal did not have free-standing jurisdiction over employment **22.18** matters derived from European law pursuant to s 2 of the European Communities Act 1972 (*Biggs v Somerset County Council* [1995] IRLR 811 at 829, approved by CA in [1996] IRLR 203). The question of whether the tribunal has jurisdiction was in any event not as simple as looking at whether the wording of the governing statute provided for the particular right or remedy claimed in the tribunal. Although in EU law Member States have autonomy over matters of domestic civil procedure (*Preston v Wolverhampton Healthcare NHS Trust* [2000] IRLR 506, para 31) tribunals and courts must be able to comply with the general principles of EU law, including specifically:

- the principle of effectiveness of national remedies (that they not be impossible or excessively difficult)
- the principle of equivalence of national remedies for similar causes of action based in domestic and European law (eg *GMB v Brennan and Sunderland City Council* [2009] ICR 479, paras 65–68 (Elias J); Case C-268/06 *Impact v Ministry of Agriculture and Food* [2008] All ER (D) 194 (*Impact*) paras 37–55; Case C-432/05 *Unibet* [2007] ECR I-2271; Case 33/76 *Rewe-Zentralfinanz and Rewe-Zentral* [1976] ECR 1989, para 5; Case 45/76 *Comet* [1976] ECR 2043, para 13; Case C-312/93 *Peterbroeck* [1995] ECR I-4599, and Case C-326/96 *Levez* [1998] ECR I-7835).

In *Brennan*, Elias J applied AG Kokott's analysis from the *Impact v Ministry of Agriculture and Food* **22.19** [2008] All ER (D) 194 case to the employment tribunal system (a couple of weeks before the ECJ followed her analysis in its judgment).

Impact was a case referred to the ECJ by the Irish Labour Court in a case brought under the Irish **22.20** legislation implementing Directive 99/70 EC, the 'Fixed Term Work Directive'.

22.21 Ireland has a similar (although not identical) system to the English employment tribunal system. The similarities are more fully fleshed out in the Opinion of AG Kokott (herself a former Labour Court judge from Germany) at paras 2, 60–63, 73, and 77:

(a) the Irish Labour Courts/Right Commissioners derive their jurisdiction wholly from statute

(b) they are the forum of priority for disputes under various pieces of Employment Regulation/legislation

(c) they have been generally presumed not to have jurisdiction to hear cases based purely on directly effective EU law rights and

(d) they generally only award costs in exceptional circumstances.

22.22 There is an important distinction between:

- the jurisdiction of tribunals under legislation which is derived solely from Parliament and domestic law (for example, the provisions on unfair dismissal in ERA 1996) and
- the jurisdiction of tribunals under legislation which implements provisions of EU law. This clearly applies to legislation such as the Fixed Term Employees (Prevention of Less Favourable Treatment) Regulations 2002 and may apply to legislation, for instance much of discrimination law, which began initially simply through national legislation, but subsequently has been covered by the Framework Directive on Equality and the Race Directive.

22.23 This newer line of case law fits in some ways rather uncomfortably with some of the older domestic case law, for example *Biggs v Somerset County Council* [1995] ICR 811, 830, EAT; *Secretary of State for Employment v Mann* [1996] ICR 197, 204; *Barber v Staffordshire County Council* [1996] ICR 376, 395; *Mensah v Northwick Park Hospital* UKEAT/711/99, para 10. These older cases stressed the first point, that the tribunal has no inherent jurisdiction other than under statute.

22.24 Before *Impact* and *Brennan*, the strictness of this older approach had already begun to weaken in cases such as *R (on the application of Finian Manson) v Ministry of Defence* [2006] ICR 355, in which the Court of Appeal held that the employment tribunal had jurisdiction to determine whether a claimant came within the scope of the Directive 97/81/EC on Part-time Workers implemented by the Part-time Workers (Prevention of Less Favourable Treatment) Regulations 2000, even where this might mean the disapplication of some of the domestic regulations. This case is now best analysed as an example of the *Impact* principle in action.

22.25 Under the older line of cases there was a strict demarcation between 'freestanding' rights in EU law, and those which had a statutory foundation under the relevant national legislation. The battle ground in many of the cases concerned Art 141 of the EC on equal treatment between men and women. The ECJ in *Impact* did not, however, draw any distinction between freestanding rights and those derived wholly from statute. The principle of effectiveness may also require the employment tribunal to have territorial jurisdiction over a case based on rights derived from EU legislation, where it would not otherwise do so (see *Duncombe v Secretary of State for Children, Schools and Families* [2010] IRLR 331 and *Bleuse v MBT Transport Ltd* [2008] IRLR 264 EAT). It is important to note that the Equality Act 2010 does not include any transnational provisions (other than in relation to employment on board ships and offshore employees). The Explanatory Note states that the intention is to leave this issue to be determined by the Tribunal. Following *Kucukdeveci* and *Duncombe*, it is likely that, where the right in the Equality Act implements rights derived from or secured in the Framework, Race, or Recast Directives, if there is jurisdiction of the English courts under the Judgments Regulations and English law applies to the contract of employment, the tribunal must have jurisdiction to determine the case, regardless of whether it would have had jurisdiction under the old discrimination statutes or under *Lawson v Serco* [2006] IRLR 289.

Time limits

22.26 One other point needs mentioning and that is the question of when time starts to run for an EU law claim where the Directive in question has not been properly transposed into domestic law. The ECJ in Case C-208/90 *Emmott v Minister for Social Welfare* [1991] ECR I-4269 held that time does not start to run until the Directive has been properly transposed and this is so even where the ECJ has delivered a judgment that the Member State is in default and that the obligations under the Directive are clear and precise. However, following the case of *R v Secretary of State for Employment, ex parte EOC* [1994] IRLR 176 and *Rankin v British Coal Corporation* [1993] IRLR 69, most commentators and practitioners have taken a cautious line. The cases suggested that the time limit for claims not already pending, whether under the EU Treaty or a Directive, should be three months from the date of the legislation coming into force. This has been confirmed in *BP Supergas v Greece* [1995] All ER 684, where the ECJ held that domestic time limits will apply in a situation where the Member State has not properly transposed a Directive.

To summarize the position, although domestic time limits will probably apply from the relevant **22.27** date, there are two separate dates to consider depending on the EU source:

(a) Where there is no direct effect, the date is that of the proper transposition of the Directive (*Cannon v Barnsley Metropolitan Borough Council* [1992] ICR 698, [1992] 2 CMLR 795; *Emmott v Minister for Social Welfare* [1993] ICR 8); if the application is held to be out of time because the employee has delayed bringing the claim until full implementation, there is a strong argument that it is just and equitable that the time limit be extended.

(b) Where there is direct effect or EU Treaty base, the date is when it becomes reasonably clear to any person affected that a claim could properly be made (*Rankin v British Coal*; *Emmott*).

As the time limits for bringing proceedings in the employment tribunal are often so short, it is par- **22.28** ticularly important to keep an eye on whether a timing point can be affected by Community law.

The general time limit for many European derived causes of action (such as sexual orientation **22.29** discrimination) is three months (plus an additional three-month extension pursuant to the Employment Act 2002 in cases caught by the Employment Act 2008 (Commencement No 1 Transitional Provisions and Savings Order 2008) and a discretionary extension when this is 'just and equitable'. The similarity to other domestic discrimination employment claims means that it is most unlikely, of itself, to be held to be contrary to the European principles of effectiveness and equivalence (see eg *Emmott and Livingstone v Hepworth Refractories plc* [1992] IRLR 63). In European claims, it is important for employment lawyers to be sensitive to the following timing points:

• The tribunal only has jurisdiction conferred on it by statute. However, the absence of a provision permitting retroactive application of the statute or regulations does not mean that claims cannot extend back to the date on which the Directive should have been implemented (*Impact*).

• In cases against public entities, the respondent cannot rely on the Member State's failure to implement a Directive on time to defeat a claimant's cause of action because to do so would permit the Member State to rely on its own wrong (*Emmott*, para 23).

• In similar cases against private entities, it is likely to be just and equitable to extend time to a claimant to when the Directive has been implemented into national law (conferring jurisdiction on the tribunal) (see *Cannon v Barnsley Metropolitan Council* [1992] ICR 698 at 704, where the principle was developed in relation to a public body).

• *Impact* also makes clear that this extension of time backwards applies both to directly effective and indirectly effective claims. However, a statute/regulation can only be disapplied if the right in the Directive has direct effect and the respondent is a public body.

Francovich claims

One type of claim under EU law which tribunals do not have jurisdiction over are claims for **22.30** tortious State liability based on a Member State's failure properly to implement EC legislation/ having committed a sufficiently serious breach of EU law (see *Secretary of State for Employment v Mann* [1997] ICR 209). Such claims are treated as being a species of the tort of breach of statutory duty, over which the tribunal has no jurisdiction (see *Spencer v Secretary of State for Work & Pensions* [2008] EWCA Civ 750, [2009] 2 WLR 593 [2008] IRLR 911 for an analysis of limitation issues).

Part B Procedure in Other Jurisdictions

D.   REFERENCES TO THE COURT OF JUSTICE OF THE EU

Discretion to refer

22.31   Article 267 of the EC TFEU declares that references to the CJEU may be made by 'any court or tribunal of a Member State'. This includes employment tribunals.

22.32   The criteria for seeking a reference are set out in the *CILFIT* case (Case 283/81 *Srl CILFIT and Lanificio di Gavardo SpA v Ministry of Health* [1982] ECR 3415, paras 22.9–22.11):

> 9 In this regard, it must in the first place be pointed out that Article 177 (now 234) does not constitute a means of redress available to the parties to a case pending before a national court or tribunal. Therefore the mere fact that a party contends that the dispute gives rise to a question concerning *the* interpretation of community law does not mean that the court or tribunal concerned is compelled to consider that a question has been raised within the meaning of Article 177 (now 234). On the other hand, a national court or tribunal may, in an appropriate case, refer a matter to the Court of Justice of its own motion.
>
> 10 Secondly, it follows from the relationship between the second and third paragraphs of Article 177 (now 234) that the courts or tribunals referred to in the third paragraph have the same discretion as any other national court or tribunal to ascertain whether a decision on a question of community law is necessary to enable them to give judgment. Accordingly, those courts or tribunals are not obliged to refer to the Court of Justice a question concerning the interpretation of Community law raised before them if that question is not relevant, that is to say, if the answer to that question, regardless of what it may be, can in no way affect the outcome of the case.
>
> 11 If, however, those courts or tribunals consider that recourse to Community law is necessary to enable them to decide a case, Article 177 (now 234) imposes an obligation on them to refer to the Court of Justice any question of interpretation which may arise.

22.33   In *HP Bulmer v J Bollinger SA* [1974] Ch 40, Lord Denning MR set out a number of factors for a court to consider when making a reference. These guidelines have been criticized, as they considerably restrict the circumstances in which a court may make a reference, and in any event have been expressly overruled by Case C-106/89 *Marleasing SA v La Comercial Internacional de Alimentacion SA* [1990] ECR I-4135. The clearest statement by the United Kingdom courts of this principle is in *R v International Stock Exchange of the United Kingdom & the Republic of Ireland Ltd, ex parte Else (1982) Ltd* [1993] 2 CMLR 677 (not an employment case), where it was said:

> In relation to the determination of germane questions of Community law the correct approach in principle of a national court (other than a court of final appeal) is quite clear: if the facts have been found and the Community law issue is critical to the court's final decision, the appropriate course is ordinarily to refer the issue to the European Court unless the national court can with complete confidence resolve the issue itself. In considering whether it can resolve the issue itself the national court must be fully mindful of the difference between national and Community legislation, of the pitfalls which face a national court venturing into what may be an unfamiliar field, of the need for uniform interpretation throughout the Community and the great advantages enjoyed by the European Court in construing Community instruments. If the national court has any real doubt, it should refer.

22.34   In the ECJ Case C-303/06 *Coleman v Attridge Law* [2008] ICR 1128 the Netherlands government sought to argue that the question was inadmissible on the basis that it did not determine the issues between the parties because the tribunal had not yet found that Ms Coleman had in fact suffered less favourable treatment or harassment because of her son's disability. The ECJ did not decline jurisdiction on this basis (paras 30–31), holding that the matter was primarily for the referring court. However, where the questions are 'manifestly unrelated to the reality or the subject matter' of the domestic proceedings the ECJ will be likely to decline jurisdiction. It is tactically important when considering whether a reference should be made to the ECJ (which can take between eighteen months and two years to return to the tribunal) whether the tribunal should make key findings of fact first in order to determine whether it is necessary to make a reference. This point is reinforced in the Information Note on References from National Courts for a Preliminary Ruling in CPR, 68PD Annex, para 19.

Form of reference

The reference takes the form of a question or questions for determination and is usually submitted **22.35** in draft form by the parties' representatives for the tribunal to add to or amend as they see fit. If facts have been agreed or decided, they should be included in the reference, along with an outline of the opposing parties' contentions, a draft of the order sought, and a clear statement of the national law (so far as it can be agreed).

There is useful and specific guidance which can be found in the CPR, Part 68PD as to the form **22.36** and content of a reference and the ECJ's information note on references from national courts for a preliminary ruling (published in the Official Journal 2005/C 143/01 and on the ECJ's website). The ECJ also provides notes for guidance to counsel available from their website, which is essential reading for any party proposing a reference or dealing with European procedure once a reference is made.

It is the normal practice of the ECJ that costs incurred on a reference are to be treated as costs **22.37** forming part of the proceedings before the national court, but the EAT has no power to award costs beyond those referred to in the rules so that no costs could in fact be awarded (according to the EAT in *Burton v British Railways Board* [1983] ICR 544).

Stays

In order to avoid substantially identical references being made in cases which raise similar or the **22.38** same issues, tribunals and courts generally order that those cases are stayed pending the outcome of the original reference (the principles are set out in *Johns v Solent* [2008] All ER (D) 18, CA, confirming the EAT [2008] IRLR 88, where it was stressed that it is not permissible for the domestic courts to speculate about the outcome of any referred case when deciding whether to stay or not).

Part B Procedure in Other Jurisdictions

23

Collective Labour Law Institutions—
The Central Arbitration Committee
and Certification Officer

SUMMARY

(1) The primary jurisdiction of the Central Arbitration Committee (CAC) is in respect of trade union recognition.

(2) The CAC may determine its own procedure and has no set of procedural rules.

(3) There is no direct appeal from the CAC in recognition cases but challenge may be made by way of an application for judicial review.

(4) The certification officer maintains a list of organizations which are trade unions or employers' associations and receives their annual returns and deals with matters in connection with political expenditure.

A. INTRODUCTION

23.01 The CAC is a permanent independent body of a judicial character established by statute (see TULR(C)A 1992, s 259(1) and (2)). Its main function now is to adjudicate on applications for statutory recognition and de-recognition of trade unions for collective bargaining purposes under Sch A1 to TULR(C)A 1992. It also has powers under the Information and Consultation of Employees Regulations 2004, SI 2004/3426, European Works Councils, the European Company Statute, and the disclosure of information for collective bargaining purposes. It can provide voluntary arbitration on a reference from ACAS. It has close ties to ACAS, who provide all its staff, equipment, and other facilities (TULR(C)A 1992, s 259(3)) and must be consulted on any appointment to its membership.

The CAC is an unusual judicial body in that it does not have any formal rules of procedure be- **23.02** cause in the primary legislation, subject to specific provisions (of which there are few), it states that it 'shall determine its own procedure' (TULR(C)A 1992, s 263(5) and s 263A(7)). In all of its jurisdictions, the CAC's approach is flexible and orientated towards practical problem solving.

B. MEMBERSHIP

Appointment to membership of the CAC is by the Secretary of State (TULR(C)A 1992, s 260(1)). **23.03** Members must be 'experienced in industrial relations' (TULR(C)A 1992, s 260(3)), and include persons who have experience as representatives of employers and persons who have experience as representatives of workers. Before making any appointment to the CAC the Secretary of State must consult ACAS and may also consult other persons (TULR(C)A 1992, s 260(3A)). Members normally have long experience in industry and are senior representatives of trade unions or employers' federations.

The Secretary of State also appoints from the members a chairman and deputy chairmen (TULR(C) **23.04** A 1992, s 260(2)) of the CAC. The CAC consists of several deputy chairmen (who conduct most of the hearings, under powers contained in s 260(4) of the TULR(C) A 1992 including well-known employment law academics) and lay members nominated by employers and unions.

The only rules on the terms of appointment of members are set out in s 261 of the TULR(C)A **23.05** 1992. Amongst other rules, no term of appointment may exceed five years, but previous membership does not prevent reappointment beyond that five-year term (s 261(2)).

C. JURISDICTION

The CAC was first established by the Employment Protection Act 1975 as a permanent and inde- **23.06** pendent industrial relations arbitration body. It succeeded what had been known as the Industrial Court. Its operation was at first quite narrowly focused and close to its precise name, that is it provided for voluntary and unilateral arbitrations. It then gained control of disclosure of information requests by trade unions (see TULR(C)A 1992, ss 183 and 184) but these are and always have been few and far between. The jurisdiction of the CAC was, however, much extended by the Employment Relations Act 1999, which introduced the compulsory trade union recognition provisions into Sch A1 to the TULR(C)A 1992 and later by the Transnational Information and Consultation of Employee Regulations 1999, SI 1999/3323, and the European Company Statute (Council Regulation (EC) 2157/2001 [2001] OJ L294/1).

Information

Sections 181 to 185 of the TULR(C)A 1992 give the right of a recognized trade union to informa- **23.07** tion from the employer for the purposes of collective bargaining, and the trade union may present a complaint to the CAC that an employer has failed to disclose the required information (s 183). If an employer then fails to disclose the necessary information the trade union may bring a further complaint under s 184 that the contracts of one or more descriptions of employees should include the terms and conditions specified in the complaint.

Union recognition

Under Sch A1 of the TULR(C)A 1992 when a union(s) seeks recognition the CAC receives the **23.08** applications under Part 1 and may make crucial decisions on the validity of the application for recognition, the bargaining unit, the method of balloting, and the method of collective bargaining. After recognition has been granted, it may need to decide whether a bargaining unit has in due course ceased to exist or to be appropriate in the particular circumstances, whether another bargaining unit is appropriate, and whether bargaining arrangements should cease to have effect (see for fuller coverage J Bowers, M Duggan, and D Reade, *The Law of Industrial Action and Trade Union Recognition* (Oxford University Press 2019)).

European Works Councils

23.09 Under the Transnational Information and Consultation of Employees Regulations 1999, claims and complaints may be made to the CAC regarding the establishment and operation of European Works Councils. Employees may request information to assist them in determining whether their employer is part of a relevant EU-wide undertaking (reg 8) and the central management of that employer may apply to the CAC for a declaration that it is not such an undertaking (reg 10). Further applications may be made under regs 15 and 23. See also the Information and Consultation of Employees Regulations 2004, SI 2004/3426.

Trade disputes

23.10 Section 212 of the TULR(C)A 1992 provides that where a trade dispute exists, the parties to that dispute may request ACAS to refer all or any of the matters in dispute to the CAC for settlement by way of arbitration.

European public limited-liability company

23.11 The CAC has a role under the European Public Limited-Liability Company Regulations 2009, SI 2009/2401, which replace Part 3 of the European Public Limited-Liability Company Regulations 2004 SI 2004/2326, and came into force on 1 October 2009. The Regulations provide for employee involvement arrangements that must apply to the company. The arrangements for employee involvement, which encompass employee information, consultation, and, in certain circumstances, participation on the board (or supervisory board) of the company, may be contained in either an employee involvement agreement (drawn up by the employee representatives of the participating companies, acting through a special negotiating body, and the competent organs of the participating companies). If no such agreement is concluded, in the 'standard' information and consultation provisions (the 'standard' rules are defined in Part 5, r 19) a complaint may be made to the CAC (reg 20). Complaints may also be made to the CAC about a failure of a company to supply information concerning mergers, the establishment of holding companies, or subsidiaries (regs 5 and 6). An individual can also apply to an employment tribunal in relation to a failure to allow time off work to a member of a special negotiating body or where such a member has suffered a detriment or been dismissed (regs 28 and 31).

D. PROCEEDINGS OTHER THAN UNDER SCHEDULE A1

23.12 When discharging its functions in any particular case (other than under Sch A1) the CAC consists of the chairman (or one of his deputies) and such other members as the chairman may direct (TULR(C)A 1992, s 263).

23.13 The chairman also has the power to call in the aid of one or more assessors and rely on their assistance (TULR(C)A 1992, s 263(2)).

23.14 The CAC has the power to sit in private if it appears expedient to do so, at the discretion of the chairman (TULR(C)A 1992, s 263(3)). Such situations are rare, and may involve the need to protect national security or commercial confidentiality. On occasions part of an application may be heard in private and the rest in public.

23.15 The chairman has the powers of an umpire to decide on any award where the CAC cannot reach a unanimous decision (TULR(C)A 1992, s 263(4)).

23.16 Subject to the above, the CAC determines its own procedures (TULR(C)A 1992, s 263(5)).

E. RECOGNITION PROCEEDINGS

There are different provisions for trade union recognition cases. When discharging its functions **23.17** in any matter under Sch A1 (its most usual fare), the CAC consists of a panel established under s 263A of the TULR(C)A 1992. The chairman establishes particular panels to deal with particular cases (TULR(C)A 1992, s 263A(3)), to consist of the chairman or a deputy chairman to chair the panel, a member whose experience is as a representative of employers, and a member whose experience is as a representative of workers (TULR(C)A 1992, s 263A(2)).

Any panel has the power to sit in private if it appears expedient to do so (TULR(C)A 1992, s **23.18** 263A(4)). Such situations are likely to be rare, and may only involve the need to protect national security or commercial confidentiality.

Where a panel cannot reach a unanimous decision on a question arising before it the decision of **23.19** the majority is held to be the decision of the panel (TULR(C)A 1992, s 263A(5)). However, if a panel cannot reach a unanimous decision on a question arising before it and there is no majority opinion, the chairman of the panel decides the question given the powers of an umpire, ie his decision is determinative of the issue.

Subject to the above, the panel determines its own procedures (TULR(C)A 1992, s 263A(7)). **23.20**

Under Sch A1 panels have a general duty to 'have regard to the object of encouraging and **23.21** promoting fair and efficient practices and arrangements in the workplace, so far as having regard to that object is consistent with applying other provisions of this Schedule is concerned' (para 171).

An application passes through various stages requiring input from the parties and the appropriate **23.22** panel. Each application is assigned a case manager who takes an active role in procedural matters and seeks to ensure that deadlines are kept to and that there should be no adjournments because of lack of preparation of necessary documents. Especially tight deadlines are set down in the statutory recognition procedure with little scope for the CAC to waive a party's failure to meet a deadline. However, these deadlines may be extended with the consent of the parties or the CAC. Case managers usually sit in at the relevant hearing but have no decision-making role.

Generally, applications to start the recognition procedure and applications at various other stages **23.23** (there are seventeen possible applications) must be made 'in such form and supported by such documentation as the CAC specifies'. Where such forms have been specified and an application is to be dealt with on paper, it will be important to comply with any requirements in relation to documentation. Both a Recognition Application Form and Employer's Questionnaire (to respond to an application) can be found on the CAC website.

Where the CAC is likely to decide a matter on paper and not by an oral hearing, it is important **23.24** that a party asks for an oral hearing if the issue is sufficiently important that the parties wish for an oral hearing. Where it appears to the panel that a hearing will be necessary, the chairman of the panel may hold a preliminary meeting in order to set out procedures and identify the issues to be resolved.

Occasionally, the CAC may appoint counsel specializing in employment law as an *amicus curiae* **23.25** (friend of the court) to address a legal point which neither side has raised or wishes to raise, and which is thought to be of significance, or where neither party is legally represented nor wishes to be so and a legal point requires to be considered. By a statement in January 2004, the chairman of the CAC explained that the practice of appointing CAC panels is not affected by the decision of the House of Lords in *Lawal v Northern Spirit Ltd* [2003] IRLR 538. In that case, it was decided that it was inappropriate for counsel to appear before panel members of the EAT with whom that counsel had previously sat as a (part-time) judge. Therefore, counsel who has appeared as an *amicus curiae* before particular members will not be prevented from appearing as counsel for a party in a later case.

23.26 Decisions of the CAC on particular issues in one case do not bind later panels in other cases. However, such decisions may be referred to as guidance upon the manner in which issues have been resolved previously.

F. HEARINGS

23.27 Cases are heard around the country, at places which are convenient to the parties in the particular matter, in hotels, country clubs, and other convenient venues. Most, however, are held in London.

23.28 The approach of the CAC is generally quite informal (although the extent of this informality depends crucially on the personality of the deputy chairman involved) and normally all sit round a single table with name plates to indicate who everyone is and his or her role.

23.29 There is often no formal divide between submissions and 'evidence', with each party being asked in turn to present their 'case'. Statements will have been exchanged between the parties at the discretion of the CAC and sent to the CAC itself in advance of the hearing. New evidence will be admitted at hearings only for good reasons and with the permission of the panel, and subject to any additional time being allowed for another party to consider it. Examination of the other side takes place with the consent of and through the deputy chair. The CAC may determine that in particular cases stricter, more conventional standards of evidence are required or that more formality in the proceedings is appropriate.

23.30 The principles of natural justice (and Art 6 of the ECHR) require that the CAC should consider any evidence put to it when deciding any particular questions, and that each side should have the opportunity to comment on the other side's evidence and submissions. Under the Transnational Information and Consultation of Employees Regulations 1999 (but not under the Sch A1 procedure) the CAC must make 'such enquiries as it sees fit' and seek out evidence (reg 38(2)). Under Sch A1, the CAC has no power to order disclosure of documents other than those required for the initial application.

G. ENFORCEMENT

23.31 The CAC does not have its own enforcement powers. However, the statutory procedures under which it has jurisdiction each provide directly or indirectly for various forms of enforcement in the civil courts and EAT.

H. CHALLENGING DECISIONS

23.32 Under reg 38(8) of the Transnational Information and Consultation Regulations 1999, there exists a right of appeal to the EAT on any question of law arising from any declaration or order of, or arising from any proceedings of the CAC under the Regulations.

23.33 By para 165A of Sch A1, parties to the recognition procedure may appeal to the employment tribunal a demand for costs made under paras 19E(3), 28(4), or 120(4).

23.34 Section 264 of the TULR(C)A 1992 applies the 'slip rule' to awards, decisions, or declarations of the CAC, giving it the power to correct any clerical mistake or error arising from an accidental slip or omission.

23.35 The only other way of challenging a CAC decision is by judicial review for which the procedure is set out in CPR, r 54, and the only grounds on which an application for judicial review will succeed is if the CAC erred in law or reached a perverse conclusion which no reasonable CAC could reach.

23.36 Where a decision to be challenged arises under Sch A1, the hearings may be very speedily arranged in order not to disrupt the strict time schedule imposed under the recognition procedure. Indeed, the CAC may not defer the ongoing timetable because an application for judicial review is made. Thus, in the case of *R v CAC, ex parte Kwik Fit Ltd* [2002] EWCA Civ 512, [2002] IRLR 395, the hearing before the Administrative Court was held within three weeks of the CAC's decision and the Court of Appeal was convened three weeks thereafter.

The claim for judicial review is brought directly against the CAC with the union potentially in- **23.37** volved as an interested party. The interested party may gain costs of the proceedings if its arguments are successful.

Parties considering a judicial review should note that the Administrative Court will be reluctant **23.38** to interfere with decisions of the CAC given that it is a specialist body in an area which is not suitable for detailed intervention by the courts (*ex p Kwik Fit Ltd*, above, see para 23.37; *R (on the application of the BBC) v CAC* [2003] EWHC 1375, [2003] ICR 1542, paras 14–16; *R (on the application of Ultraframe UK Ltd) v CAC* [2005] EWCA Civ 560, [2005] IRLR 1194, para 16; *R (NUJ) v CAC (Secretary of State for Trade and Industry intervening)* [2006] ICR 1). The CAC should not take a legalistic approach (*R (on the application of Cable & Wireless Services UK Ltd) v CAC and CWU* [2008] IRLR 425).

The CAC has a useful website at http://www.cac.gov.uk, from which application forms to the CAC **23.39** may be downloaded.

I. THE CERTIFICATION OFFICER

The certification officer is appointed by the Secretary of State for the Department for Business, **23.40** Energy and Industrial Strategy (BEIS) in consultation with ACAS under TULR(C)A 1992. He appoints his own assistants, including one for Scotland, and his staff is provided by ACAS.

The certification officer carries on duties previously imposed on the Chief Registrar of Trade **23.41** Unions and Employers' Associations under the Industrial Relations Act 1971. They are as follows:

(a) maintaining a list of organizations which are trade unions or employers' associations and receiving their annual returns under TULR(C)A 1992
(b) dealing with matters in connection with political expenditure under TULR(C)A 1992
(c) dealing with amalgamations of trade unions under the Trade Union (Amalgamations) Act 1964 and
(d) entertaining applications for breach of the requirement that a union elects its executive committee by secret ballot under TULR(C)A 1992.

In settling disputes between the union and one of its members, the certification officer often acts **23.42** on the basis of written evidence and when hearings are necessary they are informal in procedure. There is an appeal from the certification officer's decision on both fact and law to the EAT.

In *Squibb UK Staff Association v Certification Officer* [1979] IRLR 76, the certification officer was **23.43** put into the witness box and cross-examined on the validity of his decision on the granting of a certificate of independence to a trade union. The Court of Appeal considered that such practice was wrong. He was not to be treated as an opposing party, but rather as occupying a judicial position. He should not, therefore, be called upon to justify his adjudication under interrogation.

Part B Procedure in Other Jurisdictions

PART C

The Substantive Law

These chapters are designed to set out a short summary of some of the most common issues which arise in an employment tribunal. Each chapter is followed by a checklist to summarize the key points which parties in tribunal claims need to consider.

24

Dismissal

SUMMARY

(1) All employees have the right not to be wrongfully or unfairly dismissed.

(2) These rights are distinct but overlapping.

A. WRONGFUL DISMISSAL

Basic test

An employee is wrongfully dismissed if, without cause, he is dismissed without full notice or **24.01** without money in lieu of notice. The notice period is either: that set out in the contract; or the appropriate implied notice; or is determined in accordance with the statutory minimum period calculated in accordance with the employee's length of service. An employer may legitimately terminate an employee's employment without notice or money in lieu of notice if the employee has committed gross misconduct or some other serious breach of his contract of employment such as dishonesty, disobedience, or serious incompetence. The test of whether an employee has committed a sufficiently serious breach of contract is similar to the test of whether an employee's conduct or capability is such that he can be fairly dismissed (see paras 24.35–24.53).

24.02　Some employment contracts contain a clause allowing the employer summarily to end the contract provided it makes a payment in lieu of notice (PILON). Invoking this clause will normally mean that any dismissal is not wrongful, although it may still be unfair if, for example, an unfair procedure was followed, or the employer had no valid ground for terminating the contract. Once an employer has terminated a contract of employment by invoking the clause, it cannot rely on later-discovered misconduct to refuse to make the termination payment, as the payment is by that stage already due as a debt (*Cavenagh v William Evans Limited* [2012] IRLR 679, CA). Had the employer simply terminated the contract, without exercising the pay in lieu clause, the misconduct could have been taken into account under the *Boston Deep Sea Fishing* principle (see para 24.03). The employer could, however, consider arguing that such a payment to a senior employee is forfeit because the employee breached his fiduciary duties to report his misconduct, or, if the payment term is set out in a settlement agreement rather than the original contract, that the contract to terminate on payment of a PILON was void/voidable because the employer entered into it under the mistaken belief that it had no grounds to terminate the contract summarily.

Wrongful dismissal damages

24.03　If an employer, without legitimate reason, summarily terminates an employee's contract, the employee is entitled to compensation for his notice period. This is quantified by calculating the net amounts (salary and benefits) he should have received during the balance of his notice period. The first £30,000 of the total of termination payments paid to employees as damages for wrongful dismissal is normally tax free (Income Tax (Earnings and Pensions) Act 2003, ss 401–416 (see paras 36.06–36.15 and 36.24–36.26) unless it is paid pursuant to a payment in lieu of notice (PILON) clause in a contract of employment. However, from 6 April 2018 if the payment is considered in lieu of notice, whether paid pursuant to a PILON clause in an employment contract or otherwise, the payment will be taxed as earnings. Any balance above £30,000 is grossed up at the employee's marginal tax rate to arrive at the final figure. A claim can also be brought for any non-discretionary bonus or commission that would have fallen due during the notice period. Claims for discretionary bonuses will only succeed in exceptional circumstances where a court accepts that a decision to award no, or a low, bonus was irrational or perverse (*Commerzbank AG v Keen* [2007] IRLR 132, CA). In wrongful dismissal cases, an employer can justify a dismissal by reference to facts which he did not know about at the time, but discovered subsequently (*Boston Deep Sea Fishing and Ice Co v Ansell* (1888) 39 Ch D 339).

24.04　In addition, if procedural requirements such as disciplinary and warning procedures are incorporated into contracts of employment, but are ignored, this could give rise to a claim by the employee for damages representing the salary he would have received had contractual disciplinary procedures been complied with, up to the date when the employer could lawfully have terminated the contract (*Gunton v London Borough of Richmond-upon-Thames* [1980] ICR 755, CA). The breach of contract in failing to follow the contractual procedure gives rise to a different cause of action to wrongful dismissal, but not to a claim for career-long loss of earnings (*Edwards v Chesterfield Royal Hospital NHS Foundation Trust; Botham v Ministry of Defence* [2012] IRLR, 129, SC) (see para 24.86 below for further detail on this). In extreme cases, an employer who suspends an employee without any contractual right to do so, or who dismisses an employee without going through contractual disciplinary procedures, may be ordered to reverse the decision if the employee applies to the High Court for an injunction (*Mezey v South West London and St George's Mental Health NHS Trust* [2010] EWCA Civ 293, CA, where an employer proceeding under old procedures was

WRONGFUL DISMISSAL/BREACH OF CONTRACT FLOWCHART

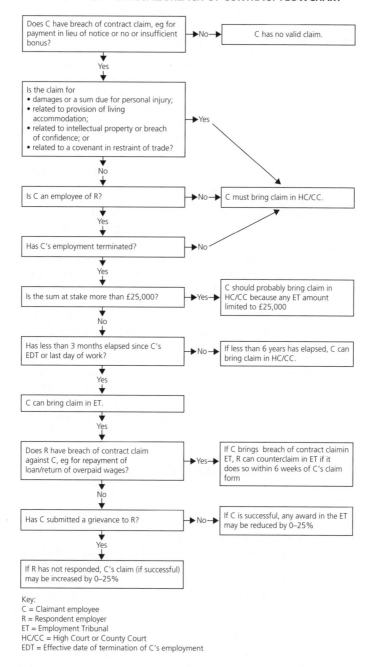

Key:
C = Claimant employee
R = Respondent employer
ET = Employment Tribunal
HC/CC = High Court or County Court
EDT = Effective date of termination of C's employment

prevented from continuing with the disciplinary process where recently-revised procedures were not being followed). If an employer dismisses an employee without notice, and by doing so deprives the employee of the benefit of statutory rights which would accrue if the notice period were worked out (eg by summarily dismissing someone whose notice period was three months after he or she had been employed for fifty weeks, thereby depriving him or her of the opportunity to claim unfair dismissal) no damages will be awarded for the loss of opportunity to bring any unfair dismissal claim (*Harper v Virgin Net Ltd* [2004] IRLR 390, CA).

Court jurisdiction in wrongful dismissal cases

24.05 Because the right to damages for wrongful dismissal is a common law right rather than a statutory right, the limitations and restrictions imposed by statute in relation to unfair dismissal do not apply. For example, there is no minimum service requirement before one can claim damages for wrongful dismissal. In addition, an employee is not entitled to damages for wrongful dismissal merely because the employer has not followed fair procedural requirements, or because any serious breach by the employee of the contract of employment was only discovered subsequent to dismissal and was not cited as the reason for dismissal (see para 24.03).

24.06 It is possible for ex-employees (only ex-employees—not present employees or former workers) to bring a wrongful dismissal claim in the employment tribunal as a breach of contract claim, rather than in the High Court or county court, although the amount of any award is subject to a maximum of £25,000 (Employment Tribunals Extension of Jurisdiction (England and Wales) Order 1994 and Employment Tribunals Extension of Jurisdiction (Scotland) Order 1994 (1994 Orders)) and no interest can be awarded if the award is paid within fourteen days after the judgment is sent to the parties (see also Chapter 35, section A). Although the compensation for wrongful dismissal and unfair dismissal overlaps to a certain extent, this will give the employee a useful additional weapon subject to two provisos: first, if a claim for wrongful dismissal is brought in the employment tribunal, the employer can counterclaim for losses it considers it has suffered as a result of the employee's breach of contract (other than where those losses have arisen as a result of a breach of the duty of confidence/fidelity by the employee) subject again to a maximum of £25,000 (1994 Orders, Art 4); and, secondly, an employee with a potentially large dismissal claim who succeeds in such a claim in the employment tribunal, where damages are limited to £25,000, or whose claim is dismissed, cannot seek to recover any excess in High Court proceedings as the issue will be *res judicata* (*Fraser v HLMAD Ltd* [2006] IRLR 687, CA), so high-earning employees would be ill-advised to bring such a claim in an employment tribunal. An employee does not have to bring a grievance before making any breach of contract claim against an employer in the employment tribunal. However, should he not have done so any award may be reduced by 0–25 per cent (TULR(C)A 1992, s 207A).

B. UNFAIR DISMISSAL

Qualifying periods

24.07 In addition to wrongful dismissal claims, many employees are entitled to claim compensation for unfair dismissal. Such a claim must generally be brought within three months of the effective date of termination of employment (EDT) (see para 24.08 for definition of EDT), although this period may be extended if a tribunal accepts it was not reasonably practicable to have done so. Only employees are able to bring unfair dismissal claims. To bring a claim for unfair dismissal, an employee must overcome certain hurdles. The most important hurdle is that, in order to be entitled to complain of unfair dismissal, generally employees must have been employed continuously for two years or more (one year for employees whose employment began before 6 April 2012). It does not matter how many hours each week they work during this period if they have two years' continuity. Continuity is not broken by annual summer holidays which fall between adjacent periods of employment where work ceases during the holiday (*Hussain v Acorn Independent College Ltd* [2011] IRLR 463, EAT—a case involving a teacher), nor where a shop working employee's employment ended because one store had closed down, and the following week he accepted an offer of employment with the same employer at another store, to start more than a clear week after the earlier employment ended (*Welton v Deluxe Retail Ltd t/a Madhouse (in administration)* [2013] IRLR 166). If an employee resigns, and then both employer and employee agree that the notice can be withdrawn, this means that the resignation never takes effect and continuity is preserved (*Chelmsford College Corporation v Teal* [2012] UKEAT 0277/11). Continuity is also preserved where an employee is dismissed, claims unfair dismissal, and is then reinstated, even where this is part of a settlement (*Lipinski v Ebbsfleet Autospray Centre Ltd* UKEAT/0288/12).

The general test is whether the employee has been continuously employed for two years by the effective date of termination of his employment (EDT). The EDT may be: **24.08**

(1) The date any notice period given expires or (if notice is less than the notice period to which the employee is statutorily entitled, the date statutory notice (see para 24.08(2)) would have expired (ERA 1996, s 97(1)(a)). If notice is given in writing, the test for determining the start date of the period within which an employee must launch unfair dismissal proceedings depends on the date when the employee receives the communication that he is dismissed, ie the date he actually reads any dismissal letter or has a reasonable opportunity to read it (*GISDA Cyf v Barratt* [2010] IRLR 1073, SC). If notice is given, but while the employee is working it out, the employer summarily dismisses the employee, or gives the employee a shorter notice period, the EDT is the date of the summary dismissal, and not the date when the original notice would have ended (*M-Choice UK Limited v Aalders* [2011] UKEAT 0227/2011; *Parker Rhodes Hickmotts Solicitors v Harvey* [2012] UKEAT 0455/11). If the employee resigns and claims constructive dismissal, the EDT is the date given in the resignation letter, even if that letter is handed in to the employer before the date on the letter (*Vasella Limited (in administrative receivership) and Anor v Eyre* [2012] UKEAT 0039/11). If the employee resigns in writing, the EDT is the date the letter was received and date stamped, not a later date which the employer said would be taken as the resignation date (*Horwood v Lincolnshire County Council* [2012] UKEAT 0462-0463/11). The date a resignation letter is received is the relevant date, even if the employer subsequently offers a cooling off period for reconsideration (*Secretary of State for Justice v Hibbert* [2013] UKEAT 0289/13, EAT).

(2) If no notice is given, and employment is not legitimately terminated for gross misconduct, the EDT, for the purposes of determining an employer's length of service, is the date on which statutory notice would have expired, had it been given on the date the employee was actually or constructively dismissed (ERA 1996, s 97(2) and (4)). Statutory notice is essentially one week, once the employee has been employed for a month, and one week per completed year of service after that, subject to a maximum of twelve weeks (ERA 1996, s 86). This is so even if payment is given in lieu of notice but dismissal takes effect immediately. Thus, if someone is dismissed after one year and 360 days' employment, the EDT will be a week later, so the person will be deemed to have continuous employment for over two years and hence be able to bring an unfair dismissal claim (*Secretary of State for Employment v Staffordshire County Council* [1989] IRLR 117, CA).

(3) The date the term of a fixed-term contract expires (unless the parties agree that the contract should continue after that date) (ERA 1996, s 97(1)(c)).

(4) If the employee is dismissed with notice, but is not required to work during the notice period (garden leave), the EDT is the date of expiry of the notice period (ie at the end of the garden leave period), even if the employee is immediately given pay for the full notice period at the start of the garden leave.

(5) The date an employee is summarily—and legitimately—dismissed for gross misconduct (ERA 1996, s 97(1)(b)). Note: if the employee successfully appeals against dismissal, the contract is regarded as re-instated as of that date—an employer's refusal to accept any contractually binding appeal may be a breach of contract capable of being accepted as a constructive dismissal (*McMaster v Antrim Borough Council* [2011] IRLR 235, Northern Ireland CA).

(6) If the employer serves notice on the employee to terminate a contract and the employee subsequently serves a counter notice terminating the contract on an earlier date, the EDT is nevertheless the date when the employer's notice would have expired.

(7) The date the employer and employee agree the employment will terminate. This is the case even if the employee has already received notice of his dismissal but then agrees an earlier termination date (*Palfrey v Transco plc* [2004] IRLR 916, EAT).

Note: Any appeal in any disciplinary procedure following dismissal is to be ignored for the purposes of estimating the EDT unless there is an express contractual provision which states that the contract will remain in force during the appeal.

GENERAL UNFAIR DISMISSAL FLOWCHART

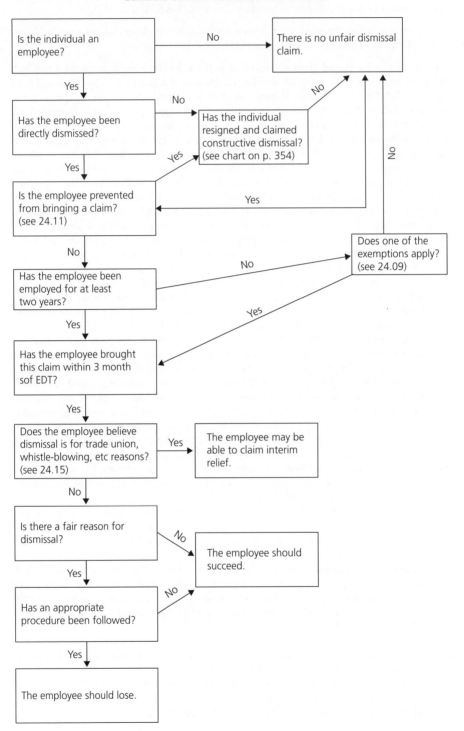

The exceptions to this general rule, where there is no qualifying period, include dismissals: **24.09**

(1) for trade union reasons (TULR(C)A 1992, s 154) or connected with union recognition (TULR(C)A 1992, Sch A1, para 162)
(2) for a health and safety reason (ERA 1996, s 108(3)(c))
(3) because of the employee's actions or proposed actions as the trustee of a relevant occupational pension scheme (ERA 1996, s 108(3)(e)) or as an employee representative for TUPE or redundancy collective consultation (ERA 1996, s 108(3)(f))
(4) for asserting a statutory right (ERA 1996, s 108(3)(g))
(5) for a pregnancy or other parental leave-related reason (ERA 1996, s 108(3)(b)
(6) for asserting rights under the Working Time Regulations 1998 (ERA, 1996, s 108(3)(dd)) or for a national minimum wage (ERA 1996, s 108(3)(gg)) or under the Tax Credits Act 1999 (ERA 1996, s 108(3)(gh))
(7) for making a protected disclosure (ERA 1996, s 108(3)(ff))
(8) for activities as a member of a European Works Council (ERA 1996, s 108(3)(hh))
(9) for asserting rights as a part-time worker or fixed-term employee, or for supporting someone else to do so (ERA 1996, s 108(3)(i) and (j))
(10) for exercising rights to accompany, or be accompanied by, workers at grievance and disciplinary hearings (Employment Relations Act 1999, s 12(4))
(11) for taking part in legitimate industrial action after properly conducted ballot, provided that at least twelve weeks have elapsed since the employee started to do so (TULR(C)A 1992, s 238A)
(12) of protected shop workers who refuse to work on a Sunday (ERA 1996, s 108(3)(d))
(13) for refusing to accept an offer to become an 'employee shareholder', giving up unfair dismissal and other rights in return for shares (ERA 1996, s 108(3)(gm))
(14) for being summoned to or attending jury service (ERA 1996, s 108(3)(aa))
(15) for exercising the right to participate in education or training accorded by ss 27 and 28 of the Education and Skills Act 2008 (ERA 1996, s 108(3)(de))
(16) for being on a trade union blacklist (ERA 1996, s 108(3)(gk))
(17) for exercising rights as an agency worker (ERA 1996, s 108(3)(q))
(18) where the employee is selected for redundancy where the principal reason was really one of those set out above (ERA 1996, s 108(3)(h))
(19) where the principal reason relates to the employee's political opinions or affiliation (ERA 1996, s 108(4)).

In all these exceptions, the key factor is the motive for dismissal: the courts will not look at whether **24.10** the employee actually has the relevant right, or whether or not that right has actually been infringed.

Excluded employees

Certain categories of employees are excluded from bringing unfair dismissal claims. These include: **24.11**

(1) Those working under illegal contracts, although if an employer persuades an employee to accept an illegal contract (for example, one which enables the employer to defraud HMRC) it may still be enforceable by the employee. The employment of an employee who makes false declarations to a foreign court to get a visitor's visa, and then works knowingly without the appropriate permit, although tainted by illegality, will not prevent an employee from suing, partly due to public policy reasons, in relation to the prevention of human trafficking (*Hounga v Allen and Anor* [2014] UKSC 47). If the employee genuinely does not realize that the contract is illegal when he enters into it, or if he has wrongly but innocently been treated as self-employed by HMRC when on a correct legal analysis he is an employee, he will still be able to rely upon the contract (*Colen v Cebrian (UK) Ltd* [2004] ICR 568, CA; *Enfield Technical Services Ltd v Payne* [2008] IRLR 500, CA). The employee's conduct in taking part in the illegal contract must be blameworthy: it is not enough for the employee just to have wrongly represented his employment status to HMRC. However, the employee will not be allowed to pursue a dismissal case where he knows that his assertion of self-employment status is unsustainable (*Connolly v Whitestone Solicitors* [2011] UKEAT 0445/10/EAT).

Part C The Substantive Law

Equally, an employee who worked under a contract for the supply of services, under which she had not paid income tax or National Insurance contributions, who then claimed she was in fact an employee during the period, failed in an unfair dismissal claim because the EAT held that her contract was tainted with illegality (*Daymond v Enterprise South Devon* EAT/ 0005/07).

(2) Those whose contracts of employment are frustrated by some circumstance unforeseen when the contract was entered into which renders performance of the contract very different from what was originally contemplated—for example, because the employee is severely incapacitated for a very long time as a result of sickness or because the employee is imprisoned (*Williams v Watsons Luxury Coaches Ltd* [1990] ICR 536, EAT).

(3) Statutorily exempt employees, such as those employed in the police service; certain Crown employees, particularly those in the armed forces; and share fishermen and people employed on board ships registered outside Great Britain (ERA 1996, ss 191–200). Note that those working on ships registered in Great Britain will be eligible to claim compensation for unfair dismissal unless they are wholly employed or resident outside Great Britain (*Diggins v Condor Marine Crewing Services Ltd* [2009] EWCA Civ 1133, CA).

(4) Those who are not employed in Great Britain. The new tests for deciding whether those not employed in Great Britain are covered by the legislation (taking the place of *Lawson v Serco Ltd* [2006] IRLR 289 HL) are:

- whether the respondent, or one of the respondents, resides or carries on business in England and Wales or in Scotland
- whether one or more of the acts or omissions complained of took place in England, Wales, or Scotland
- whether the claim relates to a contract under which work is or has been performed partly in England, Wales or Scotland or
- if the tribunal has jurisdiction to determine the claim by virtue of a connection with Great Britain which is at least partly a connection with England, Wales or Scotland (Employment Tribunal Regulations 2013, reg 8).

In looking at the issue of connection with Great Britain, cases preceding the new rules focused on whether the employment relationship had a stronger connection with Great Britain, and British employment law, than with the foreign country where the employee works (*Ravat v Halliburton Manufacturing & Services Ltd* [2012] IRLR 315, SC, where the employee could bring proceedings in Great Britain where he lived in Great Britain but worked entirely in Libya, working four weeks on, four weeks off—relevant factors included that the parties had chosen English law as the governing law of the contract, and that the employee had been told he would retain English employment rights). This was a question of fact and degree in each case. The following principles were to be applied when considering whether an employee who lives and/or works abroad is protected by British unfair dismissal legislation:

- The overarching question is whether Parliament intended unfair dismissal protection in ERA 1996, s 94 (1) to apply to a person in the claimant's circumstances.
- The general rule is that the place of employment is decisive, but, where the employment has much stronger connections with Great Britain and British employment law than with any other system of law, then the claimant will be within the scope of s 94(1) if the connection is sufficiently strong.
- A comparative exercise in which factors which point towards a connection with Great Britain are compared with the factors pointing in favour of another jurisdiction is appropriate where the claimant is employed wholly abroad. The comparison is between Great Britain and the jurisdiction in which the claimant works.
- The country in which the claimant lives is relevant. If the claimant lives as well as works abroad, an especially strong connection with Great Britain and British employment law is required before an exception can be made.
- When the claimant lives and/or works at least part of the time in Great Britain, a comparison of connections between Great Britain and the country in which he or she works is not required. All that is required is a sufficiently strong connection to enable it to be said that Parliament would

have regarded it as appropriate for a tribunal to deal with the claimant's unfair dismissal claim (*Creditsights Ltd v Dhunna* [2014] EWCA Civ 1238).

The claimant had to produce a sufficiently strong case to enable it to be said that Parliament would have regarded it as appropriate for the tribunal to deal with the claim (*Bates van Winkelhof v Clyde & Co LLP* [2012] IRLR 992, CA), where a claimant who worked largely in Tanzania, but spent over 25 per cent of her year in Great Britain, much of this being in the respondent's office, could bring proceedings in England). Claims could be brought in the UK by peripatetic employees based in Great Britain or expatriate employees whose services are performed abroad but whose work nevertheless has a close connection with a business carried on in Great Britain, such as a foreign correspondent of a British newspaper, or whose employment has a much closer connection with Great Britain and British law than any other country or system, such as teachers employed by a UK government department to teach in European schools (*Duncombe and Another v Secretary of State for Children, Schools and Families* [2011] IRLR 840, SC, where it was significant that the contracts were governed by English law, and that the work was performed in international enclaves which had no real connection with the country in which they were situated). People who conduct and engage in work overseas, even for a British employer, did not have British employment rights if they were not working for the purposes of a business carried on in Great Britain and had no strong employment connection with Great Britain (*Walker v Church Mission Society* [2011] EAT 0036/11, where a charity worker posted abroad to work in a decentralized way was not entitled to British employment rights). Prior cases may cast light on the definition of a peripatetic employee's country of employment as being where he habitually carries out work or where he can be said, in the light of all the factors which characterize the work activity, to perform the greater part of his obligations (*Koelzsch v Etat du Grand-Duché de Luxembourg* [2011] ECJ 15 March 2011 (C-29/10), where relevant factors included where work tools were situated; from where did the employee (an international lorry driver) carry out his transport tasks; where did he receive instructions and where was the work organized). The question is examined by looking at what was happening at the date of dismissal, not the date the contract was entered into (*YKK Europe Limited v Heneghan* [2010] IRLR 563, EAT, which also contains guidance on relevant factors for consideration where an employee has been absent from his expected place of work). There was an exception to this rule where allowing someone who works abroad to bring a claim in the UK was essential to enable them to enforce a right derived from European law (*Duncombe v Secretary of State for Children, Schools and Families* [2011] IRLR 840, SC—where teachers employed in continental Europe on successive fixed-term contracts could bring claims for unfair dismissal when the contracts were not renewed. Their rights derived ultimately from the Fixed Term Workers Directive).

(5) Those who are not employees, but are, say, casual workers (*Carmichael v National Power plc* [2000] IRLR 43, HL; *Ready Mixed Concrete (South East) Ltd v Minister of Pensions & National Insurance* [1968] 2 QB 497; *Redrow Homes (Yorkshire) Ltd v Wright* [2004] ICR 1126) or agency workers (*Dacas v Brook Street Bureau (UK) Limited* [2004] IRLR 358 CA; *Cable & Wireless v Muscat* [2006] IRLR 354 CA; *James v Greenwich Council* [2008] IRLR 302, CA; *Cairns v Visteon Ltd* [2007] IRLR 175, EAT; *RSA Consulting Limited v Patricia Evans* [2010] EWCA Civ 866, CA); *Tilson v Alstom Transport* [2011] IRLR 169, CA—the Courts are reluctant to imply a contract of employment in what would otherwise be an agency relationship unless it is necessary to do so, and if the parties understand that the relationship is not a contract of employment, because for example they cannot agree terms, this is a powerful pointer that no employment relationship exists. Generally the court will look to see if there is 'mutuality of obligation'—ie the court will look at the business reality considering two main issues: is the end user obliged to provide the individual with work and is the individual obliged to attend and do the work under the end user's direction and control (*Carmichael v National Power plc* [2000] IRLR 43 HL; *Ready Mixed Concrete (South East) Ltd v Minister of Pensions and National Insurance* [1968] 2 QB 497)? An essential question is whether the individual performs services for, or under the direction of, an employer in return for which he receives remuneration, or whether he is an independent provider of services who is not in a subordinate relationship with the person who has appointed him (*Jivraj v Hashwani* [2011] IRLR 827, SC, where an arbitrator was found not to be an employee). When examining the degree of control that an

employer exercises over an individual, the tribunal will look at whether the employer has, to a sufficient degree, a contractual right of control over the worker, as opposed to whether in practice the worker has day-to-day control over his own work (*White v Troutbeck SA* [2013] EWCA Civ 1171, CA). While the label used by the parties in an employment contract is not conclusive proof of the nature of the relationship, the Court will give weight to the way the parties choose to categorize the relationship where the position is otherwise uncertain (*Stringfellow Restaurants Ltd v Quashie* [2013] IRLR 99, CA; *White v Troutbeck SA* [2013] EWCA Civ 1171, CA). On some occasions, employers attempt to sidestep their obligations to those who work for them by stating that the individual does not have to perform the work personally, but can send a substitute. If this is genuine, it absolves the employer from employment obligations towards the individual. However, the court will look beyond the words of the contract, and test the reality of the situation and will conclude that a contract is a sham if it creates a false picture, as in recent 'gig economy' cases such as *Gascoigne v Addison Lee Ltd* ET/2200436/2016 and *Dewhurst v Citysprint UK Ltd* ET/220512/2016. The court will look at the position not only when the contract is made, but also at a later date if there is evidence that the parties have expressly or impliedly varied their agreement—the true agreement often being gleaned from the circumstances, not simply from any written contract, particularly where there is inequality of bargaining power (*Autoclenz Ltd v Belcher* [2011] IRLR 820, SC, where individuals who had answered advertisements calling for self-employed car valets, but who were expected to attend for work every day, and who, despite a contractual provision to the contrary, were not able to provide substitutes if they did not attend themselves, were indeed employees). Those who work under zero hours contracts are often not employees, because there is no mutuality of obligation as the employer is not bound to offer work, and the worker is not bound to accept it, unless the contract is a sham which does not reflect the true agreement between the parties (*Pulse Healthcare Ltd v Carewatch Care Services Ltd and Others* [2012] UKEAT 0123/12). In particular, in *Uber BV and Others v Aslam and Others* UKEAT/0056/17, the tribunal held that Uber drivers were workers, as Uber's claim that the drivers operated individual businesses and formed their own contract with each passenger 'was a pure fiction, which bore no relation to the real dealings and relationship between the parties'. Company shareholders who work at the company, even if they own a controlling stake in the company, may also be employees (*Secretary of State for BERR v Neufeld* [2009] IRLR 475 CA; *Stack v Ajar-Tec Ltd* [2015] EWCA Civ 46). Employees who have been seconded to third parties may, depending on the circumstances, be regarded as employed by the third party during the secondment (*Fitton v City of Edinburgh BC* UKEATS/0010/07). Even where a work-wage relationship is established and there is substantial control over what an individual can do, there may be other features to the relationship which indicate that there is no contract of employment, even during an individual engagement. Thus, a lap dancer was not an employee, in particular because the club did not pay her, rather she paid the club for the opportunity to earn money on its premises and took the financial risk (*Stringfellow Restaurants Ltd v Quashie* [2013] IRLR 99, CA). The fact that a contract can be terminated at will does not automatically mean that the individual will be a casual worker (*Drake v Ipsos Mori UK Ltd* [2012] IRLR 973, EAT), where a market researcher engaged on a succession of individual assignments, each one of which could be terminated at will on either side without its being completed, could still be an employee during the course of any particular assignment, and for a longer period if the assignments were carried out under a series of contracts of employment, as opposed to a series of contracts for services). Ministers of religion will only be employees if the parties intended the benefits and burdens of the ministry to be the subject of a legally binding agreement between them (*President of the Methodist Conference v Preston* [2013] UKSC 29, SC, where a Methodist minister was not an employee, in particular because she could not unilaterally resign from the ministry, her stipend was characterized as maintenance and support, and her rights and duties arose from her status in the Church's constitution, not from any arrangement which could be said to amount to a contract).

(6) Volunteers (*X v Mid Sussex Citizens Advice Bureau* [2013] IRLR 146, SC).

(7) Employees who have resigned, without being pressured to do so. If the employee is told he faces a disciplinary process for misconduct but agrees to resign to avoid this, or if he is

otherwise responding to a 'resign or be sacked' ultimatum, this will be regarded as a dismissal, not a resignation (*East Sussex County Council v Walker* [1972] ITR 280, NIRC; *Sandhu v Jan de Rijk Transport Ltd* [2007] ICR 1137); while an employee who resigns in the heat of the moment, who is given a reasonable cooling-off period to reconsider and does not change his mind during that period, will be held to have resigned properly, even if, after the period, he asks to rescind the resignation but is refused (*Ali v Birmingham City Council* UKEAT/0313/08, EAT).

(8) Employees who have not been dismissed (eg an employee removed from his workplace at the request of a client, for whom no alternative work had been allocated during a four-week consultation, had not been dismissed, and could therefore not claim unfair dismissal, even though the employer had alerted the employee to the possibility of dismissal if the consultation proved unsuccessful—*Mitie Security (London) Ltd v Ibrahim* UKEAT/0067/10). However, employees who are given formal notice to terminate their employment and are then re-engaged on new, less attractive terms are to be regarded as dismissed (*Darby v The Law Society of England and Wales* [2008] UKEAT 0447/08). Removal from the payroll and ceasing to pay his salary while an employee is suspended and a compromise agreement is being negotiated also amounts to dismissal (*Radecki v Kirklees Metropolitan Borough Council* [2009] EWCA Civ 298, CA), as do unambiguous words of dismissal (*Willoughby v CF Capital plc* [2011]IRLR 985, CA, where the employee was given a date for 'the termination of your existing employment contract' following a misunderstanding that the employee had agreed to transfer to an agency agreement). An employee may not have been dismissed where the employer has dismissed the employee in the heat of the moment, and then quickly withdraws the dismissal, because it had no real intention to dismiss (*Martin v Yeoman Aggregates Ltd* [1983] IRLR 49, EAT; *Barclay v City of Glasgow District Council* [1983] IRLR 313, EAT). The tribunal disapproves of the concept of 'self-dismissal', so that if an employee does not return to work after sick leave, and changes addresses without telling the employer, he will not have been dismissed unless and until the employer formally accepts the employee's breach, for example by contacting him by some means and informing him his employment is at an end (*Zulhayir v JJ Food Service Limited* [2011] UKEAT 0593/10).

(9) Employees who have resigned and are working out their notice but whose employment is subsequently terminated by their employer upon payment of the balance of the notice money due: this cannot be constructive dismissal—the cause of termination was the employee's resignation which cannot be unilaterally repudiated (*Tom Findlay & Co Ltd v Devlin* UKEATS/0071/06).

(10) Partners in partnerships or members of limited liability partnerships, unless their role within the organization is not one of true partnership/membership (*Kovats v TFO Management LLP* [2009] All ER (D) 116 (May) EAT). Members in limited liability partnerships will be workers and salaried partners may well be employees (*Tiffin v Lester Aldridge LLP* [2012] IRLR 391, CA; *Clyde & Co LLP and Anor v Bates van Winkelhof* [2014] UKSC 32).

(11) Employee shareholders—ie employees who, after 1 September 2013, have given up their rights to bring, among other things, unfair dismissal claims in exchange for fully paid-up shares in their employer worth between £2,000 and £50,000 (ERA 1996, s205A). (Note that the tax benefits associated with the employee shareholder status were withdrawn with effect from 1 December 2016.)

Constructive dismissal

The tests

If the employer has seriously breached the contract of employment, or has threatened to do so, an **24.12** employee may resign and claim constructive dismissal (s 95(1)(c) ERA). The tests are:

(1) The employer's conduct must amount to a fundamental breach of contract (*Western Excavating (ECC) Ltd v Sharp* [1978] QB 761). Unreasonable behaviour not amounting to a breach, for example, delaying the date on which salary payment is made, is not sufficient. The employer's actions will not amount to a constructive dismissal, however unreasonable, if there is an express contractual term allowing him to take that action. For example, a provision in a contract, or in a collective agreement or staff handbook, that an employer is entitled to vary shift patterns (if its terms are incorporated into the contract of employment), will enable the employer to do

so. However, the employer has a duty not to conduct itself in a manner, without reasonable or proper cause, likely to destroy or seriously damage the relationship of trust and confidence between the parties. Thus any change in shift pattern could not be wholly unreasonable, and would require reasonable prior notice (*United Bank Ltd v Akhtar* [1989] IRLR 507, EAT).

(2) The employer's breach of contract must be sufficiently important, judged objectively (*Buckland v Bournemouth University Higher Education Corporation* [2010] IRLR 445, CA), to justify the employee resigning, or must be the last in a series of less important incidents. The contractual breach need not be the principal reason for the employee's resignation, so long as it was serious enough to constitute a repudiatory breach, and played a part in the employee's decision-making process (*Wright v North Ayrshire Council* [2013] 0017/13/2706, EAT, where the employee was still constructively dismissed after her grievances had long gone unanswered, even though a key reason why she resigned was to look after a partner who had recently suffered a stroke; and *Nottingham County Council v Meikle* [2004] IRLR 703, CA). An employee need not be aware of the employer's breach of her rights at the time of resignation in order to claim that there was a repudiatory breach of contract, as a contract can be so egregiously breached that it is obvious that the reason for an employee's leaving had everything to do with that breach (*Mruke v Khan* [2018] EWCA Civ 280).

(3) An employee may rely on constructive dismissal citing a pattern of actions, the most recent of which is the 'last straw'. The last straw need not itself be a breach of contract so long as it is more than trivial and is capable of contributing to a breach of the implied term of mutual trust and confidence and has been preceded by blameworthy or unreasonable conduct in the past. This is an objective, not a subjective test (*Omilaju v Waltham Forest LBC* [2005] IRLR 35, CA). Examples of what might constitute the last straw could include a reduction in the number of hours worked, or a requirement to move to a workplace some way away, even if the contract allows such changes to be made, provided this has been preceded by previous unreasonable behaviour towards the employee. See also para 24.12(9). Wholly innocuous conduct cannot amount to a 'last straw' (*Salford NHS Primary Care Trust v Smith* [2011] 0507/10, EAT).

(4) The employee must accept the repudiatory conduct, for the employment to come to an end. The employment does not end automatically upon the repudiatory breach (*Société Générale, London Branch v Geys* [2013] IRLR 122, SC).

(5) The employee must leave in response to the breach. In any resignation letter an employee would be wise to set out the employer's breach on which he relies in resigning and claiming constructive dismissal. If the employee has indeed breached the contract, it can still be a constructive dismissal even if the employee had an ulterior motive for resigning (*Shipperley v Nucleus Information Systems Ltd* [2007] UKEAT 0340/06). However, if the resignation is simply part of a concerted exit strategy designed to enable the employee to join a new employer, perhaps unencumbered by restrictive covenants (*Tullett Prebon plc v BGC Brokers LP* [2011] EWCA Civ 131, CA) a tribunal will not regard this as constructive dismissal.

(6) The employee must act promptly in resigning following the breach or he may be deemed to have waived the breach and agreed to vary the contract. What is 'prompt' will vary according to circumstances, but will normally be within at least one or two months. In *Quigley v University of St Andrews* [2006] UKEATS 0025/05, a two-month delay was sufficient to affirm the contract, preventing the employee from arguing that he was constructively dismissed, even though he had claimed the gap was caused by the length of time it took him to consult his solicitor. Acceptance of sick pay and the giving of more extensive notice may also constitute affirmation (*Colomar Mari v Reuters Ltd* UKEAT/ 0539/13; Cockram v Air Products Plc UKEAT/ 0038/14).

(7) The employee may rely upon the conduct of anyone employed by the employer in a supervisory capacity, and not only upon the conduct of the particular person who has the power to dismiss the employee.

(8) Deliberate misconduct or bad faith is not a necessary prerequisite for the obligation of mutual trust and confidence to be destroyed (*Post Office v Roberts* [1980] IRLR 347, EAT).

(9) A common argument in constructive dismissal cases is that the employer has acted in such a way that it has breached the implied term of trust and confidence that should exist in the employment relationship. To establish breach, the employee must show conduct by the employer 'which, objectively considered, is calculated or likely seriously to undermine the

CONSTRUCTIVE DISMISSAL FLOWCHART

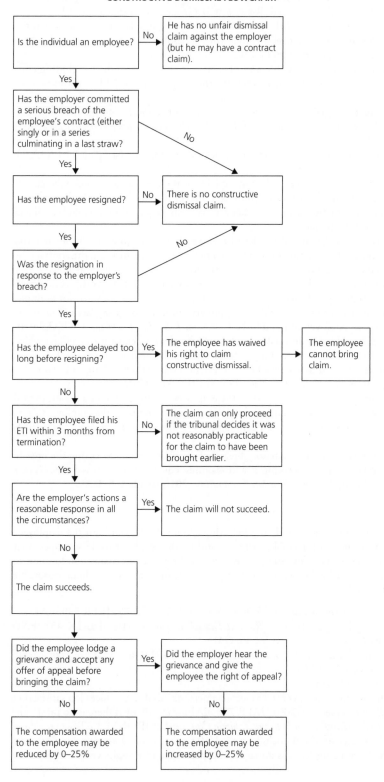

necessary trust and confidence in the employment relationship' (*Baldwin v Brighton & Hove City Council* [2007] IRLR 232, EAT; *Woods v WM Car Services (Peterborough) Ltd* [1982] IRLR 413, CA). Where breach of the implied term is raised in relation to a single act, the employment tribunal should ask itself the following questions:

- What was the conduct of the employer that is complained of?
- Did the employer have reasonable and proper cause for that conduct including consideration of whether its action was within the range of reasonable responses? And if not;
- Was the conduct complained of calculated to destroy or seriously damage the employer/ employee relationship of trust and confidence (*Fairbrother v Abbey National plc* [2007] IRLR 320, EAT)?

However, where the employee is relying on the 'last straw' doctrine (see para 24.12(3)) the relevant principles are as follows:

- The final straw act need not be of the same quality as the previous act relied on as cumulatively amounting to a breach of the implied term of trust and confidence, but it must, when taken in conjunction with the earlier acts, contribute something to that breach and be more than utterly trivial.
- Where the employee, following a series of acts which amount to a breach of the term, does not accept the breach but continues in employment, thus affirming the contract, he cannot subsequently rely on the earlier acts if the final straw is entirely innocuous.
- The final straw, viewed alone, need not be unreasonable or blameworthy conduct on the part of the employer. It need not itself amount to a breach of contract, for example, it could be an invitation to attend a disciplinary meeting following acrimonious exchanges between employer and employee (*Thornton Print Ltd v Morton* UKEAT/0090/08). However, it will be an unusual case where the 'final straw' consists of conduct which viewed objectively as reasonable and justifiable satisfies the final straw test. In 'last straw' cases, one does not need to review whether the action was within the range of reasonable responses (*GAB Robins (UK) Ltd v Triggs* [2008] IRLR 317, CA).
- An entirely innocuous act on the part of the employer cannot be the final straw, even if the employee genuinely (and subjectively) but mistakenly interprets the employer's act as destructive of the necessary trust and confidence (*Waltham Forest v Omilaju* [2005] IRLR 35, CA).

(10) An employer who has been in repudiatory breach of contract cannot, by curing the breach, preclude the employee from accepting it and claiming constructive dismissal (*Buckland v Bournemouth University Higher Education Corporation* [2010] IRLR 445, CA).

Examples

24.13 Examples of constructive dismissal include the following actions if taken without the employee's consent or without an express contractual provision entitling the employer to do so (unless that provision is wholly unreasonable—for example, requiring an employee to change job location to a considerable distance from his home, or imposing material shift patterns, without reasonable notice—see para 24.12(1)):

(1) imposing a salary reduction (*Industrial Rubber Products v Gillon* [1977] IRLR 389, EAT)

(2) materially reducing benefits (*Gillies v Richard Daniels & Co Ltd* [1979] IRLR 457, EAT; *French v Barclays Bank plc* [1998] IRLR 646, CA)

(3) reduction in status (*Lewis v Motorworld Garages Ltd* [1985] IRLR 465, CA; *Coleman v S&W Baldwin* [1977] IRLR 342, EAT)

(4) change in hours or shift patterns

(5) removing the most enjoyable or central aspect of a person's job if this reduces job satisfaction or prestige (*Hilton v Shiner Ltd* [2001] IRLR 727, EAT), particularly if there is no prior consultation (*McBride v Falkirk Football and Athletic Club* [2012] IRLR 22, EAT, where giving someone else the choice of who to include in the U19 football team, without prior discussion with the original team chooser, was a matter of constructive dismissal, even in an industry

whose management culture was autocratic: bad practice throughout an industry cannot condone what would otherwise, in other, better managed industries, be a breach of the employment relationship)

(6) moving someone from a hands-on role to a managerial one (*Land Securities Trillium Ltd v Thornley* [2005] IRLR 765, EAT)

(7) requiring someone to go on garden leave if there is no contractual provision entitling the employer to do so, but only if the contract impliedly confers a right to work on the employee, by looking at items such as whether the employee has specific and unique duties, and whether his special skills require frequent exercise to stop the employee becoming deskilled (*Christie v Johnston Carmichael* [2010] IRLR 1016, CS, where an accountant in a general tax adviser role did not have such an implied term, varying *William Hill Organisation Ltd v Tucker* [1998] IRLR 313, CA) unless the employee has been guilty of serious misconduct or has otherwise demonstrated (here by planning to direct new business opportunities to his new employer) in a serious way that he is not able or willing to work (*SG&R Valuation Services Co v Boudrais* [2008] IRLR 770, QB)

(8) imposing new restrictive covenants on an employee without going through proper procedure (*Willow Oak Developments Ltd (t/a Windsor Recruitment) v Silverwood* [2006] IRLR 607, CA)

(9) failing to bring an employee's attention to a right he holds which is about to expire, when the right has been negotiated collectively on behalf of employees, and the employee could not reasonably have been expected to be aware of the right (*Scally v Southern Health & Social Services Board* [1991] IRLR 522, HL)

(10) failing to comply with the implied 'sex equality clause' (s 66(1) Equality Act 2010) in the employee's contract by paying a female employee less than a male employee doing equal work (*BMC Software Ltd v Shaikh* UKEAT/0092/16)

(11) behaving without reasonable and proper cause in a manner likely to destroy or seriously damage the mutual relationship of trust and confidence which should exist between employer and employee, for example, by:

(a) conducting a fraudulent business (*Malik v BCCI* [1997] IRLR 462, HL)

(b) giving an employee no or a low salary rise or bonus out of all proportion to colleagues, without any justification (*Clark v Nomura International plc* [2000] IRLR 766, HC)

(c) allowing a bullying or harassing environment to persist, or failure to investigate allegations of harassment (*Bracebridge Engineering Ltd v Darby* [1990] IRLR 3, EAT)

(d) non-trivial bullying or harassment of the employee by another employee (*(1) Reed, (2) Bull Information Systems Ltd v Stedman* [1999] IRLR 299, EAT)

(e) offering an employee who has been on long-term absence from work through stress a new job in his old department, when the employee had maintained that his health problems would be exacerbated by a return to that department. There is an implied contractual term that the employer will safeguard its employee's health and safety at work. If it does not do so, it will be in breach of contract. When examining whether the employer's conduct is fair, the tribunal will look at whether, before requiring a return to the same department, the employer obtained medical reports and consulted with the employee on the medical position and on alternatives (*Thanet District Council v Webster* [2003] UKEAT 1090/01)

(f) a senior executive acting in a high-handed and aggressive manner towards employees (*Horkulak v Cantor Fitzgerald International* [2004] ICR 697, QBD)

(g) rudely and unjustly criticizing an employee in front of others (Isle of *Wight Tourist Board v Coombes* [1976] IRLR 413, EAT)

(h) accusing an employee, without foundation, of inability to do his job (*Courtaulds Northern Textile Ltd v Andrew* [1979] IRLR 84, EAT)

(i) suspending an employee (even if pursuant to a contractual right) without reasonable and proper cause (*Gogay v Hertfordshire County Council* [2000] IRLR 703, CA) or suspending him and reporting his activity to the police as a knee-jerk reaction to an event, without considering whether the employee's behaviour merited such a draconian response (*Crawford v*

Suffolk Mental Health Partnership NHS Trust [2012] IRLR 402, CA (j) maintaining suspension of an employee even though the employer has already concluded that one of two charges against the employee is unfounded (*Camden and Islington Mental Health and Social Care Trust v Atkinson* EAT/0058/07)

(k) imposing a disciplinary suspension without pay, unless the employer has the power to do so under the contract of employment

(l) giving an unjust and unmerited warning or other disciplinary sanction out of all proportion to the offence (*Stanley Cole (Wainfleet) Ltd v Sheridan* [2003] IRLR 52, EAT)

(m) failing to progress disciplinary and grievance processes fairly and promptly (*Flexman v BG International Limited* [2013] 2701998/11, ET)

(n) failing adequately to investigate a grievance; for example, a failure properly to address a complaint of overworking (which accompanied a complaint of alleged bullying) was, when looked at cumulatively in the context of earlier unreasonable actions, constructive dismissal (*GAB Robins (UK) Ltd v Triggs* [2008] IRLR 317, CA)

(o) apparent bias in conducting grievance proceedings (eg where a member of an appeal panel has publicly supported the person against whom a grievance is made—*Watson v University of Strathclyde* [2011] IRLR 458, EAT)

(p) failure to provide for an appeal against a grievance decision to be heard by a different manager from the one who made the original decision (*Blackburn v Aldi Stores Ltd* [2013] 0185/12, EAT)

(q) giving a bad reference without checking that it is fair and reasonable (*TSB Bank plc v Harris* [2000] IRLR 157, EAT)

(r) requiring an employee to relocate, without giving reasonable notice (*United Bank Ltd v Akhtar* [1989] IRLR 507, EAT)

(s) laying off employees without pay, in the absence of an express contractual provision allowing the employer to do so (*D&J McKenzie Ltd v Smith* [1976] IRLR 345, CS)

(t) failing to give an employee the necessary support to perform his functions and duties properly (*Associated Tyre Specialists (Eastern) Ltd v Waterhouse* [1976] IRLR 386, EAT)

(u) failing to cooperate with an employee in his attempts to achieve sales targets which allow him to obtain benefits under a bonus scheme (*Takacs v Barclays Services Jersey Ltd* [2006] IRLR 877, QBD—interim decision of the High Court)

(v) failing to provide a satisfactory working environment to enable the employee to work, for example, requiring people to work in an unpleasantly smoky atmosphere (*Waltons & Morse v Dorrington* [1997] IRLR 488, EAT)

(w) requiring the employee to work in unsafe conditions (*Marshall Specialist Vehicles Ltd v Osborne* [2003] IRLR 672, EAT)

(x) causing psychiatric damage by volume or character of work (*Walker v Northumberland County Council* [1995] IRLR 35, DC)

(y) in the absence of a written contractual provision entitling the employee to do so, failing to pay full wages to an employee during periods of sickness absence (*Secession Ltd (t/a Freud) v Bellingham* [2006] All ER (D) 62, EAT)

(z) refusing to provide work where a significant proportion of the employee's remuneration is based upon commission

(aa) not making reasonable adjustments to a disabled employee's job which would allow him to continue working (*Greenhof v Barnsley Metropolitan Council* [2006] IRLR 98, EAT)

(ab) making public remarks about an employee which are highly damaging to his reputation (*Clements v RDF Media Group Ltd* [2008] IRLR 207, HC)

(ac) discriminating against the employee (*Shaw v CCL Ltd* [2008] IRLR 284, EAT, where the employer unreasonably refused a woman's request to work flexibly following the birth of her child), although the fact that there has been discrimination is not determinative of the issue—it depends on the degree of discrimination (*Amnesty International v Ahmed* [2009] IRLR 884, where the employer did not unfairly dismiss a Sudanese employee whom it had technically discriminated against by following its policy not to send staff to countries in conflict where they were nationals, in the genuine and honest belief that to do so might compromise their impartiality, and endanger the employee's safety)

(ad) refusal, without reasonable and proper cause, to follow a doctor's recommendation in a Statement of Fitness to Work (fit note)

(ae) placing improper influence on a colleague to produce an untrue witness statement in defence of the employee's discrimination claims (*Singh v Moorlands Primary School* [2013] EWCA Civ 909, CA)

(af) writing to an employee when she was on sick leave for work related stress, to raise concerns with her about her employment that were not serious or urgent (*Private Medicine Intermediaries Ltd v Hodkinson* UKEAT/0134/15)

(ag) providing a false reason for dismissal, even if the employee was not aware that the reason is false when he resigned (*Rawlinson v Brightside Group Ltd* UKEAT/0142/17).

Employer's defence

Once an employee has shown there is a substantial breach going to the root of his contract of employment, the burden of proof is neutral as to whether the employee's dismissal was a reasonable response in all the circumstances, so that any 'dismissal' will be fair. The employer must show that: **24.14**

(1) it has not acted in substantial breach of contract. Conduct which will usually not amount to an event of constructive dismissal includes:

   (a) minor alterations to the employee's contractual terms;

   (b) changes allowed by the contract of employment (for example, pursuant to flexibility provisions—*White v Reflecting Roadstuds Ltd* [1991] IRLR 331, EAT)

   (c) a delay in payment of wages, if not substantial or repeated

   (d) lack of consultation over the appointment of a subordinate

   (e) telling an employee he will be dismissed at some time in the future (this is not constructive dismissal because the employer may intend to give due notice, which would not be a breach of contract)

   (f) introducing adverse changes to employees' contracts brought on in response to a necessary reorganization as the only perceived alternative to dismissing the employees (*St John of God (Care Services) Ltd v Brooks* [1992] IRLR 546, EAT)

   (g) appointing someone to an internal interview panel whom the employee perceives to be prejudiced against transsexuals when the employer did not know the employee was a transsexual (*Baldwin v Brighton & Hove City Council* [2007] IRLR 232, EAT)

   (h) conducting a grievance raised by the employee in respect of co-workers in a way the tribunal concluded was a reasonable and proper manner (*Abbey National plc v Fairbrother* [2007] IRLR 320, EAT)

   (i) the actions of a third party, even one whom the employee considered her 'overall boss', over whom the employer had no control (*Yorke v Moonlight* EAT/0025/06) or

   (j) suspending an employee but subsequently, and speedily, exonerating him of the alleged offence (*Assamoi v Spirit Pub Company Services Ltd* [2012] UKEAT 0050/11)

(2) there is a potentially fair reason for the constructive dismissals, and this reason falls within one of the potentially fair reasons set out in s 98(2) of the ERA 1996 or is some other substantial reason

(3) the employee had, unbeknown to the employer at the time, already breached the implied term of trust and confidence before the employer subsequently breached the term (*RDF Media Group plc v Clements* [2008] IRLR 207, HC, where the employee had probably disclosed confidential information to a prospective employer and had assisted the prospective employer in press briefings to put pressure on the existing employer; and *Aberdeen City Council v McNeill* [2010] IRLR 374, EAT, where an employee's serious harassment of a colleague meant that he was not able to maintain a constructive dismissal claim on the basis that the ensuing investigation was oppressive). However, this approach was doubted in *Tullett Prebon plc v BCG Brokers LP* [2010] IRLR 648, QBD; *Brandeaux Advisers Ltd v Chadwick* [2011] IRLR 224, High Court; and *McNeil v Aberdeen City Council (No 2)* [2014] IRLR 114

(4) it acted reasonably in acting in breach of contract (Cape Industrial Services Ltd v Ambler [2003] UKEAT 0950/01).

24.15   An employee's breach of a statutory duty (eg abuse of an employee's trade union rights) may not necessarily be a constructive dismissal (*Doherty v British Midland Airways Ltd* [2006] IRLR 90 EAT).

Grievance procedure

24.16   If an employee believes that he is being unfairly dismissed, the ACAS Code of Practice on Disciplinary and Grievance Procedures applies to the issue whether the employee should lodge a grievance in relation to his potential claim.

24.17   The Code sets out the five steps which should be followed without unreasonable delay. They are:

- the employee must let the employer know the nature of the grievance, in writing
- the employer must hold a meeting with the employer to discuss the grievance
- the employer must allow the employee to be accompanied at the meeting
- the employer must decide on appropriate action
- the employee should be offered the right of appeal.

24.18   If the employer fails to follow the grievance procedure, this does not make any dismissal automatically unfair. If an employee fails to follow the grievance procedure, the employee can still bring proceedings for unfair dismissal, and must do so within three months of the EDT (see para 24.08 for definition of EDT). If either party does not follow the grievance procedure (for example, if the employee does not lodge a grievance, or if the employer does not consider the grievance or does not allow the right of appeal), and if the employee wins the claim for unfair dismissal, the tribunal may adjust the compensation award up or down by up to 25 per cent either way, depending upon which party has failed to comply with the procedures. Tribunals should make such an award where there has been a failure to comply with the code which the tribunal finds is unreasonable. An award may then be granted if the tribunal considers it just and equitable in all the circumstances to make the adjustment (TULR(C)A 1992, s 207A).

C. APPLICATION FOR INTERIM RELIEF

24.19   A person who believes he has been dismissed for:

(1) trade union reasons
(2) most health and safety reasons
(3) acting as trustee of his employer's occupational pension fund
(4) acting as an employee representative in redundancy or TUPE consultations or a Working Time Regulations representative
(5) making a protected disclosure
(6) activities to do with union recognition or
(7) asserting rights to accompany or be accompanied by someone facing disciplinary or grievance proceedings may apply to an employment tribunal for interim relief (ERA 1996, s 128).

24.20   The application must be presented to an employment tribunal within seven days of the EDT (see para 24.08 for definition of EDT). For further details, please see para 3.23.

D. GROUNDS FOR DISMISSAL

24.21   In respect of all qualifying employees, an employer must show that the reason for dismissal is one of the statutorily fair reasons set out in s 98 of the ERA 1996. These are incapability, lack of qualifications, misconduct, redundancy, or breach of statutory provisions. There is also a catch-all ground of 'some other substantial reason which would justify dismissal'.

It is automatically fair to dismiss someone to safeguard national security (Employment Tribunals **24.22** Act 1996, s 10(1)) or while they are taking part in an official strike or industrial action which has lasted for over twelve weeks when all those in a similar position are dismissed, or while taking part in unofficial action (TULR(C)A 1992, ss 237–238A) but, even so, the employer must show that appropriate steps were taken and dismissal was within the range of reasonable responses (for example, that there were no suitable redeployment options, *B v BAA plc* [2005] ICR 1530, EAT).

Time for assessing the reason for dismissal in unfair dismissal cases

A dismissal must be fair, based upon the facts known to the employer either at the date the em- **24.23** ployee was given notice of his dismissal or, if there is an appeal, at the date of the announcement of the appeal decision.

Subsequently discovered conduct

While conduct discovered after notice of dismissal or announcement of any appeal cannot be used **24.24** to justify the dismissal in any unfair dismissal proceedings, it may be taken into account in the following circumstances:

(1) It may be relied upon to show the employer was reasonable in reaching any decision which it did, before dismissal, about the employee's performance or conduct.

(2) It may affect remedies. If subsequently discovered conduct is very serious, it could lead to a finding that it was not just and equitable for the tribunal to make any compensatory award at all because of the employee's conduct (see paras 32.166–32.168—but see also para 24.24(4)).

(3) If new facts arise between the notice of dismissal and the termination date which show that the employer's conduct was unwarranted, this can be relied upon by the employee to show that the ultimate dismissal was unfair and vice versa. For example, if an employer gives an employee notice of termination of his employment as a result of misconduct but, before the termination date, discovers that it was another employee who committed the acts of misconduct in question, if the employer still upholds the original employee's dismissal, this will be unfair.

(4) The employer can rely upon information relating to the original reason for dismissal received during the course of any appeal procedure even where the appeal takes place after the dismissal, though it may not use such information to introduce a fresh reason for dismissal. In these latter circumstances, if the employer wishes to rely upon the new information as a reason for dismissal, the original dismissal should be revoked upon appeal and further dismissal proceedings instituted.

Burden and standard of proof

The employer must show that the reason for dismissal is a potentially fair one. It is then for the tri- **24.25** bunal to determine whether the employer has acted reasonably in all the circumstances in treating the reason for dismissal as a sufficiently serious one to dismiss the employee (ERA 1996, ss 98(1) and 98(4)). The tribunal will look at what the operative reason for dismissal was: even if the employee has committed an act of misconduct, if relying on the misconduct as the reason for dismissal was a sham device from an employer who had other reasons to wish to terminate the employment, dismissal may still be unfair (*ASLEF v Brady* [2006] IRLR 576, EAT).

The process for establishing the reason for dismissal is as follows: **24.26**

(1) it is for the employer to prove a fair reason for his dismissal

(2) there is no burden on the employee to disprove the reason put forward by the employer, or positively to prove a different reason

(3) if the employee chooses to assert that there was a different and inadmissible reason for the dismissal (for example, making a protected disclosure) he must produce some evidence supporting his case and must challenge the employer's case

(4) the employer can defeat a claim of inadmissible reason for dismissal either by proving a different reason or by successfully contesting the employee's proposed reason

(5)   if the tribunal does not accept the employer's case, it may, but is not obliged to, accept that the reason is one put forward by the employee (*Kuzel v Roche Products Ltd* [2008] IRLR 530, CA; see also *Serco Ltd v Dahou* [2017] IRLR 81, CA).

24.27   An employment tribunal cannot substitute its own reasoning and opinions for those of the employer (*Foley v Post Office; HSBC Bank plc v Madden* [2000] IRLR 827, CA). The matter must be judged by the objective standard of the way in which a reasonable employer in that line of business of that size in those circumstances would have behaved. The tribunal must ask the question: 'Was dismissal, as a sanction, one within the range of reasonable responses to the conduct which a reasonable employer might reasonably have imposed?' It is irrelevant whether other employers (or indeed the members of the employment tribunal hearing the case) might have behaved more leniently towards the individual.

Automatically unfair grounds

24.28   Several types of dismissal are automatically unfair. These include where the principal reason for dismissal is:

(1)   *Spent convictions* Dismissal of the employee where the principal reason for the dismissal is a criminal conviction which is deemed to have been spent under the Rehabilitation of Offenders Act 1974 (Rehabilitation of Offenders Act 1974, s 4(3)(b)).

(2)   *Trade union activities* Dismissal of the employee where the principal reason for the dismissal is a reason connected with membership or non-membership of, or participation in, the activities of an independent trade union (TULR(C)A 1992, s 152). For a rare example of a case under this head, see *Evans v Open Sight* [2011] ET/3100599/11, where the employee was dismissed soon after exercising her statutory right to accompany colleagues to disciplinary hearings, and the tribunal critically examined the ostensible reason for dismissal (capability) and decided that the trigger was the representation and planned continued representation of colleagues, so that the dismissal was automatically unfair.

(3)   *Health and safety reasons* Dismissal of the employee where the principal reason is the fact he is a health and safety representative or has taken reasonable action as a result of the inadequacy of health and safety procedures or refuses to work in what he reasonably believes are dangerous surroundings (ERA 1996, s 100). This is a three-step test: (1) Were there circumstances of danger which the employee reasonably (an objective test) believed to be imminent? (2) Either did the employee take or propose to take appropriate steps to protect himself or others from the danger or did the employee take appropriate steps to communicate these circumstances to his employer by appropriate means? (3) If the answers to (1) and (2) are yes, was the employer's sole or principal reason for dismissal that the employee took or proposed to take such steps? (*Oudahar v Esporta Group Limited* [2011] IRLR 730, EAT); Note that there is no statutory maximum ceiling for compensation for dismissals on health and safety grounds (ERA 1996, s 124(1A)).

(4)   *Pension trustee* Dismissal of the employee where the principal reason is that he is trustee of a relevant occupational pension scheme (ERA 1996, s 102).

(5)   *Employee representative* Dismissal of the employee where the principal reason is that he is an employee representative performing consultation on redundancies or transfers of undertakings or that he takes part in an election for employee representatives (ERA 1996, s 103).

(6)   *Assertion of statutory right* Dismissal of the employee where the principal reason is that he has asserted statutory rights (for example, the rights to: written particulars of terms and conditions of employment; minimum statutory notice; time off, holiday, and other rights under the Working Time Regulations 1998; retain employment terms and rights following a TUPE transfer and similar rights) (ERA 1996, ss 101A and 104). This would include dismissal for the principal reason that the employee complained that her salary had not been paid on time, on the basis that she was asserting her statutory right not to have unlawful deductions made from her wages (*Elizabeth Claire Care Management Ltd v Francis* [2005] IRLR 858, EAT). The right must actually be asserted to the employer (*Ajayi and Anor v Aitch Care Homes (London) Ltd* [2012] UKEAT 0464/11, where employees who fell asleep on shift could not

claim that they were asserting a statutory right to rest breaks, if they had not earlier communicated their intention of doing so).

(7) *Family-related reasons* Dismissal of a woman where the principal reason for the dismissal is because she is pregnant or for a reason connected with pregnancy, maternity leave, adoption leave, ante-natal leave, paternity leave, shared parental leave, or compassionate leave (ERA 1996, s 99). This is so where the stated reason for dismissal is a reasonable one such as misconduct, but where the tribunal is satisfied that the real reason for dismissal relates to family matters (*Coulombeau v Enterprise Rent-a-Car (UK) Ltd* [2007] IDS Employment Law Brief 826, ET, where the tribunal found that the real reason for dismissal was the employer's view that the employee was likely to become entitled to additional leave because she was hoping to adopt a child). To succeed in arguing that the sole or principal reason for dismissal relates to paternity leave, the employee must probably show that the dismissal was caused by the paternity leave—this is a stronger test than just showing that the dismissal was associated with taking paternity leave (*Atkins v Coyle Personnel plc* [2008] UKEAT 0206/07).

(8) *Transfer of undertakings* Dismissal of the employee where the sole or principal reason for the dismissal is the transfer of an undertaking unless the employer can show that the dismissal was for an 'economic, technical or organisational reason entailing changes in the workforce' (ETO reason) (TUPE 2006, reg 7). The exception applies only if the proposed changes relate to job functions or numbers or the place where employees are employed by the employer and must apply to the particular employee who is dismissed (*Miles v Insitu Cleaning Co Ltd* [2013] UKEAT 0157/12, EAT). For examples of the application of this rule, see *Meter U Ltd v Ackroyd and Others* [2012] ICR 834, EAT; *Manchester College v Hazel and Anor* [2012] UKEAT 0642/11 and 0136/12; *Spaceright Europe Ltd v Baillavoine and Others* [2012] ICR 520, CA; and *Abellio London Ltd v Musse and Others* [2012] IRLR 360, EAT.

(9) *Industrial action* Dismissal of those taking part in official industrial action either during the first twelve weeks of the action, or (if the employee in question has stopped taking part in the industrial action) after this period (TULR(C)A 1992, s 238A(2), (3)).

(10) *Public interest disclosures* Dismissal of a person for being a 'whistle-blower' (ERA 1996, s 103A) and making a protected disclosure (see also ERA 1996, ss 43A–43K and, for example, *Street v Derbyshire Unemployed Workers' Centre* [2004] ICR 213, EAT). Note that there is no statutory maximum ceiling for compensation for dismissals on public interest disclosure grounds (ERA 1996, s 124(1A)). The law relating to the dismissal of 'whistle-blowers' is set out in more detail in Chapter 31.

(11) *Sunday working* Dismissal of a shop or betting worker, who has been continuously employed by the same employer since before 1995 and who has opted out of Sunday working, for refusing to work on a Sunday (ERA 1996, s 101).

(12) *Minimum wage* Dismissal of an employee for trying to enforce the rights of himself or others to a minimum wage (ERA 1996, s 104A).

(13) *Union recognition* Dismissal of an employee for getting involved or refusing to get involved in an application for union recognition (TULR(C)A 1992, Sch A1, para 161).

(14) *Tax credit rights* Dismissal of an employee for trying to enforce the rights of himself or others to working tax credits (formerly working families' tax credits) or disabled person's tax credits (ERA 1996, s 104B).

(15) *Accompanying colleagues at disciplinary or grievance hearings* Dismissal of an employee for accompanying or being accompanied by a colleague at a disciplinary or grievance hearing (Employment Relations Act 1999, s 12).

(16) *Part-time and fixed-term workers* Dismissal of an employee for enforcing rights under the Part-time Workers (Prevention of Less Favourable Treatment) Regulations 2000, reg 7; or the Fixed-Term Employees (Prevention of Less Favourable Treatment) Regulations 2002, reg 6.

(17) *Works Councils* Dismissal of an employee for activities in connection with European Works Councils (Transnational Information and Consultation of Employees Regulations 1999, regulation 28) or information and consultation bodies (Information and Consultation of Employees Regulations 2004, reg 30).

(18) *Flexible working request* Dismissal for exercising rights to apply for flexible working (ERA 1996, s 104C).

Part C The Substantive Law

(19) *Refusal to become employee shareholder* Dismissal of an employee who refuses to accept an offer of £2,000–£50,000-worth of paid-up shares in his employer in return for forfeiting the rights to request study or training, request flexible working, to be unfairly dismissed and to a redundancy payment (ERA 1996, s 104G and s 205A). (Note that the tax benefits associated with the employee shareholder status were withdrawn with effect from 1 December 2016.)

(20) *Study and training* Dismissal of an employee for making a statutory request to undertake study or training (ERA 1996, s 104E).

(21) *Blacklist* Dismissal of an employee whose name is on a prohibited blacklist for trade union activities (ERA 1996, s 104F).

(22) *Unfair selection for redundancy* Selection for redundancy on one of the grounds set out above (save relating to flexible working arrangements and works councils) (ERA 1996, s 105).

Special provisions relating to retirement dismissals

24.29 Retirement dismissals are now subject to the normal test of fairness of procedure set out in ERA 1996, s 98(4). However, for dismissals between 1 October 2006 and 30 September 2011 the provisions of ERA 1996, ss 98ZA–98ZH applied so that during this period:

(1) Dismissal of an employee below the age of 65, in the absence of a normal retirement age below 65, is not for retirement.

(2) Dismissal of an employee 65 or older, in the absence of a normal retirement age or at the normal retirement age, is for retirement provided the employer has told the employee of his right to request not to retire (Employment Equality (Age) Regulations 2006, Sch 6, para 2) and the dismissal takes effect on the intended date of retirement. Note: these provisions have been repealed with effect from 1 October 2011 (The Employment Equality (Repeal of Retirement Age Provisions) Regulations 2011, regs 2 and 3, repealing ERA 1996, ss 98ZA–98ZH; varying Equality Act 2010, Sch 9). From 1 October 2011, retirement is no longer a valid reason for an employer to dismiss an employee.

Written reasons for dismissal

24.30 An employee who has been continuously employed for two years or more has the right to request written reasons for his dismissal. No such continuity qualification applies if the employee is pregnant at the time of the dismissal or if she is dismissed while pregnant or during her maternity or adoption leave, when reasons should be given whether or not requested. The employer must respond to such requests within fourteen days (ERA 1996, ss 92 and 93). If the employer unreasonably fails to give reasons, it is liable to pay the employee two weeks' pay.

24.31 An employment tribunal is not bound to accept the employer's stated reason or reasons for dismissal if it finds that the reasons given conceal the true reason, but in any tribunal proceedings the employer is bound by the facts given in the stated reasons support of any dismissal, though not necessarily by the legal label given to those facts.

24.32 When considering the reasons the tribunal will seek to ensure that they are genuinely held by the employer. If the employer relies on more than one reason, he may have to prove all of them to show a fair dismissal. If the tribunal decides that the stated reason for dismissal, even where misconduct has been committed which would potentially justify a dismissal, is not the true reason, the dismissal may be unfair (*ASLEF v Brady* [2006] IRLR 576, EAT).

Fair reasons

24.33 In any dismissal action, the burden is on the employer to show the reason for dismissal. In a case of wrongful dismissal, the employer must then show that the reason is sufficiently serious to have justified the employer terminating the contract, whether he knew of the reason at the date of termination or otherwise. For unfair dismissal, the tribunal will decide:

(1) what the reason for dismissal was

(2) whether it was the actual reason why the decision to dismiss was taken and

(3) whether it was a fair reason.

Potentially fair reasons are set out in s 98 of the ERA 1996, and are: **24.34**

(1) that the employee was incapable (measured by reference to skills, aptitude, health, or any physical or mental quality) of performing the work of the kind he was currently employed by the employer to do (see paras 24.49–24.53 for incompetence and paras 24.54–24.64 for ill-health)

(2) that the employee lacked the qualifications required to perform work of the kind that he was currently employed by the employer to do (see paras 24.65–24.66)

(3) misconduct (see paras 24.35–24.48)

(4) redundancy (see Chapter 25)

(5) that if the employee were to continue to be employed in the position he held, either he or the employer would be in breach of some statutory provision (see paras 24.67–24.68)

(6) retirement before 1 October 2011 (see para 24.29) and

(7) some other substantial reason which will justify dismissal (see paras 24.69–24.71).

E. MISCONDUCT

Generally, misconduct amounts to behaviour which is unacceptable in the employment context. **24.35** Most reasonably sized employers will have a code of conduct, either in a staff manual or in an employment contract, which gives examples of misconduct with differing degrees of seriousness.

Disciplinary code

A disciplinary code may be expressly incorporated into the employee's contract of employment. If **24.36** it is, its provisions should be adhered to. In the absence of an express disciplinary code, any employment tribunal will have regard to the ACAS Disciplinary Code of Practice (see para 24.37). It will also expect any contractual disciplinary code to be along similar lines.

The ACAS Code of Practice on Disciplinary and Grievance Procedures provides that facts should **24.37** be established promptly following any disciplinary matter and an individual should be interviewed and given the opportunity to state his or her case and be advised of any rights under the procedure before a decision is made. They should have the right to be accompanied at any formal disciplinary meeting and a right of appeal (see Chapter 24, section I for further details).

Minor offences

The ACAS Code of Practice on Disciplinary and Grievance Procedures states that in the case of **24.38** minor offences the individual should in general first be given a written warning setting out the nature of the offence and the likely consequence of further offences. Further misconduct might warrant a final written warning, which should contain a statement that any one occurrence could lead to suspension or dismissal. Minor offences include lateness, taking overly long meal breaks, minor acts of insubordination or rudeness, and so on. Appeals should be available at every stage. For dismissal following minor offences, normally, spent warnings cannot be relied on as part of the cumulative process *(Diosynth Ltd v Thomson* [2006] IRLR 284, CS), but this is not a hard and fast rule where the employee has committed gross misconduct. One example of this is *Airbus UK Ltd v Webb* [2008] IRLR 309, CA, where five employees were watching television during working hours. One had a spent warning, the other four had clean disciplinary records. The fact that the employer viewed the clean records as a mitigating factor converting dismissal to a final warning for four of the employees did not make dismissal of the fifth employee unfair, where the employer viewed him differently because he had previously been subject to a final written warning, even though that warning was spent. In another case, a dismissal was found to be potentially fair on grounds of misconduct when the dismissal took into account the claimant's poor disciplinary history in general, including his expired warnings, and the claimant's manager's belief that the situation was unlikely to change (*Stratford v Auto Trail VR Ltd* EAT 0116/16) (see also para 24.115).

Gross misconduct

24.39 Any single act of gross misconduct (ie serious breach of contract) will be sufficient to justify immediate dismissal without notice, money in lieu of notice, or compensation. Employers should be consistent (*Cain v Leeds Western Health Authority* [1990] ICR 585), and impose similar sanctions for similar offences; if not, the employee given the tougher sanction may be unfairly dismissed so long as the circumstances are truly comparable (*Levenes Solicitors v Dalley* [2007] UKEAT 0330/2006). They should also act reasonably speedily in taking disciplinary action—if they delay (even while an employee is taking time off for stress) without reserving their position, they may have waived the right to dismiss summarily (*Cook v MSHK Limited* [2009] EWCA Civ 624, CA).

24.40 Misconduct involves some deliberate or reckless act or omission. Negligence or carelessness will generally be regarded as incapability (see paras 24.49–24.53).

Examples of misconduct

Refusal to obey a lawful order

24.41 Refusal to obey a lawful instruction is misconduct. The nature of the refusal and the importance of the order will determine whether the misconduct is minor or gross (*UCATT v Brain* [1981] IRLR 224, CA). To determine what is lawful, one must look at the contract and any other incorporated documents such as a collective agreement or staff handbook, and at custom and practice. If the instruction is not lawful, that fact is not necessarily decisive when deciding whether any resulting dismissal was reasonable (*Farrant v Woodroffe School* [1998] ICR 184).

24.42 Examples of refusals include:

(1) refusal to comply with safety requirements
(2) refusal to move location if the contract provides that the employee can be required to move to a proposed new site
(3) refusal to perform a task which the employee is contractually obliged to perform
(4) refusal to work reasonable overtime if the contract provides that the employees must work overtime so long as the employee is not being asked to work hours or at times that would involve a breach of the Working Time Regulations 1998
(5) refusal to give new terms of employment a trial run, after having agreed (albeit reluctantly) to do so (Robinson v Tescom Corporation EAT 0567/07).

24.43 The following acts would not amount to misconduct under this head:

(1) refusal by employees to work in dangerous conditions (and indeed a dismissal on this basis may be automatically unfair)
(2) refusal to obey an unlawful order, for example, to falsify accounts
(3) refusal to work overtime if the employee is not contractually obliged to do so
(4) refusal to accept changes in terms and conditions of employment. However, if the employer can show that the changes are justifiable because of pressing business need, the dismissal may be for some other substantial reason and so the employer would be justified in dismissing the employee
(5) frequent short-term, self-certified absences should be dealt with under the procedure set out at para 24.55, and not as misconduct.

Breaches of discipline

24.44 If the employer's disciplinary code sets out an exhaustive list of disciplinary offences, no additional offences omitted from the list may be relied upon. If the disciplinary code sets out examples only of breaches of disciplinary procedure, then items which are not set out in the list may nevertheless, if sufficiently serious, be categorized by the employer as misconduct. To justify summary dismissal, the conduct must completely undermine the trust and confidence inherent in the employment re-lationship (*Neary v Dean of Westminster* [1999] IRLR 288). An employer can rely on breach of trust and confidence where the employee evinces an intention no longer to comply with her contractual obligations. However, if the employer simply loses confidence in the employee's abilities, this will not amount to an employee's breach of contract, and will not justify a 'losing trust and confidence' ground for dismissal (*R (Shoesmith) v OFSTED and Others* [2011] IRLR, 679 CA, when the court ruled that the London Borough of Haringey had been wrong summarily to dismiss its director of children's services following a requirement for it to do so by the Secretary of State for Education after the notorious death of Baby P; the borough's concerns related to competence, and it was un-just to dismiss the director for being accountable for the death without giving her an opportunity to respond and explain).

Examples of breaches of discipline are: **24.45**

(1) drunkenness at work (provided any alcohol policy which requires an employee to seek treat-ment for his alcoholism is drawn to his attention before the event in question: *Sinclair v Wandsworth Council* [2007] UKEAT 0145/07). The employer should question whether the drunkenness is an act of misconduct or the manifestation of a long-term illness, such as bi-polar disorder, requiring medical opinion and consultation, through which the employee should be supported (*Strathclyde Regional Council v Syme* (EAT 233/79))

(2) possessing or taking illegal drugs at the workplace (or off duty, if work is safety-critical) (*Mathewson v RB Wilson Dental Laboratory Ltd* [1988] IRLR 512, EAT; *Booth v Southampton Airport Ltd* Case No 39214/81, ET)

(3) theft of employer's, colleagues', clients', or suppliers' property (*Trusthouse Forte Hotels Ltd v Murphy* [1977] IRLR 186, EAT)

(4) physical violence or fighting

(5) threatening behaviour

(6) bad language

(7) rudeness

(8) fraud, for example, falsifying timesheets, or giving false information on a curriculum vitae (for example, not disclosing a past, unspent conviction)

(9) gross insubordination

(10) failure to comply with legitimate management instructions, eg a director flouting his managing director's express instructions not to attend a particular meeting (*Annis v Eclipse Energy* [2007] All ER (D) 73, HC)

(11) working for or assisting a competitor whilst still employed, particularly where the employees are directors or have senior positions, so that they owe fiduciary duties or duties of fidelity to the employer (*Davidson and Maillou v Comparisons* [1980] IRLR 360, EAT; *Crowson Fabrics Ltd v Rider* [2008] IRLR 288, HC) (although merely seeking alternative employment even before the termination of the present contract is not unlawful: *Harris & Russell Ltd v Slingsby* [1973] IRLR 221, NIRC) and, in the absence of a contractual provision to the contrary, preparing to compete by developing a competitive product in one's spare time may not be a breach of fiduciary or other duties (*Helmet Integrated Systems v Tunnard* [2007] IRLR 126)

(12) misusing or unlawfully disclosing confidential information

(13) downloading the employer's confidential documents to a personal account, even if with a view to defending legal proceedings or disclosure to a regulator (*Brandeaux Advisers Ltd v Chadwick* [2011] IRLR 224, HC)

(14) serious computer misuse (*Spence v Department of Agriculture and Rural Development* [2011] IRLR 806, NICA)

(15) unauthorized use of or tampering with a computer (*Denco Ltd v Joinson* [1991] IRLR 63, EAT)

(16) sending an offensive email from a home computer to a colleague's home computer—privacy issues did not apply as the offending item was chain email (*Gosden v Lifeline Project Ltd* [2011] 2802731/2009/ET)

(17) taking unauthorized industrial action (but see para 24.28(9))

(18) taking bribes or secret commissions

(19) serious breach of codes of relevant professional or governing bodies

(20) failure to comply with important company policy, eg smoking on company premises (*Smith v Michelin Tyre plc* [2007] ETS 100726/07, ET) or failure to disclose and seek formal approval for work performed for third parties, even though the employee had mentioned the work to her employers (*Guernina v Thames Valley University* [2008] EWCA Civ 34, CA)

(21) refusal to give consent to disclosure of medical records when there was a contractual obligation requiring the employee to do so, even though the employee had consented to undergo a medical examination (*Chaplin v Howard Kennedy* [2009] All ER (D) 16 (Jun) EAT)

(22) failure to report a major issue of possible fraud by a supplier, because the employee was trying to resolve the issue in good faith, even though the employee had a contractual obligation to abide by the employer's risk management guidelines which required him to report any significant negative information relating to the employer (*Dunn v AAH Ltd* [2010] IRLR 709, CA)

(23) a lorry driver allowing his HGV licence to expire but still carrying dangerous loads on a lorry—hence without licence or insurance (*Wincanton plc v Atkinson and Another* [2011] UKEAT/0040/11). This was a fair reason to dismiss, because of the potentially horrific consequences, even though no harm was in fact done

(24) raising unfair and multiple baseless grievances, in bad faith or in an aggressive (not merely intemperate) manner (*Woodhouse v West North West Homes Leeds Ltd* [2013] 0007/12, EAT)

(25) an employee leaving the shop where he worked carrying goods which had not been paid for (*Stuart v London City Airport Ltd* [2013] EWCA Civ 973, CA)

(26) The expression of forthright views on issues such as gay marriage by an employee on his private facebook wall, promoting views which the employer thought were contrary to its code of conduct, did not amount to misconduct or bring the employer into disrepute—it would have been obvious to any reader that the views were for personal and social, rather than work-related purposes, and were not liable to cause offence to work colleagues. The prohibition in the employer's code of conduct rules on promoting political or religious views did not extend to a personal Facebook wall (*Smith v Trafford Housing Trust* [2013] IRLR 86, HC)

(27) poor attitude to organizational change (*Adeshina v St George's University Hospitals NHS Foundation Trust and Others* [2017] EWCA Civ 257)

(28) serious failure to comply with an implied term of the employment to report safeguarding issues, where the claimant is under a duty to assist her employer with its safeguarding duties (*Reilly v Sandwell Metropolitan Borough Council* [2018] UKSC 18). The claimant's failure to admit that she was in breach contributed to the decision to dismiss.

Criminal offences

24.46 Criminal offences should only merit dismissal if they relate in some way to the employee's duties, for example, because they show that the employee is unsuitable for performing that type of work, or because the offence damages the employees' relationship with the employer, other employees and/or customers. This is a precept of the ACAS Code of Practice on Disciplinary and Grievance Procedures (see para 31 of the Code).

24.47 Examples of criminal offences which justify dismissal are:

(1) dishonesty (fraud, theft, etc): this will normally justify dismissal unless, for example, the employee has been actively employed (ie not just on suspension) for a period

(2) sexual offences: these will justify dismissal if the employee's duties often put him in contact with women or children, especially vulnerable ones, for example, where the job is in the education or health sectors (*X v Y* [2004] IRLR 625; *P v Nottinghamshire County Council* [1992] IRLR 362, CA) but not where they are unproven and historical (*Z v A* UKEAT/0203/13 and UKEAT/0380/13)

(3) minor criminal offences which do not justify dismissal include minor drugs or traffic offences—these will not usually justify dismissal unless, for example, drug addiction affects the employee's capability or the employee's job requires a clean driving licence.

24.48 For appropriate procedure where misconduct is alleged, see paras 24.72–24.119.

F. INCOMPETENCE

If the employer honestly believes, on reasonable grounds, that the employee is incompetent, he **24.49** may dismiss him. It is, however, very rare that an employer may fairly dismiss an employee for incompetence if the employee has not had proper appraisals and warnings before a final decision is taken.

Evidence of incompetence

The employment tribunal must rely to a large extent on the evidence of the employee's superiors **24.50** in deciding whether or not an employee has been incompetent. An employer should have specific examples of incompetence, for example:

(1) failure by the employee to perform part of his duties
(2) complaints by colleagues or customers about the actions of the employee
(3) inaccuracies committed by the employee
(4) delays in finishing work by the employee
(5) inflexibility and lack of adaptability on the part of the employee (*Abernethy v Mott Hay & Anderson* [1974] IRLR 213, CA)
(6)· slovenliness or persistent carelessness on the part of the employee or
(7) negligent acts or omissions on the part of the employee.

Separate and dissimilar acts of incompetence may cumulatively be relied upon by the em- **24.51** ployer. The employee is to be judged by the standards to be expected of someone in his present job, even if he has been over-promoted by the employer: the employee cannot demand to be returned to his former position, although in these circumstances a prudent employer would seek to establish whether there are any lower grade jobs to which the employee could be transferred.

Procedure

Before dismissing the employee for incompetence, the employer will normally need to adopt the **24.52** following procedure (see also ACAS of Practice on Disciplinary and Grievance Procedures, and ACAS guidance is available at http://www.acas.org.uk/index.aspx?articleid=2179):

(1) *Appraisal* The employer should discuss with the employee the criticisms he has of the employee's performance. The employer should maintain a system to monitor the employee's progress.
(2) *Warning* The employer should write to the employee telling him where his performance is deemed to be substandard, inviting him and a representative to come to a meeting to discuss his concerns and giving him an opportunity to express his point of view and explain why he might have been performing badly. If the explanation is not satisfactory, the employer should warn the employee of the consequences of a failure to improve. This should, preferably, be in writing. The warning should set out:
   (a) where the employee has failed to meet the required standards
   (b) the time within which the employee must improve and a review date
   (c) the standard the employee must meet
   (d) any support/training the employer will provide to assist the employee
   (e) the fact that if the employee fails to improve, a further warning will be necessary (or, after the second warning that dismissal may be invoked) and
   (f) the fact that the employee has a right to appeal.
(3) *Opportunity to improve* The employer must give the employee a reasonable period within which to improve. In establishing what is reasonable one must bear in mind the nature of the job, the employee's length of service, status, and past performance. The employer should give the employee the necessary support and assistance (which can include training) to enable the employee to improve. Normally, employees should receive at least two warnings before being dismissed for poor performance (but see para 24.53).

Part C The Substantive Law

(4) An employee of previously good standing and long service will require special attention by the employer before any dismissal is made. He should be given reasonably substantial periods within which to improve unless there are very obvious reasons why the employee has suddenly become incapable, such as:

    (a) the employee's capacity to do the job is altered, for example, because of ill-health (but see Chapter 26 on disability discrimination)

    (b) the employee's job functions have altered, for example, as a result of new technology

    (c) the employee has failed to heed past warnings.

24.53 Warnings for incompetence may not be necessary in the following circumstances:

(1) gross incompetence or unsuitability

(2) incompetence which has had serious physical consequences, for example, where a pilot has incompetently landed a plane causing actual or potential injury to passengers and/or expensive equipment (*Alidair Ltd v Taylor* [1976] IRLR 420, EAT)

(3) incompetence which has serious economic consequences, for example, deliberate or reckless incompetence leading to a loss of a whole production batch

(4) incompetence where the employer reasonably believes that a warning would make no difference, for example, where an employee refuses to admit that there is any need for him to improve

(5) the incompetence of a senior employee, who should appreciate what standards are required of him and whether he matches up to those standards. The employee must, however, be in a position to know (whether from his own experience or because he has been told his work is unsatisfactory) that he may be dismissed unless his work meets the required standard.

G. ILL-HEALTH

24.54 Before dismissing an employee on the grounds of ill-health, the employer should make proper inquiry into the actual state of the employee's health, its likely duration, and its effect upon the employee's ability to perform his tasks.

Absenteeism

24.55 Where the employee takes frequent short-term, self-certificated absences, the employer should:

(1) review the employee's attendance record and the reasons given for it

(2) give the employee the opportunity to explain his attendance record (*International Sports Co Ltd v Thompson* [1980] IRLR 340, EAT)

(3) if the employee does not give a satisfactory explanation, but claims his absences are on grounds of ill-health, or if there is any reason to suspect that the absences are caused by any disability, ask him to see a doctor to consider whether medical treatment is necessary. Any genuine illness must be treated with sympathy and under normal illness procedures (see paras 24.58–24.62). However, the fact that someone is disabled does not of itself prevent the employer from dismissing him for absenteeism (*Royal Liverpool Children's NHS Trust v Dunsby* [2006] IRLR 351), although an employer should consider whether it might be a 'reasonable adjustment' to disregard disability-related absences (see paras 26.114–26.123). If there are no reasonable adjustments that can be made, then the contract may be terminated by means of frustration (*Warner v Armfield Retail and Leisure Ltd* [2013] 0376/12, EAT)

(4) if there is still no satisfactory explanation for the absences, give the employee a misconduct warning that further unwarranted absences are likely to result in dismissal

(5) interview the employee after any subsequent absence to ascertain its cause.

If there is no improvement in the attendance record, and still no valid reason for the absences, the employer may dismiss the employee.

Disability

Where the employer knew, when it engaged the employee, of the existence and extent of a dis- **24.56** ability, it is most unlikely to be able to dismiss the employee fairly by reason only of the disability; if it does, this is likely to be discrimination under the terms of the disability provisions in the EqA 2010 (*Williams v J Walter Thompson Group Ltd* [2005] IRLR 376, CA), see paras 26.64–26.78. In those circumstances, the standard of work required of the employee will be that of a disabled person to do the particular job in hand.

Where the employee becomes disabled during the course of his employment, he should be treated **24.57** in the same manner as employees suffering from other illnesses but subject always to the disability provisions of the EqA 2010, in particular in relation to the making of reasonable adjustments to the workplace (see paras 26.114–26.123).

Illness

Before taking any action regarding the employee's illness, provided the employee is not disabled **24.58** within the definition of disability provisions of the EqA 2010, s 6 and Sch 1 (see paras 26.21–26.28) the employer should take the following steps:

(1) consult the employee about the situation and ask the employee for his own views on his health and abilities (*East Lindsey District Council v Daubney* [1977] IRLR 181, EAT)
(2) where appropriate, obtain a medical opinion. This medical opinion should be more detailed than a mere expression of opinion that the employee is unfit to work, and should deal with the likelihood of an improvement in health and attendance. The employee cannot be compelled (in the absence of an express contractual term) to undergo medical examinations. Where the absences are unconnected and intermittent, or where otherwise there will be no apparent benefit from a medical review of the position, there will be no obligation to obtain medical evidence (*Lynock v Cereal Packaging Ltd* [1988] IRLR 510, EAT)
(3) examine the sickness record
(4) discuss the position again with the employee
(5) review whether there is any alternative employment which might suit the employee
(6) consider whether the employee can be 'medically retired' and granted an ill-health pension— failure to do so could render a dismissal unfair (*First West Yorkshire Ltd v Haigh* [2008] IRLR 182, EAT). The general test is that the employer must carry out a reasonable investigation and then decide whether the employee should be dismissed—a managerial and not a medical decision. A tribunal will look at whether a reasonable employer could decide, on the evidence before it, whether the employee was capable of returning to his post (*DB Schenker Rail (UK) Ltd v Doolan* [2011] EAT0053/09 EAT). The key test for whether an employer has been too precipitate in dismissing an employee for ill-health is whether a reasonable employer would have waited longer and, if so, for how much longer, whether there has been appropriate consultation with the employee, and whether reasonable steps have been taken to find out the employee's condition and prognosis. It is not necessary for the employer to pursue detailed medical examination as the decision to dismiss is not a medical question but a question to be answered in the light of the available medical advice (*BS v Dundee City Council* [2013] CSIH 91 XA 162/12, CS).

If the employee is disabled within the definition of disability in the EqA 2010, s 6 and Sch 1, but **24.59** the employer is contemplating dismissing the employee, for example because of incompetence or absenteeism, the employer must review whether any reasonable adjustments might improve the position, for example by giving training or adapting the working environment (in the case of incompetence) or changing the working hours (in the case of absenteeism), and if there are any, it should make them. Failure to do so would render a dismissal a breach of ss 20–21 of the EqA 2010.

Having formed a reasoned opinion of the employee's medical state, the employer should consider **24.60** the following factors:

(1) the nature of the illness
(2) the likelihood of it recurring

(3) the length of absences likely and the intervening spaces of good health

(4) the requirements of his business

(5) whether the employee's tasks can smoothly be done by colleagues or temporary employees while the employee is absent, bearing in mind the size of the organization

(6) the impact on colleagues of the employee's absence

(7) the employee's length of service

(8) the need for the employer to have employees of this nature in rude health (for example, deep-sea divers, heavy manual workers)

(9) whether the ill-health might cause potential problems at the workplace (for example, an epileptic may be thought unable to work with dangerous machinery or in a nightclub)

(10) whether continuing to employ the individual in his former job, or any suitable available employment, could give rise to injury for which the employer could be liable, if medical opinion is disregarded and the employee returns to work (*Liverpool Area Health Authority (Teaching) Central & Southern District v Edwards* [1977] IRLR 471, EAT)

(11) alternative employment (for example, a desk job) for the employee, even if at a reduced rate of pay. The employer is not, however, expected to create a special job for the employee but only to look to see whether he has any suitable vacancies (*Merseyside & North Wales Electricity Board v Taylor* [1975] IRLR 60, HC)

(12) whether it is possible to make adjustments to the workplace so that the employee could return to work

(13) whether the employee has exhausted his sick pay

(14) any permanent health insurance scheme maintained by the employer. The employer should generally not dismiss an employee who is still entitled to benefits under the scheme, especially if by doing so, the employee is unable to benefit from the scheme in the future. Even if the employer has an express contractual right to dismiss, the courts are likely to strive to stop the employer blocking an employee's rights under, for example, a permanent health insurance scheme

(15) whether the employee has been consulted with, whether his views have been taken into account, and whether such views have been properly balanced against a medical professional's opinion.

See, generally, *Spencer v Paragon Wallpapers Ltd* [1976] IRLR 373 and *BS v Dundee City Council* [2013] CSIH 91 XA 162/12, CS. Length of service is not automatically relevant—the issue is whether the length of service, and the manner in which the service was rendered during the period, yields inferences that indicate that the employee is likely to return to work as soon as he can (*BS v Dundee City Council* [2013] CSIH 91 XA 162/12, CS).

24.61 If it is clear, after consultation with the employee and his representative, that the employee will not within a reasonable time be able to resume his duties satisfactorily, and there are no alternative available jobs which the employee could be offered, and, for disabled employees, no reasonable adjustments that can be made to improve the position, it may be reasonable for the employer to dismiss the employee. This may be the case even where the employer's behaviour caused or contributed to the relevant incapacity, if there is no prospect of the employee being sufficiently well to return to work and the employer acted reasonably in all the circumstances (*McAldie v Royal Bank of Scotland* [2006] All ER (D) 393, EAT).

24.62 Very serious ill-health, which will either mean the employee cannot in future carry out his old role or will be absent for long periods of time (at least more than the period when the employer's sick pay scheme operates) can in rare circumstances mean that the contract terminates by frustration, and there is, therefore, no dismissal.

HIV

24.63 An employer will generally not be able to dismiss an employee who is HIV positive unless AIDS has manifested itself and prevents the employee from working properly. The employer must consider the issues set out at paras 24.58–24.62 and the disability provisions of the EqA 2010 (see Chapter 26) in the normal way. An employer will not be able to dismiss an HIV positive employee following workforce pressure (see para 24.69(4)). The employer should seek to allay unreasoned fears of any of the employee's colleagues. A person who is HIV positive or who has cancer or multiple sclerosis is now automatically regarded as disabled (EqA 2010, Sch 1, para 6).

Responsibility for absences

When considering whether the employee was unfairly dismissed on grounds of ill-health, the cause **24.64** of the ill-health is immaterial. An employer who caused the ill-health may still dismiss an employee after going through the steps in paras 24.58–24.62, but may face High Court or county court proceedings for a personal injury claim.

H. OTHER REASONS FOR DISMISSAL

Lack of qualifications

Generally, an employer has an opportunity to assess a prospective employee's qualifications before **24.65** employing him. There are therefore only limited circumstances where this ground can be relied upon, for example:

(1) where someone employed as a driver loses his driving licence or
(2) where regulations, or new and profoundly sensible employer practice, require an employee carrying out work which the original employee had previously been doing to have particular qualifications, which the original employee does not possess.

Where an employer proposes to dismiss for lack of qualifications, it should still look to see whether **24.66** there are any alternative jobs in which he can place the employee.

Illegality

If an employer is to dismiss an employee under this head the employment must genuinely be in **24.67** breach of the law. If the employer erroneously believes it is, then the dismissal may be fair for some other substantial reason but not under the heading of illegality (*Kelly v University of Southampton* [2010] UKEAT 0139/10). Examples of illegality include:

(1) the employee losing a work permit. If the employer mistakenly believes the employee does not have the appropriate work permit, this may be some other substantial reason justifying dismissal (see para 24.69) but an illegality defence can only be relied on when it would actually be illegal to continue the employment (*Klusova v London Borough of Hounslow* [2007] EWCA Civ 1127, CA) (*Baker v Abellio London Ltd* [2018] IRLR 186, EAT). However, a contract will not be regarded as illegal just because the employee is working for a lower salary than that specified on the work permit, where the application for the permit had been genuine, and there was no misrepresentation or collusion in obtaining it (*San Ling Chinese Medical Centre v Lian Wei Ji* [2009] UKEAT/0201/09). Nor will it be illegal simply because a 'right of residence' stamp in a passport has expired, so long as the employee still has a right to work in the UK, for example due to being a family member of an EEA National (*Okuoimose v City Facilities Management (UK) Ltd* [2012] UKEAT 0192/11)
(2) the employee being disqualified from driving if driving is an essential part of the job
(3) the employee no longer having relevant professional qualifications (for example, an employed solicitor or doctor who is struck off his respective professional register).

Before dismissing on the ground of illegality the employer should consider whether it has any alter- **24.68** native vacancies which it could offer the employee that the employee would not legally be disqualified from performing. The employer does not have to create a suitable position if none is available. An alternative route to dismissal may be some other substantial reason (*Nayak v Royal Mail Group Limited* [2016] UKEATS/0011/15).

Part C The Substantive Law

Some other substantial reason

24.69 Examples of this catch-all provision to justify a dismissal include:

(1) An unreasonable refusal by the employee to accept changes in the terms and conditions of his employment whose imposition is necessary for sound business reasons. The tribunal should consider whether the dismissal is in accordance with equity, for example by looking at whether management has accepted a similar pay cut, and whether or not a fair process was adopted in the negotiation of the pay cut (*Garside & Laycock Ltd v Booth* [2011] IRLR 735, EAT; *Willow Oak Developments Ltd v Silverwood* [2006] IRLR 607, CA; *Catamaran Cruisers Ltd v Williams* [1994] IRLR 386, EAT).

(2) Where a genuine business reorganization dislodges an employee: the employer must show there is economic necessity for the reorganization and be prepared to produce supporting financial accounts (*Banerjee v City & Eastern London Health Authority* [1979] IRLR 147, EAT). If the reorganization is not genuine, but a pretext for getting rid of an old employee, it will be unfair (*Oakley v The Labour Party* [1988] IRLR 34, CA). When reviewing the employer's decision, the tribunal should conduct a balancing act, taking into account the advantages to the employer of its business reorganization and the disadvantages to employees—the employer does not have to go so far as to show that the changes are vital for the survival of the business (*Glasgow City Council v Deans* [2005] UKEATS 0061/05).

(3) A personality clash if it disrupts workplace relationships (*Ezsias v N Glamorgan NHS Trust* [2011] IRLR 550, EAT). An employer should first try to establish whether the position is remediable, for example, by moving one of the employees to another department.

(4) The dismissal of the employee at the request of a third party (*Dobie v Burns International Security Services (UK) Ltd* [1984] IRLR 329, EAT). The employer must take into account, however, the potential injustice to the employee before acting on the third party's request. This will only be a fair dismissal in exceptional cases, for example, if a valued customer requires the employer to dismiss the employee (which the employer will have to prove—for example, by having a letter from the customer) (*Henderson v Connect South Tyneside Ltd* [2010] IRLR 466, EAT, where dismissal was fair in circumstances where the employer had done everything that he reasonably could to avoid or mitigate the injustice brought about by the client's stance—in this case by trying, albeit unsuccessfully, to persuade the client to change its mind, and to find alternative work for the employee; and *Bancroft v Interserve (Facilities Management) Ltd* [2013] UKEAT 0329/12, EAT). The employer should take into account issues such as the employee's length of service, work record, and potential difficulties in finding a new job (*Greenwood v Whiteghyll Plastics Ltd* [2007] UKEAT 0219/07). This ground will not help any employer who, for example, gives in to union pressure to dismiss the employee. It would be against a person's human rights under Arts 8 and 14 of the ECHR to dismiss someone who is HIV positive in response to calls to do so from the workforce, even if the reason is to secure the workforce's harmonious atmosphere (*IB v Greece* App no 552/10 (ECtHR, 3 October 2013)).

(5) The dismissal of an employee following a report by a body such as the Child Abuse Investigation Command that he may be a continuing threat to children (*A v B* [2010] IRLR 844, CA) but the employer cannot place uncritical reliance on such a report, but should check the integrity of the source and the safeguards within its internal processes concerning the accuracy of the information supplied and should where necessary seek clarification, confirmation and further information before holding a disciplinary hearing (*Leach v OFCOM* [2012] IRLR 839, CA— on the same facts as *A v B*).

(6) A breakdown of trust and confidence between employer and employee (*Perkin v St George's Healthcare NHS Trust* [2005] IRLR 93, CA, when behaviour at the disciplinary meeting was appropriately taken into account). There must be a substantial reason for a breakdown in trust and confidence, not simply a convenient label to be used if the employer is faced with difficulties in establishing a more conventional conduct reason for dismissal (*Leach v OFCOM* [2012] IRLR 839, CA).

(7) Imprisonment of the employee.

(8) The protection of the employer's business, for example, where the employee refuses to sign a reasonable restrictive covenant (*Willow Oak Developments Ltd v Silverwood* [2006] IRLR 607, CA).

(9) The dismissal of an employee who refuses to agree a new shift pattern which would have resulted in him losing substantial overtime earnings (*Scott and Co v Richardson* [2004] UKEAT 0074/04).

(10) A dismissal arising following a transfer of undertaking for an economic, technical, or organizational reason entailing changes in the workforce (*McGrath v Rank Leisure Ltd* [1985] IRLR 323, EAT).

(11) The non-renewal of a contract where the employee has been told in advance it is temporary and why (for example, because it replaces someone on maternity leave (ERA 1996, s 106(2)) or someone who is suspended on medical grounds). The employer must have specifically told the employee in writing at the outset both that he is being employed to replace such a person and that the employment will cease when the person returns to work (*Victoria and Albert Museum v Durrant* [2011] IRLR 290, EAT).

(12) The mistaken belief that the employee did not have an appropriate work permit (*Klusova v London Borough of Hounslow* [2007] EWCA Civ 1127, CA) or the right to work in the UK (*Baker v Abellio London Ltd* [2018] IRLR 186, EAT).

The following have been held not to justify dismissal: **24.70**

(1) a rumour that the employee would leave to start up a rival business
(2) the fact that a relative of the employee has been convicted of dishonesty
(3) the fact that the employee is looking for alternative employment.

No employee should be dismissed for some other substantial reason unless appropriate warning **24.71** and consultation procedures are first carried out.

I. DISCIPLINARY PROCEDURE FOR ALL DISMISSALS

Dismissal and disciplinary procedures

There are minimum procedures, set out in the ACAS Code of Practice on Disciplinary and **24.72** Grievance Procedures, which an employer is expected to adopt for all dismissals other than those by reason of redundancy or on expiry of a fixed-term contract. The EAT has confirmed that the ACAS Code is also not applicable to dismissals for some other substantial reason under s 98(1)(b) of the ERA 1996 (*Phoenix House Ltd v Stockman and Another* UKEAT/0264/15).

Failure to follow the ACAS Code of Practice on Disciplinary and Grievance Procedures may be taken **24.73** into account by an employment tribunal and may entitle the tribunal to increase or decrease any award by up to 25 per cent (depending on whose fault it was that the Code was not complied with) (TULR(C)A 1992, s 207A). Failure to follow the Code to the letter, however, will not inevitably make a dismissal unfair—whether it does so will depend upon the seriousness of the failure, and whether the employer followed a fair process overall (*Buzolli v Food Partners Limited* [2012] 0317, EAT).

The ACAS Code is short—eleven pages. It is accompanied by lengthy guidance. Tribunals are **24.74** obliged to take into account any relevant element in the Code when adjudicating on cases. They are not, however, obliged to take into account all the guidance provisions (http://www.acas.org. uk/index.aspx?articleid=2179. In an unfair dismissal context, the Code applies to all employees (not workers) who are dismissed or constructively dismissed, except in the two circumstances expressly stated in the ACAS Code: those dismissed for redundancy, or on the expiry of a fixed-term contract, and the circumstances which have subsequently been determined by the EAT, including dismissals for some other substantial reason.

The core principles of the ACAS Code are: **24.75**

• issues should be dealt with promptly
• employers should act consistently

- employers should carry out any necessary investigations to establish the facts of the case
- employers should inform employees of the basis of the problem and give them an opportunity to put their case in response before any decisions are made
- employers should allow employees to be accompanied at any formal disciplinary or grievance meeting and
- employers should allow employees the right to appeal against any formal decision.

24.76 Key elements of the ACAS Code are:

(a) Employers should have a written disciplinary policy, although it does not have to be contractual. It should give examples of unacceptable behaviour including those which might be regarded as acts of gross misconduct.

(b) Employees and, if appropriate, their representatives, should be involved in the preparation of the disciplinary policy (although they do not have to agree to it), and should know where to find it.

(c) There should be an investigation before disciplinary action is taken (see paras 24.78–24.90).

(d) The employee should be told in writing of the allegations which form the subject of any disciplinary action, preferably accompanied by any relevant documents and witness statements. The notification should invite the employee to a disciplinary meeting (see para 24.93).

(e) The disciplinary meeting should be held after the employee has had enough time to consider the position. The employee should make every effort to attend, be allowed to state his case and has the right to be accompanied at the meeting (see paras 24.91 and 24.96).

(f) After the meeting, the employer must notify the employee in writing of its decision and give the employee the opportunity to appeal.

(g) If the employee appeals, this should be dealt with impartially, without unreasonable delay, and where possible by someone different from the person who took the original decision. Employees have the right to be accompanied at any appeal meeting (see paras 24.91 and 24.96). The employer must notify the result of the appeal to the employee in writing.

(h) Where the employee is a trade union representative, in addition to the normal steps it would be advisable to discuss the matter with a trade union official, after having obtained the employee's consent to do so.

24.77 If the employer does not follow the principles set out in para 24.76 and has no reasonable reason for not having done so, any award to an employee may be uplifted by 0–25 per cent. Similarly, if the employee does not follow the process without a reasonable reason, but wins an unfair dismissal case, an award may be reduced by 0–25 per cent (TULR(C)A 1992, s 207A and see paras 32.190–32.191).

Procedure for all dismissals

Investigation

24.78 Before taking disciplinary action, the ACAS Code of Practice on Disciplinary and Grievance Procedures requires an employer to conduct a reasonable investigation into the issue (*British Home Stores Ltd v Burchell* [1978] IRLR 379, EAT—see paras 24.100–24.101). Where possible, the investigation, if for conduct issues, should be conducted by a different person from the one who takes the disciplinary decision. The employer should consider allowing the employee to be accompanied at the meeting (see paras 24.91 and 24.96 for details) (ACAS Code paras 5–8). If, unreasonably, no investigation is undertaken, any award made to the employee may be increased by 0–25 per cent.

24.79 While the ACAS Code does contemplate an employer dismissing an employee on the spot, it is only incredibly rarely that any such dismissal, without any investigation or the opportunity for the employee to explain his actions, will be fair. These exceptional circumstances must indicate that, practically, the continuance of the employment relationship is impossible. To succeed, an employer will normally be expected to have summarily dismissed the employee at the point of discovering his actions: delay may indicate that the employer has lost the right to claim immediately that the employee has committed misconduct that is so serious that he cannot continue to be employed (*McCormack v Hamilton Academical Football Club* [2012] IRLR 108, Court of Session, where the employees' use of foul and offensive language did not justify immediate, summary dismissal).

The employer should always make proper investigation of all the circumstances—failure to do **24.80** so will render the dismissal unfair (see eg *Salford Royal NHS Foundation Trust v Roldan* [2010] IRLR 721, CA, where there was conflicting evidence on a key issue, and the Court of Appeal required the employer to test the evidence where possible). The tribunal will consider whether the employer's investigation was within the reasonable range of inquiries which should be made: it must not substitute its own view of exactly what it would have done (*Sainsbury's Supermarkets Ltd v Hitt* [2003] IRLR 23, CA). Nor should it come to conclusions on disputed facts about the employee's conduct and use its own conclusions to substitute its own view for that of the employer on the reasonableness of the dismissal—such a view of facts can only be applied by tribunals when considering a remedy (*London Ambulance Services NHS Trust v Small* [2009] EWCA Civ 220). The test is whether in all the circumstances the reasonable employer would regard the investigations carried out as adequate—a question for assessment by the employment tribunal who will examine the nature and extent of the investigations and the content and reliability of what those investigations had revealed before reaching a view on whether the investigatory process is sufficient (*Sneddon v Carr-Gomm Scotland Ltd* [2012] IRLR 820, CS). It is not illegitimate to obtain covert video evidence against an employee suspected of fraudulent activity (in this case, of spending time in the gym during working hours) so to do so does not automatically render any subsequent dismissal unfair, as those committing fraudulent acts during their employment can have no expectation of privacy (*City and County of Swansea v Gayle* [2013] IRLR 768, EAT). An example of an inadequate investigation is *Martin v British Railways Board* [1991] EATS 362/91, where the employer failed to investigate an employee's claims that he had not been drunk at work but was displaying similar symptoms as a result of hypertension. However, there may be exceptional occasions where a proper investigation requires complainants to make their statements before the employees (*Dolan v Premier International Foods Ltd* [2005] All ER (D) 152, where the complainants, who were making allegations of harassment, included the employee's immediate supervisor).

Any investigation should be undertaken promptly. Where an employee is off sick with stress fol- **24.81** lowing discovery of facts which might lead to disciplinary sanction, if the employer does not begin disciplinary proceedings, without at the very least reserving its right to do so once the employee returns to work, it may find that the tribunal will hold that it has waived its right to rely on the breach as grounds for dismissal (*Cook v MSHK Ltd* [2009] EWCA Civ 624, CA).

The employer should take all necessary witness statements and examine all relevant documents. **24.82** Even if the employee has been caught red-handed committing an act of gross misconduct, it is still not sensible to dismiss the employee on the spot if any anxiety about possible harm to the employer or its employees can be dealt with by suspending the employee and then pursuing the standard statutory procedures.

How rigorous should the investigation be?

The ACAS Guide (which is not statutorily enforceable) recommends that employers give em- **24.83** ployees advance notice of an investigatory meeting and time to prepare for it. There may, however, be circumstances where such a step is not reasonable. No decisions should be taken at the meeting (ACAS Guide p 22).

Where charges which are criminal in nature have been made, and where the consequence of the **24.84** dismissal may result in loss of reputation, loss of job, loss of work permit, or possibly the prospect of securing future employment in the chosen field, a careful, conscientious, and full investigation is necessary (*A v B* [2003] IRLR 405, EAT; *Salford Royal NHS Foundation Trust v Roldan* [2010] IRLR 721, CA; *Tykocki v Royal Bournemouth and Christchurch Hospitals NHS Foundation Trust* UKEAT/0081/16) (see also para 24.103). If the employee refuses to take part in the disciplinary process for fear of prejudicing his defence in the criminal proceedings, the employer should consider whether it has sufficient evidence to justify dismissal without hearing the employee. There should be an investigation, and where doubts remain it may be appropriate for the employer to postpone the decision until it can interview the employee (*Ali v Sovereign Buses (London) Ltd* EAT/0274/06).

24.85   The investigation should make sure that reasons put forward by the employee excusing the conduct, whether the dismissal might be for reasons of misconduct or capability, are properly explored, or that there are good reasons for not doing so (eg in *City of Edinburgh Council v Dickson* [2009] UKEATS/0038/09, dismissal of an employee viewing pornographic material was unfair because the employer did not investigate, by taking occupational advice at least, the employee's claims that he was suffering from a hypoglycaemic episode and was therefore not responsible for his actions). The tribunal will take all the circumstances into account when deciding if an investigation has been appropriate (*Stuart v London City Airport Ltd* [2013] EWCA Civ 973, CA, where a legitimate belief that the account of an employee accused of theft on one ground lacked credibility rendered unnecessary the obligation thoroughly to investigate the evidence on other conflicting issues, for example by viewing CCTV footage and speaking to other witnesses. See also *Shrestha v Genesis House Association Ltd* [2015] EWCA Civ 94). If an experiment is carried out to establish the plausibility of the employee's explanation for events which occurred, which is regarded as a key part of the investigation, then a subsequent dismissal may be unfair if the employee and her representative are not given the opportunity to be present to demonstrate what she says actually happened (*Crawford and Anor v Suffolk Mental Health Partnership Trust* [2012] IRLR 402, CA).

24.86   If the employer has an established disciplinary policy, it is an implied term of the contract of employment that the employer will adhere to it unless it can establish a good reason not to do so. If it fails to do so, the High Court may grant an injunction preventing the dismissal, but only if it finds that a basis of mutual trust and confidence survives between employer and employee (*Lakshmi v Mid Cheshire Hospitals NHS Trust* [2008] IRLR 956, HC, where the court declared that the NHS Trust was in breach of contract in refusing to postpone a disciplinary hearing against a doctor until the outcome of a police investigation, in contravention of the Trust's disciplinary policy, although no injunction was granted). Injunctions in the High Court will generally only be available where there is clear evidence that the employer is in breach of contract (*West London Mental Health NHS Trust v Chhabra* [2013] IRLR 398, CA—where an investigation disclosed evidence justifying the employer's decision to convene a disciplinary meeting, so no injunction was ultimately granted). Failure to follow such a procedure only entitles the employee to a possible injunction and limited damages—it does not give the employee the right to recover loss of earnings for the balance of his career, or to cover the cost of engaging legal representation caused by the breach. Any compensation will be limited to what the employee would have earned had the correct, contractual procedure been carried out (*Edwards v Chesterfield Royal Hospital NHS Foundation Trust; Botham v Ministry of Defence* [2012] IRLR 129, SC). The employer should be responsible for the conduct of any investigation and should not rely on any parallel police investigation. It is also preferable not to have police present during any disciplinary meeting, particularly if the employee does not consent (*Read v Phoenix Preservation Ltd* [1985] IRLR 93, EAT).

24.87   Where an employee is accused of bringing an employer into disrepute by publicly making allegations against it, so that Art 10 of the European Convention on Human Rights may be engaged, the appropriate approach for the employer to adopt is:

(a) to explore whether what occurred fell within the ambit of freedom of expression

(b) if it does, to explore whether it is bound (for example because it is a public body, such as a school) to respect the exercise of that right unless it is qualified by Art 10(2)

(c) if it is bound, to identify the aim which the restriction on free speech sought to serve (eg protection of the reputation or rights of others or preventing the disclosure of information received in confidence)

(d) to satisfy itself that the restriction or penalty imposed in the light of that aim was one pre-scribed by statute or common law

(e) if so, to consider whether the restriction or penalty is proportionate and appropriate (*Hill v Governing Body of Great Tey Primary School* [2013] IRLR 274, EAT).

The employer may consider whether to suspend the employee (with pay unless the contract pro-vides otherwise) during the course of any investigation. Generally, there should be at least a pre-liminary enquiry before suspension (*Gogay v Hertfordshire County Council* [2000] IRLR 703, CA) and suspension should not be a knee-jerk reaction where there is no real risk of the conduct in question being repeated (*Crawford and Anor v Suffolk Mental Health Partnership Trust* [2012] IRLR 402, CA). If there is no contractual right to suspend, the employee may claim that suspension is an act of constructive dismissal as in *London Borough of Lambeth v Agoreyo* [2019] EWCA Civ 322 in which the Court of Appeal confirmed that the correct test for the courts to consider is whether there is reasonable and proper cause to suspend.oIn rare circumstances, where suspension is likely to be a breach of contract and unduly harsh in its effect on the employee, may obtain an injunc-tion requiring the suspension to be lifted (*Mezey v SW London and St George's Mental Health NHS Trust* [2007] IRLR 244, CA). An employer can, however, make use of witness statements made to the police in an investigation into the same subject matter; it does not have to start from scratch again provided the witnesses confirm their original statements (*Rhondda Cynon Taf County Borough Council v Close* [2008] IRLR 868, EAT). **24.88**

Witnesses should ideally be asked to deal with the following points (*Linfood Cash & Carry Ltd v Thomson* [1989] IRLR 235, EAT): **24.89**

(1) the date, time, and place of any observation or incident
(2) whether the individual had an opportunity to observe clearly what happened
(3) the details of the event
(4) any additional facts which have a bearing on the event
(5) any circumstantial evidence giving credence to the key recollections
(6) whether the individual has any reason to be biased against the employee.

Where witnesses do not wish to be identified, because they are frightened of reprisals from the em-ployee under investigation, the employer should: **24.90**

(1) take statements, ignoring the fact the witness wishes to be anonymous
(2) cover the items set out at para 24.89 plus whether the witness has suffered at the hands of the accused, or has any other reason to fabricate
(3) seek further evidence to corroborate/undermine the statement
(4) make tactful inquiries as to the probity of the witness
(5) if the witness is still not prepared to be named, decide whether the fear is justified and whether to proceed with the disciplinary action
(6) where possible ask the people taking the decision to interview the witness
(7) provide the statement, with any elements identifying the witness removed, along with any other relevant statements and documents, to the accused and his representatives. However, even this may not be required where it would be within the range of reasonable responses not to disclose the statements, even in anonymised form (*Surrey County Council v Henderson* [2005] All ER (D) 320, EAT, where the employee was alleged to have threatened serious violence against individuals, but they did not wish to be identified for fear of reprisals by the employee)
(8) if the accused raises any issues which need to be put to the witness, consider adjourning to allow the decision-maker to investigate them
(9) make full and careful notes.

Note that there is a chance that confidential witness statements may be disclosed to the employee if a court decides that doing so is necessary for the fair disposal of the case (*Arqiva Ltd v Sagoo* UKEAT/0135/06), but the employer may be able to provide copies of statements in redacted form, omitting confidential or sensitive information (*Defoe v HM Prison Service* UKEAT/0451/06).

Part C The Substantive Law

Companion

24.91 An employee has the right to be accompanied at a disciplinary meeting by a colleague or a trade union representative. The following points apply in relation to the identity of the companion:

(1) So long as the employee chooses a companion who is an employed or certified trade union official or a colleague, the identity of the particular companion does not have to be 'reasonable'. If the employer rejects the chosen companion on grounds of his/her identity, this will be a breach of s 10(3) of the ERA 1999 and the employer will be liable to compensate the employee for actual loss suffered by the breach (or if no loss, then nominal compensation of £2—*Total v GB Oils Ltd* [2013] UKEAT 0569/12 EAT).

(2) Generally, an employer is not obliged to allow the employee to be represented by a solicitor. In exceptional circumstances, where a disciplinary decision could have far-reaching consequences affecting an employee's whole career or would otherwise have a substantial impact on the determination of the employee's civil rights, the employee may be able to require to be represented by a lawyer who may also have the right to cross-examine witnesses, by reference to Art 6 of the European Convention on Human Rights (right to a fair and public hearing). In reviewing the position, the parties should review whether the proceedings in question would in fact be dispositive of the issue without any further hearing; whether they would be so influential on any further hearing that the future hearing would be bound to follow it; and whether there was any policy reason why Art 6 should not apply in the particular circumstances. Most recently, the Court of Appeal has indicated that disciplinary processes at employer/employee level do not engage Art 6, so that the right to be legally represented would not apply at that stage, even where a dismissal would have the practical result of a medical professional not being able to obtain another job as a consultant in the public or private sector, and therefore could effectively affect his right to work in his chosen profession (*Mattu v University Hospitals of Coventry and Warwickshire NHS Trust* [2012] IRLR 661 CA). This has been followed in *Ministry of Justice v Parry* [2013] ICR 311, EAT, where the EAT emphasized that Art 6 is only engaged where the disciplinary decision creates a legal, not merely a practical, barrier on the employee's employability. Other examples of cases where this principle has been discussed include the prospective dismissal of a teaching assistant for abuse of an under-age pupil, where any dismissal would need to be reported to the Secretary of State for determination whether the assistant could work in schools again—*R v Governors of X School and Y City Council* [2011] IRLR 756, SC, where the Supreme Court found that it was not proven that the proceedings would definitely result in the teaching assistant being unable to practise his profession, since it was not the last stage in the process, and that therefore he was not entitled to legal representation; and *R (on the application of Puri) v Bradford Teaching Hospitals NHS Foundation Trust* [2011] EWHC 970, HC (Admin), where legal representation was not allowed, because what was at stake was loss of a particular job, not loss of any prospect of practising one's profession. See also the obiter comments in *Kulkarai v Milton Keynes Hospital NHS Foundation Trust* [2009] EWCA Civ 789.

(3) The right to legal representation at disciplinary hearings is most unlikely to be extended to standard cases where an employee faces dismissal, even though that may have the effect of damaging the employee's career prospects (*R (on the application of Kirk) v Middlesbrough Council* [2010] IRLR 699).

The ambit of the companion's role is set out at para 24.96.

Disciplinary meeting—general

24.92 Following internal investigation, the employer should hold a disciplinary meeting. If the employer has a written procedure about the conduct of the meeting, it should be followed. If dismissal is a possible sanction, and the employer starts off using an informal procedure, this may indicate that dismissal is outside the range of reasonable sanctions available to the employer (*Sarkar v West London Health NHS Trust* [2010] IRLR 508, CA).

Notice of meeting

Once the employer has conducted its internal investigation it should ask the employee to attend **24.93**
a disciplinary meeting. In order to comply with the ACAS Code of Practice on Disciplinary and
Grievance Procedures, the notification should be in writing (see para 24.76(d)). The employee
should be told the following before the meeting:

(1) the time and place of the meeting (which should give him reasonable time to consider his response to the allegations) (note: if the employee's chosen companion is not available for the
hearing at that time and the employee proposes a reasonable alternative time within the next
five working days, the employer must postpone the hearing to the suggested time (ERA 1999,
s 10(4) and (5)), failing which the employer is liable to pay the employee up to two weeks'
pay subject to the statutory maximum pay (ie up to £525 at the rates current from 6 April
2019) (ERA 1999, s 11(3)))
(2) the fact that the meeting will be a disciplinary meeting
(3) the topics which will be discussed at the meeting. These should be set out precisely—it is rarely
permissible for an employer to dismiss for a reason not clearly put forward (*Strouthos v London
Underground Ltd* [2004] IRLR 636, CA)
(4) the fact (if it be the case) that the employer is considering dismissal as an option
(5) the right of the employee to be accompanied by a colleague or (if appropriate) trade union
representative (see para 24.91)
(6) preferably, and definitely in good time before any meeting which might lead to dismissal, provide the employee with the evidence and all key documents (for example, any investigatory
report or witness statements) which will be relied on against him. In very rare circumstances,
an employer may not need to give the employee all available evidence, provided that it has
given him sufficient to enable him properly to prepare his response (*Spence v Department of
Agriculture and Rural Development* [2011] IRLR 806, NICA).

Conduct of meeting

The meeting should, where the size of the organization allows this, be chaired by the person who will **24.94**
be responsible for taking the decision to warn or dismiss. If possible, this should not be a witness
or a complainant in the case. The decision-maker should plan the meeting in advance, and should
where possible be accompanied by a note-taker (ACAS Guidance p 19—http://www.acas.org.uk/
index.aspx?articleid=2179). In some cases, for example where the employer is small and inexperienced in employment matters, it may be reasonable for the employer to outsource the decision or an
appeal process to an external consultant (*GM Packaging v Haslem* [2014] UKEAT 0259/13, EAT)
but Human Resources must not have too much influence (*Ramphal v Department for Transport*
UKEAT/0352/14). All relevant information should be before the decision-maker (see eg *Crawford
and Anor v Suffolk Mental Health Partnership Trust* [2012] IRLR 402, CA, where an earlier version
of a key witness statement, which differed materially from a later one, was not included). Generally,
it is wise for the meeting not to proceed if the employee does not attend, but if the employee is
being obstructive and unreasonable, it may not be unfair to hold the meeting in the employee's absence (*Bashir v Sheffield Teaching Hospital NHS Foundation Trust* [2010] 0448/09, EAT, where the
employee had delayed the hearing on several occasions, and then, having said he was fully able to
present his case himself, at a reconvened meeting refused to proceed without union representation).
Ideally, the decision-maker should conduct the meeting in the following manner, although failure to
adhere to this plan will not necessarily render a dismissal unfair (see para 24.80):

(1) Identify those present.
(2) Explain the role of any companion to the employee (see para 24.96).
(3) Explain the purpose of the meeting.
(4) Outline the structure at the meeting and inform the employee and any representative that they
may ask questions or make observations at any stage, and that when the employer has set out the
allegations, the employee will have the opportunity to respond to those allegations either by calling
evidence or by argument, and to put forward any explanation or mitigating circumstances.

Part C The Substantive Law

(5) If appropriate, arrange representation for the employee. The employee should have the opportunity to be accompanied by a colleague of his choice or, in some circumstances, a trade union representative (see para 24.91).

(6) Inform the employee of the allegations being made.

(7) Make sure the employee has received all the evidence and has had a proper opportunity to consider it.

(8) The employee and/or his representative should then have an opportunity to put the employee's case, both relating to the allegations themselves and to any facts in mitigation. Note that if the employee is facing criminal prosecution, the employer must not prejudice a trial but should only give the employee the opportunity to make any statement he may volunteer: no pressure should be put upon the employee to admit guilt.

(9) If the employee asks to bring a witness to support his case, this should generally be allowed. The ACAS Guidance, in a change from what was earlier regarded as acceptable practice, suggests that all witnesses should be available at the hearing, unless it is clear that their oral evidence will not affect the substance of the complaint. If this is not practicable, then the decision-maker should put any relevant supplementary questions to the witness after the disciplinary meeting, but before making the decision (see para 24.95(5)).

(10) The employee should be asked whether there is any further evidence or inquiry which he considers could help his case and whether there are any mitigating circumstances.

(11) If an employee asks for additional questions to be put to witnesses an employer would be wise to adjourn the meeting to make further inquiries, or to ensure that those questions are put to the witnesses subsequently.

(12) The decision-maker should sum up the meeting.

(13) The meeting should be adjourned or concluded before the decision is taken.

24.95 A disciplinary procedure, although formal, is not a court of law. It used to be thought that an employee is not normally entitled to cross-examine witnesses. However, the ACAS Guidance (http://www.acas.org.uk/index.aspx?articleid=2179), which is not statutorily enforceable, suggests that if the employee wishes to do so, and notifies the employer of this fact in good time, witnesses may be cross-examined. Factors to bear in mind include the following:

(1) The decision-maker should consider whether it would be fair and reasonable to allow him to do so taking into account issues such as what cross-examination would achieve, whether it might help the employee's case, and the likely effect on witnesses (especially in a harassment or bullying case).

(2) If there is a stark difference of evidence on fact, and this fact goes to the root of the disciplinary allegation, the decision-maker should very rarely refuse to allow cross-examination. A refusal would probably only be acceptable if, for example, the witnesses, having been asked if they will attend the disciplinary hearing, have refused to do so on the basis that it would be far too stressful—perhaps because they claim to have been bullied by the employee under investigation, or because the witnesses are not employees and cannot therefore be compelled to attend.

(3) Where the person subject to the disciplinary process is a professional person, at a stage beyond employment disciplining, Art 6 of the European Convention on Human Rights (right to a fair and public hearing) may be engaged, and give the employee the right to cross-examine witnesses, particularly where their evidence is disputed by the employee, taking into account the seriousness of the allegations and the gravity of the adverse consequences to the professional's career and reputation (*R (on the application of Bonhoeffer) v General Medical Council* [2012] IRLR 37, HC, where a written statement giving (disputed) hearsay evidence of sexual abuse should have been disallowed as evidence if the accused employee was not able to cross-examine the witness).

(4) The decision-maker would be wise to give reasons for any decision refusing to allow cross-examination.

(5) if cross-examination is refused, the employer should go back to the witnesses after the disciplinary hearing and put to them any allegations made by the employee which have not already been addressed (*Santamera v Express Cargo Forwarding* [2003] IRLR 273, EAT).

If the employee is accompanied, the companion: **24.96**

(1) may (unless the employee has indicated he does not wish the companion to do so) address the hearing by putting the employee's case, summing up that case, and responding on the employee's behalf to any view expressed at the hearing
(2) may confer with the employee during the hearing
(3) may not answer questions on the employee's behalf
(4) may not act in such a way that either the employer is prevented from explaining his case or any other person is prevented from making any contribution to the hearing (ERA 1999, s 10(2)).

It may be necessary for the decision-maker to initiate further inquiries should the employee have **24.97** raised fresh issues, for example where an employee is himself suspended and has been denied the opportunity of being able to contact potentially relevant witnesses, the employer needs to make sure that it focuses as much on any potential evidence that may exculpate or point towards the employee's innocence as on the evidence directed towards proving the charges (*A v B* [2003] IRLR 405, EAT). However, the fairness of the decision is judged by what the decision-taker either knew or ought reasonably to have known (*Orr v Milton Keynes Council* [2011] IRLR 317, CA, where an employer was not to be taken to have known exculpatory facts which were known to the employee's line manager, but not passed on to the decision-taker—the key issue is whether any reasonable investigation should have unearthed the relevant facts). This principle is further demonstrated in *Royal Mail Ltd v Jhuti* [2017] EWCA Civ 1632, where the Court of Appeal determined that an employee who had made protected disclosures to her line manager was not automatically unfairly dismissed because the individual who dismissed her was unaware of those disclosures.

If the employee raises a grievance about the way the disciplinary process has been handled, the em- **24.98** ployer shall consider whether the meeting should be adjourned until the grievance is dealt with. An adjournment might be appropriate if the employee alleges that the decision-maker has a conflict of interest or if biased management have been selective in producing evidence for the meeting, or the process has been tainted by discrimination (ACAS Guidance p 22). However, it will only be in the rarest of cases that a decision to dismiss will be rendered unfair if the employer fails to complete a grievance process before taking the decision (*Samuel Smith Old Brewery (Tadcaster) v Marshall* [2010] UKEAT/0488/09).

In rare circumstances, it can be reasonable for an employer to conduct a second set of disciplinary **24.99** proceedings on the basis of the same facts as a previous hearing, for example where the original decision had been based on a superficial and fast-track, rather than a detailed disciplinary process which new management reasonably felt was an inadequate course to take. There is no rule preventing an employer from instituting fresh disciplinary proceedings, in relation to the same facts, if the first proceedings were inadequate, or following a change of management, and the doctrine of *res judicata* does not apply to disciplinary proceedings, only to court or tribunal proceedings, but the fact that a view had previously been taken by an employer that the misconduct was not so serious as to warrant dismissal would obviously be relevant factor in determining whether any subsequent dismissal on the same facts was fair. It is likely to be extremely rare for such a dismissal to be fair (*Christou v London Borough of Haringey* [2013] IRLR 379, CA).

Standard of proof

The standard of proof is a reasonable suspicion, amounting to a belief in the guilt of the employee **24.100** of that misconduct at that time. The employer must establish:

(1) the fact of his belief in the guilt of the employee
(2) that the employer had in his mind reasonable grounds on which to sustain that belief
(3) that the employer had carried out an investigation which was reasonable in all the circumstances (*British Home Stores Ltd v Burchell* [1978] IRLR 379, EAT).

The test set out above in *Burchell* has recently come under scrutiny in *Reilly v Sandwell Metropolitan Borough Council* [2018] UKSC 16, where the Supreme Court questioned its correctness in relation to s 98(4) of the ERA 1996. However, this remains the established test.

Where suspicion genuinely points to one or other of two employees, both may be dismissed (*Frames Snooker Centre v Boyce* [1992] IRLR 472).

24.101 If the employer has not acted consistently, for example, because employees had been led to believe that particular categories of conduct would be overlooked, or met with only a mild disciplinary sanction (*Hadjioannou v Coral Casinos Ltd* [1981] IRLR 352, EAT) or because in truly comparable cases one employee is dismissed while another has not been (*Securicor v Smith* [1989] IRLR 356, CA), then the dismissal is likely to be unfair. This is because it will not have passed the test in s 98(4) of the ERA 1996 that the tribunal must have regard to 'equity and the substantial merits of the case'.

Sanction

24.102 The tribunal must be satisfied that the sanction the employer has imposed is fair in all the circumstances. This must always be considered, even where the tribunal has found that the employee had committed an act of gross misconduct, as there may, for example, be mitigating factors (*Brito-Babapulle v Ealing Hospital NHS Trust* [2013] IRLR 854, EAT). The ACAS Guidance (available at http://www.acas.org.uk/index.aspx?articleid=2179) recommends that the decision-maker considers the following:

(1) whether the employer's disciplinary policy indicates what the likely penalty will be as a result of the particular misconduct

(2) the penalty imposed in similar cases in the past—though differences in the circumstances (such as where an employee who had earlier breached health and safety policy had suffered a serious injury as a result: *General Mills (Berwick) Ltd v Glowacki* [2011] 0139/11, EAT) may justify different responses, providing the employer acts within the range of reasonable responses in so doing

(3) whether the standards of other employees are acceptable, making sure that this employee is not being unfairly singled out

(4) the employee's disciplinary record (including current warnings, general work record, work experience, position, and length of service) and any mitigating circumstances which might make it appropriate to reduce the severity of the penalty. The fact that an employee is on a final warning can be taken into account by an employer, even if the most recent event is of a different nature to that which was subject to previous warnings (*Wincanton Group plc v Stone* [2013] IRLR 178, EAT), and it will be exceptional where further misconduct will not lead to dismissal. Employers should give proper value to all the relevant matters. When considering the relevance of an earlier warning, the tribunal must not put itself into the shoes of the employer and substitute its own view of the event, but should also take into account whether the warning is being challenged by internal appeal, and whether there is any particular feature relating to the earlier warning which might contextualize it. In *Bandara v British Broadcasting Corporation* UKEAT/0335/15, the EAT overturned a decision of the tribunal where it determined that the tribunal had considered circumstances which did not exist when a manifestly inappropriate warning had been given, namely it considered what would have happened in circumstances where an ordinary warning had been given. An employment tribunal should not look behind a previous warning if satisfied it was not issued for an oblique motive, was not manifestly inappropriate, and was issued in good faith (*Wincanton Group plc v Stone* [2013] IRLR 178, EAT) but may do if it appears that the warning was manifestly inappropriate—a high threshold (*Simmonds v Milford Club* [2012] UKEAT 0323/12, EAT). Even if there is suspicion a previous warning was inappropriately given, it will not be necessary to examine the point if the final act of misconduct is so serious as to justify dismissal on its own (*Adegbola v Marks and Spencer plc* [2013] EWCA Civ 634, CA). It is potentially legitimate for an employer considering whether to dismiss an employee for misconduct to rely on a final warning, even one which was the subject of an unresolved internal appeal, provided that the warning was issued in good faith, that there were at least prima facie grounds for imposing it, and that it was not manifestly inappropriate to issue it. It is not otherwise for the tribunal in an unfair dismissal case to determine whether the final warning should or should not have been given

(*Davies v Sandwell Metropolitan Borough Council* [2013] IRLR 374, CA). However, a previous warning imposed, albeit genuinely, in error because of a misunderstanding of an absence policy could render a subsequent dismissal, relying on that warning, unfair, particularly where the employer is a large one (*Sakharkar v Northern Foods Grocery Group Ltd t/a Fox's Biscuits* [2011] UKEAT 0442/10, EAT)

(5) whether the penalty is reasonable in all the circumstances

(6) whether any training or additional support or adjustments to the work are necessary.

When reviewing the employer's decision to dismiss, an employment tribunal will look at whether **24.103** the decision to dismiss is within the band of reasonable responses which a hypothetical reasonable employer might have adopted in the circumstances. The employment tribunal must not substitute its own decision for that of the employer (*Iceland Frozen Foods Ltd v Jones* [1982] IRLR 439, EAT and *Foley v Post Office*; *HSBC Bank plc v Madden* [2000] IRLR 827, CA; *Tayeh v Barchester Healthcare Ltd* [2013] IRLR 387, CA; see also para 24.27). However, this does not mean that the tribunal must always back the employer's decision—see for example *Bowater v North West London Hospitals NHS Trust* [2011] IRLR 331, CA where a tribunal had been correct to find that the decision to dismiss a nurse for making a light-hearted but ribald remark was outside the range of reasonable responses. The *Madden* test allows for a heightened standard to be adopted where the consequences of dismissal on an employee are particularly grave (*Turner v East Midlands Trains Ltd* [2013] IRLR 107, CA, where the employee was dismissed for fraud, and had argued that his right to private life (under Art 8 of the European Convention on Human Rights) was engaged. The employee had argued that the employer should therefore apply a stricter test as to whether dismissal was appropriate, in proportion to the consequences. The Court held that where Art 8 was engaged, for example where a misconduct dismissal would damage the employee's opportunity to take up further employment in the same field, or involved an allegation of immoral or criminal conduct which would harm his or her reputation, the appropriate level and scope of the investigation should be determined with a full appreciation of the gravity of the potentially adverse consequences to the employee. The issue was not one of proportionality. In this case, there was no breach: the process followed was fair under the band of reasonableness test, and Art 8 added nothing).

Notification of decision

The employee, and any representative, should be notified of the employer's decision in writing. **24.104** The employee should also be told of his right to appeal and to be accompanied to that appeal by a colleague or trade union representative. The employer should clearly specify any time limit within which the appeal should be lodged. It makes sense for notification of the right to appeal to be contained within the document recording the decision, but it is acceptable for the employee to be told of the right to appeal orally (*Aptuit (Edinburgh) Ltd v Kennedy* UKEATS/0057/06).

Appeals

If possible, the appeal body should be composed of different and more senior people from those who **24.105** made the decision to dismiss (ACAS Code of Practice on Disciplinary and Grievance Procedures).

Appeals may take into account additional facts learnt since the decision to dismiss. It used to **24.106** be thought that an appeal cannot provide justification for unfairness at a lower level unless the appeal is a comprehensive rehearing. However, this is no longer the case, where the employee is given a proper opportunity in the appeal to understand the case against him and respond appropriately. Appeal hearings cannot of themselves correct earlier procedural failures simply because the employee has not, on appeal, complained about the poor process, and the issue was not considered, or remedied, on appeal (*Crawford v Suffolk Mental Health Partnership NHS Trust* [2012] IRLR 402, CA).

Appeals should be heard promptly. An employer should not reject an appeal simply because the **24.107** employee did not comply with the contractual time limit for bringing the appeal, so long as the employee appeals within a reasonable time—to do otherwise would be contrary to the spirit of the ACAS Code.

24.108 Normally, a dismissal or resignation cannot be unilaterally withdrawn. However, by appealing, the employee may impliedly consent to any subsequent withdrawal of the dismissal by the employer. Therefore, if the appeal is upheld, the employee may not be able to claim to have been dismissed (*Brock v Minerva Dental Ltd [2007] EAT/0356/06 and Folkestone Nursing Home Ltd v Patel* UKEAT/0348/15).

24.109 If an employee fails to exercise his right of appeal the employer may be able to argue that there should be a reduction in any compensation paid because the employee has failed to mitigate his loss. A dismissed employee who does not take up an invitation to appeal may have any compensatory award reduced by 0–25 per cent (see paras 32.190–32.191).

24.110 Where there is a failure to follow a proper procedure, the tribunal will consider whether the employer has shown that the employee would have been dismissed had a fair procedure been followed.

(1) The employer may persuade the tribunal that there was a chance that, had a fair procedure been complied with, dismissal may well have occurred in any event. The dismissal will still be unfair but compensation should be reduced on *Polkey* principles (see para 24.110(2)). The court must attempt the task, however speculative, of evaluating the evidence on what might have happened had a proper procedure been followed (*Software 2000 Ltd v Andrews* [2007] ICR 825, EAT) unless evidence on this point is particularly sparse (*Clarke v Governing Body of Hastingbury School* EAT 0373/07 and 0374/07).

(2) The principles are set out in *Polkey v AE Dayton Services Ltd* [1987] IRLR 503, HL—a redundancy case. In brief, in addition to the principle set out in para 24.110(1), they are that a dismissal will be unfair if inadequate procedures are followed, unless at the time the decision was taken and bearing in mind the facts the employer actually knew, a reasonable employer could have known that conducting a procedure (in this case, there was no consultation with individual employees before they were selected for redundancy) would be useless. The tribunal must consider the action of the employer in treating the reason as sufficient to dismiss as part of its review of the manner of dismissal. It is not sufficient, to pass the *Polkey* test, for the employer to show that the result would have been the same had a proper procedure taken place.

(3) The tribunal may decide that the employment would have continued but only for a limited period, in which case compensation for loss of earnings should be restricted to the remuneration the employee would have received during this period.

(4) The tribunal may decide the employment would continue indefinitely, in which case compensation will be assessed on normal principles. This decision should only be reached where the evidence is so scant or unreliable that it should be ignored because, even with a certain amount of legitimate speculation, it is impossible to reconstruct what might have happened (*Software 2000 Ltd v Andrews* [2007] IRLR 568, EAT).

24.111 If the ACAS Code is not followed, a tribunal will have the discretion to increase or decrease any compensation award by 0–25 per cent (TULR(C)A 1992, s 207A and see paras 32.190–32.191).

J. WARNING PROCEDURE

Warnings

24.112 Except for gross misconduct, dismissal should not be the sanction for a first offence. The ACAS Code of Practice on Disciplinary and Grievance Procedures lays down, for minor offences, a three-stage warning process before dismissal: oral warning, first written warning, and final written warning, and then dismissal. The number of warnings may, however, be reduced either because of practicalities or because an offence is of a more serious nature.

24.113 Dismissal will not normally be a valid response to a first act of misconduct, unless the misconduct is potentially serious. Generally, the employer should give the employee a first (perhaps oral) warning for minor offences, and a written warning for more serious offences or subsequent offences.

Successive warnings need not relate to similar subject matter.   **24.114**

Lapsed warnings

In the absence of an express provision regarding the lapse of warnings, it is generally assumed that **24.115**
oral warnings should lapse after six months and written warnings after 6–12 months. It is normally
unreasonable to take a lapsed warning into account when deciding whether to dismiss someone
for gross misconduct: if it influences the decision, the dismissal will be unfair (*Diosynth Ltd v
Thomson* [2006] IRLR 284). However, expired warnings may influence a decision not to reduce
any appropriate sanction because of mitigating circumstances. There are limited circumstances
where lapsed warnings have been considered in determining a dismissal, and this has been deemed
fair. In *Stratford v Auto Trail VR Ltd* UKEAT/0116/16 the EAT determined that it was fair to
take expired warnings into account as part of the overall circumstances under s 98(4) of the ERA
1996. In this case, an employee was issued with a final written warning for a disciplinary offence,
following which the employer went on to dismiss the employee after consideration of his history
of expired warnings. In *NHS 24 v Pillar* UKEATS/0005/16 the EAT determined it had been fair
for the employer's investigation into misconduct, which lead to an employee's dismissal, to take
account of earlier, similar instances of misconduct by that employee which had not been treated
as disciplinary matters (and for which no formal warnings were issued), but rather had been dealt
with by way of training.

A warning subject to appeal can still be relied upon when taking action regarding a fresh offence, **24.116**
although the employer must, when deciding what weight to attach to the earlier warning, bear in
mind that it is subject to appeal.

Warnings are especially important where rules have recently been disregarded in practice. For ex- **24.117**
ample, it would be unfair to dismiss a man for sleeping on a night shift where in practice his colleagues had been doing the same, to management's knowledge, for some time and management
had not told employees that in future on-shift sleeping would be regarded as serious misconduct.
If management had not known of the custom, dismissal would have been a reasonable sanction,
provided it was applied consistently.

A warning will not be necessary in the following circumstances: **24.118**

(1) where the employer's rules clearly and reasonably spell out that a particular action will result
     in instant dismissal
(2) where the employee's conduct is likely to endanger safety
(3) where a warning would make no difference, for example, because the employee refuses to ac-
     cept he has done anything wrong
(4) where the employee knew that he was putting his job in jeopardy.

K. STRESS ISSUES PRIOR TO INVESTIGATORY/
DISCIPLINARY MEETINGS

If an employee who is subject to a disciplinary or performance procedure goes off work and claims **24.119**
he cannot attend the procedure on the grounds of stress, the employer should postpone the procedure until the employee returns or do the following—failure to do so may render any subsequent
dismissal unfair:

(1) Check the staff handbook to see if it contains procedures to follow in these circumstances. If
     it does, these should be followed. If not, the employer should:
(2) Obtain the employee's consent to his general practitioner (GP) giving the employer his or her
     opinion on:
     (a) whether the employee is fit to attend the disciplinary procedure

Part C The Substantive Law

(b) if not, when he is likely to be

(c) whether there are any steps which could be taken to enable the meeting to take place.

(3) If concerned about the GP's response, seek the employee's consent to visiting a medical practitioner chosen by the employer, who should be asked similar questions.

(4) An employee is not obliged to give consent to sharing medical information, even if his contract of employment states that he must undergo any medical examinations that the employer reasonably requests. However, if this contractual term is in place and the employee refuses to see a doctor or to allow the employer to know the doctor's opinion, the employer can proceed carefully, making his own assumptions. If the employee allows his GP to give his or her opinion, but refuses to undergo a second opinion, the employer is effectively stuck with the first opinion.

(5) Make sure that all the allegations against the employee are set out clearly, and sent to him, together with copies or (where appropriate) summaries of witness statements and documents which will be relied on.

(6) Extend the time limit for any responses.

(7) Consider providing written questions to which answers will be sought in advance of the meeting, perhaps inviting written replies and/or representations.

(8) Consider permitting the employee to be accompanied by a relative or friend in addition to any colleague from work or union representative.

(9) Hold the hearing at a neutral venue, preferably close to the employee's home.

(10) Where possible, appoint someone with little or no prior involvement with the employee to chair the meeting and make the decision.

(11) Follow any recommendations from the medical practitioners on how the meeting should be held and conducted.

(12) Offer the employee breaks during the meeting.

(13) Send the employee and his representative a copy of written reasons for the decision.

(14) Allow an extended time for appeal.

CHECKLIST OF ISSUES FOR TRIBUNAL CLAIMS CONNECTED WITH DISMISSAL

Wrongful dismissal

(1) as the employer without cause terminated the employee's contract of employment without either:

  (a) allowing the employee to work out all his notice or

  (b) following the provisions of a 'pay in lieu of notice' clause in the employment contract or

  (c) paying the employee in lieu of his salary and benefits for all of his unworked notice period?

  If so, or if the employer has acted in such a way that he has constructively dismissed the employee (see paras 24.12–24.14), the employee has been wrongfully dismissed.

(2) Is the maximum claim for £25,000 or less?

  The employment tribunal cannot award more than £25,000 damages for breach of contract. If the claim is for more, the employee might be better advised to bring proceedings in the High Court or county court (Employment Tribunals Extension of Jurisdiction (England and Wales) Order 1994, Art 10; Employment Tribunals Extension of Jurisdiction (Scotland) Order 1994, Art 10 (the 1994 Orders)). Any excess over any maximum £25,000 award cannot be recovered by a claim in the High Court see para 24.06.

(3) Was the claim brought within three months of the EDT of the employee's contract? (See para 24.08 for the definition of EDT.)

  If not, it will be out of time (1994 Orders, Art 7) and a claim should be brought in the High Court or county court.

(4) Did the employer dismiss the employee for cause, but ignoring any contractual procedural requirements such as disciplinary and warning procedures which are expressly or impliedly incorporated into

the employee's contract of employment (eg, because expressly referred to in the contract, staff hand-book, or collective agreement)?

If so, this will be wrongful dismissal (*Gunton v Richmond-upon-Thames LBC* [1980] ICR 755) but there are likely to be only two remedies:

(a) damages limited to the period between actual dismissal and the date dismissal should have taken place had proper procedures been followed or

(b) (very rarely and only if sought promptly enough) an injunction obtained in the High Court preventing the employer from terminating the employment until proper procedures are under-taken (*Robb v London Borough of Hammersmith and Fulham* [1991] ICR 514, DC).

(5) Did the employee commit a material breach of contract?

If yes, the employer has a full defence to a wrongful dismissal claim. A breach of contract may be a breach of an express term of a contract or staff manual or it may be that the employee has shown himself to be so incompetent or to have conducted himself so badly as to entitle the employer to ter-minate the contract. In essence, the tests to be applied as to whether the employee's incompetence or misconduct are sufficiently serious to justify dismissal are the same as those which apply in unfair dismissal (see paras 24.35–24.47, 24.49–24.51). The court will examine all the employee's conduct before dismissal, whether or not the employer knew of the conduct before it terminated the contract (see para 24.03).

UNFAIR DISMISSAL: GENERAL CHECKLIST

Issues

(1) Was the individual an employee (see paras 24.07 and 24.11(5))?
    If not, he has no unfair dismissal rights.

(2) Was the employee dismissed, either directly by the employer or as a result of constructive dismissal (see paras 24.12–24.14)?
    If not, for example because he has resigned (*Riordan v War Office* [1959] 3 All ER 774), without being forced to do so, he has no unfair dismissal claim.

(3) Was the employee in one of the categories which prevents him from bringing a claim for unfair dis-missal (see para 24.11)?
    If he was, then the tribunal has no jurisdiction to hear the claim.

(4) Has the employee brought his claim in time, within three months from the effective date of termin-ation of his employment (ERA 1996, s 111(2)) (see paras 3.07, 3.40–3.81, and 24.08)?
    If not he is unlikely to be allowed to pursue his claim in the employment tribunal unless the em-ployment tribunal considers it was not reasonably practicable for the case to have been brought earlier.

(5) Did the employee have the necessary continuity of service—essentially two years from the ef-fective date of termination of his employment (see para 24.08)—unless special situations apply (see para 24.09)?
    If not, in the absence of one of the special situations, he will not be able to maintain his claim.

(6) If the employee believes he has been constructively dismissed:

(a) as the employer committed a breach of contract which goes to the root of the employment re-lationship (see para 24.13 for examples) or a series of breaches culminating in a breach which is effectively the last straw (see para 24.12(3))?

(b) Did the employee resign as a result of this breach?

(c) Did the employee act promptly in resigning following the breach or last straw, so that he could not be said to have waived his rights in relation to the breach?
    If the answer to all these questions is yes, the employee will have been constructively dismissed.

(7) Does the employee believe he was dismissed for trade union, health and safety, or whistle-blowing reasons, or one of the other grounds set out in para 24.19?
    If so, he may apply for interim relief (for details, see paras 3.23, 24.19 and Chapter 31)

(8) What is the principal reason for dismissal? Is it a potentially fair reason within s 98(2) of the ERA 1996, (see para 24.33)?

If yes, the employer may have a defence to the claim.

(9) Was the principal reason for dismissal one of the automatically unfair grounds listed at para 24.28? If yes, then the employee will win his unfair dismissal claim and the tribunal will determine the appropriate remedy.

(10) Was the principal reason for dismissal one of the automatically fair grounds listed at para 24.22?

If yes, then the employee will lose his unfair dismissal claim.

(11) Did the employer make it clear why the employee was being dismissed? Was the employee continuously employed for two yearsor more (unless she is pregnant, when there is no qualifying period)? Has the employee requested written reasons for his dismissal?

If the answer to all these questions is yes, and the employer has unreasonably not provided written reasons for dismissal, the tribunal will require the employer to pay the employee two weeks' pay, and may make a declaration as to what the reasons for dismissal were (ERA 1996, ss 92 and 93) (see para 24.30).

(12) If the employer claims that the employee was dismissed for misconduct

(a) was the conduct sufficiently gross that dismissal was within the range of reasonable responses available to the employer (for examples, see paras 24.41–24.47)?

If yes, the dismissal will potentially be fair. Go to (12)(b) below.

If not, the dismissal will be unfair unless there have been previous warnings (see (12)© below).

(b) If the employer had an exhaustive list of matters which constituted gross misconduct (as opposed to a non-exclusive list giving examples of gross misconduct), was the conduct of a type on the list?

If not, any summary dismissal will be unfair.

(c) If the employee's misconduct is not so gross it justifies dismissal, has the employee previously been givenwarnings telling him that dismissal may be an option if there is further misconduct (see para 24.38 for examples of minor offences)?

If not, the employee will have been unfairly dismissed.

(d) Is there another employee who has committed similar misconduct who was not dismissed, and did not have mitigating circumstances which would militate against dismissal?

If so, dismissal will probably be unfair (see para 24.39).

(e) Was the misconduct known to the employer at the time of the dismissal? Did it form the real reason for the dismissal (see paras 24.23–24.26)?

If the answer to either question is no, the employee will have been unfairly dismissed, but his award may be reduced on the basis that it is not just and equitable to award compensation in these circumstances (see paras 32.166–32.167).

(f) Did the employer comply with the key principles of the ACAS Code of Practice on Disciplinary and Grievance Procedures (see paras 24.75–24.76)? If not, a tribunal may increase any award by 0–25 per cent (see paras 24.73 and 32.190–32.191).

(g) Did the employee comply with the key principles of the ACAS Code, see paras 24.75–24.76)? If not, but the employee wins an unfair dismissal claim, the award may be reduced by 0–25 per cent (see paras 32.190–32.191 and 32.163).

(h) Did the employer conduct an appropriate investigation into the misconduct prior to the dismissal (see paras 24.78–24.90)? If not, was there an appeal and was the failure remedied prior to the appeal decision?

If the answer to both questions is no, the employee will have been unfairly dismissed. If it is yes to either question, go to (i) below.

(i) Was the conduct of the disciplinary meeting fair (see paras 24.94–24.97)?

If not, the dismissal may be unfair unless any lapses would not have affected the outcome of the decision (see para 24.80). If it was, go to (j).

(j) Having conducted a reasonable investigation (see (12)(h)8, did the decision-maker genuinely believe, on reasonable grounds, that the employee was guilty of the misconduct (see para 24.100)?

If not, the employee will have been unfairly dismissed. If yes, go to (k)

(k) Was dismissal, given the conduct in question and the decision-maker's state of mind, within the range of reasonable responses available to the employer?

If yes, the dismissal will be fair (see paras 24.100–24.103). If not, it will be unfair.

(l)   If the procedure pre-appeal was insufficient, was the failure remedied by an appeal (see paras 24.105–24.110)?

If yes, the dismissal may be fair. If not, it will be unfair.

(13) If the employer claims that the employee wasdismissed for incompetence:

(a)(i) Had the employee had a prior warning of incompetence?(ii) If not, was the incompetence on one of those very rare occasions when it amounted to such gross negligence that the employer could not reasonably be expected to continue to employ the employee (see para 24.53)?

If yes, the employee may have been fairly dismissed. Go to (13)(d) below.

If not, the employee will have been unfairly dismissed.

(b)   Has the employee been given a warning telling him that unless there is an improvement in his performance, he may be dismissed? Is that warning still current and unexpired (see paras 24.52 and 24.112–24.118)? Has sufficient time expired to allow the employee to demonstrate an improved performance?

If the answer to all questions is yes, the employee may have been fairly dismissed. Go to (13(c) below.

If the answer is no, unless 13(a)(ii) applies, the employee will have been unfairly dismissed.

(c)   Can the employer demonstrate that it is reasonable to conclude that the employee has been incompetent, for example does he have samples of poor quality work, or details of particular incidents (see paras 24.50–24.51)?

If yes, the employee may have been fairly dismissed, provided any appropriate warning process was followed—go to 13(d) below.

If not, the employee will have been unfairly dismissed.

(d)   Did the employer comply with the key principles of the ACAS Code (see paras 24.75–24.76)? If not, a tribunal may increase any award by 0–25 per cent (see paras 32.190–32.191).

(e)   Did the employee comply with the key principles of the ACAS Code (see paras 24.75–24.76)?

If not, but the employee wins an unfair dismissal claim, the award may be reduced by 0–25 per cent (see paras 32.190–32.191 and 32.163).

(f)   Was the conduct of the pre-dismissal meeting fair (see paras 24.92–24.98)?

If not, the dismissal will probably be unfair unless any failures were minor. If it was, go to (13) (h) below.

(g)   Are there any mitigating circumstances (for example, previous good record of long-standing employment) which would militate against dismissal in favour of a further warning?

If yes, dismissal may be unfair. Go to (13)(i) below.

(h)   Was dismissal, given the incompetence in question, the conduct of the disciplinary meeting and any mitigating factors, within the band of reasonable responses open to the employer?

If yes, the dismissal will be fair (see paras 24.99–24.103).

If not, it will be unfair.

(i)   If the procedure pre-appeal was insufficient, was the failure remedied by an appeal (see paras 24.105–24.110)?

If yes, the dismissal may be fair. If not, it will be unfair.

(14) If the employer claims the employee was dismissed by reason of ill-health:

(a)   Has the employer made full inquiry (which would normally include meetings with the employee, obtaining a medical report, and examining the sickness record) about the employee's state of health (see para 24.55)?

If not, the dismissal is likely to be unfair.

(b)   Has the employer considered whether the employee is disabled and if so whether there are any reasonable adjustments he should make to allow the employee not to be at a disadvantage? If the employee is disabled and if the employer has not made reasonable adjustments (see paras 26.114–26.123) the employee may have been both discriminated against and unfairly dismissed (see paras 24.56 and 24.57).

(c)   If the employee has been persistently absent, is there any medical excuse for this? If yes, go to (14)(d) below.

If not, treat the problem as misconduct. Go back to 12.

(d)   Has the employer considered all relevant factors before deciding whether or not he wishes to dismiss the employee (see para 24.58)?

If he has, and if there are no other steps (such as alternative employment) which he could take, the employee may fairly be dismissed. Go to (14)(e) below.

(e)   Did the employee comply with the key principles of the ACAS Code (see paras 24.75–24.76)?

If not, but the employee wins an unfair dismissal claim, the award may be reduced by 0–25 per cent (see paras 32.190–32.191 and 32.163).

(f)   Did the employer comply with the key principles of the ACAS Code (see paras 24.75–24.76)?

If not, a tribunal may increase any award by 0–25 per cent (see paras 32.190–32.191).

(g)   Is the employee benefiting from permanent health insurance cover which will be withdrawn if dismissed (see para 24.60(14))?

If he is, then unless there is a clause in his contract of employment which nevertheless allows the employer to dismiss in those circumstances, any dismissal is likely to be unfair.

(h)   If the procedure pre-appeal was insufficient, was the failure remedied by an appeal (see paras 24.105–24.110)?

If yes, the dismissal, may be fair. If not, it will be unfair.

15 If the employer claims the employee has been dismissed by reason of lack of relevant qualifications, or illegality:

(a)   Can the employer demonstrate why ownership of the qualifications has become necessary (see para 24.65)?

If not, the dismissal will be unfair.

If yes, go to (15(c) below.

(b)   Can the employer demonstrate why the employment is now illegal (see para 24.67)? If no, the dismissal will be unfair. If yes, go to (15)(c) below.

(c)   Were there any alternative positions into which the employee could have been placed?

If there were, and they were not offered to the employee, the dismissal is likely to be unfair.

(d)   Did the employer comply with the key principles of the ACAS Code (see paras 24.75–30.76)? If not, a tribunal may increase the award by 0–25 per cent (see paras 32.190–32.191).

(e)   Did the employee comply with the key principles of the ACAS Code (see paras 24.75–24.76)?

If not, but the employee wins an unfair dismissal claim, any award may be reduced by 0–25 per cent (see paras 32.190–32.191 and 32.163).

(f)   If the procedure pre-appeal was insufficient, was the failure remedied by an appeal (see paras 24.105–24.110)?

If yes, the dismissal, may be fair. If no, it will be unfair.

16 If the employer claims that the employee was dismissed for redundancy, follow the checklist at Chapter 25.

17 If the employer claims that the employee was dismissed for some other substantial reason:

(a)   If the reason is to do with a business reorganization, the employer should follow a procedure similar to that described in Chapter 25.

(b)   For most other dismissals under this head, the employer should follow procedures similar to those described in 12, 13, or 14 above, whichever appears the most appropriate.

18 If the employee has been unfairly dismissed, consider remedies. Does the employee want to be re-instated or re-engaged? If he does, the tribunal must consider whether this is practicable and whether the employee has contributed to his dismissal so reinstatement or re-engagement would not be just or equitable. If it is practicable, the employment tribunal may well exercise its discretion to make the necessary order. For details of the consequences if the employer fails to reinstate or re-engage, see paras 32.31–32.38.

19 If compensation is the appropriate remedy, consider the following:

(a)   What is the actual loss the employee has suffered to date?

Calculate the loss of salary and benefits.

(b)   For how long is this likely to last in future? Does the employee have another job?

If the salary is the same or more than with the employer, the employer's liability will cease from the moment the employee gains a new and ostensibly permanent job.

1(c) If less than the old salary, how long will this continue?

(d) If there is no new job, when is the employee likely to find one and at what salary?

Further details are set out at paras 32.139–32.150.

(e) Would the employee have been dismissed fairly by the employer in the near future in any event or if a fair procedure had been followed?

If a fair procedure has not been followed, dismissal will only be fair if the employer knew at the time that the process would be useless (see para 24.110(2)). If there is doubt whether, had a proper procedure been followed, dismissal would have resulted, dismissal will be unfair, but the award can be reduced to reflect this chance. However, compensation may be reduced if the employee would have been dismissed anyway had a fair procedure been followed. The period for which the employee will be compensated will end when he would otherwise have been dismissed under a fair procedure, although any basic award will still be payable (*Polkey v AE Dayton Services Ltd* [1988] AC 344, HL) (see paras 24.110(1) and (2), and 32.169–32.177).

(f) Has the employee mitigated his loss by finding another job? If the employee has failed to take appropriate steps to find another job, would he have found alternative employment had he taken those steps?

If the answer to either question is yes, there will be no further compensation to cover the period from which the alternative employment was or should have been obtained. The only caveat to this is that if the new job carries a lower salary and benefits package, the employee may recover damages representing the difference between the old and the new for such time as the tribunal decides this discrepancy will last. For further details, see para 32.154.

(g) Did the employee contribute to his own dismissal?

If there is an element of contributory fault, the compensation payments payable to the employee will be reduced by an appropriate percentage (see Chapter 32, section G). Note that conduct arising after the dismissal or which did not cause or contribute to the dismissal cannot be taken into account (*Mullinger v Department for Work and Pensions* UKEAT/0515/05).

(h) Has the employer made any ex gratia payment to the employee?

If so, it will be taken into account in reducing the award—see Chapter 32, section H.

(i) How much compensation should be awarded for the employee's loss of statutory rights (particularly because he will have to work for two years at his new employer before he is generally entitled to claim he has been unfairly dismissed and before he is entitled to a redundancy payment)? Generally an award in the region of £300–£400 is made here.

(j) In what order should any deductions from the compensation award be made?
See paras 32.219–32.222.

(k) Should the employment tribunal add to the award on the basis that the employee has been deprived of the money due to him for a period?

The tribunal is entitled to make an allowance for loss caused by delayed payment and interest is a measure of the loss (*Melia v Magna Kansei Ltd* [2006] IRLR 117, CA).

20 In terms of evidence, it is prudent for an employer and employee facing a dispute to obtain as much as possible of the following information:

(a) identity of employer, and any associated employer, its size and administrative resources
(b) length of service of employee
(c) contractual terms—value of salary/wages and benefits, plus general contractual obligations and entitlements, for example, duties, hours worked, etc. Documents should evidence contractual terms, for example, letter of appointment, contract, amendment letters, staff handbook, collective agreement, etc. Custom and practice may, too, be relevant in the absence of express written terms
(d) any relevant disciplinary procedures
(e) the reason for any termination of employment. Is the stated reason the true reason? Was a lesser sanction appropriate?
(f) what inquiries the employer made into the allegations against the employee—for cases involving poor performance, as many example of poor performance as possible should be produced
(g) what warnings were given earlier to the employee
(h) what warning, consultation, and disciplinary meetings were held relating to the dismissal
(i) all correspondence and notes of meetings relating to the inquiries, disciplinary meetings, and dismissal
(j) whether there was an appeal. If there was, all relevant documents and notes of meetings relating to the appeal

(k) what effort has the employee made to find a new job? Has he retained details? The burden of proof is on the employer to show that the employee has not properly mitigated any loss

(l) whether it is practicable to reappoint the employee in his old or any similar job

(m) whether the employee received any settlement payment. If he did, was a legally enforceable settlement agreement completed?

25

Redundancy

SUMMARY

(1) An employer in financial difficulty often needs to reduce the number of its employees by making them redundant.

(2) Redundancy is potentially a fair reason for dismissal. In selecting those to be made redundant, the employer must act reasonably.

(3) An employee who has been employed for two years or more is entitled by statute to a redundancy payment on a sliding scale, calculated in accordance with his age and length of service.

(4) Most tribunal cases concerning redundancy revolve around: whether the people selected for redundancy are actually redundant; whether they have been selected for some unfair reason; whether proper individual consultation and/or collective consultation has been implemented; and the compensation to which any redundant person is entitled.

A. WHEN IS A PERSON REDUNDANT?

An employee is dismissed by reason of redundancy if the dismissal is attributable wholly or mainly **25.01** to the fact that the employer has ceased or intends to cease to carry on the relevant business at all, or the business in the particular place where the employee was employed; or because the requirement of the business for an employee to carry out work of a particular kind has ceased or diminished or is expected to do so (ERA 1996, s 139; *Murray v Foyle Meats Ltd* [1999] IRLR 562, HL). The commercial decision that the business needs fewer employees of a particular type rests with the employer, and the tribunal will generally not inquire into whether the employer was reasonable in taking that commercial decision, although this may be a proper subject for collective consultation with staff representatives before any final decision is taken—see para 25.16. An employer selecting people for redundancy should be able to demonstrate to a tribunal that it has reviewed the number of staff it needs to maintain the business it proposes to carry on and the positions which will thereby become vacant: if it thinks in terms of which individuals it no longer requires, this may indicate that any selection process is unfair. However, the issue has to be viewed in context: an employee of an agency who placed him to work with a specific employer named in his contract of employment was not automatically redundant when the employer no longer had any need for him, but was dismissed (*Francis v Pertemps Recruitment Partnership Ltd* [2013] 0003/13, EAT).

25.02 When a tribunal looks at the issue of redundancy it takes into consideration not only the employing company but also, in reviewing the question whether the employee should be offered alternative employment elsewhere, any associated companies.

25.03 When a whole business or office closes down there is rarely an issue whether the employee is redundant. If there is any question, it relates only to: whether there should have been any collective consultation (see paras 25.11–25.16); and (in a claim for unfair dismissal) whether associated employers have appropriate alternative work for the employee. An employee will not be made redundant if he has a mobility clause in his contract of employment and is genuinely (and with advance notice as part of the redundancy consultation procedures) relocated pursuant to this clause (*Home Office v Evans* [2008] IRLR 59, which contrasted the position here from one where employers 'dodge' between implementing contractual redundancy procedures and invoking a mobility clause). However, it is at least arguable that the behaviour of employers who exercise mobility clauses solely in order to avoid the automatic TUPE transfer of certain employees is inconsistent with TUPE principles and unfair (*Royal Mail Group Ltd v Communication Workers Union* [2009] 0338/08 EAT).

25.04 When, however, the employer is merely reducing numbers rather than closing the business altogether, problems can arise if it cannot actually show that its cost-cutting measures are the direct cause of a particular person's departure. Company restructuring which does not involve a reduction in numbers of employees or hours worked, is unlikely to involve any redundancies, although anyone losing their job as a result may have been dismissed for 'some other substantial reason' (see para 24.69(2)). An employee who is dismissed because she refused to agree to work reduced hours in response to a reduction in work available was dismissed by reason of redundancy. There is no need to have a reduction in headcount in order to have a dismissal by reason of redundancy—a reduction in the number of hours to be worked is sufficient (*Packman, t/a Packman Lucas Associates v Fauchon* [2012], IRLR 721, EAT—where the employer wanted to reduce the number of hours each bookkeeper worked, as a result of a down-turn in work and the introduction of a better software package, an employee who refused to reduce the number of hours worked was nevertheless dismissed by reason of redundancy. This case did not follow *Aylward and Others v Glamorgan Holiday Home Ltd t/a Glamorgan Holiday Hotel* [2003] UKEAT 0167/02). An employee may successfully claim unfair dismissal if he can show that no proper method of selecting people for redundancy was implemented or that there is some other motive for dismissal.

B. SELECTION OF THOSE EMPLOYEES TO BE MADE REDUNDANT

25.05 In establishing the pool from which any potentially redundant person is to be drawn, and the appropriate selection criteria, the employer must act reasonably (ERA 1996, s 98(4)). The employer must not use as its principal reason for selecting a person any facts relating to the individual's membership of or participation in the affairs of a trade union, or any other automatically unfair reason (see para 24.28 for automatically unfair reasons).

25.06 The employer must choose its own selection criteria, which must be reasonable (*Williams v Compair Maxam Ltd* [1982] IRLR 83, EAT) and followed in a consistent and unbiased way (*Dixon Stores Group v Sangster* [2004] UKEAT 0205/04). Most fair criteria would include one or more of the following factors: the type of skills and capabilities for which there is a continuing employment need, and the suitability of the individuals to perform those tasks: competence, commitment and attitude, team-working ability, health, absences, and conduct. In the past 'last in first out' has been applied as a criterion, although its use has been declining. Now, it may be unwise to adopt this as a criterion because it may disadvantage younger employees who will not have had the opportunity to build up substantial years of service, and may therefore be regarded as indirect age discrimination. However, in one of the first reported cases on the point, use of length of service as one of six criteria was upheld (*Rolls-Royce plc v Unite the Union* [2009] EWCA Civ 387, CA), because its two aims, maintenance of a stable workforce during a redundancy exercise and rewarding loyalty, while potentially discriminatory, were objectively justifiable in the particular circumstances. (See also *MacCulloch v ICI plc* [2008] IRLR 846 which discussed, but reached no conclusion on, the use of age and service in the calculation of a contractual redundancy payment, and para 25.34.) The criteria should be capable of being objectively checked, but can be weighted in favour of particular criteria (*Williams v Compair Maxam Ltd* [1982] ICR, 156, EAT, where the criterion to retain employees who 'would keep the company viable' was too subjective and unreasonable; and *Rees v Peninsula Business Services Ltd* [2006] 2401955, ET, where 'receipt of unsolicited commendations from clients' was unfair, depending entirely on luck). The application of a competency assessment normally used in a recruitment exercise is likely to be an inappropriate selection basis, as it does not take into account past appraisals or the view of those who manage the individuals—although it might be appropriate to allocate potentially redundant employees to alternative employment (*Mental Health Care (UK) Ltd v Biluan and Anor* [2013] UKEAT 0248/12).

An employer should apply the criteria carefully: a glaring inconsistency may make the selection **25.07** unfair (*Northgate HR Ltd v Mercy* [2008] IRLR 222, CA). Simply selecting on a cost-saving basis could also be unfair (*KGB Micros Ltd v Lewis*, EAT 573/90, where salesmen were unfairly selected for redundancy by comparing their overheads with their revenue generation (ie net profit per salesman) as this did not comprise an objective valuation of the salesmen's skills). If the employer cannot back up how the criteria were applied, for example by reference to previous appraisals or other records, but the marker has exercised his own judgement over a range of criteria, the process may be faulty and any selected employee may have been unfairly dismissed (*E-Zec Medical Transport Service Ltd v Gregory* UKEAT/0192/08). Employees may have a discrimination claim against employers if selection criteria are chosen or applied in a discriminatory fashion. For example, a tribunal may detect a 'young' culture in the employer as a result of failure to consider other employees, all younger than the claimant, for redundancy, and conclude that there has been age discrimination (*Court v Dennis Publishing Ltd* 2200327/07, ET); or an employer may assess employees who have taken parental leave less favourably than those who have not done so (*Riezneice v Zemkopibas Ministrija* [2013] CJEU C-7/12) and it is likely to be discriminatory to use absence as a criterion without taking into account that someone's absence may be as a result of their having a disability (*Harding v Eden Park Surgery* [2005] 1100367/05, ET); or to fail to make adjustment to scores which disadvantage a disabled person (*Dominique v Toll Global Forwarding Ltd* UK EAT/0308/13). Employers have an obligation to offer any alternative employment to an employee made redundant while on maternity leave (The Maternity and Parental Leave etc Regulations 1999, reg 10). UK legislation in fact goes further than the requirements of the Pregnant Workers Directive which does not provide that special treatment be given to pregnant workers where dismissal is unconnected with their pregnancy—see judgment of Court of Justice of the European Union in Case C-103/16 *Porras Guisado v Bankia SA and Others* (ECLI:EU:C:2018:99). An employer must not score a pregnant employee more favourably than other employees when marking her under any selection criteria—to do so may be discriminatory of, say, any men also being considered for redundancy in the exercise (*Eversheds Legal Services Ltd v De Belin* [2011] 0352/10, EAT). An employer cannot, after having applied selection criteria, then make a choice to retain one person over another who scored higher, on the basis, say, of the overall needs of the business (*Watkins v Crouch t/a Temple Bird Solicitors* [2011] IRLR 382 EAT, where a high street firm of solicitors retained a receptionist, whose skills the firm it felt it could not do without over a secretary, the tribunal ruling that if the needs could be defined with some form of certainty, then to be relied on at all 'the overall needs of the business' should have been one of the selection criteria).

In addition, the *pool* from which the employee is to be selected for redundancy needs to be ascer- **25.08** tained. A wise employer will examine the extent to which other employees are performing similar roles to the role earmarked for redundancy, the extent to which other jobs are interchangeable and whether there are employees doing similar work at other locations. Note however *Fulcrum Pharma (Europe) Ltd v Bonassera* [2010] 0198/2010, EAT, where the EAT found that the tribunal was right to have found an employer at fault for not consulting with the employee about the size of the pool, but wrong to have found that the pool necessarily consisted of two people because each had historically on occasion carried out the other's functions. The principles which guide consideration of the appropriate selection pool, set out by the EAT in *Wrexham Golf Co Ltd v Ingham* [2012] UKEAT 0190/12, are:

- It is not for the tribunal to decide whether it would have thought it fairer to act in another way: the question is whether the dismissal lay within the range of conduct which a reasonable employer could have adopted (*Williams v Compair Maxam Ltd* [1982] ICR, 156, EAT).
- The reasonable response test applies to the selection of the pool from which the redundancies are to be drawn; there may be more than one appropriate pool (*Hendy Banks City Print v Fairbrother* UKEAT/0691/04).
- There is no legal requirement that a pool should be limited to employees doing the same or similar work. The question of how the pool should be defined is primarily a matter for the employer to determine. It would be difficult for the employee to challenge it where the employer has genuinely applied its mind to the problem (*Taymech v Ryan* [1994] UKEAT 663/94).
- The tribunal is entitled, if not obliged, to scrutinize carefully the reasoning of the employer to determine if it has 'genuinely applied' its mind as to who should be in the pool.

25.09 Even if the employer has not considered whether to operate a selection pool, but has, say, nominated someone performing a unique role for redundancy, this may nevertheless be a reasonable response in the circumstances (*Taymech v Ryan* [1994] UKEAT 663/94). It may be appropriate to adopt a 'pool of one' if an employee is in a unique position (*Halpin v Sandpiper Books Ltd* [2012] UKEAT 0171/11, where an overseas office was being closed, and the employee was the only who had been sent from the UK to man it, even though there were other employees in the UK who were performing tasks that the employee was capable of performing, and had in the past performed). However, this is not always the case, particularly where the employer has not applied its mind to the problem (*Capita Hartshead Ltd v Byard* [2012] IRLR 814, EAT, where it was inappropriate to include in a pool only one of four actuaries who performed similar work, who primarily each had their own clients, although who might be substituted for each other in some circumstances such as long-term absence, just on the basis that her client basis had dwindled more than that of her colleagues).

25.10 *Bumping.* If, for example, the employer decides that he needs two fewer employees in one department, yet there are employees in another department who perform similar tasks and who, by their contracts of employment, could be required to work in the first department, then those other employees could also be subject to the same criteria for selection. This 'bumping' rule is sound practice to follow, although it is not a hard and fast rule in every case (see *Lionel Leventhal Ltd v North* [2004] UKEAT 0265/04, where on the facts of the case the employer should have considered bumping a more junior employee, even though the potentially redundant employee had not requested it—factors to consider were: how different the two jobs are; the difference in remuneration; and the qualifications of the potentially redundant employee. The extent to which an employer should consider bumping to avoid redundancy is an issue to which the band of reasonable responses test applies—see *Mirab v Mentor Graphics (UK) Limited* UKEAT/0172/17/DA. Further, an employer which is going to adopt a bumping practice should have clear reasons for having done so, such as the need to maintain key skills: if it cannot show that it considered these issues at the time, the 'bumped' employee could be unfairly dismissed (see eg *O'Reilly v Welwyn and Hatfield District Council* [1975] IRLR 334). Where there is a customary arrangement or agreed procedure about identifying the ambit of the pool, this should be followed unless the employer can show it was reasonable to depart from it (*Russell v LB Haringey* [1999] EWCA Civ 1792, CA).

C. CONSULTATION

Collective consultation

25.11 Consultation over the redundancies should take place on two levels, both the collective (where twenty or more are to be made redundant) and the individual. Section 188 of the TULR(C)A 1992 provides that where twenty or more employees at any one establishment may be made redundant (see para 25.15 for relevant time frames), the employer must consult with 'appropriate representatives'. Staff who are due to leave on the expiry of their fixed-term contracts should not be included in the headcount unless the contract is terminated by reason of redundancy before the expiry of their term, the completion of the task, or the recurrence or non-recurrence of the event specified in the contract (TULR(C)A 1992, s 282, now amended to specify accordingly; cf *University and College Union v University of Stirling* [2015] UKSC 26). The relevant definition of 'dismissal as redundant' for the purpose of collective consultation under s 188 is wider than that under the ERA 1996 and includes a dismissal for a reason not related to the individual concerned. This would encompass a dismissal where the employer has terminated the employment of and re-engaged an employee in order to effect a change to their terms and conditions of employment. The ECJ has held that employees who have resigned in response to a unilateral change by the employer to an essential element of their contract of employment (for example, pay) for a reason not related to the individual employee will be taken to be dismissed as redundant for the purpose of the EU Collective Redundancies Directive (No 98/59) and therefore should be included in the headcount (see Case C-422/14 *Pujante Rivera v Gestora Clubs Dir SL and Another* (ECLI:EU:C:2015:743)). In 2013, the EAT reinterpreted the English law and directed that the words 'at one establishment' should be deemed deleted from the legislation because they were incompatible with the EU Collective Redundancies Directive (No 98/59), so that thousands of employees who were made redundant when a substantial high street chain went into administration were all entitled to be the subject of consultation, even though some were employed in stores that individually employed fewer than twenty people, and all employees were therefore entitled to a protective award (see para 25.19) where consultation was inadequate (*USDAW v Ethel Austin Ltd (in administration) and Anor* [2013] UKEAT 0547-8/12). This was a controversial decision, which was referred by the Court of Appeal to the ECJ ([2015] IRLR 577), which restored the previously settled position that 'establishment' means the unit or entity to which the employees are assigned to carry out their duties and not the whole of the employer's business. The ECJ made similar rulings in the cases of C-182/13 *Lyttle and Others v Bluebird UK Bidco 2 Ltd* (ECLI:EU:C:2015:317) and Case C-392/13 *Cañas v Nexea Gestión Documental and Another* (ECLI:EU:C:2015:318). Although the Court of Appeal has not formally ruled following the ECJ's decision, many practitioners are advising on the basis that the EAT decision in *USDAW v Ethel Austin Ltd (in administration) and Anor* has in effect been overturned and the following paragraph sets out the position on the basis that this is the case.

There have to be twenty or more employees employed in the same establishment who may be made **25.12** redundant before collective consultation is required. The word 'establishment' is broadly defined. Where a business consists of a number of discrete workplaces, each one might be a separate 'establishment'. For example, a production unit could be an establishment if it, say, has a head of production and a substantial and specialized workforce, and is a stand-alone operation, even if it does not have any legal, economic, financial, administrative, or technological autonomy (*Athinaikim Chartopoiia AE v Panagiotidis* [2007] IRLR 284, ECJ). The ACAS Guide on How to Manage Collective Redundancies (http://www.acas.org.uk/?articleid=747) suggests that, in determining whether a workplace is an establishment, one should look at: whether it is a distinct entity; whether it has a degree of permanence and stability; whether it has the ability to carry out the tasks assigned to it; and whether it has a workforce, technical means, and organizational structure that allow it to carry out this function. In determining the establishment at which the employee works, the focus is on the physical premises at which the employee works, rather than on the organization of which it is part. Prior to the EAT decision in *USDAW v Ethel Austin Ltd (in administration) and Anor* in 2013, taking into account the relevant case law, it was thought that the Court should focus on the unit to which the workers are assigned to perform their tasks—whether the unit is capable of being an establishment, and if so, whether the employee is assigned to it. This is a factual question—the fact that an employee had a mobility clause in his contract did not necessarily mean that he was assigned to a wider unit (*Renfrewshire Council v Educational Institute of Scotland* [2013] IRLR 76, EAT).

The representatives may be representatives of a recognized trade union, if there is one, or if not they **25.13** must be employee representatives (see para 25.14). Those whom the employer plans to redeploy elsewhere in the business must be included in the headcount of those potentially redundant (*Hardy v Tourism South East* [2005] IRLR 242, EAT), as must those who voluntarily accept redundancy (*Optare Group Limited v Transport & General Workers Union* [2007] IRLR 931, EAT). However, those whose employment is due to end because of the expiry of a fixed-term contract, provided that the contract is not terminated prematurely, are not to be included within the number count (TULR(C)A 1992, s 282).

25.14 If there is already a group of employees who have been appointed or elected to represent colleagues in general in circumstances such that they have authority to receive information about and be consulted about proposed redundancy dismissals, then, in the absence of a recognized union, this group can be consulted with. If no such group exists, or if the employer does not wish to consult this group, he must consult with a group who has been specially elected by the affected employees in an election. The election must be held in the following way:

(a) The employer must make such arrangements as are reasonably practicable to ensure that the elections are fair.

(b) It is for the employer to decide:
    (i) how many representatives there should be, but they must be sufficient to represent all employee interests, having regard to the number and classes of affected employees
    (ii) whether employees of different classes should be represented by all the representatives, or just be representatives of their class and
    (iii) the length of the term of office—which must be sufficiently long to enable the representatives to remain in place until the consultation concludes.

(c) The candidates for election must be affected employees as at the election date.

(d) No affected employee must be unreasonably excluded from standing for election.

(e) All affected employees as at the election date must have the opportunity to vote.

(f) The employees must be able to vote for as many candidates as are entitled to represent them.

(g) There should be a secret ballot.

(h) Votes should be accurately counted (TULR(C)A 1992, s 188A).

However, if the employer proposes to accept all the names put forward to be representatives, no formal election needs to take place (*Phillips v Xtera Communications Limited* [2011] IRLR 724, EAT). Employers should ensure that those whom they consult have authority from the employees to receive the information and be consulted on their behalf—consulting with a body whose members expressly do not have any negotiation rights is probably inadequate (*Kelly v The Hesley Group Ltd* [2013] IRLR 514, EAT).

25.15 Consultations must begin in good time and at least 30 days before any dismissal takes effect where the employer proposes to dismiss as redundant between twenty and ninety-nine employees at one establishment within a ninety-day period, and at least forty-five days before any dismissal where the employer proposes to dismiss 100 or more employees within a ninety-day period (TULR(C)A 1992, s 188(1) and (1A)). Note that where the employer proposed to dismiss 100 or more employees before 6 April 2013, the minimum consultation period was ninety days. The dismissal 'takes effect' not on the day the employment terminates, but on the day that notice to terminate is given to the employees (*Junk v Kühnel* [2005] IRLR 310, ECJ). These time limits apply unless there are special circumstances which render it not reasonably practicable for them to be adhered to. 'In good time' does not mean 'at the earliest opportunity'. Consultation must begin when there is a real proposal to dismiss, even if the proposal is a recommendation to management which has yet to be ratified (*Leicestershire County Council v Unison* [2005] IRLR 920, EAT), although if the proposals are still at a formative stage, the fact that there is a gap between their formulation and the start of consultations will not prevent the consultation being 'in good time' so long as there is sufficient consultation before proposals are finalized (*Amicus v Nissan Motor Manufacturing (UK) Ltd* UKEAT/0184/05, where constructive negotiations began several months after proposals had been announced). Consultation may conceivably only take two weeks if that is sufficient time to produce a fair and meaningful consultation process (*Amicus v Nissan Motor Manufacturing (UK) Ltd* UKEAT/0184/05). On the other hand, it is conceivable that employees facing a substantial number of redundancies may argue that forty-five days is not in good time, because the period is insufficient for the full consultation required in the particular circumstances. The ECJ regards the obligation to consult, under Art 2 of the Collective Redundancies Directive (No 98/59), (which binds government bodies) is triggered when the employer has an intention to make redundancies, shown by the taking of a business decision that compels the employer to contemplate or plan for collective redundancies: the obligation does not arise where a decision deemed likely to lead to collective redundancies is merely contemplated and where accordingly the redundancies are only a probability (*Akavan Erityisalojen Keskusliitto AEK RY v Fujitsu Siemens Computers OY* [2009] IRLR 944, ECJ).

25.16 Consultation must be about ways of avoiding dismissals, reducing the numbers of employees to be dismissed, and mitigating the consequences of the dismissals. The employer should undertake the consultation with a view to reaching agreement with the representatives/union (TULR(C)A 1992, s 188(2)). As part of the consultation, the employer must disclose the following information, in writing, to the representatives/union:

(1) its reasons for the proposals including the business reasons behind any proposed redundancies, eg the reasons for the closure of a business (*UK Coal Mining Ltd v NUM* [2008] IRLR 4, EAT and, where the reasons are policy-related rather than commercial, *USA v Nolan* [2009] IRLR 923, EAT)
(2) the number and descriptions of employees whom it is proposed to dismiss as redundant
(3) the total number of employees of any such description employed by it at the establishment in question
(4) the proposed method of selecting the employees who may be dismissed
(5) the proposed method of carrying out the dismissals—with due regard to any agreed procedure, including the period over which the dismissals are to take effect
(6) the proposed method of calculating the amount of any redundancy payments to be made and
(7) the number of agency workers working temporarily for and under the supervision and direction of the employer; the parts of the undertaking in which those agency workers are working; and the type of work they are carrying out (TULR(C)A 1992, s 188(4)).

It is not sufficient for consultation simply to deal with matters of concern to the employees (*Kelly v the Hesley Group Ltd* [2013] IRL514, EAT).

25.17 The employer also has to give notice of the intention to effect redundancies to the Department for Business, Energy & Industrial Strategy if it proposes to make twenty or more people redundant over a ninety-day period, and must use form HR1. This must be done within similar time limits to those required for consultation with authorized representatives (see para 25.15) (TULR(C)A 1992, s 193(1)(b)). If the employer fails to submit the form, it could be convicted and fined up to level 5 on the standard scale in a magistrates' court which since 12 March 2015 is an unlimited fine (TULR(C)A 1992, s 194(1)).

25.18 If the employer has an agreement by which it has to inform and consult representatives under the Information and Consultation of Employees Regulations 2004, it need not discuss impending collective redundancies with those representatives if it tells them in writing that it will be consulting under TULR(C)A 1992, s 188 (Information and Consultation of Employees Regulations 2004, reg 20(1)(c)).

25.19 Failure to consult with authorized representatives renders the employer liable to a protective award of up to ninety days' pay for each relevant employee (a week's pay being basic salary, not including any discretionary bonus element—*Canadian Imperial Bank of Commerce v Beck* [2010] 0141/10, EAT). This is a punitive, rather than compensatory award and tribunals are required to look at the seriousness of the employer's default. A proper approach where there is no consultation at all is to start with the maximum award and then reduce it only if there are mitigating circumstances which would justify a reduction (*Susie Radin Ltd v GMB* [2004] IRLR 400, CA; *Hutchins v Permacell Finesse Ltd* EAT/0350/07). The starting point is not ninety days, however, where some consultation has taken place (*London Borough of Barnet v Unison and another* UKEAT/0191/13). Special circumstances which might reduce an award include situations where the employer is unexpectedly required by a client to take instant action to reduce resources devoted to the client's project (*Shanahan Engineering Ltd v Unite the Union* [2010] UKEAT 0411/09, where some award was still appropriate as the employer should still have attempted to consult the union before making some 50 redundancies). The award is intended to be punitive,

Part C The Substantive Law

so in determining the size of the protective award, the Court refers only to the extent of the employer's failure to consult, not any loss suffered by individual employees (*Shields Automotive Ltd v Langdon and Anor* [2013] EATS 0059/12). As a result, an award may still be made even where employees remained employed throughout the protected period and were not dismissed or under notice until that period had ended (*Cranswick Country Foods Ltd v Beall* UKEAT/0222/06). Where there are employee representatives or a recognized trade union, they must make the application for a protective award (TULR(C)A, s 189(1)). If not, a claim can be made by any of the affected employees or any employee dismissed as redundant. If a protective award is obtained by a trade union, it can only be enforced by employees in respect of whom the union is recognized and not, for example, by employees from non-recognized unions, even where they were members of the union which obtained the award (*TGWU v Brauer Coley Ltd* [2007] ICR 226, EAT). If a protective award is granted to an individual, where there is no trade union or elected representative, it applies only to that individual, and not to all other individuals in the same situation (*Independent Insurance Co Limited v Aspinall* [2011] IRLR 716, EAT).

25.20 NIC contributions are payable on all of a protective award; they are also, in principle, treated by HMRC as taxable, but subject to the £30,000 limit set out in ITEPA, ss 401–403 (see paras 36.06–36.15 and 36.24–36.26).

Individual consultation

25.21 The employer must also consult with each individual employee whom it proposes to make redundant before any decision is finalized. There are no formal rules to apply, and the ACAS Code of Practice on Disciplinary and Grievance Procedures specifically exempts redundancy dismissals from its remit. Nevertheless, an employer is expected, before any decision is taken, to go through a fair consultation procedure, warning and consulting employees at risk of redundancy, using a fair selection basis, and taking steps to minimize the redundancies by exploring redeployment with employees (*Williams v Compair Maxam Ltd* [1982] IRLR 83, EAT; *Polkey v AE Dayton Services Ltd* [1987] IRLR 503, HL).

25.22 Individual consultation will involve explaining to the employee:

- why their role is at risk of redundancy
- why they have been provisionally selected for redundancy, and what the selection criteria were. It will be unfair if the employer refuses to explain elements of its scoring in the redundancy selection exercise which are not obvious (*Pinewood Repro Ltd t/a County Print v Page* [2010] 0028/10, EAT, where the employer refused to explain its reasoning for giving the employee a low score against 'flexibility'). It is not necessary to produce the performance records of other employees, although it would be sensible to have the information to hand in an anonymized format (*Alexander v Bridgen Enterprises Ltd* [2006] IRLR 422). Failure to consult an employee who has recently moved to a commercially risky and now potentially redundant role about the possibility of moving back to her old job does not necessarily make the dismissal unfair (*Hachette Filipacchi UK Ltd v Johnson* [2006] All ER (D) 53)
- alternative roles available
- financial proposals

and giving the employee the opportunity to comment and respond before any final decision is taken (*R v British Coal Corporation and Secretary of State for Trade and Industry ex parte Price* [1994] IRLR 72, Divisional Court). If this does not happen, an employee will be likely to have been unfairly dismissed. The only reason to avoid such a finding is if the employer convinces a tribunal that, on the basis of the facts it knew at the time, it would have been futile to have adopted the procedures (per Lord Bridge in *Polkey*). In all other circumstances, the employee will be unfairly dismissed, but compensation may be reduced by the '*Polkey* reduction' if the employer can demonstrate to the tribunal that a fair procedure would have resulted in dismissal anyway (see paras 32.169–32.177). Also, if a tribunal finds that any redundancy label was a sham, masking a true (potentially unfair) reason for dismissal, it will expect the ACAS Code to be followed (see para 24.78 for consequences of failure to follow the Code).

Even if the redundancies are subject to collective consultation, it is still advisable for the em- **25.23**
ployer to conduct individual consultation with the employees, for example about available alternative employment. Failure to do so may well render any subsequent dismissal unfair.

D. ALTERNATIVE EMPLOYMENT

The employer also has a duty, if someone is provisionally selected for redundancy, to see whether **25.24**
there is any other role which might suit that particular employee, not only with the employer but
also with any associated company of the employer. If this requirement is ignored, a dismissal is
normally rendered unfair. If there are jobs, even if they are of lower status or carry lower wages
than those which apply to the employee's present job, the prospect of moving to the alternative
employment should nevertheless be raised. Where employees are potentially redundant but there
are other vacant roles available, an employer should not invite applications for the vacant roles
from the whole workforce before satisfying itself that the potentially redundant employees are not
suitable to carry out the vacant role—and the selection process for deciding on their suitability
must meet some criteria for fairness, although the test is not as stringent as those for the general
selection procedure (*Ralph Martindale v Harris* EAT/0166/07) and employers may use their judgement to appoint the most suitable candidate for the role in future (*Morgan v Welsh Rugby Union*
[2011] IRLR 376, EAT; *Samsung Electronics (UK) Ltd v Monte-D'Cruz* [2012] 0039/11, EAT). It is
sensible for an employer to inform the employee of the proposed salary and benefits of any alternative position—failure to do so may make the dismissal unfair (*Fisher v Hoopoe Finance Ltd* [2005]
0043/05, EAT). If there are any updates to the job specification for alternative employment for
which an employee is being considered, these must be drawn to the employee's attention (*Somerset
County Council v Chaloner* [2013] UKEAT0600/12, EAT). Employees on maternity leave must
be offered any suitable alternative jobs if their normal job is to be made redundant, although in
Simpson v Endsleigh Insurance Services Ltd [2010] 0544/09, EAT an employer was not obliged to
offer a London-based employee roles some distance outside London where there was no evidence
she might have been willing to relocate—the suitability of prospective vacancies is to be judged
from the perspective of an objective employer, and not from the employee's perspective. Failure
to consult an employee who had recently moved to a commercially risky and now potentially redundant role about the possibility of moving back to her old job does not necessarily make the
dismissal unfair (*Hachette Filipacchi UK Ltd v Johnson* [2006] All ER (D) 53). If there is no consideration given to alternative employment, but the employer can show it would not have appointed
the employee to the vacant position in any event, the decision to make the employee redundant
might still be regarded as fair if the breaches in procedure were not so serious as to make the decision to dismiss unreasonable (*Loosley v Social Action for Health* UKEAT/0378/06).

If there is a mobility clause in the employee's contract, entitling the employer to transfer the em- **25.25**
ployee to another work location, an employer can rely on this clause, upon giving the employee
reasonable notice of the proposed relocation, to avoid a redundancy at one site if there are equivalent vacancies elsewhere. Any employee who refuses to transfer will not have been constructively
dismissed if he refuses to transfer and resigns (*Home Office v Evans* [2008] IRLR 59, CA). This
process must be adopted from the start—an employer cannot start a redundancy process and then
evade the consequences by attempting to enforce a mobility clause (*Curling v Securicor Ltd* [1992]
IRLR 549, EAT). In exercising its rights under a mobility clause, the employer must have regard
to the duty of mutual trust and confidence. If there is no mobility clause, an employer cannot go
down this route, but must proceed as in paras 25.26–25.28.

If the employer is able to identify suitable alternative work, either within its own company or **25.26**
with an associated company, which is substantially similar to the employee's previous position and
commands a similar wage package, it is to the employer's advantage to offer such a job to the pro-
spectively redundant employee. The job offer, which should be made before termination, to start
within four weeks of the termination of the redundant job, is then generally subject to a four-week
trial period (although the trial period may be extended if the employee has further training). If the
employee accepts the job offer and continues to work after the trial period, there is no redundancy.

If, however, he refuses a suitable job offer (either immediately or during the trial period) he will lose his right to a redundancy payment unless he can show that it was reasonable for him to reject the offer. If the job is not suitable, or if the employee acts reasonably in refusing it (respectively an objective and a subjective test) the employee will still be redundant unless he accepts the job offer and continues to work normally. If the employer invites potentially redundant employees to compete for other, vacant jobs, the selection process for the new post may not be so rigorous as it is for the original redundancy/selection itself, but the employer must simply act reasonably and fairly (*British Steel plc v Slater* EAT 644196; *Ralph Martindale and Co Ltd v Harris* EAT 0166/07; *Morgan v Welsh Rugby Union* [2011] IRLR 376, EAT).

25.27 For the offer to be suitable, it must be made (orally or in writing) by the original employer or an associated employer before the employee's employment actually terminates. The new post should start within four weeks of the ending of the old one, and, if not on the same terms and conditions it is subject to an objective test of suitability. In determining this, the tribunal will review issues such as pay, status, location, and whether the new job is within the employee's skill set. If the terms and conditions differ at all from the original contract, the employee is allowed a trial period of four weeks to assess the new role, although this period may be extended by agreement.

25.28 If the terms of the new employment are suitable and the employee unreasonably refuses it, either immediately or during the trial period, he will not be entitled to a redundancy payment. Whether the employee is reasonable in refusing a job offer is a subjective test, viewed from the employee's perspective: the burden of proof is on the employer to show that the employee is behaving unreasonably (*Hudson v George Harrison Ltd* EAT/0571/02; *Executors of Everest v Cox* [1980] ICR 415). For example, an employee might reasonably refuse a job with apparently reasonable hours if it will prevent him or her from complying with childcare arrangements, or if he perceives it involves a loss of status (*Cambridge & District Co-operative Society v Ruse* [1993] IRLR 156, EAT), or because the new employment would require a nursing manager to work in a hospital when she had been working in the community for over twenty years (*Devon Primary Care Trust v Readman* [2013] EWCA Civ 1110, CA). It is relevant to consider whether the new post is overwhelmingly suitable (as opposed, say, to only marginally suitable). If the post is only marginally suitable, it will be harder for the employer to persuade a tribunal that the employee was acting unreasonably in refusing it (*Commission for Health Care Audit & Inspection v Ward* [2008] UKEAT 0579/07). The tribunal should not apply a 'range of reasonable responses' test to the question whether the employee had unreasonably refused a job offer (*Devon Primary Care Trust v Readman* [2013] EWCA Civ 1110, CA).

E. CALCULATION OF REDUNDANCY PAYMENT

25.29 The redundancy payment is calculated according to a fixed formula. Provided that the employee has been employed for a minimum of two years (or would have been if given statutory notice (ERA 1996, ss 155 and 145(5) and see para 24.08), the employee will receive a redundancy payment calculated by multiplying his weekly gross remuneration (subject to a maximum payment, which, for dismissals on or after 6 April 2019 is set at £525 and for dismissals between 6 April 2018 and 5 April 2019 is £508) by a factor determined in accordance with age and length of service. Length of service means the period from commencement of employment to the effective date of termination (EDT) (see para 24.08 for the definition of EDT). If an employee is not paid a redundancy payment, he can bring a claim in the employment tribunal (ERA 1996, s 163).

25.30 If the employee is paid less than the national minimum wage, the award will be calculated as if the employee were receiving the national minimum wage—£8.21 per hour for those aged 25 or over; £7.70 per hour for those aged 21–24; £6.15 for those aged 18–20; £4.35 per hour for 16- and 17-year-olds who are not apprentices; and £3.90 per hour for apprentices aged under 19 or in the first year of their apprenticeship with effect from 1 April 2019 (see Appendix 6 for earlier minimum wages).

25.31 In addition to the redundancy payment, each employee is entitled either to work out his contractual notice period, or to be paid money in lieu of notice.

Some employers have contractually enhanced redundancy payment programmes. These may be **25.32** included:

(1) in the employment contract itself
(2) in a collective agreement incorporated into the employment contract, even if that collective agreement had expired before the redundancy took effect (*Framptons Ltd v Badger* [2006] All ER (D) 127 (Oct), EAT) and even if the policy expressly states that it is not part of the employee's contract if the policy has been followed without exception for a substantial period to such an extent that it has acquired contractual status by custom and practice (*Peries v Wirefast Ltd* EAT/0245/06). Note that it may be possible for the employer to imply a term, via custom and practice, that payment of enhanced redundancy terms as set out in a collective agreement is conditional on the employee signing a compromise agreement, if this has been the practice, without exception, over recent years (*Garratt v Mirror Group Newspapers Ltd* [2011] IRLR 591 CA) or
(3) a staff handbook (*Keeley v Fosroc International Ltd* [2006] IRLR 961, CA; *Allen v TWR Systems Ltd* [2013] UKEAT 0083/12), provided that the term is 'apt' for inclusion (ie that it purports to confer a right, rather than being aspirational or procedural) and that it has actually been incorporated into the contract. The term may be found as one of a collection of contractual policies on the employer's intranet (*Christopher Harlow v Artemis International Corporation Limited* [2008] IRLR 629).

Employers may regularly pay enhanced redundancy payments, and if these have been consistently **25.33** applied so that a custom and practice is established, future employees may have a contractual right to equivalent payments on redundancy. The burden of proof is on the employee to demonstrate that there is a custom of enhanced payments. Questions designed to establish whether an enhanced redundancy payment scheme is included in an individual's contract of employment include:

(1) whether the policy is 'reasonable, notorious and certain' and whether the payments are all the same (if the payments are not the same, this is a pointer against custom and practice)
(2) whether the policy has been drawn to the attention of the employee, and if so was it in such a way that it indicated that the employer intended to be contractually bound by the policy. Here, the tribunal will look at industrial reality—so that publication to a trade union or a large section of the work force may imply publication to all the workforce
(3) whether the policy has been followed consistently and without exception on every occasion where there have been redundancies for a substantial period
(4) how many times the policy has been followed, and over how long a period (if many times over a long period, this is a pointer towards custom and practice)
(5) whether there is anything inconsistent in the employment contracts with the existence of a custom and practice to pay enhanced payments. If there is, then there is unlikely to be a custom and practice without evidence of an obvious intention to vary it
(6) whether payments have been made under the policy as a matter of course, or only as a result of specific negotiations, or, viewed objectively, are equally explicable on the basis that the employer is making the payments as an exercise of discretion rather than legal obligation (*Albion Automotive Ltd v Walker* [2002] EWCA Civ 946, CA; *Park Cakes Ltd v Shumba and Others* [2013] EWCA Civ 974, CA).

Enhancing the statutory minimum redundancy payments will not be regarded as age discrimin- **25.34** ation so long as the amount an employer offers to each employees is calculated in the same way, eg by applying the same multiplicand or substituting actual working wage for maximum weekly wage (Equality Act 2010, Sch 9, para 13). If the employer does not follow the pattern of the statutory scheme, for example if it increases payments according to age more sharply than the scheme, it faces the task, if challenged by younger employees, of trying to justify why the greater differentials were a proportionate means of achieving a legitimate aim, for example because younger people have fewer family responsibilities, have greater flexibility and/or are more likely to move to a new job than older people, failing which the payments may be discriminatory on the ground of age (*MacCulloch v Imperial Chemical Industries Plc* [2008] IRLR 846, EAT; *Loxley v BAE Systems Land*

Part C The Substantive Law

Systems (Munitions & Ordnance) Ltd [2008] IRLR 853, EAT; *Lockwood v Department of Work and Pensions* [2013] EWCA Civ 1195, CA, where the Court of Appeal accepted that, with limited money available, it was potentially legitimate to band payments to different age groups, and that it was impractical to assess whether an individual's needs had more in common with people from other age groups rather than her own) or possibly disability (*Odar v Baxter Deutschland GmbH* [2013] ECJ (C-152/11), where a tapering enhanced payment was found to be indirectly discriminatory on ground of disability and without objective justification). To be legitimate, the aim must be of a public interest nature, consistent with the social policy aims of the state, rather than for purely individual reasons particular to the employer (*Seldon v Clarkson, Wright & Jakes* [2012] ICR 716, SC). However, a staggered increase in enhanced pay, depending on age bracket, in a voluntary redundancy scheme was acceptable where the employer could justify it on the grounds of the public interest in facilitating and promoting employment for young people, planning the recruitment and departure of staff, and the sharing out of opportunities for advancement in a balanced manner according to age (*Lockwood v DWP* [2013] UKEAT 0094/12). It may, however, be legitimate for an employer to cap enhanced pay awards to the amount the employee would have earned until he had retired under any standard retirement age (*Kraft Foods UK Ltd v Hastie* [2010] ICR 1355, EAT. In assessing whether the employer adopted a proportionate means to achieving the legitimate aims, an holistic approach should be taken by an employment tribunal.(*McDowell v BAE Systems (Operations) Ltd* [2018] ICR 214).

25.35 An employee who is unfairly selected for redundancy will be entitled to compensation for unfair dismissal.

CHECKLIST OF ISSUES FOR TRIBUNAL CLAIMS CONNECTED WITH REDUNDANCY

1. Can the employer establish that it has or intends to close down the business where the employee works, or that the requirements of that business for employees to carry out work of a particular kind have ceased or diminished? (ERA 1996, s 139—see para 25.01.) If this cannot be established, then redundancy cannot be the reason for dismissal.

2. Were twenty or more employees potentially to be made redundant at the same establishment within ninety days or less? (TULR(C)A 1992, s 188—see para 25.15.)

    If twenty or more employees are potentially to be made redundant (or redeployed (*Hardy v Tourism South East* [2005] IRLR 242, EAT)) during this period, the employer will need to undertake collective consultation, either with a recognized trade union, or with special employee representatives. Any election for employee representatives must be fair (TULR(C)A 1992, s 188A—see para 25.14).

3. Was there a failure to consult or, where necessary, to hold a fair election of employee representatives—see para 25.19?

    If so, a claim may be brought against the employer for a protective award of up to ninety days' pay per affected employee (TULR(C)A 1992, s 189).

4. What is the reason for the employee's dismissal? Is it because his role is redundant, or is it for some other reason?

    If it is for some other reason but redundancy is given as the ostensible reason, the employee will probably have been unfairly dismissed.

5. If the employer proposed to make at least twenty employees redundant at one establishment within a ninety-day period, did he notify the Department for Business, Energy & Industrial Strategy of his intention to do so using form HR1?

    If not, the employer could be convicted in the magistrates' court and face an unlimited fine (TULR(C) A 1992, s 194(1)—see para 25.17).

6. Did the employer adopt a fair procedure leading up to the dismissal (see paras 25.05–25.10 and 25.24)? For example, have appropriate selection criteria been adopted/agreed and fairly applied?

REDUNDANCY FLOW CHART

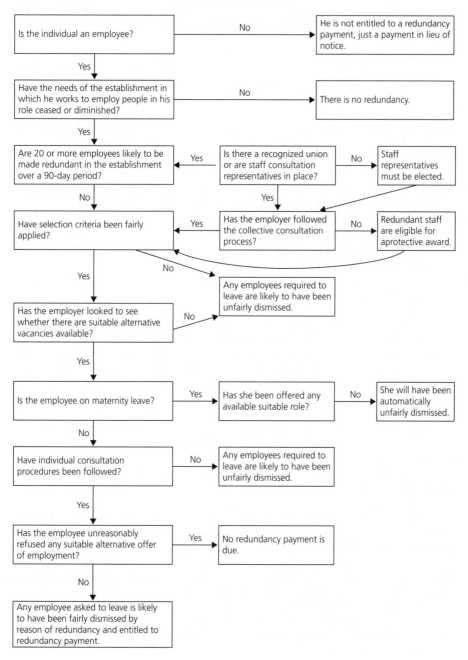

(*Williams v Compair Maxam Ltd* [1982] ICR 156, EAT and see generally for consultation obligations on an employer when dealing with union/employee representatives.)

If not, any consequent dismissal may well be (but is not bound to be—see *Grundy (Teddington) Ltd v Plummer* [1983] ICR 367) unfair.

7. Was the consultation process reasonable or was it a sham?

    If the employee can demonstrate it was a sham, for example because the employer had reached a final but not inevitable decision before the process began, he is likely to have been unfairly dismissed (*Rowell v Hubbard Group Services Ltd* [1995] IRLR 195).

8. Was the employee on maternity leave at the time of her dismissal?

    If so, and she was not (before her old employment ends) offered alternative employment if any suitable vacancy exists, she will have been automatically unfairly dismissed (Maternity and Parental Leave etc Regulations 1999, SI 1999/3312, regs 10 and 20).

9. Did the employer review whether there are any suitable alternative jobs, within the employer company or any group companies, for the employee—see paras 25.24–25.28? Did it give the employee the available information about the proposed salary and benefits attaching to the alternatives?

    If not, the dismissal may be unfair (*Vokes Ltd v Bear* [1974] ICR 1; *Avonmouth Construction Co Ltd v Shipway* [1979] IRLR 14; *Fisher v Hoopoe Finance Ltd* [2005] 0043/05, EAT).

10. Did the employee unreasonably refuse any offers of suitable alternative employment (see para 25.28)?

    If so, he will not be entitled to a redundancy payment (ERA 1996, s 141).

11. Was it appropriate for the employer to consider 'bumping' so that an employee in a potentially redundant role would be given another's job (see para 25.10)?

    If not, there may be circumstances where this failure makes the dismissal unfair (*Thomas & Betts Manufacturing Ltd v Harding* [1980] IRLR 255).

12. Was the employee selected for redundancy for an automatically unfair reason? Automatically unfair reasons are set out at para 24.28.

    If so, the redundancy will be automatically unfair (ERA 1996, s 105).

13. Did the position regarding the potential redundancy, or any suitable alternative positions, change between the date on which notice was given and the date when the redundancy takes effect?

    If so, and if the employer does not take action which might allow the employee to remain employed, the dismissal may be regarded as unfair (*Dyke v Hereford and Worcester County Council* [1989] ICR 800).

14. Was an employee who is being made redundant asked to work out his notice period or paid salary in lieu?

    If neither, he may have a claim against his employer for breach of contract. If the amount is less than £25,000 the claim may be brought under Art 3 of the Employment Tribunal (Employment Tribunals Extension of Jurisdiction) (England and Wales) Order 1994.

15. Was the employee employed for at least two years by the EDT (ie the termination date or, if no or inadequate statutory notice was given, the termination date plus this notice—see para 24.08 (ERA 1996, ss 145(5), 86, and 155))?

    If so, he is entitled to a redundancy payment calculated in accordance with s 162 of the ERA 1996. The current maximum week's pay is £525 per week for dismissals on or after 6 April 2019 and £508 per week from 6 April 2018 to 5 April 2019.

16. Did the employer have a contractually enhanced redundancy programme which is incorporated into the individuals' contracts of employment, or has he consistently applied an enhanced redundancy payment policy so that it has become custom and practice for it to be paid (see paras 25.32–25.33)?

    If so, the employee may have a contractual claim against the employer, which can be brought in the employment tribunal up to a value of £25,000, or otherwise in the High Court or county court, for receipt of the enhanced redundancy payment (Employment Tribunals Extension of Jurisdiction (England and Wales) Order 1994, Art 3).

17. Is the enhanced redundancy scheme modelled on the method for calculating statutory redundancy pay, but increased across the board by enhancing, consistently, any relevant multiplicands?

    If not, the scheme may be age discriminatory—see para 25.34.

26

Discrimination

SUMMARY

(1) The Equality Act 2010 (EqA 2010) codifies the anti-discrimination legislation into one statute.

(2) Discrimination is unlawful if it is because of the protected characteristics of age, disability, gender reassignment, marriage and civil partnership, race, religion or belief, sex, or sexual orientation.

(3) Employees and others who are in 'work like' relationships are protected against direct discrimination, combined discrimination, indirect discrimination, harassment, victimization, discrimination for a reason arising from a disability, and from a failure to make reasonable adjustments for disabled persons.

(4) Employers and principals are generally liable for the discriminatory acts of their employees and agents.

(5) There are a number of defences to claims for discrimination and exceptions to the obligation not to discriminate set out in the EqA 2010. These are largely provided for in Schedule 9 to the EqA 2010 but are also set out in other parts of the EqA 2010.

(6) Courts and tribunals recognize the difficulty complainants have in obtaining evidence of discrimination. One means of assisting claimants in gathering such evidence was by use of the statutory questionnaire procedure. However, the statutory questionnaire procedure no longer exists, s 138 of the EqA 2010 having been repealed in 2014. Even absent the statutory questionnaire procedure, complainants can question their employers in relation to detrimental treatment and ask employment tribunals to draw adverse inferences from a failure to give an appropriate response.

The main provisions of the EqA 2010 came into force on 1 October 2010. According to the Explanatory Notes issued with the Act, it is intended 'to harmonize discrimination law, and to strengthen the law to support progress on equality'. Prior to October 2010, the law was contained in a large number of statutes and statutory instruments, as well as European Directives which were themselves supported by case law. Much of the case law which predates the EqA 2010 will continue to be relevant, however, because the EqA 2010 is, for the most part, a consolidating statute which draws heavily on the pre-existing statutory provisions. There are, however, as the Explanatory Notes suggest, some substantive changes to the law which have been effected by this Act. In 2011, the Equality and Human Rights Commission produced a statutory Code of Practice relating to 'employment', which can be found online at :

http://equalityhumanrights.com/uploaded_ files/EqualityAct/employercode.pdf.

A. THE SCOPE OF DISCRIMINATION LAW IN EMPLOYMENT SITUATIONS

26.01 The law does not prohibit discrimination generally, but only in particular social situations. This chapter is concerned with the prohibition on discrimination in employment situations and quasi-employment situations. However, there are a range of 'employment situations' which are covered by the EqA 2010, relating to employees, contract workers, and office holders.

Employees

26.02 Employment is defined in s 83 of the EqA 2010 as being employment under either (1) a contract of employment, a contract of apprenticeship, or a contract personally to do work; (2) Crown employment; or (3) employment as a relevant member of the House of Commons or House of Lords staff.

26.03 The meaning of the term 'contract of employment' has been much considered as the same phrase is used in s 230 of the Employment Rights Act 1996 (ERA 1996). However, it is clear from the definition of employee in s 83 that it is much wider than the definition in s 230 of the ERA 1996 since establishing that an individual is working under a 'contract personally to do work' will suffice to establish employee status. This wording was considered by the Court of Appeal in *Gunning v Mirror Group Newspapers* [1986] IRLR 27. In that case, the proprietor of a business had entered into a commercial relationship with a newspaper to collect and distribute newspapers to newsagents. The Court of Appeal held that there was no contract personally to do work on the basis that the dominant purpose of the contract was a commercial contract for the distribution of newspapers. It mattered not whether there was any requirement under the contract to undertake some work personally. The question was whether or not the dominant purpose of the contract, taken as a whole, was for the undertaking of personal work. However, the 'dominant purpose' test set out in *Gunning* is not a test which should be universally applied. In *Jivraj v Haswani* [2011] 1 WLR 1872, the Supreme Court opined that in *Gunning* the essential question which the court was asking itself by the application of the 'dominant purpose' test was: was the contract for the provision of services by an independent contractor who was not an 'employee' or was it a contract where a person agreed to work under the control or subordination of another and therefore was an employee? The Supreme Court found this to be the appropriate test drawing on the jurisprudence of the ECJ set out in *Allonby v Accrington and Rossendale College* [2004] IRLR 224 and as applied by the House of Lords in *Percy v Church of Scotland Board of National Mission* [2005] UKHL 73. In *Jivraj* itself, the Supreme Court applied this test and came to the conclusion that an arbitrator was not an employee for the purposes of the discrimination legislation because arbitrators did not work under the direction of the parties to an arbitration.

Although, for the most part, domestic law requires a 'contract' between employer and employee to **26.04** exist, in order that a person is in employment for the purposes of s 83 of the EqA 2010, European law has no such requirement. In contrast, European law focuses on whether the putative employee has agreed personally to perform services, and whether the putative employee is in a subordinate position to the putative employer: *Halawi v WDFG UK Limited* [2015] IRLR 50. The EqA 2010 has to be read, of course, to give effect to the underlying European Directives which it implements and, as such, it may be that there is no longer a strict requirement for a contract in order that the s 83 of the EqA 2010 definition is satisfied.

There is a series of cases considering whether or not the holders of certain offices are workers **26.05** for the purposes of what is now s 83 of the EqA 2010. For example, the position of special constables was considered in *Sheikh v Chief Constable of Greater Manchester Police* [1989] ICR 373; the position of associate ministers in the Church of Scotland was considered in *Percy v Church of Scotland Board of National Mission* [2005] UKHL 73; and the position of judges was considered (in relation to the test of employment in the Part-Time Workers (Less Favourable Treatment) Regulations 2000) by the ECJ and the Supreme Court in *O'Brien v Ministry of Justice* [2013] IRLR 315, [2012] IRLR 421. As set out above, it was determined in *Jivraj v Haswani* [2011] UKSC 40 that arbitrators are not 'employees' for the purposes of the discrimination legislation.

Neither the European Directives nor the EqA 2010 prohibits discrimination against those who **26.06** are unpaid volunteers since the concepts of 'occupation' and 'employment' in those Directives are not apt to cover such unpaid volunteers: see *X v Mid Sussex Citizens Advice Bureau* [2013] IRLR 146 (SC).

Employees (and applicants to become employees) are protected by the EqA 2010 from: **26.07**

(a) discrimination (whether direct, indirect, or for a reason associated with a disability) and victimization in the arrangements made for deciding to whom to offer employment, the terms on which that employment is offered, and/or by not offering employment: see s 39(1) EqA 2010
(b) discrimination (whether direct, indirect or for a reason associated with a disability) and victimization in the terms of employment, in the way that an employee is afforded access to opportunities for promotion, transfer or training or for receiving any other benefit, facility or service: see EqA 2010, s 39(2)(a) and (b)
(c) discrimination (whether direct, indirect or for a reason associated with a disability) and victimization by dismissal (see EqA 2010, s 39(2)(c) and further s 39(7) of the EqA 2010, which provides that dismissal includes the concept of constructive dismissal where an employee resigns in response to a repudiatory breach of contract on the part of the employer) and by the occasioning of any other detriment (see EqA 2010, s 39(2)(d)). For the meaning of the term 'detriment' see *Ministry of Defence v Jeremiah* [1980] QB 87, *Jiad v Byford* [2003] EWCA Civ 135, *Shamoon v Chief Constable of the Royal Ulster Constabulary (Northern Ireland)* [2003] UKHL 11, and *Clamp v Aerial Systems* [2004] All ER (D) 259. Detriment must be assessed from the point of view of the employee in question, need not be financial, but must be

Part C The Substantive Law

material and substantial in the sense that the act complained of must not be trivial or amount to an unjustified sense of grievance on the part of the employee

(d) harassment: see EqA 2010, s 40

(e) a failure to make reasonable adjustments: see EqA 2010, s 39(5).

Contract workers

26.08 Contract workers also fall within the scope of the discrimination legislation by reason of s 41 of the EqA 2010. A contract worker is a person who is employed by one person but works for another person ('the principal'). The contract worker must work for the principal pursuant to an agreement between his employer and the principal: see s 41(5) EqA 2010. There is, however, no need to show a relationship of control between the 'principal' and the worker, although where there is control of the worker by the 'principal' it will be easier for employment tribunals to find that an individual is a contract worker: see *Leeds City Council v Woodhouse* [2010] IRLR 625 As such, the provision is designed to provide protection for agency workers who otherwise would likely fall outside the scope of the discrimination legislation.

26.09 Although s 41(5) of the EqA 2010 requires a contract between the principal and the employer of the contract worker, it is likely that more complex contractual arrangements whereby there is a chain of contracts as between the contract worker and the principal will suffice: see *MHC Consulting Services Limited v Tansell* [2000] ICR 789.

26.10 Contract workers are provided with protection from:

(a) discrimination (whether direct, indirect, or for a reason associated with a disability) and victimization as to the terms on which the principal allows the worker to do the work or by not allowing the worker to do or to continue doing the work, in the way the principal affords the worker access to opportunities for receiving a benefit, facility, or service, and/or by subjecting the worker to any detriment: see EqA 2010, s 41(1) and (3)

(b) harassment: see EqA 2010, s 41(2)

(c) a failure to make reasonable adjustments: see EqA 2010, s 41(4).

Police officers

26.11 Police officers do not work under any contract of employment or other contract of personal service: see *Fisher v Oldham Corporation* [1930] 2 KB 364; *Attorney General for New South Wales v Perpetual Trustee* [1955] AC 457; and *Sheikh v Chief Constable of Greater Manchester* [1990] 1 QB 637. However, by s 42 of the EqA 2010 the office of police constable (save for those employed at the Civil Nuclear Constabulary and the Serious Organised Crime Agency, Scottish Police Services Authority, or the Scottish Crime and Drugs Enforcement Agency, as to which see s 42(3)–(6) of the EqA 2010) is deemed to be employment:

(a) by the chief officer in respect of any act done by the chief officer in relation to the police constable

(b) by the responsible authority in respect of any act done by the authority in relation to a police constable: see EqA 2010, s 42(1).

There are similar provisions made for police cadets in s 42(2) of the EqA 2010.

26.12 It follows that the scope of the protection afforded to employees under EqA 2010 will also apply to police officers. Although at one time there was a question as to whether or not police officers would be able to mount effective challenges to the termination of their offices using the discrimination legislation because of the principles of judicial proceedings immunity (see *Heath v Commissioner of the Police of the Metropolis* [2005] IRLR 301) the Supreme Court has now confirmed that police officers are entitled to bring discrimination claims in relation to the termination of their offices because the principles of judicial proceedings immunity have to give way to the right to bring discrimination claims, afforded to police officers by EU law: see *P v Commissioner of the Police of the Metropolis* [2018] IRLR 66.

Partnerships and LLPs

Pursuant to ss 44 and 45 of the EqA 2010, partnerships and LLPs and proposed partnerships and **26.13**
LLPs are prohibited from:

(a) discriminating against or victimizing a person in the arrangements they make for deciding to
whom to offer a position as a partner; on the terms on which they offer a position as a partner;
or by not offering a person a position as a partner: see EqA 2010, ss 44(1) and (5) and 45(1)
and (5)

(b) discriminating against or victimizing a partner as to the terms of partnership; in the way access is afforded to opportunities for promotion, transfer, or training or for receiving any other
benefit, facility, or service; by expulsion; or by subjecting a partner to any other detriment: see
ss 44(2) and (6) and 45(2) and (6) of the EqA 2010

(c) harassing partners or applicants for partnership: see EqA 2010, ss 44(3) and (4) and 45(3)
and (4)

(d) failing to make reasonable adjustments (to accommodate disabled persons): see EqA 2010, ss
44(7) and 45(7).

Even corporate members of LLPs (such as companies) can bring claims under these provisions: *EAD* **26.14**
Solicitors LLP v Abrams [2015] IRLR 978.

Barristers and advocates

Pursuant to ss 47 and 48 of the EqA 2010, barristers and advocates are prohibited from: **26.15**

(a) discriminating, victimizing, or harassing applicants for pupillage or tenancy and/or pupils and
tenants themselves: see EqA 2010, ss 47(1)–(6) and 48(1)–(6) and

(b) failing to make reasonable adjustments (in accommodate disabled persons): see EqA 2010, ss
47(7) and 48(7).

Office holders

Additionally, the EqA 2010 prohibits discrimination as against office holders. These may be either: **26.16**

(a) personal office holders. A personal office is defined by s 49(3) of the EqA 2010 as an office or
post to which a person is appointed to discharge a function personally under the direction of
another person and in respect of which that office holder is entitled to remuneration or

(b) public office holders. A public office is defined by s 50(2) of the EqA 2010 as an office or post
which is made by a member of the executive, in relation to which appointment is made on the
recommendation of or subject to the approval of a member of the executive, or an office or
post appointment to which is made on the recommendation of, or subject to the approval of
the House of Commons, the House of Lords, the National Assembly for Wales, or the Scottish
Parliament.

The following are unlawful: **26.17**

(a) discrimination or victimization (by a person who has the power to make an appointment to
an office) in relation to the appointment to such offices: see EqA 2010, ss 49(3) and (5) and
50(3) and (5)

(b) discrimination or victimization (by a relevant person, defined by s 52 of the EqA 2010, and
who will be, for example, in the case of a complaint about the terms of appointment, the
person who set those terms, or in the case of termination of an appointment, the person who
had the power to terminate the appointment) in relation to the terms of appointment to such
an office; the way in which access is afforded to opportunities for promotion, transfer, training,
or the receiving of any other benefit, facility, or service; or by terminating the appointment of
the office holder subjecting the office holder to any other detriment: see EqA 2010, ss 49(6)
and (8) and 50(6)–(7) and (9)–(10). Holders of offices appointed on the recommendation or
subject to the approval of one of the Houses of Parliament and/or the National Assembly for

Part C The Substantive Law

411

Wales and/or the Scottish Parliament are not protected from termination of their offices: see EqA 2010, s 50(7)(c) and (10)(c)

(c) discrimination or victimization in relation to recommendations to the appointment to an office: see EqA 2010, s 51

(d) harassment in relation to an office holder or person seeking appointment to the office: see EqA 2010, ss 49(4) and (7) and 50(4) and (8)

(e) failing to make reasonable adjustments by a person who has the power to appoint or by a 'relevant person': see EqA 2010, ss 49(9) and 50(11).

Other entities

26.18 The EqA 2010 also prevents discrimination, victimization, harassment, and a failure to make reasonable adjustments by:

(a) qualifications bodies: see EqA 2010, s 53. For a discussion of what amounts to a qualifying body see *Reverend Canon Pemberton v Right Reverend Inwood, formerly acting Bishop of Southwell and Nottingham* [2017] IRLR 211;

(b) trade organizations: see EqA 2010, s 570. In particular, s 57(7) defines a trade organization, and the corresponding provisions in the pre-EqA 2010 legislation were considered in *National Federation of Self-Employed and Small Businesses Limited v Philpott* [1997] IRLR 340 and *Medical Protection Society v Sadek* [2004] EWCA Civ 865;

(c) employment service providers including providers of vocational training and employment agencies: see EqA 2010, ss 55 to 56.

B. THE PROTECTED CHARACTERISTICS

26.19 Section 4 of the EqA 2010 sets out nine protected characteristics. These are the 'grounds' upon which it is unlawful to discriminate against those who fall within the scope of the discrimination legislation. The protected characteristics are (1) age; (2) disability; (3) gender reassignment; (4) marriage and civil partnership; (5) pregnancy and maternity; (6) race; (7) religion or belief; (8) sex; and (9) sexual orientation. The meaning of each of the protected characteristics is considered in turn.

Age

26.20 Age is considered in s 5 of the EqA 2010. That section states that, in the EqA 2010, a reference to a person who has the protected characteristic of age is a reference to 'a person of a particular age group'. Thereafter, 'age group' is defined in s 5(2) of the EqA 2010 as referring to a group of persons defined by reference to age, whether by reference to a particular age or to a range of ages. As such, 'age' could mean, in relation to a person who was aged 31, any of the following (on a non-exhaustive basis) (a) the age of 31; or (b) the age group of people in their 30s; or (c) the age group of people under the age of 40; or (d) the age group of people over the age of 21.

Disability

26.21 Disability is defined in s 6 of the EqA 2010 as being where a person has a physical or mental impairment and that impairment has a substantial and long-term adverse effect on the person's ability to carry out normal day-to-day activities. This is substantially the same definition as was found in s 1 of the Disability Discrimination Act 1995 (DDA 1995). In addition to s 6 of the EqA 2010, it is necessary to have regard to the provisions of Schedule 1 to the EqA 2010, which sets out further explanation as to the component parts of the definition of disability.

26.22 In *Goodwin v The Patent Office* [1999] IRLR 4, the EAT gave guidance to employment tribunals as to the correct approach to establishing whether or not a person has a disability. The EAT suggested that there were four questions which employment tribunals should have regard to: first, whether or not a mental or physical impairment exists at all; secondly, whether or not that impairment has an adverse effect on the ability of an individual to carry out normal day-to-day activities; thirdly, whether or not any adverse effect was substantial; finally, whether or not any substantial adverse effect was long term.

The term 'impairment' is not defined in the EqA 2010 but is a broad term. For example, there is no **26.23** need to identify an underlying fault or defect in order for a physical impairment to exist. A physical impairment can be the effects of an illness even where it is impossible to identify the root cause of the illness: *College of Ripon and York St. John v Hobbs* [2002] EWCA Civ 1074. As to mental impairments, it used to be the case that it was necessary to identify a clinically well-recognized mental impairment such that mere references to 'stress' or 'depression' would not suffice: *Morgan v Staffordshire University* [2002] IRLR 190. However, in *Dunham v Ashford Windows* [2005] ICR 1584 the EAT found that a person could have a mental impairment which did not amount to a mental illness. Furthermore, it is noteworthy that *Morgan v Staffordshire University* was determined at a time when the DDA 1995 included a provision which required a mental impairment to be clinically well recognized. That provision was removed from the DDA 1995 in December 2005 and has not been included in the EqA 2010. Notwithstanding the removal of that provision, the EAT in *J v DLA Piper UK LLP* [2010] IRLR 936 found that it could still be legitimate for employment tribunals to draw a distinction between 'clinical depression' on the one hand, and stress or anxiety brought on by adverse circumstances on the other hand. The EAT observed that, while it would be difficult to elucidate the boundaries of each of these concepts in theoretical terms, in practical terms, any depression which satisfied the other elements of the test for disability was likely to be a form of 'clinical depression' such that it would satisfy the requirement of 'impairment'. Certain impairments, such as an addiction to alcohol, nicotine, or any other substance are deemed not to be impairments for the purposes of the EqA 2010: see the Equality Act 2010 (Disability) Regulations 2010.

Whether or not the impairment has an adverse effect on the ability of an individual to carry out **26.24** normal day-to-day activities will require a consideration of what the individual is able to do and the way in which the individual is able to do it, as against what would be the case if the individual did not have the relevant impairment. The focus should be on what the individual cannot do rather than upon what the individual can do: *Leonard v Southern Derbyshire Chamber of Commerce* [2001] IRLR 19. It follows that the fact that an individual is able to attend work and undertake the duties of his or her job, will not mean that the individual is not a disabled person: see *Law Hospitals NHS Trust v Rush* [2001] IRLR 611; *Ekpe v Metropolitan Police Commissioner* [2001] IRLR 605, and *Paterson v Metropolitan Police Commissioner* [2007] ICR 1522. Similarly, it might be necessary to consider what normal day-to-day activities an individual is able to carry out in the working environment where the working environment exacerbates the individual's impairment: *Cruickshank v VAW Motorcast Limited* [2002] IRLR 24. Under the DDA 1995, it was necessary to look at a statutory list of capacities to determine whether or not an impairment had an effect on a person's ability to carry out normal day-to-day activities. That list does not appear in the EqA 2010 and therefore it is likely that normal day-to-day activities will be given a wider construction.

In determining the effect that an impairment has on the ability of an individual to carry out normal **26.25** day-to-day activities, the 'deduced effect' must be considered. That means that the effects of any measures taken to treat or correct an impairment, such as medication, must be discounted: see para 5 of Schedule 1 to the EqA 2010. However, where the effect of corrective measures was to restore the ability of an individual to carry out normal day-to-day activities such that the corrective measures were no longer required, an individual would not then be able to assert that he continued to have an impairment which caused an adverse effect on his ability to carry out normal day-to-day activities on the basis that, without the corrective measures, the adverse effect would have continued: *Abadeh v British Telecommunications plc* [2001] ICR 156.

In order to be long term, the effects of an impairment must have lasted for at least twelve months, **26.26** must be likely to last for at least twelve months, or must be likely to last for the rest of the life of a person. However, para 2 of Schedule 1 to the EqA 2010 makes provision for the situation where an impairment is recurrent. Where the substantial adverse effect (on a person's ability to carry out normal day-to-day activities) of an impairment is likely to recur, it is treated for the purposes of s

6 of the EqA 2010 as though it were continuing. The meaning of 'likely' was investigated by the House of Lords in *SCA Packaging Ltd v Boyle* [2009] IRLR 746. 'Likely' was determined to mean 'could well happen' rather than 'more likely than not'. The latter formulation had previously been considered to be the correct approach following the decision of the EAT in *Swift v Chief Constable of Wiltshire Constabulary* [2004] IRLR 540. Further, in considering whether the effects of an impairment are 'long term' in might be necessary to consider the effects of secondary conditions which an impairment has given rise to: see *Patel v Oldham Metropolitan Borough Council* [2010] IRLR 280.

26.27   There are certain impairments which are deemed to be disabilities, without more. A severe disfigurement is deemed to give rise to substantial adverse effect on the ability of a person to carry out normal day-to-day activities: para 3 of Schedule 1 to the EqA 2010. Further, cancer, HIV, and multiple sclerosis are each deemed to be disabilities by virtue of para 6 of Schedule 1 to the EqA 2010. Further, where a person has a progressive condition which is likely to result in that person having an impairment satisfying the definition of disability in s 6 of the EqA 2010, that person is deemed to have a disability.

26.28   The Office for Disability Issues issued guidance on matters to be taken into account in determining questions relating to the definition of disability in 2010 http://odi.dwp.govuk/docs/wor/new/ea-guide.pdf. That guidance provides useful examples of the sort of factual questions which are likely to be determined in employment tribunals in assessing whether or not a person is disabled within the meaning of s 6 of the EqA 2010.

Gender reassignment

26.29   Gender reassignment is defined as a protected characteristic by s 7 of the EqA 2010. A person has that protected characteristic where that person is proposing to undergo, is undergoing, or has undergone a process, or part of a process, for the purpose of reassigning the person's sex by changing physiological or other attributes of sex. Section 7(2) then provides that where a person has the protected characteristic of gender reassignment, that person is referred to, in the remainder of the EqA 2010 as a 'transsexual person'.

Civil partnership and marriage

26.30   Section 8(1) of the EqA 2010 provides that a person who is married or is a civil partner has the protected characteristic of marriage or civil partnership. It is apparent from the wording of s 8 of the EqA 2010 that a person who is not married or does not have a civil partner cannot be said to have this protected characteristic. Similarly, a person who is divorced could not be said to have this protected characteristic. There have been few cases dealing with discrimination because of marital status. However, the leading case is now *Hawkins v Atex Group Limited* [2012] IRLR 807. In that case, Underhill J was at pains to stress that this ground of discrimination occurs where a married person is treated less favourably than a non-married person, rather than because a person is married to a particular person. On the facts of that case, the chief executive officer of a company had appointed his wife as corporate marketing director in breach of an instruction that no further member of his family ought to be appointed to the company. Underhill J explained that in order to amount to direct discrimination because of marriage, a woman would have to be dismissed because she was *married*, rather than because she was married to *a particular man*. Accordingly, it was held that the proper approach to the comparator question in a marital discrimination case was to consider the treatment that a married person received as against that which would have been afforded to a 'common law spouse' or 'partner'.

Pregnancy and maternity

26.31   Pregnancy and maternity are identified as protected characteristics by s 4 of the EqA 2010. The general scheme of the EqA 2010 (prohibiting direct and indirect discrimination at ss 13 and 19 of the EqA 2010) is modified in the case of pregnancy. The law of pregnancy discrimination is therefore considered immediately below.

By s 18 of the EqA 2010, it is unlawful to discriminate against a woman in the 'protected period' **26.32** in relation to a pregnancy of hers, either:

(a) because of the pregnancy (see *Interserve FM Limited v Tuleikyte* [2017] IRLR 615) or

(b) because of an illness suffered by the woman as a result of the pregnancy. This provision replicates the law settled at European level in cases such as *Brown v Rentokil Limited* [1998] All ER (EC) 791, [1998] ECR I– 4185.

The 'protected period' is defined by s 18(6) of the EqA 2010 as beginning when the pregnancy be- **26.33** gins, and ending where the woman has the right to ordinary and additional maternity leave at the end of the additional maternity leave period or (if earlier) when the woman returns to work. Where the woman does not have the right to ordinary and additional maternity leave, the protected period will end at the end of the period of two weeks beginning with the end of the pregnancy (which reflects the period of compulsory maternity leave). As to the definitions of these periods of maternity leave, see the Maternity and Parental Leave Regulations 1999, SI 1999/3312 (which are unaffected by the EqA 2010).

Section 18(3) to (4) of the EqA 2010 prohibits discrimination on grounds of maternity leave by **26.34** stating that a person discriminates against a woman if he treats her unfavourably because she is on compulsory maternity leave or because she is seeking to exercise, has exercised, or sought to exercise the right to ordinary or additional maternity leave. Presumably this prohibition (and/ or the prohibition in s 18(2) of the EqA 2010) will continue to prohibit discrimination where the 'effective cause' of the unfavourable treatment was the pregnancy or taking of maternity leave: see, for example, *O'Neill v Governors of St Thomas More RCVA Upper School* [1997] ICR 33; *Rees v Apollo Watch Repairs plc* [1996] ICR 466; *Abbey National v Formoso* [1999] IRLR 222; and *Lewis Woolf Griptight Limited v Corfield* [1997] IRLR 432.

Section 18 does not require any comparison in the case of pregnancy or maternity discrimination. **26.35** This reflects the settled law of the ECJ as set out in *Webb v EMO Air Cargo (UK) Limited* [1994] ICR 770 and *Dekker v Stichting VJV-Centrum Plus* 177/88 [1990] ECR I-3941, [1992] ICR 325, although note the decision of the Court of Appeal in *Madarassy v Nomura International plc* [2007] EWCA Civ 33, where Mummery LJ opined that while a comparator was not necessary in pregnancy cases, the use of a comparator might still be helpful in order to test why unfavourable treatment was occasioned.

Where a decision to discriminate is taken within the 'protected period' but is not implemented **26.36** until after that period, it will be treated as having been done in the 'protected period': see EqA 2010, s 18(5).

It is unclear whether or not claims for 'pregnancy discrimination' not covered by s 18 of the EqA **26.37** 2010 could be brought by way of a claim under s 13 of the EqA 2010. Section 18(7) of the EqA 2010 prevents a claim for sex discrimination being pursued under s 13 of the EqA 2010, where the discrimination occurs in the protected period and is pregnancy discrimination or discrimination by reason of a pregnancy-related illness, or whenever the discrimination occurs, when it is by reason of a woman taking or seeking to take advantage of a maternity leave right. However, the above appears to leave a *lacuna*, namely, discrimination because of pregnancy or pregnancy-related illness which takes place outside of the protected period (for example, a woman who was dismissed on her return to work and therefore outside the protected period, but was dismissed by reason of her pregnancy, or a woman who was dismissed by reason of an apparent pregnancy when she was not, in fact, pregnant). As such, although s 18(2) of the EqA 2010 appears to set out the law in relation to pregnancy discrimination (see eg, EqA 2010, s 25(5)), s 18(2) of the EqA 2010 is limited to a prohibition on discrimination within the 'protected period'. It might be argued that such claims can be pursued under s 13 of the EqA 2010. Similarly, it might be that some acts of unfavourable treatment which are related to maternity or pregnancy are too remote in order to fall within the prohibitions in s 18(2) to (4) of the EqA 2010, which require the unfavourable treatment to be 'because' of pregnancy or maternity leave. Arguably, a claim could be pursued under s 13 of the EqA 2010 in any event.

Part C The Substantive Law

26.38 It should be noted, however, that the prohibition on discrimination on grounds of pregnancy or maternity does not protect women who are on maternity leave from being deprived of the benefits of the (non-contractual) terms of their employment relating to pay (see Schedule 9, Part 3, para 17(1) of the EqA 2010) save for:

(a) maternity-related pay including maternity-related pay that is increase-related (meaning that where, for example, a woman receives 90 per cent of her salary by way of maternity pay, and her salary would have been increased but for her taking maternity leave, the woman should receive 90 per cent of the increased salary from the date that the increase would have occurred, rather than 90 per cent of the former salary). As to this provision see the jurisprudence of the ECJ as set out in *Caisse Nationale D'Assurance Vieillesse Des Travailleurs Salariés v Thibault* C-136/95 [1999] ICR 160 and *Land Brandenburg v Sass* C-284/02 [2005] IRLR 147

(b) pay in respect of times when the woman is not on maternity leave and

(c) pay by way of bonus in respect of times when the woman is on compulsory maternity leave. This reflects the jurisprudence of the ECJ as set out in *Lewen v Denda* [2000] IRLR 67 and discussed by Burton J in *Equal Opportunities Commission v Secretary of State for Trade and Industry* [2007] EWHC 483.

26.39 In seeking to avoid pregnancy discrimination, regard should also be had to the provisions of the Management of Health and Safety at Work Regulations 1999, SI 1999/3242 (which implement the Pregnant Workers' Directive (92/85) and which are unaffected by the EqA 2010). It was suggested in *Hardman v Mallon* [2002] IRLR 516 that a failure to conduct a pregnancy risk assessment as is required by reg 16 of those Regulations amounted to sex discrimination. However, the courts have narrowed the application of this provision in a series of cases: see *New Southern Railways Limited v Quinn* [2006] IRLR 266; *Madarassy v Nomura International plc* [2007] IRLR 246; and *O'Neill v Buckinghamshire County Council* [2010] IRLR 384.

26.40 Employers must, in seeking to avoid discrimination claims, not treat pregnant women, or women absent from work on maternity leave, in a disproportionately more favourable manner than their male colleagues. In *Eversheds Legal Services Limited v De Belin* [2011] IRLR 448 the EAT upheld a decision of an employment tribunal that the employer had discriminated against a male employee by affording more favourable treatment to a colleague who was absent from work on maternity leave. In that case, when completing a redundancy selection exercise, the employer had given the woman the maximum score on one criterion which could only be measured in relation to employees who were at work, and therefore could not be measured in the case of the pregnant woman who was absent from work on maternity leave. The EAT took the view that the more proportionate way of dealing with the problem was for the employer to measure that criterion in the case of the woman from the period before she went on maternity leave.

Race

26.41 Section 9(1) of the EqA 2010 defines the protected characteristic of race as including (a) colour, (b) nationality, and (c) ethnic or national origins. Further, by s 9(2)(b) of the EqA 2010 a reference to persons who share a colour, nationality, and/or ethnic or national origins is a reference to persons of the same racial group and by s 9(3) of the EqA 2010 a racial group is a group of persons defined by reference to race. It follows therefore, that discrimination against group who share the protected characteristic of 'race' and therefore amount to a 'racial group', will amount to discrimination because of race. However, by s 9(4) of the EqA 2010, the fact that a racial group comprises two or more distinct racial groups does not prevent it constituting a racial group.

26.42 The Explanatory Note to the EqA 2010 provides the following examples by way of explanation:

(a) colour includes being black or white

(b) nationality includes being a British, Australian, or Swiss citizen

(c) ethnic or national origins include being from a Roma background or of Chinese heritage

(d) a racial group could be 'black Britons' which would encompass those people who are both black and who are British citizens.

The meaning of race and racial groups has been considered by the courts in a number of cases de- **26.43**
termined under the Race Relations Act 1976 (RRA 1976). For example, in *Mandla v Dowell Lee*
[1983] 2 AC 548 Lord Fraser considered that, in order to constitute an ethnic group for the purposes of the RRA 1976, the group must regard itself as a distinct community by reason of certain
characteristics. It is essential that there is a long shared history, of which the group is conscious as
distinguishing it from other groups and the memory of which keeps it alive and that the group has
a cultural tradition of its own, including family and social customs and manners, often but not
necessarily associated with religious observance. In addition, there will commonly be other characteristics which will help to distinguish the group from the secondary community:

(a) either a common geographical origin, or descent from a small number of common ancestors
(b) a common language, not necessarily peculiar to the group
(c) a common literature peculiar to the group
(d) a common religion different from that of the neighbouring groups or from the general community surrounding it
(e) a sense of being a minority or being an oppressed or a dominant group within a larger
community.

On the facts, the Sikhs were held to be an ethnic group for the purposes of the RRA 1976.

Consequently, Jews have been held to be members of a racial group: see *Seide v Gillette Industries* **26.44**
[1980] IRLR 427 and *R v The Governing Body of JFS and the Admissions Appeal Panel* [2009]
UKSC 15, [2010] IRLR 136 (where a criterion was applied in order for a child to be admitted
to a faith school that the prospective pupil's mother should have been Jewish by birth or should
have converted to Judaism under the auspices of an Orthodox synagogue). Similarly, gypsies have
been held to be members of racial group in the sense that they are members of the Romany race.
However, a reference to 'travellers' is not a reference to gypsies: see *Commission for Racial Equality
v Dutton* [1989] IRLR 8. Rastafarians are not a racial group since, although they are a separate
group with identifiable characteristics, they have not established a separate identity by reference
to their ethnic origins: see *Dawkins v Department for the Environment* [1983] IRLR 284. In *BBC
Scotland v Souster* [2001] IRLR 150 the claimant was dismissed from his job as a television pre-
senter on Scottish television and claimed that his dismissal was because he was English. The Court
of Session accepted that the claimant could complaint that he had been discriminated against on
grounds of his English nationality since the words 'national origins' in the RRA 1976 were not
limited to nationality alone. Therefore, English and Scottish could be national origins even though
individuals who were English or Scottish would describe their nationality as British. In any event,
nationality was not limited to current citizenship since a person could change his or her citizenship by acquiring or adopting a different citizenship. The decision in *Souter* echoes the decision in
Tejani v The Superintendent Registrar for the District of Peterborough [1986] IRLR 502, where it was
held that the term national origins refers to 'the nation' in the sense of race and not in the sense of
citizenship.

In *Jyske Finans A/S v Ligebehandlingsnaenet* [2017] IRLR 665, the CJEU considered that the con- **26.45**
cept of 'ethnic origins' in the Race Directive has in its origins the idea of societal groups marked
in particular by common nationality, religious faith, language, cultural and traditional origins and
backgrounds. Country of birth might be relevant to ethnicity but would not always be determinative or even relevant to the concept of 'ethnic origins'.

In *Chandhok v Tirkey* [2015] IRLR 195 the EAT held that discrimination because of a person's **26.46**
'caste' might, in some circumstances, be covered by the EqA 2010 if it could be brought within the
provisions prohibiting discrimination on the basis of 'ethnic origins'. The EAT noted that there was
no universally accepted definition of 'caste' but that aspects of 'caste' could be related to 'descent'
and therefore could be covered by the prohibition on discrimination because of a person's 'ethnic
origins'.

However, in *Onu v Akwiwu* [2016] ICR 756 the Supreme Court declined to find that discrimin- **26.47**
ation on the basis of a person's immigration status amounted to race or nationality discrimination.

Although a person's immigration status would be linked to their race or nationality, the two were not one and the same. There were many non-British nationals living in the UK who were not in the vulnerable position that the claimants in that case found themselves in by reason of their immigration status.

Religion or belief

26.48 Section 10 of the EqA 2010 defines religion as meaning 'any religion' and belief as meaning 'any religious or philosophical belief'. Section 10 provides explicitly that the protected characteristic extends to those who do not have a particular religion or belief. It follows that the protected characteristic of religion or belief includes:

(a) religion
(b) a religious belief and
(c) philosophical belief.

26.49 The meaning of 'religion' has yet to be considered by the case law relating to the EqA 2010, although it is likely that a broad definition would be adopted. In other legal contexts, broad definitions have been adopted: see *R(on the application of Hodkin and Another) v Registrar General of Births, Deaths and Marriages* [2014] 1 All ER 737, where Scientology was held to be a religion on the basis that it was 'a spiritual or non-secular belief system, held by a group of adherents, which claims to explain mankind's place in the universe and relationship with the infinite, and to teach its adherents how they are to live their lives in conformity with the spiritual understanding associated with the belief system'. The ACAS guidelines on religion and belief in the workplace (which were released following the bringing into law of the Employment Equality (Religion or Belief) Regulations 2003, SI 2003/1660) suggest that matters such as collective worship and a clear belief system might be relevant as well as a 'profound belief affecting he way of life or view of the world'. This is supported by the Explanatory Notes to the EqA 2010, which state that:

(a) the definition is intended to be 'in line' with the protection afforded by Art 9 of the European Convention on Human Rights
(b) a religion must have a clear structure and belief system
(c) examples of religions for the purposes of s 10 of the EqA 2010 are 'the Baha'i faith, Buddhism, Christianity, Hinduism, Islam, Jainism, Judaism, Rastafarianism, Sikhism and Zoroastrianism'.

26.50 The definition of religious belief was considered in the context of Art 9 of the European Convention on Human Rights in *R (on the application of Williamson) v Secretary of State for Education & Employment* [2001] EWHC Admin 960. In that case, it was argued that certain provisions of the Education Act 1996 had to be read so as to permit corporal punishment in schools because corporal punishment was in line with the religious beliefs of a certain group of Christian teachers and parents. Lord Nicholls of Birkenhead stated that:

> When the genuineness of a claimant's professed belief is an issue in the proceedings the court will inquire into and decide this issue as a question of fact. This is a limited inquiry. The court is concerned to ensure an assertion of religious belief is made in good faith: 'neither fictitious, nor capricious, and that it is not an artifice', to adopt the felicitous phrase of Iacobucci J in the decision of the Supreme Court of Canada in *Syndicat Northcrest v Anselem* (2004) 241 DLR (4th) 1, 27, para 52. But, emphatically, it is not for the court to embark on an inquiry into the asserted belief and judge its 'validity' by some objective standard such as the source material upon which the claimant founds his belief or the orthodox teaching of the religion in question or the extent to which the claimant's belief conforms to or differs from the views of others professing the same religion. Freedom of religion protects the subjective belief of an individual. As Iacobucci J also noted, at p 28, para 54, religious belief is intensely personal and can easily vary from one individual to another. Each individual is at liberty to hold his own religious beliefs, however irrational or inconsistent they may seem to some, however surprising.

26.51 Accordingly, a belief can be a religious belief even it is only held by one person. Elias P, giving the judgment of the EAT in *Eweida v British Airways* [2009] ICR 3030 stated:

> Accordingly, it is not necessary for a belief to be shared by others in order for it to be a religious belief, nor need a specific belief be a mandatory requirement of an established religion for it to qualify as a religious

belief. A person could, for example, be part of the mainstream Christian religion, but hold additional beliefs which are not widely shared by other Christians, or indeed shared at all by anyone.

However, it should be noted that in a claim of indirect discrimination, where, as in that case, the individual wanted to manifest a religious belief in a particular manner (for example, by wearing a cross) that it will be necessary to show that more than one person holds the particular belief in question or wants to manifest the belief in that way in order to show that persons holding a particular religious belief are placed at a 'particular disadvantage'. In the Court of Appeal [2010] IRLR 322, Sedley LJ stated that it was impossible for the Court to conclude that the views of one 'solitary believer' were shared by others when 'fellow-believers elsewhere in society may accord different degrees of importance to the same manifestation of faith'.

26.52 In a series of domestic cases, the Court of Appeal attempted to distinguish between the holding of a particular religious belief on the one hand, and the manifestation of that particular belief on the other hand:

(a) in *Islington London Borough Council v Ladele* [2009] ICR 387 (EAT) and [2010] IRLR 154 (CA) the EAT and Court of Appeal considered the case of a civil registrar who refused to perform civil partnership ceremonies or to register civil partnerships. The EAT, whose decision was upheld by the Court of Appeal, held that in instructing Ms Ladele to conduct civil partnerships, the Council had not directly discriminated against Ms Ladele. Ms Ladele had not been treated in the way she had because of any religious belief which she held, but rather because of the manner in which she manifested those religious beliefs. Ms Ladele's claim was properly a claim for indirect discrimination but on the facts of this case, the Council's legitimate aim of implementing its 'dignity for all' policy was proportionate and therefore its conduct was justified

(b) in *McFarlane v Relate Avon Limited* [2010] IRLR 196 (EAT) and [2010] IRLR 872, where a counsellor refused to provide psycho-sexual counselling to same-sex couples and was dismissed, Laws LJ, refusing permission to appeal, stated that he was bound by the decision of the Court of Appeal in *Ladele* but went onto state, at para 22 of his judgment:

> In a free constitution such as ours there is an important distinction to be drawn between the law's protection of the right to hold and express a belief and the law's protection of that belief's substance or content. The common law and ECHR Article 9 offer vigorous protection of the Christian's right (and every other person's right) to hold and express his or her beliefs. And so they should. By contrast they do not, and should not, offer any protection whatever of the substance or content of those beliefs on the ground only that they are based on religious precepts. These are twin conditions of a free society.

26.53 However, subsequently *Eweida, Ladele,* and *McFarlane*'s cases were considered (together) by the ECtHR in *Eweida v United Kingdom* [2013] IRLR 231. The Court held that the manifestation of a religious belief was protected by Art 9 of the ECHR provided that there was a sufficiently close and direct nexus between the act said to manifest the belief and the underlying belief. In all three cases, the individuals were found to be manifesting their religious beliefs so as to engage Art 9. The outcomes in each of the cases therefore turned on whether the UK's failure to prevent the interference with the individuals' Art 9 rights could be justified. There was found to be a breach of Art 9 only in the *Eweida* case, and not in the cases of *Ladele* and *McFarlane*.

26.54 Article 9 of the ECHR cannot be enforced directly in the employment tribunal. However, the Court of Appeal considered the application of Art 9 of the ECHR to the refusal of a worker to work on Sundays, by reason of deeply held religious conviction, in *MBA v Mayor and Burgesses of the London Borough of Merton* [2014] IRLR 145. It was alleged that the requirement to work on Sundays was indirectly discriminatory. The Court held that in assessing the question of justification, the employment tribunal should have regard to the complainant's Art 9 right to religious freedom. Article 9 made it illegitimate for the employment tribunal to consider, as part of the proportionality analysis, that not all Christians had an objection to Sunday working.

26.55 In *Azmi v Kirklees Metropolitan Borough Council* [2007] ICR 1154 the requirement that a teaching assistant keep her face uncovered when teaching children was held to place Muslim women at a particular disadvantage but was held to be justified on the facts of that case. Similarly, the CJEU has held that a prohibition on the wearing of Islamic headscarves arising out of a policy prohibiting the wearing of religious signs in the workplace would not amount to direct discrimination and might well be justifiable (and therefore not indirectly discriminatory). It might be supported by the legitimate aim of displaying political, philosophical, and religious neutrality and would be proportionate, provided it was only applied to customer facing employees: see *Achbita v G4S Secure Solutions* [2017] IRLR 466.

26.56 The term 'philosophical belief' has also been the subject of consideration by the EAT in a series of recent cases. In *McClintock v Department for Constitutional Affairs* [2008] IRLR 29 the EAT considered that the appropriate test was whether the putative philosophical beliefs 'have sufficient cogency, seriousness, cohesion and importance and are worthy of respect in a democratic society'. In that case it was held that the complainant, who considered that he could not place children for adoption with same-sex couples, did not have a 'philosophical belief' on the basis that his belief was little more than an opinion which was held albeit the complainant recognized that it could change depending upon the state of the evidence available.

26.57 The law has been further developed by the decision of the EAT in *Grainger v Nicholson* [2010] ICR 360. In that case, Burton J considered that the following were the hallmarks of a 'philosophical belief' which was protected by s 10 of the EqA 2010: (a) the belief must be genuinely held; (b) it must be a belief and not, as in McClintock, an opinion or viewpoint based on the present state of information available; (c) it must be a belief as to a weighty and substantial aspect of human life and behaviour; (d) it must attain a certain level of cogency, seriousness, cohesion, and importance; (e) it must be worthy of respect in a democratic society, be not incompatible with human dignity and not conflict with the fundamental rights of others. Burton J went onto reject further proposed limitations on the scope of 'philosophical belief' that were put forward in argument. In so doing, Burton J confirmed that (1) a philosophical belief need not be widely held and can be a philosophical belief it is only held by one person; (2) a political philosophy could qualify as a philosophical belief provided it satisfied the requirements set out above; (3) a philosophical belief could be based on science. In *General Municipal and Boilermakers Union v Henderson* [2015] IRLR 451, the ET accepted that a person being a 'left-wing democratic socialist' was a protected belief. That conclusion was not challenged before the EAT.

26.58 The Explanatory Notes to the EqA 2010 state that 'beliefs such as humanism and atheism would be beliefs for the purposes of this provision but adherence to a particular football team would not be'.

26.59 The definition of 'philosophical belief', and in particular the requirement that the belief must be worthy of respect in a democratic society under the EqA 2010, is notably different from the protection offered to persons or associations by Art 11 of the ECHR. In *Redfearn v United Kingdom* [2013] IRLR 51 the ECtHR held that the Art 11 protection extended to views which 'offend, shock or disturb'.

Sex

26.60 Section 11 of the EqA 2010 defines references to sex as references to a man or a woman. Further, s 13(6) of the EqA 2010 (a) includes within the definition of sex (or more specifically less favourable treatment of a woman), the fact that a woman is breast feeding; but (b) excludes from the definition of sex the special treatment of women connected with pregnancy or childbirth.

26.61 Prior to the implementation of the EqA 2010, much of the case law defining the scope of the prohibition on sex discrimination related to whether such prohibition could include (1) pregnancy: see, for example, *Webb v EMO Air Cargo (UK) Limited* [1994] ICR 770; (2) transsexuals: see *P v S* [1996] All ER (EC) 397; and (3) homosexuals: see *Grant v South West Trains Limited* [1998] IRLR 206 and *Pearce v Governing Body of Mayfield School* [2003] IRLR 512. However, each of these is now a protected characteristic in its own right: see EqA 2010, s 4.

Sexual orientation

26.62 Sexual orientation is defined by s 12 of the EqA 2010 as a person's sexual orientation towards persons of the same sex, persons of the opposite sex, or persons of either sex. The definition is limited, therefore, to sexual orientation to another person such that, for example, a sexual orientation towards animals is not included within the definition.

It is unclear to what extent sexual behaviour can fall within the definition of sexual orientation. **26.63** While, on the face of it, sexual behaviour does not fall within that definition, in *R v Secretary of State for Trade and Industry and Christian Action Research Education* [2004] IRLR 430. Richards J considered that sexual behaviour was a mere manifestation of a sexual orientation and therefore, it was suggested, that it would fall within the definition when read in accordance with Art 8 of the European Convention on Human Rights (as required by s 3 of the Human Rights Act 1998). However, this must be read alongside the more recent domestic jurisprudence which suggests that in the context of religious belief, manifestations of a belief are unlikely to be protected by the anti-discrimination legislation (*McFarlane v Relate Avon Limited* [2010] IRLR 872 and the contrasting views of the ECtHR as expressed in *Eweida v United Kingdom* [2013] IRLR 231).

C. PROHIBITED CONDUCT

We now turn to consider the conduct which is prohibited by the EqA 2010. The vast majority **26.64** of cases which are considered by employment tribunals are cases of direct discrimination, but the EqA 2010 also prohibits indirect discrimination, victimization, and harassment, as well as discrimination arising from a disability and failure to make reasonable adjustments for disabled persons.

Direct discrimination

Direct discrimination is defined in s 13 of the EqA 2010 as being differential treatment because **26.65** of a protected characteristic. This gives rise to a two-stage test in order to identify the existence of direct discrimination:

(a) was a person treated less favourably than an actual or hypothetical comparator was or would have been treated in circumstances that were the same or not materially different and
(b) if so, was that less favourable treatment because of a protected characteristic?

The first of these questions often requires the identification of an actual or hypothetical com- **26.66** parator. The identification of such a comparator has, as its purpose, the test of whether or not that comparator would have been treated any differently than the complainant has been treated. Section 23 of the EqA 2010 provides that where a comparison is to be made, there must be 'no material difference between the circumstances relating to each case'. This language was considered by the House of Lords in *Shamoon v Chief Constable of the Royal Ulster Constabulary* [2003] UKHL 11, [2003] ICR 337, in which Lord Rodger considered that the relevant circumstances were all of the circumstances which the putative discriminator had in his mind at the time that he did the act or omission complained of, save for the relevant protected characteristic. It is often difficult, therefore, for complainants to find an actual comparator in cases of direct discrimination since it is unusual to find another individual who is exactly the same position as the complainant. Invariably, there are a large number of interlocking reasons as to why employers act in the manner in which they do. However, differences which are merely features of the different protected characteristics will not amount to a difference in the material circumstances for the purposes of s 23. As such, in *Lockwood v Department of Work and Pensions* [2013] IRLR 941, where an employer had paid lower redundancy payments to younger employees on the basis that younger employees were likely to have lesser financial commitments and were more likely to react easily and rapidly to the loss of their jobs, the Court of Appeal held that there were no material differences other than age, as between younger and older employees. Of course, the manner in which others have been treated, even where those others cannot be considered as actual comparators, is likely to provide helpful evidence as to how a hypothetical comparator might have been treated.

The requirement of comparison contained within the words 'less favourably' (used in s 13(1) **26.67** of the EqA 2010) demonstrates that unreasonable treatment in and of itself cannot amount to

Part C The Substantive Law

discrimination. This has been confirmed by the House of Lords in *Glasgow City Council v Zafar* [1998] 2 All ER 953 and by the Court of Appeal in *Bahl v Law Society* [2004] EWCA 1070.

26.68 The selection of the comparator is the responsibility of the complainant although, even if the relevant comparator is not appropriate, a tribunal may go on to consider the treatment of the complainant as against a hypothetical comparator: see *Balamoody v UK Central Council for Nursing, Midwifery and Health Visiting* [2001] EWCA Civ 2097.

26.69 In pursuing a claim for sexual orientation discrimination, a person in a civil partnership (within the meaning of the Civil Partnership Act 2004) will be able to compare himself with a married person: see EqA 2010, s 23(3). However, prior to the coming into force of the Civil Partnership Act 2004 on 5 December 2005, it was not unlawful sexual orientation discrimination to provide benefits to married couples but not to others who were not married: see para 18 of Schedule 9 to the EqA 2010.

26.70 If an employment tribunal finds that there has been less favourable treatment it must go on to consider the second question identified above, namely, the reason for that less favourable treatment. There are two separate and distinct questions: see *Madden v Preferred Technical Group CHA Limited* [2004] EWCA Civ 1178.

26.71 Prior to the implementation of the EqA 2010, the pre-existing discrimination legislation used the words 'on grounds of' (or variations of this formulation) in relation to the question of causation. This gave rise to a number of difficult questions. First, there was a debate in the authorities as to whether or not the test of causation was a 'but for' test or whether it required a consideration of motivation. In *James v Eastleigh Borough Council* [1990] 2 AC 751, where pensioners were entitled to use a swimming pool for free with the effect that men between the ages of 60 and 65 had to pay for use of the swimming pool whereas women did not (because of the different retirement ages), the House of Lords resolved that a 'but for' test was the appropriate test. Had Mr James been a woman, he would not have to pay for use of the local authority swimming pool and therefore he had been treated less favourably on grounds of his sex. However, in *Dhatt v McDonalds Hamburgers* [1991] ICR 238 the Court of Appeal found that Mr Dhatt had not been discriminated in circumstances where he had been dismissed for failing to provide evidence of a work permit. The Court of Appeal distinguished the *James* case on the basis that Parliament had placed an obligation on employers to ensure that their workers were working lawfully. This would suggest, therefore, that a 'but for' test is not the appropriate test and that it is necessary to consider the motivation of the putative discriminator. The 'but for' test of discrimination has also been rejected in cases such as *Martin v Lancehawk Limited (t/a European Telecom Solutions)* [2004] All ER (D) 400 and *Chief Constable of West Yorkshire Police v Khan* [2001] UKHL 48, where it was held that the proper test of causation required an examination of the motivation of the putative discriminator. However, the dicta in these cases are difficult to reconcile with the proposition that motivation is irrelevant in considering the question of direct discrimination: see *R v Birmingham City Council ex parte Equal Opportunities Commission* [1989] IRLR 173.

26.72 The question has been most recently considered by the EAT in *Amnesty International v Ahmed* [2009] IRLR 884 and the Supreme Court in *R v The Governing Body of JFS and the Admissions Appeal Panel* [2009] UKSC 15, [2010] IRLR 136, where a similar analysis of the law was adopted. The majority of the Supreme Court in the *JFS* case held that:

(a) there are some cases in which it is self-evident that discrimination is taking place because the mental processes of the putative discriminator include reference to a protected characteristic. In such cases it is not necessary to examine the motives of a putative discriminator at all. *James v Eastleigh Borough Council* was said to be a case of this type

(b) where discrimination is not obvious, it is necessary to examine the motivation of a putative discriminator but only in order to determine whether or not treatment is being afforded because of the relevant protected characteristic

(c) those are the only circumstances in which motivation is relevant to the question of discrimination. It follows that a good motive does not amount to a defence to a claim of direct discrimination.

The Court of Appeal confirmed in *CLFIS (UK) Limited v Reynolds* [2015] IRLR 562 that it was the **26.73** motivation of the putative discriminator that was the relevant question. As such, a person will not discriminate where he is innocent of any discriminatory motivation, even where he is influenced by information supplied or views expressed by another employee whose motivation is discriminatory.

The second matter of controversy which the old wording of the anti-discrimination legislation gave **26.74** rise to, was the concept of associative or transferred discrimination. It was held that, for example, under the RRA 1976, a person did not have to hold the protected characteristic themselves in order to be discriminated against. For example, where a person was not permitted to enter a bar because of the race of a companion, both individuals had been discriminated against on 'racial grounds': see *Showboat Entertainment Centre v Owens* [1984] ICR 65, *Weathersfield v Sergeant* [1999] ICR 425, and *Coleman v Attridge Law* [2008] ICR 1128. It follows that a person who was dismissed because of the race of his or her partner would be protected by the antidiscrimination legislation.

In the EqA 2010, the 'on grounds of' wording was replaced by a requirement that less favourable **26.75** treatment is *because* of the relevant protected characteristic. The effect of this change is likely to be that:

(a) causation will continue to be assessed in the manner set out by the Supreme Court in the *JFS* decision

(b) an expansion in the scope of associative or transferred discrimination will apply in respect of all of the protected grounds (whereas previously it was questionable as to whether there was scope for the doctrine of transferred discrimination operating in the cases of at least sex discrimination, and possibly age discrimination and disability discrimination).

The protected characteristic does not have to be the only reason for the treatment in question **26.76** provided that it is the substantial or effective cause of that treatment: see *R v Commission for Racial Equality ex parte Westminster City Council* [1984] ICR 770 and *Nagarajan v London Regional Transport* [1999] IRLR 572.

Proving direct discrimination can be difficult for complainants since direct discrimination is rarely **26.77** overt. However, by s 136(2) of the EqA 2010: 'if there are facts from which the court could decide, in the absence of any other explanation, that a person (A) contravened the provision concerned, the court must hold that the contravention occurred'; and then by s 136(3) of the EqA 2010: 'but subsection (2) does not apply if A shows that A did not contravene the provision'. The effect is that there is a two-stage process:

(a) First, it must be considered whether or not there are facts from which a court could draw the inference that a discriminatory act had been committed. At this stage, the burden of proof lies with the complainant: see *Efobi v Royal Mail Group* [2019] EWCA Civ 18 and *Ayodele v Citilink Ltd* [2018] ICR 748.

(b) Secondly, whether or not there is a non-discriminatory explanation which can be advanced by the respondent such that the inference of discrimination should not be drawn.

The leading authorities on the shifting burden of proof are *Barton v Investec Henderson Crosthwaite* **26.78** *Securities Limited* [2003] ICR 1205; *Igen v Wong* [2005] ICR 931; *Laing v Manchester City Council* [2006] IRLR 748; *Madarassy v Nomura International plc* [2007] IRLR 246; *Hewage v Grampian Health Board* [2012] IRLR 491; and *IPC Media Limited v Millar* [2013] IRLR 707. The following propositions can be derived from those authorities:

(a) In order to establish a prima facie case of discrimination, primary facts from which an employment tribunal could draw the inference that the complainant was treated less favourably because of a protected ground, must be established. At the first stage, the tribunal must find, therefore, a prima facie case that the complainant was treated less favourably because of a protected ground and not merely that the same was a possibility: see *Madarassy* Accordingly, it is not enough to shift the burden of proof if all that can be shown is a difference in protected characteristic and a difference in treatment. Such facts only demonstrate the mere possibility of discrimination: see *Igen v Wong* and *Madarassy* at para 65.

(b) At the first stage, the employment tribunal is entitled to consider all the factual evidence adduced by both the parties: see *Laing* and *Madarassy*. As was stated by Mummery LJ at para 71 of the decision in *Madarassy*:

> Section 63A(2) does not expressly or impliedly prevent the tribunal at the first stage from hearing, accepting or drawing inferences from evidence adduced by the respondent disputing and rebutting the complainant's evidence of discrimination. The respondent may adduce evidence at the first stage to show that the acts which are alleged to be discriminatory never happened; or that, if they did, they were not less favourable treatment of the complainant; or that the comparators chosen by the complainant or the situations with which comparisons are made are not truly like the complainant or the situation of the complainant; or that, even if there has been less favourable treatment of the complainant, it was not on the ground of her sex or pregnancy.

(c) An alternative approach which an employment tribunal might adopt is to simply to ask why the treatment was afforded to the complainant. If facts from which the tribunal could draw the inference that the reason for her treatment was a protected ground, then the analysis will move to the second stage: see the speech of Lord Nicholls of Birkenhead in *Shamoon v Chief Constable of the Royal Ulster Constabulary*.

(d) At the second stage the burden of proof will shift to the respondent to the proceedings to provide an explanation for the treatment of the complainant. The explanation must be a clear and non-discriminatory explanation and must be supported by evidence given that the evidence is likely to be in the hands of respondent: see *Igen v Wong*.

(e) Some authorities stress that it is important not to over analyse the burden of proof provisions. In *Hewage*, Lord Hope stated that the provisions 'have nothing to offer where the tribunal is in a position to make positive findings on the evidence one way or the other'. Similar remarks were made by Underhill J in *Martin v Devonshires Solicitors* [2011] ICR 352 and in *IPC Media Limited v Millar* [2013] IRLR 707.

26.79 In addition to the above, the following should be noted with regard to direct discrimination:

(a) Direct discrimination because of age (but no other protected characteristic) can be justified as being a proportionate means of achieving a legitimate aim: see s 13(2) of the EqA 2010. However, direct age discrimination (in contrast to indirect discrimination) can only be justified by employers having regard to (i) legitimate objectives of a public interest nature; (ii) legitimate aims which are consistent with the social policy aims of the state; and (iii) proportionate means of achieving legitimate aims: see *Seldon v Clarkson Wright & Jakes* [2012] UKSC 16, [2012] IRLR 590. In that case, the Supreme Court noted that the Court of Justice of the European Union has recognized two legitimate objectives in relation to age discrimination (in *Fuchs and Another v Land Hessen* [2011] IRLR 1043 and *Rosenbladt v Oellerking Gebäudereinigungs mbH* [2012] All ER (EC) 288). Those are, first, intergenerational fairness (such as the need to facilitate access to employment in relation to younger generations) and, secondly, dignity (such as the need to avoid dismissing older employees because of incapacity and underperformance).

(b) It is not unlawful to treat a disabled person more favourably than a non-disabled person: see EqA 2010, s 13(3).

(c) Segregation amounts to less favourable treatment because of race: see EqA 2010, s 13(5).

(d) It is not unlawful to treat a woman more favourably in connection with pregnancy or childbirth: see EqA 2010, s 13(6).

(e) It may amount to direct discrimination to reveal the existence of a person's protected characteristic to another, where that person wanted it to be kept a secret provided that the reason why the revelation is made, is because of the protected characteristic. The obvious example of such conduct is 'outing' a person of a particular sexual orientation. However, such a claim will be unlikely to succeed where the person's sexual orientation is widely known: see *Grant v HM Land Registry* [2011] IRLR 748.

Combined discrimination

26.80 Section 14 of the EqA 2010 provides that it is unlawful to treat a person less favourably because of a combination of the following protected characteristics: age, disability, gender reassignment, race, religion or belief, sex, or sexual orientation. The protected characteristics of marriage and civil partnership and pregnancy and maternity are, therefore, excluded from the list of characteristics which may be combined. In contrast to the other forms of prohibited conduct, s 14 did not come into effect on 1 October 2010, and will come into effect on a date to be appointed.

Combined discrimination, occurs, therefore, when a person is treated less favourably, not because **26.81** they hold any particular protected characteristic but because of a combination of protected characteristics. The explanatory notes to the EqA 2010 give as an example:

> A bus driver does not allow a Muslim man onto her bus, claiming that he could be a 'terrorist'. While it might not be possible for the man to demonstrate less favourable treatment because of either protected characteristic if considered separately, a dual discrimination claim will succeed if the reason for his treatment was the specific combination of sex and religion or belief, which resulted in him being stereotyped as a potential terrorist.

It follows that it will be no defence to a claim of combined discrimination to show that there was **26.82** no discrimination because of either of the protected characteristics alone, and this is made plain by s 13(3) of the EqA 2010. However, where it is shown that the treatment of the complainant was not because of either or both of the protected characteristics, then a claim of combined discrimination will fail: see EqA 2010, s 14(4).

Indirect discrimination

Indirect discrimination occurs where everybody is treated in the same way, but the conse- **26.83** quences of treating everybody in the same way impact disparately on those holding a protected characteristic. Lady Hale put it as follows at para 25 of her judgment in *Essop v Home Office* [2017] IRLR 558: 'indirect discrimination assumes equality of treatment ... but aims to achieve a level playing field'. Indirect discrimination is made unlawful by s 19 of the EqA 2010, which provides that a person discriminates against another person if the person applies a provision, criterion, or practice (PCP) in relation to a protected characteristic in the following circumstances:

(a) the putative discriminator applies the PCP or would apply the PCP to persons irrespective of whether they have the protected characteristic
(b) it puts those who hold a particular protected characteristic at a particular disadvantage because: (i) there is disparity of treatment; and (ii) that disparity is related to the difference in protected characteristic
(c) it puts the complainant at that disadvantage
(d) it cannot be justified as being a proportionate means of achieving a legitimate aim.

Indirect discrimination is prohibited by s 19 of the EqA 2010 in respect of all of the protected **26.84** characteristics with the exception of pregnancy and maternity.

The meaning of a PCP was considered by the EAT in *Starmer v British Airways plc* [2005] IRLR **26.85** 862 in the context of the Sex Discrimination Act 1975. In that case, the EAT considered that the term 'provision' was apt to include any requirement or condition. Furthermore, the EAT considered that a PCP might be applied in circumstances where, on the face of it, a single management decision had been made in respect of an employee. The EAT considered that a 'provision' or 'practice' could be said to be applied in respect of a one-off management decision if the same decision would have been made in respect of other employees in similar circumstances. According to the Court of Appeal in *GMB v Allen* [2008] EWCA Civ 810, [2008] IRLR 690, less favourable treatment (where the same is not unlawful as being direct discrimination) can amount to a PCP. This proposition seems doubtful, however, having regard to the statutory language which requires the neutral application of a PCP (see EqA 2010, s 19(2)(a)).

The circumstances in which a PCP places those holding a protected characteristic at a particular dis- **26.86** advantage are many and varied. As Lady Hale explained in *Essop v Home Office* [2017] IRLR 558:

> *They could be genetic, such as strength or height. They could be social, such as the expectation that women will bear the greater responsibility for caring of the home and family than will men. They could be traditional*

employment practices, such as the division between 'women's jobs' and 'men's jobs' or the practice or starting at the bottom of an incremental pay scale. They could be another PCP, working in combination with the one at issue …

In considering whether or not the PCP puts those holding a particular protected characteristic to a particular disadvantage, a statistical approach will sometimes be of assistance. However, after the implementation of the EqA 2010 it is no longer necessary to adopt such an approach: see *Homer v Chief Constable of West Yorkshire Police* [2012] IRLR 601 and *Games v University of Kent* [2015] IRLR 202. Indeed, in *Homer*, the Supreme Court suggested that all that it was necessary for an employment tribunal to consider was whether or not persons who had a particular protected characteristic suffered a disadvantage by the application of a PCP when compared to others who did not share the protected characteristic. In that case, it was held that the implementation of a PCP which required that a person had to hold a law degree in order to progress to a particular level in a pay and grading structure was potentially indirectly discriminatory in relation to a person's age, because on the facts of that case, the complainant would not be able to complete a law degree before he was forced to retire. However, where a statistical approach is adopted, the following case law sets out the proper approach to statistical analysis:

(a) First an employment tribunal must consider the appropriate pool for comparison. Although there may be various pools which are appropriate, the starting point is to consider those to whom the employer has applied or would apply the PCP: see *London Underground v Edwards (No 2)* [1998] IRLR 364 and *Jones v University of Manchester* [1993] ICR 474.

(b) While there may be various pools which are appropriate, a pool cannot be drawn by bringing within it those who have no interest in the benefit on offer: see *Chaudhury v British Medical Association* [2007] EWCA Civ 788 and *Rutherford v Secretary of State for Trade and Industry* [2006] UKHL 19. As such, in *Rutherford*, where it was alleged that the employment rights legislation which, at that time, removed the right to claim unfair dismissal from those over the age of 65, the majority of the House of Lords stated that the appropriate pool for comparison could not include those under the age of 65 since those people had no interest in the benefit on offer.

(c) In some cases it will be impossible to draw a pool at all by the nature of the PCP which is alleged to have been applied: see *Lord Chancellor v Coker* [2001] IRLR 116.

(d) Once a pool for comparison has been drawn, then those who are able to comply with the PCP and those who are not must be considered according to whether or not they hold the protected characteristic in question. However, whether there is sufficient disparity for a tribunal to conclude that those holding a particular protected characteristic are put at a particular disadvantage will be a matter for the employment tribunal. As such, in *London Underground v Edwards* the Court of Appeal upheld the decision of an employment tribunal which found that women were placed at a particular disadvantage by a set of working practices on the basis that only one woman could not comply (amounting to 95.2 per cent of the pool) whereas all the men (and therefore 100 per cent of the pool) could comply.

(e) It will be easier to find 'particular disadvantage' in relation to a protected characteristic where there is a disparity occurring historically or over a long period of time: see *R v Secretary of State for Employment ex parte Seymour-Smith* [1999] ICR 447 (ECJ) and [2000] ICR 244 (House of Lords).

26.87 The PCP must put persons having a particular protected characteristic at a 'group disadvantage'. It is not enough that the complainant is put at a disadvantage. As such, in *Eweida v British Airways* [2010] EWCA Civ 80, the complainant's claim of indirect discrimination because of her religious belief manifested in the wearing of a crucifix failed, because the PCP applied by British Airways was found not to put Christians at a particular disadvantage, but rather, only the complainant herself. On the other hand, in addition to group disadvantage, the PCP must also place the individual at the disadvantage suffered by group. The precise requirements of individual disadvantage in this context are under consideration in *Essop*.

26.88 As well as putting those holding a protected characteristic at a 'group disadvantage' the PCP must also place the individual complainant at the same disadvantage. However, an individual is placed at that same disadvantage merely by showing that the application of the PCP disadvantages the complainant in the same way as it disadvantages the group. It is not necessary to identify why the disadvantage arises at group/individual level so as to seek to find correlation between them: see *Essop v Home Office* [2017] IRLR 558.

A PCP which puts those holding a protected characteristic to a particular disadvantage will not **26.89** be unlawful if it can be justified as being a proportionate means of achieving a legitimate aim. In *Bilka-Kaufhaus GmbH v Weber von Hartz* [1986] IRLR 317 the ECJ considered the question of the justification of indirect discrimination and stated that an employer could only establish a justification defence if the measures 'correspond to a real need on the part of the [employer], are appropriate with a view to achieving that objective in question and are necessary to that end'. Justification was described in *Hampson v Department of Education and Science* [1989] IRLR 69 as requiring the striking of an objective balance between the discriminatory effects of a requirement or condition and the reasonable needs of the enterprise.

As such: **26.90**

(a) The greater the group disadvantage, the more difficult it will be to justify the discriminatory effect: see *MBA v Mayor and Burgesses of the London Borough of Merton* [2014] IRLR 145 (Elias LJ at paras 31–32).

(b) There is no question of the application of a band of reasonable responses test as is seen in the application of the employment protection legislation: see *Hardys & Hansons plc v Lax* [2005] EWCA Civ 846.

(c) Issues of cost can be relevant in establishing a defence of justification although they are unlikely, of themselves, to amount to a legitimate aim: see *Woodcock v Cumbria Primary Care Trust* [2012] IRLR 491 and *Cross v British Airways* [2006] IRLR 804. That said, where cost is relevant to the question of justification, it is not necessary for the employer to establish cost saving as a matter of absolute necessity in the sense that without the cost saving in question the employer would have become insolvent: *HM Land Registry v Benson* [2012] IRLR 373.

(d) Where there is a less discriminatory manner of achieving the legitimate aim relied upon by an employer, it will be fatal to the employer's defence of justification. However, it does not follow that the PCP will be justified where a legitimate aim can only be achieved in one way: see *Islington London Borough Council v Ladele* [2010] IRLR 211. If a legitimate aim can only be justified by disproportionate means, it will not be justified: see *GMB v Allen* [2008] EWCA Civ 810.

(e) It is not necessary for the employer to have subjectively considered that the PCP was a proportionate means of achieving a legitimate aim at the time although *ex post facto* justifications put forward in support of a PCP will be scrutinized closely by an employment tribunal: *R (Elias) v Secretary of State for Defence* [2006] EWCA Civ 1293.

(f) Where an employer has recognized that a PCP is indirectly discriminatory and cannot be justified, it will be very difficult to continue with such a policy even on a transitional basis: see *Pulham v London Borough of Barking & Dagenham* [2010] ICR 333 and *Bainbridge v Redcar & Cleveland Borough Council* [2008] IRLR 776.

(g) Human rights derived from the ECHR may be relevant to the justification analysis. As such, in *MBA v Mayor and Burgesses of the London Borough of Merton* [2014] IRLR 145 the Court of Appeal held that it was inappropriate for the employment tribunal to have taken into account, in assessing the question of justification, the fact that an objection to Sunday working was not a core component of the Christian belief. To take that into account did not have sufficient regard to the complainant's Art 9 ECHR right to freedom of religious belief.

Although the test for indirect discrimination must be applied in each case, examples of PCPs which **26.91** have been found to be indirectly discriminatory on grounds of sex include:

(a) a requirement or policy that people should be a certain height

(b) treatment that disadvantages workers with young children (which may also discriminate on the grounds of marital status) in particular, inflexibility in relation to flexible working, for example, part-time and home working, or job sharing (*Bilka-Kaufhaus GmbH v Weber von Hartz*

Part C The Substantive Law

[1987] ICR 110; *Clymo v Wandsworth Borough Council* [1989] ICR 250; *Robinson v Oddbins Ltd* [1996] 27 DCLD 1; *Lockworth v Crawley Warren Group Ltd* [2001] IDS Employment Law Brief 680, EAT)

(c) a requirement or practice that candidates should have a long period of previously uninterrupted working—which tends to exclude women who have taken time off work to look after children

(d) a requirement or practice that applicants should be aged 25 to 35 (which excludes many women with young children) (*Price v Civil Service Commission and the Society of Civil and Public Servants* [1978] IRLR 3)

(e) a requirement that employees should work long and uncertain hours (*London Underground Ltd v Edwards (No 2)* [1998] IRLR 364 and *Ministry of Defence v DeBique* [2010] IRLR 471).

26.92 The shifting burden of proof provision in s 136 of the EqA 2010 applies to claims for indirect discrimination as it does to direct discrimination (see para 26.77). The burden of proof in cases of indirect discrimination has not been a matter which has troubled the courts a great deal, but it was considered in the context of a claim for equal pay in *Nelson v Carillion Services* [2003] IRLR 428. In that case, the Court of Appeal held that the burden of proof rests on the complainant to show the existence of the relevant PCP and that it placed those having a protected characteristic at a particular disadvantage, and, further, that it placed the complainant at a particular disadvantage. At that stage, the burden of proof shifted to the employer to show that the PCP could be justified as being a proportionate means of achieving a legitimate aim. The employer also bears the burden of showing (should he wish to advance such an argument) that any apparent disparity in treatment is unrelated to a particular protected characteristic: see *Naeem v Secretary of State for Justice* [2016] IRLR 118 and *Essop v Home Office (UK Border Agency)* [2015] IRLR 724.

Discrimination arising from a disability

26.93 Disabled persons are granted another level of protection pursuant to s 15 of the EqA 2010 in that they are protected from unfavourable treatment arising in consequence of the disability where the same cannot be shown to be a proportionate means of achieving a legitimate aim.

26.94 In order to understand this provision it is important to consider the history of the DDA 1995 That Act contained protection from what came to be known as 'disability related discrimination': where a disabled person was treated less favourably for a reason relating to a disability rather than the disability itself. An example of such less favourable treatment can be found in the Court of Appeal's decision in *Clark v Novacold* [1999] IRLR 318. In that case, an employee was dismissed from work by reason of ill-health absence caused by a back injury. The employee was not being treated less favourably because of the back injury itself but rather because it caused him to be absent from work: a disability related reason. It followed that the correct comparator was a person who was present at work, rather than a non-disabled person who was also absent from work. However, in *London Borough of Lewisham v Malcolm* [2008] UKHL 43 the House of Lords overruled *Clark v Novacold* in stating that the proper comparator in the *Clark v Novacold* situation was a non-disabled person who was absent from work. It followed that there was very little difference, if any, between disability related discrimination and direct disability discrimination.

26.95 Section 15 of the EqA 2010 overturned the decision in *Malcolm* (see *Hall v Chief Constable of West Yorkshire Police* [2015] IRLR 893), with the effect that, where a disabled person is treated less favourably than he or she would otherwise be treated by reason of something arising in consequence of the disability, an act of discrimination will have occurred (subject to the defence of justification).

26.96 In assessing whether or not the elements of s 15 of the EqA 2010 are made out, employment tribunals should consider:

(a) whether there is unfavourable treatment

(b) whether such treatment occurs because of 'something' which arises in consequence of the complainant's disability

(c) whether the treatment can be justified.

'Unfavourable treatment' has its own meaning and is not to be equated to either 'detriment' or 'less **26.97** favourable treatment'. It does not arise where a person is afforded an advantage merely because the advantage was not greater: see *Williams v Trustees of Swansea University Pension & Assurance Scheme* [2017] IRLR 882. In assessing whether or not the treatment occurs because of 'something' arising in consequence of the complainant's disability, the 'something' need not be the sole or main cause of the treatment. It is enough that the 'something' had a significant influence on the unfavourable treatment: see *Pnaiser v NHS England* [2016] IRLR 170. The test of justification set out in s 15(1)(b) of the EqA 2010 is the well-known test in the discrimination sphere: the treatment must be a proportionate means of achieving a legitimate aim. It is noteworthy that this is, on the face of it, a different test to the band of reasonable responses test which previously applied under the DDA 1995 in respect of disability related discrimination: see *Jones v The Post Office* [2001] ICR 805. However, in *O'Brien v Bolton St. Catherine's Academy* [2017] IRLR 547 the Court of Appeal considered that in considering the question of justification in a s 15 claim, tribunals might afford a substantial degree of respect to the decision of the decision maker as to his reasonable needs, provided he has acted rationally and reasonably. It should not be forgotten that it is 'the treatment' which must be justified rather than any particular policy or procedure applied by the employer. As such, where an employer applies a sickness absence management procedure, the employer may be required to justify the steps taken under the procedure rather than merely justifying the existence of the procedure as a whole: see *Buchanan v Chief Constable of the Police of the Metropolis* [2016] IRLR 918.

Pursuant to s 15(2) of the EqA 2010, an employer will have a defence to this type of claim in cir- **26.98** cumstances where that person did not know and could not reasonably be expected to know that the disabled person had a disability.

Harassment

Harassment is made unlawful by s 26 of the EqA 2010 Harassment includes three separate torts: **26.99**

(1) harassment which is related to a protected characteristic
(2) sexual harassment and
(3) less favourable treatment arising out of sexual harassment.

Harassment relating to protected characteristics arises where a person engages in unwanted con- **26.100** duct which is related to the protected characteristics of age, disability, gender reassignment, race, religion or belief, sex, or sexual orientation and which has the purpose or effect violating the dignity of the complainant or creating an intimidating, hostile, degrading, humiliating, or offensive environment for the complainant.

The EqA 2010 has widened the scope of liability by using the language 'related to' rather than 'on **26.101** grounds of' in relation to the question of causation. As to the differences between these two formulations see the analysis of Burton J in *Equal Opportunities Commission v Secretary of State for Trade and Industry* [2007] EWHC 483.

The provision prohibiting harassment related to a protected characteristic (or at any rate the cor- **26.102** responding provision in the Race Relations Act 1976) was subjected to analysis by the EAT in *Richmond Pharmacology v Dhaliwal* [2009] IRLR 336. The following can be drawn from the judgment:

(a) harassment which is related to a protected characteristic requires findings that (1) there was unwanted conduct; (2) that the conduct had the purpose or effect of either violating the dignity of the complainant or creating an intimidating, hostile, degrading, humiliating, or offensive environment for the complainant; (3) that the conduct was for a reason related to a protected characteristic
(b) that there is a part objective test in relation to the effect of any unwanted conduct (which is now found in s 26(4) of the EqA 2010). Liability should not exist merely because it had an unforeseen effect of violating the dignity of the complainant or creating an intimidating, hostile, degrading, humiliating, or offensive environment for the complainant. In order for liability to

Part C The Substantive Law

429

exist, it should be reasonable that that effect has occurred having regard to the unwanted conduct in question. However, in assessing that objective criterion, it is necessary to have regard to the subjective feelings of the complainant as well as all the circumstances of the case

(c) at para 22 the EAT observed that:

> not every racially slanted adverse comment or conduct may constitute the violation of a person's dignity. Dignity is not necessarily violated by things said or done which are trivial or transitory, particularly if it should have been clear that any offence was unintended. While it is very important that employers, and tribunals, are sensitive to the hurt that can be caused by racially offensive comments or conduct (or indeed comments or conduct on other grounds covered by the cognate legislation to which we have referred), it is also important not to encourage a culture of hypersensitivity or the imposition of legal liability in respect of every unfortunate phrase.

26.103 It is now clear that in the case of harassment relating to a protected characteristic, it is not necessary for the complainant to hold the protected characteristic. In *English v Thomas Sanderson Blinds Limited* [2009] ICR 543 the Court of Appeal held that harassment had occurred in circumstances where an employee who was not homosexual and who was known not to be homosexual was subjected to homophobic abuse because he had attended boarding school and had lived in Brighton. However, it was held in *Peninsula Business Services v Baker* [2017] IRLR 394 that the law did not prohibit harassment on the basis of a mere (unproven) claim that a person holds a protected characteristic (in that case, disability).

26.104 An actual dismissal (but not a constructive dismissal) is capable of being an act of harassment: see *Urso v Department of Work and Pensions* [2017] IRLR 304.

26.105 As to sexual harassment, acts of a sexual nature which have the effect of violating the dignity of the complainant or creating an intimidating, hostile, degrading, humiliating, or offensive environment for the complainant are prohibited. The EqA 2010 does not provide any definition of 'acts of a sexual nature'.

26.106 Where a person is treated less favourably because of their submission to or rejection of sexual harassment or harassment related to gender reassignment or sex, then that will amount to harassment pursuant to s 26(3) of the EqA 2010.

26.107 The potential liability of employers for acts of harassment committed by third parties on employees has had something of a chequered history:

(a) Originally, it was held that an employer could not be liable for the acts of third party harassment: see *Pearce v Governing Body of Mayfield School* [2003] IRLR 512 (in which the House of Lords concluded that the decision in *Burton v De Vere Hotels* [1996] IRLR 596 was wrongly decided).

(b) However, this changed in the context of sex discrimination after the judgment of Burton J in *Equal Opportunities Commission v Secretary of State for Trade and Industry* [2007] EWHC 483. In the case, Burton J held that the Equal Treatment Directive 2002/73/EC required the possibility of liability where an employer subjected an employee to harassment by knowingly failing to protect that employee from repeated harassment by a third party, such as a customer and supplier. Amendments were made to the Sex Discrimination Act 1975 in the light of Burton J's judgment.

(c) When the EqA 2010 was implemented, the changes which had been made to the law relating to sex discrimination (in the light of the Burton J judgment) were applied to all protected characteristics by s 40 of the EqA 2010. In particular, by s 40(2) of the EqA 2010, an employer was liable for the harassing acts of third parties where an employee was harassed in the course of his/her employment and where the employer had not taken such steps as were reasonably practicable to prevent the third party from committing the act of harassment. That was qualified, however, by s 40(3) of the EqA 2010, which provided that an employer was only liable in circumstances where the employer was aware that the employee concerned had been harassed by third parties on two previous occasions during the course of that person's employment.

(d) From 1 October 2013, however, ss 40(2) to (4) of the EqA 2010 have been repealed: see s 65 of the Enterprise and Regulatory Reform Act 2013. This would appear to take the law back to the position as set out by the House of Lords in *Pearce v Governing Body of Mayfield School* [2003] IRLR 512 and therefore would appear to raise (again) the problem of adequate implementation of the Equal Treatment Directive, which was raised by Burton J in *Equal Opportunities Commission v Secretary of State for Trade and Industry* [2007] EWHC 483.

Victimisation

Victimization is prohibited by s 27 of the EqA 2010. This prohibits retaliation by employers **26.108** where the employee (or an associated person: see *Thompson v London Central Bus Company* [2016] IRLR 9) has done a protected act or where it is considered that a person has done or may do a protected act.

The following are protected acts: **26.109**

(a) bringing proceedings under EqA 2010
(b) giving evidence or information in connection with proceedings under the EqA 2010. It follows that the giving of a witness statement would be sufficient to amount to a protected act: see *Kirby v National Probation Service for England and Wales (Cumbria Area)* [2006] IRLR 508
(c) doing any other thing for the purposes of or in connection with proceedings under the EqA 2010
(d) making an allegation that a person has contravened the EqA 2010. One *lacuna* in this provision is that where the allegation that is made is not in breach of the EqA 2010, for example, because it was committed outside the scope of employment of an employee such that an employer was not vicariously liable for the act in question, or it was committed in an area which is outside the geographical scope of the EqA 2010, the act will not be protected: see *Waters v Metropolitan Police Commissioner* [1997] IRLR 589.

An act will not amount to a protected act, however, where the allegation, evidence, or information **26.110** made or given is false and given or made in bad faith: see EqA 2010, s 27(3). As such, employment tribunals must ask whether the allegation, evidence, or information made or given was in accordance with the truth or facts (see *HM Prison Service v Ibimidun* [2008] IRLR 940) and whether it was made for some ulterior motive so that it could be said to have been made in bad faith (see *Street v Derbyshire Unemployed Workers' Centre* [2004] IRLR 687 for a consideration of the meaning of the term 'good faith' within the meaning of the Public Interest Disclosure Act 1998).

Where a protected act has been done, or where it is considered that a protected act has been done **26.111** or may be done, then individuals are protected from suffering detriment occasioned because of that protected act. In this context, the authorities dealing with the question of causation in cases of direct discrimination will be relevant. In particular, it should be noted that:

(a) it is not appropriate to apply a 'but for' test: see *Chief Constable of West Yorkshire Police v Khan* [2001] UKHL 48; *Martin v Devonshires Solicitors* [2011] ICR 352; and *Woods v Pasab Limited* [2013] IRLR 305
(b) the protected act need not be the whole reason for the victimization provided it is a substantial and effective cause: see *Nagarajan v London Regional Transport* [1999] IRLR 572.

Difficult questions of causation arise where a complainant has been subjected to detriment in response **26.112** to the making of an allegation of discrimination. In such cases, it might be important to distinguish between the allegation of discrimination itself and the manner in which the complaint is made. The manner in which the complaint is made (or other features, a past history of the making of false complaints) may give rise to features 'genuinely separable' from the allegation of discrimination itself: see *Martin v Devonshires Solicitors* [2011] ICR 352 and *Woods v Pasab Limited* [2013] IRLR 305. However, it should be noted that the EAT gave guidance in *Woodhouse v West North West Homes Leeds Limited* [2013] IRLR 773 that employment tribunals should treat *Martin v Devonshires Solicitors* as an exceptional case.

Prior to the implementation of the EqA 2010, there was some debate as to the steps which an **26.113** employer could take in litigation in order to protect itself without victimizing the complainant.

In *Chief Constable of West Yorkshire Police v Khan* [2001] UKHL 48 it was held that the taking of honest and reasonable steps in litigation could not amount to victimization of a complainant. In that case, the employer had refused to provide a reference. The matter was reconsidered in *Derbyshire v St. Helens Metropolitan Borough Council* [2007] UKHL 16. In that case, the employer had written to its employees in an attempt to persuade them to settle complaints of equal pay and pointing out the effects that succeeding in those complaints would have on the employer and the complainants' colleagues. Lady Hale stressed, in her opinion in that case, that the appropriate question to consider was whether or not a detriment had been suffered, rather than whether or not the taking of honest and reasonable steps in litigation was by reason of a protected act.

26.114   A rather different approach was taken by the EAT in *South London & Maudsley NHS Trust v Dathi* [2008] IRLR 350. In that case it was held that a series of letters sent in the context of proceedings were the subject of the doctrine of absolute immunity from suit since they had come into existence for the purposes of the proceedings. This approach was followed in *Parmar v East Leicester Medical Practice* [2011] IRLR 641. However, the Court of Appeal stressed in *Singh v Governing Body of Moorlands Primary School* [2013] IRLR 820 that there are limits to the judicial immunity principle. The Court held that the 'core immunity from suit' with regard to judicial proceedings applied to the giving of evidence (in that witnesses should not be deterred from giving evidence in court) as well as to statements of case and other documents which were placed before the court or which came into existence for the purposes of the proceedings. That immunity could be extended, but only where such extension was necessary in order to prevent the core immunity from being outflanked. In particular, immunity did not extend, on the facts of that case, to an allegation that undue pressure had been placed on a witness to give evidence in proceedings. That allegation related to the manner in which evidence had been gathered, not to the content of the evidence itself. In addition, it has long been established that the conduct of litigation can be taken into account in deciding whether to make an award of aggravated damages: see *Zaiwalla & Co v Walia* [2002] IRLR 697.

26.115   The shifting burden of proof provision in s 136 of the EqA 2010 applies to complaints of victimization (see para 26.77). The complainant will have to show that a protected act was done, that a detriment was suffered. The ET will have to find a prima facie case that the detriment was occasioned because of the protected act. The burden of proof will then shift to the employer to show a non-discriminatory reason for the treatment in question.

Failure to make reasonable adjustments

26.116   The EqA 2010 requires employers to make reasonable adjustments in relation to disabled persons in certain circumstances.

26.117   By s 21(1) of the EqA 2010, a failure to comply with the first, second, or third requirements amounts to a failure to comply with the duty to make reasonable adjustments and by s 21(2) of the EqA 2010, such a failure amounts to discrimination. Those requirements are set out at s 20(3) to (5) of the EqA 2010:

(1) The first requirement in s 20(3) is a requirement that, where a provision, criterion, or practice of A's puts a disabled person at a substantial disadvantage in relation to a relevant matter in comparison with persons who are not disabled, A should take such steps as it is reasonable to have to take to avoid the disadvantage.

(2) The second requirement (s 20(4) is a requirement that, where a physical feature puts a disabled person at a substantial disadvantage in relation to a relevant matter in comparison with persons who are not disabled, such steps as it is reasonable to have to take to avoid the disadvantage should be taken.

(5) The third requirement (s 20(5) is a requirement that, where a disabled person would, but for the provision of an auxiliary aid, be put at a substantial disadvantage in relation to a relevant matter in comparison with persons who are not disabled, such steps as it is reasonable to have to take to provide the auxiliary aid should be taken.

The statutory provisions in ss 20 and 21 of the EqA 2010 are supplemented by Sch 8 to the EqA 2010 in defining the scope of the duty to make reasonable adjustments regarding employees and workers.

The first and second requirements mirror those which were previously found in s 4A of the DDA **26.118** 1995. The proper approach for employment tribunals to adopt in such cases was considered by the EAT in *Environment Agency v Rowan* [2008] IRLR 20. The EAT considered that before making a finding that an employer falls under a duty to make reasonable adjustments, employment tribunals must consider a number of matters. Those are:

(a) the provision, criterion, or practice (PCP) applied by or on behalf of the employer or
(b) the physical feature of premises occupied by the employer
(c) the identity of non-disabled comparators (where appropriate) and
(d) the nature and extent of the substantial comparative disadvantage suffered by the employee in comparison to non-disabled persons. In this regard, the fact that a disabled person and a non-disabled person would suffer the same disadvantage in the same circumstances, does not mean that the disabled person will not suffer a substantial comparative disadvantage, if those circumstances are more likely to apply to him than to a non-disabled person. The comparison exercise is not, therefore, the same exercise as in a direct discrimination case: see *Griffiths v Secretary of State for Work and Pensions* [2016] IRLR 216.

Where those steps are satisfied, the employer falls under a duty to make reasonable adjustments. **26.119** S 18B of the DDA 1995 provided further guidance as to the sort of matters that should be considered when considering whether or not a particular adjustment is reasonable. Those matters were:

(a) the extent to which the step concerned would prevent the effect in relation to which the duty is imposed
(b) the practicability of taking the step
(c) the cost of taking the step
(d) the extent of the employer's financial resources
(e) the availability of financial assistance with regard to the taking of the step
(f) the nature of the undertaking and the size of its resources and
(g) where the step was to be taken in relation to a private household, the extent to which it would disrupt that household or disturb any person residing there. That list has not been reproduced in the EqA 2010.

However, presumably these matters will continue to be highly relevant in determining whether or not a particular adjustment is reasonable. Furthermore, provision is made in s 22 of the EqA 2010 for the possibility of Regulations which will further define the scope of the duty to make reasonable adjustments.

Further, s 18B(2) of the DDA 1995 set out a list of steps which a person might need to take in **26.120** order to comply with the duty to make reasonable adjustments. Those were (a) making adjustments to premises; (b) allocating some of the disabled person's duties to another person; (c) transferring him to fill an existing vacancy (including one at a more senior level, having regard to the decision of the House of Lords in *Archibald v Fife Council* [2004] ICR 954 and note that subsequent authority has suggested that it would not be a reasonable adjustment to create a new post for a disabled person: *Tarbuck v Sainsbury's Supermarkets* [2006] IRLR 664, but it may be a reasonable adjustment to swap an employee's position with another employee: *Chief Constable of South Yorkshire Police v Jelic* [2010] IRLR 744); (d) altering his hours of working or training; (e) assigning him to a different place of work or training; (f) allowing him to be absent during working or training hours for rehabilitation, assessment, or treatment; (g) giving, or arranging for, training or mentoring (whether for the disabled person or any other person); (h) acquiring or modifying equipment; (i) modifying instructions or reference manuals; (j) modifying procedures for testing or assessment; (k) providing a reader or interpreter; and (l) providing supervision or other support. Although much will depend on the individual facts of any particular case, these steps are still likely to be regarded as reasonable steps for employers take as regards disabled persons. A 'step' can be anything which would modify or qualify the PCP in question and should not be given a narrow meaning: see *Griffiths v Secretary of State for Work and Pensions* [2016] IRLR 216.

26.121 The burden of proof provided for in s 136 of the EqA 2010 will apply to claims of this nature and the tribunal will have to find:

(a) the application of a PCP

(b) the existence of comparative substantial disadvantage

(c) the sort of reasonable adjustments which could have been made and were not made.

The burden of proof will then shift to the employer to establish that the adjustments put forward by the claimant were either made or were not reasonable: see *Project Management Institute v Latif* [2007] IRLR 579.

26.122 It has been held in a number of cases, such as *Tarbuck v Sainsbury's Supermarkets Limited* [2006] IRLR 664 and *Spence v Intype Libra Limited* UKEAT/0617/06/JOJ, that a failure to consult as to the making of adjustments does not, in and of itself, amount to an independent breach of the duty to make reasonable adjustments. In these cases, the EAT observed that employers who do consult are more likely to comply with the duty to make reasonable adjustments, but a failure to consult cannot logically amount to a breach of the duty in and of itself.

26.123 The third requirement was found in the DDA 1995 but not in relation to discrimination in the workplace. The Explanatory Notes to the EqA 2010 give an example of the provision of auxiliary aids:

> The organiser of a large public conference knows that hearing impaired delegates are likely to attend. She must therefore consider how to make the conference accessible to them. Having asked delegates what adjustments they need, she decides to engage BSL/English interpreters, have a palantypist and an induction loop to make sure that the hearing impaired delegates are not substantially disadvantaged.

26.124 The EqA 2010 provides at para 20 of Sch 8 to the EqA 2010 that a person is not subject to a duty to make reasonable adjustments if he does not know and could not reasonably be expected to know, in the case of job applicants, that a disabled person is or may be an applicant for the work in question and, in any other case, that a disabled person has a disability and is likely to be placed at the disadvantage referred to in the first, second, or third requirement. As such, if an employer does not know either that a disabled person is, in fact, disabled, or does not know that the effects of the disability are likely to give rise to a substantial comparative disadvantage, then the employer is under no duty to make reasonable adjustments: see *Rideout v TC Group* [1998] IRLR 628 and *Alam v Secretary of State for Work and Pensions* [2010] IRLR 283. In assessing whether or not an employer knew of an employee's disability, the employment tribunal should focus on whether or not the employer knew of the relevant facts, namely: (i) an impairment; (ii) which has a substantial and long-term adverse effect; (iii) on a person's ability to carry out normal day-to-day activities. Employers need to make their own determination in relation to this and cannot simply rely on the conclusions of an occupational health adviser: see *Gallop v Newport City Council* [2014] IRLR 211.

26.125 The concept of associative discrimination does not apply to claims for reasonable adjustments. As such, a complainant cannot allege that his employer should have made adjustments to assist him in caring for another disabled person: see *Hainsworth v Ministry of Defence* [2014] IRLR 728.

Other prohibited acts

26.126 The following examples of 'ancillary conduct' are also made unlawful by the EqA 2010:

(a) Committing an act of discrimination or harassment after the termination of the contract of employment or other relevant relationship where the discrimination arises out of and is closely connected to that relationship: see *Relaxion Group plc v Rhys-Harper* [2003] IRLR 484; *Metropolitan Police Commissioner v Shoebridge* [2004] ICR 1690; and s 108 of the EqA 2010. Notwithstanding the wording of s 108(7) of the EqA 2010, the Court of Appeal has held that post-termination victimization is unlawful under the EqA 2010: see *Rowstock v Jessemey*

[2014] IRLR 448. Where, after the termination of an employment relationship, an employer is re-organized, a successor body cannot be liable for discrimination against an individual that was never its employee: see *Butterworth v Police and Crime Commissioner's Office for Greater Manchester* [2016] IRLR 280.

(b) Instructing, causing, or inducing contraventions of Parts 3 to 7 of the EqA 2010 or s 108(1) or (2) of the EqA 2010 (which relate to relationships that have ended) or s 112(1) of the EqA 2010 (which relates to aiding contraventions). Together these are termed 'basic contraventions' of the EqA 2010: see EqA 2010, s 111(1). Proceedings in respect of breaches of this provision may be taken by either (1) the 'victim' of the unlawful act where that person is subjected to a detriment; (2) the person who is induced, caused, or instructed to commit an unlawful act where that person is subjected to a detriment; and (3) the Commission for Equality and Human Rights. However, liability pursuant to s 111 of the EqA 2010 is constrained to cases where the person instructing, causing, or inducing a basic contravention is in a position to commit a basic contravention himself in relation to the person instructed, caused, or induced to commit a basic contravention. As such, employers will be liable for instructing, causing, or inducing their employees to commit basic contraventions of the EqA 2010.

(c) Knowingly aiding another person to commit basic contraventions of the Act: see EqA 2010, s 112. The House of Lords considered the words 'knowingly aiding' in *Hallam v Avery* [2001] UKHL 15 In that case the police had provided to a local authority information that a wedding might be a 'gypsy wedding'. The local authority had reacted by imposing constraints on the wedding which would not have otherwise been imposed. As such, to have knowingly aided the local authority in its discriminatory act, the police would have had to have had some participation in the process which led to the local authority's decision. A failure to investigate an act of harassment could not amount to knowingly aiding that act to occur: see *May and Baker v Okerago* [2010] IRLR 394.

(d) Where an employee or agent undertakes an act which renders their employer vicariously liable for a contravention of the EqA 2010, then that employee or agent will be in breach of s 110 of the EqA 2010 and will be liable as though he were primarily liable for the breach of the EqA 2010 (as his employer or agent was): see s 110(6) of the EqA 2010. The effect of this section is that a complainant can pursue both employer and employee and principal and agent and seek the remedies provided for in Part 9 of the EqA 2010, in respect of a discriminatory act contrary to the EqA 2010.

D. VICARIOUS LIABILITY OF EMPLOYERS AND PRINCIPALS FOR DISCRIMINATORY ACTS

A large number of employers are companies who cannot commit discriminatory acts themselves (as corporate bodies) but act instead through their employers or agents. The EqA 2010 makes provision for this by providing, at s 109(1) to (2) of the EqA 2010 that employers/principals will be liable for the discriminatory acts of their employees and agents: see *Peninsula Business Services v Baker* [2017] IRLR 394 as to the requirement that the act of the employee/agent must be a discriminatory act.   **26.127**

Employers

Section 109(1) of the EqA 2010 provides that anything done by a person in the course of his employment will also be deemed to have been done by the employer. The words are to be interpreted as words of everyday speech and are not to be constrained by reference to the common law principles of vicarious liability: see *Jones v Tower Boot Co Limited* [1997] IRLR 168.   **26.128**

The scope of acts done in the course of an employee's employment (prior to the implementation of the EqA 2010) was, however, unclear. For example, while in *Chief Constable of Lincolnshire Constabulary v Stubbs* [1999] ICR 547 the EAT found that acts of discrimination which occurred in the pub after work were done in the course of employment on the basis that the drinks were   **26.129** organized by the employer as a 'leaving party' and were therefore a mere extension of the work-place, in *Sidhu v Aerospace Composite Technology Limited* [2000] IRLR 602 the Court of Appeal found that acts of discrimination which occurred during an employer-organized 'away day' at a theme park were not committed within the course of employment. It follows that whether or not an employer is vicariously liable for the acts of its employees which do not fall squarely within the employment relationship will be highly fact sensitive.

Principals and agents

26.130 Principals will also be liable for the discriminatory acts of their agents by reason of s 109(2) of the EqA 2010, where those acts are done with the authority of the principal. The relationship of agency required by the anti-discrimination legislation in order to fix a principal with liability has been suggested to be the common law concept of agency of a fiduciary relationship where the agent can bind the principal in contract: see *Yearwood v Commissioner of Police of the Metropolis* [2004] ICR 1660 and *May and Baker v Okerago* [2010] IRLR 394. However, doubts have been expressed as to whether *Yearwood* was correctly decided and the Court of Appeal declined to offer a conclusive de-termination in relation to this issue in *Kemeh v Ministry of Defence* [2014] IRLR 377. Nonetheless, it is likely that a person who operates a contract on behalf of another will be within the common law concept of agency. As such, a contract worker would act as the agent of a person in acting as a line manager of employees or other contract workers of that person and/or in imposing discip-linary sanctions on such a person: see *Chief Constable of Cumbria v McGlennon* [2002] ICR 1156.

26.131 The concept of 'acting with authority' relates to the nature of the act in which the discrimination occurred. It will be no defence for a principal to allege that he had not given the agent authority to commit the said act in a discriminatory manner: see *Lana v Positive Action Training in Housing (London) Limited* [2001] IRLR 501 and *Kemeh v Ministry of Defence* [2014] IRLR 377.

26.132 It is noteworthy that the statutory defence set out at s 109(4) of the EqA 2010 does not appear to apply as between principals and agents, although the contrary was suggested (erroneously in the view of the editors of this work) in *Victor-Davis v London Borough of Hackney* UKEAT/1269/01.

E. DEFENCES TO DISCRIMINATION CLAIMS

26.133 There are a raft of exceptions and defences to discrimination claims set out in the EqA 2010. Many of them are specific to particular causes of action. The discussion which follows could not, there-fore, be exhaustive. However, it sets out the main exceptions to the prohibition on discrimination and defences which are likely to be considered by employment tribunals.

The statutory defence

26.134 As set out above, employers will be vicariously liable for the discriminatory acts of their employees which are done in the course of their employment. However, employers are given a defence by s 109(4) of the EqA 2010 in circumstances where they have taken all reasonable steps to prevent their employees from doing the discriminatory act in question or from doing 'anything of that de-scription'. This is a similar provision to that found under the discrimination legislation prior to the implementation of the EqA 2010 save that the 'old wording' required the employer to have taken such steps as were 'reasonably practicable'. There is no requirement of causation however. Even if the taking of such steps would not have prevented the discriminatory acts in question, the employer will not be able to make out the 'statutory defence': *Canniffe v East Riding of Yorkshire Council* [2000] IRLR 555.

Illegality

26.135 The laws prohibiting discrimination are a series of statutory torts. As such, the common law of il-legality (in the context of tortious claims) applies to the discrimination legislation. The test set out in *Hall v Woolston Hall Leisure* [2001] ICR 99 is that a claim will fail for illegality in circumstances where the complainant's claim is so closely connected or inextricably bound up or linked with the unlawful conduct that to permit the claim to proceed would be for the court or tribunal to condone the unlawful conduct. As such, where employees have been engaged in tax evasion or complicit in the tax evasion of their employer, it is unlikely that there could be a successful illegality defence. Where an employment situation is unlawful 'from top to bottom' by reason of an employee having no right to work lawfully in the United Kingdom, an illegality defence may be successful: *Vakante v Governing Body of Addey and Stanhope School* [2003] ICR 290. However, the rules relating to illegality are rules of public policy and are therefore capable of being applied flexibly. Accordingly, where a person is working illegally because he or she is the victim of human trafficking then public policy will not permit the operation of the defence of illegality: *Hounga v Allen* [2014] IRLR 811, *Patel v Mirza* [2016] UKSC 42.

The general genuine occupational requirement defence

Prior to the implementation of the EqA 2010, there were a series of genuine occupational require- **26.136** ment defences taking different forms in the Sex Discrimination Act 1975 and Race Relations Act 1976. In contrast, the EqA 2010 has created a general genuine occupational requirement defence in para 1 of Sch 9 to the EqA 2010. That will apply where having regard to the nature or context of the work:

(a) an occupational requirement exists
(b) that occupational requirement is a proportionate means of achieving a legitimate aim
(c) the person to whom the requirement is applied does not meet the requirement or the putative discriminator has reasonable grounds for not being satisfied that the person meets it. This final limb does not apply, however, where the protected characteristic in question is sex: see para 1(4) of Sch 9 to the EqA 2010.

However, the defence is only a defence to the following contexts in which discrimination can **26.137** occur: (1) the arrangements made in deciding to whom to offer employment; (2) a refusal to offer employment; (3) the way in which a person is afforded access to opportunities for promotion, transfer, or training or for receiving any other benefit, facility, or service; (4) dismissal. It follows that the defence cannot be argued in respect of discriminatory terms and conditions of employment, nor subjecting a person to a detriment.

Furthermore, the defence only applies in respect of discrimination and does not apply to victim- **26.138** ization claims or failures to make reasonable adjustments claims.

The defence applies to employees as well as contract workers, partners, and office holders. **26.139**

It might be argued that the defence comes very close to providing for a justification defence to **26.140** certain claims of direct discrimination although it is constrained somewhat by the fact that the genuine occupational requirement in question must have regard to the nature or context of the work in question. In *Bougnaoui v Micropole SA* [2017] IRLR 447 it was held by the CJEU that the general genuine occupational requirement defence found in the Framework Directive must be based on the objective requirements of the job, rather than subjective requirements, such as the need to take account of the views or a particular customer.

The organized religion genuine occupational requirement

Pursuant to para 2 of Sch 9 to the EqA 2010, there are exceptions from the prohibition on certain **26.141** forms of discrimination where:

(a) the employment in question is for the purposes of organized religion
(b) a requirement is imposed which engages the compliance or non-conflict principle
(c) the person to whom the requirement is applied does not meet it or the putative discriminator has reasonable grounds for considering that he or she does not meet it.

However, this genuine occupational requirement defence only applies to requirements: (1) to be a **26.142** particular sex; (2) not to be a transsexual person; (3) not to be married or a civil partner; (4) not to

Part C The Substantive Law

be married to, or a civil partner of, a person who has a living former spouse or civil partner; (5) relating to the circumstances in which marriage or civil partnership came to an end; (6) relating to sexual orientation: see para 2(4) of Sch 9 to the EqA 2010.

26.143 The compliance principle is 'engaged' if it is applied so as to comply with the doctrines of the religion: para 2(5) of Sch 9 to the EqA 2010. The non-conflict principle is 'engaged' if, because of the nature of the context of the employment, the requirement is applied so as to avoid conflicting with the strongly held convictions of a significant number of the religion's followers: para 2(6) of Sch 9 to the EqA 2010.

26.144 A similar genuine occupational requirement defence which was found in the Employment Equality (Sexual Orientation) Regulations 2003, SI 2003/1661 was considered on a judicial review application by Richards J in *R v Secretary of State for Trade and Industry and Christian Action Research Education* [2004] IRLR 430. The genuine occupational requirement defence was found not to be an unlawful derogation from the Framework Directive (2000/78/EC) in that case but in order to do so, Richards J gave a narrow construction to the wording. In particular:

(a) the expression 'for the purposes of organized religion' was narrower than being employed in a religious organization. As such, a teacher in a faith school was not employed for the purposes of organized religion

(b) the tests that a requirement so as 'to comply with the doctrines of the religion' and 'to avoid conflicting with the strongly held religious convictions of a significant number of the religion's followers' were to be construed narrowly and would be difficult to overcome.

26.145 A somewhat more expansive construction was given to the legislation, however, in *Reverend Canon Pemberton v Right Reverend Inwood, formerly acting Bishop of Southwell and Nottingham* [2017] IRLR 211. HHJ Eady QC held that employment as a chaplain within the NHS was employment for the purposes of organized religion. In considering the 'compliance principle', HHJ Eady QC considered that 'doctrines' meant the teachings or beliefs of the religion and might include, in the context of the Church of England, a belief that marriage was between one man and one woman.

Other requirements relating to religion and belief

26.146 There is a genuine occupational requirement defence where a requirement to be a particular religion is applied where having regard to the ethos and the nature or context of the work it can be shown that:

(a) it is an occupational requirement and

(b) the requirement can be justified as being a proportionate means of achieving a legitimate aim and

(c) the person to whom the requirement is applied does not meet it or there are reasonable grounds for believing that the person does not meet it.

This defence is found at para 3 of Sch 9 to the EqA 2010.

Positive discrimination

26.147 The EqA 2010 makes 'positive discrimination' lawful in certain circumstances. In particular, s 158 provides that, where persons who share a protected characteristic and (1) suffer a disadvantage connected to that characteristic; or (2) have needs that are different from persons who do not share that protected characteristic; or (3) participation in an activity in relation to that protected characteristic is disproportionately low; the EqA 2010 does not prohibit the taking of action which is a proportionate means of achieving a legitimate aim of:

(a) overcoming or minimizing the disadvantage in question or

(b) meeting the needs in questions or

(c) enabling or encouraging participation in the activity.

Further, s 159 provides that, where persons who share a protected characteristic and (1) suffer a **26.148** disadvantage connected to that characteristic; or (2) participation in an activity in relation to that protected characteristic is disproportionately low; Part 5 of the EqA 2010 (which relates to work) does not prevent the taking of action with the aim of overcoming or minimizing the disadvantage or participating in the activity where that action is treating a person more favourably in relation to his recruitment or promotion than another person who does not hold the protected characteristic in question. This section did not come into effect with the rest of the EqA 2010 on 1 October 2010, but came into force on 6 April 2011.

Section 159 is constrained by s 159(4) by three requirements: **26.149**

(a) the person treated more favourably must be as qualified to be recruited or promoted as the 'comparator'
(b) the employer does not have a policy of treating persons who share the protected characteristic more favourably in connection with recruitment or promotion than persons who do not share it
(c) taking the action is a proportionate means of achieving the aim of encouraging or enabling persons sharing the protected characteristic of overcoming or minimizing the disadvantage or participating in the activity.

National security

Section 192 of the EA provides that there will be no contravention of the EqA 2010 where a person **26.150** does something for the purposes of national security and it is proportionate for that purpose. It is noteworthy that the requirement of proportionality has been introduced in order to justify the national security exception. Presumably, in the light of the reasoning of the ECJ in *Johnston v Chief Constable of the Royal Ulster Constabulary* [1987] ICR 83, the use of this exception will be scrutinized carefully by courts and tribunals since it is a derogation from the principle of equal treatment provided for in the Directives which underpin the prohibition on discrimination provided for in the EqA 2010.

Benefits provided to the public

Where an employer provides benefits, facilities, or services to the public and provides the same **26.151** benefits to its employees, contract workers, partners, or office holders, it will not be liable for a breach of ss 39(2) and (4) (relating to employees), 41(1) and (3) (relating to contract workers), 44(2) and (6), 45(2) and (6) (relating to partnerships and LLPs), and 50(6), (7), (9), and (10) in respect of the provision of such benefits, pursuant to para 19 of Sch 9 to the EqA 2010, provided that:

(a) the benefit, facility, or service provided does not differ in a material respect to that provided to the public
(b) the provision of the benefit, facility, or service is not regulated by the terms of the complainant's contract of employment or other terms on which the complainant undertakes work (such as the terms of partnership or the terms of the complainant's appointment to the relevant office)
(c) the benefit, facility, or service does not relate to training: see para 19(3) of Sch 9 to the EqA 2010.

Discrimination in compliance with the law

Where anything is done **26.152**

(a) in pursuance of an enactment
(b) in pursuance of an instrument made by a member of the executive under an enactment
(c) to comply with a requirement imposed by a member of the executive by virtue of an enactment
(d) in pursuance of arrangements made by or with approval of, or for the time being approved by a Minister of the Crown or
(e) to comply with a condition imposed by a Minister of the Crown,

then a person does not contravene Part 5 of the EqA 2010 (EqA 2010, ss 39 to 83, which relate to work) by doing anything which would discriminate against another person because of that person's nationality, or by applying a PCP which relates to the ordinary place of residence of the other person or the length of time which the other person has been present, resident, or outside the United Kingdom: see para 1 of Sch 23 to the EqA 2010.

26.153   This exception is a narrow one, since the words 'in pursuance of' are confined to acts done which are necessary to perform an express obligation. It is not enough that there is a statutory discretion to do the act in question: see *Hampson v Department of Education and Science* [1990] ICR 511. Where discrimination is required by an enactment then the discriminator may be afforded a defence by s 191 and Sch 22 to the EqA 2010.

Defences to age discrimination claims

26.154   Part 2 of Sch 9 to the EqA 2010 sets out a number of defences which are specific to age discrimination claims. In summary, those are:

(a)   certain benefits which are based on length of service are excluded from the scope of the provisions relating to age discrimination: see para 10 of Sch 9 to the EqA 2010. This provision was applied in the context of a service related criterion in the selection of individuals for redundancy in *Rolls Royce v Unite* [2009] IRLR 576

(b)   the lawfulness of the development rate of the national minimum wage is preserved by para 11 of Sch 9 to the EqA 2010

(c)   the basing of enhanced redundancy payments on length of service in the same manner as the Employment Rights Act 1996 bases the calculation of the statutory redundancy payment is not unlawful by reason of para 13 of Sch 9 to the EqA 2010

(d)   the restriction of the availability of insurance or associated financial products, to the period prior to the employee reaching the normal retirement age or 65: see para 14 of Sch 9 to the EqA 2010

(e)   provisions relating to child care for children of a particular age group: see para 15 of Sch 9 to the EqA 2010

(f)   a power provided to Ministers of the Crown to use 'practices, actions or decisions' based on age regarding contributions to personal pension schemes: see para 16 of Sch 9 to the EqA 2010.

26.155   There is no longer an exception to the obligation not to discriminate because of age, by retiring those at or over the age of 65. This provision which was previously found in Part 2 of Sch 9 to the EqA 2010 was repealed by the Employment Equality (Repeal of Retirement Age Provisions) Regulations 2011 with effect from 6 April 2011. Note, however, the transitional provisions in those Regulations.

Other defences

26.156   The following defences also exist under the EqA 2010:

(a)   There is an exception from the anti-discrimination legislation provided for at para 4 of Sch 9 to the EqA 2010 where the armed forces apply a requirement that a person must be a man or a requirement that a person may not be a transsexual in order to serve in the armed forces. However, such a requirement must be a proportionate means of ensuring the combat effectiveness of the armed forces. Again, having regard to the decision of the ECJ in *Johnston v Chief Constable of the Royal Ulster Constabulary* [1987] ICR 83 it is likely that this exception will be narrowly construed.

(b)   There is a defence to discrimination on the ground of sexual orientation in relation to the differential treatment of same sex spouses or civil partners in relation to accessing benefits, facilities or services where the relevant right accrued before the Civil Partnership Act 2004 came into effect: see para 18 of Sch 9 to the EqA 2010. The scope of this defence and its compatibility with the Framework Directive was considered by the Supreme Court in the context of survivors pensions in *Walker v Innospec Limited* [2017] IRLR 928.

(c)   There are defences in relation to sports and charities at ss 193 to 195 of the EqA 2010.

F. DISCRIMINATION CLAIMS AND QUESTIONS

Section 138 of the EqA 2010 made provision for statutory questionnaires to be issued by a person **26.157** who considered that a contravention of the EqA 2010 had occurred in relation to them. However, s 66 of the Enterprise and Regulatory Reform Act 2013 provided for the repeal of s 138 of the EqA 2010 and s 138 of the EqA 2010 ceased to be law from April 2014.

The questionnaire procedure recognized that complainants often have difficulty in proving dis- **26.158** crimination cases (and particularly cases of direct discrimination) because what is at issue is the motivation of the putative discriminator in committing the act or omission which is said to be discriminatory.

Notwithstanding the repeal of s 138, complainants who feel they have been discriminated against **26.159** can and should still ask questions of their employer (or other putative discriminator). Indeed, prior to the implementation of the EqA 2010, the EAT had held that employment tribunals could draw inferences from a failure to answer questions in documents that did not satisfy the form requirements of the statutory questionnaire process: see *Dattani v Chief Constable of West Mercia Police* [2005] IRLR 267. This continues to be the case; it reflects the position in the general law that courts and tribunals may draw such inferences from the evidence as are appropriate. As such, even after the repeal of s 138 of the EqA 2010, where questions from a complainant are unanswered or are inadequately answered, there is still scope for employment tribunals to draw adverse inferences as to a person's discriminatory motivation. Plainly, however, only appropriate inferences can and should be drawn: *D'Silva v NATFHE* [2008] IRLR 412.

Complainants should use any questionnaire process carefully and thoughtfully. Although it **26.160** can often be tempting to ask a large number of questions in order to 'cast the net' as wide as possible, a more focused approach is often more revealing, is less likely to be dismissed by a respondent on the basis that it is disproportionate, and is more likely to encourage employment tribunals to draw adverse inferences from failures to answer or from evasive or equivocal answers.

G. TERRITORIAL JURISDICTION

Prior to the implementation of the EqA 2010, the appellate courts had developed a body of **26.161** law dealing with the territorial jurisdiction of the employment tribunals to consider breaches of the anti-discrimination legislation based on the statutory provisions found at, for example, s 8 of the Race Relations Act 1976, s 10 of the Sex Discrimination Act 1975, and s 68 of the Disability Discrimination Act 1995 (although there were similar provisions in the Employment Equality Regulations of 2003 and 2006 which prohibited discrimination on grounds of sexual orientation, religion or belief, and age). In short, those provisions provided that an employee was to be regarded as in employment at an establishment in Great Britain in circumstances where:

(a) he did his work wholly or mainly in Great Britain or

(b) he did his work wholly outside of Great Britain but the employer (1) had a place of business at an establishment in Great Britain; and (2) the work carried out by the employee was for the purposes of the business carried on at that establishment; and (3) the employee was ordinarily resident in Great Britain either at the time when he applied for or was offered the employment or at any time during the course of the employment.

A body of settled case law had grown in relation to these provisions: see *Saggar v Ministry of Defence* **26.162** [2005] IRLR 618; *Williams v University of Nottingham* [2007] IRLR 660; and *Tradition Securities and Futures SA v X* [2009] ICR 88. However, this was somewhat cast into doubt by the decision of the EAT in *Ministry of Defence v Wallis* [2010] IRLR 1035. In that case, it appeared plain that the employee concerned could not bring a claim for discrimination in the employment tribunal because she had not at

Part C The Substantive Law

any time been 'ordinarily resident' in Great Britain. However, Underhill P applied the decisions in *Bleuse v MBT Transport Limited* [2008] IRLR 264 and *Duncombe v Secretary of State for Children, Schools and Families* [2009] EWCA Civ 1355 (which suggested that tribunals should apply an expansive conception of territorial jurisdiction having regard to the need for complainants to be able to adequately enforce rights derived from EU law) so as effectively to 'read out' of s 10 of the Sex Discrimination Act 1975 the need for a person to be 'ordinarily resident' in Great Britain. Underhill P found that the 'duty of consistent interpretation' in European law required him to make such a determination. See also para 23 of the EAT's judgment in *Pervez v Macquarie Bank Limited* [2011] IRLR 284.

26.163   The EqA 2010 contains few provisions dealing with territorial jurisdiction. The Explanatory Notes to the EqA 2010 state that 'the Act leaves it to tribunals to determine whether the law applies, depending for example on the connection between the employment relationship and Great Britain'. There are specific provisions which provide for work on ships and hovercrafts (s 81 of the EqA 2010) and in relation to offshore work (s 82 of the EqA 2010).

26.164   In *R (on the application of Hottak) v Secretary of State for Foreign and Commonwealth Affairs* [2016] EWCA Civ 438, the Court of Appeal held that the approach adopted in relation to s 94 of the Employment Rights Act 1996 and as adumbrated by Lord Hoffmann in *Lawson v Serco* [2006] UKHL 3 and developed in *Duncombe v Secretary of State for Children Schools and Families (No 2)* [2011] ICR 1312 and *Ravat v Halliburton Manufacturing & Services Limited* [2012] 2 All ER 905 ought to be applied to the EqA 2010. However, because of the decision in *Ministry of Defence v Wallis* [2010] IRLR 1035, employment tribunals will have to have regard to the expansive conception of territorial jurisdiction provided for in *Bleuse v MBT Transport Limited* [2008] IRLR 264 and *Duncombe v Secretary of State for Children, Schools and Families* [2009] EWCA Civ 1355.

H. LIMITATION

26.165   Section 123 of the EqA 2010 provides that proceedings before an employment tribunal brought (pursuant to s 120 of the EqA 2010) in relation to a contravention of Part 5 of the EqA 2010 (which is the Part of the EqA 2010 relating to work) should be brought within a period of three months starting with the date of the act to which the complaint relates or such other period as the employment tribunal thinks just and equitable. For a summary of the principles applicable in relation to just and equitable extensions of time see *Virdi v Metropolitan Police Commissioner* [2007] IRLR 24 Two qualifications to that proposition are that:

(a)   conduct which extends over a period is to be treated as done at the end of the period: see s 123(3)(a) of the EqA 2010 and

(b)   omissions to act are treated as occurring when the person in question decided to omit to do the act in question. A person will be taken to have omitted to do something when he does an act inconsistent with it or on the expiry of the period in which he might have been reasonably expected to do the act: see s 123(3)(b) and (4) of the EqA 2010 and *Matuszowicz v Kingston-upon-Hull City Council* [2009] IRLR 288.

26.166   It follows that respondents to discrimination claims have a limitation defence. For a detailed discussion of the principles in relation to time limits, see Chapter 3.

CHECKLIST FOR CLAIMS OF DISCRIMINATION BASED ON SEX (TO INCLUDE MARITAL/CIVIL PARTNERSHIP AND GENDER REASSIGNMENT), RACE, RELIGION, OR BELIEF, AND SEXUAL ORIENTATION

1   Is the complainant employed under a contract of service or of apprenticeship or a contract personally to execute any work or labour?: see ss 39 and 83 of the EqA 2010. If not, does he fall under any of the quasi-employment situations set out in Part V of the EqA 2010? If not, he may not have the protection of the legislation.

2   Does the general genuine occupational requirement defence set out at para 1 of Sch 9 to the EqA 2010 apply and is the requirement applied a proportionate means of achieving a legitimate aim? If so, the complainant will not have a claim.

3   Does the complainant work wholly outside Great Britain, or does the complainant work on a ship or hovercraft or work otherwise offshore? If so, the complainant may not be able to pursue a claim.

4   If claiming sex discrimination, is the complainant claiming about special treatment to women in connection with pregnancy and childbirth? If so, he may be excluded from claiming: see s 13(6) of the EqA 2010.

5   Does the claim relate to something done for the purposes of national security and if so, is it proportionate for that purposes? If so, the complainant may not have a claim: see s 192 of the EqA 2010. Is the complainant employed in the armed forces? If so and the claim is that a requirement was imposed which prevented women or transsexuals from serving, there may be no claim if that requirement was a proportionate means of ensuring the combat effectiveness of the armed forces: see para 4 of Sch 9 to the EqA 2010.

6   Do any of the following defences apply?

   (a)   illegality

   (b)   the discrimination is in relation to benefits provided to an employee, contract worker, partner, or office holder and the employer also provides the benefit, facility, or service to the public: see para 19 of Sch 9 to the EqA 2010

   (c)   the discrimination is in compliance with the law: see para 1 of Sch 23 to the EqA 2010

   (d)   the claim is in relation to organized religion and the compliance or non-conflict principles are engaged in relation to requirements to be of a particular sex, or not to be a transsexual person, or not to be married or a civil partner or a person who has a living former spouse or civil partner, or in relation to the circumstances in which a marriage or civil partnership came to an end, or relating to sexual orientation: see para 2 of Sch 9 to the EqA 2010

   (e)   the claim is in relation to an occupation requirement that a person must be of a particular religion where, having regard to the ethos and the nature and context of the work, that can be shown to be a proportionate means of achieving a legitimate aim.

   If so, the complainant may not have a claim.

7   Is the complainant an employee, temporary worker, supplied by an employment agency, or a worker and claiming sex discrimination or race discrimination or discrimination based on religion or belief or sexual orientation in respect of the areas listed below?

   (a)   arrangements for recruitment

   (b)   recruitment advertisements

   (c)   contractual benefits, but only where discrimination is on grounds other than sex

   (d)   non-contractual benefits

   (e)   occupational pension schemes (race, marital status, gender reassignment, religion or belief, sexual orientation only)

   (f)   opportunities for promotion and transfer

   (g)   training opportunities (save in a case where positive training of particular groups is allowed, as to which see ss 158 to 159 of the EqA 2010)

   (h)   harassment

   (i)   grounds for dismissal

   (j)   claims by employees in relation to their treatment after the termination of employment as long as the act complained of arose from the employment relationship or was closely connected with it

   (k)   other detriments.

   If so, the complainant could have a claim under the relevant provisions of the EqA 2010.

8   In direct discrimination cases, has the employee received the less favourable treatment because of the relevant protected characteristic? If so, and the employee can convince the tribunal on the balance of probabilities that this is the case the employee concerned may have a claim for direct discrimination: see ss 13, 39, and 136 of the EqA 2010.

9   Can the employer show on the balance of probabilities that the protected characteristic was not the reason for less favourable treatment? If not, the employer may not be able to defend an allegation of direct discrimination: see ss 13 and 136 of the EqA 2010.

10 In cases of combined discrimination, the same approach will apply in relation to the combination of the relevant protected characteristics: see s 14 of the EqA 2010.

11 Has the complainant been subject to unwanted conduct which has the purpose or effect of violating another person's dignity or creating an intimidating, hostile, degrading, humiliating, or offensive environment for them? Can the conduct, having regard to all the circumstances, including, in particular, the perception of the victim, reasonably be considered as having that effect? If so, the complainant may have a claim of harassment for a reason relating to the protected characteristic: see s 26 of the EqA 2010.

12 Is the complainant subject to a provision, criterion, or practice which is applied to everyone but which subjects those holding a protected characteristic to a particular disadvantage, and does the employee who is claiming suffer that disadvantage? If so, the employee concerned may have a claim for indirect discrimination: see s 19 of the EqA 2010.

13 To prove whether a provision, criterion, or practice amounts to indirect discrimination (which obligation is on the claimant having regard to s 136 of the EqA 2010 and *Nelson v Carillion Services Ltd* [2003] IRLR 428):

(a) identify the criteria for selection

(b) identify the relevant pool of potential candidates

(c) divide the pool into those who satisfy the criteria and those who do not, and consider whether the members of the minority group are under-represented in the group which satisfies the criteria in comparison with the statistics and over-represented in the group which does not satisfy the criteria

(d) does the group which is over-represented suffer disadvantage as a result of the imposition of the provision, criteria, or practice, and does the employee complaining suffer that disadvantage? If so, it is potentially discriminatory.

14 Can the employer show that the conditions which have been imposed are a proportionate means of achieving a legitimate aim or that any group disadvantage is entirely unrelated to the protected characteristic? If so, the employer may have a defence to a claim of indirect discrimination. In considering this, the employer will need to ask the following questions:

(a) What is the legitimate aim? Non-exhaustive examples of legitimate aims are:

(i)   economic factors such as business needs and efficiency

(ii) the health, welfare, and safety of the individual

(iii) the particular training requirements of the job.

(b) Does the legitimate aim correspond with a real need of the business? It should do and not simply be cheaper.

(c) What is proportionate?

(i)   it must actually contribute to the legitimate aim

(ii) the discriminatory effect should be significantly outweighed by the importance and benefits of the legitimate aim

(iii) the employer should have no reasonable alternative to the action it is taking.

15 Has the complainant been treated less favourably than others because that person threatens to bring proceedings, to give evidence or information, to take any action or to make any allegations concerning the employer under the discrimination legislation? If so, the complainant may have a claim of victimization as long as the allegation was not false and was made in good faith: see s 27 of the EqA 2010.

16 Has the complainant brought the claim in the employment tribunal during employment or within three months of the act complained of? If not, the complainant's claim is likely to be out of time, unless it forms part of a continuing act: see s 123 of the EqA 2010.

CHECKLIST FOR DISABILITY DISCRIMINATION

1 Is the complainant employed under a contract of service or of apprenticeship or a contract personally to execute any work or labour? If not, does he fall under any of the quasi-employment situations set out in Part V of the EqA 2010?

2 Is the complainant an employee who works outside Great Britain or an employee who works on a ship or hovercraft? If so, he may not have a claim under the EqA 2010.

3 Does the general genuine occupational requirement defence set out at para 1 of Sch 9 to the EqA 2010 apply and is the requirement applied a proportionate means of achieving a legitimate aim? If so, the complainant will not have a claim.

4 Does the claim relate to something done for the purposes of national security and if so, is it proportionate for those purposes? If so, the complainant may not have a claim: see s 192 of the EqA 2010.

5 Do any of the following defences apply?

   (a) illegality

   (b) the discrimination is in relation to benefits provided to an employee, contract worker, partner, or office holder and the employer also provides the benefit, facility, or service to the public: see para 19 of Sch 9 to the EqA 2010

   (c) the discrimination is in compliance with the law: see para 1 of Sch 23 to the EqA 2010.

   If so, the complainant may not have a claim.

6 Does the complainant have a disability, ie a physical or mental impairment which has a substantial and long-term adverse effect on the employee's ability to carry out his normal day-to-day activities? See s 6 and Sch 1 to the EqA 2010.

7 Has the complainant been treated less favourably by someone than he treats or would treat a person not having that particular disability whose relevant circumstances, including his abilities, are the same as or not materially different from, those of the disabled person? If so, the complainant may have a claim of direct discrimination: see s 13 of the EqA 2010.

8 Has the complainant been treated less favourably for a combination of two reasons including disability and another protected characteristic? If so, the complainant may have a claim for combined discrimination.

9 In harassment cases, has the complainant been subject to unwanted conduct related to the disability, which has the purpose or effect of violating another person's dignity or creating an intimidating, hostile, degrading, humiliating, or offensive environment for them? If so, the complainant may have a claim of harassment.

10 Is the complainant subject to a provision, criterion, or practice which is applied to everyone but which subjects those holding a protected characteristic to a particular disadvantage, and does the employee who is claiming suffer that disadvantage? If so, the employee concerned may have a claim for indirect discrimination: see s 19 of the EqA 2010.

11 To prove whether a provision, criterion, or practice amounts to indirect discrimination (which obligation is on the claimant having regard to s 136 of the EqA 2010 and *Nelson v Carillion Services Ltd* [2003] IRLR 428):

   (a) identify the criteria for selection

   (b) identify the relevant pool of potential candidates

   (c) divide the pool into those who satisfy the criteria and those who do not, and consider whether the members of the minority group are under-represented in the group which satisfies the criteria in comparison with the statistics and over-represented in the group which does not satisfy the criteria

   (d) does the group which is over-represented suffer disadvantage as a result of the imposition of the provision, criteria, or practice, and does the employee complaining suffer that disadvantage? If so, it is potentially discriminatory.

12 Can the employer show that the conditions which have been imposed are a proportionate means of achieving a legitimate aim or that any group disadvantage is entirely unrelated to the protected characteristic? If so, the employer may have a defence to a claim of indirect discrimination.

13 Has the complainant received less favourable treatment for a reason associated with his disability? If so, the complainant may have a claim of disability discrimination: see s 15 of the EqA 2010. The respondent will have a defence if he can show that his treatment of the complainant amounted to a proportionate means of achieving a legitimate aim.

14 Has the employer complied with its duty to take steps as are reasonable to prevent substantial disadvantage to a disabled person in relation to the application of PCPs, the physical features of premises

and/or the provision of auxiliary aids? If not, the complainant will have a claim: see s 21 of the EqA 2010.

15 Has the complainant been treated less favourably than others because that person has brought proceedings for disability discrimination against another person under the EqA 2010, given information or evidence in relation to such a claim, otherwise done anything under the EqA 2010 in relation to the employer or alleged that the employer has breached the EqA 2010 or believes the employer intends to do so? If so, the complainant may have a claim for victimization, as long as the allegation was not false and/or provided that the allegation was made in good faith: see s 27 of the EqA 2010.

16 Has the complainant been subject to unwanted conduct which has the purpose or effect of violating another person's dignity or creating an intimidating, hostile, degrading, humiliating, or offensive environment for them? Can the conduct, having regard to all the circumstances, including, in particular, the perception of the victim, reasonably be considered as having that effect? If so, the complainant may have a claim of harassment for a reason relating to the disability: see s 26 of the EqA 2010.

17 Is the employer unaware of the disability or the effects of the disability? This will potentially be a defence to claims of reasonable adjustments: see Sch 8 to the EqA 2010. Further, lack of knowledge as to the existence of a disability will be a good defence to a claim of direct discrimination or combined discrimination.

18 Has the complainant brought the claim in the employment tribunal during employment or within three months of the act complained of? If not, the complainant's claim is likely to be out of time.

CHECKLIST FOR CLAIMS OF AGE DISCRIMINATION

1 Is the complainant employed under a contract of service or of apprenticeship or a contract personally to execute any work or labour: see ss 39 and 83 of the EqA 2010? If not, does he fall under any of the quasi-employment situations set out in Part V of the EqA 2010? If not, he may not have the protection of the legislation.

2 Does the general genuine occupational requirement defence set out at para 1 of Sch 9 to the EqA 2010 apply and is the requirement applied a proportionate means of achieving a legitimate aim? If so, the complainant will not have a claim.

3 Does the complainant work wholly outside Great Britain, or does the complainant work on a ship or hovercraft or work otherwise offshore? If so, the complainant may not be able to pursue a claim.

4 Does the claim relate to something done for the purposes of national security and if so, is it proportionate for that purposes? If so, the complainant may not have a claim: see s 192 of the EqA 2010. Is the complainant employed in the armed forces?

5 Do any of the following defences apply?

   (a) illegality
   (b) the discrimination is in relation to benefits provided to an employee, contract worker, partner of office holder and the employer also provides the benefit, facility of service to the public: see para 19 of Sch 9 to the EqA 2010
   (c) the discrimination is in compliance with the law: see para 1 of Sch 23 to the EqA 2010.

   If so, the complainant may not have a claim.

6 Is the complainant claiming age discrimination about one of the areas below?

   (a) arrangements for recruitment
   (b) contractual and non-contractual benefits (including occupational pension schemes)
   (c) opportunities for promotion and transfer and training
   (d) harassment
   (e) grounds for dismissal
   (f) claims by employees in relation to their treatment after the termination of employment as long as the act complained of arose from the employment relationship or was closely connected with it
   (g) vocational training.

   If so, the EqA 2010 prohibits discrimination because of age in these areas.

7 Would the employee have received the same treatment from the employer or potential employer because of age (or apparent age)? If so, the employee concerned may have a claim for direct discrimination: see s 13 of the EqA 2010.

8 Is the complainant subject to a provision, criterion, or practice which is applied to everyone but which disadvantages those in a specific age group and does the employee who is claiming suffer that disadvantage? If so, the employee concerned may have a claim for indirect discrimination: see s 19 of the EqA 2010.

9 Can the employer show that the direct or indirect discrimination is a proportionate means of achieving a legitimate aim or that any group disadvantage is entirely unrelated to the protected characteristic? In considering this, the employer will need to ask the following questions:

(a) What is a legitimate aim? In the case of direct discrimination this will have to be an aim which protects 'intergenerational fairness' or 'dignity'. Non-exhaustive examples of legitimate aims (insofar as indirect discrimination is concerned) are:

(i) economic factors such as business needs and efficiency
(ii) the health, welfare, and safety of the individual
(iii) the particular training requirements of the job.

(b) Does the legitimate aim correspond with a real need of the business? It should do and not simply be cheaper.

(c) What is proportionate?

(i) it must actually contribute to the legitimate aim
(ii) the discriminatory effect should be significantly outweighed by the importance and benefits of the legitimate aim
(iii) the employer should have no reasonable alternative to the action it is taking.

10 Was the complainant treated less favourably because of a combination of age and another protected characteristic? If so, the complainant may have a claim for combined discrimination: see s 14 of the EqA 2010.

11 Has the complainant been subject to unwanted conduct which has the purpose or effect of violating another person's dignity or creating an intimidating, hostile, degrading, humiliating, or offensive environment for them? Can the conduct, having regard to all the circumstances, including, in particular, the perception of the victim, reasonably be considered as having that effect? If so, the complainant may have a claim of harassment for a reason relating to age: see s 26 of the EqA 2010.

12 Has the complainant been treated less favourably than others because that person threatens to bring proceedings, to give evidence or information, to take any action, or to make any allegations relating to age discrimination? If so, the complainant may have a claim for victimization as long as the allegation was not false and was made in good faith: see s 27 of the EqA 2010.

13 Does one of the other exceptions to liability under Part 2 of Sch 9 to the EqA 2010 apply? These are set out at para 26.152 above.

14 Has the complainant brought the claim in the employment tribunal during employment or within three months of the act complained of? If not, the complainant's claim is likely to be out of time.

27

Equal Pay: Law and Procedure

SUMMARY

(1) The Equality Act 2010 (EqA 2010) prohibits discrimination in relation to terms and conditions of employment as between men and women. It does so by use of the implication of a 'sex equality clause' into the contracts of employees (as defined by s 83 of the EqA 2010).

(2) The EqA is underpinned by European law found in both the Treaty of Rome (as amended by the Lisbon Treaty) and a number of European Directives.

(3) In an equal pay situation, a complainant must be able to identify an actual comparator who is engaged on like work: work rated as equivalent or work of equal value to the complainant.

(4) There is a separate procedural regime in relation to equal pay complaints where the comparator relied upon is said to have been undertaking work of equal value to the work of the complainant.

(5) An equal pay claim will not be successful if the employer can point to a material factor (MF) as between the complainant and the comparator which explains that pay differential, provided that the material factor is not itself either directly or indirectly discriminatory.

(6) Once it is established that a complainant can identify a proper comparator and the employer has no material factor defence, the EqA 2010 operates so as to modify any term in the contract of the complainant so that it is as favourable as that in the contract of the comparator.

(7) The EqA 2010 also applies to pension schemes where a 'sex equality rule' is implied into the scheme rules.

(8) There are various provisions in the EqA 2010 which are designed to eliminate the 'gender pay gap' by prohibiting secrecy in pay practices and by requiring companies to undergo gender pay 'audits'.

A. INTRODUCTION TO THE LAW OF EQUAL PAY

Until October 2010 the law of equal pay was contained, for the most part, in the Equal Pay Act **27.01** 1970 (EqPA 1970). The EqA 2010 has been in force since 1 October 2010 and has replaced the EqPA 1970. For the most part, the pre-existing case law will remain relevant in interpreting the EqA 2010.

The current law relating to equal pay can then, for the most part, be found in Chapter 3 of Part 5 **27.02** of the EqA 2010. However, importantly, the EqA 2010 is underpinned by Art 157 of the Treaty on the Functioning of the European Union (TFEU), which was formerly Art 141 of the Treaty of Rome (which itself was formerly Art 119 of the Treaty of Rome). That Treaty Article provides that:

> Each Member State shall during the first stage ensure and subsequently maintain the application of the principle that men and women should receive equal pay for equal work.

In addition to Art 157, Directive No 2006/54/EC (the Consolidating Directive) which replaced **27.03** Directive No 75/117 (the Equal Pay Directive) and Directive No 76/207 (the Equal Treatment Directive) from 15 August 2009 sets out EU law in relation to equal pay. Art 14 of the Consolidating Directive provides:

> There shall be no direct or indirect discrimination on grounds of sex in the public or private sectors, including public bodies, in relation to:
>
> ...
>
> (c) employment and working conditions, including dismissals, as well as pay as provided for in Article 141 of the Treaty ...

Article 157 has been held to be directly effective and can therefore be relied upon by individuals **27.04** to enforce the right directly before national courts. However, employment tribunals as statutory bodies only have the jurisdiction to adjudicate over particular statutory complaints. As such, the claim for equal pay will always be brought under Chapter 3 of Part 5 of the EqA 2010. However, those parts of the statute which are inconsistent with the Article will be disapplied by the employment tribunal: see *Scullard v Knowles* [1996] IRLR 344 In addition, both Art 157 and the provisions of the Consolidating Directive will be used in order to assist in construing the domestic legislation: see, for example, *Marleasing SA v La Comercial Internacional de Alimentacion SA* [1990] ECR I-4135.

The Equality and Human Rights Commission has produced a statutory Code of Practice relating **27.05** to equal pay, which can be found at http://equalityhumanrights.com/uploaded_files/EqualityAct/ equalpaycode.pdf.

The equal pay regime is very different to the other mechanisms by which discrimination is prohib- **27.06** ited in the EqA 2010. In particular, the equal pay regime does not make discrimination a 'statutory tort' in the way that the other discrimination machinery regulates behaviour in the workplace. Instead, it implies into every relevant contract a sex equality clause. That sex equality clause has the effect of equalizing any less favourable term or condition of employment as between a complainant and a comparator, provided that the employer cannot defend a claim by pointing to a non-discriminatory difference as between the employment situation of the complainant and the comparator. Appropriate comparators are those who are engaged on either (1) like work; (2) work rated as equivalent; or (3) work of equal value.

Part C The Substantive Law

27.07 A number of important differences as between the regime prohibiting sex discrimination in relation to terms and conditions of employment and those prohibiting other forms of discrimination thereby arise, such as:

(a) in order for the sex equality clause to operate, it is necessary to have a real comparator of the opposite sex, whereas, in the case of any other form of discrimination, a hypothetical comparator is sufficient: contrast *Walton Centre for Neurology & Neurosurgery NHS Trust v Bewley* [2008] ICR 1047 with *Balamoody v UK Central Council for Nursing, Midwifery and Health Visiting* [2001] EWCA Civ 2097

(b) whereas an 'ordinary' discrimination complaint must be brought within three months of the act complained of (subject to the possibility of an extension of time), a complaint of equal pay must be brought within six months of the end of the relevant employment (and there is no possibility of an extension of time but the complainant will be permitted to recover pay arrears for six years): contrast ss 120 and 129 of the EqA 2010

(c) whereas complainants in 'ordinary' discrimination cases can and do routinely recover awards for injury to feelings, such awards are not available in complaints of equal pay: see *Degnan v Redcar and Cleveland Borough Council* [2005] IRLR 504.

B. THE SCOPE OF THE LAW OF EQUAL PAY

27.08 Section 64 of the EqA 2010 sets out the scope of the law of equal pay. It applies where a person:

(a) is employed (as to which see s 83(2) of the EqA 2010, which defines employment as 'employment under a contract of employment, a contract of apprenticeship or a contract personally to do work') or

(b) holds a public or personal office.

There is a wealth of case law setting out what is meant by the definition in s 83(2) of the EqA 2010: as to which see the discussion at paras 26.02–26.07.

27.09 However, in order to fall under Chapter 3 of Part 5 of the EqA 2010, the complaint must not only be brought by an employee or office holder but must also be a sex discrimination complaint in relation to the terms and conditions of employment (or upon which an office is held) by the complainant. If the complaint is other than a sex discrimination complaint based on the terms and conditions of employment, it should be presented under Chapter 1 of Part 5 of the EqA 2010 (and in the case of employees, under s 39 of the EqA 2010).

27.10 This 'dividing line' is set out in s 70 of the EqA 2010, which provides that:

(a) by s 70(1) and (3) the provisions prohibiting discrimination in relation to contractual terms and benefits have no effect where a term is modified by the equal pay provisions (or would be modified but for the operation of the MF defence) and

(b) discrimination in relation to less favourable terms and conditions of employment as between complainants and comparators is not sex discrimination by reason of s 70(2).

These provisions provide, therefore, that the prohibition on discrimination in relation to terms and conditions of employment in Chapter 1 of Part 5 of the EqA 2010 cannot give rise to a claim for sex discrimination because the complaint is properly a complaint of equal pay and that, where the equal pay provisions in Chapter 3 of Part 5 of the EqA 2010 apply, no claim for sex discrimination lies.

27.11 These provisions are similar to provisions which were set out in the EqPA 1970 and the Sex Discrimination Act 1975 (SDA 1975). The relationship between the SDA 1975 and the EqPA 1970 was considered in the Scottish Courts in *Hoyland v Asda Stores* [2006] IRLR 468. In that case, Asda operated a discretionary bonus scheme based on profit for those employees with six months' continuous service. Maternity leave was treated as absence for the purpose of calculating bonus payments, and as such, in 2002, Mrs Hoyland who had been absent on maternity leave, had her bonus payment reduced accordingly. She issued a claim in the tribunal. The claim was dismissed and the same was upheld by the EAT. The matter was appealed to the Court of Session by Mrs Hoyland. The Court of Session dismissed the appeal agreeing with the employment tribunal and the EAT that the matter fell within s 6(6) of the SDA 1975 (which excluded from the SDA claims relating to monetary benefits regulated by the contract of employment), notwithstanding that the bonus in question was said to be a 'discretionary bonus' rather than a contractual bonus. At para 14 of the judgment:

> While we recognise that the word 'discretionary' is used by the employer in referring to the bonus scheme, that can be construed as relating only to the amount being paid in any one year and we recognise that the tribunal found, as a matter of fact, that every employee received a bonus. We have no doubt that that entitlement, if it be such in law, arose out of the contract of employment and is regulated by it in the sense that but for the existence of the contract of employment the bonus would not be paid and it is therefore being paid as a consequence of its very existence. It does not seem to us to be necessary for s 6(6) to have any application in a given situation that the entitlement in question should be part of the formal contract of employment. This conclusion reflects the dichotomy between equal pay and equal treatment, and avoids an employer being exposed to double jeopardy.

Hoyland is a difficult case because although it was clear that the bonus in question would not have **27.12** been paid but for the contract of employment in question, that could be said of almost any contractual benefit. The bonus was a discretionary bonus in relation to which there was no contractual right and so it is difficult to see how the provisions of the EqPA 1970 (as now found in Chapter 3 of Part 5 of the EqA 2010) could have any effect.

A more coherent analysis of this area of law (in the view of the editors of this work) was offered **27.13** by the Court of Appeal in *Hosso v European Credit Management Limited* [2012] IRLR 235 In that case, the claimant wished to complain about the award of share options to her, which she alleged to be discriminatory. There was no contractual right to the award of share options, although there was a discretionary share option scheme. The claimant was out of time to present a complaint under the SDA 1975 and therefore sought to present a complaint about the alleged discriminatory award of share options, as an equal pay complaint under EqPA 1970. The Court of Appeal held that the claimant had no valid equal pay complaint. The reason why was that there was no contractual clause governing the award of share options and which could be modified or regulated by the 'equality clause'; the share option scheme was entirely discretionary, not contractual. This leaves open the question as to whether or not the exercise of a contractual discretion could give rise to an equal pay complaint. *Hoyland* would suggest that it could, but Stanley Burnton LJ considered in *Hosso* that it could not (see para 29 of *Hosso*). Mummery LJ did not offer a view as to this question in *Hosso* (see para 51), preferring to leave it open for future argument.

There is a major difference between the regime put in place by the EqPA 1970 and the SDA 1975 **27.14** and the regime under the EqA 2010 by reason of s 71 of the EqA 2010. That section provides that where a term or condition of employment relates to pay but the sex equality clause has no effect (presumably, either because a comparator cannot be identified or because a MF defence was successful) a sex discrimination complaint or complaint of combined discrimination can still be pursued under ss 13 and/or 14 of the EqA 2010. The effect of this provision is that, therefore, complaints about unequal contractual terms relating to pay (in distinction to complaints about other less favourable terms) can be pursued as ordinary direct discrimination complaints with the effect that a hypothetical comparator could be relied upon in such claims. The Explanatory Notes to the EqA 2010 make this plain by stating, referring to s 71 of the EqA 2010, that:

> The section replaces similar provision in the Sex Discrimination Act 1975 which ensured that the sole remedy in respect of claims made about sex discrimination in contractual pay matters was obtained through the Equal Pay Act 1970. This required that the comparator be a real person. This section however contains a new provision designed to allow claims to be brought where a person can show evidence of direct sex discrimination or dual discrimination (where sex is one of the protected characteristics in the combination) in relation to contractual pay but is unable to gain the benefit of a sex equality clause due to the absence of a comparator doing equal work.

This is an important expansion in the protection afforded by the law relating to sex discrimination and equal pay.

27.15 There are no provisions setting out the limits of the territorial application of the EqA 2010. However, it was held in *R(on the application of Hottak) v Secretary of State for Foreign and Commonwealth Affairs* [2016] EWCA Civ 438 that tribunals should apply the sort of test adumbrated by Lord Hoffmann in the context of the employment protection legislation in *Lawson v Serco* [2006] UKHL 3 and as developed in *Ravat v Halliburton Manufacturing & Services Limited* [2012] 2 All ER 905. However, because the right to equal pay is a right founded in European law, the expansive conception of territorial jurisdiction identified and developed in *Bleuse v MBT Transport Limited* [2008] IRLR 264, *Duncombe v Secretary of State for Children, Schools and Families* [2009] EWCA Civ 1355, and *Ministry of Defence v Wallis* [2010] IRLR 1035 will also be relevant.

C. COMPARATORS

27.16 The scheme in Chapter 3 of Part 5 of the EqA 2010 which prohibits unequal pay practices and unequal practices in relation to other terms and conditions of employment has, as its foundation, the identification by the complainant of a real comparator of the opposite sex who is engaged on 'equal work' to that of the complainant: see s 64 of the EqA 2010.

27.17 'Equal work' is defined by s 65 of the EqA 2010 as:

(a) like work
(b) work rated as equivalent or
(c) work of equal value.

Like work

27.18 Work is regarded as amounting to like work where it is 'broadly similar' and any differences as to the work are not of practical importance in relation to the terms of the person's contract of employment or other relevant contract: see s 65(2) of the EqA 2010. Further, when considering differences between the work of a complainant and a comparator, it is necessary to have regard to the frequency with which differences between their work occur and the nature and extent of those differences: see s 65(3) of the EqA 2010.

27.19 The practical reality of the work undertaken will be considered by the employment tribunal rather than the strict wording of a particular job description, albeit that any job description will be important evidentially. In *Eaton Limited v Nuttall* [1977] ICR 272 the EAT commented that:

> In considering whether there is like work, though the most important point is what the man does and what the woman does, the circumstances in which they do it should not be disregarded. One of the circumstances properly to be taken into account is the degree of responsibility involved in carrying out the task.

27.20 Circumstances may indicate, then, that work which at first sight would appear to be broadly similar, is not in fact 'like work'. For example, in *Thomas v National Coal Board* [1987] ICR 757 it was held that a male canteen worker on a permanent night-shift was not employed on like work with female day-shift canteen workers having regard to differences between the different shifts.

Work rated as equivalent

27.21 Work is rated as equivalent where a job evaluation study gives the work an equal value in relation to the demands made on the worker: see s 65(4)(a) of the EqA 2010. As such, where a job evaluation study has been completed and the woman's work and her chosen comparator's work have been awarded the same grade, the woman may claim equivalence with that comparator. The job of each worker covered by the study must be valued in terms of the demands which are made upon the worker under various objective headings. For example, typical headings are:

(a) mental ability
(b) emotional demands
(c) numeracy skills

(d) literacy skills

(e) manual dexterity

(f) levels of responsibility including supervisory function.

It is necessary to look at the job evaluation study as a whole in order to determine whether or not **27.22** two jobs can be regarded as equivalent. For example, in *Springboard Sunderland Trust v Robson* [1992] ICR 554, the EAT held that two employees had been rated as equivalent on a study because they had been given the same grade at the end of the study, notwithstanding that they had obtained different marks in different sections of the study.

The EqA 2010 provides a mechanism for complainants to challenge a job evaluation study where **27.23** a job evaluation study is 'sex specific'. Such a study will be 'sex specific' if it sets different values for men than it sets for women. In those circumstances it is necessary to consider what the job evaluation study would have shown had it not been tainted by discrimination. If (had it not been tainted by discrimination) the job evaluation study would have rated the complainant's work as equivalent to that of her comparator, then the complainant will have established equivalence pursuant to s 65(4)–(5) of the EqA 2010.

Work of equal value

In circumstances where a woman is not employed to undertake like work with her comparator and **27.24** has not been rated as equivalent, the woman may allege that she is employed on work which is of equal value in terms of the demands placed upon her: see s 65(6) of the EqA 2010.

The claim under s 65(6) of the EqA 2010 cannot be pursued by a woman in circumstances where **27.25** a job evaluation study has been completed by the employer which has come to the conclusion that the work undertaken by the complainant and her comparator is not of equal value (see s 131(5)–(6) of the EqA 2010) unless the job evaluation study discriminated because of sex or was otherwise unsuitable: see s 131(6) 2010. A job evaluation study discriminates because of sex in circumstances where 'a difference (or coincidence) between values that the system sets on different demands is not justifiable regardless of the sex of the person on whom the demands are made': see s 131(7).

It has been held, as a matter of European law, that a complainant can claim equal pay with a **27.26** comparator where that complainant is employed to undertake work of greater value to the work undertaken by that comparator: see *Murphy v Bord Telecom Eireann* [1988] ICR 445 and *Redcar & Cleveland Borough Council v Bainbridge* [2007] IRLR 91.

The range of permissible comparators

Complainants may compare themselves with comparators: **27.27**

(a) (where the complainant is an employee) for the purposes of s 79 of the EqA 2010 who are employees and who are employed by the same employer or an associated employer (which could include employees of subsidiary companies or LLPs, parent companies or LLPs, or those under common control: see *Glasgow City Council v Unison Claimants* [2014] IRLR 532) and at the same establishment (see *City of Edinburgh Council v Wilkinson* [2012] IRLR 202 as to the meaning of the 'same establishment') or at different establishments where common terms of employment apply as between the establishments either generally or in relation to the complainant and her comparator. As to what is meant by common terms of employment see *Leverton v Clwyd County Council* [1989] ICR 33; *British Coal Corporation v Smith* [1996] IRLR 404; *North Yorkshire County Council v Ratcliffe* [1994] IRLR 342; *City of Edinburgh Council v Wilkinson* [2012] IRLR 202; and *North v Dumfries and Galloway Council* [2013] IRLR 737. In *North* it was held that the proper question was whether or not, if a comparator was employed at the same establishment as the woman, even if in fact that was not a 'real possibility', the comparator would be employed on common terms of employment with those on which the woman was employed. If so, then the comparator is a proper comparator for the purposes of s 79 of the EqA 2010

(b) (where the complainant is an office holder) for the purposes of the EqA 2010, pursuant to s 79 of the EqA 2010, who are office holders and where the person responsible for paying the complainant is also responsible for paying the comparator

(c) for the purposes of Art 141 of the Treaty of Rome (now Art 157 TFEU), whose terms and conditions of employment derive from a single source: see *Lawrence v Regent Office Care Limited* [2003] ICR 1092 and *Robertson v Department for Environment, Food & Rural Affairs* [2005] EWCA Civ 138. In *Glasgow City Council v Unison Claimants* [2014] IRLR 532 the Court of Session found that a 'single source' could exist where a local authority had established two limited liability partnerships to carry out some of its functions, where there was a close relationship between the local authority and the LLP and where the local authority controlled the LLP.

It is likely that the 'single source test' which is applied for the purposes of Art 141 of the Treaty of Rome and Art 157 of the TFEU is narrower than the test found in s 79 of the EqA 2010. However, s 79 should not be constrained by the single source test notwithstanding the rules that suggest that domestic legislation should be construed consistently with related European legislation. The scope of EU law does not prevent Member States of the EU from providing greater protection in domestic legislation. As such, legislation should not be 'read down' so as to ensure compliance with the Treaty of Rome (now the TFEU), even though it might be 'read up': see *North Cumbria Acute Hospitals NHS Trust v Potter and Others* [2009] IRLR 176 (at paras 78 to 79).

27.28 It is clear that complainants and their comparators do not have to be employed contemporaneously. This was set out in *Macarthy's Ltd v Smith* [1981] QB 180 and was confirmed by the Court of Appeal in the context of TUPE transfers in *Gutridge v Sodexo* [2009] IRLR 721. That position has now been codified by s 64(2) of the EqA 2010.

27.29 However, it had been held under the EqPA 1970 that complainants cannot rely on successors in their post as comparators: see *Walton Centre for Neurology & Neurosurgery NHS Trust v Bewley* [2008] ICR 1047. The reasoning in that case may be susceptible to challenge, however, by reason of s 64(2) of the EqA 2010. In any event, a hypothetical comparator may be invoked in relation to pay discrimination where the complaint is pursued as a complaint of direct discrimination or combined discrimination having regard to s 71 of the EqA 2010.

27.30 Complainants can also 'piggyback' on the claims of other claimants as a result of the decision of the EAT in *Llewellyn v Hartlepool Borough Council* [2009] ICR 1426 In that case, a group of male complainants were permitted to compare themselves with female employees who, on the face of it had the same terms and conditions of employment as the male complainants, but whose terms and conditions were modified by the operation of the sex equality clause, the female employees having brought equal value complaints relying on other employees as comparators. However, the EAT held in that complaint, which was brought under EqPA 1970, that the requirement for a real comparator meant that the 'piggy-backing' male employees could only compare themselves with the female employees (whose terms had been modified by the equality clause) for the period in which the female employees had been successful in their claims of equal pay.

D. THE MATERIAL FACTOR DEFENCE

27.31 Section 69 of the EqA 2010 sets out the material factor (MF) defence (formerly known as the genuine material factor or GMF defence) and provides that the sex equality clause has no effect as between the terms of the woman's contract and the terms of the men's contract where it is shown that the disparity is:

(a) because of a material factor

(b) that material factor is not directly discriminatory

(c) that material factor is not indirectly discriminatory in the sense that it does not:

    (i) place persons of the same sex at a particular disadvantage when compared to persons of the opposite sex who are doing equal work

    (ii) where the factor cannot be justified as a proportionate means of achieving a legitimate aim.

Material factor

It follows that where a complainant is able to establish that he or she is employed on like work, **27.32** work rated as equivalent, or work of equal value with a real comparator, the sex equality clause will not operate on the complainant's contract of employment where the employer is able to rely on the defence set out in s 69 of the EqA 2010, namely, that the difference in pay as between the claimant and comparator can be explained by reference to a material factor other than sex.

In *Rainey v Greater Glasgow Health Board* [1987] AC 224, Lord Keith of Kinkel set out the hurdles **27.33** which an employer would have to overcome in seeking to establish the material factor defence:

> The difference must be 'material', which I would construe as meaning 'significant and relevant', and it must be between 'her case and his'. Consideration of a person's case must necessarily involve consideration of all circumstances of that case. There may well go beyond what is not very happily described as 'the personal equation'; i.e. the personal qualities by way of skill, experience or training which the individual brings to the job. Some circumstances may on examination prove to be not significant or not relevant, but others may do so, though not relating to the personal qualities of the employee. In particular, where there is no question of intentional sex discrimination whether direct or indirect (and there is none here) a difference which is connected with economic factors affecting the efficient carrying on of the employer's business or other activity may well be relevant.

Similarly, in *Glasgow City Council v Marshall* [2000] IRLR 272 Lord Nicholls of Birkenhead stated: **27.34**

> The scheme of the Act is that a rebuttable presumption of sex discrimination arises once the genderbased comparison shows that a woman, doing like work or work rated as equivalent or work of equal value to that of a man, is being paid or treated less favourably than the man. The variation between her contract and the man's contract is presumed to be due to the difference of sex. The burden passes to the employer to show that the explanation for the variation is not tainted with sex. In order to discharge this burden the employer must satisfy the tribunal on several matters. First, that the proffered explanation, or reason, is genuine, and not a sham or pretence. Second, that the less favourable treatment is due to this reason. The factor relied upon must be the cause of the disparity. In this regard, and in this sense, the factor must be a 'material' factor, that is, a significant and relevant factor. The factor must be 'material' in a causative sense, rather than in a justificatory sense. Third, that the reason is not 'the difference of sex', which is apt to embrace any form of sex discrimination, whether direct or indirect. Fourth, that the factor relied upon is or, in a case within section 1(2)(c), may be a 'material' difference, that is, a significant and relevant difference, between the woman's case and the man's case.

> An employer who proves the absence of sex discrimination, direct or indirect, is under no obligation to prove a 'good' reason for the pay disparity. If there is any evidence of sex discrimination, such as evidence that the difference in pay has a disparately adverse impact on women, the employer will be called upon to satisfy the tribunal that the difference in pay is objectively justifiable. But if the employer proves the absence of sex discrimination, he is not obliged to justify the pay disparity.

It follows that an employer must, in order to succeed in a MF defence, show that: **27.35**

(a) the reason put forward is not a sham or pretence: as to this, see *Hartlepool Borough Council v Dolphin* [2009] IRLR 168 and *Bury Metropolitan Borough Council and Others v Hamilton and Others* [2011] IRLR 358 (affirmed by the Court of Appeal in *City of Sunderland v Brennan* [2012] IRLR 507)
(b) the reason explains the differential
(c) the reason is a significant and relevant difference between the woman's case and the man's case
(d) the reason is not the difference in sex itself (and is not therefore directly or indirectly discriminatory).

The following factors are regularly used by employers as material factors upon which to base the **27.36** section 69 of the EqA 2010 defence:

(a) *Market forces* (albeit that these can be tainted by historic discrimination: see *Ratcliffe v North Yorkshire County Council* [1995] IRLR 439 and *Newcastle upon Tyne Hospitals NHS Foundation Trust v Armstrong (No 2)* [2010] ICR 674).
(b) *Incremental pay scales*. In *Cadman v Health and Safety Executive* [2006] IRLR 969, the ECJ held that, as a general rule, incremental pay scales depending on length of service and seniority

were likely to amount to material factors which were not required to be justified unless there was evidence capable of giving rise to serious doubts that a length of service criterion is appropriate to achieve the legitimate aim of rewarding experience. The Court of Appeal has held in *Wilson v Health & Safety Executive* [2010] ICR 302 that length of service criteria, however, should be treated like any other material factor and that the employer should be required to justify them in an indirect discrimination case once the complainant has satisfied the requirement of showing disparate impact. See also the decision of the EAT in *Secretary of State for Justice v Bowling* [2012] IRLR 382.

(c) *Certain reasons personal to the comparator, such as ability, skills, or even nepotism* (see eg *Coker v Lord Chancellor's Department* [2001] ICR 507, in which it was held that nepotism and discrimination were distinct and separate concepts).

(d) *Differences in collective bargaining arrangements* (although note that it may be difficult to justify pay differentials by reference to different collective bargaining arrangements alone and absent other justificatory factors: see *Kenny v Minister for Justice, Equality and Law Reform* [2013] IRLR 463 and *Enderby v Frenchay Health Authority* [1993] IRLR 591).

(e) *The red circling of the salary of an employee or employees for historic reasons*, although where red circling continues recognized historic discrimination it may be difficult for an employer to suggest that it is a non-discriminatory material factor: see *Bainbridge v Redcar & Cleveland Borough Council* [2008] EWCA Civ 885, *Haq v Audit Commission* [2013] IRLR 206 and *Glasgow City Council v Unison* [2017] IRLR 739. It should be noted that the EqA 2010 has made specific provision for 'pay protection' in s 69(3) of the EqA 2010 by stating that 'the long-term objective of reducing inequality between men's and women's terms of work is always to be regarded as a legitimate aim'. However, in making use of 'red circling' or 'pay protection' schemes, employers should be wary that the scheme does have as its aim, the long-term reduction of inequality and further, that any such scheme is proportionate to achieving that legitimate aim having regard to the discriminatory impact of the scheme.

(f) *Differential shift working*: see *Blackburn v Chief Constable of West Midlands Police* [2009] IRLR 135.

(g) *The introduction of a London weighting*.

(h) *Mistake*. However, repeated mistakes which reveal a pattern are likely to be viewed by an employment tribunal with suspicion.

27.37 The longer the period over which it is sought to rely on at least some of the MFs referred to above, the more difficult it may be for the employer to do so. For example, an employment tribunal is liable to view with some suspicion the salary of an employee which has been red circled with no effort at conversion: see *Home Office v Bailey* [2005] IRLR 757.

Justifying material factor defences

27.38 There has been a debate in both domestic and European law as to the extent to which it is necessary to justify any difference in pay as between a claimant and that claimant's comparator. The position recognized in domestic law was set out by the EAT (Elias P presiding) in the case of *Villalba v Merrill Lynch & Co Inc* [2006] IRLR 437.

27.39 In *Villalba* (a case involving bonus payments based on performance assessments) the claimant argued that any difference in pay as between a claimant and her chosen comparator had to be justified by reason of the ECJ's decision in *Brunnhofer v Bank der Osterreichischen Postparkasse AG* [2001] IRLR 571. The EAT did not accept the argument of the claimant and, in so doing, restated the position in domestic law and European law as follows (references are to paragraphs of the EAT judgment):

(a) once a woman demonstrates that her job is either like work, or work of equal value to that of her chosen male comparator, there is a rebuttable presumption of sex discrimination: see para 104

(b) it is then for the employer to rebut that presumption: see para 104;

(c) in rebutting that presumption, an employer must show the tribunal that the difference in treatment is not expressly on grounds of sex in the sense that it does not amount to direct sex discrimination: see para 115

(d) in addition, pay arrangements might be tainted by sex discrimination in circumstances where they are indirectly discriminatory. Indirect discrimination might be said to exist where:

(i)   there is a difference in treatment which, while not directly on grounds of sex, results from the adoption of a provision, criterion, or practice which adversely affects women. Treating part-time workers less favourably is an example of this form of indirect discrimination and the adoption of such a provision, criterion, or practice must be justified: see para 116

(ii) where cogent, relevant, and sufficiently compelling statistics demonstrate that women suffer a disparate impact when compared with men, there is an irrebuttable presumption of sex discrimination, even though it may not be possible to identify what has caused the disparity. This is the *Enderby v Frenchay Health Authority* [1993] IRLR 591 form of indirect discrimination. In these circumstances, any difference must be justified.

It follows from this analysis that in the ordinary case it will not be necessary to justify any differ- **27.40** ence in pay as between a claimant and her chosen comparator. In the ordinary case, if an employer points to a material factor other than sex which explains the difference in pay, the employer will have made out the s 69 of the EqA 2010 defence. However, in some circumstances an employer might have to justify a difference in pay. Those circumstances are where the factor relied upon by the employer as a material factor to explain the difference in pay, can be said to be indirectly discriminatory in either the standard 'provision, criterion, or practice' sense, or in the *Enderby* sense.

The EAT concluded, therefore, as to the argument that every difference in pay had to be justified: **27.41**

> The elimination of discrimination on grounds of sex cannot in our view begin to require objective justification for differences in pay in circumstances where the employer has satisfactorily rebutted direct sex discrimination and there is no independent evidence of any kind to show that sex has had any influence on the difference in pay. It is only in the language of Lewis Carroll that such a pay differential not tainted in any way by sex could be rendered unlawful under provisions which outlaw sex discrimination. It could of course be rendered unlawful under a wider principle of fair wages which entitled the tribunals to become wage setting bodies, but that is not the law.

Since *Villalba* it has been accepted in a series of cases including *Middlesbrough Borough Council v* **27.42** *Surtees* [2007] IRLR 869 and *Bury Metropolitan Borough Council and Others v Hamilton and Others* [2011] IRLR 358 (affirmed by the Court of Appeal in *City of Sunderland v Brennan* [2012] IRLR 507) that it is not necessary to justify all pay disparities. There can be no need to justify where a pay disparity is not directly discriminatory nor prima facie indirectly discriminatory.

As such, the stages of analysis under the s 69 of the EqA 2010 MF defence are: **27.43**

(a) Is the factor a significant and relevant difference explaining the difference in pay between the claimant and her chosen comparator?

(b) If so, is that factor directly discriminatory?

(c) If not, can it be shown to be indirectly discriminatory in the 'classic sense' or in the *Enderby* sense in the sense of placing one sex at a disadvantage when compared to another?

(d) If so can it be justified as being a proportionate means of achieving a legitimate aim?

The *Armstrong* defence

A gloss might possibly be added to the above as a result of a series of decisions. In *Armstrong v* **27.44** *Newcastle upon Tyne NHS Hospital Trust* [2005] EWCA Civ 1608, the Court of Appeal determined that where the material factor relied upon was unrelated to gender, there was no need for the employer to justify the differential in pay. This was surprising since it had always been assumed that where a material factor defence was relied upon which was not directly discriminatory, but which nonetheless put one sex at a particular disadvantage when compared to another, that the employer would be required to justify the differential in pay.

27.45 The *Armstrong* defence was analysed by the EAT (Elias P presiding) in both *Villalba* and in *Middlesbrough Borough Council v Surtees* [2007] IRLR 869. In *Villalba*, the EAT thought that the Court of Appeal in *Armstrong* had simply been wrong and had overlooked the impact of the ECJ's *Enderby* decision. However, in the *Surtees* case the EAT accepted the submission of the employers that a non-sex based explanation for a difference in pay would be a complete answer to an equal pay claim and would prevent it being established that any material factor defence relied upon was tainted with discrimination (whether direct or indirect) such that the employer would not be called upon to justify the difference in treatment. The EAT suggested, however, that the sort of non-sex based explanation of discrimination which would prevent any consideration of the question of indirect discrimination would be very rare. At para 54 of the judgment, the following was suggested as such an example:

> it may be shown that a particular group of workers (group A) has always been paid less than another group (group B) even although the jobs are of equal value. If both groups were originally predominantly male, but group B has over time become mainly female (such as might well be the case with lawyers or academics, at least in certain fields), a tribunal might readily be satisfied that despite the current adverse effect, there is no proper basis for inferring prima facie discrimination, whether based on historical stereotyping or otherwise. The factors leading to the difference in pay may be long established but the history suggests that they do not have their roots in sex discrimination but have operated independently of the sex of the job holders.

27.46 The matter was considered again by the Court of Appeal in *Gibson v Sheffield City Council* [2010] IRLR 311, a case involving local authority bonus schemes. A majority of the Court of Appeal considered that the *Armstrong* defence did exist in law and that an employer would avoid the need to justify a pay disparity where it was shown that the disparity was unrelated to sex. Smith LJ, in the majority, considered that Elias J had identified one example of the application of the *Armstrong* defence in the *Surtees* case. She considered that there may be other applications of that defence (although no other applications were referred to in any of the judgments of the Court). However, the dissenting judgment of Pill LJ considered that, in accordance with the view of Elias J in *Villalba*, the *Armstrong* defence could not exist in law because of the decision of the ECJ in *Enderby*. The view of Smith LJ (as expressed in *Gibson*) was considered to be the correct view by a differently constituted Court of Appeal in *City of Sunderland v Brennan* [2012] IRLR 507.

27.47 It might be argued that the EqA 2010, at s 69(1)–(2), put in place a scheme which left no room for the *Armstrong* defence on the basis that where it is shown that one sex is put at a particular disadvantage by the application of a material factor, that material factor will have to be justified: see s 69(1)(b). It might also be argued that the effect of the decision of the Supreme Court in *Essop and Others v Home Office* [2017] IRLR 558 is to cast doubt on the existence of the *Armstrong* defence. Lady Hale stated at para 24 that:

> *in none of the various definitions of indirect discrimination, is there any express requirement for an explanation of the reasons why a particular PCP puts one group at a disadvantage when compared with others ... There is no requirement in the Equality Act 2010 that the claimant show why the PCP puts one group sharing a particular protected characteristic at a particular disadvantage when compared with others. It is enough that it does.*

Armstrong was cited in argument before the Supreme Court but was not referred to in Lady Hale's judgment.

E. BURDEN OF PROOF

27.48 The burden of proof in claims for equal pay operates as follows:

(a) It is for the complainant to identify a proper comparator.

(b) It is for the complainant to identify a disparity in pay as between her terms and conditions of employment and those of the comparator.

(c) Once a proper comparator has been identified, the burden shifts to the employer to show that the disparity was because of a material factor. The employer must show that:

    (i)   the material factor relied upon is not a sham or pretence

    (ii) the material factor relied upon explains the differential.

(d) Thereafter, the complainant must show that the material factor is prima facie directly discriminatory (by showing facts from which the inference could be drawn in the absence of an adequate explanation that the material factor was the difference in sex) or prima facie indirectly discriminatory, either

    (i)   in the sense that material factor amounts to the application of a provision, criterion, or practice which places one sex at a particular disadvantage when compared to another or

    (ii) in the *Enderby* sense that the statistics themselves allow an inference to be drawn: see *Bury Metropolitan Borough Council and Others v Hamilton and Others* [2011] IRLR 358 (at paras 14 and 16 of the judgment) (affirmed by the Court of Appeal in *City of Sunderland v Brennan* [2012] IRLR 507). In that case, this form of discrimination was referred to as 'tainting by numbers'.

(e) If the complainant cannot show a prima facie case of direct or indirect discrimination, then the material factor defence will succeed, irrespective of whether or not a pay disparity can be justified: *Tyldesley v TML Plastics* [1996] IRLR 395.

(f) If the complainant is able to show a prima facie case of direct discrimination, the burden will fall on the employer to show that the material factor was not directly discriminatory in any sense whatsoever: see para 14 of the judgment in *Bury Metropolitan Borough Council and Others v Hamilton and Others* [2011] IRLR 358 (affirmed by the Court of Appeal in *City of Sunderland v Brennan* [2012] IRLR 507).

(g) If the complainant can show a prima facie case of indirect discrimination the employer might be able to avoid the need to justify the pay differential by relying upon the *Armstrong* defence, although, even if such a defence does exist in law, there is likely to be little practical scope for its application.

(h) If the employer is unable to rely on the *Armstrong* defence, he must show that that the differential is justified as being a proportionate means of achieving a legitimate aim: see *Nelson v Carillion Services Limited* [2003] ICR 1256.

27.49 It should be noted, however, that the decision in *Nelson* has been subjected to a good deal of criticism on the basis that s 69 of the EqA 2010 (and its predecessor, s 1(3) of the EqPA 1970) places the burden of proof in relation to the establishment of a material factor defence on the employer and that, therefore, the employer should have to show both that the material factor relied upon is not directly discriminatory or indirectly discriminatory. In *Bainbridge v Redcar & Cleveland Borough Council* [2008] EWCA Civ 885, the court accepted the force of this argument but felt it unnecessary to determine the question of burden of proof for the purposes of that appeal.

F. THE OPERATION OF THE EQUALITY CLAUSE

27.50 Once it has been established that a woman is employed alongside a male comparator, that the comparator has more favourable terms and conditions of employment than the woman, and the employer cannot rely upon the defence of material factor, then the equality clause which is deemed to be included in contracts by virtue of s 66(1) of the EqA 2010 will operate.

27.51 The equality clause operates so as to:

(a) modify any clause which is less favourable in the woman's contract than a corresponding clause in a man's contract so that it is not less favourable

(b) include within the woman's contract a corresponding clause, if it does not already include such a clause: see s 66(2) of the EqA 2010.

27.52 A claimant then, is able to bring an action before an employment tribunal or county court (subject to the possibility of strike-out: see s 128 of the EqA 2010) to recover damages in respect of any breach of a term of the claimant's contract of employment as modified by the equality clause. The operation of the equality clause was considered by the EAT (Phillips P presiding) in *Sorbie v Trust Houses Forte Hotels Ltd* [1976] IRLR 371. In that case, the claimants, who were waitresses and were paid 85p per hour, sought to compare themselves with a male comparator who had been engaged on like work with the claimants (and who had been paid 97½p per hour for that work) but had ceased to be so engaged because he had been promoted to be the supervisor of the claimants. The argument was taken by the employers that the claimants could only rely on their chosen comparator to found an action for damages/a declaration for the period prior to his promotion. In rejecting this argument, the EAT reasoned:

> One then goes on to see what the effect as prescribed is, and it is that that term, so identified, in the appellants' contracts shall be treated, as so modified, as not to be less favourable. It seems to us that the way it is treated, as so modified, is to strike out 85p and to substitute 97½p. Upon an application made to an Industrial Tribunal under s. 2—where we think there is power to grant a declaration, or to order the payment of arrears of remuneration, or damages in respect of contravention—the situation is that the Industrial Tribunal, if it so applies s. 1 (2)(a)(i), will find that the contracts of the appellants when modified contains a clause under which they are entitled to remuneration at the rate of 97½p. In other words, once the section is applied and the contract is modified, there is then a contract providing remuneration at that rate. It seems to us that the true way of looking at it is that that contract remains so modified until something else happens, such as a further agreement between the parties, a further collective agreement, or a further statutory modification by reason of a further operation of the equality clause. For that reason we think that the Industrial Tribunal came to a wrong conclusion. It seems to us that when making the Order under s. 2 the Industrial Tribunal has to take the contract of employment as so modified, with the consequence in this case that after 29 December, unless and until there is some such further change, the remuneration continues at the rate of 97½p.

27.53 As such, it would appear that the sex equality clause provided for in s 66 of the EqA 2010 does not 'float over the contract' until an application is made to the employment tribunal. On the contrary, the clause operates so as to modify a discriminatory contractual term immediately albeit that such modification would have subsequently to be declared by an employment tribunal and any breach of the modified pay clause would be remedied by an employment tribunal on an application pursuant to Chapter 3 of Part 5 of the EqA 2010.

27.54 This analysis is supported by the decision of the Court of Appeal in *Gutridge v Sodexo* [2009] IRLR 721, in which the Court of Appeal held that the terms of a contract of employment were modified immediately so as to remain modified by the application of TUPE 2006 in the period after the transfer had taken place. The analysis is further supported by the reasoning of the EAT in *Llewellyn v Hartlepool Borough Council* [2009] ICR 1426, in which it was held that 'piggybacking' male complainants could rely, as comparators, on female employees whose terms and conditions of employment had been modified by the operation of the sex equality clause.

27.55 The sex equality clause will operate in relation to a 'corresponding' term in the contract of employment of the comparator. Under the EqPA 1970, it was unclear whether or not a 'term by term' approach was appropriate, or whether the terms in the contract of employment could be considered 'in the round'. In *Hayward v Cammell Laird Shipbuilders Limited* [1988] ICR 464, the House of Lords considered that each term had to be considered in isolation. However, in *Degnan v Redcar & Cleveland Borough Council* [2005] IRLR 615 the Court of Appeal took a rather different view and determined that, in considering bonus payments made to certain groups of employees, allowances had to be factored in, as all these payments related to a single term of the contract. As such, the Court considered the total amount payable to the claimants as compared to the total amount payable to the comparators in determining whether there was any disparity of treatment. It is difficult to reconcile the decisions in *Hayward* and *Degnan*, even though *Degnan* was expressed to be consistent with the decision in *Hayward*. *Hayward* has, however, been followed by the Court of Appeal in *St Helen's and Knowsley Hospitals NHS Trust v Brownbill and Others* [2011] EWCA Civ 903, where the Court of Appeal suggested that, because the EqPA 1970 strove to ensure that women and men worked under equal terms, the focus of the court should be on each term, rather than on the total amount of pay received.

G. THE PROCEDURE IN AN EQUAL PAY CLAIM AND THE EQUAL VALUE RULES

Equal pay claims are started in the normal manner by submitting an ET1 claim form. Two or more **27.56** complainants may present their claims on the same form if they are based on the same set of facts (ETR 2013, r 9). This can be particularly useful in equal pay cases, where there are likely to be numerous claimants in the same position. However, care should be taken in submitting multiple claims on one ET1 in equal pay cases. In *Farmah v Birmingham City Council* [2017] IRLR 785, Lewis J held that claims would not be based on the same set of facts and therefore would not be able to be submitted on the same ET1 where: (i) claimants were undertaking different work to one another; (ii) claimants sought to compare their work with different comparators undertaking different work; and (iii) male claimants wished to make contingent claims (contingent, that is, on the success of claims brought by female claimants). Where claims are wrongly included on the same ET1, r 6 of the ETR 2013 provides for a discretion on the part of employment judges to waive irregularities. Lewis J considered the sort of factors which are likely to be relevant to the exercise of that discretion, in the context of equal pay claims, in *Farmah*. Where there are multiple claimants, the parties may agree that lead claimants be identified. These should be as representative as possible of all the issues to be determined by the tribunal in the particular series of cases.

Time limits

The time limit for bringing a claim is usually six months from the last date of employment: see **27.57** EqA 2010, s 129. The relevant consideration is neither the end of the job nor the employee leaving the employer but the end of the contract in respect of which the equality clause has been breached. *National Power v Young* [2001] IRLR 32 is authority for the proposition that time does not run from the end of a particular job, the tribunal having found (or proceeded on the assumption) that the claimant was employed under the same contract throughout each job change. Where a TUPE transfer takes place, it appears that time may run on a claim for equal pay from the date of the TUPE transfer since, although TUPE 2006 preserves rights and continuity of service, for the purposes of the EqA 2010 the relevant employment has ended. The scope of the principle is, however, unclear: see *Powerhouse Retail v Burroughs* [2006] IRLR 381; *Unison v Allen* [2007] IRLR 975; and *Sodexo Ltd v Gutridge* [2009] IRLR 721.

The tribunal has no discretion to extend the time limit, but ss 129 to 130 of the EqA 2010 provide **27.58** for some modifications to the time limit in specified circumstances:

(1) A concealment case, in which the employer deliberately concealed from the complainant any fact (referred to as a qualifying fact in s 130 of the EqA 2010) which is relevant to the proceedings and without which he or she could not reasonably have been expected to institute proceedings: the time limit is six months from the day on which the claimant discovered the fact (or could with reasonable diligence have discovered it).
(2) An incapacity case, in which the claimant had an incapacity at any time during the six months after (a) the last date of employment, or (b) where an incapacity case is combined with a concealment case, the six-month period following the discovery of the qualifying fact or six months from the date upon which, with reasonable diligence, the qualifying fact could have been discovered: the time limit is six months from the day on which the claimant ceased to have the incapacity.
(3) A stable employment case, in which the proceedings related to a period during which a stable employment relationship subsisted between the claimant and the employer, notwithstanding that the period includes any time after the ending of a contract of employment when no further contract of employment is in force: the time limit is six months from the date on which the stable employment relationship ended (see *Preston v Wolverhampton Healthcare NHS Trust* [2004] IRLR 96 and *Slack v Cumbria County Council* [2009] IRLR 463).
(4) A standard case, which is a case not falling within any of the other categories: the time limit is six months from the last date of employment.

27.59 Claims brought between 1 October 2004 and 5 April 2009 required an employee to raise a statutory grievance before commencing the claim: see EA 2002, s 32 and *Suffolk Mental Health Partnership NHS Trust v Hurst* [2009] IRLR 12. However, from 6 April 2009 s 32 of the EA 2002, has been repealed. Transitional provisions state that where the facts giving rise to a claim began before 6 April 2009 and continued after that date and a grievance or a claim is brought on or before 4 October 2009, then EA 2002, s 32 will continue to apply. Otherwise, the requirement to raise a grievance will no longer apply.

Questionnaires

27.60 S 138 of the EqA 2010 made provision for statutory questionnaires to be issued by a person who considers that a contravention of the EqA 2010 has occurred in relation to them. However, s 66 of the Enterprise and Regulatory Reform Act 2013 provided for the repeal of s 138 of the EqA 2010 and it ceased to be law from April 2014. Questions can still be asked of employers however and appropriate inferences can be drawn from the failure of employers to answers questions asked: see *Dattani v Chief Constable of the West Mercia Police* [2005] IRLR 267.

Equal value claims

27.61 While like work and work rated as equivalent claims are dealt with under the ordinary tribunal rules, equal value claims are subject to a special procedure because of the particular evidential difficulties in comparing the value of two jobs which may be entirely different. An equal value claim is commenced in the ordinary manner, but the determination of the question of equal value is subject to the Equal Value Rules (see below), which facilitate the commissioning of a report from an independent expert, if the tribunal considers it to be necessary in the particular case(s). ACAS maintains a list of independent experts for this purpose and designates an independent expert to a case when the tribunal directs that one is to be appointed.

27.62 The Employment Tribunals (Equal Value) Rules of Procedure (EV Rules) are contained in Sch 3 to the 2013 Regulations. They modify and supplement the general tribunal rules in certain respects, and are designed to be operated only by judges who specialize in equal pay cases. The EV Rules take effect subject to the tribunal's general case management powers and that, therefore, a tribunal may decide to conduct an equal value case in a manner other than as suggested by the EV Rules: *JD Baldwin v Haberdashers Monmouth School for Girls* (unreported, 15 November 2007, EAT).

27.63 The overall aim of the EV Rules is to reduce the excessive delays which had become customary in equal value cases. The Annex to the EV Rules sets out an 'indicative timetable' of twenty-five weeks for cases not involving an independent expert and thirty-seven weeks for those involving an independent expert. This timetable, however, applies only to the period from presentation of the claim form to determination of the question of equal value, and therefore resolution of a whole claim may take significantly longer if the claim is brought on alternative bases and/or the respondent seeks to rely on a material factor defence. It is noteworthy that the timetable is only indicative. The very large series of cases involving local authorities and the NHS largely located in the North East in the mid-2000s has suggested that it is difficult to fulfil the timetable in practice where very large claims are brought raising a wide variety of issues.

Stage 1 equal value hearing

27.64 If there is a dispute as to whether the work is of equal value, the tribunal must convene a stage 1 equal value hearing. From 6 April 2009, an employment judge sitting alone may hear a stage 1 hearing. The tribunal must give the parties reasonable notice of the date of a stage 1 hearing (EV Rules, r 1(4)). The following steps must be taken at the stage 1 hearing (EV Rules, r 3(1)):

(1) If the work of the claimant and that of the comparator have been given different values on a job evaluation study, the tribunal must strike out the equal value claim at the stage 1 hearing unless it has reasonable grounds for suspecting that the evaluation was made on a system which discriminated because of sex or is 'otherwise unreliable' (EqA 2010, s 131(6); see also

Bromley v H & J Quick Ltd [1988] IRLR 249 and *Paterson v Islington London Borough Council* [2004] UKEAT 0347_ 03_ 2304). Before a claim is struck out for this reason, the claimant shall be permitted to make representations to the tribunal in relation to the job evaluation study and s 131(6) of the EqA 2010. There is no need for the tribunal to send a written notice to the claimant in circumstances where the claimant has been given the opportunity to make oral representations to the tribunal (see EV Rules, r 3(2)).

(2) Determine whether or not to require an independent expert to prepare an expert report to be considered at a 'stage 2 equal value hearing'. If the tribunal decides not to require an independent expert to prepare a report on the question, it shall fix a date for a final hearing (see EV Rules, r 3(2)).

(3) Before deciding whether to appoint an independent expert, the tribunal may, on application by a party, hear evidence and submissions as to the question of whether or not the respondent can make out a material factor defence under s 69 of the EqA 2010 (see EV Rules, r 3(3)).

(4) The tribunal must make standard orders as follows, unless it considers it inappropriate to do so (EV Rules, r 4):

(a) Within fourteen days of the stage 1 hearing: the claimant shall disclose in writing to the respondent the name of any comparator or such information as enables the comparator to be identified by the respondent, and the period of comparison.

(b) Within twenty-eight days of the stage 1 hearing: where the claimant has not disclosed the name of the comparator to the respondent and the respondent has been provided with sufficient detail to be able to identify the comparator, the respondent shall disclose in writing the name of the comparator to the claimant. In addition, the parties shall provide each other with written job descriptions for the claimant and any comparator. The parties shall identify to each other in writing the facts which they consider to be relevant to the question.

(c) The respondent shall grant access to the claimant and his or her representative to its premises for them to interview any comparator.

(d) Within fifty-six days of the stage 1 hearing: the parties shall present to the tribunal a joint agreed statement in writing of (i) job descriptions, (ii) relevant facts, and (iii) facts on which the parties disagree and a summary of their reasons for disagreeing.

(e) At least fifty-six days prior to the hearing: the parties shall disclose to each other, to any experts, and to the tribunal written statement of any facts on which they intend to rely in evidence at the hearing.

(f) At least twenty-eight days prior to the hearing: the parties shall present to the tribunal a statement of facts and issues on which the parties agree and on which they disagree and a summary of the reasons for disagreeing.

(5) The tribunal may add to, vary, or omit any of the standard orders.

Stage 2 equal value hearing

A stage 2 hearing is only held where the tribunal has decided to require an independent expert **27.65** to prepare a report. Its purpose is for the tribunal to make a determination of facts on which the parties cannot agree. That determination will bind the tribunal at the final hearing. The facts determined by the tribunal and any agreed facts are then provided to the independent expert for the purposes of preparing the report: EV Rules, r 6. The tribunal will provide the parties reasonable notice of the stage 2 equal value hearing.

The tribunal must also make the following orders, unless it considers it inappropriate to do so (EV **27.66** Rules, r 7), although the tribunal may add to, vary, or omit any of the standard orders where it considers it appropriate to do so:

(1) The independent expert shall prepare a report and send copies to the tribunal and to the parties by a specified date.

(2) The independent expert shall prepare the report on the basis of the facts provided to him or her by the tribunal and on no other facts.

27.67 The tribunal will also, usually, fix a date for the final hearing at the stage 2 equal value hearing.

The independent expert

27.68 EV Rules, r 5 provides that:

> Where the Tribunal has decided to require an independent expert to prepare a report on the question, it may at any stage of the proceedings, on its own initiative or on the application of a party, order the independent expert to assist the Tribunal in establishing the facts on which the independent expert may rely in preparing the report.

27.69 EV Rules, r 10 provides that:

(a) the tribunal shall restrict expert evidence to that which it considers is reasonably required to resolve the proceedings

(b) an expert shall have a duty to assist the tribunal on matters within the expert's expertise. This duty overrides any obligation to the person from whom the expert has received instructions or by whom the expert is paid

(c) the permission of the tribunal is required to instruct an expert. No expert report can be relied upon unless it is disclosed to all other parties twenty-eight days before the final hearing

(d) where an independent expert has been required to prepare a report on the question, the tribunal shall not admit evidence of another expert on the question unless such evidence is based on the facts relating to the question. If the tribunal considers it inappropriate to do so, any such expert report shall be disclosed to all parties and to the tribunal on the same date on which the independent expert is required to send his report to the parties and to the tribunal

(e) if an expert (who is not an independent expert) does not comply with the EV Rules, or any order made by the tribunal, then the tribunal may order that the evidence of the expert shall not be admitted

(f) where two or more parties wish to submit expert evidence on a particular issue, the tribunal may order that the evidence on that issue is to be given by one joint expert only and if the parties wishing to instruct the joint expert cannot agree an expert, the tribunal may select an expert.

27.70 The duties and powers of the independent expert are set out in r 9(1) and (2) of the EV Rules, and include:

(a) a duty to assist the tribunal in furthering the overriding objective

(b) a duty to comply with the requirements of the EV Rules and any orders

(c) a duty to keep the tribunal informed of any delay in complying with any order

(d) a duty to comply with the timetable set by the tribunal insofar as it is reasonably practicable

(e) a duty to inform the tribunal on request of progress in the preparation of the report

(f) a duty to prepare a report on the question based on the facts relating to the question and send it to the parties (subject to the rules relating to national security proceedings)

(g) a duty to make him or herself available to attend hearings.

27.71 The independent expert may make an application for any order or for a hearing as though he were a party to proceedings (EV Rules, r 9(3)). The tribunal may, after giving the independent expert the opportunity to make representations, withdraw instructions from the expert. If it does so, the tribunal may determine the question itself or instruct a different expert (EV Rules, r 9(4)). Where an independent expert is disinstructed, he shall return to the tribunal all documentation and work in progress. Such work must be in a form which the tribunal is able to use and may be used by the tribunal in proceedings (EV Rules, r 9(5)).

27.72 Where an expert report has been produced, any party or expert may put written questions to the expert which shall be answered within twenty-eight days, provided that (i) the questions may only be put once; (ii) they shall be put within twenty-eight days of the date on which the parties were sent the report; (iii) the questions must be put for the purpose of clarifying the factual basis of the report; (iv) the questions must be copied to all other parties and experts involved in the proceedings at the same time as they are sent to the expert: EV Rules, r 11. Where an expert fails to reply to the questions asked, the tribunal may debar reliance on the expert's evidence: EV Rules, r 11(4).

The hearing

At the substantive hearing the tribunal will determine whether the work of the claimant and that **27.73** of the comparator are of equal value. Where an independent expert's report has been prepared, the report must be admitted in evidence unless the tribunal determines that the report is not based on 'the facts relating to the question' (ie the facts determined at the stage 2 hearing). If the report is not admitted the tribunal may determine the question itself or require another independent expert to prepare a report. The tribunal may refuse to admit evidence of facts or hear submissions on issues which have not been disclosed to the other party as required by the EV Rules, or as are required by the tribunal's orders.

The EV Rules remove the ability formerly in the rules for a party to challenge the admissibility of **27.74** the independent expert's report on the basis that it is not 'satisfactory'. The independent expert's time and public funds will thus be less often wasted by the report being declared inadmissible, although the tribunal may still hear submissions on whether it should adopt the conclusions of the report and may hear expert evidence on this.

Equal pay claims and the civil courts

The EqA 2010 appears to envisage the possibility of claims for equal pay being pursued in the **27.75** civil courts as breach of contract claims. However, the court has the power to strike out such a claim where it can be more conveniently dealt with in the employment tribunal: see s 128 of the EqA 2010. This gives rise to the question of whether claims which would otherwise have been out of time in the employment tribunal can be pursued as breach of contract claims in the county court taking advantage of the longer limitation period provided for in relation to contract claims in the Limitation Act 1980. This question was considered in *Ashby and Others v Birmingham City Council* [2011] IRLR 473. The judge at first instance considered that it was more convenient for the claims to be dealt with in the employment tribunal having regard to the specialist knowledge of judges and the specialist rules of procedure, even though the claims could not be pursued in the employment tribunal at all because they were out of time and there was no possibility of an extension of time. However, that was overturned on appeal by Slade J: see [2011] IRLR 473. Slade J applied jurisprudence developed in the context of the rules of *forum conveniens* (and in particular the principles applicable of staying claims brought in one jurisdiction where there was a more appropriate foreign jurisdiction). Slade J considered, therefore, that it was imperative before striking out claims that there was a consideration as to whether there was a good reason for pursuing them in the county court rather than the employment tribunal (such as, because the employees in question were not aware of their rights during the employment tribunal time limit). In *Abdullah v Birmingham City Council* [2011] IRLR 309, Mr C Edelman QC (sitting as a deputy judge in the Queen's Bench Division) refused to strike out a series of equal pay complaints. He considered that claims for equal pay could be brought in either the employment tribunal or the county court and that it could not be said to be more convenient to pursue such claims in the employment tribunal, where they were out of time in that forum. The decision of Mr Edelman QC was upheld in the Court of Appeal [2012] IRLR 116 and in the Supreme Court [2013] IRLR 38. The Supreme Court held that it would be an exceptional case where the civil courts could strike out an equal pay case which could not be heard by the employment tribunal (because of the more stringent time limits operating in the employment tribunal). The strike-out provisions in the EqPA 1970 and in the EqA 2010 were intended to govern mixed claims (which involved equal pay elements as well as other elements), which had been presented in the civil courts but where it would be more convenient for the employment tribunal to deal with the equal pay aspect of the complaint, having regard to its specialist knowledge and procedures.

Where equal pay proceedings are instituted in the employment tribunal (and where there are **27.76** no parallel proceedings in the civil courts), the employment tribunal will have no power to stay proceedings so that they may be litigated in the civil courts, even where the employment tribunal considers the civil courts to be the more appropriate jurisdiction: see *Asda Stores Limited v Brierley* [2016] IRLR 709.

H. APPLICATIONS OF THE LAW OF EQUAL PAY

The pensions litigation

27.77 One area in which there have been huge numbers of equal pay claims relates to pension schemes that have, historically, had rules which have prevented part-time employees from joining them. Indeed, it was perhaps in recognition of this that the EqPA 1970 as originally drafted did not include pensions and retirement rights within its ambit. However, a statutory scheme had to be reconsidered in the light of a series of appellate and ECJ decisions.

27.78 The attack on the exclusion of pensions from the ambit of the equal pay legislation began with the decision of the ECJ in *Bilka-Kaufhaus GmbH v Webber von Hartz* C-170/84 [1986] IRLR 317. In that case, the ECJ held that the right to be a member of an occupational pension scheme came within the concept of equal pay as found in Art 141 of the Treaty of Rome (as it then was). Further, in *Barber v Guardian Royal Exchange Assurance Group* C-262/88 [1990] ICR 616, the ECJ found that the entitlement to benefits under an occupational pension scheme (whether contributory or non-contributory) fell within the concept of pay as found in Art 141 (as it was). The ECJ reasoned that pensions are nothing more than pay, the receipt of which is deferred until retirement: see *Ten Oever v Stichting Bedrijfspenssionfonds Voor Het Glazenwassers En Schoonmaakbedrijf* C-109/91 [1995] ICR 74. These decisions meant that, pursuant to Art 119 (as it then was), there was an obligation not to discriminate in terms of both:

(a) access to an occupational pension scheme and
(b) benefits received pursuant to an occupational pension.

Because of the potentially far reaching effects of the *Barber* decision, the ECJ took the unusual step of restricting the ambit of the decision to those benefits accrued under an occupational scheme relating to periods of service after 17 May 1990—the date of the *Barber* decision.

27.79 As a result of these decisions, the UK was forced to enact the Occupational Pension Schemes (Equal Access to Membership) Regulations 1995, SI 1995/1215, and subsequently the Pensions Act 1995. These statutory schemes were similar to the schemes set out in the EqPA 1970 but regulated access to and benefits obtained under occupational pension schemes.

27.80 It is well established in European law that, where part-time employees are subjected to less favourable treatment than is afforded to full-time employees, that such treatment is likely indirectly to discriminate against women: see *R v Secretary of State for Employment ex parte Seymour Smith* [2000] IRLR 263. In reliance upon these decisions, the ECJ held in *Vroege v NCIV Instituut Voor Volkshuisvesting BV* [1994] IRLR 651 and *Fisscher v Voorhuis Hengelo BV* [1994] IRLR 662 that an occupational pension scheme which excluded part-time workers from its ambit would be indirectly discriminatory. All of the above gave rise to a large number of claims which, collectively, have become known as the *Preston v Wolverhampton* litigation.

27.81 The *Preston* litigation (and its associated cases) arises from the rules set out above and concerns claims by thousands of workers, most of whom were working in the public sector, who allege that they have been discriminated against indirectly on the basis that they have been excluded from their employer's pension scheme by reason of being part-time workers. These claims are founded on what was Art 141 as interpreted by the *Barber* decision, since a number of them predate the Pensions Act 1995.

27.82 In *Preston v Wolverhampton Healthcare NHS Trust (No 1) and (No 2)* [2000] IRLR 506 and [2001] IRLR 237, the ECJ and House of Lords considered a number of procedural questions which the litigation had thrown up in relation to time limits. This led to substantial amendment of the

EqPA 1970, which has been retained in ss 129 and 130 of the EqA 2010. However, in *Preston v Wolverhampton Healthcare NHS Trust (No 3)* [2005] ICR 222, the EAT considered the applicable principles as to whether or not there would, in fact, be a breach of the 'equality clause' in particular factual situations arising out of the part-time workers cases. The EAT concluded that:

(a) The equality clause is breached where part-time employees are excluded from a pension scheme, in relation to which, membership is compulsory for full-time employees. Where a claim is advanced on this basis, it does not matter whether or not the claimant would have joined the pension scheme had it been made available to her. The sex discrimination arises from the unequal access to the scheme: see *Copple v Littlewoods Plc* [2012] IRLR 121.

(b) There can be no breach of the equality clause where membership of a pension scheme is obligatory for full-time employees but optional for part-time employees on the basis that it is not less favourable for an employee to have optional access to a pension scheme as opposed to being compulsorily placed in that pension scheme: see *Copple v Littlewoods Plc* [2012] IRLR 121.

(c) Where an employer removed a qualifying hours threshold in relation to membership of an occupational pension scheme but failed to inform his employees, there could only be liability in two situations:

(i) liability might arise where there was a policy of concealment on the part of the employer, directed at part-time employees of 'discouragement, dissuasion, misinformation or a practical denial of membership rights', and where such policy had the effect of dissuading a female employee from joining the scheme

(ii) liability might arise by reason of a failure to inform employees of valuable contractual rights, not pursuant to the equal pay provisions in the Pensions Act 1995 but, alternatively, under the law of contract itself. Indeed, the House of Lords held in *Scally v Southern Health & Social Services Board* [1991] ICR 771 that there was a duty 'on the employer to bring it to his attention to render efficacious the very benefit which the contractual right to purchase added years was intended to confer ...'. As such, where an inequality in access to a pension scheme was removed, the *Scally* implied term would come into effect at that time such that there was a contractual obligation on an employer to inform employees of their contractual right to join the pension scheme and/or to 'buy back' years in respect of periods of service where there was unequal access to the scheme.

Further, in the *Preston* line of cases, the appellate courts have grappled with the difficult question **27.83** of the interaction between the Transfer of Undertakings (Protection of Employment) Regulations 1981 and the right to equal pay: see *Powerhouse Retail v Burroughs* [2006] IRLR 381. Where there has been a TUPE transfer, time, in respect of an equal pay pensions claim, runs from the date of that transfer. The position is the same, irrespective of whether or not the claim is a pensions claim or other type of equal pay claim: see *Gutridge v Sodexo* [2009] IRLR 721.

The EqA 2010 has attempted to codify this complex area of law. The following is a summary of the **27.84** provisions of the EqA 2010 in relation to pensions claims:

(a) where a complaint relates to discriminatory access to the pension scheme or discriminatory terms of the pension scheme a complaint can be pursued as a breach of the 'sex equality rule' provided for in s 67 of the EqA 2010. However:

(i) claims in relation to discriminatory access to pensions schemes cannot be pursued in relation to pensionable service prior to 8 April 1976: see s 67(9) of the EqA 2010, which reflects the date of the decision in *Defrenne v Sabena* [1976] ECR 455 (which held that Art 119 of the Treaty of Rome (now Art 157 of the TFEU) was directly effective and thus gave rise to the possibility of bringing claims in relation to discriminatory access to pension schemes prior to the enactment of the Pensions Act 1995. However, in that case, the Court indicated that its ruling should not be applied retrospectively)

(ii) (ii) claims in relation to discriminatory terms of pension schemes cannot be pursued in relation to pensionable service prior to 17 May, 1990—the date of the decision in *Barber v Guardian Royal Exchange Assurance Group* [1991] 1 QB 344

Part C The Substantive Law

(b) trustees and managers of occupational pension schemes are entitled to alter the scheme rules so as to comply with a sex equality rule: see s 68 of the EqA 2010.

27.85 In addition, s 61 of the EqA 2010 provides for pension schemes to include a non-discrimination rule which prohibits discrimination, victimization, and harassment by 'responsible persons' (such as scheme managers and trustees) as against members of an occupational pension scheme.

27.86 The Employment Tribunals Service maintains a part-time pensions section of its website upon which a series of bulletins can be found http://webarchive.nationalarchives.gov.uk/20110207135458/ http://www.employmenttribunals.gov.uk/PartTimeWorkers/informationBulletins.htm. These bulletins provide a useful summary of the relevant law and the case management of the part-time pensions claims.

Maternity

27.87 Pregnant women who are absent from work as a result of having taken maternity leave are not, in general terms, entitled to the benefit of a sex equality clause so as to claim equal pay with men, since pregnancy has been held to be a unique state which renders it impossible for a woman to compare herself with a (non-pregnant) man: see *Gillespie v Northern Health and Social Services Board* [1996] IRLR 214.

27.88 However, in *Lewen v Denda* [2000] IRLR 67 the ECJ considered that position of the payment of bonuses during a period of maternity leave. That case related to a complaint by Mrs Lewen that she had not been entitled to payment of a Christmas bonus by reason of the fact that she had been on maternity leave. The ECJ considered that:

(a) Article 141 of the Treaty of Rome (as it then was) precluded an employer from excluding a woman from the payment of a Christmas bonus where, as at the payment date, she was on maternity leave but where the bonus related to a period actually worked by the said employee prior to her taking maternity leave

(b) Article 141 of the Treaty of Rome (as it then was) would not prevent an employer from excluding a woman on maternity leave from payment of a Christmas bonus where the bonus was subject merely to the condition that the employee in question was in active employment on the date that the bonus was awarded

(c) where a bonus payment related to the previous year of work, there was nothing in Art 141 (as it then was) which prevented an employer from reducing a bonus payment pro rata to reflect the fact that an individual had been on maternity leave during the year in which the bonus payment accrued

(d) where a bonus payment related to the previous year of work, Art 141 would, however, preclude an employer from taking into account periods of compulsory maternity leave so as to reduce a bonus payment pro rata.

27.89 Indeed, the ECJ stated at paras 41 and 42 of the judgment, referring to compulsory maternity leave, that:

> As to whether periods for the protection of mothers (in which they are prohibited from working) must be taken into account, it must be held that they are to be assimilated to periods worked.

> Indeed, to exclude periods for the protection of mothers from the periods worked for the purpose of awarding a bonus retroactively as pay for work performed would discriminate against a female worker simply as a worker since, had she not been pregnant, those periods would have had to be counted as periods worked.

27.90 In addition, in *Alabaster v Woolwich plc and Secretary of State for Social Security* [2004] IRLR 486, a further clarification of the decision in *Gillespie* was made by the ECJ. In *Alabaster*, it was stated that, where the maternity pay which a woman receives is determined by reference to her full pay, pay rises which take place (or would have taken place) during the period of maternity leave should be reflected in the maternity pay received by the woman.

These decisions have been codified in the EqA 2010 at ss 73 and 74. In summary, a maternity **27.91** equality clause is implied into the contract of employment of a woman which operates as follows:

(a) where maternity pay is calculated by reference to basic pay, any increase to the basic pay of a woman during a period of maternity leave should be reflected in a proportionate increase in maternity pay: see EqA 2010 s 74(1)–(5)

(b) any pay or bonus payments which would have been made to a woman before or after a period of ordinary maternity leave or during a period of compulsory maternity leave should be paid, irrespective of the fact that the woman had taken maternity leave: see EqA 2010, s 74(6)–(7)

(c) any increase in pay which the woman would have received had she not been absent from work on maternity leave should be awarded to the woman on her return to work: see EqA 2010, s 74(8).

Section 75 of the EqA 2010 provides for a maternity equality rule to be implied into an occupational **27.92** pension scheme. That rule entitles a woman who is on maternity leave to continued membership of an occupational pension scheme and where a woman is in receipt of maternity pay, the woman is entitled to continue to accrue rights as though she were being paid her usual salary, even though the woman is only required to make contributions to the scheme based on the maternity pay actually received.

I. OTHER RELEVANT PROVISIONS OF THE EQUALITY ACT 2010

The EqA 2010 also contains provisions: **27.93**

(a) which prohibit 'gagging clauses' in contracts of employment which would prevent the employee from disclosing information about their terms and conditions of employment: see s 77 of the EqA 2010. The provision is designed to encourage the exchange of information about pay as between colleagues in the workplace so as to discourage employers from introducing or maintaining discriminatory pay practices;

(b) providing the power for government to introduce Regulations requiring employers who have 250 or more employees to undertake 'pay gap audits': see s 78 of the EqA 2010. On 6 April, 2017, the Equality Act 2010 (Gender Pay Gap Information) Regulations 2017 came into force. Those regulations require the annual publication of certain information in relation to 'gender pay gaps' for 'relevant employers'.

CHECKLIST FOR EQUAL PAY CLAIMS

1 Is the complainant employed under a contract of service or of apprenticeship or a contract personally to execute any work or labour, or a personal or public office holder? If not, the claim for equal pay may not be able to be pursued: see s 64 of the EqA 2010.

2 Does the complainant work wholly outside Great Britain? If so, he may not be able to bring an equal pay claim although it should be noted that the EqA 2010 contains no provisions in relation to its territorial scope and as such it is not clear what approach the courts will take to this issue.

3 Does the claim relate to a contractual term relating to, for example:
(a) pay
(b) bonuses
(c) concessions and benefits in kind
(d) terms in collective agreements
(e) general contractual provisions such as those regarding holidays, sickness benefits, and hours?
If so, it will fall within Chapter 3 of Part 5 of the EqA 2010.

4 Was there a difference in terms and conditions of employment, for example, is there a difference in:
(a) pay
(b) hours of work

Part C The Substantive Law

    (c)   method of allocation of bonuses or size of bonuses

    (d)   incentive payments

    (e)   concessions and benefits in kind such as advantageous loans, mortgage repayment allowances, participation in insurance schemes, or share option schemes

    (f)   provisions in collective agreements, in respect of the above matters, incorporated into the contracts of employment

    (g)   terms relating to holidays, sickness benefits, and other contractual provisions?

    If so, the complainant may have an equal pay claim under Chapter 3 of Part 5 of the EqA 2010.

5 Is there a comparator who is a genuine individual, and not a hypothetical comparator? If there is no actual comparator (other than in maternity cases), an equal pay claim cannot be pursued under Chapter 3 of Part 5 of the EqA 2010. However, a sex discrimination claim might be pursued under Chapter 1 of Part 5 of the EqA 2010: see EqA 2010, s 71.

6 Did the comparator work at the same establishment as the claimant? See EqA 2010, s 79. This is a question of fact, depending upon the following factors

    (a)   the degree of exclusive occupation of the premises

    (b)   the degree of permanence of the arrangements

    (c)   the organization of workers—whether they are organized as part of one group, or in separate and distinct entities

    (d)   how the administration is organized—if there is central administration and the head office runs several sites, such as building sites, those sites are likely to be part of the same establishment. If each site is separately run, such as branches of a chain of shops, each site is likely to be a separate establishment.

    (*Barley v Amey Roadstone Corp Ltd (No 2)* [1977] IRLR 299, in the context of a protective award under TULR(C)A 1992, but applicable here.)

7 If the comparator is not working at the same establishment, is he working at an establishment where broadly similar terms and conditions apply for the relevant class of employee? This must be the case, for example, where a collective agreement applies to both establishments (*Leverton v Clwyd County Council* [1989] ICR 33). If similar terms and conditions apply, the establishments may be owned by associated companies and not only by the employer.

8 Where the differences identified in the pay of workers performing like work or work of equal value cannot be attributed to a single source (even where the employer is the same), the claim does not come within the legislation (or Art 157 of the TFEU) since there is no body which is responsible for the inequality and which could restore equal treatment (*Lawrence v Regent Office Care Ltd* [2000] IRLR 822; *Robertson v Department for Environment, Food and Rural Affairs* [2005] IRLR 363; *Armstrong v Newcastle upon Tyne NHS Hospital Trust* [2006] IRLR 124).

9 Was the comparator engaged upon like work, work rated as equivalent, or work of equal value? As to this, see EqA 2010, s 65.

10 Can the employer show that, even where the two individuals are engaged in like work, or if their work is rated as equivalent under a job evaluation scheme, that where there is a variation between the woman's contract and the man's contract, the variation is genuinely due to a material factor between the two cases, but is a material difference which causes the *whole* of the difference? If so, the employee's claim will fail. If the difference only explains part of the variation, then the employee's claim will succeed as to the unexplained part: see EqA 2010, s 69.

11 If the employer is able to show that a difference in pay can be explained by reference to a material factor, is that factor directly or indirectly discriminatory? See EqA 2010, s 69(1) to (2). Where the application of the factor puts one sex at a particular disadvantage when compared to another, then the employer will be required to justify the factor as being a proportionate means of achieving a legitimate aim.

12 Has the complainant brought a grievance in relation to her claim? If not, the complainant may not be able to bring a claim in the employment tribunal (EA 2002, s 32 and the Employment Act 2002 (Dispute Resolution) Regulations 2004, reg 15). Note that the requirement to raise a grievance will not apply after 6 April 2009 save for in circumstances where the facts giving rise to the claim began before that date and the claim has been commenced or a grievance raised before 4 October 2009.

13 Has the complainant brought the claim in the employment tribunal during employment or within six months of the termination of the contract in relation to which the claim arises in a standard case? See ss 129 to 130 of the EqA 2010. Is the case a concealment case or an incapacity case?

14 If the claim is out of time in the employment tribunal, can it be pursued in the county court, having regard to the limitation period of six years set out in the Limitation Act 1980?

Part C The Substantive Law

28

Unlawful Deductions from Wages

SUMMARY

(1) Deductions by an employer from a worker's wages will be unlawful unless certain statutory requirements are fulfilled.

(2) Wages has a wide meaning and includes any fee, bonus, commission, holiday pay, or other emolument which is payable in connection with the worker's employment.

A. GENERAL PAY OBLIGATIONS

28.01 A worker's entitlement to be paid, when, and how much is generally governed by the contract of employment. Statute intervenes in the following ways:

(a) an employer's right to make certain deductions from salary is circumscribed by statute, mainly ss 13–27 of the ERA 1996 sections (see the remainder of this chapter);

(b) by prescribing a minimum level of pay under the National Minimum Wage Act 1998 (not dealt with in this book);

(c) by not differentiating between men and women as to pay (see Chapters 26 and 27).

B. DEDUCTIONS FROM WAGES

28.02 The provisions contained in ss 13 to 27 of the ERA 1996 apply to the wider category of individuals defined as 'workers' (see para 1 of the checklist below).

28.03 During the course of employment the employer can only make the following deductions from the workers' wages:

(a) Deductions required or authorized by statute such as PAYE and national insurance contributions or a relevant provision of the employee's contract (ERA 1996, s 13(1)(a)).

(b) Any deduction to which the worker has previously signified in writing his agreement or consent prior to it being made (ERA 1996, s 13(1)(b)).

(c) Any payment to a third party to which the employee has consented in writing (ERA 1996, s 14(4)).

(d) Any deductions made within a reasonable time for reimbursement of previous overpayments of wages or expenses (ERA 1996, s 14(1)).

(e) Any deductions made on account of a worker's participation in industrial action (including not only pay but also any damages suffered by the employer as a result of the industrial action) (ERA 1996, s 14(5)).

(f) Any payments the employer is required by statute to make to a public authority following an appropriate determination (ERA 1996, s 14(3)).

(g) Any sums the employer is required to pay pursuant to an attachment of earnings order made by the court (ERA 1996, s 14(6)).

The word 'wages' is very widely defined and includes fees, bonuses, commissions, and holiday pay **28.04** (including statutory holiday pay pursuant to the Working Time Regulations 1998: see *Her Majesty's Revenue and Customs v Stringer* [2009] UKHL 31), statutory sick pay, statutory maternity, paternity, and adoption pay, as well as some more esoteric statutory payments (ERA 1996, s 27(1)), but not (usually) pay in lieu of notice (*Delaney v Staples* [1992] ICR 483).

The EAT and appellate courts have attempted to limit wages claims to straightforward situations **28.05** where an employer is alleged to have paid a sum due on the face of the contract. As such, although bonuses fall within the definition of wages as set out in s 27 of the ERA 1996, a discretionary bonus which had yet to be determined and which, therefore, was not an identifiable sum, would not be recoverable under Part II of the ERA 1996 (*Farrell Matthews & Weir v Hansen* [2005] IRLR 160 and *Adcock v Coors Brewers Ltd* [2007] IRLR 440). Claims in respect of these matters ought properly to be pursued as claims in contract for unliquidated damages either in the employment tribunal or in the civil courts. However, the Court of Appeal has confirmed that an employment tribunal is entitled to construe the express terms of an employment contract to determine whether or not wages are properly payable for the purposes of Part II of the ERA 1996: *Agarwal v. Cardiff University* [2018] EWCA Civ 1434.

Special provisions apply in the retail industry, where, even if the worker has consented in writing **28.06** to deductions being made, deductions in any period to compensate for stock deficiencies or cash shortages (or any payments the employee is required to make as a result of deficiencies or shortages) cannot exceed 10 per cent of the worker's gross wages for the relevant period (ERA 1996, ss 17–22 (not included in this book)).

If the employer wrongfully makes deductions from pay or makes no payment whatsoever, the **28.07** worker may complain to an employment tribunal within three months (subject to any extension of time in relation to which, see para 3.54 ff) of the relevant deduction, or of the last deduction in the series, seeking an order for payment of the sums due (ERA 1996, s 23). A 'series' of deductions is unlikely to exist or continue, however, where there are gaps between the deductions of more than three months: see *Bear Scotland Limited v Fulton* [2015] ICR 221. The worker may also, if he so wishes, bring proceedings in a county court or High Court for damages for breach of contract but cannot recover more than once in respect of any particular deduction.

CHECKLIST FOR UNLAWFUL DEDUCTION CLAIMS

1 Was or is the claimant a worker, ie someone who works under a contract of employment or any other contract, whether express or implied and (if it is express) whether oral or in writing whereby the individual undertakes to perform personally any work or services for another party to the contract whose status is not by virtue of the contract that of a client or customer of any profession or business undertaking carried on by the individual? If so, the individual can bring this claim (ERA 1996, s 230(3), s 13(1)).

2 Was or is the worker working in retail employment? If so, refer to the provisions of ERA 1996, ss 17–22 (not included in this book).

3 Was the deduction made from the wages of the worker, that is, a fee, bonus, commission, holiday pay, or other emolument referable to the employment, whether payable under the contract or not; statutory sick pay; statutory maternity pay; statutory paternity pay; statutory adoption pay; a guarantee payment; any payment for time off for carrying out trade union duties; any remuneration on suspension on medical or maternity grounds; any sums payable in pursuance of an order for reinstatement or re-engagement; any payment made under an order for interim relief leading to the continuation of

the employment; any remuneration under a protective award (ERA 1996, s 27(1))? If it was, consider the question of deductions below.

4   Was the deduction made from payment in lieu of notice owed to the worker? Such a payment probably does not qualify as wages and therefore the claimant will not have a claim (*Delaney v Staples* [1992] ICR 483).

5   Is the sum properly claimable as wages? If the tribunal will be required to construe the employment contract, to imply terms into the contract or to consider whether there has been an appropriate exercise of a contractual discretion, then it is unlikely that the sum can be claimed as wages.

6   Was the payment an advance under an agreement for a loan or an advance of wages; payment in respect of expenses incurred by the employee in carrying out his employment; any payment by way of pension, allowance, or gratuity in connection with the worker's retirement or compensation for loss of office; any payment referable to the worker's redundancy or any payment to the worker otherwise than in his capacity as a worker? Such payments do not qualify as wages and therefore the claimant will not have a claim (ERA 1996, s 27(2)).

7   Was the deduction for tax or national insurance contributions made pursuant to relevant provision of the employee's contract, made with the employee's written consent, as a result of an overpayment of wages, as a result of industrial action, required by statute to be made to a public authority, or required to be made pursuant to an attachment of earnings order? If so, it is probably an allowed deduction and the claimant will not have a claim (ERA 1996, ss 13(1), (14)).

8   Was the claim brought within three months of the relevant deduction or the last in a series of deductions (ERA 1996, s 23(2) and (3))? If a series of deductions is relied upon, are there gaps of more than three months between the deductions so as to prevent a series existing?

9   Has the employer failed to make a payment which the employment tribunal then orders it to make? If so, the employer will be unable to recover the payment from the worker subsequently, even where the employer has the right to recover it (ERA 1996, s 25(4)).

29

Transfer of Undertakings

Part C The Substantive Law

SUMMARY

(1) Employees working in an undertaking which is transferred are entitled to certain protections.
(2) Various changes to TUPE 2006 were implemented by the Collective Redundancies and Transfer of Undertakings (Protection of Employment) (Amendment) Regulations 2014 (2014 TUPE Amendment Regulations). These changes begin to apply from various dates between January 2014 and July 2014.

When an undertaking is transferred by one party to another, the Transfer of Undertakings (Protection **29.01** of Employment) Regulations 2006, SI 2006/246 (TUPE 2006) operate so as to preserve, to a substantial extent, the employee's statutory and contractual employment rights which he had before the transfer. TUPE 2006 implements Council Directive 2001/23/EC, which is commonly referred to as the 'Acquired Rights Directive'. They revoke the Transfer of Undertakings (Protection of Employment) Regulations 1981 (TUPE 1981). Although they are similar to TUPE 1981, they take advantage of certain policy options conferred by the Directive. TUPE 2006 applies to any relevant transfer that takes place on or after 6 April 2006. The government has issued guidance to accompany TUPE 2006: 'Employment Rights on the Transfer of an Undertaking—A Guide to the 2006 TUPE Regulations for Employees, Employers and Representatives' (Government Guidance). Whilst this is not legally binding, it will no doubt be referred to by the courts and employment tribunals.

A. DEFINITION OF 'TRANSFER' AND 'UNDERTAKING'

TUPE 2006 applies to a transfer of an 'undertaking' or business or to a part of an undertaking **29.02** or business situated, prior to the transfer, in the United Kingdom where there is a transfer of an economic entity which retains its identity (TUPE 2006, reg 3(1)(a). As to transfers outside of the UK and outside of the European Union see *Holis Metal Industries v GMB* [2008] IRLR 187). 'Economic' is defined as an organized grouping of resources which has the objective of pursuing an economic activity whether central or ancillary. Under TUPE 1981, an 'undertaking' was not expressly defined, and much case law has been devoted to determining its meaning (*Sanchez Hidalgo v Asociacion de Servicios Aser* [1999] IRLR 136; *Cheeseman v R Brewer Contracts Ltd* [2001] IRLR 144; *ECM (Vehicle Delivery Service) Ltd v Cox* [1999] IRLR 559).

29.03 The test pursuant to TUPE 2006 is likely to be similar to that established by this case law and, indeed, this case law is referred to in the Government Guidance on TUPE 2006. The Government Guidance also states that business transfers covered by TUPE 2006 are those 'where there is an identifiable set of resources (which includes employees) assigned to the business or part of the business which is transferred and that set of resources retains its identity after the transfer'. In relation to the transfer of part of a business:

> the resources do not need to be used exclusively in the transferring part of the business and by no other part. However, where resources are applied in a variable pattern over several parts of a business, then there is less likelihood that a transfer of any individual part of a business would qualify as a business transfer under [TUPE 2006].

A 'transfer' includes a sale, conditional sale, grant, transfer, or assignment of a lease or some other contract, or a transfer by way of gift. A sale of shares and a mere sale of bare assets is unlikely to amount to a transfer of undertaking (*Initial Supplies Ltd v McCall* 1992 SLT 67; *Brookes v Borough Care Services* [1998] IRLR 636, albeit these cases were under TUPE 1981 but confirmed in the Government Guidance. See also the decision of the EAT in *The Print Factory (London) 1991 v Millam* [2007] IRLR 526 and the decision of the High Court in *ICAP Management Services Limited v Berry* [2017] IRLR 811, which indicate that the mere fact of a share sale does not preclude a relevant transfer taking place by other means.) The fact that employees are not taken on does not prevent TUPE applying in certain circumstances (see eg the decision of the Court of Appeal in *RCO Support Services v Unison* [2002] IRLR 401 and *ECM v Cox* [1999] IRLR 559).

29.04 Additionally, TUPE 2006 will apply to a 'service provision change'. This is now expressly set out in TUPE 2006 at reg 3(1)(b). A service provision change is, in effect, an initial outsourcing (TUPE 2006, reg 3(1)(b)(i)), a second round tender (TUPE 2006, reg 3(1)(b)(ii)), and a contracting back in (TUPE 2006, reg 3(1)(b)(iii)), which, prior to that event, is an organized grouping of employees situated in Great Britain which has the principal purpose of carrying out the activities on behalf of the client. A service provision change will not occur where the client intends the activities to be related to a specific event or a task of short-term duration (see *Robert Sage Limited v O'Connell* [2014] IRLR 428; *ICTS UK Limited v Mahdi* [2016] IRLR 113), and the activities must not consist wholly or mainly of the supply of goods for the customer's use (TUPE 2006, reg 3(3)): see *Pannu v Geo W King Limited* [2012] IRLR 193. The Government Guidance makes it clear that there must be an identifiable group of employees providing the service, and gives the example of a courier service which uses different employees each day as an example of where this test would not be satisfied. See also *Eddie Stobart v Moreman* [2012] IRLR 356, in which Underhill J held that in order for there to be an organized grouping of employees, the employer had to deliberately or intentionally arrange for a group of employees to service a particular client. In that case, although a group of employees principally worked for a particular client, that was a matter of happenstance, rather than any deliberate or intentional decision on the part of the employer to organize the grouping in that way. See also *Seawell Limited v Ceva Freight (UK) Limited* [2013] IRLR 726 but note *Mustafa v Trek Highways Services Limited* [2016] IRLR 326, in which the EAT held that there was no requirement for employees to be working immediately before the service provision change in order to amount to an 'organized grouping'. It is also clear that 'service provision' can consist of just one employee: *Rynda (UK) Limited v Rhijnsburger* [2015] IRLR 394. Difficulties can arise where, upon a transfer, there is fragmentation of a service: see *Kimberley Group Housing Limited v Hambley* [2008] IRLR 682 and *Clearsprings Management Limited v Ankers* [2009] All ER (D) 261. Further difficulties can arise in assessing whether or not the activities carried out before and after the putative transfer are fundamentally or essentially the same, so as to engage the service provision change legislation: see *Metropolitan Resources v Churchill Dulwich* [2009] IRLR 700; *Enterprise Management Services Limited v Connect-Up* [2012] IRLR 190; *SNR Denton UK LLP v Kirwan* [2012] IRLR 966 and *Salvation Army Trustee Co v Bahi* [2017] IRLR 410. A service provision change will not occur where the client to which the services are being provided changes: see *Hunter v McCarrick* [2013] IRLR 26 and *SNR Denton UK LLP v Kirwan* [2012] IRLR 966. However, in certain circumstances a service provision change will occur even though there are several 'clients': *Ottimo Property Services Limited v Duncan* [2015] IRLR 806. (The TUPE Amendment Regulations 2014 have amended

TUPE 2006 so as to make it clear, in the context of a service provision change, that the appropriate test is whether or not the activities pre and post transfer 'are fundamentally the same': see reg 3(2A) TUPE 2006.) The multi-factoral test set out in *Cheesman* does not apply when considering whether or not a service provision change has occurred: *Metropolitan Resources v Churchill Dulwich* [2009] IRLR 700.

TUPE 2006 will not apply to a transfer of an administrative function between public administrations or a reorganization of a public administration (TUPE 2006, reg 3(5) and see *Law Society of England & Wales v Secretary of State for Justice* [2010] IRLR 407). However, the Cabinet Office's Statement of Practice 'Staff Transfers in the Public Sector' may apply separate regulations, and give employees similar rights to TUPE 2006. **29.05**

A transfer under TUPE can be effected by a series of two or more transactions (TUPE 2006, reg 3(4)). The actual date of the transfer is determined by when, in fact, the responsibility as employer for carrying on the business or the unit transferred moves from the transferor to the transferee (*Celtec Ltd v Astley* [2005] IRLR 647). **29.06**

Under TUPE 1981, there used to be an exception to the normal rule that when a transfer takes place is where a business is 'hived down' by a receiver or liquidator of a company, who may transfer a viable part of the business to a wholly owned subsidiary in the hope of making that part of the business more saleable to others. This exception no longer applies and this will be a transfer under TUPE 2006, provided the statutory definition is met. **29.07**

B. WHICH EMPLOYEES?

TUPE 2006 only applies to people who are employed, under a contract of employment or apprenticeship (TUPE 2006, reg 2(1)), in the undertaking by the transferor *immediately before* the transfer or would have been so employed, if he had not been dismissed for an automatically unfair reason in accordance with reg 7(1) (TUPE 2006, reg 4(3)), although employees dismissed before the transfer but reinstated on appeal after the transfer will transfer pursuant to TUPE: see *Salmon v Castlebeck Care (Teesdale) Limited* [2015] IRLR 189. Therefore, it is important to look carefully at whether the transferor and the employer are one and the same and to check which part of the business the employees are actually working in. If the employee was employed by another group company rather than the transferor, then the court may not look behind the formal legal position so TUPE 2006 may not apply to this employee (*Michael Peters Ltd v (1) Farnfield, (2) Michael Peters Group plc* [1995] IRLR 190; *Sunley Turriff Holdings Ltd v Stuart Lyle Thomson* [1995] IRLR 184; *Duncan Webb Offset (Maidstone) Ltd v Cooper* [1995] IRLR 633; *The Print Factory (London) 1991 v Millam* [2007] EWCA Civ 322, [2007] ICR 1331 (although these are all cases relating to TUPE 1981)). **29.08**

It is necessary to consider whether the employee works in the undertaking or part of the business that is transferred. Factors under TUPE 1981 which would have shown that he is working in the relevant part of the undertaking are: that his contract of employment specifically assigns him to that part of the business (although this will not be decisive); that he is regarded as part of the human stock or permanent workforce of that business or part of the business, for example, he spends all his time working in that part of the business; that he values his work in that part of the business above his work in other areas; or that the cost of employing him is charged to that part of the business. If these factors are in favour of the employee being employed in the relevant part of the business it will not matter that there is a mobility clause in the contract which in theory allows the transferor to move the employee. Unless the transferor actually exercises his right to move the employee prior to the transfer he will be treated as if employed in the relevant part (Case 186/83 *Botzen v Rotterdamsche Droogdok Maatschappij BV* [1985] ECR 519; *CPL Distribution v Todd* [2003] IRLR 28; *Jakowlew v Nestor Primecare Services Limited* [2015] IRLR 813). Under TUPE 2006, the Government Guidance makes it clear that those who are temporarily assigned to the business will not transfer—and whether someone is temporarily assigned will depend on a number **29.09** of factors, such as the length of time the employee has been there and whether a date has been set for the employee's return or reassignment. The mere fact that an employee has resigned his employment will not mean that his assignment to part of the business is a temporary assignment: *Marcroft v Heartland (Midlands) Limited* [2011] IRLR 599. However, where an employee is absent from work and is permanently unable to return to work, he may not be assigned to a transferring part of the business: see *BRT Managed Services Limited v Edwards* [2015] IRLR 994. The EAT considered that the *Botzen* principles ought to apply in the context of a service provision change: see *Kimberley Group Housing Limited v Hambley* [2008] IRLR 682.

29.10 Further, if the employee expressly informed either the transferor or transferee prior to the transfer that he objects to the transfer (which must mean a refusal to consent to it, at the least) the employee will not transfer; his employment will be deemed to terminate on the transfer of the undertaking, but that termination will usually not be regarded as a dismissal by the transferor (TUPE 2006, reg 4(7) and (8)). The exception to this is where the transfer would involve a substantial and detrimental change to his working conditions when the employee can still be treated as if they have been dismissed (TUPE 2006, reg 4(9)). See para 29.18 in relation to the protection afforded to the employee in these circumstances. Although reg 4(7) only usually operates before the relevant transfer takes place (see, for example, *Capita Health Solutions v McLean* [2008] IRLR 595, where it was held that an agreement that an employee would work for the transferee for a short period did not amount to an objection), where the employees are not made aware of the identity of the transferee prior to the transfer, the employees will be permitted to object to the transfer, so as to prevent the operation of reg 4(1) and (2), even after the transfer has taken place: see *New ISG Limited v Vernon* [2008] IRLR 115.

C. WHAT PROTECTION?

29.11 When an undertaking is transferred, TUPE 2006 provides that any contract of employment of any person employed by the transferor and assigned to the undertaking shall have effect as if originally made between the person so employed and the transferee (TUPE 2006, reg 4(1)). More particularly, the transferee takes over all the transferor's rights, powers, duties, and liabilities under the employment contracts so that after a transfer, any wrongful act committed by the transferor is deemed to have been done by the transferee, and similarly any breach of duty on the part of the employee before a transfer is deemed to have been a breach of duty to the transferee (TUPE 2006, reg 4(2)). The purpose of TUPE is therefore to preserve rights rather than to create new rights: see *Jackson v Computershare Investor Services plc* [2008] IRLR 80.

29.12 The exception to the above is where the transfer to the transferor is subject to:

(a) relevant insolvency proceedings, where the obligation to pay certain amounts due to the employee will not transfer, for example, arrears in pay, statutory redundancy pay, payment in lieu of notice, holiday pay, or the basic award of compensation for unfair dismissal. These sums will instead be met by the Secretary of State through the National Insurance Fund (TUPE 2006, reg 8) provided that the obligation to pay such sums has accrued before the date of the relevant transfer: *Pressure Coolers v Molloy* [2011] IRLR 630. A relevant insolvency procedure is defined at reg 8(6) as insolvency proceedings which have been opened in relation to the transferor, not with a view to the liquidation of the assets of the transferor and are under the supervision of an insolvency practitioner. According to the Government Guidance on TUPE 2006, this is intended to cover any collective insolvency procedures in which the whole or part of the business or undertaking is transferred to another entity as a going concern. It does not cover winding up by either creditors or members where there is no such transfer. The EAT gave guidance as to the definition of 'relevant insolvency proceedings' under TUPE 2006, reg 8 in *Secretary of State for Trade & Industry v Slater* [2007] IRLR 928. It appears, notwithstanding the decision of the EAT in *Oakland v Wellswood (Yorkshire) Limited* [2009] IRLR 250 (EAT), that 'pre pack administrations' will engage reg 8(6) TUPE 2006 such that there will be a 'relevant transfer' and consequent transfer of obligations to a transferee in relation to such employees (other than in relation to those obligations set out above which will be assumed by the Secretary of State and the National Insurance Fund). Regulation 8(7) of TUPE 2006, on the other hand, will not apply to 'pre pack administrations': see *OTG Limited and Others v Barke and Others* [2011] IRLR 247; *Key2Law (Surrey) Ltd v De'Antiquis* [2012] IRLR 212; and *Federatie Nederlandse Vakereniging and Others v Smallsteps BV* [2017] IRLR 852;

(b) bankruptcy proceedings or analogous insolvency proceedings where regs 4 and 7 TUPE 2006 do not apply at all by virtue of reg 8(7). As set out above, in the light of the decision of the EAT in *OTG Limited and Others v Barke and Others* [2011] IRLR 247 and the Court of Appeal in *Key2Law (Surrey) Ltd v De'Antiquis* [2012] IRLR 212, liquidations will fall within the scope of reg 8(7) of TUPE 2006 but 'pre pack administrations' will not.

29.13 All aspects of the employee's contract of employment and rights connected with that contract of employment are transferred save for criminal liability (TUPE 2006, reg 4(6)) and the rights concerning occupational pension schemes. Occupational pension schemes are specifically excluded from any transfer (TUPE 2006, reg 10). An occupational pension scheme is defined by reference to s 1 of the Pension Schemes Act 1993 as a pension scheme established by an employer for employees of a certain description for the purpose of providing benefits to, amongst others, persons of that description. It does not include a personal pension scheme, which is broadly a scheme registered and established in accordance with the Finance Act 2004. It is only those parts of the occupational pension scheme which relate to benefits for old age, invalidity, or survivors which shall be exempted from transfer; all other rights and obligations will transfer (TUPE 2006, reg 10(2) and see *Beckmann v Dynamco Whicheloe Macfarlane* [2002] IRLR 578, *Martin v South Bank University* [2004] IRLR 74; and *Procter & Gamble Co v Svenska Cellulosa Aktiebolaget SCA* [2012] IRLR 733. In the *Procter & Gamble* case, it was held that benefits payable prior to retirement age did transfer pursuant to TUPE 2006 but not those benefits payable after retirement age). TUPE 2006 now makes it clear that an employee will not have a claim as a result of a failure to transfer rights under an occupational pension scheme where that failure comes within reg 10 and took place after 6 April 2006 (TUPE 2006, reg 10(3)). However, where transferred employees were entitled to participate in an occupational pension scheme prior to the transfer, the transferee employer must establish a minimum level of pension provision for the transferred employees, which requires the transferee employer to match employee contributions, up to 6 per cent of salary, into a stakeholder pension or to offer an equivalent alternative (Pensions Act 2004).

29.14 Regulation 4(1) and (2) has the following effect:

(a) If the transferor fails to pay the employee's wages, the employee can sue the transferee to recover the underpayment save where the transfer is subject to relevant insolvency proceedings (see para 29.12).

(b) If the transferor dismissed the employee before the transfer, because of the transfer, and for a reason which was not an economic, technical, or organizational reason entailing changes in the workplace, the employee can claim reinstatement or compensation for unfair dismissal and any other outstanding liabilities from the transferee (TUPE 2006, regs 4(3) and 7(1)) (see also para 29.15).

(c) If the transferor has discriminated against an employee on grounds of sex or race prior to the transfer (even where that discrimination took place when he was employed under a previous contract of employment) liability for that discrimination will transfer to the transferee.

(d) If the transferor was negligent towards the employee prior to the transfer, the employee can claim against the transferee in respect of that negligence and, potentially, under any connected insurance (*Martin v Lancashire County Council; Bernadone v Pall Mall Services Group* [2000] IRLR 487).

(e) If the employee has committed acts of misconduct for which he has or has not been given warnings, or if he has been given warnings for incapability, the transferee may rely upon such misconduct or warnings when considering subsequent stages in any disciplinary procedure affecting that employee.

(f) If the employee's contract of employment contains restrictive covenants, these will transfer, but their scope will be limited to protecting the undertaking transferred; they will not be construed as protecting the rest of the transferee's business as well (*Morris Angel & Son Ltd v Hollande* [1993] IRLR 169).

(g) The employee is generally deemed to have continuous employment so far as his statutory and contractual employment rights are concerned. These will include the right not to be unfairly dismissed, the right to redundancy or statutory maternity payments, and maternity rights.

(h) The rule applies to both express and implied contractual provisions. It also applies to collective agreements (TUPE 2006, reg 5). A customary arrangement or agreed procedure for selection of employees for redundancy would be deemed to be carried over. Until recently, it was unclear whether a transferee could be bound by new collective agreements entered into after the transfer and to which the transferee was not a party so as to require, for example, a transferee to 'track' pay rates according to changes to a national collective agreement to which the transferee is not a party, after the transfer. The ECJ has held in *Parkwood Leisure Limited v Alemo-Herron* [2013] IRLR 744 that a 'dynamic approach' of this kind was precluded by the European directives which underpin TUPE 2006 since those directives not only seek to protect employees but also to strike a fair balance between the interests of employees and transferees (see also *Werhof v Freeway Traffic Systems GmbH* [2006] IRLR 400). By the TUPE Amendment Regulations 2014, the government has amended TUPE 2006 so as to make it clear that *Parkwood Leisure Limited v Alemo-Herron* [2013] IRLR 744 is good law (see TUPE 2006, reg 4A) and to enable transferees to vary terms in collective agreements within one year of the transfer, provided that the variation is no less favourable to the employee than the provisions which previously applied (see TUPE 2006, reg 4(5B)). That is not to say, however, that there is no scope for the dynamic approach, where the parties have contractually bound themselves to such an approach: see *Asklepios Kliniken Langen-Seligenstadt GmbH v Felja* [2017] IRLR 653.

(i) Share options, profit shares, bonus or equivalent schemes transfer, even if on a normal construction the provisions do not easily transfer. However, in that case the employee only has the right to participate in a scheme of 'substantial equivalencies, but one which is free from unjust, absurd or impossible features' (*Unicorn Consultancy Services v Westbrook* [2000] IRLR 80; *MITIE Management Ltd v French* [2002] IRLR 512).

(j) In relation to liability for a protective award in relation to a failure by the transferor to inform and consult, see para 29.29.

29.15 Any employee who has worked for one year for either the transferor or transferee, and whether or not in the undertaking or elsewhere, who is dismissed where the sole or principal reason for the dismissal is the transfer itself, or a reason connected with the transfer which was not an economic, technical, or organizational reason (ETO reason) entailing changes in the work force, is deemed to have been automatically unfairly dismissed (TUPE 2006, reg 7(1)(5)). If, however, the dismissal is not because of the transfer, but for a justifiable reason, such as gross misconduct, it will not be automatically unfair. Dismissals may be because of the transfer even where a potential transferee has not been identified as at the date of the dismissal: see *Spaceright Europe Limited v Baillavoine* [2012] IRLR 111.

29.16 There is a defence to this rule where the dismissal is as a result of an ETO reason entailing changes in the workforce of either the transferor or the transferee (TUPE 2006, reg 7(2)). The reason may apply to a dismissal which takes place either before or after the relevant transfer but the reason must be connected with the conduct or running of the business. Thus, dismissals carried out by the transferor at the insistence of the transferee, or dismissals whose main purpose is to raise the sale price of the business, would not have sufficient economic reason to justify fair termination of employment. For example, where an administrator dismissed employees with the aim of making a business more attractive to a potential purchaser, then this is unlikely to give rise to an ETO reason: see *Spaceright Europe Limited v Baillavoine* [2012] IRLR 111. However, where the aim of the dismissal is to save the business this may qualify for the defence (see *Kavanagh v Crystal Palace FC (2000) Limited* [2014] IRLR 139) but only where, for example, the business was overstaffed, inefficient in terms of sales, and insolvent, and there was no collusion between seller and buyer: see *Thomson v SCS Consulting Ltd* [2001] IRLR 801. In determining the reason for the dismissal in question, the reasoning of the person taking the decision must be analysed. As such, where an administrator took the decision to dismiss employees, it is his reasoning which must be considered: see *Dynamex Friction Limited v Amicus* [2008] IRLR 515. The reason must entail changes in the workforce; that is, a diminution of number of staff or a substantial reorganization: see *Berriman v Delabole Slate Ltd* [1985] IRLR 305 and *The Manchester College v Hazel and Another* [2014] IRLR 392. In assessing whether or not there has been a diminution in the number of staff, regard should only be had to whether or not the number of employees in the relevant workforce has reduced. Regard should not be had to staff employed by contractors or franchisees: see *Meter U Limited v Ackroyd* [2012] IRLR 367. At one time it was unclear whether a change in location of a workforce would amount to an ETO reason. However, the government has amended TUPE 2006 by the TUPE Amendment Regulations 2014 to make it clear that a change in location can amount to an ETO reason (TUPE 2006, reg 7(3A)). Even if a sufficient ETO reason does exist, the employer must still act fairly towards the employee and must follow all the appropriate procedures (TUPE 2006, reg 7(3)(b)).

29.17 Claims for TUPE-related unfair dismissals must be brought within the relevant time limits under the substantive legislation, that is usually within three months of the effective date of termination.

29.18 An employee who has resigned in response to a substantial change in working conditions to their material detriment and whose contract is or would otherwise be transferred in accordance with reg 4(1), will be treated as if he had been dismissed and could bring a claim for unfair dismissal (TUPE 2006, reg 4(9)). This provision was considered by the EAT in *Tapere v South London and Maudsley NHS Trust* [2009] IRLR 972, where it was held that a change in working conditions to the material detriment of an employee was simply a detrimental change which was not immaterial. The provision was also considered in *London Limited v Musse* [2012] IRLR 360, where the EAT noted that a change in 'working conditions' did not necessarily involve a change in contractual conditions. However, where a reg 4(9) dismissal can be established, the dismissal will not necessarily be automatically unfair; it will be for the employee to prove that it is. Also, the employee will not be entitled to any damages in respect of a failure by the employer to pay the employee in respect of a notice period which he has failed to work (TUPE 2006, reg 4(10)). The Government Guidance states that a substantial change in working conditions could be a major relocation of the work place, or the withdrawal of a right to a tenured post. This protection is in addition to the employee's common law right to claim constructive dismissal (TUPE 2006, reg 4(11)).

29.19 An employee also has additional protection under TUPE 2006 where the transferor or, more usually, the transferee varies the terms and conditions of employment of the employee. Any variation of contract where the sole or principal reason is the transfer itself or a reason connected with the transfer that is not an ETO reason entailing changes in the workforce shall be void (TUPE 2006, reg 4(4)). Variations for an ETO reason entailing changes in the workforce or a reason unconnected with the transfer will, however, be valid (TUPE 2006, reg 4(5)). See para 29.15 for a discussion of what constitutes an ETO reason entailing changes in the workforce. Note, however, that the Government Guidance states categorically that a desire to harmonize terms and conditions cannot constitute an ETO reason entailing changes in the workforce. Variations of contract will also be valid where those variations are purely beneficial to the employee(s) who are subject to the relevant transfer: see *Regent Security Services Limited v Power* [2008] IRLR 66.

29.20 Where the employee is employed in an undertaking which, at the time of the transfer, is subject to relevant insolvency proceedings, the protection in relation to variation of the contract of employment is different. Variations to the contract will be valid where they are agreed with appropriate representatives, who are either trade union representatives or, if there are none, elected representatives (TUPE 2006, reg 9(1) and (2)). Where the representatives are not trade union representatives, in addition to agreeing the variation with the appropriate representatives, the employer must obtain agreement in writing, signed by each of the representatives, and, before it is signed, provide all employees to whom it is intended to apply on the date on which it is intended to come into effect with copies of the text of the agreement and such guidance as those employees might reasonably require in order to understand it fully (TUPE 2006, reg 9(5)). For a variation to come within the scope of this additional flexibility, the sole or principal reason for it must be the transfer itself or a reason connected with the transfer which is not an ETO reason entailing changes in the

Part C The Substantive Law

workforce and it must be designed to safeguard employment opportunities by ensuring the survival of the undertakings or business (TUPE 2006, reg 9(7)).

29.21 By the TUPE Amendment Regulations 2014, the government has amended the Trade Union and Labour Relations (Consolidation) Act 1992 so as to provide that collective redundancy consultation which takes place prior to a relevant transfer, counts (in certain circumstances) for the purposes of satisfying ss 188 to 189 of the Trade Union and Labour Relations (Consolidation) Act 1992.

D. TRADE UNIONS

29.22 TUPE 2006 also operates to transfer over any recognition agreement between the transferor and a recognized independent trade union but only where the transferred organized grouping of resources or employees maintains an identity distinct from the remainder of the transferee's undertaking (TUPE 2006, reg 6(1)). See also para 29.14(h) in relation to collective agreements.

E. DUTY TO INFORM AND CONSULT

29.23 Both the transferor and the transferee must notify representatives of employees who may be affected by the impending transfer of certain information and, if measures may be taken which could affect the employees, they also have consultation obligations (TUPE 2006, reg 13). As to the meaning of 'affected employees' see *Unison v Somerset County Council* [2010] IRLR 207 and *I Lab Facilities Limited v Metcalfe* [2013] IRLR 605 (in which it was held that an employee indirectly affected by a relevant transfer would not be an affected employee).

29.24 Representatives for these purposes are, where a trade union is recognized in relation to the employees, representatives of the trade union, or, if not, representatives elected by the employees generally or specifically for the purposes of consultation under TUPE 2006 (TUPE 2006, reg 13(3)). However, by the TUPE Amendment Regulations 2014, the government has amended TUPE 2006 by inserting reg 13A so that micro-businesses (those with fewer than ten employees) can consult directly with affected employees where there are no appropriate representatives in place (in relation to TUPE transfers which take place on or after 31 July 2014).

29.25 If it is necessary to hold elections for the representatives, arrangements for elections must:

(a) be fair
(b) ensure that there are sufficient representatives to represent the interests of all the employees
(c) identify the term for which the employee representatives shall be in office
(d) ensure the candidates are affected employees and that no one is excluded from standing
(e) equally, that all are able to vote
(f) ensure that the election is conducted so as to secure that so far as reasonably practicable those voting do so in secret and the votes given are accurately counted (TUPE 2006, reg 14(1)).

29.26 The transferor must inform the employee representatives of the following matters:

(a) The fact that the transfer is to take place.
(b) The approximate date for the proposed transfer.
(c) The reason for the proposed transfer.
(d) The legal, economic, and social implications of the transfer for the affected employees.
(e) Any measure which it is envisaged the transferor or the transferee will take as a result of the transfer or, if no such measures will be taken, that fact. 'Measure' means an action which the transferor or transferee has a present plan to implement, and does not include a vague idea for the future (TUPE 2006, reg 13(2); *Institution of Professional Civil Servants v Secretary of State for Defence* [1987] IRLR 373).

However, the transferor cannot be required by reg 13(2) of TUPE 2006 to give a warranty as to the accuracy of the information given to the employee representatives or recognized trade union. Provided the transferor provides information which it genuinely considers to be accurate and the transferor's view as to the legal implications of the transfer is a considered view, then the transferor will not have fallen foul of the requirements of reg 13(2) of TUPE 2006: see *Royal Mail Group v Communications Workers Union* [2009] IRLR 1046. In the light of the decisions of the EAT in *Cable Realisations Limited v GMB Northern* [2010] IRLR 42 and *Todd v Strain* [2011] IRLR 11, the obligation to inform pursuant to reg 13(2) arises even where no measures are envisaged for the purposes of reg 13(6). In *Cable Realisations Limited v GMB Northern*, the EAT explained that one such purpose for the obligation to inform arising pursuant to reg 13(2), even where no measures were envisaged which would engage the obligation to consult under reg 13(6) was that the parties may wish to engage in voluntary consultation as to other matters. Further, it was pointed out by the EAT in *Todd v Strain* that any other construction would give rise to an absurdity because where no measures were envisaged for the purposes of reg 13(6), the transferor would not even be under an obligation to inform employee representatives of the fact and date of any proposed transfer.

29.27 If measures are to be taken by either the transferor or the transferee which may affect the employee, the employer must consult with the employee representatives of his employees and consider the views expressed by the employee representatives with a view to seeking the representatives' agreement to them, before reaching a final decision to implement those measures (TUPE 2006, reg 13(6)). For this purpose, where the transferee intends to take measures that will affect transferring staff, he is obliged to give information in relation to such measures to the transferor so that the transferor can inform his employees and consult with his employees (TUPE 2006, reg 13(4)). The employer must discuss those measures with the representatives with an open mind and make every effort to secure the representatives' agreement to what is proposed and to accommodate their objections. The employer must consider any representations, reply to them, and, if they are to be rejected, state the reasons for doing so.

29.28 If the transferor fails to inform the representatives of the material facts, or if the representatives are not consulted about any measures which may be taken, the representatives may within three months of the transfer bring a complaint in an employment tribunal for a declaration and appropriate compensation for the failure to consult. The maximum award is thirteen weeks' pay for each of the affected employees. The award is intended to be punitive rather than compensatory and the statutory maximum in respect of 'a week's pay' set out in s 227 of the ERA 1996 does not apply: see *Sweetin v Coral Racing* [2006] IRLR 252 and *Zaman v Kozee Sleep Products Limited t/a Dorlux Beds UK* [2011] IRLR 196. An award for failure to comply with the duty to inform and consult can be made against either the transferor, or the transferee. Where an award is made against the transferor, if, after being given notice, the transferee failed to provide information on time regarding any measures it proposed to take as a result of the transfer, or failed to consult about such measures, the transferee may also be liable (TUPE 2006, regs 15 and 16). However, there can be no obligation on the transferee to consult after the transfer: see *UCATT v Amicus* [2009] ICR 852.

29.29 A claim for failure to inform and consult under regs 15 and 16 can only be pursued by an employee himself, where there are no employee representatives or a recognized trade union within the meaning of reg 13(3) TUPE 2006. Otherwise, the claim must be pursued by those employee representatives or recognized trade union: see *Nationwide Building Society v Benn* [2010] IRLR 922.

29.30 The regulations expressly provide that the transferee and the transferor will be jointly liable for a failure to inform and consult. The transferee will be liable for its failure and will also be jointly and severally liable with the transferor for any failure by it (TUPE 2006, reg 15(7) to (9)). However, claims can only be pursued by transferring employees against the transferor employer (and not the transferee employer): see *Allen v Morrisons Facilities Services Limited* [2014] IRLR 514, where the claim related to the transferee's failure to comply with its reg 13(2)(d) of the TUPE 2006 duty. The transferor employer can then join the transferee to proceedings pursuant to reg 15(5) of TUPE 2006.

Part C The Substantive Law

F. DISCLOSURE OF 'EMPLOYEE LIABILITY INFORMATION'

29.31 TUPE 2006 introduces new obligations on the transferor to produce certain information to the transferee within certain specified timeframes (TUPE 2006, regs 11 and 12).

29.32 The obligation is in respect of any person employed by the transferor who is assigned to the organized grouping of resources or employees that is the subject of the transfer (TUPE 2006, reg 11(1)). The information must be notified in writing or some other readily accessible form. The information which must be provided is:

(a) the identity and age of the employee
(b) the statutory particulars of employment
(c) any information in relation to a disciplinary or grievance procedure which would come within the terms of the statutory dispute resolution procedures within the previous two years
(d) information about any actual or pending court or tribunal case within the last two years
(e) information about any collective agreement (TUPE 2006, reg 11(2)).

29.33 It was the law that the employee liability information had to be up-to-date (it had to date from no more than fourteen days before the date on which it was provided) and had to be notified no more than fourteen days before the transfer (TUPE 2006, reg 11(3) and (6)). However, TUPE 2006 has been amended by the TUPE Amendment Regulations 2014 so that the information must be provided 28 days before the transfer for TUPE transfers which take place after 1 May 2014: see TUPE 2006, reg 11(6).

29.34 If the transferor fails to provide the information in accordance with reg 11, the transferee may present a complaint to the employment tribunal within three months of the relevant transfer. The employment tribunal may make a declaration and award compensation (TUPE 2006, reg 12(1), (2), and (3)). The minimum award to be made by the employment tribunal shall be £500 per employee. Otherwise, the compensation should take into account the loss suffered by the transferee and the terms of any contract between the transferor and the transferee (TUPE 2006, reg 12(4) and (5)).

CHECKLIST FOR TUPE-RELATED CLAIMS

The checklist below is relevant to any claims (unfair dismissal, unlawful deduction, contractual claim, discrimination) where additional protection afforded by TUPE 2006 may be applicable.

Qualifying employee?

1 Is the relevant individual employed under a contract of service or of apprenticeship? If not, for example where the individual is a worker or otherwise employed under a contract for services or a partner in a partnership, TUPE 2006 will not apply (TUPE 2006, reg 2(1)).

2 Was the employee employed by the transferor or some other entity, for example, another company in the same group? If employed by another company in the group, TUPE 2006 may not apply (see para 29.08).

3 Was the employee temporarily assigned to the organized grouping of resources which was transferred? If yes, TUPE 2006 may not apply to him (see para 29.09).

4 Was the employee employed by the transferor in the undertaking immediately before the relevant transfer took place (ie before serious negotiations began between the parties leading to the transfer)? Subject to the next paragraph, unless they were, TUPE 2006 will not apply (TUPE 2006, reg 4(1)).

5 Was the employee dismissed prior to the transfer, because of the transfer or for a reason connected with the transfer which was not an economic, technical, or organizational reason? If so, TUPE 2006 will apply and liability for the individual's contract of employment will, nonetheless, be deemed to be transferred to the transferee of the business (TUPE 2006, reg 4(3)).

6   Was the employee dismissed prior to the transfer for some reason unconnected with the transfer, whether or not that reason is ultimately valid, such as misconduct? If so, TUPE 2006 will not apply and the employee's only remedy is against the transferor (TUPE 2006, reg 4(3)).

7   Did the employee carry on working for the transferor after the transfer? If so, even if the employee expressly agrees with the transferor that he would continue to work for the transferor, this will not necessarily preclude him from claiming that TUPE 2006 applies and that, in fact, their employment has or should have been transferred to the transferee (TUPE 2006, reg 18).

Qualifying undertaking?

1   1 Is the undertaking:

(a)   in the United Kingdom prior to the transfer? If not, TUPE 2006 will not apply (TUPE 2006, reg 3(1))

(b)   a transfer of shares in a company so that the only change is the identity of the shareholders and not the identity of the employing company? If so, TUPE 2006 will probably not apply, even where the share sale route is adopted to avoid the application of TUPE 2006

(c)   a transfer of assets only? For example, the sale of a building, where all the employees of the seller continue to work for the seller in a different building. If so, TUPE will not apply (TUPE 2006, reg 3(2))

(d)   a non-commercial entity, for example, a non-profit-making body? Even if it is, TUPE 2006 will still apply

(e)   a transfer of administrative functions between public administrators or a reorganization of a public administration? If so, TUPE 2006 will not apply (TUPE 2006, reg 3(5) and see *Law Society of England and Wales v Secretary of State for Justice* [2010] IRLR 407) but other similar provisions may apply

(f)   an organized grouping of resources which has the objective of pursuing an economic activity, whether or not that activity is central or ancillary, which is sufficiently structured to amount to an undertaking and so that an undertaking has actually transferred to the putative transferee? If it is, TUPE 2006 will apply.

2   Some or all of the following factors have to be proven before the test set out at para 1(f) above will be satisfied. It is necessary to consider all the factors characterizing the transaction in question, but each is a single factor and none is to be considered in isolation.

(a)   Do the parties believe that TUPE 2006 applies?

(b)   Do tangible assets, such as buildings or movable property, transfer? (TUPE 2006, reg 3(6)(b)).

(c)   Do intangible assets, such as copyright, goodwill, customers, operational resources, etc transfer? (TUPE 2006, reg 3(6)(b)).

(d)   Are the majority of employees taken over by the new employer (or would they be if the transferee was not avoiding the obligations under TUPE 2006)?

(e)   Are the activities organized and carried on in a similar way before and after the transfer?

(f)   Is there any suspension of the business or activities?

(g)   Is the transfer effected by a series of two or more transactions? No matter, TUPE 2006 can still apply (TUPE 2006, reg 3(6)(a)).

(h)   Do any assets transfer, or is it only people? No matter, TUPE 2006 will still apply if the undertaking is labour intensive, retains its identity, and satisfies other of the criteria (TUPE 2006, reg 3(6)(b)).

3   Is the transfer a service provision change, that is an outsourcing, insourcing, or retender? If so, TUPE 2006 may apply, subject to the following points (TUPE 2006, reg 3(1)(b)):

(a)   Does the service provision change involve an organized grouping of employees situated in Great Britain with its principal purpose of carrying out the activities on behalf of the client? If so, TUPE 2006 may apply (TUPE 2006, reg 3(3)(a)(i)).

(b)   Is the service provision intended to be in connection with a specific event or a task of short duration? If so, TUPE 2006 will not apply (TUPE 2006, reg 3(3)(a)(ii)).

(c)   Is the service provision wholly or mainly concerned with the supply of goods for the client's use? If so, TUPE 2006 will not apply (TUPE 2006, reg 3(3)(b)).

(d)   Does the service provision change involve a change in activities and/or fragmentation of activities. If so, TUPE 2006 may not apply.

Qualifying claim?

4   Does the claim relate to one of the following (on a non-exhaustive basis), which occurred before the transfer, with regard to:

    (a) a failure to pay wages?

    (b) a dismissal because of or for a reason connected with the transfer?

    (c) discrimination which occurred before transfer?

    (d) negligence by the employer against the employee?

    (e) the employee's continuity of employment?

    (f) share option, profit shares, bonus, or equivalent shares?

    (g) if the other components of TUPE 2006 have been met, the transferee will be liable for the payment and/or will have to maintain the same terms as with the transferor save where the transfer is subject to relevant insolvency proceedings, where the obligation to pay certain payments will not transfer.

5   Does the claim relate to a matter which does not transfer, such as old age pension benefits and/or a claim which is unconnected with the contract of employment? If so, TUPE 2006 is unlikely to apply.

30

Contractual Employment Issues

SUMMARY

(1) Contract forms the basis of the employment relationship. Claims may arise out of that contractual relationship.

(2) Employees may bring claims for unpaid remuneration under their contracts of employment. Claims may be brought for breach of contract based upon the implied duty of mutual trust and confidence but these cannot include claims in respect of the manner of an employee's dismissal.

(3) Employers may bring claims based upon the express and implied duties of the contract of employment. Aside from claims for damages, such breaches may form the basis for claims for injunctive relief against a former employee.

(4) Breach of contract claims may arise on the termination of employment in circumstances where either the employer or the employee has wrongfully purported to terminate the contract summarily on the basis of an alleged repudiatory breach of contract by the other party.

(5) It is clear that both an employer and an employee may decline to accept the repudiatory breach of the other and elect to keep the contract alive for the period of notice. Neither party will be able to compel either the giving of or the performance of work.

(6) The employee may be subject to post-termination restraints. These may include restraints in respect of the employer's confidential information extending beyond an employer's trade secrets. Such restraints are in restraint of trade and will be void and unenforceable unless they are no more onerous than is reasonably necessary to protect the employer's legitimate protectable interests.

A. INTRODUCTION

Employment disputes outside the forum of the employment tribunal typically derive from the contract of employment itself. Some claims will be within the jurisdiction of the employment tribunal: see Chapter 8 and Chapter 20 at paras 20.10 ff. Employment law protection is conventionally built upon the form of the contractual relationship between the contracting parties. Employee   **30.01** rights attach to contracts of service, whereas certain rights that are afforded to workers will attach additionally to certain contractual relationships beyond a contract of service. Whatever the form of the contractual relationship, certain contractual rights will be actionable in the civil courts. The employment tribunal has a limited jurisdiction for employees to bring breach of contract claims, capped at a maximum award of £25,000.

30.02 Actions based upon the contract of employment before the civil courts typically fall into four broad categories:

(a) Employee claims arising out of the course of the employment relationship, for example claims for unpaid wages or bonus. Such claims include claims for personal injury, embracing claims for harassment and stress. Such claims are, however, outside the scope of this book.

(b) Employer claims brought in respect of the employee's breach of the terms of their employment during the course of the employment.

(c) Actions for breach of contract arising out of the termination or the threatened termination of the employment relationship.

(d) Claims in relation to the breach of post-termination restrictions, normally including claims for injunctive relief.

B. UNPAID WAGES AND REMUNERATION

30.03 In the most straightforward case, an employee may bring a claim for unpaid remuneration before the civil courts. In the case of wages or defined commission, this may be an action in debt for the unpaid amounts. Such claims are more typically brought as unlawful deduction from wages claims before the employment tribunal, see Chapter 28. The failure to pay the defined amount is also a breach of contract and the claim may be framed as a breach of contract.

30.04 It is now clear that equal pay claims may also be brought in the civil courts, relying on the implied contractual equality clause, so that the claim becomes one for a declaration and the consequent payment of unpaid salary and interest. The practical advantage of such claims is that they may rely on the longer contractual limitation period of six years rather than the six-month limitation period in the employment tribunal (*Birmingham City Council v Abdulla and Others* [2012] UKSC 47).

30.05 Claims may also be brought for remuneration which is not expressly defined under the contract of employment. These are typically claims for discretionary remuneration in the form of bonus. The starting point for such claims will be the contract itself, the terms of which may provide for the method of calculation of bonus, or may contain provisions narrowing or widening the scope of the discretion. Even in the absence of such provisions, when the discretion appears absolute, it will be subject to the implied duty of mutual trust and confidence. Thus the exercise of the discretion in bad faith or where there has been a capricious exercise of the discretion, will be a breach of the implied term of mutual trust and confidence (*Commerzbank A G v Keen* [2006] EWCA Civ 1536, [2007] IRLR 132). The Supreme Court in *Braganza v BP Shipping Ltd* [2015] UKSC 17, [2015] ICR 449 concluded that and employer had acted in breach in reaching a decision on whether a death in service benefit should be paid without cogent evidence to support the decision.

30.06 There is an implied duty of trust and confidence, which is implied within the contract of employment, that the employer will not without reasonable and proper cause conduct itself in a manner calculated and likely to destroy or seriously damage the relationship of confidence and trust between employer and employee (*Malik v Bank of Credit and Commerce International SA* [1997] IRLR 462, [1997] 3 All ER 1). This may form the basis of claims arising out of the employment relationship. However, with the exception of claims for unpaid notice pay, the common law has been limited in its development so that there is no general basis for actionable losses arising out of dismissal (*Johnson v Unisys Ltd* [2001] IRLR 279, [2001] ICR 480, HL) and any remedies for the unfairness of a decision to dismiss must rest within the parameters set by the statutory scheme of protection. This is sometimes referred to as the *Johnson v Unisys* 'exclusion zone'. Where there are breaches of contract arising out of the employee's treatment but they do not amount to dismissal then claims for breach of contract may still be brought, for example in the case of breach of a contractual disciplinary policy falling short of dismissal itself (*Eastwood v Magnox Electric plc* and *McCabe v Cornwall County Council* [2004] UKHL 35, [2004] ICR 1064, [2004] IRLR 733). The precise boundary between actionable claims for breach of contract and the *Johnson v Unisys* 'exclusion zone' remains one which is open to argument and was not clarified with certainty by the Supreme Court in *Edwards v Chesterfield Royal Hospital NHS Foundation Trust* [2011] UKSC 58, [2012] IRLR 129, [2012] ICR 201.

C. CLAIMS BY EMPLOYERS ARISING OUT OF THE COURSE OF EMPLOYMENT

These claims do not normally arise during the continuity of the employment relationship but typically arise when the employment relationship is ending or has ended. Here the employer may claim that the employee has previously acted in breach of the contractual duties of their employment. **30.07**

During the course of employment the employee, even absent express contractual provision, is subject to an implied term of their contract of employment that they will well and faithfully serve their employer, the implied duty of fidelity. The contract of employment may expressly articulate that duty and amplify it. Even negligence on the part of the employee, of sufficiently serious, may be a breach justifying summary dismissal, see *Adesokan v Sainsbury's Supermarkets Ltd* [2017] ICR 590. **30.08**

In the case of more senior employees, the duties of their employment may, by reason of the contract obligations of their employment, be subject to more onerous fiduciary duties which require them to act in the best interests of the employer, even placing the employer's interests above their own; see *Ranson v Customer Systems Ltd* [2012] IRLR 769, CA. These may require the employee to disclose his or her own wrongdoing, as well as that of the employee's colleagues. Senior employees who pursuant to their employment hold statutory director roles will additionally be subject to the duties imposed upon directors by the Companies Act 2006. **30.09**

The contract will normally provide for express contractual obligations in relation to the employer's confidential information. As explained further below, these typically extend both during and after the employment relationship. **30.10**

Arguments about whether the employee was in breach of these obligations may arise where the employer is seeking to defend a claim for constructive or wrongful dismissal where it is asserted that earlier, latterly discovered, conduct on the part of the employee would have justified summary dismissal (*Boston Deep Sea Fishing and Ice Co Ltd v Ansell* (1888) 39 ChD 339). **30.11**

Occasionally, it may be that the employer asserts that the breach of the contract has given the employee, or the employee's new employer, an unfair 'head start' in the operation of a competing business, for example where a current employee recruits among colleagues for a new employer, or uses confidential information for the purposes of competition. Here, the employer may seek a form of injunction known as a 'springboard' injunction to restrain the employee, and potentially the new employer, from operating the competing business to nullify the unfair head start (*QBE Management Services Ltd v Dymoke* [2012] EWHC 80, [2012] IRLR 458). **30.12**

D. CLAIMS ARISING OUT OF THE TERMINATION OF EMPLOYMENT

Claims by employees

Where an employee's contract has been terminated without the required notice, whether the notice period expressly provided in the contract or that implied by the ERA, an action will lie for damages for wrongful dismissal. Such damages fall to be calculated on the basis of the net earnings of the employee for the notice period, net, that is, of tax and national insurance (*British Transport* **30.13**

Commission v Gourley [1956] AC 185, [1955] 3 All ER 796). The employee's claims are conventionally limited to the notice period, that being the period over which the employer could have lawfully terminated the contract, and damages are therefore assessed on the basis of the remuneration which would have been received had the employer lawfully terminated the contract: see *Lavarack v Woods of Colchester Ltd* [1967] 1 QB 278, [1966] 3 All ER 683, CA. See further paras 24.03–24.04.

30.14 In conventional contractual analysis, such a breach of contractual election would entitle the innocent party to have the right to elect to accept the breach, discharging further performance of the contract (this would crystallize a claim for damages), or the innocent party may choose to affirm the contract, seeking to keep it alive. There had been an argument that the personal nature of employment contracts meant than an employee, oddly not an employer, was forced to accept the termination of the contract. In *Geys v Société Générale* [2012] UKSC 63, [2012] IRLR 122, the Supreme Court held that the concept of 'automatic' termination did not apply to contracts of employment and that, as with other contracts, the innocent party was entitled to make an election. Thus, faced with a wrongful repudiatory breach of their contract, the innocent employee could elect to keep the contract alive and bring a claim for salary as it fell due. The employer would thus be unable to bring the employment relationship to an end until it had terminated the contract in accordance with its provisions. In the case of *Geys*, this was by way of a payment in lieu of notice (PILON) under the contract, which had the effect of lawfully terminating the contract, although not until the employer had met the contractual conditions for its payment and communicated this to the employee. From the employee's perspective, not accepting the breach but electing to keep the contract alive will mean that the duty to mitigate does not arise and, as in *Geys*, the employee may be entitled to continue to receive benefits which are reliant on the continuation of the employment relationship.

30.15 Whilst an employee may elect to keep the contract alive faced with a repudiatory breach on the part of the employer, an employee is not able to seek an injunction from the civil courts to compel the employer to provide work or to permit the employee to perform his employment. This reflects the long-standing principle that the courts will not enforce by order of specific performance a contract for personal performance. Despite that approach, a body of jurisprudence has built around the enforcement of contractual disciplinary procedures with the granting of injunctions to compel compliance with procedures, even to the extent of requiring suspensions to be lifted. This has particularly evolved in the field of medical practitioners who are subject to contractual disciplinary procedures (see eg *Mezey v South West London & St George's Mental Health NHS Trust* [2010] EWCA Civ 293, [2010] IRLR 512). The grant of such injunctions is not, however, limited to medical practitioners; see by way of example *Lew v Board of Trustees of United Synagogue* [2011] EWHC 1265 (QB), [2011] IRLR 664, but threatened or continuing breach of contract is necessary.

Claims by employers

30.16 The reverse position for the employer is that of the employee who, in repudiatory breach of contract, purports to leave without the required notice to terminate his contract of employment or otherwise acts in breach of the duties of his contract. Here, it is the employer who may choose between electing to accept the employee's breach, with the consequent immediate termination of the contract, or asserting that the contract remains alive. Whilst the employer also cannot compel specific performance of the contract, so that the employee is compelled to work for the employer, it may be able to obtain an injunction to restrain the employee from entering into employment with another person for the period over which lawful notice should have been given to terminate the contract (*Evening Standard Co Ltd v Henderson* [1987] IRLR 64, [1987] ICR 588, CA). The price for the employer is the requirement that it continues to make the payments and confer the benefits under the contract for the duration of the notice period. To deprive the employee of such benefits would itself be a breach and would further impermissibly force the employee to return to his duties, which is not permitted because this would be indirectly ordering specific performance of the contract of service.

The employee may choose to return to work for the duration of his notice period but it is more **30.17** likely that the employer will have invoked a contractual power to place the employee on 'garden leave'. It may not always be necessary for there to be an express power to place the employee on 'garden leave' as there may be no 'right to work' under the contract (*William Hill Organisation Ltd v Tucker* [1998] IRLR 313, CA). The conduct of an employee threatening to act in breach of their obligations may also give rise to an implied right to place the employee on 'garden leave' (*Standard Life Health Care Ltd v Gorman* [2010] IRLR 233, CA), but typically such a power is expressly included within the contract of employment. Where an employer seeks to enforce such a term so that the employee is removed from the pursuit of the economic activity of their employment, and this may be done where the employee has lawfully given notice, the doctrine of restraint of trade will be engaged and a court may decline to grant an injunction for all or part of the period of 'garden leave'. This is considered below.

Constructive dismissal or summary dismissal

This analysis assumes that the argument is simply whether or not the appropriate notice has been **30.18** given or PILON has been made to terminate the contract. There may be an argument about whether the contract has been terminated by one party's conduct, which is accepted by the other as a repudiatory breach of contract. In the case of acceptance by an employee, this would be a constructive dismissal. In the case of such repudiatory conduct by an employee, the employer would be entitled to terminate the employment without notice. This is a summary dismissal.

In the case of constructive dismissal, the employee might point to breach of a specific term, such **30.19** as the failure to pay wages, as amounting to a repudiatory breach. The employee relies on the employer's conduct, either from a single event or a succession of events, as giving rise to a breach of the implied contractual duty on the employer that it will not without reasonable and proper cause conduct itself in a manner calculated and likely to destroy or seriously damage the relationship of confidence and trust between employer and employee (*Malik v Bank of Credit and Commerce International SA* [1997] IRLR 462, [1997] 3 All ER 1).

The present decided authority is that such a breach on the part of the employer discharges the **30.20** employee from the continuing obligations of their contract of employment, including any post-employment obligations to which they would otherwise be subject (*General Billposting Co Ltd v Atkinson* [1909] AC 118, HL). It is therefore not uncommon for there to be an issue within proceedings for injunctive relief to enforce such obligations as to whether the employee had been entitled to treat themselves as being constructively dismissed. It should be noted that this principle is not the same as that which is applied in cases of breach of contract other than of employment (*Photo Production Ltd v Securicor Transport Ltd* [1980] AC 827). In *Rock Refrigeration Ltd v Jones* [1997] 1 All ER 1, [1996] IRLR 675, CA, some *dicta* of the Court of Appeal suggested that *General Billposting* might be apt for review, but for the present it remains the settled law.

E. POST-TERMINATION RESTRAINTS

One specific area of contractual disputes is that of post termination restraints. These are provisions **30.21** within the contract of employment, occasionally in separate agreements, which seek to restrain an employee after the end of the employment relationship. These clauses may be the subject of a claim for breach of contract and damages. However, they are frequently the subject of actions for injunctive relief to restrain the threatened or continuing breach of the term. Actions before the court normally include applications for interim injunctions to preserve the position until a trial of the claim. It is common for the courts to order an expedited trial process for the hearing of such claims so that the issues can be resolved before the expiry of the period of the restraint.

Part C The Substantive Law

30.22 Post-termination restraints may take a variety of forms but can conveniently be grouped into three categories:

(a) Clauses which seek to restrain the employee from competitive activities. These may restrain the employee from soliciting or dealing with the clients or suppliers of the former employer for a period of time. Sometimes such clauses may seek to restrain the employee from being employed in a competitive business for a period of time.

(b) Clauses which restrain the employee from disclosing or using information which was confidential to the former employer.

(c) Clauses which restrain the former employee from inducing their former colleagues to leave the employer and occasionally from employing such former colleagues.

30.23 All of these clauses impose a restraint on the activities of an employee after the end of the employment relationship. Putting to one side for the moment the position of confidential information, the other restraints are subject to the common law doctrine of restraint of trade (*Office Angels Ltd v Rainer-Thomas* [1991] IRLR 215). This doctrine reflects the public interest in ensuring the economic freedom for persons to exercise their skill and calling. Under the doctrine, restraints are void and unenforceable, even though they form part of the contract, unless they are no wider than reasonably necessary to protect the employer's legitimate interests. The principles were conveniently summarized in *TFS Derivatives Limited v Morgan* [2005] IRLR 246:

> In assessing reasonableness, there is essentially a three-stage process to be undertaken. Firstly, the court must decide what the covenant means when properly construed. Secondly, the court will consider whether the former employers have shown on the evidence that they have legitimate business interests requiring protection in relation to the employee's employment. In this case, it will be seen later on, the defendant concedes that TFS have demonstrated on the evidence legitimate business interests to protect in respect of its customer connection, confidential information and the integrity or stability of the workforce, although the extent of the confidential information is in dispute in relation to its shelf life and/or the extent to which it is either memorable or portable. Thirdly, once the existence of legitimate protectable interests has been established, the covenant must be shown to be no wider than is reasonably necessary for the protection of those interests. Reasonable necessity is to be assessed from the perspective of reasonable persons in the position of the parties as at the date of the contract, having regard to the contractual provisions as a whole and to the factual matrix to which the contract would then realistically have been expected to apply.

30.24 The burden then rests upon the employer to show that there is a protectable interest and that the restriction is no more onerous than is reasonably necessary to protect the particular interest. It will be noted that whether or not a clause is justified will be determined at the point at which the contract was entered into. Even if subsequent events mean that the covenant may be reasonable at the date of enforcement (for example, if the employee is promoted into a more sensitive role), the covenant will be void if it was unenforceable at the date of the contract (*Patsystems v Neilly* [2012] IRLR 979, QB). Enforceability at the date of the contract does not guarantee enforcement by the court at the point of alleged breach; it will additionally be necessary for the employer to show that it has legitimate protectable interests at the date of enforcement.

30.25 The commonly recognized forms of protectable interest are (1) trade connections, in the form of customer and supplier connections, (2) the integrity of the workforce, although this is limited to senior employees, and (3) confidential information. It will be noted that typically the confidentiality of an employer's information is subject to specific provision under the contract of employment but it is recognized that the difficulties of enforcement may lead to the preservation of the confidentiality of the information justifying post-termination restraints, even constraints restraining involvement in competitive activities.

30.26 In each case, it will fall to the former employer to establish the existence of the legitimate protectable interest in its business and that the former employee could interfere with those protectable interests by unfairly exploiting an advantage they have acquired in the course of their employment. For example, in the case of restrictions in respect of the solicitation of customers, the former employee must have dealt with those customers or have knowledge of confidential information which applied to them which they could unfairly misuse. In the case of former colleagues, it is necessary for the employee to have known the individuals or to have access again to confidential information which would enable them to unfairly seek to persuade them to leave the employer. In each case, a post-termination restraint that simply seeks to restrain a former employee from competition, which does not involve the unfair exploitation of an advantage which the employee has derived from his employment, will be void.

As noted from the passage in *TFS Derivatives*, even if a clause legitimately seeks to protect a legit- **30.27** imate protectable interest by restraining a former employee from unfairly exploiting an advantage they acquired in the course of their employment, the restraint must still meet the reasonableness test. The clause must do no more than is adequate to protect the particular interest. In particular, the court will closely examine the length of the restriction and whether it is longer than is neces- sary to protect the employer's legitimate interests. In this regard it is rare for covenants in excess of twelve months to be enforceable and, in many cases, only shorter periods are justifiable.

In construing the contract, the court will seek to give effect to the intention of the parties and that **30.28** will lean the court to an interpretation which renders the clause enforceable in the case of ambi- guity (*Turner v Commonwealth and British Minerals Ltd* [2000] IRLR 114, CA). The court will not, however, strain the construction of a clause or rewrite a clause to make it enforceable. Thus, in *Prophet PLC v Huggett* [2014] EWCA Civ 1013, the Court of Appeal declined to adopt a pur- posive approach to the construction of a clause so as to cure the literal meaning, which rendered the clause ineffective. It is possible for parts of a covenant to be declared void with the remainder remaining intact but only if the offending promise can be identified as a separate promise (*Mason v Provident Clothing and Supply Co Ltd* [1913] AC 724, HL). At the time of writing *Mason* has been reviewed by the Supreme Court in an appeal in the case of *Egon Zenhnder Ltd v Tillman* [2018] ICR 881, Judgment is awaited.

Confidentiality obligations merit separate treatment. Restrictions on the disclosure of the employer's **30.29** information following the termination of employment are also a form of post-termination re- straint. Even absent such contractual restraints, certain forms of information will be subject to ob- ligations in equity. In particular, confidential information that is so confidential that it can properly be described as a trade secret may not be used or disclosed by a former employee (*Faccenda Chicken Ltd v Fowler* [1986] IRLR 69, [1986] ICR 297). The information which may properly be described as trade secrets is very narrow and typically the employer will seek to define under the contract of employment further classes of information to which duties of confidentiality will attach. There are limits to the scope of such restrictions. In particular, imposing restraints on employees' use of information to the extent of restraining the exploitation of their skill and experience, rather than the misuse of specific information, will again be in restraint of trade. Indeed, the suggestion in the Court of Appeal in *Caterpillar Logistics Services Ltd v de Crean* [2012] IRLR 410, CA is that, broad confidentiality obligations being subject to the doctrine of restraint of trade, confidential information falling short of trade secrets should be protected by suitably worked post-termination restraints on competitive activity. In particular, knowledge of confidential information, particularly on the part of senior employees, may justify restraining the employee from engaging in any com- petitive activity at all for a period of time (*Thomas v Farr plc* [2007] EWCA Civ 118, [2007] IRLR 419, [2007] ICR 932, CA).

As noted above, it is common for employers to include within their contracts of employment **30.30** 'garden leave' provisions, which may be enforced to ensure that the employee does not enter into other employment, whilst at the same time preventing the employee from performing their duties. Where the employer has protectable interests the use of 'garden leave' will form one of the methods of protecting those interests together with post-termination restraints. As noted, the effect of the 'garden leave' provision is also to prevent the employee from pursuing their skill or calling and the doctrine of restraint of trade is engaged. Employers will typically provide under the contract of employment for the period for which an employee was on 'garden leave' to be set off against the period of the post-termination restraints. The absence of such a provision is not fatal to the post- termination restraints under a contract but this may impact on the court's discretion whether to grant injunctive relief (*Credit Suisse Asset Management Ltd v Armstrong* [1996] IRLR 450, [1996] ICR 882).

Part C The Substantive Law

31

Whistle-blowing

SUMMARY

(1) The ERA 1996 provides protection for employees and workers who have made protected disclosures. For these purposes the definition of worker is an extended one.

(2) A protected disclosure is a qualifying disclosure which is made in defined circumstances. A qualifying disclosure is a disclosure of information which, in the reasonable belief of the discloser, is made in the public interest and tends to show that one or more relevant failures has occurred, is occurring, or is likely to occur. The requirements for protection of a qualifying disclosure depend upon the person to whom the disclosure is made.

(3) The protection is twofold. Dismissal of an employee is automatically unfair if the reason (or principal reason) for dismissal is that the employee made a protected disclosure. It is unlawful to subject an employee or worker to detriment on the ground that they have made a protected disclosure.

A. INTRODUCTION

31.01 Statutory protection for whistle-blowers dates back to the Public Interest Disclosure Act 1998 (PIDA 1988), which introduced new provisions into ERA 1996: Part IVA, s 47B, and s 103A. The legislation underwent major changes in 2013, introduced in the Enterprise and Regulatory Reform Act 2013 (ERRA 2013).

31.02 In outline, the structure of the legislation is as follows:

(a) The term 'whistle-blower' does not appear in the legislation. Protection is given to employees and workers who have made a 'protected disclosure' as defined in s 43A of the ERA.
(b) The protection is twofold:
  (i) Dismissal of an employee is automatically unfair if the reason (or principal reason) for the dismissal is that the employee made a protected disclosure: ERA, s 103A.
  (ii) A worker has the right not to be subjected to any detriment done on the ground that the worker has made a protected disclosure: ERA, s 47B.
(c) For the purposes of protection from detriment, the term 'worker' bears an extended definition: ERA, s 43K.

The ERRA 2013, in force from 25 June 2013, changes the legislative framework in the following **31.03** key ways:

(a) It is now necessary for the worker/employee to have made the disclosure reasonably believing it to be in the public interest.

(b) Good faith is *not* a necessary ingredient though it can affect remedy. Compensation may be reduced by up to 25 per cent where good faith is impugned successfully.

(c) Where a worker is subjected to a detriment on grounds of having made a protected disclosure by a co-worker or by an agent of the employer, the employer may be vicariously liable, and the co-worker or agent himself may be liable.

Despite these changes, the effectiveness of the legal protection for whistle-blowers remained **31.04** under review by the government. In June 2014, the government concluded, after consultation, that there was a need for further reform. The government noted that the statutory regime in place was aimed at protecting those who had *already* suffered a detriment or been dismissed, rather than preventing detriment from arising at all. The government issued guidance and created a model whistle-blowing policy as well as pushing for organizational and cultural change. The list of prescribed persons to whom a disclosure may be made has been expanded and close attention has been brought to bear on the health care sector, in the wake of the Francis report ('Freedom to Speak Up', Sir Robert Francis QC, February 2015). On 14 June 2017, the House of Commons published a useful briefing paper, 'NHS whistle-blowing procedure in England'. The financial services sector has also been active in this area. From September 2016, under new rules published by the Prudential Regulation Authority (PRA) and the Financial Conduct Authority (FCA), banks and other financial institutions were obliged to appoint a whistle-blowers' champion (a senior manager with designated responsibility) and to inform all staff how to raise concerns. For a more detailed treatment of this subject, see Jeremy Lewis, John Bowers, Martin Fodder, and Jack Mitchell, *Whistle-blowing: Law and Practice* (3rd edn, Oxford University Press 2017).

B. PERSONS PROTECTED

Protection from unfair dismissal is afforded to employees (ERA, s 103A). Protection from detri- **31.05** ment is afforded to workers (ERA, s 47B).

For the purpose of s 103A, 'employee' bears its normal meaning as set out in s 230(1) of the ERA. **31.06** Worker bears an extended meaning for the purposes of s 47B. The definition of 'worker' is to be found in s 43K of the ERA. It encompasses all those persons who are workers under s 230(3) ie employees and workers as defined for the purposes of other parts of the ERA, that is a person who has entered into or works under

> any other contract, whether express or implied and (if it is express) whether oral or in writing, whereby the individual undertakes to do or perform personally any work or services for another party to the contract whose status is not by virtue of the contract that of a client or customer of any profession or business undertaking carried on by the individual.

However, the definition in s 43K goes beyond s 230(3), to include certain contract workers supplied by third parties (s 43K(1)(a)), and those who would fall within the s 230(3) definition, but for the requirement that services be provided personally (s 43K(1)(b)).

Further, s 43K(1)(ba)–(d) makes special provision for persons in particular work relationships: for **31.07** example, doctors, dentists, and opticians working for the NHS, trainees on work experience, and servants of the Crown. Those categories have been amended, with effect from 25 June 2013, by the ERRA 2013. Section 43KA makes specific detailed provisions for the application of whistle-blowing protection to the police.

Section 20 of the ERRA 2013 included a power allowing the government to amend the definition **31.08** of worker by regulation, ie without having to enact primary legislation. Sub-section 20(7) of the ERRA 2013 inserts a new s 43K(4) into the ERA, which gives the Secretary of State the power to amend by order the definition of 'workers', even if the 'workers' in question may not fall within the definition of 'worker' set out in s 230 of the ERA. Further, a category of individuals cannot be removed from the definition of worker by this mechanism unless the Secretary of State is satisfied that there are no longer any individuals falling within the category. Pursuant to the Protected Disclosures (Extension of Meaning of Worker) Order 2015, student nurses and midwives are expressly deemed to be 'workers' for the purpose of the ERA, consistent with a drive to encouraging whistle-blowing within the NHS.

31.09 In *Day v Lewisham and Greenwich NHS Trust* [2016] IRLR 415, the EAT held that a specialist doctor in medical training who worked under an employment contract with an NHS Trust could not bring a claim for detriment against his training body, which did not fall within any of the categories set out in s 43K of the ERA. This was overturned by the Court of Appeal, which applied a purposive approach to the construction of the ERA (see [2017] ICR 917 (CA)). It held that, notwithstanding the doctor was a worker vis-à-vis the NHS trust which engaged him, and that s 43K(1)(a) of the ERA states in express terms that it only applies when s 230(3) of the ERA does not, the words 'as against a given respondent' should be read into the statute. Accordingly, the extended definition of an employer provided for at s 43K(2)(a) could apply to Health Education England. Meanwhile, the draft Employment Rights Act 1996 (NHS Recruitment—Protected Disclosure) Regulations 2017 are currently the subject of consultation and include Health Education England, a national training body, as an 'NHS employer'.

31.10 In *McTigue v University Hospital Bristol NHS Foundation Trust* UKEAT/0354/15/JOJ, the claimant worked under a contract of employment with an agency and held an honorary contract with the NHS Trust, which was terminated. The tribunal had to consider whether the claimant satisfied the terms of s 43K(1)(a)(ii) because the terms on which she was engaged to work were, or were in practice, 'substantially determined' by the NHS Trust as the end user. The employment tribunal struck out the claim, finding that the NHS Trust did not, but the EAT (Simler P) allowed the appeal, clarifying that it was not necessary for the claimant to prove that the NHS Trust determined her terms to the same or a greater extent than her agency did; merely, that it substantially determined the terms on which she was engaged to do the work. Where both the agency and the NHS Trust 'substantially determined' the terms of her engagement, the NHS Trust could still be treated as her 'employer' for the purposes of s 43K(2)(a) of the ERA. This is consistent with *Day*.

31.11 In *Clyde & Co LLP & Anor v Bates Van Winkelhof* [2012] IRLR 992, CA, it was held that a partner in an LLP was not a worker for the purposes of her s 47B ERA claim; the concept of being both employer and worker at one and the same time was not feasible and the necessary hierarchical aspect of the relationship between a worker and the employer would also be missing.

31.12 In *BP Plc v Elstone and Anor* [2010] IRLR 558 (EAT), Langstaff J held that it was not necessary for a worker to be working for the same employer at the time of making a protected disclosure and of suffering a detriment.

31.13 The Court of Appeal held in *Gilham v Ministry of Justice* [2017] IRLR 23 that judges are office-holders, not workers, and therefore are not protected in relation to whistle-blowing.

C. PROTECTED DISCLOSURE

31.14 Determining whether a protected disclosure has been made depends on a number of issues, including the nature of the information disclosed, to whom it was disclosed, and the state of mind of the person making the disclosure.

31.15 Section 43A of the ERA provides that a protected disclosure means a qualifying disclosure which is made by a worker in the circumstances set out in ss 43C–43H. Section 43B defines 'qualifying disclosure'. Each of ss 43C to 43H provides requirements for a qualifying disclosure to be protected, depending upon the person to whom the disclosure is made. Broadly speaking, one determines first whether the information disclosed is, by its nature, a qualifying disclosure; and one then goes on to determine whether that qualifying disclosure is protected in the particular circumstances in which it was made.

It is desirable for tribunals to analyse the constituent elements of a protected disclosure separately: *Easwaran v St George's University of London*, UKEAT/0167/10, 24 June 2010, EAT. **31.16**

Qualifying disclosure

Section 43B of the ERA provides that a qualifying disclosure is any 'disclosure of information' which, in the 'reasonable belief' of the worker making the disclosure, is 'made in the public interest' and 'tends to show' one or more 'relevant failures'. **31.17**

The requirement that the worker reasonably believes that disclosure of the relevant failure is in the public interest was introduced by the ERRA 2013 with effect from 25 June 2013. Prior to that amendment, the worker needed, for the purposes of establishing a qualifying disclosure, simply to have the relevant reasonable belief as to what the information tended to show. **31.18**

Relevant failures

Relevant failures are listed at s 43B(1)(a)–(f): **31.19**

(a) that a criminal offence has been committed, is being committed or is likely to be committed
(b) that a person has failed, is failing or is likely to fail to comply with any legal obligation to which he is subject
(c) that a miscarriage of justice has occurred, is occurring, or is likely to occur
(d) that the health or safety of any individual has been, is being, or is likely to be endangered
(e) that the environment has been, is being, or is likely to be damaged or
(f) that information tending to show any matter falling within any one of the preceding paragraphs has been, or is likely to be, deliberately concealed.

It is immaterial whether the relevant failure occurred, occurs, or would occur in the United Kingdom or elsewhere, and whether the law applying to it is the law of the United Kingdom or any other country or territory: s 43A(2). **31.20**

A disclosure is not a qualifying disclosure if the person making the disclosure commits an offence by making it: s 43A(3). **31.21**

It is common for claimants to rely on what may be seen as a 'catch-all' provision in s 43B(1)(b) of the ERA (failure to comply with a legal obligation). Under the regime that applied until June 2013, it was established that the relevant legal obligation may be the worker's own contract: *Parkins v Sodexho* [2002] IRLR 110. The EAT held in *Parkins* that an employee may make a protected disclosure when he complains that his employer is in breach of the employee's own contract of employment. That decision paved the way for many whistle-blowing claims which concerned only private disputes as to employer and employee's legal rights, with no real element of public interest involved. Such disputes were widely acknowledged not to be within the intended scope of PIDA. The amendment (introduced by the ERRA 2013) that the worker reasonably believes disclosure to be in the public interest is intended to exclude such 'private' disputes from the scope of the legislation, though it remains to be seen what effect the amendment will have: see para 31.33 below. **31.22**

It is not necessary that the person who is believed to have failed to comply with a legal obligation is the same person as the respondent to the complaint of victimization because the statutory language simply refers to 'a person': *Hibbins v Hesters Way Neighbourhood Project* [2009] IRLR 198 (EAT). **31.23**

Disclosure of information

The starting point is whether there has been a disclosure of information. This has been distinguished from a mere allegation or statement of opinion. In *Cavendish Munro Professional Risk Management Ltd v Geduld* [2010] ICR 325 (EAT), a letter from a solicitor instructed by a complainant was held by Slade J not to convey facts but merely to state an allegation or position adopted on behalf of the employee, which was not sufficient. Arguably, this was extended even further in *Goode v Marks and Spencer plc* UKEAT/0442/09, 15 June 2010. In that case, the EAT held that the tribunal was entitled to find that expressing an opinion about a proposal with which the claimant plainly disagreed **31.24** did not amount to a disclosure of information; it was a disclosure of opinion alone. Slade J again found against the claimant in *Smith v London Metropolitan University* [2011] IRLR 884 (EAT) on the basis that the grievance submitted by the claimant, about his workload, to the university employer did not amount to a disclosure of information as opposed to the making of allegations.

31.25 This may, however, be seen as the high-water mark of the restrictive approach to construing a disclosure of information, with more recent EAT decisions emphasizing the need for a careful and contextual approach: see eg *Western Union Payment Services UK Limited v Anastasiou* UKEAT/ 0135/13/LA and [2014] UKEAT 0135_ 13_ 1205 and *Kilraine v London Borough of Wandsworth* [2016] UKEAT 0260_ 15_ 2601 11.

31.26 A statement may be a disclosure of information, even if the recipient already knows the information. Where the person receiving the information is already aware of it, bringing the information to the attention of that person constitutes a disclosure of information (ERA, s 43L(3)).

31.27 A disclosure made after employment has ended may still attract protection: *Onyango v Berkeley Solicitors* [2013] IRLR 338 (EAT). A detriment, which occurs post termination, can also be relied on following *Woodward v Abbey National plc* [2006] IRLR 677, CA.

Reasonable belief as to what the information tends to show

31.28 The worker must reasonably believe, at the time of the disclosure, that the disclosure in question 'tends to show' one or more relevant failures. The worker need not believe that the information he discloses actually establishes that there has been a relevant failure, nor need he prove that there has been a relevant failure as a matter of fact. He need not, for the purposes of s 43B, have a belief that the allegations are substantially true (although for a qualifying disclosure to be protected in some circumstances this may be a necessary additional element: see ss 43F, 43G, 43H). It is sufficient that he reasonably believes the information 'tends to show' a relevant failure: *Babula v Waltham Forest College* [2007] ICR 1045, para 1026 (Wall LJ). This is an important distinction, and reflects the fact that often a whistle-blower will have information which is incomplete and imperfect, but which nonetheless gives rise to real concern as to a relevant failure.

31.29 The Court of Appeal held in *Babula* that the appropriate test was whether the employee's subjective belief was objectively reasonable. A reasonable mistake will not operate so as to disqualify the disclosure: *Darnton v University of Surrey* [2003] IRLR 133 (EAT).

31.30 What is reasonable will be judged both objectively and subjectively, having regard to the circumstances as known to the worker. See *Korashi v Abertawe Bro Morgannwg University Local Health Board* [2012] IRLR 4 (EAT); see also *Royal Cornwall Hospitals NHS Trust v Watkinson* UKEAT/ 0378/10, EAT. It will be relevant to consider the following questions:

(a) What did the worker/employee subjectively believe?
(b) Was that belief objectively reasonable having regard to their personal circumstances?

31.31 Where there is more than one disclosure, the need for the relevant reasonable belief applies to each and every disclosure, and a general belief in the gist of them is insufficient (see *Korashi*).

31.32 The information which may be the subject of a qualifying disclosure includes not only information tending to show that a relevant failure has occurred, is occurring, or is likely to occur. The meaning of likelihood of future failures was addressed by the EAT in *Kraus v Penna* [2004] IRLR 260. Although *Kraus* was disapproved in some respects by the Court of Appeal in *Babula*, its approach to likelihood was not disapproved. 'Likely' requires more than a possibility. The worker must have a reasonable belief that the information disclosed tends to show that a relevant failure is probable or more probable than not. However, it may be that the approach in *Kraus* is open to challenge on the basis of authorities which suggest that the meaning of 'likely' may change dependent on context, and that in some contexts it does not mean 'more likely than not': see *Cream Holdings Ltd v Banerjee* [2005] 1 AC 253, *SCA Packaging Ltd v Boyle* [2009] ICR 1056.

Reasonable belief that disclosure is in the public interest

Since the amendment introduced by the ERRA 2013, the worker making the disclosure must hold **31.33** a reasonable belief, at the time of making it, that the disclosure was in the public interest. No statutory definition of public interest has been introduced by ERRA 2013, nor is there any guidance as to how the phrase is to be interpreted. As mentioned above, the purpose of the amendment was to undo the effect of *Parkins v Sodexho*. In July 2013, the Department for Business Innovation and Skills stated that the purpose of the change was to reinstate the original intended scope of protection, ie in respect of matters raised genuinely in the public interest and not simply private contract disputes in respect of which claimants were (anecdotally) using the whistle-blowing legislation to leverage uncapped compensation (BIS Call for Evidence on the Whistle-blowing Framework, July 2013). The effect of the amendment is that the requirement of a reasonable belief that disclosure is in the public interest applies to each of the relevant failures, not just to those under s 43B(1)(b).

The Court of Appeal, in an important decision, considered the meaning of 'public interest' in **31.34** *Chesterton Global Limited and Anor v Nurmohamed* [2017] EWCA Civ 979 (CA). The claimant argued that his employer had manipulated accounts resulting in lower commission payments to him and, as it happened, to another ninety-nine senior managers. It was argued by the employer that his complaint was effectively personal and not a matter he had raised in the reasonable belief that it was in the public interest. However, the EAT held that the public interest test was satisfied on the basis that the other managers were a section of the public who would be affected: [2015] ICR 920, [2015] IRLR 614, EAT. The Court of Appeal held that a number of factors could and should be taken into account in determining whether a disclosure was made in 'the public interest' in the reasonable belief of the maker, even where there was a personal interest in making it. It held that absolute rules were inapposite and a multifactorial approach was to be adopted in considering whether a disclosure that related to a breach of a worker's own contract of employment or personal interest was made in the public interest within the statutory test provided:

(a) the numbers in the group of people whose interests were served by the making of the disclosure
(b) The nature of the wrongdoing
(c) the identity of the wrongdoer and
(d) The nature of the interests and the extent to which they are affected by the disclosure.

The Court of Appeal did not give any of these factors greater or lesser weight and did not require tribunals to do so either.

Circumstances in which a qualifying disclosure is protected

A qualifying disclosure is protected if it is made in the circumstances provided for by one of ss **31.35** 43C–43H:

(a) section 43C: disclosure to the worker's employer, or other responsible person
(b) section 43D: disclosure to a legal adviser
(c) section 43E: disclosure to a minister of the Crown
(d) section 43F: disclosure to a prescribed person
(e) section 43G: disclosure in other cases
(f) section 43H: disclosure of exceptionally serious failure.

The sections have been described as a 'three tiered disclosure regime' (see *Street v Derbyshire* **31.36** *Unemployed Workers Centre* [2005] ICR 97, para 5 (Auld LJ)). The first tier (ss 43C–43E) relates to disclosures to the employer, or to a person otherwise responsible for the matter to which the disclosure relates, or to the worker's legal advisers. These sections impose the least stringent requirements for a qualifying disclosure to be protected. The second tier is disclosure to a regulatory body (s 43F). The third tier (ss 43G and 43H) relates to wider disclosures, including to the media; this tier imposes the most stringent requirements in order for a qualifying disclosure to be protected.

In practice, the most common disclosures giving rise to litigation are those under s 43C. A qualifying **31.37** disclosure made by a worker to his employer will be a protected disclosure, as will a qualifying disclosure made to a person in accordance with a procedure whose use is authorized by the employer.

Section 43C also gives protection to a qualifying disclosure to a person other than the employer where the worker reasonably believes that (i) the relevant failure relates solely or mainly to the conduct of that person, or (ii) the person has legal responsibility for the matter to which the relevant failure relates.

31.38 None of ss 43C–43E imposes additional requirements in relation to the nature of the disclosure in order for it to be protected. Good faith in the making of the disclosure is no longer a requirement since the ERRA 2013 amendments (see below). Section 43F imposes a requirement that the worker believes the information disclosed and any allegation contained in it to be substantially true. Sections 43G and 43H each provides substantial additional requirements.

31.39 Section 43G is the section under which a disclosure to the media may possibly be protected. In cases where a disclosure is made to someone other than a person falling within ss 43C–43F, its provisions require detailed consideration. Each of the conditions summarized below must be satisfied:

(a) The worker must believe that the information disclosed and any allegations contained within it are substantially true.

(b) The worker must not make the disclosure for the purposes of personal gain.

(c) One of the conditions in s 43(2) must be met. Those are in outline: a reasonable belief in detriment if disclosure is made to the employer; a reasonable belief that evidence will be concealed or destroyed if disclosure is made to the employer; that disclosure of substantially the same information has already been made to the employer or under s 43F.

(d) In all the circumstances of the case it must be reasonable for the worker to make the disclosure. Section 43G(3) sets out a number of factors to which particular regard shall be had in determining whether it was reasonable to make the disclosure.

31.40 By s 43H a qualifying disclosure to any person is protected if the relevant failure is of an 'exceptionally serious nature' and:

(a) the worker believes that the information disclosed and any allegations contained within it are substantially true

(b) the worker does not make the disclosure for the purposes of personal gain

(c) in all the circumstances of the case it is reasonable to make the disclosure. The only specific factor to which regard must be had in determining reasonableness is the identity of the person to whom the disclosure was made.

Good faith

31.41 Prior to the changes introduced to the ERA by s 18 of the ERRA 2013, for a qualifying disclosure to be protected under any of ss 43C, 43E, 43F, 43G, and 43H of the ERA, the disclosure needed to be made in good faith. Where the employee's motive was undirected at righting the wrongs identified in the legislation, but amounted to an ulterior motive unconnected with the statutory objectives, the disclosure was not in good faith: *Street v Derbyshire Unemployed Workers' Centre* [2005] ICR 97, CA. It was for the employer to prove a lack of good faith (see *Bachnak v Emerging Markets Partnership (Europe) Ltd* UKEAT/0288/05, 27 January 2006, EAT).

31.42 Now there is no requirement of good faith. However, tribunals are now empowered to reduce compensation in any case where the protected disclosure was not made in good faith if it is considered just and equitable to do so in all the circumstances: ss 49(6A) and 123(6A) of the ERA. The maximum reduction is 25 per cent. In an unfair dismissal case, the reduction may only be applied to the compensatory award, not the basic award.

31.43 Accordingly, while the case law in this area is yet to develop following the new legislative scheme, it is clear that Parliament envisages that there will be a case where a disclosure is made in the public interest, but an employee nonetheless lacks good faith and will be able to get past the threshold for liability, but can be 'punished' by a reduction to any award of compensation. While conceptually difficult to imagine, the possibility remains of a case in which a good faith reduction is appropriate (with or without any reduction for contributory fault under s 123 of the ERA, which is also possible), although the authors suspect that it will require extreme and unique facts given the primary aim to protect and encourage whistle-blowing and the introduction of the public interest test. One hypothetical situation may be the whistle-blower who is, himself, directly implicated in the wrongdoing in question.

D. PROHIBITED ACTS AND REMEDIES

Dismissal

Dismissal of an employee is unfair if the reason (or if more than one, the principal reason) for dismissal is that the employee made a protected disclosure (s 103A). If the prohibited reason is established the dismissal is automatically unfair, without the need to consider reasonableness in all the circumstances. Selection for redundancy (where the redundancy affects more than one person) for the reason of having made a protected disclosure is also automatically unfair (s 105(1)). **31.44**

Establishing the reason for dismissal

Section 103A of the ERA does not stipulate upon whom the burden of proof lies as to the reason for dismissal. Where an employee has less than a year's continuous service, it has been held that it is the employee who bears the burden of establishing that the dismissal is for the proscribed reason: *Smith v Hayle Town Council* [1978] IRLR 413 (CA). **31.45**

Where an employee has the requisite continuous service, the position is different, as addressed by the Court of Appeal in *Kuzel v Roche Products Ltd* [2008] ICR 199 (CA). Without sufficient service, the employee bringing a claim of this type is still required to establish that he comes within the jurisdiction of the tribunal: *Ross v Eddie Stobart Ltd* [2013] UKEAT 0068_ 13_ 0808. **31.46**

In an 'ordinary' unfair dismissal claim, the employer bears the legal burden of proving the reason for dismissal. However, in a s 103A case, a failure on the part of the employer to prove its reason does not mean that the tribunal will necessarily accept the s 103A reason. If the claimant raises a prima facie case for the s 103A reason, and the respondent fails to prove its own alleged reason, the tribunal may infer that the s 103A reason was the true reason for dismissal. However, it is open to the respondent to satisfy the tribunal on the available evidence that the s 103A reason was not the true reason. At no stage is it for an employee with qualifying service to prove the s 103A reason. Further, in most cases, the outcome is unlikely to turn on the burden of proof, but rather, as emphasized by Lord Justice Mummery in *Kuzel*, on findings of fact. **31.47**

It is now reasonably clear that in establishing the reason for dismissal, the tribunal is concerned with the reason in the mind of the person who is dismissing, although someone who has sought to influence the outcome or process may be liable at an earlier stage of events, pursuant to a detriment claim: *CLFIS (UK) Ltd v Reynolds* [2015] IRLR 562, CA; *Royal Mail Ltd v Jhuti* [2018] IRLR 251. However, the Court of Appeal has confirmed that the decision-maker's belief as to whether or not a disclosure is protected is completely irrelevant in determining a claim under s 103A of the ERA: *Croydon Health Services NHS Trust v Beatt* [2017] IRLR 748. **31.48**

Cases in which the protected disclosure is said to provide the background to a sequence of events leading to dismissal but not the reason can be difficult to categorize. It seems that 'but for' cases, that is to say where dismissal would not have occurred but for the disclosure, fall on one side of the line and can be separated from the statutory test in s 103A of the ERA: *Shinwari v Vue Entertainment Ltd* [2015] UKEAT 0394_ 14_ 1203. Further, providing that the tribunal scrutinizes the reason with care, there is no additional hurdle of exceptionality for an employer to meet where the reason for dismissal is connected to or arises from the disclosures made in the sense of giving rise to a dysfunctional working relationship: *Panayiotou v Chief Constable Paul Kernaghan and Another* [2014] IRLR 500, EAT. **31.49**

Enforcement and remedy

31.50 A claim under s 103A proceeds as a claim for unfair dismissal under s 111 The time limits are the same as for any other claim for unfair dismissal. However, a claim under s 103A differs from an 'ordinary' unfair dismissal claim in a number of respects:

(a) there is no qualifying service threshold before an employee is entitled to bring a claim (s 108(3))

(b) there is no cap on the compensatory award (s 124(1A))

(c) a claim under s 103A is one of the types of claim in which an order for interim relief may be made (s 128(1)) (see further paras 32.40–32.48).

Detriment claims

31.51 By s 47B a worker has a right not to be subjected to any detriment by any act, or any deliberate failure to act, by his employer done on the ground that the worker has made a protected disclosure.

Detriment

31.52 In *Pinnington v Swansea City Council* [2005] ICR 685 (CA), Mummery LJ explained that once it is established that there has been a protected disclosure, there are four further elements of the cause of action: (1) that she was subjected to a detriment; (2) that she was subjected to detriment 'by any act, or any deliberate failure to act'; (3) the act or failure to act was that of the employer; and (4) it was on the ground that the worker had made a protected disclosure.

31.53 Section 47B(2) excludes from the definition of detriment the dismissal of an employee. A claim in relation to such a dismissal must be brought under s 103A.

31.54 The term 'detriment' in this context is not defined by statute but has over many years been taken to mean the same as in discrimination law (see eg *Woodward v Abbey National plc* [2006] IRLR 677 (Ward LJ)). Under the discrimination legislation detriment is given a wide meaning, see *Shamoon v Chief Constable of the Royal Ulster Constabulary (Northern Ireland)* [2003] ICR 337 (HL) at paragraphs 34 and 35 (Lord Hope): 'by reason of the act or acts complained of a reasonable worker would or might take the view that he had thereby been disadvantaged in the circumstances in which he had thereafter to work'. There is no requirement that the detriment be substantial; though this question will obviously be relevant to the assessment of damages. An unjustified sense of grievance will not suffice.

31.55 A detriment may occur after the end of the employment relationship: see *Woodward v Abbey National plc* [2006] IRLR 677, where the claimant suffered detriments several years after termination of her employment, including the employer's refusal or failure to provide a reference for her. There must be a sufficient connection or relationship between the employment and the detriment, however the exact nature and limits of that relationship is left unclear by *Woodward*.

Liability for detriments inflicted by co-workers or agents

31.56 Section 19 of the ERRA 2013 introduced amendments, contained in s 47B(1A)–47B(1E) of the ERA, which extend the scope of protection from detriment to include detriment by another worker of the employer, in the course of his employment; or by an agent acting with the employer's authority (s 47B(1A)). A claim for detriment in such circumstances is actionable against both the employer and the co-worker or agent. It is also actionable in principle as against non-executive directors in a personal capacity, the EAT having given s 47B(1a) of the ERA a wide construction in *International Petroleum Limited and Others v Osipov and Others* (EAT/0058/17/DA). In *Osipov* the claimant brought a s 103A claim against the employer and asserted that the two non-executive directors named as individual respondents had been instrumental in the decision to dismiss and hence subjected him to detriment constituted in the dismissal itself. Though an unusual case, on the right facts this could open up a substantial avenue of litigation against individual respondents.

The Court of Appeal agreed that claims could be brought against individuals in *Timis and another v Osipov* [2018] EWCA Civ 232.

Where a worker is subjected to detriment by anything done as mentioned in s 47B(1A), that thing **31.57** is treated as done by the worker's employer (s 47B(1B)); the employer need not have knowledge of or approve the acts of its workers or agents in order to be liable (s 47B(1C)). The employer is afforded a statutory defence to vicarious liability, in line with other similar formulations in discrimination law. Thus if the employer took all reasonable steps to prevent the worker from perpetrating the act in question (whether the specific act or acts of that description) the employer will not be liable (ERA, s 47B(1D)).

The co-worker or agent is also afforded a statutory defence if he does the proscribed act in reliance **31.58** on a statement by his employer that the detriment does not contravene the Act and it is reasonable to have relied on that statement: s 47B(1E) of the ERA. The employer's liability is unaffected by this.

'On the ground that'

A relevant detriment gives rise to a claim if it is inflicted 'on the grounds that' the worker made a **31.59** protected disclosure. On a complaint of contravention of s 47B it is for the employer to show the ground on which any act, or deliberate failure to act, was done (s 48(2)). This requires consideration of the reason why the employer acted (or deliberately failed to act). The test is whether the protected disclosure was a significant influence on the act or deliberate failure to act; an influence is significant if it is more than trivial: *Fecitt and Others v NHS Manchester* [2012] ICR 372 (CA). Careful consideration of the reason for action (or deliberate failure of action) is required. As *Fecitt* itself illustrates, a distinction may be drawn between, on the one hand, the disclosure itself and, on the other, matters such as the consequence of disclosure, the manner of disclosure, or steps associated with the disclosure. See also *Bolton School v Evans* [2006] IRLR 500; and *Martin v Devonshires Solicitors* [2011] ICR 352.

Enforcement and remedy

Enforcement of the right not to be subjected to a detriment follows the same model as that which **31.60** applies to other rights not to suffer detriment in employment (see Part V of the ERA 1996). The enforcement provisions are set out in ss 48 and 49. By s 48(1A) a worker may present a claim to an employment tribunal that he has been subjected to a detriment in contravention of s 47B (ie on the ground that he has made a protected disclosure). Time limits are set out in s 48(3), and follow the same model as for unfair dismissal.

Where a claim of detriment contrary to s 47B is made out, the tribunal shall make a declaration **31.61** to that effect and may make an award of compensation. The amount of any compensation shall be such as the tribunal considers just and equitable in all the circumstances having regard to (a) the infringement to which the complaint relates; and (b) any loss which is attributable to the infringement (s 49). Section 49 goes on to provide that the loss shall be taken to include any expenses reasonably incurred by the complainant in consequence of the infringement; and loss of any benefit which he might reasonably have been expected to have had but for the infringement. The award of damages may include an award for pecuniary loss (past and/or future), and may include an award for injury to feelings, awarded on a similar basis to such awards in discrimination claims (see Chapter 26).

In *Small v Shrewsbury & Telford Hospitals NHS Trust* [2017] EWCA Civ 882 the Court of Appeal **31.62** emphasized that, in a case in which the evidence suggests that a claimant should be compensated in damages for stigma and loss of future prospects then, even if such damages are not expressly pursued by a claimant, it is incumbent upon the tribunal to consider making such an award after hearing from the parties. It is worth bearing in mind that the claimant had adduced substantial witness evidence, which squarely suggested that he may be entitled to *Chagger* damages, albeit that he had not expressly formulated such a claim as a litigant in person.

E. PROTECTED DISCLOSURES AND CONTRACTUAL DUTIES

31.63 Section 43J provides that any provision in a relevant agreement is void in so far as it purports to preclude the worker from making a protected disclosure. The section applies to any agreement between a worker and his employer (whether in the worker's contract or not), including an agreement to refrain from instituting or continuing any proceedings under the ERA or any proceedings for breach of contract.

31.64 Where a settlement agreement is negotiated, there is no difficulty in reaching an agreement to settle a claim in relation to a protected disclosure that has been made, but the section would operate to invalidate a term of the agreement which sought to prevent further protected disclosures from being made.

PART D

Remedies

Remedies for Unfair Dismissal

Part D Remedies

SUMMARY

(1) An award of unfair dismissal compensation is normally made up of a basic award and a compensatory award.

(2) An additional award of between twenty-six and fifty-two weeks' pay will be awarded where an employer fails to comply with an order for reinstatement or re-engagement unless it was not practicable to comply with such an order.

(3) An application for interim relief (interim reinstatement or re-engagement) may be made in specific circumstances; for example, dismissals relating to union membership reasons, dismissals relating to carrying out health and safety responsibilities, and 'whistle-blowing' dismissals.

(4) The basic award is calculated in accordance with a statutory formula which is similar to a redundancy payment except that there is no minimum or maximum age requirement.

(5) The compensatory award is calculated in accordance with s 123(1)–(3) of the ERA 1996 and is based on the financial loss suffered by the claimant as a consequence of dismissal insofar as this is attributable to the actions of the employer, subject to the statutory maximum referred to below.

(6) The assessment of future loss involves a consideration of both 'old job facts' involving a consideration of how long the old job was likely to continue and, where there is a continuing loss, 'new job facts', whether the claimant is likely to find a new job, if so when and how long the loss is likely to continue.

(7) Compensation for injured feelings may not be recovered as part of the compensatory award.

(8) The compensatory award may be limited where an employment tribunal considers this to be 'just and equitable', for example, where the dismissal is held to be unfair for some technical procedural reason but would have been fair but for this procedural error.

(9) Depending on the circumstances, the options available to the tribunal are to make no award, to limit the award to a period of time, to make an assessment of the outcome on a percentage chance basis, or to refuse to speculate on the outcome and make a full award.

(10) The compensatory award may also be limited where the employee has failed to mitigate his or her loss and may be reduced for contributory fault as a result of blameworthy conduct by the employee which contributed to the dismissal.

(11) There is power to increase or reduce the compensatory award by up to 25 per cent where there is an 'unreasonable' failure by the employee to comply with the ACAS Code of Practice on Discipline and Grievances at Work (2009).

(12) There is power to reduce the compensatory award by up to 25 per cent in whistle-blowing cases where the protected disclosure was not made in good faith.

(13) The statutory maximum, currently £86,444 or fifty-two weeks' pay, is applied after the quantification of the award under s 124 of the ERA 1996.

A. INTRODUCTION

32.01 The remedies for unfair dismissal are set out in ss 112–124 of the ERA 1996.

32.02 An award of unfair dismissal compensation is usually made up of a basic award (ERA 1996, ss 119–120) and a compensatory award (ERA 1996, ss 123–124). However, where an employment tribunal makes an order for reinstatement or re-engagement pursuant to s 113 of the ERA 1996, , and an employer fails to comply with such an order, the tribunal has the power to make an additional award (ERA 1996, s 117).

32.03 Each of the statutory awards is subject to prescribed statutory maxima. In the case of the basic and additional awards, these are reviewed annually and increased or decreased by statutory instrument in line with changes in the RPI index. The new rates are normally announced and laid before Parliament in early December and come into force with effect from 1 February the following year (ERelA 1999, s 34). In the case of the compensatory award, the minimum increase may not be less than the median annual earnings and the maximum may not be more than three times annual median earnings (ERRA 2013, s 15).

B. REINSTATEMENT AND RE-ENGAGEMENT ORDERS

32.04 Where a complaint of unfair dismissal is successful, the tribunal is required to explain to the claimant the orders for reinstatement or re-engagement that may be made under s 113 of the ERA

1996, , the circumstances in which they may be made, and to ask the claimant whether he or she wishes the tribunal to make such an order (ERA 1996, s 112(2)). If the claimant does wish the tribunal to make such an order, it may do so (ERA 1996, s 112(3)).

A failure to consider making such an order where it is requested by the claimant may amount to **32.05** an error of law (*Cruickshank v London Borough of Richmond* EAT/483/97 and *King v Royal Bank of Canada (Europe) Ltd* [2012] IRLR 280). The requirements of s 113 of the ERA 1996 are mandatory and a failure to explain the orders amounts to an error of law (*Pirelli General Cable Works Ltd v Murray* [1979] IRLR 190) but this may not apply in certain situations, ie *Richardson v Walker* EAT/312/79, where the claimant had found a new job, and *Pratt v Pickford Removals Ltd* EAT/43/86, where the complainant contributed 100 per cent to the dismissal. A failure to comply with these provisions does not render the decision on compensation a nullity (*Cowley v Manson Timber Ltd* [1995] IRLR 153).

Duty to give reasons

The tribunal must give its reasons for making or refusing such an order and in particular the reasons **32.06** why it considers the order to be practicable or otherwise (*Port of London Authority v Payne* [1992] IRLR 447, EAT and *Clancy v Cannock Chase Technical College & Parkers* [2001] IRLR 331).

The orders

An employment tribunal is empowered to make two types of orders: an order for reinstatement **32.07** (ERA 1996, s 114) or an order for re-engagement (ERA 1996, s 115). (In this chapter they will be referred to collectively as 're-employment orders'.)

An order for reinstatement is an order that the employer shall treat the complaint in *all* respects **32.08** as if he had not been dismissed (ERA 1996, s 114). This involves the claimant being reinstated in his or her previous job on the same terms. However, care must be taken to analyse what the claimant's previous job was. In *McBride v Scottish Police Authority* [2016] UKSC 27 the claimant was a fingerprint expert who for some years prior to her unfair dismissal had worked on limited duties, in that she was excluded from court duties. After finding her to have been unfairly dismissed, the employment tribunal made an order for reinstatement to the job of '(non-court going) fingerprint expert'. The Court of Session Inner House found this to be an alteration to her contractual duties, and therefore not a permissible reinstatement order. The Supreme Court overturned that decision: the employment tribunal had not imposed a contractual limitation on the claimant in its reinstatement order; it had simply recognized a practical limitation on the scope of her work caused by circumstances beyond her control or that of her employer. An order for re-engagement is an order, on such terms as the employment tribunal may decide, that the complainant be engaged by the employer, or by a successor of the employer, or by an associated employer, in employment comparable to that from which he was dismissed or other suitable employment (ERA 1996, s 115). However, in *British Airways plc v Valencia* [2014] IRLR 683, the EAT ruled that it is not open to a tribunal to order reinstatement under the guise of a re-engagement order, so a tribunal erred in ordering the claimant to be re-engaged in the same role when it declined to order reinstatement because of the high level of contributory fault.

In exercising its discretion whether to make an order, the tribunal must first consider whether to **32.09** make an order for reinstatement and, in so doing, the tribunal must take into account:

(a) whether the complainant wishes to be reinstated
(b) whether it is practicable for the employer to comply with an order for reinstatement and
(c) where the complainant has caused or contributed to some extent to the dismissal, whether it would be just to order reinstatement (ERA 1996, s 116(1)(a)).

If the tribunal decides not to make an order for reinstatement, it must then consider whether to **32.10** make an order for re-engagement and, if so, on what terms (ERA 1996, s 116(2)).

32.11 In so doing the tribunal must take into account:

(a) any wish expressed by the complainant as to the nature of the order to be made

(b) whether it is practicable for the employer (or a successor or an associated employer) to comply with an order for re-engagement and

(c) where the complainant caused or contributed to some extent to the dismissal, whether it would be just to order his re-engagement and (if so) on what terms (ERA 1996, s 116(3)).

These factors are looked at in greater detail below.

Wishes of complainant

32.12 No order can be made if the claimant does not want to be reinstated or re-engaged which accounts in part for the small number of orders that are made (ERA 1996, s 112(2) and (3)).

Practicability of compliance

32.13 The practicability of compliance is an important factor in determining whether such an order should be made. It is also relevant to the issue of enforcement of such an order: a tribunal must consider this factor at both stages and cannot postpone its consideration until the enforcement stage (*Port of London Authority v Payne* [1994] IRLR 9). The practicability of reinstatement or re-engagement is determined at the time of the remedies hearing (*King v Royal Bank of Canada (Europe) Ltd* [2012] IRLR 280) or, more unusually, if submissions on practicability are received after the remedies hearing, at the time the order would take effect (*Rembiszewski v Atkins Ltd* EAT/0402/11). The fact that the claimant was dismissed for redundancy is not conclusive as to the availability of suitable vacancies at the time of the remedies hearing.

32.14 In deciding whether a re-employment order is practicable, the tribunal should consider whether, having regard to the employment relations realities of the situation, it is capable of being put into effect with success (*per* Stephenson LJ in *Coleman and Stephenson v Magnet Joinery Ltd* [1974] IRLR 343). What is 'practicable' should not be equated with what is 'possible' and, in this context, the tribunal may take into account the impact the order has on other staff (*Meridian Ltd v Gomersall* [1977] IRLR 425). However, mere inexpediency is no bar to re-employment (*Qualcast (Wolverhampton) Ltd v Ross* [1979] IRLR 98) but re-engagement should not be used as a means of imposing a duty to search and find a generally suitable vacancy irrespective of actual vacancies (*Lincolnshire County Council v Lupton* [2016] IRLR 576).

32.15 It should also be remembered that the tribunal is only required to 'take into account' the issue of practicability at this stage and therefore the tribunal's assessment on the issue of practicability is provisional (*McBride v Scottish Police Authority* [2016] IRLR 633) as the issue will be considered again at the enforcement stage (para 32.35). It is not uncommon for tribunals to make an order to test whether or not employer claims of impracticability are justified (*Timex Corporation Ltd v Thomson* [1981] IRLR 522 and *Freemans plc v Flynn* [1984] IRLR 486). A tribunal may therefore make an order where an employer claims that there is no vacancy (*Electronic Data Processing Ltd v Wright* 1986 IRLR 8) or where the reason for dismissal was redundancy (*Polkey v AE Dayton Services* [1988] AC 344, [1987] IRLR 503) or where there has been a substantial *Polkey* reduction (see para 32.171) (*Arriva North London Ltd v Eleftheriou* (EAT/0272/12)). But such orders are unlikely where the employer believes that the employee is incapable of doing the job or has a genuine fear that the employee will not be able to do the job without endangering those in his care (*ILEA v Gravett* [1988] IRLR 497). An order is also unlikely where there has been a fundamental loss of trust between the parties (*Nothman v London Borough of Barnet (No 2)* [1980] IRLR 65), particularly where the employer is small and the job involves a close working relationship (*Enessy Co SA (t/a The Tulcan Estate) v Minoprio* [1978] IRLR 489). Indeed, it has been suggested that such a re-employment order will only be made in the rarest of cases where there has been a breakdown in trust and confidence (*Wood Group Heavy Industrial Turbines Ltd v Crossan* [1998] IRLR 680) and the employer genuinely believes this to be so on a rational basis (*United Lincolnshire*

Hospitals NHS Foundation Trust v Farren [2017] ICR 513). But there are no hard and fast rules: for example, in *Oasis Community Learning v Woolf* (EAT/0364/12) the fact that the claimant had accused colleagues of fabricating evidence against her was held not to be a bar against re-engagement in a different location. In addition, tribunals should not necessarily conclude that re-employment is impracticable because of the claimant's conduct of litigation (*Cruickshank v London Borough of Richmond* EAT/483/97). It is open to a tribunal to order a disabled claimant to be re-engaged on different terms where an employer has failed to comply with its duty to make reasonable adjustment under s 20 of the EqA 2010 (*Great Ormond Street Hospital for Children NHS Trust v Patel* EAT/0085/07).

Permanent replacements

Reinstatement or re-engagement is not necessarily considered impracticable simply because **32.16** the employer has taken on a permanent replacement. S 116(5) of the ERA 1996 provides that where an employer has engaged a permanent replacement, this shall not be taken into account in deciding whether or not to make a re-employment order unless 'it was not practicable for [the employer] to arrange for the dismissed employee's work to be done without engaging a permanent replacement' or the employer engaged the replacement 'after the lapse of a reasonable period without having heard from the dismissed employee that he wished to be reinstated or re-engaged', and at the time the replacement was taken on, 'it was no longer reasonable for [the employer] to have the dismissed employee's work to be done except by a permanent replacement' (ERA 1996, s 116(6)).

The effect of s 116 of the ERA 1996 is that the employer will be required to dismiss a permanent **32.17** replacement if an order is made unless the proviso referred to above applies. The effect of this provision appears to have been overlooked by the EAT in *Cold Drawn Tubes Ltd v Middleton* [1992] IRLR 160.

Contributory fault

Tribunals are also required to consider whether re-employment is just in the light of the **32.18** employee's contributory conduct. The test to be applied is the same as under s 123(6) of the ERA 1996 (*Boots Company Ltd v Lees-Collier* [1986] ICR 728), ie the conduct involved must be blameworthy (see paras 32.198 ff). However, a finding of contributory conduct does not rule out the possibility of a re-employment order being made although such an order is unlikely where the employee is substantially to blame for the dismissal (*Nairne v Highlands and Islands Fire Brigade* [1989] IRLR 366). In such circumstances, the tribunal must consider whether it is 'just' to make such an order and, if so, to consider its terms. It is important not to conflate the two statutory questions. Furthermore, where a tribunal declines to make a reinstatement order in such circumstances, it will not normally be just to order re-engagement, as in *British Airways plc v Valencia* [2014] IRLR 685, where the tribunal had found the claimant 85 per cent to blame for his dismissal.

Other factors

In addition to these requirements, a tribunal may take into account other factors in deciding **32.19** whether or not to make a re-employment order. For example, in *Port of London Authority v Payne*, the EAT thought that the tribunal should have taken into account the claimants' ability to repay the severance payments they had received from their employers. Similarly tribunals may take into account the impact the order would have on employment relations generally (*Coleman v Magnet Joinery Ltd* [1974] ICR 46) or the personal relationships with other employees (*Intercity East Coast Ltd v McGregor* EAT/473/96: reinstatement was not practicable because of the acrimonious relationship between employee and supervisor to which the employee had contributed) but this may not carry the same weight where re-engagement is ordered at a different location (*Oasis Community Learning v Woolf* EAT/0364/12).

Part D Remedies

Terms of the order

Reinstatement

32.20 Section 114(2) of the ERA 1996 provides that, on making an order for reinstatement, the tribunal must specify:

(a) any amount payable by the employer in respect of any benefit which the complainant might reasonably be expected to have had but for the dismissal (including arrears of pay) for the period between the date of termination of employment and the date of reinstatement

(b) any rights and privileges (including seniority and pension rights) which must be restored to the employee and

(c) the date by which the order must be complied with.

32.21 The amount under s 114(2)(a) is based on what the claimant would actually have earned during the period between dismissal and reinstatement. The tribunal can therefore require the employer to award full back pay, holiday pay, etc between the date of dismissal and reinstatement. This may include improvements in terms and conditions which have taken place in the interim (ERA 1996, s 114(3)). There is no statutory limit on the amount which the tribunal can award in this regard as the statutory limit in s 124 of the ERA 1996 does not apply to awards under s 114(2).

32.22 However, in calculating the amount payable by the employer, tribunals must deduct the payments set out in s 114(4) of the ERA 1996, namely:

(a) wages in lieu of notice or any *ex gratia* payment received by the employee from the employer in respect of the period between the date of termination and the date of reinstatement (see *Butlers v British Railways Board* EAT/510/89)

(b) any payments received by the employee in respect of employment with another employer in the same period and

(c) such other benefits as the tribunal thinks fit in the circumstances.

No deduction should be made for contributory fault or a failure to mitigate (*City & Hackney Health Authority v Crisp* [1990] IRLR 47).

32.23 The Employment Protection (Recoupment of Jobseeker's Allowance and Income Support) Regulations 1996, SI 1996/2349 apply to the award.

Re-engagement

32.24 Section 115(2) of the ERA 1996 provides that, on making an order for re-engagement, the tribunal must specify:

(a) the identity of the employer

(b) the nature of the employment

(c) the remuneration for the employment

(d) any amount payable by the employer in respect of any benefit which the complainant might reasonably be expected to have had but for the dismissal (including arrears of pay) for the period between the date of termination of employment and the date of re-engagement

(e) any rights and privileges (including seniority and pension rights) which must be restored to the employee and

(f) the date by which the order must be complied with.

32.25 The tribunal is under a duty to state the terms of re-engagement. In effect, this means that it must write a new contract for the parties. It will not comply with the statutory requirements, if it leaves the parties to decide the terms of re-engagement (*Pirelli General Cable Works Ltd v Murray* [1979] IRLR 190) or leave the parties to agree the nature of the work and the rate of pay (*Stena Houlder Ltd v Keenan* EATS/543/93). The terms of the order must be sufficiently precise to be capable of being put into effect with success. For an order to state that the employment had to be 'comparable' was not adequate to identify specifically and with precision into what role the claimant was to be re-engaged (*Lincolnshire County Council v Lupton* [2016] IRLR 576).

Other than in cases where the claimant is found to have contributed to the dismissal, the tribunal **32.26** is required to order re-engagement on such terms which are, so far as is reasonably practicable, as favourable as reinstatement (ERA 1996, s 116(4)) but the tribunal cannot order re-engagement on terms that are *more* favourable than if the employee had been reinstated (*Rank Xerox (UK) Ltd v Stryczek* [1995] IRLR 568). It is unclear whether the tribunal can require the employer to make reasonable adjustments to '/the employment where a dismissal is held to be both unfair and in breach of the Equality Act 2010'.

The order should specify the place of employment and the nature of employment (*Rank Xerox* **32.27** *(UK) Ltd v Stryczek* [1995] IRLR 568) and the date by which the order should be complied with (*Pirelli General Cable Works Ltd v Murray* [1979] IRLR 190).

The tribunal is entitled to award the full amount of back pay which has accrued between dismissal **32.28** and the date when the order will take effect and the claimant may also recover compensation for any improvements in such terms and conditions between the date of dismissal and the date on which the order takes effect, although there is no authority on this point. There is no statutory limit on the amount the tribunal can award in this regard (ERA 1996, s 124(3)).

Credit must be given for payments that have been made to the claimant since dismissal such **32.29** as wages in lieu, *ex gratia* payments, and any payments made by a new employer (ERA 1996, s 115(3)) but no deduction should be made for a failure to mitigate (*City & Hackney Health Authority v Crisp* [1990] IRLR 47).

The 1996 Recoupment Regulations (see Chapter 34) apply to the award. **32.30**

Enforcing a re-employment order

The statutory provisions distinguish between partial compliance with the tribunal's order and **32.31** non-compliance.

Partial compliance by employer

Section 117(1) of the of the ERA 1996 provides that if an order for reinstatement or re-engagement **32.32** is made and the complainant is reinstated or re-engaged but the terms of the order are not complied with, then the tribunal 'shall make an award of compensation'. In such circumstances, the amount of the award 'shall be such as the tribunal thinks fit having regard to the loss sustained by the complainant in consequence of the failure to comply fully with the terms of the order' (ERA 1996, s 117(2)). So where, for example, the employer fails to pay the arrears of pay due to the employee, the tribunal may order the employer to pay the arrears even if this exceeds the statutory maximum (ERA 1996, s 124(3)) but in relation to the other matters set out in s 114(2) or 115(2) of the ERA 1996, the tribunal can only award compensation up to the statutory maximum, £86,444 or fifty-two weeks' pay (para 32.228) from 6 April 2019. There is no power to make an additional award in these circumstances.

Non-compliance by employer

Section 117(3) of the ERA 1996 provides that if the claimant is not reinstated or re-engaged, the **32.33** tribunal is required, subject to the defence of impracticability, to make an additional award as well as a standard award of compensation for unfair dismissal calculated in accordance with ss 118–127 of the ERA 1996. Reinstatement on different terms from that ordered by the tribunal amounts to noncompliance (*Artisan Press Ltd v Srawley and Parker* [1986] IRLR 126).

Non-compliance by employee

Where the tribunal finds that the claimant has unreasonably prevented an order under s 114 or **32.34** s 115 of the ERA 1996 from being complied with, it must treat the employee's conduct in this regard as a failure to mitigate under s 123(4) of the ERA 1996 (ERA 1996, s 117(8)).

Defence of impracticability

32.35 No additional award is payable if the employer can show that 'it was not practicable to comply with the order' (ERA 1996, s 117(4)(a)).

32.36 In determining whether the defence is made out, the tribunal is not restricted to considering the events which have taken place since the order was made. The tribunal may take account of all the relevant facts both before and after the date of the order (*Freemans plc v Flynn* [1984] IRLR 486). The employer therefore has a second opportunity to raise the objections raised in the first place to the order being made because, as stated at para 32.13, those objections do not necessarily prevent the order from being made. Employers are not under a duty to create a special job for the employee to do or to dismiss existing employees to enable them to re-employ the complainant (*Freemans plc v Flynn* [1984] IRLR 486). Subject to the rules on 'permanent replacements', it will not be practicable to comply with the order if this would result in over-manning or a redundancy situation (*Cold Drawn Tubes Ltd v Middleton* [1992] IRLR 160). Furthermore, whilst the tribunal will scrutinize the employer's reasons for failing to comply with the order, due weight should be given to the commercial judgment of management and the employer cannot be expected to explore every avenue which ingenuity might suggest (*Payne v Port of London Authority* [1994] IRLR 9).

Additional award

32.37 The additional award is fixed by s 117(3)(b) of the ERA 1996 as an amount of not less than twenty-six weeks' pay and not more than fifty-two weeks' pay, subject to the statutory maximum. Where the 'effective date of termination' is on or after 6 April 2019, the statutory limit on a week's pay is £525. Where the 'effective date' is prior to 6 April 2019, the statutory limit on a week's pay was £505. (The rules on the calculation of a week's pay are summarized at para 32.57.)

32.38 The additional award is a penalty for non-compliance with the order and therefore the most important factor in deciding how much to award is the employer's conduct. The more serious the violation, the higher the award, but where it is found that, even though it was practicable to comply, the employer faced genuine difficulties, the award may be lower (*Morganite Electrical Carbon Ltd v Donne* [1987] IRLR 363). Another relevant factor is the extent to which the employer has complied with the ancillary parts of the order, for example that he has paid any of the back-pay due to the employee. The tribunal may also take into account the extent to which the compensatory award compensates the employee for the financial loss suffered, whether the employee has taken steps to mitigate the loss (although no specific reduction should be made for this reason), the extent to which the employee contributed to the dismissal and, possibly, the injury to feelings suffered by the employee as a result of the dismissal, see *Morganite Electrical Carbon v Donne* and *Mabrizi v National Hospital for Nervous Diseases* [1990] IRLR 428.

Relationship between additional and compensatory award

32.39 Where an employer fails to comply with an order for reinstatement and re-engagement, the tribunal is empowered to make an award in respect of arrears of pay and other matters specified in s 114(2)(a) and s 115(2)(d) of the ERA 1996 in excess of the statutory maximum, but in those circumstances if the award of arrears exceeds the combined total of the compensatory award and the additional award, it is not open to the tribunal also to make an additional award and a compensatory award (*Selfridges Ltd v Malik* [1997] IRLR 577; *Parry v National Westminster Bank plc* [2005] IRLR 193). This is likely to be significant in the light of the new cap placed on the compensatory award (para 32.228).

C. INTERIM RELIEF

32.40 An application for interim relief may be made where a claimant claims that the principal reason for his or her dismissal is one or more of the following reasons:

> (i) union membership reasons pursuant to s 152(1)(a) and (c) of the TULR(C)A 1992 and s 104F(a) and (b) of the ERA 1996 (blacklists) (as provided for by ERA 1996, s 128(1)(b)),

(ii)   taking part in union activities pursuant to s 152(1)(b) of the TULR(C)A 1992,

(iii) making use or proposing to make use of trade union services at an appropriate time pursuant to s 152(1)(ba) of the TULR(C)A 1992,

(iv) failing to accept an offer to give up union membership or collective bargaining rights pursuant to s 152(1)(bb) of the TULR(C)A 1992,

(v)   acting in a representative capacity under the Working Time Regulations 1998 pursuant to s 101A(d) of the ERA 1996 (as provided for by ERA 1996, s 128(1)(a)(i)),

(vi) performing the functions of a pension fund trust pursuant to s 102 of the ERA 1996 (as provided for by ERA 1996, s 128(1)(a)(i)),

(vii) acting as an employee representative pursuant to s 103 of the ERA 1996 (as provided for by ERA 1996, s 128(1)(a)(i)),

(viii) making a 'protected disclosure' pursuant to s 103A of the ERA 1996 (as provided for by ERA 1996, s 128(1)(a)(i)),

(ix) taking action to prevent or support union recognition pursuant to para 161(2) of Sch A1 to the TULR(C)A 1992 (as provided for by ERA 1996, s 128(1)(a)(ii)).

32.41 The procedure in trade union cases is set out in ss 161–163 of the TULR(C)A 1992. The procedure in whistle-blowing and the other types of claim referred to above is set out in ss 128–129 of the ERA 1996.

32.42 An application for interim relief must be made within seven days of the effective date of dismissal (TULR(C)A 1992, s 161(2); ERA 1996, s 128(2)). In the case of dismissal for union membership, it must be supported by a certificate in writing signed by an authorized official of the independent trade union of which the employee was or had proposed to become a member, stating that there are reasonable grounds for supposing that the reason or principal reason for dismissal was the one alleged in the complaint (TULR(C)A 1992, s 161(3)). There is no equivalent requirement in the ERA 1996. On receipt of the application, the employment tribunal is under a statutory duty to determine the matter 'as soon as practicable', although the employer must be given at least seven days' notice of the hearing (TULR(C)A 1992, s 161(2); ERA 1996, s 128(4)). Furthermore, where it is proposed to join the trade union as a party to the proceedings, the union must be given at least three days' notice of the hearing (TULR(C)A 1992, s 162(3)). The tribunal may postpone the hearing in special circumstances (TULR(C)A 1992, s 162(4); ERA 1996, s 128(5)).

32.43 If at the hearing of the application for interim relief, the tribunal is satisfied that it is likely that, on determining the complaint to which the application relates, the tribunal will find that the reason for the claimant's dismissal was one or more of the prohibited reasons referred to in para 32.40, it must announce its findings and explain to both parties its powers under s 163 of the TULR(C)A 1992 and s 129 of the ERA 1996.

32.44 Broadly, these are:

(a) if the employer is willing to reinstate the employee, to order interim reinstatement until the case is heard or settled (TULR(C)A 1992, s 163(4); ERA 1996, s 129(3)(a))

(b) if the employer is willing to re-engage the employee, to order interim re-engagement until the case is heard or settled (TULR(C)A 1992, s 163(5); ERA 1996, s 129(3))

(c) if the employer is unwilling to reinstate or re-engage the employee, to order that the contract of employment shall continue in force, irrespective of whether it has been terminated until the case is heard or settled (TULR(C)A 1992, ss 163(6) and 164(2); ERA 1996, s 130(1)). The tribunal is required to specify in its order 'the amount which is to be paid by the employer to the employee' (TULR(C)A 1992, s 164(2); ERA 1996, s 130(2)), although in making the order it will take account of any payment made by the employer such as payment in lieu of notice (TULR(C)A 1992, s 164(5) and (6); ERA 1996, s 130(5) and (6)).

32.45 On the application of either party, the tribunal may 'at any time between the making of an order' under these provisions and 'the determination or settlement of the complaint, revoke or vary its order on the ground of a relevant change in circumstances' (TULR(C)A 1992, s 165; ERA 1996, s 131).

Part D Remedies

32.46 The penalty for a failure to comply with the terms of a continuation order is set out in s 166 TULR(C)A 1992 and s 132 ERA 1996. This s provides that if, on the application of an employee, the tribunal is satisfied that the employer has failed to comply with an order of continuation of the contract, for example by not paying the employee the amount stated under the order, the tribunal is required to determine the amount of pay owed by the employer and order that the sum due is paid to the employee by way of additional compensation at the 'full' hearing. In cases where the employer has failed to comply with some other aspect of the tribunal's order, for example in relation to pension rights or similar matters, the tribunal may award such compensation as it considers just and equitable in the circumstances.

32.47 In effect these provisions enable the tribunal to ensure that the employee is either reinstated or reengaged or suspended on full pay until the case is resolved. Any sums paid under these orders are not recoverable in the event that the employee loses the substantive complaint of unfair dismissal (*Initial Textile Services v Rendell* EAT/383/91).

32.48 As stated in para 32.43, such an order will only be made if the employment tribunal is satisfied that the complaint of automatic unfair dismissal for one or more of the prohibited reasons set out in para 32.40 is 'likely' to succeed. In *Taplin v C Shippam Ltd* [1978] ICR 1068, in which it was alleged that the claimant was dismissed for taking part in trade union activities, the EAT held that 'likely' meant that the claimant had a 'pretty good' chance of success. The same approach was applied by the EAT in *Raja v Secretary of State for Justice* [2010] All ER (D) 134, a whistle-blowing case, in which it was stated that a claimant should show 'specific reason why his prospects of success are sufficiently strong to make interim relief appropriate'. More recently in *Ministry of Justice v Sarfraz* [2011] IRLR 562, the EAT ruled that a pretty good chance of success involves a significantly higher degree of likelihood than a 51 per cent chance of success. This contrasts with the interpretation given to the word 'likely' by the House of Lords in *SCA Packaging Ltd v Boyle* [2009] IRLR 746, where in the context of the definition of 'disability' for the purpose of a disability discrimination claim, it was stated that the word 'likely' meant 'could well happen', a lower standard. But the approach in both *Taplin* and *Sarfraz* had been confirmed by the EAT in *London City Airport Ltd v Chako* [2013] IRLR 610, where the EAT described the task to be undertaken by the employment tribunal to be 'an expeditious summary assessment as to how the matter looks to him on the material that he or she has'. Perhaps more significantly, in practical terms, the likelihood of success must be established in relation to each element of the claim. So, for example, in a protected disclosure dismissal, the tribunal must be satisfied that the disclosure is both a qualifying disclosure pursuant to s 43B of the ERA 1996 and that it is a protected disclosure pursuant to s 43A of the ERA 1996.

D. COMPENSATION FOR UNFAIR DISMISSAL

32.49 Section 112 of the ERA 1996 provides that if no order for reinstatement or re-engagement is made under s 113, the tribunal shall make an award of compensation for unfair dismissal calculated in accordance with ss 118–127 of the ERA 1996, to be paid by the employer to the employee.

32.50 The unfair dismissal award consists of a basic award calculated in accordance with ss 119–122 of the ERA 1996, and a compensatory award calculated in accordance with ss 123, 124, 124A, and 126 of the ERA 1996.

E. BASIC AWARD

Calculating the basic award

32.51 Section 119(1) of the ERA 1996 provides that the basic award shall be calculated by:

(a) determining the period, ending with the effective date of termination during which the employee has been continuously employed

(b) reckoning backwards from the end of that period the number of years of employment falling within that period and

(c) allowing the appropriate amount for each of those years of employment.

The statutory formula is subject to a maximum of twenty years of employment. Thus, the maximum award is thirty weeks' pay (ERA 1996, s 119(3)), although this is not subject to any statutory age limit.

Section 119(2) of the ERA 1996 defines the 'appropriate amount' as: **32.52**

(a) one and a half week's pay for a year of employment in which the employee was not below the age of forty-one

(b) one week's pay for a year of employment (not within para (a)) in which he was not below the age of twenty-two and

(c) half a week's pay for a year of employment not within para (a) or (b).

This formula has not been changed as a result of the implementation of the Employment Equality (Age) Regulations 2006 (EEAR 2006), SI 2006/1031 or the Equality Act 2010 (EqA 2010).

Effective date of termination

The effective date of termination is defined in s 97 of the ERA 1996. Where an employer summarily **32.53** dismisses an employee or gives him less than the period of notice guaranteed by the statutory provisions, the effective date of termination is the date on which the statutory period of notice would have expired had it been given (ERA 1996, s 97(2)(b)). Similarly, if an employee is constructively dismissed, the effective date of termination is extended by the statutory period of notice (ERA 1996, s 97(4)). However, where the employer gives notice which is equivalent to or greater than the statutory minimum, the effective date of termination is the date on which the notice expires (ERA 1996, s 97(2)).

Age

The statutory provisions make it clear that years which span the twenty-second or forty-first year do **32.54** count. However, in accordance with the statutory provisions, a year of employment is a complete year. This is calculated by working backwards from the effective date of termination. Therefore, only complete years of service which occur after the relevant anniversary are calculated at the higher rate. A year which spans the relevant anniversary is not treated as a complete year of service for this purpose, and therefore falls to be calculated at the lower rate.

There is no minimum or lower age limit or upper age limit (EEAR 2006, Sch 8, Part 2, para 25 **32.55** and EqA 2010, Sch 9, para 13). The previous provisions which provided for the scaling down of the award in the 64th year have been repealed by the EEAR 2006 (Sch8, Part 2, para 27) and EqA 2010 (Sch 9, para 13).

A week's pay

For the purpose of calculating the basic award, the calculation date, (ie the date on which a week's **32.56** pay is calculated) is defined in s 226 (3) and (6) of the ERA 1996:

(a) where statutory notice was not given but should have been given, the date by which notice is extended pursuant to s 97(2) or (4) of the ERA 1996 or, otherwise

(b) the date when notice is given if the employer gives statutory notice or is given statutory notice by the employee (ERA 1996, s 226(6)).

The rules for calculating a week's pay are set out in ss 220–229 of the ERA 1996 and may be sum- **32.57** marized as follows:

(a) The rules governing the calculation of a week's pay depend on whether or not the employment is one with normal working hours. There is no comprehensive definition of normal working hours but, in general, employments which follow a fixed pattern of work will be treated as

Part D Remedies

employment with normal working hours. This will include time workers, piece workers, and most shift workers, but employees whose hours of work fluctuate with the demands of the business are likely to be treated as having no normal working hours.

(b) In most cases, the crucial issue is what hours count as *normal* working hours. This is based on the minimum number of hours of work the employer guarantees by the terms of the contract. Overtime hours do not normally count unless overtime is guaranteed and required to be worked (*Lotus Cars Ltd v Sutcliffe* [1982] IRLR 381).

(c) Not all payments received by employees count towards a week's pay. Most contractual payments do count such as wages, salaries, shift bonuses, and productivity bonuses, but overtime payments will not count unless these form part of an employee's normal working hours or the employment is one with no normal working hours.

(d) The calculation is based on an employee's gross earnings (ie earnings before the deduction of tax and national insurance).

(e) There are four different ways of calculating a week's pay. In the case of most workers (time workers) a week's pay is simply the amount which they earn during the normal working week but the rules are complicated in relation to piece workers, shift workers, and those who have no normal working hours.

32.58 The amount of a week's pay which counts towards a basic award is currently capped at £525 per week where the effective date of termination is on or after 6 April 2019. Where the 'effective date' is prior to 6 April 2019, the statutory limit on a week's pay was £505. The current maximum basic award is £15,750.

Example

An employee aged 30 earning £525 per week is dismissed after working for an employer for six years. The basic award is 6 x 1 x £525 = £3,150.

Minimum basic award

32.59 Generally, there is no minimum basic award. However, statute does provide for a minimum basic award in the situations of union-related, health and safety, and whistle-blowing dismissals. Where employees are dismissed for reasons which are regarded as unfair under ss 152 and 153 of the TULR(C)A 1992 or s 100(1)(a) and (b) and s 103 of the ERA 1996, the statutory minimum is £6,408 where the effective date of termination is on or after 6 April 2019. This is reviewed annually as increased or decreased in line with s 34 of the Employment Relations Act 1999.

Redundancy dismissals

32.60 An employee is not entitled to receive both a basic award and a redundancy payment. In cases of redundancy, therefore, the redundancy payment is deducted from the basic award (ERA 1996, s 122(4)). (As to the calculation of the redundancy award to be deducted, see the redundancy ready reckoner at page 843.) However, such a deduction will not be made if the tribunal finds that redundancy was not the real reason for dismissal (*Boorman v Allmakes Ltd* [1995] IRLR 553).

32.61 This general exclusion does not apply in two situations: the first is where an employee is selected for redundancy in breach of s 153 of the TULR(C)A 1992, ie for a reason related to trade union membership, or where a workers' representative is selected for redundancy for carrying out health and safety duties pursuant to s 100(1)(a) and (b), and ss 101A(d), 102(1), and 103 of the ERA 1996. In such circumstances, an employee is entitled to a minimum basic award as well as a redundancy payment (TULR(C)A 1992, s 159; ERA 1996, s 120(1)). The second is where the principal reason for dismissal is redundancy but the employee is ineligible for a redundancy payment because he has: (a) unreasonably refused an offer of suitable employment (ERA 1996, s 141(2)); or (b) unreasonably terminated or given notice to terminate a trial period (ERA 1996, s 141(4)(d)); or (c) had his contract renewed or is re-engaged under a new employment contract pursuant to s 141(1) of the ERA 1996, so that there is no dismissal. In such circumstances the employee is entitled to a basic award of two weeks' pay (ERA 1996, s 121).

Reducing the basic award

The basic award may be reduced or further reduced where any conduct of the claimant before dismissal (or, where the dismissal was with notice, before the notice was given) was such that it would be 'just and equitable' to reduce or further reduce the award (ERA 1996, s 122(2)).   **32.62**

The power to reduce the basic award for conduct is therefore wider than the power to reduce the   **32.63**
compensatory award for contributory fault (*Optikinetics Ltd v Whooley* EAT/1275/97 and *Frith Accountants Ltd v Law* [2014] IRLR 510, discussed at para 32.199) because *any* conduct may be taken into account (including misconduct which was not known at the time of dismissal), even though it did not contribute to the dismissal in a causative sense (*Parker Foundry Ltd v Slack* [1992] IRLR 11) but the case law relating to what amounts to 'blameworthy' conduct for this purpose is still relevant in considering whether it is just and equitable to reduce the award (see para 32.209). The conclusion that the claimant is 100 per cent responsible for the dismissal and that it is just and equitable to reduce the basic award to nil is 'unusual' but a 'permissible' one (*Steen v ASP Packaging Ltd* [2014] ICR 56).

Unreasonable refusal of offer of reinstatement

The basic award may also be reduced by such extent as the tribunal considers just and equitable   **32.64**
having regard to its finding that the employee 'has unreasonably refused an offer by the employer which (if accepted) would have the effect of reinstating the complainant in all respects as if he had not been dismissed' (ERA 1996, s 122(1)). This provision will apply only where the employer makes an offer which complies with the statutory provisions for reinstatement. An offer of a different job or the same job on less favourable terms would appear to be insufficient (*Artisan Press Ltd v Srawley and Parker* [1986] IRLR 126). Otherwise, the factors in determining when it is unreasonable to turn down such an offer are similar to those referred to in mitigation cases (see para 32.151). Such a reduction will normally be made where the employee is found to have acted unreasonably, but a tribunal is not bound to make a reduction if it feels that this would not be just and equitable (see *Muirhead & Maxwell Ltd v Chambers* EAT/516/82, where the employee turned down the offer because he feared victimization).

Restrictions in minimum award dismissals

Special statutory rules apply to the reduction in the basic award in union membership cases and   **32.65**
other cases where there is a minimum award. No reduction or further reduction in the basic award should be made where the employee's conduct amounts to a breach of a requirement to be a union member or non-member, or to take part in trade union activities. Tribunals should ignore a refusal to comply with a requirement to make a payment in lieu of union subscriptions or an objection to deduction from pay for that purpose. It is hard to imagine a case where the employee would be held to have acted in a blameworthy manner in relation to a dismissal under ss 152 and 153 of the TULR(C)A 1992. Furthermore, as a general rule there can be no reduction in the basic award where the reason or principal reason for dismissal is redundancy. However, the restriction does not apply where an employee is entitled to receive a minimum basic award (see para 32.59). In such circumstances, the minimum basic award can be reduced for contributory fault but the reduction applies only to so much of the basic award as is payable under s 120 of the ERA 1996. An employee with two years' service who earns £525 per week and is selected for redundancy for union-related reasons would normally be entitled to a redundancy payment of £1,050 but is entitled to a minimum basic award of £6,408 and is therefore entitled to an award of £5,358. Any reduction for pre-dismissal blameworthy conduct would be limited to £1,050.

Other deductions

The basic award is a statutory award and therefore may only be reduced where this is permitted by   **32.66**
statute (*Cadbury Ltd v Doddington* [1977] IRLR 982); it cannot therefore be reduced where the employee failed to mitigate his loss (*Lock v Connell Estate Agents Ltd* [1994] IRLR 44) or where the tribunal considers it just and equitable (*Sahil v KoresNordic (GB) Ltd* EAT/379/90). But it has

been held that where an *ex gratia* payment is specifically referable to the employee's statutory right to unfair dismissal compensation (ie the payment is specifically referable to the basic and compensatory awards), it is open to the employer to argue that it has paid the basic award in full, and any compensation ordered may thereby be further diminished in accordance with the guidance at para 32.215 (*Chelsea Football Club and Athletic Co Ltd v Heath* [1981] IRLR 73; cf *Pomphrey of Sittingbourne Ltd v Reed* EAT/457/94, where the payment was referred to as a payment in lieu of notice and therefore was not a defence to statutory liability). Whether the payment is referable to the statutory provision is a question of construction in each case.

F. THE COMPENSATORY AWARD

PART 1 ASSESSING THE LOSS

General principles

32.67 The compensatory award will usually make up the largest part of the award of compensation for unfair dismissal. Section 123(1) of the ERA 1996 provides that:

> Subject to the provisions of this section and sections 124 [124A and 126], the amount of the compensatory award shall be such amount as the tribunal considers just and equitable in all the circumstances having regard to the loss sustained by the complainant in consequence of the dismissal in so far as that loss is attributable to action taken by the employer.

32.68 This provision gives employment tribunals a wide discretion over the assessment of the compensatory award. Where the claim is relatively small, tribunals are likely to approach the task with a minimum amount of technicality. In the past, this approach has been encouraged by the EAT and the Court of Appeal. In *Fougère v Phoenix Motor Co Ltd* [1976] IRLR 259, the EAT stressed that tribunals are 'bound by necessity to operate in a rough and ready manner and to paint the picture with a broad brush', rather than as skilled cost accountants or actuaries (although it should be noted that these decisions preceded the increase in the compensatory award). If the circumstances so justify, the brush can be reasonably broad: for example, in *Basildon Academies v Amadi* (EAT/0343/14), the claimant was Nigerian and his work visa was only valid for a limited period of time. The tribunal concluded that this meant he would have severe difficulties in finding work and awarded four years' loss of earnings. The EAT recognized that the award was 'arbitrary' but acknowledged that a degree of arbitrariness was inevitable on the facts because if the claimant's visa was not renewed he would have to return to Nigeria and there was no evidence as to his earnings potential there. The tribunal was entitled to have regard to the fact that the claimant could not reasonably have been expected to have achieved any earnings up to the date of the hearing and would suffer future loss for a period of at least four years. Nonetheless, the discretion must be exercised on some rational basis: in *Norton Tool Co Ltd v Tewson* [1973] 1 All ER 183, the NIRC stated that the discretion conferred by s 123(1) of the ERA 1996 must be exercised 'judiciously and upon the basis of principle' and a tribunal must set out its reasons in sufficient detail to show the principles it has applied in making its assessment. This case was decided when the statutory maximum was significantly lower and tribunals are now required to provide a table showing how the sum has been calculated or a description of the manner in which it has been calculated as part of its duty to give reasons pursuant to r 62(5) of the Employment Tribunals (Constitution & Rules of Procedure) Regulations 2013.

Compensation, not punishment

32.69 Generally, the object of the compensatory award is to compensate the claimant but not to punish or express disapproval of the employer's policies (*Lifeguard Assurance Ltd v Zadrozny* [1977] IRLR 56).

32.70 There are two possible exceptions to the general principle that the award should be based strictly on the financial loss suffered by the claimant. First it is well established that a claimant is entitled to be compensated for the loss of statutory rights (see para 32.142). Secondly, it has been established that, as a matter of justice and equity, claimants are normally entitled to receive a minimum award equivalent to their notice pay (*Norton Tool Co Ltd v Tewson* [1973] 1 All ER 183; *TBA Industrial Products Ltd v Locke* [1984] IRLR 48; *Babcock FATA Ltd v Addison* [1987] IRLR 173), although it would appear that this exception does not apply where the claimant is employed under a fixed term contract (*Isleworth Studios Ltd v Rickard* [1988] IRLR 137). These latter decisions are now open to doubt in the light of the EAT ruling in *Hardy v Polk Ltd* [2004] IRLR 420 and *Morgans v Alpha Plus Security Ltd* [2005] IRLR 234, both decisions of Burton P. In the latter case in particular, the EAT considered that the earlier interpretations were inconsistent with the approach taken by the House of Lords in the *Dunnachie* case that compensation should only be awarded to cover actual financial loss suffered by the claimant. But these recent EAT rulings were not followed by the EAT in *Voith Turbo Ltd v Stowe* [2005] IRLR 228 (presided over by Judge McMullen QC). The approach of Burton P was followed by the EAT majority in *Langley v Burlo* [2006] IRLR 460 The EAT's reasoning, based on the *Dunnachie* ruling, was rejected when the *Burlo* case went to the Court of Appeal ([2007] IRLR 145), even though the outcome, what the Court of Appeal calls the 'pay point' (the correct rate of pay), namely that the claimant's loss during her eight-week notice period should be calculated on the statutory sick pay rate rather than her normal rate of pay, was upheld. Mummery LJ (with whom Leveson LJ agreed) refused to resolve the conflict in case law on this issue, whereas Smith LJ cast doubt on the principle of whether it is good employment practice for an employer to pay an amount equivalent to a payment in lieu. Nonetheless, at the time of writing, it would appear that whilst it remains good employment practice to make a payment in lieu of notice, a failure to do so will not necessarily result in a minimum award of a sum equivalent to such a payment. The *Norton Tool* principle does not apply to constructive dismissals (*Stuart Peters Ltd v Bell* [2009] IRLR 941).

Remoteness

The employer is liable for all financial loss which flows directly from the dismissal provided it is 'attributable to the employer's actions' (see *Royal Court Hotel v Cowans* EAT/48/84), but compensation cannot be recovered if the loss suffered by the employee is too remote, ie if it does not arise as a 'consequence of dismissal' and/or is not 'attributable to the employer's action' (ERA 1996, s 123(1)). **32.71**

It has been argued that the employer's liability ceases once the claimant finds a new job or undergoes a period of training. In some cases the EAT has accepted this argument and adopted a relatively strict approach to the issue of causation (see *Courtaulds Northern Spinning Ltd v Moosa* [1984] IRLR 43 and *Simrad Ltd v Scott* [1997] IRLR 147) but in *Dench v Flynn & Partners* [1998] IRLR 63, the Court of Appeal adopted a more liberal interpretation of s 123(1) of the ERA 1996 and held that, as a matter of justice and equity, loss consequent upon dismissal does not necessarily cease when the claimant finds a new job at an equivalent or higher salary if that job turns out to be temporary. The effect of the *Dench* decision is to focus on whether it is just and equitable for the claimant to recover compensation for continuing loss if the claimant, having lost the new job, is out of work at the time of the remedies hearing. The *Dench* principle was followed by the EAT in *Cowen v Rentokil Initial Facility Services (UK) Ltd* (EAT/0473/07). Relevant factors will include the nature of the new job, whether it was intended to be temporary or permanent, how long the new employment lasted, the reasons for the claimant leaving, and whether the claimant is able to bring an unfair dismissal claim against the new employer. The *Dench* principle applies to all elements of the award, so it is wrong in principle for an employment tribunal to conclude that a new job meant that the claimant had no claim in respect of continuing loss regarding loss of earnings but could claim for loss of pensions when she subsequently lost the new job since either the loss ceases in these circumstances or it does not (*Aegon UK Corp Services Ltd v Roberts* [2009] IRLR 1042). The position would have been different if the employment tribunal had not found, as a matter of causation, that the loss came to an end when Ms Roberts found her new job. **32.72**

A similar approach has been applied to cases where the employee elects to retrain rather than look for a new job. In such circumstances, a tribunal must also consider the question of mitigation **32.73** (see para 32.144) as well as the issue of causation. In *Simrad Ltd v Scott* [1997] IRLR 147, it was successfully argued that the employer's liability ceases under s 123(1) of the ERA 1996, where an individual chooses to undergo a period of training prior to embarking on a new career since any subsequent loss can no longer be attributed to the employer's action. But in *Khanum v IBC Vehicles Ltd* EAT/785/98 and *Larkin v Korean Airlines Ltd* EAT/1241/98 the EAT ruled that the claimant's decision to embark on a training course for a new career did not preclude the claimant from recovering compensation from her old employers for the loss suffered thereafter and this approach would appear to be consistent with the Court of Appeal's ruling in *Dench v Flynn & Partners* above.

32.74 Loss under s 123(1) of the ERA 1996 can only be awarded if it is sustained by the claimant as a 'consequence of the dismissal'. In *GAB Robins (UK) Ltd v Triggs* [2008] IRLR 317 the Court of Appeal ruled that an employee's loss under s 123(1) of the ERA 1996 does not cover financial loss arising as a result of personal injury caused by the employer's actions prior to dismissal. In support of its analysis, the Court relies on the House of Lords' ruling in *Eastwood v Magnox Electric plc and McCabe v Cornwall County Council* [2004] IRLR 733, where it was held that where an employer's pre-dismissal conduct is in breach of the duty of trust and confidence, this could give rise to an action for damages in the ordinary courts, even if compensation could not be awarded for such loss in an employment tribunal as a result of the House of Lords' ruling in *Johnson v Unisys Ltd* [1999] IRLR 279. On the facts in *Triggs*, the Court of Appeal ruled that the employment tribunal was wrong to direct that compensation could be awarded for future loss of earnings arising after the claimant's constructive dismissal caused by the employer's repudiatory breaches of the implied duty of trust and confidence, as the dismissal arose as a result of the employee's acceptance of the breach and therefore the loss was not consequent upon dismissal. It is unclear how far the court's ruling extends beyond the particular circumstances of that case, but on its face it would appear to substantially limit the compensation which can be claimed by an employee who suffers illness as a result of an employer's pre-dismissal conduct which leads to a complaint of constructive dismissal. However, much will depend on the act which constitutes the 'last straw' and the scope of the *Johnson* exclusion. For example, in *Gebremariam v Ethiopian Airlines Enterprise (t/a Ethiopian Airlines)* [2014] IRLR 354, the EAT held that the *Johnson* exclusion did not apply to acts of the employer that related to a decision to dismiss which is not carried through but which the employee then chooses to treat as sufficient to ground a complaint of constructive dismissal. For the same reason it would appear that the principle in *Triggs* does not apply to a direct dismissal (see para 32.141). Furthermore, the position would appear to be different in any event if the illness is caused by the dismissal itself (see para 32.141). In *Wood v Mitchell SA Ltd* (EAT 0018/10) the EAT ruled that the employment tribunal was wrong to treat the claimant's post dismissal illness as the 'cut off' point for an award of compensation. The tribunal should have assessed how long the employment would have lasted but for the dismissal and then assessed the value of lost pay and benefit during the period of sickness. This could have included compensation for loss of any sick pay and notice pay he would have received during that period.

32.75 In the rather unusual circumstances of *Sheffield Forgemasters International Ltd v Fox* [2009] IRLR 192 the EAT ruled that the employment tribunal had not erred in holding that the receipt of incapacity benefit did not preclude the claimants from obtaining compensation for loss of earnings during the same period. This was because the wording of s 30A of the Social Security Contributions and Benefits Act 1992 (and the Social Security (Incapacity for Work) (General) Regulations 1995), which determined the eligibility for incapacity benefit, did not preclude the individual from obtaining paid employment during the relevant period when benefit was payable. However, credit would have to be given for the value of such benefits received during that period (see para 32.186).

Industrial pressure disregarded

32.76 Section 123(5) of the ERA 1996 provides that, in assessing the compensatory award, an employment tribunal should take no account of 'any pressure which. by calling, organising, procuring, or financing a strike or other industrial action or threatening to do so, was exercised on the employer to dismiss the employee'. The assessment of compensation must be determined 'as if no pressure had been exercised'.

Meaning of loss

'Loss' is normally limited to financial or economic loss. It does not extend to non-pecuniary loss **32.77** such as injury to health or injury to feelings (*Dunnachie v Kingston Upon Hull City Council* [2004] IRLR 727).

The principal heads of compensation were identified by the National Industrial Relations Court **32.78** (NIRC)—now the Employment Appeal Tribunal—in *Norton Tool Co Ltd v Tewson* [1973] 1 All ER 183 as follows:

(a)   immediate loss of earnings, ie the loss of earnings between the date of dismissal and the date of the hearing
(b)   future loss of earnings, ie anticipated loss of earnings in the period following the hearing
(c)   loss arising from the manner of dismissal and
(d)   loss of statutory rights.

Although the *Norton Tool* case refers to loss of earnings (and in many cases loss of earnings will **32.79** make up the most substantial part of the claim), compensation may also be claimed for loss of benefits including loss of pensions (see para 32.98). Furthermore, by s 123(2) of the ERA 1996, loss is also taken to include '(a) any expenses reasonably incurred by the complainant in consequence of the dismissal, and (b) loss of any benefit which he might reasonably be expected to have had but for the dismissal'. Special provision is made for the loss of any entitlement or potential entitlement to a redundancy payment (see para 32.117).

Proof of loss

Whilst it is the duty of the tribunal to raise each of the heads of compensation referred to **32.80** above (*Tidman v Aveling Marshall Ltd* [1977] IRLR 218), it is up to the claimant to particularize the sums claimed. This point was stressed by the EAT in *Adda International Ltd v Curcio* [1976] IRLR 425, where, in the context of a claim for future loss of earnings, Bristow J said (at 427): 'The industrial tribunal must have something to bite on, and if an applicant produces nothing for it to bite on he will only have himself to thank if he gets no compensation for loss of future earnings'.

The claimant should come to the tribunal well prepared, with evidence which shows what his or **32.81** her loss is under each heading of compensation. It is now standard practice for a claimant to be required to prepare a schedule of loss prior to the hearing and, in more complex cases, for this to be updated shortly before the hearing. Failure to make a claim under one of the heads or to quantify a particular type of loss cannot normally be remedied on appeal (*UBAF Bank Ltd v Davis* [1978] IRLR 442).

Any relevant information which is not in the possession of the claimant should be obtained by **32.82** way of a request for further information or (if necessary) an order for disclosure. This will be particularly important in relation to a claim for loss of pension rights where much of the relevant information is likely to be in the employer's possession or control (see, for example, *Benson v Dairy Crest Ltd* EAT/192/89). Once the claimant has produced evidence of loss, in practical terms, the evidential burden will then switch to the employer if the employer wishes to challenge the sums claimed by the claimant.

Calculating the period of loss

The normal rule is that the claimant's loss is determined at the date of the remedies hearing, which **32.83** may or may not be the same date as the liability hearing. This rule applies even where the assessment of compensation is delayed because of an appeal to the EAT against the ruling on liability (*Ging v Ellward Lancs Ltd* (1978) 12 ITR 265 and *Gilham v Kent County Council* [1986] IRLR 56), although it is now quite common for tribunals to assess compensation even if an appeal is pending. In *NCP Services Ltd v Topliss* (EAT 0147/09), the EAT extended this principle to cases where there is an appeal against a financial award, ruling that in such circumstances it was 'just and equitable' that the award be calculated as at the date of the remitted hearing. However, it is clear from the Court of Appeal's ruling in *Griffin v Plymouth Hospital NHS Trust* [2014] IRLR 962 that much will depend on the terms of the remission: in *Griffin*, the 'first' appeal had been remitted by the EAT for the tribunal to consider what earnings Ms Griffin would have received on the basis of its earlier findings that she would have found new employment after a year (although she would not have returned to the same level of earnings for twelve years). There had been no challenge to this finding. But by the time of the remitted hearing, she claimed that the one-year estimate proved to be over optimistic and therefore wished to adduce further evidence on that point. However, the tribunal refused to admit the fresh evidence. The tribunal's judgment on this point was confirmed by the Court of Appeal. Underhill LJ referred to the statement of principle by Lord Wilberforce in *Mitchell v Mulholland* [1971] AC 666, that 'fresh evidence ought not to be admitted when it bears upon matters falling with the field or area of uncertainty in which the trial judge's estimate has previously been made' (as effectively was the case in relation to the estimate of future employment in the present case). This was the inevitable result of a system of law based on a 'once and for all' assessment and also was in the interests of finality of litigation. However, Underhill LJ stated that he could conceive of cases where evidence of subsequent events had to be admitted for purpose 'A' and it was then arguably impracticable not to admit it also for purpose 'B', even if it would not have been admissible if that was its sole purpose. Furthermore, it should be noted that where there is an immediate change in circumstances, it may be open to the parties to apply for a reconsideration (para 32.232).

32.84 As the NIRC pointed out in the *Norton Tool* case (see para 32.78), the compensation claim falls within two periods: the loss from the date of dismissal to the date of the hearing, and future loss.

Loss between the date of dismissal and the date of the hearing

32.85 The tribunal will first assess the loss between the date of dismissal and the date of the hearing. Subject to mitigation, that loss will normally come to an end when the claimant has found a permanent new job on an equivalent remuneration package. It has been argued that where the claimant has found a permanent new job on a higher salary between the date of dismissal and the remedies hearing, the claimant should give credit for the payments received between the date when the claimant commenced the new job and the date of the hearing (ie these sums should be set off against any loss claimed during the period when the claimant was out of work), but this argument was rejected by the EAT in *Lytlarch Ltd (t/a The Viceroy Restaurant) v Reid* EAT/296/90, and *Fentimans v Fluid Engineering Products Ltd* [1991] IRLR 151. In the latter case, the EAT justified its decision on the basis that if this were the case employees would be discouraged from mitigating their loss by finding new employment prior to the tribunal hearing and, as a matter of justice and equity, it would be unjust for the employer's liability to be reduced 'to a fraction of the loss sustained by the complainant during his period of unemployment'. On the other hand, it may be argued that 'justice and equity' work both ways and that on a strict application of the 'financial loss' principle, the claimant should give credit for all the payments received between dismissal and the date of the hearing. Furthermore, it could also be argued that the approach in these cases is inconsistent with the more flexible approach of the Court of Appeal in *Dench v Flynn and Partners* (para 32.72). It remains to be seen whether *Fentimans* is upheld in the future. If the new employment is of a temporary or uncertain nature, the tribunal is not necessarily required to set off the additional payments received during that period of employment against future loss (*Islam Channel Ltd v Ridley* EAT/0083/09).

32.86 A related issue is the extent to which a claimant has to account for payments received during the notice period. As noted at para 32.70, there is a conflict of authority on this point: in *Hardy v Polk Ltd* and *Morgans v Alpha Plus Security Ltd*, the EAT ruled that credit must be given for all payments received during the notice period, but in *Voith Turbo Ltd v Stowe*, the EAT relied on early authorities to conclude that the claimant should always, as a matter of good employment relations, receive compensation for loss of notice pay and should not be required to give credit for any payments received during that period. It was thought that this conflict of authority was resolved by the EAT's ruling in *Langley v Burlo* [2006] IRLR 460, but the issue has been left open by the Court of Appeal. It would seem that on the 'narrow' interpretation of the *Norton Tool* case adopted by the Court of Appeal in *Burlo* (referred to in para 32.70), the current position is that credit need not be given for payment received during the notice period.

Monetary losses

Compensation can be claimed for pay or the loss of any benefit which can be valued in money **32.87** terms and which forms part of an employee's remuneration package. Common examples of such types of loss include:

(a) pay
(b) notice pay
(c) holiday pay
(d) bonus and commission
(e) pension
(f) redundancy pay
(g) stock options
(h) company cars and petrol allowances
(i) accommodation
(j) company loans and mortgages
(k) childcare costs
(l) medical and other health insurance
(m) food
(n) telephones and other electronic equipment
(o) travel concessions
(p) clothing allowances or free goods
(q) club membership.

The object of the compensatory award is 'to compensate and compensate fully, but not to award **32.88** a bonus' (see *Norton Tool Co Ltd v Tewson* [1973] 1 All ER 183 (Sir John Donaldson)). As stated above, the burden is on the claimant to quantify the loss suffered as a result of the dismissal, and any claims made should be set out in the 'schedule of loss' (para 32.81).

Guidance on how to quantify some of the more typical types of claim is given below. **32.89**

Pay

As the EAT points out in *Brownson v Hire Services Shops Ltd* [1978] IRLR 73, 'other things **32.90** being equal, the first thing you lose in consequence of being dismissed is what you would have got in your pay packet'. Pay for this purpose means all payments which are included in the 'pay packet' whether payable under the contract of employment as of right or otherwise (ie overtime pay) excluding the payment of genuine tax-free reimbursement of expenses (*Tradewinds Airways Ltd v Fletcher* [1981] IRLR 272). Pay is assessed on actual earnings as a net figure, ie after deduction of tax and national insurance. It has been held, at employment tribunal level, that a claimant may be compensated for the loss of working tax credits received in the course of employment (*Mosse v Hastings & Rother Voluntary Association for the Blind* ET Case No 1103096/06/NW).

Normally the calculation is straightforward but difficulties can arise where the claimant's pay **32.91** varies from week to week due to output or as a result of fluctuating payments such as tips, bonuses, and commission. In such circumstances, the normal practice is for tribunals to work out the average amount an employee was earning over the twelve weeks prior to dismissal, but it is open to the claimant or the respondent to put forward some different reference period or to award a lump sum.

32.92 The rate of pay is the contractual rate. It is for the tribunal to resolve any disputes relating to the correct rate based on what the claimant should have been receiving at that time (*Kinzley v Minories Finance Ltd* [1987] IRLR 490).

32.93 The claimant is entitled to be compensated for any pay rises which take place or are likely to take place over the period of the award. In *Leyland Vehicles Ltd v Reston* [1981] IRLR 19 the EAT ruled that a pay increase awarded after the calculation date could not be included in the basic award even if it was backdated. The same principle applies to the additional award but in assessing the compensatory award a tribunal can take into account any pay increase awarded up to the date of the hearing, including a backdated increase and any increase which the employee might reasonably be expected to have had but for the dismissal. This may also include a future pay rise provided there is a high probability that, 'in conformity with company policy, the company would increase the salary of an employee' in the period of assessment (*York Trailer Co Ltd v Sparkes* [1973] IRLR 348).

Notice pay

32.94 Notice pay can be awarded as part of the claimant's lost earnings in the compensatory award (*TBA Industrial Products Ltd v Locke* [1984] IRLR 48). If there are doubts about the solvency of the respondent, it is advisable to invite the tribunal to make a separate award for notice pay as, in the event of the respondent's insolvency, statutory notice pay is recoverable from the Secretary of State under Part XII of the ERA 1996, whereas the compensatory award is not (ERA 1996, s 184(1)(b)) (see Chapter 34).

Holiday pay

32.95 Holiday pay can be recovered as part of the compensatory award (*Tradewinds Airways Ltd v Fletcher* [1981] IRLR 272), although a claimant cannot be compensated twice for the same loss and therefore such an award is unusual. Again, if there are doubts about the solvency of the respondent, it is advisable to invite the tribunal to make a separate award for holiday pay as in the in the event of the respondent's insolvency, up to six week's holiday pay is recoverable from the Secretary of State under Part XII of the ERA 1996, whereas the compensatory award is not (ERA 1996, s 184(1)(c)).

Bonus and commission

32.96 An important difference between a claim for wrongful dismissal and unfair dismissal is that in an unfair dismissal compensation claim it is not necessary to show that the claimant has a contractual right to the sum claimed as a claim will lie for the loss of any benefit which the claimant 'might reasonably be expected to have had but for the dismissal' (ERA 1996, s 123(2)(b)). Claims can be made for lost bonuses and commission payments on this basis.

32.97 However, it is still necessary to show, on a balance of probabilities, that the claimant had an 'expectation' of receiving such a payment and that that expectation was 'reasonable'. Such an expectation may be generated by the terms of the contract or by representations made to the claimant at an interview or in the employee handbook or at an appraisal. Furthermore, in relation to bonuses, even where a reasonable expectation is established, there may still be difficulties in quantifying the amount of the bonus, particularly where the scheme is completely discretionary. Tribunals may also base their awards on a 'percentage chance' approach if liability is established (*Allied Maples Group Ltd v Simmons & Simmons* [1995] 1 WLR 1602). The task may be easier where a bonus is a group bonus linked to targets where the evidence shows that the targets were achieved. Where the bonus is based on individual performance, evidence of bonuses paid to other people may set an appropriate benchmark. Quantification problems may also arise in relation to commission payments, although the rate of commission is likely to be stated in the scheme itself.

Pension

32.98 The right to recover compensation for pension loss was established by the NIRC in *Copson v Eversure Accessories Ltd* [1974] IRLR 247. (It is also an established head of claim in discrimination cases (see *Ministry of Defence v Mutton* [1996] ICR 590).) However, as the EAT pointed out in *Benson v Dairy Crest Ltd* EAT/192/89, it can be one of the most difficult areas to quantify.

There are three main types of pension arrangement in the UK: state, personal, and occupational. **32.99** The starting point is to identify the type of occupational scheme under consideration. Employers commonly provide two types of pension: a defined contributions scheme (for example a money purchase scheme); or a defined benefits scheme (or final salary scheme). If the employee is not required to make a contribution, this is known as a 'non-contributory' scheme. A defined benefits scheme aims to provide a certain pension benefit on retirement and the level of contributions will be the amount necessary to fund that benefit. The level of benefit is expressed as a specified fraction of the employee's salary at or near retirement (normally one sixtieth in the private sector and one eightieth in the public sector) multiplied by the years of pensionable service. In a defined contribution scheme, the scheme defines the contributions made by the employer and (if appropriate) any made by the employee. On retirement the employee receives the pension which can be bought by the redemption of those contributions (sometimes by way of an annuity).

In addition, in recent years personal pension plans have become popular as have 'stakeholder' **32.100** pensions. More recently, following the recommendations of the Turner report, the Pensions Act 2008 introduced a new approach by which most workers would be enrolled automatically (known as 'auto-enrolment) into a qualifying pension scheme. The government set up the National Employment Savings Trust (NEST) for this purpose. This formally commenced in October 2012 but was not fully implemented until February 2018. These are all varieties of defined contributions schemes. In a personal pension plan an employer and employee (or one or other) contributes to a private pension plan with an insurance company or other pension provider and the final pension on retirement will be an annuity purchased from the accumulated contributions.

Quite apart from these provisions, there are pensions payable by the State. These can consist of a **32.101** basic state pension, a graduated retirement benefit, and an additional state pension payable under the State Earnings Related Pension Scheme known as SERPS or a State Second Pension (S2P).

In *Copson v Eversure Accessories Ltd* [1974] IRLR 247, the NIRC held that compensation for pen **32.102** sion loss falls to be considered under two heads: past loss and future loss. However, there may be cases where it may not be appropriate to make an award at all.

Guidance on how to quantify an award for loss of pension right is given in the booklet 'Employment **32.103** Tribunals: Principles for Compensating Pension Loss' (referred to as the 'Principles') which was published in August 2017. This has succeeded the earlier guidance *Compensation for Loss of Pension Rights: Employment Tribunals*, first published in 2003 but revised in 2004, which was withdrawn in 2015 following the Court of Appeal's ruling in *Griffin v Plymouth Hospital NHS Trust* [2014] IRLR 962, as it was no longer reliable. The new 'guidance' has been prepared by a working group of experienced employment judges. The aim is to achieve justice, simplicity, proportionality and, pragmatism and flexibility. As the President of Employment Tribunals points out, the 'Principles' do not have the 'force of law'. Furthermore, as also recognized by the President, tribunals are not bound to apply the guidelines (*Bingham v Hobourn Engineering Ltd* [1992] IRLR 298) and it is open to the parties to call their own expert actuarial evidence if they wish to do so (*Port of Tilbury (London) Ltd v Birch* [2005] IRLR 92), although tribunals must have regard to the Principles. At the time of writing, it remains to be seen whether and to what extent the Principles are approved by the appellate court. The principles can be downloaded from https://www.judiciary.gov. uk/pubnlications/employment-rules-and-legislation-practice-direction (for England and Wales) and https://www.judiciary.gov.uk/publications/direction-for-employment-tribunals-scotland (for Scotland).

Summary of key concepts

The key concepts set out in the Principles may be summarized as follows: **32.104**

(i) It is assumed in the absence of evidence to the contrary that where a claimant has not accrued significant occupational pension rights, the claimant will retire at the state pension age. By contrast if a claimant has accrued significant occupational pension rights in a scheme with a normal retirement age below state pension age, the tribunal will assume retirement at the scheme's normal retirement age in the absence of evidence to the contrary. It will be for the tribunal to determine what level of benefit is 'significant'.

(ii) The Principles explain the difference between gross income and net income, which is relevant when assessing both loss of earnings (and how this is affected by tax relief on pension contributions and types of pensions tax relief that may be applied and loss of pension rights'). The Principles also explain how awards of compensation are 'grossed up' in accordance with the so-called '*Gourley* principles' (see para 32.233).

(iii) The Principles explain the operation of the new state pension system and provide a framework for calculating loss of state pension rights under the new system.

(iv) In so far as loss of occupational pension rights are concerned, the Principles identify a category of 'simple' cases. In such cases, the tribunal will use the contributions method to assess a claimant's net pension loss (see below).

(v) The Principles seek to identify a category of 'complex' cases for which the contributions method is not suited. The Principles describe a 'seven steps' model by which loss will be ascertained in these complex cases (see below).

(vi) The Principles suggest that it may be appropriate in complex cases for a two-stage remedy hearing to be conducted (see below).

(vi) Specific guidance is offered in relation to specific public sector schemes in Appendix 1 and worked examples of the principles in operation are given in Appendix 3.

State pension

32.105 Dismissal interrupts an individual's national insurance contributions record but in most cases the interruption will not be sufficiently long to result in a loss of what the Principles call 'NSP' benefits. In rare cases, there may be a loss where an individual fails to reach the necessary thirty-five qualifying years, and the Principles recommend at para 3.49 that an approach based on the Ogden Tables may be used to calculate such a loss.

Pension loss in defined contributions schemes

32.106 In relation to defined contributions schemes and personal pension schemes/aut-enrolment (which is specifically addressed in Chapter 4 of the Principles), the calculation of past and future loss (see paras 32.108 and 32.109) is normally relatively straightforward as it is based on the loss of the employer's contributions to the scheme up to the date of the hearing and (if appropriate) beyond, subject to the guidance on the calculation on future loss set out below and the other rules on deductions. The Principles state that this method will invariably be used where the claimants lost pension rights relate to a defined contributions scheme. It is arguable that where the sums would have been paid into a fund, some allowance should be made for the increase in the value of the fund between the date of dismissal and the date of the hearing (although a tribunal may well ignore this if the change is minimal). If the claimant suffers any kind of penalty for leaving the scheme early, this will be recoverable as compensation.

Pension loss in defined benefit schemes (final salary schemes)

32.107 Unless the claimant is covered by a private scheme which confers greater benefits than the State scheme there will be no loss, although there may be a loss of S2P during any period of unemployment. Furthermore, even where the claimant is covered by a pension scheme, there may be no loss if the claimant does not qualify for a pension under the rules of the scheme within the period covered by the award (*Manning v R&H Wale (Export) Ltd* [1979] ICR 433) or if the claimant's rights are valueless.

32.108 The first type of potentially compensatable loss is *past loss*, that is the loss up to the date of dismissal. The reason why this loss arises is that the pension loss suffered by the individual is based on the salary the individual would have earned on the date of retirement rather than at the date of leaving. This type of loss is referred to as 'loss of enhancement of accrued pension rights'. However, in calculating this loss, allowance must be made for the fact that deferred pensions are now revalued in line with the statutory requirements of either the rise in the RPI or 5 per cent per annum compound interest (whichever is the lower) and this will reduce the amount of loss. This would appear to be an over-estimate bearing in mind current inflation rates. There is no past loss if the claimant is offered the opportunity to transfer the full value of the accrued pension into a new fund provided that this takes into account any projected increases in salary (*Freemans plc v Flynn* [1984] IRLR 486 and *Yeats v Fairey Winches Ltd* [1974] IRLR 362). In this context, it should be borne in mind that employees leaving occupational pension schemes have the right to a 'transfer value' equivalent to the cash equivalent of the benefits to which the member leaving early would have been entitled had he or she remained in the scheme. However, there is no obligation to provide for projected increases in salary, so where there is a transfer value it will be necessary to check whether there is a residual loss. Most schemes make provision for the return of contributions if the employee leaves the scheme before completing two years of service. Allowance must be made for the return of contributions, although this does not compensate the claimant for the value of the lost contributions in pension terms (*Willment Bros v Oliver* [1979] IRLR 393). At the very least compound interest should be awarded on those contributions. The duty to mitigate may also be relevant to the assessment of past pension loss. For example, an employee may be found to have failed to mitigate his loss where the employee elects for a return of contributions instead of a deferred pension (as the latter is the more valuable benefit) but the question whether this amounts to a failure to mitigate will depend on the facts (see *Sturdy Finance v Bardsley* [1979] IRLR 65). Allowance must also be made for the possibility of *withdrawal*.

32.109 Compensation may also be awarded for *future loss* of pension rights. Future loss for this purpose is divided between loss from the date of dismissal to the date of the hearing and future loss beyond the date of the hearing. Where, by the time of the hearing, the claimant has found a new job with equivalent pension benefits or is likely to do so in the near future and the period of 'future' loss is relatively short, a tribunal may well only award the loss of pension contributions over the period of loss (see para 32.108). Indeed, the tribunal may even conclude that there is no loss where the new and old schemes are equivalent (*Sturdy Finance v Bardsley* [1979] IRLR 65). Where the new scheme is less beneficial, the tribunal will have to assess the consequential loss to the employee bearing in mind the need to consider issues relating to 'new job facts' referred to at para 32.159 and other relevant conditions of employment such as a higher salary. Credit must be given for future pension benefits from the new pension scheme, whether it is a final salary scheme or a money purchase scheme (*Network Rail Infrastructure Ltd v Booth* EAT/0071/06/ZT). Tribunals must also consider the possibility of *withdrawal* (see para 32.110) and make allowance for future pension contributions by the employee (if the scheme was non-contributory or contributions were at a lower rate) and the *accelerated receipt* of the payment (see para 32.228).

Risk of withdrawal

32.110 The possibility of withdrawal, ie the chance that the claimant might have left the scheme and therefore suffered some loss in any event, has to be discounted both in relation to the calculation of past loss and future loss. In addition, it may be argued in the current environment that the employer might have closed the scheme in any event (see *Glen Dimplex UK Ltd v Burrows* EAT/0265/03, where a tribunal decision was overturned by the EAT for not considering this issue). Relevant factors will include the state of the business (ie the risk of future redundancy) and personal factors relating to the individual such as the chance of leaving on health grounds or for reasons relating to career development. The figure for future withdrawal may be the same or higher than the risk for past loss, although it is often the same. A failure to consider the possibility of withdrawal amounts to an error of law (*Manpower Services Ltd v Hearne* [1982] IRLR 281). It is suggested that this will still be relevant in 'complex' cases where an Ogden table approach is used as the Ogden Tables do not take account of all of these factors.

Methods of calculating the loss: (i) contributions method

32.111 There are a number of different ways of putting a value on past and future pension loss. The most straightforward is the *contributions method* which defines the loss in terms of the lost contributions made by the employer during the period of the award. The Principles acknowledge that this simple method is the most appropriate method in straightforward cases where the loss is relatively small, for example where loss is limited for *Polkey* reasons (see para 32.171), where the claimant has found a new job with an equivalent scheme or where, overall, the pay and benefits in the 'new' job are better than in the 'old'. The Principles suggest in this context that, 'as a rule of thumb', 'six months would very likely be a short period; twelve months would probably still be short; 18 months and above would arguably not be short'. Three examples of simple DB cases are given in Appendix 3. The 'Principles' acknowledge that the 'contributions' method is not appropriate in more complex cases.

Method of calculating the loss in 'complex' cases

32.112 It is recognized that the 'contributions method' is not appropriate in 'complex' cases. In this context the Presidential 'guidance' states that 'a case will be a complex one if the claimant's lost pension rights derive from a defined benefits scheme (including final salary schemes and CARE Schemes) and the loss is for a longer period'. Furthermore, 'complex cases include, but are not limited to career long loss cases'. The Principles themselves refer to 'complex' cases as being cases where 'the period of loss cannot be categorized as short or which for some other reason, involve a potentially significant quantifiable loss'. Beyond this, understandably the 'Principles' are less clear when it comes to identify what is meant by a 'complex' cases but it is suggested that these are likely to be cases where the 'contribution method' would leave the Claimant substantially under-compensated, where the period of future loss is substantial (see *Clancy v Cannock Chase Technical College* [2001] IRLR 331). The previous guidelines at para 4.14 referred to three factors which favoured the application of the 'substantial method' (and these may still be helpful in identifying complex cases: first, the length of time the claimant has been employed; secondly the 'stability' of the employment; and, thirdly, whether the claimant has reached the age where she/he is less likely to be moving on to 'pastures' new. What these factors have in common is that they all increase the likelihood that the employee would, but for the dismissal, still have been an active member of the scheme at retirement. The problem is that these assumptions, particularly the assumption of employment stability, may no longer be as relevant as they used to be, even for those who work in the public sector. This was recognized by the Court of Appeal in *Griffin v Plymouth Hospital NHS Trust* [2010] IRLR 962. In that case, the Court of Appeal suggested that where there is evidence that the employee would probably have changed jobs within a short period, then the previous 'simplified' approach should apply. On the other hand, the fact that final salary schemes are no longer so common in the private sector means that employees even with relatively short periods of service may still suffer substantial pension loss if they are dismissed and it can be shown that they were likely to remain in their employment. It was previously recognized that the previous substantial loss approach is not confined to cases involving a career-long loss (*Griffin v Plymouth Hospital NHS Trust* [2014] IRLR 962). In *Orthet Ltd v Vince-Cain* [2004] IRLR 857 the EAT considered that the substantial loss approach may be more appropriate where the period of loss is likely to be more than two years. Similarly, in *Sibbit v The Governing Body of St Cuthbert's Catholic Primary School* (EAT/0070/10), the EAT indicated that the substantial loss approach is appropriate where a claimant is in employment which is of a stable nature, had been employed for a considerable time (twenty-three years), and her employment was unlikely to be affected by the economic cycle. An employment tribunal will err if it fails to consider properly which of the two approaches is appropriate. So, for example, in *Griffin*, where the employment tribunal applied the simplified approach, the Court of Appeal observed that the employment tribunal had 'failed to engage with the general question to which [4.13] of the [2003] guidelines is directed'. The Court remitted the case with a direction that the substantial loss approach applied in the light of the fact that Ms Griffin was an employee who had specialist skills for which the principal (if not the only) market was the NHS and therefore she was likely to remain in the NHS for the whole of her career, even though she was only 34.

Methods of calculating loss in complex cases: Using the Ogden Tables

32.113 The Principles anticipate that the most common method which will be used to calculation loss in 'complex' cases is a method based on the Ogden tables. The relevant tables are set out in Appendix

2. Six examples are given of calculations in complex cases in Appendix 3. The Principles state that an Ogden table approach will involve seven steps:

(i) the first step is to identify what the claimant's net pension income would have been at their retirement age if dismissal had not occurred

(ii) the second step is to identify what the claimant's net pension income will be at their retirement age in the light of their dismissal

(iii) the third step is to deduct the result of step 2 from the result of step 1 which produces a figure for net annual loss of pension benefits

(iv) the fourth step is to identify the period over which that net annual loss is to be awarded using the Ogden tables to identify a multiplier. The Ogden tables are reproduced in Appendix 2

(v) the fifth step is to multiply the multiplicand by the multiplier, which produces the capital value of the loss

(vi) the sixth step is to check the lump sum position and perform a separate calculation if required

(vii) the seventh step is to take account of the other sums awarded by the tribunal and gross up the compensation awarded.

The Principles acknowledge that the award may be further enhanced if the claimant is entitled to a lump sum payment or has the benefit of a death in service insurance as part and parcel of the pension scheme (which is not uncommon in public sector schemes). The Principles give further guidance on how this is to be calculated. Detailed information in relation to each of these steps can be found in Chapter 5 of the Principles. In relation to steps one and two it should be noted that where the claimant has found a new job and has the benefit of a money purchase scheme, or the tribunal concludes this is likely, then the calculation should take account of the income the claimant will receive from the new pension. For example, in *Network Rail Infrastructure Ltd v Booth* EAT/0071/06/ZT, the EAT ruled that the employment tribunal had erred in law because, having found that the claimant was likely to find comparable employment with the benefit of a money purchase scheme, it failed to make this assessment. The result was an 'obvious injustice conferring a windfall upon the employee'. The EAT observed that there may be 'some dispute about the best way in which credit can be given for future pension benefits, but what cannot be in doubt is that in a system which is designed to assess loss actually flowing from the unlawful act, credit must properly be given in one way or another'. Furthermore, in relation to step four, the Ogden tables for pension loss only make allowance for mortality (see para 30 of the commentary on the Ogden Tables) and therefore it may be necessary to make a further reduction for the risk of withdrawal to take account of the factors referred to in para 32.110 above.

Methods of calculating loss in complex cases: other alternatives

The Principles acknowledge that the parties there may be cases where the parties wish to use an alternative method to the Ogden tables and in such circumstances the parties may wish to instruct an expert to assess the loss. This will involve valuing the capital cost of buying an annuity which would yield an equivalent pension which the employee would have had but for the dismissal and from this to deduct what the claimant has received (*John Millar & Sons v Quinn* [1974] IRLR 107) and will involve obtaining an actuarial valuation of what the claimant has lost under the scheme taking account of the periods of both past loss and future loss. **32.114**

Contributory fault

The normal rules on contributory fault (see para 32.198) apply to the sums awarded for loss of pension rights (*Port of Tilbury (London) Ltd v Birch* [2005] IRLR 92). **32.115**

Case management of claims for pension loss

The Principles give new guidance as to the procedure that should be applied by tribunals in approaching claims for pension loss. The first change is that parties will be invited at an early stage to identify whether or not the claim is likely to involve a significant award for pension loss. It will no longer be sufficient for a professional party to state in a schedule of loss that pension loss is to be confirmed. However, this is not quite as prescriptive as it sounds: tribunals have published a new **32.116** standard form agenda which deals with pension loss in para 3.5. This requires the claimant in cases of dismissal to confirm whether or not he/she was a member of an occupational pension scheme and if so whether it was a defined benefits scheme or a defined contribution scheme? Where the calculation of loss is likely to be 'complex', for example, in cases involving civil servants, teacher, nurses, doctors, academics, and firefighters, the issue of pension loss will not be addressed at the same hearing as liability. Such cases will involve at least one remedy hearing, but the Principles raise the possibility of two remedies hearing being held in some 'complex' cases: the first to determine all other issues relating to remedy (including submission on whether the Ogden approach should apply to the calculation of pension loss) and the second hearing to determine pension loss itself if the parties are not able to agree a figure either by themselves or possibly through judicial mediation or assessment. In addition, specific guidance is given on the disclosure of pension-related information including the rate of employee/employer contributions, details of ancillary benefits such as death in service benefits, normal retirement age under the scheme, in a defined contributions scheme, the current value of the invested funds, in a defined benefits scheme, the value of accrued benefits (particularly where the scheme has closed) and also in relation to future accruals, whether this is based on final salary, CARE, or some other design, and also whether there is provision for a lump sum. It will also be necessary to disclosure a statement of the claimant's projected benefits and ideally a statement of projected benefits if dismissal had not occurred that may help quantify the impact of various withdrawal factors, a statement of benefits from any new employment and disclosure of pay slips setting out deductions to seek to identify the respective contributions of employer and employee.

Redundancy pay

32.117 Where a redundancy payments scheme is more generous than the statutory scheme, compensation may be claimed for the loss of this benefit pursuant to s 123(3) of the ERA 1996, which provides that 'the loss referred to [in s 123(1) ERA 1996], shall be taken to include in respect of any loss of (a) any entitlement or potential entitlement to a payment on account of dismissal by reason of redundancy (whether in pursuance of Part XI or otherwise), or (b) any expectation of such a payment'. This provision, on which there is a dearth of authority, means that a claim can be made where there is a contractual right to an enhanced redundancy payment (or otherwise) or where there is a reasonable expectation of such a payment, ie where such a payment formed part of a collective agreement. The right to claim compensation in such circumstances was recognized by the EAT in *Lee v IPC Business Press Ltd* [1984] ICR 306, where it was said that:

> if it is shown that there was a term in the contract between Mr Lee and the company which was binding on the company and meant that, if Mr Lee was made redundant, he was entitled as a matter of contract to more than the statutory redundancy payment, that is something which he had lost as a result of being unfairly dismissed and it is one of the things which the industrial tribunal should be able to take into account in arriving at their award of compensation if any.

32.118 Such a claim can clearly be made where an employee is unfairly dismissed on grounds of redundancy but it is arguable that it can also be made where the employee would (or might) have been made redundant during the compensation period.

Stock options

32.119 It has become common for senior staff to be granted stock options as part of an employee incentive package. There are a number of different schemes recognized by HM Revenue & Customs (HMRC) including Share Incentive Plans, approved SAYE Option Schemes, approved Company Share Option Schemes, and Enterprise Management Incentive Schemes.

32.120 The value of these schemes will vary depending on their nature. In *Leonard v Strathclyde Buses Ltd* [1998] IRLR 693, the EAT accepted that compensation could be awarded for the loss in value caused by the premature sale of stock options. The claimants successfully recovered the difference between the share price on termination and the share price they would have received but for their unfair dismissal.

32.121 Compensation may be awarded for the loss of the option itself provided the employment tribunal is satisfied that the claimant would have been granted such an option but for the dismissal

(*O'Laoire v Jackel International Ltd* [1991] IRLR 170), ie that there was a real and substantial chance that the claimant would have been granted the option. In *Timothy James Consulting Ltd v Wilton* [2015] IRLR 368, the EAT, applying *Allied Maples Group Ltd v Simmons* [1995] 1 WLR 1602 and *Wellesley Partners LLP v Withers LLP* [2014] EWHC 556, upheld an employment tribunal's ruling not to award compensation at all for the loss of a chance to buy equity in the company on the basis that the claimant had not established that there had been a substantial chance of her securing equity in the company and that the value of the prospective equity had been 'purely speculative'. Importantly, the tribunal had found that the company would not be sold in the 'foreseeable future' and there was also real uncertainty about what the sale price would be when the business was sold. It was therefore impossible, on a balance of probabilities, to assess the 'loss of the chance' as claimed by the claimant. Even where the option has been granted, the loss may be difficult to quantify and prove where there is no more than a mere promise to grant such an option in the future. Nonetheless, where possible, tribunals should seek to place a value on these rights. In *Casey v Texas Homecare Ltd* EAT/632/87, an employment tribunal declined to estimate the value of an employee's share option because it was too 'speculative and indefinite'. The EAT held that this was wrong and, on the basis of the evidence presented to it, awarded £1,000 after making allowance for the chance that the share price might fall. As the EAT recognized in *Selective Beauty (UK) Ltd v Hayes* UKEAT/0582/04/SM, not referred to in *Wilton*, this can involve a separate assessment of any uncertainties connected with the future exercise of share options, including an assessment of the likelihood of flotation, the likely value of the shares on flotation, and the likelihood that the claimant would have purchased some, or all, of the shares.

Company cars and petrol allowances

Compensation may be awarded for the loss of private use of a company car. The position is different if the car is used exclusively for business purposes or if private use is minimal (as, for example, where the employee has use of a 'pool' car for business purposes). In such circumstances, little or no compensation will be awarded. On the other hand, the award will be greater if, in addition to the use of the car, the employee also receives free maintenance, tax, insurance, and petrol. **32.122**

There is no single or universal method of valuing the loss of the use of a car. Indeed, in many cases, tribunals do not always give any clear indication of their reasons for making an award or the method used in choosing a particular figure. In the past, some tribunals have awarded a conventional figure of between £40 and £120 per week for the loss of this benefit depending on the type of car but much will depend on the evidence presented to the employment tribunal. Three methods are commonly used. **32.123**

AA and RAC estimates: One common method of establishing the value of being provided with a company car is to estimate the weekly costs of running a particular type of car based on the AA or RAC estimates which are published annually. This method was used in *Shove v Downs Surgical plc* [1984] 1 All ER 7, where £10,000 was awarded for the loss of a company Daimler over a thirty-month period and allowance was made for the ratio of business use to private use. Some employers have their own motor mileage allowances, which may also form the basis of a valuation. Adjustments may need to be made if the employee contributes to the running costs of the car. **32.124**

HMRC scales: Another method of valuing the benefit of a company car is to rely on the scale charges drawn up by HMRC for tax purposes. The scale charges are based on the cylinder capacity and age of the car or in the case of a more expensive car, its original market value and its age. The problem with this approach is that the scales have been devised with a view to valuing the benefit for tax purposes and, to some extent, reflect changes in government policy on this issue. The use of the scales was rejected in *Shove v Downs Surgical plc* [1984] 1 All ER 7 for this reason. **32.125**

Cost of hire and other methods: Another possible way of valuing the loss of a company car is for the employee to buy or hire a car and claim a proportion of the cost from the employer. This approach was relied on by the claimant in *Nohar v Granitstone (Galloway) Ltd* [1974] ICR 273, where the tribunal awarded the difference between the cost of purchase and resale. However, it is open to employers to argue that this over-values the benefit and fails to make allowance for factors such as depreciation or the hirer's profit. A variant on this method, where the car is purchased on hire **32.126**

Part D Remedies

purchase, is to award the claimant a proportion of the outstanding hire purchase payments (see *S&U Stores v Wormleighton* EAT/477/77, where the EAT described this approach as 'unscientific' but not 'unreasonable').

32.127 Increasingly, employers are offering staff a car allowance or a travel allowance as an alternative to providing a company car. Compensation may be recovered for the loss of this allowance.

Accommodation

32.128 Compensation may be awarded for the loss of rent-free or subsidized accommodation. This has become a more valuable benefit in the light of the increases in the cost of accommodation (whether rented or bought). Clearly no compensation will be awarded if the claimant pays the market rent (*Nohar v Granitstone (Galloway) Ltd* [1974] ICR 273).

32.129 There is no single or universal method of valuing this benefit. The most favourable method from the claimant's point of view is the open market value of the accommodation (see eg *Butler v J Wendon & Son* [1972] IRLR 15, where the open market rental of a tied cottage was assessed at £3 a week). Evidence of open market values may be obtained from surveyors or local estate agents or even advertisements in the local newspapers for comparable property. The more favourable method for employers is the cost of providing suitable alternative accommodation. This method is commonly used where the claimant has found new accommodation at the time of the hearing and the award is based on the difference between the two (*Lloyd v Scottish Cooperative Wholesale Society* [1973] IRLR 93). Where the claimant buys a property rather than looking for suitable rented accommodation, it is arguable that the award should be based on a discounted proportion of the mortgage payment or alternatively the interest element in the mortgage over the period of the award but there are no reported cases where this approach has been adopted.

Company loans and mortgages

32.130 Some employers, particularly in the financial sector, offer their staff the benefit of interest-free (or reduced) loans or subsidized mortgages. The loss of such a perk may be recovered as part of the compensatory award. The problem is how to put a cash value on the benefit. In theory, the assessment should be fairly straightforward—the claimant's loss is the difference between the subsidy received and the market rate for the mortgage and the loan—but tribunals often opt for a broad brush approach rather than a mathematical quantification of the award. For example, in *UBAF Bank Ltd v Davis* [1978] IRLR 442, the tribunal awarded Mr Davis a lump sum of £2,000 for all the privileges he had lost as a result of his dismissal rather than the amount he said he would have to pay if he took out a mortgage from a high street building society.

Childcare costs

32.131 It is not uncommon for employers to offer either free childcare in the workplace or make a contribution to childcare costs. Where an employer does this, the loss may be claimed as part of the compensatory award. From an employer's point of view, the simplest way of calculating the loss will be the cost of providing the benefit to the employer, but from the employee's point of view, the loss will be based on the 'reasonable' cost of providing equivalent childcare. Where the employer makes a contribution to the childcare costs, the financial loss will be the loss of that contribution (*Visa International Ltd v Paul* [2004] IRLR 42).

Medical and other health insurance

32.132 Private medical insurance is also a common benefit. Often the employer's 'group' scheme will also make provision for the employee's family and children. From an employer's point of view, the most favourable way of valuing this benefit is the cost of providing it to the employee. The problem from an employee's point of view, however, is that the cost to the employee of finding equivalent cover may be higher because the employer is able to gain the advantage of being a 'group' purchaser and therefore the value to the employee is the cost of alternative equivalent provision. The same principles apply to claims for loss of death in service benefits and other forms of life assurance.

However, in *Knapton v ECC Card Clothing Ltd* [2006] IRLR 756 the EAT ruled that compensa- **32.133** tion is only recoverable for the loss of such benefits if the claimant has actually suffered the loss, for example as a result of death or illness, or has bought such cover. Where, as in *Knapton*, the claimant survived for the period covered by the award and did not take out life assurance cover during that period, there was no financial loss up to the date of the hearing and therefore compensation could not be awarded for the loss of life assurance. On the other hand, where either the claimant does suffer the loss through death or illness, the award may be substantial. For example, in *Fox v British Airways plc* [2013] IRLR 812, the claimant's estate recovered £85,000 as compensation for a death in service benefit where the claimant died very shortly after his dismissal. However, the Court of Appeal observed that in most cases an award would be based on the cost of obtaining insurance to provide equivalent benefits.

Food

Some employers have their own staff catering facilities: sometimes the meals are provided free of **32.134** charge but more often they are subsidized. The loss of this perk has been claimed in a number of cases where on the evidence the value of the benefit was substantial.

Telephone, mobile, laptop, and other electronic equipment

Sometimes employers pay for the rental and telephone/mobile charges. Compensation may be re- **32.135** covered for the value of this benefit (see *Dundee Plant Hire v Riddler* EAT/377/88, where £160 was awarded for the free use of a telephone covering both the rental and telephone charges). Claimants wishing to make such a claim would need to produce evidence of the rental fee and relevant bills showing the value of private use of the phone or mobile or other electronic equipment.

Expenses

Section 123(2)(a) of the ERA 1996 provides that the assessment of loss also includes any expenses **32.136** reasonably incurred as a result of the dismissal. However, in relation to such claims, the tribunal must be satisfied:

(a) the expenses were incurred as a result of dismissal
(b) the expenses were reasonably incurred
(c) the sums incurred were reasonable in themselves.

Costs associated with finding a new job are the most common kind of expenses awarded by tri- **32.137** bunals. For example, the cost of attending interviews (*Leech v Berger, Jensen & Nicholson Ltd* [1972] IRLR 58) and, in appropriate cases, removal expenses and relocation costs (*Lloyd v Scottish Cooperative Wholesale Society* [1973] IRLR 93) and even estate agents' fees and legal costs (*Daykin v IHW Engineering Ltd* COIT 1440/117 and *United Freight Distribution Ltd v McDougall* EATS/ 218/94, where £500 was awarded to cover the legal fees necessary to sell the claimant's house).

In addition, tribunals have allowed employees to recover some of the costs incurred in setting up **32.138** a business where this was considered a reasonable way of mitigating the loss flowing from the dismissal. For example, in *Gardiner-Hill v Roland Berger Technics Ltd* [1982] IRLR 498, the claimant successfully recovered £500 of expenses which he had incurred in setting up a business.

Legal costs associated with the tribunal hearing itself, however, are not recoverable as part of the **32.139** compensatory award (*Raynor v Remploy* [1973] IRLR 3). (For the rules on legal and preparatory costs, see Chapter 12.)

Non-monetary loss

Manner of dismissal

As stated above, in *Dunnachie v Kingston Upon Hull City Council* [2004] IRLR 727 the House of **32.140** Lords decided that the loss contemplated by s 123(1) of the ERA 1996 does not include compensation for injury to health or injury to feelings. Nonetheless, compensation for financial loss may

Part D Remedies

be awarded where the manner of dismissal means that the claimant is likely to be at a disadvantage in the labour market or causes psychological injury which prevents the claimant from looking for a new job (*John Millar & Sons v Quinn* [1974] IRLR 107; *Devine v Designer Flowers Wholesale Florist Sundries Ltd* [1993] IRLR 517; *Vaughan v Weighpack Ltd* [1974] IRLR 105).

32.141 The correct approach to such situations was clarified by the Court of Session in *Dignity Funerals Ltd v Bruce* [2005] IRLR 189, where a tribunal declined to award the claimant compensation for reactive depression which was allegedly caused by the dismissal but did take this into account in its award for future loss. Confirming the correctness of the tribunal's approach, the Court of Session said that if it could be shown that the depressive illness was caused by the dismissal and it was this that prevented the claimant from working, then a full award of compensation for future loss of earnings should be made. On the other hand, where the dismissal is merely one of two or more concurrent causes of the claimant's loss or where the dismissal was a cause of the loss for only part of the period, a tribunal should consider what sum is 'just and equitable' to award and 'in all likelihood' this would be less than the full amount of the wages claimed by way of future loss. However, it is important to stress that such loss must be a consequence of the dismissal: losses arising from a series of events leading up to 'last straw' type constructive dismissal will not be recoverable. So, for example, in *GAB Robins (UK) Ltd v Triggs* [2008] IRLR 317 the Court of Appeal overturned the EAT's ruling that an employee was entitled to recover compensation for her loss of earnings for breaches of the duty of trust and confidence which preceded her constructive dismissal as such a loss was not a consequence of her dismissal. The claimant was therefore not entitled to recover compensation for 'wrongs already inflicted on her' as part of the tribunal's award of compensation for unfair dismissal. It may prove difficult to apply the Court's approach to cases where the loss of earning capacity is primarily, or substantially, a consequence of the final act which caused the constructive dismissal. In such circumstances, the approach in the *Dignity Funerals* case is still likely to be relevant.

Loss of statutory rights

32.142 A fixed award is normally made for the loss of statutory rights (ie the need to re-qualify for statutory protection against unfair dismissal and other statutory rights). In *SH Mufett v Head* [1986] IRLR 488, the EAT held that this should be in the region of £100 (although these days the conventional sum is closer to £400). A sum can also be claimed for the loss of other employment rights such as the loss of statutory notice. In *Daley v AE Dorset (Almar Dolls) Ltd* [1981] IRLR 385, the EAT suggested that this should be fixed at half the employee's statutory entitlement at the time of dismissal, although a tribunal which awards more than this conventional amount will not necessarily err in law (*Arthur Guinness Son & Co (GB) Ltd v Green* [1989] IRLR 288). A 'Daley' award will normally only be made where the claimant has lost the protection afforded by a long notice period which will take an equally long period to re-establish.

32.143 On the other hand, a tribunal will not necessarily err in law if it makes no award for loss of statutory rights (*Harvey v Institute of the Motor Industry (No 2)* [1995] IRLR 416), particularly where the loss is too remote (ie if it is found that the employee is unlikely to be on the labour market for some time due to illness (*Gourley v Kerr* EAT/692/81), for some other reason such as retraining (*Pagano v HGS* [1976] IRLR 9), or the claimant is going to become self-employed). The award may also be refused where the claimant has a relatively short period of service with the previous employer and has quickly found a new job.

PART 2 THE DUTY TO MITIGATE AND FUTURE LOSS

The duty to mitigate

32.144 Section 123(4) of the ERA 1996 provides that in ascertaining the loss to be awarded under s 123(1) of the ERA 1996, a tribunal 'shall apply the same rule concerning the duty of a person to mitigate his loss as applies to damages recoverable under the common law of England and Wales or (as the case may be) Scotland'. The common law duty to mitigate distinguishes between the duty to mitigate in law and in fact. Mitigation in law means that the claimant should not recover damages for any loss which could reasonably have been avoided. Mitigation in fact means that the claimant must give credit for any benefit received as a consequence of the respondent's breach (see para 32.186). Evidence of any attempt to mitigate (whether successfully or otherwise) should be included in the 'schedule of loss'.

General principles

In the context of unfair dismissal law, the duty to mitigate in law means that the claimant must take **32.145** reasonable steps to minimize the loss by finding another job or, as Donaldson J put it in *Archibold Freightage Ltd v Wilson* [1974] IRLR 10: 'It is the duty of an employee who has been dismissed to act as a reasonable man would do if he had no hope of receiving compensation from his previous employer'. Similarly, in *Wilding v British Telecommunications plc* [2002] IRLR 524, the Court of Appeal held that the steps taken by the employee must be reasonable as a claimant cannot recover compensation for any loss which he could have avoided by taking reasonable steps. But, as the EAT points out in *Cooper Contracting Ltd v Lindsey* (EAT/0184/15), the fact that the claimant has not taken one reasonable step does not necessarily mean that there has been a failure to mitigate loss.

The burden of proving a failure to mitigate is on the employer (as the wrongdoer): *Fyfe v Scientific* **32.146** *Furnishing Ltd* [1989] IRLR 331 (as it is at common law: *Bessenden Properties Ltd v JK Corness* [1974] IRLR 338) and confirmed in *Cooper Contracting Ltd v Lindsey* (EAT/0184/15). This means that an employment tribunal will not be obliged to make such a finding if no evidence is put forward by the employer. The employment tribunal is not required to fill the 'evidential vacuum': *Ministry of Defence v Hunt* [1996] ICR 554 There is some inconsistency in the case law as to whether the reasonableness of a claimant's attempts to mitigate loss are judged objectively, subjectively, or by the standard of a 'reasonable employee'. The Court of Appeal's ruling in *Wilding v British Telecommunications plc* (para 32.145) appears to support the latter, although Sedley LJ suggested that tribunals should consider whether the claimant's behaviour fell within a range of reasonable employee responses. As stated above, it is for the respondent to show that the claimant has acted unreasonably and the standard should not be too demanding. The employment tribunal should consider all the circumstances including the claimant's views. As Langstaff P pointed out in *Cooper*: 'he [the claimant] is not to be put on trial as if the losses were his fault when the central cause is that act of the wrongdoer'. The question of what is 'unreasonable' is essentially one of fact and pre-eminently one to be determined by the employment tribunal whose decision will only be overturned on appeal if it is shown to have misdirected itself in law or reached a decision to which no reasonable tribunal could have come. A failure to consider the issue of mitigation will, however, amount to an error of law (*Morganite Electrical Carbon Ltd v Donne* [1987] IRLR 363).

In *Savage v Saxena* [1998] IRLR 182, the EAT suggested that an employment tribunal should ask **32.147** itself the following questions in relation to mitigation of loss: (1) what steps should the claimant have taken to mitigate his or her loss? and (2) on what date would such steps have produced an alternative income? Having answered those questions, the award should be reduced accordingly. The way tribunals assess the deduction is set out in para 32.185.

Limits to the duty to mitigate

The duty to mitigate only arises after dismissal. This may be relevant to offers of re-employment **32.148** made prior to the termination of employment such as in *Gilham v Kent County Council* [1986] IRLR 56; *Trimble v Supertravel Ltd* [1982] IRLR 451; and *McAndrew v Prestwick Circuits Ltd* [1988] IRLR 514. There is nothing to prevent the employer from renewing such an offer after dismissal.

Similarly, employees will not be held to be in breach of their duty to mitigate by not pursuing an **32.149** internal grievance prior to their dismissal or resignation (*Seligman & Latz Ltd v McHugh* [1979] IRLR 130). A failure to pursue an internal appeal may be in breach of the duty to mitigate where such an appeal stands a good prospect of success. In *Hoover Ltd v Forde* [1980] ICR 239 the award was reduced by 50 per cent for this reason, but contrast *William Muir (Bond 9) Ltd v Lamb* [1985] IRLR 95, where the award was not reduced because the appeal involved too many 'imponderable

Part D Remedies

factors' and therefore the employee did not act unreasonably. These cases must now be seen in the light of the more general power to increase or reduce the award of compensation as a result of a breach of the ACAS Code (para 32.196).

Unreasonable refusal of offer of reinstatement

32.150 In certain circumstances, the claimant may be required to accept an offer of re-employment by his or her old employer in mitigation of loss (see *Martin v Yeoman Aggregates Ltd* [1983] IRLR 49) or even apply for vacant positions at his or her former employer (*Kelly v University of Southampton* EAT 0139/10).

32.151 In *Wilding v British Telecommunications plc* [2002] IRLR 524, a disability discrimination case, the Court of Appeal suggested that in applying the general principles referred to above to such an offer, it is necessary to consider the circumstances in which the offer was made and refused, the attitude of the former employer, the way in which the employee had been treated, and all the surrounding circumstances including the employee's state of mind. The Court advised tribunals not to be too stringent on the expectation of the employee. A relevant factor will include the timing of the offer. Normally it will not be unreasonable to turn down an offer made a long time after the dismissal, but as the *Wilding* case shows—where the offer was made after liability was established—there are no hard and fast rules (see also *Debique v MOD* (EOR December 2011, Issue 219), a discrimination case, where the claimant was found to have acted unreasonably in turning down an offer of redeployment made during the claimant's notice period to a position where her childcare needs could be more easily accommodated and therefore was held not to be entitled to compensation for loss of earnings). Another relevant factor is the clarity of the offer: the claimant may be reasonable in turning down an offer which is vague or unclear, but this will depend on the circumstances as it may be more 'reasonable' to ask the employer to clarify the terms. Other relevant factors include the reason for dismissal, the reasonableness of the dismissal, and in particular the impact it had on the relationship of trust which may be critical. It may be more reasonable to turn down an offer of reinstatement if the claimant has found a new job by the time it is made (*Yetton v Eastwoods Froy Ltd* [1966] 3 All ER 353; *How v Tesco Ltd* [1974] IRLR 194). Similar considerations apply to offers of re-engagement in alternative positions. Additional relevant factors will include the similarity of the positions and the length of time the claimant has been unemployed. In a TUPE situation, a claimant will not be treated as having acted unreasonably in turning down an offer of continued employment on inferior terms as this would defeat the intent of the TUPE Regulations 2006 (*F&G Cleaners Ltd v Saddington* [2012] IRLR 892).

Unreasonable refusal of early retirement

32.152 It may be open to an employer to argue that employees who unreasonably turn down an offer of early retirement on generous terms in redundancy or ill-health dismissals have failed to mitigate their loss, but employees will not necessarily act unreasonably in turning down such an offer. For example, in *Fyfe v Scientific Furnishing Ltd* [1989] IRLR 331, the employment tribunal held that the applicant was unreasonable in turning down a generous offer of an early retirement package made after he was dismissed, but the decision was overturned by the EAT on the grounds that the employer had not explained its offer in clear terms and had not given the applicant sufficient time to think about it. Furthermore, it should be remembered that the duty to mitigate only arises after dismissal (see para 32.144), so any pre-dismissal offer is irrelevant for this purpose.

Alternative employment

32.153 In most cases, the main issue will be whether the claimant has taken reasonable steps post-dismissal to find alternative employment with a new employer. As stated above, whether a claimant has acted reasonably in this regard is largely a question of fact and the citation of authority in this context is therefore mainly of illustrative value (*Bessenden Properties Ltd v JK Corness* [1974] IRLR 338). Much will depend on the state of the labour market and the personal characteristics of the employee. For example, an employee who is elderly or in poor health may experience particular difficulty in finding a new job and this is recognized by the tribunal (as are other discriminatory factors in the labour market). Claimants are expected not to turn down reasonable offers of alternative employment. However, this does not mean that they have to accept the first job offer that is made to them. As the NIRC said in *AG Bracey v Iles* [1973] IRLR 210:

> it may not be reasonable to take the first job that comes along. It may be much more reasonable, in the interests of the employee and of the employer who has to pay compensation, that he should wait a little time. He must, of course, use the time well and seek a better paid job which will reduce his overall loss and the amount of compensation which the previous employer ultimately will have to pay.

It should be observed that these comments were made at a time of high employment and the reasonableness of the claimant's behaviour needs to be considered in the context of the prevailing labour market. Claimants who have been out of work for some time may be required to be more flexible in their approach to job search both in relation to the level of pay (and terms and conditions) and the nature of the work they are looking for. Issues of relocation draw significant differences in response from tribunals: some tribunals expect the claimant to be willing to relocate whereas others less so (see *Ramsay v WB Anderson & Son Ltd* [1974] IRLR 164). The job search should extend to temporary or part-time work where the outlook for permanent employment is bleak (*Hardwick v Leeds Area Health Authority* [1975] IRLR 319).

Setting up a business or becoming self-employed

If there is no suitable alternative employment available, it is possible to mitigate loss by setting **32.154** up a business or becoming self-employed but it is for the tribunal to decide whether this was reasonable in the particular circumstances. The leading case on this point is *Gardiner-Hill v Roland Berger Technics Ltd* [1982] IRLR 498, where a former managing director aged 55 decided to set up his own business after being out of work for more than six and a half months. Furthermore, if the decision to set up the business was reasonable, the employee will not be penalized if the business subsequently fails (*Blick Vessels & Pipework Ltd v Sharpe* EAT/681/84). In *Cooper Contracting Ltd v Lindsey* (EAT/0184/15), the EAT upheld that tribunal's ruling that it was not unreasonable for the claimant, a carpenter, to return to self-employment after his dismissal (having previously been self-employed for eight years) on the basis that he could not work further afield on building sites for health, safety, and family reasons.

Retraining

Similarly, tribunals will not necessarily penalize claimants who decide to improve their skills by **32.155** retraining, thereby increasing their prospects of finding alternative employment. Again, much will depend on the state of the labour market and the length of the particular course. Tribunals are more sympathetic to short-term or part-time courses (*Sealy v Avon Aluminium Co Ltd* EAT/516/78) than long-term academic courses (*Holroyd v Gravure Cylinders Ltd* [1984] IRLR 259). It is more difficult to show that it was reasonable to embark on a long-term course which involves a career change, but there are no hard and fast rules. For example, in *Khanum v IBC Vehicles* EAT/785/98, the tribunal found that it was reasonable for the complainant to take up a place at Luton University to study for a computer systems degree because she considered it would be difficult to find employment without it. The EAT dismissing the appeal agreed, noting that there were special factors supporting this decision. Similarly, in *Orthet Ltd v Vince-Cain* [2004] IRLR 857, a sex discrimination case, the EAT held that the tribunal had not erred in law in awarding compensation covering the whole period of a four-year training course to become a dietician.

Future loss

The more difficult task is to assess the award for future loss. This will often be a highly speculative **32.156** exercise. Nonetheless, an employment tribunal is under a statutory duty to assess what is just and equitable and this may involve making a prediction based on the evidence it has heard. A tribunal cannot be allowed to 'opt out' of that task simply because the task is a difficult one and may involve speculation (*Scope v Thornett* [2007] IRLR 155). If the claimant has found a new job by the time of the hearing where the remuneration package is either equivalent to or better than the old job, then there will be no future loss. On the other hand, the task will be less straightforward where the new job is less well paid (or the overall package is less generous) or the claimant is still unemployed at the time of the hearing. This will involve having to assess how long the loss is likely to continue, which entails consideration of what the EAT in *Kingston Upon Hull City Council v Dunnachie (No 3)* [2003] IRLR 843 called 'old job facts' and 'new job facts'.

Old job facts

32.157 'Old job facts' include whether the claimant would have remained in the job anyway and, if so, for how long? Overall, this will involve a reasonable assessment based on the evidence as to how long the employment would have lasted. So, for example, in *Scope v Thornett* [2007] IRLR 155 the employment tribunal was entitled to have considered how long the employment relationship would have lasted in the light of the relationship problems between the claimant and one of her colleagues but had not given adequate reasons for its conclusion that the employment would have come to an end after six months. In the absence of evidence to the contrary, it should be assumed that the claimant would have wished to have stayed in the old job (*Chagger v Abbey National plc* [2010] IRLR 47) and that it would be exceptional to conclude that the claimant would have left the job voluntarily. In *Wardle v Credit Agricole Corporate & Investment Bank* [2011] IRLR 604, the Court of Appeal, following *Chagger* (above) stated that it was wrong for the employment tribunal to have reduced its award by 80 per cent on the basis of a generalized assumption that there was an 80 per cent chance that the claimant would have left his job in any event. Elias LJ observed that, in general, such evidence is unlikely to assist the tribunal is assessing the loss. Nonetheless there may be factors whether personal (such as health, family situations, or relocation) or economic (such as new technology, fall-off in orders, lay-offs, redundancies), which should on the available evidence (including the experience of the tribunal itself), be taken into account. Similarly, the ET is entitled to consider whether the claimant would have taken early retirement or considered a change of career. It is also entitled to consider whether the claimant would have been promoted and whether his or her level of earnings would have gone up or remained stable (other than by reference to the cost of living).

32.158 In considering these questions tribunals should take into account the actual consequence (as well as the hypothetical issues referred to above). For example, if a business is closed, employees who are unfairly dismissed at an earlier date cannot recover compensation for any loss they suffer beyond the date of closure unless they are able to persuade the tribunal that the closure is not genuine (*Gilham v Kent County Council* [1986] IRLR 56; *James W Cook & Co (Wivenhoe) Ltd v Tipper* [1990] IRLR 386).

New job facts

32.159 'New job facts' include whether the claimant is likely to find a new job at all? If so, when and at what salary? (This will involve considering issues of mitigation.) How long is any pay differential likely to last? Is the claimant likely to change jobs to one which is better paid? Is the claimant likely to be promoted? Are the earnings in the new job likely to be stable, subject to cost of living increases, or will they improve? Whilst these issues will inevitably involve a degree of speculation on the part of the tribunal, it is wrong in principle for a tribunal to simply pluck a figure from the air in determining its award for future loss (*NCP Services Ltd v Topliss* (EAT 0147/09)).

32.160 In considering these factors, tribunals will take account of the personal characteristics of the claimant such as the claimant's age, skill, and qualifications. For example, in *Cartiers Superfoods Ltd v Laws* [1978] IRLR 315, the EAT held that the tribunal was entitled to take into account the claimant's age, the prospects of her having a child, and of being relocated to another part of the country in awarding future loss over a three-year period as these considerations were all relevant in considering the likely period of future loss (although tribunals must take care not to make discriminatory assumptions in making allowance for these contingencies).

Age may be an important factor when a claimant is nearing retirement age (*Isle of Wight Tourist* **32.161** *Board v Coombes* [1976] IRLR 413), particularly where this is combined with a poor state of health (*Fougère v Phoenix Motor Co Ltd* [1976] IRLR 259) or some other disadvantage in the labour market (*Brittains Aborfield Ltd v Van Uden* [1977] IRLR 211), although age of itself may become less relevant, particularly following the abolition of the maximum statutory retirement age with effect from 1 October 2011 (Employment Equality (Repeal of Retirement Age Provisions) Regulations 2011 (SI 2011/1069)).

Tribunals will take into account the local and national state of the labour market in the light of **32.162** any specific evidence which is presented to it. Where the tribunal relies on its own knowledge of the local labour market, the tribunal should give the parties an opportunity to comment on that knowledge (*Hammington v Berker Sportcraft Ltd* [1980] ICR 248).

Subject to the guidance given by the EAT in *Dunnachie*, it is open to the tribunal to award com- **32.163** pensation for the remainder of the claimant's working life if the tribunal is satisfied that the claimant will not work again, or will not work again in an equally remunerative employment, or has to undergo a change of career and thereby suffers a career-long loss as in *Chagger v Abbey National Plc* [2010] IRLR 47. Such awards are rare (see also *Kerley v New Forest Bakeries Ltd* ET Case No 7405/83, where a 59-year-old baker with no experience of any other trade was awarded compensation until retirement; *Barrel Plating and Phosphating Co Ltd v Danks* [1976] IRLR 262, where the evidence showed that the claimant would have worked beyond normal retirement age and the compensation was assessed accordingly) and should be regarded as 'exceptional' (*Wardle v Credit Agricole Corporate & Investment Bank* [2011] IRLR 604). Indeed, where an employment tribunal concludes that there is a 50 per cent or greater chance that the claimant will find alternative employment within a specific period of time, the award should be limited to that period. So, in *Wardle*, the employment tribunal was found to have erred in awarding compensation for the remainder of the claimant's working life when it was 'sure' that the claimant would find an equivalent job within a defined period of time (albeit one that the tribunal had defined in percentage terms).

In broad terms, support for two different approaches may be found in the decided case law: first, **32.164** the use of a 'multiplier' which takes account of contingencies referred to above and, secondly, the use of actuarial tables such as the Ogden Tables.

Use of multiplier

Some tribunals have used a basic multiplier, ie a figure in terms of weeks, months, or years, which **32.165** reflects the employee's likely continuing loss of earnings and have then deducted or made allowance for the contingencies (referred to above) (see, for example, *Cartiers Superfoods Ltd v Laws* [1978] IRLR 315; *Tidman v Aveling Marshall Ltd* [1977] IRLR 218; and *Morgan Edwards Wholesale Ltd v Francis* EAT/205/78). Where such a multiplier is used, tribunals need not apply it with the same precision as a cost accountant or a skilled actuary (*Fougère v Phoenix Motor Co Ltd* [1977] IRLR 259).

Use of actuarial tables

More recently some claimants have relied on actuarial tables such as the Ogden Tables in support **32.166** of their claims for future loss. The Ogden Tables, which are updated periodically, are usually used in personal injury cases, and provide a multiplier to be used for calculating future loss of earnings up to retirement age (and beyond, if pension loss is appropriate) where a severely injured claimant will never be able to work again in his or her chosen field and therefore will be in either less remunerative employment or unable to work for the rest of his or her working life. The current tables for 2017–2018 assess the loss of life (Tables 1–2) or up to a retirement age of 50, 55, 60, or 65 (Tables 3 to 14) and make allowance for accelerated payments, for mortality rates, and other contingencies such as the risk of periods of non-employment and absence from the workforce because of sickness but not for other risks more directly associated with the employment relationship, such as the possibility that the level of earnings may have been affected by periods of illness (as opposed to absence from the workforce through sickness) or ceasing to work to care for children or other dependants. Nor do the tables allow for specific risks associated with the particular employment such as redundancy. The circumstances in which the Ogden Tables (or other actuarial tables) may be used in the calculation of unfair dismissal compensation were considered by the EAT in *Kingston Upon Hull City Council v Dunnachie (No 3)* [2003] IRLR 843, where it was held that the Ogden Tables (or any other similar such table which may be devised) should only be relied upon by an employment tribunal where it is satisfied that having considered the 'old job facts' and 'new job facts', the loss is likely to extend over the remainder of the claimant's life (ie a career-long loss) analogous to the circumstances where the table is used in personal injury claims. As stated in para 32.157, in the light of the guidance in *Wardle v Credit Agricole Corporate & Investment Bank* [2011] IRLR 604, such cases are likely to be rare. An example of such a case referred to by the EAT is *Kennard v Royal British Legion Industries* ET Case No 1100479/2001/R, where a disabled employee, aged 58, who was unfairly selected for redundancy, recovered compensation for the rest of his working life. Another example is *Chagger*, where there was strong evidence of a career long loss [2010] IRLR 47. Furthermore, for the reasons given above, the Ogden Tables do not take account of the many contingencies which fall to be discounted in the calculation of loss in an unfair dismissal claim and therefore even in those unusual cases where it is appropriate to use the Tables to calculate future loss, it will still be necessary to discount other contingencies such as specific risks associated with the particular individual or the particular employment. The EAT also warns of other 'dangers' of using actuarial tables such as: (a) difficulties in calculating loss of earnings over the relevant period as the differential may be variable, (b) the failure to address issues relating to tax and mitigation, and (c) the risk of double counting. Furthermore, it should be noted that the EAT's decision in *Dunnachie (No 3)* is not intended to apply to the calculation of pension loss where an actuarial method is used if the 'substantial loss' method is relevant to the calculation of pension loss. Similar points are made by the EAT in *Abbey National Plc v Chagger* [2009] IRLR 86 at page 104, where Underhill J makes it clear that even in a case where it is appropriate to use the Ogden Tables, it will never be right to use the multiplier taken from the main Tables without considering any 'contingencies' (referred to above), which the tables do not reflect.

32.167 It should be stressed that a tribunal has considerable discretion to award what is appropriate in the particular circumstances of the case. Although many tribunals limit their award to a fixed period of around twelve months based on their perception of the labour market, they are not bound to do so and, subject to the statutory maximum, compensation may be awarded for such period as the tribunal considers appropriate in the circumstances (see *Morganite Electrical Carbon Ltd v Donne* [1987] IRLR 363, where an award of thirty weeks up to the date of the hearing and fifty-two weeks thereafter was not considered excessive).

PART 3 DEDUCTIONS AND REDUCTIONS

The statutory provisions

32.168 The compensatory award may be reduced where:

(a) the employment tribunal finds that the conduct of the employee caused or contributed to the dismissal (ERA 1996, s 123(6))

(b) the employee is shown to have failed to mitigate his or her loss (ERA 1996, s 123(4))

(c) the employment tribunal considers it just and equitable to limit the award for some other reason (ERA 1996, s 123(1))

(d) the employee has failed to comply with the requirements of the ACAS Code (TULR(C)A 1992, s 207A(3)).

32.169 The compensatory award may also be reduced where a redundancy payment exceeds the statutory maximum (ERA 1996, s 123(7)), and where an *ex gratia* payment is received by the employee.

32.170 The grounds on which the compensatory award may be reduced or limited are considered in greater detail below.

'Just and equitable' reduction

General principles

Section 123(1) of the ERA 1996   **32.171**

> does not provide that regard should be had only to the loss resulting from the dismissal being unfair. Regard must be had to that, but the award must be just and equitable in all the circumstances, and it cannot be just and equitable that a sum should be awarded in compensation when in fact the employee has suffered no injustice by being dismissed[:]

(see *W Devis & Sons v Atkins* [1977] IRLR 314 (Viscount Dilhorne)). This principle has become particularly important since the House of Lords' ruling in *Polkey v AE Dayton Services* [1988] AC 344, [1987] IRLR 503, where the House of Lords held that the so-called 'any difference' rule did not apply to liability but that the degree of injustice suffered by the claimant was relevant to compensation. In *Audere Medical Services Ltd v Sanderson* EAT/0409/12, the EAT confirmed that the so-called *Polkey* principle also applies to cases where the dismissal is found to be automatically unfair, for example, whistle-blowing cases.

In *Tele-Trading Ltd v Jenkins* [1990] IRLR 430 the Court of Appeal stated that it may be just and   **32.172** equitable to make no award where:

(a)   at the time of the application to the employment tribunal, the employer can show that the employee is in fact guilty of the misconduct alleged against him or some other serious misconduct (see also *Polkey v AE Dayton Services Ltd* [1987] IRLR 503, 506–508 (Lord Mackay)) or

(b)   the employer would or might have fairly dismissed the employee if a thorough and just investigation had been conducted prior to the dismissal, whether or not the employee is guilty of the alleged misconduct (see also *Polkey v AE Dayton Services Ltd* [1987] IRLR 503, 508–509 (Lord Bridge)).

Dishonest behaviour

Category (a) cases cover situations where the evidence clearly establishes dishonest behaviour,   **32.173** or other serious misconduct, on the part of the employee even if the behaviour in question was not known at the time of dismissal (as in *Devis*). It is not entirely clear whether category (a) cases also allow an employer to put forward an alternative reason for dismissal as a basis for limiting the award of compensation, ie to argue that even if dismissal for reason 'A' was unfair, it would have been fair to dismiss for reason 'B' on the facts as known at the time of dismissal and that therefore compensation should be limited accordingly. There is some support for this view in *McNee v Charles Tenant & Co Ltd* EAT/338/90, and *Melia v Magna Kansei Ltd* [2005] IRLR 449, where Burton P considered that it was consistent with the ruling in *Devis v Atkins*, but in *Trico-Folberth Ltd v Devonshire* [1989] IRLR 396 the Court of Appeal appears to have held that it is not just and equitable to limit the compensatory award where the employers could have dismissed for another reason. However, the Court of Appeal's ruling may also be justified on the alternative basis that the findings made by the employment tribunal did not establish that the employers would have dismissed the claimant on the alternative ground. The point therefore remains arguable.

The rule in Polkey

Category (b) cases (which are the more common) are cases where the employer seeks to argue that   **32.174** dismissal would have been a reasonable response if a proper procedure had been followed, ie where there has been some relatively minor procedural irregularity. For example, where there is a failure to consult in a redundancy dismissal or there is some minor procedural irregularity in a misconduct dismissal. However, this argument will not succeed where the employer is unable to show that the dismissal would have been fair had a fair procedure been followed, for example there is insufficient evidence of the employee's guilt, as in *Tele-Trading Ltd v Jenkins* [1990] IRLR 430, or dismissal would not have been a reasonable response on the basis of the evidence (see *Panama v London Borough of Hackney* [2003] IRLR 278). It should therefore be assumed that 'the employer would have acted fairly though it did not do so beforehand' (*Hill v Governing Body of Great Tey Primary School* [2013] IRLR 275).

Distinction between procedure and substance?

32.175   At one time, it was suggested that category (b) arguments would only apply where the error was one of procedure rather than one of substance (see *Steel Stockholders (Birmingham) Ltd v Kirkwood* [1993] IRLR 515), ie that it might be open to a tribunal to limit or make no award where there had been a failure to consult in a redundancy case but not where the defect related to the selection criteria used to select those to be made redundant. However, the position has since been clarified by the Court of Session's ruling in *King v Eaton Ltd (No 2)* [1998] IRLR 686, where the Court stated that the distinction between 'procedural' and 'substantive' errors may be of some practical use in deciding whether it is realistic or practicable or just and equitable to embark upon an attempt to reconstruct a hypothesis to assess what would have happened had the error not occurred. Where the lapse is procedural, 'it may be relatively straightforward to envisage what would have been if procedures had stayed on track', whereas if what went wrong was more fundamental (or substantive), 'it may be more difficult to envisage what track one would be on, in the hypothetical situation of the unfairness not having occurred'. If in a particular case such as *O'Dea v ISC Chemicals Ltd* [1995] IRLR 599, it is possible to say that the claimant would have been made redundant or dismissed for some other reason in any event, or the tribunal is able with a degree of certainty to reach such a conclusion on a percentage chance basis, then there is no reason why the *Polkey* principle should be limited to procedural errors alone. However, where (to follow the analogy in *King*) the process has been completely derailed, an employment tribunal will not necessarily be required to speculate on the outcome because, as the Court recognized in *King*, this would involve embarking 'upon a sea of speculation where the opinions of witnesses could have no reliable factual starting point'. The Court of Session's approach to this question was approved by the Court of Appeal in *Lambe v 186K Ltd* [2004] EWCA Civ 1045. The Court stressed that the distinction between procedural and substantive defects was not helpful as the real issue is whether or not it is possible for the tribunal to reach a reasoned conclusion on the issue. A reduction will be upheld where adequate reasons are given. So in *Gover v Propertycare Ltd* an employment tribunal did not err in limiting its award to four months' loss of earnings as this represented the period which it would have taken for the employers to consult properly over a proposed variation in contractual commission. The EAT's decision dismissing the appeal (EAT/0458/05/2J) was subsequently confirmed by the Court of Appeal ([2006] EWCA Civ 286).

32.176   The tribunal should therefore ask itself: Could the employer have fairly dismissed and, if so, what were the chances that the employer would have done so? In *Ministry of Justice v Parry* [2013] ICR 311, the EAT ruled that this was not simply a 'yes/no' distinction but involved considering, on the balance of probabilities, the chance of what would have happened. The chances may be at the extreme (certainty that it would have dismissed, or certainty it would not), although more usually will fall somewhere on a spectrum between these two extremes. The tribunal is not answering the question of what it would have done if it were the employer; it is assessing the chances of what another person (the actual employer) would have done (*Hill v Governing Body of Great Tey Primary School* [2013] IRLR 275).

32.177   In summary, therefore, the options open to tribunals in category (b) cases are as follows:

(a) to make no award

(b) to limit the award to a particular period of time

(c) to make an assessment of the outcome on a percentage chance basis. In *Ministry of Justice v Parry* [2013] ICR 311, the EAT ruled that this could range from zero to 100 per cent

(d) to refuse to speculate on the outcome and make a full award. (See *Software 2000 Ltd v Andrews* [2007] IRLR 568, where the principles are usefully summarized by Elias P. It should be noted, however, that this case predates the repeal of section 98A(2) of the ERA 1996, and therefore some of the guidance is no longer applicable.)

However, it is not open to a tribunal to combine options (b) and (c). In *Zebrowski v Concentric Birmingham Ltd* EAT 0245/16, the EAT held that the tribunal had erred when it found that there was a 60 per cent chance that the employer would have dismissed had it followed a fair procedure and at the same time limited the award to two months from the date of dismissal. It would, however, have been open to the tribunal to limit its award to two months on mitigation grounds and reduce that award by 60 per cent.

The tribunal is under a duty to consider whether or not it should limit its award for these **32.178** reasons and a failure to do so may be grounds for appeal (*Wolseley Centres Ltd v Simmons* [1994] ICR 503). If the employer seeks to contend that the award should be limited for one or more of these reasons, the employer should call evidence in support of this contention. However, a tribunal must have regard to all the evidence when making the assessment, including any evidence given by the employee (*Software 2000 Ltd v Andrews* [2007] IRLR 568). The parties should then be given an opportunity to make representations on the nature and the extent of what is sometimes referred to as a *Polkey* reduction (*Market Force (UK) Ltd v Hunt* [2002] IRLR 863). As with the assessment of future loss, sometimes this will involve an element of speculation but the employment tribunal should not shy away from this task if there is sufficient evidence to form a rational conclusion (*Eversheds Legal Services Ltd v De Belin* [2011] IRLR 448). Difficult issues may sometimes arise in the application of the *Polkey* principle to TUPE cases. In *London Borough of Hillingdon v Gormanley and Others* (EAT/0169/14), the EAT overturned an employment tribunal's refusal to apply *Polkey* to a situation where the tribunal concluded that the local authority would not have terminated its contract with the claimant's previous employer if it had realized that this would have caused the claimant's contract to transfer to it under TUPE and therefore awarded the full loss suffered by the claimant. The EAT ruled that there was no evidence to support the tribunal's conclusion and no submissions had been made to that effect. The conclusion therefore amounted to impermissible speculation: the tribunal should have asked itself the question for how long would the claimant have been employed had he not been unfairly dismissed rather than what would have happened had the council not terminated the contract with its contractors. Whilst this also involved an element of speculation, applying *De Belin* (above), the tribunal should have answered that question in the light of the evidence.

Some illustrations of category (b) cases

The application of these principles is particularly relevant to the assessment of compensation in **32.179** redundancy dismissals where the dismissal is held unfair on procedural grounds such as a failure to consult or warn of impending redundancy, but it should be emphasized that the principles apply to any type of dismissal.

It is also important to bear in mind the nature and significance of the procedural defect. For **32.180** example, in *Parker v D&J Tullis Ltd* EAT/306/91, the tribunal concluded that, although the dismissal was unfair because the employers failed to show the witness statement of the employee who had witnessed the incident which led to the dismissal, the outcome would have been the same if the statement had been shown and therefore made no award (see also *Slaughter v C Brewer & Sons Ltd* [1990] IRLR 426, where a similar approach was taken to an ill-health case). In redundancy dismissals where there has been a failure to consult but the tribunal considers that the outcome would have been the same even if there had been proper consultation (ie where dismissal is inevitable), tribunals will often limit the award to the length of time it would have taken for such proper consultation to take place (*Mining Supplies (Longwall) Ltd v Baker* [1988] IRLR 417). The length of time will depend on the particular circumstances but a period of between fourteen days and one month is common (*Abbotts v Wesson Glynwed Steels Ltd* [1982] IRLR 51). A period of six weeks was considered excessive in the *Baker* case referred to above. A similar period may be appropriate if the tribunal is satisfied that the employee would have rejected an offer of alternative employment had it been made (*Lambe v 186K Ltd* [2004] EWCA Civ 1045). However, there are no hard and fast rules: in *Elkouil v Coney Island* [2002] IRLR 174 the EAT held that the tribunal had erred in limiting the compensatory award to two weeks where the employers had been aware of the redundancy situation some ten weeks earlier. The EAT held that, had the claimant been made aware of the risk of redundancy at an earlier stage,

Part D Remedies

he would have had a longer opportunity to find himself a new job and therefore substituted an award for a ten-week period.

32.181 On the other hand, a full award will be made if it is clear that the employee would have been retained if proper consultation had taken place. The position is more complicated if dismissal is a possible but not an inevitable outcome. In some cases, tribunals will adopt a percentage chance approach as in *Hough v Leyland DAF Ltd* [1991] IRLR 194, where the EAT upheld a tribunal's ruling that compensation should be reduced by 50 per cent to take account of the chance that the employee would have been retained. In *Rao v Civil Aviation Authority* [1992] IRLR 203, an illness case, it was held by both the EAT and the Court of Appeal that there was only a 20 per cent chance that the applicant would have kept his job if the employers would have postponed their decision on his future pending the outcome of further treatment for a back problem and accordingly reduced the award by 80 per cent, and in *O'Dea v ISC Chemicals Ltd* [1995] IRLR 599, the Court of Appeal held that the applicant had a 20 per cent chance of being retained and reduced the award by 80 per cent. A percentage chance approach may also be used in assessing the chances of the claimant obtaining alternative employment at the same or a lower salary. Where the alternative employment is based on a lower salary, then the percentage should be applied to that salary from the date when the employee would have started the new job (*Red Bank Manufacturing Ltd v Meadows* [1992] IRLR 209). In other cases, as stated above, particularly where different criteria would have been used, a tribunal may be unwilling to speculate on the outcome and will make a full award. *King v Eaton (No 2)* referred to at para 32.175 is an example of such a case.

Time-limited awards

32.182 It is open to tribunals to limit the award to a specific period of time if it considers that it was inevitable that the claimant would have been fairly dismissed within that period. For example, in *Winterhalter Gastronom Ltd v Webb* [1973] IRLR 120, the tribunal limited the compensatory award to three months because even if the claimant had received a final warning, it felt that 'he would not have been able to hold down the job in the future'. Similarly, in *O'Donoghue v Redcar & Cleveland Borough Council* [2001] IRLR 615, the Court of Appeal upheld an employment tribunal's decision to award six months' salary to the claimant on the basis that she would have been fairly dismissed at that time because of her divisive and antagonistic approach to her colleagues. A tribunal may also limit its award if the evidence shows that the claimant would have been made redundant or there was a risk of redundancy (for example *Youngs of Gosport Ltd v Kendell* [1977] IRLR 433, where the award was limited to nine months for this reason). As indicated above, such a risk may be assessed on a percentage chance basis where appropriate (see *O'Donoghue*, where the court did not rule out the possibility that the risk of future dismissal could be assessed in percentage terms, although it rejected the argument that the tribunal should have done this in the case before it). Where an employee has resigned and is dismissed during the notice period, the award will be limited to the unexpired period of notice (see *Ford v Milthorn Toleman Ltd* [1980] IRLR 30). It is also possible that a tribunal retains a residual discretion to limit the award for other inequitable conduct, although the reductions in the reported cases may be justified for one or more of the reasons considered below. However, a tribunal may not take account of conduct which takes place after dismissal. For example, in *Soros and Soros v Davidson* [1994] IRLR 264, the EAT held that the tribunal was wrong to take account of the fact that the applicant had allegedly sold confidential information about his employment to national newspapers after he had left his employment.

Impact of age discrimination legislation

32.183 Since April 2011, there has been no statutory default retirement age. It remains open to employers to justify the imposition of a contractual retirement age. But, even where an upper age limit is justified, ordinary unfair dismissal compensation claims may arise where the dismissal is found to be unfair for procedural or other reasons, although it is likely that awards will be limited under s 123(1) of the ERA 1996, for the reasons explained in paras 32.166–32.182.

Mitigation in law

An award of compensation may be limited to a specific period where the claimant is found to have **32.184** failed to mitigate his or her loss, pursuant to s 123(4) of the ERA 1996 in accordance with the principles set out in para 32.182 .

Assessing the deduction

There is no specific statutory guidance on how the deduction for a failure to mitigate should be **32.185** calculated. The normal approach is to decide when the employee would have found other work and limit the compensatory award accordingly (*Savage v Saxena* [1998] IRLR 182). If the tribunal concludes that the job will be less well paid, this will be reflected in the award for continuing loss (*Smith, Kline & French Laboratories Ltd v Coates* [1977] IRLR 276 and *Peara v Enderlin Ltd* [1979] ICR 804). Tribunals should not, however, reduce the award on a percentage basis as they do in assessing contributory fault or making a *Polkey* reduction.

Credit for payments received

In assessing the loss suffered by the claimant, it is necessary to give credit for any payment or the **32.186** value of benefits received since dismissal. The treatment of *ex gratia* payments is considered at para 32.218.

Remoteness

It is open to an employment tribunal to refuse to give credit for certain payments and benefits **32.187** which an employee receives after dismissal on the basis that the sums are either too remote or arise independently of the employer's wrong. In *Justfern Ltd v Skaife D'Ingerthorpe* [1994] IRLR 164, the EAT upheld a tribunal's decision that the claimant need not give credit for an educational grant which the claimant had received to attend a training course. The same principle is likely to apply to payments received by an employee under a private insurance scheme (*Parry v Cleaver* [1970] AC 1). Similarly, credit need not be given for payments received from the former employer's pension scheme as such payments are considered to be either analogous to payments from private insurance or are treated as collateral benefits (*Knapton v ECC Card Clothing Ltd* [2006] IRLR 756, EAT).

Payments in lieu

In the absence of an express or an implied agreement to the contrary, credit should be given for **32.188** any payment in lieu of notice (*Babcock FATA Ltd v Addison* [1987] IRLR 173) but note that the position in Scotland may be different (*Finnie v Top Hat Frozen Foods Ltd* [1985] IRLR 365).

Payments received from the new employer

As a general rule, credit must also be given for any payment received from new employment since **32.189** dismissal, including income from part-time employment (*Justfern Ltd v Skaife D'Ingerthorpe* [1994] IRLR 164). But this rule is subject to two provisos:

(1) For the reasons explained in para 32.85, a claimant is not required to give credit for any payments or benefits received after the claimant has found permanent new employment.
(2) Previously, there was a conflict of case law as to the extent that a claimant must account for payments received during the notice period (see para 32.70). In *Hardy v Polk Ltd* [2004] IRLR 420 and *Morgans v Alpha Plus Security Ltd* [2005] IRLR 234, the EAT ruled that credit should be given for such payments but in *Voith Turbo Ltd v Stowe* [2005] IRLR 228, the EAT decided that normally such payments should be ignored as a matter of good employment relations. The approach of Burton P was followed by the EAT in *Langley v Burlo* [2006] IRLR 460 but was doubted by the Court of Appeal in the same case ([2007] IRLR 145). The court ruled that, on what it called a narrow interpretation of the NIRC's ruling in *Norton Tool Co Ltd v Tewson* [1973] 1 All ER 183, a claimant was not required to give credit for payments received from the new employer during the notice period (see para 32.86).

Part D   Remedies

Settlement payments

32.190 In *Optimum Group Services plc v Muir* [2013] IRLR 339, the EAT ruled that the employment tribunal was wrong not to deduct a payment the claimant had received in settlement of his claims against the transferee in a TUPE case when assessing his compensation claim against the transferor (the tribunal having found that there was no TUPE transfer and therefore upheld the unfair dismissal claim against the transferor). The EAT reasoned that as the award for unfair dismissal is compensatory in nature, the tribunal should not award a sum in excess of the loss actually suffered by the claimant and that what was 'just and equitable' only became relevant once the loss had been assessed. Accordingly, the settlement payment fell to be deducted in the assessment of the loss suffered by the claimant. The fact that this would result in a windfall benefit to the transferor (whose liability to pay compensation would be reduced was not relevant).

Tax rebates

32.191 Where, as a result of the dismissal, an employee is entitled to a tax rebate, the employer may argue that the amount of the award should be reduced to reflect this. Conversely, where the dismissal occurs towards the end of a tax year, the claimant may argue that account should be taken of the fact that had the correct process been followed, the dismissal might have occurred in the next tax year, leaving the claimant with a claim to a rebate.

32.192 This issue has led to a number of conflicting decisions from the EAT ranging from the view that the tax implications should be completely ignored (*Adda International Ltd v Curcio* [1976] IRLR 425) to the view that compensation should be awarded for the loss of a rebate and by implication credit should be given for any rebate received (*Lucas v Laurence Scott Electromotors Ltd* [1983] IRLR 61). The current position would appear to be that the tax implications should be ignored unless the sums involved are substantial (*MBS Ltd v Calo* [1983] IRLR 189).

Are state benefits deductible?

32.193 State benefits which are recoverable under the Employment Protection (Recoupment of Job Seeker's Allowance and Income Support) Regulations 1996, SI 1996/2349 (Recoupment Regulations) (see Chapter 34) are not deducted from the compensatory award for losses which arise up to the date of the hearing as these form part of the 'monetary' award to which the Recoupment Regulations apply. This includes job seeker's allowance and income support (*Savage v Saxena* [1998] IRLR 182). Claimants would not be eligible for such benefits for the period covered by an award for future loss.

32.194 Other state benefits such as invalidity or disability benefit and incapacity benefit are deductible in full (*Morgans v Alpha Plus Security Ltd* [2005] IRLR 234). It is unclear what impact the Court of Appeal's ruling in *Burlo v Langley* [2007] IRLR 145 (referred to in para 32.70) has on this decision. Furthermore, it is unclear whether the ruling in *Morgans* applies to all state benefits. For example, in the earlier case of *Savage v Saxena* [1998] IRLR 182, the Scottish EAT ruled that housing benefit should not be deducted because it would not be just and equitable for employers to benefit from such payments.

Power to adjust the award

32.195 The power to increase or to reduce the award for a failure to comply with the Statutory Disputes Procedure, referred to in previous editions of this book, was repealed with effect from 6 April 2009 by s 3 of the Employment Act 2002. This inserted what was then a new s 207A(2) and (3) into the TULR(C)A 1992.

32.196 Section 207A(2) of the TULR(C)A 1992 empowers (but does not require) the employment tribunal to increase the compensatory award by such amount as it considers 'just and equitable' up to a maximum of 25 per cent where the employer 'unreasonably' fails to comply with the ACAS Code of Practice 2009 by, for example, failing to follow a fair disciplinary procedure. As stated above, s 124A(a) of the ERA 1996 provides that the increase applies before any reduction is made for contributory fault under s 123(6) of the ERA 1966, or the payment of an enhanced redundancy payment under s 123(7). The power to adjust the award does not apply to a redundancy or a SOSR dismissal (*Phoenix House Ltd v Stockman* [2016] IRLR 848).

Whistle-blowers

With effect from 25 June 2013, where the reason or principal reason for the dismissal is that the **32.197** complainant made a protected disclosure and it appears to the tribunal that the disclosure was not made in good faith, the tribunal may, if it considers it just and equitable in the circumstances to do so, reduce the award by up to 25 per cent (ERA 1996, s 123(6A)). It is not entirely clear whether this reduction should be made (if it is made at all) before or after the reduction for contributory fault as there is no equivalent to s 124A of the ERA 1996, but it is likely that the reduction should take place after the reduction for contributory fault as s 123(6A) of the ERA 1996, follows s 123(6) and, where applicable, would appear to justify a further reduction in addition to that for contributory fault. A tribunal may conclude that a disclosure was not made in good faith where an ulterior motive was the dominant or predominant motive for the disclosure (*Street v Derbyshire Unemployed Workers' Centre* [2004] IRLR 687). This provision applies to dismissals which take place after 25 June 2013.

G. CONTRIBUTORY FAULT

Section 123(6) of the ERA 1996 provides that where a tribunal finds that the dismissal was to any **32.198** extent caused or contributed to by an action of the claimant, it shall reduce the amount of the compensatory award by such proportion as it considers just and equitable having regard to that finding.

Contributory conduct

As far as the compensatory award is concerned, the statutory provisions make clear that the award **32.199** may only be reduced where the conduct genuinely causes or contributes to the dismissal. For example, in *Hutchinson v Enfield Rolling Mills* [1981] IRLR 318, the EAT held that the tribunal was wrong to take into account the claimant's political views and the fact that the employers regarded him as a troublemaker. The EAT said that the only relevant factors are those which led to the dismissal. The principle was reiterated by the EAT in *Lindsay v General Contracting Ltd (t/a Pik a Pak Home Electrical)* EAT/1096/00 and 1126/00, where the claimant was found to have been unfairly dismissed for union membership-related reasons but the tribunal had reduced the award for unrelated conduct. However, tribunals may take into account subsidiary reasons which contributed to the decision to dismiss as in *Robert Whiting Designs Ltd v Lamb* [1978] ICR 89. The question of causation has to be approached in a robust manner: it is only if a tribunal has abdicated its responsibility or has approached the matter in a wrong way or has reached a wholly perverse conclusion that a finding as to causation can be upset on appeal (*Frith Accountants Ltd v Law* [2014] IRLR 510). Nonetheless, difficult questions of causation may arise in constructive dismissal cases (para 32.208) as this will involve a consideration of whether the claimant contributed to the events which give rise to the complaint of constructive dismissal, as illustrated by the ruling in the *Frith Accountants* case, where the EAT held the tribunal was entitled to conclude that the claimant's conduct had not so caused let alone contributed to her dismissal. Conduct which occurs post-dismissal such as conduct in the notice period or a failure to appeal (*Hoover Ltd v Forde* [1980] ICR 239) cannot be relied on as this does not cause or contribute to the dismissal. However, it should be noted that previously a failure to appeal could lead to a reduction in the award under s 31(2) of the EA 2002. This provision was repealed when the Employment Act 2008 came into force.

In *Optikinetics Ltd v Whooley* EAT/1275/97, the EAT helpfully summarized the case law on reduc- **32.200** tions for contributory fault as follows:

(a) The claimant must be found to have acted in a culpable, blameworthy, or wholly unreasonable manner.
(b) The tribunal's inquiry in this regard should be directed solely at the conduct of the claimant, not the employer.

(c) The conduct must be known to the employer prior to the dismissal and have been the cause of it.

(d) Once blameworthy conduct is established, a tribunal is bound to reduce the award by such amount as it considers just and equitable, although the tribunal retains a complete discretion over the amount of the reduction and may in some circumstances conclude that the behaviour was too trivial to justify any reduction.

(e) It is open to the tribunal to reduce the basic and compensatory awards by different amounts.

(f) Appellate courts will rarely interfere with a tribunal's assessment of a reduction for contributory fault.

Conduct of the claimant

32.201 In deciding whether there should be a reduction for contributory fault, tribunals are concerned with the conduct of the claimant rather than the employer. In *Parker Foundry Ltd v Slack* [1992] IRLR 11 the court upheld the tribunal's decision to reduce the award by 50 per cent for contributory fault where the claimant had been dismissed for fighting and rejected the argument that the tribunal should have taken into account the conduct of another employee who had also been involved in the fight.

Blameworthy conduct

32.202 A reduction for contributory fault should only take place if the claimant has acted in a culpable or blameworthy or wholly unreasonable manner. This was established by the Court of Appeal in *Nelson v BBC (No 2)* [1979] IRLR 346, at 351 (Brandon LJ), who stated:

> The concept does not, in my view, necessarily involve any conduct of the complainant amounting to a breach of contract or a tort. It includes, no doubt, conduct of that kind. But it also includes conduct which, while not amounting to a breach of contract or a tort, is nevertheless perverse or foolish, or, if I may use the colloquialism, bloody-minded. It may also include action which, though not meriting any of those more pejorative epithets, is nevertheless, unreasonable in all the circumstances. I should not, however, go so far as to say that all unreasonable conduct is necessarily culpable or blameworthy; it must depend on the degree of unreasonableness involved.

32.203 The issue whether or not the conduct in question amounts to blameworthy conduct is therefore largely a question of fact for a tribunal to determine and a tribunal's decision is unlikely to be overturned on appeal unless it misdirects itself in law or reaches a perverse decision on the facts (*Hollier v Plysu Ltd* [1983] IRLR 260). The conduct involved is judged objectively: it is irrelevant for this purpose whether the employee fully appreciates the extent of the blameworthy conduct (*Ladbroke Racing Ltd v Mason* [1978] IRLR 49), although this may be relevant in determining the extent of the reduction. The blameworthy conduct may be that of the claimant or his agents (see *Allen v Hammett* [1982] IRLR 89, where the applicant was held responsible for the negligent advice given to him by his solicitor).

32.204 Most misconduct will be regarded as blameworthy. The following have all been so regarded: dishonesty, a breach of the company's rules, going on holiday or returning late without permission, soliciting customers for a rival business or working for a rival outside normal working hours, a poor attendance record, conduct setting back recovery from illness, failing to reply to a letter requiring an employee to attend a disciplinary hearing or a medical review. However, the way the claimant respond to allegations at a disciplinary interview or hearing, does not normally justify a reduction for contributory fault (*British Steel Corporation v Williams* EAT/776/82, *Sidhu v Superdrug Stores plc* (EAT/0244/06). Furthermore, such a reduction will only be made if there is sufficient evidence of such misconduct before the employment tribunal (*Tele-Trading Ltd v Jenkins* [1990] IRLR 430).

32.205 Tribunals should not reduce compensation for contributory fault where employees are unfairly dismissed for taking part in industrial action as industrial action of itself is not blameworthy conduct applying *Courtaulds Northern Spinning Ltd v Moosa* [1984] IRLR 43 (see *Crosville Wales Ltd v Tracey (No 2)* [1997] IRLR 691, HL, [1996] IRLR 91, CA). This reflects Parliament's intention that tribunals should not be involved in weighing up the merits of an employment dispute. However, the Court of Appeal and House of Lords in *Tracey* made clear that a reduction for contributory fault can be made if the conduct involved goes beyond mere participation in the industrial action, ie intimidatory conduct.

Tribunals are also reluctant to find blameworthy conduct where an employee is dismissed for capability-related reasons unless the employee was to blame for the performance which led to his dismissal. In *Kraft Foods Ltd v Fox* [1977] IRLR 43, the EAT drew a distinction between actions over which an employee has control and those outside his control. As regards the former, the claimant may be found to have contributed to his dismissal (see *Sutton & Gates (Luton) Ltd v Boxall* [1978] IRLR 486, where the EAT gave examples of laziness, idleness, or negligence where a reduction for contributory fault may be justified). But as regards the latter types of 'true capability dismissals', the claimant will not normally be to blame and therefore compensation should not normally be reduced for contributory fault. As the EAT put it, 'if an employee is incompetent or incapable and cannot, with the best will in the world measure up to the job, it seems to us to be wrong to say that that condition of incapacity is a contributory factor to his dismissal'. **32.206**

Similarly, compensation will not normally be reduced for contributory fault in ill-health dismissals unless there is some aspect of the claimant's behaviour which justifies it, ie a failure to undergo a medical examination or refusal to provide a medical report (*Slaughter v C Brewer & Sons Ltd* [1990] IRLR 426) or acting in a manner which harms recovery (*A Links Ltd v Rose* [1991] IRLR 353). **32.207**

The same principles apply to constructive dismissal cases. This was initially doubted in *Holroyd v Gravure Cylinders Ltd* [1984] IRLR 259, where the EAT said such a reduction should only be made in exceptional circumstances. However, in *Morrison v Amalgamated Transport and General Workers Union* [1989] IRLR 361 the Northern Ireland Court of Appeal disagreed and stated that insofar as *Holroyd* purported to lay down a general principle or rule of law, it was wrongly decided and the *Morrison* decision has since been followed and approved by the EAT in *Polentarutti v Autokraft Ltd* [1991] IRLR 457 and *Frith Accountants Ltd v Law* [2014] IRLR 510. In the latter case, Langstaff J stressed that it would be unusual for an employee to be found to have caused or contributed to his dismissal in a constructive dismissal because constructive dismissal is based on the repudiatory conduct of the employer, but there was no test of 'exceptionality'. **32.208**

Amount of reduction

Once the claimant's conduct has been found to be blameworthy, the tribunal will consider the extent to which it is just and equitable to reduce the award for this reason. **32.209**

In *Hollier v Plysu Ltd* [1983] IRLR 260, the Court of Appeal endorsed the EAT's guidance as to how tribunals should approach this task. The EAT suggested that there were four types of cases: **32.210**

(1) where the employee is wholly to blame for the dismissal, compensation could be reduced by 100 per cent
(2) where the employee is largely to blame, the award should be reduced by 75 per cent
(3) where both parties are equally to blame, the award should be reduced by 50 per cent
(4) where the employee is slightly to blame, the award should be reduced by 25 per cent.

The EAT has also acknowledged that there may be cases where the degree of blameworthiness is so small that it may not be appropriate to make a reduction at all (see *Lindsay v General Contracting Ltd (t/a Pik a Pak Home Electrical)* EAT/1096/00 and 1126/00 and *York v Brown* EAT/262/84). **32.211**

Although the EAT's guidance in *Hollier* was endorsed by the Court of Appeal, the court stressed that the question of apportionment should be approached by tribunals with a 'broad common sense view of the situation' and that appellate courts should not intervene unless a tribunal has misunderstood or misconstrued the statutory provisions or come to a decision to which no reasonable tribunal could have come. A failure to refer to the guidelines in itself will not justify an appeal. **32.212**

As stated above, it is open to a tribunal to reduce the award by 100 per cent for contributory fault but, as Chadwick LJ pointed out in *Friend v Civil Aviation Authority* [2001] IRLR 819, such a reduction is only appropriate in exceptional circumstances where the tribunal is satisfied that the employee was wholly to blame for the dismissal and it is just and equitable to make such a reduction **32.213**

Part D Remedies

(eg *Maris v Rotherham Borough Council* [1974] IRLR 147, where the claimant made a fraudulent expenses claim and *Chaplin v Rawlinson* [1999] ICR 553, where the dismissal for urinating on a consignment of wheat was held to be procedurally unfair but a 100 per cent reduction was justified). Such a reduction will not normally be justified where any procedural irregularity which was the cause of the unfair dismissal judgment is significant (see *Gibson v British Transport Docks Board* [1982] IRLR 228).

32.214 Tribunals must generally ignore industrial pressure in assessing compensation (ERA 1996, s 123(5)) but this does not prevent a tribunal from reducing the award for contributory fault where the employee was to blame for the actions which led to the industrial pressure. For example, in *Colwyn Borough Council v Dutton* [1980] IRLR 420, the tribunal found that the applicant's dismissal was the result of industrial pressure and was therefore unfair but the award was reduced for contributory fault because the cause of the industrial pressure was that his driving was so bad. Apart from this restriction, the assessment of contributory fault is a matter for the tribunal itself to determine on the evidence (*London Ambulance Services NHS Trust v Small* [2009] IRLR 564).

Consistent reduction of awards

32.215 Normally a tribunal will reduce the basic and compensatory award for contributory fault by the same amount (*G M McFall & Co Ltd v Curran* [1981] IRLR 455; *RSPCA v Crudden* [1986] IRLR 83, *University of Sunderland v Drossou* EAT/0341/16)) but, in exceptional circumstances, it may be appropriate to reduce the awards by different amounts (see *Les Ambassadeurs Club v Bainda* [1982] IRLR 5, where the EAT upheld a decision to reduce the compensatory award by 70 per cent but not to reduce the basic award at all). In this context, it should be noted that the power to reduce the basic award is wider than the power to reduce the compensatory award (see para 32.63).

32.216 The reduction for contributory fault takes place before applying the statutory ceiling on the compensatory award (*Walter Braund (London) Ltd v Murray* [1991] IRLR 100).

Relationship with 'just and equitable principle'

32.217 It is open to the tribunal to both limit an award under s 123(1) of the ERA 1996 and to reduce it for contributory fault. The tribunal should first consider whether or not it wishes to limit its award and then consider a reduction for contributory fault if this is appropriate (*Rao v Civil Aviation Authority* [1994] IRLR 240).

H. *EX GRATIA* PAYMENTS

32.218 It is not uncommon for employers to make an *ex gratia* payment in addition to any payment which an employee is entitled to receive on dismissal. For this purpose, an *ex gratia* payment is one which the employer pays without legal obligation to do so.

32.219 The case law on *ex gratia* payments is surprisingly confusing. The current position is that the claimant must normally give credit for all post-dismissal payments (*Digital Equipment Co Ltd v Clements (No 2)* [1998] IRLR 134). Where the payment is made under legal obligation such as a payment in lieu of notice, this will be taken into account in assessing the loss under s 123(1) of the ERA 1996 (*Heggie v Uniroyal Ltd* [1999] IRLR 802); (specific statutory provision is made for enhanced contractual redundancy payments, see para 32.221). The same will normally be true of an *ex gratia* payment (*Horizon Holiday Ltd v Grassi* [1987] IRLR 371; *Babcock FATA Ltd v Addison* [1987] IRLR 173) or payments made by mistake (*Boorman v Allmakes* [1995] IRLR 553), but in *Chelsea Football Club & Athletic Co Ltd v Heath* [1981] IRLR 73, the EAT ruled that where an *ex gratia* payment was expressly made with reference to the statutory liability for unfair dismissal compensation, the payment may be set off against the basic award and any excess may be set off against the final award of compensation. The case law therefore suggests that there is a distinction between *ex gratia* payments made as a goodwill gesture at the time of dismissal and payments made before a hearing on account of or without admission of liability. This issue is important because if the payment is not brought into account until the end of the process, the respondent will receive full credit for the total payment made to the claimant as in redundancy cases (see para 32.226).

Not all *ex gratia* payments fall to be deducted from the compensatory award. For example, in **32.220** *Babcock FATA Ltd v Addison* [1987] IRLR 173, the applicant recovered compensation for the loss of an *ex gratia* payment which he would have received if he had been dismissed at the same time as his colleagues some fifteen months later when the employer's business was closed. Similarly, in *Roadchef Ltd v Hastings* [1988] IRLR 142, the EAT held that the tribunal was correct not to deduct an *ex gratia* payment which the employee would have received even if he had not been dismissed. The same reasoning was applied to the non-deduction of a bonus payment which an employee would have received had he remained in employment during the period covered by the award (*Quiring v Hill House International School* EAT/500/88, but contrast *DCM Optical plc v Stark* EAT/0124/04, where a retention payment was held to be deductible and *Rushton v Harcross Timber & Building Supplies Ltd* [1993] IRLR 254, where an *ex gratia* redundancy payment was held to be deductible).

Contractual redundancy payments

Section 123(7) of the ERA 1996 provides that **32.221**

> If the amount of any payment made by the employer to the employee on the ground that the dismissal was by reason of redundancy exceeds the amount of the basic award that would be payable that excess goes to reduce the amount of the compensatory award.

So, for example, if the employer pays an enhanced redundancy payment to the claimant on dismissal, then the amount of the enhanced payment may be set off against the compensatory award. In *Digital Equipment Ltd v Clements* [1998] IRLR 134 the Court of Appeal ruled that such a payment should be set off against the loss which makes up the compensatory award (see 'Order of reductions' para 32.224).

Accelerated payment

Where an award is made for future loss of earnings and benefits, a deduction should be made for the **32.222** accelerated receipt of the payment so as to ensure that the claimant is not put in a better position than would have been the case had the payment been received as and when it falls due (*York Trailer Co Ltd v Sparkes* [1973] IRLR 348). Such a reduction need not be made if the award for future loss is relatively small as it will be in many cases (*Les Ambassadeurs Club v Bainda* [1982] IRLR 5).

There is no established method of calculating the reduction. Prior to the Court of Appeal's ruling **32.223** in *Brentwood Bros (Manchester) Ltd v Shepherd* [2003] IRLR 364, it was not uncommon for tribunals simply to reduce the overall award for future loss by the prevailing discount rate in personal injury cases (which with effect from 20 March 2017 is minus 0.75 per cent, having been reduced from 2.5 per cent to take account of the rate of inflation). In *Shepherd*, a sex discrimination and unfair dismissal case, the tribunal awarded two and half years' loss of earnings and ten years' loss of pension rights. It then reduced the award by 5 per cent to take account of the fact of accelerated receipt. The Court of Appeal held that the tribunal had erred in making a single reduction of 5 per cent, pointing out that the conventional discount is based on an annual yield rather than a cumulative yield.

Order of reductions

In *Digital Equipment Co Ltd v Clement (No 2)* [1998] IRLR 134 the Court of Appeal ruled that **32.224** the order in which the reductions should be made depends on whether or not the dismissal is for redundancy.

In ordinary cases, the correct approach is as follows: **32.225**

(a) to calculate the loss suffered by the claimant
(b) to give credit for payments received on or since dismissal

    (c) to make a *Polkey* reduction (if appropriate)

    (d) to reduce the award for contributory fault.

32.226 In redundancy cases, the correct approach is as follows:

    (a) to calculate the loss suffered by the claimant

    (b) to give full credit for any payments received by the claimant

    (c) to make a *Polkey* reduction (if appropriate)

    (d) to reduce the award for contributory fault

    (e) to set off any enhanced redundancy payment made by the employer.

32.227 This means that the employer gets full credit for any enhanced redundancy payment made on the termination of employment. However, the position is slightly different where the award is increased or decreased pursuant to the statutory provisions referred to in paras 32.195–32.196. In such circumstances, s 124A of the ERA 1996 provides that the increase or decrease should take place before any reduction for contributory fault or credit is given for an enhanced redundancy payment. It is unclear whether such an increase or reduction should be made before or after a *Polkey* reduction. The better view is that it should be made *after* the *Polkey* reduction as the actual loss is only determined at that stage.

Statutory maximum, interest, and the power to review

The statutory maximum

32.228 The compensatory award is subject to a prescribed statutory maximum. As a result of the powers conferred on the Secretary of State by s 15 of the Enterprise and Regulatory Reform Act 2013, the Unfair dismissal (Variation of the Limit of Compensatory Award) Order 2013 SI No 2013/1949) provides that, with effect from 29 July 2013, the maximum compensatory award for the year beginning 1 February 2013 shall be the lower of £86,444 (with effect from 6 April 2019) or fifty-two weeks' pay. A week's pay is determined in accordance with the provisions of chapter 2 of Part 14 of the ERA 1996. The rules are summarized in para 32.57. The statutory cap on a week's pay in s 227 of the ERA 1996 does not apply for this purpose. The provisions do not apply where the effective date of termination, as defined by s 97 of the ERA 1996 , took place before 29 July 2013. This is reviewed annually and is increased (or decreased) in line with the formula set out in ERRA 2013, s 15, which provides that the minimum increase is the amount by which median average earnings has increased and the maximum is three times median annual earnings. The new rate is normally announced in December and is varied by way of a statutory instrument laid before Parliament. The new rate comes into force with effect from 6 April of the following year, ie it applies to dismissals *after* that date.

32.229 Section 124(5) of the ERA 1996 provides that the statutory maximum is applied *after* the quantification of the award under s 123 of the ERA 1996. This means that the statutory maximum is only applied after the total loss is assessed and reduced in accordance with the provisions of ss 123 and 124A of the ERA 1996 (*McCarthy v British Insulated Callenders Cables plc* [1985] IRLR 94 and *Walter Braund (London) Ltd v Murray* [1991] IRLR 100).

32.230 The statutory maximum does not apply to dismissals which are found to be automatically unfair under s 100 of the ERA 1996, (automatic unfair dismissal for health and safety reasons), s 103A (automatic unfair dismissal for making a protected disclosure), s 105(3) (automatic unfair redundancy selection for health and safety reasons) or s 105(6A) (automatic unfair redundancy selection for making a protected disclosure) (ERA 1996, s 124(1A)).

Interest

32.231 Interest is not automatically added to the assessment of loss (for interest on employment tribunal awards, see Chapter 35, para 35.01). However, in *Melia v Magna Kansei Ltd* [2005] IRLR 449, the EAT held that it may be appropriate in some cases to compensate the claimant for the depreciation in the value of lost earnings between dismissal and judgment by applying the same premium as that used in making a deduction for an accelerated payment. The EAT's ruling has been confirmed by the Court of Appeal ([2006] IRLR 117). It has been suggested that, alternatively, the 'loss' in such circumstances may be calculated, by analogy to personal injury awards, either at half the appropriate rate of interest (*Dexter v Courtaulds Ltd* [1984] 1 All ER 70) or full interest from the mid-date of the period of loss until judgment (*Prokop v Department of Health and Social Security* [1985] CLY 1037). It remains to be seen whether these alternatives are accepted by employment tribunals.

Power to reconsider

It is possible to apply to the employment tribunal to reconsider its judgment where it is in the **32.232** interests of justice to do so. Where the application for reconsideration is based on new evidence, it is likely that it will be necessary to show (as it was prior to the introduction of the new 2013 ET rules) that the 'new' evidence could not have been known or reasonably foreseen at the time of the hearing. In exceptional circumstances, awards for future loss have been set aside and varied where there has been a fundamental change of circumstances within a short time of the hearing. For example, in *Dicker v Seceurop Ltd* EAT/554/84 the employers successfully applied for a review when the claimant unexpectedly found a new job two days after the hearing. Similarly, in *Bateman v British Leyland* [1974] IRLR 101, the claimant successfully applied for a review when he lost his new job two weeks after the hearing. In both cases, the tribunal considered that the fundamental basis of the decision had been falsified to a sufficiently substantial extent to invalidate the assessment (*Yorkshire Engineering Co Ltd v Burnham* [1974] ICR 77).

I. GROSSING UP

Where an award exceeds the tax threshold for lump sum payments (currently £30,000) (Income **32.233** Tax (Earnings and Pensions) Act 2003, ss 401, 402, and 403), the award will be taxable. This means that any such award falls to be 'grossed up' in accordance with the principles in *Shove v Downs Surgical plc* [1984] 1 All ER 7. The principle of 'grossing up' also applies to any part of the award made for pension loss (para 32.107) unless gross figures are used to calculate the award (*Chief Constable of Northumbria v Erichsen* (EAT/0027/15)). The impact of taxation is considered in greater detail in Chapter 36.

33

Remedies in Discrimination Cases

SUMMARY

(1) Where an employment tribunal finds a complaint of unlawful discrimination well founded it must, if it considers it just and equitable, make one of the following orders: a declaration, award of compensation, and/or a recommendation.

(2) The amount of compensation is assessed 'in like manner as any other claim in tort or (in Scotland) in reparation for breach of statutory duty'. The award may therefore include compensation for injury to feelings and, if appropriate, injury to health.

(3) An award for injury to feelings can be made where it is shown that the unlawful discrimination caused such an injury. Awards (inclusive of uprating) range from a minimum band of between £900 and £8,600, to a middle band of between £8,600 and £25,700, to a maximum band of between £25,700 and £42,900, depending on the gravity of the unlawful act and the employer's reaction to it (though these bands should be uprated in accordance with Presidential Guidance).

(4) An award for injury to health can be made where it is shown that the unlawful discrimination caused such an injury. The award depends on the severity of the injury, ie whether it is classified as severe, moderately severe, moderate, or minor, having regard to the Judicial Studies Board Guidelines.

(5) Awards for injury to feelings and awards for injury to health should be uprated by 10 per cent in line with the Court of Appeal's guidance in *Simmons v Castle* [2012] EWCA Civ 1039.

(6) Aggravated damages may be awarded where the discriminator has acted in a highhanded, malicious, insulting, or oppressive manner. The award must be compensatory, not punitive.

(7) In exceptional circumstances, exemplary damages may be awarded where there has been 'oppressive, arbitrary or unconstitutional action' by the state (or state employers).

(8) The award of compensation may be increased or decreased if the employment tribunal considers it 'just and equitable' up to a maximum of 25 per cent where the respondent or claimant fails to comply with the ACAS Code of Practice.

(9) Compensation may also be awarded for indirect discrimination in discrimination cases in prescribed circumstances irrespective of whether a 'provision, criterion or practice' (PCP) is applied intentionally or not.

(10) An employment tribunal has the power to make a recommendation that the respondent take action within a specified period for the purpose of obviating or reducing the adverse effect of any matter to which the proceedings relate both in relation to the claimant and any other person. A failure to comply with such a recommendation may lead to an increase in the award of compensation.

A. INTRODUCTION

Compensation is the primary, though not the only, remedy open to an employee who is the victim of unlawful discrimination. **33.01**

Compensation can be recovered under the Equality Act 2010 (EqA 2010) where a claimant successfully brings a claim against a respondent in respect of one or more of the following 'protected characteristics' (or, where appropriate, in cases of combined discrimination under EqA 2010, s 14) namely: **33.02**

(a) age
(b) disability
(c) gender reassignment
(d) marriage and civil partnership
(e) race
(f) religion or belief
(g) sex
(h) sexual orientation.

Compensation may also be awarded under the following regulations: **33.03**

(a) Part-time Workers (Prevention of Less Favourable Treatment) Regulations 2000, SI 2000/1551 (PTWR 2000)
(b) Fixed-term Employees (Prevention of Less Favourable Treatment) Regulations 2002, SI 2002/2034 (FTER 2002).

No statutory limit

There is no statutory limit to the amount of compensation which can be made in complaints of unlawful discrimination. There is also no statutory limit on awards made under what was s 132 of the EqPA 1970 (now EqA 2010), the PTWR 2000, or the FTER 2002. **33.04**

Part D Remedies

B. COMPENSATION FOR DIRECT DISCRIMINATION AND VICTIMIZATION

General principles

33.05 Where an employment tribunal finds a complaint of unlawful discrimination well founded, it may make one or more of the following orders:

(a) an order declaring the rights of the claimant and respondent in relation to the act (or acts) to which the complaint relates

(b) an order requiring the respondent to pay to the claimant compensation of an amount corresponding to any damages he could have been ordered to pay by a county court or by a sheriff court (in Scotland) if the complaint had fallen within the jurisdiction of one or other of those courts

(c) a recommendation that the respondent within a specified period takes specified steps for the purpose of obviating or reducing the adverse effect of any matter to which the proceedings relate on either the claimant or any other person (EqA 2010, s 124(2), (3)).

Remedies are discretionary

33.06 These remedies, including compensation for discrimination, are not automatic. S 124(2) of the EqA 2010 specifically states that, where there has been a contravention of the Act, the employment tribunal 'may' make one of the orders referred to above. There is no specific guidance as to how this discretion is to be exercised.

33.07 Case law under the previous statutory provisions suggested that whilst motive and intention are not relevant to liability in a complaint of direct discrimination, they may in certain circumstances be relevant to the issue of remedy (see *O'Neill v Governors of St Thomas More Roman Catholic Voluntary Aided Upper School* [1997] ICR 33 (Mummery J) and *Chief Constable of Manchester v Hope* [1999] ICR 338, where a majority of the EAT allowed an appeal against an award of £750 for injury to feelings on the basis that the tribunal did not consider whether it was 'just and equitable' to make such an award in the particular circumstances; alternatively the majority considered that the award was perverse). A similar approach may be followed in applying the discretion given to tribunals under s 124(2) of the EqA 2010.

Claim to be assessed 'as any other claim in tort'

33.08 The amount of compensation 'corresponds to the amount which could be awarded by a county court or sheriff court under section 119' (EqA 2010, s 124(6)). This includes any remedy which could be granted by the High Court in proceedings in tort (or in the sheriff court, proceedings by way of reparation) (EqA 2010, s 119(2), (3)).

33.09 Unlike unfair dismissal cases, the amount of the award itself is not based on what the tribunal considers just and equitable in the particular circumstances (*Hurley v Mustoe (No 2)* [1983] ICR 422). Instead, the general principle is that, as far as possible, claimants should be put in the same position they would have been in but for the unlawful act (*Ministry of Defence v Wheeler* [1998] IRLR 23 and *Chagger v Abbey National plc* [2010] IRLR 47).

33.10 In broad terms, the tort principles on causation and remoteness thus apply to the assessment of compensation in discrimination cases. The discriminator must therefore take his victim as he finds him (the 'eggshell skull' principle) as discriminatory behaviour affects people in different ways. This principle is of particular relevance in claims for injury to feelings as individuals will react differently to being the victims of discrimination but may also be relevant to the issue of mitigation.

33.11 At common law, compensation will only be recoverable for injury which is reasonably foreseeable but in *Essa v Laing Ltd* [2004] ICR 746 the Court of Appeal, by a majority, ruled that this principle does not apply to all statutory torts and held that it did not apply to discrimination claims involving harassment. It was therefore open to a victim of harassment to claim compensation for any loss which flows directly from the discriminatory act. It is unclear whether the Court's ruling applies to all types of discrimination claims as, arguably, the majority's reasoning is based on the intentional nature of the particular behaviour in that case (racial abuse).

Furthermore, even if the reasoning does apply more generally, tribunals may still have to grapple **33.12** with difficult issues of causation as illustrated by the ruling in *Bullimore v Pothecary Witham Weld (No 2)* [2011] IRLR 18. In that case, the EAT had to consider the respondent's continuing liability for a discriminatory reference which had been held to amount to unlawful victimization by the employment tribunal (whose decision was affirmed by the EAT [2010] IRLR 572). The respondent unsuccessfully argued that its liability ended as a result of a further act of unlawful victimization when the claimant's prospective employer made their job offer conditional on the claimant undergoing a probationary period as a result of the content of the earlier discriminatory reference. It was said that this further act of unlawful victimization broke the 'chain of causation' and that the respondent was not liable for the consequential financial loss. The EAT, at page 21 (paras 18–21) of the judgment, rejected this argument for three reasons: first there was no rule that the free choice of the subsequent tortfeasor necessarily broke the chain of causation. Nor was there a rule that a subsequent tortious act necessarily broke the chain of causation as some of the leading cases in tort have held the original tortfeasor liable for the subsequent actions of a third party. Secondly, it was foreseeable that the prospective employer might react in the way it did on receipt of the reference and, even if that reaction itself amounted to unlawful discrimination, that reaction was a 'direct and natural consequence of the supply of the information', and finally, as a matter of

> policy and fairness, the Respondent ought to be plainly liable' in such circumstances because 'where an employer or (ex-employer) gives, for an illegitimate reason, an adverse reference which leads to a prospective future employer deciding not to make, or to withdraw, a job offer to a candidate it is hard to see why that consequence should not attract compensation from the original employer: so far from being remote, it seems to us to be both close and direct.

Particular difficulties may arise when it comes to assessing compensation for injury to feelings and injury to health as the complainant can only be compensated for the injury caused by the discriminatory act (see para 33.35).

It is also well established that the tribunal's award must be based on the loss caused by the substantive complaint (or complaints) it upholds (*Chapman v Simon* [1994] IRLR 124), although sometimes it may be appropriate to take into account the findings made on the evidence in determining the extent of the injury to feelings (*British Telecommunications plc v Reid* [2004] IRLR 327). **33.13**

Awards against individual respondents

Awards can be made against individual named respondents (*Gbaja-Biamila v DHL International* **33.14** *(UK) Ltd* [2000] IRLR 730; *Armitage, Marsden and HM Prison Service v Johnson* [1997] ICR 275, where two prison officers were ordered to pay £500 respectively; and *HM Prison Service v Salmon* [2001] IRLR 425, where a named individual was ordered to pay £1,000). The statutory basis for such an awarded, as confirmed by the EAT in *London Borough of Hackney v Sivanandan and Others* [2011] IRLR 740, is that the individual, or individuals, who carry out such an act are treated as 'aiding' the discriminatory act under what is now EqA 2010, s 110(1) and are therefore individually liable for those act(s).

Where a group of employers are jointly and severally liable for the discriminatory act (either **33.15** directly or vicariously), there is no power to apportion liability between the various employers. Previously in *Way v Crouch* [2005] IRLR 603, the EAT had suggested that there was power to apportion liability under the Civil Liability (Contribution) Act 1978 But in *(1) Bungay (2) Paul v (1) Saini (2) Chandel (3) All Saints Haque Centre (In Compulsory Liquidation)* [2011] EqLR 1130, the EAT confirmed the doubts expressed in *Sivanandan* [2011] IRLR 740, that there is no such power. The EAT held that, in the particular circumstances, a group of employers were jointly and severally liable for a discriminatory act. The EAT's ruling was confirmed by the Court of Appeal's ruling in *Sivanandrum* [2013] 2 All ER 940. Giving the leading judgment, Mummery LJ stated that the apportionment argument under the 1978 Act was 'misconceived' because the 1978 Act is not about apportioning liability between the respondent and the claimant: it is about proceedings between joint tortfeasors to recover the amount for which a joint tortfeasor has been found liable to pay the claimant. However, as stated in para 33.14, the EAT in *Sivanandan* [2011] IRLR 740 recognized that the position may be different 'where the injury caused by different acts of discrimination is "divisible", [where] a tribunal can and indeed should apportion to each discriminator responsible for the part of the damage caused by him'. It should also be noted that, in the light of the EAT's subsequent ruling in *Brennan and Others v (1) Sunderland City Council, (2) GMB and Unison* (2012) ICR 1183, an equal pay case referred to at para 33.83 below, it is doubtful whether proceedings could be brought by joint tortfeasors in the High Court to apportion such liability between each other in discrimination cases because tribunals have exclusive jurisdiction to determine complaints of unlawful discrimination in employment.

C. COMPENSATION FOR NON-FINANCIAL LOSS

33.16 An important difference between compensation claims for unlawful discrimination and unfair dismissal, is that, regarding compensation for unlawful discrimination, s 119(4) of the EqA 2010 expressly provides for compensation for injury to feelings to be recoverable.

33.17 In addition, the tortious basis of awards for unlawful discrimination means that awards may be made for injury to health, aggravated damages, and, in exceptional circumstances, exemplary damages. Each element award should not be seen in isolation as the overall award of compensation for non-financial loss should not be excessive (*Commissioner of Police of the Metropolis v Shaw* UKEAT/ 0125/11).

33.18 It was suggested in *Skyrail Oceanic v Coleman* [1981] ICR 864 and *Alexander v Home Office* [1988] ICR 685 that such an award can only be made where the claimant knows the act which led to the injury to be discriminatory, although there is nothing in the statutory provisions to support such a requirement, but in *Taylor v XLN Telecom Ltd* [2010] IRLR 499 the EAT ruled that a claimant is entitled to recover compensation for any injury to feelings and psychiatric injury attributable to the discriminatory act irrespective of the claimant's knowledge of the discriminatory motivation of the employer.

Injury to feelings

33.19 An award for injury to feelings includes compensation for loss of congenial employment (*Ministry of Defence v Cannock* [1994] ICR 918) but, in England and Wales, such an award does not include aggravated damages (*Scott v Commissioners of Inland Revenue* [2004] IRLR 713). In *Commissioner of Police of the Metropolis v Shaw* UKEAT/0125/11, the EAT has suggested that in England and Wales, compensation for aggravated damages (see para 33.38) should form part of an award of compensation for injury to feelings, as is done in Scotland, but acknowledged that the practice was too well established to be changed by the EAT.

33.20 An award for injury to feelings will not be made automatically: it is for the claimant to show that such injury has been suffered as a result of the unlawful act (*Ministry of Defence v Cannock* [1994] ICR 918). However, the burden on the claimant is not a heavy one and the matter of hurt feelings may be simply stated. Tribunals should readily infer such injury in race discrimination cases (*Orthet Ltd v Vince-Cain* [2004] IRLR 857). It is then for the tribunal to consider the extent of the injury (*Murray v Powertech (Scotland) Ltd* [1992] IRLR 257). In *The Sash Window Workshop Ltd and Another v King* [2015] IRLR 348, an age discrimination case, the EAT ruled that the fact that the claimant could have been dismissed at any time was irrelevant to his right not to have been dismissed for an unlawfully discriminatory reason and the hurt he suffered as a consequence of that treatment. The tribunal had therefore erred by discounting the hurt feelings suffered by the claimant as a consequence of his forced retirement on grounds of age on an impermissible basis and had failed properly to assess the anger, upset, and humiliation that this had caused to him.

Range of awards for injury to feelings

Translating hurt feelings, such as upset, anxiety, frustration, and humiliation, into an award is **33.21** inevitably a somewhat artificial exercise but employment tribunals have to do the best they can on the evidence before them. The general policy considerations which tribunals should take into account were summarized by Smith J in *Armitage, Marsden and HM Prison Service v Johnson* [1997] ICR 275:

(a) Awards for compensation for injury to feelings are compensatory. They should be just to both parties. They should compensate fully without punishing the tortfeasor. Feelings of indignation should not be allowed to inflate the award.

(b) Awards should not be too low as that would diminish respect for the policy of anti-discrimination legislation. Society has condemned discrimination and awards must ensure that it is seen to be wrong. On the other hand, awards should be restrained as excessive awards may be seen as the way to untaxed riches.

(c) Awards should bear some broad general similarity to the range of awards in personal injury cases.

(d) In exercising their discretion, tribunals should remind themselves of the value in everyday life of the sum they have in mind. This can be done by reference to purchasing power or by reference to earnings.

(e) Tribunals should have regard to the need to retain public respect for the level of awards made.

More specific guidance on the categorization of awards was given by the Court of Appeal in *Vento* **33.22** *v Chief Constable of West Yorkshire Police* [2003] ICR 318, where an award of £50,000 was reduced to £18,000 Three broad bands of award were identified which have now been reviewed and uprated by the EAT in *Da'Bell v NSPCC* [2010] IRLR 19. In 2017, the awards have were uprated by way of Presidential Guidance following consultation.

The rates as from 20 March 2018 are: **33.23**

(a) a lower band of between £900 and £8,600 in 'less serious cases' where the unlawful act is isolated or one-off (see also *Sharifi v Strathclyde Regional Council* [1992] IRLR 259 and *Deane v London Borough of Ealing* [1993] IRLR 209)

(b) a middle band of between £8,600 and £25,700 for 'serious cases which do not merit an award in the highest band'

(c) an upper band of between £25,700 and £42,900 for the 'most serious' cases where there has been a 'lengthy campaign of harassment'. The Presidential guidance recognizes that in highly exceptional cases, awards may exceed the upper limit. (These figures make some allowance for the 10 per cent uplift recommended by the Court of Appeal in *Simmons v Castle* (discussed at para 33.37 below) and also take account of the fact that the range of figures approved in *Da'Bell* require some uprating in line with the RPI. It has now been recommended that these figures are automatically increased in line with the RPI.)

The Presidential Guidance was approved by the Court of Appeal in *Durrant v Chief Constable of* **33.24** *Avon and Somerset Constabulary* [2018] IRLR 263, a non-employment case. However, it has been stated that the previous *Vento* guidance, on which the Presidential Guidance is based, 'was not intended to be applied like rules of law' (see *Gilbank v Miles* [2006] IRLR 538 (Arden LJ)) and in *Bullimore v Pothecary Witham Weld (No 2)* [2011] IRLR 18 the EAT held that an employment tribunal's failure explicitly to uprate its award for non-pecuniary loss in 'today's money' did not necessarily amount to an error of law (although it should be noted that the tribunal's decision in that case preceded the review in *Da'Bell*). The issue of categorization and assessment is largely a matter for the tribunal's discretion and an appellate tribunal or court should not intervene unless the tribunal misdirects itself in law or reaches a perverse decision. An award may be challenged where it is manifestly excessive, as in *Vento*, or insufficient to represent the degree of harm suffered. In *Gilbank*, the Court of Appeal did not consider an award of £25,000 for injury to feelings to be 'manifestly excessive' as the tribunal was entitled to take the view that the circumstances of the case, which involved deliberate, intentional, and repeated harassment of a pregnant employee, justified an award at the top of the upper band. But, in *Doshoki v Draeger* [2002] IRLR 340 an award for

Part D Remedies

taunts of a racial nature ('oh shut up Ayatolla') was increased from £750 to £4,000, which was described as 'very close to the bottom' of the range. On the other hand, in *Kemeh v Ministry of Defence* [2014] IRLR 377, the Court of Appeal considered that an award of £12,000 for a racist remark ('shut up, you dumb black bastard') made by a line manager, who was a sergeant, to a black British Army cook was 'manifestly excessive' and reduced it to £6,000.

33.25 Where there is more than one act of unlawful discrimination, a tribunal may use a global approach in assessing injury to feelings rather than make a separate award for each complaint as it may be unrealistic to make a separate award for each act of discrimination particularly where the acts form a pattern of conduct (*ICTS (UK) Ltd v Tchoula* [2000] ICR 1191).

33.26 Such a 'global' approach will only be appropriate if either more than one type of unlawful discrimination arises out of the same facts or the act relied on is part of an overall pattern of behaviour. Where, as in *Al Jumard v Clwyd Leisure Ltd* [2008] IRLR 345, complaints of different forms of discrimination (ie race, sex, disability) are made arising out of *separate* acts of discrimination, the employment tribunal should at least start by considering the appropriate award in relation to each act of discrimination. The EAT points out that the level of award should not necessarily be the same for different forms of discrimination as the offence, humiliation, or upset may vary if, for example, the act is one of deliberate racial discrimination as contrasted with a 'thoughtless' failure to comply with the duty to make reasonable adjustments under the Disability Discrimination Act. Furthermore, the EAT states that at the end of the exercise, a tribunal should stand back to ensure that the overall award is 'proportionate' and that there has not been 'double counting'.

33.27 In some cases, it may be relevant to take into account the nature of the employment, ie whether the employment was full-time or part-time. In *Orlando v Didcot Power Stations Sports and Social Club* [1996] IRLR 262, the EAT observed that a 'person who unlawfully loses an evening job may be expected to be less hurt and humiliated than a person who loses their entire professional career'.

33.28 In principle, it is open to a tribunal to make an award for both injury to feelings and injury to health (see para 33.32), provided compensation is not awarded twice for the same loss (*HM Prison Service v Salmon* [2001] IRLR 425).

33.29 In making its award a tribunal should ignore the fact that the claimant will receive interest on the award (*Ministry of Defence v Cannock* [1994] ICR 918) or that the claimant may be fairly dismissed at some future date (*O'Donoghue v Redcar and Cleveland Borough Council* [2001] IRLR 615).

33.30 The EAT has held that awards for non-pecuniary loss such as injury to feelings are not taxable and therefore should not be grossed up (*Orthet Ltd v Vince-Cain* [2004] IRLR 857 and *Timothy James Consulting Ltd v Wilton* [2015] IRLR 368). In support of this approach it has been strongly argued by Caspar Glynn QC (ELA *Briefing* March 2016) that the reasoning in *Wilton* in particular is correct and that substantial awards (or settlements) for injury to feelings fall within the tax exclusion of s 406(b) of the ITEPA 2003, as a payment on 'account of injury or disability of an employee' and therefore is not taxable. But in *Moorthy v HMRC* (Upper Tier Tribunal) (Tax and Chancery Chamber), the Upper Tier Tribunal [2016] IRLR 258 confirmed the ruling of the First Tier Tax Tribunal (Tax Chamber) [2015] IRLR 4 that a settlement agreement which includes a payment in respect of injury to feelings was not exempted by s 406(b) of the ITEPA 2003, that the payment amounted to a payment 'received directly or indirectly in consideration or in consequence of, or otherwise in connection with the termination of employment' and that both EAT rulings are wrongly decided. Subject to any further appeal, this means that awards for injury to feelings at least where the injury is caused by the termination of employment are covered by ss 401, 403, and 404 of the ITEPA 2003, and are taxable. Although that ruling has been reversed by the Court of Appeal [2018 IRLR 860], the Upper Tier Tribunal's ruling has been put on a statutory footing by amending s 406(2) of the ITEPA 2003 which came into effect from 6 April 2018 and provides that injury includes psychiatric injury but does not include injured feelings and therefore such awards are taxable.. This has two important implications: first, any awards for injury to feelings made by tribunals should, in appropriate cases, be grossed up (para 33.90) and, secondly, settlements which seek to apportion compensation to injury to feelings will be ineffective if the total exceeds

£30,000. It is unclear what impact (if any) these rulings have on awards for injury to feelings which predate dismissal and therefore are not linked to the termination of employment within the meaning of s 401 of the ITEPA 2003 but it is suggested that in so far as it is possible to distinguish between the two, such awards are not taxable. Support for this view is to be found in *Oti-Obihara v Commissioners for HM Revenue & Customs* [2011] IRLR 386, which suggests that payments made for injury to feelings in such circumstances are not taxable and *A v Commissioners for HM Revenue* [2015] IRLR 692, where it was held that a compensation payment not linked to termination was not taxable under s 62 of the ITEPA 2003. It is also unclear whether the reasoning in *Moorthy* also applies to awards for injury to health but it is arguable that such an award falls within the exclusion in s 406(b) of the ITEPA 2003, and this is supported by the proposed amendment (referred to above). The impact of taxation is considered in greater detail in Chapter 36.

Awards for injury to feelings are fact specific but the *Equal Opportunities Review* (EOR) annual review of compensation in 2015, published in September and October 2016 (EOR 270), reports that the average award for injury to feelings including aggravated damages increased from 2014 by 23 per cent to £10,027 (the median award was £9,000, although there are significant variations depending on the type of protected characteristic asserted by the claimant. So, for example, in disability cases, the average award for injury to feelings in cases of dismissals involving a failure to make reasonable adjustments was £12,025 (although in cases not involving dismissal, the average was £10,320). In the previous year's survey (EOR 259, 260, and 261) the average in age discrimination was £12,300 and there were just two cases where awards were made for injury to feelings in religious discrimination cases: in one the award was £10,000 and in the other it was £3,000. No further information has been published since 2016. **33.31**

Injury to health

The right of a complainant to bring a claim for injury to health (apart from or in addition to, a claim for injury to feelings) caused by an unlawful act of discrimination was recognized by the Court of Appeal in *Sheriff v Klyne Tugs (Lowestoft) Ltd* [1999] ICR 1170. **33.32**

As stated above, compensation for injury to health may be claimed where the injury is a direct consequence of the discriminatory act and need not be reasonably foreseeable (*Essa v Laing Ltd* [2004] ICR 746). It is for the claimant to prove injury to health as a result of a discriminatory act. Where there is no specific medical evidence to support such a claim the award for injury to feelings should reflect general stress and emotional upset suffered by the claimant (*HM Prison Service v Salmon* [2001] IRLR 425) and tribunals may refuse to award additional compensation for injury to health in such circumstances. **33.33**

The most common form of personal injury claim in discrimination cases involves psychiatric injury. Awards are often made with reference to the Judicial College's *Guidelines for the Assessment of General Damages in Personal Injury Cases* (14th edn, 2017). According to these guidelines, relevant factors to be taken into account in valuing such damage include the injured person's ability to cope with life and work, the effect on the injured person's relationships, the extent of treatment and future vulnerability, prognosis, whether medical help is being sought, the nature of the abuse, and its duration. As with all awards, these awards may be uprated in line with inflation. The figures quoted below include the 10 per cent uplift recommended by the Court of Appeal in *Simmons v Castle* (discussed at 33.36 below). **33.34**

There are four categories of award for psychiatric injury: **33.35**

(1) Severe (£48,080–£101,470, where the injury is severe and the prognosis is very poor.
(2) Moderately severe (£16,720–£48,080), where there are significant problems in relation to the above factors but where the prognosis is more optimistic.
(3) Moderate (£5,130–£16,720), where there has been a significant improvement and the prognosis is good.
(4) Less severe (£1,350–£5,130), where the illness is of limited duration such as temporary anxiety and the extent to which daily activities and sleep were affected.

The same four categories of awards apply in cases of post-traumatic stress disorder:

(1) Severe (£52,490–£88,270); such cases will involve permanent effects and all aspects of the claimant's life will be badly affected.

(2) Moderately severe (£20,290–£52,490), where the prognosis indicates a better prospect of recovery but the effects are still likely to cause significant disability for the foreseeable future.

(3) Moderate (£7,170–£20,290), where the claimant has largely recovered and any continuing effect will not be grossly disabling.

(4) Less severe (£3,460–£7,170), where the claimant has 'virtually' made a full recovery within one to two years and only minor symptoms will persist over a longer period.

33.36 However, a discount should be made where the illness is not solely attributable to the discriminatory conduct, for example, where there is some pre-existing medical history or there are other contributory factors. In *HM Prison Service v Salmon* [2001] IRLR 425 compensation for psychiatric injury was reduced by 25 per cent on the basis that the depressive illness suffered by the claimant was not entirely caused by the unlawful discrimination suffered by the claimant. Whilst the discriminator must take the claimant as it finds him or her, it does not automatically follow that if somebody was liable to suffer depression or another psychiatric injury, then the extent to which that might have been caused by non-tortious causes should necessarily be eliminated if it is possible (on the medical evidence) to distinguish between the tortious cause and the non-tortious cause. In other words, if it is possible to divide the cause or causes of the injury then, as in *Salmon*, the employment tribunal should attempt to do so (*Olayemi v Athena Medical Centre and Ors* (EAT/0140/15)). This principle also applies to disability discrimination cases provided the injury is divisible: the issue for the employment tribunal is how far the injury or any aggravation to the injury was caused by the discriminatory conduct and an employment tribunal will err in law if it fails to address this issue (*BAE Systems (Operations) Ltd v Konczak* [2014] IRLR 676). Further guidance on the proper approach to this issue has been given by the Court of Appeal in *Konczak* [2017] IRLR 893. The court ruled that a tribunal should try to identify a rational basis on which the harm can be apportioned between the part caused by the employer's wrong and the part which is not so caused. This, says the court, is not so much a question of causative contribution as the divisibility of the harm. The question is whether the tribunal can identify, however broadly, a particular part of the suffering which is due to the wrong. The Court acknowledges that this distinction is easier to apply in a case of physical injury than psychiatric injury but where (as stated above), there is evidence of a pre-existing illness for which the employer is not responsible, the award should be limited to the extent to which that injury has been aggravated by the wrong. On the other hand, where as in *Konczak* itself such an analysis is not possible, then a full award for the injury will be justified and, in *Konczak*, the tribunal was not perverse in so concluding.

Simmons v Castle uplift

33.37 In *Simmons v Castle* [2013] 1 WLR 1239, a personal injury case, the Court of Appeal ruled that following Jackson LJ's review of civil litigation costs, there should be a 10 per cent uplift in the level of general damages in civil claims. Prior to the Court of Appeal's ruling in *De Souza v Vinci Construction (UK) Ltd* [2017] IRLR 844, there was a series of conflicting EAT rulings as to whether this uplift also applies to awards for injury to feelings. In *Cadogan Hotel Partners Ltd v Ozo*g (EAT 001/14), the EAT held that it did. This approach was followed by Simler J in *The Sash Windows Workshop Ltd and Another v King* [2015] IRLR 344. In two subsequent cases, however, *Chawla v Hewlett Packard* [2015] IRLR 536 and *Pereira de Souza v Vinci Construction UK Ltd* [2015] ICR 103, the EAT ruled that the uplift to civil damages did not apply in discrimination cases and that the two earlier rulings should not be followed. This ruling was overturned by the Court of Appeal in *De Souza*, where the court ruled that that the Simmons ruling does apply to awards for injury to feelings and awards for injury to health. The figures referred to in paras 33.23 and 33.35 above are inclusive of the uplift.

Aggravated damages

33.38 Aggravated damages are recoverable in discrimination claims in England and Wales. (This does not apply in Scotland where aggravated damages are not known to the law of delict but aggravating factors are taken into account in determining the award for injury to feelings.) The circumstances in which an award for aggravated damages may be made were summarized by Judge Burke in *Singh v University Hospital NHS Trust* EAT/1409/01 as follows:

(a) Aggravated damages may only be awarded in a case in which it is established that the discriminator has acted in a high-handed, malicious, insulting, or oppressive manner in committing the discriminatory act or the way it was handled (*Alexander v Home Office* [1988] ICR 685).

(b) While any discrimination is offensive and regrettable and may be potentially very distressing, the requirements set out in *Alexander* involve some special element in the conduct of the discriminator which takes the case beyond the ordinary run of discrimination cases. The fact that the victim is upset or distressed or even injured in his health as a result of the discrimination is not enough.

(c) It is a matter for the tribunal of fact in each case to decide whether, if the discriminator has acted in a high-handed, malicious, insulting, or oppressive manner, the case is one in which aggravated compensation should be awarded.

(d) Aggravated damages may be awarded even if the injury to feelings award is in the lower band.

(e) The award must be compensatory, not punitive.

More recently in *Commissioner of Police of the Metropolis v Shaw* [2012] IRLR 291, a whistle-blowing case that also applies equally to discrimination claims, Underhill P stated that the circumstances attracting an award of aggravated damages fell into three categories: **33.39**

(a) the manner in which the wrong was committed which encompasses the circumstances set out in 33.38(a) above

(b) the motive of the discriminator, ie where the discriminatory conduct is based on prejudice or animosity or which is spiteful, vindictive, or intended to wound in contrast with behaviour which is caused by ignorance or insensitivity (although in such cases the claimant must be aware of the motive)

(c) the subsequent conduct of the employer, such as the manner in which a grievance was investigated or where at trial the respondent conducts the proceedings in an unnecessarily offensive manner by, for example, oppressive or unjustified intrusive cross-examination (though the observations of Slade J in *Ministry of Defence v Fletcher* [2010] IRLR 25 should be noted in this context).

The following are examples of circumstances where aggravated damages have been awarded: **33.40**

(a) where an employer failed to investigate a complaint of racial discrimination and failed to apologize (*Armitage, Marsden and HM Prison Service v Johnson* [1997] ICR 275)

(b) where the respondent attempted to cover up and trivialize the discriminatory acts (*HM Prison Service v Salmon* [2001] IRLR 425)

(c) where the respondent conducted the tribunal proceedings in an inappropriate and intimidatory manner (*Zaiwalla & Co v Walia* [2002] IRLR 697 and *Ministry of Defence v Fletcher* [2010] IRLR 25)

(d) where the respondent failed to give satisfactory answers in reply to a statutory discrimination questionnaire (*City of Bradford Metropolitan Council v Arora* [1989] IRLR 442)

(e) where the respondent promoted the perpetrator of an allegedly discriminatory act before completing its investigation (*British Telecommunications plc v Reid* [2004] IRLR 327). There is also some suggestion in this case that the conduct of the investigation itself and unreasonable delay may also be aggravating factors.

In *Shaw* [2012] IRLR 291, Underhill P observed that the large majority of awards of aggravated damages have been in the range of £5,000 to £7,500; although it is unclear whether he intended to establish some kind of tariff, many tribunals have adopted this approach in practice. In this context, it should be noted that some of the awards in earlier cases have not been uprated in line with inflation and to date there has been no equivalent authority to *Vento* (para 33.22) identifying the relevant range of awards.

Relationship between non-pecuniary awards

33.41 Where awards for injury to feelings, aggravated damages, and injury to health are made, there is an inevitable risk of the claimant being compensated twice (or more) for the same loss. Where this can be demonstrated, it will amount to an error of law. For example, in *Ministry of Defence v Fletcher* [2010] IRLR 25 the tribunal was found to have erred in the amounts it awarded for injury to feelings, aggravated damages, and exemplary damages. Similarly, in *Commissioner of Police of the Metropolis v Shaw* [2012] IRLR 291 the EAT held that an award of £20,000 for aggravated damages was outside the recognized range for such award and it was also anomalous that an award of aggravated damages should exceed the award for injury to feelings. In making the award, the tribunal had made a number or errors, including focusing entirely on the seriousness of the respondent's conduct rather than on the impact on the claimant and thereby introducing a punitive element to its award.

Exemplary damages

33.42 In *Kuddus v Chief Constable of Leicestershire Constabulary* [2002] 2 AC 122, it was held that exemplary damages are recoverable if compensation is insufficient to punish the wrongdoer and if the conduct is either (a) oppressive, arbitrary, or unconstitutional action by agents of the government, or (b) where the respondent's conduct has been calculated to make a profit which may exceed the compensation payable to the claimant. Contrary to the EAT's ruling in *Deane v London Borough of Ealing* [1993] IRLR 209 that exemplary or punitive damages could not be awarded under the RRA 1976, the EAT has ruled both in *Ministry of Defence v Fletcher* [2010] IRLR 25 and *London Borough of Hackney v Sivanandan and Others* [2011] IRLR 740 that it is open to a tribunal to make such an award in an appropriate case.

33.43 Nonetheless, the *Kuddus* ruling is likely to have limited application in discrimination cases. In *Ministry of Defence v Fletcher* [2010] IRLR 25 the EAT has confirmed that exemplary damages may be awarded in category (a) but only where the wrongdoing was 'conscious and contumelious' as exemplary damages are reserved for the worst cases of the oppressive use of power by public authorities. Perhaps surprisingly the EAT, in overturning the tribunal's award, found this not to be established in *Fletcher*. The EAT further opined that an award of £50,000 exemplary damages was excessive in any event, not least because awards at this level were reserved for cases of wrongful arrest and false imprisonment. The EAT would have been minded to award £7,500 had it considered the case to be one where such an award was appropriate and indicated that, in deciding how much to award as exemplary damages, a tribunal should have regard to comparable awards in other torts. Similarly, in *Sivanandan*, the EAT ruled an award of exemplary damages was not justified where the Council, on the advice of counsel, had failed to take disciplinary action against an employee who was found to discriminated against the claimant as this could not be regarded as 'oppressive conduct' in the sense identified in *Kuddus* (although the EAT indicated that the failure to take such action in appropriate circumstances might justify an award of aggravated damages).

33.44 Exemplary or punitive damages are not available under the Equal Treatment Directive (*Ministry of Defence v Meredith* [1995] IRLR 539), although this decision may be open to review in the light of the subsequent developments in domestic law.

D. FINANCIAL LOSS

33.45 Compensation may be recovered for any financial loss flowing from the discriminatory act. As stated above, at least in cases of direct and intentional discrimination, claimants do not have to prove that the loss was reasonably foreseeable provided it can be shown to be a direct consequence of the discriminatory act.

Types of loss

33.46 Loss covers pecuniary loss as well as loss of benefits and expenses. In general, the types of recoverable loss are the same as in an unfair dismissal claim.

Earnings will include loss of pay, overtime, commission, and bonuses. The loss is assessed net **33.47** rather than gross. Compensation may also be recovered for the loss of benefits such as private health care, private use of company car, pension, share schemes, travel concessions, loan facilities, clothing allowances and free goods, free accommodation, subsidized meals, and childcare costs. Compensation may also be awarded for the loss of the opportunity to be promoted to a higher position (*Ministry of Defence v Cannock* [1994] ICR 918).

Such losses are quantified in the same manner as in an unfair dismissal claim. For example, the **33.48** tribunal's pension guidelines referred to at para 32.103 also apply to the quantification of loss in discrimination claims.

Compensation claims can also be made for any expenses flowing from the discriminatory act. **33.49** These can sometimes include medical expenses associated with treatment for recovery from the discriminatory act.

Calculating the loss

The process of calculating loss is also similar to that in an unfair dismissal claim. The loss will con- **33.50** sist of the past loss up to the date of the hearing and future loss thereafter.

Although there is no equivalent power to ERA 1996, s 123(1) to limit the award for just and equit- **33.51** able reasons, it will still be necessary for the tribunal to consider the principles in *Kingston Upon Hull City Council v Dunnachie (No 3)* [2003] IRLR 843 in the calculation of future loss, ie 'old job facts' and 'new job facts'. Tribunals often have to consider whether the claimant would have remained in his or her employment but for the discrimination, ie whether the claimant would have left voluntarily or involuntarily at some future date or would have come back to work after the birth of a child or would have moved to another job or would have worked in the same job until retirement. In *Chagger v Abbey National Plc* [2010] IRLR 47 and *Wardle v Credit Agricole Corporate & Investment Bank* [2011] IRLR 604 the Court of Appeal gives detailed guidance on how these issues should be approached including the circumstances in which it will be appropriate to make an award for career long loss. The Court in *Chagger* also confirmed that the EAT's ruling (at [2009] IRLR 86) that it is open to a tribunal to apply a *Polkey*-type limitation in discrimination cases where it can be shown that the claimant would have lost his job in any event for a lawful reason. For example, in *Chagger's* case it was argued that Chagger would have been made redundant even if the redundancy selection criteria had been applied in a non-discriminatory manner as he was one of two people in the redundancy pool. The failure to consider this issue in a proper manner amounts to an error of law (*Eversheds Legal Services Ltd v De Belin* [2011] IRLR 448 (see para 32.178). Furthermore, where the award is limited for *Polkey*-related reasons, or on the basis of 'old job facts' (see para 32.157), it is still open to a tribunal, applying *Chagger*, to award compensation for the 'stigma' caused by the discriminatory dismissal (para 33.60 below).

Statistical information may be admissible on the issue of job mobility. As Mummery LJ pointed **33.52** out in *Vento v Chief Constable of West Yorkshire Police* [2003] ICR 318, 328:

> The question requires a forecast to be made about the course of future events. It has to be answered on the basis of the best assessment that can be made on the relevant material available to the court. That includes statistical material, such as that produced to the tribunal showing the percentage of women who have in the past continued to serve in the police force until the age of retirement.

The tribunal was therefore entitled to conclude that but for the discriminatory dismissal, there was a 75 per cent chance that the claimant, a probationary constable, would have stayed with the force until her retirement age of 55. However, in *Wardle v Credit Agricole Corporate & Investment Bank* [2011] IRLR 604 the Court of Appeal stated that if, contrary to its primary ruling, the claimant was entitled to compensation for the rest of his working life (see para 32.157), the employment tribunal had erred in reducing compensation by 80 per cent on the basis that there was an 80 per cent chance that he would have left the job in any event. The Court accepted that some reduction should be made for the 'vicissitudes of life', such as the possibility that the claimant would have been fairly dismissed or might have given up employment for other reasons but, for the reasons given in *Chagger* (para 69), in the absence of specific evidence, this should not be readily inferred and therefore a 80 per cent reduction was too high.

33.53 Given the inevitable uncertainty involved in making such an assessment on an all-or-nothing basis, tribunals will often quantify the loss in percentage terms or on a loss of a chance basis (*Ministry of Defence v Wheeler* [1998] IRLR 23). Where there are a number of contingent possibilities, the correct approach is to accumulate the percentage chance of each event occurring (*Ministry of Defence v Hunt* [1996] ICR 544, ie in that case there was a 75 per cent chance that she would have returned after her first child). This may need to be combined with making a percentage assessment of other contingencies, such as a pay rise.

33.54 The tribunal may also need to take into account the risk of future dismissal. For example, in *O'Donoghue v Redcar and Cleveland Borough Council* [2001] IRLR 615 the Court of Appeal held that the tribunal was entitled to find that although the claimant had been unfairly dismissed and victimized on the grounds of sex, it was inevitable that her divisive and antagonistic attitude towards her colleagues would have led to her dismissal within six months and to limit its award accordingly. There is a difference between the approach taken by a tribunal in a discrimination case in relation to this issue from that in an unfair dismissal case: in the former the tribunal is solely concerned with the behaviour of the actual employer whereas in the latter, a tribunal may take into account the actions of a reasonable employer (*Abbey National v Formoso* [1999] ICR 222).

33.55 It is not entirely clear what bearing a future unfair dismissal has on an award of compensation for unlawful discrimination. In *HM Prison Service v Beart (No 2)* [2005] IRLR 171 the EAT, relying on the principle that a tortfeasor may not benefit from his wrong, concluded that a subsequent unfair dismissal does not break the chain of causation and that the claimant is entitled to recover full compensation for unlawful discrimination in these circumstances. The Court of Appeal upheld the EAT's ruling ([2005] IRLR 568) on the basis that, in the particular circumstances of that case, the 'second wrong' namely the unfair dismissal did not break the chain of causation. Rix LJ pointed out that all that happened was that the employer had committed two discrete wrongs in respect of which the statute provided a cap for one but not the other. Critically, in *Beart* the employment tribunal had found in relation to her discrimination claim that if the claimant had been redeployed (as recommended by an internal report), she would 'probably still have been employed' by the employer (ie there was a continuing loss) and that in relation to her unfair dismissal claim, the tribunal had found that the allegations of misconduct were unproven (ie there was no valid reason for dismissal). However, the Court of Appeal recognized that the position may be different if the employee 'commits a repudiatory breach of his own contract', ie if there is a 'new intervening act', either before or after the unlawful discriminatory act. In such circumstances, a subsequent dismissal for a valid and lawful reason may well break the chain of causation with the potential result that in such a situation, the award should be limited to the current maximum for unfair dismissal even if it is held unfair for procedural reasons, although there is no direct authority on the point.

Credit for payments received and *ex gratia* payments

33.56 The rules on giving credit for earnings and benefits received are the same as in unfair dismissal cases including the deduction of State benefits from the award paid to the claimant (*Chan v Hackney LBC* [1997] ICR 1014) but not benefits which are paid to the claimant's household or children (*Vento v Chief Constable of West Yorkshire Police* [2002] IRLR 177, EAT). Collateral benefits such as pension benefits should also normally be ignored but credit should be given for past or future payments received under a private health insurance scheme as these are not regarded as collateral benefits (*Atos Origin IT Services UK Ltd v Haddock* [2005] IRLR 20).

33.57 Credit should be given for any *ex gratia* payment received in calculating the loss before applying the percentage chance reduction (see *Ministry of Defence v Hunt* [1996] ICR 544 and *Ministry of Defence v Wheeler* [1998] ICR 242).

Mitigation

The normal common law principles on mitigation apply to the assessment of compensation. **33.58** Claimants are under a duty to mitigate each and every head of loss and cannot expect to profit from the unlawful discrimination. Whether the claimant has in fact mitigated his or her loss will be determined in accordance with the guidelines at paras 32.144–32.151 and will depend on the facts of each case.

The loss will come to an end if the tribunal considers that the claimant has or should have found **33.59** a new job at an equivalent rate of remuneration. This should be considered before the application of the multiplier or the percentage loss of a chance (*Ministry of Defence v Hunt* [1996] IRLR 139). For example, if the claimant earned £800 a week and finds a new job earning £500 a week, the net loss of £300 a week and the percentage chance will be applied to that figure (see also *Ministry of Defence v Wheeler* [1998] IRLR 23).

Future handicap in the labour market

Given that the award for unlawful discrimination is assessed in like manner as any other claim **33.60** in tort, it is open to a claimant to recover compensation for any future handicap in the labour market. This is often referred to as a 'Smith and Manchester award' after the case *Smith v Manchester Corporation* (1974) 17 KIR 1. In making its assessment, the tribunal will have to quantify the risk that the claimant will suffer such damage in the labour market. In *Moeliker v Reyrolle & Co Ltd* [1976] ICR 253, the Court of Appeal suggested a two-stage approach in relation to such claims: where the claimant is in work at the time of the remedies hearing, the first question is whether there is a 'substantial' or real risk that the claimant will lose his job before the estimated end of his working life. If so, the second question is for the tribunal to assess and quantify that risk having regard to the degree of risk itself, the time in which it might materialize, and the factors which may influence the claimant's chances of finding another job at all or one which is equally well paid. The power to award 'stigma' compensation, based on the loss suffered by a claimant who is at a disadvantage in the labour market for a discriminatory reason, has been accepted by the Court of Appeal in *Chagger v Abbey National plc* [2010] IRLR 47, where it is suggested that a notional sum may be awarded for such loss. But in *Denysenko v Credit Suisse Securities (Europe) Ltd* (ET/3200840/2008), an employment tribunal, basing itself on the *Smith v Manchester Corporation* approach (referred to above) awarded the claimant one year's salary amounting to US$600,000 to reflect the disadvantage to her banking career she had suffered as a result of her employer's unlawful sex discrimination and the stigma associated with her dismissal for discriminatory reasons.

In *Chagger v Abbey National Plc* [2010] IRLR 47 the Court of Appeal recognized that this might **33.61** include alleged stigma associated with the fact that the claimant had complained of discrimination against his former employer. The Court (Elias LJ) rejected the argument that the claimant should be required to bring such a 'victimization' claim against prospective employers who had rejected him, saying that the primary liability rested with the original employer. The Court recognized that such claims are difficult to prove and in many cases such loss would account for the difficulty the complainant might face in mitigating his loss and would therefore be reflected in a higher award of compensation for future loss of earnings. However, the Court recognized that, in exceptional cases, for example, where loss was limited for a *Polkey*-style reason, a tribunal might be justified in making a separate award of stigma compensation. Furthermore, in *Small v The Shrewsbury and Telford Hospitals NHS Trust* [2017] IRLR 889, in remitting the matter for further consideration by the tribunal, the Court of Appeal ruled that on the evidence raised by the claimant, the tribunal should have considered making an award of 'stigma' compensation where the award for future loss was limited by 'old job facts' for example that the employment would have come to an end after a relatively short period, even though the point was not raised by the claimant and in certain circumstances, such an award may be quite substantial (see para 33.61 above).

Part D Remedies

Dismissals which are both discriminatory and unfair

33.62 Compensation cannot be recovered twice for a dismissal which is discriminatory and unfair (ERA 1996, s 126). Where a dismissal is held to be both discriminatory and unfair, the tribunal should award compensation under the relevant discrimination legislation in order to give to the claimant full compensation, although it is still open to the tribunal to make a basic award (*D'Souza v London Borough of Lambeth* [1997] IRLR 677). On the other hand, if the dismissal is discriminatory but fair, no award will be made for financial loss, although an award can be made for non-pecuniary loss (*Lisk-Carew v Birmingham City Council* [2004] 2 All ER (D) 215).

Accelerated payment

33.63 The award of compensation for future loss falls to be discounted to make allowance for the accelerated receipt of the payment unless the sums involved are so small as to make this unnecessary. The case law in relation to discounts for accelerated payment is considered at para 32.222.

Power to adjust the award

33.64 The previous powers to adjust the award in the Employment Act 2002 were repealed by the Employment Act 2008 but tribunals have a discretion to increase or reduce an award by such amount as is considered 'just and equitable' up to 25 per cent where there is an 'unreasonable' failure to comply with the ACAS Code of Practice 2009 (TULR(C)A 1992, s 207A) (see para 32.195). There is no longer a requirement to increase the award by a minimum amount. Whilst tribunals have a wide discretion over the amount of any increase, it has been established that in considering what is 'just and equitable' regard should be had to the overall level of the award (*Abbey National plc v Chagger* [2010] IRLR 47 and *Wardle v Credit Agricole Corporate and Investment Bank (No 2)* [2011] IRLR 604).

33.65 It has also been suggested that it may be open to reduce an award for unlawful discrimination for contributory fault pursuant to the Law Reform (Contributory Negligence) Act 1945, although it may be questioned whether a claimant can contribute to unlawful discrimination by his or her conduct (*Way v Crouch* [2005] IRLR 603).

Overall size of awards

33.66 Compensation for a discriminatory dismissal must be adequate (*Marshall v Southampton & SW Hampshire Area Health Authority (No 2)* [1993] ICR 893). In most cases, there is nothing wrong in principle with tribunals simply adding up the awards made under each head and awarding the total (including interest) (*Ministry of Defence v Hunt* [1996] IRLR 139) but in *Ministry of Defence v Cannock* [1994] ICR 918 the EAT stressed that awards should not be excessive and there is further support for this view in *Vento v Chief Constable of West Yorkshire Police* [2003] IRLR 102, CA.

E. COMPENSATION FOR INDIRECT DISCRIMINATION

33.67 Section 124(4) and (5) of the EqA 2010 defines the circumstances in which compensation may be awarded for indirect discrimination. Section 124(4) provides that compensation may be awarded for indirect discrimination if the tribunal is satisfied that 'the provision, criteria or practice was not applied with the intention of discriminating against the complaint'. However, s 124(5) further provides that, even in the absence of such an intention, an award can be made if the tribunal 'considers' whether (a) to make a declaration, or (b) to make a recommendation under s 124(2)(a) or (c). In practical terms, this restriction is unlikely to prevent tribunals from awarding compensation where a claim for indirect discrimination is upheld.

33.68 The new statutory provisions are, in effect, in the same form as s 65(1B)) of the SDA 1975 and apply to all forms of discrimination. There have been no reported cases on this provision.

F. RECOMMENDATIONS

Introduction

Section 124(c) of the EqA 2010 empowers a tribunal to make an 'appropriate' recommendation **33.69** where it upholds the complaint. Again, the remedy is discretionary. The current power, as amended by s 2(1) of the Deregulation Act (DA) 2015 to make an 'appropriate' recommendation is such that the respondent must take within a specified period 'specified steps for the purpose of obviating or reducing the adverse effect on the complainant of any matter to which the proceedings relate'. The previous provision empowering tribunals to make recommendations in relation to 'other persons' who may have been affected by the discriminatory behaviour has been repealed where proceedings commenced after 1 October 2015.

Scope of the power to make recommendations

The power given to tribunals under the previous provisions was considered to be 'extremely **33.70** wide' (*Vento v Chief Constable of West Yorkshire Police* [2002] IRLR 177, EAT). For example, the tribunal may make a recommendation that the employer should make arrangements for racial awareness training if this is appropriate in the circumstances (*Southwark London Borough v Ayton* EAT/0515/03). Similarly, a recommendation that the employer should consider its behaviour and discuss the tribunal's findings with certain named employees where the employer was in 'institutional denial' was upheld by the EAT in the *Vento (No 2)* case (para 33.22) (although the appeal was allowed against a further recommendation that the police officers should apologize to the claimant and the Deputy Chief Constable should report on whether or not the relevant officers were willing to apologize). Much will of course depend on the nature of the complaint: for example, in *Clark v East London Bus & Coach Co Ltd* (Case no 3203484/100), a disability case, recommendations were made concerning the claimant's rota pattern and rest days and that he should be provided with an appropriate room to test his blood sugar levels and take medication. In *Atos Origin IT Services UK Ltd v Haddock* [2005] IRLR 20, the EAT considered that as an alternative to making an award for future loss, it could recommend that the employer should continue to employ the claimant to his normal retirement age to enable him to claim benefits under a private health insurance scheme.

While the discretion must be exercised in a judicial manner, it is arguable that the power given to **33.71** tribunals by the EqA 2010 is significantly wider as it extends to any specified step which, as stated above, is recommended for the purpose of obviating or reducing the adverse effect of any matter to which the proceedings relate. So, for example, it may well be open to a tribunal to make a recommendation in the form rejected by the EAT in *Vento (No 2)* (para 33.22) if it considered this to be appropriate. In addition, a recommendation can now be made to assist other potential victims of discriminatory practices in addition to the claimant.

The removal of the reference to the step or steps being 'practicable' may cast doubt on the cor- **33.72** rectness of some of the previous cases. For example, under the previous law it was held that the power does not permit tribunals to order the employer to increase the claimant's wages as this should be considered in determining the award of damages (*Irvine v Prestcold* [1981] IRLR 281). Similarly, it was previously held that the power did not permit tribunals to order that the claimant is appointed to the next available vacancy as this would be unfair to other candidates (*Noone v North West Regional Health Authority (No 2)* [1988] IRLR 530) or, for the same reason, to order the claimant's promotion (*Sharma v British Gas* [1991] IRLR 101). These cases are now open to doubt, although doubtless it will be argued that a recommendation is not 'appropriate' in such circumstances.

Furthermore, a recommendation is unlikely to be made if it is 'completely impracticable' as this **33.73** is unlikely to be seen as obviating or reducing the adverse effect of the discriminatory act (*Leeds Rhinos Rugby Club v Sterling* EAT/267/01) or if it is too general to obviate or reduce the adverse effect of the discriminatory act (*Bayoomi v British Railways Board* [1981] IRLR 431, where the claimant had left the employment by the time of the tribunal hearing) unless the recommendation would assist others.

33.74 Whilst the power to make a recommendation is used sparingly, an EOR survey in EOR 232 found that the most common recommendation is for training to be provided within a specified time frame. This is confirmed in EOR 270. Another common recommendation is for an employer's equal opportunities policy to be reviewed, updated, and circulated. In one case, the tribunal recommended that a warning should be removed from the claimant's record and in another a public authority was required to apologize to the claimant by way of a press release. A follow-up EOR survey published in 2013 found that of the ten recommendations made in 2013, seven had wider implications and required the employer to take action to address discrimination generally with no particular reference to the individual claimant but these cases, and many of those referred to in the EOR 2014 survey, no longer apply since the power to make wider recommendations has been repealed (see para 33.69).

Enforcement

33.75 There is no power to enforce a recommendation as such but where, without reasonable excuse, the respondent fails to comply with an 'appropriate' recommendation, the tribunal may either increase the amount of compensation previously awarded or (if no award was made) make an award of compensation (EqA 2010, s 124(7)).

G. EQUALITY OF TERMS

Equality clause

33.76 An employee's right to equal pay (referred to in the EqA as 'equality of terms') takes effect by way of operation of an equality clause, which is implied by s 66(1) of the EqA 2010 into the contract of employment. An equality clause is a provision which relates to terms of a contract (whether concerned with pay or not) under which a woman is employed (EqA 2010, s 66(2)) and modifies the terms of that contract. The equality clause also applies to a term relating to membership of or rights under an occupational pension scheme (EqA 2010, s 66(3)) and also to certain 'equality' terms (EqA 2010, s 73) which apply during maternity leave (EqA 2010, s 74). A detailed consideration of these provisions lies outside the scope of this chapter.

Remedies

33.77 The remedies available to the employee are therefore the same as those in any claim for breach of contract. Normally, this will involve a claim for damages for breach of contract (EqA 2010, s 132(2)(b)) but either side may apply for a declaration (EqA 2010, s 132(2)(a)) and possibly an injunction (although this remedy is not available in the employment tribunal). Where the equality clause has the effect of modifying any of the terms which relate to wages within the meaning of s 27(1) in Part 2 of the ERA 1996, a claim may be brought under those provisions for the recovery or non-payment of such wages.

33.78 Special provisions apply to claims relating to a breach of an equality clause or rule brought by pension members (EqA 2010, s 134). If the tribunal finds that there has been such a breach it has power to grant a declaration as regards the rights of the claimant and respondent in relation to the matters to which the proceedings relate (EqA 2010, s 134(2)(a)) and to order an award by way of arrears of benefits or damages or any other amount in relation to the complaint (EqA 2010, s 134(2)(b)). However, where membership of the pension scheme is voluntary, no award will be made unless the evidence shows that the claimant would have joined the scheme (*Copple v Littlewoods plc* [2012] IRLR 121).

33.79 A claim under the EqA 2010 is a financial claim only. Compensation cannot be recovered for non-economic loss such as injury to feelings, aggravated damages, and/or exemplary damages (*Council of City of Newcastle upon Tyne v Allen* [2005] IRLR 504).

Arrears date

The normal period for a 'standard case' for which arrears of remuneration or damages may be **33.80** claimed is six years before the day on which the proceedings were initiated (EqA 2010, s 132(4)) or five years in Scotland. However, in *Bainbridge v Redcar & Cleveland Borough Council (No 2)* [2007] IRLR 494, the EAT has ruled that employees whose jobs are rated equivalent under a job evaluation scheme do not have the right to seek compensation going back up to six years, unless they have also established a right to equal pay in one or more of the other ways provided for under the statutory provisions (ie they can show that their jobs were of equal value during the relevant period). The ruling, which has been criticized as being inconsistent with the earlier decisions in *Dibro Ltd v Hore* [1990] IRLR 129, *Avon County Council v Foxall* [1989] IRLR 435, and *McAuley v Eastern Health and Social Services Board* [1991] IRLR 467, means that the outcome of a Job Evaluation Scheme (JES) need not be backdated beyond the date on which it came into force.

Special provision is made for a 'stable work' case (EqA 2010, s 130(3)); a 'concealment case' (EqA **33.81** 2010, s 130(4)); and an 'incapacity case', of which there are three types (EqA 2010, s 130(7), (8), (9)). In such circumstances, the arrears date is the date of the contravention (EqA 2010, s 132(4)).

Similar provisions apply in claims for arrears brought by pension members where in a standard case **33.82** arrears may be awarded for six years (EqA 2010, s 134(5)), or five years in Scotland, and, in a concealment case, from the date on which the breach first occurred (EqA 2010, s 134(5)).

No apportionment

In *Brennan and Others v (1) Sunderland City Council and (2) GMB and Unison* (2013) ICR 1183, **33.83** the EAT held that, in a claim for equal pay under the EqA 2010, there is no power for an employment tribunal to determine claims for contribution under the Civil Liability (Contribution) Act 1978 or to apportion liability between the parties under that Act. The EAT also indicated that the High Court would not have jurisdiction to determine such a claim.

H. COMPENSATION FOR PART-TIME WORKERS
AND FIXED-TERM EMPLOYEES

Special provision is made for complaints under PTWR 2000 and FTER 2002. **33.84**

Where a tribunal finds a complaint presented to it under PTWR 2000 or FTER 2002 well founded, **33.85** it shall take such of the following steps as it considers just and equitable:

(a) make a declaration as to the rights of the complainant and the employer in relation to the matters to which the complaint relates
(b) order the employer to pay compensation to the complainant
(c) recommend that the employer takes, within a specified period, action appearing to the tribunal to be reasonable, in all the circumstances of the case, for the purpose of obviating or reducing the adverse effect on the complainant of any matter to which the complaint relates (PTWR 2000, reg 8(7); FTER 2002, reg 7(7)).

Where a tribunal awards compensation, the amount of the compensation is such as the tribunal **33.86** considers just and equitable in the circumstances having regard to (a) any infringement to which the complaint relates, and (b) any loss which is attributable to the infringement, having regard, in the case of an infringement conferred by reg 5 of the PTWR 2000 , to the pro rata principle, except where it is inappropriate to do so (PTR 2000, reg 8(9); FTER 2002, reg 7(8)).

Loss is taken to include any expenses reasonably incurred by the complainant in consequence of **33.87** the infringement and loss of any benefit which he might reasonably be expected to have had but for the infringement (PTWR 2000, reg 8(1); FTER 2002, reg 7(11)) but the loss does not include injury to feelings as a result of the less favourable treatment (PTWR 2000, reg 8(11); FTER 2002, reg 7(10)). The awards may be reduced for contributory conduct (PTWR 2000, regulation 8(13); FTER 2002, reg 7(13)).

33.88 The normal rules on mitigation apply to the assessment of loss under both regulations (PTWR 2000, reg 8(12); FTER 2002, reg 7(11)).

33.89 There is no statutory cap on the amount of compensation that can be awarded.

I. TAX

33.90 As stated above, there is no statutory limit to the amount of compensation which can be made in a complaint of unlawful discrimination but where, in a dismissal case, the award exceeds the tax threshold for lump sum payments (currently £30,000) (Income Tax (Earnings and Pensions) Act 2003, ss 401 and 403), the award is potentially taxable. This means that any such award falls to be 'grossed up' in accordance with the principles in *Shove v Downs Surgical plc* [1984] 1 All ER 7. Where an award for pension loss is calculated on the 'substantial loss' approach (para 32.112), the award should normally be grossed up unless it is calculated on gross salary (*Chief Constable of Northumbria Police v Erichsen* (EAT/0027/15). The process of 'grossing up' can be more complicated where the claimant is a high earner and useful guidance is given in the *Presidential Guidance on 'Principles for calculating Pension Loss* (4th edn, August 2017) 22–25. The impact of taxation is considered in greater detail in Chapter 36.

34

Recoupment of Benefits

SUMMARY

(1) Some awards made by a tribunal may be subject to deductions in respect of certain social security payments received by the claimant: jobseeker's allowance, income-related employment and support allowance, income support, and universal credit. The deduction is of benefits paid to the claimant either to the date his loss ceased or to the date of the tribunal hearing or reserved decision, whichever is the earlier.

(2) If the claimant has been in receipt of certain of these benefits, any receipts are ignored for the purpose of deciding the compensation due to the claimant: the claimant retains the benefits, but the respondent deducts an equivalent amount from the compensation due to the claimant and sends it direct to Job Centre Plus.

(3) If the tribunal reduces an award for contributory fault or brings the award down to the statutory cap, the amount of recoupment will be reduced by the same proportion.

(4) A claimant can challenge the tribunal's decision on the recoupment certificate by notice to the Department for Work and Pensions.

(5) The Recoupment Regulations do not apply to out-of-court settlements.

A. INTRODUCTION

The Employment Protection (Recoupment of Jobseeker's Allowance and Income Support) Regulations **34.01** 1996, SI 1996/2349 are intended to ensure that a dismissed employee is not compensated twice over for the same loss, by social security benefit and unfair dismissal compensation, and that the State can recover from the employer certain benefits previously paid to the successful claimant.

B. WHEN APPLICABLE

The Recoupment Regulations only apply to jobseeker's allowance and income support (regula- **34.02** tion 4(1)), and, by virtue of regulation 5 of the Social Security (Miscellaneous Amendments) (No 5) Regulations 2010 and regulation 50 of the Universal Credit (Consequential, Supplementary,

Incidental and Miscellaneous Provisions) Regulations 2013, to income-related employment and support allowance and universal credit. They apply where the claimant has claimed any of these allowances, whether or not he has received them (regulation 4(8)). Universal credit will eventually replace various income-related benefits, including job-seeker's allowance, income support, and employment and support allowance, as well as other state benefits which are not income-related. Only those universal credit payments which relate to the recipient's earned income will be subject to the recoupment provisions.

34.03 Other forms of benefit (for example, contributory employment support allowance and disability living allowance) must be deducted in their entirety from the amount of any compensatory award. This is because receipt of other benefits is regarded as a form of mitigation of loss (*Morgans v Alpha Plus Security Ltd* [2005] IRLR 234, EAT). In *Olayemi v Athena Medical Centre & Anor* (UKEAT/0140/15/LA) the EAT confirmed that housing benefit should not be deducted from an award as the related housing benefit legislation enables later re-assessment and claw back of this benefit in the event of an award for loss of earnings from employment.

34.04 The Recoupment Regulations apply to any of 'the payments described in column 1 of the table contained in the Schedule to these Regulations' (regulation 3(1)(a)). These include, but are not limited to, payments of unfair dismissal compensation, payments upon an order for re-engagement or reinstatement, payments where a reinstatement or re-engagement order is not complied with, protective awards, and guarantee payments. They do not apply to awards of compensation for any form of discrimination or to redundancy payments. The full description of payments to be made by a respondent to a claimant following an employment tribunal decision, to which the Recoupment Regulations apply, is set out at paras 34.14 *et seq.*

C. THE WORKING OF THE SCHEME

34.05 When a tribunal makes an award of compensation to a claimant, it must not take into account, when deciding the appropriate level of compensation, any income support, income-related employment and support allowance, jobseeker's allowance, or universal credit which has been sought by or paid to the claimant. Instead, when the tribunal makes an award of compensation where the Regulations apply, it must set out (regulation 4(3)):

(a) the monetary award
(b) the amount of any 'prescribed element'
(c) the dates of the period to which the prescribed element relates
(d) the amount, if any, by which the monetary award exceeds the prescribed element.

34.06 The 'prescribed element' of the compensation is defined in regulation 3(1)(a) as being so much of the relevant monetary award as is attributable to loss of wages or arrears of pay or to the amounts found due to the claimant for a period before the conclusion of the tribunal proceedings. The conclusion of the tribunal proceedings is the date that the judgment making any compensatory award is given: if orally, on the date of the relevant hearing; and if judgment is reserved and the decision sent to the parties in writing, on the date when it is sent (regulation 2(3)). Where benefits are to be deducted from a protective award (where a tribunal orders an employer to pay its employees remuneration for a protected period because it failed to consult a union or staff representatives in good time or at all on a redundancy or transfer of employment, pursuant to s 189 of the TULR(C)A 1992 or reg 15 of TUPE 2006), the relevant period ends on the final day of the period covered by the protective award.

34.07 In essence, the prescribed element is:

(a) any arrears of pay in respect of a period before the conclusion of the tribunal proceedings
(b) any compensation for loss of wages in respect of this period
(c) any sum ordered to be paid by the employer under a protective award.

34.08 If a tribunal reduces an award on account of the claimant's contributory fault, or to take into account any statutory maximum limit (eg to bring any substantial award of compensation for unfair dismissal down to the statutory maximum compensation limit, which, where the effective date of dismissal is on or after 6 April 2018, is £83,682 (or fifty-two weeks' pay, if lower) the element of benefit which is to be recouped is correspondingly reduced (reg 4(2)). Therefore if, for example, there has been a 25 per cent reduction in an award of compensation for unfair dismissal because of contributory fault, only 75 per cent of the job-seeker's allowance, income-related employment and support allowance, income support, or universal credit which the employee has received during the relevant period will be subject to the recoupment provisions. The correct procedure is for the tribunal first to assess the compensatory award; secondly, to reduce it to the statutory maximum or for any element of contributory fault, and finally to reduce the prescribed element by the same proportion (*Tipton v West Midlands Cooperative Society (No 2)* EAT/859/86; *Mason v (1) Wimpey Waste Management Ltd, (2) Secretary of State for Employment* [1982] IRLR 454).

34.09 Where the employer has made an *ex gratia* payment, this must be apportioned across all heads of compensation (save any basic award) which the claimant is awarded. The relevant amount should then be notionally added to any heads of compensation which are subject to the Regulations (*Digital Equipment Co Ltd v Clements (No 2)* [1998] IRLR 134, CA). For the purpose of calculating the prescribed element, it is only necessary to apportion the payment as to part against the earnings from dismissal to hearing, and the remaining part against any other losses lumped together.

D. EXPLANATION OF RECOUPMENT

34.10 If the tribunal announces the remedy to be given to a claimant at a hearing, it must explain to the parties the consequences of any recoupment award. All written decisions—whether confirming an oral award or amounting to a reserved judgment—must also contain a similar explanation.

E. NOTIFICATION TO THE DEPARTMENT FOR WORK AND PENSIONS

34.11 Where the tribunal is satisfied that the claimant has claimed or received jobseeker's allowance, income-related employment and support allowance, income support, or universal credit, and where he is to be awarded compensation to which the Recoupment Regulations apply (see para 34.04) it must send material information to the Department for Work and Pensions. The information must be sent as soon as reasonably practicable after the first announcement of the decision (whether orally or in writing) (regs 4(5) and (5)(1)).

34.12 For all relevant payments save those which relate to a protective award, the secretary of the tribunal sends the Department for Work and Pensions the information set out in reg 4(3) (see para 34.05).

34.13 Where jobseeker's allowance or income support is to be recouped against a protective award, the particulars to be supplied to the Department for Work and Pensions are:

(a) the date when the decision was announced orally, or, if the decision was reserved, the date on which it was sent to the parties
(b) the location of the tribunal
(c) the name and address of the employer
(d) the description of the employees to whom the protective award relates and
(e) the dates of the protected period (reg 5(1)).

F. DUTIES OF THE EMPLOYER

34.14 The prescribed element of any award to an employee is initially ring-fenced. The employer should retain the prescribed element from the award to the employee until the Department for Work and Pensions has either served a notice on the employer, copied to the employee, requiring the employer to forward the money to it, or else has notified the employer that it does not intend to serve such a notice.

34.15 If a recoupment notice is served on the employer, this operates as an instruction to the employer to pay, by way of deduction out of the sum due under the award, the recoupable amount to the Department for Work and Pensions. If the Department does not make an order for recoupment, the whole of the monetary sum awarded shall be paid to the employee.

34.16 If the respondent fails to pay this recoupable amount to the Department for Work and Pensions, this can be recovered from the respondent as a debt (reg 8(11)).

> *Worked example*
>
> A claimant is awarded compensation of £8,000. The prescribed element within this award is £5,000.
>
> The claimant has received income support of £2,000.
>
> (a) The respondent should pay the claimant £3,000 immediately (ie the amount of the award less the prescribed element).
> (b) The respondent should retain £5,000, pending receipt of information from the Department for Work and Pensions as to whether or not it intends to exercise its recoupment rights.
> (c) If the Department for Work and Pensions notifies the employer it does wish to recoup against £2,000 income support, the employer must send £2,000 to the Department for Work and Pensions, and £3,000 (being the balance of the prescribed element) to the employee.
> (d) If the Department for Work and Pensions notifies the employer it does not propose to exercise any recoupment rights, then the entire prescribed element of £5,000 should be sent to the employee.

G. APPEALS

34.17 A claimant may appeal against the calculation of the amount specified in the recoupment notice as the amount of jobseeker's allowance, income-related employment and support allowance, income support, or universal credit which he has been paid or is due for the period. Notice of the appeal must be given in writing to the Department for Work and Pensions within twenty-one days of the date upon which the Department's recoupment notice was served on him. This time limit can be extended by the Department for Work and Pensions for 'special reasons'. An appeal of this nature does not affect the respondent's duty to pay the recoupable amount specified in the Department for Work and Pensions' notice to the employer.

34.18 Where the claimant appeals, the Department for Work and Pensions will review its decision. The claimant then has a right of appeal to the Appeals Service tribunal against this decision.

34.19 If it is determined, either on review or on appeal, that the amount recovered by the Department for Work and Pensions from the respondent under the Recoupment Regulations exceeds the total amount paid by way of jobseeker's allowance, income-related employment and support allowance, income support, or universal credit, the Department shall pay the employee an amount equal to the excess (reg 10(4)).

H. CONSEQUENCES OF A SUCCESSFUL APPEAL AGAINST THE ORIGINAL JUDGMENT

34.20 If the original judgment, which gave rise to the recoupment exercise, is set aside in whole or in part on appeal, further adjustments occur. If the Department for Work and Pensions has by the time of any appeal or rehearing recovered any amount by way of recoupment of benefits, it shall repay the employer (or as appropriate the employee) all or part of the amount recovered as it is satisfied should properly be made having regard to the decision given on appeal or re-hearing (reg 10(4)).

I. BENEFITS OF SETTLEMENT

The recoupment provisions do not apply where a sum is paid by way of settlement of a dispute. **34.21** This may be before or after a finding of unfair dismissal is made. In this way there may be greater scope for settlement of unfair dismissal claims than other monetary claims, since what an employer may be prepared to pay by way of settlement may be less than the total of any potential monetary award, but greater than the amount the employee would receive after recoupment.

Worked example

In the situation described at para 34.16, if the claim were settled outside court on a payment of £7,000, this would advantage both employer and employee. The employer would pay out £7,000 instead of £8,000. The employee would receive £7,000 instead of £6,000.

Part D Remedies

35

Interest on Employment
Tribunal Awards

SUMMARY

(1) Interest accrues on employment tribunal awards. The current rate of interest is 8 per cent.

(2) There are different rules for discrimination awards (in the period between the act of discrimination and the calculation date) where interest can be ordered from the date of the act of discrimination (injury to feeling awards) or a mid-point date between the act of discrimination and the calculation date.

A. INTEREST ON AWARDS GENERALLY

35.01 The Employment Tribunals (Interest) Order 1990, SI 1990/479 (1990 Order) provides that where the whole or part of a sum of money has been awarded in a claim interest accrues from the day after the judgment is sent to the parties at the rate specified in s 17 of the Judgments Act 1838. However, no interest shall be payable at all if the full amount of the award is paid within fourteen days of the date on which the judgment was sent to the parties.

35.02 Interest accrues on the sum net of any recoupment, tax, or national insurance.

35.03 Where there is a review or appeal, interest still accrues from the original decision but on such lesser or greater sum as is appropriate (1990 Order, Arts 5, 6, 7, and 11).

35.04 Where there is an appeal from a decision on liability and the appellate tribunal makes a monetary award the relevant decision is that of the appellate court (1990 Order, Art 8).

35.05 Finally, where a tribunal has made a declaration as to rights under a contract, interest is only payable if there was an obligation to pay the sum before the employment tribunal's decision. The Order came into force on 1 April 1990, but also applies to cases decided before that date, save that 1 April 1990 is deemed to be the date of the employment tribunal's decision.

35.06 In terms of the interest rate, it is that specified under s 17 of the Judgments Act 1838. Since 1 April 1993, this has been 8 per cent.

Previous editions of this text set out the regime in force prior to 29 July 2013 (and which **35.07**
still applies to claims presented to the employment tribunal on or before 28 July 2013).
In short, in relation to post-judgment interest, the position differed as between discrimination complaints (where the position was broadly the same as that set out above) and non-
discrimination complaints (where interest ran from forty-two days from the sending of the
judgment to the parties): see the Employment Tribunals (Interest on Awards in Discrimination
Cases) (Amendment) Regulations 2013 and the Employment Tribunals (Interest) Order
(Amendment) Order 2013.

B. INTEREST ON DISCRIMINATION AWARDS

The EqA 2010 includes provision for enabling employment tribunals to order the payment of **35.08**
interest in circumstances where an award is made pursuant to EqA 2010. Section 139 of the EqA
2010, however, is simply a provision permitting the making of Regulations and as at the date of
writing no such Regulations have been laid before Parliament. Until such time as Regulations are
laid before Parliament, the power to award interest will continue to be governed by the Employment
Tribunals (Interest on Awards in Discrimination Cases) Regulations 1996 (as amended).

The Employment Tribunals (Interest on Awards in Discrimination Cases) Regulations 1996

The Employment Tribunals (Interest on Awards in Discrimination Cases) Regulations 1996, SI **35.09**
1996/2803 give tribunals the power to award interest in EqPA 1970, SDA 1975, RRA 1976,
and DDA 1995 cases and cases under SOR 2003, RBR 2003, and EEAR 2006. This is something that the tribunal is obliged to consider: whether or not the applicant asks for interest (1996
Regulations, reg 2(1)(b)). Curiously, reg 1(2) has not been amended to make reference to the
EqA 2010.

Regulation 3(1) of the 1996 Regulations provides that interest is to be calculated as simple interest, **35.10**
accruing from day to day at the following rates:

(a) the rate specified in the Special Investment Account under r 27(1) of the Court Fund Rules
     1987, SI 1987/821 (currently 0.5 per cent), where the claim was presented to the employment
     tribunal on or before 28 July 2013 or
(b) the rate specified in s 17 of the Judgments Act 1838 (currently 8 per cent), where the claim in
     question was presented to the employment tribunal on or after 29 July 2013.

Where the rate of interest varies during the period for which interest is to be calculated, the median
or average of the rates may be applied as the tribunal considers appropriate.

Injury to feelings

Regulation 6(1)(a) of the 1996 Regulations provides that the period of an award of interest under **35.11**
this heading begins at the date of the act of discrimination complained of and ends on the day on
which the tribunal calculates compensation.

Other awards

In awards of interest under other headings, reg 6(1)(b) provides that interest is calculated from **35.12**
the period beginning on the 'mid-point date' and ends on the date of calculation of compensation—the 'mid-point date' is the date halfway through the period beginning on the date of the act
of discrimination and ending on the date of calculation. The EAT has held, in *Ministry of Defence
v Cannock* [1994] ICR 918, that no interest can be awarded for future loss, for example pension
losses.

Part D Remedies

'Serious injustice' discretion

35.13 Regulation 6(3) of the 1996 Regulations permits tribunals to calculate interest using a different formula where 'serious injustice' would result from the normal calculation methods. An example can be found in *Cannock*, where the losses had been incurred many years earlier.

35.14 The tribunal must state the total amount of interest awarded and, where the amount cannot be agreed by the parties, it must set out a table showing its methodology (reg 7(1)) and if no interest is awarded the tribunal must give its reasons.

Special investment account rate of interest

35.15 The special investment account rate of interest under r 27(1) of the Court Fund Rules 1987, SI 1987/821 has varied over time as follows:

Date from which rate applied	Rate of interest
1 October 1991	10.25%
1 February 1993	8%
1 August 1999	7%
1 February 2002	6%
1 February 2009	3%
1 June 2009	1.5%
1 July 2009	0.5%
29 July 2013	Although the rate of interest has continued to be 0.5%, for claims presented on or after this date, the Special Investment Account rate has ceased to be relevant.

35.16 After the discrimination award has been made, interest is payable at the judgments rate in accordance with the scheme outlined above and set out in the 1990 Order.

36

Tax and Termination Payments and Employment Tribunal Awards

Part D Remedies

SUMMARY

(1) Payments made to employees on the termination of their employment may be taxed as earnings.

(2) Only if payments are not taxed as earnings do payments made in connection with the termination of their employment enjoy the £30,000 allowance.

(3) Settlement agreements settling employment disputes may be structured to ensure that the payment of the legal expenses of the former employee does not fall to be taxed as a termination payment.

(4) Tribunal awards will be taxed as appropriate depending on the underlying nature of the sum awarded.

(5) Where tribunal awards fall to be taxed as termination payments they should be 'grossed up' so as to ensure that the employee receives their true net loss.

(6) Changes took place to the taxation of termination payments with effect from April 2018. As a consequence, PILON payments will be subject to Tax and National Insurance whether or not they are made under a contractual power.

A. INTRODUCTION

36.01 The Income Tax (Earnings and Pensions) Act 2003 (ITEPA 2003), and in particular s 401(1), which is contained in Part 6 of Chapter 3 of the Act, has an impact on the payments made in connection with the termination of employment (collectively referred to in this chapter as 'termination payments') and on awards made by the tribunal and the courts. Section 401 contains a £30,000 tax free 'exemption' for certain termination payments. Changes began taking effect from 6 April 2018, which significantly impacted upon the operation and scope of the £30,000 'exemption'.

36.02 Reference is made in the course of this chapter to the HM Revenue & Customs (HMRC) Employment Income Manual which can be found on the HMRC website, http://www.hmrc.gov.uk/index.htm. This provides helpful guidance from HRMC's perspective as to their approach to the tax treatment of settlement agreements and tribunal awards. Where settlement agreements are being negotiated which involve potential issues of taxation, it is advisable to seek advanced guidance from HRMC as to their view of the proper tax treatment of the proposed agreement. All references in this chapter are references to the ITEPA unless indicated to the contrary.

36.03 In order properly to understand the taxation of termination payments, it is necessary to consider first some basic concepts about the operation of the tax regime and how it potentially impacts on termination payments. Only if having considered the other tax provisions under which a payment to an employee could be taxed, does the payment in question fall to be taxed as a termination payment. Whether the payment is a termination payment has important consequences for National Insurance (NI) as the NI scheme does not presently have an equivalent provision so that sums which are taxable under s 401 are not fully subject to employers' or employees' National Insurance contributions (NICs). The treatment of NICs on termination payments is the subject of legislative changes which will not fully take effect until 2020 from which point employer's NIC will be payable on payments above the present £30,000 threshold.

B. THE STRUCTURE OF THE TAXATION OF EMPLOYEES

36.04 A detailed consideration of the tax regime is beyond the scope of this chapter but the potential sections of the ITEPA under which a payment made to, or benefit conferred on, an employee may be taxed are as follows:

(1) Whether the payments are earnings, and as such are taxable under Part 3 Chapter 1 of the Act;
(2) Whether these are taxable benefits under the benefit code (Part 3, Chapters 2–11 of the Act);
(3) Whether they are payments for restrictive covenants and fall to be taxable under Part 3 of Chapter 12 of the Act;
(4) Whether they are payments from employer-financed retirement benefits schemes and fall to be taxable under Part 6 of Chapter 2 of the Act;
(5) And finally, if none of the foregoing, then whether the payments fall within the provision for the taxation of termination payments under Part 6 of Chapter 3 of the Act.

In respect of each payment or benefit, it will depend upon the nature and purpose of the particular payment or benefit.

C. TAXATION OF SUMS PAID ON TERMINATION OR UNDER SETTLEMENT AGREEMENTS

Payment taxable as earnings

36.05 A contractual payment made as remuneration or reward for services falls to be taxed as earnings from the employment, under s 62. It is possible that a sum that is provided to be paid under a contract of employment, as payable at the termination of the contract of employment, is properly considered to be remuneration for past services. If a payment can properly be considered to be such a payment, then it is taxed as income from the employment. The correct approach appears to be that any sum that is stipulated for payment under the terms of the contract of service falls to be considered to be part of the remuneration for the employment, because payment is made to the individual by reason of their capacity as an employee. For reasons considered below, this does not extend to non-statutory contractual redundancy schemes.

Payments on termination

Of particular concern here are payments in connection with the termination of the employment **36.06** relationship if those payments were contractually provided for or are paid as a reward for services. This may depend on the manner in which the employment relationship has been terminated. It may be terminated with notice or in breach of contract.

If the employment is terminated with notice, the employee may or may not be required to work **36.07** her notice. In either case, the wages that are paid or the benefits enjoyed over the notice period are subject to tax and NI in the same way as they have been throughout the employment.

If the employment is terminated in breach of contract, then the employee's claim is for damages **36.08** and these, if paid, are not paid under the contract of employment and therefore are not treated as earnings. This assumes that the employee accepts the breach, following the decision of the Supreme Court in *Geys v Société Générale* [2012] UKSC 63, [2012] IRLR 122, and the employee may assert that the contract remains alive. In these circumstances, it would seem to follow that payments would continue to be treated as if paid under notice.

Payments in lieu of notice (PILON)

Changes have been made to the tax treatment of PILON from 6 April 2018. Previously the tax **36.09** treatment of PILON depended on whether there was a contractual clause permitting the employer to make a PILON. This reflects the analysis of termination by use of payment in lieu clauses in *Delaney v Staples* [1992] 1 All ER 944. Other payments made under the contract on termination, even if triggered by redundancy, were taxed as earnings and subject to NI in the same way, *Hayward v HMRC* [2012] UKFTT 431 (TC). If there is no clause in the contract permitting the employer to terminate the contract, the termination of the contract without notice is a breach of contract. The sum that the employer pays by way of PILON is then a form of damages and does not flow from the contract. The position had been, for terminations before 6 April 2018, that the payment made was not be taxed as earnings.

New ss 402A to 402E have been added to address the payment of PILON from 6 April 2018. **36.10** The provisions are complex and even on their face give rise to some immediate ambiguities. These provisions apply to termination awards which are defined under s 402A(1) as a payment or other benefit received directly or indirectly in consideration of or in consequence of or otherwise in connection with the termination of person's employment. The payments to which Chapter 3 applies. Where an employer makes a termination award it is necessary to consider the award as if split into two elements. One element is the basic pay which the employee would have received for any part of the notice period that is not served, called the 'post-employment notice pay', that element is subject to normal tax and national insurance, both employer and employee. Basic pay is defined under s 402(D)(7). The remainder may benefit from the treatment of termination payments and the £30,000 exemption. Section 402D defines how post-employment notice pay is calculated.

It is first necessary to identify the 'trigger date', this either the date on which the employment **36.11** ended (if not a notice case) or the day notice is given (if it is a notice case): s 402E(2). A notice case is one in which the employer or employee gives notice to the other to terminate the employment: s 402E(3). One then considers the minimum notice that should have been given by the employer: s 402E(4). The post-employment notice period is then the period beginning with the last day of the employment and ending with the earliest lawful termination date: s 402E(5). In cases in which the employee works the whole of their notice period or they are placed on garden leave for the whole of their notice period the post-employment notice period will be zero.

36.12 It is then necessary to calculate the post-employment notice pay; this is calculated by the use of the formula ((BP x D)/P)—T where BP is the employee's basic pay, as calculated under s 420D(7), in respect of the last pay period of the employee's employment before the trigger date, P is the number of days in that pay period and D is the number of days in the post-employment notice period, or months if so expressed in the contract: s 402D(6). The practical effect of this part of the calculation is then to determine the proportion of the pay which would otherwise would have been paid over the notice period that has not been paid as part of the notice period. Thus in a full PILON situation the figure will be the full basic pay, as defined, for the notice period. T then is total amount of any payment or benefit received in connection with the termination of employment which is not taxed as a termination payment because it is taxable as earnings under Chapter 1 of Part 3, but is not pay in respect of holiday entitlement for a period before the employment ends and is not a bonus payable for the termination of the employment, s 402D(1). In the case of the exercise of a contractual PILON clause T would be the PILON payment which, on the existing law, would have been taxed under Chapter 1 of Part 3. The quantum of the lost post-employment notice pay would, in a normal contractual PILON case, be the same as T, the PILON that has been subject to tax and NI.

36.13 To take then some simple examples: an employee is entitled to a gross monthly salary of £4,000 and three months' notice. They are not given notice but in breach of contract a PILON payment is made rolled up into a lump sum payment of £20,000. Prior to 2018, this would not have been taxed. Under the new regime BP is £4,000, D is 3 and P is 1 and T is nil, as none of the payments would be taxed under s 401(1). The post-employment notice pay is then £12,000. In the same example, if the employee was required only to work one month's notice when his employment is terminated with a payment of £12,000, BP is £4,000 x 2 (D) / 1(P) – nil (T) = £8,000. Thus, the post-employment notice pay is £8,000. In both cases the post-employment notice pay would be subject to tax and national insurance as taxable income, and only the balance would fall within the £30,000 threshold. The practical effect is that it is not possible to avoid a PILON being taxed as earnings, even if it is paid in breach of contract. As a PILON paid in breach of contract may have adverse consequences for the enforcement of post termination restrictions, they may now have little to commend them.

36.14 It should be noted that these provisions only apply in relation to payments and benefits which are taxable as termination payments under Chapter 3 and not if the payments or benefits are otherwise chargeable to tax under other provisions. The considerations below as to whether payments might be otherwise chargeable to tax have to be considered first. It would also logically follow that if the PILON is the exercise of a contractual power then it is subject to tax as earnings, as was previously the case. However, there appears to some confusion as to the construction of s 402D in that it might mean that it could apply if the contractual PILON payment differed from the sum calculated under s 402D, if for example the figure calculated under s 402D was higher than the contractual PILON payment. One area where this may arise is in the context of an employee who has sacrificed salary, under s 402D the unsacrificed salary may, arguably, have to be used as the basis of the calculation. It is anticipated that HMRC will provide guidance on the point, although the initial guidance does not appear to have addressed some of the difficult issues which have been posed by the legislative changes. Statutory redundancy payments are excluded from the calculation of the termination award and post-employment notice pay, s 402C. Statutory payments are therefore paid with the benefit of the £30,000 exemption as are approved contractual payment equal to or less than the amount which would have been due if a redundancy payment had been payable, s 402C(2). Contractual or voluntary redundancy payments which exceed this fall to be considered under this analysis and thus an element accounting for PILON will be taxed.

36.15 This has assumed that the employer has given notice, it may be that the employer has dismissed for gross misconduct without any payment. If that is justified then there is no tax issue, but what if there is a dispute and the issue is resolved by a settlement payment or an award by a court or tribunal of damages for breach of contract. Under the former law even if there had been a PILON clause in the contract the payment would not be taxed as earnings: *Cerberus Software v Rowley* [2001] IRLR 160. But now it would appear that it is necessary to consider whether an element of the settlement falls within the definition of post-employment notice pay. This will depend on the interpretation of s 402E(2) to (7) and whether in such a situation the employment was to be treated as terminated with notice for the purposes of s 402(4). This is presently not clear. The same issue may arise with an employee who treats themselves as being constructively dismissed, if their claims are settled should they be treated as if notice had been given and the PILON taxation provisions applied? Historically, a parallel may be drawn with the confusion which arose on the issue of discretionary PILON clauses following *Richardson v Delaney* [2001] IRLR 663, on which HMRC subsequently provided some guidance in *Tax Bulletin* 63 (February 2003). It is to be hoped that HMRC will similarly provide guidance to clarify the position, but the cautious approach will be to treat an element of the settlement sum, equivalent to basic pay for the applicable notice period, as being subject to tax and national insurance in the normal way.

36.16 If the contract was for a fixed term, or determined by the occurrence of a specific task or event, and the contract is terminated with a termination award at an earlier point the post-employment notice pay is calculated as the basic period over the period between the termination of the employment and the date when the contract would have expired: s 402(D)(8) and (9).

36.17 Prior to the changes introduced from 6 April 2018 the focus had been on whether there was a PILON clause in the contract of employment, as is frequently the case, and the employer had exercised that power. Occasionally, the contractual basis for the PILON may be found in another document but still has contractual effect. For example, in *SCA Packaging Ltd v HM Customs & Excise* [2007] EWHC 270, a memorandum agreed with the unions was found to have been incorporated into the contracts of employment of employees with the consequence that payments in lieu of notice were paid under the contracts and were subject to tax and NI. It should also be noted that at one stage HMRC would argue that there was an implied term for PILON where employers habitually made PILON payments. This is a difficult argument to maintain in the face of an express term for notice. HMRC, in *Tax Bulletin* 63, accepted this to be the case but outlined a separate argument styled as 'Autopilon', where the practice of PILON has become an automatic response, even though there is no express contractual clause. HMRC's position is then that, if the payments are 'Autopilons', they become taxable as earnings. Whatever the legal merit of this argument, the advice was that employers should be cautious about making habitual customary PILON payments where there is no express PILON in the contract. The changes in the tax treatment of PILONs appear to make this a sterile consideration unless the payments being made are greater than the amounts which fall to be treated as the post-employment notice pay under the new regime.

36.18 Where there is a contractual PILON clause, if there is a discretion as to whether to make the PILON, then it will for the employer to elect if it decides to do so, but if it does the payment will be taxable as earnings: *EMI Group Electronics Ltd v Coldicott* [1999] STC 803, [1999] IRLR 630, CA.

Benefits

36.19 If the payment which has been made is not taxable as income from the employment, the next question is whether it is taxable under the benefit codes under the Act as benefits given to an employee by reason of his employment, which may be enjoyed during the period of employment. This may be applicable to benefits which continue to be enjoyed under a notice period pursuant to a settlement agreement. Thus, if under the settlement agreement it is agreed that the employee will continue to enjoy the free gym membership that he would have continued to have enjoyed over the period of his notice, then this benefit will continue to be taxed as it would have been during the employment. Additionally, there are specific taxation provisions in relation to the write-off of employment related loans (s 188(2)), the discharge of notional loans in respect of the acquisition of shares (s 195(3)), the disposal of shares for more than market value (s 199(4)), and in respect of gains from non-approved share options (Part 7 of Chapter 5).

Part D Remedies

The new PILON provisions do not seek to tax benefits which would have been enjoyed over the lost notice period.

Restrictive covenants

36.20 Section 225 of the Act brings into play as taxable income payments made for the giving of restrictive covenants. This may embrace the typical covenants restraining such matters as competition, solicitation, and the use of confidential information. HMRC's interpretation of the section is wider and embraces the restraint of future action more generally. This was the subject of particular concern a number of years ago, when the Revenue used this section as the basis of an argument that any compromise agreement which included the typical clause providing that the payment was made in full and final settlement constituted a restriction on the employee's future activities, and therefore the entire payment came into tax under this provision. In practical terms, the issues were resolved by Statement of Practice 3/96, under which HMRC stated that the affirmation of existing restrictive covenants will not cause s 225 to be engaged; neither will the compromise agreement stating that the termination package is made in full and final settlement of all outstanding claims nor stating that the employee agrees not to commence or continue legal proceedings bring the payment within the scope of s 225, even though those provisions restrain future action.

36.21 It follows that, where there is merely an affirmation that existing restrictive covenants under the contract of employment are still in force, this falls in with consideration of tax liability on the whole agreement and is not caught by s 225. However, it should be noted that it would appear to be HMRC's view that, if specific consideration is attached to the restatement of the covenants or to the agreement to discontinue proceedings (see *Appellant v Inspector of Taxes* [2001] STC (SCD) 21), then the sum so allocated will fall outside the scope of the Statement of Practice and be taxable under s 225.

36.22 If, by agreement, the covenants are recast or modified, then payment made for that variation would be taxable under s 225. In order to avoid all payments made under the agreement being taxed under s 225, on the basis that it is not possible to apportion the consideration, it is sensible to provide separate consideration for those new or modified covenants. As to the amount of such consideration, whilst contractually the adequacy of the consideration is not an issue, there may be questions as to whether the division of consideration is a sham. Accordingly, it would be appropriate to attribute a more than nominal payment to the new or modified clauses.

36.23 Many settlement agreements include provisions requiring confidentiality and/or restraining the employee from making derogatory remarks about their former employer. In such cases, as they potentially also fall within the scope of s 225, a cautious approach is to provide separate consideration for these promises too.

Benefits from employer-financed retirement benefit schemes

36.24 Contributions to registered pensions schemes may be made tax free, even if part of termination arrangements. This does not extend to PILONs if the payment is made as a result of a contractual PILON paid into a registered pensions scheme; these will still be subject to s 62 and tax and National Insurance. There are annual and lifetime allowances for contributions to registered pension schemes. Contributions to employer-financed retirement benefit schemes, not being contributions to registered pension schemes, will be taxed as part of the disguised remuneration rules in Part 7A of the ITEPA.

36.25 Additionally, lump sum payments and/or benefits paid on or in anticipation of retirement are included in ss 393 and 394 of Part 6 of Chapter 2 of the Act. The effect of this is that, if a payment is made in connection with retirement, then it will be taxable under this provision as earnings in the year in which the payment is received. HMRC's view of what comprises retirement may be perceived to be a broad one. There may be close scrutiny of whether, for example, there was a genuine redundancy situation and whether payments made to an individual genuinely reflected redundancy practice. The breadth of the HMRC's view as to whether there has been a payment in connection with retirement is set out by way of example in paragraph EIM15300 of its Employment Income Manual:

Situation	Retirement position
A long-service employee leaves to take a senior executive position in another company at the age of 60.	The employee has retired.
A division of the company is sold and the 55-year-old manager responsible for running it leaves to take a job with the purchaser.	The manager has retired.
A person in his 50s has a heart attack and is advised by his doctor to leave and seek a less stressful position.	If the person were re-employed in an entirely different capacity with the same employer or finds employment with another employer, we would generally accept the member had retired early from the original employment (possibly on ill-health grounds or possibly on normal early retirement grounds—depending on scheme rules and exact medical advice).
	But if the ex gratia payment made is purely consolation for loss of health that results in the premature termination of employment, it would not be regarded as made in connection with retirement (see EIM15044).
An employee aged 35 is involved in an accident and suffers disabilities that make it impossible to continue with the job.	A lump sum paid on retirement solely by reason of disability from an accident is not taxable as a benefit from an employer-financed retirement benefits scheme (see EIM15044).
An employee aged 50 leaves to take a job nearer home to be able to nurse her aged parents.	Employee has retired.

HMRC's view of a 'scheme' is equally broad and may embrace a decision or payment in accordance **36.26** with a policy. It will be evident that, in the case of a settlement agreement that makes a payment in connection with the genuine settlement of a claim or that is a redundancy payment following a genuine redundancy situation, ss 393 and 394 will not be engaged. The focus is likely to be where there is an *ex gratia* payment being made to an employee who is leaving employment or where the payment is made in anticipation of the employee's retirement.

Termination payments within Part 6 Chapter 3

If the payment which is being made to the former employee is not taxable under any of the above **36.27** provisions, then it potentially falls within the scope of s 401. Section 401 provides that payments and other benefits not otherwise chargeable to tax which are received in connection with:

(a) the termination of a person's employment or
(b) any change in the duties of or emoluments from a person's employment

are chargeable to tax under this section and, if so, to the extent that their amount exceeds £30,000.

It will be noted that s 401 includes 'benefits' as defined at s 402: **36.28**

For the purposes of this section a 'benefit' includes anything which, if received for performance of the duties of the employment

(a) would be taxable earnings of their employment, or
(b) would be such earnings apart from earnings only exemption.

36.29 If then, under a settlement agreement, the employer agreed to confer a benefit on the employee, for example the provision of continued health cover, it is necessary to consider the reason for the benefit. If it was a benefit which the employee would have been entitled to receive under the contract over the notice period, then it would be taxed as normal. If it is being conferred just on termination, in a case where there has been a breach of contract, then it will be taxed as a benefit but under s 401. Thus, if the employer allowed the employee to keep a company vehicle or purchase it at a reduced price, then that benefit will have to be brought into account for tax purposes under s 401. The taxable value of the benefit will fall to be taken in account in applying the £30,000 relief, subject to the considerations above as to PILON payments.

Redundancy payments

36.30 Where the employee was made redundant, statutory redundancy payments are brought into the scope of Part 6 of Chapter 3 by s 309(3): they would fall within the £30,000 exemption but use up part of the tax free allowance. Contractual redundancy payments are not treated as earnings but are payments within Part 6 of Chapter 3: *Mairs v Haughey* [1994] 1 AC 303, Statement of Practice 1/94. Contractual payments may be subject to scrutiny so as to ensure that such schemes are not used as a sham to conceal deferred remuneration, rather than being payments in compensation for the loss of employment. As noted above, if the contractual or voluntary redundancy payment is made in respect of a termination after 6 April 2018, it will be necessary to consider whether any element had to be treated as a payment in respect of an unworked notice period.

Payments in connection with death, disability, and personal injury

36.31 Where a payment is a termination payment or a benefit which falls in principle to be taxed under s 401, it will be exempted from taxation under that provision if the payment is made in connection with termination by reason of the death of an employee or on account of an injury to, or disability of, an employee: s 406. If, therefore, a sum is paid to an employee in compensation because he is unable to continue in employment because of an injury he has sustained, it is not taxed under s 401. It would appear to be the case that this might be a case of where the old learning on PILON clauses paid in breach of contract applies, as the new regime for the taxation of PILON payments only applies in relation to payments taxed under s 401. It should also be noted that the changes from 6 April 2018 also amend this section to make it clear that, whilst psychiatric injury is included in the exemption, injury to feelings is not. Prior to this amendment there had been a debate about whether payments for injury to feelings made in connection with the termination of employment fell within s 406. This debate was resolved by the Court of Appeal, which held, in *Moorthy v HMRC* [2018] EWCA Civ 847, that injury to feelings awards did fall within the exception under s 406. However, the April 2018 changes now render that decision academic for the future.

Legal expenses

36.32 There had been a long-standing Extra Statutory Concession (ESC81) which provided for relief in respect of the payment of legal expenses. This was put on a statutory basis by the Enactment of Extra-Statutory Concessions Order 2011 (SI 2011/1037). There was some concern that the scope of that provision was limited to compromise agreements and did not apply to COT3 agreements. The Revenue confirmed that the passing of this SI had not removed the previous Extra Statutory Concession, which applied the same conditions but embraced COT3 agreements. Further amendments were made to embrace the change in language to settlement agreements, and the form of the section which applies to payments after 6 April 2013 is as follows:

> 413A Exception for payment of certain legal costs
>
> (1) This Chapter does not apply to a payment which meets conditions A and B.
> (2) Condition A is that the payment meets the whole or part of legal costs incurred by the employee exclusively in connection with the termination of the employee's employment.

(3) Condition B is that either—

    (a) the payment is made pursuant to an order of a court or tribunal, or

    (b) the termination of the employee's employment results in a settlement agreement between the employer and the employee and—

        (i) the settlement agreement provides for the payment to be made by the employer, and

        (ii) the payment is made directly to the employee's lawyer.

(4) In this s—

…

'legal costs' means fees payable for the services and disbursements of a 'lawyer'.

(4) The amendments made by this article have effect in relation to payments made on or after 6th April 2011.

36.33 The Extra Statutory Concession was typically used to cover the legal costs of the independent adviser in a compromise agreement. Occasionally, the exemption has been used to cover costs incurred by an employee in pursuing litigation, but it should be noted that the concession only extends to legal costs incurred exclusively in connection with the termination of employment. If an employee has incurred legal costs that do not fall within the Extra Statutory Concession, it is not possible to deduct these as deductible expenses on the computation of the employee's tax liability: *Wardle v The Commissioners for Her Majesty's Revenue & Customs* [2013] UKFTT 599 (TC).

Counselling

36.34 There are further concessions in respect of modest specified costs in connection with counselling, outplacement, and retraining courses. There are specific statutory concessions in respect of these if they meet the requirements of ss 310 and 311; otherwise, they would fall to be benefits taxed as part of the termination payment.

Repayment of expenses to the employer

36.35 An employee whose employment contract requires repayment of certain expenses if the employment terminates will not normally be entitled to a deduction in calculating employment income for amounts paid to a former employer. Thus, where an employer provides free training to an employee but the employee is required to reimburse the cost of the training if the employee leaves, no deduction for the reimbursement is available (*Hinsley v HMRC* [2006] STC (SCD) 63 (SpC 569)).

D. THE CONSEQUENCES FOR THE EMPLOYER OF THE APPLICATION OF SECTION 401

36.36 It is important to consider the consequences for an employer of making an error in considering the tax status of a payment. If the entire payment should have been taxable then it is likely that HMRC will turn to the employer first and seek to recover the tax not accounted for on the basis that tax, and possibly NI, should have been deducted under PAYE.

36.37 If s 401 applies, the first £30,000 will be exempt from tax, subject to the PILON provisions considered above. Thereafter, it is taxed for the purposes of income tax but not NI. This will be the subject of change from 6 April 2020, when it is planned that all termination payments above £30,000 will be subject to employer's NI. The legislation to implement this change will be published in the course of 2019. Returning to the present scheme, typically the employer will have issued the P45 and, prior to 6 April 2011, the employer would have deducted tax at the basic rate, leaving the employee to pay any further tax that was due following the filing of the tax return. Since 6 April 2011, the cash flow advantage has been reversed and employers must now apply a specific code, the OT Code, which taxes the employee at the applicable rates and may, because of the treatment of the personal allowance, result in the employee having to recoup overpaid tax at the end of the year rather than pay it then. It should also be noted that changes made from 6 April 2018 also included a power, s 404B, for the Treasury to vary the £30,000 threshold by regulations.

E. TAXATION OF TRIBUNAL AWARDS

36.38 The preceding parts of this chapter have set out the structure of the taxation payments with particular reference to settlement agreements reached so as to effect the termination of the employment. The tax treatment of awards is addressed below. This topic is, however, relevant to the question of settlement agreements in that, where a sum is paid in settlement of a claim, the HMRC's approach is to consider the tax status of the underlying claim and treat the settlement payment accordingly. It follows that a consideration of the tax treatment of tribunal awards may have important consequences for the tax treatment of any payment in settlement of the claim, whether or not it is paid under a settlement agreement.

Unlawful deduction from wages

36.39 The HMRC guidance on this is that, as with a debt claim in the civil courts, the sums recovered are sums due under the contract of employment and, therefore, when paid by the employer they should be subject to tax and NI. This would require the award of the sums gross so that the employee was not disadvantaged. It is the author's experience that this is not, however, the universal practice amongst employment tribunals, where some tribunals make awards in respect of unlawful deduction from wages on a net loss basis. In practical terms, employees may not find the employer deducting tax and NI in paying the award, but claimants ought to seek the gross sum and require the payment of the employer's NI due on the sums, as well as ensuring the proper tax treatment of their own payment.

Unfair dismissal

Reinstatement or re-engagement

36.40 Whilst it is a remedy that is not frequently granted, an employee may be seeking reinstatement or re-engagement by the former employer. If an order is made for either of these reliefs, then the claimant is likely to seek additional compensation in the form of compensation for the lost salary for the period from dismissal to re-engagement or reinstatement. What is the nature of this payment? The HMRC's approach to this was to regard these payments as earnings from employment and thus taxable as earnings and, therefore, subject to the normal incidence of the PAYE and NI as salary paid to the employee. However, in *Wilson v Clayton* [2004] EWCA Civ 1657, [2005] IRLR 108, where a consent agreement had been reached reinstating an employee and agreeing a figure for compensation, the Court of Appeal held that this was not an emolument of employment but was a sum paid in consequence of the dismissal. The payment would therefore fall to be taxed under s 401. The proper approach would then appear to be to calculate the net loss of earnings, that being the earnings which the employee would have earned over the period after tax. The NI rules are different and NI is payable on the sums paid. Even in relation to the application of the tax exemption, if the sum awarded exceeds the £30,000 allowance, it will be taxed under s 401. It should be noted that the allowance applies only once, so a payment such as a redundancy payment which the employee has already received will have used up part of the allowance. If the compensation payable is taxable under s 401, then it should be 'grossed up' to such amount as will leave the employee, after the deduction of tax under s 401, with his true net loss. This is considered further below in the context of unfair dismissal compensation.

Compensation for unfair dismissal

36.41 If the tribunal decides to award compensation by way of the basic and compensatory awards, this is treated as a form of damages: it is not treated as earnings. This compensation element falls under s 123 of the Employment Rights Act 1996 (ERA 1996) and falls to be such amount as the tribunal considers just and equitable in all the circumstances, having regard to the loss sustained by the complainant in consequence of the dismissal, insofar as that loss is attributable to action taken by the employer. Typically, in assessing the compensatory award, whilst a modest award will be made for loss of statutory rights, the primary basis for the payment of any award will be the earnings lost as a consequence of the employee's loss of his employment, and potentially the loss of pension benefits and other benefits of his employment, going forward until he is likely to mitigate his losses. These are conventionally calculated on a basis which is net of the tax and NI that would have been paid had the claimant remained in employment. This is in accordance with the compensatory principle of placing the employee in the position he would have been in had the dismissal not occurred: *British Transport Commission v Gourley* [1956] AC 185, [1955] 3 All ER 796. Under *Gourley*, if the damages are not themselves taxed, but the original payment would have been, the damages are assessed on the basis of what the claimant would have received after the deduction of, in the case of employees, tax and NI.

The tribunal's award will, however, be taxable under s 401, because it is being paid by the employer in connection with the termination of employment. Thus, when a tribunal makes an award, when the employer makes payment it should deduct tax applying s 401. Therefore, to the extent that the award exceeds £30,000, or the appropriate lesser balance of the allowance if part has already been utilized, the claimant will be taxed. Because the compensation was assessed on a net loss basis, the practical effect would be that the employee would have been taxed twice, although HMRC will not have received tax twice. The correct approach then is to calculate, on a net earnings basis, the total compensation and, to the extent that it is taxable under s 401, 'gross up' the award so that, after the incidence of tax under s 401, the employee is left with his true net loss. Thus, if the employee is awarded £50,000 compensation for unfair dismissal, and he has not previously used any of the £30,000 tax relief, the employer, in paying the award, would have to deduct tax as a termination payment on £20,000. If the employee was a basic rate tax payer in the year the award was made, the applicable rate would be 20 per cent. To ensure the claimant was left with his intended net award, the tribunal would need to gross up the award to £55,000. When the 20 per cent tax is deducted under s 401 from the £25,000 above £30,000, the claimant would receive the intended net award of £50,000. The practical difficulty is that the only flexibility the tribunal has as to increasing the award is to account for the incidence of tax in the compensatory element. In the case of unfair dismissal, that award is of course subject to a cap on the maximum compensatory award. This raises the question of whether it is possible for the tribunal to award a sum that is grossed up so as to exceed the cap where the employee, after deduction of tax under s 401, will be left with his true net loss beneath the cap. The EAT has held in *Hardie Grant London Ltd v Aspden* [2011] UKEAT 0242/11/0311 that the statutory cap is applied after the net award has been 'grossed up'. This has the unfortunate consequence that, even where an employee's net loss of earnings exceeds the cap, the employee will never receive even the maximum compensation figure because he will be taxed upon the sum he receives. This may be even more unfortunate in some cases; for example, in the case of an employee who has low earnings but received a large compensatory payment for loss of membership of a final salary pension, where the employee may find that he is a higher rate taxpayer in respect of part of the tribunal's award when he normally would not be. **36.42**

If the dismissal is on grounds where the cap on compensation does not apply, for example dismissal on the grounds that the employee made a public interest disclosure, then the net loss may be 'grossed up' to take account fully of the impact of tax under s 401. It will readily be appreciated in the case of large awards and the present top rate of tax of 45 per cent, that the grossing up exercise may dramatically increase the size of the award. **36.43**

From the employee's position, as he will have tax deducted in order to ensure that he has his true net loss, it is important to have regard to the need to gross up the award to account for the incidence of tax under s 401. Although concerned with a wrongful dismissal claim in the High Court, the same principles apply and useful assistance on the process of 'grossing up' can be found in the decision of *Shove v Downs Surgical PLC* [1984] 1 All ER 7, [1984] ICR 532. **36.44**

It is now additionally necessary to add the complexity of the post-employment notice payment provisions considered above. This will be a relevant consideration if the dismissed employee was dismissed without serving all of his notice period. It would appear then that it may be, and the **36.45**

Part D Remedies

position is not yet clear, that the tribunal award has an element which has to be calculated applying the rules for the taxation of PILONs. This would again reduce the amount which the employee was receiving from the amount of the compensation as calculated on a net basis and would require specific grossing up to account for this incidence of tax. The cautious approach is to assume that the PILON taxation rules would apply. It would follow that, if an employee was unfairly dismissed without notice and was compensated in this respect by the tribunal, whether as damages for wrongful dismissal or compensation for unfair dismissal, it is necessary to work out the tax treatment as if the employer had made the payment with the taxation of the two elements identified above and the different tax liabilities for the employee being addressed. It is then necessary to gross up the awards, subject to the applicable cap, to ensure that the claimant is left with the true net loss after the deduction of this tax.

Wrongful dismissal claims

36.46 Where the wrongful dismissal claim is brought within the tribunal's contractual jurisdiction the same principles apply. The net loss should be determined applying the *Gourley* principle, and the award grossed up to account for the potential taxation of the award under s 401. As noted, this claim will embrace lost notice and, it would appear, although the construction of the section is not clear, that it is necessary for terminations after 6 April 2018 for the employer to deduct tax on the award as if the PILON had been paid by the employer under the new regime. The grossing up of the award should then take this tax into account. The same problem of grossing up above the cap arises here, the cap being £25,000.

Awards in relation to discrimination

36.47 The basis of compensation is that the act of discrimination is treated as a statutory tort and the objective is to put the employee in the position she would have been in had the unlawful conduct not taken place. The compensation may include compensation for injury to feelings and personal injuries. In addition, it may take a variety of forms of economic loss, reflective of lost earnings or pension rights. Where the employee suffered discrimination in the past, for example because she was not appointed to a post, then there may be historic compensation. Another example of this would be if a bonus was not paid to an employee for a discriminatory reason or the discretion, as to the amount of the bonus, was found to have been exercised upon a discriminatory basis. More typically, there may be a situation where the employment relationship has been terminated in circumstances where the tribunal has found that there were acts of discrimination that led to the dismissal. The tax treatment of any award that a tribunal may make in such circumstances will depend into which of the foregoing categories the case falls.

No termination discrimination

36.48 Dealing first with the question of the discriminatory suppression of earnings, or possibly harassing conduct: the HMRC stated at paragraph EIM12965 of the Employment Income Manual that compensation payments for discrimination other than those related to termination, which are taxable under s 401, are not subject to tax. In practical terms, this would mean that the calculation of compensation should simply be on the basis of net loss, ie to place the claimant in the position she would have been in had the discrimination not occurred, and there is no need to gross up the award to account for the incidence of tax.

36.49 One can see this approach being applied in *Yorkshire Housing v Cuerden* UKEAT/0397/09/SM, where the EAT held that a tribunal ought not to have grossed up the injury to feelings element and the personal injury award because they related to pre-termination discrimination and therefore were not taxable as a termination payment. The interest that the tribunal may award in such a discrimination claim would also fall not to be taxed, as it is part of the award. The changes to the tax treatment of injury to feelings awards considered above do not apply here as they are concerned with payment made in connection with the termination of employment.

Equal pay

It would appear to be the case that the treatment of awards under the equal pay legislation is **36.50** different. It is quite clear here that the effect of a successful Equal Pay Act claim is to cause the equality clause in the claimant's contract of employment to lead to the variation of her remuneration to be equal to that of her comparator. The claim is then a contractual one for unpaid salary, and therefore the award should be gross and the unpaid salary should be taxed as earnings, with NI being paid. The large-scale equal pay litigation of the last few years has led to specific guidance within the HMRC Employment Income Manual EIM02530 The HMRC position is that payment of the award, and any settlement sum in compromise of the claim, are taxable as earnings. They should not be taxed as if paid in the year in which any lump sum of arrears or settlement is paid, but should be taxed on the basis of the tax which would have been paid had the sums been paid in the periods to which the claim relates. The employer should operate a special PAYE procedure to calculate tax arising in each year covered by the settlement or award.

Discrimination and termination

Different considerations arise in the context of an employee whose employment has been termin- **36.51** ated. In this regard, useful assistance is provided by the Special Commissioner's decision of *Walker v Adams* [2001] STC 101. This concerned an award under the anti-religious discrimination in Northern Ireland. The tribunal had found that the employee was constructively dismissed and had been so because he had been discriminated against on the grounds of his religion. The tribunal made an award consisting of injury to feelings and future loss of earnings. Interestingly, it made the award on the basis of gross earnings and no consideration appears to have been given to the question of the incidence of tax before the tribunal. The HMRC considered that the award was taxable under the predecessor to s 401. This was contested by the claimant. The HMRC before the Special Commissioner conceded that the part of the award that related to injury to feelings should not be the subject of taxation under s 401. The HMRC set out at paragraph EIM12965 of the Employment Income Manual the basis upon which it made the concession which, as noted below, is not one that it presently adopts generally on injury to feelings awards. The Special Commissioner upheld the HMRC's view, concluding that the payment was subject to s 401 as the discrimination had caused the termination of the contract and the compensation awarded by the tribunal was therefore paid in consequence of or otherwise in connection with the termination of office. Even on this basis, the claimant had a degree of windfall as the calculation would have given him the benefit of the £30,000 exemption on an award which had been calculated on a gross basis. It follows from the reasoning in the earlier sections of this chapter that the correct approach is to calculate the lost earnings, then, on the *Gourley* basis, make a notional tax deduction to calculate the position that the employee would have been in had the discrimination not occurred, ie looking to see the net loss. Then, having reached that figure, the incidence of tax on the award itself should be considered, and an exercise in 'grossing up' undertaken, so that the sum awarded is the net loss after the incidence of tax under s 401. The sum to be grossed up would appear to be the total award, including any interest awarded, as it is the total award which will fall to be considered for the purposes of tax as a termination payment. It is of note that the EAT appears to have followed the *Walker* decision in *Orthet v Vince Cain* [2004] IRLR 857, as did the First-tier Tribunal (Tax Chamber) in *Oti-Obihara v Commissioners for HM Revenue & Customs* [2010] UKFTT 568 (TC), [2011] IRLR 386. Because the sum is paid in one tax year, the 'gross up' exercise can significantly increase the quantum of the award. One could have an employee who had never been a higher rate taxpayer in herr life being a higher rate taxpayer on this one sum. This can make an enormous difference in the quantum of the award. It should further be noted that what would need to be grossed up is the entirety of the taxable award, including any interest the tribunal may have awarded. Because all of the award may fall to be considered as to having been paid in connection with the termination, it is the global sum of the award which should be grossed up. Thus, the EAT in *Yorkshire Housing v Cuerden* [2010] UKEAT/10397/09/SM concluded that sums awarded in respect of pension and interest as compensation arising from a dismissal all had to be grossed up to account for the incidence of tax under s 401. It is also necessary to consider the application of the tax under the taxation of unserved notice period, as considered above, to ensure that if compensation is treated as including an element taxable as a PILON under the new regime, that the appropriate grossing up is undertaken for this element.

Injury to feelings

36.52 As noted in *Walker v Adams*, the HMRC appears to have conceded that the injury to feelings element of the award did not fall to be taxed under s 401. The Employment Income Manual makes clear a basis for the concession that maintains that the HMRC does not consider this to be the case where the injury to feelings arises from termination of employment. In that case, the HMRC's position is that the payment is still in connection with the termination of employment and that it falls to be taxed under s 401; as noted above in *Moorthy v HMRC*, the HMRC's approach was found to be wrong but the law has now changed: from April 2018, injury to feelings awards made in connection with the termination of employment will be taxed as termination payments.

Protective awards

36.53 Protective awards under ss 188 and 190 of the Trade Union and Labour Relations (Consolidation) Act 1992 (TULR(C)A 1992) merit some special consideration. These awards relate to the employer's failure to consult prior to making collective redundancies. The effect of the award is to require the employer to pay remuneration over the period of the protective award for those dismissed by reason of the redundancy. At first blush one might consider that, as this provision provides for remuneration to be paid as under the contract of employment for the period of the protective award, this would fall to be subject to being taxed as earnings. This point was considered in *Mimtec Ltd v Inland Revenue* [2001] STC 101, a Special Commissioner's decision. The case actually concerned payments made in lieu of their entitlement to consultation to employees who were made redundant following a merger. The HMRC sought to argue that the payments made in lieu of the consultation process were earnings and taxable as such because of the concept of remuneration being paid over a protected period. The Special Commissioner held that they were not so taxable. The payments were not made for the individual employees acting as or being an employee. It was considered whether the payments would have been taxable as earnings if they had been paid as a protective award. It was held that they would not have been because, although referable, if the employment had continued this did not change the fact that they were not paid under the contract but under the statute. The sum would not then be chargeable as earnings. It would follow, as the liability arises because of the termination of the employee's contract for redundancy, it should be treated as a termination payment and taxed under s 401 The position in respect of National Insurance is different, however, and National Insurance contributions are payable on the full amount of the protective award, even though it is taxed under s 401 in respect of income tax.

Compensation for failure to inform and consult under TUPE

36.54 This raises an interesting question about the parallel provisions of the consultation regime for TUPE transfers, although there is no specific guidance from the HMRC on this. Here of course the payment is unrelated to the termination of the employment. It would appear to follow that it is arguable that the compensation for TUPE is not taxable, albeit that it is paid calculated on gross weekly earnings.

36.55 However, in an unrelated case, *Kuehne & Nagel Drinks Logistics Ltd, Stott & Joyce v HMRC* [2009] UKFTT 379 (TC), it has been held that the continuation of employment under TUPE does not apply for the tax regime and that transfer is the termination of the former employment for tax purposes. This might form the basis for an argument that compensation paid to those who transfer is compensation payable in connection with the termination of their employment. However, even this argument, if advanced, would not appear to apply to affected employees who do not transfer.

F. INTERNATIONAL ASPECTS

Finally, a further relief to the taxation of termination payments under s 401 concerns employees **36.56** who have been working overseas for part of their period of employment. Under s 413 of the ITEPA 2003, a payment was exempted from s 401 if it is in connection with foreign service and one of a number of specified conditions was met. This relief is limited from 6 April 2018, except in relation to seafarers, for UK resident employees at the date of termination.

Part D Remedies

37

Insolvency and Employment Law

SUMMARY

(1) There is a core distinction between liquidation and administration. Compulsory liquidation causes the termination of the employment of staff but in administration, at least initially, employment continues.

(2) Administration is a particular form of insolvency proceedings where the objective is to endeavour to keep the business trading. A number of administrations involve 'pre-pack' where the sale of the assets is already in contemplation at the point of appointment.

(3) Liquidation by court order is a bar to the initiation and continuation of proceedings, although the court's permission can be sought to proceed. In the case of administration, permission is needed to start or continue proceedings.

(4) Administrators are deemed to adopt contracts of employment after fourteen days of their appointment if employment has been maintained. The employee liabilities will then enjoy priority and, in the case of an administrative receiver, they will become personally liable to an extent.

(5) Employees are preferential creditors in respect of certain debts and are also entitled to certain guaranteed debts from the National Insurance Fund.

(6) Insolvency impacts on the operation of the Transfer of Undertakings (Protection of Employment) Regulations 2006, although the impact will be limited in the typical case of a transfer occurring when the transferor is in administration.

A. INTRODUCTION

37.01 The insolvency of the employer impacts both upon the continued employment of employees and the claims that they may have against their employer. Insolvency additionally has particular consequences for the application of the Transfer of Undertakings (Protection of Employment) Regulations 2006 (TUPE 2006).

This chapter provides a broad overview of the topic looking at the form and structure of insolvency **37.02** with specific focus upon the practical issues which employees face in these circumstances.

B. STRUCTURE OF LEGISLATION

The core legislative provisions remain the Insolvency Act 1986 (IA 1986) and the Insolvency Rules **37.03** 1986. The IA 1986 embraces both individual and corporate insolvency. The focus of this chapter is on corporate insolvency, rather than individual bankruptcy.

A core distinction, which carries particular significance, is the division between liquidation and ad- **37.04** ministration. Liquidation is concerned with the termination of the existence of a corporate entity whereas administration is concerned with the attempt to keep a business or parts of a business alive whilst realizing value for the business.

Liquidation

Liquidation is not synonymous with insolvency. A company may be liquidated in circumstances **37.05** where it is not insolvent, for example, if the shareholders desire simply to terminate a corporate entity. The present focus is, however, where liquidation is prompted by the insolvency of the company.

Compulsory liquidation

This is liquidation upon the order of the court consequent upon the presentation of a petition to **37.06** wind the company up. Such a petition may be presented by the company or its directors or by the creditors of a company. The classic basis for the winding up of a company by its creditors is that the company is unable to discharge its debts.

The effect of the order for the winding up of the company is to stay any court actions against the **37.07** company, and permission is needed from the court before actions can be commenced, or continued, against the company: section 130(2) of the IA 1986.

In a compulsory liquidation, the function of liquidator is, in most cases, initially performed by **37.08** the Official Receiver. Where there are significant assets, an insolvency practitioner will usually be appointed to act as liquidator in place of the Official Receiver, either at a meeting of creditors convened for the purpose or directly by the Secretary of State. Where an insolvency practitioner is not appointed, the Official Receiver remains as liquidator.

Where a compulsory liquidation follows immediately on an administration, the court may appoint **37.09** the former administrator to act as liquidator. An administrator may also subsequently act as liquidator in a creditors' voluntary liquidation.

Voluntary liquidation

Here a company is voluntarily wound up as a consequence of a shareholder resolution. This may **37.10** take the form of a members' or creditors' voluntary winding up of the company.

A members' voluntary liquidation is under the control of the shareholders, and a creditors' **37.11** one is in the control of the creditors. In the case of insolvency, it will be a creditors' voluntary liquidation.

A company entering liquidation is likely to cease trading immediately upon the liquidator's **37.12** appointment.

Administration

The object of administration of companies was to avoid liquidation of the business if possible. For **37.13** practical purposes, most administrations lead to a sale of the assets of the company and the liquidation of the corporate entity. Administrators may be appointed either by the court, by the directors, or by the shareholders. In the case of administrators not appointed by the court, it is still necessary for formal documentation to be filed with the court.

37.14 Where the administrator is appointed by the court, the appointment will only be made if a court is satisfied that the company is or is likely to be unable to pay its debts: para 11(a) of Sch B1 to the IA 1986. Similarly, where the appointment is by the company or its directors there must be a statutory declaration that the company is or is likely to become unable to pay its debts. In either case it is apparent that the procedure is indeed an insolvency procedure. There is a distinction between administration and bankruptcy proceedings/compulsory liquidation, in that administration extends not only to where the company is unable to pay its debts as they fall due, but also where it is likely to be unable to do so.

37.15 Where the administrator is appointed by the holder of a qualifying floating charge there is no express provision for either the court to be satisfied that the company is unable to pay its debts or for a declaration to this effect. However, the appointment can only be made where the charge has become enforceable (para 16 of Sch B1 to the IA 1986) and there must be a declaration to this effect and that the purposes of the administration can be achieved (para 18 of Sch B1). In effect, therefore, the power arises where the company has been unable to repay sums secured by the charge. The procedure can still therefore be properly regarded as an insolvency procedure.

37.16 There may have been negotiations and proposals for the sale of assets of the business, sometimes to a 'Newco', before the appointment of the administrator. This is known as a 'pre-pack'.

Receivership

37.17 There are a variety of forms of receiver. Contractual receivers are typically appointed under the terms of a security device, such as a charge or floating charge, for the receiver to be appointed to take charge of the company in order to manage it so as to secure and realize the security—the contractual receiver acting as agent of the company for the purpose of managing its affairs to realize the security.

37.18 Administrative receivers are a particular statutory form of contractual receivers who have been appointed in relation to a whole company under the terms of a floating charge: s 29 of the IA 1986. They must be insolvency practitioners. They were given specific enhanced duties and powers under the IA 1986.

37.19 The ability to appoint administrative receivers is limited and, typically, the procedure adopted is that of administration.

Voluntary arrangements

37.20 A voluntary arrangement is a proposal presented by the directors of a company to a nominee who is an insolvency practitioner. The insolvency practitioner may, if he considers there are prospects of success for the proposal, summon a meeting of shareholders and creditors to vote on the proposal. The approval of the voluntary arrangement secures protection for the company from claims. This is a company voluntary arrangement.

C. THE IMPACT ON LEGAL PROCEEDINGS

37.21 As noted above, compulsory court liquidation will provide a bar to continuation or initiation of proceedings (s 130(2) of the IA 2006) unless the court gives permission for the proceedings to be commenced or continued.

37.22 Voluntary liquidation and the appointment of receivers does not act as a bar to proceedings.

37.23 Administration is different in that whilst permission is needed for the commencement or continuation of proceedings against a company in administration, this may be given either by the administrator or the court: para 43(6) of Sch B1 to the IA 1986. Legal proceedings include a claim before the employment tribunal: *Carr v British International Helicopters Ltd* [1994] IRLR 212.

Proceedings commenced without permission are not a nullity but are subject to the stay. Faced then with an expiring time limit, a claimant should issue a claim, even if it has not been possible to previously obtain consent. The consent, if required from the court, must be sought from the court which made the relevant insolvency order.

It is not a given in either the case of compulsory liquidation or administration that permission is granted. **37.24** In the case of liquidation, the court will consider if it is fair and right to allow the claims to proceed or be brought: *New Cap Reinsurance Corp Ltd v HIH Casualty & General Insurance Ltd* [2002] EWCA Civ 300. In the case of administration, the court will balance the interests of the applicant against those of the other creditors but it appears that it is only in exceptional circumstances that monetary claims will be given permission (see *Unite the Union and others v Nortel Networks (UK) Ltd (in administration)* [2010] EWHC 82, [2010] IRLR 1042). If permission is not granted, then the applicants will have to seek to prove any debts in the insolvency. It is clear from *Nortel* that claims may be proved in insolvency, even if liability has not been established; this includes claims for compensation for discrimination.

D. INSOLVENCY AND THE EFFECT ON CONTRACTS OF EMPLOYMENT

Liquidation

The effect of the making of a winding up order by a court, compulsory liquidation, is that from the **37.25** date of the publication of the order all the employees of the company are automatically dismissed with immediate effect: *Re General Rolling Stock Co, Chapman's case* (1866) LR 1 Eq 346. This is a breach of the employees' contract of employment, because they have been deprived of their notice. They will, however, have to prove their damages claims within the liquidation.

It should, however, be noted that it is possible as a consequence of the Enterprise Act 2002 **37.26** for an order for the winding up of a company to be converted into an administration. In that case, the administrator may wish to continue the employment of some employees, although the effect is that they have been dismissed on the making of the order but there is a consensual re-engagement.

The position of voluntary winding up is different, whether it be a members' or creditors' winding **37.27** up. This does not have the effect of automatically terminating the contracts of employees. The liquidator who is appointed pursuant to the voluntary winding up does, however, have limited power to continue managing the company purely for the purposes of the beneficial winding up of the company: s 87 of the IA 1986. This has the consequence that the employment of the employees will probably be terminated early in the liquidation.

Receivers

As noted, a contractual receiver appointed under the terms of a security document will be ap- **37.28** pointed as an agent of the company to conduct its affairs. Thus, dismissal would not be the normal consequence of the appointment. A different position may arise where the appointment of a receiver is inconsistent with the continued performance of certain employees' duties such as that of the managing director, in that it may be a repudiatory breach of the employee's contract of employment for their powers to have been removed by the appointment of a receiver.

The situation regarding a court appointed receiver is different—the position is the same as if a **37.29** winding up order is made by the court.

Administrators

The appointment of an administrator does not terminate contracts; an administrator acts as an **37.30** agent of the company and the purpose is, if possible, the rescue of the company as a going concern: para 69 of Sch B1 to the IA 1986. Administration normally involves the administrators continuing the operation of the business concerned, which will require some or all of the employees of the company to be retained. Where such an administrator is appointed, they will be taken to have adopted the contract of employment of an employee if they maintain that employment for fourteen days (para 99(5) of Sch B1). If the contract is adopted, the effect of para 99(5) is to give priority to sums payable in respect of 'wages or salary'. The term 'wages or salary' has an extended definition (para 99(6)) so as to include holiday pay, sick pay, payment in lieu of holiday, sums treated as earnings for the purposes of social security, and contributions to an occupational pension scheme. Matters occurring before adoption of the contract are excluded.

37.31 This has the practical effect that administrators will seek to reduce overheads by dismissing senior employees early in the administration.

37.32 Similar provision is made in respect of an administrative receiver (ss 44(2), (2A)–(2D) of the IA 1986).

37.33 If an administrator (who does not generally undertake personal liability) adopts the contracts, the 'qualifying liabilities' under the contracts incurred before adoption will rank in priority to the administrator's fees and expenses. The 'qualifying liabilities' are wages and salary, holiday and sick pay, and contributions to occupational pension schemes: para 99(5) of Sch B1. From the point of adoption, the qualifying liabilities rank as expenses of the administration and therefore enjoy a priority that ranks above that of their own remuneration and expenses (para 99(3), (4) of Sch B1).

37.34 Liabilities for protective awards under s 189 of the Trade Union and Labour Relations (Consolidation) Act 1992 (TULR(C)A 1992) (failure to consult on dismissal for redundancy) do not enjoy priority under para 99(5) and (6) of Sch B1 to the IA 1986. They do not fall within para 99(6)(d) (sums which would be treated as earnings for a period for the purposes of an enactment about social security) and are therefore outside the definition of 'wages or salary' (*Krasner (administrator of Huddersfield Fine Worsteds Ltd) v McMath* [2005] EWCA Civ 1072, [2006] ICR 205, [2005] IRLR 995). This principle is not affected by the decision of the Court of Appeal in *Haine v Day* [2008] EWCA Civ 626, [2008] IRLR 642, that contingent rights to such protective awards may be provable in company liquidations. Payments in lieu of notice are also not 'wages or salary', neither are damages for wrongful dismissal: *Re Leeds United* FC [2007] EWHC 1761 (Krasner J), or statutory redundancy payments: *Re Allders Department Stores Ltd* [2005] EWHC 172.

37.35 In the case of administrative receivers, if they adopt contracts of employment after fourteen days, then they become personally liable in respect of 'qualifying liabilities' in relation to any contracts of employment they enter into in the course of their duties (s 44(1)(b) of the IA 1986).

Preferential debts

37.36 The claims of employees would rank as those of unsecured creditors. They are, however, given preferential debt status in respect of certain claims. Such debts will be paid after the discharge of the expenses of the insolvency and the secured debts other than those secured by a floating charge. These protections extend to administrations and voluntary arrangements.

37.37 Under s 386 and Sch 6 of the IA 1986, various categories of employee debt are given preferential status, subject to a maximum total claim of £800 (excluding accrued holiday remuneration, which is uncapped). Beyond that sum the employee will rank with other unsecured creditors. The preferential debts include:

(a) Remuneration owed in respect of the whole or part of the four months prior to the relevant date (for example, in the case of a liquidation the date of the winding up order). Statutory redundancy payments or unfair dismissal awards are not given preferential status. The 'relevant date' is defined in s 387 by reference to various events in the progress of a corporate or individual insolvency.

(b) Amounts owed by way of accrued holiday remuneration.

(c) Guarantee payments, time off for ante-natal care and carrying out trade union activities.

(d) Remuneration under a protective award on redundancy in respect of the period before the insolvency.

E. 'GUARANTEED DEBTS'

37.38 In addition, there are sums guaranteed from the National Insurance Fund: see Part XI of Chapter VI of the Employment Rights Act 1996 (ERA 1986), for the recovery from the National Insurance Fund of redundancy payments (and like payments) on insolvency of the employer. The scheme is operated by the Redundancy Payments Office (RPO). If the conditions for payment are made out, then the Secretary of State will pay the employee the 'guaranteed debts'. Applications for payment are made to the RPO by the submission of a form RP1.

37.39 The debts are defined as follows (s 184 of the ERA 1996); a week's pay is presently subject to the current cap of £508 for any one week per item, according to s 186 of the Act:

(1) This Part applies to the following debts—
    (a) any arrears of pay in respect of one or more (but not more than eight) weeks,
    (b) any amount which the employer is liable to pay the employee for the period of notice required by section 86(1) or (2) or for any failure of the employer to give the period of notice required by section 86(1),
    (c) any holiday pay—
        (i) in respect of a period or periods of holiday not exceeding six weeks in all, and
        (ii) to which the employee became entitled during the twelve months ending with the appropriate date,
    (d) any basic award of compensation for unfair dismissal, and
    (e) any reasonable sum by way of reimbursement of the whole or part of any fee or premium paid by an apprentice or articled clerk.
(2) For the purposes of subsection (1)(a) the following amounts shall be treated as arrears of pay—
    (a) a guarantee payment,
    (b) any payment for time off under Part VI of this Act or section 169 of the Trade Union and Labour Relations (Consolidation) Act 1992 (payment for time off for carrying out trade union duties etc),
    (c) remuneration on suspension on medical grounds under section 64 of this Act and remuneration on suspension on maternity grounds under section 68 of this Act, and
    (d) remuneration under a protective award under section 189 of the Trade Union and Labour Relations (Consolidation) Act 1992.

37.40 An employee's entitlement to payment of the 'guaranteed debt' from the Fund is dependent upon certain conditions being met (s 182):

If, on an application made to him in writing by an employee, the Secretary of State is satisfied that—
(a) the employee's employer has become insolvent,
(b) the employee's employment has been terminated, and
(c) on the appropriate date the employee was entitled to be paid the whole or part of any debt to which this Part applies,

the Secretary of State shall, subject to section 186 which imposes the financial cap on the debt, pay the employee out of the National Insurance Fund the amount to which, in the opinion of the Secretary of State, the employee is entitled in respect of the debt.

37.41 The rights accorded by Part XII are then available only when the employer is formally insolvent as defined in s 183 ERA 1996. An employer is not 'insolvent' as defined merely because he is unable to pay debts as they fall due. It is essential for one limb or another of s 183(2) or (3) to be satisfied. Section 183(2) is the test for an individual employer and s 183(3) that for a corporate employer. It cannot just be assumed that an individual or a company is insolvent (as defined). There is no burden on the Secretary of State to disprove insolvency should the matter come before an employment tribunal; the onus is on a claimant seeking to make a claim against the Secretary of State to establish by direct evidence that the statutory test is satisfied: *Secretary of State for Trade & Industry v Walden* [2000] IRLR 168, EAT.

37.42 For a corporate entity, insolvency is defined to be, in broad terms, if a winding up order has been made or a resolution passed (s 183(3)(a)); if the company is in administration (s 183(3)(aa)); if a receiver has been appointed (s 183(3)(b)); or if a voluntary arrangement has been proposed and approved for the company (s 183 (3)(c)).

37.43 The employee's employment must have been terminated: s 182(b).

37.44 The debt must then have been due on the appropriate date, which is defined under s 185 In the case of arrears of pay, this is typically the date on which the employer became insolvent. In the case of other debts, including unfair dismissal and protective awards, the date will be the later of a number of defining events.

37.45 Despite the absence of protection under the statutory scheme, a dismissed employee may be entitled to prove in the liquidation in respect of a sum payable under a statutory cause of action, even though it was not a debt at the date of the liquidation. In *Haine v Day* [2008] EWCA Civ 626, [2008] IRLR 642 the Court of Appeal held that where employees were dismissed in breach of the consultation obligation in TULR(C)A 1992, s 188, they were entitled, in the liquidation, to prove for the amount of their protective awards, even though the claims had not been determined by a tribunal.

37.46 If payment of the debt is refused by the RPO then the employee's remedy is an application to the tribunal claiming that they have not been paid or that they have been paid too little: s 188(1) ERA 1996. The claim must be brought, subject to a possible reasonably practicable extension, within three months of the communication of the decision of the Secretary of State. The claim is brought against the Secretary of State. If the tribunal finds that the Secretary of State ought to have made the payment. then it makes a declaration to that effect: s 188(3).

F. PENSION ENTITLEMENTS

37.47 Under the Pension Schemes Act 1993, sums may be paid from the National Insurance Fund in respect of unpaid contributions to a pension scheme: s 124 of the Pension Schemes Act.

37.48 Again the application is made to the Secretary of State with the possibility of a claim for a declaration before the tribunal if payment is not refused.

G. TUPE AND INSOLVENCY

37.49 TUPE 2006 has particular relevance to insolvency where the sale of the business or part of the business may raise the question of a transfer for the purposes of TUPE.

37.50 Whether there has been a transfer for the purposes of TUPE 2006 will be determined by the normal application of the Regulations: see Chapter 29. In implementing Directive 2001/23/EC by TUPE 2006, the government gave effect to provisions within the Directive, which enabled Member States to limit the operation of the Regulations in cases of liquidation.

Regulation 8(6) and (7) TUPE

37.51 In short, reg 8 of TUPE 2006 divides insolvency proceedings into two different types. It was plainly intended by the drafters that any corporate insolvency would fall into one type or the other. For these purposes, reg 8(6) and (7) define the two types of insolvency proceedings in the following ways:

> (6) In this regulation 'relevant insolvency proceedings' means insolvency proceedings which have been opened in relation to the transferor *not with a view to liquidation of the assets of the transferor* and which are under the supervision of an insolvency practitioner;
>
> (7) Regulations 4 and 7 do not apply to any relevant transfer where the transferor is the subject of bankruptcy proceedings or any analogous insolvency proceedings *which have been instituted with a view to the liquidation of the assets of the transferor* and are under the supervision of an insolvency practitioner. (emphasis added)

37.52 As can be seen from the above, the distinction between the two types is whether the insolvency proceedings have been instituted with a view to the liquidation of the assets of the transferor, or not. In overview, where a transferor is insolvent, TUPE 2006 seeks to exclude the effect of the Regulations in two main ways:

(a) The most extensive exception from the effect of TUPE is carved out (by reg 8(7)) for insolvency proceedings 'with a view to liquidation' and which are 'under the supervision of an insolvency practitioner'. In such circumstances, reg 4 (transfer of rights and liabilities) and reg 7 (protection from dismissal) are excluded altogether. However, the remaining provisions in relation to information and consultation continue to apply; thus a liability may be acquired even if the contracts of the employees are not transferred;

(b) There is a lesser relaxation of the requirements of TUPE 2006 in relation to 'relevant insolvency proceedings', where they are opened 'not with a view to liquidation' of the transferor's assets. This lesser carve out of TUPE is contained in reg 8(2)–(5). In short:

   (i) There is provision for certain core debts (those considered above under Chapter VI of Part X and Part XII ERA 1996) to remain the liability of the transferor and to be claimable from the Secretary of State without the need to show a dismissal (reg 8(2)–(5)).

   (ii) Although reg 4 (automatic transfer of rights and liabilities) is not disapplied, there is a greater freedom for the transferor or transferee, or the insolvency practitioner, to negotiate valid variations in employment contracts provided for in reg 9 TUPE 2006. The procedure is not a simple one and requires existing consultative structures or the election of representatives, so it is open to question how frequently this will be followed.

There has been legal debate as to whether reg 8(7) of TUPE 2006 can apply in administration, particularly in the circumstances of a 'pre-pack', where it is always contemplated that the business may be sold as a going concern on appointment. In *Oakland v Wellswood (Yorkshire) Ltd* [2009] IRLR 25, the EAT upheld a tribunal decision that administration was a form of insolvency proceedings analogous to bankruptcy and it was a factual issue as to whether the administrator had been appointed with a view to the liquidation of the assets of the transferor. The issue has returned to the EAT in a number of test cases and, in *OTG Ltd v Barke* [2011] IRLR 272, the EAT rejected the 'fact-based approach' adopted in *Oakland* and held that an 'absolute approach' should apply. The EAT held that administration cannot amount to proceedings instituted with a view to liquidation as this goes against the express wording of the insolvency legislation that establishes the administration procedure. This severely limits the effect of reg 8(7), although it will remain the case that those purchasing from administrators where there is held to have been a transfer will be able to take the benefit of the guarantee payments in respect of the core debts: see *Pressure Coolers Ltd v Molloy* [2011] IRLR 630. The decision of the EAT in *OTG* was upheld by the Court of Appeal in *Key2Law (Surrey) Ltd v De'Antiquis* [2011] EWCA Civ 1567. Key2Law sought to appeal to the Supreme Court but its appeal was struck out for failure to comply with conditions on the appeal. The decision of the Court of Appeal therefore remains the binding authority on the issue, although the issue remains open before the Supreme Court.

37.53

Appendix 1
Selected Legislation

RULES

The Employment Appeal Tribunal Rules 1993

(SI 1993/2854)

Citation and commencement[1]

1.—(1) These Rules may be cited as the Employment Appeal Tribunal Rules 1993 and shall come into force on 16th December 1993.

(2) As from that date the Employment Appeal Tribunal Rules 1980, the Employment Appeal Tribunal (Amendment) Rules 1985 and the Employment Appeal Tribunal (Amendment) Rules 1988 shall be revoked.

Interpretation

[2.—(1) In these rules—[2]

'the 1992 Act' means the Trade Union and Labour Relations (Consolidation) Act 1992;

'the 1996 Act' means the Employment Tribunals Act 1996;

'the 1999 Regulations' means the Transnational Information and Consultation of Employees Regulations 1999;

['the 2004 Regulations' means the European and Public Limited-Liability Company Regulations 2004;][3]

['the Information and Consultation Regulations' means the Information and Consultation of Employees Regulations 2004;][4]

['the 2007 Regulations' means the Companies (Cross-Border Mergers) Regulations 2007;][5]

'the Appeal Tribunal' means the Employment Appeal Tribunal established under section 87 of the Employment Protection Act 1975 and continued in existence under section 20(1) of the 1996 Act and includes the President, a judge, a member or the Registrar acting on behalf of the Tribunal;

'the CAC' means the Central Arbitration Committee;

'the Certification Officer' means the person appointed to be the Certification Officer under section 254(2) of the 1992 Act;

'costs officer' means any officer of the Appeal Tribunal authorised by the President to assess costs or expenses;

'Crown employment proceedings' has the meaning given by section 10(8) of the 1996 Act;

['document' includes a document delivered by way of electronic communication;[6]

'electronic communication' shall have the meaning given to it by section 15(1) of the Electronic Communications Act 2000;]

'excluded person' means, in relation to any proceedings, a person who has been excluded from all or part of the proceedings by virtue of—

(a) a direction of a Minister of the Crown under rule 30A(1)(b) or (c); or

(b) an order of the Appeal Tribunal under rule 30A(2)(a) read with rule 30A(1)(b) or (c);

'judge' means a judge of the Appeal Tribunal nominated under section 22(1)(a) or (b) of the 1996 Act and includes a judge nominated under section 23(2) of, or a judge appointed under section 24(1) of, the 1996 Act to be a temporary additional judge of the Appeal Tribunal;

['legal representative' shall mean a person, including a person who is a party's employee, who—[7]

(a) has a general qualification within the meaning of the Courts and Legal Services Act 1990;

(b) is an advocate or solicitor in Scotland; or

---

[1] References within these rules to industrial tribunals were amended to read employment tribunals by the Employment Rights (Dispute Resolution) Act 1998 (c 8), s 1.

[2] Substituted by SI 2001/1128, r 2.

[3] Inserted by SI 2004/2526, r 2(1).

[4] Inserted by SI 2004/3426, reg 41.

[5] Inserted by SI 2007/2974, reg 64(1).

[6] Inserted by SI 2004/2526, r 2(1).

[7] Inserted by SI 2004/2526, r 2(1).

(c) is a member of the Bar of Northern Ireland or a [Solicitor of the Court of Judicature of Northern Ireland].[8]

'member' means a member of the Appeal Tribunal appointed under section 22(1)(c) of the 1996 Act and includes a member appointed under section 23(3) of the 1996 Act to act temporarily in the place of a member appointed under that section;

['national security proceedings' shall have the meaning given to it in [regulation 3 of the Employment Tribunals (Constitution and Rules of Procedure) Regulations 2013][9]][10]

'the President' means the judge appointed under section 22(3) of the 1996 Act to be President of the Appeal Tribunal and includes a judge nominated under section 23(1) of the 1996 Act to act temporarily in his place;

'the Registrar' means the person appointed to be Registrar of the Appeal Tribunal and includes any officer of the Tribunal authorised by the President to act on behalf of the Registrar;

'the Secretary of Employment Tribunals' means the person acting for the time being as the Secretary of the Central Office of the Employment Tribunals (England and Wales) or, as may be appropriate, of the Central Office of the Employment Tribunals (Scotland);

'special advocate' means a person appointed pursuant to rule 30A(4).

['writing' includes writing delivered by means of electronic communication;][11]

(2) [...][12]

(3) Any reference in these Rules to a person who was the [claimant] or, as the case may be, the respondent in the proceedings before an employment tribunal includes, where those proceedings are still continuing, a reference to a person who is the [claimant] or, as the case may be, is the respondent in those proceedings.][13]

[Overriding objective

2A.—(1) The overriding objective of these Rules is to enable the Appeal Tribunal to deal with cases justly.[14]

(2) Dealing with a case justly includes, so far as practicable—

(a) ensuring that the parties are on an equal footing;

(b) dealing with the case in ways which are proportionate to the importance and complexity of the issues;

(c) ensuring that it is dealt with expeditiously and fairly; and

(d) saving expense.

(3) The parties shall assist the Appeal Tribunal to further the overriding objective.]

[Institution of appeal

3.—(1) Every appeal to the Appeal Tribunal shall, subject to paragraphs (2) and (4), be instituted by serving on the Tribunal the following documents[15]—

(a) a notice of appeal in, or substantially in, accordance with Form 1, 1A or 2 in the Schedule to these rules;

[(b) in the case of an appeal from a judgment of an employment tribunal a copy of any claim and response in the proceedings before the employment tribunal or an explanation as to why either is not included; and][16]

[(c) in the case of an appeal from a judgment of an employment tribunal a copy of the written record of the judgment of the employment tribunal which is subject to appeal and the written reasons for the judgment, or an explanation as to why written reasons are not included;][17]

---

8 Amended by the Constitutional Reform Act 2005, s 59(5), Sch 11, Pt 3, para 5.
9 Substituted by SI 2013/1693, r 2.
10 Inserted by SI 2004/2526, r 2(1).
11 Inserted by SI 2004/2526, r 2(1).
12 As amended by SI 2004/2526, r 2.
13 As amended by SI 2004/2526, r 2.
14 Inserted by SI 2004/2526, r 3.
15 Substituted by SI 2001/1128, r 3.
16 Substituted by SI 2004/2526, r 4.
17 Substituted by SI 2004/2526, r 4.

Appendix 1 Selected Legislation: Rules

    (d) in the case of an appeal made pursuant to regulation 38(8) of the 1999 Regulations [or regulation 47(6) of the 2004 Regulations] [or regulation 35(6) of the Information and Consultation Regulations] [or regulation 57(6) of the 2007 Regulations] from a declaration or order of the CAC, a copy of that declaration or order[; and][18]

    [(e) in the case of an appeal from an order of an employment tribunal a copy of the written record of the order of the employment tribunal which is subject to appeal and (if available) the written reasons for the order;[19]

    (f) in the case of an appeal from a decision or order of the Certification Officer a copy of the decision or order of the Certification Officer which is subject to appeal and the written reasons for that decision or order.]

[(2) In an appeal from a judgment or order of the employment tribunal in relation to national security proceedings where the appellant was the claimant—[20]

    (i) the appellant shall not be required by virtue of paragraph (1)(b) to serve on the Appeal Tribunal a copy of the response if the response was not disclosed to the appellant; and

    (ii) the appellant shall not be required by virtue of paragraph (1)(c) or (e) to serve on the Appeal Tribunal a copy of the written reasons for the judgment or order if the written reasons were not sent to the appellant but if a document containing edited reasons was sent to the appellant, he shall serve a copy of that document on the Appeal Tribunal.]

(3) The period within which an appeal to the Appeal Tribunal may be instituted is—

    [(a) in the case of an appeal from a judgment of the employment tribunal—[21]

      (i) where the written reasons for the judgment subject to appeal—

        (aa) were requested orally at the hearing before the employment tribunal or in writing within 14 days of the date on which the written record of the judgment was sent to the parties; or

        (bb) were reserved and given in writing by the employment tribunal 42 days from the date on which the written reasons were sent to the parties;

      (ii) in an appeal from a judgment given in relation to national security proceedings, where there is a document containing edited reasons for the judgment subject to appeal, 42 days from the date on which that document was sent to the parties; or

      (iii) where the written reasons for the judgment subject to appeal—

        (aa) were not requested orally at the hearing before the employment tribunal or in writing within 14 days of the date on which the written record of the judgment was sent to the parties; and

        (bb) were not reserved and given in writing by the employment tribunal 42 days from the date on which the written record of the judgment was sent to the parties;]

    [(b) in the case of an appeal from an order of an employment tribunal, 42 days from the date of the order;][22]

    (c) in the case of an appeal from a decision of the Certification Officer, 42 days from the date on which the written record of that decision was sent to the appellant;

    (d) in the case of an appeal from a declaration or order of the CAC under regulation 38(8) of the 1999 Regulations [or regulation 47(6) of the 2004 Regulations] [or regulation 35(6) of the Information and Consultation Regulations] [or regulation 57(6) of the 2007 Regulations], 42 days from the date on which the written notification of that declaration or order was sent to the appellant.[23]

(4) In the case of [an appeal from a judgment or order of the employment tribunal in relation to national security proceedings], the appellant shall not set out the grounds of appeal in his notice of appeal and shall not append to his notice of appeal the [written reasons for the judgment] of the tribunal.[24]

(5) In [an appeal from the employment tribunal in relation to national security proceedings] in relation to which the appellant was the respondent in the proceedings before the employment tribunal, the appellant shall, within the period described in paragraph (3)(a), provide to the Appeal Tribunal a document setting

---

[18] As amended by SI 2004/2526, r 4; SI 2004/3426, reg 41; and SI 2007/2974, reg 64(2).
[19] Inserted by SI 2004/2526, r 4.
[20] Substituted by SI 2004/2526, r 4.
[21] Substituted by SI 2004/2526, r 4.
[22] Substituted by SI 2004/2526, r 4.
[23] As amended by SI 2004/2526, r 4; SI 2004/3426, reg 41; and SI 2007/2974, reg 64(2).
[24] As amended by SI 2004/2526, r 4.

out the grounds on which the appeal is brought.[25] (6) In [an appeal from the employment tribunal in relation to national security proceedings] in relation to which the appellant was the [claimant] in the proceedings before the employment tribunal—[26]

(a) the appellant may, within the period described in [paragraph 3(a)(ii) or (iii) or paragraph 3(b), whichever is applicable,] provide to the Appeal Tribunal a document setting out the grounds on which the appeal is brought; and

(b) a special advocate appointed in respect of the appellant may, within the period described in [paragraph 3(a)(ii) or (iii) or paragraph 3(b), whichever is applicable,] or within 21 days of his appointment, whichever is later, provide to the Appeal Tribunal a document setting out the grounds on which the appeal is brought or providing supplementary grounds of appeal.

[(7) Where it appears to a judge or the Registrar that a notice of appeal or a document provided under paragraph (5) or (6)—[27]

(a) discloses no reasonable grounds for bringing the appeal; or

(b) is an abuse of the Appeal Tribunal's process or is otherwise likely to obstruct the just disposal of proceedings,

he shall notify the Appellant or special advocate accordingly informing him of the reasons for his opinion and, subject to [paragraph (10)],[28] no further action shall be taken on the notice of appeal or document provided under paragraph (5) or (6).]

[(7ZA) Where a judge or the Registrar has taken a decision under paragraph (7), and also considers that the notice of appeal or document provided under paragraph (5) or (6) is totally without merit, the judge or Registrar may order that the appellant or special advocate is not entitled to have the matter heard before a judge under paragraph (10), with such order to be included as part of the notice issued under paragraph (7).][29]

[(7A) In paragraphs (7)[, (7ZA)][30] and (10) reference to a notice of appeal or a document provided under paragraph (5) or (6) includes reference to part of a notice of appeal or document provided under paragraph (5) or (6).][31]

(8), (9) […][32]

[(10) [Subject to paragraph (7ZA), where][33] notification has been given under paragraph (7) and within 28 days of the date the notification was sent, an appellant or special advocate expresses dissatisfaction in writing with the reasons given by the judge or Registrar for his opinion, he is entitled to have the matter heard before a judge who shall make a direction as to whether any further action should be taken on the notice of appeal or document under paragraph (5) or (6).]][34]

Service of notice of appeal

4.—[(1) On receipt of notice under rule 3, the Registrar shall seal the notice with the Appeal Tribunal's seal and shall serve a sealed copy on the appellant and on—[35]

(a) every person who, in accordance with rule 5, is a respondent to the appeal; and

(b) The Secretary of [Employment Tribunals] in the case of an appeal from an [employment tribunal]; or

(c) the Certification Officer in the case of an appeal from any of his decisions; or

(d) the Secretary of State in the case of an appeal under […] Chapter II of Part IV of the 1992 Act [or Part XI of the Employment Rights Act 1996] to which he is not a respondent[; or

(e) the Chairman of the CAC in the case of an appeal from the CAC under regulation 38(8) of the 1999 Regulations [or regulation 47(6) of the 2004 Regulations] [or regulation 35(6) of the Information and Consultation Regulations] [or regulation 57(6) of the 2007 Regulations].[36]

Appendix 1 Selected Legislation: Rules

---

[25] As amended by SI 2004/2526, r 4.
[26] As amended by SI 2004/2526, r 4.
[27] Substituted by SI 2004/2526, r 4.
[28] Substituted by SI 2013/1693, r 3(a).
[29] Inserted by SI 2013/1693, r 3(b).
[30] Inserted by SI 2013/1693, r 3(c).
[31] Inserted by SI 2004/2526, r 4.
[32] Revoked by SI 2013/1693, r 3(d).
[33] Substituted by SI 2013/1693, r 3(e).
[34] Substituted by SI 2004/2526, r 4.
[35] As amended by SI 2001/1128, r 4.
[36] As amended by SI 2004/2526, r 5; SI 2004/3426, reg 41; and SI 2007/2974, reg 64(2).

[(2) On receipt of a document provided under rule 3(5)—

    (a) the Registrar shall not send the document to a person in respect of whom a Minister of the Crown has informed the Registrar that he wishes to address the Appeal Tribunal in accordance with rule 30A(3) with a view to the Appeal Tribunal making an order applicable to this stage of the proceedings under rule 30A(2)(a) read with 30A(1)(b) or (c) (exclusion of a party or his representative), at any time before the Appeal Tribunal decides whether or not to make such an order; but if it decides not to make such an order, the Registrar shall, subject to sub-paragraph (b), send the document to such a person 14 days after the Appeal Tribunal's decision not to make the order; and

    (b) the Registrar shall not send a copy of the document to an excluded person, but if a special advocate is appointed in respect of such a person, the Registrar shall send a copy of the document to the special advocate.

(3) On receipt of a document provided under rule 3(6)(a) or (b), the Registrar shall not send a copy of the document to an excluded person, but shall send a copy of the document to the respondent.]

Respondents to appeals

5   The respondents to an appeal shall be—[37]

    (a) in the case of an appeal from an [employment tribunal] or of an appeal made pursuant to [section 45D, 56A, 95, 104 or 108C] of the 1992 Act from a decision of the Certification Officer, the parties (other than the appellant) to the proceedings before the [employment tribunal] or the Certification Officer;

    (b) in the case of an appeal made pursuant to [section 9 or 126] of the 1992 Act from a decision of the Certification Officer, that Officer;

    [(c) in the case of an appeal made pursuant to regulation 38(8) of the 1999 Regulations [or regulation 47(6) of the 2004 Regulations] [or regulation 35(6) of the Information and Consultation Regulations] [or regulation 57(6) of the 2007 Regulations] from a declaration or order of the CAC, the parties (other than the appellant) to the proceedings before the CAC.][38]

Respondent's answer and notice of cross-appeal

6.—(1) The Registrar shall, as soon as practicable, notify every respondent of the date appointed by the Appeal Tribunal by which any answer under this rule must be delivered.

(2) A respondent who wishes to resist an appeal shall, [subject to paragraph (6), and] within the time appointed under paragraph (1) of this rule, deliver to the Appeal Tribunal an answer in writing in, or substantially in, accordance with Form 3 in the Schedule to these Rules, setting out the grounds on which he relies, so, however, that it shall be sufficient for a respondent to an appeal referred to in rule 5(a) [or 5(c)] who wishes to rely on any ground which is the same as a ground relied on by the [employment tribunal][, the Certification Officer or the CAC] for making the [judgment,] decision[, declaration] or order appealed from to state that fact in his answer.[39]

(3) A respondent who wishes to cross-appeal may[, subject to paragraph (6),] do so by including in his answer a statement of the grounds of his cross-appeal, and in that event an appellant who wishes to resist the cross-appeal shall, within a time to be appointed by the Appeal Tribunal, deliver to the Tribunal a reply in writing setting out the grounds on which he relies.[40]

(4) The Registrar shall serve a copy of every answer and reply to a cross-appeal on every party other than the party by whom it was delivered.

(5) Where the respondent does not wish to resist an appeal, the parties may deliver to the Appeal Tribunal an agreed draft of an order allowing the appeal and the Tribunal may, if it thinks it right to do so, make an order allowing the appeal in the terms agreed.

[(6) In [an appeal from the employment tribunal in relation to national security proceedings], the respondent shall not set out the grounds on which he relies in his answer to an appeal, nor include in his answer a statement of the grounds of any cross-appeal.][41]

---

[37] As amended by SI 2001/1128, r 5.
[38] As amended by SI 2004/2526, r 6; SI 2004/3426, reg 41; and SI 2007/2974, reg 64(2).
[39] As amended by SI 2001/1128, r 6 and SI 2004/2526, r 7.
[40] As amended by SI 2001/1128, r 6.
[41] As amended by SI 2004/2526, r 7.

[(7) In [an appeal from the employment tribunal in relation to national security proceedings] in relation to which the respondent was not the [claimant] in the proceedings before the employment tribunal, the respondent shall, within the time appointed under paragraph (1), provide to the Registrar a document, setting out the grounds on which he intends to resist the appeal, and may include in that document a statement of the grounds of any cross-appeal.[42]

(8) In [an appeal from the employment tribunal in relation to national security proceedings] in relation to which the respondent was the [claimant] in the proceedings before the employment tribunal—[43]

(a) the respondent may, within the time appointed under paragraph (1) provide to the Registrar a document, setting out the grounds on which he intends to resist the appeal, and may include in that document a statement of the grounds of any cross-appeal; and

(b) a special advocate appointed in respect of the respondent may, within the time appointed under paragraph (1), or within 21 days of his appointment, whichever is the later, provide to the Registrar a document, setting out the grounds, or the supplementary grounds, on which the respondent intends to resist the appeal, and may include in that document a statement of the grounds, or the supplementary grounds, of any cross-appeal.

(9) In [an appeal from the employment tribunal in relation to national security proceedings], if the respondent, or any special advocate appointed in respect of a respondent, provides in the document containing grounds for resisting an appeal a statement of grounds of cross-appeal and the appellant wishes to resist the cross-appeal—[44]

(a) where the appellant was not the [claimant] in the proceedings before the employment tribunal, the appellant shall within a time to be appointed by the Appeal Tribunal deliver to the Tribunal a reply in writing setting out the grounds on which he relies; and

(b) where the appellant was the [claimant] in the proceedings before the employment tribunal, the appellant, or any special advocate appointed in respect of him, may within a time to be appointed by the Appeal Tribunal deliver to the Tribunal a reply in writing setting out the grounds on which the appellant relies.

(10) Any document provided under paragraph (7) or (9)(a) shall be treated by the Registrar in accordance with rule 4(2), as though it were a document received under rule 3(5).

(11) Any document provided under paragraph (8) or (9)(b) shall be treated by the Registrar in accordance with rule 4(3), as though it were a document received under rule 3(6)(a) or (b).]

[(12) Where it appears to a judge or the Registrar that a statement of grounds of cross-appeal contained in [the][45] respondent's answer or document provided under paragraph (7) or (8)—[46]

(a) discloses no reasonable grounds for bringing the cross-appeal; or

(b) is an abuse of the Appeal Tribunal's process or is otherwise likely to obstruct the just disposal of proceedings,

he shall notify the [respondent][47] or special advocate accordingly informing him of the reasons for his opinion and, subject to [paragraph (16)],[48] no further action shall be taken on the statement of grounds of cross-appeal.

[(12A) Where a judge or the Registrar has taken a decision under paragraph (12), and also considers that the statement of grounds of cross-appeal contained in the respondent's answer or document provided under paragraph (7) or (8) is totally without merit, the judge or Registrar may order that the respondent is not entitled to have the matter heard before a judge under paragraph (16), with such order to be included as part of the notice issued under paragraph (12).][49]

(13) In paragraphs (12)[, (12A)][50] and (16) reference to a statement of grounds of cross-appeal includes reference to part of a statement of grounds of cross-appeal.

(14), (15) [...][51]

---

[42] Inserted by SI 2001/1128, r 6 and amended by SI 2004/2526, r 7.
[43] As amended by SI 2004/2526, r 7.
[44] As amended by SI 2004/2526, r 7.
[45] Inserted by SI 2013/1693, r 4(a)(i).
[46] Inserted by SI 2004/2526, r 7.
[47] Substituted by SI 2013/1693, r 4(a)(ii).
[48] Substituted by SI 2013/1693, r 4(a)(iii).
[49] Inserted by SI 2013/1693, r 4(b).
[50] Inserted by SI 2013/1693, r 4(c).
[51] Revoked by SI 2013/1693, r 4(d).

(16) [Subject to paragraph (12A), where][52] notification has been given under paragraph (12) and within 28 days of the date the notification was sent, a respondent or special advocate expresses dissatisfaction in writing with the reasons given by the judge or Registrar for his opinion, he is entitled to have the matter heard before a judge who shall make a direction as to whether any further action should be taken on the statement of grounds of cross-appeal.]

Disposal of appeal

7.—(1) The Registrar shall, as soon as practicable, give notice of the arrangements made by the Appeal Tribunal for hearing the appeal to—

(a) every party to the proceedings; and

(b) the Secretary of [Employment Tribunals] in the case of an appeal from an [employment tribunal]; or

(c) the Certification Officer in the case of an appeal from one of his decisions; or

(d) the Secretary of State in the case of an appeal under [Part XI of the Employment Rights Act 1996] or Chapter II of Part IV of the 1992 Act to which he is not a respondent[; or[53]

(e) the Chairman of the CAC in the case of an appeal from a declaration or order of, or arising in any proceedings before, the CAC under regulation 38(8) of the 1999 Regulations] [or regulation 47(6) of the 2004 Regulations] [or regulation 35(6) of the Information and Consultation Regulations] [or regulation 57(6) of the 2007 Regulations].[54]

(2) Any such notice shall state the date appointed by the Appeal Tribunal by which any [interim] application must be made.[55]

Application in respect of exclusion or expulsion from, or unjustifiable discipline by, a trade union

8 Every application under section 67 or 176 of the 1992 Act to the Appeal Tribunal for:

(a) an award of compensation for exclusion or expulsion from a trade union; or

(b) one or both of the following, that is to say—

(i) an award of compensation for unjustifiable discipline;

(ii) an order that the union pay to the applicant an amount equal to any sum which he has paid in pursuance of any such determination as is mentioned in section 64(2)(b) of the 1992 Act;

shall be made in writing in, or substantially in, accordance with Form 4 in the Schedule to these Rules and shall be served on the Appeal Tribunal together with a copy of the decision or order declaring that the applicant's complaint against the trade union was well-founded.

9 If on receipt of an application under rule 8(a) it becomes clear that at the time the application was made the applicant had been admitted or re-admitted to membership of the union against which the complaint was made, the Registrar shall forward the application to the Central Office of [Employment Tribunals].[56]

Service of application under rule 8

10 On receipt of an application under rule 8, the Registrar shall seal it with the Appeal Tribunal's seal and shall serve a sealed copy on the applicant and on the respondent trade union and the Secretary of [Employment Tribunals].[57]

Appearance by respondent trade union

11.—(1) Subject to paragraph (2) of this rule, a respondent trade union wishing to resist an application under rule 8 shall within 14 days of receiving the sealed copy of the application enter an appearance in, or substantially in, accordance with Form 5 in the Schedule to these Rules and setting out the grounds on which the union relies.

(2) Paragraph (1) above shall not require a respondent trade union to enter an appearance where the application is before the Appeal Tribunal by virtue of having been transferred there by an [employment

---

[52] Substituted by SI 2013/1693, r 4(e).

[53] As amended by SI 2001/1128, r 7.

[54] As amended by SI 2004/2526, r 8; SI 2004/3426, reg 41; and SI 2007/2974, reg 64(2).

[55] As amended by SI 2004/2526, r 8.

[56] Substituted by the Employment Rights (Dispute Resolution) Act 1998, s 1(2)(b).

[57] Substituted by the Employment Rights (Dispute Resolution) Act 1998, s 1(2)(b).

tribunal][58] and, prior to that transfer, the respondent had entered an appearance to the proceedings before the [employment tribunal].[59]

12 On receipt of the notice of appearance under rule 11 the Registrar shall serve a copy of it on the applicant.

Application for restriction of proceedings order

13 Every application to the Appeal Tribunal by the Attorney General or the Lord Advocate under [section 33 of the 1996 Act] for a restriction of proceedings order shall be made in writing in, or substantially in, accordance with Form 6 in the Schedule to these Rules, accompanied by an affidavit in support, and shall be served on the Tribunal.[60]

Service of application under rule 13

14 On receipt of an application under rule 13, the Registrar shall seal it with the Appeal Tribunal's seal and shall serve a sealed copy on the Attorney General or the Lord Advocate, as the case may be, on the Secretary of [Employment Tribunals][61] and on the person named in the application.

Appearance by person named in application under rule 13

15 A person named in an application under rule 13 who wishes to resist the application shall within 14 days of receiving the sealed copy of the application enter an appearance in, or substantially in, accordance with Form 7 in the Schedule to these Rules, accompanied by an affidavit in support.

16 On receipt of the notice of appearance under rule 15 the Registrar shall serve a copy of it on the Attorney General or the Lord Advocate, as the case may be.

[16A. [...]][62]

[Applications under regulation 33(6) of the 2004 Regulations

16AA. Every application under regulation 33(6) of the 2004 Regulations [or regulation 22(6) of the Information and Consultation Regulations][63] [or regulation 53(6) of the 2007 Regulations][64] [or regulation 20(7), 21(6) or 21A(5) of the 1999 Regulations][65] shall be made by way of application in writing in, or substantially in, accordance with Form 4B in the Schedule to these Rules and shall be served on the Appeal Tribunal together with a copy of the declaration referred to in regulation 33(4) of [the 2004 Regulations or regulation 22(4) of the Information and Consultation Regulations][66] [or regulation 53(4) of the 2007 Regulations][67] [or the decision referred to in regulation 20(4), 21(4) or 21A(3) of the 1999 Regulations],[68] or an explanation as to why none is included.][69]

[Service of application under rule 16AA

16B. On receipt of an application under rule 16AA, the Registrar shall seal it with the Appeal Tribunal's seal and shall serve a sealed copy on the applicant and on the respondent.][70]

[Appearance by respondent

16C. A respondent wishing to resist an application under rule [...][71] [16AA][72] shall within 14 days of receiving the sealed copy of the application enter an appearance in, or substantially in, accordance with Form 5A in the Schedule to these Rules and setting out the grounds on which the respondent relies.][73]

---

[58] Substituted by the Employment Rights (Dispute Resolution) Act 1998, s 1(2)(a).
[59] Substituted by the Employment Rights (Dispute Resolution) Act 1998, s 1(2)(a).
[60] As amended by SI 2001/1128, r 8.
[61] Substituted by the Employment Rights (Dispute Resolution) Act 1998, s 1(2)(b).
[62] Inserted by SI 2001/1128, r 9 Revoked by SI 2010/1088, regs 2, 30(1), (2).
[63] Inserted by SI 2004/3426, reg 41(c)(i).
[64] Inserted by SI 2007/2974, reg 64(3).
[65] Inserted by SI 2010/1088, regs 2, 30(1), (3).
[66] Substituted by SI 2004/3426, reg 41 (c)(ii).
[67] Inserted by SI 2007/2974, reg 64(3).
[68] Inserted by SI 2010/1088, regs 2, 30(1), (3).
[69] Inserted by SI 2004/2526, r 9.
[70] Substituted by SI 2010/1088, regs 2, 30(1), (4).
[71] Revoked by SI 2010/1088, regs 2, 30(1), (5).
[72] Inserted by SI 2004/2526, r 10.
[73] Inserted by SI 2001/1128, r 9.

Appendix 1 Selected Legislation: Rules

[16D. On receipt of the notice of appearance under rule 16C the Registrar shall serve a copy of it on the applicant.]⁷⁴

Disposal of application

17.—(1) The Registrar shall, as soon as practicable, give notice to the parties to an application under rule 8[, 13[[…]⁷⁵ or 16AA]⁷⁶]⁷⁷ of the arrangements made by the Appeal Tribunal for hearing the application.

(2) Any such notice shall state the date appointed by the Appeal Tribunal by which any [interim]⁷⁸ application must be made.

[Non-payment of fee

17A.—

(1) The Registrar must strike out an appeal, and must notify each party that the appeal has been struck out, where—
  (a) upon receipt of a notice of appeal, or following a direction by the Appeal Tribunal that a matter proceed to an oral hearing, the Lord Chancellor has issued a notice to an appellant specifying that a fee is payable; and
  (b) the appellant has not paid the fee or presented a remission application on or before the date specified in that notice.

(2) Where an appeal has been struck out under paragraph (1), the appeal may be reinstated by the Registrar if—
  (a) the appellant applies to have the appeal reinstated; and
  (b) the fee specified in the Lord Chancellor's notice has been paid or a remission application has been presented and accepted.

(3) The Registrar must strike out an appeal, and must notify each party that the appeal has been struck out, where—
  (a) after consideration of a remission application the Lord Chancellor has issued a notice to an appellant specifying that a fee is payable; and
  (b) the appellant has not paid the fee on or before the date specified in that notice.

(4) Where an appeal has been struck out under paragraph (3) the appeal may be reinstated by the Registrar if—
  (a) the appellant applies to have the appeal reinstated; and
  (b) the fee specified in the Lord Chancellor's notice has been paid.

(5) An application for reinstatement under paragraph (2) or (4) is deemed to be an interim application for the purposes of rule 20.]⁷⁹

Joinder of parties

18 The Appeal Tribunal may, on the application of any person or of its own motion, direct that any person not already a party to the proceedings be added as a party, or that any party to proceedings shall cease to be a party, and in either case may give such consequential directions as it considers necessary.

Interlocutory applications

19.—(1) An [interim]⁸⁰ application may be made to the Appeal Tribunal by giving notice in writing specifying the direction or order sought.

(2) On receipt of a notice under paragraph (1) of this rule, the Registrar shall serve a copy on every other party to the proceedings who appears to him to be concerned in the matter to which the notice relates and shall notify the applicant and every such party of the arrangements made by the Appeal Tribunal for disposing of the application.

---

⁷⁴ Inserted by SI 2001/1128, r 9.
⁷⁵ Revoked by SI 2010/1088, regs 2, 30(1), (6).
⁷⁶ Substituted by SI 2004/2526, r 11.
⁷⁷ Substituted by SI 2001/1128, r 10.
⁷⁸ Substituted by SI 2004/2526, r 12.
⁷⁹ Inserted by SI 2013/1693, r 5.
⁸⁰ Substituted by SI 2004/2526, r 12.

[Disposal of interim applications[81]

20.—(1) Every interim application made to the Appeal Tribunal shall be considered in the first place by the Registrar who shall have regard to rule 2A (the overriding objective) and, where applicable, to rule 23(5).

(2) Subject to sub-paragraphs (3) and (4), every interim application shall be disposed of by the Registrar except that any matter which he thinks should properly be decided by the President or a judge shall be referred by him to the President or judge who may dispose of it himself or refer it in whole or in part to the Appeal Tribunal as required to be constituted by section 28 of the 1996 Act or refer it back to the Registrar with such directions as he thinks fit.

(3) Every interim application for a restricted reporting order shall be disposed of by the President or a judge or, if he so directs, the application shall be referred to the Appeal Tribunal as required to be constituted by section 28 of the 1996 Act who shall dispose of it.

(4) Every interim application for permission to institute or continue or to make a claim or application in any proceedings before an employment tribunal or the Appeal Tribunal, pursuant to section 33(4) of the 1996 Act, shall be disposed of by the President or a judge, or, if he so directs, the application shall be referred to the Appeal Tribunal as required to be constituted by section 28 of the 1996 Act who shall dispose of it.]

Appeals from Registrar

21.—(1) Where an application is disposed of by the Registrar in pursuance of rule 20(2) any party aggrieved by his decision may appeal to a judge and in that case [...] the judge may determine the appeal himself or refer it in whole or in part to the Appeal Tribunal as required to be constituted by [section 28 of the 1996 Act].[82]

(2) Notice of appeal under paragraph (1) of this rule may be given to the Appeal Tribunal, either orally or in writing, within five days of the decision appealed from and the Registrar shall notify every other party who appears to him to be concerned in the appeal and shall inform every such party and the appellant of the arrangements made by the Tribunal for disposing of the appeal.

Hearing of interim applications

22.—(1) The Appeal Tribunal may, subject to [any direction of a Minister of the Crown under rule 30A(1) or order of the Appeal Tribunal under rule 30A(2)(a) read with rule 30A(1),] and, where applicable, to rule 23(6), sit either in private or in public for the hearing of any [interim] application.[83]

(2) [...][84]

Cases involving allegations of sexual misconduct or the commission of sexual offences

23.—(1) This rule applies to any proceedings to which [section 31 of the 1996 Act] applies.[85]

(2) In any such proceedings where the appeal appears to involve allegations of the commission of a sexual offence, the Registrar shall omit from any register kept by the Appeal Tribunal, which is available to the public, or delete from any order, judgment or other document, which is available to the public, any identifying matter which is likely to lead members of the public to identify any person affected by or making such an allegation.

(3) In any proceedings to which this rule applies where the appeal involves allegations of sexual misconduct the Appeal Tribunal may at any time before promulgation of its decision either on the application of a party or of its own motion make a restricted reporting order having effect, if not revoked earlier by the Appeal Tribunal, until the promulgation of its decision.

(4) A restricted reporting order shall specify the persons who may not be identified.

[(5) Subject to paragraph (5A) the Appeal Tribunal shall not make a full restricted reporting order unless it has given each party to the proceedings an opportunity to advance oral argument at a hearing, if they so wish.][86]

---

[81] Substituted by SI 2004/2526, r 13.
[82] As amended by SI 2001/1128, r 12.
[83] As amended by SI 2001/1128, r 13 and SI 2004/2526, r 14.
[84] Repealed by SI 2001/1128, r 13.
[85] As amended by SI 2001/1128, r 14.
[86] Substituted by SI 2004/2526, r 15.

[(5A) The Appeal Tribunal may make a temporary restricted reporting order without a hearing.[87]

(5B) Where a temporary restricted reporting order has been made the Registrar shall inform the parties to the proceedings in writing as soon as possible of:

    (a) the fact that the order has been made; and

    (b) their right to apply to have the temporary restricted reporting order revoked or converted into a full restricted reporting order within 14 days of the temporary order being made.

(5C) If no such application is made under subparagraph (5B)(b) within the 14 days, the temporary restricted reporting order shall lapse and cease to have any effect on the fifteenth day after it was made. When such an application is made the temporary restricted reporting order shall continue to have effect until the Hearing at which the application is considered.]

(6) Any [...] hearing shall, subject to [any direction of a Minister of the Crown under rule 30A(1) or order of the Appeal Tribunal under rule 30A(2)(a) read with rule 30A(1),] or unless the Appeal Tribunal decides for any of the reasons mentioned in rule 29(2) to sit in private to hear evidence, be held in public.[88]

(7) The Appeal Tribunal may revoke a restricted reporting order at any time where it thinks fit.

(8) Where the Appeal Tribunal makes a restricted reporting order, the Registrar shall ensure that a notice of that fact is displayed on the notice board of the Appeal Tribunal at the office in which the proceedings in question are being dealt with, on the door of the room in which those proceedings are taking place and with any list of the proceedings taking place before the Appeal Tribunal.

(9) In this rule, 'promulgation of its decision' means the date recorded as being the date on which the Appeal Tribunal's order finally disposing of the appeal is sent to the parties.

[Restricted reporting orders in disability cases[89]

23A.—(1) This rule applies to proceedings to which section 32(1) of [the] [1996 Act] applies.[90]

(2) In proceedings to which this rule applies the Appeal Tribunal may, on the application of the complainant or of its own motion, make a restricted reporting order having effect, if not revoked earlier by the Appeal Tribunal, until the promulgation of its decision.

(3) Where the Appeal Tribunal makes a restricted reporting order under paragraph (2) of this rule in relation to an appeal which is being dealt with by the Appeal Tribunal together with any other proceedings, the Appeal Tribunal may direct that the order is to apply also in relation to those other proceedings or such part of them as it may direct.

(4) Paragraphs (5) to (9) of rule 23 apply in relation to the making of a restricted reporting order under this rule as they apply in relation to the making of a restricted reporting order under that rule.]

Appointment for direction

24.—(1) Where it appears to the Appeal Tribunal that the future conduct of any proceedings would thereby be facilitated, the Tribunal may (either of its own motion or on application) at any stage in the proceedings appoint a date for a meeting for directions as to their future conduct and thereupon the following provisions of this rule shall apply.

(2) The Registrar shall give to every party in the proceedings notice of the date appointed under paragraph (1) of this rule and any party applying for directions shall, if practicable, before that date give to the Appeal Tribunal particulars of any direction for which he asks.

(3) The Registrar shall take such steps as may be practicable to inform every party of any directions applied for by any other party.

(4) On the date appointed under paragraph (1) of this rule, the Appeal Tribunal shall consider every application for directions made by any party and any written representations relating to the application submitted to the Tribunal and shall give such directions as it thinks fit for the purpose of securing the just, expeditious and economical disposal of the proceedings, including, where appropriate, directions in pursuance of rule 36, for the purpose of ensuring that the parties are enabled to avail themselves of opportunities for conciliation.

---

[87] Inserted by SI 2004/2526, r 15.

[88] As amended by SI 2001/1128, r 14 and SI 2004/2526, r 15.

[89] Inserted by SI 1996/3216, r 2.

[90] As amended by SI 2001/1128, r 15.

(5) Without prejudice to the generality of paragraph (4) of this rule, the Appeal Tribunal may give such directions as it thinks fit as to—

    (a) the amendment of any notice, answer or other document;

    (b) the admission of any facts or documents;

    (c) the admission in evidence of any documents;

    (d) the mode in which evidence is to be given at the hearing;

    (e) the consolidation of the proceedings with any other proceedings pending before the Tribunal;

    (f) the place and date of the hearing.

(6) An application for further directions or for the variation of any directions already given may be made in accordance with rule 19.

Appeal Tribunal's power to give directions

25   The Appeal Tribunal may either of its own motion or on application, at any stage of the proceedings, give any party directions as to any steps to be taken by him in relation to the proceedings.

Default by parties

26.—[(1)][91] If a respondent to any proceedings fails to deliver an answer or, in the case of an application made under section 67 or 176 of the 1992 Act[, section 33 of the 1996 Act[,] [92]][93] [regulation 20, 21 or 21A of the 1999 Regulations],[94] [[…][95] regulation 33 of the 2004 Regulations][96] [[…][97] regulation 22 of the Information and Consultation Regulations][98] [or regulation 53 the 2007 Regulations],[99] a notice of appearance within the time appointed under these Rules, or if any party fails to comply with an order or direction of the Appeal Tribunal, the Tribunal may order that he be debarred from taking any further part in the proceedings, or may make such other order as it thinks just.

[(2) An order made by the Appeal Tribunal under paragraph (1) may include, but is not limited to, an order that all or part of an appeal or answer is to be struck out.

(3) An appeal or answer, or part of an appeal or answer, may not be struck out unless the party in question has been given a reasonable opportunity to make representations, either in writing, or if requested by the party, at a hearing.][100]

Attendance of witnesses and production of documents

27.—(1) The Appeal Tribunal may, on the application of any party, order any person to attend before the Tribunal as a witness or to produce any document.

[(1A) Where—

    (a) a Minister has at any stage issued a direction under rule 30A(1)(b) or (c) (exclusion of a party or his representative), or the Appeal Tribunal has at any stage made an order under rule 30A(2)(a) read with rule 30A(1)(b) or (c); and

    (b) the Appeal Tribunal is considering whether to impose, or has imposed, a requirement under paragraph (1) on any person,

the Minister (whether or not he is a party to the proceedings) may make an application to the Appeal Tribunal objecting to the imposition of a requirement under paragraph (1) or, where a requirement has been imposed, an application to vary or set aside the requirement, as the case may be. The Appeal Tribunal shall hear and determine the Minister's application in private and the Minister shall be entitled to address the Appeal Tribunal thereon. The application shall be made by notice to the Registrar and the Registrar shall give notice of the application to each party.][101]

(2) No person to whom an order is directed under paragraph (1) of this rule shall be treated as having failed to obey that order unless at the time at which the order was served on him there was tendered to him a sufficient sum of money to cover his costs of attending before the Appeal Tribunal.

---

[91] Paragraph (1) numbered by SI 2013/1693, r 6(1).

[92] Substituted by SI 2004/2526, r 17(1).

[93] Substituted by SI 2001/1128, r 16.

[94] Substituted by SI 2010/1088, regs 2, 30(1), (7).

[95] Revoked by SI 2004/3426, reg 41(d)(i).

[96] Inserted by SI 2004/2526, r 17(2).

[97] Revoked by SI 2007/2974, reg 64(4).

[98] Inserted by SI 2004/3426, reg 41(d)(ii).

[99] Inserted by SI 2007/2974, reg 64(4).

[100] Inserted by SI 2013/1693, r 6(2).

[101] Inserted by SI 2001/1128, r 17.

Oaths

28 The Appeal Tribunal may, either of its own motion or on application, require any evidence to be given on oath.

Oral hearings

29.—(1) Subject to paragraph (2) of this rule and to [any direction of a Minister of the Crown under rule 30A(1)(a) or order of the Appeal Tribunal under rule 30A(2)(a) read with rule 30A(1)(a),][102] an oral hearing at which any proceedings before the Appeal Tribunal are finally disposed of shall take place in public before, where applicable, such members of the Tribunal as ([section 28 of the 1996 Act][103]) the President may nominate for the purpose.

[(2) Notwithstanding paragraph (1), the Appeal Tribunal may sit in private for the purpose of hearing evidence from any person which in the opinion of the Tribunal is likely to consist of—

 (a) information which he could not disclose without contravening a prohibition imposed by or by virtue of any enactment;

 (b) information which has been communicated to him in confidence or which he has otherwise obtained in consequence of the confidence reposed in him by another person; or

 (c) information the disclosure of which would, for reasons other than its effect on negotiations with respect to any of the matters mentioned in section 178(2) of the 1992 Act, cause substantial injury to any undertaking of his or in which he works.][104]

[Duty of Appeal Tribunal concerning disclosure of information

30 When exercising its functions, the Appeal Tribunal shall ensure that information is not disclosed contrary to the interests of national security.][105]

[Proceedings in cases concerning national security

30A.—(1) A Minister of the Crown (whether or not he is a party to the proceedings) may, if he considers it expedient in the interests of national security, direct the Appeal Tribunal by notice to the Registrar to—

 (a) sit in private for all or part of particular Crown employment proceedings;

 (b) exclude any party who was the [claimant][106] in the proceedings before the employment tribunal from all or part of particular Crown employment proceedings;

 (c) exclude the representatives of any party who was the [claimant][107] in the proceedings before the employment tribunal from all or part of particular Crown employment proceedings;

 (d) take steps to conceal the identity of a particular witness in particular Crown employment proceedings.

(2) The Appeal Tribunal may, if it considers it expedient in the interests of national security, by order—

 (a) do [in relation to particular proceedings before it][108] anything of a kind which the Appeal Tribunal can be required to do [in relation to particular Crown employment proceedings][109] by direction under paragraph (1) of this rule;

 (b) direct any person to whom any document (including any decision or record of the proceedings) has been provided for the purposes of the proceedings not to disclose any such document or the content thereof—

 (i) to any excluded person;

 (ii) in any case in which a direction has been given under paragraph (1)(a) or an order has been made under paragraph (2)(a) read with paragraph (1)(a), to any person excluded from all or part of the proceedings by virtue of such direction or order; or

 (iii) in any case in which a Minister of the Crown has informed the Registrar in accordance with paragraph (3) that he wishes to address the Appeal Tribunal with a view to the Tribunal making

---

[102] Substituted by SI 2001/1128, r 18(a)(i).
[103] Substituted by SI 2001/1128, r 18(a)(ii).
[104] Substituted by SI 2001/1128, r 18(b).
[105] Substituted by SI 2001/1128, r 19.
[106] Substituted by SI 2004/2526, r 16.
[107] Substituted by SI 2004/2526, r 16.
[108] Inserted by SI 2005/1871, r 2(a).
[109] Inserted by SI 2005/1871, r 2(b).

an order under paragraph (2)(a) read with paragraph (1)(b) or (c), to any person who may be excluded from all or part of the proceedings by virtue of such an order, if an order is made, at any time before the Appeal Tribunal decides whether or not to make such an order;

(c) take steps to keep secret all or part of the reasons for any order it makes.

The Appeal Tribunal shall keep under review any order it makes under this paragraph.

(3) In any proceedings in which a Minister of the Crown considers that it would be appropriate for the Appeal Tribunal to make an order as referred to in paragraph (2), he shall (whether or not he is a party to the proceedings) be entitled to appear before and to address the Appeal Tribunal thereon. The Minister shall inform the Registrar by notice that he wishes to address the Appeal Tribunal and the Registrar shall copy the notice to the parties.

(4) In any proceedings in which there is an excluded person, the Appeal Tribunal shall inform the Attorney General or, in the case of an appeal from an employment tribunal in Scotland, the Advocate General for Scotland, of the proceedings before it with a view to the Attorney General (or, as the case may be, the Advocate General), if he thinks it fit to do so, appointing a special advocate to represent the interests of the person who was the [claimant][110] in the proceedings before the employment tribunal in respect of those parts of the proceedings from which—

(a) any representative of his is excluded;

(b) both he and his representative are excluded; or

(c) he is excluded, where he does not have a representative.

(5) A special advocate shall have a general qualification within the meaning of section 71 of the Courts and Legal Services Act 1990, or, in the case of an appeal from an employment tribunal in Scotland, shall be—

(a) an advocate; or

(b) a solicitor who has by virtue of section 25A of the Solicitors (Scotland) Act 1980 rights of audience in the Court of Session or the High Court of Justiciary.

(6) Where the excluded person is a party to the proceedings, he shall be permitted to make a statement to the Appeal Tribunal before the commencement of the proceedings, or the part of the proceedings, from which he is excluded.

(7) Except in accordance with paragraphs (8) to (10), the special advocate may not communicate directly or indirectly with any person (including an excluded person)—

(a) (except in the case of the Appeal Tribunal or the party who was the respondent in the proceedings before the employment tribunal) on any matter contained in the documents referred to in rule 3(5), 3(6), 6(7) or 6(8)(b); or

(b) (except in the case of a person who was present) on any matter discussed or referred to during any part of the proceedings in which the Appeal Tribunal sat in private pursuant to a direction of the Minister under paragraph (1)(a) or an order of the Appeal Tribunal under paragraph (2)(a) read with paragraph (1)(a).

(8) The special advocate may apply for directions from the Appeal Tribunal authorising him to seek instructions from, or otherwise to communicate with, an excluded person—

(a) on any matter contained in the documents referred to in rule 3(5), 3(6), 6(7) or 6(8)(b); or

(b) on any matter discussed or referred to during any part of the proceedings in which the Appeal Tribunal sat in private as referred to in paragraph (7)(b).

(9) An application under paragraph (8) shall be made by presenting to the Registrar a notice of application, which shall state the title of the proceedings and set out the grounds of the application.

(10) The Registrar shall notify the Minister of an application for directions under paragraph (8) and the Minister shall be entitled to address the Appeal Tribunal on the application.

(11) In these rules, in any case in which a special advocate has been appointed in respect of a party, any reference to a party shall (save in those references specified in paragraph (12)) include the special advocate.

(12) The references mentioned in paragraph (11) are those in rules 5 and 18, the first and second references in rule 27(1A), paragraphs (1) and (6) of this rule, the first reference in paragraph (3) of this

---

[110] Substituted by SI 2004/2526, r 16.

rule, rule 34(1), the reference in item 4 of Form 1, and in item 4 of Form 1A, in the Schedule to these Rules.][111]

Drawing up, reasons for, and enforcement of orders

31.—(1) Every order of the Appeal Tribunal shall be drawn up by the Registrar and a copy, sealed with the seal of the Tribunal, shall be served by the Registrar on every party to the proceedings to which it relates and—

  (a) in the case of an order disposing of an appeal from an [employment tribunal][112] or of an order under [section 33 of the 1996 Act],[113] on the Secretary of the [Employment Tribunals];[114] [...][115]

  (b) in the case of an order disposing of an appeal from the Certification Officer, on that Officer;

  [(c) in the case of an order imposing a penalty notice under [regulation 20, 21 or 21A of the 1999 Regulations],[116] [[...][117] regulation 33 of the 2004 Regulations][118] [[...][119] regulation 22 of the Information and Consultation Regulations][120] [or regulation 53 the 2007 Regulations],[121] on the Secretary of State; or

  (d) in the case of an order disposing of an appeal from the CAC made under regulation 38(8) of the 1999 Regulations, on the Chairman of the CAC].[122]

(2) [Subject to rule 31A,][123] the Appeal Tribunal shall, on the application of any party made within 14 days after the making of an order finally disposing of any proceedings, give its reasons in writing for the order unless it was made after the delivery of a reasoned judgment.

(3) Subject to any order made by the Court of Appeal or Court of Session and to any directions given by the Appeal Tribunal, an appeal from the Tribunal shall not suspend the enforcement of any order made by it.

[Reasons for orders in cases concerning national security

31A.—(1) Paragraphs (1) to (5) of this rule apply to the document setting out the reasons for the Appeal Tribunal's order prepared under rule 31(2) or any reasoned judgment of the Appeal Tribunal as referred to in rule 31(2), in any particular Crown employment proceedings in which a direction of a Minister of the Crown has been given under rule 30A(1)(a), (b) or (c) or an order of the Appeal Tribunal has been made under rule 30A(2)(a) read with rule 30A(1)(a), (b) or (c).

(2) Before the Appeal Tribunal gives its reasons in writing for any order or delivers any reasoned judgment, the Registrar shall send a copy of the reasons or judgment to the Minister.

(3) If the Minister considers it expedient in the interests of national security, he may—

  (a) direct the Appeal Tribunal that the document containing its reasons for any order or its reasoned judgment shall not be disclosed to any person who was excluded from all or part of the proceedings and to prepare a further document setting out the reasons for its order, or a further reasoned judgment, but with the omission of such reasons as are specified in the direction; or

  (b) direct the Appeal Tribunal that the document containing its reasons for any order or its reasoned judgment shall not be disclosed to any person who was excluded from all or part of the proceedings, but that no further document setting out the Appeal Tribunal's reasons for its order or further reasoned judgment should be prepared.

(4) Where the Minister has directed the Appeal Tribunal in accordance with paragraph (3)(a), the document prepared pursuant to that direction shall be marked in each place where an omission has been made. The document may then be given by the Registrar to the parties.

---

[111] Substituted by SI 2001/1128, r 19.
[112] Substituted by the Employment Rights (Dispute Resolution) Act 1998, s 1(2)(a).
[113] Substituted by SI 2001/1128, r 20(a).
[114] Substituted by the Employment Rights (Dispute Resolution) Act 1998, s 1(2)(b).
[115] Revoked by SI 2001/1128, r 20(b).
[116] Substituted by SI 2010/1088, regs 2, 30(1), (8).
[117] Revoked by SI 2004/3426, reg 41(d)(ii).
[118] Inserted by SI 2004/2526, r 18.
[119] Revoked by SI 2007/2974, reg 64(4).
[120] Inserted by SI 2004/3426, reg 41(d)(ii).
[121] Inserted by SI 2007/2974, reg 64(4).
[122] Inserted by SI 2001/1128, r 20(c).
[123] Inserted by SI 2001/1128, r 20(d).

(5) The Registrar shall send the document prepared pursuant to a direction of the Minister in accordance with paragraph (3)(a) and the full document without the omissions made pursuant to that direction—

    (a) to whichever of the appellant and the respondent was not the [claimant][124] in the proceedings before the employment tribunal;

    (b) if he was not an excluded person, to the person who was the [claimant][125] in the proceedings before the employment tribunal and, if he was not an excluded person, to his representative;

    (c) if applicable, to the special advocate; and

    (d) where there are proceedings before a superior court relating to the order in question, to that court.

(6) Where the Appeal Tribunal intends to take steps under rule 30A(2)(c) to keep secret all or part of the reasons for any order it makes, it shall send the full reasons for its order to the persons listed in subparagraphs (a) to (d) of paragraph (5), as appropriate.][126]

Registration and proof of awards in respect of exclusion or expulsion from, or unjustifiable discipline by, a trade union

32.—(1) This rule applies where an application has been made to the Appeal Tribunal under section 67 or 176 of the 1992 Act.

(2) Without prejudice to rule 31, where the Appeal Tribunal makes an order in respect of an application to which this rule applies, and that order—

    (a) makes an award of compensation, or

    (b) is or includes an order of the kind referred to in rule 8(b)(ii), or both, the Registrar shall as soon as may be enter a copy of the order, sealed with the seal of the Tribunal, into a register kept by the Tribunal (in this rule referred to as 'the Register').

(3) The production in any proceedings in any court of a document, purporting to be certified by the Registrar to be a true copy of an entry in the Register of an order to which this rule applies shall, unless the contrary is proved, be sufficient evidence of the document and of the facts stated therein.

Review of decisions and correction of errors

33.—(1) The Appeal Tribunal may, either of its own motion or on application, review any order made by it and may, on such review, revoke or vary that order on the grounds that—

    (a) the order was wrongly made as the result of an error on the part of the Tribunal or its staff;

    (b) a party did not receive proper notice of the proceedings leading to the order; or

    (c) the interests of justice require such review.

(2) An application under paragraph (1) above shall be made within 14 days of the date of the order.

(3) A clerical mistake in any order arising from an accidental slip or omission may at any time be corrected by, or on the authority of, a judge or member.

[(4) The decision to grant or refuse an application for review may be made by a judge.][127]

[General power to make costs or expenses orders

34.—(1) In the circumstances listed in rule 34A the Appeal Tribunal may make an order ('a costs order') that a party or a special advocate, ('the paying party') make a payment in respect of the costs incurred by another party or a special advocate ('the receiving party'). [128]

(2) For the purposes of these Rules 'costs' includes fees, charges, disbursements and expenses incurred by or on behalf of a party or special advocate in relation to the proceedings, including the reimbursement allowed to a litigant in person under rule 34D. In Scotland, all references to costs or costs orders (except in the expression 'wasted costs') shall be read as references to expenses or orders for expenses.

(3) A costs order may be made against or in favour of a respondent who has not had an answer accepted in the proceedings in relation to the conduct of any part which he has taken in the proceedings.

---

[124] Substituted by SI 2004/2526, r 16.
[125] Substituted by SI 2004/2526, r 16.
[126] Inserted by SI 2001/1128, r 21.
[127] Inserted by SI 2004/2526, r 19.
[128] Substituted by SI 2004/2526, r 20.

(4) A party or special advocate may apply to the Appeal Tribunal for a costs order to be made at any time during the proceedings. An application may also be made at the end of a hearing, or in writing to the Registrar within 14 days of the date on which the order of the Appeal Tribunal finally disposing of the proceedings was sent to the parties.

(5) No costs order shall be made unless the Registrar has sent notice to the party or special advocate against whom the order may be made giving him the opportunity to give reasons why the order should not be made. This paragraph shall not be taken to require the Registrar to send notice to the party or special advocate if the party or special advocate has been given an opportunity to give reasons orally to the Appeal Tribunal as to why the order should not be made.

(6) Where the Appeal Tribunal makes a costs order it shall provide written reasons for doing so if a request for written reasons is made within 21 days of the date of the costs order. The Registrar shall send a copy of the written reasons to all the parties to the proceedings.]

[When a costs or expenses order may be made

34A.—(1) Where it appears to the Appeal Tribunal that any proceedings brought by the paying party were unnecessary, improper, vexatious or misconceived or that there has been unreasonable delay or other unreasonable conduct in the bringing or conducting of proceedings by the paying party, the Appeal Tribunal may make a costs order against the paying party.[129]

(2) The Appeal Tribunal may in particular make a costs order against the paying party when—

(a) he has not complied with a direction of the Appeal Tribunal;

(b) he has amended its notice of appeal, document provided under rule 3 sub-paragraphs (5) or (6), Respondent's answer or statement of grounds of cross-appeal, or document provided under rule 6 sub-paragraphs (7) or (8); or

(c) he has caused an adjournment of proceedings.

[(2A) If the Appeal Tribunal allows an appeal, in full or in part, it may make a costs order against the respondent specifying the respondent pay to the appellant an amount no greater than any fee paid by the appellant under a notice issued by the Lord Chancellor.][130]

(3) Nothing in paragraph (2) [or (2A)][131] shall restrict the Appeal Tribunal's discretion to award costs under paragraph (1).]

[The amount of a costs or expenses order

34B.—(1) Subject to sub-paragraphs (2) and (3) the amount of a costs order against the paying party can be determined in the following ways:[132]

(a) the Appeal Tribunal may specify the sum which the paying party must pay to the receiving party;

(b) the parties may agree on a sum to be paid by the paying party to the receiving party and if they do so the costs order shall be for the sum agreed; or

(c) the Appeal Tribunal may order the paying party to pay the receiving party the whole or a specified part of the costs of the receiving party with the amount to be paid being determined by way of detailed assessment in the High Court in accordance with the Civil Procedure Rules 1998 or in Scotland the Appeal Tribunal may direct that it be taxed by the Auditor of the Court of Session, from whose decision an appeal shall lie to a judge.

(2) The Appeal Tribunal may have regard to the paying party's ability to pay when considering the amount of a costs order.

(3) The costs of an assisted person in England and Wales shall be determined by detailed assessment in accordance with the Civil Procedure Rules.]

[Personal liability of representatives for costs

34C.—(1) The Appeal Tribunal may make a wasted costs order against a party's representative.[133]

(2) In a wasted costs order the Appeal Tribunal may disallow or order the representative of a party to meet the whole or part of any wasted costs of any party, including an order that the representative repay to his client any costs which have already been paid.

---

[129] Inserted by SI 2004/2526, r 21.
[130] Inserted by SI 2013/1693, r 7(a).
[131] Inserted by SI 2013/1693, r 7(b).
[132] Inserted by SI 2004/2526, r 21.
[133] Inserted by SI 2004/2526, r 21.

(3) 'Wasted costs' means any costs incurred by a party (including the representative's own client and any party who does not have a legal representative):

   (a) as a result of any improper, unreasonable or negligent act or omission on the part of any representative; or

   (b) which, in the light of any such act or omission occurring after they were incurred, the Appeal Tribunal considers it reasonable to expect that party to pay.

(4) In this rule 'representative' means a party's legal or other representative or any employee of such representative [...].[134]

(5) Before making a wasted costs order, the Appeal Tribunal shall give the representative a reasonable opportunity to make oral or written representations as to reasons why such an order should not be made. The Appeal Tribunal may also have regard to the representative's ability to pay when considering whether it shall make a wasted costs order or how much that order should be.

(6) When the Appeal Tribunal makes a wasted costs order, it must specify in the order the amount to be disallowed or paid.

(7) The Registrar shall inform the representative's client in writing—

   (a) of any proceedings under this rule; or

   (b) of any order made under this rule against the party's representative.

(8) Where the Appeal Tribunal makes a wasted costs order it shall provide written reasons for doing so if a request is made for written reasons within 21 days of the date of the wasted costs order. The Registrar shall send a copy of the written reasons to all parties to the proceedings.]

[Litigants in person and party litigants

34D.—(1) This rule applies where the Appeal Tribunal makes a costs order in favour of a party who is a litigant in person.[135]

(2) The costs allowed under this rule must not exceed, except in the case of a disbursement, two-thirds of the amount which would have been allowed if the litigant in person had been represented by a legal representative.

(3) The litigant in person shall be allowed—

   (a) costs for the same categories of—

      (i) work; and

      (ii) disbursements,

     which would have been allowed if the work had been done or the disbursements had been made by a legal representative on the litigant in person's behalf;

   (b) the payments reasonably made by him for legal services relating to the conduct of the proceedings;

   (c) the costs of obtaining expert assistance in assessing the costs claim; and

   (d) other expenses incurred by him in relation to the proceedings.

(4) The amount of costs to be allowed to the litigant in person for any item of work claimed shall be—

   (a) where the litigant in person can prove financial loss, the amount that he can prove he had lost for the time reasonably spent on doing the work; or

   (b) where the litigant in person cannot prove financial loss, an amount for the time which the Tribunal considers reasonably spent on doing the work at the rate of £25.00 per hour;

(5) For the year commencing 6th April 2006 the hourly rate of £25.00 shall be increased by the sum of £1.00 and for each subsequent year commencing on 6 April, the hourly rate for the previous year shall also be increased by the sum of £1.00.

(6) A litigant in person who is allowed costs for attending at court to conduct his case is not entitled to a witness allowance in respect of such attendance in addition to those costs.

(7) For the purpose of this rule, a litigant in person includes—

   (a) a company or other corporation which is acting without a legal representative; and

   (b) in England and Wales a barrister, solicitor, solicitor's employee or other authorised litigator (as defined in the Courts and Legal Services Act), who is acting for himself; and

   (c) in Scotland, an advocate or solicitor (within the meaning of the Solicitors (Scotland) Act 1980) who is acting for himself.

---

[134] Revoked by SI 2013/1693, r 8.

[135] Inserted by SI 2004/2526, r 21.

Appendix 1 Selected Legislation: Rules

(8) In the application of this rule to Scotland, references to a litigant in person shall be read as references to a party litigant.]

Service of documents

35.—(1) Any notice or other document required or authorised by these Rules to be served on, or delivered to, any person may be sent to him by post to his address for service or, where no address for service has been given, to his registered office, principal place of business, head or main office or last known address, as the case may be, and any notice or other document required or authorised to be served on, or delivered to, the Appeal Tribunal may be sent by post or delivered to the Registrar—

(a) in the case of a notice instituting proceedings, at the central office or any other office of the Tribunal; or

(b) in any other case, at the office of the Tribunal in which the proceedings in question are being dealt with in accordance with rule 38(2).

(2) Any notice or other document required or authorised to be served on, or delivered to, an unincorporated body may be sent to its secretary, manager or other similar officer.

(3) Every document served by post shall be assumed, in the absence of evidence to the contrary, to have been delivered in the normal course of post.

(4) The Appeal Tribunal may inform itself in such manner as it thinks fit of the posting of any document by an officer of the Tribunal.

(5) The Appeal Tribunal may direct that service of any document be dispensed with or be effected otherwise than in the manner prescribed by these Rules.

Conciliation

36 Where at any stage of any proceedings it appears to the Appeal Tribunal that there is a reasonable prospect of agreement being reached between the parties [or of disposal of the appeal or a part of it by consensual means],[136] the Tribunal may take such steps as it thinks fit to enable the parties to avail themselves of any opportunities for conciliation, whether by adjourning any proceedings or otherwise.

Time

37.—(1) The time prescribed by these Rules or by order of the Appeal Tribunal for doing any act may be extended (whether it has already expired or not) or abridged, and the date appointed for any purpose may be altered, by order of the Tribunal.

[(1A) Where an act is required to be done on or before a particular day it shall be done by 4 pm on that day.][137]

(2) Where the last day for the doing of any act falls on a day on which the appropriate office of the Tribunal is closed and by reason thereof the act cannot be done on that day, it may be done on the next day on which that office is open.

(3) An application for an extension of the time prescribed for the doing of an act, including the institution of an appeal under rule 3, shall be heard and determined as an [interim][138] application under rule 20.

[(4) An application for an extension of the time prescribed for the institution of an appeal under rule 3 shall not be heard until the notice of appeal has been served on the Appeal Tribunal.][139]

Tribunal offices and allocation of business

38.—(1) The central office and any other office of the Appeal Tribunal shall be open at such times as the President may direct.

(2) Any proceedings before the Tribunal may be dealt with at the central office or at such other office as the President may direct.

Non-compliance with, and waiver of, rules

39.—(1) Failure to comply with any requirements of these Rules shall not invalidate any proceedings unless the Appeal Tribunal otherwise directs.

---

[136] Inserted by SI 2004/2526, r 22.
[137] Inserted by SI 2004/2526, r 23(1).
[138] Substituted by SI 2004/2526, r 23(2).
[139] Inserted by SI 2001/1128, r 23.

(2) The Tribunal may, if it considers that to do so would lead to the more expeditious or economical disposal of any proceedings or would otherwise be desirable in the interests of justice, dispense with the taking of any step required or authorised by these Rules, or may direct that any such steps be taken in some manner other than that prescribed by these Rules.

(3) The powers of the Tribunal under paragraph (2) extend to authorising the institution of an appeal notwithstanding that the period prescribed in rule 3(2) may not have commenced.

Transitional provisions

40.—(1) Where, prior to 16th December 1993, an [employment tribunal][140] has given full written reasons for its decision or order, those reasons shall be treated as extended written reasons for the purposes of rule 3(1)(c) and rule 3(2) and for the purposes of Form 1 in the Schedule to these Rules.

(2) Anything validly done under or pursuant to the Employment Appeal Tribunal Rules 1980 shall be treated as having been done validly for the purposes of these Rules, whether or not what was done could have been done under or pursuant to these Rules.

SCHEDULE

[RULE 3 FORM 1

Notice of Appeal from Decision of Employment Tribunal

1   The appellant is (*name and address of appellant*).[141]

2   Any communication relating to this appeal may be sent to the appellant at (*appellant's address for service, including telephone number if any*).

3   The appellant appeals from (*here give particulars of the judgment, decision or order of the employment tribunal from which the appeal is brought including the location of the employment tribunal and the date*).

4   The parties to the proceedings before the employment tribunal, other than the appellant, were (*name and addresses of other parties to the proceedings resulting in judgment, decision or order appealed from*).

5   Copies of—
   (a) the written record of the employment tribunal's judgment, decision or order and the written reasons of the employment tribunal;
   (b) the claim (ET1);
   (c) the response (ET3); and/or (*where relevant*);
   (d) an explanation as to why any of these documents are not included; are attached to this notice.

6   If the appellant has made an application to the employment tribunal for a review of its judgment or decision, copies of—
   (a) the review application;
   (b) the judgment;
   (c) the written reasons of the employment tribunal in respect of that review application; and/or;
   (d) a statement by or on behalf of the appellant, if such be the case, that a judgment is awaited are attached to this Notice. If any of these documents exist but cannot be included, then a written explanation must be given.

7   The grounds upon which this appeal is brought are that the employment tribunal erred in law in that (*here set out in paragraphs the various grounds of appeal*).

Signed: Date:

NB.—The details entered on your Notice of Appeal must be legible and suitable for photocopying or electronic scanning. The use of black ink or typescript is recommended.]

Appendix 1 Selected Legislation: Rules

---

[140] Substituted by the Employment Rights (Dispute Resolution) Act 1998, s 1(2)(a).
[141] Substituted by SI 2005/1871, r 3.

[Rule 3 Form 1A]

Notice of Appeal from the CAC Made Pursuant to Regulation 38(8) of the Transnational Information and Consultation of Employees Regulations 1999, [[...][142] regulation 47(6) of the European Public Limited-Liability Company Regulations 2004][143] [[...][144] regulation 35(6) of the Information and Consultation of Employees Regulations 2004][145] [or regulation 57(6) of the Companies (Cross-Border Mergers) Regulations 2007][146]

1 The appellant is (name and address of appellant).
2 Any communication relating to this appeal may be sent to the appellant at (appellant's address for service, including telephone number if any).
3 The appellant appeals from (here give particulars of the decision, declaration or order of the CAC from which the appeal is brought including the date).
4 The parties to the proceedings before the CAC, other than the appellant, were (names and addresses of other parties to the proceedings resulting in decision appealed from).
5 A copy of the CAC's decision, declaration or order appealed from is attached to this notice.
6 The grounds upon which this appeal is brought are that the CAC erred in law in that (here set out in paragraphs the various grounds of appeal).

Date

Signed][147]

Rule 3 Form 2

Notice of Appeal from Decision of Certification Officer

1 The appellant is (name and address of appellant).
2 Any communication relating to this appeal may be sent to the appellant at (appellant's address for service, including telephone number if any).
3 The appellant appeals from (here give particulars of the order or decision of the Certification Officer from which the appeal is brought).
4 The appellant's grounds of appeal are: (here state the grounds of appeal).
5 A copy of the Certification Officer's decision is attached to this notice.

Date

Signed

Rule 6 Form 3

[Appeal from decision of employment tribunal/certification officer]

Respondent's Answer[148]

1 The respondent is (name and address of respondent).
2 Any communication relating to this appeal may be sent to the respondent at (respondent's address for service, including telephone number if any).
3 The respondent intends to resist the appeal of (here give the name of appellant). The grounds on which the respondent will rely are (the grounds relied upon by the [employment tribunal][149]/ Certification Officer for making the [judgment,][150] decision or order appealed from) (and) (the following grounds): (here set out any grounds which differ from those relied upon by the [employment tribunal][151] or Certification Officer, as the case may be).
4 The respondent cross-appeals from (here give particulars of the decision appealed from).
5 The respondent's grounds of appeal are: (here state the grounds of appeal).

Date

Signed

---

[142] Revoked by SI 2004/3426, reg 41(e)(i).
[143] Inserted by SI 2004/2526, r 25(1).
[144] Revoked by SI 2007/2974, reg 64(5).
[145] Inserted by SI 2004/3426, reg 41(e)(ii).
[146] Inserted by SI 2007/2974, reg 64(5).
[147] Inserted by SI 2001/1128, r 24.
[148] Inserted by SI 2005/1871, r 3(b)(i).
[149] Substituted by the Employment Rights (Dispute Resolution) Act 1998, s 1(2)(a).
[150] Inserted by SI 2005/1871, r 3(b)(ii).
[151] Substituted by the Employment Rights (Dispute Resolution) Act 1998, s 1(2)(a).

RULE 8 FORM 4

Application to the Employment Appeal Tribunal for Compensation for Exclusion or Expulsion from a Trade Union or for Compensation or an Order in respect of Unjustifiable Discipline

1   My name is My address is
2   Any communication relating to this application may be sent to me at (state address for service, including telephone number, if any).
3   My complaint against (state the name and address of the trade union) was declared to be well-founded by (state tribunal) on (give date of decision or order).
4   (Where the application relates to exclusion or expulsion from a trade union) I have not been admitted/ re-admitted* to membership of the above-named trade union and hereby apply for compensation on the following grounds.
    (Where the application relates to unjustifiable discipline) The determination infringing my right not to be unjustifiably disciplined has not been revoked./The trade union has failed to take all the steps necessary for securing the reversal of things done for the purpose of giving effect to the determination.*

(*Delete as appropriate)

Date

Signed

NB.—A copy of the decision or order declaring the complaint against the trade union to be well-founded must be enclosed with this application.

[FORM 4A][...][152]

[RULE 16AA FORM 4B

[Applications under Regulation 33 of the European Public Limited-Liability Company Regulations 2004 [or regulation 22 of the Information and Consultation of Employees Regulations 2004][153] [or regulation 53 of the Companies (Cross-Border Mergers) Regulations 2007][154] [or regulation 20, 21 or 21A of the 1999 Regulations][155]

1   The applicant's name is (name and address of applicant)
2   Any communication relating to this application may be sent to the applicant at (applicant's address for service, including telephone number if any).
3   The application is made against (state identity of respondent)
4   The address of the respondent is
5   The Central Arbitration Committee made a declaration [or decision (delete which does not apply)][156] in my favour on [] (insert date) and I request the Employment Tribunal to issue a penalty notice in accordance with regulation 33 of the European Public Limited-Liability Company Regulations 2004 [or regulation 22 of the Information and Consultation of Employees Regulations 2004 [or regulation 53 of the Companies (Cross-Border Mergers) Regulations 2007][157] [or regulation 20, 21 or 21A of the Transnational Information and Consultation of Employees Regulations 1999][158] (delete which does not apply)].[159]

Date.....................................

Signed.................................][160]

Appendix 1 Selected Legislation: Rules

---

[152] Inserted by SI 2001/1128, r 25 Revoked by SI 2010/1088, regs 2, 30(1), (9)(a).
[153] Inserted by SI 2004/3426, reg 41(f)(i).
[154] Inserted by SI 2007/2974, reg 64(6)(a).
[155] Inserted by SI 2010/1088, regs 2, 30(1), (9)(b).
[156] Inserted by SI 2010/1088, regs 2, 30(1), (9)(c).
[157] Inserted by SI 2007/2974, reg 64(6)(b).
[158] Inserted by SI 2010/1088, regs 2, 30(1), (9)(c).
[159] Inserted by SI 2004/3426, reg 41(f)(ii).
[160] Inserted by SI 2004/2526, r 25(2).

RULE 11 FORM 5

Notice of appearance to Application to Employment Appeal Tribunal for Compensation for Exclusion or Expulsion from a Trade Union or for Compensation or an Order in respect of Unjustifiable Discipline

1   The respondent trade union is (name and address of union).

2   Any communication relating to this application may be sent to the respondent at (respondent's address for service, including telephone number, if any).

3   The respondent intends to resist the application of (here give name of the applicant). The grounds on which the respondent will rely are as follows:

4   (Where the application relates to exclusion or expulsion from the trade union, state whether or not the applicant had been admitted or re-admitted to membership on or before the date of application.) (Where the application relates to unjustifiable discipline, state whether—

    (a) the determination infringing the applicant's right not to be unjustifiably disciplined has been revoked; and

    (b) the trade union has taken all the steps necessary for securing the reversal of anything done for the purpose of giving effect to the determination.)

Date

Signed

Position in union

[RULE 16C FORM 5A

Notice of Appearance to the Employment Appeal Tribunal under [Regulation 20, 21 or 21A of the Transnational Information and Consultation of Employees Regulations 1999 or Regulation 20(6) of the European Public Limited-Liability Company (Employee Involvement) (Great Britain) Regulations 2009 or Regulation 22(6) of the Information and Consultation of Employees Regulations 2004 or Regulation 53(6) of the Companies (Cross-Border Mergers) Regulations 2007][161]

1   The respondent is (name and address of respondent).

2   Any communication relating to this application may be sent to the respondent at (respondent's address for service, including telephone number, if any).

3   The respondent intends to resist the application of (here give the name or description of the applicant). The grounds on which the respondent will rely are as follows: (give particulars, set out in paragraphs and making reference to the specific provisions in the Transnational Information and Consultation of Employees Regulations 1999 [or European Public Limited-Liability Company (Employee Involvement) (Great Britain) Regulations 2009 or Information and Consultation of Employees Regulations 2004 or Companies (Cross-Border Mergers) Regulations 2007][162] alleged to have been breached).

Date

Signed]

Position in respondent company or undertaking:

(Where appropriate give position in respondent central or local management or position held in relation to respondent Works Council)][163]

RULE 13 FORM 6

Application to the Employment Appeal Tribunal Under [Section 33 of the 1996 Act][164] *for a Restriction of Proceedings Order*

1   The applicant is (the Attorney General/Lord Advocate).

2   Any communication relating to this application may be sent to the applicant at (state address for service, including telephone number).

---

[161] Substituted by SI 2010/1088, regs 2, 30(1), (9)(d).
[162] Inserted by SI 2010/1088, regs 2, 30(1), (9)(e).
[163] Inserted by SI 2001/1128, r 26.
[164] Substituted by SI 2001/1128, r 27.

3   The application is for a restriction of proceedings order to be made against (state the name and address of the person against whom the order is sought).

4   An affidavit in support of the application is attached.

Date

Signed

RULE 15 FORM 7

Notice of appearance to Application to the Employment Appeal Tribunal under [section 33 of the 1996 Act][165] for a Restriction of Proceedings Order

1   The respondent is (state name and address of respondent).

2   Any communication relating to this application may be sent to the respondent at (respondent's address for service, including telephone number, if any).

3   The respondent intends to resist the application. An affidavit in support is attached to this notice.

Date

Signed

Appendix 1 Selected Legislation: Rules

---

[165] Substituted by SI 2001/1128, r 27.

The Employment Tribunals (Constitution and Rules of Procedure) Regulations 2013

SI 2013/1237

Citation and commencement

1.—(1) These Regulations may be cited as the Employment Tribunals (Constitution and Rules of Procedure) Regulations 2013 and the Rules of Procedure contained in Schedules 1, 2 and 3 may be referred to, respectively, as—
(a) the Employment Tribunals Rules of Procedure 2013;
(b) the Employment Tribunals (National Security) Rules of Procedure 2013; and
(c) the Employment Tribunals (Equal Value) Rules of Procedure 2013.
(2) This regulation and regulations 3 and 11 come into force on 1st July 2013 and the remainder of these Regulations (including the Schedules) come into force on 29th July 2013.

Revocation

2   Subject to the savings in regulation 15 the Employment Tribunals (Constitution and Rules of Procedure) Regulations 2004 are revoked.

Interpretation

3   Except in the Schedules which are subject to the definitions contained in the Schedules, in these Regulations—
'2004 Regulations' means the Employment Tribunals (Constitution and Rules of Procedure) Regulations 2004;
'appointing office holder' means, in England and Wales, the Lord Chancellor, and in Scotland, the Lord President;
'Employment Tribunals Act' means the Employment Tribunals Act 1996;
'Lord President' means the Lord President of the Court of Session;
'national security proceedings' means proceedings in relation to which a direction is given, or an order is made, under rule 94 of Schedule 1;
'President' means either of the two presidents appointed from time to time in accordance with regulation 5(1);
'Regional Employment Judge' means a person appointed or nominated in accordance with regulation 6(1) or (2);
'Senior President of Tribunals' means the person appointed in accordance with section 2 of the Tribunals, Courts and Enforcement Act 2007;
'Tribunal' means an employment tribunal established in accordance with regulation 4 and, in relation to any proceedings, means the Tribunal responsible for the proceedings in question, whether performing administrative or judicial functions;
'Vice President' means a person appointed or nominated in accordance with regulation 6(3) or (4).

Establishment of employment tribunals

4   There are to be tribunals known as employment tribunals.

President of Employment Tribunals

5.—(1) There shall be a President of Employment Tribunals, responsible for Tribunals in England and Wales, and a President of Employment Tribunals, responsible for Tribunals in Scotland, appointed by the appointing office holder.
(2) A President shall be—
(a) a person who satisfies the judicial-appointment eligibility condition within the meaning of section 50 of the Tribunals, Courts and Enforcement Act 2007 on a 5-year basis;
(b) an advocate or solicitor admitted in Scotland of at least five years standing; or
(c) a member of the Bar of Northern Ireland or solicitor of the Supreme Court of Northern Ireland of at least five years standing.
(3) A President may at any time resign from office by giving the appointing officer holder notice in writing to that effect.

(4) The appointing officer holder may remove a President from office on the ground of inability or misbehaviour, or if the President is adjudged to be bankrupt or makes a composition or arrangement with his creditors.

(5) Where a President is unable to carry out the functions set out in these Regulations, those functions may be discharged by a person nominated by the appointing office holder (save that any nomination in relation to England and Wales shall be made by the Lord Chief Justice following consultation with the Senior President of Tribunals, rather than by the Lord Chancellor).

(6) The Lord Chief Justice may nominate a judicial office holder (as defined in section 109(4) of the Constitutional Reform Act 2005) to exercise his functions under this regulation.

Regional Employment Judges and the Vice President

6.—(1) The Lord Chancellor may appoint Regional Employment Judges.

(2) The President (England and Wales) or the Regional Employment Judge for an area may nominate an Employment Judge to discharge the functions of the Regional Employment Judge for that area.

(3) The Lord President may appoint a Vice President.

(4) The President (Scotland) or the Vice President may nominate an Employment Judge to discharge the functions of the Vice President.

(5) Appointments and nominations under this regulation shall be from the salaried[166] Employment Judges on the panel referred to in regulation 8(2)(a).

Responsibilities of the Presidents, Regional Employment Judges and Vice President

7.—(1) The President shall, in relation to the area for which the President is responsible, use the resources available to—

(a) secure, so far as practicable, the speedy and efficient disposal of proceedings;

(b) determine the allocation of proceedings between Tribunals; and

(c) determine where and when Tribunals shall sit.

(2) The President (England and Wales) may direct Regional Employment Judges, and the President (Scotland) may direct the Vice President, to take action in relation to the fulfilment of the responsibilities in paragraph (1) and the Regional Employment Judges and Vice President shall follow such directions.

Panels of members for tribunals

8.—(1) There shall be three panels of members for the Employment Tribunals (England and Wales) and three panels of members for the Employment Tribunals (Scotland).

(2) The panels of members shall be—

(a) a panel of Employment Judges[167] who satisfy the criteria set out in regulation 5(2) and are appointed by the appointing office holder;

(b) a panel of persons appointed by the Lord Chancellor after consultation with organisations or associations representative of employees; and

(c) a panel of persons appointed by the Lord Chancellor after consultation with organisations or associations representative of employers.

(3) Members of the panels shall hold and vacate office in accordance with the terms of their appointment, but may resign from office by written notice to the person who appointed them under paragraph (2), and any member who ceases to hold office shall be eligible for reappointment.

(4) The President may establish further specialist panels of members referred to in paragraph (2) and may select persons from those panels to deal with proceedings in which particular specialist knowledge would be beneficial.

Composition of tribunals

9.—(1) Where proceedings are to be determined by a Tribunal comprising an Employment Judge and two other members, the President, Vice President or a Regional Employment Judge shall select—

(a) an Employment Judge; and

(b) one member from each of the panels referred to in regulation 8(2)(b) and (c), and for all other proceedings shall select an Employment Judge.

Appendix 1 Selected Legislation: Rules

---

[166] As amended by SI 2014/271, r 2.
[167] As amended by S1 2014/271, r 3.

(2) The President, Vice President or a Regional Employment Judge may select him or herself as the Employment Judge required under paragraph (1).

(3) The President, Vice President or a Regional Employment Judge may select from the appropriate panel a substitute for a member previously selected to hear any proceedings.

(4) This regulation does not apply in relation to national security proceedings (see regulation 10(2)).

National security proceedings—panel of members and composition of tribunals

10.—(1) The President shall select—

(a) a panel of persons from the panel referred to in regulation 8(2)(a);

(b) a panel of persons from the panel referred to in regulation 8(2)(b); and

(c) a panel of persons from the panel referred to in regulation 8(2)(c), who may act in national security proceedings.

(2) Where proceedings become national security proceedings, the President, Vice President or a Regional Employment Judge shall—

(a) select an Employment Judge from the panel referred to in paragraph (1)(a) and may select him or herself; and

(b) where the proceedings are to be determined by a Tribunal comprising an Employment Judge and two other members, select in addition one member from each of the panels referred to in sub-paragraphs (b) and (c) of paragraph (1).

Practice directions

11.—(1) The President may make, vary or revoke practice directions about the procedure of the Tribunals in the area for which the President is responsible, including—

(a) practice directions about the exercise by Tribunals of powers under these Regulations (including the Schedules); and

(b) practice directions about the provision by Employment Judges of mediation, in relation to disputed matters in a case that is the subject of proceedings, and may permit an Employment Judge to act as mediator in a case even though they have been selected to decide matters in that case.

(2) Practice directions may make different provision for different cases, different areas, or different types of proceedings.

(3) Any practice direction made, varied or revoked shall be published by the President in an appropriate manner to bring it to the attention of the persons to whom it is addressed.

Power to prescribe

12.—(1) The Secretary of State may prescribe—

(a) one or more versions of a form which shall be used by claimants to start proceedings in a Tribunal;

(b) one or more versions of a form which shall be used by respondents to respond to a claim before a Tribunal; and

(c) that the provision of certain information on the prescribed forms is mandatory.

(2) It is not necessary to use a form prescribed under paragraph (1) if the proceedings are—

(a) referred to a Tribunal by a court;

(b) proceedings in which a Tribunal will be exercising its appellate jurisdiction; or

(c) proceedings brought by an employer under section 11 of the Employment Rights Act 1996.

(3) The Secretary of State shall publish the prescribed forms in an appropriate manner to bring them to the attention of prospective claimants, respondents and their advisers.

Application of Schedules 1 to 3

13.—(1) Subject to paragraph (2), Schedule 1 applies to all proceedings before a Tribunal except where separate rules of procedure made under the provisions of any enactment are applicable.

(2) Schedules 2 and 3 apply to modify the rules in Schedule 1 in relation, respectively, to proceedings which are—

(a) national security proceedings; or

(b) proceedings which involve an equal value claim (as defined in rule 1 of Schedule 3).

Register and proof of judgments

14.—(1) The Lord Chancellor shall maintain a register containing a copy of all judgments and written reasons issued by a Tribunal which are required to be entered in the register under Schedules 1 to 3.

(2) The Lord Chancellor shall delete any entry in the register six years from the date of judgment.

(3) A document purporting to be certified by a member of staff of a Tribunal to be a true copy of an entry of a judgment in the register shall, unless the contrary is proved, be sufficient evidence of the document and its contents.

Transitional provisions

15.—(1) Subject to paragraphs (2) and (3), these Regulations and the Rules of Procedure contained in Schedules 1 to 3 apply in relation to all proceedings to which they relate.

(2) Where a respondent receives from a Tribunal a copy of the claim form before 29th July 2013, rules 23 to 25 of Schedule 1 do not apply to the proceedings and rule 7 of Schedule 1 to the 2004 Regulations continues to apply.

(3) Where in accordance with Schedules 3 to 5 of the 2004 Regulations, a notice of appeal was presented to a Tribunal before 29th July 2013, Schedule 1 does not apply to the proceedings and Schedule 3, 4 or 5, as appropriate, of the 2004 Regulations continues to apply.

Jo Swinson
Parliamentary Under Secretary of State for Employment Relations and Consumer Affairs
Date   Department for Business, Innovation and Skills

SCHEDULE 1

REGULATION 13(1)

THE EMPLOYMENT TRIBUNALS RULES OF PROCEDURE

CONTENTS

Introductory and General

Starting a Claim

The Response to the Claim

Appendix 1 Selected Legislation: Rules

INTRODUCTORY AND GENERAL

Interpretation

1.—(1) In these Rules—
  'ACAS' means the Advisory, Conciliation and Arbitration Service referred to in section 247 of the Trade Union and Labour Relations (Consolidation) Act 1992;
  'claim' means any proceedings before an Employment Tribunal making a complaint;
  'claimant' means the person bringing the claim;
  'Commission for Equality and Human Rights' means the body established under section 1 of the Equality Act 2006;
  'complaint' means anything that is referred to as a claim, complaint, reference, application or appeal in any enactment which confers jurisdiction on the Tribunal;
  'Employment Appeal Tribunal' means the Employment Appeal Tribunal established under section 87 of the Employment Protection Act 1975 and continued in existence under section 135 of the Employment Protection (Consolidation) Act 1978 and section 20(1) of the Employment Tribunals Act; 'electronic communication' has the meaning given to it by section 15(1) of the Electronic Communications Act 2000;
  'employee's contract claim' means a claim brought by an employee in accordance with articles 3 and 7 of the Employment Tribunals Extension of Jurisdiction (England and Wales) Order 1 or articles 3 and 7 of the Employment Tribunals Extension of Jurisdiction (Scotland) Order 1994;
  'employer's contract claim' means a claim brought by an employer in accordance with articles 4 and 8 of the Employment Tribunals Extension of Jurisdiction (England and Wales) Order 1994 or articles 4 and 8 of the Employment Tribunals Extension of Jurisdiction (Scotland) Order 1994; 'Employment Tribunal' or 'Tribunal' means an employment tribunal established in accordance with regulation 4, and in relation

to any proceedings means the Tribunal responsible for the proceedings in question, whether performing administrative or judicial functions;

'Employment Tribunals Act' means the Employment Tribunals Act 1996;

'Equality Act' means the Equality Act 2010;

'full tribunal' means a Tribunal constituted in accordance with section 4(1) of the Employment Tribunals Act;

'Health and Safety Act' means the Health and Safety at Work etc. Act 1974;

'improvement notice' means a notice under section 21 of the Health and Safety Act;

'levy appeal' means an appeal against an assessment to a levy imposed under section 11 of the Industrial Training Act 1982;

'Minister' means Minister of the Crown;

'prescribed form' means any appropriate form prescribed by the Secretary of State in accordance with regulation 12;

'present' means deliver (by any means permitted under rule 85) to a tribunal office;

'President' means either of the two presidents appointed from time to time in accordance with regulation 5(1);

'prohibition notice' means a notice under section 22 of the Health and Safety Act;

'Regional Employment Judge' means a person appointed or nominated in accordance with regulation 6(1) or (2);

'Register' means the register of judgments and written reasons kept in accordance with regulation 14;

'remission application' means any application which may be made under any enactment for remission or part remission of a Tribunal fee;

'respondent' means the person or persons against whom the claim is made;

'Tribunal fee' means any fee which is payable by a party under any enactment in respect of a claim, employer's contract claim, application or judicial mediation in an Employment Tribunal;

'tribunal office' means any office which has been established for any area in either England and Wales or Scotland and which carries out administrative functions in support of the Tribunal, and in relation to particular proceedings it is the office notified to the parties as dealing with the proceedings;

'unlawful act notice' means a notice under section 21 of the Equality Act 2006;

'Vice President' means a person appointed or nominated in accordance with regulation 6(3) or (4);'writing' includes writing delivered by means of electronic communication.

(2) Any reference in the Rules to a Tribunal applies to both a full tribunal and to an Employment Judge acting alone (in accordance with section 4(2) or (6) of the Employment Tribunals Act).

(3) An order or other decision of the Tribunal is either—

    (a) a 'case management order', being an order or decision of any kind in relation to the conduct of proceedings, not including the determination of any issue which would be the subject of a judgment; or

    (b) a 'judgment', being a decision, made at any stage of the proceedings (but not including a decision under rule 13 or 19), which finally determines—

        (i) a claim, or part of a claim, as regards liability, remedy or costs (including preparation time and wasted costs); or

        (ii) any issue which is capable of finally disposing of any claim, or part of a claim, even if it does not necessarily do so (for example, an issue whether a claim should be struck out or a jurisdictional issue).

Overriding objective

2 The overriding objective of these Rules is to enable Employment Tribunals to deal with cases fairly and justly. Dealing with a case fairly and justly includes, so far as practicable—

    (a) ensuring that the parties are on an equal footing;

    (b) dealing with cases in ways which are proportionate to the complexity and importance of the issues;

    (c) avoiding unnecessary formality and seeking flexibility in the proceedings;

    (d) avoiding delay, so far as compatible with proper consideration of the issues; and

    (e) saving expense.

A Tribunal shall seek to give effect to the overriding objective in interpreting, or exercising any power given to it by, these Rules. The parties and their representatives shall assist the Tribunal to further the overriding objective and in particular shall co-operate generally with each other and with the Tribunal.

Alternative dispute resolution

3   A Tribunal shall wherever practicable and appropriate encourage the use by the parties of the services of ACAS, judicial or other mediation, or other means of resolving their disputes by agreement.

Time

4.—(1) Unless otherwise specified by the Tribunal, an act required by these Rules, a practice direction or an order of a Tribunal to be done on or by a particular day may be done at any time before midnight on that day. If there is an issue as to whether the act has been done by that time, the party claiming to have done it shall prove compliance.

(2) If the time specified by these Rules, a practice direction or an order for doing any act ends on a day other than a working day, the act is done in time if it is done on the next working day. 'Working day' means any day except a Saturday or Sunday, Christmas Day, Good Friday or a bank holiday under section 1 of the Banking and Financial Dealings Act 1971.

(3) Where any act is required to be, or may be, done within a certain number of days of or from an event, the date of that event shall not be included in the calculation. (For example, a response shall be presented within 28 days of the date on which the respondent was sent a copy of the claim: if the claim was sent on 1st October the last day for presentation of the response is 29th October.)

(4) Where any act is required to be, or may be, done not less than a certain number of days before or after an event, the date of that event shall not be included in the calculation. (For example, if a party wishes to present representations in writing for consideration by a Tribunal at a hearing, they shall be presented not less than 7 days before the hearing: if the hearing is fixed for 8th October, the representations shall be presented no later than 1st October.)

(5) Where the Tribunal imposes a time limit for doing any act, the last date for compliance shall, wherever practicable, be expressed as a calendar date.

(6) Where time is specified by reference to the date when a document is sent to a person by the Tribunal, the date when the document was sent shall, unless the contrary is proved, be regarded as the date endorsed on the document as the date of sending or, if there is no such endorsement, the date shown on the letter accompanying the document.

Extending or shortening time

5   The Tribunal may, on its own initiative or on the application of a party, extend or shorten any time limit specified in these Rules or in any decision, whether or not (in the case of an extension) it has expired.

Irregularities and non-compliance

6   A failure to comply with any provision of these Rules (except rule 8(1), 16(1), 23 or 25) or any order of the Tribunal (except for an order under rules 38 or 39) does not of itself render void the proceedings or any step taken in the proceedings. In the case of such non-compliance, the Tribunal may take such action as it considers just, which may include all or any of the following—

(a) waiving or varying the requirement;

(b) striking out the claim or the response, in whole or in part, in accordance with rule 37;

(c) barring or restricting a party's participation in the proceedings;

(d) awarding costs in accordance with rules 74 to 84.

Presidential Guidance

7   The Presidents may publish guidance for England and Wales and for Scotland, respectively, as to matters of practice and as to how the powers conferred by these Rules may be exercised. Any such guidance shall be published by the Presidents in an appropriate manner to bring it to the attention of claimants, respondents and their advisers. Tribunals must have regard to any such guidance, but they shall not be bound by it.

STARTING A CLAIM

Presenting the claim

8.—(1) A claim shall be started by presenting a completed claim form (using a prescribed form) in accordance with any practice direction made under regulation 11 which supplements this rule.

(2) A claim may be presented in England and Wales if—
  (a) the respondent, or one of the respondents, resides or carries on business in England and Wales;
  (b) one or more of the acts or omissions complained of took place in England and Wales;
  (c) the claim relates to a contract under which the work is or has been performed partly in England and Wales; or
  (d) the Tribunal has jurisdiction to determine the claim by virtue of a connection with Great Britain and the connection in question is at least partly a connection with England and Wales.
(3) A claim may be presented in Scotland if—
  (a) the respondent, or one of the respondents, resides or carries on business in Scotland;
  (b) one or more of the acts or omissions complained of took place in Scotland;
  (c) the claim relates to a contract under which the work is or has been performed partly in Scotland; or
  (d) the Tribunal has jurisdiction to determine the claim by virtue of a connection with Great Britain and the connection in question is at least partly a connection with Scotland.

Multiple claimants

9   Two or more claimants may make their claims on the same claim form if their claims are based on the same set of facts. Where two or more claimants wrongly include claims on the same claim form, this shall be treated as an irregularity falling under rule 6.

Rejection: form not used or failure to supply minimum information

10.—(1) The Tribunal shall reject a claim if—
  (a) it is not made on a prescribed form; or
  (b) it does not contain all of the following information—
      (i) each claimant's name;
      (ii) each claimant's address;
      (iii) each respondent's name;
      (iv) each respondent's address.
(2) The form shall be returned to the claimant with a notice of rejection explaining why it has been rejected. The notice shall contain information about how to apply for a reconsideration of the rejection.

Rejection: absence of Tribunal fee or remission application

11.—(1) The Tribunal shall reject a claim if it is not accompanied by a Tribunal fee or a remission application.
(2) Where a claim is accompanied by a Tribunal fee but the amount paid is lower than the amount payable for the presentation of that claim, the Tribunal shall send the claimant a notice specifying a date for payment of the additional amount due and the claim, or part of it in respect of which the relevant Tribunal fee has not been paid, shall be rejected by the Tribunal if the amount due is not paid by the date specified.
(3) If a remission application is refused in part or in full, the Tribunal shall send the claimant a notice specifying a date for payment of the Tribunal fee and the claim shall be rejected by the Tribunal if the Tribunal fee is not paid by the date specified.
(4) If a claim, or part of it, is rejected, the form shall be returned to the claimant with a notice of rejection explaining why it has been rejected.

Rejection: substantive defects

12.—(1) The staff of the tribunal office shall refer a claim form to an Employment Judge if they consider that the claim, or part of it, may be—
  (a) one which the Tribunal has no jurisdiction to consider; or
  (b) in a form which cannot sensibly be responded to or is otherwise an abuse of the process.
(2) The claim, or part of it, shall be rejected if the Judge considers that the claim, or part of it, is of a kind described in sub-paragraphs (a) or (b) of paragraph (1).
(3) If the claim is rejected, the form shall be returned to the claimant together with a notice of rejection giving the Judge's reasons for rejecting the claim, or part of it. The notice shall contain information about how to apply for a reconsideration of the rejection.

Reconsideration of rejection

13.—(1) A claimant whose claim has been rejected (in whole or in part) under rule 10 or 12 may apply for a reconsideration on the basis that either—
  (a) the decision to reject was wrong; or
  (b) the notified defect can be rectified.
(2) The application shall be in writing and presented to the Tribunal within 14 days of the date that the notice of rejection was sent. It shall explain why the decision is said to have been wrong or rectify the defect and if the claimant wishes to request a hearing this shall be requested in the application.
(3) If the claimant does not request a hearing, or an Employment Judge decides, on considering the application, that the claim shall be accepted in full, the Judge shall determine the application without a hearing. Otherwise the application shall be considered at a hearing attended only by the claimant.
(4) If the Judge decides that the original rejection was correct but that the defect has been rectified, the claim shall be treated as presented on the date that the defect was rectified.

Protected disclosure claims: notification to a regulator

14 If a claim alleges that the claimant has made a protected disclosure, the Tribunal may, with the consent of the claimant, send a copy of any accepted claim to a regulator listed in Schedule 1 to the Public Interest Disclosure (Prescribed Persons) Order 1999 'Protected disclosure' has the meaning given to it by section 43A of the Employment Rights Act 1996.

THE RESPONSE TO THE CLAIM

Sending claim form to respondents

15 Unless the claim is rejected, the Tribunal shall send a copy of the claim form, together with a prescribed response form, to each respondent with a notice which includes information on—
  (a) whether any part of the claim has been rejected; and
  (b) how to submit a response to the claim, the time limit for doing so and what will happen if a response is not received by the Tribunal within that time limit.

Response

16.—(1) The response shall be on a prescribed form and presented to the tribunal office within 28 days of the date that the copy of the claim form was sent by the Tribunal.
(2) A response form may include the response of more than one respondent if they are responding to a single claim and either they all resist the claim on the same grounds or they do not resist the claim.
(3) A response form may include the response to more than one claim if the claims are based on the same set of facts and either the respondent resists all of the claims on the same grounds or the respondent does not resist the claims.

Rejection: form not used or failure to supply minimum information

17.—(1) The Tribunal shall reject a response if—
  (a) it is not made on a prescribed form; or
  (b) it does not contain all of the following information—
    (i) the respondent's full name;
    (ii) the respondent's address;
    (iii) whether the respondent wishes to resist any part of the claim.
(2) The form shall be returned to the respondent with a notice of rejection explaining why it has been rejected. The notice shall explain what steps may be taken by the respondent, including the need (if appropriate) to apply for an extension of time, and how to apply for a reconsideration of the rejection.

Rejection: form presented late

18.—(1) A response shall be rejected by the Tribunal if it is received outside the time limit in rule 16 (or any extension of that limit granted within the original limit) unless an application for extension has already been made under rule 20 or the response includes or is accompanied by such an application (in which case the response shall not be rejected pending the outcome of the application).

(2) The response shall be returned to the respondent together with a notice of rejection explaining that the response has been presented late. The notice shall explain how the respondent can apply for an extension of time and how to apply for a reconsideration.

Reconsideration of rejection

19.—(1) A respondent whose response has been rejected under rule 17 or 18 may apply for a reconsideration on the basis that the decision to reject was wrong or, in the case of a rejection under rule 17, on the basis that the notified defect can be rectified.

(2) The application shall be in writing and presented to the Tribunal within 14 days of the date that the notice of rejection was sent. It shall explain why the decision is said to have been wrong or rectify the defect and it shall state whether the respondent requests a hearing.

(3) If the respondent does not request a hearing, or the Employment Judge decides, on considering the application, that the response shall be accepted in full, the Judge shall determine the application without a hearing. Otherwise the application shall be considered at a hearing attended only by the respondent.

(4) If the Judge decides that the original rejection was correct but that the defect has been rectified, the response shall be treated as presented on the date that the defect was rectified (but the Judge may extend time under rule 5).

Applications for extension of time for presenting response

20.—(1) An application for an extension of time for presenting a response shall be presented in writing and copied to the claimant. It shall set out the reason why the extension is sought and shall, except where the time limit has not yet expired, be accompanied by a draft of the response which the respondent wishes to present or an explanation of why that is not possible and if the respondent wishes to request a hearing this shall be requested in the application.

(2) The claimant may within 7 days of receipt of the application give reasons in writing explaining why the application is opposed.

(3) An Employment Judge may determine the application without a hearing.

(4) If the decision is to refuse an extension, any prior rejection of the response shall stand. If the decision is to allow an extension, any judgment issued under rule 21 shall be set aside.

Effect of non-presentation or rejection of response, or case not contested

21.—(1) Where on the expiry of the time limit in rule 16 no response has been presented, or any response received has been rejected and no application for a reconsideration is outstanding, or where the respondent has stated that no part of the claim is contested, paragraphs (2) and (3) shall apply.

(2) An Employment Judge shall decide whether on the available material (which may include further information which the parties are required by a Judge to provide), a determination can properly be made of the claim, or part of it. To the extent that a determination can be made, the Judge shall issue a judgment accordingly. Otherwise, a hearing shall be fixed before a Judge alone.

(3) The respondent shall be entitled to notice of any hearings and decisions of the Tribunal but, unless and until an extension of time is granted, shall only be entitled to participate in any hearing to the extent permitted by the Judge.

Notification of acceptance

22 Where the Tribunal accepts the response it shall send a copy of it to all other parties.

EMPLOYER'S CONTRACT CLAIM

Making an employer's contract claim

23 Any employer's contract claim shall be made as part of the response, presented in accordance with rule 16, to a claim which includes an employee's contract claim. An employer's contract claim may be rejected on the same basis as a claimant's claim may be rejected under rule 12, in which case rule 13 shall apply.

Notification of employer's contract claim

24 When the Tribunal sends the response to the other parties in accordance with rule 22 it shall notify the claimant that the response includes an employer's contract claim and include information on how to submit a response to the claim, the time limit for doing so, and what will happen if a response is not received by the Tribunal within that time limit.

Responding to an employer's contract claim

25 A claimant's response to an employer's contract claim shall be presented to the tribunal office within 28 days of the date that the response was sent to the claimant. If no response is presented within that time limit, rules 20 and 21 shall apply.

INITIAL CONSIDERATION OF CLAIM FORM AND RESPONSE

Initial consideration

26.—(1) As soon as possible after the acceptance of the response, the Employment Judge shall consider all of the documents held by the Tribunal in relation to the claim, to confirm whether there are arguable complaints and defences within the jurisdiction of the Tribunal (and for that purpose the Judge may order a party to provide further information).

(2) Except in a case where notice is given under rule 27 or 28, the Judge conducting the initial consideration shall make a case management order (unless made already), which may deal with the listing of a preliminary or final hearing, and may propose judicial mediation or other forms of dispute resolution.

Dismissal of claim (or part)

27.—(1) If the Employment Judge considers either that the Tribunal has no jurisdiction to consider the claim, or part of it, or that the claim, or part of it, has no reasonable prospect of success, the Tribunal shall send a notice to the parties—

(a) setting out the Judge's view and the reasons for it; and

(b) ordering that the claim, or the part in question, shall be dismissed on such date as is specified in the notice unless before that date the claimant has presented written representations to the Tribunal explaining why the claim (or part) should not be dismissed.

(2) If no such representations are received, the claim shall be dismissed from the date specified without further order (although the Tribunal shall write to the parties to confirm what has occurred).

(3) If representations are received within the specified time they shall be considered by an Employment Judge, who shall either permit the claim (or part) to proceed or fix a hearing for the purpose of deciding whether it should be permitted to do so. The respondent may, but need not, attend and participate in the hearing.

(4) If any part of the claim is permitted to proceed the Judge shall make a case management order.

Dismissal of response (or part)

28.—(1) If the Employment Judge considers that the response to the claim, or part of it, has no reasonable prospect of success the Tribunal shall send a notice to the parties—

(a) setting out the Judge's view and the reasons for it;

(b) ordering that the response, or the part in question, shall be dismissed on such date as is specified in the notice unless before that date the respondent has presented written representations to the Tribunal explaining why the response (or part) should not be dismissed; and

(c) specifying the consequences of the dismissal of the response, in accordance with paragraph (5) below.

(2) If no such representations are received, the response shall be dismissed from the date specified without further order (although the Tribunal shall write to the parties to confirm what has occurred).

(3) If representations are received within the specified time they shall be considered by an Employment Judge, who shall either permit the response (or part) to stand or fix a hearing for the purpose of

deciding whether it should be permitted to do so. The claimant may, but need not, attend and participate in the hearing.

(4) If any part of the response is permitted to stand the Judge shall make a case management order.

(5) Where a response is dismissed, the effect shall be as if no response had been presented, as set out in rule 21 above.

Case Management Orders and Other Powers

Case management orders

29 The Tribunal may at any stage of the proceedings, on its own initiative or on application, make a case management order. The particular powers identified in the following rules do not restrict that general power. A case management order may vary, suspend or set aside an earlier case management order where that is necessary in the interests of justice, and in particular where a party affected by the earlier order did not have a reasonable opportunity to make representations before it was made.

Applications for case management orders

30.—(1) An application by a party for a particular case management order may be made either at a hearing or presented in writing to the Tribunal.

(2) Where a party applies in writing, they shall notify the other parties that any objections to the application should be sent to the Tribunal as soon as possible.

(3) The Tribunal may deal with such an application in writing or order that it be dealt with at a preliminary or final hearing.

Disclosure of documents and information

31 The Tribunal may order any person in Great Britain to disclose documents or information to a party (by providing copies or otherwise) or to allow a party to inspect such material as might be ordered by a county court or, in Scotland, by a sheriff.

Requirement to attend to give evidence

32 The Tribunal may order any person in Great Britain to attend a hearing to give evidence, produce documents, or produce information.

Evidence from other EU Member States

33 The Tribunal may use the procedures for obtaining evidence prescribed in Council Regulation (EC) No. 1026/2001 of 28 May 2001 on cooperation between the courts of the Member States in the taking of evidence in civil or commercial matters.

Addition, substitution and removal of parties

34 The Tribunal may on its own initiative, or on the application of a party or any other person wishing to become a party, add any person as a party, by way of substitution or otherwise, if it appears that there are issues between that person and any of the existing parties falling within the jurisdiction of the Tribunal which it is in the interests of justice to have determined in the proceedings; and may remove any party apparently wrongly included.

Other persons

35 The Tribunal may permit any person to participate in proceedings, on such terms as may be specified, in respect of any matter in which that person has a legitimate interest.

Lead cases

36.—(1) Where a Tribunal considers that two or more claims give rise to common or related issues of fact or law, the Tribunal or the President may make an order specifying one or more of those claims as a lead case and staying, or in Scotland sisting, the other claims ('the related cases').

(2) When the Tribunal makes a decision in respect of the common or related issues it shall send a copy of that decision to each party in each of the related cases and, subject to paragraph (3), that decision shall be binding on each of those parties.

(3) Within 28 days after the date on which the Tribunal sent a copy of the decision to a party under paragraph (2), that party may apply in writing for an order that the decision does not apply to, and is not binding on the parties to, a particular related case.

(4) If a lead case is withdrawn before the Tribunal makes a decision in respect of the common or related issues, it shall make an order as to—

(a) whether another claim is to be specified as a lead case; and

(b) whether any order affecting the related cases should be set aside or varied.

Striking out

37.—(1) At any stage of the proceedings, either on its own initiative or on the application of a party, a Tribunal may strike out all or part of a claim or response on any of the following grounds—

(a) that it is scandalous or vexatious or has no reasonable prospect of success;

(b) that the manner in which the proceedings have been conducted by or on behalf of the claimant or the respondent (as the case may be) has been scandalous, unreasonable or vexatious;

(c) for non-compliance with any of these Rules or with an order of the Tribunal;

(d) that it has not been actively pursued;

(e) that the Tribunal considers that it is no longer possible to have a fair hearing in respect of the claim or response (or the part to be struck out).

(2) A claim or response may not be struck out unless the party in question has been given a reasonable opportunity to make representations, either in writing or, if requested by the party, at a hearing.

(3) Where a response is struck out, the effect shall be as if no response had been presented, as set out in rule 21 above.

Unless orders

38.—(1) An order may specify that if it is not complied with by the date specified the claim or response, or part of it, shall be dismissed without further order. If a claim or response, or part of it, is dismissed on this basis the Tribunal shall give written notice to the parties confirming what has occurred.

(2) A party whose claim or response has been dismissed, in whole or in part, as a result of such an order may apply to the Tribunal in writing, within 14 days of the date that the notice was sent, to have the order set aside on the basis that it is in the interests of justice to do so. Unless the application includes a request for a hearing, the Tribunal may determine it on the basis of written representations.

(3) Where a response is dismissed under this rule, the effect shall be as if no response had been presented, as set out in rule 21.

Deposit orders

39.—(1) Where at a preliminary hearing (under rule 53) the Tribunal considers that any specific allegation or argument in a claim or response has little reasonable prospect of success, it may make an order requiring a party ('the paying party') to pay a deposit not exceeding £1,000 as a condition of continuing to advance that allegation or argument.

(2) The Tribunal shall make reasonable enquiries into the paying party's ability to pay the deposit and have regard to any such information when deciding the amount of the deposit.

(3) The Tribunal's reasons for making the deposit order shall be provided with the order and the paying party must be notified about the potential consequences of the order.

(4) If the paying party fails to pay the deposit by the date specified the specific allegation or argument to which the deposit order relates shall be struck out. Where a response is struck out, the consequences shall be as if no response had been presented, as set out in rule 21.

(5) If the Tribunal at any stage following the making of a deposit order decides the specific allegation or argument against the paying party for substantially the reasons given in the deposit order—

(a) the paying party shall be treated as having acted unreasonably in pursuing that specific allegation or argument for the purpose of rule 76, unless the contrary is shown; and

(b) the deposit shall be paid to the other party (or, if there is more than one, to such other party or parties as the Tribunal orders),

otherwise the deposit shall be refunded.

(6) If a deposit has been paid to a party under paragraph (5)(b) and a costs or preparation time order has been made against the paying party in favour of the party who received the deposit, the amount of the deposit shall count towards the settlement of that order.

Non-payment of fees

40.—(1) Subject to rule 11, where a party has not paid a relevant Tribunal fee or presented a remission application in respect of that fee the Tribunal will send the party a notice specifying a date for payment of the Tribunal fee or presentation of a remission application.

(2) If at the date specified in a notice sent under paragraph (1) the party has not paid the Tribunal fee and no remission application in respect of that fee has been presented—

    (a) where the Tribunal fee is payable in relation to a claim, the claim shall be dismissed without further order;

    (b) where the Tribunal fee is payable in relation to an employer's contract claim, the employer's contract claim shall be dismissed without further order;

    (c) where the Tribunal fee is payable in relation to an application, the application shall be dismissed without further order;

    (d) where the Tribunal fee is payable in relation to judicial mediation, the judicial mediation shall not take place.

(3) Where a remission application is refused in part or in full, the Tribunal shall send the claimant a notice specifying a date for payment of the Tribunal fee.

(4) If at the date specified in a notice sent under paragraph (3) the party has not paid the Tribunal fee, the consequences shall be those referred to in sub-paragraphs (a) to (d) of paragraph (2).

(5) In the event of a dismissal under paragraph (2) or (4) a party may apply for the claim or response, or part of it, which was dismissed to be reinstated and the Tribunal may order a reinstatement. A reinstatement shall be effective only if the Tribunal fee is paid, or a remission application is presented and accepted, by the date specified in the order.

RULES COMMON TO ALL KINDS OF HEARING

General

41 The Tribunal may regulate its own procedure and shall conduct the hearing in the manner it considers fair, having regard to the principles contained in the overriding objective. The following rules do not restrict that general power. The Tribunal shall seek to avoid undue formality and may itself question the parties or any witnesses so far as appropriate in order to clarify the issues or elicit the evidence. The Tribunal is not bound by any rule of law relating to the admissibility of evidence in proceedings before the courts.

Written representations

42 The Tribunal shall consider any written representations from a party, including a party who does not propose to attend the hearing, if they are delivered to the Tribunal and to all other parties not less than 7 days before the hearing.

Witnesses

43 Where a witness is called to give oral evidence, any witness statement of that person ordered by the Tribunal shall stand as that witness's evidence in chief unless the Tribunal orders otherwise. Witnesses shall be required to give their oral evidence on oath or affirmation. The Tribunal may exclude from the hearing any person who is to appear as a witness in the proceedings until such time as that person gives evidence if it considers it in the interests of justice to do so.

Inspection of witness statements

44 Subject to rules 50 and 94, any witness statement which stands as evidence in chief shall be available for inspection during the course of the hearing by members of the public attending the hearing unless the Tribunal decides that all or any part of the statement is not to be admitted as evidence, in which case the statement or that part shall not be available for inspection.

Timetabling

45 A Tribunal may impose limits on the time that a party may take in presenting evidence, questioning witnesses or making submissions, and may prevent the party from proceeding beyond any time so allotted.

Hearings by electronic communication

46 A hearing may be conducted, in whole or in part, by use of electronic communication (including by telephone) provided that the Tribunal considers that it would be just and equitable to do so and provided that the parties and members of the public attending the hearing are able to hear what the Tribunal hears and see any witness as seen by the Tribunal.

Non-attendance

47 If a party fails to attend or to be represented at the hearing, the Tribunal may dismiss the claim or proceed with the hearing in the absence of that party. Before doing so, it shall consider any information which is available to it, after any enquiries that may be practicable, about the reasons for the party's absence.

Conversion from preliminary hearing to final hearing and vice versa

48 A Tribunal conducting a preliminary hearing may order that it be treated as a final hearing, or vice versa, if the Tribunal is properly constituted for the purpose and if it is satisfied that neither party shall be materially prejudiced by the change.

Majority decisions

49 Where a Tribunal is composed of three persons any decision may be made by a majority and if it is composed of two persons the Employment Judge has a second or casting vote.

Privacy and restrictions on disclosure

50.—(1) A Tribunal may at any stage of the proceedings, on its own initiative or on application, make an order with a view to preventing or restricting the public disclosure of any aspect of those proceedings so far as it considers necessary in the interests of justice or in order to protect the Convention rights of any person or in the circumstances identified in section 10A of the Employment Tribunals Act.

(2) In considering whether to make an order under this rule, the Tribunal shall give full weight to the principle of open justice and to the Convention right to freedom of expression.

(3) Such orders may include—
   (a) an order that a hearing that would otherwise be in public be conducted, in whole or in part, in private;
   (b) an order that the identities of specified parties, witnesses or other persons referred to in the proceedings should not be disclosed to the public, by the use of anonymisation or otherwise, whether in the course of any hearing or in its listing or in any documents entered on the Register or otherwise forming part of the public record;
   (c) an order for measures preventing witnesses at a public hearing being identifiable by members of the public;
   (d) a restricted reporting order within the terms of section 11 or 12 of the Employment Tribunals Act.

(4) Any party, or other person with a legitimate interest, who has not had a reasonable opportunity to make representations before an order under this rule is made may apply to the Tribunal in writing for the order to be revoked or discharged, either on the basis of written representations or, if requested, at a hearing.

(5) Where an order is made under paragraph (3)(d) above—
   (a) it shall specify the person whose identity is protected; and may specify particular matters of which publication is prohibited as likely to lead to that person's identification;
   (b) it shall specify the duration of the order;
   (c) the Tribunal shall ensure that a notice of the fact that such an order has been made in relation to those proceedings is displayed on the notice board of the Tribunal with any list of the proceedings taking place before the Tribunal, and on the door of the room in which the proceedings affected by the order are taking place; and
   (d) the Tribunal may order that it applies also to any other proceedings being heard as part of the same hearing.

(6) 'Convention rights' has the meaning given to it in section 1 of the Human Rights Act 1998.

WITHDRAWAL

End of claim

51   Where a claimant informs the Tribunal, either in writing or in the course of a hearing, that a claim, or part of it, is withdrawn, the claim, or part, comes to an end, subject to any application that the respondent may make for a costs, preparation time or wasted costs order.

Dismissal following withdrawal

52   Where a claim, or part of it, has been withdrawn under rule 51, the Tribunal shall issue a judgment dismissing it (which means that the claimant may not commence a further claim against the respondent raising the same, or substantially the same, complaint) unless—

(a)   the claimant has expressed at the time of withdrawal a wish to reserve the right to bring such a further claim and the Tribunal is satisfied that there would be legitimate reason for doing so; or

(b)   the Tribunal believes that to issue such a judgment would not be in the interests of justice.

PRELIMINARY HEARINGS

Scope of preliminary hearings

53.—(1) A preliminary hearing is a hearing at which the Tribunal may do one or more of the following—

(a)   conduct a preliminary consideration of the claim with the parties and make a case management order (including an order relating to the conduct of the final hearing);

(b)   determine any preliminary issue;

(c)   consider whether a claim or response, or any part, should be struck out under rule 37;

(d)   make a deposit order under rule 39;

(e)   explore the possibility of settlement or alternative dispute resolution (including judicial mediation).

(2) There may be more than one preliminary hearing in any case.

(3) 'Preliminary issue' means, as regards any complaint, any substantive issue which may determine liability (for example, an issue as to jurisdiction or as to whether an employee was dismissed).

Fixing of preliminary hearings

54   A preliminary hearing may be directed by the Tribunal on its own initiative following its initial consideration (under rule 26) or at any time thereafter or as the result of an application by a party. The Tribunal shall give the parties reasonable notice of the date of the hearing and in the case of a hearing involving any preliminary issues at least 14 days' notice shall be given and the notice shall specify the preliminary issues that are to be, or may be, decided at the hearing.

Constitution of tribunal for preliminary hearings

55   Preliminary hearings shall be conducted by an Employment Judge alone, except that where notice has been given that any preliminary issues are to be, or may be, decided at the hearing a party may request in writing that the hearing be conducted by a full tribunal in which case an Employment Judge shall decide whether that would be desirable.

When preliminary hearings shall be in public

56   Preliminary hearings shall be conducted in private, except that where the hearing involves a determination under rule 53(1)(b) or (c), any part of the hearing relating to such a determination shall be in public (subject to rules 50 and 94) and the Tribunal may direct that the entirety of the hearing be in public.

FINAL HEARING

Scope of final hearing

57 A final hearing is a hearing at which the Tribunal determines the claim or such parts as remain outstanding following the initial consideration (under rule 26) or any preliminary hearing. There may be different final hearings for different issues (for example, liability, remedy or costs).

Notice of final hearing

58 The Tribunal shall give the parties not less than 14 days' notice of the date of a final hearing.

When final hearing shall be in public

59 Any final hearing shall be in public, subject to rules 50 and 94.

DECISIONS AND REASONS

Decisions made without a hearing

60 Decisions made without a hearing shall be communicated in writing to the parties, identifying the Employment Judge who has made the decision.

Decisions made at or following a hearing

61.—(1) Where there is a hearing the Tribunal may either announce its decision in relation to any issue at the hearing or reserve it to be sent to the parties as soon as practicable in writing.

(2) If the decision is announced at the hearing, a written record (in the form of a judgment if appropriate) shall be provided to the parties (and, where the proceedings were referred to the Tribunal by a court, to that court) as soon as practicable. (Decisions concerned only with the conduct of a hearing need not be identified in the record of that hearing unless a party requests that a specific decision is so recorded.)

(3) The written record shall be signed by the Employment Judge.

Reasons

62.—(1) The Tribunal shall give reasons for its decision on any disputed issue, whether substantive or procedural (including any decision on an application for reconsideration or for orders for costs, preparation time or wasted costs).

(2) In the case of a decision given in writing the reasons shall also be given in writing. In the case of a decision announced at a hearing the reasons may be given orally at the hearing or reserved to be given in writing later (which may, but need not, be as part of the written record of the decision). Written reasons shall be signed by the Employment Judge.

(3) Where reasons have been given orally, the Employment Judge shall announce that written reasons will not be provided unless they are asked for by any party at the hearing itself or by a written request presented by any party within 14 days of the sending of the written record of the decision. The written record of the decision shall repeat that information. If no such request is received, the Tribunal shall provide written reasons only if requested to do so by the Employment Appeal Tribunal or a court.

(4) The reasons given for any decision shall be proportionate to the significance of the issue and for decisions other than judgments may be very short.

(5) In the case of a judgment the reasons shall: identify the issues which the Tribunal has determined, state the findings of fact made in relation to those issues, concisely identify the relevant law, and state how that law has been applied to those findings in order to decide the issues. Where the judgment includes a financial award the reasons shall identify, by means of a table or otherwise, how the amount to be paid has been calculated.

Absence of Employment Judge

63 If it is impossible or not practicable for the written record or reasons to be signed by the Employment Judge as a result of death, incapacity or absence, it shall be signed by the other member or members (in the case of a full tribunal) or by the President, Vice President or a Regional Employment Judge (in the case of a Judge sitting alone).

Consent orders and judgments

64 If the parties agree in writing or orally at a hearing upon the terms of any order or judgment a Tribunal may, if it thinks fit, make such order or judgment, in which case it shall be identified as having been made by consent.

When a judgment or order takes effect

65 A judgment or order takes effect from the day when it is given or made, or on such later date as specified by the Tribunal.

Time for compliance

66 A party shall comply with a judgment or order for the payment of an amount of money within 14 days of the date of the judgment or order, unless—
   (a) the judgment, order, or any of these Rules, specifies a different date for compliance; or
   (b) the Tribunal has stayed (or in Scotland sisted) the proceedings or judgment.

The Register

67 Subject to rules 50 and 94, a copy shall be entered in the Register of any judgment and of any written reasons for a judgment.

Copies of judgment for referring court

68 Where the proceedings were referred to the Tribunal by a court a copy of any judgment and of any written reasons shall be provided to that court.

Correction of clerical mistakes and accidental slips

69 An Employment Judge may at any time correct any clerical mistake or other accidental slip or omission in any order, judgment or other document produced by a Tribunal. If such a correction is made, any published version of the document shall also be corrected. If any document is corrected under this rule, a copy of the corrected version, signed by the Judge, shall be sent to all the parties.

RECONSIDERATION OF JUDGMENTS

Principles

70 A Tribunal may, either on its own initiative (which may reflect a request from the Employment Appeal Tribunal) or on the application of a party, reconsider any judgment where it is necessary in the interests of justice to do so. On reconsideration, the decision ('the original decision') may be confirmed, varied or revoked. If it is revoked it may be taken again.

Application

71 Except where it is made in the course of a hearing, an application for reconsideration shall be presented in writing (and copied to all the other parties) within 14 days of the date on which the written record, or other written communication, of the original decision was sent to the parties or within 14 days of the date that the written reasons were sent (if later) and shall set out why reconsideration of the original decision is necessary.

Process

72.—(1) An Employment Judge shall consider any application made under rule 71 If the Judge considers that there is no reasonable prospect of the original decision being varied or revoked (including, unless there are special reasons, where substantially the same application has already been made and refused), the application shall be refused and the Tribunal shall inform the parties of the refusal. Otherwise the Tribunal shall send a notice to the parties setting a time limit for any response to the application by the other parties and seeking the views of the parties on whether the application can be determined without a hearing. The notice may set out the Judge's provisional views on the application.
(2) If the application has not been refused under paragraph (1), the original decision shall be reconsidered at a hearing unless the Employment Judge considers, having regard to any response to the notice provided under paragraph (1), that a hearing is not necessary in the interests of justice. If the reconsideration proceeds without a hearing the parties shall be given a reasonable opportunity to make further written representations.

Appendix 1 Selected Legislation: Rules

(3) Where practicable, the consideration under paragraph (1) shall be by the Employment Judge who made the original decision or, as the case may be, chaired the full tribunal which made it; and any reconsideration under paragraph (2) shall be made by the Judge or, as the case may be, the full tribunal which made the original decision. Where that is not practicable, the President, Vice President or a Regional Employment Judge shall appoint another Employment Judge to deal with the application or, in the case of a decision of a full tribunal, shall either direct that the reconsideration be by such members of the original Tribunal as remain available or reconstitute the Tribunal in whole or in part.

Reconsideration by the Tribunal on its own initiative

73 Where the Tribunal proposes to reconsider a decision on its own initiative, it shall inform the parties of the reasons why the decision is being reconsidered and the decision shall be reconsidered in accordance with rule 72(2) (as if an application had been made and not refused).

COSTS ORDERS, PREPARATION TIME ORDERS AND WASTED COSTS ORDERS

Definitions

74.—(1) 'Costs' means fees, charges, disbursements or expenses incurred by or on behalf of the receiving party (including expenses that witnesses incur for the purpose of, or in connection with, attendance at a Tribunal hearing). In Scotland all references to costs (except when used in the expression 'wasted costs') shall be read as references to expenses.

(2) 'Legally represented' means having the assistance of a person (including where that person is the receiving party's employee) who—
   (a) has a right of audience in relation to any class of proceedings in any part of the Senior Courts of England and Wales, or all proceedings in county courts or magistrates' courts;
   (b) is an advocate or solicitor in Scotland; or
   (c) is a member of the Bar of Northern Ireland or a solicitor of the Court of Judicature of Northern Ireland.

(3) 'Represented by a lay representative' means having the assistance of a person who does not satisfy any of the criteria in paragraph (2) and who charges for representation in the proceedings.

Costs orders and preparation time orders

75.—(1) A costs order is an order that a party ('the paying party') make a payment to—
   (a) another party ('the receiving party') in respect of the costs that the receiving party has incurred while legally represented or while represented by a lay representative;
   (b) the receiving party in respect of a Tribunal fee paid by the receiving party; or
   (c) another party or a witness in respect of expenses incurred, or to be incurred, for the purpose of, or in connection with, an individual's attendance as a witness at the Tribunal.

(2) A preparation time order is an order that a party ('the paying party') make a payment to another party ('the receiving party') in respect of the receiving party's preparation time while not legally represented. 'Preparation time' means time spent by the receiving party (including by any employees or advisers) in working on the case, except for time spent at any final hearing.

(3) A costs order under paragraph (1)(a) and a preparation time order may not both be made in favour of the same party in the same proceedings. A Tribunal may, if it wishes, decide in the course of the proceedings that a party is entitled to one order or the other but defer until a later stage in the proceedings deciding which kind of order to make.

When a costs order or a preparation time order may or shall be made

76.—(1) A Tribunal may make a costs order or a preparation time order, and shall consider whether to do so, where it considers that—
   (a) a party (or that party's representative) has acted vexatiously, abusively, disruptively or otherwise unreasonably in either the bringing of the proceedings (or part) or the way that the proceedings (or part) have been conducted; or
   (b) any claim or response had no reasonable prospect of success.

(2) A Tribunal may also make such an order where a party has been in breach of any order or practice direction or where a hearing has been postponed or adjourned on the application of a party.

(3) Where in proceedings for unfair dismissal a final hearing is postponed or adjourned, the Tribunal shall order the respondent to pay the costs incurred as a result of the postponement or adjournment if—

  (a) the claimant has expressed a wish to be reinstated or re-engaged which has been communicated to the respondent not less than 7 days before the hearing; and

  (b) the postponement or adjournment of that hearing has been caused by the respondent's failure, without a special reason, to adduce reasonable evidence as to the availability of the job from which the claimant was dismissed or of comparable or suitable employment.

(4) A Tribunal may make a costs order of the kind described in rule 75(1)(b) where a party has paid a Tribunal fee in respect of a claim, employer's contract claim or application and that claim, counterclaim or application is decided in whole, or in part, in favour of that party.

(5) A Tribunal may make a costs order of the kind described in rule 75 (1)(c) on the application of a party or the witness in question, or on its own initiative, where a witness has attended or has been ordered to attend to give oral evidence at a hearing.

Procedure

77 A party may apply for a costs order or a preparation time order at any stage up to 28 days after the date on which the judgment finally determining the proceedings in respect of that party was sent to the parties. No such order may be made unless the paying party has had a reasonable opportunity to make representations (in writing or at a hearing, as the Tribunal may order) in response to the application.

The amount of a costs order

78.—(1) A costs order may—

  (a) order the paying party to pay the receiving party a specified amount, not exceeding £20,000, in respect of the costs of the receiving party;

  (b) order the paying party to pay the receiving party the whole or a specified part of the costs of the receiving party, with the amount to be paid being determined, in England and Wales, by way of detailed assessment carried out either by a county court in accordance with the Civil Procedure Rules 1998, or by an Employment Judge applying the same principles; or, in Scotland, by way of taxation carried out either by the auditor of court in accordance with the Act of Sederunt (Fees of Solicitors in the Sheriff Court)(Amendment and Further Provisions) 1993, or by an Employment Judge applying the same principles;

  (c) order the paying party to pay the receiving party a specified amount as reimbursement of all or part of a Tribunal fee paid by the receiving party;

  (d) order the paying party to pay another party or a witness, as appropriate, a specified amount in respect of necessary and reasonably incurred expenses (of the kind described in rule 75(1) (c)); or

  (e) if the paying party and the receiving party agree as to the amount payable, be made in that amount.

(2) Where the costs order includes an amount in respect of fees charged by a lay representative, for the purposes of the calculation of the order, the hourly rate applicable for the fees of the lay representative shall be no higher than the rate under rule 79(2).

(3) For the avoidance of doubt, the amount of a costs order under sub-paragraphs (b) to (e) of paragraph (1) may exceed £20,000.

The amount of a preparation time order

79.—(1) The Tribunal shall decide the number of hours in respect of which a preparation time order should be made, on the basis of—

  (a) information provided by the receiving party on time spent falling within rule 75(2) above; and

  (b) the Tribunal's own assessment of what it considers to be a reasonable and proportionate amount of time to spend on such preparatory work, with reference to such matters as the complexity of the proceedings, the number of witnesses and documentation required.

(2) The hourly rate is £33 and increases on 6 April each year by £1.

(3) The amount of a preparation time order shall be the product of the number of hours assessed under paragraph (1) and the rate under paragraph (2).

When a wasted costs order may be made

80.—(1) A Tribunal may make a wasted costs order against a representative in favour of any party ('the receiving party') where that party has incurred costs—

  (a) as a result of any improper, unreasonable or negligent act or omission on the part of the representative; or

(b) which, in the light of any such act or omission occurring after they were incurred, the Tribunal considers it unreasonable to expect the receiving party to pay. Costs so incurred are described as 'wasted costs'.

(2) 'Representative' means a party's legal or other representative or any employee of such representative, but it does not include a representative who is not acting in pursuit of profit with regard to the proceedings. A person acting on a contingency or conditional fee arrangement is considered to be acting in pursuit of profit.

(3) A wasted costs order may be made in favour of a party whether or not that party is legally represented and may also be made in favour of a representative's own client. A wasted costs order may not be made against a representative where that representative is representing a party in his or her capacity as an employee of that party.

Effect of a wasted costs order

81 A wasted costs order may order the representative to pay the whole or part of any wasted costs of the receiving party, or disallow any wasted costs otherwise payable to the representative, including an order that the representative repay to its client any costs which have already been paid. The amount to be paid, disallowed or repaid must in each case be specified in the order.

Procedure

82 A wasted costs order may be made by the Tribunal on its own initiative or on the application of any party. A party may apply for a wasted costs order at any stage up to 28 days after the date on which the judgment finally determining the proceedings as against that party was sent to the parties. No such order shall be made unless the representative has had a reasonable opportunity to make representations (in writing or at a hearing, as the Tribunal may order) in response to the application or proposal. The Tribunal shall inform the representative's client in writing of any proceedings under this rule and of any order made against the representative.

Allowances

83 Where the Tribunal makes a costs, preparation time, or wasted costs order, it may also make an order that the paying party (or, where a wasted costs order is made, the representative) pay to the Secretary of State, in whole or in part, any allowances (other than allowances paid to members of the Tribunal) paid by the Secretary of State under section 5(2) or (3) of the Employment Tribunals Act to any person for the purposes of, or in connection with, that person's attendance at the Tribunal.

Ability to pay

84 In deciding whether to make a costs, preparation time, or wasted costs order, and if so in what amount, the Tribunal may have regard to the paying party's (or, where a wasted costs order is made, the representative's) ability to pay.

DELIVERY OF DOCUMENTS

Delivery to the Tribunal

85.—(1) Subject to paragraph (2), documents may be delivered to the Tribunal—
  (a) by post;
  (b) by direct delivery to the appropriate tribunal office (including delivery by a courier or messenger service); or
  (c) by electronic communication.

(2) A claim form may only be delivered in accordance with the practice direction made under regulation 11 which supplements rule 8.

(3) The Tribunal shall notify the parties following the presentation of the claim of the address of the tribunal office dealing with the case (including any fax or email or other electronic address) and all documents shall be delivered to either the postal or the electronic address so notified. The Tribunal may from time to time notify the parties of any change of address, or that a particular form of communication should or should not be used, and any documents shall be delivered in accordance with that notification.

Delivery to parties

86.—(1) Documents may be delivered to a party (whether by the Tribunal or by another party)—
   (a) by post;
   (b) by direct delivery to that party's address (including delivery by a courier or messenger service);
   (c) by electronic communication; or
   (d) by being handed personally to that party, if an individual and if no representative has been named in the claim form or response; or to any individual representative named in the claim form or response; or, on the occasion of a hearing, to any person identified by the party as representing that party at that hearing.

(2) For the purposes of sub-paragraphs (a) to (c) of paragraph (1), the document shall be delivered to the address given in the claim form or response (which shall be the address of the party's representative, if one is named) or to a different address as notified in writing by the party in question.

(3) If a party has given both a postal address and one or more electronic addresses, any of them may be used unless the party has indicated in writing that a particular address should or should not be used.

Delivery to non-parties

87 Subject to the special cases which are the subject of rule 88, documents shall be sent to non-parties at any address for service which they may have notified and otherwise at any known address or place of business in the United Kingdom or, if the party is a corporate body, at its registered or principal office in the United Kingdom or, if permitted by the President, at an address outside the United Kingdom.

Special cases

88 Addresses for serving the Secretary of State, the Law Officers, and the Counsel General to the Welsh Assembly Government, in cases where they are not parties, shall be issued by practice direction.

Substituted service

89 Where no address for service in accordance with the above rules is known or it appears that service at any such address is unlikely to come to the attention of the addressee, the President, Vice President or a Regional Employment Judge may order that there shall be substituted service in such manner as appears appropriate.

Date of delivery

90 Where a document has been delivered in accordance with rule 85 or 86, it shall, unless the contrary is proved, be taken to have been received by the addressee—
   (a) if sent by post, on the day on which it would be delivered in the ordinary course of post;
   (b) if sent by means of electronic communication, on the day of transmission;
   (c) if delivered directly or personally, on the day of delivery.

Irregular service

91 A Tribunal may treat any document as delivered to a person, notwithstanding any non-compliance with rules 86 to 88, if satisfied that the document in question, or its substance, has in fact come to the attention of that person.

Correspondence with the Tribunal: copying to other parties

92 Where a party sends a communication to the Tribunal (except an application under rule 32) it shall send a copy to all other parties, and state that it has done so (by use of 'cc' or otherwise). The Tribunal may order a departure from this rule where it considers it in the interests of justice to do so.

MISCELLANEOUS

ACAS

93.—(1) Where proceedings concern an enactment which provides for conciliation, the Tribunal shall—
   (a) send a copy of the claim form and the response to an ACAS conciliation officer; and
   (b) inform the parties that the services of an ACAS conciliation officer are available to them.

(2) Subject to rules 50 and 94, a representative of ACAS may attend any preliminary hearing.

National security proceedings

94.—(1) Where in relation to particular Crown employment proceedings a Minister considers that it would be expedient in the interests of national security, the Minister may direct a Tribunal to—

    (a) conduct all or part of the proceedings in private;

    (b) exclude a person from all or part of the proceedings;

    (c) take steps to conceal the identity of a witness in the proceedings.

  (2) Where the Tribunal considers it expedient in the interests of national security, it may order—

    (a) in relation to particular proceedings (including Crown employment proceedings), anything which can be required to be done under paragraph (1);

    (b) a person not to disclose any document (or the contents of any document), where provided for the purposes of the proceedings, to any other person (save for any specified person).

    Any order made must be kept under review by the Tribunal.

  (3) Where the Tribunal considers that it may be necessary to make an order under paragraph (2) in relation to particular proceedings (including Crown employment proceedings), the Tribunal may consider any material provided by a party (or where a Minister is not a party, by a Minister) without providing that material to any other person. Such material shall be used by the Tribunal solely for the purposes of deciding whether to make that order (unless that material is subsequently used as evidence in the proceedings by a party).

  (4) Where a Minister considers that it would be appropriate for the Tribunal to make an order under paragraph (2), the Minister may make an application for such an order.

  (5) Where a Minister has made an application under paragraph (4), the Tribunal may order—

    (a) in relation to the part of the proceedings preceding the outcome of the application, anything which can be required to be done under paragraph (1);

    (b) a person not to disclose any document (or the contents of any document) to any other person (save for any specified person), where provided for the purposes of the proceedings preceding the outcome of the application.

  (6) Where a Minister has made an application under paragraph (4) for an order to exclude any person from all or part of the proceedings, the Tribunal shall not send a copy of the response to that person, pending the decision on the application.

  (7) If before the expiry of the time limit in rule 16 a Minister makes a direction under paragraph (1) or makes an application under paragraph (4), the Minister may apply for an extension of the time limit in rule 16.

  (8) A direction under paragraph (1) or an application under paragraph (4) may be made irrespective of whether or not the Minister is a party.

  (9) Where the Tribunal decides not to make an order under paragraph (2), rule 6 of Schedule 2 shall apply to the reasons given by the Tribunal under rule 62 for that decision, save that the reasons will not be entered on the Register.

  (10) The Tribunal must ensure that in exercising its functions, information is not disclosed contrary to the interests of national security.

Interim relief proceedings

95 When a Tribunal hears an application for interim relief (or for its variation or revocation) under section 161 or section 165 of the Trade Union and Labour Relations (Consolidation) Act 1992 or under section 128 or section 131 of the Employment Rights Act 1996, rules 53 to 56 apply to the hearing and the Tribunal shall not hear oral evidence unless it directs otherwise.

Proceedings involving the National Insurance Fund

96 The Secretary of State shall be entitled to appear and be heard at any hearing in relation to proceedings which may involve a payment out of the National Insurance Fund and shall be treated as a party for the purposes of these Rules.

Collective agreements

97 Where a claim includes a complaint under section 146(1) of the Equality Act relating to a term of a collective agreement, the following persons, whether or not identified in the claim, shall be regarded as the persons against whom a remedy is claimed and shall be treated as respondents for the purposes of these Rules—

    (a) the claimant's employer (or prospective employer); and

(b) every organisation of employers and organisation of workers, and every association of or representative of such organisations, which, if the terms were to be varied voluntarily, would be likely, in the opinion of an Employment Judge, to negotiate the variation.

An organisation or association shall not be treated as a respondent if the Judge, having made such enquiries of the claimant and such other enquiries as the Judge thinks fit, is of the opinion that it is not reasonably practicable to identify the organisation or association.

Devolution issues

98.—(1) Where a devolution issue arises, the Tribunal shall as soon as practicable send notice of that fact and a copy of the claim form and response to the Advocate General for Scotland and the Lord Advocate, where it is a Scottish devolution issue, or to the Attorney General and the Counsel General to the Welsh Assembly Government, where it is a Welsh devolution issue, unless they are a party to the proceedings.

(2) A person to whom notice is sent may be treated as a party to the proceedings, so far as the proceedings relate to the devolution issue, if that person sends notice to the Tribunal within 14 days of receiving a notice under paragraph (1).

(3) Any notices sent under paragraph (1) or (2) must at the same time be sent to the parties.

(4) 'Devolution issue' has the meaning given to it in paragraph 1 of Schedule 6 to the Scotland Act 1998 (for the purposes of a Scottish devolution issue), and in paragraph 1 of Schedule 9 to the Government of Wales Act 2006 (for the purposes of a Welsh devolution issue).

Transfer of proceedings between Scotland and England & Wales

99.—(1) The President (England and Wales) or a Regional Employment Judge may at any time, on their own initiative or on the application of a party, with the consent of the President (Scotland), transfer to a tribunal office in Scotland any proceedings started in England and Wales which could (in accordance with rule 8(3)) have been started in Scotland and which in that person's opinion would more conveniently be determined there.

(2) The President (Scotland) or the Vice President may at any time, on their own initiative or on the application of a party, with the consent of the President (England and Wales), transfer to a tribunal office in England and Wales any proceedings started in Scotland which could (in accordance with rule 8(2)) have been started in England and Wales and in that person's opinion would more conveniently be determined there.

References to the Court of Justice of the European Union

100 Where a Tribunal decides to refer a question to the Court of Justice of the European Union for a preliminary ruling under Article 267 of the Treaty on the Functioning of the European Union, a copy of that decision shall be sent to the registrar of that court.

Transfer of proceedings from a court

101 Where proceedings are referred to a Tribunal by a court, these Rules apply as if the proceedings had been presented by the claimant.

Vexatious litigants

102 The Tribunal may provide any information or documents requested by the Attorney General, the Solicitor General or the Lord Advocate for the purpose of preparing an application or considering whether to make an application under section 42 of the Senior Courts Act 1981, section 1 of the Vexatious Actions (Scotland) Act 1898 or section 33 of the Employment Tribunals Act.

Information to the Commission for Equality and Human Rights

103 The Tribunal shall send to the Commission for Equality and Human Rights copies of all judgments and written reasons relating to complaints under section 120, 127 or 146 of the Equality Act. That obligation shall not apply in any proceedings where a Minister of the Crown has given a direction, or a Tribunal has made an order, under rule 94; and either the Security Service, the Secret Intelligence Service or the Government Communications Headquarters is a party to the proceedings.

Application of this Schedule to levy appeals

104 For the purposes of a levy appeal, references in this Schedule to a claim or claimant shall be read as references to a levy appeal or to an appellant in a levy appeal respectively.

Appendix 1 Selected Legislation: Rules

Application of this Schedule to appeals against improvement and prohibition notices

105.—(1) A person ('the appellant') may appeal an improvement notice or a prohibition notice by presenting a claim to a tribunal office—

(a) before the end of the period of 21 days beginning with the date of the service on the appellant of the notice which is the subject of the appeal; or

(b) within such further period as the Tribunal considers reasonable where it is satisfied that it was not reasonably practicable for an appeal to be presented within that time.

(2) For the purposes of an appeal against an improvement notice or a prohibition notice, this Schedule shall be treated as modified in the following ways—

(a) references to a claim or claimant shall be read as references to an appeal or to an appellant in an appeal respectively;

(b) references to a respondent shall be read as references to the inspector appointed under section 19(1) of the Health and Safety Act who issued the notice which is the subject of the appeal.

Application of this Schedule to appeals against unlawful act notices

106 For the purposes of an appeal against an unlawful act notice, this Schedule shall be treated as modified in the following ways—

(a) references in this Schedule to a claim or claimant shall be read as references to a notice of appeal or to an appellant in an appeal against an unlawful act notice respectively;

(b) references to a respondent shall be read as references to the Commission for Equality and Human Rights.

SCHEDULE 2

REGULATION 13(2)

THE EMPLOYMENT TRIBUNALS (NATIONAL SECURITY) RULES OF PROCEDURE

Application of Schedule 2

1.—(1) This Schedule applies to proceedings in relation to which a direction is given, or order is made, under rule 94 and modifies the rules in Schedule 1 in relation to such proceedings.

(2) References in this Schedule to rule numbers are to those in Schedule 1.

(3) The definitions in rule 1 apply to terms in this Schedule and in this Schedule—

'excluded person' means, in relation to any proceedings, a person who has been excluded from all or part of the proceedings by virtue of a direction under rule 94(1)(b) or an order under rule 94(2)

(a) (read with rule 94(1)(b)).

Serving of documents

2 The Tribunal shall not send a copy of the response to any excluded person.

Witness orders and disclosure of documents

3.—(1) Where a person or their representative has been excluded under rule 94 from all or part of the proceedings and a Tribunal is considering whether to make an order under rule 31 or 32, a Minister (whether or not he is a party to the proceedings) may make an application to the Tribunal objecting to that order. If such an order has been made, the Minister may make an application to vary or set aside the order.

(2) The Tribunal shall hear and determine the Minister's application in private and the Minister shall be entitled to address the Tribunal.

Special advocate

4.—(1) The Tribunal shall inform the relevant Law Officer if a party becomes an excluded person. For the purposes of this rule, 'relevant Law Officer' means, in relation to England and Wales, the Attorney General, and, in relation to Scotland, the Advocate General.

(2) The relevant Law Officer may appoint a special advocate to represent the interests of a person in respect of those parts of the proceedings from which—

(a) a person's representative is excluded;

(b) a person and their representative are excluded;

(c) a person is excluded and is unrepresented.

(3) A special advocate shall be a person who has a right of audience in relation to any class of proceedings in any part of the Senior Courts or all proceedings in county courts or magistrates' courts, or shall be an advocate or a solicitor admitted in Scotland.

(4) An excluded person (where that person is a party) may make a statement to the Tribunal before the commencement of the proceedings or the relevant part of the proceedings.

(5) The special advocate may communicate, directly or indirectly, with an excluded person at any time before receiving material from a Minister in relation to which the Minister states an objection to disclosure to the excluded person ('closed material').

(6) After receiving closed material, the special advocate must not communicate with any person about any matter connected with the proceedings, except in accordance with paragraph (7) or

(9) or an order of the Tribunal.

(7) The special advocate may communicate about the proceedings with—

  (a) the Tribunal;

  (b) the Minister, or their representative;

  (c) the relevant Law Officer, or their representative;

  (d) any other person, except for an excluded person or his representative, with whom it is necessary for administrative purposes to communicate about matters not connected with the substance of the proceedings.

(8) The special advocate may apply for an order from the Tribunal to authorise communication with an excluded person or with any other person and if such an application is made—

  (a) the Tribunal must notify the Minister of the request; and

  (b) the Minister may, within a period specified by the Tribunal, present to the Tribunal and serve on the special advocate notice of any objection to the proposed communication.

(9) After the special advocate has received closed material, an excluded person may only communicate with the special advocate in writing and the special advocate must not reply to the communication, except that the special advocate may send a written acknowledgment of receipt to the legal representative.

(10) References in these Regulations and Schedules 1 and 2 to a party shall include any special advocate appointed in particular proceedings, save that the references to 'party' or 'parties' in rules 3, 6(c), 22, 26, 34, 36(2), 36(3), the first reference in rule 37, 38, 39, 40, 41, 45, 47, 64, 74 to 84, 86, 96 and 98(3) shall not include the special advocate.

Hearings

5.—(1) Subject to any order under rule 50 or any direction or order under rule 94, any hearing shall take place in public, and any party may attend and participate in the hearing.

(2) A member of the Administrative Justice and Tribunals Council shall not be entitled to attend any hearing conducted in private.

Reasons in national security proceedings

6.—(1) The Tribunal shall send a copy of the written reasons given under rule 62 to the Minister and allow 42 days for the Minister to make a direction under paragraph (3) below before sending them to any party or entering them onto the Register.

(2) If the Tribunal considers it expedient in the interests of national security, it may by order take steps to keep secret all or part of the written reasons.

(3) If the Minister considers it expedient in the interests of national security, the Minister may direct that the written reasons—

  (a) shall not be disclosed to specified persons and require the Tribunal to prepare a further document which sets out the reasons for the decision, but omits specified information ('the edited reasons');

  (b) shall not be disclosed to specified persons and that no further document setting out the reasons for the decision should be prepared.

(4) Where the Minister has directed the Tribunal to prepare edited reasons, the Employment Judge shall initial each omission.

(5) Where a direction has been made under paragraph (3)(a), the Tribunal shall—

  (a) send the edited reasons to the specified persons;

  (b) send the edited reasons and the written reasons to the relevant persons listed in paragraph (7); and

  (c) where the written reasons relate to a judgment, enter the edited reasons on the Register but not enter the written reasons on the Register.

(6) Where a direction has been made under paragraph (3)(b), the Tribunal shall send the written reasons to the relevant persons listed in paragraph (7), but not enter the written reasons on the Register.

(7) The relevant persons are–
  (a) the respondent or the respondent's representative, provided that they were not specified in the direction made under paragraph (3);
  (b) the claimant or the claimant's representative, provided that they were not specified in the direction made under paragraph (3);
  (c) any special advocate appointed in the proceedings; and
  (d) where the proceedings were referred to the Tribunal by a court, to that court.
(8) Where written reasons or edited reasons are corrected under rule 69, the Tribunal shall send a copy of the corrected reasons to the same persons who had been sent the reasons.

Schedule 3

Regulation 13(2)

The Employment Tribunals (Equal Value) Rules of Procedure

Application of Schedule 3

1.—(1) This Schedule applies to proceedings involving an equal value claim and modifies the rules in Schedule 1 in relation to such proceedings.
(2) The definitions in rule 1 of Schedule 1 apply to terms in this Schedule and in this Schedule—'comparator' means the person of the opposite sex to the claimant in relation to whom the claimant alleges that his or her work is of equal value;
  'equal value claim' means a claim relating to a breach of a sex equality clause or rule within the meaning of the Equality Act in a case involving work within section 65(1)(c) of that Act;
  'the facts relating to the question' has the meaning in rule 6(1)(a);
  'independent expert' means a member of the panel of independent experts mentioned in section 131(8) of the Equality Act;
  'the question' means whether the claimant's work is of equal value to that of the comparator; and 're- port' means a report required by a Tribunal to be prepared in accordance with section 131(2) of the Equality Act.
(3) A reference in this Schedule to a rule, is a reference to a rule in this Schedule unless otherwise provided.
(4) A reference in this Schedule to 'these rules' is a reference to the rules in Schedules 1 and 3 unless otherwise provided.

General power to manage proceedings

2.—(1) The Tribunal may (subject to rules 3(1) and 6(1)) order—
  (a) that no new facts shall be admitted in evidence by the Tribunal unless they have been disclosed to all other parties in writing before a date specified by the Tribunal (unless it was not reasonably practicable for a party to have done so);
  (b) the parties to send copies of documents or provide information to the independent expert;
  (c) the respondent to grant the independent expert access to the respondent's premises during a period specified in the order to allow the independent expert to conduct interviews with persons identified as relevant by the independent expert;
  (d) when more than one expert is to give evidence in the proceedings, that those experts present to the Tribunal a joint statement of matters which are agreed between them and matters on which they disagree.
(2) In managing the proceedings, the Tribunal shall have regard to the indicative timetable in the Annex to this Schedule.

Conduct of stage 1 equal value hearing

3.—(1) Where there is a dispute as to whether one person's work is of equal value to another's (equal value being construed in accordance with section 65(6) of the Equality Act), the Tribunal shall conduct a hearing, which shall be referred to as a 'stage 1 equal value hearing', and at that hearing shall—
  (a) strike out the claim (or the relevant part of it) if in accordance with section 131(6) of the Equality Act the Tribunal must determine that the work of the claimant and the comparator are not of equal value;

(b) determine the question or require an independent expert to prepare a report on the question;

(c) if the Tribunal has decided to require an independent expert to prepare a report on the question, fix a date for a further hearing, which shall be referred to as a 'stage 2 equal value hearing'; and

(d) if the Tribunal has not decided to require an independent expert to prepare a report on the question, fix a date for the final hearing.

(2) Before a claim or part is struck out under sub-paragraph (1)(a), the Tribunal shall send notice to the claimant and allow the claimant to make representations to the Tribunal as to whether the evaluation contained in the study in question falls within paragraph (a) or (b) of section 131(6) of the Equality Act. The Tribunal shall not be required to send a notice under this paragraph if the claimant has been given an opportunity to make such representations orally to the Tribunal.

(3) The Tribunal may, on the application of a party, hear evidence and submissions on the issue contained in section 69 of the Equality Act before determining whether to require an independent expert to prepare a report under paragraph (1)(b).

(4) The Tribunal shall give the parties reasonable notice of the date of the stage 1 equal value hearing and the notice shall specify the matters that are to be, or may be, considered at the hearing and give notice of the standard orders in rule 4.

Standard orders for stage 1 equal value hearing

4.—(1) At a stage 1 equal value hearing a Tribunal shall, unless it considers it inappropriate to do so, order that—

(a) before the end of the period of 14 days the claimant shall—

  (i) disclose in writing to the respondent the name of any comparator, or, if the claimant is not able to name the comparator, disclose information which enables the respondent to identify the comparator; and

  (ii) identify to the respondent in writing the period in relation to which the claimant considers that the claimant's work and that of the comparator are to be compared;

(b) before the end of the period of 28 days—

  (i) where the claimant has not disclosed the name of the comparator to the respondent under sub-paragraph (a) and the respondent has been provided with sufficient detail to be able to identify the comparator, the respondent shall disclose in writing the name of the comparator to the claimant;

  (ii) the parties shall provide each other with written job descriptions for the claimant and any comparator;

  (iii) the parties shall identify to each other in writing the facts which they consider to be relevant to the question;

(c) the respondent shall grant access to the respondent's premises during a period specified in the order to allow the claimant and his or her representative to interview any comparator;

(d) the parties shall before the end of the period of 56 days present to the Tribunal an agreed written statement specifying—

  (i) job descriptions for the claimant and any comparator;

  (ii) the facts which both parties consider are relevant to the question;

  (iii) the facts on which the parties disagree (as to the fact or as to the relevance to the question) and a summary of their reasons for disagreeing;

(e) the parties shall, at least 56 days before the final hearing, disclose to each other, to any independent or other expert and to the Tribunal written statements of any facts on which they intend to rely in evidence at the final hearing; and

(f) the parties shall, at least 28 days before the final hearing, present to the Tribunal a statement of facts and issues on which the parties are in agreement, a statement of facts and issues on which the parties disagree and a summary of their reasons for disagreeing.

(2) The Tribunal may add to, vary or omit any of the standard orders in paragraph (1).

Involvement of independent expert in fact finding

5 Where the Tribunal has decided to require an independent expert to prepare a report on the question, it may at any stage of the proceedings, on its own initiative or on the application of a party, order the independent expert to assist the Tribunal in establishing the facts on which the independent expert may rely in preparing the report.

Conduct of stage 2 equal value hearing

6.—(1) Any stage 2 equal value hearing shall be conducted by a full tribunal and at the hearing the Tribunal shall—

    (a) make a determination of facts on which the parties cannot agree which relate to the question and shall require the independent expert to prepare the report on the basis of facts which have (at any stage of the proceedings) either been agreed between the parties or determined by the Tribunal (referred to as 'the facts relating to the question'); and

    (b) fix a date for the final hearing.

(2) Subject to paragraph (3), the facts relating to the question shall, in relation to the question, be the only facts on which the Tribunal shall rely at the final hearing.

(3) At any stage of the proceedings the independent expert may make an application to the Tribunal for some or all of the facts relating to the question to be amended, supplemented or omitted.

(4) The Tribunal shall give the parties reasonable notice of the date of the stage 2 equal value hearing and the notice shall draw the attention of the parties to this rule and give notice of the standard orders in rule 7.

Standard orders for stage 2 equal value hearing

7.—(1) At a stage 2 equal value hearing a Tribunal shall, unless it considers it inappropriate to do so, order that—

    (a) by a specified date the independent expert shall prepare his report on the question and shall (subject to rule 13) send copies of it to the parties and to the Tribunal; and

    (b) the independent expert shall prepare his report on the question on the basis only of the facts relating to the question.

(2) The Tribunal may add to, vary or omit any of the standard orders in paragraph (1).

Final hearing

8.—(1) Where an independent expert has prepared a report, unless the Tribunal determines that the report is not based on the facts relating to the question, the report of the independent expert shall be admitted in evidence.

(2) If the Tribunal does not admit the report of an independent expert in accordance with paragraph (1), it may determine the question itself or require another independent expert to prepare a report on the question.

(3) The Tribunal may refuse to admit evidence of facts or hear submissions on issues which have not been disclosed to the other party as required by these rules or any order (unless it was not reasonably practicable for a party to have done so).

Duties and powers of the independent expert

9.—(1) When a Tribunal makes an order under rule 3(1)(b) or 5, it shall inform that independent expert of the duties and powers under this rule.

(2) The independent expert shall have a duty to the Tribunal to—

    (a) assist it in furthering the overriding objective set out in rule 2 of Schedule 1;

    (b) comply with the requirements of these rules and any orders made by the Tribunal;

    (c) keep the Tribunal informed of any delay in complying with any order (with the exception of minor or insignificant delays in compliance);

    (d) comply with any timetable imposed by the Tribunal in so far as this is reasonably practicable;

    (e) when requested, inform the Tribunal of progress in the preparation of the report;

    (f) prepare a report on the question based on the facts relating to the question and (subject to rule 13) send it to the Tribunal and the parties; and

    (g) attend hearings.

(3) The independent expert may make an application for any order or for a hearing to be held as if he were a party to the proceedings.

(4) At any stage of the proceedings the Tribunal may, after giving the independent expert the opportunity to make representations, withdraw the requirement on the independent expert to prepare a report. If it does so, the Tribunal may itself determine the question, or it may require a different independent expert to prepare the report.

(5) When paragraph (4) applies the independent expert who is no longer required to prepare the report shall provide the Tribunal with all documentation and work in progress relating to the proceedings

by a specified date. Such documentation and work in progress must be in a form which the Tribunal is able to use and may be used in relation to those proceedings by the Tribunal or by another independent expert.

Use of expert evidence

10.—(1) The Tribunal shall restrict expert evidence to that which it considers is reasonably required to resolve the proceedings.

(2) An expert shall have a duty to assist the Tribunal on matters within the expert's expertise. This duty overrides any obligation to the person from whom the expert has received instructions or by whom the expert is paid.

(3) No party may call an expert or put in evidence an expert's report without the permission of the Tribunal. No expert report shall be put in evidence unless it has been disclosed to all other parties and any independent expert at least 28 days before the final hearing.

(4) In proceedings in which an independent expert has been required to prepare a report on the question, the Tribunal shall not admit evidence of another expert on the question unless such evidence is based on the facts relating to the question. Unless the Tribunal considers it inappropriate to do so, any such expert report shall be disclosed to all parties and to the Tribunal on the same date on which the independent expert is required to send his report to the parties and to the tribunal.

(5) If an expert (other than an independent expert) does not comply with these rules or an order made by the Tribunal, the Tribunal may order that the evidence of that expert shall not be admitted.

(6) Where two or more parties wish to submit expert evidence on a particular issue, the Tribunal may order that the evidence on that issue is to be given by one joint expert only and if the parties wishing to instruct the joint expert cannot agree an expert, the Tribunal may select an expert.

Written questions to experts (including independent experts)

11.—(1) When an expert has prepared a report, a party or any other expert involved in the proceedings may put written questions about the report to the expert who has prepared the report.

(2) Unless the Tribunal agrees otherwise, written questions under paragraph (1)—
   (a) may be put once only;
   (b) must be put within 28 days of the date on which the parties were sent the report;
   (c) must be for the purpose only of clarifying the factual basis of the report; and
   (d) must be copied to all other parties and experts involved in the proceedings at the same time as they are sent to the expert who prepared the report.

(3) An expert shall answer written questions within 28 days of receipt and the answers shall be treated as part of the expert's report.

(4) Where a party has put a written question to an expert instructed by another party and the expert does not answer that question within 28 days, the Tribunal may order that the party instructing that expert may not rely on the evidence of that expert.

Procedural matters

12.—(1) Where an independent expert has been required to prepare a report, the Tribunal shall send that expert notice of any hearing, application, order or judgment in the proceedings as if the independent expert were a party to those proceedings and when these rules or an order requires a party to provide information to another party, such information shall also be provided to the independent expert.

(2) There may be more than one stage 1 or stage 2 equal value hearing in any case.

(3) Any power conferred on an Employment Judge by Schedule 1 may (subject to the provisions of this Schedule) in an equal value claim be carried out by a full tribunal or an Employment Judge.

National security proceedings

13 Where in an equal value claim a direction is given, or order is made, under rule 94 of Schedule 1—
   (a) any independent expert appointed shall send a copy of any report and any responses to written questions to the Tribunal only; and
   (b) before the Tribunal sends the parties a copy of a report or answers which have been received from an independent expert, it shall follow the procedure set out in rule 6 of Schedule 2 as if that rule referred to the independent expert's report or answers (as the case may be) instead of written reasons, except that the independent expert's report or answers shall not be entered on the Register.

Appendix 2
Practice Directions and Guidance

Practice Direction
(Employment Appeal Tribunal—Procedure) 2013

1 Introduction and Objective

1.1 This Practice Direction ('PD') supersedes all previous Practice Directions. It comes into force on Monday 29 July 2013.

1.2 The following statutory provisions apply to the way appeals are handled at the Employment Appeal Tribunal ('the EAT'), whenever those appeals were begun:

a) Employment Tribunals Act 1996 ('ETA 1996');

b) the Employment Appeal Tribunal Rules 1993 (SI 1993/2854) (as amended by the Employment Appeal Tribunal (Amendment) Rules 2001 (SI 2001/1128 and 2001/1476), the Employment Appeal Tribunal (Amendment) Rules 2004 (SI 2004/2526), and the Employment Appeal Tribunal (Amendment) Rules 2013 (SI 2013/1693)) ('the Rules').

1.3 Where the Rules do not otherwise provide, the following procedure will apply to all appeals to the EAT.

1.4 By s30(3) of the ETA 1996 the Employment Appeal Tribunal ('the EAT') has power, subject to the Rules, to regulate its own procedure. In so doing, the EAT regards itself as subject in all its actions to the duties imposed by Rule 2A. It will seek to apply the overriding objective when it exercises any power given to it by the Rules or interprets any Rule.

1.5 The overriding objective of this PD is to enable the EAT to deal with cases justly. Dealing with a case justly includes, so far as is practicable:

1.5.1 ensuring that the parties are on an equal footing;

1.5.2 dealing with the case in ways which are proportionate to the importance and complexity of the issues;

1.5.3 ensuring that it is dealt with expeditiously and fairly;

1.5.4 saving expense.

1.6 Dealing with a case justly also includes safeguarding the resources of the EAT so that each case gets its fair share of available time, but no more.

1.7 The parties are required to help the EAT to further the overriding objective.

1.8 Where it is appropriate to the EAT's jurisdiction, procedure, unrestricted rights of representation and restricted costs regime, the EAT is guided by the Civil Procedure Rules. So, for example:

1.8.1 For the purpose of serving a valid Notice of Appeal under Rule 3 and para. 3 below, when an Employment Tribunal decision is sent to parties on a Wednesday, that day does not count when calculating time limits, and the Notice of Appeal must arrive at the EAT before, or by 4.00pm on, the Wednesday 6 weeks (i.e. 42 days) later.

1.9 The provisions of this PD are subject to any specific directions which the EAT makes in any particular case. Otherwise, the directions set out below must be complied with in all appeals from Employment Tribunals. In national security appeals and appeals from the Certification Officer and the Central Arbitration Committee, the Rules set out the separate procedures to be followed and the EAT will normally give specific directions.

1.10 In this PD any reference to the date of an order shall mean the date stamped upon the relevant order by the EAT ('the seal date').

1.11 The parties can expect the EAT normally to have read the documents (or the documents indicated in any essential reading list if permission is granted under para. 8.3 below for an enlarged appeal bundle) in advance of any hearing.

2 Basis of Appeal

2.1 Since the ETA provides that appeal lies only on a 'question of law', the parties must expect any decision of fact made by an employment Tribunal, Certification Officer or Central Arbitration Committee to be decisive.

2.2 It is not an error of law for a Tribunal, judge, CO or CAC to reach a decision which one party to the case thinks should have been differently made. The appeal is not a rehearing of the case. The Employment Tribunal must be shown to have made an error of law.

2.3 If a party is in any doubt about whether a point is one of law or not, legal advice should be sought. The EAT cannot and does not give legal advice to any party.

3 Institution of Appeal: What should be in a Notice of Appeal

3.1 The Notice of Appeal must be, or be substantially, in accordance with Form 1 (in the amended form annexed to this Practice Direction) or Forms 1A or 2 of the Schedule to the Rules. It must identify the date of the judgment, decision or order being appealed. Copies of the judgment, decision or order appealed against must be attached, as must be the Employment Tribunal's written reasons, together with a copy of the claim (ET1) and the response (ET3), or if not, a written explanation for the omission of the reasons, ET1 and ET3 must be given. It must include a postal address at or through which the appellant can be contacted. A Notice of Appeal without such documentation will not be validly presented.

3.2 If the appellant has made an application to the Employment Tribunal for a reconsideration of its judgment or decision, a copy of that application should accompany the Notice of Appeal together with the judgment and written reasons of the Employment Tribunal in respect of that reconsideration application, or a statement, if such be the case, that a judgment is awaited.

3.3 If any of these documents cannot be included, a written explanation must be given. The appellant should also attach (where they are relevant to the appeal) copies of any orders (including case management orders) made by the Employment Tribunal, CO or CAC.

3.4 Where written reasons of the Employment Tribunal are not attached to the Notice of Appeal, either (as set out in the written explanation) because a request for written reasons has been refused by the Employment Tribunal or for some other reason, an appellant must, when presenting the Notice of Appeal, apply in writing to the EAT to exercise its discretion to hear the appeal without written reasons or to exercise its power to request written reasons from the Employment Tribunal, setting out the full grounds of that application.

3.5 The Notice of Appeal must clearly identify the point(s) of law which form(s) the ground(s) of appeal from the judgment, decision or order of the Employment Tribunal to the EAT. It should also state the order which the appellant will ask the EAT to make at the hearing.

3.6 A Notice of Appeal should be no longer than the making of a clear statement of the ground of appeal requires. This must be sufficient for a judge looking at the Notice of Appeal to know what the error(s) of law is/are said to be, but except in the case of a perversity appeal or one which complains about the conduct and/or bias of the Employment Tribunal (see para. 13 below) should be no longer: in any case, it should not set out detailed argument and citation from case law unless this is essential for understanding.

3.7 If it appears to the judge or Registrar that a Notice of Appeal or an application gives insufficient grounds of, or lacks clarity in identifying, a point of law, the judge or Registrar may postpone any further consideration of the Appeal pending the appellant's amplification or clarification of the Notice of Appeal or the receipt of further information from the Employment Tribunal.

3.8 Perversity Appeals: an appellant may not state as a ground of appeal simply words to the effect that 'the judgment or order was contrary to the evidence', or that 'there was no evidence to support the judgment or order', or that 'the judgment or order was one which no reasonable Tribunal could have reached and was perverse' unless the Notice of Appeal also sets out full particulars of the matters relied on in support of those general grounds.

3.9 Where it appears that the Notice of Appeal or any part of it (a) discloses no reasonable grounds for bringing the appeal, or (b) is an abuse of the Employment Appeal Tribunal's process or is otherwise likely to obstruct the just disposal of proceedings, Rules 3(7)–(10) give a judge or the Registrar power to decide that no further action shall be taken on the appeal. The Rules specify the rights of the appellant and the procedure to be followed. The appellant can request an oral hearing before a judge to reconsider the decision.

3.10 A party cannot 'reserve a right' to amend, alter or add, to a Notice of Appeal or a respondent's Answer. No party has the right to amend any Notice of Appeal or Answer without the prior permission of the EAT. Any application for permission to amend must be made as soon as practicable and must be accompanied by a draft of the amended Notice of Appeal or amended Answer which makes clear the precise amendments for which permission is sought.

3.11 Where an application is made for permission to institute or continue relevant proceedings by a person who has been made the subject of a Restriction of Proceedings Order pursuant to s33 of ETA 1996, that application will be considered on paper by a judge, who may make an order granting, refusing or otherwise dealing with such application on paper.

4 Fees Payable on Appeal

This section is no longer applicable following R (on the application of UNISON) v Lord Chancellor [2017] UKSC 51

5 Time for Instituting Appeals

5.1 The time within which an appeal must be instituted depends on whether the appeal is against a judgment or against an order, direction or decision of the Employment Tribunal.

5.2 If the appeal is against an order, direction or decision, the appeal must be instituted within 42 days of the date of the order, direction or decision. The EAT will treat a Tribunal's refusal to make an order or decision as itself constituting an order direction or decision. The date of an order direction or decision is the date when the order direction or decision was sent to the parties, which is normally recorded on or in the order direction or decision.

5.3 If the appeal is against a Judgment, the appeal must be instituted within 42 days from the date on which the written record of the Judgment was sent to the parties. However, in three situations the time for appealing against a Judgment will be 42 days from the date when written reasons for the Judgment were sent to the parties. This will be the case if (and only if) (1) written reasons were requested orally at the hearing before the Tribunal or (2) written reasons were requested in writing within 14 days of the date on which the written record of the judgment was sent to the parties or (3) the Tribunal itself reserved its reasons and gave them subsequently in writing. Time will not be extended where a request to the Tribunal for written reasons is made out of time (whether or not such request is granted). The date of the written record of the Judgment and of the written reasons for the Judgment is the date when they are sent to the parties, which is normally recorded on or in the written record and the written reasons.

5.4 The time limit referred to in paras. 5.1 to 5.3 above applies even though the question of remedy and assessment of compensation by the Employment Tribunal has been adjourned or has not been dealt with and even though an application has been made to the Employment Tribunal for a reconsideration.

5.5 An application for an extension of time for appealing cannot be considered until a Notice of Appeal in accordance with para. 3 above has been presented with the EAT.

5.6 Any application for an extension of time for appealing must be made as an interim application to the Registrar, who will normally determine the application after inviting and considering written representations from each side. An interim appeal lies from the Registrar's decision to a judge. Such an appeal must be notified to the EAT within 5 working days of the date when the Registrar's decision was sent to the parties: this means that where, for example, the Registrar's decision is sent to the parties on a Wednesday, any appeal against it must be received no later than 4pm. on the following Wednesday [See para. 1.8.1 above].

5.7 In determining whether to extend the time for appealing, particular attention will be paid to whether any good excuse for the delay has been shown and to the guidance contained in the decisions of the EAT and the Court of Appeal, as summarised in cases such as *United Arab Emirates v Abdelghafar* [1995] ICR 65, *Aziz v Bethnal Green City Challenge Co Ltd* [2000] IRLR 111, and *Jurkowska v HLMAD Ltd* [2008] ICR 841.

5.8 It is not usually a good reason for late presentation of a Notice of Appeal that (a) an application for litigation support from public funds has been made, but not yet determined; or that support is being sought from, but has not yet been provided by, some other body, such as a trade union, employers' association or the Equality and Human Rights Commission; (b) that the appellant was waiting for the result of an application for reconsideration (c) that negotiations between the parties were occurring.

5.9 In any case of doubt or difficulty, a Notice of Appeal should be presented in time and an application made to the Registrar for directions.

6 Interim Applications

6.1 Interim applications should be made in writing (no particular form is required) and will be initially referred to the Registrar who after considering the papers may deal with the case or refer it to a judge. The judge may dispose of it or refer it to a full EAT hearing. Parties are encouraged to make any such applications at a Preliminary Hearing ('PH') or an Appointment for Directions if one is ordered (see paras. 11.8–11.19 and 12.4 below).

6.2 Unless otherwise ordered, any application for extension of time will be considered and determined as though it were an interim application to the Registrar, who will normally determine the application after inviting and considering written representations from each side.

6.3 An interim appeal lies from the Registrar's decision to a judge. Such an appeal must be notified to the EAT within five days of the date when the Registrar's decision was sent to the parties.

7 The Right to Inspect Certain Documents and to Take Copies

7.1 Any document presented to the Central Office of the EAT in London or in the EAT office in Edinburgh in any proceedings before the EAT shall be stamped with the seal of the EAT showing the date (and time, if received after 4.00 pm) on which the document was presented.

7.2 Particulars of the date of delivery at the London or Edinburgh EAT office of any document for filing or presentation together with the time, if received after 4.00pm, the date of the document and the title of the appeal of which the document forms part of the record shall be entered in the list of registered cases kept in London and in Edinburgh or in the file which forms part of the list of registered cases.

7.3 Any person shall be entitled during office hours by appointment to inspect and request a copy of any of the following documents filed or presented to the London or Edinburgh EAT office, namely:

7.3.1 any Notice of Appeal or respondent's Answer or any copy thereof;

7.3.2 any judgment or order given or made in court or any copy of such judgment or order.

7.4 Any other document may be inspected only with the permission of the EAT, which may be granted for proper reason on an application.

7.5 A copying charge per page will be payable for those documents mentioned in paras. 7.3 and 7.4 above.

7.6 Nothing in this Direction shall be taken as preventing any party to an appeal from inspecting and requesting a copy of any document filed or presented to the EAT office in London or Edinburgh before the commencement of the appeal, but made with a view to its commencement.

8 Papers for use at the Hearing

8.1 It is the responsibility of the parties or their advisers to prepare a core bundle of papers (see paras. 8.3–8.6 below) for use at any hearing. Ultimate responsibility lies with the appellant, following consultation with other parties. The bundle must include only those exhibits (productions in Scotland) and documents used before the Employment Tribunal which are considered to be necessary for the appeal. It is the duty of the parties or their advisers to ensure that only those documents are included which are (a) relevant to the point(s) of law raised in the appeal and (b) likely to be referred to at the hearing. It is also the responsibility of parties to retain copies of all documents and correspondence, including hearing bundles, sent to EAT. Bundles (see para. 8.3 below) used at one EAT hearing will not be retained by the EAT for a subsequent hearing.

8.2 The documents in the core bundle should be numbered by item, then paginated continuously and indexed, in the following order:

8.2.1 Judgment, decision or order appealed from and written reasons

8.2.2 Sealed Notice of Appeal

8.2.3 Respondent's Answer if a Full Hearing ('FH'), respondent's Submissions if a PH

8.2.4 ET1 claim (and any Additional Information or Written Answers)

8.2.5 ET3 response (and any Additional Information or Written Answers)

8.2.6 Questionnaire and Replies, if any (discrimination and equal pay cases)

8.2.7 Relevant orders, judgments and written reasons of the Employment Tribunal

8.2.8 Relevant orders and judgments of the EAT

8.2.9 Affidavits and Employment Tribunal comments (where ordered)

8.2.10 Any documents agreed or ordered (subject to para. 8.3 below).

8.3 Other documents necessary for and relevant to the appeal, which were referred to at the Employment Tribunal may follow in the core or a supplementary bundle, if the total pages additional to the documents set out in para. 8.2–8.2.9 do not exceed 50 No bundle containing more than 50 such additional pages should be agreed or lodged without the permission of the Registrar or order of a judge which will not be granted without the provision of an essential reading list as soon as practicable thereafter. If permitted or ordered, further pages should follow, with consecutive pagination, in an additional bundle or bundles if appropriate.

8.4 All documents must be legible and unmarked.

8.5 For PH cases (see para. 11.8 below), Appeals from Registrar's Order, Rule 3(10) hearings, or Appointments for Directions: the appellant must prepare and present two copies (four copies if the judge has directed a sitting with lay members) of the bundle as soon as possible after service of the Notice of Appeal and no later than 28 days prior to the date fixed for the hearing, unless otherwise directed.

8.6 For FH cases (see para. 11.20 below): the parties must co-operate in agreeing a bundle of papers for the hearing. By no later than 28 days prior to the date fixed for the hearing, unless otherwise directed, the appellant is responsible for ensuring that two copies (four copies if the judge has directed a sitting with lay members) of a bundle agreed by the parties is presented to the EAT.

8.7 For Fast Track FH cases: the bundles should be presented as soon as possible and (unless the hearing date is within seven days) in any event within seven days after the parties have been notified that the case is expedited.

Appendix 2 Practice Directions and Guidance

8.8 In the event of disagreement between the parties or difficulty in preparing the bundles, the Registrar may give appropriate directions, whether on application in writing (on notice) by one or more of the parties or of his/her own initiative.

8.9 In no case other than those subject to Rule 30A (Proceedings in cases concerning national security) will the EAT accept documents or communications on the basis that they are to be confidential to the EAT and are not to be disclosed to another party. All documents presented by one party are disclosable to the other(s), and the parties must expect that to be the case.

9 Evidence before the Employment Tribunal

9.1 An appellant who considers that a point of law raised in the Notice of Appeal cannot be argued without reference to evidence given (or not given) at the Employment Tribunal, the nature or substance of which does not, or does not sufficiently, appear from the written reasons, must ordinarily submit an application with the Notice of Appeal. The application is for the nature of such evidence (or lack of it) to be admitted, or if necessary for the relevant parts of the employment judge's notes of evidence to be produced. If such application is not so made, then it should be made:

9.1.1 if a PH is ordered, in the skeleton argument or written submissions presented prior to such PH; or

9.1.2 if the case is listed for FH without a PH, then within 14 days of the seal date of the order so providing.

9.1.3 Any such application by a respondent to an appeal, must, if not made earlier, accompany the respondent's Answer.

9.2 The application must explain why such a matter is considered necessary in order to argue the point of law raised in the Notice of Appeal or respondent's Answer. The application must identify:

9.2.1 the issue(s) in the Notice of Appeal or respondent's Answer to which the material is relevant;

9.9.2 the names of the witnesses whose evidence is considered relevant, alternatively the nature of the evidence the absence of which is considered relevant;

9.2.3 (if applicable) the part of the hearing when the evidence was given;

9.2.4 the gist of the evidence (or absence of evidence) alleged to be relevant; and

9.2.5 (if the party has a record of the evidence), saying so and by whom and when it was made, or producing an extract from a witness statement given in writing at the hearing.

9.3 The application will be considered on the papers, or if appropriate at a PH, by the Registrar or a judge. The Registrar or a judge may give directions for written representations (if they have not already been lodged), or may determine the application, but will ordinarily make an order requiring the party who seeks to raise such a matter to give notice to the other party(ies) to the appeal/cross-appeal. The notice will require the other party(ies) to co-operate in agreeing, within 21 days (unless a shorter period is ordered), a statement or note of the relevant evidence, alternatively a statement that there was no such evidence. All parties are required to use their best endeavours to agree such a statement or note.

9.4 In the absence of such agreement within 21 days (or such shorter period as may be ordered) of the requirement, any party may make an application within seven days thereafter to the EAT, for directions. The party must enclose all relevant correspondence and give notice to the other parties. The directions may include: the resolution of the disagreement on the papers or at a hearing; the administration by one party to the others of, or a request to the employment judge to provide, information; or, if the EAT is satisfied that such notes are necessary, a request that the employment judge produce his/her notes of evidence either in whole or in part.

9.5 If the EAT requests any documents from the employment judge, it will supply copies to the parties upon receipt.

9.6 In an appeal from an Employment Tribunal which ordered its proceedings to be tape recorded, the EAT will apply the principles above to any application for a transcript.

9.7 A note of evidence is not to be produced and supplied to the parties to enable the parties to embark on a 'fishing expedition' to establish grounds or additional grounds of appeal or because they have not kept their own notes of the evidence. If an application for such a note is found by the EAT to have been unreasonably made or if there is unreasonable lack of co-operation in agreeing a relevant note or statement, the party behaving unreasonably is at risk of being ordered to pay costs.

10 Fresh Evidence and New Points of Law

10.1 Usually the EAT will not consider evidence which was not placed before the Employment Tribunal unless and until an application has first been made to the Employment Tribunal against whose judgment the appeal is brought for that tribunal to reconsider its judgment. Where such an application has been made, it is likely that unless a judge of the EAT dismisses the appeal as having no reasonable prospect of success the judge will stay (or sist) any further action on that appeal until the result of the reconsideration is known.

The Employment Tribunal as the fact-finding body, which has heard relevant witnesses, is the appropriate forum to consider 'fresh evidence' and in particular the extent to which (if at all) it would or might have made a difference to its conclusions. It remains open to an intending appellant to contend that there has been an error of law if the Employment Tribunal is in error of law in refusing to reconsider its decision, and if so then to refer to evidence which was not placed before the Employment Tribunal at the time it made its initial decision but was placed before that Tribunal for the purposes of seeking or hearing a reconsideration of its decision.

10.2 Subject to para. 10.1, where an application is made by a party to an appeal to put in, at the hearing of the appeal, any document which was not before the Employment Tribunal, and which has not been agreed in writing by the other parties, the application and a copy of the documents sought to be admitted should be presented to the EAT with the Notice of Appeal or the respondent's Answer, as appropriate. The application and copy should be served on the other parties. The same principle applies to any oral evidence not given at the Employment Tribunal which is sought to be adduced on the appeal. The nature and substance of such evidence together with the date when the party first became aware of its existence must be disclosed in a document, where appropriate a witness statement from the relevant witness with signed statement of truth, which must be similarly presented to the EAT and served.

10.3 In exercising its discretion to admit any fresh evidence or new document, the EAT will apply the principles set out in Ladd v Marshall [1954] 1WLR 1489, having regard to the overriding objective, i.e.:

10.3.1 the evidence could not have been obtained with reasonable diligence for use at the Employment Tribunal hearing;

10.3.2 it is relevant and would probably have had an important influence on the hearing;

10.3.3 it is apparently credible.

Accordingly, the evidence and representations in support of the application must address these principles.

10.4 A party wishing to resist the application must, within 14 days of its being sent, submit any representations in response to the EAT and other parties.

10.5 The application will be considered by the Registrar or a judge on the papers (or, if appropriate, at a PH) who may stay (or sist) the appeal in accordance with para. 10.1, determine the issue or give directions for a hearing or may seek comments from the employment judge. A copy of any comments received from the employment judge will be sent to all parties.

10.6 If a respondent intends to contend at the FH that the appellant has raised a point which was not argued below, the respondent shall say so:

11.5.1 if a PH has been ordered, in writing to the EAT and all parties, within 14 days of receiving the Notice of Appeal;

11.5.2 if the case is listed for a FH without a PH, in a respondent's Answer. In the event of dispute the employment judge should be asked for his/her comments as to whether a particular legal argument was deployed.

11 The Sift of Appeals: Case Tracks and Directions

11.1 Once a Notice of Appeal has been received, properly instituted, and any applicable fee has been paid or remission has been granted within time, it will be sifted by a judge or the Registrar who will consider the Notice of Appeal and, if appropriate, obtain any additional information so as to determine

(a) whether it discloses any reasonable ground for bringing an appeal; (see further para. 11.4 below)

(b) if so, whether the whole or only part of the grounds of appeal should be argued before a Full Hearing;

(c) if not, whether the appeal is wholly without merit (in which case there is no right for the appellant to an oral hearing before a judge at the EAT, though this does not remove any right to appeal to the Court of Appeal);

11.1.1 The EAT will deal with applications in order, and parties must not expect their appeal to take precedence over any other unless there are truly exceptional circumstances.

11.2 If the Notice of Appeal does or might disclose a reasonable ground or grounds, the judge deciding the sift will determine the most effective case management of the appeal. This will be to allocate the relevant ground(s) of appeal for further consideration at a Preliminary Hearing (PH), or for determination at a Full Hearing (FH), and in either case to give appropriate directions.

11.3 The judge or Registrar may also stay (or sist in Scotland) the appeal for a period, normally 21 days, pending the making or the conclusion of an application by the appellant to the Employment Tribunal for a reconsideration (if necessary out of time) or pending the response by the Employment Tribunal to an invitation from the judge or Registrar to clarify, supplement or give its written reasons.

Appendix 2 Practice Directions and Guidance

11.4   An appeal will not be treated as showing any reasonable ground for bringing the appeal insofar as it is an abuse of the process or otherwise likely to obstruct the just disposal of the matters in issue between the parties.

11.5   Reasons will be sent and within 28 days the appellant may request an oral hearing (known as a 'Rule 3(10) hearing') before a judge unless the judge determining the sift has ruled that the appeal is wholly without merit.

11.6   At a Rule 3(10) hearing the judge may confirm the earlier decision or order that the appeal proceeds in whole or in part to a PH or FH, giving appropriate directions. These directions may permit an amendment to be made to the grounds of appeal. Such a proposed amendment should wherever practicable be made available in writing at the hearing or on the same day, and will not take effect unless the judge has approved it.

11.7   A hearing under Rule 3(10), including judgment and any directions, will normally last not more than one hour including time for oral judgment to be given.

Preliminary Hearings (PHs)

11.8   The purpose of a PH is to determine whether any of the grounds in the Notice of Appeal raise a point of law which gives:

11.8.1   reasonable grounds to appeal i.e. a reasonable prospect of success at a FH; or

11.8.2   that for some other compelling reason the appeal should be heard e.g. that the appellant seeks a declaration of incompatibility under the Human Rights Act 1998; or to argue that a decision binding on the EAT should be considered by a higher court.

11.9   Prior to the PH there will be automatic directions. These include sending the Notice of Appeal to the respondent(s) to the appeal. The direction may order but in any event will enable the respondent(s) to present and serve, within 14 days of the seal date of the order (unless otherwise directed), concise written submissions in response to the Notice of Appeal, dedicated to showing that there is no reasonable prospect of success for all or any grounds of any appeal. Those submissions will be considered at the PH.

11.10   If the respondent to the appeal intends to serve a cross-appeal this must be accompanied by written Notice to that effect which must be presented and served within 14 days of service of the Notice of Appeal. The respondent to the appeal must make clear whether it is intended to advance the cross-appeal:

11.10.1 in any event (an unconditional cross-appeal); or

11.10.2 only if the Appellant succeeds (a conditional cross-appeal).

In either case the respondent is entitled to attend the PH, which will also amount to a PH of the cross-appeal, and make submissions.

11.11   All parties will be notified of the date fixed for the PH. In the normal case, unless ordered otherwise, only the Appellant and/or a representative should attend to make submissions to the EAT on the issue whether the Notice of Appeal raises any reasonable ground for bringing an appeal, though it is open to the Respondent to observe the proceedings, and though a respondent will not normally be permitted to take part in them may with the permission of the court do so if the judge considers it desirable. Any written submissions as referred to in para. 11.9 above will be considered at the PH.

11.12   If the appellant does not attend, the appeal may nevertheless be dealt with as above on written submissions, and be dismissed wholly or in part or allowed to proceed.

11.13   The PH, including judgment and directions, will normally last no more than one hour. Arguments should be carefully planned so that this time is not exceeded; if it is, the Appeal Tribunal may impose a guillotine on further argument, in order to ensure that the case does not take a share of the Appeal Tribunal's resources which is disproportionate to that taken by other appeals yet to be heard.

11.14   The sift procedure will be applied to cross-appeals as well as appeals. If satisfied that the appeal (and/or the cross-appeal) should be heard at a FH on all or some of the grounds of appeal, the EAT will give directions relating to, for example, a time estimate, any application for fresh evidence, a procedure in respect of matters of evidence before the Employment Tribunal not sufficiently appearing from the written reasons, the exchange and lodging of skeleton arguments and an appellant's Chronology, and bundles of documents and authorities.

11.15   Permission to amend a Notice of Appeal (or cross-appeal) may be granted at a PH:

11.15.1 If the proposed amendment is produced at the hearing, then, if such amendment has not previously been notified to the other parties, and the appeal (or cross-appeal) might not have been permitted to proceed but for the amendment, the opposing party(ies) will have the opportunity to apply on notice to vary or discharge the permission to proceed, and for consequential directions as to the hearing or disposal of the appeal or cross-appeal.

11.15.2 A draft amendment should wherever practicable be made available at the PH or on the same day unless otherwise directed.

11.16 If not satisfied that the appeal, or any particular ground of it, should go forward to a FH, the EAT at the PH will dismiss the appeal, wholly or in part, and give a judgment setting out the reasons for doing so.

11.17 If an appeal is permitted to go forward to an FH on all grounds, a reasoned judgment will not normally be given.

11.18 Parties who become aware that a similar point is raised in other proceedings at an Employment Tribunal or the EAT are encouraged to co-operate in bringing this to the attention of the Registrar so that consideration can be given to the most expedient way of dealing with the cases, in particular to the possibility of having two or more appeals heard together.

11.19 If an appeal is permitted to go forward to an FH, a listing category will be assigned i.e.:
P (recommended to be heard in the President's list);
A (complex, and raising point(s) of law of public importance); B (any other cases).
The President reserves the discretion to alter any relevant category as circumstances require.

Full Hearings (FHs)

11.20 If a judge or the Registrar decides to list the case for an FH s/he will consider appropriate directions, relating for example to amendment, further information, a procedure in respect of matters of evidence at the Employment Tribunal not sufficiently appearing from the written reasons, allegations of bias, apparent bias or improper conduct, provisions for skeleton arguments, appellant's Chronology and bundles of documents and of authorities, time estimates and listing category (as set out in para. 11.19 above).

11.21 The EAT aims to hear FH cases in the order in which they are received.
However, there are times when it is expedient to hear an appeal as soon as it can be fitted into the list. Appeals thus fast-tracked, at the discretion of a judge or the Registrar, will normally fall into the following cases:

11.21.1 appeals where the parties have made a reasoned case on the merits for an expedited hearing;

11.21.2 appeals against interim orders or decisions of an Employment Tribunal, particularly those which involve the taking of a step in the proceedings within a specified period, for example adjournments, further information, amendments, disclosure, witness orders;

11.21.3 appeals on the outcome of which other applications to the Employment Tribunal or the EAT or the civil courts depend;

11.21.4 appeals in which a reference to the European Court of Justice (ECJ), or a declaration of incompatibility under the Human Rights Act 1998, is sought;

11.21.5 appeals involving reinstatement, re-engagement, or interim relief.

11.22 Category B cases estimated to take two hours or less may also be fast-tracked.

12 Further Fees, Respondent's Answer and Directions

12.1 Fees no longer apply.

12.2 Once a fee has been paid, the EAT will send the Notice of Appeal, with any amendments which have been permitted, and any submissions or skeleton argument lodged by the appellant, to all parties who are respondents to the appeal. Within 14 days of the seal date of the order (unless otherwise directed), respondents must present to the EAT and serve on the other parties a respondent's Answer. If it contains a cross-appeal, the cross-appellant must within 14 days of service (unless otherwise directed), pay any fee which is due in respect of the cross-appeal (or apply for remission). The Appellant must present and serve a Reply. The Answer must show how the Respondent would wish the EAT to deal with the appeal if the Appellant succeeds: see para. 3.5 above.

12.3 A respondent to the appeal who wishes to resist the appeal and/or to cross-appeal, but who has not delivered a respondent's Answer as directed by the Registrar, or otherwise ordered, may be barred from taking part in the appeal unless permission is granted to serve an Answer out of time.

12.4 After presentation and service of the respondent's Answer and of any Reply to a cross-appeal, the Registrar may, where necessary, invite applications from the parties in writing, on notice to all other parties, for directions, and may give any appropriate directions on the papers or may fix a day when the parties should attend on an Appointment for Directions.

12.5 A judge may at any time, upon consideration of the papers or at a hearing, make an order requiring or recommending consideration by the parties or any of them of compromise, conciliation, mediation or, in particular, reference to ACAS.

13 Complaints about the Conduct of the Employment Tribunal Hearing or Bias

13.1   An appellant who intends to complain about the conduct of the Employment Tribunal (for example bias, apparent bias or improper conduct by the employment judge, any lay members or any material procedural irregularity at the hearing) must include in the Notice of Appeal full particulars of each complaint made.

13.2   An appeal which is wholly or in part based on such a complaint will be sifted by a judge or the Registrar as set out in para. 11.1 above. The judge or Registrar may postpone a decision on the sift, and direct that the appellant or a representative provide an affidavit or statement setting out full particulars of all allegations of bias or misconduct relied upon, and/or may enquire of the party making the complaint whether it is intended to proceed with it and may draw attention to para. 13.6 below.

13.3   If a decision is taken at the sift to proceed further with the appeal, the EAT may take the following steps prior to any hearing within a time-limit set out in the relevant order:

13.3.1   require the appellant or a representative to provide, if not already provided, an affidavit or statement as set out in para. 13.2 above;

13.3.2   require any party to give an affidavit or to obtain a witness statement from any person who has represented any of the parties at the Tribunal hearing, and any other person present at the Tribunal hearing or a relevant part of it, giving their account of the events set out in the affidavit of the appellant or the appellant's representative. For this purpose, the EAT will provide copies of any affidavits received from or on behalf of the appellant to any other person from whom an account is sought;

13.3.3   seek comments, upon all affidavits or witness statements received, from the employment judge of the Employment Tribunal from which the appeal is brought and may seek such comments from any lay members of the Tribunal. For this purpose, copies of all relevant documents will be provided by the EAT to the employment judge and, if appropriate, the lay members; such documents will include any affidavits and witness statements received, the Notice of Appeal and other relevant documents;

13.3.4   the EAT will on receipt supply to the parties copies of all affidavits, statements. and comments received.

13.4   A respondent who intends to make such a complaint must include such particulars as set out in paras. 13.1 and 13.2 above:

13.4.1   in the respondent's Answer

13.4.2   or in the cross-appeal referred to in para. 11.5 above, or,

13.4.3   where a PH is ordered in the absence of a cross-appeal, in written submissions, as referred to in para. 11.9 above.

A similar procedure will then be followed as in para. 13.3 above.

13.5   In every case which is permitted to go forward to an FH the EAT will give appropriate directions, ordinarily on the papers after notice to the appellant and respondent, as to the procedure to be adopted at, and material to be provided to, the FH; such directions may be given at any stage but particularly at the sift stage or at a PH.

13.6   Parties should note the following:

13.6.1   The EAT will not permit complaints of the kind mentioned above to be raised or developed at the hearing of the appeal unless this procedure has been followed.

13.6.2   The EAT recognises that employment judges and Employment Tribunals are themselves obliged to observe the overriding objective and are given wide powers and duties of case management (see Employment Tribunal (Constitution and Rules of Procedure) Regulations 2004 (SI No 1861)), so appeals in respect of conduct of Employment Tribunals which is in exercise of those powers and duties, are the less likely to succeed.

13.6.3   Unsuccessful pursuit of an allegation of bias or improper conduct, particularly in respect of case management decisions, may put the party raising it at risk of an order for costs against them.

14 Case Management

14.1   Consistent with the overriding objective, the EAT will seek to give directions for case management so that the appeal can be dealt with quickly, or better considered, and in the most effective and just way.

14.2   Applications and directions for case management will usually be dealt with on the papers at the sift stage by a judge, or by the Registrar with an appeal to a judge.

14.3   Any party seeking directions must serve a copy on all parties.

14.4   Directions may be given at any stage, before or after the registration of a Notice of Appeal. An order made will contain a time for compliance, which must be observed or be the subject of an application by any party to vary or discharge it, or to seek an extension of time. Otherwise, failure to comply with an order in time or at all may result in the EAT exercising its power under Rule 26 to strike out the appeal, cross-appeal or respondent's Answer, to debar the party from taking any further part in the proceedings or to make any other order it thinks fit, including an award of costs. The power to strike out an appeal, cross-appeal or answer to an appeal will not be exercised without the party subject to it being sent notification that the power may be exercised: but a notice stating that 'unless … (a particular step is taken by a certain time). the appeal (or a specified part of it) will be struck out' is sufficient notification for this purpose, and if the step is not taken before the time specified has elapsed the consequential strike-out will occur automatically.

14.5 Any application to vary or discharge an order, or to seek an extension of time, must be presented to the EAT and served on the other parties within the time fixed for compliance. Such other parties must, if opposing the application and within 14 days (or such shorter period as may be ordered) of receiving it, submit their representations to the EAT and the other parties.

14.6 An application to amend a Notice of Appeal or respondent's Answer must include the text of the original document with any changes clearly marked and identifiable, for example with deletions struck through in red and the text of the amendment either written or underlined in red. Any subsequent amendments will have to be in a different identifiable colour. Where provided from a computer print-out, the deleted wording should be struck through, and new wording put in italics. Where re-amendment is made, the new wording must be in bold italics or a distinctive and easily readable font.

15 Listing of Appeals

15.1 Estimate of Length of Hearing: All parties are required to ensure that the estimates of length of hearing (allowing for the fact that the parties can expect the EAT to have pre-read the papers and for deliberation and the giving of a judgment) are accurate when first given. This is of particular importance in any case in which it is directed that lay members should sit. Lay members of the EAT are part-time members. They attend when available on pre-arranged dates. They do not sit for continuous periods. Consequently, appeals which run beyond their estimated length have to be adjourned part-heard (often with substantial delay) until a day on which the judge and members are all available again. Any change in such estimate, or disagreement with an estimate made by the EAT on a sift or at a PH, is to be notified immediately to the Listing Officer.

15.2 The estimate should include time for judgment to be considered and delivered orally on the day of hearing.

15.3 If the EAT concludes that the hearing is likely to exceed the estimate, or if for other reasons the hearing may not be concluded within the time available, it may seek to avoid such adjournment by placing the parties under appropriate time limits in order to complete the presentation of the submissions within the estimated or available time.

15.4 A judge may at any time during any hearing, and with a view to achieving the overriding objective, require submissions to take place in whatever order the judge considers appropriate, and within whatever time limit seems fit. It will not be a legitimate objection that different time limits are prescribed for different parties: where this happens, it will be with a view to ensuring overall fairness.

15.5 The EAT will normally consult the parties on dates, and will accommodate reasonable requests if practicable, but is not bound to do so. Once the date is fixed, the appeal will be set down in the list. A party finding that the date which has been fixed causes serious difficulties may apply to the Listing Officer for it to be changed, having first notified all other parties entitled to appear on the date, of their application and the reasons for it.

15.6 Parties receiving such an application must, as soon as possible and within seven days, notify the Listing Officer of their views.

15.7 In addition to this fixed date procedure, a list ('the warned list') may be drawn up. Cases will be placed in such warned list at the discretion of the Listing Officer or may be so placed by the direction of a judge or the Registrar. These will ordinarily be short cases, or cases where expedition has been ordered. Parties or their representatives will be notified that their case has been included in this list, and as much notice as possible will be given of the intention to list a case for hearing, when representations by way of objection from the parties will be considered by the Listing Officer and if necessary on appeal to the Registrar or a judge. The parties may apply on notice to all other parties for a fixed date for hearing.

15.8 Other cases may be put in the list by the EAT with the consent of the parties at shorter notice: for example, where other cases have been settled or withdrawn or where it appears that they will take less time than originally estimated. Parties who wish their cases to be taken as soon as possible and at short notice should notify the Listing Officer. Representations by way of objection may be made by the parties to the Listing Officer and if necessary by appeal to a judge or the Registrar.

15.9 Each week an up-to-date list for the following week will be prepared, including any changes which have been made, in particular specifying cases which by then have been given fixed dates. The list appears on the EAT website.

16 Skeleton Arguments

16.1   Paras. 16.2 to 16.12 of the Practice Direction do not apply to an appeal heard in Scotland, unless otherwise directed in relation to that appeal by the EAT.

16.2   Skeleton arguments must be provided by all parties in all hearings, unless the EAT is notified by a party or representative in writing that the Notice of Appeal or respondent's Answer or relevant application contains the full argument, or the EAT otherwise directs in a particular case. It is the practice of the EAT for all the members to read the papers in advance. A well-structured skeleton argument helps the EAT and the parties to focus on the point(s) of law required to be decided and so makes the oral hearing more effective.

16.3   The skeleton argument should be concise and should identify and summarise the point(s) of law, the steps in the legal argument and the statutory provisions and authorities to be relied upon, identifying them by name, page and paragraph and stating the legal proposition sought to be derived from them. It is not, however, the purpose of the skeleton argument to argue the case on paper in detail. A skeleton argument where possible should be in print, rather than handwritten, using A4 paper, 12-point typescript, arranged in consecutively numbered paragraphs each separated from the other by a double space, and in a standard readable font.

16.4   The parties should be referred to by name or as they appeared at the Employment Tribunal i.e. Claimant (C) and Respondent (R).

16.5   The skeleton argument should state the form of order which the party will ask the EAT to make at the hearing: for example, in the case of an appellant, whether the EAT will be asked to remit the whole or part of the case to the same or to a different Employment Tribunal, or whether the EAT will be asked to substitute a different decision for that of the Employment Tribunal.

16.6   The appellant's skeleton argument must unless dispensed with by direction of the Registrar or a judge be accompanied by a Chronology of events relevant to the appeal which, if possible, should be agreed by the parties. That will normally be taken as an uncontroversial document, unless corrected by another party or the EAT. It is good practice to give references to paragraphs in the ET Judgment or pages in the EAT bundle.

16.7   Unless impracticable, the skeleton argument should be prepared using the pagination in the index to the appeal bundle. In a case where a note of the evidence at the Employment Tribunal has been produced, the skeleton argument should identify the parts of the record to which that party wishes to refer.

16.8   Represented parties should give the instructions necessary for their representative to comply with this procedure within the time limits.

16.9   The fact that conciliation or settlement negotiations are in progress in relation to the appeal does not excuse delay in lodging and exchanging skeleton arguments.

16.10 A skeleton argument may be lodged by the appellant with the Notice of Appeal or by the respondent with the respondent's Answer.

16.11 Skeleton arguments must (if not already so lodged):

16.11.1 be lodged at the EAT not less than 10 days (unless otherwise ordered) before the date fixed for the PH, appeal against Registrar's Order, Rule 3 (10) hearing or Appointment for Directions; or, if the hearing is fixed at less than seven days' notice, as soon as possible after the hearing date has been notified, and unless otherwise directed be provided to the other party(ies)

16.11.2 be lodged at the EAT, and exchanged between the parties, not less than 14 days before the FH;

16.11.3 in the cases either fast-tracked or in the warned list be lodged at the EAT and exchanged between the parties as soon as possible and (unless the hearing date is less than seven days later) in any event within seven days after the parties have been notified that the case is expedited or in the warned list.

16.12 Failure to follow this procedure may lead to a postponement of an appeal or to dismissal for noncompliance with the PD pursuant to Rule 26, and to an award of costs. The party in default may also be required to attend before the EAT to explain their failure. It will always mean that the defaulting party must immediately despatch any delayed skeleton argument to the EAT by hand or by fax or by email to londoneat@hmcts.gsi.gov.uk or, as appropriate, edinburgheat@hmcts.gsi.gov.uk and (unless notified by the EAT to the contrary) bring to the hearing sufficient copies (a minimum of 4, or 6 if the Judge is sitting with Lay Members) of the skeleton argument and any authorities referred to unless they are contained in the 'familiar authorities' bundle details of which are given on the EAT website. The EAT staff will not be responsible for supplying or copying other authorities on the morning of the hearing.

16.13 **Scotland: Skeleton Arguments** Skeleton arguments are considered particularly helpful to the EAT. Subject to any direction specific to a particular case, parties are at liberty to present a skeleton argument to the EAT. If they do so, however, they must serve a copy on every other party at the same time as presenting it to the EAT; and since the purpose is to indicate to the EAT in advance of a hearing how the argument is to be developed, in enough time for the judge (and members, if any) to consider it before the hearing, it should be presented at least 7 days prior to the day appointed for the hearing. Any skeleton argument presented later than that may not be read, and the party presenting it will lose the advantage of it. A party is entitled to present a skeleton argument even if the opposing party does not choose to do so.

17 Authorities

General

17.1 It is undesirable for parties to cite the same case from different sets of reports. The parties should, if practicable, agree which report will be used at the hearing. Where the Employment Tribunal has cited from a report it may be convenient to cite from the same report.

17.2 The parties must co-operate in agreeing a list of authorities.

17.3 It is the responsibility of a party wishing to cite any authority to provide photocopies for the use of each member of the Tribunal and photocopies or at least a list for the other parties. All authorities should be indexed and incorporated in an agreed bundle.

17.4 For those parties who are represented, best practice is to use photo or online copies of formal reports, such as the ICR's or IRLR's rather than those available from other on-line sources. These reports have head notes and are more useful to the Court than other electronic copies of the same case. The reports should be presented in a bundle, in chronological order, because that assists the Court in seeing how the law has developed. Relevant passages on which a party intends to rely should be side-lined and/or highlighted clearly. If ring binders are used, they should be properly tabulated.

17.5 Some familiar authorities are so frequently cited to the Appeal Tribunal that sufficient copies of those authorities for any hearing will be maintained at the Tribunal in every court. This will avoid unnecessary work for the parties, and avoid overuse of paper and copying resources. A list of such cases will be maintained on the website of the Appeal Tribunal, and any case on the list should not be photocopied. It may be relied on if necessary in argument before the Appeal Tribunal (which may refer to the maintained copy), and if so it will be sufficient for the party relying upon it to identify the principle contended for, or said to be inapplicable, by reference to the paragraph number(s) of the report.

17.6 Parties should note that in the Practice Direction in respect of civil appeals in England and Wales issued by the Lord Chief Justice and Heads of Division on 23rd. March 2012 (which parties should consider applicable to appeals to the EAT in England and Wales, subject only to necessary adaptations) it is directed that in the cases to which it relates reference should be made to no more than 10 authorities unless the scale of the appeal warrants more extensive citation. The same general principle applies to the Employment Appeal Tribunal in both Scotland and England/Wales. Cases should set out legal principle, rather than be merely illustrative of an application of it. Parties must be prepared to justify more extensive citation of authority.

PH Cases

17.7 If it is thought necessary to cite any authority at a PH, appeal against Registrar's Order, Rule 3(10) hearing or Appointment for Directions, two copies should be provided for the EAT (four copies if a judge is sitting with members) no less than 10 days before the hearing, unless otherwise ordered: and additional copies for any other parties notified. All authorities should be bundled, indexed and incorporated in one bundle as set out above.

17.8 The parties are reminded that the Employment Appeal Tribunal will expect them to identify authorities which stand in opposition to their case on the question of law raised in the appeal, just as much as those which favour it.

18 Disposal of Appeals by Consent

18.1 An appellant who wishes to abandon or withdraw an appeal should notify the other parties and the EAT immediately. If a settlement is reached, the parties should inform the EAT as soon as possible. The appellant should submit to the EAT a letter signed by or on behalf of the appellant and signed also by or on behalf of the respondent, asking the EAT for permission to withdraw the appeal and to make a consent order in the form of an attached draft signed by or for both parties dismissing the appeal, together with any other agreed order sought.

18.2 If the other parties do not agree to the proposed order the EAT should be informed. Written submissions should be lodged at the EAT and served on the parties. Any outstanding issue may be determined on the papers by the EAT, particularly if it relates to costs, but the EAT may fix an oral hearing to determine the outstanding matters in dispute between the parties.

18.3 If the parties reach an agreement that the appeal should be allowed by consent, and that an order made by the Employment Tribunal should be reversed or varied or the matter remitted to the Employment Tribunal on the ground that the decision contains an error of law, it is usually necessary for the matter to be heard by the EAT to determine whether there is a good reason for making the proposed order. On notification by the parties, the EAT will decide whether the appeal can be dealt with on the papers or by a hearing at which one or more parties or their representatives should attend to argue the case for allowing the appeal and making the order that the parties wish the EAT to make.

18.5 If the application for permission to withdraw an appeal is made close to the hearing date the EAT may require the attendance of the Appellant and/or a representative to explain the reasons for delay in making a decision not to pursue the appeal.

19 Appellant's Failure to Present a Response

19.1 If the appellant in a case did not present a response (ET3) to the Employment Tribunal and did not apply to the Employment Tribunal for an extension of time for doing so, or applied for such an extension and was refused, the Notice of Appeal must include particulars directed to the following issues, namely whether:

19.1.1 there is a good excuse for failing to present a response (ET3) and (if that be the case) for failing to apply for such an extension of time; and

19.1.2 there is a reasonably arguable defence to the claim (ET1).

19.2 In order to satisfy the EAT on these issues, the appellant must present at the EAT, together with the Notice of Appeal, a witness statement explaining in detail the circumstances in which there has been a failure to serve a response (ET3) in time or apply for such an extension of time, the reason for that failure and the facts and matters relied upon for contesting the claim (ET1) on the merits. There should be exhibited to the witness statement all relevant documents and a completed draft response (ET3).

20 Hearings

20.1 Where consent is to be obtained from the parties pursuant to s28(3) of the ETA 1996 to an appeal commencing or continuing to be heard by a judge together with only one lay member, the parties must, prior to the commencement or continuation of such hearing in front of a two-member court, themselves or by their representatives each sign a form containing the name of the one member remaining, and stating whether the member is a person falling within s28(1)(a) or (b) of the ETA 1996.

20.2 **Video and Telephone Hearings:** facilities can exceptionally be arranged for the purpose of holding short PHs or short Appointments for Directions by video or telephone link, upon the application (in writing) of an appellant or respondent who, or whose representative, has a relevant disability (supported by appropriate medical evidence). Such facilities will only be made available for a hearing at which the party or, if more than one party will take part, both or all parties is or are legally represented. An application that a hearing should be so held will be determined by a judge or the Registrar, and must be made well in advance of the date intended for the hearing, so that arrangements may be made. So far as concerns video conferencing facilities, they may not always be available, dependent on the location of the parties; as for telephone hearings or, especially, telephone conferencing facilities, consideration may need to be given as to payment by a party or parties of any additional expenditure resulting.

20.3 Hearings will not normally be recorded, except for the giving of any judgment. Parties are reminded that they are NOT permitted to make any video or audio recording nor take any photograph of the proceedings except with the express prior consent of the judge at the hearing, for which good reason must be shown, and that it is a contempt of court to do so, the penalties for which include fines and imprisonment.

21 Handing Down of Judgments

England and Wales

21.1 When the EAT reserves judgment to a later date, the parties will be notified of the date when it is ready to be handed down. It is not necessary for a party or representative to attend.

21.2 The judgment will be pronounced without being read aloud, by the judge who presided or by another judge, on behalf of the EAT. The judge may deal with any application or may refer it to the judge and/ or the Tribunal who heard the appeal, whether to deal with on the papers or at a further oral hearing on notice. Applications for permission to appeal should be made pursuant to para. 25 below. Applications for costs should be made pursuant to para. 22.2 below.

21.3 Transcripts of unreserved judgments at a PH, appeals against Registrar's Orders, Appointment for Directions and Rule 3(10) hearings will not (save as below) be produced and provided to the parties:

21.3.1 Where an appeal, or any ground of appeal, is dismissed in the presence of the appellant, no transcript of the judgment is produced unless, within 14 days of the seal date of the order, either party applies to the EAT for a transcript, or the EAT of its own initiative directs that a judgment be transcribed (in circumstances such as those set out in para. 21.4.2 below).

21.3.2 Where an appeal or any ground of appeal is dismissed in the absence of the appellant, a transcript will be supplied to the appellant.

21.3.3 Where an appeal is allowed to go forward to a PH or an FH, reasons will be given, either in the form of a short judgment or in a note made by the judge of the reasons for permitting the appeal to go forward. If a judgment is given orally, it will be transcribed, and a transcript provided to the parties unless the judge considers a written note of his reasons is sufficient. The transcript, or note, whichever is the case will be provided to all parties to the appeal.

21.4 Transcripts of unreserved judgments at an FH: where judgment is delivered at the hearing, no transcript will be produced and provided to the parties unless:

21.4.1 either party applies for it to the EAT within 14 days of that hearing;

21.4.2 the EAT of its own initiative directs that the judgment be transcribed, e.g. where it is considered that a point of general importance arises or that the matter is to be remitted to, or otherwise continued before, the Employment Tribunal; or

21.4.3 a party is not present at the hearing of the appeal.

21.5 Where judgment at either a PH or an FH is reserved, and later handed down in writing, a copy is provided to all parties, and to recognised law reporters. It will at the discretion of the judge be provided in advance on suitable undertakings as to confidentiality for the purpose of correcting any obvious errors of transcription or expression: the reasoning is not open to revision unless a review (see Rule 33) is applied for and granted. The parties may apply in advance of the handing down in respect of costs, or permission to appeal, and unless it is otherwise directed that application will normally be dealt with on paper without an oral hearing.

Scotland

21.6 Judgments are often reserved in Scotland and will be handed down as soon as practicable thereafter on a provisional basis to both parties who will thereafter have a period of 14 days to make any representations with regard to expenses, leave to appeal or any other relevant matter. At the expiry of that period or after such representations have been dealt with, whichever shall be the later, an order will be issued to conform to the original judgment.

EAT Website

21.7 All FH judgments which are transcribed or handed down will be posted on the EAT website. Any other judgment may be posted on the EAT website if so directed by the Registrar or a Judge.

22 Costs (referred to as Expenses in Scotland)

22.1 In this PD 'costs' includes legal costs, expenses, allowances paid by the Secretary of State and payment in respect of time spent in preparing a case. Such costs may relate to interim applications or hearings or to a PH or FH. The Rules provide also that where a fee has been paid for bringing an appeal which succeeds a costs order may be made which is no greater than the amount of the fee (and it is open to the EAT at the same time to order that where a fee has been paid to bring that case before an Employment Tribunal costs may additionally be awarded which are no greater than the amount of any fee so paid).

22.2 An application for costs must be made either during or at the end of a relevant hearing, or in writing to the Registrar within 14 days of the seal date of the relevant order of the EAT or, in the case of a reserved judgment, as provided for in para. 22.4 below, copied to all parties.

22.3 The party seeking the order must state the legal ground on which the application is based and the facts on which it is based and, by a schedule or otherwise, show how the costs have been incurred. If the application is made in respect of only part of the proceedings, particulars must be given showing how the costs have been incurred on that specific part. If the party against whom the order is sought wishes the EAT to have regard to means and/or an alleged inability to pay, a witness statement giving particulars and exhibiting any documents must be served on the other party(ies) and presented to the EAT. Further directions may need to be given by the EAT in such cases.

22.4 Such application may be resolved by the EAT on the papers, provided that the opportunity has been given for representations in writing by all relevant parties, or the EAT may refer the matter for an oral hearing, and may assess the costs either on the papers or at an oral hearing, or refer the matter for detailed assessment.

22.5 **Wasted Costs:** An application for a wasted costs order must be made in writing, setting out the nature of the case upon which the application is based and the best particulars of the costs sought to be recovered.

Such application must be presented to the EAT and served upon the party(ies) who will pay the costs/expenses if the application succeeds. Further directions may need to be given by the EAT in such cases.

22.6 Where the EAT makes any costs order by decision on the papers it shall provide written reasons for so doing. If such order is made at a hearing, then written reasons will be provided if a request is made at the hearing or within 21 days of the seal date of the costs order. The Registrar shall send a copy of the written reasons to all the parties to the proceedings.

23 Remission of Cases to the Employment Tribunal

23.1 Where the EAT orally makes an order remitting the case or part of it to an Employment tribunal for further or re-hearing, the parties must immediately raise any uncertainty they or any of them have as to the precise scope of the remission, for it is this which defines the jurisdiction of the Tribunal on the remitted issues. The scope of the remission will be recorded in the Order following the hearing. It is the obligation of each party to ensure that the scope as there set out corresponds with their understanding and to raise the question without delay if it appears not to do so.

23.2 If at a later hearing before an Employment Tribunal an issue arises as to the scope of remission, the Tribunal may invite the EAT to give whatever clarification is thought necessary, and if given this will be conclusive.

24 Review

24.1 Where an application is made for a review of a judgment or order of the EAT, it will normally be considered by the judge or judge and lay members who heard the appeal in respect of which the review is sought, who may exercise any power of case management as seems appropriate. If the original judgment or order was made by the judge together with lay members, then the judge may, pursuant to Rule 33, consider and refuse such application for review on the papers. If the judge does not refuse the application, he or she may make any relevant further order, but will not grant the application without notice to the opposing party and reference to the lay members, for consideration with them, either on paper or in open court. A request to review a judgment or order of the EAT must be made within 14 days of the seal date of the order, or must include an application, for an extension of time, with reasons, copied to all parties.

25 Appeals from the EAT

Appeals Heard in England and Wales

25.1 An application to the EAT for permission to appeal to the Court of Appeal must be made (unless the EAT otherwise orders) at the hearing or when a reserved judgment is handed down or in writing within seven days thereafter as provided in para. 21.5 above. If not made then, or if refused, or unless the EAT otherwise orders, any such applications must be made to the Court of Appeal within 21 days of the sealed order. An application for an extension of time for permission to appeal may be entertained by the EAT where a case is made out to the satisfaction of a judge or Registrar that there is a need to delay until after a transcript is received (expedited if appropriate) or for other good reason. Applications for an extension of time for permission to appeal should however normally be made to the Court of Appeal.

25.2 The party seeking permission must state the point of law to be advanced and the grounds.

Appeals Heard in Scotland

25.3 An application to the EAT for permission to appeal to the Court of Session must be made within 42 days of the date of the hearing where judgment is delivered at that hearing: if judgment is reserved, within 42 days of the date the transcript was sent to parties.

25.4 The party seeking permission must state the point of law to be advanced and the grounds.

26 Conciliation

26.1 Pursuant to Rule 36 and the overriding objective, the EAT encourages alternative dispute resolution.

26.2 In all cases the parties should, and when so directed must, consider conciliation of their appeals. The Registrar or a judge may at any stage make such a direction and require the parties to report on steps taken, but not the substance, to effect a conciliated settlement with the assistance of an ACAS officer notified by ACAS to the EAT.

THE HONOURABLE MR JUSTICE LANGSTAFF

PRESIDENT

Dated: 29 July 2013

EAT Practice Statement: Notices of Appeal and Skeleton Arguments, June 2015

Introduction

1 Too many notices of appeal are simply too long. If a Notice of Appeal is too long, focus on what really matters can easily be lost. Justice then suffers. A change of culture is needed.

2 Parties should realise that short, well-directed notices of appeal are usually more persuasive than long ones. The more points an appeal raises, the more it suggests that none is a very good one.

What Grounds in a Notice of Appeal Should Look Like

3 Notices of appeal should be set out in numbered paragraphs, in line with the forms set out in the EAT Rules 1993, rule 3 and Schedule. The grounds are contained within the notice.

4 There is no right to appeal except on a point of law. A point of law should be easy to identify in a few words. Whatever the paragraph numbering of the surrounding text is, the grounds of appeal themselves:

   a. (a) should begin with the heading 'Numbered Grounds' and be numbered consecutively, starting at (1);

   b. (b) each be headed by a brief description—underlined or in bold or both—of the point of law relied on (e.g. 'Misinterpreted Section XX of the Equality Act 2010'; 'Reached a decision on a point which had not been argued'; etc.) followed only by what is needed to enable a Judge of the EAT to understand the point;

   c. (c) should (except in the case of appeals alleging either perversity or bias) usually occupy in total no more than 2 sides of A4 paper;

   d. (d) in the case of appeals alleging either perversity or bias, or both, should comply with paragraph 3.8 (perversity) or paragraph 13 (bias) of the EAT Practice Direction 2013;

   e. (e) should not include any quotation from either the Tribunal judgment under appeal (which can and will be read by the EAT) or any authority (though if it is important and relevant to refer to an authority, the reference should allow it to be identified, and the relevant page and paragraph number should be stated);

   f. (f) should not contain any footnote, nor incorporate any other document.

5 If introductory, or further explanatory, text is considered desirable in addition to the grounds themselves, it should in most appeals be short, and should avoid making a complaint about the judgment of the Tribunal which is not made as one of the numbered grounds. Notices of Appeal are not meant to be skeleton arguments though it is permissible for enough to be said to persuade a judge at the EAT who considers the appeal on paper that it shows a reasonable ground for appealing.

Respondent's Answer

6 A Respondent to an appeal is not obliged to respond in any answer to contentions made in any text which accompanies the notice of Appeal. Unless it has additional reasons to add, it is enough simply to say it relies on the Reasons of the Tribunal. Additional reasons to support the Decision, if any, should be stated shortly.

What will happen if Notices of Appeal do not follow these Directions

7 (a) A judge may send them back to be shortened and resubmitted. Any delay caused by this will be regarded as that party's responsibility (though will not itself result in the appeal being ruled to be out of time). (b) A preliminary hearing may be directed, for the Appellant alone to attend, to persuade the EAT there is reasonable ground for the appeal. Any expense, inconvenience and delay caused by this is the Appellant's sole responsibility. (c) In some cases, the failure may be regarded as unreasonable conduct of litigation and expose the Appellant to a risk of costs.

Why is this Practice Statement Needed?

8 An appeal which is too long risks losing focus. There are other consequences too. Too long a Notice of Appeal invites too lengthy a Respondent's answer. This in turn can add to the length of hearings. This takes up time, to the disadvantage of the parties and to other cases which are also entitled to be heard in good time. It costs money where at least one party pays to be represented, not only in the additional length of a hearing, but because longer Notices and Answers may be thought by those who prepare them to justify higher charges.

9 It is particularly unfair for litigants in person to have to try to work out from a mass of material what appeal point is really being made, when it could be simply and clearly stated.

10 The judges of the EAT consider that Notices of Appeal have become longer and longer in recent times, and less helpful as a result.

11 Other senior courts have found the same, and taken similar steps e.g. the Commercial Court (*Tchenguiz v Grant Thornton* [2015] EWHC 405) and Court of Appeal (*Standard Bank PLC v Via Mat International Ltd* [2013] EWCA Civ 490), and this has been echoed in the EAT (e.g. in *Salmon v Castlebeck Care (Teesdale) Ltd* [2014] UKEAT/0304/14 (10 December 2014)).

Skeleton Arguments

12 Skeleton arguments are not expected to be full written arguments, but instead are intended to provide the framework within which oral submissions will be made, and should be as short as the nature of the case permits. In particular they should not be lengthy just because the judgment under appeal is lengthy.

13 They should refer to the decision or judgment under appeal, identifying the paragraphs of the judgment where an error of law may be detected or point of law arise; and the argument should correspond to the numbered grounds set out in the Notice of Appeal.

14 It is often helpful to include citations to relevant legislation and authorities (i.e. case law) which are critical to the argument, though it is sufficient to identify these by adequate reference. As well as giving the reference, there should be a concise statement of what the legislation relevantly provides, and the legal principle for which a case is being cited.

15 The argument should be self-contained: though it may give references for relevant legal authorities, it should not incorporate arguments set out in other documents by adopting them.

Mr. Justice Langstaff, President, E.A.T. 13 May 2015

ET Presidential Practice Direction—Presentation of Claims (England and Wales), December 2016

1   This Presidential Practice Direction, which sets out the methods by which a completed form may be presented, is made in accordance with the provisions of Regulation 11 of the Employment Tribunals (Constitution & Rules Procedure) Regulations 2013 The Practice Direction has effect on and from 14 December 2016.

2   Rule 8(1) of Schedule 1 of the Employment Tribunals (Constitution and Rules of Procedure) Regulations 2013 ('the Rules') is in the following terms:

Presenting the claim

8.—(1) A claim shall be started by presenting a completed claim form (using a prescribed form) in accordance with any practice direction made under regulation 11 which supplements this rule.

3   For the purpose of this Presidential Practice Direction, 'claims' are defined by R 1 of the Rules as any proceedings before an employment tribunal making a complaint. A 'complaint' is also clarified as anything that is referred to as a claim, complaint, reference, application, or appeal in any enactment which confers jurisdiction on the tribunal.

Methods of starting a claim

4   A completed claim form may be presented to an employment tribunal in England & Wales:

Online by using the online form submission service provided by Her Majesty's Courts and Tribunals Service, accessible at www.employmenttribunals.service.gov.uk.

By post to: Employment Tribunal Central Office (England & Wales), PO Box 10218, Leicester, LE1 8EG.

A claim may also be presented in person to an Employment Tribunal Office listed in the schedule to this Practice Direction.

5   Fees no longer apply.

6   The Presidential Practice Direction dated 10 March 2016 is hereby revoked.

Brian Doyle

President, Employment Tribunals (England and Wales)

Dated: 14 December 2016

Additional Information for the Assistance of Individuals Who Wish to Present Claims

The following information does not form part of this Practice Direction but is provided for the assistance of those who wish to present claims ('claimants').

1   Fees no longer apply.

2   Fees no longer apply.

3   The speediest and most efficient method of presenting a claim will normally be by using the online submission service. The online system will assist in calculating the fee which is due, will ensure that a claimant does remember to pay or apply for help with fees (since it will not allow the claim to be submitted otherwise), and will reach the fee processing centre very quickly. It also leaves no room for doubt about when the claim was presented since this is recorded electronically. That may be important if the claim is being presented close to the end of the limitation period. An electronic version of the claim form can be found at www.employmenttribunals.service.gov.uk.

Schedule

Region	Address
London Central	Victory House 30–34 Kingsway London WC2B 6EX
London East	2nd Floor Anchorage House 2 Clove Crescent London E14 2BE
London South	Montague Court 101 London Road West Croydon CR0 2RF
Midlands West	9th Floor Centre City Tower 7 Hill Street Birmingham B5 4UU

Appendix 2 Practice Directions and Guidance

Region	Address
Midlands East	Nottingham Justice Centre Carrington Street Nottingham NG2 1EE
Newcastle	2nd Floor, Kings Court Earl Grey Way Royal Quays North Shields Tyne & Wear NE29 6AR
North West	Alexandra House 14–22 The Parsonage Manchester M3 2JA
South East	Huntingdon Law Courts and Tribunals Centre Walden Road Huntingdon Cambridgeshire PE29 3DW
South East	3rd Floor Radius House 51 Clarendon Road Watford Hertfordshire WD17 1HP
South West	Bristol Civil and Family Justice Centre 2 Redcliff Street Bristol BS1 6GR
Wales	Caradog House 1–6 St Andrews Place Cardiff CF10 3BE
Yorkshire and Humber	4th Floor City Exchange 11 Albion Street Leeds LS1 5ES

ET Presidential Guidance (England and Wales)—General Case Management, March 2014

The Guidance is issued on the thirteenth day of March 2014 under the provisions of Rule 7 of the first schedule to the Employment Tribunals (Constitution and Rules of Procedure) Regulation 2013 ('the Rules').

Note:

Whilst the Tribunals in England and Wales must have regard to such Guidance they will not be bound by it and have the discretions available to them as set out in the Rules as to how they would apply the various Case Management provisions.

This Presidential Guidance in relation to General Case Management matters does not supersede or alter any other Presidential Guidance.

Hyperlinks are provided for the examples set out below. Those hyperlinks and the information provided are a guide to parties but are not binding upon the Tribunal in England and Wales. If parties require advice in such matters they should take such advice separately.

Background

1   The overriding objective set out in Rule 2 applies.
2   Rule 29 of the Rules permits a Tribunal to make Case Management Orders. The particular powers subsequently identified in the Rules do not restrict the general power contained in Rule 29.
3   Any Case Management Order may vary, suspend or set aside any earlier Case Management Order where that is necessary in the interests of justice, in particular where a party affected by the earlier Order did not have a reasonable opportunity to make representations before it was made.
4   Rule 30 specifies details of how an application for a Case Management Order is made generally. Rules 31, 32, 34, 35, 36, and 37 deal with specific instances where Case Management Orders may be made.
5   Rule 38 deals specifically with the situation where Unless Orders can be made.
6   Rule 39 deals with the provision relating to Deposit Orders.
7   The Rules generally contain other Case Management provisions, for example Rule 45 in relation to timetabling.
8   In applying the provisions of the Rules this guidance attempts to set out the procedure, processes and considerations that will normally apply in the circumstances specified below.

Action by Parties:

9   Whilst any application for a Case Management Order can be made at the hearing or in advance of the hearing, it should ordinarily be made in writing to the Employment Tribunal office dealing with the case or at a Preliminary Hearing which is dealing with Case Management issues.
10   Any such application should be made as early as possible.
11   Where the hearing concerned has been fixed, especially with agreement by the parties, that matter will be taken into account by the Employment Judge considering the application
12   The application should state the reason why it is made; why it is considered to be in accordance with the overriding objective to make the Case Management Order applied for; and where a party applies in writing, they should notify the other parties or other representatives if they have them that any objections should be sent to the Tribunal as soon as possible.
13   All relevant documents should be provided with the application
14   If the parties are in agreement that should also be indicated in the application to the Tribunal.

Examples

15   These are examples of Case Management situations:
    15.1   Disclosure of documents and preparing bundles
    15.2   Witness statements
    15.3   Amendment to the claim and response including adding and removing parties
    15.4   Disability
    15.5   Remedy
    15.6   Costs
    15.7   Timetabling
    15.8   Concluding cases without a hearing
    15.9   Judicial Mediation

Appendix 2 Practice Directions and Guidance

16 Where the parties' circumstances or contact details have changed. such changes should be notified to the Tribunal and the other parties immediately.

Action by the Employment Judge

17 Where the appropriate information has been supplied then the Employment Judge will deal with the matter as soon as practicable. If any information has not been supplied an Employment Judge may request further relevant information which will have the effect of delaying consideration of the application.

18 The decision of the Employment Judge will be notified to all parties as soon as practicable after the decision has been made

19 Orders are important. Non-compliance with them may lead to sanctions. Therefore, if a party is having difficulty in complying with such an Order they should discuss it with the other parties and then apply to the Tribunal to vary the Order.

Agenda for Preliminary Hearing

20 In preparation for a Preliminary Hearing concerned with Case Management matters the Tribunal will often send out an agenda to the parties in advance of such Preliminary Hearing. The agenda should be completed in advance of that Preliminary Hearing and returned to the Tribunal. If possible, it should be agreed by the parties. A copy of the current form of agenda can be found at Agenda for Case Management at Preliminary Hearing.

13th March 2014
David J Latham
President

Disclosure of Documents and Preparing Bundles

1   The Tribunal often orders that the parties must co-operate to prepare a set of documents for the hearing. Even if no formal order is made, the Tribunal prefers that documentary evidence is presented in one easily accessible set of documents (often known as 'the hearing bundle') with everyone involved in the hearing having an identical copy.

Why have an agreed set of documents?

2   Early disclosure of documents helps the parties see clearly what the issues are and prepare their witness statements and their arguments. There is no point in withholding evidence until the hearing as this serves only to delay and to add to the costs and may put you at risk of having your case struck out.

3   Agreeing a set of documents means that all parties agree which documents are relevant and the Tribunal will need to see. It does not mean they agree what the documents mean.

4   It avoids problems at a hearing when a party produces a document which the other party has not seen before. This is unfair and may lead to the hearing being delayed or adjourned, which is costly to all concerned and may result in the offending party paying the costs of the adjournment.

5   An agreed set—rather than each party bringing their own set of documents to the hearing-prevents uncertainty and delay at the hearing.

What is the disclosure of documents?

6   Disclosure is the process of showing the other party (or parties) all the documents you have which are relevant to the issues the Tribunal has to decide. Although it is a formal process (governed by the Civil Procedure Rules), it is not hostile but requires co-operation in order to ensure that the case is ready for hearing.

7   Relevant documents may include documents which record events in the employment history, for example a letter of appointment, statement of particulars or contract of employment; notes of a significant meeting such as a disciplinary interview, a resignation or dismissal letter or even electronic and social media documents. The claimant may have documents to disclose which relate to looking for and finding alternative work.

8   Any relevant document in your possession (or which you have the power to obtain) which is or may be relevant to the issues must be disclosed. This includes documents which may harm your case as well as those which may help it. To conceal or withhold a relevant document is a serious matter.

9   A party is usually not required to give a copy of a 'privileged' document, for example something created in connection with the preparation of a party's Tribunal case (such as notes of interviews with witnesses); correspondence between a party and their lawyers; correspondence between parties marked 'without prejudice' or part of discussions initiated on a 'without prejudice' basis with a view to settlement of the matters in issue or records of exchanges with ACAS.

How and when does disclosure take place?

10   The process should start and be completed as soon as possible. A formal order for disclosure of documents usually states the latest date by which the process must be completed.

11   In most cases, the respondent (usually the employer) has most or all of the relevant documents. This often makes it sensible for the respondent to take the lead in disclosure. Each party prepares a list of all relevant documents they hold and sends it as soon as possible to the other party.

12   Sometimes the parties meet and inspect each other's documents. More commonly they agree to exchange photocopies of their documents in the case, which should be 'clean' copies.

How is the hearing bundle produced?

13   They then co-operate to agree the documents to go in the bundle, which should contain only documents to be mentioned in witness statements or cross-examined upon at the hearing and which are relevant to the issues in the proceedings. If there is a dispute about what documents to include, the disputed documents should be put in a separate section or folder and this should be referred to the Tribunal at the start of the hearing.

14   One party—often the respondent, because it is more likely to have the necessary resources—then prepares the documents in a proper order (usually chronological), numbers each page ('pagination') and makes sufficient sets of photocopies which are stapled together, tagged or put into a ring binder.

Appendix 2 Practice Directions and Guidance

15   Each party should have at least one copy and the Tribunal will need 5 copies for a full Tribunal panel or 3 copies if the Employment Judge is to sit alone (one copy for the witness table, one for each member of the Tribunal and one to be shown to the public, where appropriate). The Tribunal's copies must be brought to the hearing and should not be sent to the Tribunal in advance, unless requested.

Are the documents confidential?

16   All documents and witness statements exchanged in the case are to be used only for the hearing. Unless the Tribunal orders otherwise, they must only be shown to a party and that party's adviser/representative or a witness (insofar as is necessary). The documents must not be used for any purpose other than the conduct of the case.

17   Since it is a public hearing, the Tribunal will enable persons present at the hearing to view documents referred to in evidence before it (unless it orders otherwise).

Witness Statements

1   The Tribunal often orders witness statements to be prepared and exchanged. Even if no formal order is made, the Tribunal generally prefers evidence to be presented by means of written statements. These are normally read in advance by the Tribunal so that they stand as the evidence in chief (the main evidence before questions are put in cross-examination), without being read out loud by the witness.

Why prepare witness statements?

2   It helps to write down what you have to say in evidence. You often remember much more and feel more comfortable when giving evidence having done so.

3   Early exchange of statements enables the parties to know the case they have to meet and what the issues are going to be. All the relevant evidence will come out at the hearing and there is nothing to gain (and much to lose) by withholding it until then.

4   Preparation of witness statements helps the Tribunal identify the issues and ensure that the case is completed in the time allowed.

How should a statement be set out and what should it contain?

5   It is easier for everyone if the statement is typewritten or word-processed (although a clear and legible handwritten statement is acceptable) with each page numbered.

6   The statement should be in logical numbered paragraphs. It should cover all the issues in the case and set out fully what the witness has to tell the Tribunal about their involvement in the matter, usually in date order.

7   The statement should be as full as possible because the Tribunal might not allow the witness to add to it, unless there are exceptional circumstances and the additional evidence is obviously relevant.

8   When completed, it is good practice for the statement to be signed particularly if the witness is unavailable to attend the hearing, and a copy should be provided to the other party. You should bring 5 copies with you to the hearing if there is a full Tribunal panel and 3 copies if the Employment Judge is to sit alone (one copy for the witness table, one for each member of the Tribunal and one to be shown to the public, where appropriate).

9   If you realise that your statement has left out something relevant when you receive the other party's statements, you should make a supplementary statement and send it immediately to the other party -but you do not need to comment on or respond to every point in the other side's statements or repeat what you said originally.

How should a statement be exchanged?

10   When the statements are ready, a copy should usually be sent to the other side, whether or not their statements have been received or are ready to be exchanged.

11   Exchange at the same time is the norm, but it is not always appropriate. In some cases, it makes sense for the claimant's witness statement to be sent first. The respondent will then know exactly what case has to be answered. This avoids irrelevant statements being taken from witnesses who are not needed. In other cases, however, it may make sense for the respondent's statements to be sent first. Any particular directions made by the Tribunal must be followed.

12   Unless there is a different date fixed, the exchange of statements should be completed by no later than two weeks before the hearing.

Appendix 2 Practice Directions and Guidance

Amendment to the claim and response including adding and removing parties

Amendment

1 Amendment means changing the terms of the claim or response. This note concentrates on amendments to the claim. The tribunal can allow amendments but will generally only do so after careful consideration and taking the views of the other parties. In some cases, a hearing may be necessary to decide whether to allow an amendment.

2 Generally speaking minor amendments cause no difficulties. Sometimes the amendment is to give more detail. There may have been a typographical error, or a date may be incorrect. The tribunal will normally grant leave to amend without further investigation in these circumstances.

3 More substantial amendments can cause problems. Regard must be had to all the circumstances, in particular any injustice or hardship which would result from the amendment or a refusal to make it. If necessary, leave to amend can be made conditional on the payment of costs by the claimant if the other party has been put to expense as a result of a defect in the claim form.

4 The Tribunal in deciding whether to grant an application to amend must carry out a careful balancing exercise of all of the relevant factors, having regard to the interests of justice and the relative hardship that will be caused to the parties by granting or refusing the amendment.

5 Relevant factors would include: -

    (1) The Amendment to be Made—applications can vary from the correction of clerical and typing errors to the addition of facts, the addition or substitution of labels for facts already described and the making of entirely new factual allegations which change the basis of the existing claim. The Judge must decide whether the amendment applied for is a minor matter or a substantial alteration, describing a new complaint. 11/07/2014

    (2) Time Limits—if a new complaint or cause of action is intended by way of amendment, the Tribunal must consider whether that complaint is out of time and, if so, whether the time limit should be extended. Once the amendment has been allowed, and time taken into account, then that matter has been decided and can only be challenged on appeal. An application for leave to amend when there is a time issue should be dealt with at a preliminary hearing to address a preliminary issue and to allow all parties to attend, to make representations and possibly even to give evidence.

    (3) The Timing and Manner of the Application –An application can be made at any time as can an amendment even after Judgment has been promulgated. Allowing an application is an exercise of a discretion. A party will need to show why the application was not made earlier and why it is being made at that time. An example which may justify a late application is the discovery of new facts or information from disclosure of documents.

6 The tribunal draws a distinction between amendments as follows: -

    (1) those that seek to add or substitute a new claim arising out of the same facts as the original claim; and

    (2) those that add a new claim entirely unconnected with the original claim

7 In deciding whether the proposed amendment is within the scope of an existing claim or constitutes an entirely new claim, the entirety of the claim form must be considered

8 **Re-labelling**—Labelling is the term used for the type of claim in relation to a set of facts. Usually, mislabelling does not prevent the relabelled claim being introduced by amendment. Seeking to change the nature of the claim may seem significant but very often all that is happening is a change of label. For instance, a claimant may describe his claim as for a redundancy payment when, in reality, he or she may be claiming that they were unfairly dismissed. If the claim form includes facts from which such a claim can be identified, the tribunal as a rule, adopts a flexible approach and grants amendments that only change the nature of the remedy claimed.

There is a fine distinction between raising a claim which is linked to an existing claim and raising a new claim for the first time. In the leading case the claimant tried to introduce an automatically unfair dismissal claim on the specific ground of his trade union activity in addition to the ordinary unfair dismissal claim in his claim form. The appeal court refused the amendment because the facts originally described could not support the new claim. Furthermore, there would be a risk of hardship to the employer by increased costs if the claimant was allowed to proceed with this new claim.

9 While there may be a flexibility of approach to applications to relabel facts already set out there are limits. Claimants must set out the specific acts complained of as tribunals are only able to adjudicate on specific

complaints. A general complaint in the claim form will therefore not suffice. Further, an employer is entitled to know the claim he has to meet.

10   **Time Limits**—the tribunal will give careful consideration in the following contexts: -

(1)   The fact that the relevant time limit for presenting the new claim has expired will not exclude the discretion to allow the amendment. In one case a Tribunal allowed the amendment of a claim form complaining of race discrimination to include a complaint of unfair dismissal. The appeal court upheld the Tribunal's decision although the time limit for unfair dismissal had expired. The facts in the claim form were sufficient to found both complaints and the amendment would neither prejudice the respondent nor cause it any injustice.

(2)   It will not always be just to allow an amendment even where no new facts are pleaded. The Tribunal must balance the injustice and hardship of allowing the amendment against the injustice and hardship of refusing it. Where for instance a claimant fails to provide a clear statement of a proposed amendment when given the opportunity through case management orders to do so, an application at the hearing may be refused because of the hardship that would accrue to the respondent.

11   **Seeking to add new ground of complaint**

(1)   The tribunal looks for a link between the facts described in the claim form and the proposed amendment. If there is no such link, the claimant will be bringing an entirely new cause of action.

(2)   In this case, the Tribunal must consider whether the new claim is in time.

(3)   The tribunal will take into account the tests for extending time limits—

(a)   the just and equitable formula in discrimination claims; and

(b)   the not reasonably practicable formula in most other claims;

(c)   the specific time limits in redundancy claims; and

(d)   the special time limits in equal pay claims.

12   **Adding a new party** The Tribunal may of its own initiative, or on the application of a party, or person wishing to become a party, add any other person as a party by adding them or substituting them for another party. This can be done if it appears that there are issues between that person and any of the existing parties falling within the jurisdiction of the Tribunal which it is in the interests of justice to have determined in the proceedings.

Adding or removing parties

13   These are some of the circumstances which give rise to addition of parties:

(1)   Where the claimant does not know, possibly by reason of a business transfer situation, who is the correct employer to be made respondent to the claim.

(2)   Where individual respondents, other than the employer, are named in discrimination cases on the grounds that they have discriminated against the claimant and an award is sought against them.

(3)   Where the respondent is a club or an unincorporated association and it is necessary to join members of the governing body.

(4)   Where it is necessary in order to decide a claim which involves a challenge to a decision of the relevant Secretary of State. The Secretary of State is responsible by statute for certain sums of money in different insolvency situations. The tribunal decides if a refusal to pay is correct, provided conditions are met in relation to timing.

14   Asking to add a party is an application to amend the claim. The tribunal will have to consider the type of amendment sought. The amendment may deal with a clerical error, add factual details to existing allegations, or add new labels to facts already set out in the claim. The amendment may if allowed make new factual allegations which change or add to an existing claim. The considerations set out above in relation to amendments generally apply to these applications.

15   When you apply to add a party you should do so promptly. You should therefore set out clearly in your application the name and address of the party you wish to add and why you say they are liable for something you have claimed. You should further explain when you knew of the need to add the party and what action you have taken since that date.

16   The Tribunal may also remove any party apparently wrongly included. A party who has been added to the proceedings should apply promptly after the proceedings are served on them if they wish to be removed.

17   A party can also be removed from the proceedings if the claimant has settled with them, or no longer wishes to proceed against them.

18   The Tribunal may permit any person to participate in proceedings on such terms as may be specified in respect of any matter in which that person has a legitimate interest. This could involve where they will be liable for any remedy awarded, as well as other situations where the findings made may directly affect them.

Appendix 2 Practice Directions and Guidance

Disability

1   Disabled and disability are words in common use. In discrimination cases in Employment Tribunals, disability has a particular meaning.

The Meaning of Disability

2   The Equality Act 2010 provides that a person has a disability if:
They have a physical or mental impairment and the impairment has a substantial and long term adverse effect on their ability to carry out normal day to day activities.

3   A disabled person may be a person who has or who has had a disability.

4.1 What matters is whether, at the date or during the period of any discrimination, the claimant had a physical impairment or impairments, and if so what it was or what they were A mental impairment or impairments and if so what it is or what they were.

4.2 If neither, whether the claimant had at any time in the past, a physical or mental impairment or impairments in the past and if so, what, when and for how long.

4.3 The Tribunal will have to consider whether any impairment adversely affects or affected the claimant's ability to carry out normal day to day activities.

Day to Day Activities

5   Relevant day to day activities are not necessarily work activities but may be. Although the list is not exhaustive, the following are included:
Mobility
Manual dexterity
Physical co-ordination
Continence
Ability to lift, carry or otherwise move everyday objects
Speech, hearing or eyesight
Memory or ability to concentrate, learn or understand
Perception of the risk of physical danger

Substantial Adverse Effect

6   In considering whether an impairment has or would be likely to have a substantial adverse effect the parties and the Tribunal should: -
Ignore any measures especially medical treatment or the use of any prosthesis or other aid except spectacles or contact lenses.
Think about what the claimant cannot do or can only do with difficulty rather than what he or she can do.

7.1 Care has to be taken to decide whether any adverse effect was minor or trivial and relevant is any substantial adverse effect.

7.2 A Tribunal will need to be satisfied that at the date or during the period of any discrimination the substantial adverse effect had either lasted or was likely to last at least 12 months in total or for the remainder of the claimant's life.

7.3 If, at the date of any discrimination an impairment existed but did not at the time have a substantial adverse effect but there has been such an adverse effect in the past, the Tribunal will need to consider whether recurrence of any substantial adverse effect is likely and, if so, when.

7.4 A severe disfigurement is treated as having a substantial adverse effect.

7.5 A progressive condition which results in an impairment which has/had an adverse effect on normal day to day activities but was no more than minor or trivial, the Tribunal will consider whether any progressive condition is likely eventually to cause a substantial adverse effect.

Conditions which always amount to disability

8   Certain medical conditions namely cancer, HIV infection and multiple sclerosis are each a disability.

Conditions which cannot amount to disability

9   Certain conditions are NOT to be treated as disabilities, these are:—
   •   Addiction to alcohol, nicotine or any other substance, unless the addiction was originally the result of the administration of medically prescribed drugs or other medical treatment;
   •   A tendency to set fire;

- A tendency to steal;
- A tendency to physical or sexual abuse of others;
- Exhibitionism;
- Voyeurism;
- Seasonal allergic rhinitis—which includes, for example, hay fever BUT the condition can be taken into account if it aggravates the effect of another condition.

Guidance

10   For assistance see the Guidance on Matters to be Taken into Account in Determining Questions relating to the Definition of Disability—see link. The Equality Act 2010 Guidance on the Definition of Disability—see link and the website of the Equality and Human Rights Commission—see link.

Evidence

11.1   A claimant may be able to provide much of the information required without medical reports. A claimant may be able to describe their impairment and its effects on their ability to carry out normal day to day activities.

11.2   Sometimes medical evidence may be required. For instance, where there is a dispute about whether the claimant has a particular disability or where an impairment is under effective control by medication or treatment.

11.3   The question then to be answered is what effects the impairment would have if the medication was withdrawn. Once more, a claimant may be able to describe the effects themselves but respondents frequently call for some medical evidence in support.

11.4   Claimants must expect to have to agree to the disclosure of relevant medical records or occupational health records.

11.5   Few people would be happy to disclose all of their records or for disclosure to be given to too many people. Employment Judges are well used to such difficulties and will limit documents to be disclosed and the people to whom disclosure should be made. It can be remembered as well that in proceedings disclosure in general is for use only in the proceedings and not for sharing with outsiders.

11.6   Even after a claimant's description of their impairment and disclosure of documents respondents may dispute that they are disabled. If that happens the intervention of an Employment Judge may be necessary. Possibilities include: -

11.6.1   That the claimant has to agree to undergo medical examination by a doctor or specialist chosen and paid for by the respondent.

11.6.2   The claimant agrees to provide further medical evidence at their own expense.

11.6.3   The claimant and respondent may agree to get a report jointly. That would involve sharing the decision as to who to appoint, the instructions to be given and the cost of any report. This may be most effective course but neither party may in the end be bound by the findings of the report even if they agree to this course of action.

11.6.4   It can be expensive to obtain medical evidence. Limited financial assistance may be available but whether it is granted is a matter which only a member of the administrative staff of the Tribunal can decide. Any application for such assistance should be made to the manager of the relevant regional office.

11.6.5   Care should be taken to decide whether a medical report is necessary at all. For instance, if a claimant has epilepsy which is well controlled by medication then medical evidence may be unnecessary for a Tribunal to consider what effect would follow if the medication was not taken.

11.6.6   Claimants must remember that they have the burden of proving that they are disabled. They may be satisfied that they can do this, perhaps with the assistance of the records of the General Practitioner and their own evidence.

Appendix 2 Practice Directions and Guidance

Remedy

What is remedy?

1   After a tribunal has decided whether the claimant's claim succeeds it will consider how a successful party should be compensated. This part of the judgment is called 'Remedy'. Sometimes it is done immediately after the merits judgment, but in long or complex cases it may be adjourned to another day.

2   The tribunal has different powers for each different type of claim. It must calculate loss and order an appropriate remedy for each part of a successful claim. Accurate and often detailed information from both parties is needed to make correct calculations and issue a judgment which is fair to all, but sometimes the tribunal can only estimate the loss, for example for how long a party may be out of work.

Different types of remedy

3   For some claims the only remedy is to order the employer to pay a sum of money—for example wages due, holiday and notice pay.

4   For unfair dismissal the tribunal may:
   • order the employer to 'reinstate' the dismissed employee, which is to put them back in their old job, as if they had not been dismissed; or to 'reengage' them, which is to employ them in a suitable different job. In each case the tribunal may order payment of lost earnings etc.
   • If those orders are not sought by the claimant or are not practicable, it may order the employer to pay compensation, calculated in two parts: a 'Basic Award', which is calculated in a similar way to a redundancy payment, and a 'Compensatory Award', which is intended to compensate the employee for the financial loss suffered.

5   In claims of unlawful discrimination, the tribunal may;
   • make a declaration setting out the parties' rights; and/or
   • order compensation to be paid by the employer and/or fellow workers who have committed discriminatory acts, but if the employer can show that it has taken all reasonable steps to prevent employees from committing such acts (called the 'Statutory Defence') the only award which can be made is against the fellow worker, not the employer; and/or
   • make a recommendation, such as for the claimant's colleagues or managers to be given training to ensure that discrimination does not happen again.

Mitigation

6   All persons who have been subjected to wrongdoing are expected to do their best, within reasonable bounds, to limit the effects on them. If the tribunal concludes that a claimant has not done so, it must reduce the compensation so that a fair sum is payable. The tribunal will expect evidence to be provided by claimants about their attempts to obtain suitable alternative work; and by respondents who consider that the claimant has not tried hard enough, about other jobs which the claimant could have applied for. (See 'Information needed for the tribunal to calculate remedy' below.)

Statement of Remedy

7   The tribunal will usually order the claimant to make a calculation showing how each amount claimed has been worked out (eg x weeks' pay at £y per week). Sometimes this is called a 'Schedule of Loss'. As tribunals are expected to calculate remedy for each different type of loss—sometimes called 'Heads of Loss' or 'Heads of Damage'—the statement should show how much is claimed under each head. If the claimant has received state benefits it should also specify the type of benefit, the dates of receipt, the amount received and the claimant's national insurance number. (See also 'Recoupment' below.)

8   Typical heads of loss include;
   • wages due
   • pay in lieu of notice, where no, or inadequate, notice was given
   • outstanding holiday pay
   • a basic award or redundancy payment
   • past loss of earnings
   • future loss of earnings
   • loss of future pension entitlements
   • in discrimination cases:
     injury to feelings
     aggravated or exemplary damages, (which are rare)

damages for personal injury—but only when the act of discrimination is the cause of the claimant becoming ill

- any tribunal fee paid

9 The tribunal will usually order the statement to be produced early in the proceedings, as it can help in settlement negotiations and when considering mediation, and when assessing the length of the hearing. It should however be updated near to the hearing date.

Submissions on *Polkey* and Contributory Fault

10 If an employee has been dismissed but the employer has not followed a proper procedure (such as the ACAS Code), tribunals will follow the guidance in *Polkey v AE Dayton Services Limited* and subsequent cases and consider whether, if a fair procedure had been followed, the claimant might still have been fairly dismissed, either at all, or at some later time. This question is often shortened to '*Polkey*'. There are also cases where the dismissal may be procedurally unfair but the employee's own conduct has contributed to the position they now find themselves in. This is called 'contributory conduct'.

11 Where either or both of these are relevant, the tribunal will reduce the compensation awarded by an appropriate percentage in each case. This means that there may be two reductions, which, where there has been really serious misconduct, could be as high as 100 per cent, so that nothing would be payable.

12 Generally the tribunal will decide these issues at the same time as it reaches its decision on the merits of the claim, and sometimes at a separate remedy hearing. It should explain at the start of the hearing which of those options it will follow, but if it does not, then the parties should ask for clarification of when they are expected to give evidence and make submissions (see separate guidance on 'Timetabling') on these matters.

Injury to Feelings

13 In discrimination cases and some other detriment claims, tribunals may award a sum of money to compensate for injury to feelings. When they do so they must fix fair, reasonable and just compensation in the particular circumstances of the case, bearing in mind that compensation is designed to compensate the injured party not to punish the guilty one, and that awards should bear some relationship to those made by the courts for personal injury.

14 They follow guidelines first given in *Vento v Chief Constable of West Yorkshire Police*, which have since been updated by *Da Bell v NSPCC* and *Simmons v Castle*, but are still referred to as the 'Vento' Guidelines. They identify three broad bands of compensation for injury to feelings as distinct from psychiatric or personal injury:

- The lower band is for less serious acts of discrimination. Awards in this band are currently between £660 and £6,600.
- The middle band is for cases which are more serious but do not come into the top band. These awards tend to be from £6,600 to £19,800.
- The top band is for the most serious cases such as where there has been a lengthy campaign of harassment. These awards are between £19,800 and £33,000, but are relatively rare. A case would have to be highly exceptional for any sum higher than this to be awarded.

15 Tribunals will expect claimants to explain in their statement of remedy which Vento band they consider their case falls in, and will also expect both parties to make submissions on this during the hearing.

Information needed for the tribunal to calculate remedy.

16 This varies in each case dependent on what is being claimed. Each party should look for, provide to the other, and include in the bundle, copies of any of these which could help the tribunal with any necessary calculations in their case:

- Copy contract of employment or statement of terms & conditions with the old employer, including the date the claimant started work, and details of any pension scheme
- Copy pay slips for the last 13 weeks in the old employment or any other document showing the claimant's gross and net pay
- Proof of any payments actually made by the employer, such as a redundancy payment or pay in lieu of notice
- Any document recording the day s/he last actually worked
- Any document explaining how many days/hours per week the claimant worked
- Any document explaining how overtime is paid
- Any document recording when the holiday year starts
- Any document recording when holiday has been taken in that year and what has been paid for those days
- Any documents setting out the terms of the former employer's pension scheme
- Any document showing the claimant's attempts to find other work
- Copy contract of employment and pays slips for any new job
- Documents such as bank statements if losses for bank charges are claimed

- Medical reports or 'Fit' notes if unable to work since dismissal
- Any document showing that jobs were/are available in the locality for which the claimant could have applied.

17 The witness statements should tell the tribunal which parts of these documents are important and why. Providing enough information to the tribunal at an early stage could help to promote a settlement and so avoid a hearing.

Is all loss awarded?

18 For claims such as unpaid wages, holiday and notice pay the tribunal will order the difference between what should have been paid and what has actually been paid. Wages and holiday pay are usually calculated gross, but pay in lieu of notice is usually calculated net of tax and national insurance. The judgment should specify whether each payment ordered has been calculated gross or net.

19 In the case of unfair dismissal there are several limits (called statutory caps) on what can be awarded:
- For the basic award there is a maximum sum for a week's pay, which, for dismissals on or after 1 February 2013, is £450 per week. It is usually increased each year.
- For the compensatory award there are two separate limits. The first is an overall maximum, which for dismissals on or after 1 February 2013 is £74,200 and usually increases each year. However, under the Unfair Dismissal (Variation of the Limit of Compensatory Award) Order 2013, where the dismissal took effect on or after 29 July 2013 (subject to rules about the minimum notice having been given) the maximum which can be awarded to any individual is one year's salary.
- There is no limit to the maximum compensatory award where the reason for the dismissal was that the claimant made a Public Interest Disclosure, or complained of certain Health and Safety related matters, and no limit to an award for discrimination, as long as it genuinely compensates for loss actually incurred as a result of the discrimination.

Grossing up

20 The rules on when tax is payable on awards made by tribunals are too complex for inclusion here. When it is clear that the claimant will have to pay tax on the sum awarded, the tribunal will award a higher figure, calculated so that tax can be paid and the claimant will receive the net sum which properly represents the loss. This calculation is called 'grossing up'.

Interest

21 There are two separate situations where interest is relevant.

22 Firstly, when a tribunal calculates compensation for discrimination, it is obliged to consider awarding interest. If it decides to do so, it calculates interest from the date of the act of discrimination up to the date of the calculation, except for interest on lost wages, where the calculation is done from the middle of that period (as that is simpler than calculating interest separately on each missing wage but leads to a roughly similar result). The tribunal will then include that interest in the award made. For claims presented on or after 29 July 2013 the rate of interest is 8 per cent. For claims presented before that date, it is 0.5 per cent.

23 In addition, interest of 8 per cent is payable on awards for all claims if they are not paid when due. In respect of all claims presented on or after 29 July 2013 interest is calculated from the day after the day upon which the written judgment was sent to the parties, unless payment is actually made within the first 14 days, in which case no interest is payable. For claims presented before 29 July, interest is payable 42 days after the day upon which the written judgment was sent to the parties.

24 Employment Tribunals play no part in enforcing payment of the awards they make. That is done by the civil courts, who issue separate guidance on how to enforce payments.

Recoupment

25 For some claims, such as unfair dismissal, if the claimant has received certain state benefits the tribunal is obliged to ensure that the employer responsible for causing the loss of earnings reimburses the State for the benefits paid. In those cases, the tribunal will order only part of the award to be paid to the claimant straight away, with the rest set aside until the respondent is told by the State how much the benefits were. The respondent then pays that money to the State and anything left over to the claimant. This is called 'recoupment'. The judge should set out in the judgment whether or not recoupment applies, and if it does, how much of the award is set aside for recoupment purposes. If either party is in any doubt about recoupment, they should ask the Judge to explain how it affects them.

Costs

26 See the separate guidance on 'Costs'

Costs

1 The basic principle is that employment tribunals do not order one party to pay the costs which the other party has incurred in bringing or defending a claim. However, there are a number of important exceptions to the basic principle as explained below.

What are costs?

2 'Costs' means some or all of the fees, charges, payments or expenses incurred by a party in connection with the tribunal case. It includes Tribunal fees (since these are not part of any remedy awarded) and the expenses incurred by a party or witness in attending a hearing.

What orders for payment of costs can be made?

3 There are three different types of payment orders: costs orders; preparation time orders (sometimes referred to as PTOs); wasted costs orders. These specific terms have the following meanings.

4 A costs order generally means that a party is ordered to pay some or all of the costs paid by the other party to its legal representatives (barristers and solicitors) or to its lay representative. No more than the hourly rate of a preparation time order, see paragraph 17 below, can be claimed for a lay representative. Separately, costs orders can be made for a party's Tribunal fees and expenses reasonably and proportionately incurred by a party or witness in attending a hearing.

5 Preparation time orders are for payment in respect of the amount of time spent working on the case by a non-represented party, including its employees or advisers, but not the time spent at any final hearing.

6 Wasted costs orders are for payment of costs incurred by a party as a result of any improper, unreasonable or negligent act or failure to act by a representative or for costs incurred after such act where it would be unreasonable to expect the party to bear them. They require payment by a representative to any party, including the party represented by the payer.

When may orders for costs and preparation time be made?

7 Apart from costs orders for Tribunal fees and the attendance of witnesses or parties at hearings, a party cannot have both a costs order and a preparation time order made in its favour in the same proceedings. So it is often sensible for a Tribunal in the course of the proceedings (for example, at a preliminary hearing) to decide only that an order for payment will be made, but to leave to the end of the case the decision about which type of order and for how much.

8 Orders for payment of costs or for preparation time may be made on application by a party, a witness (in respect of their expenses) or on the Tribunal's initiative, up to 28 days after the end of the case. If judgment on the claims is given at a hearing, it will usually be sensible to make any application for costs or PTOs then, in order to avoid delay and the additional cost of getting everyone back for another hearing. The circumstances when payment orders may be made are as follows.

9 If an employer in unfair dismissal proceedings requires an adjournment to obtain evidence about the possibility of re-employment, the tribunal must order the employer to pay the costs of the adjournment provided: the claimant notified the desire to be re-employed at least seven days before the hearing; the employer cannot prove a special reason why it should not pay.

10 A party may be ordered to pay costs or preparation time to the other party, without any particular fault or blame being shown, where:
  - the paying party has breached an order or practice direction; or
  - an adjournment or postponement is granted at the request of or due to the conduct of the paying party; or
  - the receiving party had paid a Tribunal fee for a claim and has wholly or partly won the claim.

11 A party may be ordered to pay costs in the form of the expenses incurred or to be incurred by a witness attending a hearing, without any particular fault or blame being shown. The order may be in favour of or against the party who called the witness. It may be made on the application of a party, the witness or at the Tribunal's own initiative and may be payable to a party or to the witness.

12 A party may be ordered to pay costs or preparation time to the other party where the Tribunal considers that:
  - a party has acted vexatiously, abusively, disruptively or otherwise unreasonably in bringing or defending the proceedings or in its conduct of the proceedings; or
  - the claim or response had no reasonable prospect of success.

13 The circumstances described at paragraph 11 require a tribunal to consider first whether the criteria for an order are met. Each case will turn on its own facts, but examples from decided cases are that it could

be unreasonable where a party has based the claim or defence on something which is untrue (sometimes called 'a lie'). That is not the same as something which they have simply failed to prove, nor does it mean something they reasonably misunderstood. Abusive or disruptive conduct would include insulting the other party or its representative or sending numerous unnecessary e-mails. If the criteria are met, the Tribunal is at the threshold for making an order and will decide whether it is appropriate to order payment. It will consider any information it has about the means of the party from whom payment is sought, the extent of any abusive or unreasonable conduct and any factors which seem to indicate that the party which is out-of-pocket should be reimbursed. For example, sometimes it becomes clear that a party never intended to defend on the merits (that is, for example, whether the claimant was unfairly dismissed), but pretended that it was doing so until the last minute, causing the claimant to use his lawyer more, before conceding what was really always obvious.

When may a wasted costs order be made?

14 A Tribunal may consider making a wasted costs order of its own initiative or on the application of any party, provided the circumstances described at paragraph 6 above are established. This is a very rare event. When it happens, usually a party will seek costs from the other party and, in the alternative, wasted costs from that party's representative. The representative from whom payment is sought is entitled to notice and so is the party—because they may need separate representation at this costs hearing.

Amount of costs, preparation time and wasted costs orders

15 Broadly speaking, costs orders are for up to the amount of legal fees and related expenses reasonably incurred, based on factors like the significance of the case, the complexity of the facts and the experience of the lawyers who conducted the litigation for the receiving party.

16 In addition to costs for witness expenses and Tribunal fees, the Tribunal may order any party to pay costs:
   - up to £20,000, by forming a broad-brush assessment of the amounts involved, working from a schedule of legal costs or, more frequently and in respect of lower amounts, just, for example, the fee for the barrister at the hearing;
   - calculated by a detailed assessment in the County Court or by an Employment Judge, up to an unlimited amount;
   - in any amount agreed between the parties.

17 Preparation time orders are calculated at the rate of £33 per hour (until April 2014, when the rate increases by £1 as every April) for every hour which the receiving party reasonably and proportionately spent preparing for litigation. This requires the Tribunal to bear in mind matters such as the complexity of the proceedings, the number of witnesses and extent of documents.

18 Wasted costs orders are calculated like costs orders, amount wasted by the blameworthy (as at paragraph 6) conduct of the representative.

19 When considering the amount of an order, information about a person's ability to pay may be considered, but the Tribunal may make a substantial order even where a person has no means of payment. Examples of relevant information are: the person's earnings, savings, other sources of income, debts, bills and necessary monthly outgoings.

Timetabling

1   The overriding objective means that each case should have its fair share of available time, but no more, otherwise other cases would be unjustly delayed. Also, each party must have a fair share of the time allowed for the hearing of their case.

What is timetabling?

2   Each party has a duty to conduct the case so that wherever possible the tribunal can complete the case within the time allowed. Failing to do that may mean a delay of many weeks, and also that other cases waiting to be heard might be delayed. To avoid the risk of this happening the tribunal sometimes divides up the total time allowed for a hearing into smaller blocks of time to be allowed for each part of the hearing. This is called 'timetabling'. It is necessary in particularly long or complicated hearings, or sometimes where a party has no experience of conducting hearings.

How and when is timetabling done?

3   Judges estimate the amount of time to be allowed for a hearing based on all the information they have when the hearing is listed. In straightforward cases that might be when the claim first comes in, or when the response arrives; in complex cases it is often done at a preliminary hearing.

4   For very short cases it is rare for a formal timetable to be issued, although for a hearing of one day it might be helpful for the judge and parties to agree at the beginning of the hearing roughly how long they expect each of the various stages to take. For longer or complex hearings, a timetable is often decided in consultation with the parties at a preliminary hearing, or at the start of the hearing itself.

5   Fairness does not always mean that the hearing time must be divided equally between the parties or each witness. For example, the party giving evidence first, (in unfair dismissal cases usually the employer, but in discrimination cases often the employee) will often have to explain the relevance of the documents referred to, which requires time. Also, some witnesses might have to give evidence about many separate incidents, whereas others just one short conversation. If an interpreter is required, extra time has to be allowed. The tribunal will take these things into account when estimating how long the evidence of each witness should take.

6   The tribunal will set the timetable using its own experience, but the Judge will often ask for the parties' views on how long each stage of the hearing might take.

7   The stages involved in a typical hearing are:
   • At the start the tribunal should, if this has not been done before, make sure that everybody understands the questions the tribunal has to answer (called 'Identifying the Issues') and check that everyone has copies of all of the documents etc.
   • Often the tribunal will then read the witness statements and any pages in the agreed bundle of documents to which they refer.
   • Each witness is then questioned on their own statement (called 'cross-examination') and the tribunal may also ask questions. A specific time may be allocated for questions in respect of each witness.
   • When the evidence is finished, each party is entitled to make 'submissions', which means to summarise the important evidence in their case and to highlight any weak parts of the other side's case, and also to refer the tribunal to any legal authorities which might be relevant. Although each party has the right to make submissions, they are not obliged to do so.
   • After submissions, the tribunal will reach its decision. Sometimes it needs to 'retire' (which means to leave the tribunal room) in order to consider everything that has been said. The length of time it needs to do this might just be a few minutes in a simple straightforward case or may be days in a very long case.
   • The tribunal will then tell the parties what has been decided and why (called 'delivering judgment'). This might be done orally—that is by telling the parties in the tribunal room -or, if the decision is made later, then it may be sent in writing.
   • After delivering judgment, the tribunal will, if the claim succeeds, hear evidence about the claimant's loss. The parties may then make submissions on what award is necessary.
   • The tribunal may then have to retire again to decide on remedy. It will then deliver its judgment on remedy either orally, or reserve it and send it later in writing.
   • Lastly the tribunal might have to consider orders in respect of fees or any costs matters. Orders for costs are, however, rare. It will then give judgment with reasons on those matters, again either orally or in writing.

8   If a party believes that the time estimate for the whole or any part of the hearing is wrong, the tribunal will expect them to say so as soon as possible. Waiting till the day before the hearing or the start of it, to

ask for extra time, is not helpful. It can save time to try to agree a more accurate estimate and then to ask the tribunal to change the timetable.

What can a party do to assist the Tribunal to keep to the timetable?

9   It is helpful for each party to make a list, for their own use, of the questions to be asked about each of the issues in the case. It is also useful to decide which of the questions are the most important, so that if time is running out the really important questions can be asked, even if others have to be abandoned.

10   Being able to find and quote the page number of the relevant documents in the bundle can save a lot of time. Asking questions using words the witness will understand, so that less time is wasted having to explain what is being asked, also saves time. A series of short precise questions is generally better than one long complicated one. They take less time to ask and answer, and are easier for the tribunal to understand and for everyone to take a note of.

11   There is nothing to be gained by asking the same question several times, or 'arguing' with the witness. That will just waste the time allowed. The purpose of asking questions is not to try to make the witness agree with the questioner, but to show the tribunal which side's evidence is more likely to be accurate. If necessary the tribunal can be reminded in submissions at the end of the case that, for example, the witness would not answer a question, or gave an answer which was not believable, or which was not consistent with a document in the bundle etc. An explanation of why your evidence is more reliable can be given at that stage.

What if the time allowed is exceeded?

12   The parties must try to conclude their questioning of each witness, and their submissions, within the time limit allocated. Usually the judge will, when time is nearly up, remind a party of how long they have left. If a party does not finish in time, they run the risk that the tribunal may stop their questioning of that witness, which is sometimes called 'guillotining' the evidence. This is not a step tribunals like to take, but sometimes it is necessary, especially if one side takes so long that they might prevent the other side from having a fair opportunity to ask their own questions. If later witnesses take less time than expected, it might be possible to 're-call' the witness who did not have enough time.

Concluding cases without a hearing

1   A claim or response which has been accepted may be disposed of by the tribunal at a number of stages before the final hearing. This paper sets out most of the situations generally encountered and refers you to the relevant rules.

Rejection at issue

2   A claim may be rejected by an Employment Judge at the time of issue under Rule 12 if it is one which the tribunal has no jurisdiction to consider. It may also be rejected under this rule if it is not in a form to which the respondent can sensibly respond, or is otherwise an abuse of process. The claimant may apply for reconsideration of that rejection by a Judge within 14 days on the grounds that it is wrong or that the defect can be rectified. Unless the claimant asks for a hearing the issue is decided on paper by the Employment Judge. If there is a hearing only the claimant attends.

Failure to respond and Rule 21 judgment

3   If no response is received within the prescribed time the tribunal considers whether a judgment can be issued under Rule 21 on the available material. A judge may seek further information from the claimant or order a hearing. The respondent will receive notice of the hearing but will only be allowed to participate in the hearing to the extent permitted by the judge.

Notice under Rule 26 after response received

4   If a response is accepted the tribunal conducts an initial consideration of the claim form and response under rule 26 If the judge considers that the Tribunal has no jurisdiction to hear the claim, or that it, or the response, has no reasonable prospect of success, notice will be sent to the parties setting out the judge's view and the reasons for it and ordering that the claim or response (or part) shall be dismissed on a date specified unless the claimant or respondent has before that date written to explain why that should not happen.

5   If no representations are received the claim or response or the relevant part will be dismissed. If representations are received, they will be considered by a judge who will either permit the claim or response to proceed, or fix a hearing for the purposes of deciding whether it should be permitted to do so. Such a hearing may consider other matters in relation to preparing the case for hearing.

Preparation for the final hearing

6   If the judge directs the case is to proceed to hearing orders will normally be made under rule 29 to prepare for the hearing which is listed. These may include disclosure of documents and exchange of witness statements. Failure to comply with these orders may lead to sanctions as set out below.

Striking out under Rule 37

7   Under rule 37 the tribunal may strike out all or part of a claim or response on a number of grounds at any stage of the proceedings, either on its own initiative, or on the application of a party. These include that it is scandalous or vexatious or has no reasonable prospect of success, or the manner in which the proceedings have been conducted has been scandalous, unreasonable or vexatious. Non-compliance with the rules or orders of the tribunal is also a ground for striking out, as is the fact that the claim or response is not being actively pursued. The fact that it is no longer possible to have a fair hearing is also ground for striking out. In some cases, the progress of the claim to hearing is delayed over a lengthy period. Ill health may be a reason why this happens. This means that the evidence becomes more distant from the events in the case and eventually a point may be reached where a fair hearing is no longer possible. Before a strike out on any of these grounds a party will be given a reasonable opportunity to make representations in writing or request a hearing. The tribunal does not use these powers lightly and will often hold a hearing before taking this action.

8   In exercising these powers the Tribunal follows the overriding objective seeking to deal with cases justly and expeditiously and in proportion to the matters in dispute. In some cases, parties apply for strike out of the opponent at every perceived breach of the rules. This is not a satisfactory method of managing a case and such applications are rarely successful. The outcome is often further orders by the tribunal to ensure the case is ready for the hearing.

9   It follows that before a claim or response is struck out you will receive a notice explaining what is being considered and what you should do. If you oppose the proposed action you should write explaining why and seeking a hearing if you require one.

Unless order under Rule 38

10   The Tribunal may, in order to secure compliance with an order for preparation of the case, make an 'unless order' under rule 38 which will specify that, if it is not complied with, the Claim or Response or part of it shall be dismissed without further order. The party may apply, within 14 days of the date that the order was sent, to have the order set aside or for time for compliance to be extended. If the party does not comply with the order the case is struck out without further order. A party may also apply after dismissal for the claim or response to be reinstated.

Deposit orders under Rule 39

11   The Tribunal has power under rule 39 to order that a deposit be paid on the ground that a specific allegation or argument has little reasonable prospect of success. If such an order is made the deposit must be paid in the time specified as a condition of continuing to advance the allegation or argument. If the party fails to pay the deposit by the date specified, the allegation to which the deposit relates is struck out.

Hearing Fee: Rule 40

12   Fees no longer apply.

13   Fees no longer apply.

Withdrawal under Rule 51

14   When a claimant withdraws the claim comes to an end. The tribunal must issue a dismissal judgment under rule 52 unless for some reason this is inappropriate. Often the settlement of a claim includes that the claimant withdraws and a dismissal judgment is made.

Compromise contracts and ACAS

15   Section 203 of the Employment Rights Act 1996 and section 144 of the Equality Act restrict contracting out of the provisions of these two Acts. Claims can be settled using an ACAS conciliator to produce a COT3 agreement or where legal advice is available to the claimant a compromise or settlement agreement.

Conclusion

16   In the absence of one of the outcomes outlined above the case will be determined at a final hearing following consideration of the evidence and law by a tribunal.

Appendix 2 Practice Directions and Guidance

Judicial Mediation

Explanatory Note to the Parties

1 Alternative Dispute Resolution is a priority for the Government. Judicial mediation is seen as one of the possible ways to achieve this. The Employment Tribunals operate a scheme in all regions in England and Wales.

2 Judicial mediation involves bringing the parties in a case together for a mediation preliminary hearing. The judicial mediation is conducted by a trained Employment Judge, who remains neutral and tries to assist the parties to resolve their dispute. The Employment Judge will help to identify issues in dispute, but will not make a decision about the case, nor give an opinion on the merits of the case. The role of the Employment Judge as mediator is to help the parties find ways to resolve their dispute by mutual agreement. Resolution is not limited to the remedies available at a hearing.

3 Whilst judicial mediation is part of the process of resolving employment disputes, it is an alternative to a Tribunal hearing, but not an alternative to ACAS conciliation. ACAS and the judiciary of the Employment Tribunals work collaboratively in relation to judicial mediation. The statutory duty placed on ACAS is not compromised by the process, and ACAS and the judiciary remain independent of each other at all times.

4 There are no restrictions on the jurisdictions that will be considered for judicial mediation, although it is unlikely that equal pay claims will normally be suitable for this process.

5 An important factor in assessing suitability is whether there is an ongoing employment relationship.

6 Whilst cases suitable for judicial mediation are identified in a number of different ways, identification is usually by an Employment Judge at a preliminary hearing for case management purposes. At that preliminary hearing, suitability for judicial mediation is considered, the parties advised of the possibility of an offer of judicial mediation, their interest (or otherwise) noted, and normal case management orders and directions made.

7 If the parties agree to consider an offer of judicial mediation, the file will be passed to the Regional Employment Judge, who will apply agreed criteria and determine whether the case qualifies for an offer of judicial mediation. An offer of judicial mediation is normally made at a telephone preliminary hearing with the parties when timetables for the mediation will be set, a stay or variation of the existing case management orders made if necessary, and the dates for the judicial mediation agreed. Agreement will also be reached on the issues for the judicial mediation (which may be wider than those determinable by a Tribunal at a hearing), who will attend the mediation (which must include people empowered to make decisions), and any requirements of the parties for the conduct of the mediation.

8 It is not possible to offer judicial mediation in all cases because of resource constraints and suitability of the issues to mediation. Parties are notified if an offer cannot be made.

9 Provided that the offer of judicial mediation is accepted by all parties, the matter proceeds to a one or two-day mediation.

10 The judicial mediation will be carried out by an experienced Employment Judge trained in mediation. A facilitative mediation technique is adopted and applied.

11 The judicial mediation is held in private and in circumstances which are entirely confidential with appropriate facilities made available. The contents or the events at a judicial mediation may not be referred to at any subsequent hearing. The Employment Judge mediating will play no further role in the case should it proceed to a hearing.

12 The judiciary of the Employment Tribunals may, on occasions, and with the prior consent of the parties, contact ACAS to reactivate conciliation, either during, or at the end, of the judicial mediation. This contact is usually by telephone conference call with the parties and an appropriate ACAS officer.

13 If there are any matters of concern or any explanation required then please write to the Regional Employment Judge for clarification.

Agenda for Case Management at Preliminary Hearing

Rules 29–40 and 53–56 Employment Tribunals Rules of Procedure 2013

You may be assisted by reading Presidential Guidance—General Case Management It may help the efficient management of the case if you complete this agenda, as far as it applies, and send it to every other party and the Tribunal to arrive at least 7 days before the preliminary hearing ('ph'). A completed agreed agenda is particularly helpful.

1 Parties

1.1	Are the names of the parties correct? Is the respondent a legal entity? If not, what is the correct name?	
1.2	Should any person be joined or dismissed as a respondent? If yes, why?	

2 The claim and response

2.1	What complaints (claims) are brought? This should be just the complaint title or head (eg unfair dismissal). If any are withdrawn, say so.	
2.2	Is there any application to amend the claim or response? If yes, write out what you want it to say. Any amendment should be resolved at the ph, not later.	
2.3	Has any necessary additional information been requested? If not, set out a limited, focussed request and explain why the information is necessary. If requested, can the relevant information be provided for the ph? If so, please do.	

3 Remedy

3.1	If successful, what remedy does the claimant seek? This means eg compensation or reinstatement (where that is possible) etc.	
3.2	What is the financial value of the monetary parts of the remedy? All parties are encouraged to be realistic.	
3.3	Has a schedule of loss been prepared? If so, please provide a copy.	
3.4	Has the claimant started new work? If yes, when?	

Appendix 2 Practice Directions and Guidance

703

4 The issues

4.1	What are the issues or questions for the Tribunal to decide?	
	It is usually sensible to set this out under the title of the complaint/s	
4.2	Are there any preliminary issues which should be decided before the final hearing?	
	If yes, what preliminary issues?	
	Can they be added to this preliminary hearing? If not, why not?	

5 Preliminary hearings

5.1	Is a further preliminary hearing needed for case management?	
	NB This should be exceptional.	
	If so, for what agenda items?	
	For how long?	
	On what date?	
5.2	Is a further substantive preliminary hearing required to decide any of the issues at 4.1?	
	If so, for which issues?	
	How long is needed? Possible date/s?	

6 Documents and expert evidence

6.1	Have lists of documents been exchanged?	
	If not, date/s for exchange of lists	
6.2	Have copy documents been exchanged?	
	If not, date/s or exchange of copies:	
	• for any further preliminary hearing	
	• for the final hearing	
6.3	Who will be responsible for preparing	
	• index of documents?	
	• the hearing bundles?	
	Date for completion of this task and sending a copy to the other parties?	

| 6.4 | Is this a case in which medical evidence is required?

Why?

Dates for

• disclosure of medical records
• agreeing any joint expert
• agreeing any joint instructions
• instructing any joint expert
• any medical examination
• producing any report
• asking questions of any expert
• making any concessions | |

7 Witnesses

| 7.1 | How many witnesses will each party call?

Who are those witnesses?

Why are they needed? | |
| 7.2 | Should witness statements be:

- exchanged on the same date?
- provided sequentially?

Dates for exchange:

• for further preliminary hearing
• for the final hearing | |

8 The hearing(s)

| 8.1 | Time estimate for final hearing, with intended timetable.

Is a separate hearing necessary for remedy? If yes, why? | |
| 8.2 | Dates to avoid (with reasons) or to list. Any dates pre-listed by the Tribunal? | |

9 Other preparation

9.1	Should there be admissions and/or agreed facts? If yes, by what date/s?	
9.2	Should there be a cast list? From whom and when?	
9.3	Should there be a chronology? From whom and when?	

Appendix 2 Practice Directions and Guidance

| 9.4 | Are there special requirements for any hearing?

(eg interpreter, hearing loop, evidence by video, hearing partly in private under rule 50)

If yes, give reasons. | |

10 Judicial mediation

10.1	Is this a case that might be suitable for judicial mediation?	
10.2	Are the parties interested in the possibility of judicial mediation?	
10.3	JUDICIAL USE ONLY	Judge to consider whether judicial mediation criteria are met; if so, discuss with the parties; record/direct their responses. Refer to REJ, if appropriate

11 Any other matters

ET Presidential Guidance (England and Wales)—Rule 3 Protocol on Judicial Assessments, October 2016

1 This Presidential Guidance is issued on 3 October 2016 under the provisions of Rule 7 of the First Schedule to the Employment Tribunals (Constitution and Rules of Procedure) Regulations 2013 ('the Employment Tribunals Rules of Procedure').

2 The employment tribunals in England and Wales must have regard to such Presidential Guidance, but they shall not be bound by it.

3 Rule 2 of the Employment Tribunals Rules of Procedure provides that the overriding objective of the Rules is to enable employment tribunals to deal with cases fairly and justly.

4 Dealing with a case fairly and justly includes, so far as practicable—(a) ensuring that the parties are on an equal footing; (b) dealing with cases in ways which are proportionate to the complexity and importance of the issues; (c) avoiding unnecessary formality and seeking flexibility in the proceedings; (d) avoiding delay, so far as compatible with proper consideration of the issues; and (e) saving expense.

5 A tribunal shall seek to give effect to the overriding objective in interpreting, or exercising any power given to it by, the Rules. The parties and their representatives shall assist the tribunal to further the overriding objective and in particular shall cooperate generally with each other and with the tribunal.

6 Rule 3 of the Employment Tribunals Rules of Procedure provides that a tribunal shall, wherever practicable and appropriate, encourage the use by the parties of the services of ACAS, judicial or other mediation, *or other means of resolving their disputes by agreement.*

7 Having regard to r 2 and r 3, this Presidential Guidance adopts a Protocol for an Employment Judge conducting a Judicial Assessment of a claim and a response as part of a preliminary hearing (case management) held under r 53(1)(a) of the Employment Tribunals Rules of Procedure.

8 The Protocol is appended to this Presidential Guidance (together with some Questions and Answers for the parties). It provides a formal framework for the preliminary consideration of the claim and response with the parties that is already often an important part of a preliminary hearing (case management) in defining the issues to be determined at a final hearing.

9 It is not anticipated that it will lead to longer preliminary hearings or to an increase in the number of preliminary hearings conducted by electronic communications under r 46 It will be particularly helpful, but not exclusively so, where a party to a claim is not professionally represented at the preliminary hearing (case management).

Judge Brian Doyle

President

Employment Tribunals (England & Wales)

3 October 2016

Appendix to the Presidential Guidance Protocol
for Judicial Assessment

Introduction

1 This protocol sets out the basis on which the employment tribunals will offer to parties the facility of Judicial Assessment of their cases.

The aims and purpose of Judicial Assessment

2 Judicial Assessment is an impartial and confidential assessment by an Employment Judge, at an early stage in the proceedings, of the strengths, weaknesses and risks of the parties' respective claims, allegations and contentions.

3 The statutory basis for the offer is Rule 3 of the Employment Tribunals Rules of Procedure 2013, which provides that 'A Tribunal shall wherever practicable and appropriate encourage the use by the parties of the services of ACAS, judicial or other mediation, or other means of resolving their disputes by agreement.'

4 Although the purpose of Judicial Assessment is to encourage parties to resolve their dispute by agreement, it is not envisaged that settlement discussions will necessarily occur during the Judicial Assessment itself.

5 Employment tribunal proceedings are costly of parties' time and resources. They are stressful for parties and witnesses. Almost every case entails risks for both parties.

6 An early assessment of the case by an Employment Judge may assist the parties in identifying what the case is really about, what is at stake, and may clarify and narrow the issues and encourage settlement. This may lead to resolution of the case by agreement between the parties before positions become entrenched and costs excessive, or may shorten and simplify the scope of hearings.

7 This reflects the overriding objective of the employment tribunals to deal with cases justly, speedily, and cost-effectively (r 2). Judicial Assessment is particularly valuable in view of the lack of information and advice available to parties in employment tribunal cases, many of whom are unrepresented.

Identification of suitable cases

8 Judicial Assessment will generally be offered at the first case management hearing in the proceedings. It will take place after the issues have been clarified and formal case management orders made in the first part of the case management hearing.

9 Most cases of any complexity which are listed for a case management hearing on service of proceedings will be suitable for Judicial Assessment. However, the following (non-exclusive) factors may render the case unsuitable for an offer of Judicial Assessment:
   • there are multiple claimants not all of whom request Judicial Assessment
   • a party is insolvent
   • High Court or other proceedings exist or are intimated.

Initial formalities

10 Written information about Judicial Assessment will be available to parties in all cases listed for an initial case management hearing.

11 The parties are encouraged to inform the tribunal in advance of the case management hearing that they wish to have Judicial Assessment in their case. This will enable the Employment Judge to prepare for the process and to make sure that sufficient time is available on the day. However, even if the parties have made no request in advance, the Employment Judge, in suitable cases, may offer Judicial Assessment during the case management hearing.

12 Judicial Assessment will almost invariably take place at the initial case management hearing. This reflects the need for it to happen at an early stage in the proceedings. It will not generally be offered later in the proceedings.

13 If Judicial Assessment is expected to take place, the case management hearing may be listed in person rather than by telephone conference call if it is envisaged that the necessary in-depth discussion could not take place in a telephone conference call. However, the Employment Judge will have the discretion to conduct a Judicial Assessment by telephone or other electronic communication means in appropriate

cases. Sufficient time will be allocated to the case management hearing (generally up to two hours, depending always on the nature of the case).

14 It is a requirement for Judicial Assessment that the parties freely consent to it. Whilst the Employment Judge will explain the advantages of Judicial Assessment, no pressure should ever be placed on any party to agree to it.

15 The information provided to the parties in advance will make clear that Judicial Assessment is strictly confidential. This will be repeated by the Employment Judge before the Judicial Assessment takes place.

16 Although anything said in the Judicial Assessment might be used in subsequent 'without prejudice' discussions between the parties, or in a Judicial Mediation, the views expressed by the Employment Judge are non-attributable and must be kept strictly confidential. They must not be disclosed to third parties, other than advisers, as having been expressed by the Employment Judge, or attributed or identified as the views of the Employment Judge in subsequent proceedings, including the final hearing. Unless the parties agree to these conditions, Judicial Assessment will not take place.

The conduct of the Judicial Assessment

17 Judicial Assessment involves evaluating the strength of the parties' cases. Employment Judges will use their skill and experience in doing this, whilst remaining wholly impartial. Whilst recognizing that evidence will not have been heard, Employment Judges may, when appropriate, give indications about the possible outcome of the case.

18 Judicial Assessment is not the same as Judicial Mediation. An outcome of Judicial Assessment may be that a case is listed for Judicial Mediation. Judicial Assessment is indicative in nature and will involve a practical assessment of the case by the Employment Judge. Judicial Mediation is facilitative, has the aim of assisting the parties to achieve a resolution of the issues between them without giving any indication of prospects of success, and is usually allocated a full day of the employment tribunal's time.

19 It is possible that the Judicial Assessment process will lead to immediate settlement negotiations between the parties. This is not the primary purpose of Judicial Assessment, but will be encouraged if it occurs, and time will be made available for it.

20 The Judicial Assessment must only be conducted after the issues between the parties have been fully clarified and case management orders made in the usual way at the case management hearing. The Judicial Assessment is not a way of avoiding the discipline of a properly conducted case management hearing and indeed is dependent upon the process.

21 If the parties consent, the Employment Judge may then give an assessment of the liability and/or remedy aspects of the case. It will be made clear that the assessment is provisional and that the employment tribunal hearing the case may come to a different view. In conducting the assessment the Employment Judge must make it clear that they are assessing the case on the state of the allegations and not evaluating the evidence, which has not been heard or seen, and assessing provisionally the risks as to liability and, typically, brackets of likely compensation on remedy. The Employment Judge will encourage parties to approach the process with an open mind and to be prepared to enter into the assessment pragmatically and to be receptive and listen to the Employment Judge's views.

22 The Judicial Assessment will be conducted with a view to assisting eventual settlement of all or part of the claim. If the parties express the wish to enter into immediate settlement negotiations, this may be encouraged but care must be taken to make sure that unrepresented parties have time to think and to consider any offer, and are advised that if an offer is made, they should take time to reflect upon it.

23 Judicial Assessment of parties' cases must be provisionally and guardedly expressed because no evidence will have been heard. Employment Judges must recognize that parties may not fully understand the distinction between a provisional indication and the eventual result of the case.

24 The Employment Judge may make his or her own notes of the Judicial Assessment. These will not be placed on the case file and the parties will be informed that such notes are kept only as the Employment Judge's record and will not be distributed to them or to any third parties.

25 The Employment Judge who conducted the Judicial Assessment will normally not then be involved in any part of the proceedings which may entail final determination of the parties' rights (except that they may conduct any subsequent Judicial Mediation). This is to encourage full and frank assessment of the claim and ensure public trust in the confidentiality and impartiality of the evaluation. This does not preclude involvement in day to day case management of the proceedings, including, in particular, case management hearings.

Action following the Judicial Assessment

26 In some cases, a settlement may be reached at the Judicial Assessment. Any settlement will be recorded by one of the following means:
- ACAS COT3
- Formal settlement agreement between the parties
- Consent judgment by the tribunal
- Conditional withdrawal and dismissal of the claim upon payment within an agreed period.

27 More usually, the parties will wish to consider their positions following the Judicial Assessment. If the parties agree, a Judicial Mediation may be listed. Otherwise, the Employment Judge will remind the parties of the availability of the conciliation services of ACAS.

Records

28 Each employment tribunal region will keep a record of the number of Judicial Assessments and settlements in cases where Judicial Assessments have been conducted and will provide a report monthly to the President as evidence of the use and effectiveness of the facility and for judicial training and development.

Judicial Assessment

Questions and Answers for the parties

Not every case is suitable for Judicial Assessment. It is in the discretion of the Employment Judge whether to offer Judicial Assessment

What is Judicial Assessment?

Judicial Assessment is a service offered by the employment tribunals to assess the strengths, weaknesses, and risks of the parties' respective claims, allegations, and contentions on liability and remedy, at an early stage on an impartial and confidential basis. If all parties and the Employment Judge agree, the Judicial Assessment will take place at the end of the private case management hearing. The service is optional and the Employment Judge cannot decide anything about your case at a Judicial Assessment.

Why might I want to consider taking part in a Judicial Assessment?

Judicial Assessment may save time and expense if it leads to a settlement. The first part of your case management hearing will clarify the issues between the parties and set a timetable to ensure that the case is ready for a full hearing. This involves a great deal of work over the coming weeks and months (organizing documents and witness statements and having other evidence ready such as medical reports). Preparation for a hearing is expensive and time consuming for all parties. The Employment Judge will normally arrange a full hearing, which may be in several months' time. It may involve several days or weeks in tribunal, depending on the complexity of the case.

Judicial Assessment may lead to an early settlement of the proceedings.

How is the Judicial Assessment different from the first part of the private preliminary hearing?

Judicial Assessment is strictly confidential and will involve the Judge giving a provisional assessment of the case.

What does 'Confidential' mean?

The parties cannot give details of the assessment to anyone other than advisers.

Although anything said in the Judicial Assessment might be used in subsequent 'without prejudice' discussions between the parties or in a Judicial Mediation, the views expressed by the Employment Judge are non-attributable and must be kept strictly confidential. They must not be disclosed to third parties, other than advisers, as having been expressed by the Employment Judge, or attributed or identified as the views of the Employment Judge in subsequent proceedings, including the final full merits hearing. Unless the parties agree to these conditions, Judicial Assessment will not take place.

The Judge's notes will be kept separate from the case file and if the case proceeds to a full hearing the tribunal will not see those notes.

What does 'without prejudice' mean?

Anything said during the Judicial Assessment may not be referred to in correspondence or at subsequent hearings.

Such statements are inadmissible evidence. They include offers of settlement and what is said leading up to and to explain such offers. They are made with view to settling the case and are without prejudice to the parties' position at a full merits hearing. They include anything said by the Employment Judge during the Judicial Assessment.

What is an assessment?

The Employment Judge in the Judicial Assessment may express a provisional view on the strengths and weaknesses of parts of the case without having heard any evidence, but by considering the law and what parties say about their cases. The Employment Judge will use his or her skill and experience in the assessment, whilst remaining wholly impartial. The assessment may identify possible ranges of compensation for remedy if liability is established. The purpose of the provisional assessment is to help the parties to resolve their differences by way of settlement. The eventual outcome at the hearing may be different from the Employment Judge's assessment.

An assessment is not legal advice nor does it relieve a party from the need to take legal advice.

Will the Judge always offer a Judicial Assessment?
There is no presumption that an Employment Judge will offer a Judicial Assessment. The Employment Judge will take into account the time available and matters that might mean settlement is difficult or impossible. These might include where a party is insolvent or bankrupt, other proceedings exist or the parties indicate an intention to commence other proceedings, or the parties express a view that the case cannot be settled.

Is there any fee payable for a Judicial Assessment?
No.

What do I have to do if I want a Judicial Assessment?
You should indicate your interest in the box on the case management agenda for the case management hearing and bring it to the case management hearing or send it in advance to the tribunal. A Judicial Assessment will only take place if all parties agree.

How can a case settle at a Judicial Assessment?
There are four ways in which this can happen:
- ACAS may be contacted to produce a conciliated settlement (normally recorded by way of an ACAS COT3 agreement).
- There may be a formal settlement agreement between the parties (often called a compromise agreement).
- There may be a consent judgment by the Employment Judge.
- There may be conditional withdrawal and dismissal of the claim upon payment within an agreed period.

What if the case does not settle at a Judicial Assessment?
The case will proceed as ordered at the case management hearing. The Employment Judge will not normally be involved in any part of the proceedings which may entail a final determination of the parties' rights, but the Employment Judge may conduct any subsequent judicial mediation and is not precluded from day to day case management, including any further case management hearing. It is still open to the parties to agree to Judicial Mediation, if offered. The services of ACAS are available to the parties at any time.

Appendix 3
Codes of Practice

ACAS Code of Practice 1: Disciplinary and Grievance Procedures (2015)

Foreword

The Acas statutory Code of Practice on discipline and grievance is set out at paras 1 to 47 on the following pages. It provides basic practical guidance to employers, employees and their representatives and sets out principles for handling disciplinary and grievance situations in the workplace. The Code does not apply to dismissals due to redundancy or the non-renewal of fixed term contracts on their expiry. Guidance on handling redundancies is contained in Acas' guide 'Handling small-scale redundancies: a step-by-step guide' and in its advisory booklet 'How to manage large-scale redundancies'.

The Code is issued under section 199 of the Trade Union and Labour Relations (Consolidation) Act 1992 and was laid before both Houses of Parliament on 16 January 2015. It comes into effect by order of the Secretary of State on 11 March 2015 and replaces the Code issued in 2009.

A failure to follow the Code does not, in itself, make a person or organisation liable to proceedings. However, employment tribunals will take the Code into account when considering relevant cases. Tribunals will also be able to adjust any awards made in relevant cases by up to 25 per cent for unreasonable failure to comply with any provision of the Code. This means that if the tribunal feels that an employer has unreasonably failed to follow the guidance set out in the Code they can increase any award they have made by up to 25 per cent. Conversely, if they feel an employee has unreasonably failed to follow the guidance set out in the code they can reduce any award they have made by up to 25 per cent.

Employers and employees should always seek to resolve disciplinary and grievance issues in the workplace. Where this is not possible employers and employees should consider using an independent third party to help resolve the problem. The third party need not come from outside the organisation but could be an internal mediator, so long as they are not involved in the disciplinary or grievance issue. In some cases, an external mediator might be appropriate.

Many potential disciplinary or grievance issues can be resolved informally. A quiet word is often all that is required to resolve an issue. However, where an issue cannot be resolved informally then it may be pursued formally. This Code sets out the basic requirements of fairness that will be applicable in most cases; it is intended to provide the standard of reasonable behaviour in most instances.

Employers would be well advised to keep a written record of any disciplinary or grievances cases they deal with.

Organisations may wish to consider dealing with issues involving bullying, harassment or whistleblowing under a separate procedure.

More comprehensive advice and guidance on dealing with disciplinary and grievance situations is contained in the Acas booklet, 'Discipline and grievances at work: the Acas guide'. The booklet also contains sample disciplinary and grievance procedures. Copies of the guidance can be downloaded from the ACAS website at www.acas.org.uk/discipline.

Unlike the Code employment tribunals are not required to have regard to the Acas guidance booklet. However, it provides more detailed advice and guidance that employers and employees will often find helpful both in general terms and in individual cases.

Introduction

1   This Code is designed to help employers, employees and their representatives deal with disciplinary and grievance situations in the workplace.
    • Disciplinary situations include misconduct and/or poor performance. If employers have a separate capability procedure they may prefer to address performance issues under this procedure.

If so, however, the basic principles of fairness set out in this Code should still be followed, albeit that they may need to be adapted.
- Grievances are concerns, problems or complaints that employees raise with their employers. The Code does not apply to redundancy dismissals or the non-renewal of fixed term contracts on their expiry.

2   Fairness and transparency are promoted by developing and using rules and procedures for handling disciplinary and grievance situations. These should be set down in writing, be specific and clear. Employees and, where appropriate, their representatives should be involved in the development of rules and procedures. It is also important to help employees and managers understand what the rules and procedures are, where they can be found and how they are to be used.

3   Where some form of formal action is needed, what action is reasonable or justified will depend on all the circumstances of the particular case. Employment tribunals will take the size and resources of an employer into account when deciding on relevant cases and it may sometimes not be practicable for all employers to take all of the steps set out in this Code.

4   That said, whenever a disciplinary or grievance process is being followed it is important to deal with issues fairly. There are a number of elements to this:
- Employers and employees should raise and deal with issues promptly and should not unreasonably delay meetings, decisions or confirmation of those decisions.
- Employers and employees should act consistently.
- Employers should carry out any necessary investigations, to establish the facts of the case.
- Employers should inform employees of the basis of the problem and give them an opportunity to put their case in response before any decisions are made.
- Employers should allow employees to be accompanied at any formal disciplinary or grievance meeting.
- Employers should allow an employee to appeal against any formal decision made.

Discipline

Keys to handling disciplinary issues in the workplace

Establish the facts of each case

5   It is important to carry out necessary investigations of potential disciplinary matters without unreasonable delay to establish the facts of the case. In some cases, this will require the holding of an investigatory meeting with the employee before proceeding to any disciplinary hearing. In others, the investigatory stage will be the collation of evidence by the employer for use at any disciplinary hearing.

6   In misconduct cases, where practicable, different people should carry out the investigation and disciplinary hearing.

7   If there is an investigatory meeting this should not by itself result in any disciplinary action. Although there is no statutory right for an employee to be accompanied at a formal investigatory meeting, such a right may be allowed under an employer's own procedure.

8   In cases where a period of suspension with pay is considered necessary, this period should be as brief as possible, should be kept under review and it should be made clear that this suspension is not considered a disciplinary action.

Inform the employee of the problem

9   If it is decided that there is a disciplinary case to answer, the employee should be notified of this in writing. This notification should contain sufficient information about the alleged misconduct or poor performance and its possible consequences to enable the employee to prepare to answer the case at a disciplinary meeting. It would normally be appropriate to provide copies of any written evidence, which may include any witness statements, with the notification.

10   The notification should also give details of the time and venue for the disciplinary meeting and advise the employee of their right to be accompanied at the meeting.

Hold a meeting with the employee to discuss the problem

11   The meeting should be held without unreasonable delay whilst allowing the employee reasonable time to prepare their case.

12   Employers and employees (and their companions) should make every effort to attend the meeting. At the meeting the employer should explain the complaint against the employee and go through the evidence that has been gathered. The employee should be allowed to set out their case and

answer any allegations that have been made. The employee should also be given a reasonable opportunity to ask questions, present evidence and call relevant witnesses. They should also be given an opportunity to raise points about any information provided by witnesses. Where an employer or employee intends to call relevant witnesses they should give advance notice that they intend to do this.

Allow the employee to be accompanied at the meeting

13 Workers have a statutory right to be accompanied by a companion where the disciplinary meeting could result in:
   • a formal warning being issued; or
   • the taking of some other disciplinary action; or
   • the confirmation of a warning or some other disciplinary action (appeal hearings).

14 The statutory right is to be accompanied by a fellow worker, a trade union representative, or an official employed by a trade union. A trade union representative who is not an employed official must have been certified by their union as being competent to accompany a worker. Employers must agree to a worker's request to be accompanied by any companion from one of these categories. Workers may also alter their choice of companion if they wish. As a matter of good practice, in making their choice workers should bear in mind the practicalities of the arrangements. For instance, a worker may choose to be accompanied by a companion who is suitable, willing and available on site rather than someone from a geographically remote location.

15 To exercise the statutory right to be accompanied workers must make a reasonable request. What is reasonable will depend on the circumstances of each individual case. A request to be accompanied does not have to be in writing or within a certain timeframe. However, a worker should provide enough time for the employer to deal with the companion's attendance at the meeting. Workers should also consider how they make their request so that it is clearly understood, for instance by letting the employer know in advance the name of the companion where possible and whether they are a fellow worker or trade union official or representative.

16 If a worker's chosen companion will not be available at the time proposed for the hearing by the employer, the employer must postpone the hearing to a time proposed by the worker provided that the alternative time is both reasonable and not more than five working days after the date originally proposed.

17 The companion should be allowed to address the hearing to put and sum up the worker's case, respond on behalf of the worker to any views expressed at the meeting and confer with the worker during the hearing. The companion does not, however, have the right to answer questions on the worker's behalf, address the hearing if the worker does not wish it or prevent the employer from explaining their case.

Decide on appropriate action

18 After the meeting decide whether or not disciplinary or any other action is justified and inform the employee accordingly in writing.

19 Where misconduct is confirmed or the employee is found to be performing unsatisfactorily it is usual to give the employee a written warning. A further act of misconduct or failure to improve performance within a set period would normally result in a final written warning.

20 If an employee's first misconduct or unsatisfactory performance is sufficiently serious, it may be appropriate to move directly to a final written warning. This might occur where the employee's actions have had, or are liable to have, a serious or harmful impact on the organisation.

21 A first or final written warning should set out the nature of the misconduct or poor performance and the change in behaviour or improvement in performance required (with timescale). The employee should be told how long the warning will remain current. The employee should be informed of the consequences of further misconduct, or failure to improve performance, within the set period following a final warning. For instance that it may result in dismissal or some other contractual penalty such as demotion or loss of seniority.

22 A decision to dismiss should only be taken by a manager who has the authority to do so. The employee should be informed as soon as possible of the reasons for the dismissal, the date on which the employment contract will end, the appropriate period of notice and their right of appeal.

23 Some acts, termed gross misconduct, are so serious in themselves or have such serious consequences that they may call for dismissal without notice for a first offence. But a fair disciplinary process should always be followed, before dismissing for gross misconduct.

24 Disciplinary rules should give examples of acts which the employer regards as acts of gross misconduct. These may vary according to the nature of the organisation and what it does, but might include things such as theft or fraud, physical violence, gross negligence or serious insubordination.

25 Where an employee is persistently unable or unwilling to attend a disciplinary meeting without good cause the employer should make a decision on the evidence available.

Provide employees with an opportunity to appeal

26 Where an employee feels that disciplinary action taken against them is wrong or unjust they should appeal against the decision. Appeals should be heard without unreasonable delay and ideally at an agreed time and place. Employees should let employers know the grounds for their appeal in writing.

27 The appeal should be dealt with impartially and wherever possible, by a manager who has not previously been involved in the case.

28 Workers have a statutory right to be accompanied at appeal hearings.

29 Employees should be informed in writing of the results of the appeal hearing as soon as possible.

Special cases

30 Where disciplinary action is being considered against an employee who is a trade union representative the normal disciplinary procedure should be followed. Depending on the circumstances, however, it is advisable to discuss the matter at an early stage with an official employed by the union, after obtaining the employee's agreement.

31 If an employee is charged with, or convicted of a criminal offence this is not normally in itself reason for disciplinary action. Consideration needs to be given to what effect the charge or conviction has on the employee's suitability to do the job and their relationship with their employer, work colleagues and customers.

Grievance

Keys to handling grievances in the workplace

Let the employer know the nature of the grievance

32 If it is not possible to resolve a grievance informally employees should raise the matter formally and without unreasonable delay with a manager who is not the subject of the grievance. This should be done in writing and should set out the nature of the grievance.

Hold a meeting with the employee to discuss the grievance

33 Employers should arrange for a formal meeting to be held without unreasonable delay after a grievance is received.

34 Employers, employees and their companions should make every effort to attend the meeting. Employees should be allowed to explain their grievance and how they think it should be resolved. Consideration should be given to adjourning the meeting for any investigation that may be necessary.

Allow the employee to be accompanied at the meeting

35 Workers have a statutory right to be accompanied by a companion at a grievance meeting which deals with a complaint about a duty owed by the employer to the worker. So this would apply where the complaint is, for example, that the employer is not honouring the worker's contract, or is in breach of legislation.

36 The statutory right is to be accompanied by a fellow worker, a trade union representative or an official employed by a trade union. A trade union representative who is not an employed official must have been certified by their union as being competent to accompany a worker. Employers must agree to a worker's request to be accompanied by any companion from one of these categories. Workers may also alter their choice of companion if they wish. As a matter of good practice, in making their choice workers should bear in mind the practicalities of the arrangements. For instance, a worker may choose to be accompanied by a companion who is suitable, willing and available on site rather than someone from a geographically remote location.

37 To exercise the right to be accompanied a worker must first make a reasonable request. What is reasonable will depend on the circumstances of each individual case. A request to be accompanied does not have to be in writing or within a certain timeframe. However, a worker should provide enough time for the employer to deal with the companion's attendance at the meeting. Workers should also consider how they make their request so that it is clearly understood, for instance by letting the employer know in advance the name of the companion where possible and whether they are a fellow worker or trade union official or representative.

38 If a worker's chosen companion will not be available at the time proposed for the hearing by the employer, the employer must postpone the hearing to a time proposed by the worker provided that the alternative time is both reasonable and not more than five working days after the date originally proposed.

39 The companion should be allowed to address the hearing to put and sum up the worker's case, respond on behalf of the worker to any views expressed at the meeting and confer with the worker during the hearing. The companion does not however, have the right to answer questions on the worker's behalf, address the hearing if the worker does not wish it or prevent the employer from explaining their case.

Decide on appropriate action

40 Following the meeting decide on what action, if any, to take. Decisions should be communicated to the employee, in writing, without unreasonable delay and, where appropriate, should set out what action the employer intends to take to resolve the grievance. The employee should be informed that they can appeal if they are not content with the action taken.

Allow the employee to take the grievance further if not resolved

41 Where an employee feels that their grievance has not been satisfactorily resolved they should appeal. They should let their employer know the grounds for their appeal without unreasonable delay and in writing.

42 Appeals should be heard without unreasonable delay and at a time and place which should be notified to the employee in advance.

43 The appeal should be dealt with impartially and wherever possible by a manager who has not previously been involved in the case.

44 Workers have a statutory right to be accompanied at any such appeal hearing.

45 The outcome of the appeal should be communicated to the employee in writing without unreasonable delay.

Overlapping grievance and disciplinary cases

46 Where an employee raises a grievance during a disciplinary process the disciplinary process may be temporarily suspended in order to deal with the grievance. Where the grievance and disciplinary cases are related it may be appropriate to deal with both issues concurrently.

Collective grievances

47 The provisions of this code do not apply to grievances raised on behalf of two or more employees by a representative of a recognised trade union or other appropriate workplace representative. These grievances should be handled in accordance with the organisation's collective grievance process.

Equality Act 2010

Guidance on Matters to be Taken into Account in Determining Questions Relating to the Definition of Disability

STATUS AND PURPOSE OF THE GUIDANCE

This guidance is issued by the Secretary of State under section 6(5) of the Equality Act 2010 In this document, any reference to 'the Act' means the Equality Act 2010.

This guidance concerns the definition of disability in the Act. Section 6(5) of the Act enables a Minister of the Crown to issue guidance about matters to be taken into account in determining whether a person is a disabled person. The guidance gives illustrative examples.

This guidance does not impose any legal obligations in itself, nor is it an authoritative statement of the law. However, Schedule 1, paragraph 12 to the Act requires that an adjudicating body[1] which is determining for any purpose of the Act whether a person is a disabled person, must take into account any aspect of this guidance which appears to it to be relevant.

This guidance applies to England, Wales and Scotland. Similar, but separate, guidance applies to Northern Ireland.

PART I
INTRODUCTION

The Equality Act 2010

1   The Equality Act 2010 prohibits discrimination against people with the protected characteristics that are specified in section 4 of the Act. Disability is one of the specified protected characteristics. Protection from discrimination for disabled people applies to disabled people in a range of circumstances, covering the provision of goods, facilities and services, the exercise of public functions, premises, work, education, and associations. Only those people who are defined as disabled in accordance with section 6 of the Act, and the associated Schedules and regulations made under that section, will be entitled to the protection that the Act provides.

Using the guidance

2   This guidance is primarily designed for adjudicating bodies which determine cases brought under the Act. The definition of who is a disabled person for the purposes of the Act is a legal definition and it is only adjudicating bodies which can determine whether a person meets that definition. However, the guidance is also likely to be of value to a range of people and organisations as an explanation of how the definition operates.

3   In the vast majority of cases there is unlikely to be any doubt whether or not a person has or has had a disability, but this guidance should prove helpful in cases where the matter is not entirely clear.

4   The definition of disability has a number of elements. The guidance covers each of these elements in turn. Each section contains an explanation of the relevant provisions of the Act which supplement the basic definition. Guidance and illustrative examples are provided where relevant. Those using this guidance for the first time should read it all, as each part of the guidance builds upon the part(s) preceding it.

5   Throughout the guidance, descriptions of statutory provisions in the legislation are immediately preceded by bold text and followed by a reference to the relevant provision of the Act or to regulations made under the Act. References to sections of the Act are marked 'S'; references to schedules are marked 'Sch'; and references to paragraphs in schedules are marked 'Para'.

[1] Schedule 1, Para 12 defines an 'adjudicating body' as a court, tribunal, or a person (other than a court or tribunal) who may decide a claim relating to a contravention of Part 6 (education).

Appendix 3   Codes of Practice

Other references to 'disability'

6   The definition of disability set out in the Act and described in this guidance is the only defin-
     ition relevant to determining whether someone is a disabled person for the purposes of the Act.
     References to 'disability' or to mental or physical impairments in the context of other legislation
     are not relevant to determining whether someone is a disabled person under this Act and should be
     disregarded.

7   There is a range of services, concessions, schemes and financial benefits for which disabled people
     may qualify. These include, for example: local authority services for disabled people; the Blue Badge
     parking scheme; tax concessions for people who are blind; and disability-related social security bene-
     fits. However, each of these has its own individual eligibility criteria and qualification for any one of
     them does not automatically confer entitlement to protection under the Act, nor does entitlement
     to the protection of the Act confer eligibility for benefits, or concessions. Similarly, a child who has
     been identified as having special educational needs is not necessarily disabled for the purposes of
     the Act.

8   In order to be protected by the Act, a person must meet the Act's definition of disability as
     explained below.

PART 2

GUIDANCE ON MATTERS TO BE TAKEN INTO ACCOUNT IN DETERMINING
QUESTIONS RELATING TO THE DEFINITION OF DISABILITY
Section A: General

Main elements of the definition of disability

A1   The Act defines a disabled person as a person with a disability. A person has a disability for the
     purposes of the Act if he or she has a physical or mental impairment and the impairment has
     a substantial and long-term adverse effect on his or her ability to carry out normal day-to-day
     activities (**S6(1)**).

A2   This means that, in general:
     • the person must have an impairment that is either physical or mental (see paragraphs A3 to A8);
     • the impairment must have adverse effects which are substantial (see Section B);
     • the substantial adverse effects must be long-term (see Section C); and
     • the long-term substantial adverse effects must be effects on normal day-to-day activities (see
       Section D).
     This definition is subject to the provisions in **Schedule 1 (Sch1)**.

Meaning of 'impairment'

A3   The definition requires that the effects which a person may experience must arise from a physical or mental
     impairment. The term mental or physical impairment should be given its ordinary meaning. In many
     cases, there will be no dispute whether a person has an impairment. Any disagreement is more likely to
     be about whether the effects of the impairment are sufficient to fall within the definition. Even so, it may
     sometimes be necessary to decide whether a person has an impairment so as to be able to deal with the
     issues about its effects.

A4   Whether a person is disabled for the purposes of the Act is generally determined by reference to the
     effect that an impairment has on that person's ability to carry out normal day-to-day activities. It
     is not possible to provide an exhaustive list of conditions that qualify as impairments for the pur-
     poses of the Act. Any attempt to do so would inevitably become out of date as medical knowledge
     advanced.

A5   It is important to remember that not all impairments are readily identifiable. While some impair-
     ments, particularly visible ones, are easy to identify, there are many which are not so immediately
     obvious.

A6   A disability can arise from a wide range of impairments which can be:
     • sensory impairments, such as those affecting sight or hearing;
     • impairments with fluctuating or recurring effects such as rheumatoid arthritis, myalgic encephalitis
       (ME)/chronic fatigue syndrome (CFS), fibromyalgia, depression and epilepsy;
     • progressive, such as motor neurone disease, muscular dystrophy, forms of dementia and
       lupus (SLE);

- organ specific, including respiratory conditions, such as asthma, and cardiovascular diseases, including thrombosis, stroke and heart disease;
- developmental, such as autistic spectrum disorders (ASD), dyslexia and dyspraxia;
- learning difficulties;
- mental health conditions and mental illnesses, such as depression, schizophrenia, eating disorders, bipolar affective disorders, obsessive compulsive disorders, as well as personality disorders and some self-harming behaviour;
- produced by injury to the body or brain.

A7 It may not always be possible, nor is it necessary, to categorise a condition as either a physical or a mental impairment. The underlying cause of the impairment may be hard to establish. There may be adverse effects which are both physical and mental in nature. Furthermore, effects of a mainly physical nature may stem from an underlying mental impairment, and vice versa.

A8 It is not necessary to consider how an impairment is caused, even if the cause is a consequence of a condition which is excluded. For example, liver disease as a result of alcohol dependency would count as an impairment, although an addiction to alcohol itself is expressly excluded from the scope of the definition of disability in the Act. What it is important to consider is the effect of an impairment not its cause—provided that it is not an excluded condition. See also paragraph A12 (exclusions from the definition).

> **A woman has obesity which gives rise to impairments such as mobility restrictions and breathing difficulties. She is unable to walk more than 50 yards without having to rest.**
>
> **A man has borderline moderate learning difficulties which have an adverse impact on his short-term memory and his levels of literacy and numeracy. For example, he cannot write any original material, as opposed to slowly copying existing text, and he cannot write his address from memory.**
>
> **It is the effects of these impairments that need to be considered, rather than the underlying conditions themselves.**
>
> **Persons with HIV infection, cancer and Multiple Sclerosis.**

A9 The Act states that a person who has cancer, HIV infection or multiple sclerosis (MS) is a disabled person. This means that the person is protected by the Act effectively from the point of diagnosis. (Sch1, Para 6). See also paragraphs B16 to B19 (progressive conditions).

Persons deemed to be disabled

A10 The Act provides for certain people to be deemed to meet the definition of disability without having to show that they have an impairment that has (or is likely to have) a substantial, adverse, long-term effect on the ability to carry out normal day-to-day activities. Regulations provide for a person who is certified as blind, severely sight impaired, sight impaired or partially sighted by a consultant ophthalmologist to be deemed to have a disability.[2]

A11 Anyone who has an impairment which is not listed in A9 and A10 will need to meet the requirements of the definition as set out in paragraph A1 in order to demonstrate that he or she has a disability under the Act. (But see paragraph A17 for details of some people who are treated as having had a past disability.)

Exclusions from the definition

A12 Certain conditions are not to be regarded as impairments for the purposes of the Act. These are:
- addiction to, or dependency on, alcohol, nicotine, or any other substance (other than in consequence of the substance being medically prescribed);
- the condition known as seasonal allergic rhinitis (e.g. hayfever), except where it aggravates the effect of another condition;
- tendency to set fires;
- tendency to steal;
- tendency to physical or sexual abuse of other persons;
- exhibitionism;
- voyeurism.

---

[2] The reference to blind and partially sighted persons includes people who were certified under the Disability Discrimination (Blind and Partially Sighted Persons) Regulations 2003 (S.I. 2003/712). Those provisions are to be consolidated in revised regulations. [Details of those regulations will be added.]

Appendix 3 Codes of Practice

A13 The exclusions apply where the tendency to set fires, tendency to steal, tendency to physical or sexual abuse of other persons, exhibitionism, or voyeurism constitute an impairment in themselves. The exclusions also apply where these tendencies arise as a consequence of, or a manifestation of, an impairment that constitutes a disability for the purposes of the Act.

A young man has Attention Deficit Hyperactivity Disorder (ADHD) which manifests itself in a number of ways, one of which is exhibitionism. The disorder, as an impairment which has a substantial and long-term adverse effect on the young person's ability to carry out normal day-to-day activities, would be a disability for the purposes of the Act. However, the young man is not entitled to the protection of the Act in relation to any discrimination he experiences as a consequence of his exhibitionism, because that is an excluded condition under the Act.

A14 Also, disfigurements which consist of a tattoo (which has not been removed), non-medical body piercing, or something attached through such piercing, are to be treated as not having a substantial adverse effect on the person's ability to carry out normal day-to-day activities.[3]

A15 A person with an excluded condition may nevertheless be protected as a disabled person if he or she has an accompanying impairment which meets the requirements of the definition. For example, a person who is addicted to a substance such as alcohol may also have depression, or a physical impairment such as liver damage, arising from the alcohol addiction. While this person would not meet the definition simply on the basis of having an addiction, he or she may still meet the definition as a result of the effects of the depression or the liver damage.

People who have had a disability in the past

A16 The Act says that, except for the provisions in Part 12 (Transport[4]) and section 190 (improvements to let dwelling houses), the provisions of the Act also apply in relation to a person who previously has had a disability as defined in paragraphs A1 and A2 (S6(4) and Sch1, Para 9). This means that someone who is no longer disabled, but who met the requirements of the definition in the past, will still be covered by the Act. For example, a woman who, four years ago, experienced a mental illness that had a substantial and long-term adverse effect on her ability to carry out normal day-to-day activities, but who has experienced no recurrence of the condition, is still entitled to the protection afforded by the Act, as a person with a past disability.

A17 A particular instance of someone who is treated under the Act as having had a disability in the past is someone whose name was on the register of disabled persons under provisions in the Disabled Persons (Employment) Act 1944[5] on both 12 January 1995 and 2 December 1996 The Disability Discrimination Act 1995 provided for such people to be treated as having had a disability in the past, and those provisions are being saved so that they still apply.

Disability as a particular protected characteristic or as a shared protected characteristic

A18 Certain provisions in the Act apply where a person has a particular protected characteristic. For example, Schedule 1 paragraph 1 provides that it is not discrimination, under a range of work provisions, for it to be a requirement of the job that the job holder has a protected characteristic. The Act states that, in relation to the protected characteristic of disability, a reference to a person with a particular protected characteristic is a reference to a person who has a particular disability (S6(3)).

A charitable organisation that provides services to people with HIV Aids has a vacancy for a counsellor for whom personal experience of being HIV positive is a genuine occupational requirement. The requirement is to have a particular protected characteristic

---

[3] Provisions in The Disability Discrimination (Meaning of Disability) Regulations 1996 are to be consolidated in revised regulations. [Details of those regulations will be added.]

[4] Covering: taxis etc; public service vehicles and rail transport.

[5] The Disability Discrimination Act 1995 (DDA) provided that any individual who was registered as a disabled person under the Disabled Persons (Employment) Act 1944 and whose name appeared on the register both on 12 January 1995 and 2 December 1996 was treated as having a disability for during the period of three years starting on 2 December 1996 (when the DDA employment provisions came into force). This applied regardless of whether the person met the DDA definition of a disabled person during that period. Following the end of the three-year transitional period, those persons who were treated by this provision as being disabled are now treated as having a disability in the past. This provision is being preserved for the purposes of the Equality Act 2010.

which in this instance is the particular disability of having been diagnosed as being HIV positive.

A 19 Some provisions in the Act, for example those relating to single characteristic associations, apply where persons share a protected characteristic. The Act states that, in relation to the protected characteristic of disability, a reference to persons who share a particular characteristic is a reference to persons who have the same disability (S6(3)).

A group of people with hearing impairments forms a private club that provides advice, support and recreational activities specifically for people who share that particular impairment. For the purposes of the Act, a reference to people who share a protected characteristic would, in this instance, be people who have hearing impairments.

Section B: Substantial

Meaning of 'substantial adverse effect'

B1 The requirement that an adverse effect on normal day-to-day activities should be a substantial one reflects the general understanding of disability as a limitation going beyond the normal differences in ability which may exist among people. A substantial effect is one that is greater than the effect which would be produced by the sort of physical or mental conditions experienced by many people which have only 'minor' or 'trivial' effects (this is stated in the Act, S212(1)). This section looks in more detail at what 'substantial' means. It should be read in conjunction with Section D which considers what is meant by 'normal day-to-day activities'.

The time taken to carry out an activity

B2 The time taken by a person with an impairment to carry out a normal day-to-day activity should be considered when assessing whether the effect of that impairment is substantial. It should be compared with the time it might take a person who did not have the impairment to complete an activity.

A ten-year-old child has cerebral palsy. The effects include muscle stiffness, poor balance and uncoordinated movements. The child is still able to do most things for himself, but he gets tired very easily and it is harder for him to accomplish tasks like eating and drinking, washing, and getting dressed. Although he has the ability to carry out everyday activities such as these, everything takes longer compared to a child of a similar age who does not have cerebral palsy. This amounts to a substantial adverse effect.

The way in which an activity is carried out

B3 Another factor to be considered when assessing whether the effect of an impairment is substantial is the way in which a person with that impairment carries out a normal day-to-day activity. The comparison should be with the way that the person might be expected to carry out the activity if he or she did not have the impairment.

A person who has obsessive compulsive disorder follows a complicated ritual of hand washing. When preparing a simple meal, he washes his hands carefully after handling each ingredient and each utensil. A person without the disorder might wash his or her hands at appropriate points in preparing the meal, for example after handling raw meat, but would not normally do this after every stage in the process of preparation.

Cumulative effects of an impairment

B4 An impairment might not have a substantial adverse effect on a person's ability to undertake a particular day-to-day activity in isolation, but its effects on more than one activity, taken together, could result in an overall substantial adverse effect.

B5 For example, a person whose impairment causes breathing difficulties may, as a result, experience minor effects on the ability to carry out a number of activities such as getting washed and dressed, preparing a meal, or travelling on public transport. But taken together, the cumulative result would amount to a substantial adverse effect on his or her ability to carry out these normal day-to-day activities.

A man with depression experiences a range of symptoms that include a loss of energy and motivation that makes even the simplest of tasks or decisions seem quite difficult. For example, he finds it difficult to get up in the morning, get washed and dressed, and

Appendix 3 Codes of Practice

prepare breakfast. He is forgetful and cannot plan ahead. As a result, he has often run out of food before he thinks of going shopping again. Household tasks are frequently left undone, or take much longer to complete than normal. Together, the effects amount to a substantial adverse effect.

B6 A person may have more than one impairment, any one of which alone would not have a substantial effect. In such a case, account should be taken of whether the impairments together have a substantial effect overall on the person's ability to carry out normal day-to-day activities. For example, a minor impairment which affects physical co-ordination and an irreversible but minor injury to a leg which affects mobility, when taken together, might have a substantial effect on the person's ability to carry out certain normal day-to-day activities. The cumulative effect of more than one impairment should also be taken into account when determining whether the effect is long-term, see section C.

Effects of behaviour

B7 Account should be taken of how far a person can reasonably be expected to modify his or her behaviour to prevent or reduce the effects of an impairment on normal day-to-day activities. If a person can reasonably be expected to behave in such a way that the impairment ceases to have a substantial adverse effect on his or her ability to carry out normal day-to-day activities, the person would no longer meet the definition of disability. For example, when considering modification of behaviour, it would be reasonable to expect a person who has back pain to avoid extreme activities such as parachuting. It would not be reasonable to expect him or her to give up, or modify, more normal activities that might exacerbate the symptoms; such as moderate gardening, shopping, or using public transport.

B8 Account should also be taken of where a person avoids doing things which, for example, cause pain, fatigue or substantial social embarrassment; because of a loss of energy and motivation. It would **not** be reasonable to conclude that a person who employed an avoidance strategy was not a disabled person. In determining a question as to whether a person meets the definition of disability it is important to consider the things that a person cannot do, or can only do with difficulty, rather than focusing on those things that a person can do.

> **In order to manage her condition, a woman with a persistent stammer uses coping strategies, such as avoiding using the telephone, not giving verbal instructions at work, limiting social contact outside her immediate family, and avoiding challenging situations with service providers. As a consequence, it may not be readily obvious that she has an impairment which adversely affects her ability to carry out normal day-to-day activities.**
>
> **In determining whether she meets the definition of disability, consideration should be given to the extent to which it is reasonable to expect her to place such restrictions on her working and domestic life.**

B9 In some cases, people have coping strategies which cease to work in certain circumstances (for example, where someone who has dyslexia is placed under stress). If it is possible that a person's ability to manage the effects of an impairment will break down so that effects will sometimes still occur, this possibility must be taken into account when assessing the effects of the impairment. See also paragraphs B11 to B15 (effects of treatment), paragraph C9 (likelihood of recurrence) and D9 (indirect effects).

Effects of environment

B10 Environmental conditions may exacerbate the effect of an impairment. Factors such as temperature, humidity, lighting, the time of day or night, how tired the person is, or how much stress he or she is under, may have an impact on the effects. When assessing whether adverse effects are substantial, the extent to which such environmental factors are likely to exacerbate the effects should, therefore, also be considered. See also paragraphs C5 to C8, meaning of 'long-term' (recurring or fluctuating effects).

> **A woman has had rheumatoid arthritis for the last three years and has difficulty carrying out day-to-day activities such as walking, undertaking household tasks, and getting washed and dressed. The effects are particularly bad during autumn and winter months when the weather is cold and damp. Symptoms are mild during the summer months.**

The effect on ability to carry out normal day-to-day activities fluctuates according to the weather conditions, but because the effect of the impairment is likely to recur, this person meets the definition of disability requirement on the meaning of 'long-term' (Sch1, Para 2(2)).

Effects of treatment

B11 The Act provides that, where an impairment is subject to treatment or correction, the impairment is to be treated as having a substantial adverse effect if, but for the treatment or correction, the impairment is likely to have that effect. In this context, 'likely' should be interpreted as meaning 'could well happen'. The practical effect of this provision is that the impairment should be treated as having the effect that it would have without the measures in question (Sch1, Para 5(1)). The Act states that the treatment or correction measures which are to be disregarded for these purposes include, in particular, medical treatment and the use of a prosthesis or other aid (Sch1, Para 5(2)).

B12 This provision applies even if the measures result in the effects being completely under control or not at all apparent. Where treatment is continuing it may be having the effect of masking or ameliorating a disability so that it does not have a substantial adverse effect. If the final outcome of such treatment cannot be determined or if it is known that removal of the medical treatment would result in either a relapse or a worsened condition, it would be reasonable to disregard the medical treatment in accordance with paragraph 5 of Schedule 1.

B13 For example, if a person with a hearing impairment wears a hearing aid the question as to whether his or her impairment has a substantial adverse effect is to be decided by reference to what the hearing level would be without the hearing aid. Similarly, in the case of someone with diabetes which is being controlled by medication or diet, or the case of a person with depression which is being treated by counselling, whether or not the effect is substantial should be decided by reference to what the effects of the condition would be if he or she were not taking that medication or following the required diet, or were not receiving counselling (the so-called 'deduced effects').

B14 The Act states that this provision does not apply to sight impairments to the extent that they are capable of correction by spectacles or contact lenses. In other words, the only effects on the ability to carry out normal day-to-day activities which are to be considered are those which remain when spectacles or contact lenses are used (or would remain if they were used). This does not include the use of devices to correct sight which are not spectacles or contact lenses (Sch1, Para 5(3)).

B15 Account should be taken of where the effect of the continuing medical treatment is to create a permanent improvement rather than a temporary improvement. For example, a person who develops pneumonia may be admitted to hospital for treatment including a course of antibiotics. This cures the impairment and no effects remain. See also paragraph C10, regarding medical or other treatment that permanently reduces or removes the effects of an impairment.

Progressive conditions

B16 Progressive conditions are subject to the special provisions set out in Sch1, Para 8 These provisions provide that a person with a progressive condition is to be regarded as having an impairment which has a substantial adverse effect on his or her ability to carry out normal day-to-day activities before it does so. A person who has a progressive condition, will be treated as having an impairment which has a substantial adverse effect from the moment any impairment resulting from that condition first has some adverse effect on his or her ability to carry out normal day-to-day activities, provided that in the future the adverse effect is likely to become substantial. Medical prognosis of the likely impact of the condition will be the normal route to establishing protection under this provision. The effect need not be continuous and need not be substantial. (See also paragraphs C5 to C8 on recurring or fluctuating effects). The person will still need to show that the impairment meets the requirements of Sch1, Para 2 (meaning of long-term).

B17 Examples of progressive conditions to which the special provisions apply include systemic lupus erythematosis (SLE), various types of dementia, rheumatoid arthritis, and motor neurone disease. This list, however, is not exhaustive.

A young boy aged 8 has been experiencing muscle cramps and some weakness. The effects are quite minor at present, but he has been diagnosed as having muscular dystrophy. Eventually it is expected that the resulting muscle weakness will cause substantial adverse effects on his ability to walk, run and climb stairs. Although there is no substantial adverse effect at present, muscular dystrophy is a progressive condition, and this child will still be entitled to the protection of the Act under the special provisions in Sch1, Para 8 of the Act if it can be shown that the effects are likely to become substantial.

A woman has been diagnosed with lupus (SLE) following complaints to her GP that she is experiencing mild aches and pains in her joints. She has also been feeling generally unwell, with some flu-like symptoms. The initial symptoms do not have a substantial adverse effect on her ability to carry out normal day-to-day activities. However, SLE is a progressive condition, with fluctuating effects. She has been advised that the condition may come and go over many years, and in the future the effects may become substantial, including severe joint pain, inflammation, stiffness, and skin rashes. Providing it can be shown that the effects are likely to become substantial, she will be covered by the special provisions in Sch1, Para 8 She will, however, still need to meet the 'long-term' condition of the definition in order to be protected by the Act.

B18   As explained in paragraph A9, the Act provides for a person with one of the progressive conditions of cancer, HIV and multiple sclerosis to be a disabled person from the point at which they have that condition, so effectively from diagnosis.

B19   A person with a progressive condition which has no effect on day-to-day activities because it is successfully treated (for example by surgery) may still be covered by Sch1, Para **8** where the effects of that treatment give rise to a further impairment which does have an effect on normal day-to-day activities. For example, treatment for the condition may result in an impairment which has some effect on normal day-to-day activities and the effects of that impairment are likely to become substantial in the future.

A man has an operation to remove the colon because of progressing and uncontrollable ulcerative colitis. This is a treatment that is fairly routine for severe colitis. The operation results in his no longer experiencing adverse effects from the colitis. He requires a colostomy, however, which means that his bowel actions can only be controlled by a sanitary appliance. The effect of the incontinence should be taken into account as an effect arising from the original impairment.

B20   Whether the effects of any treatment can qualify for the purposes of Sch1, Para 8 will depend on the circumstances of the individual case.

Severe disfigurements

B21   The Act provides that where an impairment consists of a severe disfigurement, it is to be treated as having a substantial adverse effect on the person's ability to carry out normal day-to-day activities. There is no need to demonstrate such an effect (Sch1, Para 3). Regulations provide that a disfigurement which consists of a tattoo (which has not been removed) is not to be considered as a severe disfigurement. Also excluded is a piercing of the body for decorative purposes including anything attached through the piercing.[6]

B22   Examples of disfigurements include scars, birthmarks, limb or postural deformation (including restricted bodily development), or diseases of the skin. Assessing severity will be mainly a matter of the degree of the disfigurement. However, it may be necessary to take account of where the disfigurement in question is (e.g. on the back as opposed to the face).

Section C: Long-term

Meaning of 'long-term effects'

C1   The Act states that, for the purpose of deciding whether a person is disabled, a long-term effect of an impairment is one:
   • which has lasted at least 12 months; or
   • where the total period for which it lasts, from the time of the first onset, is likely to be at least 12 months; or
   • which is likely to last for the rest of the life of the person affected (Sch1, Para 2).

---

[6] See footnote 3.

For the purpose of deciding whether a person has had a disability in the past, a long-term effect of an impairment is one which lasted at least 12 months (Sch1, Para 9).

C2 The cumulative effect of related impairments should be taken into account when determining whether the person has experienced a long-term effect for the purposes of meeting the definition of a disabled person. The substantial adverse effect of an impairment which has developed from, or is likely to develop from, another impairment should be taken into account when determining whether the effect has lasted, or is likely to last at least twelve months, or for the rest of the life of the person affected.

> A woman developed a breathing condition that arose following a lung infection which had lasted seven months. The condition and the lung infection each had a substantial adverse effect on the woman's ability to carry out normal day-to-day activities. The breathing condition itself lasted some ten months. As the condition arose from, and therefore was related to, the lung infection, the effects of each should be aggregated when considering whether the disability was long-term. As the total period over which the effects lasted was in excess of twelve months, the long-term element of the definition of disability was met.

> However, where a person experiences, over a long period, adverse effects arising from two separate and unrelated conditions, for example a lung infection and a leg injury, these effects should not be aggregated.

Meaning of 'likely'

C3 The meaning of 'likely' is relevant when determining whether an impairment has a long-term effect (Sch1, Para 2(1)), but also when determining whether an impairment has a recurring effect (Sch1, Para 2(2)) or how an impairment should be treated for the purposes of the Act when the effects of that impairment are controlled or corrected by treatment or behaviour (Sch1, Para 5(1)). In this context, 'likely', should be interpreted as meaning that it could well happen, rather than it is more probable than not that it will happen.

C4 In assessing the likelihood of an effect lasting for 12 months, account should be taken of the total period for which the effect exists. This includes any time before the point at which the alleged incident of discriminatory behaviour which is being considered by the adjudicating body occurred. Account should also be taken of both the typical length of such an effect on an individual, and any relevant factors specific to this individual (for example, general state of health or age).

Recurring or fluctuating effects

C5 The Act states that, if an impairment has had a substantial adverse effect on a person's ability to carry out normal day-to-day activities but that effect ceases, the substantial effect is treated as continuing if it is likely to recur. (In deciding whether a person has had a disability in the past, the question is whether a substantial adverse effect has in fact recurred.) Conditions with effects which recur only sporadically or for short periods can still qualify as impairments for the purposes of the Act, in respect of the meaning of 'long-term' (Sch1, Para 2(2)). See also C3 (meaning of likely).

C6 For example, a person with rheumatoid arthritis may experience substantial adverse effects for a few weeks after the first occurrence and then have a period of remission. See also example at B10 If the substantial adverse effects are likely to recur, they are to be treated as if they were continuing. If the effects are likely to recur beyond 12 months after the first occurrence, they are to be treated as long-term. Other impairments with effects which can recur, or where effects can be sporadic, include Menières disease and epilepsy as well as mental health conditions such as schizophrenia, bipolar affective disorder, and certain types of depression, though this is not an exhaustive list. It should be noted that some impairments with recurring or fluctuating effects may be less obvious in their impact on the individual concerned than is the case with other impairments where the effects are more constant.

> A young man has bipolar affective disorder, a recurring form of depression. The first episode occurred in months one and two of a 13-month period. The second episode took place in month 13 This man will satisfy the requirements of the definition in respect of the meaning of long-term, because the adverse effects have recurred beyond 12 months after the first

occurrence and are therefore treated as having continued for the whole period (in this case, a period of 13 months).

A woman has two discrete episodes of depression within a ten-month period. In month one she loses her job and has a period of depression lasting six weeks. In month nine she suffers a bereavement and has a further episode of depression lasting eight weeks. Even though she has experienced two episodes of depression she will not be covered by the Act. This is because, as at this stage, the effects of her impairment have not yet lasted more than 12 months after the first occurrence, and there is no evidence that these episodes are part of an underlying condition of depression which is likely to recur beyond the 12-month period.

C7 It is not necessary for the effect to be the same throughout the period which is being considered in relation to determining whether the 'long-term' element of the definition is met. A person may still satisfy the long-term element of the definition even if the effect is not the same throughout the period. It may change: for example, activities which are initially very difficult may become possible to a much greater extent. The effect might even disappear temporarily. Or other effects on the ability to carry out normal day-to-day activities may develop and the initial effect may disappear altogether.

C8 Regulations specifically exclude seasonal allergic rhinitis (e.g. hayfever) except where it aggravates the effects of an existing condition.[7] For example, this may occur in some cases of asthma. See also paragraph A12 (exclusions).

Likelihood of recurrence

C9 Likelihood of recurrence should be considered taking all the circumstances of the case into account. This should include what the person could reasonably be expected to do to prevent the recurrence. For example, the person might reasonably be expected to take action which prevents the impairment from having such effects (e.g. avoiding substances to which he or she is allergic). This may be unreasonably difficult with some substances. In addition, it is possible that the way in which a person can control or cope with the effects of an impairment may not always be successful: for example, because a routine is not followed or the person is in an unfamiliar environment. If there is an increased likelihood that the control will break down, it will be more likely that there will be a recurrence. That possibility should be taken into account when assessing the likelihood of a recurrence. See also paragraphs B7 to B9 (effects of behaviour, including coping strategies and medical advice), paragraph B10 (environmental effects); paragraphs B11 to B15 (effect of treatment); and C3 (meaning of likely).

A woman experiences stress-related anxiety. She is able to manage her workload and meet normal deadlines provided that she avoids too much responsibility. She achieves this through careful monitoring of her workload and regular supervision by her manager. She can cope with the symptoms of her condition most of the time, provided that she is not exposed to stressful situations.

The possibility that she might be exposed to stressful situations should be taken into account when deciding whether there is a likelihood of recurrence.

C10 If medical or other treatment is likely to permanently cure a condition and therefore remove the impairment, so that recurrence of its effects would then be unlikely even if there were no further treatment, this should be taken into consideration when looking at the likelihood of recurrence of those effects. However, if the treatment simply delays or prevents a recurrence, and a recurrence would be likely if the treatment stopped, as is the case with most medication, then the treatment is to be ignored and the effect is to be regarded as likely to recur.

Assessing whether a past disability was long-term

C11 The Act provides that a person who has had a disability within the definition is protected from some forms of discrimination even if he or she has since recovered or the effects have become less than substantial. In deciding whether a past condition was a disability, its effects count as long-term if they lasted 12 months or more after the first occurrence, or if a recurrence happened or continued

---

[7] See footnote 3.

until more than 12 months after the first occurrence (S6(4) and Sch2, Para 2). For the forms of discrimination covered by this provision see paragraph A16. For examples of how this provision works, see paragraph C6.

Section D: Normal day-to-day activities

D1 The Act looks at a person's impairment and whether it substantially affects the person's ability to carry out normal day-to-day activities.

Meaning of 'normal day-to-day activities'

D2 The Act does not define what is to be regarded as a 'normal day-to-day activity'. It is not possible to provide an exhaustive list of day-to-day activities, although guidance on this matter is given here and illustrative examples of when it would, and would not, be reasonable to regard an impairment as having a substantial adverse effect on the ability to carry out normal day-to-day activities are shown in the Appendix. In general, day-to-day activities are things people do on a regular or daily basis, and examples include shopping, reading and writing, having a conversation or using the telephone, watching television, getting washed and dressed, preparing and eating food, carrying out household tasks, walking and travelling by various forms of transport, and taking part in social activities.

D3 The term 'normal day-to-day activities' is not intended to include activities which are normal only for a particular person, or a small group of people. In deciding whether an activity is a normal day-to-day activity, account should be taken of how far it is normal for a large number of people, and carried out by people on a daily or frequent and fairly regular basis. In this context, 'normal' should be given its ordinary, everyday meaning.

D4 A normal day-to-day activity is not necessarily one that is carried out by a majority of people. For example, it is possible that some activities might be carried out only, or more predominantly, by people of a particular gender, such as applying make-up or using hair curling equipment, and cannot therefore be said to be normal for **most** people. They would nevertheless be considered to be normal day-to-day activities.

Work-related and other specialised activities

D5 Normal day-to-day activities do not include work of any particular form because no particular form of work is 'normal' for most people. In any individual case, the activities carried out might be highly specialised. For example, carrying out delicate work with specialised tools may be a normal working activity for a watch repairer, whereas it would not be normal for a person who is employed as a semi-skilled worker. The Act only covers effects which go beyond the normal differences in skill or ability.

D6 The same is true of other specialised activities such as playing a musical instrument to a high standard of achievement; taking part in a particular game or hobby where very specific skills or level of ability are required; or playing a particular sport to a high level of ability, such as would be required for a professional footballer or athlete.

D7 However, many types of work or specialised hobby, sport or pastime may still involve normal day-to-day activities. For example; sitting down, standing up, walking, running, verbal interaction, writing, making a cup of tea, using everyday objects such as a keyboard, and lifting, moving or carrying everyday objects such as chairs.

> **A woman plays the piano to a high standard, and often takes part in public performances. She has developed carpal tunnel syndrome in her wrists, an impairment that adversely affects manual dexterity. She can continue to play the piano, but not to such a high standard, and she has to take frequent breaks to rest her arms. This would not of itself be an adverse effect on a normal day-to-day activity. However, as a result of her impairment she also finds it difficult to operate a computer keyboard and cannot use her PC to send emails or write letters. This is an adverse effect on a normal day-to-day activity.**

> **A man works in a warehouse, loading and unloading heavy stock. He develops heart problems and no longer has the ability to lift or move heavy items of stock at work. Lifting and moving such unusually heavy types of item is not a normal day-to-day activity. However, he is also unable to lift, carry or move moderately heavy everyday objects such as chairs, either at work or around the home. This is an adverse effect on a normal day-to-day activity.**

Appendix 3 Codes of Practice

D8 The effects experienced by a person as a result of environmental conditions, either in the workplace or in another location where a specialised activity is being carried out, should not be discounted simply because there may be a work-related or other specialised activity involved. It is important to consider whether there may also be an adverse effect on the ability to carry out a normal day-to-day activity.

> **A middle-aged man works in a factory where chemical fumes cause him to have breathing difficulties, and this has made it impossible for him to continue to do his job. He has been diagnosed with occupational asthma, which has a substantial adverse effect while he is at work. As a result, he is no longer able to work where he would continue to be exposed to the fumes. Even in a non-work situation he finds any general exertion difficult and this adversely affects his ability to carry out normal day-to-day activities like lifting and carrying everyday objects. The effects fluctuate, and when he is not at work his asthma attacks are very infrequent. Although the substantial effect is only apparent while at work, the man is able to demonstrate that his impairment has an adverse effect on normal day-to-day activities.**

Indirect effects

D9 An impairment may not directly **prevent** someone from carrying out one or more normal day-to-day activities, but it may still have a substantial adverse long-term effect on how he or she carries out those activities. For example:

- pain or fatigue: where an impairment causes pain or fatigue in performing normal day-to-day activities the person may have the ability to do something but suffer pain in doing so; or the impairment might make the activity more than usually fatiguing so that the person might not be able to repeat the task over a sustained period of time. See also paragraphs B7 to B9 (effects of behaviour);

> **A man has had chronic fatigue syndrome for several years and although he has the physical capability to walk and to stand, he finds these very difficult to sustain for any length of time because of the overwhelming fatigue he experiences. As a consequence, he is restricted in his ability to take part in normal day-to-day activities such as travelling, so he avoids going out socially, and works from home several days a week. Therefore, there is a substantial adverse effect on normal day-to-day activities.**

- medical advice: where a person has been advised by a medical practitioner or other health professional, as part of a treatment plan, to change, limit or refrain from a normal day-to-day activity on account of an impairment or only do it in a certain way or under certain conditions. See also paragraphs B11 to B15 (effects of treatment).

> **A woman who works as a teacher develops sciatic pain which is attributed to a prolapsed inter-vertebral disc. Despite physiotherapy and traction her pain became worse. As part of her treatment plan her doctor prescribes daily pain relief medication and advises her to avoid repetitive bending or lifting, and to avoid carrying heavy items. This prevents her from carrying out a range of normal day-to-day activities such as shopping.**

Children with a disability

D10 Regulations provide that an impairment to a child under six years old is to be treated as having a substantial and long-term adverse effect on the ability of that child to carry out normal day-to-day activities where it would normally have a substantial and long-term adverse effect on the ability of a person aged six years or over to carry out normal day-to-day activities.[8]

D11 Children aged six and older are subject to the normal requirements of the definition.

> **A six-year-old child has been diagnosed as having autism. He has difficulty communicating through speech and in recognising when someone is happy or sad. Without a parent or carer with him he will often try to run out of the front door and on to the road to look at the wheels of parked or sometimes passing cars, and he has no sense of danger at all. When going somewhere new or taking a different route he can become very anxious.**

---

[8] See footnote 3.

This amounts to a substantial adverse effect on his ability to carry out normal day-to-day activities, even for such a young child.

D12 Part 6 of the Act provides protection for disabled pupils and students by preventing discrimination against them at school or in post-16 education because of, or for a reason related to, their disability. A pupil or student must satisfy the definition of disability as described in this guidance in order to be protected by Part 6 of the Act. The duties for schools in the Act are designed to dovetail with duties under the Special Educational Needs (SEN) framework which are based on a separate definition of special educational needs. Further information on these duties can be found in the SEN Code of Practice and the Equality and Human Rights Commission's Code of Practice for Education.

Examples of children in an educational setting where their impairment has a substantial and long-term adverse effect on ability to carry out normal day-to-day activities:

A 10-year-old girl has learning difficulties. She has a short attention span and has difficulties remembering facts from one day to the next. She can read only a few familiar words and has some early mathematical skills. To record her work in class she needs to use a tape recorder, pictures and symbols.

A 14-year-old boy has been diagnosed as having attention deficit hyperactivity disorder (ADHD). He often forgets his books, worksheets or homework. In class he finds it difficult to concentrate and skips from task to task forgetting instructions. He often fidgets and makes inappropriate remarks in class or in the playground.

In both of these examples reading, writing and participating in activities in class and/or in the playground, which are all normal day-to-day activities, are adversely affected to a substantial degree.

Adverse effects on the ability to carry out normal day-to-day activities

D13 This section provides guidance on what should be taken into account in deciding whether a person's ability to carry out normal day-to-day activities might be restricted by the effects of that person's impairment. The examples given are purely illustrative and should not in any way be considered as a prescriptive or exhaustive list.

D14 In the Appendix, examples are given of circumstances where it would be reasonable to regard the adverse effect on the ability to carry out a normal day-to-day activity as substantial. In addition, examples are given of circumstances where it would not be reasonable to regard the effect as substantial. In these examples, the effect described should be thought of as if it were the only effect of the impairment.

D15 The examples of what it would, and what it would not, be reasonable to regard as substantial adverse effects on normal day-to-day activities are indicators and not tests. They do not mean that if a person can do an activity listed then he or she does not experience any substantial adverse effects: the person may be affected in relation to other activities, and this instead may indicate a substantial effect. Alternatively, the person may be affected in a minor way in a number of different activities, and the cumulative effect could amount to a substantial adverse effect. See also paragraphs B4 to B6 (cumulative effects).

D16 The examples describe the effect which would occur when the various factors described in Sections A, B and C have been allowed for, including for example the effects of a person's making such modifications of behaviour as might reasonably be expected, or of disregarding the impact of medical or other treatment.

D17 Some of the examples in this section show how an adverse effect may arise from either a physical or a mental impairment. Where illustrations of both types of impairment have not been given, this does not mean that only one type of impairment could result in that particular effect. Regard should be given to the fact that physical impairments can result in mental effects—for example, a person with a physical impairment may, because of pain or fatigue, experience difficulties in concentrating. Similarly, mental impairments can have physical manifestations—for example, a person with a mental impairment may experience difficulty in carrying out activities that involve mobility.

D18 The effect of a person's physical or mental impairment may make it difficult for him or her to carry out such day-to-day activities as: getting around unaided or using a normal means of transport; leaving home with or without assistance; walking a short distance; climbing stairs;

Appendix 3 Codes of Practice

travelling in a car or completing a journey on public transport; sitting, standing, bending, or reaching; or getting around in an unfamiliar place.

A young man with severe anxiety and symptoms of agoraphobia is unable to go out because he fears being outside in open spaces and gets panic attacks in stressful situations such as shopping or travelling on a route that is less than familiar.

A woman with Downs Syndrome has learning difficulties, and finds difficulty in travelling unaccompanied because she often gets lost in areas that are slightly unfamiliar.

A man with Menière's disease experiences dizziness and nausea. This restricts his ability to move around within his home without some form of support.

In these cases, the effects of the impairment have a substantial adverse effect on the ability to carry out normal day-to-day activities.

D19 The effect of a person's impairment may make it substantially difficult for him or her to carry out normal day-to-day activities that involve things like picking up or manipulating small objects, operating a range of equipment manually, or communicating through writing or typing on standard machinery. Loss of function in the dominant hand would be expected to have a greater effect than equivalent loss in the non-dominant hand.

A man with tenosynovitis experiences significant pain in his hands and lower arms when undertaking repetitive tasks such as using a keyboard at home or work, peeling vegetables, and writing.

The impairment substantially adversely affects the man's ability to carry out normal day-to-day activities.

D20 A person's physical or mental impairment may have a substantial adverse affect on their ability to co-ordinate their movements or carry out more than one normal day-to-day activity in unison, such as walking and using hands at the same time. In the case of a child, it is necessary to take account of the level of achievement which would be normal for a person of a similar age.

A young man who has dyspraxia experiences a range of effects which include difficulty co-ordinating physical movements. He is frequently knocking over cups and bottles of drink and cannot combine two activities at the same time, such as walking while holding a plate of food upright, without spilling the food.

It would be reasonable to regard this as a substantial adverse effect on normal day-to-day activities.

D21 Some impairments may affect the ability to control urination and/or defecation. Account should be taken of the frequency and extent of the loss of control when considering whether a person's ability to carry out normal day-to-day activities is adversely affected.

A young woman has developed colitis, an inflammatory bowel disease. The condition is a chronic one which is subject to periods of remission and flare-ups. During a flare-up she experiences severe abdominal pain and bouts of diarrhoea. This makes it very difficult for her to travel, go shopping, or go to work as she must ensure she is always close to a lavatory.

This has a substantial adverse effect on her ability to carry out normal day-to-day activities.

D22 A person's impairment may have a substantial adverse effect on their ability to carry everyday objects that might include such items as books, a kettle of water, bags of shopping, a briefcase, an overnight bag, a chair or other piece of light furniture.

A man with achondroplasia has unusually short stature, and arms which are disproportionate in size to the rest of his body. He has difficulty lifting or manipulating everyday items like a vacuum cleaner, or bulky items of household furniture, and has difficulty opening moderately heavy doors, and operating revolving barriers at the entrance to some buildings.

It would be reasonable to regard this as a substantial adverse effect on normal day-to-day activities.

D23 Account should be taken of the extent to which, as a result of either a physical or mental impairment, a person may have the ability to speak, hear or see, but may nevertheless be substantially adversely affected in carrying out normal day-to-day activities.

For example, account should be taken of how far a person is able to speak clearly at a normal pace and rhythm and to understand someone else speaking normally in the person's native language. It is necessary to consider any effects on speech patterns or which impede the acquisition or processing of a person's native language, for example by someone who has had a stroke.

> **A man has had a stammer since childhood. He does not stammer all the time, but his stammer can appear, particularly in telephone calls, to go beyond the occasional lapses in fluency found in the speech of people who do not have the impairment. However, this effect can often be hidden by his coping strategy. He tries to avoid making or taking telephone calls where he believes he will stammer, or he does not speak as much during the calls. He sometimes tries to avoid stammering by substituting words, or by inserting extra words or phrases.**

> **A six-year-old boy has verbal dyspraxia which adversely affects his ability to speak and make himself clear to other people, including his friends and teachers at school.**

> **A woman has bipolar disorder. Her speech sometimes becomes over-excited and irrational, making it difficult for others to understand what she is saying.**

> **In these cases it would be reasonable to regard these effects as substantial adverse effects on the person's ability to carry out normal day-to-day activities.**

D24 Account should be taken of effects where the level of background noise is within such a range and of such a type that most people would be able to hear adequately. If a person uses a hearing aid or similar device, what needs to be considered is the effect that would be experienced if the person were not using the hearing aid or device.

> **A woman has tinnitus which interferes with, and makes it difficult for her to hear or understand normal conversations, to the extent that she cannot hear and respond to what a supermarket checkout assistant is saying if the two people behind her in the queue are holding a conversation at the same time.**

> **This has a substantial adverse effect on her ability to carry out the normal day-to-day activity of shopping.**

D25 If a person's sight is corrected by spectacles or contact lenses, or could be corrected by them, what needs to be considered is any adverse effect that the visual impairment has on the ability to carry out normal day-to-day activities which remains while he or she is wearing such spectacles or lenses.

D26 If a person's eyesight is impaired sufficiently to lead to certification as a blind, severely sight impaired, sight impaired or partially sighted by a consultant ophthalmologist he or she is deemed to be a disabled person,[9] and does not need to prove that he or she has an impairment which has a substantial and long-term adverse effect on his or her ability to carry out normal day-to-day activities.

D27 Account should be taken of the possible effects on a person who has monocular vision, particularly if the sight in the remaining eye is compromised in any way.

> **A man has retinitis pigmentosa (RP), a hereditary eye disorder which affects the retina. In RP sight loss is gradual but progressive. It is unusual for people with RP to become totally blind – most retain some useful vision well into old age. In this case the man has difficulty seeing in poor light and experiences a marked reduction in his field of vision (referred to as tunnel vision). As a result, he often bumps into furniture and doors when he is in an unfamiliar environment, and can only read when he is in a very well-lit area.**

> **It would be reasonable to conclude that the effects of his impairment have a substantial adverse effect on his ability to carry out normal day-to-day activities.**

[9] See footnote 2.

Appendix 3 Codes of Practice

D28 Account should be taken of whether the person's impairment substantially affects his or her ability to carry out normal day-to-day activities such as remembering to do things, organising their thoughts, planning a course of action and carrying it out, taking in new knowledge, and understanding spoken or written information. This includes considering whether the person has cognitive difficulties or learns to do things significantly more slowly than a person who does not have an impairment.

D29 Account should also be taken of whether the person has persistent and significant difficulty in carrying out day-to-day activities such as reading and understanding text in their native language despite adequate educational opportunities, or in reading and understanding straight-forward numbers. An impairment can have an adverse effect on a person's ability to understand human non-factual information and non-verbal communication such as body language and facial expressions. Account should be taken of how this in turn can cause difficulties in normal day-to-day activities which require a person to understand and follow verbal instructions.

> **A man has Asperger's syndrome, a form of autism, and this causes him to have difficulty communicating with people. He finds it hard to understand non-verbal communications such as facial expressions, and non-factual communication such as jokes. He takes everything that is said very literally, and therefore has difficulty in making or keeping friends or developing close relationships. He is given verbal instructions during office banter with his manager, but his ability to understand the instruction is impaired because he is unable to isolate the instruction from the social conversation.**

> **A woman with bipolar affective disorder is easily distracted. This results in her frequently not being able to concentrate on performing an activity like making a sandwich without being distracted from the task. Consequently, it takes her significantly longer than a person without the disorder to complete the task.**

> **It would be reasonable to regard these impairments as having a substantial adverse effect on normal day-to-day activities.**

D30 Account should be taken of whether the impairment has an effect on a person's estimation or assessment of physical danger, including danger to personal well-being. This can include consideration, for example, of whether the person is inclined to neglect basic functions such as eating, drinking, sleeping, keeping warm or personal hygiene; reckless behaviour which puts the person or others at risk; or excessive avoidance behaviour without a good cause.

> **A man has had paranoid schizophrenia for five years, and one of the effects of this impairment is an inability to make proper judgements about activities that may result in a risk to his personal safety. For example, he will walk into roads without checking if cars are coming. This makes normal day-to-day activities such as shopping very difficult.**

> **A woman has had anorexia, an eating disorder, for two years and the effects of her impairment restrict her ability to properly carry out the normal day-to-day activity of eating.**

> **In these cases, it would be reasonable to regard these impairments as having a substantial adverse effect on the person's ability to carry out normal day-to-day activities.**

Appendix

An illustrative and non-exhaustive list of factors which, if they are experienced by a disabled person, **it would be reasonable** to regard as having a substantial adverse effect on normal day-to-day activities:

Whether a person satisfies the definition of a disabled person for the purposes of the Act will depend upon the full circumstances of the case. That is, whether the substantial adverse effect of the impairment on normal day-to-day activities is long-term.

- Difficulty in travelling a short journey as a passenger in a vehicle, because, for example, it would be painful getting in and out of a car, or sitting in a car for even a short time; the person has a frequent need for a lavatory; or perhaps, as a result of a mental impairment, the person would become distressed while in the car.
- A total inability to walk, or difficulty walking other than at a slow pace or with unsteady or jerky movements.

- Difficulty in going up or down steps, stairs or gradients; for example, because movements are painful, uncomfortable or restricted in some way.
- Difficulty using one or more forms of public transport; for example, as a result of physical restrictions, pain or fatigue, or as a result of a mental impairment.
- Difficulty going out of doors unaccompanied; for example, because the person has a phobia.
- Difficulty co-ordinating the use of a knife and fork at the same time.
- Difficulty preparing a meal because of problems doing things like opening cans or other packages; peeling vegetables; lifting saucepans; and opening the oven door.
- Difficulty opening doors which have door knobs rather than lever handles, or gripping handrails on steps or gradients.
- Difficulty pressing the buttons on keyboards or keypads at the same speed as someone who does not have an impairment.
- Difficulty in dealing with buttons and fasteners when dressing and activities associated with toileting.
- Ability to pour hot water into a cup to make a cup of tea only with unusual slowness or concentration.
- Difficulty placing food into one's own mouth with a fork or spoon, without unusual concentration or assistance.
- Inability to place a key in a lock without unusual concentration or requiring assistance.
- Infrequent loss of control of the bowels, if it is entirely unpredictable and leads to immediate major soiling.
- Loss of control of the bladder while asleep at least once a month.
- Frequent minor faecal incontinence or frequent minor leakage from the bladder, particularly if it is unpredictable.
- Difficulty picking up objects of moderate weight with one hand.
- Difficulty opening a moderately heavy door.
- Difficulty carrying a moderately loaded tray steadily.
- Difficulty giving clear basic instructions orally to colleagues or providers of a service.
- Difficulty asking specific questions to clarify instructions.
- Taking longer than someone who does not have an impairment to say things.
- Difficulty hearing someone talking at a sound level which is normal for everyday conversations, and in a moderately noisy environment.
- Difficulty hearing and understanding another person speaking clearly over the voice telephone (where the telephone is not affected by bad reception.
- Difficulty hearing or understanding normal conversations because of interference caused by auditory hallucinations as a result of a mental impairment.
- Inability to see to pass the eyesight test for a standard driving test (however where this is corrected by glasses, this is not a substantial adverse effect).
- Difficulty recognising by sight a known person across a moderately-sized room (unless this can be corrected by glasses).
- Inability to distinguish any colours at all.
- Difficulty reading ordinary newsprint (unless this can be corrected by reading glasses).
- Difficulty walking safely without bumping into things (unless this can be corrected by glasses).
- Intermittent loss of consciousness and associated confused behaviour.
- Persistent difficulty in remembering the names of familiar people such as family or friends.
- Difficulty in adapting after a reasonable period to minor changes in work routine.
- Persistent and significant difficulty with reading.
- Persistent difficulty in remembering the spelling and meaning of words in common usage.
- Considerable difficulty in following a short sequence such as a simple recipe or a brief list of domestic tasks.
- Significant difficulty taking part in normal social interaction or forming social relationships.
- Disordered perception of reality.
- Difficulty in safely operating properly-maintained equipment.
- Persistent difficulty crossing a road safely.
- Persistent failure to nourish oneself, where nourishment is available.
- Inability to recognise the physical dangers of touching an object which is very hot or cold.

An illustrative and non-exhaustive list of factors which, if they are experienced by a disabled person, it would not be reasonable to regard as having a substantial adverse effect on normal day-to-day activities:

- Experiencing some discomfort as a result of travelling in a car for a journey lasting more than two hours.
- Experiencing some tiredness or minor discomfort as a result of walking unaided for a distance of about 1.5 kilometres or one mile.
- Inability to undertake activities requiring delicate hand movements, such as threading a small needle.
- Inability to reach typing speeds standardised for secretarial work.
- Inability to pick up a single small item, such as a pin.
- Simple clumsiness.
- Inability to catch a tennis ball.
- Infrequent (less than once a month) loss of control of the bladder while asleep.
- Infrequent and minor leakage from the bladder.
- Incontinence in a very young child who would not be expected to be able to control urination and/or defecation.
- Inability to carry heavy luggage without assistance.
- Inability to move heavy objects without a mechanical aid, such as moving a heavy piece of furniture without a trolley.
- Inability to articulate fluently due to a lisp or other minor speech impediment.
- Inability to speak in front of an audience simply as a result of nervousness.
- Inability to be understood because of having a strong accent.
- Inability to converse in a language which is not the speaker's native language.
- Inability to hold a conversation in a very noisy place, such as a factory floor, a pop concert or alongside a busy main road.
- Inability to sing in tune.
- Inability to read very small or indistinct print without the aid of a magnifying glass.
- Inability to distinguish a known person across a substantial distance (e.g. across the width of a football pitch).
- Simple inability to distinguish between red and green, which is not accompanied by any other effect such as blurring of vision.
- Occasionally forgetting the name of a familiar person, such as a colleague.
- Inability to concentrate on a task requiring application over several hours.
- Some shyness or timidity.
- Inability to fill in a long, detailed, technical document without assistance.
- Inability to read at faster than normal speed.
- Minor problems with writing or spelling.
- Fear of significant heights.
- Underestimating the risk associated with dangerous hobbies, such as mountain climbing.
- A person consciously taking a higher than normal risk on their own initiative, such as persistently crossing a road when the signals are adverse, or driving fast on highways for own pleasure.
- Underestimating risks—other than obvious ones—in unfamiliar workplaces.

ACAS Code of Practice on Settlement Agreements (under section 111A of the Employment Rights Act 1996)

Foreword

The Acas statutory Code of Practice set out in paragraphs 1 to 24 on the following pages is designed to help employers, employees and their representatives understand the implications of section 111A of the Employment Rights Act (ERA) 1996 for the negotiation of settlement agreements (formerly known as compromise agreements) before the termination of employment. In particular, it explains aspects of the confidentiality provisions associated with negotiations that take place to reach such agreements. The Code does not cover all aspects of settlement agreements. Further guidance on settlement agreements can be found in the Acas booklet '*Settlement Agreements: A Guide*' which also offers more detailed guidance on the confidentiality provisions set out in section 111A.

The Code is issued under section 199 of the Trade Union and Labour Relations (Consolidation) Act 1992 and comes into effect by order of the Secretary of State on 29 July 2013. Failure to follow the Code does not, in itself, make a person or organisation liable to proceedings, nor will it lead to an adjustment in any compensation award made by an employment tribunal. However, employment tribunals will take the Code into account when considering relevant cases.

The discussions that take place in order to reach a settlement agreement in relation to an existing employment dispute can be, and often are, undertaken on a 'without prejudice' basis. This means that any statements made during a 'without prejudice' meeting or discussion cannot be used in a court or tribunal as evidence. This 'without prejudice' confidentiality does not, however, apply where there is no existing dispute between the parties. Section 111A of the ERA 1996 has therefore been introduced to allow greater flexibility in the use of confidential discussions as a means of ending the employment relationship. Section 111A, which will run alongside the 'without prejudice' principle, provides that even where no employment dispute exists, the parties may still offer and discuss a settlement agreement in the knowledge that their conversations cannot be used in any subsequent unfair dismissal claim. It is the confidentiality aspect of section 111A that is the specific focus of this Code.

Throughout this Code the word 'should' is used to indicate what Acas considers to be good employment practice, rather than legal requirements. The word 'must' is used to indicate where something is a legal requirement.

The Code of Practice

Introduction

1   This Code is designed to help employers, employees and their representatives understand the law relating to the negotiation of settlement agreements as set out in section 111A of the Employment Rights Act (ERA) 1996 In particular it gives guidance on the confidentiality provisions associated with negotiations about settlement agreements and on what constitutes improper behaviour when such negotiations are taking place.

2   Settlement agreements are only one way of handling potentially difficult employment situations. Problems in the workplace are best resolved in open conversations, including, where appropriate, through the use of performance management, or informal and formal disciplinary or grievance procedures.

What are settlement agreements?

3   Settlement agreements are legally binding contracts which can be used to end the employment relationship on agreed terms. Their main feature is that they waive an individual's right to make a claim to a court or employment tribunal on the matters that are specifically covered in the agreement. Settlement agreements may be proposed prior to undertaking any other formal process. They usually include some form of payment to the employee by the employer and may also include a reference.

4   For a settlement agreement to be legally valid the following conditions must be met:
(a) The agreement must be in writing;

(b) The agreement must relate to a particular complaint or proceedings;[10]

(c) The employee must have received advice from a relevant independent adviser[11] on the terms and effect of the proposed agreement and its effect on the employee's ability to pursue that complaint or proceedings before an employment tribunal;

(d) The independent adviser must have a current contract of insurance or professional indemnity insurance covering the risk of a claim by the employee in respect of loss arising from that advice;

(e) The agreement must identify the adviser;

(f) The agreement must state that the applicable statutory conditions regulating the settlement agreement have been satisfied.

5   Settlement agreements are voluntary. Parties do not have to agree them or enter into discussions about them if they do not wish to do so. Equally the parties do not have to accept the terms initially proposed to them. There can be a process of negotiation during which both sides make proposals and counter proposals until an agreement is reached, or both parties recognise that no agreement is possible.

Settlement agreement discussions and section 111A of the ERA 1996

6   Section 111A of the ERA 1996 provides that offers to end the employment relationship on agreed terms (i.e. under a settlement agreement) can be made on a confidential basis which means that they cannot be used as evidence in an unfair dismissal claim to an employment tribunal. Under section 111A, such pre-termination negotiations can be treated as confidential even where there is no current employment dispute or where one or more of the parties is unaware that there is an employment problem. Section 111A can also apply to offers of a settlement agreement against the background of an existing dispute, although in such cases the 'without prejudice' principle can also apply.

7   There are, however, some exceptions to the application of section 111A. Claims that relate to an automatically unfair reason for dismissal such as whistleblowing, union membership or asserting a statutory right are not covered by the confidentiality provisions set out in section 111A. Neither are claims made on grounds other than unfair dismissal, such as claims of discrimination, harassment, victimisation or other behaviour prohibited by the Equalities Act 2010, or claims relating to breach of contract or wrongful dismissal. Throughout this Code there are a number of references to unfair dismissal. These references should be read in general as subject to the exceptions set out in this paragraph.

8   The confidentiality provisions of section 111A are, additionally, subject to there being no improper behaviour. Guidance on what constitutes improper behaviour is contained in paragraphs 17 and 18 of this Code. Where there is improper behaviour, anything said or done in pretermination negotiations will only be inadmissible as evidence in claims to an employment tribunal to the extent that the tribunal considers it just. In some circumstances, for instance where unlawful discrimination occurs during a settlement discussion, this may itself form the basis of a claim to an employment tribunal.

9   Where there has been some improper behaviour for these purposes this does not mean that an employer will necessarily lose any subsequent unfair dismissal claim that is brought to an employment tribunal. Equally, the fact that an employer has not engaged in some improper behaviour does not mean that they will necessarily win any subsequent unfair dismissal claim brought against them.

10 Where the parties sign a valid settlement agreement, the employee will be unable to bring an employment tribunal claim about any type of claim which is listed in the agreement. Where a settlement agreement is not agreed, an employee may bring a subsequent claim to an employment tribunal but where this claim relates to an allegation of unfair dismissal the confidentiality provisions of section 111A of the ERA 1996 will apply.

---

10 Simply saying that the agreement is in 'full and final settlement of all claims' will not be sufficient to contract out of employment tribunal claims. To be legally binding for these purposes, a settlement agreement has to state specifically the claims that it is intended to cover.

11 The independent adviser can be a qualified lawyer; a certified and authorized official, employee or member of an independent trade union; or a certified and authorized advice centre worker.

Reaching a settlement agreement

11 Settlement agreements can be proposed by both employers and employees although they will normally be proposed by the employer. A settlement agreement proposal can be made at any stage of an employment relationship. How the proposal is made can vary depending on the circumstances. It may be helpful if any reasons for the proposal are given when the proposal is made. Whilst the initial proposal may be oral, one of the requirements for a settlement agreement to become legally binding is that the agreement must ultimately be put in writing (see paragraph 4).

12 Parties should be given a reasonable period of time to consider the proposed settlement agreement. What constitutes a reasonable period of time will depend on the circumstances of the case. As a general rule, a minimum period of 10 calendar days should be allowed to consider the proposed formal written terms of a settlement agreement and to receive independent advice, unless the parties agree otherwise.

13 The parties may find it helpful to discuss proposals face-to-face and any such meeting should be at an agreed time and place. Whilst not a legal requirement, employers should allow employees to be accompanied at the meeting by a work colleague, trade union official or trade union representative. Allowing the individual to be accompanied is good practice and may help to progress settlement discussions.

14 Where a proposed settlement agreement based on the termination of the employment is accepted, the employee's employment can be terminated either with the required contractual notice or from the date specified in the agreement. The details of any payments due to the employee and their timing should be included in the agreement.

Improper behaviour

15 If a settlement agreement is being discussed as a means of settling an existing employment dispute, the negotiations between the parties can be carried out on a 'without prejudice' basis. 'Without prejudice' is a common law principle (i.e. non-statutory) which prevents statements (written or oral), made in a genuine attempt to settle an existing dispute, from being put before a court or tribunal as evidence. This protection does not, however, apply where there has been fraud, undue influence or some other 'unambiguous impropriety' such as perjury or blackmail.

16 Section 111A of the ERA 1996 offers similar protection to the 'without prejudice' principle in that it provides that any offer made of a settlement agreement, or discussions held about it, cannot be used as evidence in any subsequent employment tribunal claim of unfair dismissal. Unlike 'without prejudice', however, it can apply where there is no existing employment dispute. The protection in section 111A will not apply where there is some improper behaviour in relation to the settlement agreement discussions or offer.

17 What constitutes improper behaviour is ultimately for a tribunal to decide on the facts and circumstances of each case. Improper behaviour will, however, include (but not be limited to) behaviour that would be regarded as 'unambiguous impropriety' under the 'without prejudice' principle.

18 The following list provides some examples of improper behaviour. The list is not exhaustive:
   (a) All forms of harassment, bullying and intimidation, including through the use of offensive words or aggressive behaviour;
   (b) Physical assault or the threat of physical assault and other criminal behaviour;
   (c) All forms of victimisation;
   (d) Discrimination because of age, sex, race, disability, sexual orientation, religion or belief, transgender, pregnancy and maternity and marriage or civil partnership;
   (e) Putting undue pressure on a party. For instance:
      (i) Not giving the reasonable time for consideration set out in paragraph 12 of this Code;
      (ii) An employer saying before any form of disciplinary process has begun that if a settlement proposal is rejected then the employee will be dismissed;
      (iii) An employee threatening to undermine an organisation's public reputation if the organisation does not sign the agreement, unless the provisions of the Public Interest Disclosure Act 1998 apply.

19 The examples set out in paragraph 18 above are not intended to prevent, for instance, a party setting out in a neutral manner the reasons that have led to the proposed settlement agreement, or factually stating the likely alternatives if an agreement is not reached, including the possibility of starting a disciplinary process if relevant. These examples are not intended to be exhaustive.

Appendix 3 Codes of Practice

20 In situations where there is no existing dispute between the parties, the 'without prejudice' principle cannot apply but section 111A can apply. In these circumstances the offer of, and discussions about, a settlement agreement will not be admissible in a tribunal (in an unfair dismissal case) so long as there has been no improper behaviour. Where an employment tribunal finds that there has been improper behaviour in such a case, any offer of a settlement agreement, or discussions relating to it, will only be inadmissible if, and in so far as, the employment tribunal considers it just.

21 Where there is an existing dispute between the parties, offers of a settlement agreement, and discussions about such an agreement, may be covered by both the 'without prejudice' principle and section 111A. The 'without prejudice' principle will apply unless there has been some 'unambiguous impropriety'. As the test of 'unambiguous impropriety' is a narrower test than that of improper behaviour, this means that pretermination negotiations that take place in the context of an existing dispute will not be admissible in a subsequent unfair dismissal claim unless there has been some 'unambiguous impropriety'.

22 In court or tribunal proceedings other than unfair dismissal claims, such as discrimination claims, section 111A does not apply. In these cases, the 'without prejudice' principle can apply where there is an existing dispute at the time of the settlement offer and discussions, meaning that these will not be admissible in evidence unless there has been some 'unambiguous impropriety'.

What if a settlement agreement cannot be agreed?

23 If a settlement agreement is rejected and the parties still wish to resolve the dispute or problem that led to the offer being made then some other form of resolution should be sought. Depending on the nature of the dispute or problem, resolution might be sought through a performance management, disciplinary or grievance process, whichever is appropriate. The parties cannot rely on the offer of a settlement agreement or any discussions about the agreement as being part of this process.

24 It is important that employers follow a fair process, as well as the other principles set out in the Acas discipline and grievance Code of Practice, because, if the employee is subsequently dismissed, failure to do so could constitute grounds for a claim of unfair dismissal.

Appendix 4
Financial Information

Income Tax Rates

	2012/13 £	2013/14 £	2014/15	2015/16	2016/17	2017/18
Basic rate (20%)*	0–34,370	0–32,010	0–31,865	0–31,785	0–32,000	0–33,500
Higher rate (40%)*	34,371–150,000	32,011–150,000	31,866–150,000	31,786–150,000	32,001–150,000	33,500–150,000
Additional Rate (50% but 45% from 2013–2014 tax year)	150,000+	150,000+ (45%)	150,000+	150,000+	150,000+	150,000+

Personal Allowances and Reliefs

	2012/13 £	2013/14 £	2014/15 £	2015/16 £	2016/17 £	2017/18 £
Personal allowance	8,105	10,500	10,000	10,600	11,000	11,500
Blind person's allowance	2,100	2,160	2160	2,290	2290	2,320
Income limit for personal allowance	100,000	100,000	100,000	100,000	100,000	100,000

NI Contributions

Employers' Rates

2012–13		2013–14		2014–15		2015–16		2016–17		2017-18	
Below £107	Nil	Below £109	Nil	Below £111	Nil	Below £112	Nil	Below £112	Nil	Below £113	Nil
£107–£144	0%	£109–£148	0%	£111–£153	0%	£112–£156	0%	£112–£156	0%	£113–£157	0%
£144–£817	13.8%	£149–£797	13.8%	£153–£770	13.8%	£156–£770	13.8%	£156–£827	13.8%	£157–£866	13.8%
£817+	13.8%	£797+	13.8%	£770+	13.8%	£770+	13.8%	£827+	13.8%	£866+	13.8%

Employees' Standard Rates

2012/2013		2013/2014		2014/2015		2015/2016		2016/2017		2017/2018	
First £144	Nil	First £149	Nil	First £111	Nil	First £112	Nil	First £112	Nil	First £113	Nil
				£112– £153	0%	£112– £155	0%	£112– £155	0%	£113– £157	0%
£144– 817	12%	£149– 797	12%	£153– £805	12%	£156– £815	12%	£156– £827	12%	£157– £866	12%
£817+	2%	£797+	2%	£805+	2%	£815+	2%	£827+	2%	£866+	2%

Employees' Class 2 Contributions

2012/13	2013/14	2014/15	2015/16	2016/17
£2.65	£2.70	£2.75	£2.80	£2.80

Main Social Security Benefits

Jobseeker's Allowance (updated in April)

Rate for adult dependants in brackets

2012/13	2013/14	2014/15	2015/16	2016/17	2017/18
£71.00 (25+ yr-olds)	£71.70 (25+ yr-olds)	£72.40 (25+ yr-olds)	£73.10 (25+ yr-olds)	£73.10 (25+ yr-olds)	£73.10 (25+ yr-olds)
£56.25 (under 25 yr-olds)	£56.80 (under 25 yr-olds)	£57.35 (under 25 yr-olds)	£57.90 (under 25 yr-olds)	£57.90 (under 25 yr-olds)	£57.90 (under 25 yr-olds)

The jobseeker's allowance came into force on 7 October 1996 and replaces both income support and unemployment benefit.

Incapacity Benefit (before 1995 known as Sickness Benefit) (updated in April)

Weeks	2012/13	2013/14	2014/15	2015/16	2016/17	2017/18
1–28	£74.80	£76.45	£78.50	£79.45	£79.45	£80.25
29–52	£88.55	£90.50	£92.95	£94.05	£94.05	95.00
52+	£99.15	£101.35	£104.10	£105.35	£105.35	106.40

Appendix 4 Financial Information

Statutory Sick Pay (updated in April)

The amount of SSP depends upon the level of gross earnings.

2012/13	2013/14	2014/15	2015/16	2016/17	2017/18
£85.85	£86.70	£87.55	£88.45	£88.45	£89.35

Statutory Maternity Pay

2012/13	2013/14	2014/15	2015/16	2016/17	2017/18
90% of average weekly earnings for 6 weeks and then £135.45 (if lower) for 33 weeks	90% of average weekly earnings for 6 weeks and then £136.78 (if lower) for 33 weeks	90% of average weekly earnings for 6 weeks and then £138.18 (if lower) for 33 weeks	90% of average weekly earnings for 6 weeks and then £139.58 (if lower) for 33 weeks	90% of average weekly earnings for 6 weeks and then £139.58 (if lower) for 33 weeks	90% of average weekly earnings for 6 weeks and then £140.98 (if lower) for 33 weeks

AA Motoring Costs Tables 2014

Petrol Cars Running Costs 2014

	Purchase price of the car when new:				
	Up to £13,000	£13,000 to £18,000	£18,000 to £25,000	£25,000 to £32,000	Over £32,000
Standing charges per year, £					
VED (Road Tax)	110	145	180	283	609
Insurance	360	409	481	571	762
Cost of capital	203	251	355	494	877
Depreciation	1190	2156	2611	3672	6974
Breakdown cover	50	50	50	50	50
Standing charges only: £	1913	3011	3678	5070	9271
Standing charges as pence per mile					
at 5,000 miles per year	37.78	59.36	72.51	99.93	182.64
at 10,000	19.13	30.11	36.78	50.70	92.71
at 15,000	13.07	20.65	25.21	34.78	63.67
at 20,000	10.16	16.13	19.69	27.18	49.84
at 25,000	8.22	13.08	15.96	22.04	40.43
at 30,000	6.89	10.97	13.39	18.49	33.93
Petrol *	10.84	13.12	14.55	16.22	18.04
Tyres	1.37	1.57	1.94	2.32	3.35

	Purchase price of the car when new:				
	Up to £13,000	£13,000 to £18,000	£18,000 to £25,000	£25,000 to £32,000	Over £32,000
Service labour costs	2.10	2.07	2.09	2.04	2.34
Replacement parts	2.24	2.39	2.25	2.73	3.34
Parking and tolls	2.00	2.00	2.00	2.00	2.00
Running costs only: p.	18.56	21.14	22.83	25.31	29.06
* NB: Petrol at 129.0 pence per litre For each penny more or less, add or take away:					
	0.08	0.10	0.11	0.13	0.14
Total of standing and running costs as pence per mile					
at 5,000 miles per year	56.34	80.51	95.34	125.24	211.70
at 10,000	37.68	51.26	59.60	76.01	121.78
at 15,000	31.63	41.79	48.04	60.09	92.73
at 20,000	28.72	37.28	42.52	52.49	78.91
at 25,000	26.78	34.22	38.79	47.35	69.50
at 30,000	25.45	32.12	36.22	43.80	62.99

Diesel Cars Running Costs 2014

	Up to £16,000	£16,000 to £22,000	£22,000 to £26,000	£26,000 to £36,000	Over £36,000
Standing charges per year, £					
VED (Road Tax)	30	110	180	180	361
Insurance	424	499	511	601	771
Cost of capital	245	325	429	541	823
Depreciation	1705	2426	2618	3373	5197
Breakdown cover	50	50	50	50	50
Standing charges only: £	2454	3411	3788	4745	7203
Standing charges as pence per mile					
at 5,000 miles per year	48.40	67.24	74.71	93.55	141.98
at 10,000	24.54	34.11	37.88	47.45	72.03
at 15,000	16.81	23.38	25.95	32.53	49.40
at 20,000	13.12	18.27	20.25	25.41	38.61
at 25,000	10.63	14.81	16.41	20.60	31.31
at 30,000	8.92	12.42	13.76	17.28	26.26
Running costs, pence per mile					

Appendix 4 Financial Information

	Up to £16,000	£16,000 to £22,000	£22,000 to £26,000	£26,000 to £36,000	Over £36,000
Diesel Fuel *	9.28	10.20	12.65	12.88	16.79
Tyres	1.15	1.49	2.06	2.02	2.87
Service labour costs	2.10	2.14	2.29	2.24	2.76
Replacement parts	2.73	2.43	2.53	2.99	3.44
Parking and tolls	2.00	2.00	2.00	2.00	2.00
Running costs only: p.	17.26	18.25	21.54	22.14	27.85

* NB Fuel at: 137.0 pence per litre For each penny more or less, add or take away:

	0.07	0.07	0.09	0.09	0.12

Total of standing and running costs as pence per mile

at 5,000 miles per year	65.66	85.49	96.25	115.69	169.83
at 10,000	41.80	52.36	59.41	69.59	99.88
at 15,000	34.08	41.64	47.49	54.67	77.26
at 20,000	30.39	36.52	41.79	47.55	66.47
at 25,000	27.90	33.06	37.94	42.74	59.16
at 30,000	26.18	30.67	35.30	39.42	54.11

Extract from Judicial College *Guidelines for the Assessment of General Damages in Personal Injury Cases*

(14th edn, 2017)

4 PSYCHIATRIC AND PSYCHOLOGICAL DAMAGE

This chapter covers those cases where there is a recognisable psychiatric injury. In part (A) of this chapter some of the brackets contain an element of compensation for post-traumatic stress disorder. This is of course not a universal feature of cases of psychiatric injury and hence a number of the awards upon which the brackets are based did not reflect it. Where it does figure any award will tend towards the upper end of the bracket. Cases where post-traumatic stress disorder is the sole psychiatric condition are dealt with in part (B) of this chapter. Where cases arise out of sexual and/or physical abuse in breach of parental, family or other trust, involving victims who are young and/ or vulnerable, awards will tend to be at the upper end of the relevant bracket to take into account (A)(vii) below.

Where the psychiatric injury arises out of the death of a close relative, e.g. a child, spouse or parent, awards will tend to fall into (A)(c) or (B)(c) below unless the long- term prognosis is especially poor then an award within (A)(b) or (B)(b) may be appropriate.

(A) Psychiatric Damage Generally

The factors to be taken into account in valuing claims of this nature are as follows:

(i) the injured person's ability to cope with life, education and work;

(ii) the effect on the injured person's relationships with family, friends and those with whom he or she comes into contact;

(iii) the extent to which treatment would be successful;

(iv) future vulnerability;

(v) prognosis;

(vi) whether medical help has been sought;

(vii) Claims relating to sexual and physical abuse usually include a significant aspect of psychiatric or psychological damage. The brackets discussed in this chapter provide a useful starting point in the assessment of general damages in such cases. It should not be forgotten, however, that this aspect of the injury is likely to form only part of the injury for which damages will be awarded. Many cases include physical or sexual abuse and injury. Others have an element of false imprisonment. The fact of an abuse of trust is relevant to the award of damages. A further feature, which distinguishes these cases from most involving psychiatric damage, is that there may have been a long period during which the effects of the abuse were undiagnosed, untreated, unrecognised or even denied. Aggravated damages may be appropriate.

(a) **Severe** £43,710 to £92,240 (with 10% uplift £48,080 to £101,470)

In these cases the injured person will have marked problems with respect to factors (i) to (iv) above and the prognosis will be very poor.

(b) **Moderately Severe** £15,200 to £43,710 (with 10% uplift £16,720 to £48,080)

In these cases there will be significant problems associated with factors (i) to (iv) above but the prognosis will be much more optimistic than in (a) above. While there are awards which support both extremes of this bracket, the majority are somewhere near the middle of the bracket. Cases of work-related stress resulting in a permanent or long-standing disability preventing a return to comparable employment would appear to come within this category.

(c) **Moderate** £4,670 to £15,200 (with 10% uplift £5,130 to £16,720)

While there may have been the sort of problems associated with factors (i) to (iv) above there will have been marked improvement by trial and the prognosis will be good.

(d) Less Severe   £1,220 to £4,670 (with 10% uplift £1,350 to £5,130)

The level of the award will take into consideration the length of the period of disability and the extent to which daily activities and sleep were affected. Cases falling short of a specific phobia or disorder such as travel anxiety when associated with minor physical symptoms may be found in the Minor Injuries chapter.

(B) Post-Traumatic Stress Disorder

Cases within this category are exclusively those where there is a specific diagnosis of a reactive psychiatric disorder following an event which creates psychological trauma in response to actual or threatened death, serious injury or sexual violation. The guidelines below have been compiled by reference to cases which variously reflect the criteria established in the 4th and then 5th editions of *Diagnostic and Statistical Manual of Mental Disorders* (DSM IV TR and DSM 5). The symptoms may include nightmares, flashbacks, sleep disturbance, avoidance, mood disorders, suicidal ideation and hyper- arousal. Symptoms of hyper- arousal can affect basic functions such as breathing, pulse rate and bowel and/ or bladder control.

(a) Severe   £47,720 to £80,250 (with 10% uplift £52,490 to £88,270)

Such cases will involve permanent effects which prevent the injured person from working at all or at least from functioning at anything approaching the pre-trauma level. All aspects of the life of the injured person will be badly affected.

(b) Moderately Severe   £18,450 to £47,720 (with 10% uplift £20,290 to £52,490)

This category is distinct from (a) above because of the better prognosis which will be for some recovery with professional help. However, the effects are still likely to cause significant disability for the foreseeable future. While there are awards which support both extremes of this bracket, the majority are between £22,930 and £29,590 (£25,220 and £32,550 accounting for 10% uplift).

(c) Moderate   £6,520 to £18,450 (with 10% uplift £7,170 to £20,290)

In these cases the injured person will have largely recovered and any continuing effects will not be grossly disabling.

(d) Less Severe   £3,150 to £6,520 (with 10% uplift £3,460 to £7,170)

In these cases a virtually full recovery will have been made within one to two years and only minor symptoms will persist over any longer period.

Table of statutory redundancy entitlement—Redundancies on or after 1.10.06

Age (years)	Service (years)																		
	2	3	4	5	6	7	8	9	10	11	12	13	14	15	16	17	18	19	20
18	1	1½																	
19	1	1½	2	2½															
20	1	1½	2	2½	3														
21	1	1½	2	2½	3	3½													
22	1	1½	2	2½	3	3½	4												
23	1½	1	2½	3	3½	4	4½	5											
24	2	2½	3	3½	4	4½	5	5½	6										
25	2	3	3½	4	4½	5	5½	6	6½	7									
26	2	3	4	4½	5	5½	6	6½	7	7½	8								
27	2	3	4	5	5½	6	6½	7	7½	8	8½	9							
28	2	3	4	5	6	6½	7	7½	8	8½	9	9½	10						
29	2	3	4	5	6	7	7½	8	8½	9	9½	10	10½	11					
30	2	3	4	5	6	7	8	8½	9	9½	10	10½	11	11½	12				
31	2	3	4	5	6	7	8	9	9½	10	10½	11	11½	12	12½	13			
32	2	3	4	5	6	7	8	9	10	10½	11	11½	12	12½	13	13½	14		
33	2	3	4	5	6	7	8	9	10	11	11½	12	12½	13	13½	14	14½	15	
34	2	3	4	5	6	7	8	9	10	11	12	12½	13	13½	14	14½	15	15½	16
35	2	3	4	5	6	7	8	9	10	11	12	13	13½	14	14½	15	15½	16	16½
36	2	3	4	5	6	7	8	9	10	11	12	13	14	14½	15	15½	16	16½	17
37	2	3	4	5	6	7	8	9	10	11	12	13	14	15	15½	16	16½	17	17½
38	2	3	4	5	6	7	8	9	10	11	12	13	14	15	16	16½	17	17½	18

Age (years)	Service (years)																		
	2	3	4	5	6	7	8	9	10	11	12	13	14	15	16	17	18	19	20
39	2	3	4	5	6	7	8	9	10	11	12	13	14	15	16	17	17½	18	18½
40	2	3	4	5	6	7	8	9	10	11	12	13	14	15	16	17	18	18½	19
41	2	3	4	5	6	7	8	9	10	11	12	13	14	15	16	17	18	19	19½
42	2½	3½	4½	5½	6½	7½	8½	9½	10½	11	12½	13½	14½	15½	16½	17½	18½	19½	20½
43	3	4	5	6	7	8	9	10	11	12	13	14	15	16	17	18	19	20	21
44	3	4½	5½	6½	7½	8½	9½	10½	11½	12½	13½	14½	15½	16½	17½	18½	19½	20½	21½
45	3	4½	6	7	8	9	10	11	12	13	14	15	16	17	18	19	20	21	22
46	3	4½	6	7½	8½	9½	10½	11½	12½	13½	14½	15½	16½	17½	18½	19½	20½	21½	22½
47	3	4½	6	7½	9	10	11	12	13	14	15	16	17	18	19	20	21	22	23
48	3	4½	6	7½	9	10½	11½	12½	13½	14½	15½	16½	17½	18½	19½	20½	21½	22½	23½
49	3	4½	6	7½	9	10½	12	13	14	15	16	17	18	19	20	21	22	23	24
50	3	4½	6	7½	9	10½	12	13½	14½	15½	16½	17½	18½	19½	20½	21½	22½	23½	24½
51	3	4½	6	7½	9	10½	12	13½	15	16	17	18	19	20	21	22	23	24	25
52	3	4½	6	7½	9	10½	12	13½	15	16½	17½	18½	19½	20½	21½	22½	23½	24½	25½
53	3	4½	6	7½	9	10½	12	13½	15	16½	18	19	20	21	22	23	24	25	26
54	3	4½	6	7½	9	10½	12	13½	15	16½	18	19½	20½	21½	22½	23½	24½	25½	26½
55	3	4½	6	7½	9	10½	12	13½	15	16½	18	19½	21	22	23	24	25	26	27
56	3	4½	6	7½	9	10½	12	13½	15	16½	18	19½	21	22½	23½	24½	25½	26½	27½
57	3	4½	6	7½	9	10½	12	13½	15	16½	18	19½	21	22½	24	25	26	27	28
58	3	4½	6	7½	9	10½	12	13½	15	16½	18	19½	21	22½	24	25½	26½	27½	28½
59	3	4½	6	7½	9	10½	12	13½	15	16½	18	19½	21	22½	24	25½	27	28	29
60	3	4½	6	7½	9	10½	12	13½	15	16½	18	19½	21	22½	24	25½	27	28½	29½
61*	3	4½	6	7½	9	10½	12	13½	15	16½	18	19½	21	22½	24	25½	27	28½	30

Appendix 5
Forms and Precedents

For a specimen Settlement Agreement see Chapter 5

Employment Tribunal

THE CLAIM

The Claim Form ET1

The form can be found on the ETS website at <http://www.gov.uk/employment-tribunals/make-a-claim>.

The form can also be completed online. For more details about the completion of the claim form see Chapter 2.

Specimen Grounds of Complaint

Claim alleging constructive unfair dismissal

IN THE [   ] EMPLOYMENT TRIBUNAL   <u>Claim No</u>

BETWEEN:

MISS A

<u>Claimant</u>

-and-

XYZ IT SYSTEMS LIMITED

<u>Respondent</u>

RIDER TO ET1

---

1. The Respondent carries on business as a provider of bespoke IT solutions to commercial clients. The Claimant was employed as a sales representative between 6 January 2017 and 22 March 2019.
2. It was an implied term of the Claimant's contract of employment that the Respondent would not, without reasonable cause, act in a manner calculated or likely to destroy or seriously damage the relationship of trust and confidence between the employer and employee.
3. The Claimant's role involved two distinct functions. First, generating 'sales leads' through cold calling companies with whom the Respondent had no previous contact, such contact was deemed to be successful if the potential client agreed to a meeting with the Respondent's representatives. Secondly, the Claimant would form part of a two-person team, along with a technical expert, who attended such meetings and attempted to persuade the client to agree to buy a system from the Respondent. It was the Respondent's policy that, where a sales lead was generated by a particular representative, they would normally attend the meeting. However, if the meeting could not be arranged to fit in with that individual's availability, another representative would be designated by the sales manager to attend.
4. The Claimant was paid two monthly bonuses based on the number of successful cold calls she made and the value of the contracts signed as a result of her sales meetings. The Claimant and other sales representatives were given individual targets for each of these bonuses.
5. When the Claimant commenced employment the sales manager she reported to was Mr B. During the first six months of her employment the Claimant met all her targets. At her six-month appraisal Mr B complimented her performance and indicated that she had a bright future within the Respondent's organization.
6. In March 2017, Mr B left the company and was replaced by Mr C. Mr C had a very different style of management to Mr C and he sought to achieve results by intimidating the sales staff. During the period July 2017 to February 2018 Mr C increasingly singled out the Claimant. In particular:
   (a) Mr C frequently swore in the office, and would direct this at the Claimant.
   (b) Mr C told the Claimant that she was 'crap' at sales and didn't understand the Respondent's products. He repeated this in front of other employees.
   (c) Mr C never gave the Claimant the opportunity to go to sales meetings that other representatives could not attend. Whenever possible he removed her sales meetings and gave them to other employees. This resulted in a decrease in the value of contracts agreed by the Claimant and she began to fail to meet her targets.
   (d) Mr C unreasonably increased the Claimant's targets, thereby 'setting her up to fail'. Other employees' targets remained the same.
7. On 23 February 2019 the Claimant discovered that Mr C had asked another employee to attend a scheduled sales meeting with a company called 123 Ltd the following week. 123 Ltd is a large educational publisher with offices all over the country, if they were to agree to allow the Respondent to replace their IT system it would be an extremely valuable contract. The Claimant had made contact

with 123 Ltd and developed the relationship over several weeks, she believed that she would be attending the sales meeting.

8. The Claimant went to Mr C's office to challenge him in relation to the 123 Ltd meeting. Mr C confirmed that he had asked another employee, Ms D, to attend the sales meeting. He said that the reason for this was that he was not confident that the Claimant had the skills or experience to manage such a potentially large order. The Claimant said that she disagreed that Ms D was any more able than her to successfully conduct the meeting. The Claimant said she believed that Mr C unfairly favoured Ms D.

9. At this point Mr C began to shout at the Claimant. He told her that she was 'always whinging' and that she was 'useless' and should be glad that she still had a job. He said that he would be 'a fool' to send her to such an important meeting as the 123 Ltd meeting and continued to shout at her for about five minutes. The Claimant was reduced to tears by Mr C's outburst. She ran out of his office and immediately left the building.

10. Mr C's actions, on behalf of the Respondent, both separately and cumulatively, amounted to repudiatory breaches of the implied term of trust and confidence in the Claimant's contract of employment.

11. The following day, in response to the Respondent's repudiatory breach, the Claimant resigned in writing giving one month's notice as required by her contract. The Claimant made it clear in the letter that she considered that she had been left with no option but to resign due to Mr C's unacceptable treatment of her. The Respondent and Claimant agreed that she would take the notice as garden leave.

12. The Claimant also raised a grievance in her letter of resignation. The grievance was heard on 5 March 2019 and subsequently rejected. The appeal was heard on 29 March 2019 and was also rejected.

13. In all the circumstances the Claimant claims that she was constructively dismissed by the Respondent, and that such dismissal was unfair. The Claimant claims compensation for unfair dismissal.

[*Name*]

[*Date*]

Claim alleging discrimination on grounds of sex and maternity

IN THE [   ] EMPLOYMENT TRIBUNAL   <u>Claim No</u>

BETWEEN:

MRS A

<u>Claimant</u>

-and-

R & R

A FIRM

<u>Respondent</u>

RIDER TO ET1

1. The Claimant was employed by the Respondent as a marketing executive from 1 December 2015 until her dismissal on 16 May 2018. The Respondent employed eight marketing executives in its marketing department.

2. In December 2016 the Claimant told her manager, Mr B, that she was pregnant. Mr B said 'congratulations' but then added that this was not the best timing as three other members of the department were either on maternity leave or shortly to commence maternity leave.

3. Prior to the Claimant commencing maternity leave two new, male, marketing executives joined the team. In the months preceding the start of her maternity leave the Claimant noticed that many of her clients were handed over to the new marketing executives and that she was left with very little to do.

4. The Claimant commenced maternity leave on 13 March 2017. The Claimant took full ordinary and additional maternity leave, as she was entitled to do, and returned to work on 12 March 2018.

5. When the Claimant returned to work none of the marketing executives remained on maternity leave. The total number of marketing executives now numbered ten, of which four were female. The Claimant was not given her previous client accounts to look after and found she had relatively little work to do. The other marketing executives, particularly the male ones, were very busy and were working long hours.

6. On or around 30 March 2018 Mr B called a meeting of all the marketing executives. Mr B said that the department needed to make cost savings and that it would perhaps be necessary to make a redundancy. Mr B asked if anyone would be prepared to reduce their hours but none of the executives volunteered to do this. Mr B did not ask whether anyone would be prepared to take voluntary redundancy.

7. The Claimant was invited to a meeting with Mr B on 4 April 2018 and informed her that she could be accompanied at that meeting. The Claimant attended the meeting with Miss C, a colleague. At the meeting, the Claimant was told that she had been provisionally selected for redundancy.

8. The Claimant was presented with a 'score sheet' which showed only her scores and appeared to show marks out of ten for length of service, qualifications, appraisal outcomes, attendance/timekeeping and performance. The Claimant was unable properly to argue against the scores she had been given without being able to compare herself to other employees. The Claimant had scored only 5 out of 10 for performance and argued that she would have scored higher if proper account had been taken of the fact that she had been absent on maternity leave and had not been given the same level of work as others before and afterwards.

9. The meeting was adjourned for approximately 10 minutes. Mr B returned and said that, in light of the Claimant's comments, he would increase her 'qualifications' mark from 4 to 5 out of 10 Mr B then said that the Claimant's score remained the lowest and said that he was terminating her contract by reason of redundancy on six weeks' notice.

10. The Claimant received a letter dated 4 April 2018 confirming Mr B's decision and informing her of her right to appeal. The Claimant appealed and argued that the redundancy process was a sham and merely designed to allow the Respondent to terminate her employment, or alternatively, that she had been unfairly selected for redundancy because of her maternity leave. The appeal was unsuccessful.

11. In the circumstances, the Claimant claims that the Respondent unlawfully discriminated against her on grounds of pregnancy and/or on grounds that she was seeking to exercise, or had exercised, her statutory right to maternity leave. The following acts of discrimination are relied upon:
    (a) Mr B requiring the Claimant to 'hand over' her accounts to new marketing executives prior to commencing her maternity leave.
    (b) Mr B failing to give the Claimant her accounts or equivalent accounts on her return to work following maternity leave.
    (c) The Claimant's dismissal.

12. Further, or in the alternative, the Claimant claims that the acts set out at paragraph 11(a) to (c) above are acts of direct sex discrimination.

13. Further, or in the alternative, the Claimant claims that her dismissal was automatically unfair under s 99 of the Employment Rights Act 1996 ('ERA') and regulation 20 of the Maternity and Parental Leave etc Regulations 1999, that is, that the dismissal was for a reason connected with:
    (a) the fact that she took or availed herself of the benefits of, ordinary maternity leave; further or alternatively,
    (b) the fact that she took additional maternity leave.

14. The Claimant's primary case is that her position was not redundant as defined by s 139 ERA, and redundancy was not the reason for dismissal. The Respondent decided, as a result of her pregnancy and maternity leave, that it wished to dismiss the Claimant, and that the alleged redundancy was contrived to achieve this end.

15. In the alternative, should the ET find that there was a genuine redundancy, the Claimant was unfairly selected for redundancy by reason of her pregnancy and maternity leave and her dismissal was automatically unfair.

16. Further or in the alternative, should the ET find that dismissal was by reason of redundancy, and was not connected with the Claimant's pregnancy and maternity leave, the dismissal was nevertheless unfair as the Claimant was not adequately consulted, was not subject to objective selection criteria and was not offered any alternative employment.

17. The Claimant seeks a declaration that she has been discriminated against on grounds of sex and unfairly dismissed and appropriate compensation.

[*Name*]

[*Date*]

Claim alleging discrimination on grounds of age and disability and whistle-blowing

IN THE [   ] EMPLOYMENT TRIBUNAL   <u>Claim No</u>

BETWEEN:

MR A

<u>Claimant</u>

-and-

R ESTATE AGENTS LIMITED

<u>Respondent</u>

RIDER TO ET1

The Parties

1. The Claimant is employed by the Respondent as a sales assistant.
2. The Claimant's date of birth is 10 December 1955.
3. The Respondent is an estate agency and property management company operating within the residential sales and letting market in the Manchester area.

The Claimant's disability

4. In 2002 the Claimant was involved in a road traffic accident which resulted in serious injuries being sustained to both of his legs. The Claimant's injuries continue to constitute a physical impairment which has a substantial effect on his ability to carry out day-to-day activities and, in particular, upon his mobility. The Claimant walks with a pronounced limp and requires rest breaks when walking distances beyond around 200 metres. The Claimant can negotiate stairs only with extreme difficulty and pain and takes much longer to do so than an able-bodied person. As a result of his injuries, the Claimant can no longer drive.
5. In the premises, at all material times the Claimant was a disabled person within the meaning of the Equality Act 2010 ('EA').
6. The Respondent was at all times aware of the Claimant's disability.
   (a) The Claimant informed Mr B of the Respondent of his disability during his interview on 4 March 2009;
   (b) The Claimant's impairment is in any event obvious and apparent.

The Claimant's role

7. The Claimant was appointed to the role of sales assistant by letter dated 6 March 2009. His appointment commenced on 4 April 2009. From the commencement of his employment the Claimant's place of work was the Respondent's offices at 14 Hillside Road, Manchester ('Hillside Road'). The role was a part-time role working 9am to 1.30pm Monday to Friday.

The move to Riverside House

8. In or around November 2017 the Claimant and other employees were informed that they would be relocated to the Respondent's offices at Riverside Road, Salford ('Riverside House'). No consultation took place as to this relocation. The relocation took effect on 5 January 2018.
9. The offices at Riverside House were only accessible via a flight of 35 stairs. The Claimant experienced great difficulty accessing Riverside House via the flight of stairs.
10. On 5 January 2018 Mr B told the Claimant that he recognised the stairs would cause problems for the Claimant. Mr B indicated that he envisaged installing a stairlift, subject to obtaining quotes in relation to that work. Mr B informed the Claimant that he felt it appropriate that the Claimant change his hours to work from 9am to 6pm on two days and then from 9am to 1.30pm on a third day in order to reduce the number of times that the Claimant had to come into the office (and therefore use the stairs) in any given week. The Claimant reluctantly agreed to this on the basis that it would be for a short time only.

11. From 6 January 2018 the Claimant worked at Riverside House attending for full days on Mondays and Thursdays and half days on Wednesdays. The Respondent has failed to take any steps to install a stairlift.

The employment of Miss C

12. In or around October 2017 the Respondent employed another office assistant, Miss C.

13. On numerous occasions from October 2017 onwards, Miss C made age-specific disparaging comments, both to the Claimant's face and to other employees. These included 'old git', 'grand-daddy' and 'slaphead'. Various junior members of the sales negotiation team particularly Mr D, Mr E and Miss F, also began to use these terms.

14. Mr B was at all material times aware of the disparaging comments, and sent an email to all members of staff on 18 January 2018 reminding them that conduct should be professional and appropriate at all times. However, the Respondent took no further steps to stop the comments, which continued, a fact of which Mr B of the Respondent was aware.

Breach of Estate Agency Act 1979

15. On or about 15 December 2017 it came to the Claimant's attention that one of the sales negotiators, Mr D, had failed to pass on an offer from a potential property purchaser to the vendor. The Claimant raised this with Mr D. Mr D said 'Be cool, grandad, sometimes you've got to let them sweat a bit to get the best deal'.

16. As a result of the information referred to in the previous paragraph, the Claimant believed (on reasonable grounds) that:
    (a) Mr D was deliberately failing to pass on an offer from a purchaser to a vendor;
    (b) The failure to do so constitutes an undesirable practice within the Estate Agents Act 1979 and the Estate Agents (Undesirable Practices) (No 2) Order 1991 and thus Mr D was failing to comply with his legal obligations towards his clients.

Meeting 24 January 2018

17. At the Claimant's request, the Claimant had a meeting with Mr B on 24 January 2018. In the meeting, the Claimant raised the following matters:
    (a) He complained about the age-related harassment that he had suffered at the hands of the above-mentioned employees and asked that action be taken in this respect.
    (b) He asked what progress had been made in respect of a stairlift.
    (c) He requested to return to his previous hours, and/or to be permitted to work from Hillside Road.
    (d) He informed Mr B about Mr D's actions in respect of failing to inform vendors of offers made by prospective purchasers.

18. The Claimant's disclosure at paragraph 17(d) above was a protected disclosure within s 43A Employment Rights Act 1996 ('ERA').
    (a) The Claimant disclosed information which, in his reasonable belief was in the public interest and tended to show that a person had failed to comply with a legal obligation, within the meaning of s 43B(1)(b) ERA; and
    (b) The disclosure was made to the Claimant's employer, within s 43C(1) ERA.

19. Further, or in the alternative, in raising the matters referred to in paragraph 17(a)– (c) the Claimant alleged that the Respondent and its employees had committed acts which would be in contravention of the EA as discriminatory on grounds of both age and disability. The Claimant's actions in raising the said matters were protected acts for the purposes of s 27 EA.

20. The Respondent has failed to take any or any adequate steps to remedy the matters complained of by the Claimant.

Meeting 31 January 2018

21. The Claimant was asked by Mr B to attend a further meeting on 31 January 2018 The Claimant was not told what this meeting was about, nor was he offered the opportunity to be accompanied.

22. At the meeting on 31 January 2018 Mr B informed the Claimant that he was concerned that the Claimant's performance had been deteriorating in recent weeks and cited two allegations that the Claimant had failed to diarise appointments with the result that appointments were missed. Mr B informed the Claimant that he was to be given a formal written warning and that this would be kept on file. At the end of the meeting Mr B gave the Claimant a pre-prepared warning letter.

23. The allegations which formed the subject matter of the warning were false and without foundation.
24. The Respondent conducts an annual pay review on 28 February each year. As a result of having a written warning on his record, under the Respondent's remuneration policy, the Claimant was eligible for a pay increase of only 1.5 per cent. The Claimant's pay increase would otherwise have been 3.5 per cent.

Grievance procedure

25. The Claimant wrote a letter to Mr B dated 2 February 2018 which was stated to be both an appeal against the written warning and a grievance letter in respect of disability discrimination, age discrimination and detriment on the grounds of making a protected disclosure.
26. Mr B met with the Claimant to hear his grievance on 16 February 2018, the grievance was rejected. The Claimant appealed the rejection and this was heard on 21 March 2018 by Mr G, the Managing Director of the Respondent. The appeal was rejected.

Claims

Disability discrimination
27. The stairs in Riverside House placed the Claimant at a substantial disadvantage compared to people without his disability. The Respondent failed to make reasonable adjustments to alleviate this disadvantage by:
   (a) failing to install a stairlift or similar device.
   (b) failing to permit the Claimant to work from Hillside Road.
28. The Respondent has failed in its duty to the Claimant under s 20 EA and has therefore discriminated against the Claimant under s 21 EA.
29. The implementation of these reasonable adjustments would have allowed him to revert to his original contractual hours.
30. Further or in the alternative, the Respondent has discriminated against the Claimant on grounds of his disability under s 13 EA by:
   (a) changing the Claimant's hours from five mornings per week to two days and one morning per week; and/or
   (b) requiring the Claimant to relocate to Riverside House.
31. Further or in the alternative, the Respondent's actions in issuing him with an unjustified written warning on 31 January 2018 was by reason, or in part by reason, of the allegations of disability discrimination made by the Claimant to Mr B at the 24 January 2018 meeting and therefore constitutes unlawful discrimination by way of victimisation contrary to s 27 EA.

Age discrimination
32. The actions of Miss C, Mr D, Mr E and Miss F, as outlined above constituted unlawful harassment on the grounds of age under s 26 EA. The Respondent is liable for such harassment by virtue of s 109 EA.
33. The Claimant further contends that the Respondent's actions in issuing him with an unjustified written warning on 31 January 2018 was by reason, or in part by reason, of the allegations of age discrimination made by the Claimant to Mr B at the 24 January 2018 meeting and therefore constitutes unlawful discrimination by way of victimisation contrary to s 27 EA.

Protected disclosure
34. The Claimant further contends that the Respondent's actions in issuing him with an unjustified written warning on 31 January 2018 was by reason, or in part by reason, of the allegations made by the Claimant to Mr B at the 24 January 2018 meeting in respect of Mr D's professional conduct. In the premises, the Claimant has suffered a detriment on the ground that he had made a protected disclosure contrary to s 47B ERA.

Remedy
35. The Claimant seeks declarations that he has been subject to discrimination and/or victimisation and/or detriment on grounds of making a protected disclosure as set out above.
36. The Claimant seeks a recommendation that the Respondent shall, within such time as the Tribunal determines to be appropriate, relocate the Claimant to the Hillside Road office and/or install a stairlift or similar apparatus in the Riverside House office.

37. By reason of the matters aforesaid the Claimant has suffered loss and damage. The Claimant seeks compensation in respect of each of his claims. In particular, the Claimant claims:
   (a) Compensation for injury to feelings.
   (b) Compensation in respect of financial loss resulting from his failure to obtain a 3.5 per cent pay increase.
   (c) Compensation in respect of anticipated financial loss resulting from his failure to obtain a 3.5 per cent pay increase.

[Name]

[Date]

THE RESPONSE

The Response Form ET3

The form can be found on the ETS website at <http://www.employmenttribunals.service.gov.uk/employment-tribunal-response>.

This applies in the vast majority of cases. The response can also be completed online. Further details of the response can be found in Chapter 4.

Specimen Grounds of Response

Response to claim of constructive unfair dismissal

IN THE [   ] EMPLOYMENT TRIBUNAL   <u>Claim No</u>

BETWEEN:

MISS A

<u>Claimant</u>

-and-

XYZ IT SYSTEMS LIMITED

<u>Respondent</u>

RIDER TO ET3

---

1. References to paragraph numbers are references to the Claimant's Rider to ET1.
2. Paragraph 1, 2, 3 and 4 of the ET1 are admitted.
3. Paragraph 5 of the ET1 is admitted. However, the Respondent's policy is to set easily obtainable targets in the first six months of employment to encourage new sales representatives and recognise the fact that it takes some time to build up a list of contacts which will ultimately result in a stream of potential business.
4. As to the appraisal conducted by Mr B in June 2017, Mr B did compliment the Claimant in relation to her cold-calling ability, but noted a concern that she appeared to have some difficulty in turning the opportunities she created into sales. The appraisal records that this is an area for further monitoring and development.
5. As to paragraph 6:
    (a) It is admitted that Mr B left the company and was replaced by Mr C in March 2018.
    (b) It is denied that Mr C 'sought to achieve results by intimidating the sales staff'.
    (c) It is admitted that Mr C occasionally swore in the office. It is denied that this was specifically directed at the Claimant or was such that a reasonable person would find it offensive. The Claimant made no complaint about this language until her resignation and has herself been known to use similar language on occasion.
    (d) Mr C quickly identified problems with the Claimant's performance. She had not met her targets for July and August in respect of contracts agreed and was still performing at the level expected of new starters. Mr C had several discussions with the Claimant where she accepted these problems and resolved to try to improve.
    (e) It is denied that Mr C ever told the Claimant she was 'crap'.
    (f) As the Claimant continued to perform well in cold-calling, Mr C was concerned that perhaps her lack of in-depth knowledge of the products was causing problems at the meeting stage. This was confirmed by technical staff who had accompanied the Claimant to meetings. Mr C addressed this by increasing the Claimant's cold-calling targets for November and December and reducing her contracts target. He also arranged for her to spend two afternoons with technical staff to develop a further understanding of the business. The Claimant did not indicate any objection to these proposals.
    (g) It is denied that the objective in increasing the Claimant's cold-calling target was to set her up to fail, rather it was to protect her ability to earn whilst recognising that neither she nor the company were benefiting from her poor performance in sales meetings.
    (h) As a result of this policy, Mr C did arrange for certain opportunities generated by the claimant through cold-calling to be handled at the meeting stage by other employees. Mr C also allowed the Claimant to continue to attend meetings so as to develop her skills in this area.
6. As to paragraph 7, on or around 22 February 2019 it came to Mr C's attention that the Claimant had diarised to attend a sales meeting with 123 Ltd. It is admitted that this was a contact established by the Claimant and admitted and averred that this was potentially an extremely important and valuable contract for the Respondent. Mr C therefore asked another sales representative to take on this meeting.

7. Paragraphs 8 and 9 are denied, save that it is admitted that the Claimant came to Mr C's office to challenge him in relation to the 123 Ltd meeting. The Claimant appeared very angry. The Claimant asked Mr C if it was correct that she was no longer going to the 123 Ltd meeting. He confirmed that it was and began to provide an explanation. The Claimant refused to listen to Mr C's explanation and instead told him that she hated working for the Respondent and that she had only taken the job because she believed she would earn huge bonuses. The Claimant told Mr C that she intended to resign. Mr C asked the Claimant to think about her decision overnight and explained that he felt that she could still develop into a successful sales representative. The Claimant agreed to do this. The Claimant had become tearful as she told Mr C that she wished to resign.

8. It is denied that Mr C shouted at the Claimant or said that she was 'whinging', 'useless' or a 'fool'. There was no discussion as to the identity of another person who would conduct the meeting in place of the Claimant.

9. For the reasons set out above, paragraph 10 is denied.

10. Mr C had told the Claimant that she could take the rest of the afternoon off, and understood that she returned to her desk to collect her handbag and then left the office.

11. As to paragraph 11, it is admitted that the Claimant tendered her resignation the following day and that she claimed that Mr C's conduct had left her with no option but to resign. Mr C called the Claimant and asked her if she would like any more time to reconsider her decision and she said that she already had another job and that she would not wish to return to the Respondent. It is admitted that both parties agreed the Claimant would serve her notice as garden leave.

12. Paragraph 12 is admitted, the Respondent conducted a full investigation and concluded that there was no evidence that Mr C had acted in anything other than an appropriate manner towards the Claimant.

13. Paragraph 13 is denied.
    (a) There was no breach of the implied term of trust and confidence as alleged by the Claimant or at all.
    (b) Further or in the alternative, the Claimant did not resign in response to any breach of contract on the part of the Respondent, but resigned to pursue other employment opportunities.
    (c) Further or in the alternative, if the ET find that the Claimant was constructively dismissed, such dismissal was due to the Claimant's capability and was a fair dismissal.
    (d) Further or in the alternative, if the ET find that the Claimant was unfairly dismissed, the Claimant contributed to her dismissal and that her compensation should be reduced accordingly.
    (e) Further or in the alternative, if the ET find that the Claimant was unfairly dismissed, it is likely that the Claimant would have been fairly dismissed and/or would have resigned in any event within a short period and that her compensation should be assessed accordingly.

[*Name*]

[*Date*]

Appendix 5 Forms and Precedents

Response to claim alleging discrimination on grounds of sex and maternity

IN THE [   ] EMPLOYMENT TRIBUNAL   <u>Claim No</u>
BETWEEN:

MRS A

<u>Claimant</u>

-and-

R & R A FIRM

<u>Respondent</u>

RIDER TO ET3

---

1. References to paragraph numbers are references to the Claimant's Rider to ET1.
2. The first sentence of paragraph 1 is admitted. It is admitted that from the commencement of the Claimant's employment until November 2016 the headcount of the marketing department was eight. In September 2016, in response to significant new business, the Respondent decided to increase the headcount to 10. The new marketing executives, Mr D and Mr E, began work in October and November 2016 respectively.
3. As to paragraph 2, it is admitted that the Claimant informed the Respondent, through Mr B, of her pregnancy in December 2016 and that Mr B congratulated her. The remainder of paragraph 2 is denied. In fact, the Respondent's position with regard to employees on maternity leave was as follows:
    (a) Ms F had commenced maternity leave in February 2016 She had informed the Respondent that she did not intend to return to work and a permanent replacement had been recruited in June 2016.
    (b) Ms G was on maternity leave and due to return in June 2017. An employee had been hired to cover this maternity leave on a temporary contract. Ms G returned as planned and this employee left.
    (c) Ms H was due to commence maternity leave on 6 January 2017. Temporary cover was arranged forMs H. Ms H ultimately informed the company that she did not wish to return and the employee covering her role, Ms I, was offered a permanent role.
4. Save that it is admitted that Mr D and Mr E joined the team in late 2016, as set out above, paragraph 3 is denied. Some clients from each member of the team were transferred to Mr D and Mr E, as they had been recruited to reduce the workload of other team members, the Claimant was not treated any differently in this respect from other team members. A temporary employee, Ms J, was engaged from 27 February 2017 to cover the Claimant's maternity leave, there was therefore a two-week handover period during which the Claimant introduced Ms J to her clients.
5. Paragraph 4 is admitted.
6. Save that it is admitted that the headcount of the marketing department was 10, as it had been since autumn 2016, paragraph 5 is denied. Five of the marketing executives at this time were female. The Claimant was given her three most important previous clients—X Ltd, Y Ltd and Z Ltd. All the executives were relatively quiet at this time as two very large contracts had been lost in February 2018.
7. It was apparent to the Respondent in February 2018 that the loss of the two large contracts meant that it would be uneconomic to sustain a marketing department of ten people. Mr B worked for around six weeks attempting to secure other business before concluding that the Respondent would need to reduce personnel costs.
8. Paragraph 6 is admitted. The Respondent does not make enhanced redundancy payments, its experience is that in these circumstances voluntary redundancy is not attractive to employees. The employees were asked about reducing their hours and about any other suggestions.
9. Following the meeting Mr B decided that there was no alternative but to make one member of the team redundant. He constructed an assessment matrix and obtained advice from a human resources consultancy as to the appropriateness of the criteria used. The categories were as set out in the Claimant's paragraph 8. In relation to performance, this was based on feedback on file from clients.

10. Mr B was aware that the Claimant had been on maternity leave and this did not result in her having a reduced score in any category. In relation to performance, the Respondent considered feedback received prior to the Claimant's maternity leave and assumed that she would have continued to receive this level of feedback had she been undertaking the role in the period of her maternity leave.

11. The Claimant received an overall score of 22 out of 50 The next lowest score was 28.

12. Paragraph 7 is admitted.

13. As to paragraph 8, the Claimant and Mr B had an extensive discussion around her scores and the Claimant accepted most of them. It is admitted that the Claimant was not shown the scores of other employees but the Respondent contends that such an approach was neither necessary nor appropriate. Mr B explained that the Claimant had been assessed on her previous performance as if this was replicated throughout the period of her maternity leave. The Claimant received 5 out of 10 because she had significant neutral feedback and a small amount of negative feedback from the period prior to her maternity leave.

14. As to paragraph 9, in discussing her qualifications the Claimant noted that she had recently passed a further module in a professional marketing distance learning course. This had not appeared on her personnel file and Mr B accordingly increased her score in this area by one mark. The Claimant's total score following the meeting was therefore 23 out of 50 and she remained the lowest scoring employee by some margin. Mr B therefore verbally dismissed the Claimant on notice.

15. Paragraph 10 is admitted. It is denied that there was any foundation in the Claimant's allegations relating to the reasons for dismissal. The letter dated 4 April 2018 also set out the Claimant's entitlement to a statutory redundancy payment which was paid with her final wage.

16. For the reasons set out above, the reason for the Claimant's dismissal was redundancy and that the dismissal was fair in all the circumstances.

17. For the reasons set out above, it is denied that Mr B's instructions to the Claimant regarding the management of her clients either before or after her maternity constituted less favourable treatment, whether on the grounds of sex or pregnancy/maternity status.

18. Further, insofar as the Claimant's claim relates to actions undertaken by Mr B prior to her maternity leave, the claim is out of time and it would not be just and equitable for the ET to extend time. The ET therefore has no jurisdiction to hear this claim.

19. For the reasons set out above, paragraphs 11–16 are denied.

20. The Respondent carried out reasonable consultation with the Claimant. Objective criteria were used to select for redundancy, and were fairly applied. There were no vacancies at the time of the Claimant's dismissal.

21. The Respondent denies that the Claimant is entitled to any remedy as claimed or at all.

[*Name*]

[*Date*]

Response to claim alleging discrimination on grounds of age
and disability and whistle-blowing

IN THE []   EMPLOYMENT TRIBUNAL   <u>Claim No</u>
BETWEEN:

MR A

<u>Claimant</u>

-and-

R ESTATE AGENTS LIMITED

<u>Respondent</u>

RIDER TO ET3

Introduction

1. References to paragraph numbers are references to paragraphs contained within the Claimant's Rider to ET1.
2. Paragraphs 1–3 are admitted.
3. The Respondent is a small company currently employing 16 employees, 14 of which are based at Riverside House and two at Hillside Road.
4. Paragraph 4 is not admitted, as the Respondent does not have detailed knowledge of the Claimant's medical history and medical condition. It is, however, admitted, that the Claimant is, and was at all material times, a disabled person within the meaning of the Equality Act 2010 ('EA') and that the Respondent had knowledge of such.
5. For the reasons set out above, paragraphs 5 and 6 are admitted.
6. Paragraph 7 is admitted. The Claimant's role was specifically to provide administrative support to the Respondent's sales and lettings negotiations.

The move to Riverside House

7. As to paragraph 8, it is admitted that the Claimant and other employees were relocated to Riverside House on 5 January 2018 It is denied that there was no consultation in relation to this move. There were regular meetings and discussions between the employees and management in the period between October and December 2017. These meetings addressed inter alia the issue of accessibility at Riverside House. Mr B offered to visit Riverside House with the Claimant in advance of the relocation in order to properly assess the difficulties the new location would present, but the Claimant refused to undertake such a visit.
8. Paragraph 9 is admitted.
9. As to paragraph 10, it is admitted that the Claimant and Mr B had a private discussion on 5 January 2018 regarding accessibility. It is further admitted that Mr B agreed to investigate the cost and practicality of installing a stairlift. It is denied that Mr B suggested to the Claimant that he should change his hours as described. The Claimant suggested this change. Mr B agreed to this change in hours solely in order to assist the Claimant.
10. Save that the start date and hours of work are admitted, paragraph 11 is denied. Mr B took steps to obtain quotes from three suppliers as to fitting a stairlift. Each supplier expressed concerns about the age of the building and the physical structure of the staircase. One supplier said that he could not undertake the work, the other two quotes were £15,000 and £18,000 respectively. The two companies which did provide quotes each estimated that it would take at least four months before they would be able to carry out the work.
11. The Respondent envisages continued expansion necessitating a further office move in around 18 months to 2 years. Taking into account the high price of the work, the fact that the Respondent is a small business with a modest turnover, and the relatively short time for which the Respondent is likely to remain in occupation of Riverside House, it is the Respondent's case that the installation of a stairlift is not a reasonable adjustment in all the circumstances.

The employment of Miss C

12. Paragraph 12 is admitted.

13. Paragraph 13 is denied. The Respondent conducted extensive interviews with the employees in question as part of the grievance process and could find no evidence of disparaging comments having been made.

14. Paragraph 14 is denied. Mr B was never aware of any disparaging comments made by the named members of staff, or any other member of staff, towards the Claimant. Mr B was aware that the Claimant on several occasions made inappropriate personal comments regarding Miss C's dress and appearance. Miss C has several body piercings and the Claimant was in the habit of telling her that she looked 'like the nails section in B&Q'.

15. During early January 2018 Mr B became aware of a culture among the sales assistants and some sales negotiators of making inappropriate comments about customers and deliberately keeping people waiting on the telephone. It was this which caused Mr B to send the email dated 18 January 2018.

Breach of Estate Agents Act 1979

16. Paragraphs 15 and 16 are denied, save that it is admitted that had Mr D acted in the manner alleged by the Claimant, this would constitute a breach of his legal obligations under the Estate Agents Act 1979 and subordinate legislation.

Meeting 24 January 2018

17. As to paragraph 17, it is admitted that a meeting took place between the Claimant and Mr B on the 24 January 2018.
    (a) It is admitted that the Claimant made a general complaint that he had been 'called names' related to his age by Miss C. It is denied that the Claimant made this allegation against any employee other than Miss C.
    (b) It is admitted that the Claimant asked what progress had been made in respect of the stairlift.
    (c) It is denied that the Claimant requested to return to his previous hours but admitted that he asked if it would be possible to work from Hillside Road.
    (d) It is denied that the Claimant raised any issue at all in respect of Mr D's alleged actions or in respect of the professional conduct of any sales negotiator.

18. Paragraph 18 is denied.

19. To the extent that the allegations made were restricted to those set out above, paragraph 19 is admitted.

20. Paragraph 20 is denied:
    (a) Mr B had an informal meeting with Miss C where she admitted that she did not get on with the Claimant but denied using age-specific disparaging terms. Mr B took the view that this was a simple clash of personalities and asked both employees to act respectfully towards one another.
    (b) Mr B informed the Claimant that he was waiting for quotes in respect of the stairlift, which was correct at that time.
    (c) Mr B explained to the Claimant that it would not be possible for him to work from Hillside Road. That office had been reduced to only two sales negotiators and all the administration systems had been relocated. There was not a sufficient requirement for administrative support to provide the Claimant with work at Hillside Road.
    (d) As set out above, the Claimant raised no issue in respect of regulatory breach and so this point was not addressed.

Meeting 31 January 2018

21. Paragraphs 21 and 22 are admitted.

22. Paragraph 23 is denied. The Claimant had recorded appointments in the diary for two clients, X and Y, on 25 and 27 January 2018. The appointments are recorded in the Claimant's handwriting, which is distinctive. The appointments should both have been recorded on the 26 January. As a result, the client attended the appointments and nobody from the Respondent attended. Both clients called to complain. Mr and Mrs X were looking to place their property on the market and subsequently did so with another agent, without agreeing to another appointment with the Respondent. The Respondent therefore lost a potentially valuable client as a result of the Claimant's mistake.

23. Save that it is admitted that the Respondent conducts a pay review on 28 February each year, paragraph 24 is denied. In the 2017 pay review the majority of employees received a 1.5 per cent pay

increase. Only two employees, who had performed particularly well, received a 3.5 per cent increase. The Claimant would have received a pay increase of 1.5 per cent regardless of the written warning.

24. At the conclusion of this meeting the Claimant informed Mr B of the matters set out at paragraph 15 of the Rider to ET1 This disclosure was therefore made, for the first time, after the Claimant had received the written warning.

25. It is denied that the disclosure was a qualifying disclosure within s 43B Employment Rights Act 1996 ('ERA'). It is denied that the Claimant believed, or had reasonable grounds to believe that the information he disclosed tended to show a breach of a legal obligation. The Claimant was aware at the time of his disclosure that the content of his disclosure was not true.

26. Further or in the alternative, it is denied that the allegation was made in accordance with s 43C ERA because it is denied that the allegation was made by the Claimant in the belief that it was in the public interest. The allegation was made in response to the Claimant having received a written warning. For these reasons it is denied that the disclosure is a protected disclosure within s 43A ERA. Further, for the same reasons it is denied that the allegation was made in good faith by the Claimant.

Grievance procedure

27. Paragraphs 25 and 26 are admitted.

Claims

Disability discrimination

28. As to paragraph 27, it is admitted that the stairs at Riverside house placed the Claimant at a substantial disadvantage compared to people without his disability. For the reasons set out above, it is denied that either of the adjustments proposed by the Claimant were, or are, reasonable.

29. Paragraph 28 is denied for the reasons set out above.

30. Paragraph 29 is admitted, save that it is denied the adjustments were, or are, reasonable.

31. Paragraph 30 is denied. As to 30(a), this change was proposed by the Claimant who has never asked to revert to his original hours. In any event, it is the Respondent's case that this change in hours was an appropriate adjustment to accommodate the Claimant's disability following the relocation to Riverside House. As to 30(b), it is denied that this relocation constitutes discrimination against the claimant. Further or in the alternative, to the extent that it would otherwise constitute such discrimination the requirement to relocate was justified in all the circumstances.

32. Paragraph 31 is denied. The Respondent's actions in issuing the Claimant with a written warning were for the reasons set out above.

Age discrimination

33. Paragraph 32 is denied for the reasons set out above. In the event that the Tribunal find that the Claimant has been subjected to harassment the Respondent admits that it is vicariously liable for the actions of the employees and does not rely on the statutory defence set out at s 109(4) EA.

34. For the reasons set out in paragraph 31 above, paragraph 33 is denied.

Protected disclosure

35. Paragraph 34 is denied. The Respondent's case is that:
   (a) The Claimant made the disclosure relied upon subsequent to the treatment complained of, further or in the alternative;
   (b) The disclosure is not a protected disclosure, for the reasons set out above, further or in the alternative;
   (c) In any event, the written warning was issued solely for the reasons set out above.

Remedy

36. For the reasons set out above it is denied that the Claimant is entitled to any remedy as claimed in paragraphs 35–37 or at all.

[Name]

[Date]

Employment Appeal Tribunal (EAT)

NOTICE OF APPEAL

[See Form 1, Schedule 1 to the Employment Appeal Tribunal Rules 1993, SI 1993/2854 as substituted by SI 2005/1871.]

Notice of Appeal from Decision of Employment Tribunal

1. The appellant is [*name* and *address of the appellant*].
2. Any communication relating to this appeal may be sent to the appellant at [*appellant's address for service, including telephone number if any*].
3. The appellant appeals from [*here give particulars of the judgment, decision or order of the employment tribunal from which the appeal is brought including the location of the employment tribunal* and *the date*].
4. The parties to the proceedings before the employment tribunal, other than the appellant, were [*names* and *addresses of other parties to the proceedings resulting in judgment, decision or order appealed from*].
5. Copies of—
   (a) the written record of the employment tribunal's judgment, decision or order and the written reasons of the employment tribunal;
   (b) the claim (ET1);
   (c) the response (ET3); and/or (where relevant)
   (d) an explanation as to why any of these documents are not included;
   are attached to this notice.
6. If the appellant has made an application to the employment tribunal for a review of its judgment or decision, copies of—
   (a) the review application;
   (b) the judgment;
   (c) the written reasons of the employment tribunal in respect of that review application; and/or
   (d) a statement by or on behalf of the appellant, if such be the case, that a judgment is awaited are attached to this Notice. If any of these documents exist but cannot be included, then a written explanation must be given.
7. The grounds upon which this appeal is brought are that the employment tribunal erred in law in that [*here set out in paragraphs the various grounds of appeal*].

Signed. . . . .

Date. . . . .

N.B. The details entered on your Notice of Appeal must be legible and suitable for photocopying. The use of black ink or typescript is recommended.

RESPONDENT'S ANSWER

[See Form 3, Schedule 1 to the Employment Appeal Tribunal Rules 1993, SI 1993/2854 as amended by SI 2005/1871.]

Appeal from decision of employment tribunal/certification officer—Respondent's Answer

1. The respondent is [*name* and *address of respondent*].
2. Any communication relating to this appeal may be sent to the respondent at [*respondent's address for service, including telephone number if any*].
3. The respondent intends to resist the appeal of [*here give the name of appellant*]. The grounds on which the respondent will rely are [the grounds relied upon by the employment tribunal/ Certification Officer for making the judgment, decision or order appealed from] [and] [the following grounds]:
   [*here set out any grounds which differ from those relied upon by the employment tribunal or Certification Officer, as the case may be*].

Appendix 5 Forms and Precedents

4. The respondent cross-appeals from
    [*here give particulars of the decision appealed from*].
5. The respondent's grounds of appeal are:
    [*here state the grounds of appeal*].

Date

Signed

High Court and County Court

THE CLAIM

Claim Form N1

The N1 claim form, reproduced below, can be found at http://hmctsformfinder.justice.gov.uk/HMCTS/FormFinder.do.

Specimen Claim Form Endorsement: Wrongful Dismissal

Where Particulars of Claim are to be served with the Claim Form, it is sufficient to say in the Claim Form 'Particulars of Claim attached'. Where Particulars of Claim are to be served at a later date, brief particulars should be inserted in the space provided on the second page of the Claim Form.

For example:

'The Claimant's claim is for wrongful dismissal, in breach of a contract of employment made between the Claimant and the Defendant dated [*date*].

The Claimant claims damages and interest pursuant to section 35A Senior Courts Act 1981.

The Claimant expects to recover more than £25,000.'

[*Note 1*: CPR, r 16.3 requires a statement of value to assist the court in allocation. The valuation brackets are: not more than £10,000; more than £10,000 but not more than £25,000; more than £25,000. For claims involving damages for personal injury, see CPR, r 16.3(4).

Note 2: in a county court claim, interest should be claimed under s 69 of the County Courts Act 1984.]

Specimen Particulars of Claim: Wrongful Dismissal

IN THE HIGH COURT OF JUSTICE	CLAIM No.
QUEEN'S BENCH DIVISION	
BETWEEN	

A	Claimant
— and—	
B	Defendant

PARTICULARS OF CLAIM

1. The Defendant is a limited company carrying on business in the manufacture, sale and distribution of electronic components.
2. The Claimant was employed by the Defendant from [*date*] as a Sales Manager.
3. The terms of the Claimant's employment are set out in a written contract of employment made between the Claimant and the Defendant and dated [*date*] ('the Contract'). A copy of the Contract is attached to these Particulars of Claim.

   There were (amongst others) the following express terms of the Contract:

   3.1. The Claimant's salary was £[] per annum.

   3.2. The Claimant was entitled to benefits as follows:

   [*insert details of other benefits provided for by the contract insofar as relevant to losses during the notice period, for example bonus, share options, car, insurance, private health care, etc*]

   3.3. By clause [], the period of notice to be given by either the Claimant or the Defendant to terminate the Claimant's employment was three months.

4. On [*date*], in breach of contract, the Defendant summarily dismissed the Claimant. At about 16.00 on [*date*] the Claimant was called to a meeting with []. The Claimant was told that he was dismissed with immediate effect and was given a letter dated the same date confirming the same. The Claimant was not given three months', or any, notice as required by clause [] of the contract.

5. By reason of the Defendant's breach of contract the Claimant has suffered loss and damage.

PARTICULARS OF LOSS

5.1. The Defendant was not entitled to terminate the Claimant's employment summarily. The Defendant could only have terminated the Claimant's employment lawfully by giving three months' notice under clause []. The Claimant has lost the benefit of the remuneration and other benefits he was entitled to and would have received from the Defendant during a three months' notice period.

5.2. A schedule of loss is attached to this statement of case.

6. Further, at the date of termination of his employment the Claimant was owed arrears of salary in respect of the months [insert details], in the sum of £[]. The Defendant has not paid the Claimant the said arrears or any part thereof.

7. The Claimant is entitled to and claims interest pursuant to section 35A of the Senior Courts Act 1981, at the Judgments Act rate of 8 per cent (or alternatively at such rates as the court shall find fit):

7.1 On the arrears of salary from [*date salary due*] to the date hereof, in the sum of £[], and there after continuing at a daily rate of £[]; or, alternatively for such periods as the court finds fit. A calculation of interest due until the date hereof is attached to these Particulars of Claim.

7.2 On such damages as are awarded to him for breach of contract at the Judgment Act rate of 8 per cent from [*date*]; or, alternatively, at such rate and for such period as the court finds fit.

AND the Claimant claims:

1 The sum of £[] arrears of salary.

2 Damages for wrongful dismissal.

3 Interest pursuant to section 35A of the Senior Courts Act 1981 as set out at paragraph 7 above.

[Signature of Draftsman]

STATEMENT OF TRUTH

The Claimant believes that the facts stated in these Particulars of Claim are true.

I am duly authorized by the Claimant to sign this statement.

[Full Name]

[Date]

Signed

Solicitor,

of [ ]

Solicitors for the Claimant

[In a county court claim, interest should be claimed under s 69 of the County Courts Act 1984.]

THE DEFENCE

Specimen Defence: Wrongful Dismissal

IN THE HIGH COURT OF JUSTICE   CLAIM No.

QUEEN'S BENCH DIVISION

BETWEEN

A	Claimant
— and—	
B	Defendant

DEFENCE

1. Paragraphs 1 and 2 of the Particulars of Claim are admitted.
2. The Contract referred to in paragraph 3 is admitted. The Defendant will refer to the Contract at trial for its full meaning and effect.
3. It is admitted that the Claimant was summarily dismissed on [*date*]. It is admitted that the dismissal was without notice.
4. Prior to the termination of the Claimant's employment, on dates between [*date*] and [*date*], the Claimant had submitted false expenses claims, in the total sum of £500, to the Defendant in respect of expenses which had not been incurred by the Claimant and/or in respect of items which were not legitimate business expenditure incurred in the course of the Defendant's business. A schedule of the said expenses claims is attached to this Defence. The submission of the said claims was gross misconduct on the part of the Claimant.
5. In the premises the Defendant was entitled to dismiss the Claimant summarily, and it is denied that the dismissal was in breach of contract as alleged or at all.
6. The Defendant disputes the Claimant's assessment of the value of the claim. A counter schedule is attached to this Defence.
7. It is denied that the Claimant is entitled to the alleged or any relief.

[Signature of Draftsman]

STATEMENT OF TRUTH

The Defendant believes that the facts stated in this Defence are true.

I am duly authorized by the Defendant to sign this statement.

[Full Name]

[Date]

Signed

Solicitor,

of [   ]

Solicitors for the Defendant

Appendix 6
Tables

Contents

Current and Recent Maximum Awards

Complaint	Detail	Limit 6 April 2018 to 5 April 2019	Limit 6 April 2019 to 5 April 2020
Unfair dismissal			
Basic award (ERA 1996, s 119)	Based on week's pay and length of service	£15,240	£15,750
Maximum week's pay (ERA 1996, ss 220–229)		£508	£525
Minimum basic award (TULR(C)A 1992 ss 152–153; ERA 1996, ss 100, 101A, 102, 103)	Applies on dismissals for health and safety, union, workforce/employee representative or pension trustee reasons	£6,203	£6,408
Compensatory award (ERA 1996, ss 123–124)	Most dismissals	£83,682 (or 52 weeks' pay if lower)	£86,444 (or 52 weeks' pay, if lower)
	Dismissals for health and safety/protected disclosure reasons	Unlimited	Unlimited
Additional award (ERA 1996, s 117)	26–52 weeks' pay	£13,208 to £26,416	£13,650 to £27,300
Redundancy payment (ERA 1996, s 162)	Based on week's pay, age and length of service	£15,240	£15,750
Guarantee pay per day (ERA 1996, ss 30–31)		£28 a day (subject to a maximum of 5 days or £140 in any three months)	£29 a day (subject to a maximum of 5 days or £145 in any three months)
Contract claims in employment tribunal			
Employment Tribunals (Extension of Jurisdiction) Order 1994		£25,000	£25,000
Insolvency payments (ERA 1996, s 184)			
Arrears of pay	Up to 8 weeks' pay	£4064	£4,200
Notice pay	Up to 12 weeks' pay	£6096	£6,300
Holiday pay	Up to 6 weeks' pay	£3048	£3,150
Redundancy payment	See above	£15,240	£15,750
Consultation/Notification rights			
Protective award (TULR(C)A 1992, s 192)	Up to 90 days' pay	Unlimited	Unlimited

Complaint	Detail	Limit 6 April 2018 to 5 April 2019	Limit 6 April 2019 to 5 April 2020
Failure to comply with information and consultation obligations (TUPE 2006, reg 15)	Up to 13 weeks' pay	Unlimited	Unlimited
Failure to comply with information and consultation provisions (ICER 2004)		£75,000	£75,000
Failure to allow right to be accompanied (ERA 1999, s 11)	Up to 2 weeks' pay	£1,016	£1,050
Discrimination		Unlimited	Unlimited
Flexible working			
Failure to follow procedure (ERA 1996, s 80H) (FWR 2014, reg 6)	Up to 8 weeks' pay	£4,064	£4,200

Past Awards Limits

Complaint	Limit	Limit	Limit	Limit	Limit	Limit	Limit	
	1 February 2010 to 31 January 2011	1 February 2011 to 31 January 2012	1 February 2012 to 31 January 2013	1 February 2013 to 5 April 2014	6 April 2014 to 5 April 2015	6 April 2015 to 5 April 2016	6 April 2016 to 5 April 2017	6 April 2017 to 5 April 2018
Unfair dismissal								
Basic award (ERA 1996, s 119)	£11,400	£12,000	£12,900	£13,500	£13,920	£14,250	£14,370	£14,670
Maximum week's pay (ERA 1996, ss 220–229)	£380	£400	£430	£450	£464	£475	£479	£489
Minimum basic award (TULR(C)A 1992 ss 152–167; ERA 1996, ss 100, 101A, 102, 103)	£4,700 min.	£5,000 min.	£5,300 min.	£5,500	£5,676	£5,807	£5,853	£5,970
Compensatory award (ERA 1996, ss 123–124)	£65,300	£68,400	£72,300	£74,200	£76,574	£78,335	£78,962	£80.541
Additional award (ERA 1996, s 117)	£19,760	£20,800	£22,360	£23,400	£24,128	£24,700	£24,908	25,428
Redundancy payment (ERA 1996, s 162)	£11,400	£12,000	£12,900	£13, 500	£13,920	£14,250	£14,370	£14,670
Guarantee pay per day (ERA 1996, ss 30–31)	£21.20	£22.20	£23.50	£24.20	£25	£26	£26	£27
Insolvency payments								
Week's pay for insolvency debts (ERA 1996, s 18H)	£380	£400	£430	£450	£464	£475	£479	£489

National Minimum Hourly Wage

National Minimum Hourly Wage from 1 April 2019 to 31 March 2020

Age	From April 2019
Apprentices	**£3.90**
under 18	£4.35
18–20	£6.15
21–24	£7.70
National Living Wage* (25 and above)	£8.21

*applicable from 1.04.16

Past National Minimum Hourly Wages

Age	From October 2009	From October 2010	From October 2011	From October 2012	From October 2013	From October 2014	From October 2015	From October 2016	From April 2017	From April 2018
Apprentices	—	£2.50	£2.60	£2.65	£2.68	£2.73	£3.30	£3.40	£3.50	£3.70
under 18	£3.57	£3.64	£3.68	£3.68	£3.72	£3.79	£3.87	£4.00	£4.05	£4.20
18–20	£4.83	£4.92	£4.98	£4.98	£5.03	£5.13	£5.30	£5.55	£5.60	£5.90
21+	£5.80	£5.93	£6.08	£6.19	£6.31	£6.50	£6.70	£6.95	£7.05	£7.38
25+								£7.20	£7.50	£7.83

Appendix 6 Tables

Time Limits

Qualifying Periods and Time Limits

Note that in some cases, time limits will also be extended through participation in the ACAS early conciliation scheme.

Employment right and statutory provision	When complaint must be made	Qualifying period	Discretionary power to extend time limit
Equal pay/Equality of terms: EqA 2010, s 127	Whilst working or within 6 months of leaving employment/stable employment/discovery or could with reasonable diligence have discovered of a qualifying fact in a concealment case/cessation of incapacity: EqA 2010, s 129	None	None
Discrimination in employment: EqA 2010, s 120	(i) 3 months from the date when the discriminatory act was done/6 months for complaints within armed forces. An act that extends over a period, as opposed to a one-off act, is treated as done at the end of the period: EqA 2010, s 123	None	Just and equitable: EqA 2010, s 123
Appeal from EHRC unlawful act notice	6 weeks from service of notice: EA 2006, s 21(5)	None	None
Written particulars of employment: ERA 1996, ss 1–4	While working or within 3 months of employee leaving: ERA 1996, s 11(4)(a)	Employee should be provided with statement no later than 2 months after employment begins: s 1(2); employees with less than 1 month's service do not qualify: s 198	Reasonably practicable: s 11(4)(b)
Itemized pay statement: ERA 1996, s 8	While working or within 3 months of employee leaving: ERA 1996, s 11(4)(a)	None	Reasonably practicable: s 11(4)(b)
Unlawful deduction from wages: ERA 1996, s 23	3 months from date of deduction (or last in a series of deductions) made: s 23(2)–(3)	None	Reasonably practicable: s 23(4)
Guarantee payments: ERA 1996, ss 28–35	3 months from the day the guarantee payment should have been made: ERA 1996, s 34(2)(a)	1 month: s 29	Reasonably practicable: s 34(2)(b)

Employment right and statutory provision	When complaint must be made	Qualifying period	Discretionary power to extend time limit
Detriment in health and safety cases: ERA 1996, ss 44, 48, 49	3 months from act complained of: s 48(3)(a)	None	Reasonably practicable: s 48(3)(b)
Detriment in connection with time off work for study or training: ERA 1996, s 47A	3 months from act complained of: s 48(3)(a)	None	Reasonably practicable: s 48(3)(b)
Time off for public duties: ERA 1996, ss 50–51	3 months from the date when failure to permit time off occurred: s 51(2)(a)	None	Reasonably practicable: s 51(2)(b)
Time off to look for work or training on redundancy: ERA 1996, s 52	3 months from the date of refusal: s 54(2)(a)	2 years: s 52(2)	Reasonably practicable: s 54(2)(b)
Time off for ante-natal care: ERA 1996, s 55	3 months beginning with the day of the relevant appointment for ante-natal care: s 57(2)(a)	None	Reasonably practicable: s 57(2)(b)
Right to remuneration on suspension on medical grounds: ERA 1996, ss 64–65	3 months from the date payment during suspension was due: s 70(2)(a)	1 month: s 65(1)	Reasonably practicable: s 70(2)(b)
Paid time off for employee representative (or candidate in an election as such an employee representative) for the purpose of consultation in relation to collective redundancies or the transfer of an undertaking or to undergo training in relation to their functions: ERA 1996, ss 61(1) and 62	3 months from the date when the failure to permit time off occurred: s 63(2)(a)	None	Reasonably practicable: s 63(2)(b)
Claim for remuneration on suspension from work on maternity grounds: ERA 1996, ss 68 and 70(1)	3 months beginning with date of failure to pay: s 70(2)(a)	None	Reasonably practicable: s 70(2)(b)
Written reasons for dismissal: ERA 1996, s 92	3 months from the effective date of termination: s 93(3) when read with s 111(2)(a)	2 years	Reasonably practicable: s 93(3) when read with s 111(2)(b)

Employment right and statutory provision	When complaint must be made	Qualifying period	Discretionary power to extend time limit
Unfair dismissal in connection with health and safety functions: ERA 1996, s 100	3 months from effective date of termination: s 111(2)(a)	None: s 108(3)(c)	Reasonably practicable: s 111(2)(b)
Unfair dismissal of a shop or betting worker for refusing to work on a Sunday: ERA 1996, s 101	3 months from effective date of termination: s 111(2)(a)	None: s 108(3)(d)	Reasonably practicable: s 111(2)(b)
Unfair dismissal in connection with leave for family reasons: ERA 1996, s 99	3 months from effective date of termination: s 111(2)(a)	None: s 108(3)(b)	Reasonably practicable: s 111(2)(b)
Unfair dismissal for a reason connected with WTR 1998: ERA 1996, s 101A	3 months from effective date of termination: s 111(2)(a)	None: s 108(3)(dd)	Reasonably practicable: s 111(2)(b)
Unfair dismissal for performing occupational pension trustee functions or those as an employee representative: ERA 1996, ss 102–103	3 months from effective date of termination: s 111(2)(a)	None: s 108(3)(e) and (f)	Reasonably practicable: s 111(2)(b)
Unfair dismissal related to making a protected disclosure: ERA 1996, s 103A	3 months from effective date of termination: s 111(2)(a)	None: s 108(3)(ff)	Reasonably practicable: s 111(2)(b)
Unfair dismissal in connection with asserting a statutory right: ERA 1996, s 104	3 months from effective date of termination: s 111(2)(a)	None: s 108(3)(g)	Reasonably practicable: s 111(2)(b)
Detriment to shop or betting worker for refusing Sunday work: ERA 1996, s 45	3 months from effective date of termination or act complained of: s 48(3)(a)	None	Reasonably practicable: s 48(3)(b)
Unfair dismissal related to national minimum wage: ERA 1996, s 104A	3 months from effective date of termination: s 111(2)(a)	None: s 108(3)(gg)	Reasonably practicable: s 111(2)(b)
Unfair dismissal in connection with suspension on medical grounds: ERA 1996, s 64(2) when read with s 108(2)	3 months from effective date of termination	1 month: s 108(2)	Reasonably practicable: s 111(2)(b)
Interim relief on a complaint under ERA 1996, ss 100, 101A, 102, 103, 103A or under TULR(C)A 1992, Sch A1, para 161(2): ERA 1996, s 128	7 days immediately following EDT, s 128(2)	None	None except potentially in case of fraud

Employment right and statutory provision	When complaint must be made	Qualifying period	Discretionary power to extend time limit
Unfair dismissal: ERA 1996, s 98	(i) Before effective date of termination if employee is dismissed with notice: ERA 1996, s 111(3), or (ii) within 3 months from effective date of termination (s 111(2)(a)) but (iii) in the case of unfair selection of strikers for re-engagement, 6 months from claimant's day of dismissal: TULR(C)A 1992, s 239(2)	2 years: s 108(1)	Reasonably practicable: s 111(2)(b)
Interim relief in health and safety cases: ERA 1996, s 100	7 days after effective date of termination: s 128(2)	None	None except potentially in the case of fraud
Redundancy payment: ERA 1996, ss 135–170	Within 6 months of the relevant date defined in ERA 1996, s 164. This is similar to the effective date of termination	2 years: s 115,	Just and equitable: ERA 1996, s 164(2). Can be extended to one year in case of death of employee s 176(7)
Payments on insolvency of employer: ERA 1996, ss 182–190	3 months from date of communication of Secretary of State's decision: s 188(2)(a)	Each of the payments claimed are dependent upon qualifying periods	Reasonably practicable: s 188(2)(b)
Unfair dismissal in connection with transfer of an undertaking: TUPE 2006, reg 7	3 months from the effective date of termination: ERA 1996, s 111(2)(a)	2 years	Reasonably practicable: ERA 1996, s 111(2)(b)
Failure to notify transferee of employee liability information: TUPE 2006, reg 11	3 months from date of transfer: reg 12(2)(a)	None	Reasonably practicable: reg 12(2)(b)
Consultation and provision of information on transfer of undertaking: TUPE 2006, regs 13 and 14	3 months from the date of the relevant transfer: reg 15(12)(a)	None	Reasonably practicable: reg 15(12)
Failure to pay compensation ordered by employment tribunal in respect of failure to consult on a transfer of undertakings: TUPE 2006, reg 15(7)	3 months from the employment tribunal's decision: reg 15(12)(b)	None	Reasonably practicable: reg 15(12)
Unlawful deduction from wages: ERA 1996, ss 13–27	3 months from date of last deduction (ie date payment was contractually due): s 23(2) and (3)	None	Reasonably practicable: s 23(4)

Employment right and statutory provision	When complaint must be made	Qualifying period	Discretionary power to extend time limit
Unjustifiable discipline by a union: TULR(C)A 1992, ss 64–66	3 months starting with date of decision: s 66(2)(a)	None	Reasonably practicable or if delay is wholly or partly attributable to reasonable attempts to appeal a decision: s 66(2)(b)
Application for compensation after successful s 66 complaint: TULR(C)A 1992, s 67	Not before 4 weeks and not later than 6 months starting with the date of the employment tribunal's decision: s 67(3)	None	None
Unauthorized deduction of union member's subscriptions: TULR(C)A 1992, ss 68, 68A	3 months from date of deduction: s 68A(1)(a)	None	Reasonably practicable: s 68A(1)(b)
Refusal of employment because of union membership: TULR(C)A 1992, s 137	3 months from date of refusal: s 139(1)(a)	None	Reasonably practicable: s 139(1)(b)
Refusal of services of employment agency because of union membership: TULR(C)A 1992, s 138	3 months from date of refusal: s 139(1)(a)	None	Reasonably practicable: s 139(1)(b)
Right not to receive inducements relating to union membership and activities or collective bargaining: TULR(C)A 1992, ss 145A and 145B	3 months from inducement (or last in a series of inducements): s 145C	None	Reasonably practicable: s 145C(b)
Detriment on grounds related to union membership or activities: TULR(C)A 1992, ss 146–151	3 months from the date on which there occurred the action complained of or, where that action is part of a series of similar actions, from the last of those actions: s 147(1)(a)	None	Reasonably practicable: s 147(1)(b)
Unfair dismissal in connection with trade union membership and activities: TULR(C)A 1992, ss 152 and 153	3 months from effective date of termination: ERA 1996, s 111(2)(a)	None	Reasonably practicable: ERA 1996, s 111(2)(b)
Right of employee representative (or candidate or participant in election of employee representative) in respect of consultation over transfer of undertaking or collective redundancies not to suffer detriment: ERA 1996, s 47(1) and (1A)	3 months from the date on which there occurred the action complained of. If the act is one of a series of similar acts, then the date of the last such act: s 48(3)(a)	None	Reasonably practicable: s 48(3)(b)

Employment right and statutory provision	When complaint must be made	Qualifying period	Discretionary power to extend time limit
Unfair dismissal on account of employee being an employee representative (or candidate or participant in election of employee representative) in respect of consultation over transfer of undertaking or collective redundancies: ERA 1996, s 103	3 months from effective date of termination: s 111(2)(a)	None: s 108(2)(f)	Reasonably practicable: s 111(2)(b)
Interim relief in dismissal for trade union membership and activities: TULR(C)A 1992, s 161	7 days from the effective date of termination: s 161(2)	None	None unless fraud involved
Time off for trade union activities and duties and for union learning representatives: TULR(C)A 1992, ss 168, 168A, 169 and 170	3 months from the date when failure to permit time off for union activities or to pay remuneration, occurred: TULR(C)A 1992, s 171(a)	None	Reasonably practicable: s 171(b)
Unlawful exclusion or expulsion from trade union: TULR(C)A 1992, s 174	6 months from the date of expulsion for initial complaint: s 175(a); following which an application may be made for compensation between 4 weeks and 6 months after the date of a declaration by employment tribunal: s 176(3)	None	Reasonably practicable: s 175(b)
Consultation with recognized union over redundancy: TULR(C)A 1992, s 188	Before the proposed dismissal or 3 months from the date on which the last dismissal takes effect: s 189(5)(a) and (b)	None	Reasonably practicable: s 189(5)(c)
Protective award claim by trade union for failing to consult over redundancies: TULR(C)A 1992, s 192	3 months from the date when the complaint of failure to pay was made: s 192(2)(a)	None	Reasonably practicable: s 192(2)(b)
Unfair dismissal in connection with official industrial action: TULR(C)A 1992, ss 238 and 238A	6 months from date of dismissal—where contract terminated by notice, date on which employer's notice given and in any other case, the EDT: s 238(5) when read with s 239(2)(a)	None: s 239(1)	Reasonably practicable: s 239(2)(b)
Levy appeal: Employment Tribunals (Constitution and Rules of Procedure) Regulations 2013, Sch 1, r 104	None	None	None

Employment right and statutory provision	When complaint must be made	Qualifying period	Discretionary power to extend time limit
Appeal against health & safety improvement notice: Employment Tribunals (Constitution and Rules of Procedure) Regulations 2013, Sch 1, r 105	21 days from date of service of notice: Sch 1, r 105(a)	None	Reasonably practicable: Sch 1, r 105(b)
Right of safety representatives to take time off to perform functions/for training: SRCR 1977, r 4(2)	3 months from failure: r 11(2)	None	Reasonably practicable: r 11(2)
Paid time off for pension scheme trustees to undergo training: ERA 1996, ss 58–60	3 months from the date when the failure to permit time off occurred: s 60(2)(a)	None	Reasonably practicable: s 60(2)(b)
Employee's contract claim: ETEJ (E&W) O 1994; ETEJ (S) O 1994, para 3	In employment tribunal, 3 months beginning with EDT or if no EDT, last working day: para 7 In county court/High Court, 6 years from breach of contract (12 years in the case of a deed)	None	Reasonably practicable: para 7(c)
Employer's contract claim: ETEJ (E&W) O 1994; ETEJ (S) O 1994	In employment tribunal, 6 weeks beginning with date of receipt by employer of employee's claim: para 8 In county court/High Court, 6 years from breach of contract (12 years in the case of a deed)	None	Reasonably practicable
Right to daily rest: WTR 1998, reg 10	3 months from the date when the right should have been permitted: reg 30(2)(a)	None	Reasonably practicable: reg 30(2)(b)
Right to weekly rest: WTR 1998, reg 11	3 months from the date when the right should have been permitted: reg 30(2)(a)	None	Reasonably practicable: reg 30(2)(b)
Right to rest breaks: WTR 1998, reg 12	3 months from the date when the right should have been permitted: reg 30(2)(a)	None	Reasonably practicable: reg 30(2)(b)
Right to compensatory rest in cases where regulations modified or excluded: WTR 1998, reg 24	3 months from the date when the right should have been permitted: reg 30(2)(a)	None	Reasonably practicable: reg 30(2)(b)
Right to annual leave: WTR 1998, reg 13	3 months from the date when the right should have been permitted: reg 30(2)(a)	None	Reasonably practicable: reg 30(2)(b)
Right to payment in lieu of holiday on termination of employment: WTR 1998, reg 14(2)	3 months from the date when the payment should have been made: reg 30(2)(a)	None	Reasonably practicable: reg 30(2)(b)

Employment right and statutory provision	When complaint must be made	Qualifying period	Discretionary power to extend time limit
Right to pay during annual leave: WTR 1998, reg 16(1)	3 months from the date when the payment should have been made: reg 30(2)(a)	None	Reasonably practicable: reg 30(2)(b)
Failure to allow access to records: NMWA 1998, s 11	3 months from end of 14 days from receipt of production notice or 3 months from agreed later date: s 11(3)(a) and (b)	None	Reasonably practicable: s 11(4)
Detriment arising from enforcement of rights: NMWA 1998, s 24	3 months beginning with date of act or failure	None	Reasonably practicable
Appeal against notice of underpayment: NMWA 1998, s 19C	28 days following date of service of notice: s 19C(3)	Not applicable	None
Failure or threat to fail to comply with right to be accompanied at a disciplinary or grievance hearing: ERelA 1999, s 10	3 months beginning with date of failure or threat: s 11(2)(a)	None	Reasonably practicable: s 11(2)(b)
Time off for members of European Works Council, etc: TICER 1999, reg 25	3 months beginning with date when time off should have been allowed or day taken off: reg 27(2)(a)	None	Reasonably practicable: reg 27(2)(b)
Detriment relating to membership of EWC, etc: TICER 1999, reg 31	3 months beginning with last date of less favourable treatment or detriment	None	Reasonably practicable: s 48(3) ERA 1996
Right not to be treated less favourably as a part-time worker: PTWR 2000, reg 5	3 months starting from date of less favourable treatment: reg 8(2)	None	Just and equitable: reg 8(3)
Right of part-time worker to receive written statement of reasons for less favourable treatment: PTWR 2000, reg 6	Not applicable	None	Not applicable (this is not a claim – settlement is used in evidence)
Unfair dismissal or right not to suffer detriment related to a part-time worker status: PTWR 2000, reg 7	3 months starting from date of last act or failure to act: reg 8(2)	None	Just and equitable: reg 8(3)

Appendix 6 Tables

787

Appeal Time Limits

Employment right and statutory provision	When application must be made	Discretionary power to extend time limit
Reconsideration of employment tribunal decision: Employment Tribunals (Constitution and Rules of Procedure) Regulations 2013, Sch 1, r 71	14 days from date decision sent to parties: r 71	None
Appeal from employment tribunal decision or order	42 days from date full written reasons for decision or order were sent: EAT Rules 1993, r 3(3)	May be extended or abridged under broad power in r 37, but no specific power
Review of EAT decision or order: EAT Rules, r 33	Within 14 days of the order: r 33(2)	General discretion to extend time under EAT Rules, r 37
Appeal from EAT to Court of Appeal: ETA 1996, s 37	Application for permission to appeal must be made at hearing or in case of reserved judgment within 7 days of being handed down/given in writing: para 21.5 EAT Practice Direction 2013 If not made then/ refused or unless otherwise ordered appeal must be made to Court of Appeal within 21 days of the sealed order: para 25.1 EAT Practice Direction 2013	See para 25.1 EAT Practice Direction 2013

Index

Material contained in the Appendices is referenced with page numbers